VOLUME 524   NOVEMBER 1992

THE ANNALS

of The American Academy *of* Political
and Social Science

RICHARD D. LAMBERT, *Editor*
ALAN W. HESTON, *Associate Editor*

POLITICAL ISLAM

Special Editors of this Volume

CHARLES E. BUTTERWORTH

University of Maryland
College Park

I. WILLIAM ZARTMAN

School of Advanced International Studies
Johns Hopkins University
Washington, D.C.

Ⓢ SAGE PUBLICATIONS   *NEWBURY PARK   LONDON   NEW DELHI*

THE ANNALS

© 1992 *by* The American Academy *of* Political *and* Social Science

2 8511

Editorial Office: 3937 Chestnut Street, Philadelphia, PA 19104.

For information about membership* (individuals only) and subscriptions (institutions), address:

SAGE PUBLICATIONS, INC.
2455 Teller Road
Newbury Park, CA 91320

From India and South Asia,		*From the UK, Europe, the Middle*
write to:		*East and Africa, write to:*
SAGE PUBLICATIONS INDIA Pvt. Ltd.		SAGE PUBLICATIONS LTD
P.O. Box 4215		6 Bonhill Street
New Delhi 110 048		London EC2A 4PU
INDIA		UNITED KINGDOM

SAGE Production Staff: LINDA GRAY, LIANN LECH, and JANELLE LeMASTER
*Please note that members of The Academy receive THE ANNALS with their membership.
Library of Congress Catalog Card Number 91-67480
International Standard Serial Number ISSN 0002-7162
International Standard Book Number ISBN 0-8039-4687-2 (Vol. 524, 1992 paper)
International Standard Book Number ISBN 0-8039-4686-4 (Vol. 524, 1992 cloth)
Manufactured in the United States of America. First printing, November 1992.

Information about membership rates, institutional subscriptions, and back issue prices may be found on the facing page.

Advertising. Current rates and specifications may be obtained by writing to THE ANNALS Advertising and Promotion Manager at the Newbury Park office (address above).

Claims. Claims for undelivered copies must be made no later than three months following month of publication. The publisher will supply missing copies when losses have been sustained in transit and when the reserve stock will permit.

Change of Address. Six weeks' advance notice must be given when notifying of change of address to ensure proper identification. Please specify name of journal. Send address changes to: THE ANNALS, c/o Sage Publications, Inc., 2455 Teller Road, Newbury Park, CA 91320.

The American Academy of Political and Social Science

3937 Chestnut Street   Philadelphia, Pennsylvania 19104

Origin and Purpose. The Academy was organized December 14, 1889, to promote the progress of political and social science, especially through publications and meetings. The Academy does not take sides in controverted questions, but seeks to gather and present reliable information to assist the public in forming an intelligent and accurate judgment.

Meetings. The Academy occasionally holds a meeting in the spring extending over two days.

Publications. THE ANNALS is the bimonthly publication of The Academy. Each issue contains articles on some prominent social or political problem, written at the invitation of the editors. Also, monographs are published from time to time, numbers of which are distributed to pertinent professional organizations. These volumes constitute important reference works on the topics with which they deal, and they are extensively cited by authorities throughout the United States and abroad. The papers presented at the meetings of The Academy are included in THE ANNALS.

Membership. Each member of The Academy receives THE ANNALS and may attend the meetings of The Academy. Membership is open only to individuals. Annual dues: $42.00 for the regular paperbound edition (clothbound, $60.00). California residents must add 7.25% sales tax on all orders ($45.05 paperbound; $64.35 clothbound). Add $9.00 per year for membership outside the U.S.A. Members may also purchase single issues of THE ANNALS for $13.00 each (clothbound, $18.00). California residents: $13.94 paperbound, $19.31 clothbound. Add $1.50 for shipping and handling on all prepaid orders.

Subscriptions. THE ANNALS (ISSN 0002-7162) is published six times annually—in January, March, May, July, September, and November. Institutions may subscribe to THE ANNALS at the annual rate: $132.00 (clothbound, $156.00). California institutions: $141.57 paperbound, $167.31 clothbound. Add $9.00 per year for subscriptions outside the U.S.A. Institutional rates for single issues: $24.00 each (clothbound, $29.00). California institutions: $25.74 paperbound, $31.10 clothbound.

Second class postage paid at Thousand Oaks, California, and additional offices.

Single issues of THE ANNALS may be obtained by individuals who are not members of The Academy for $17.00 each (clothbound, $26.00). California residents: $18.23 paperbound, $27.89 clothbound. Add $1.50 for shipping and handling on all prepaid orders. Single issues of THE ANNALS have proven to be excellent supplementary texts for classroom use. Direct inquiries regarding adoptions to THE ANNALS c/o Sage Publications (address below).

All correspondence concerning membership in The Academy, dues renewals, inquiries about membership status, and/or purchase of single issues of THE ANNALS should be sent to THE ANNALS c/o Sage Publications, Inc., 2455 Teller Road, Newbury Park, CA 91320. Telephone: (805) 499-0721; FAX/Order line: (805) 499-0871. *Please note that orders under $30 must be prepaid.* Sage affiliates in London and India will assist institutional subscribers abroad with regard to orders, claims, and inquiries for both subscriptions and single issues.

Printed on recycled, acid-free paper

THE ANNALS

of The American Academy *of* Political *and* Social Science

RICHARD D. LAMBERT, *Editor*
ALAN W. HESTON, *Associate Editor*

─────────────── **FORTHCOMING** ───────────────

WHITE-COLLAR CRIME
Special Editors: Gilbert Geis and Paul Jesilow
Volume 525   January 1993

FREE TRADE IN THE WESTERN HEMISPHERE
Special Editor: Sidney Weintraub
Volume 526   March 1993

RELIGION IN THE NINETIES
Special Editor: Wade Clark Roof
Volume 527   May 1993

See page 3 for information on Academy membership and
purchase of single volumes of **The Annals.**

CONTENTS

BOOK DEPARTMENT CONTENTS

SOCIOLOGY

ECONOMICS

PREFACE

Political Islam has been seen by some as the successor to the Communist threat, a creeping mobilization that confronts the "Great Satan" of Western civilization and modernization. To others, it is nothing to worry about—merely an inherent aspect of religious practice wherever there are Muslims. This study aims to steer a careful path between these two inadequate perceptions.

Islam is, indeed, a religious belief that covers all aspects of life and denies the validity of any philosophical separation between "church" and state. *"Islam din wa dawla"* ("Islam is religion and state") is a basic precept subscribed to by all Muslims as part of their faith. But the fact that this identity contains two distinct elements in its predicate indicates that those elements are actually separate, and the ultimate relation between the two can take many variations. Otherwise, there would be no concern at the present time —as opposed to other periods in history—over the political forms of Islam.

On the other hand, some of the ways in which political Islam manifests itself at the end of the twentieth century are specifically anti-Western, consciously revolutionary, avowedly antisecularist and antimodernist, even intentionally violent. Probably the biggest contradiction within this extreme form of political Islam is the fact that it consists not of a single movement but of a plethora of groups and liaisons divided above all by national origins. Within different countries, even the most extreme forms differ widely; moreover, when particular groups have been totally successful in seizing power, none of the governments they have formed resembles any other. Indeed, like any religious movement, the desire to foster unity and orthodoxy proves to be the greatest guarantee of division and heterodoxy.

Somewhere in the broad terrain between the normal and the extreme form of religion and politics in Islam lies the reality of the phenomenon under investigation. Its manifestations are varied and contradictory, and no single expression can be taken as evidence of the nature of the whole. There are peaceful Islamic intellectual circles and violent terrorist groups, political parties that have won and lost by pursuing the democratic process and those dedicated to eradicating the democratic regime by which they seek to come to power. Similarly, there are interpreters and adherents who profess to live by the unchanged Word of the seventh century, just as there are those who seek new meanings appropriate to the twentieth. The articles presented in this volume bring that diversity to light; they identify the nuances within its stark threat and the myriad details of its current practices.

None of the articles focuses on the everyday beliefs of the millions of Muslims around the world as these relate to their personal perception of themselves and of God. There is no reason to do so, for their God is universally

8

recognized to be the same as the God of Jews and Christians, and it is acknowledged that human understanding of this God derives initially from the same scriptural sources while going beyond them to provide a newer and somewhat different revelation. Though these commonalities and differences of belief are not addressed here, they should be kept in mind. After all, they form the basis for the political manifestation of the religion that is the subject of investigation.

At the outset, some definitional distinctions appear warranted. The term "fundamentalism" is avoided in the following articles primarily because it is objected to by the subjects of study themselves as a Christian—and therefore inappropriate—term. There might be some value to using it, nonetheless, since a single term would underline the fact that literal application of past scripture to current daily life is an element present in many religions—an element present in various strengths at various times and thus not just a variation applied to Islam. On the other hand, a specific term highlights the specific features of this particular tendency, and so the term "Islamicist" is used to refer to those who strive to bring politics into line with Islamic precepts. "Islamic," by contrast, is used to refer to religious and specifically Quranic prescriptions, and "Muslim" is used to refer merely to the general practice of the religion without any particular implication of either politics or piety.

The articles forming this study are about political Islam, the religiously based efforts of some Muslims to relate to state power. In bringing out the specific nature of the common subject, our coauthors define and analyze political Islam in several different ways. Thus the following 14 articles fall into six general groupings: political Islam viewed across time, nonofficial manifestations of political Islam, official attitudes to and ways of dealing with political Islam, political Islam empowered, accounts of political Islam apart from the Middle East, and the interplay between culture and politics with respect to political Islam.

Differently stated, the study attempts to offer a survey of Islamic attitudes and practices at the hand of the state both in instances where governments have become Islamic and those where they seek to control the expression of Islamicist tendencies. It also looks at Islamic organizations that govern their own affairs as fraternities and independent societies outside of direct state control or opposition. In addition, it examines oppositional forms of political Islam, either as the low-culture form of religion opposed to the official or high-culture version, or as parties and movements designed to seize power by various means in order to create an Islamic political order. Moreover, focusing on the way Islamic regimes interact with Islamic groups seeking to have a greater say in rule or with non-Islamic groups calling for greater recognition, the study examines the state and the larger community both in general and in particular. Finally, it considers what is theoretically involved in calling for greater attention to empowering Islam.

POLITICAL ISLAM ACROSS TIME

In the article that opens this study, Ira M. Lapidus looks at Middle Eastern states over time. Though he notes how influential Islam was in the premodern era, Lapidus argues that it has little national sway today. Tracing the development of two Islamic paradigms for rule, he urges that most states in the Middle East have now opted for a political life in which Islam is relegated to private practice and thus deprived of influence over official political life.

Charles E. Butterworth agrees with the way Lapidus views the influence of Islam on Middle Eastern politics in the premodern era, but he then seeks to discover what those calling for a greater Islamic role in politics today have in mind. Arguing that there is nothing new about such a demand, Butterworth sketches a general history of political discourse within the Islamic tradition to buttress his point and proposes a novel way for proponents of liberal democracy to reassess their criticism of unabashedly Islamic regimes.

NONOFFICIAL MANIFESTATIONS OF POLITICAL ISLAM

Taking issue with recent journalistic attempts to capture popular Islam, Patrick D. Gaffney proposes that we begin by looking at the way Islam has evolved through history. His analysis leads him to distinguish between official and popular Islam and thus to emphasize the way the populace has had recourse to Sufism, rather than activism, over the ages. He concludes by noting that popular Islam now seems to point in two directions. First, it serves as the basis for a comprehensive teaching advanced by those who would challenge the present status quo; second, it continues to capture the lived experiences of the masses of Muslims, that is, the populace.

Militant Islamic movements in Algeria, Tunisia, Libya, the Occupied Territories, and Lebanon are the focus of Mary-Jane Deeb's article. She begins by noting five broad conditions that seem to be common to all of these movements, then turns to a detailed consideration of how each has emerged. In the course of her presentation, she notes the concepts and causes embraced by each and strives to discern how these also link the different movements.

Casting an eye on the way Sufi brotherhoods have functioned in West Africa, North Africa, Russia, the Sudan, and Egypt in the last century as well as in this one, John Obert Voll shows how they have preserved Islamic piety and how they represent popular expressions of Islam. Like Patrick Gaffney, Voll sees the Sufi brotherhoods as offering significant solace to the populace at times when Islam was out of favor by providing a sense of continuity. In his article, Voll explains the origins and functions of several brotherhoods, then details the way some have come to play a role in the growing move toward the Islamization of society and politics.

OFFICIAL ATTITUDES TO POLITICAL ISLAM

Nazih N. Ayubi paints a broad picture of Islam empowered. Looking at the role of the 'ulama' in a number of different regimes that proclaim themselves Islamic, he first sketches the major differences between Sunnite and Shiite regimes, then turns to a consideration of the way non-Muslim minorities are treated in all Islamic states. To make his argument more persuasive, Ayubi turns from time to time to recent history and even looks back to medieval jurisprudence. A salient feature of his article is his intelligent use of recent analyses from the pens of scholars living in the Arab Middle East and writing in Arabic.

In contrast, Shahrough Akhavi looks at two particular cases of how proponents of Islam discern its relationship to political power. In Egypt, about ten years ago, the leader of al-Azhar issued a formal religious reply to a pamphlet written by the revolutionary leader implicated in Sadat's assassination. Noting how the religious leader sought in this instance to defend secular rule, urging that in Egypt it was perfectly compatible with the aspirations of Muslims, Akhavi contrasts that writing with Khomeini's powerful *Islamic Government*, the treatise meant to justify the Islamic regime that he intended as the proper Islamic replacement for the rule of the Shah.

POLITICAL ISLAM EMPOWERED

Ibrahim A. Karawan denies the existence of a monolithic model of Islamic government or governance. Insisting that it makes more analytic sense to speak of a diversity of Islamic regimes, he shows that the Islamic regimes of Saudi Arabia, Iran, the Sudan, and Pakistan evince three different types of regime: a conservative dynastic regime, a populist authoritarian regime, and a military authoritarian regime. Karawan is, nonetheless, equally intent upon noting that all three share in using religious symbolism to gain legitimacy.

Identifying himself as "neither a Western politician nor an Algerian army officer" but as a somewhat theoretical academic, Lahouari Addi considers what changes must take place in contemporary Islamic societies for an Islamicist polity to be formed. His reflections center on the missed opportunity of the Islamic Salvation Front in Algeria, on what might have been and at what price. In the process, he notes the tensions between the conditions for democracy based on political parties and a regime—calling itself popular or not—based on the conviction that it rules in accordance with divine will.

POLITICAL ISLAM OUTSIDE THE MIDDLE EAST

Four articles are devoted to instances of political Islam in countries outside of the Middle East. Vitaly Naumkin discusses the way Islam managed to survive in Central Asia and other parts of the former USSR under the Communist regime and pays special attention to the role of the local *'ulama'*. Though not well educated in Islamic doctrine, they succeeded in carrying on a tradition that has now come into its own. Indeed, under the right conditions, Naumkin thinks we could well see Islamicists coming to power in Kazakhstan, Tadzhikistan, and Uzbekistan.

The focus of John Hunwick's article is Nigeria. He discusses the relationship of Islam to politics within that nation since it became independent in 1960. Religion first appeared on the political scene in 1977 when proposals to create a federal *shari'a* court unleashed protest from Christian members of the Constituent Assembly on the draft constitution. Since then, Muslims and Christians have become increasingly polarized, and Hunwick predicts that Nigeria will continue to be plagued by religious violence.

Alain-Gérard Marsot's article focuses on the role of Islam in the politics of Asia. He notes first that the majority of Muslims live in Asia, not the Middle East. For him, Islamic resurgence is a response to the global issue of modernization and development. Recounting the history of the spread of Islam to Asia, Marsot discusses the events that first encouraged conversion to Islam, namely, the spread of Islam, European colonialism, and population patterns.

Rémy Leveau addresses the issue of immigration from North Africa to Europe and the problems created as a new culture seeks to take root in an older, established one. Islamic identity remains powerful within the Maghrebian community in Europe, and this sometimes creates tensions between those who demand cultural and religious recognition and the state, which—due to historical precedents such as the Iranian revolution—fears political Islam. Leveau concludes by suggesting that a European communitywide immigration policy should be established, in part to filter and slow immigration from the South and in part to end the discrimination against Muslims currently practiced in Europe.

THE CULTURE AND POLITICS OF POLITICAL ISLAM

I.William Zartman's concluding article addresses the issue of the confrontation between political Islam and Western democracy. He traces the modern resurgence of political Islam to problems facing states that have adopted Western, secular, and materialistic polities. Insisting that there is no inherent incompatibility between Islam and democracy since Islam does not prescribe how rulers should be chosen but only that they should be pious, he concedes that some currents of political Islam nonetheless monopolize the national religion and allow only those subscribing to what they deem the true path a place in power.

CHARLES E. BUTTERWORTH

I. WILLIAM ZARTMAN

ANNALS, *AAPSS*, 524, November 1992

The Golden Age:
The Political Concepts of Islam

By IRA M. LAPIDUS

ABSTRACT: The present role of Islam in Middle Eastern politics is not a continuation but a reconstruction of the historical paradigms. In the premodern era, there were two Islamic paradigms. One was of an integral state and society unified under the political and moral leadership of a charismatic religious teacher; the other, of a society divided between state and religious institutions and differentiated political and religious elites, the latter being the custodians of the true Islam. The second tradition made room for purely secular monarchical concepts and a secular political culture. In the modern era, the historical Islamic paradigms have little influence on state formation. Even the avowedly Islamic states do not really hark back to the past but represent, for the most part, contemporary national states appealing to a new concept of national-state Islam.

Ira M. Lapidus is professor of history and chairman of the Center for Middle Eastern Studies at the University of California at Berkeley. Author of Muslim Cities in the Later Middle Ages; A History of Islamic Societies *and other works, he is a past president of the Middle East Studies Association of North America and has been a fellow of the National Endowment for the Humanities, the Center for Advanced Study in the Behavioral Sciences, and other institutions.*

THE Islamic revival is once again of urgent importance. Now, in the midst of a worldwide Muslim struggle over the role that Islam should play in contemporary societies, we are faced with compelling questions: How much does this revival reflect the desire to return to a golden age of the Muslim past? How much is it a contemporary phenomenon? Indeed, what is the Islamic and, in particular, the Middle Eastern political heritage, and what is its impact in the present?

THE FIRST GOLDEN AGE

The Middle Eastern Islamic heritage provides not one but two basic constellations of historical society, two golden ages, two paradigms, each of which has generated its own characteristic repertoire of political institutions and political theory. The first is the society integrated in all dimensions, political, social, and moral, under the aegis of Islam. The prototype is the unification of Arabia under the leadership of the Prophet Muhammad in the seventh century. The Prophet brought together the Meccans who left their home to join his community, the Medinans who accepted Islam, individual Arabians who emigrated to Medina, fractions of clans, converts made among the aristocratic families of Mecca, and various tribes in western Arabia; he unified a disparate and fragmented population into a single community. The Prophet functioned, on the one hand, as an economic and political leader and, on the other, as an exemplar of individual righteousness and morality. In this community, no distinction was made between religion and religious authority and the state and secular authority.[1]

The concept of an undifferentiated political religious community was carried over from the Prophet to the early caliphs. The Rashidun, who ruled from 632 to 660, did not inherit the Prophet's capacity to receive revelation, but their authority to implement and execute revealed law was considered as great as his authority to pronounce it.[2] Most Muslims, though for different reasons, believe that the first civil war (656-60), brought this authority to an end and that ever after the office of the caliphate was corrupted. The Shiites believe that it fell into the hands of inappropriate successors, for only Ali and the family of Ali could rightfully be caliphs; the Sunnites accept the actual historical succession but believe that later rulers were secular, self-serving kings—neither true caliphs nor true representatives of the community bequeathed by the Prophet.

Nonetheless, this image of the Prophetic community has inspired ever-renewed movements to restore the wholeness of the umma (community of Muslims). Shiites and Kharijites have struggled to restore the leadership of the rightful Imam. Repeatedly, Sunnite reformers have risen up to overthrow corrupt governments and set up a state committed to an Islamic morality. Sufi heroes have at-

1. W. Montgomery Watt, *Muhammad at Mecca* (New York: Oxford University Press, 1953); *Muhammad at Medina* (New York: Oxford University Press, 1955).

2. Patricia Crone and Martin Hinds, *God's Caliph* (New York: Cambridge University Press, 1986).

tempted to establish their authority, acting self-consciously in imitation of the Prophet. These reformers, like the Prophet himself, commonly found their supporters in tribal or other factionalized societies. Like the Prophet, they attempted to integrate individuals, families, clans, lineages, and clientele groups into a unified body. Such movements include, in North Africa, the Fatimids, the Almoravids, the Almohads, and the Sa'di and Alawite dynasties in Morocco; the Safavid dynasty in Iran; and, throughout the Muslim world, Berber Zawaya lineages, Evliadi among Turkomans, and Sufi-led movements such as the Sanusiyya. All of these movements exemplify the impulse to re-create, under religious leadership, the ideal community exemplified in the first golden age of Islam.[3] Nowadays, neo-Islamic movements, still inspired by the same underlying concept, take up the old ideal. Now this ideal, however, is supported not by tribal and rural communities but by the urban petite bourgeoisie, petty traders, craftspeople, *bazaaris*, and mobile and sometimes déraciné students.

THE SECOND GOLDEN AGE

The second historical paradigm is the imperial Islamic society, built not on Arabian or tribal templates but on the differentiated structures of previ-

3. On revivalist movements, see Ira M. Lapidus, *A History of Islamic Societies* (New York: Cambridge University Press, 1988), pp. 257-59, 563-68; John Voll, *Islam: Continuity and Change in the Modern World* (Boulder, CO: Westview Press, 1982); Fazlur Rahman, *Islam* (Chicago: University of Chicago Press, 1979), pp. 193-224.

ous Middle Eastern societies. By the advent of Islam, Middle Eastern societies had already been organized into differentiated tribal, state, and church institutions. After the Arab conquests, the early caliphate underwent a similar differentiation. Tribal armies were displaced by newly recruited client forces who were expected to be more dependent upon, loyal to, and obedient to their rulers; and tribal chiefs were replaced by administrative cadres drawn from the conquered populations. At the same time, the caliphate was transformed from the charismatic succession to the religious authority of the Prophet into an imperial institution and a regime governed not by religious norms but by the laws of political survival. As the caliphate took on an increasingly secularized political identity, the religious heritage of the Prophet came to be embodied in his companions and their disciples and successors, scholars, and holy men. Eventually, the caliphs retained only a nominal role as the official representatives of Islam and the official fount of state and religious authority, while the Muslim populace came to be organized into schools of law, theological sects, Shiite communities, Sufi lineages, and brotherhoods representing the legacy of the Prophet.

Such religious groups were commonly independent of state regimes. Most withdrew from participation in government and were concerned with community solidarity, worship, education, law, personal morality, and the upholding of the symbols of Islam. While religious scholars maintained their aspiration for an ideal society in which state and community were integrated as in the time of the Prophet, they were not actually committed to bringing it about in practice. In return for state support, they commonly legitimized reigning governments and taught acceptance and submission to the common people.

By the eleventh century, Middle Eastern states and religious communities were highly differentiated. States were officially committed to the defense and patronage of Muslim worship, education, law, and *jihad*, but they were not inherently Islamic institutions. It was widely recognized that these states operated on the basis of non-Islamic legitimation. Conquering regimes, be they Arab or Turkish, looked back to tribal ancestry as the basis of dynastic legitimacy. By the cultivation of local languages, poetic traditions, architectural motifs, musical themes, and cultic practices, Middle Eastern states asserted independence from Islam and identified themselves as cosmopolitan, imperial, and patrimonial regimes legitimated by non-Muslim civilization.[4]

Thus, despite the common statement that Islam is a total way of life defining political as well as social and family matters, most Muslim societies did not conform to this ideal. They were in fact built around separate institutions of state and religion.

The separation of state and religion yields a second image of the golden age of Islam. This image is embedded in the Ottoman empire; it is an image of a world-conquering empire, establishing the dominion of Islam over all peoples and fulfilling the Islamic "providence" or "manifest destiny" to rule the world. This was a golden era of security, preeminence, and world domination. This was a golden age also because the Ottoman empire upheld the true practice of Islam. It was the protector and patron, indeed the organizer and master, of the scholars and holy men who managed Muslim education, Muslim legal and judicial affairs, and Muslim worship.[5]

The practical tradition of separation of state and religion also generated a sociopolitical theory. Muslim political theorists, such as al-Baqillani, al-Mawardi, and Ibn Taimiyya, devised a theory of the caliphate that symbolized the ideal existence of the unified *umma*, while at the same time allowing for historical actualities. The conclusion of their theorizing was that the state was not a direct expression of Islam but a secular institution whose duty it was to uphold Islam. The community of scholars and holy men were the ones who truly carried on the legacy of the Prophet.[6]

4. Lapidus, *History of Islamic Societies*, pp. 137-80; A.K.S. Lambton, *Theory and Practice in Medieval Persian Government* (London: Variorum Reprints, 1980); H. Busse, *Chalif und grosskönig, die Buyiden im Iraq* (Beirut: Franz Steiner Verlag, 1969).

5. On the Ottoman empire, see Halil Inalcik, *The Ottoman Empire: The Classical Age, 1300-1600* (London: Weidenfeld & Nicolson, 1973); H.A.R. Gibb and Harold Bowen, *Islamic Society and the West* (New York: Oxford University Press, 1954, 1957).

6. Yusuf Ibish, *The Political Doctrine of al-Baqillani* (Beirut: American University Press, 1966); al-Mawardi, *Les Statuts gouvernementaux*, trans. E. Fagnan (Algiers: Adolph Jourdan, 1915); Ibn Taymiya, *Ibn Taymiya on Public and Private Law in Islam* (Beirut: Khayats, 1968); Henri Laoust, *Essai sur les doctrines sociales et politiques de Taki-d-Din Ahmad b. Tamiya* (Cairo: L'Institut française d'archéologie orientale, 1939).

In this tradition, the realm of Islamic authenticity lies within the soul of the individual and in the relations of individuals to each other within small communities. This is the Islam that sees holiness and religion as incompatible with state power. Politics are expected to be violent and corrupt. The control of the state is justified only by conquest; obedience is legitimated by the need to submit, to minimize further warfare, and to prevent anarchy in society, but the state cannot embody a religious ideal. This renunciation of political utopianism may help explain some cases of acquiescence to patrimonial regimes and the relative weakness of democratic or other secular utopian movements in the present-day Middle East.

THE NON-ISLAMIC
POLITICAL HERITAGE

This second paradigm allows for a differentiated nonreligious concept of political authority. Alongside the Islamic concept of the caliph as the upholder of Islam, there is a concept of political rationality inherently valid in its own terms as a source of political behavior. This level of political thinking is expressed in the Persian political heritage in which the ruler is the shadow of God on earth and bears a divine authority independent of religion. He both upholds order and serves as a moral example to his subjects. Rulership and statehood, in a sense, serve a religious purpose apart from Islam and apart from the spokesmen of the religious establishment.[7]

7. On Persian political theory, see E.I.J. Rosenthal, *Political Thought in Medieval Is-*

Furthermore, behind the formal and literary concepts of the state and the ruler, there were also working assumptions, axioms, and premises about the nature and organization of political power that did not reach the level of formal theory but are nonetheless crucial to understanding Middle Eastern politics. One is that state power is not an expression of the total society but rather the prerogative of certain individuals or groups. Control of the state belonged to certain families, tribes, dynasties, or military castes. Not only did some groups rule over others, but elites and subjects were of a totally different standing. Government was the prerogative of the one and not of the other. In Middle Eastern societies, there was a caste-like bifurcation between the military elite and the subject population.[8]

A further assumption of Middle East political systems was that, within the ruling elite and between the ruling elite and the various segments of the subject population, the exercise of political power was organized through networks of clients and retainers. These networks were bound together by subjective obligations, such as the oath of allegiance or gratitude, rather than by legal or

lam (New York: Cambridge University Press, 1958); al-Jahiz, *Le livre de la couronne*, trans. Charles Pellat (Paris: Société d'édition "Les belles lettres," 1954); Nizam al-Mulk, *The Book of Government or Rules for Kings*, trans. H. Darke, 2d ed. (London: Routledge & Kegan Paul, 1960); Kai Ka'us b. Iskandar, *A Mirror for Princes: The Qabus Nama*, trans. Reuben Levy (New York: E. P. Dutton, 1951).

8. On the rulers and the ruled, see Gibb and Bowen, *Islamic Society and the West*, passim.

other formal, institutional, or hierarchical considerations.[9]

Between rulers and subjects, political power was brokered by intermediary notables. For example, in the Mamluk empire of Egypt and Syria, state-appointed governors cultivated local notables, appointed them to offices, contributed to their religious and charitable causes, and organized public works in return for cooperation in maintaining public order and facilitating taxation. The governors similarly cultivated ties with youth gangs, fraternities, and the populace of town quarters.[10] In Middle Eastern societies with a strong tribal component, Sufis played the intermediary role. Muslim holy men—sometimes charismatic teachers, sometimes the custodians of local shrines, sometimes the members of holy lineages, sometimes affiliated with brotherhoods—facilitated the selection of tribal chiefs, mediated disputes, organized long-distance trade, and otherwise helped in the administration of rural populations.[11]

9. For example, see Roy Mottahedeh, *Loyalty and Leadership in an Early Islamic Society* (Princeton, NJ: Princeton University Press, 1980).

10. Ira M. Lapidus, *Muslim Cities in the Later Middle Ages*, 2d ed. (New York: Cambridge University Press, 1984).

11. On the social and political functions of Sufism, see Lapidus, *History of Islamic Societies*, pp. 168-72, 254-57, 261-64. For further examples, see V. N. Basilov, "Honour Groups in Traditional Turkmenian Society," in *Islam in Tribal Societies: From the Atlas to the Indus*, ed. A. A. Ahmed and D. M. Hart (London: Routledge & Kegan Paul, 1984), pp. 220-43; Julia Clancy-Smith, "Saints, Mahdis and Arms: Religion and Resistance in Nineteenth-Century North Africa," in *Islam, Politics, and Social Movements*, ed. Edmund Burke and Ira M. Lapidus (Berkeley: University of California

Thus we have not one but two paradigms, two concepts of the Muslim golden age. One looks to a unified state and society under the leadership of the caliph, whose authority extends to all realms of personal and public concern. This is the integralist conception of Islam. The second, in both its classic and Ottoman versions, tacitly recognizes the institutional division between the structures of state and religion. In this paradigm, Muslims look to the religious sphere for personal and communal fulfillment, to Islam as a personal and social ethos and not a concept or institution of the political regime. Finally, the differentiation of state and religion allows for an imperial and secular notion of the state and for the incorporation of Middle Eastern but not Islamic institutions and concepts into the theory, legitimation, and operation of political regimes.

ISLAM IN THE MODERN ERA

The modern era has brought a radical transformation of political and social institutions and inevitably of the ideas that shape, accompany, and reflect these institutions. There is a renewed struggle over the role that Islam should play in the constitution of contemporary Muslim societies. The role of the historical culture is being reconstructed by political struggle. There are two main arenas for the contestation over Islamic and traditional political values: the domain of the state, its definition, legit-

Press, 1988), pp. 60-80; Charles C. Stewart with E. K. Stewart, *Islam and Social Order in Mauritania* (New York: Oxford University Press, 1973).

imation, and institutional organization; and the domain of the civil or nonstate society.

THE ISLAMIC STATES

In the domain of the state, the avowedly Islamic states are a conspicuous minority. Only Saudi Arabia, Morocco, Iran, and Pakistan today profess to be legitimated or regulated by Islamic norms. The contemporary Islamic states, however, do not simply return to either of the two traditional paradigms. Absent from contemporary political rhetoric is any appeal to the concept of the caliphate.

Saudi Arabia and Morocco are in many ways closest to the traditional image of Islamic states and Muslim rulers. This is due to the continuity of premodern regimes. The Saudi state was founded in the eighteenth century by the alliance of a religious reformer, deliberately copying the precedents of the Prophet, and a tribal chieftain, using allegiance to the principles of reformed Islam, as the basis of an integrated state. The Saudi state continues to use Islam as the basis of its legitimacy, reinforced by the seizure of Mecca and Medina in 1926, by control and patronage of the pilgrimage, and by the sponsorship of international Islamic educational, missionary, and political activities. Combining religious teaching with the formation of a polity transcending tribal groups, the Saudi state seems to repeat the early Islamic experience, but the community of the Prophet was based upon his sole leadership, while the Saudi state is based on a separation of authority and an alliance between religious and secular chieftains. While the Saudi rulers have tried to take on the religious aura of imams, there remains a lingering division between political authority vested in the state and religious authority vested in the 'ulama'—the descendants of ibn 'Abd al-Wahhab.[12]

The Moroccan regime is also based on the Islamic identity of the monarch, who is considered a caliph, an executor and defender of Islam, a personal descendant of the Prophet, a bearer of Sufi virtues, a charismatic holy man, and a dispenser of *baraka*, of God's blessing in the world. He is the high priest of the great Moroccan Islamic festivals such as the birthday of the Prophet and the celebration at the end of Ramadan. Like the Saudi regime, the Moroccan government is one of the few Middle Eastern or Islamic states to have survived the colonial era and the transition to the national state. It survives because the French helped preserve the monarchy as a vehicle of colonial control, while the sultans managed to maintain themselves as the personification of Moroccan national identity. While the sultan continues to bear the Islamic marks of legitimacy, his political power is actually based on

12. R. Bailey Winder, *Saudi Arabia in the 19th Century* (New York: Octagon Books, 1965); J. S. Habib, *Ibn Sa'ud's Warriors of Islam: The Ikhwan of Najd and Their Role in the Creation of the Sa'udi Kingdom* (Leiden: E. J. Brill, 1978); William Ochsenwald, "Saudi Arabia and the Islamic Revival," *International Journal of Middle East Studies*, 13:271-86 (1981).

the administrative strength of a modern territorial national state.[13]

Similarly, Islamic Iran is not built on a return to past models but rather on a radically new concept of the Islamic state. The Islamic Republic of Iran is based on a modern type of national state, constructed between 1925 and 1979, on the same organizational bases and secular concepts as Turkey. It differs in that it was the one Middle Eastern country in which the religious elites remained a powerful social and political force, antagonistic to the state elites; laid claim to direct political authority; and were able to mobilize mass support to overthrow the state. The Iranian Islamic republic, much as it is Islamic in identity, remains a national state in terms of its institutional bureaucratic structure and the kinds of economic and political policies it pursues.[14]

So Pakistan, despite its nominal Islamic affiliation, is also a modern national state. It originates in an Islam that has been defined in nationalist political terms but excludes the personal and moral dimensions of Muslim religiosity. The leaders of the movement to establish an independent Pakistan were entirely secularized in their education and life-styles and had no commitment to Islam in

the traditional personal or local communal sense. Their rhetoric was Muslim in form, but the content was wholly nationalistic.

A nationalist concept of Pakistan expressed in religious and Muslim rather than in secular terms was necessary for various reasons. First, religiously based nationalism was the only rhetorical solution to the political dilemma of the Muslim elites of the Indian subcontinent. They used Islam to differentiate themselves from the Hindu Indian nationalist movement and to carve out a domain in which Muslim military and bureaucratic chieftains and Muslim merchant leaders would have a territory of their own and a more favorable opportunity to maintain their position in the postcolonial era. Second, Islam was essential to unify a population divided by tribal, ethnic, linguistic, caste, and local differences.[15]

13. Abdullah Laroui, *Les origines sociales et culturelles du nationalism marocain, 1830-1912* (Paris: F. Maspero, 1977); J. P. Halstead, *Rebirth of a Nation: The Origins and Rise of Moroccan Nationalism, 1912-1944* (Cambridge, MA: Harvard University Press, 1967).
14. Nikki R. Keddie, *Roots of Revolution: An Interpretive History of Modern Iran* (New Haven, CT: Yale University Press, 1981); H. Algar, *Religion and State in Iran, 1785-1906: The Role of the Ulama in the Qajar Period* (Berkeley: University of California Press, 1972);

idem, "The Oppositional Role of the Ulama in Twentieth-Century Iran," in *Scholars, Saints and Sufis*, ed. Nikki R. Keddie (Berkeley: University of California Press, 1972), pp. 231-55; S. Akhavi, *Religion and Politics in Contemporary Iran: Clergy-State Relations in the Pahlavi Period* (Albany: State University of New York Press, 1980); Said A. Arjomand, "Shi'ite Islam and the Revolution in Iran," *Government and Opposition*, 16:293-316 (1981); idem, "Traditionalism in Twentieth-Century Iran," in *From Nationalism to Revolutionary Islam*, ed. Said A. Arjomand (New York: Macmillan in association with St. Anthony's College, Oxford, 1984), pp. 195-232; idem, *The Turban for the Crown* (New York: Oxford University Press, 1988).
15. Leonard Binder, *Religion and Politics in Pakistan* (Berkeley: University of California Press, 1961); R. S. Wheeler, *The Politics of Pakistan* (Ithaca, NY: Cornell University Press, 1970).

THE SECULAR NATIONAL STATES

Apart from these cases of Islam refashioned, it is striking how little influence the historical Islamic traditions have had on modern state formation. The Islamic heritage is no longer invoked, is largely ignored, and is sometimes expressly repudiated. In the great waves of state building that followed World War I and World War II, old empires were liquidated and replaced by new national states built around secular cultural identities. In Turkey, Tunisia, Egypt, Syria, Iraq, and Jordan, Islam was disestablished. It is no longer the officially supported religion of the state. Though these states sometimes give special consideration to Muslim symbols and Muslim practices, Islam no longer legitimates the state and no longer defines its moral and social vision. All of these states abolished the *millet* system and set up secular educational and judicial systems, which actually compete with the primary functions of Islam. Muslim religious life, in general, became separated from state institutions and flourishes as a differentiated element of the "civil society."[16]

The Turkish state was the most radical example of modern secularization. The republic of Ataturk was founded on nationalist and republican principles and undertook a veritable cultural revolution to liquidate the attachment of the Turkish people to their Islamic past. It included changing the script in which Turkish was written so as to make the Ottoman language inaccessible. Muslim religious organizations were disestablished; formal instruction of Islam was abolished; changes in style of dress were mandated; and a new legal code replaced the *shari'a*. Perhaps the most important change was the increased scope given for the participation of women in public life. All of these transformations, including the idea of constitutional government, the standards of technical, social, and political modernity, and the concept of the total mobilization of society to reach its economic and political goals, were of European inspiration.[17]

Furthermore, these states strive for secular national identities. The nationalist concept did not rise spontaneously from the people or the historical culture but came into being as the preferred doctrine of opposition intelligentsia in the late nineteenth and early twentieth centuries. The primary reason for the adoption of nationalism was that Middle Eastern intelligentsias wanted to reject the political dominance of an older generation of Ottoman or Qajar imperial rulers and the moral dominance of Islam. Furthermore, nationalism served to articulate domestic opposition to European colonial rule precisely because Europeans accepted it as the basis of political society. Thus

16. Lapidus, *History of Islamic Societies*, pp. 571-717; idem, "Islam and Modernity," in *Patterns of Modernity*, ed. S. N. Eisenstadt (London: Frances Pinter, 1989), pp. 89-115; Michael S. Hudson, *Arab Politics: The Search for Legitimacy* (New Haven, CT: Yale University Press, 1977).

17. R. D. Robinson, *The First Turkish Republic* (Cambridge, MA: Harvard University Press, 1965); Lord Kinross, *Ataturk: The Rebirth of a Nation* (London: William Morrow, 1964).

nationalism conveniently expressed the opposition of a new elite both to the older imperial and religious elites of their own societies and to their colonial rulers.

Nationalism also had another, symbolic importance. For cosmopolitan, mobile, educated persons who had been taken out of the matrix of small, family-centered communities and launched into the world of cities, international contacts, foreign languages, and global political concerns, the concept of a national state became a homeland of the mind. For people who no longer belonged to the older order, and for whom the colonial political societies could offer only positions of subordination to a foreign elite, nationalism defined a new identity.

With the formation of modern states and the coming of independence, nationalism was diffused from the elites to the masses. For these masses, now subject to new state regimes bent on the social and economic transformation of their societies, nationalism would again serve as a concept replacing loyalties to more parochial family, village, and religious associations.[18]

18. On Turkish nationalism, see D. Kushner, *The Rise of Turkish Nationalism 1876-1908* (London: Frank Cass, 1977); Ziya Gökalp, *Turkish Nationalism and Western Civilization* (New York: Columbia University Press, 1959). On Arab nationalism, see Albert Hourani, *Arabic Thought in the Liberal Age* (New York: Cambridge University Press, 1983); Sylvia Haim, ed., *Arab Nationalism: An Anthology* (Berkeley: University of California Press, 1976); Zeine N. Zeine, *The Emergence of Arab Nationalism* (Delmar, NY: Caravan Books, 1973); C. E. Dawn, *From Ottomanism to Arabism: Essays on the Origins of Arab Nationalism* (Urbana: Illinois University Press, 1973);

For the masses, nationalism takes elements of the traditional culture borrowed from linguistic, ethnic, tribal, and religious identities and fuses them into a new concept of political identity. We find fused into Arab nationalism the Arabic language and its literary achievements, the saga of the Arab conquests and the early Arab empires, tribal and family ties that are still traced back to pre-Islamic Arabia, and, of course, the Arab identification with Islam.

Still, nationalism is not an age-old concept but a modern synthesis of elements of cultural traditions that previously did not belong together. In the Middle Eastern past, national, ethnic, or linguistic identities had never been important bases for political solidarity. Before the modern era, Middle Eastern peoples defined political loyalty in terms of family, lineage, or tribal ties, in terms of clientele obligations, in terms of religious affiliation, and in terms of service to the state. While Middle Eastern cultures recognized that there were important linguistic and ethnic differences between populations, these differences were never the basis of political action.

ISLAMIC ORIENTATIONS IN MODERN SOCIETIES

Still, in the contempory situation there is a subtle, if negative, role for

Philip S. Khoury, *Urban Notables and Arab Nationalism: The Politics of Damascus, 1860-1920* (New York: Cambridge University Press, 1983); William Cleveland, *The Making of an Arab Nationalist: Ottomanism and Arabism in the Life and Thought of Sati' al-Husri* (Princeton, NJ: Princeton University Press, 1971).

Islam and for the historical political culture in shaping the general orientations, attitudes, dispositions, and practices of Middle Eastern states. The historical orientations within Islamic culture may affect the role of modern states in economic development. For example, an important strand in the Islamic tradition may contribute indirectly to the limited commitment of many contemporary Middle Eastern regimes to economic development. Both rulers and subjects often expect the state to be concerned with the maintenance of power and the exploitation of their populations, but not necessarily with economic development as the primary goal. These expectations may also reflect the traditional attitude of Muslim societies that high status is gained from education, piety, or power, to which money may contribute but is not the defining component. As opposed to European cultures, where the accumulation of wealth was the central value and was validated by high status for successful merchants and entrepreneurs, in Middle Eastern societies maintenance of power and religious piety seem to have been the dominant values.

Furthermore, modern states can be seen as an expression of the historical separation of state and Islam. This separation allows the state to be a purely political and power-based entity. Stripped of its Islamic functions, the modern state no longer has a transcending importance as the locus of ultimate values and is no longer expected to fulfill the ultimate religious yearnings of its subjects and citizens. All hope of salvation has been concentrated in the nonstate realm, in the religiocivil community, and in personal piety. This leads again, in practice, to an acceptance of the state as necessary for political power, military security, and public order, but it removes the expectation that the state itself can be a source of worldly justice and dignity. Utopian expectations that the state can embody genuine secular democratic, socialist, or egalitarian ideals are also subverted.

In these circumstances, not the Islamic but the "unspoken premises" of the Middle Eastern cultural tradition come to the fore. Many Middle Eastern states are authoritarian, military, and patrimonial regimes run by means of clienteles. For example, many features of the Turkish republic and the Ataturk program may be derived from the patrimonial premises of the Ottoman empire. In present-day Syria and Iraq, one may see a similar assumption of state power by small cliques operating through clienteles, and the continuation of the traditional expectation that the state is the prerogative of segmented elites.

Many factors help perpetuate the grip of patrimonial premises upon modern statecraft. Not only past cultural orientations but also the continuation into the modern era of small and insecure bourgeoisies, weak landowning classes, and tribal and factional divisions within society all combine to perpetuate institutional features and cultural assumptions that derive from the unspoken Middle Eastern political tradition.

ISLAM AND IDENTITY

While Islam has a limited role in the construction of contemporary national states, it has a pervasive importance in the constitution of civil society, society outside the state, and, therefore, a profound potential for the reconstruction of modern states in Islamic or neo-Islamic terms. Despite the success of secular national states, Middle Eastern identities have never been fully secularized. Rather Islam has been parochialized in national terms. Today nationalism is the single most important bearer of Islam. For example, the concept of Turkish national identity includes kinship to the Turks of Inner Asia, the Hittite ancestry of Turkish peoples in Anatolia, a history of the dominance of Turkish-speaking military elites, and also the historical allegiance of Turkish peoples to Islam. Latent Islamic identifications are the ultimate basis of Turkish national identity. In Turkey, Greeks, Armenians, and Jews, though Turkish speaking, have not been accepted as part of the nation. What makes Turks Turks, in the minds of many, is Islam, just as what makes Arabs Arabs for many Arabs is being Muslim. Much of the emotional power of nationalism in the Middle East is derived from the capacity of Islam to signify social solidarity and channel the force of Muslim faith into national commitments.[19]

In some cases Islam enters into the formation of national identity in a more direct way. Since the nineteenth century, throughout North Africa, Islamic reformism has been particularly important in overcoming parochial, localistic identifications and creating a broader sense of identity among the populations of Tunisia, Algeria, and Morocco. The reform movements created a new universal standard of religious values and religious practices; they stressed the importance of education, literate knowledge, and responsible commitment to Islamic social goals. These sentiments helped create a sense of commonality and political solidarity and became the basis of national identifications throughout North Africa.[20]

Islam continues to define national identities precisely because it remains the basis of local community life and personal religious belief. There are strong trends in all Middle Eastern countries toward new types of Islamic communal activities. Ethnic associations, religious congregations, welfare associations, charities, discussion groups, educational organizations, women's groups, economic cooperatives, and paramilitary training organizations have become more common.[21]

19. See note 18. See also James Piscatori, *Islam in a World of Nation-States* (New York: Cambridge University Press, 1986).

20. On Islam and nationalism in North Africa, see Ali Merad, *Le reformisme musulman en Algerie de 1923 à 1940* (Paris: Mouton, 1967); P. Shinar, "The Historical Approach of the Reformist 'Ulama' in the Contemporary Maghrib," *Asian and African Studies* (Jerusalem), 7:181-210 (1971); Abdullah Laroui, *Les origines du nationalisme marocain*; J. P. Halstead, *Rebirth of a Nation*; E. E. Evans-Pritchard, *The Sanusi of Cyrenaica* (New York: Oxford University Press, 1949).

21. See Morroe Berger, *Islam in Egypt Today* (New York: Cambridge University Press, 1970); Gilles Kepel, *Muslim Extremism in Egypt* (Berkeley: University of California Press, 1985).

Furthermore, even where Islamic movements are not strongly organized, Islam remains important as a personal or private religion. While it no longer regulates the public world, it continues to be vital to people's ethical and psychological needs. In highly secularized Middle Eastern societies, Islam becomes more and more a quest for meaning without being linked to political purposes. In these milieus, a new kind of Islamic community emerges, one that is based on personal piety rather than on commitment to political institutions, and an Islam of private belief and private social identity that is dissociated from the communal political matrix in which such identity was once embedded.[22]

This reconstruction of Islam has important implications for political and social behavior. First, Islam, especially in its reformist and revivalist versions, is the basis for a more fully self-disciplined and self-directed autonomous personality. The neo-Islamic movements seem to cultivate in their members a sense of social responsibility, moral dynamism, and an active engagement in the affairs of the society with a view to Islamizing contemporary Muslim populations. They provide through religious identity a sense of dignity, self-esteem, and self-discipline. This focusing of individual loyalties upon religious values is a critical factor in mobilizing people for moral, social, and political action.

Finally, and perhaps most important, Islam is the basis of political opposition movements. These movements appeal precisely to the excluded elements in the formation of modern political states, to the petite bourgeoisie or *bazaaris*, and sometimes to workers, students, and rural migrants to cities; they have a new urban class base in contrast to the historically rural character of reformist movements. They try to define the principles of a new Muslim morality by going back to the Quran and the *sunna*, but their idea is not to create a prescriptive program of detailed rules for behavior but to find general values to allow people living in new social conditions to reorganize their daily lives. These movements also attempt to meet the need for social solidarity in disorganized populations. They build up extensive networks of cells or chapters and mosques, schools, clinics, clubs, cooperative workshops, and industries. Ultimately, they aspire to the creation of an Islamic state.

Yet the goals of many of these movements are not, strictly speaking, political. The movements are not committed to particular institutions or to political principles such as democracy and equality. They are concerned rather with individual morality and ethical behavior, and to them the state is simply the force that encourages or requires the people to adhere to Islamic norms. The true domain of Islam is still the righteous small community and the ethical individual.

22. For postmodern Islam, see Lapidus, *History of Islamic Societies*, pp. 551-70, 879-917.

ANNALS, *AAPSS*, 524, November 1992

Political Islam:
The Origins

By CHARLES E. BUTTERWORTH

ABSTRACT: Seeking to understand why Islamicists prize the non-democratic and even nonliberal political rule to be found in revelation-based politics, the article first considers the older Arabic and Islamic analysis of political regimes and their goals. Then it investigates why, in a more recent past, thoughtful thinkers within that same cultural milieu called for independence while endorsing non-democratic and nonliberal regimes. Finally, it suggests why thinkers today continue to do the same. The goal is not to apologize for Islamicist doctrines in the present or in the recent or distant past but to point to the problems with current Western analyses and critiques of political Islam.

Professor of government and politics at the University of Maryland, College Park, Charles E. Butterworth specializes in medieval Islamic political philosophy. His publications include critical editions of most of the Middle Commentaries written by Averroes on Aristotle's logic; translations of books and treatises by Averroes, Alfarabi, and Alrazi, as well as Maimonides; and studies of different aspects of the political teaching of these and other thinkers in the ancient, medieval, and modern traditions of philosophy.

BEFORE rushing to castigate as benighted, backward, and hopelessly illiberal those Middle Eastern peoples who long to govern themselves by religious laws and thus to ensure a higher level of communal moral decency, we modern Westerners would do well to pause and reflect momentarily on our own cultural origins. Though now almost universally rejected in the West as a valid description of the proper attitude toward government and its functionaries, the following admonition once held great sway among faithful Christians:

Let every soul be subject to the governing authorities. For there is no authority except from God, and those that exist have been instituted by God. Therefore the one resisting authority goes against what God has appointed, and resisters will incur judgment.[1]

Nor is it all that different from the injunction laid upon pious Muslims:

Oh, you who believe, obey God and obey the Apostle and those charged with authority among you. If you disagree among yourselves about anything, refer it to God and the Apostle.[2]

1. See Rom. 13:1-2; here and in what follows, the translation is my correction of the Revised Standard Version. The next two verses (13:3-4) explain why Paul insists so adamantly on obedience to authority: "For rulers are not a terror to good conduct, but to bad. Would you have no fear of the one who is in authority? Then do what is good, and you will receive his approval. For he is God's servant for your good. But if you do wrong, be fearful, for he does not bear the sword in vain; he is the servant of God to execute His wrath on the wrongdoer." The rest of the exhortation (13:5-7) is also worth considering.
2. See Quran 4:59; the translation is my own.

Not until sometime after Marsilius of Padua (c. 1275-1342) were Paul's strictures forsaken and the famous advice offered by Jesus about distinguishing between the things belonging to Caesar and those belonging to God raised to the elevated rank it occupies today.[3] Though of a piece with the prophet Samuel's dire predictions about the harsh demands a king would make upon his subjects,[4] Jesus' suggestion is not consonant with the larger Old Testament teaching about the need for the faithful to let themselves be guided in all matters by God. Nonetheless, by the late fourteenth or fifteenth century, we Westerners began to turn away from the notion that political authority is divinely inspired. Whatever the reasons for that change—deeper understanding of the base demands of politics on rulers, however honorable their intentions; conviction that political and temporal concerns differ

3. See Matt. 22:15-22: "Then the Pharisees went and took counsel how to entangle him in his talk. And they sent their disciples to him, along with the Herodians, saying, 'Teacher, we know that you are true, teach the way of God truthfully, and concern yourself about no one; for you do not regard the rank of men. Tell us, then, what do you think: Is it lawful to pay taxes to Caesar, or not?' But Jesus, aware of their malice, said, 'Why do you test me, you hypocrites? Show me the money for the tax.' And they brought him a dinar. And Jesus said to them, 'Whose likeness and inscription is this?' They said, 'Caesar's.' Then he said to them, 'Render, then, Caesar's things to Caesar and the things that are God's to God.' When they heard it, they were astonished; and they went away and left him." Note especially verse 21, that is, the next to the last sentence. See also Matt. 17:24-27 and compare with Mark 12:13-17, esp. 17, and Luke 20:19-26, esp. 25. Again, the translation is my correction of the Revised Standard Version.
4. See 1 Sam. 8:10-21, 1-9.

radically from spiritual and moral ones; doubt about the existence of a divine or natural order—it finds a clear and all too familiar expression in the middle of the eighteenth century with Rousseau's famous, albeit completely unsubstantiated, assertion that "man is born free."[5]

It is the major sentiment standing behind our repugnance for political regimes that take their bearing from revelation, that is, for regimes that are or would be self-consciously Islamicist. Convinced that natural human freedom—and the equality that necessarily accompanies it—must be respected and preserved by a political regime if it is to be deemed legitimate, we condemn those regimes that aim at instilling moral virtues and sacrificing human liberty for a higher goal.[6] Although particular actions—for example, Ayatollah Khomeini's sentence of death against Salman Rushdie—or promises of actions to be taken—such as the Algerian Islamic Salvation Front's declaration that once in power it would put an end to the very democratic systems that allowed it to come to power—reveal all too clearly the lack of patience that Islamicist regimes have for the freedoms and procedures we Westerners hold to be essential hallmarks of good government, it is

also utterly manifest that, precisely because those hallmarks are merely procedural, they are not the only guarantors of good government.

For this reason, it is appropriate to inquire why others prize the nondemocratic and even nonliberal political rule that is to be found in revelation-based politics. To this end, I propose first to consider the older Arabic and Islamic analyses of political regimes and their goals. Then I will explain why, in a more recent past, thoughtful thinkers within that same cultural milieu called for independence while endorsing nondemocratic and nonliberal regimes. Finally, I will suggest why thinkers today continue to do the same. There is no intent here to apologize for Islamicist doctrines in the present or in the recent or distant past, for such apologetics would serve no purpose. If anything, my approach merely points to the failure in current Western analysis of political Islam to pay sufficient attention to the rhetorical transformations that arguments for something like an Islamic regime have undergone in the course of history as the character of the audience addressed has changed over time and as the goal pursued by the various speakers has been altered.

THE DISTANT PAST

There is little need to insist that Islam offers as much practical as it does spiritual guidance to the faithful. Whether we look back to the community founded by the Prophet Muhammad while he was in Medina (622-30) or to the way it was continued during the two years after he

---

5. See Jean-Jacques Rousseau, *Social Contract*, bk. 1, chap. 1. The complete phrase reads: "Man is born free, and everywhere he is in chains" (my translation). *Social Contract* was published in 1762.

6. See, for example, Leonard Binder, *Islamic Liberalism: A Critique of Development Ideologies* (Chicago: University of Chicago Press, 1988), pp. 1-4; also Francis Fukuyama, *The End of History and the Last Man* (New York: Free Press, 1992), passim.

returned to Mecca, whether we think about the tradition of the four rightly guided caliphs (632-61)—the first successors to Muhammad—or about the caliphs who guided the Umayyad (661-750), Abbasid (750-1258), and Spanish Umayyad (756-1031) empires, or whether we consider the princes and commanders who ruled the Arab and Berber dynasties in Spain and North Africa (1031-1492) and the sultans who ruled the Ottoman empire (1453-1918), we see political rule linked with religion. From the very opening of the Quran and the plea that the Lord of the universe show the faithful the straight path to the assurance that He has made of Muslims "a balanced nation that [they] may be witnesses to people" and on to the promise that He will bring victory to those who enter His religion, the close link between Islam and power is evident.[7]

During the Golden Age of Islam, referred to in this *Annals* issue in the article by Ira Lapidus, numerous thinkers argued that Islam should be joined to politics. Nominally, of course, it was joined. The rulers were supposed to represent a continuation of the Prophet Muhammad's rule; they were his successors and, as such, something like the vicegerents of God. Yet, as Lapidus notes, there was a great gap between intention and achievement, between what was supposed to be and what actually was. Jurists, theologians, and philosophers sought in their writings as well as in their deeds to resolve this discrepancy. They addressed them-

selves to a small, but learned, audience, namely, to individuals schooled in the sciences of Islam (the sayings and deeds of the Prophet, jurisprudence, and theology), in grammar as well as in poetry and literature, and in philosophical writings.

The jurists and theologians strove to make revealed doctrine more apparent. With a jurist like al-Mawardi (c. 985-1058), this resulted in explanations of the qualities needed for a person to become a caliph, the ways matters of state could be administered without infringing on revealed laws, or the conditions that must be met for military incursions to be in accordance with Quranic strictures. Neither al-Mawardi nor any of his fellow jurists raised the larger questions of whether it was appropriate to change political rule itself or how a wise ruler might expand the liberty of his subjects. In the writings of a sometime theologian like al-Ghazali (1058-1111), we find a defense of doctrines of the faith and attacks upon groups and individuals whose thinking appeared to threaten the well-being of the community. Even in his efforts to quicken religious faith, the emphasis is on particular issues— above all, on morals—rather than on how a ruler intent upon following in the path of the Prophet might best fashion his regime. Furthermore, in speaking about moral improvement, al-Ghazali dwells on personal endeavor; he pays no attention to how laws or institutions might shape moral conduct.

For reflections on the goals of political life and how a regime might be structured to achieve them, we must

7. See Quran 1:2-4, 5; 2:143; 110:1-2; the translation is mine.

turn to the philosophers. Our best guides in such matters are Alfarabi (870-950), Avicenna (980-1037), and Averroes (1126-98), not least because they dare to look back beyond the advent of Islam to the wisdom of Greece in order to suggest what can make political life best. In looking back, however, they never forget the importance of revelation and its influence on politics.

Alfarabi draws attention to this new phenomenon in his *Enumeration of the Sciences* by setting forth two accounts of political science. Both presuppose the validity of the traditional separation between the practical and the theoretical sciences, but neither is adequate for the radically new situation created by the appearance of revealed religion. The first account puts forth a political science that is simply practical.[8] It begins abruptly, not be defining political science and its general scope or what it consists of, but by stating what political science investigates, namely, the distinctively human things: voluntary actions and ways of life. The investigation looks back to what leads to these actions and ways of life

as well as forward to why the actions are performed.

The first political science thus provides a general overview of individual and civic human morality without ever leaving the immediate domain in which humans find themselves. At no point does it look beyond human beings and human things. This first political science also shows why political association is beneficial. In addition, it sets forth the general guidelines that thoughtful individuals can use to judge between different regimes.

The second account of political science goes beyond the practical limits of the first without presenting a fully theoretical political science. Indeed, even though this political science is said to include the "theoretical and practical sciences," such exclusive attention is paid to what it has to say about actions that nothing is said about how it handles opinions, especially the theoretical opinions set forth in religion.[9] Alfarabi designates it at first as political philosophy, explaining that it is limited to investigating general rules and to giving general descriptions or patterns for determining the voluntary actions and ways of life it investigates. This second political science starts, then, from where the first political science left off; it presupposes the investigations already undertaken by the first political science and moves from them to the formulation of general rules and patterns.

From this sketch it should be manifest that neither the first nor the second account of political science in

8. See 'Uthman Amin, ed., *Ihsa' al-'Ulum li-al-Farabi* (Cairo: Dar al-Fikr al-'Arabi, 1949). Fauzi Najjar has translated the work into English; see *Enumeration of the Sciences* in *Medieval Political Philosophy: A Sourcebook*, ed. Ralph Lerner and Muhsin Mahdi (New York: Free Press of Glencoe, 1963), pp. 22-30. The following interpretation develops a suggestion made by Muhsin Mahdi in "Science, Philosophy, and Religion in Alfarabi's *Enumeration of the Sciences*," in *The Cultural Context of Medieval Learning*, ed. J. E. Murdoch and E. D. Sylla (Dordrecht: B. Reidel, 1975), pp. 113-47, esp. pp. 144-45. The first account of political science occurs in *Enumeration of the Sciences*, 102:4-104:15.

9. The second account is set forth in *Enumeration of the Sciences*, 104:16-107:4.

the *Enumeration of the Sciences* can lead to the kind of rulership or to the royal craft needed for the new phenomenon of revealed religion. Nor can either speak about the opinions or actions that the jurisprudence and theology of revealed religion address. Such a rulership or royal craft can come only from a political science that would both combine theoretical and practical sciences along with prudence and show how they are to be ordered in the soul of the ruler. This kind of political science would be more theoretical than the one first set forth in the *Enumeration of the Sciences* and go beyond the understanding of the sciences presupposed in the second one, an understanding that is based on what has preceded in the *Enumeration of the Sciences*.[10] In his other writings—most notably in his *Book of Religion*, but also in the *Political Regime*, the *Aphorisms of the Statesmen*, and the *Principles of the Opinions of the Inhabitants of the Virtuous City*—Alfarabi develops this broader political science. It speaks of religious beliefs as opinions and of acts of worship as actions and notes that both are prescribed by a supreme ruler or prophet for a community.

Opening with a discussion of religion centered in political community, then moving to political science, the *Book of Religion*[11] presents Alfarabi's

restructuring of political science. As in the *Enumeration of the Sciences*, two accounts are provided, but here they are preceded by an account of virtuous religion. It begins with a description of a supreme ruler whose goals are similar to those of the Prophet and an analysis of his prescriptions. The reasons for everything done by this supreme ruler are traced back to philosophy so incessantly that religion appears to depend on philosophy, theoretical as well as practical. Similarly, the art of jurisprudence, presented as providing for what the supreme ruler did not accomplish before his death, is portrayed as both dependent on practical philosophy and a part of political science.[12] Obliged to say something about practical philosophy, Alfarabi complies by again offering two accounts of political science. The deficiencies of the first resemble those that came to light in the *Enumeration of the Sciences*, but the second account provides what is needed by presenting a political science that can offer a comprehensive view of the universe and indicate what kind of practical acumen permits the one who possesses this understanding, either the supreme ruler or a successor endowed with all of his qualities, to rule wisely. Able to explain the various ranks of all the beings, it also stresses the importance of religion for uniting the citizens and for helping them attain the virtues that prolong decent political life.[13]

This view of the harmony between good government and the activity of the Prophet finds similar expression

10. See Mahdi, "Science, Philosophy, and Religion," p. 137.

11. See Alfarabi, *Kitab al-Millah wa Nusus Ukhra*, ed. Muhsin Mahdi (Beirut: Dar al-Mashriq, 1968). An English translation of this work by Charles E. Butterworth is in the new edition of *Medieval Political Philosophy: A Sourcebook*, ed. Ralph Lerner and Muhsin Mahdi (New York: Free Press of Glencoe, forthcoming).

12. See *Book of Religion*, paras. 5, 10.

13. See ibid., paras. 15-27, esp. para. 27 end.

in Avicenna's most extensive discussion of politics, that set forth at the very end of the *Metaphysics* in his *Shifa*.[14] It differs from any of the accounts to be found in Alfarabi because Avicenna is silent on the different sorts of virtuous and vicious regimes, rulerships, and civic communities. He says nothing about what distinguishes them or how to bring them about. He is equally silent about what would cause each one to cease to exist and how each one might be transformed into one opposed to it. Political science for Avicenna, at least insofar as it is presented here, centers around an explanation of the political characteristics of prophecy and divine law.

Nonetheless, the attention he gives those two subjects leads him to raise questions fundamental to politics: the nature of law, the purpose of political community, the need for sound moral life among the citizens, the importance of providing for divorce as well as for marriage, the conditions for just war, the considerations that lie behind penal laws, and the goal of human life. Avicenna's description of the way the political community arises and the provisions made for it by a ruler as wise as a prophet shows why traditional Islamic political rule is praiseworthy and alludes to what is wrong with regimes that prize freedom, the pursuit of wealth, or conquest rather than adherence to moral virtue. To underline his purpose, Avicenna constantly refers to the ruler who sets down the laws he praises here as one who gives "traditional law" (calling this lawgiver a *sannin* and his law *sunna*) or as one who gives "divine law" (calling this lawgiver a *shari'* and his law *shari'a*).

For reasons too involved to discuss here, Averroes perceives his task differently from either of his two predecessors. Seeing the pursuit of philosophy threatened in his day and saddened by the bickering between the proponents of different religious factions or sects, he attempts to show why philosophical investigation was warranted by the divine law. In the most famous of his works, *The Decisive Treatise*, he likens the lawgiver to a physician: just as the latter strives to preserve the health or cure sicknesses of the body, so does the former for the soul.[15] The lawgiver, like the physician, knows what preserves health and prevents sickness. He understands what good health is and how it can be achieved as well as how to preserve it. Because those whom he seeks to heal do not understand these things, he speaks to them in language they can understand. He no more enters into the details or the premises of his actions than the physician does of his. To gain the people's acceptance of his prescriptions, he uses whatever kind of speech the people can most readily understand—again, as does the physician.

---

14. See Avicenna, *Kitab al-Shifa, al-Ilahiyyat*, ed. G. Anawati and S. Zayid (Cairo: al-Hai'a al-'Amma li-Shu'un al-Matabi' al-Amiriyya, 1960). The discussion of politics occurs in bk. 10, chaps. 1-5.

15. See Averroes, *Kitab Fasl al-Maqal*, ed. George F. Hourani (Leiden: E. J. Brill, 1959). An English translation by Hourani is to be found in *Medieval Political Philosophy* (1963), pp. 163-86. For what follows, see the translation by Charles E. Butterworth forthcoming in the new edition of *Medieval Political Philosophy*, paras. 53-56.

The problem, notes Averroes, is that many jurists and theologians do not understand that the lawgiver or prophet spoke indirectly and thus try to explain things to the people that only confuse them. By this analogy, Averroes shows why one cannot interpret all the words of the Prophet literally and points to the need for those so qualified to investigate the health and sickness of the soul as well as the ways to preserve or attain the one and avoid or repel the other. To do so is to understand the Prophet's goal with respect to the people for whom he legislated, for the Prophet's prescriptions are his laws, and they presuppose political community. Like Alfarabi and Avicenna before him, then, Averroes seeks to preserve philosophical inquiry because it provides the understanding and explanation of what is sound about that legislation.

None of these philosophers explicitly rails against the rulers of the day, although Averroes does suggest on occasion that things are not as good as they might be in "these cities in this time of ours."[16] Their goal is not to urge radical change or to cajole actual rulers to act better by offering advice about how to rule, but to show what goals are to be pursued by a good ruler and what conduces to the achievement of those goals. For them, the purpose of living together in community is to acquire the human excellences impossible to at-tain in solitary existence, and they investigate how the prescriptions of the Prophet as well as the practices traditionally derived from them lead to these excellences. Because the goal of association is excellence, intellectual as well as moral, rule by one who has such excellence is preferable. Though it is admittedly difficult to find rulers so qualified, rule by such a one remains the standard. Similarly, the pursuit of excellence—not the pursuit of freedom, wealth, or conquest—remains the standard. The philosophers of the Arabic or Islamic distant past stand out as guides to that goal, guides ever cognizant of its arduous demands and abundant riches. Moreover, acutely aware of the intellectual and moral differences between individuals and the groups they constitute, these philosophers see no reason to expect much from popular government.

THE RECENT PAST

Apart from Ibn Khaldun and perhaps Mulla Sadra, political reflection in the Arabic or Islamic tradition languished during the next six and a half centuries. Philosophical speculation was focused on metaphysical questions and issues of personal morality. When it did turn to politics, it usually took the form of particular advice to rulers and was directed to questions that would help them preserve their own reign. Only with the advent of Jamal al-Din al-Afghani (1837-97) does it return to the larger questions raised by Alfarabi, Avicenna, and Averroes.

Al-Afghani is troubled by the weakness that characterizes the Is-

16. This occurs above all in his *Commentary on Plato's "Republic"*; see Charles E. Butterworth, *Philosophy, Ethics, and Virtuous Rule: A Study of Averroes' Commentary on Plato's "Republic"* (Cairo: American University in Cairo Press, 1986), pp. 12-13, 87-88.

lamic world in his day. Dominated by Western imperialist powers, even in their own lands, Arab and Muslim rulers seem to have lost all memory of the grandeur and greatness that were once theirs and to have no idea of how they might regain their former rank. His challenge to thoughtful Muslims, first formulated in lectures to university audiences and then distributed in occasional articles read by an educated few, won him the sympathy of Muhammad 'Abduh (1849-1905). These two eventually joined forces to launch—from Paris, because no Arab or Muslim country would tolerate al-Afghani's presence —a short-lived journal known as al-'Urwa al-wuthqa (The most solid link). In it, they argue vigorously for independence from foreign domination but see no reason to replace monarchic rule with popular government. It is their conviction that the Arab and Muslim populaces are not yet sufficiently disciplined to govern themselves well and thus still need the tutelage of a ruler who will train them in the skills needed for self-government.[17] Their total silence elsewhere in their writings about the possibility of future self-rule need not be taken as evidence that the promise here is no more than a diplomatic ploy to preserve the goodwill of otherwise sympathetic Westerners. Indeed, al-Afghani's generous concession to Ernest Renan that philosophy and religion must always be in conflict also strengthens the case for

postponing democracy, for he makes it clear that Middle Eastern peoples will not soon be ready to forsake religious guidance.[18]

The same theme is developed more extensively by 'Abduh. In fact, he bases his own political teaching on an attempt to explain the reasonableness of letting political life be guided by Islamic precepts. His famous Risalat al-tawhid (Treatise on unity) presents a coherent exposition of how Islam helps human beings to live together in society so that they may eventually attain the happiness intended for them by the Creator. 'Abduh focuses on the assistance that God offers mankind by sending prophets who show us how to get along in political community. By drawing our attention to something higher than self-preservation or immediate gain, they teach us how to work together without harming one another or causing evil. In learning to honor such a higher Being, we are prompted to love one another as fellow creatures of that Being, to control our desires, redirect our passions, and regulate our actions. Almost like another Alfarabi, 'Abduh explains what prompts the opinions the prophets ask us to believe and the actions they urge us to perform.

Whereas al-Afghani addresses his explanations to anyone who will listen, even to the supremely confident readers of the Journal des débats, his primary audience is those learned Near and Middle Easterners, Mus-

17. See "Madi al-umma wa hadiruha wa 'ilaj 'ilaliha" [The nation's past, its present, and the treating of its ills], in al-'Urwa al-wuthqa (Cairo: Dar al-'Arabi, 1957), pp. 13-21; al-Afghani, "al-Hukuma al-istibdadiyya" [Despotic government], Misr, 2/33 (1879).

18. See Ernest Renan, "L'Islamisme et la science," Journal des débats, 30 Mar. 1883; Jamal al-Din al-Afghani, "Réponse à M. Renan," ibid., 18 May 1883; Ernest Renan's own reply to al-Afghani in ibid., 19 May 1883.

lim or Christian, who suffer the degradation of imperialist rule. Even so, his references are primarily Muslim, and the past age of glory he recalls is distinctly one of Muslim hegemony. That tendency is taken further by 'Abduh, with his emphasis on the soundness of living according to Islamic precepts; but the audience is still a learned one. With Hasan al-Banna (1906-49), as with Abu al-A'la al-Mawdudi (1903-80) before him, the audience and the teaching change radically. Both speak to the masses, al-Mawdudi in order to defend Islam and to show how easily it can be applied to all problems of daily life, al-Banna in order to reform Muslims and to awaken them to what they can be as self-reliant and fully conscious followers of their faith. The change in audience and in goal are reflected in the quality of the arguments both offer, namely, ones far more rhetorical and hortatory than analytical or measured.

Each sees a need for founding an Islamic political regime. Al-Mawdudi considers it the only rule under which Muslims can live freely and fully as Muslims and thus deems it essential that the Quranic provisions for personal and communal virtue be implemented. For al-Banna, it makes no sense to deny Muslims the right to national liberation natural to all peoples; moreover, only a Muslim regime can fight against the atheism, pursuit of pleasure, self-centeredness, and relentless profit seeking that he believes will destroy all of Western society. In addition, each is responsible for the formation of groups that seek to carry out the teachings of the founder. Yet whereas the Islamic

groups patterned on al-Mawdudi's teaching arose almost accidentally, Hasan al-Banna founded the Muslim Brotherhood from the very beginning in order to spread his call to other Muslims more readily and more efficiently.

THE ISSUE BEFORE US

The spokesmen for Islamic government who succeed al-Mawdudi and al-Banna share with them the desire to speak to a larger audience and the willingness to make popular arguments. But instead of railing against non-Muslim and Western colonial or imperialist powers, these spokesmen denounce the Muslim rulers who came to power after Near and Middle Easterners were moved to act on the teachings of al-Afghani, 'Abduh, al-Mawdudi, and al-Banna. Whereas al-Mawdudi and al-Banna simply ignore the philosophical teachings of the distant tradition on which al-Afghani and 'Abduh are only too happy to rely for guidance as well as for evidence of a rich cultural past, new spokesmen such as Sayyid Qutb (1906-66) and Ruhollah Khomeini (1900-89) dismiss the older philosophers as having been too influenced by a foreign tradition to be of any assistance in an authentic Muslim undertaking. Though they thereby demonstrate that they have learned nothing from Averroes' *Decisive Treatise* and its famous rebuke of al-Ghazali for this same error, they are not in the least concerned. Their goals are to defend Islam against the aspersions cast upon it by Westerners who have failed to understand its merits, to bring about a thorough moral change in Muslims themselves, and to achieve truly Islamic self-rule rather than an imitation of socialism, as in the Egypt of Nasser combated by Qutb, or an unbridled capitalist consumerism, as in the Iran of the Shah as portrayed by Khomeini.

Now others too numerous to name follow the lead of Qutb and Khomeini. Shahrough Akhavi discusses Egypt's 'Abd al-Salam Faraj in his contribution to this volume, and Mary-Jane Deeb speaks of Tunisia's Rached Ghannouchi, Lebanon's Muhammad Hussain Fadhlallah, and Ahmad Yassin, the founder of Hamas in the Occupied Territories. Even were we to add the names of Egypt's Shaykh Kishk and Mustafa Mahmoud, the list would still not be exhausted. All those now calling for Islamic politics share the desire to replace errant rulers who have failed to enforce or to abide by the teachings of Islamic divine law, the shari'a, as well as to improve the material and spiritual well-being of fellow Muslims through encouraging their closer adherence to Islamic precepts. But despite opportunities for practical reflection afforded by current instances of Islamic rule in nations as diverse as Pakistan, Saudi Arabia, and Iran, these spokesmen have yet to set forth clear ideas about how Islamic government should function. Their rhetoric, addressed now more than ever to the unlearned masses of citizens, speaks only of what might be and ignores the practical, procedural issues of how these goals are to be reached without harming citizens along the way. It also ignores the major question of how to provide for

prudent decisions once the goal of Islamic government has been reached. To some extent, the failure to address such issues is also a result of overriding concern with reaching the goals.

Yet, properly understood, it is against precisely this tendency to ignore procedural safeguards that Western criticism of political Islam is addressed. There are other objections, of course. We in the West are more concerned with safeguarding freedom than with providing for citizen virtue. That is partly due to a prevailing confusion about what ought to be called virtue, one that has its roots in the thinkers to whom we turn for guidance about classical liberalism. Though they teach us that the greatest goods are life, liberty, and the pursuit of either property or happiness, they have little to say about the pursuit of virtue. Similarly, the high regard in which we hold life and freedom leads us to look dimly on coercive inducements to virtuous conduct—especially when those inducements threaten life or limb.

To the latter kind of procedural objections, proponents of Islamic government have a ready answer: the penalties are meant to serve as vivid signs that there are boundaries or limits that human conduct should not transgress, and before the divine law that calls for such penalties is instituted, Muslims subject to them must undergo a thorough moral reform. For such thinkers—and those in this path are only too happy to cite the teaching of Hasan al-Banna with approval—the basic preliminary to an official return to Islamic law must be a thorough moral reform of the citizenry carried out at all levels of society. But the Western criticism is not merely procedural, at least not in this sense. It goes deeper, for it raises the very question of whether moral improvement is the proper concern of government or not. Until at least the days of Muhammad 'Abduh, the philosophical foundations for considering moral improvement a proper concern of government were clear; since then, the cogent philosophical defense tends to have been rejected, but the theological one goes back to basically the same principles.

When all of these objections have been met, there is still another reason behind the Western criticism of political Islam. Whatever Western attitudes are today about imperialism and colonialism, it is clear that the West still considers itself as deserving to set the tempo for the rest of the world to follow. Patent as this is in the title and basic premise of Fukuyama's best-seller or in Binder's acknowledged presupposition that the whole world—and especially the Islamic part of it—must become politically liberal, it also prevails in the analyses of those who seek to explain what is truly fearful about calls for political Islam. Shireen T. Hunter insists, for example, that we should not consider these calls or the movements they engender as aberrations "in the social, economic, and political development of the Muslim world" that will soon pass away but should rather be alarmed about "the fundamentalists' animosity toward the great-power domination of the

present international order."[19] To this there are only two replies. One calls for greater tolerance with respect to the basic presuppositions of those who look to religion for guidance and thus serves as an especially appealing rejoinder to the proponents of liberalism.[20] The other, set forth here, points to the goals sought by those in favor of Islamicism and argues for their validity both because they are part of a higher understanding of politics that we Westerners once embraced and because the political liberalism we now follow has not shown them to be without benefit but merely difficult to achieve.

19. See Shireen T. Hunter, "Islamic Fundamentalism: What It Really Is and Why It Frightens the West," *SAIS Review*, 6:189-91, 199-200 (1986). See also R. Hrair Dekmejian, "Anatomy of Islamic Revival: Legitimacy Crisis, Ethnic Conflict, and the Search for Islamic Alternatives," *Middle East Journal*, 34:1-3 (1980); Lucien S. Vandenbroucke, "Why Allah's Zealots? A Study of the Causes of Islamic Fundamentalism in Egypt and Saudi Arabia," *Middle East Review*, 16:32, 38 (1983); Raymond A. Hinnebusch, Jr., *Egyptian Politics under Sadat: The Post-Populist Development of an Authoritarian-Modernizing State* (Cambridge: Cambridge University Press, 1985), pp. 199-200; Hassan Bakr A. Hassan, "Islamic Revivalism and Its Impact on the Middle East and the Superpowers," in *Culture and International Relations*, ed. Jongsuk Chay (New York: Praeger, 1990), pp. 207-8.

20. See Mona Abul-Fadl, *Islam and the Middle East: The Aesthetics of a Political Inquiry* (Herndon: International Institute of Islamic Thought, 1990), pp. 38-39 and passim. In this light, Rousseau's single negative dogma needed in civil religion is instructive; see *Social Contract*, bk. 4, chap. 8, last three paras.

ANNALS, *AAPSS*, 524, November 1992

Popular Islam

By PATRICK D. GAFFNEY

ABSTRACT: The current wave of religiously motivated protest movements throughout the Islamic world has frequently been associated with popular Islam. This concept of a popular, as opposed to an official, practice has deep roots, however, extending back to the formative period of the Muslim tradition. Classically, the emergence of a clerical elite defined in terms of their functions in the fields of law, education, and administration as well as religion coincided with the rise of a parallel folk piety inspired by Sufism which adapted Islam to local circumstances. The sweeping changes of the last two centuries have undermined many of the old religious institutions belonging to both these spheres. But the overall structures of social relations have largely remained within the context of the nation-state. With few and short-lived exceptions, rural peasants and urban masses who continue to regard Islam as the primary basis for their identity have not responded positively to the summons of the current revival. On the other hand, Islamicists, despite divisions among themselves, have established their importance. Popular Islam persists therefore as a vital concept pointing in two directions.

Patrick D. Gaffney is currently an associate professor in the Department of Anthropology and a faculty fellow at the Kroc Institute for International Peace Studies at the University of Notre Dame. He has conducted extensive field research, especially in Egypt. His publications include articles on the ethnography of Islamic preaching, the history of religious bureaucracies, the function of mosques, social movements, popular culture, and human rights.

THE term "popular Islam" suggests a variety of meanings across different fields of discourse. Most generally, it occurs as a term of contrast. It describes one set of phenomena presumably associated with the populace or the masses over against another set joined to the elite. On another level, however, as a unit of analysis, popular Islam also serves as a symbolic index for the assertion of authority. It is evoked with respect to such contested areas as orthodoxy, authenticity, legitimacy, social justice, modernity, alignment, popularity, and accountability.

With respect to the sociopolitical aspects of religion, the term appears with both of these connotations. In most classical contexts, referring to beliefs and practices as popular usually denotes complexes held to be aberrant, such as the veneration of saints; the use of amulets, charms, and oracles; or the often spectacular performances of certain Sufi brotherhoods. This conservative approach typically dismisses these activities as products of ignorance or superstition. The late shaykh of al-Azhar, Dr. Abd al-Halim Mahmud, for instance, held popular Islam to be a sort of oxymoron. It consisted simply of abuses, which he disparaged as "the religion of the streets," which needed reform.

For those who study religion from an anthropologically informed perspective, the term is essentially neutral, conveying empirical facts. In general, "popular Islam" alludes to the derivative and synthetic patterns of the little tradition characteristic of communities on the periphery rather than at the center of a putative Islamic civilization. The category includes those forms of Islamic expression typical of the commoners in urban neighborhoods, villages, or tribal settings. Presumably it reflects the adaptations of localized social structures and indigenous cultural values to the so-called great tradition of the literate, urban upper class, which supposedly embodies the normative standard.

Increasingly, however, the term "popular Islam" has prompted considerable debate over its definition and its usefulness. Nevertheless, most scholars continue to agree on the importance of distinguishing between what Abdul Hamid el-Zein has called different "Islams" even while controversy persists over terminology, methods, and interpretation.[1]

More recently, popular Islam has arisen as a concept of major significance in discussions of the ideological, social, political, and economic tensions that currently challenge many regimes and to some extent the entire international order of the contemporary Middle East. Here, in addition to serving as a term of description and analysis with sometimes contradictory applications, popular Islam is frequently connected with various militant groups that manifest this link in all manner of names, titles, and slogans. Explicit evocations of a "popular" base by Arabic designa-

1. Abdul Hamid el-Zein, "Beyond Ideology and Theology: The Search for the Anthropology of Islam," in *Annual Review of Anthropology*, ed. Bernard J. Siegel (Palo Alto, CA: Annual Reviews, 1977), pp. 227-54; J.D.Y. Peel and C. C. Steward, eds., *"Popular Islam" South of the Sahara* (Manchester: Manchester University Press, 1985); Jacques Waardenburg, "Official and Popular Religion in Islam," *Social Compass*, 25(3-4):315-41 (1978).

tions such as "popular front" (*jabha sha'biyya*) or, in Persian, of the "masses" (*tudeh*) are usually avoided since they are tainted as Marxist vocabulary. But Islamicist groups often project an equivalent image of populism by resort to other phrases.

For instance, names may connote the broadest possible appeal regardless of a group's limited scope or the exclusive nature of its actual membership. Illustrations include Hizballah, or Party of God, a militant nucleus of marginalized Lebanese Shiites; Jama'at al-Muslimin, or Society of Muslims, a tiny clandestine band once operating in Upper Egypt; and Ittijah al-Islami, or Islamic Trend, a Tunisian protest movement made up largely of students, young intellectuals, and middle-class businessmen. Thus popular Islam has come to be variously identified with the perceived properties of everything signaled by Islamic fundamentalism.

Unfortunately, this largely journalistic or propagandistic use of popular Islam has severely reduced the concept's richness and its protean implications on several scores. First, it has led to an overall shrinking of focus. As a result, use of the term frequently encourages mistaken impressions of uniformity, continuity, or even inevitability with regard to events billed as Islamic in quite different settings. Sometimes wildly distorted misunderstandings of both historical forces and sociological scale follow. The naive anticipation, widely echoed a decade ago, of a Middle Eastern domino effect, with the Islamic Republic in Iran as the ready paradigm advancing ineluctably upon other lands, exemplified this myopia.

Second, the conflation of popular Islam with a quite small number of actual revolutionary elements tends to freeze the elusive and dynamic aspects represented by the concept. It flattens into one dimension the many facets of consciousness and the diverse avenues for mobilization relevant to the long-established contrast between popular and official Islam. Furthermore, it overlooks the fluid character of the relationships that define this pairing not as static entities but as formal institutions and informal frameworks that may change places over time, that may depend upon and reinforce each other, or that may fuse and eventually reappear only to divide again along new lines.

Finally, to confine a discussion of popular Islam to "sacred rage" (*ghadba li-allah*) risks both confusion and diversion. It invites the drawing of false conclusions based on errors of the sort that Georg Simmel warned against as the misplacing of the "teleological accent." To single out a few banner incidents chosen on the basis of the size of the headlines they generate often feeds an impression that politicized Islam is the reason behind the general instability throughout the region, whereas, in fact, this perception mistakes effect for cause.

ISLAM AS POPULAR AND OFFICIAL

The relation of Islamic militancy to the uncertain status quo is indirect. While dissident activism expressed in religious terms does pose an acknowledged security dilemma, this movement is far more the result than the origin of these troubles. Islamic resurgence represents a reaction to a tangled history of regional domestic interaction that has left the peoples of the Middle East generally feeling fragmented, violated, frustrated, and demoralized. The causes of these problems are revealed not in the tactics of any particular confrontation, but in the contradictions between ideals and expectations, on the one hand, and present life circumstances, on the other.

Because Islam by definition encompasses both the mundane and the spiritual, it is not surprising that it should play a central and public role among Muslims. What is remarkable is the changing character of the Islam that asserts these moral and political prerogatives. Clearly, the right to represent Islam and to speak authoritatively in its name is now contested by differing parties. Some view the outcome of this struggle in uncompromising and absolutist terms, including, not infrequently, the sounding of millennial evocations naming the Madhi or, for Shiites, the Imam.

But the language of Islam is also deeply embedded in the fabric of both official functions and everyday activity. Virtually all Muslim nations prescribe Islam as the state religion, and they directly subsidize mosques together with their clergy, as well as religious schools, publications, and special festivals. Thus to presuppose that popular Islam as a concept always belongs on one side or the other of a given crisis situation, whether it be the government—as in Iran, the Sudan, Libya, and Saudi Arabia—or the opposition—as in Algeria, Tunisia, Egypt, and Syria—is to deprive

the term at the outset of a great deal of its potential value.

To recover the usefulness of the contrast between these two levels, one high and the other low, requires therefore a pulling back from the contemporary barricades and the stridency of rhetorical battlegrounds. Assuming this more detached perspective, the background of this conventional dualism can be traced in two directions.

First, in doctrinal terms, the revealed texts themselves specify a division within the *umma*, that is, the idealized community, on the basis of piety. In the Quran (49:14-17), for instance, an explicit distinction is made between "Muslims" (*muslimun*) and "believers" (*mu'minun*). The former epithet refers to those who have technically converted by proclaiming their submission to God and his Prophet but who are lax in the performance of faith's duties. The latter term denotes those who have dedicated themselves wholly in obedience to carrying out the will of the creator. Believers are declared morally superior to mere Muslims. Interestingly, in its original context this dichotomy also includes a social marker, for these verses are addressed in reproach specifically to bedouins.

Second, this dualism asserts itself historically. Comparable divisions arose after the death of the Prophet that specify social gradations based on the closeness of followers to the Messenger of God when he lived. The measure for such status was understood to entail one's biography and behavior as modeled on the Prophet's words and deeds. But piety was also implicit in one's knowledge of those remembered precedents that came to be known as traditions (*hadith*). As the Islamic imperium rapidly expanded, bringing with it the complexities of governing an extensive polyglot realm, the rivalries of tensions within that first generation of Muslims that had been redirected outward began to resurface within the community. Civil war erupted, shattering the pristine unity of the *umma*.

After defeating the legitimists who had supported Ali, the fourth and last of the Rightly Guided Caliphs, the triumphant Umayyads established a dynasty in Damascus based as much on tribal loyalties as on religion. Only after this rupture did a self-conscious corpus of Islamic norms begin to emerge, replacing the earlier "silent" living practice. Remarking on this development, Fazlur Rahman points to it as the pivotal moment in Islamic history, when "the Sunna was being explicitly formulated not only in respect to its content but also in the concept of the Sunna itself."[2] Simultaneously and by consequence, the opposing concept of innovation, or *bid'a*, was also gaining definite doctrinal and jural status.

The codification of the *sunna*, which together with the Quran constitutes the two sources of the *shari'a*, or "Islamic law," occurred over the next three centuries. Accompanying this process was the forging of the great legal and theological sciences specific to Islam. A distinct social class of scholars trained in these disciplines also began to establish itself. Increasingly, its members assumed important functions throughout urban Islamic society, especially in the fields of law, education, and administration, in addition to religion. By the eleventh century, a vast system with the *madrasa*, or "school," as its core institution had evolved into the formation of the *'ulama'*, or "scholars," as a corporate status group comparable to the clergy of medieval Europe. This learned elite constituted the origin of what has since become known as establishment or official Islam.

LEGALISTIC AND MYSTICAL AUTHORITY

Theories of political order formulated in the classical era tend to portray the *'ulama'* as responsible for assuring that no ruler acts in a way that prevents the application of the *shari'a*. As the guardians, arbiters, and teachers of the law, they embodied the aspiration for a just and virtuous community even while caliphs from roughly the tenth century onward saw their authority steadily usurped by successions of military chiefs and provincial autocrats. Thus, as the Abbasid empire waned and finally collapsed, these religio-juridical specialists continued to represent the source of Islamic legitimacy for any power elite. This role had several public ritual elements. As preachers, they regularly confirmed a ruler's authority by pronouncing his name in an obligatory blessing at the Friday sermon. Likewise, by custom, they ratified the loyalty of the people upon the inauguration of new ruler through an oath known as the *bai'a*.

2. Fazlur Rahman, *Islam* (Garden City, NY: Doubleday, 1968), p. 60.

During this same period, while these men of the pen flourished, separate yet parallel developments were occurring among the rural and lower classes. For the Muslim masses, the legalistic refinements of the 'ulama' grew increasingly remote and irrelevant to their needs. Coinciding with the rise of sophisticated Islamic jurisprudence and speculative theology, a second trend had taken root that concentrated directly on the spiritual and mystical dimensions of Islam. Thus, throughout the same long summer and autumn of the Abbasid golden age, an extensive Sufi tradition was also being elaborated.

Marked by its own distinctive beliefs, institutions, and forms of organization, often fusing with other lines of solidarity such as kin groups, village and neighborhood bonds, or guild membership, this Sufi ethos came to permeate the entire fabric of popular life. Open to inspiration from Jewish, Christian, Gnostic, Hindu, and animist sources, while always borrowing freely from the learning of 'ulama' who were themselves frequently drawn by the charisma and lore of the salahun, or "holy men," Sufism produced a satisfying vision of divine-human relations. In fact, in many settings, its teachings and ritual practices all but engulfed the legalistic form of religion. It was primarily through Sufism and not the shari'a that Islam spread gradually across central Asia, into the subcontinent, to Indonesia, and across sub-Saharan Africa.

Moreover, Sufism, in addition to its abundant esoteric and introspective features, produced its own coherent, if sometimes implicit, theories on the use and abuse of power. One such subterranean doctrine asserts that the world is governed by unseen holy men whose authority derives from their proximity to the Prophet, his family, and his friends. Those who succeed in winning and maintaining the favor of these saints find that their patron not only guides and protects them but bestows blessings that may include miracles.[3]

Concomitant with these notions is the belief that certain rulers are placed in power and then sustained through similar mystical patronage. Amounting to a claim of divine right, this conviction is central among Shiites for whom the "hidden Imam" acts as a determinant political idea. But it also plays a formidable role, notably during crises situations, in the popular appeal of King Hassan of Morocco, for example, or King Hussein of Jordan, both of whom cite pedigrees as descendants of the Prophet.[4]

Finally, this bifurcation is widely reflected in Islam's great philosophical heritage. Alfarabi, Avicenna, Averroes, and others who built upon the ethics and politics of Greeks typically characterize the "city" as divided into two distinct orders, "the elect few and the common masses" (al-khassa wa al-'amma). Likewise, the seminal thesis of Ibn Khaldun

3. Edward B. Reeves, *The Hidden Government: Ritualism, Clientism, and Legitimation in Northern Egypt* (Salt Lake City: University of Utah Press, 1990); Clifford Geertz, *Islam Observed: Religious Development in Morocco and Indonesia* (Chicago: University of Chicago Press, 1968).

4. Dale F. Eickelman, "Religion in Polity and Society," in *The Political Economy of Morocco*, ed. I. William Zartman (New York: Praeger, 1987), pp. 84-97.

rests on the dyadic interaction of two populations, that of the desert and that of the city, which undergo cyclic transformations through the changing structures of their solidarity.[5]

ISLAM AS A
POLITICAL IDEOLOGY

The dramatic spread of the Ottoman empire out of Anatolia starting in the early sixteenth century only exacerbated Islam's dichotomous character. The two-tiered quality of its society was formalized in the evolution of sultanism, which drew clear boundaries between an elite stratum consisting of the court, with its appended military and its civilian administration, over against a popular stratum made up of the administered. These stark divisions were reinforced by numerous markings. Historians of Turkish literature point, for instance, to the gap that separated palace culture, which was "esoteric both in language and subject matter . . . comprehensible to but a selected few . . . unconcerned with the happenings of day to day life," from a "folk" culture in local vernaculars.[6]

Law was likewise partitioned. The *shari'a* or its functional derivative, which was understood popularly as Islam, served as the moral foundation for ordinary community relationships while a second system of *qanun* laws emanated from the Sul-

5. E.I.J. Rosenthal, *Political Thought in Medieval Islam* (New York: Cambridge University Press, 1962).

6. Walter Andrews, *Poetry's Voice, Society's Song* (Seattle: University of Washington Press, 1985), p. 16, cited in Serif Mardin, "The Just and the Unjust," *Daedalus*, 120(3):118 (1991).

tan, the great lawgiver. An economic border also split the society in that Ottoman officials did not pay taxes, whereas, with few exceptions, all others did. Ottoman clergy were also bifurcated. However, as the empire declined in the face of external pressures from European imperialism and internal ethnic and regional assertiveness, their status, especially at the upper tier of the societal gulf, began to erode markedly.

Even while the clergy's traditional role as intermediaries between the elite and the masses persisted, the *'ulama'* as a learned class were steadily losing their rapport with the wider populace. Their place as advocates for justice on the part of the community was being taken over by others whose authority rested not on their academic competence but on their spiritual leadership within the realm of the popular brotherhoods.

The sweeping transformations that brought an uneasy end to Ottoman hegemony in the nineteenth and twentieth centuries also had a profound impact on the social contours of religion. Most decisive was the mass appeal of nationalism, which was variously grafted onto Islam during the colonial period. A host of initiatives urged reforms in order to revive the *umma* and to check the overwhelming advance of Western influence and exploitation seen as undermining the integrity of traditionally Muslim lands. This surge of nationalist enthusiasm began with secular elites, such as the Young Turks, who sought to strengthen and modernize their own societies through education, industry, political change, and social progress modeled along Western lines. But the rhetoric of the spokesmen for this new future was thoroughly steeped in such Islamic ideals as liberty, justice, unity, honor, responsibility, order, and *maslaha* or "public welfare."[7]

This translation of aspirations, rooted in the idiom of religion made into a political ideology articulated by an emerging indigenous elite, prompted fundamental changes in many spheres including the diminution of many attitudes and practices that were long synonymous with popular Islam. The meteoric decline of the influence of Sufi organizations that coincided with the ascent of the nationalist agenda has been seen by many as a process of virtually direct conversion. Marshall Hodgson has remarked, for instance, that the "toning down of all of the more emotional, and much of the more collective side of religion [meant that] as emotions were withdrawn from cult, they were invested in politics."[8]

POPULAR ISLAM
AND NATIONALISM

In many cases this redirecting of fervor from the spiritual to earthly rituals spurred armed conflicts. Rebellions

and liberation struggles have brought *jihad* and the modern iconography of revolution (*thawra*) together in the forging of "popular" regimes in the Middle East. At times, allegedly grass-roots religious movements attained power—such as was claimed in Pakistan, Saudi Arabia, Libya, and lately Iran—so that a "purified" or "reformed" religious practice is, at least initially, formally installed.

But this purported reshaping of popular Islam into a lasting political system has inevitably failed. The realities of inequality, underdevelopment, ethnic and sectarian division, lack of opportunity, unemployment, poverty, factionalism, corruption, censorship, autocratic rule, and disregard for human rights have arisen out of the crucible of postcolonial Third World experience to dash the original exalted hopes at least for the many have-nots. Just as nationalism has brought about independence, as well as the political fragmentation of the Islamic world, so, too, colonial rule and its successor, the world market system, have brought some tokens of modernity along with a degrading economic dependency and moral vulnerability.

These complex processes also dealt catastrophic blows to the traditionally sanctioned structures that had bridged the gap between popular and official Islam. As the monopolies held by the religious establishment over such fields as education, welfare services, and the courts ended, and as they lost control of their once considerable resources, derived from mortmain trusts known as *waqf*, their political relevance dimmed as well. With nationalism supplanting reli-

7. Serif Mardin, *The Genesis of Young Ottoman Thought: A Study in the Modernization of Turkish Political Ideas* (Princeton, NJ: Princeton University Press, 1962); J. M. Ahmad, *The Intellectual Origins of Egyptian Nationalism* (New York: Oxford University Press, 1960); Tamara Sonn, *Between Qur'an and Crown: The Challenge of Political Legitimacy in the Arab World* (Boulder, CO: Westview Press, 1990).

8. Marshall G. S. Hodgson, *The Venture of Islam: The Gunpowder Empires and Modern Times* (Chicago: University of Chicago Press, 1974), 3:285.

gion as the focus for loyalty, the perennial distinction between popular and official Islam seemed to slip from view. First, collective energy was fixed on the expulsion of foreign masters whose illegitimacy was most fully demonstrated in their exclusion from the *umma*, now constituted as the burgeoning nation. Then later, in the 1950s and 1960s, the immediacies of economic and social development combined with regional hostilities, particularly broad support for the struggle of the Palestinians, caused the older divisions to pass into the background.

Of course, a variety of specifically Islamic reform efforts accompanied this crystallizing of political nationalism, exhibiting two general tendencies. One of these, later dubbed Islamic modernism, envisaged the prevailing European ideas of progress, liberty, justice, equality, and scientific education as entirely compatible with Islam and it sought to transplant them onto Muslim soil. Its founding visionary, Shaykh Rifaʻa al-Tahtawi (1801-73), is credited with having masterfully invested the banal term for "birthplace" (*watan*) with a new meaning as the equivalent to the French "*patrie*." In his influential writings, he incorporated all the ardor, pride, and loyalty of European patriotism in Islam, coining the axiom which has since become proverbial: "Love of country is a branch of the faith."

The second was a conservative countermove intent upon resisting the perceived alien and hostile values imported from the West. Wahhabism, in its many variants, represents this effort, which had perhaps its most

forceful leader in Hasan al-Banna, who started the Society of the Muslim Brothers. He called upon Muslims to throw off the debilitating encrustations that had sullied their communal life and resulted in defeat and degradation. They were to draw inspiration directly from the purity of early Islam, establishing an "Islamic nation" (*watan Islami*) through the comprehensive application of the *shariʻa*. By doing so, he insisted, Muslims would regain the strength and prosperity of that blessed original era when the community was united and Islam reigned triumphant.

Neither Islamic modernism nor its traditionalist counterpart, which came to be known broadly as Islamic fundamentalism, were ever really mass movements. Both, however, strongly influenced public opinion, especially among the educated youth and *evolués* who had earlier embraced the cause of nationalism but continued to ask questions about its ultimate direction. Both also contributed to the general restlessness that mounted through the middle of this century as the anticipated benefits of national independence in both moral and material terms were constantly postponed. Through newspapers, books, and pamphlets, but most cogently through the spread of a distinctly modern form of association, the *jamaʻiyya*, or "voluntary benevolent society," the tenets of a loosely conceived Islamic alternative were advanced. These practical and highly flexible associations served as a channel for local religiously motivated initiatives to establish schools, clubs, cooperatives, welfare services, and, most notably, mosques.

It has been the rapidly accelerating increase in the number of mosques sponsored by these associations that has lately charged with extraordinary significance a double classification system that had been evolving quietly throughout this century. In brief, while details vary from country to country, a general distinction has emerged that defines mosques as either belonging to the government (*masjid hukumi*) or as independent or, as it is often translated, somewhat misleadingly, "private" (*masjid ahli*).

In theory, this distinction points to the agency that subsidizes and therefore administers the mosque. But practically, the difference for Muslims in recent decades has revolved more around the two types of preachers involved. In the first case, it is a religious functionary, trained in an official institute and then appointed and supervised by the state. Those who preach in independent mosques, by contrast, are chosen by a given mosque's patron, which in the case of a *jama'iyya*, is its congregation. Thus mosques of this second type have often provided platforms for dissent in the absence of other public vehicles for effective protest.

But it gravely oversimplifies matters to say that this distinction between mosques reproduces the contrast of official and popular Islam. For, in fact, many prominent Islamicist spokesmen hold pulpits in government mosques, where they preach sermons brimming with half-submerged cues conveying unmistakable sympathy for increasing Islamization. Most are moderates, but not all, including the renowned Shaykh Abd al-Hamid Kishk of Cairo. Although long banned from his country's broadcast media and frequently restrained in other ways, including occasional arrest, not only does this pyrotechnic orator, known for his barbed and defiant indictments of officials, continue to preach regularly before crowds of thousands at a government mosque, but his sermons on bootlegged cassette recordings enjoy a colossal circulation from Marrakech to Muscat.[9]

ISLAMIC STATES AND MUSLIM CITIZENS

Seen in retrospect, the Six Day War of 1967 was the cataclysm that toppled the collective confidence in the golden promises of nationalism throughout the Islamic world. In confronting the humiliation, the deprivation, and the utter perplexity that followed what seemed an incomprehensible military defeat, an incisive moral verdict was discerned. In the 1970s, the Islamicist agenda began to find a newly receptive public especially among that same educated class that had imbibed the imported tonics of liberating socialism or liberal capitalism, only to find them toxic.[10] Many were inclined to return to religious imperatives and they re-

9. Gilles Kepel, *Muslim Extremism in Egypt: The Prophet and Pharaoh* (Berkeley: University of California Press, 1985), pp. 172-90; Johannes J. G. Jansen, *The Neglected Duty: The Creed of Sadat's Assassins and Islamic Resurgence in the Middle East* (New York: Macmillan, 1986), pp. 121-50.

10. Jalal Al-i Ahmad, *Occidentosis: A Plague from the West* (Berkeley, CA: Mizan Press, 1984).

sponded favorably to the refurbished slogan of the Muslim Brothers, "Islam is the solution."

Numerous regimes sought to co-opt this groundswell while some leaders attempted to harness it for short-term political motives. Sadat was one of the latter as he encouraged Islamicist consolidation and activism in the early 1970s as a foil to the strong Arab socialist cadres on campuses, within the party, and in professional syndicates. But by the late 1970s, in Egypt and elsewhere, after Islamicist forces had far exceeded their limited usefulness to those in power, it had become extremely difficult to contain the mounting enthusiasm. This trend has since continued, although not by the repetition of Iran's unique experience.

Thus Saad Eddin Ibrahim, reviewing trends in the 1980s, has concluded that "religious popularism is proving to be the functional equivalent of Nasser's national socialism."[11] But the mobilization this experienced observer here calls "popularism" must not be confounded with popular Islam in the broadest sense. For to do so would be to ignore vital differences in the historical context of these two movements and to presuppose a "privileging of ideology" at the expense of attention to social dynamics that supply the concept of popular Islam with its greatest advantages.[12]

Clearly, those currently claiming to speak for Islam in political contests regard themselves as representatives of the moral authority rooted in a united community of believers. The state, presumably, is their adversary. But this perception of a solid bloc of Islamicists in conflict with a fixed opponent, the government, can be quite misleading. For one thing, such a static view renders bizarre or literally incoherent a sequence of headlines such as "Algeria Chooses Islam"[13] when noting election returns, only to be followed shortly thereafter with "Algeria Sends Muslims a Message"[14] when reporting that the Islamic Salvation Front had been suppressed. Here, references to the rulers, the nation, the religion, and some of its adherents collide in a free-for-all of semantic slippage.

In fact, not only does the Islamicist movement remained divided along the familiar lines of traditionalism and modernism already noted, but many positions have grown more radical. Islamic fundamentalists have been increasingly influenced by theorists such as Abd al-Salam Yasin of Morocco, Umr Abd al-Rahman of Egypt, and Sa'id Hawwa of Syria, who have gone beyond the view of Sayyid Qutb in his judgment that our times are a match for or worse than the *jahiliyya*, that is, the age of ignorance prior to the coming of Islam. They draw the implication that all "human government" is blasphemous, that piety requires revolution, and, in the

11. Saad Eddin Ibrahim, "Egypt's Islamic Activism in the 1980's," *Third World Quarterly*, 10:684 (1988).

12. Edmund Burke III, "Islam and Social Movements: Methodological Reflections," in *Islam, Politics and Social Movements*, ed. Edmund Burke III and Ira Lapidus (Berkeley: University of California Press, 1988), p. 26.

13. *New York Times*, 3 Jan. 1992.
14. *Chicago Tribune*, 18 Jan. 1992.

extreme, that present leaders can be deemed in the condition of apostasy.[15]

Islamic modernists, on the other hand, pressing for the opening and restructuring of their societies, demand greater political participation, reform through decentralization, broader economic liberalization, a priority upon social justice, and more pluralism and tolerance. Taking democratization or, in Islamic terms, *shura* or "consultation" as their chief demand, they seek to restore confidence in government after decades of discredited military regimes. Furthermore, they tend to regard themselves, being the leading proponents of this delicate transformation, as at least implicitly the most suitable candidates to effect its eventual realization.

WHICH ISLAM IS UNDERGOING A REVIVAL?

But it is important to note that neither of the variously shaded components of this movement draws pervasive or consistent support from the masses. In fact, the general perception among the rural poor has been that issues such as the veiling of women, interest-free banking, the banning of alcohol, the closing of nightclubs, and regular attendance at mosques, which preoccupy the urban Islamicists, are virtually irrelevant to them. Rather, as al-Sadiq al-Mahdi has cogently put it, "the masses have always regarded Islam as the basis of their identity [and] the source of their morality."[16] In their

view, it is the elite who have fallen prey to foreign acculturation and the West's corrupting models of development. If an Islamic revival is needed somewhere, it is not among those who have never fallen away from it in the first place.

Furthermore, the heavy emphasis of Islamicists on the refuting of the godless, alien, unjust, and immoral contents of so many modern "isms" points to another perceived deficiency of the movement, namely, its penchant for negativism. While it has proven capable of opposing programs and denying legitimacy to regimes, it has never succeeded in elaborating concrete and constructive alternatives upon which Islamic activists themselves could agree. In part, surely, this shortcoming stems from the unresolved contradictions within the movement itself. But looking from the bottom up, this inability may also be evidence of another sort of cleavage.

The use of Islam as a political discourse that brings together liberals and conservatives, radicals and reactionaries across regional and generational lines may itself be a key factor in the exclusion of the masses from this movement. Insofar as these activists have arrogated to themselves the symbols of Islam as indicative of the popular will, they presume to translate the aspirations of the lower classes into political force. On the other hand, the fact that the masses resist cooperation and seem largely unmoved or even alienated by these processes might also suggest that those for whom Islam has always been "the basis of their identity" do

15. Shireen T. Hunter, ed., *The Politics of Islamic Revivalism* (Bloomington: Indiana University Press, 1988).

16. Al-Sadiq al-Mahdi, "Islam—Society and Change," *Voices of Resurgent Islam*, ed.

John L. Esposito (New York: Oxford University Press, 1983), p. 231.

not feel themselves summoned by the major themes of this revival. In this sense, the inability of Islamicists to clarify their message, whether it is the "corrupt" elite or the "backward" masses who have deserted Islam, stands as a primary liability on both fronts.

Since activists can effectively unify only around dissent, their ranks have frequently been broken by government moves that co-opt or suppress selected parts of the movement. But at the same time, by refusing to recognize the deeply felt legitimacy of popular Islam among those with an undisturbed assurance of their relative moral integrity, Islamicists distance themselves from the very population they claim to represent. In the end, therefore, in the eyes of "the rural majority in Islamic countries . . . revivalists are one segment of the elite doing battle with another segment of the elite, while unjustly condemning the masses as deficient religiously."[17]

But this general disinterest on the part of the masses in an essentially urban struggle against corruption and tyranny should not be taken for mere social stagnation or inertia. In fact, in addition to the massive rates of migration and dislocation affecting rural populations, life everywhere in the countryside is rapidly being drawn into an ever tighter web of economic interdependency, political centralization, and cultural syncretism. Popular Islam as a set of distinct practices and beliefs continues

17. Abdulwahab Saleh Babeair, "Contemporary Islamic Revivalism: A Movement of a Moment," *Journal of Arab Affairs*, 9:137 (1990).

therefore to change. The old ways marked by folkloric rituals with their aura of magic around localized devotional centers have long been giving way, albeit at times reluctantly, to patterns of observance more in conformity with the *sunna*.

But this considerable upgrading of Islamic expression may not indicate a comparable shift in the structure of societal relations. The corps of juroreligious scholars of old who functioned as intermediaries between multiple levels of a highly stratified society have, for all practical purposes, disappeared. In the nationalist vision of a society built on equality, the *'ulama'* has become superfluous as rational bureaucracies have replaced primary relationships of kinship and patronage.

In this sense, the emergence of a new and increasingly institutionalized Islamic voice occupying the moral and political space between the populace and the governing elite may offer an important clue as to how the current Islamic resurgence or revival is authentic in its own way. It is not necessarily doomed just because it has not incited the sudden arousal of popular Islam from its presumed fourteen centuries of slumber. Rather, its achievement has been the restoration, however incomplete and experimental, of a composite of self-consciously committed guardians, instructors, preachers, and arbiters who define their social responsibility in terms of their privileged relation to the *shari'a*. This reestablishment and reconfiguration of the *'ulama'*, in mixed clerical and lay garb, who assume the right, however disparate their opinions, to speak authoritatively in the name of the *umma*, suggest that the current movement belongs as much to Islam's past as to its future. But by the same token, it argues strongly for retaining the concept of popular Islam rather than discarding it any time soon.

ANNALS, *AAPSS*, 524, November 1992

Militant Islam and
the Politics of Redemption

By MARY-JANE DEEB

ABSTRACT: Militant Islam has emerged in the 1980s and 1990s as a major political force to be contended with in the Middle East. It is characterized by its readiness to use violence and by the challenge it constitutes to existing political institutions. This article looks at the conditions under which five militant Islamic movements in Algeria, Tunisia, Libya, Lebanon, and the Gaza Strip and on the West Bank have emerged as a political force, and the concepts they have used to mobilize public support and to create a mass base for themselves in order to challenge leaders or governments in power. The conditions include political stagnation and the weakening of central authority, economic stagnation leading to the decline in standards of living, deteriorating security conditions, pervasiveness of Western culture, and secular states and leaders perceived as antagonistic to Islamic movements. The leaders of these movements do not portray themselves as revolutionaries trying to create a new society but rather as saviors trying to rescue the old society from self-destruction. Their ideology is an ideology of redemption.

Mary-Jane Deeb is academic director of the Omani Program at the School of International Service at the American University, Washington, D.C. She received her Ph.D. in international relations from the School of Advanced International Studies, Johns Hopkins University, and is the author of Libya's Foreign Policy in North Africa, *and coauthor with M. K. Deeb of* Libya since the Revolution: Aspects of Social and Political Development.

MILITANT Islam has emerged in the 1980s and 1990s as a major political force to be contended with in the Middle East. It is characterized by its readiness to use violence and by the challenge it constitutes to existing political institutions. Although ideologically it may not differ greatly from the earlier and somewhat more moderate Islamic movements, it is more aggressive in propounding and attempting to implement its ideas. The overwhelming success of the Islamic Salvation Front (FIS) in December 1991 in the first free elections since independence in Algeria highlights the significance of this new trend. Iran has been a Shiite Islamic republic for more than a decade, and in the Sudan the first military-Islamic government in the modern history of the Middle East came to power in 1989 by means of a coup that overthrew a democratically elected government.

This article looks at the conditions under which five Arab militant Islamic movements have emerged as a political force and at the concepts they have used to mobilize public support and to create a mass base of support for themselves in order to challenge leaders or governments in power. The basic thesis is that militant Islamic movements emerge under certain specific conditions that enable them to capture a broad audience and they capitalize on those conditions to create an ideology of redemption wherewith all societal problems can be resolved through religion.[1]

1. The specific conditions under which Shiite militant movements emerge are discussed in Juan R. I. Cole and Nikki R. Keddie, eds.,

CONDITIONS FOR THE RISE OF MILITANT ISLAM

Militant Islam has emerged under five broad conditions: the first is political stagnation and the weakening of central authority. This could be due to a loss of legitimacy with a change of leadership, as in the case of Tunisia; the failure of the ruling party to fulfill its promises or to live up to the expectations of the people, as in Algeria; the regional and international isolation of the Libyan leadership; an inability to control the political events or prevent the breakdown of law and order, as in Lebanon; or the inability of the Palestine Liberation Organization (PLO) leaders to achieve any significant gain for Palestinians despite the enormous costs of the *intifada* for the Arab population of the West Bank and Gaza.

The second condition for the emergence of Islamic militancy has been economic stagnation and decline and/or a growing gap between the haves and the have-nots. In all five cases—in Algeria, Tunisia, Libya,

Shi'ism and Social Protest (New Haven, CT: Yale University Press, 1986). Others have looked at the conditions under which Islamic movements emerge in North Africa; see, for instance, Susan Walz, "Islamist Appeal in Tunisia," *Middle East Journal*, vol. 40 (1986); Jean-Claude Vatin, "Popular Puritanism versus State Reformism: Islam in Algeria," in *Islam in the Political Process*, ed. James P. Piscatori (New York: Cambridge University Press, 1983). Abdelkader Zghal sees the Islamicist phenomenon as "a component of the ideology and the dynamics of nationalist movements." Zghal, "The New Strategy of the Movement of the Islamic Way: Manipulation or Expression of Political Culture," in *Tunisia: The Political Economy of Reform*, ed. I. William Zartman (Boulder, CO: Lynne Rienner, 1991), p. 206.

Lebanon, and the West Bank and Gaza—life became harder, unemployment increased, as did inflation, while major shortages in commodities and housing occurred and even accessibility to good health care was severely reduced. Higher education was no longer a guarantee of employment, and even the number of jobs abroad declined as did remittances to families dependent on them for survival. In Lebanon the misery was compounded by a war that impoverished large sections of the population and destroyed houses and places of work. Militant Islamic movements emerged in the 1980s as a direct outcome of the war.

The third condition under which militant Islamic movements have thrived has been a deteriorating security situation that could be caused by external or internal factors or both. In Tunisia, Israelis attacked PLO headquarters twice, and Libya supported a very serious armed attack on Gafsa; Libya was bombed by the United States in 1986 and suffered a major military defeat by Chad in 1987; Algerian-Moroccan relations were tense throughout the 1980s over the Western Sahara; insecurity was prevalent in Gaza and on the West Bank, exacerbated by the *intifada* and the Israeli reaction to it. In Lebanon the civil war threatened everyone in the country, and the air raids by Israel culminating in the 1982 invasion of Lebanon were the ultimate security threat.

What was perceived as an even greater threat to the Muslim populations of the Middle East was the insidious invasion of the region by Western culture and values. Every

night, Maghrebi television broadcast shows from Europe depicting a way of living that was different but fast becoming the model of the good life for North Africans. Western and Jewish culture were the dominant cultures in Israel, where Arab and Islamic cultures were disparaged. In Lebanon, the dominant culture by the mid-1970s in Beirut had become Western, with shops carrying the latest in fashion, music, books, and newspapers from the West; the restaurants, cafes, and nightclubs being similar to those on the other side of the Mediterranean; and the most prestigious academic institutions being American or French.

In every case, finally, the governments in power were perceived as encouraging this cultural change and as being themselves secular or paying only lip service to Islam. In Algeria, Libya, and Tunisia, the governments were seen as attempting to separate religion from politics and as harassing and persecuting Islamic organizations and their leaders. The PLO's leadership was always secular, with Christian and Muslim leaders sharing power and formulating policy for the rest of the movement. In Lebanon, the president was Christian, and the Muslim leaders came from traditional bourgeois and notable families who were westernized and secular.

It is under those conditions that strong militant Islamic movements emerged throughout the southern Mediterranean claiming to be able to save Muslims from the political, economic, social, and cultural problems they were facing in their bewildering and fast-changing societies.

THE POLITICS
OF REDEMPTION

There is nothing new in such movements. Max Weber, in "The Economic Ethic of the World Religions," noted:

The conception of the idea of redemption as such is very old, if one understands by it a liberation from distress, hunger, drought, sickness, and ultimately from suffering and death. Yet redemption attained a specific significance only where it expressed a systematic and rationalized "image of the world" and represented a stand in the face of the world.[2]

The militant Islamic movements that emerged in the region in the last decade and a half offered to save Muslims from those very conditions that had enabled them to mobilize public opinion in the first place. They did not portray themselves as revolutionaries trying to create a new society but rather as saviors trying to save the old society from self-destruction. This may explain why they look back to a golden age to which they wish to return, rather than forward to a new age that they want to create. In the final analysis, the two processes may be the same, and the retrospective movement may be as revolutionary as the forward-looking one, but, at the outset at least, the conception of what each is trying to achieve is different.

RELIGION AND
POLITICS IN ALGERIA

Although Islam became the religion of the state under the new Algerian Constitution after independence,

the *shari'a*, or Islamic law, was not made an integral part of the legal system of the state, nor were Muslim jurists allowed to play an independent role in legislative matters on the national level. Instead, a minister of religious affairs was appointed by the Algerian leaders to head a bureaucratic organization that had the final authority to appoint or dismiss clergymen, review Friday sermons, administer religious endowments, control religious publications, and set up Islamic institutions of higher learning.[3]

In 1964, an Islamic militant group, al-Qiyam (Values), with links to the Algerian Muslim Brothers, emerged and became a precursor of the Islamic fundamentalists of the 1980s. It called for a more visible role for Muslim practices in society and opposed Western cultural manifestations in clothing and entertainment in Algeria.[4] One of its leaders, Muhammad Khider, was a founding member of the National Liberation Front (FLN), who had broken away from the party and set up the nucleus of an opposition to Ben Bella and

2. H. H. Gerth and C. Wright Mills, eds., *From Max Weber: Essays in Sociology* (London: Routledge & Kegan Paul, 1964), p. 280.

3. For a discussion of the role of Islam in Algerian society, see Jean-Claude Vatin, *L'Algérie politique: Histoire et société*, 2d ed. (Paris: Presses de la Fondation Nationale des Sciences Politiques, 1983); Christiane Souriau, ed., *Le Maghreb musulman en 1979* (Paris: Centre National de la Recherche Scientifique, 1981); Ali Merad, *Le réformisme musulman en Algérie de 1925 à 1940* (Paris: Mouton, 1967); Susan E. Marshall, "Islamic Revival in the Maghreb: The Utility of Tradition for Modernizing Elites," *Studies in Comparative International Development*, 14:95-108 (1979).

4. Raymond Vallin, "Muslim Socialism in Algeria," *Man, State and Society in the Contemporary Maghrib* (New York: Praeger, 1973), p. 56.

later to Boumedienne. The movement was eventually suppressed by the Boumedienne regime, and Khider was assassinated in 1967.

By the end of the 1970s, Ahl al-Da'wa (People of the Call), an autonomous Islamic movement with strong links to the original al-Qiyam movement, began to voice the dissatisfaction of many Algerians with state policies and with the direction they were taking the country.[5] But it was only after the death of Boumedienne in 1978 and the emergence of an Islamic republic in Iran the following year that the movement became organized and active.[6]

In the early 1980s, the members of al-Da'wa took over mosques that had been under government control for two decades, and when government security forces attempted to stop the takeover—in Laghouat, in 1981, for instance—bloody clashes erupted and resulted in a number of casualties. University campuses witnessed pitched battles between Muslim fundamentalists and left-wing students. These confrontations culminated in the death of a student on the Ben Aknoun campus of the University of Algiers in November 1982.[7]

5. For an analysis of Islam and the state at that juncture, see Jean Leca and Jean-Claude Vatin, *L'Algérie politique, institutions et régime* (Paris: Fondation Nationale des Sciences Politiques, 1975), pp. 304-31.

6. For an excellent discussion of the impact of Boumedienne's policy on the Islamic fundamentalist movement in Algeria, see Hugh Roberts, "Radicalism and the Dilemma of Algerian Nationalism: The Embattled Arians of Algiers," *Third World Quarterly*, vol. 10 (1988).

7. John P. Entelis, *Algeria: The Revolution Institutionalized* (Boulder, CO: Westview Press, 1986), p. 87.

This event led the government of Chadli Bendjedid, whose policy toward al-Da'wa activities had hitherto been rather tolerant, to clamp down. During the rest of the 1980s, the Algerian state began a systematic campaign to undermine the movement by arresting its leaders, conducting police raids on the homes of suspected members, and branding them in the mass media as "criminals" and "agitators."[8] Three of the leaders arrested were clergymen and founding members of the FIS.

In October 1988, riots broke out in the Bab al-Oued sector of Algiers over government austerity measures to cut state subsidies on some basic commodities. The riots spread quickly to the rest of the capital, to Oran, Constantine, Annaba, Blida, Tiarret, and Sinya, and beyond to Tizi-Ouzou in the Berber Kabylie region. Demonstrators were protesting the high unemployment, the shortage of basic consumer goods, and the unavailability of affordable housing in the cities. The armed forces brought in to quell the riots were unable to restore law and order for 10 days, at the end of which more than 150 people were reported dead, over a thousand injured, and an estimated 3000 arrested.[9]

Although the riots were not initiated by Islamic militants, these militants tried to exploit the disturbances to mobilize support for their views. Two days after the riots broke out, several thousand young Muslim

8. See Mary-Jane Deeb, "Algeria," in *Religion in Politics: A World Guide*, ed. Stuart Mews (Harlow, Essex: Longman Group, 1989), pp. 6-9.

9. *Le Monde*, 15 Oct. 1988.

fundamentalists demonstrated in the Belcourt District of Algiers, while the army attempted to keep them away from demonstrations in other sectors of the city. When the riots were over, President Bendjedid met with Muslim fundamentalist leaders. They condemned acts of violence and sabotage and submitted a number of proposals for economic and social reforms including a demand that Islam constitute the basis of all such reforms.

In February 1989, a new constitution was approved in Algeria. Among other things, it permitted the creation of "associations of a political character."[10] In March 1989, the first Algerian Islamic political party, the FIS, was proclaimed in Kouba, a suburb of Algiers, and was officially legalized in September 1989.[11] It had a consultative council, or *shura*, made up of 14 members, some of whom were very important Islamic leaders in Algeria. In June 1990, the first test of strength took place between the FLN and the FIS in local elections for the 1539 municipal councils and the 48 provincial assemblies. The Islamicists won 54 percent of the vote as compared to the FLN's 28 percent, giving them control of 850 municipalities, including those of major urban centers such Algiers, Constantine, and Oran. On 25 May 1991, on the eve of general legislative elections,

10. See the analysis in Robert Mortimer, "Islam and Multiparty Politics in Algeria," *Middle East Journal*, 45:578-79 (1991).

11. For an excellent analysis of Algerian politics at the end of the 1980s, see Robert A. Mortimer, "Algeria after the Explosion," *Current History*, 89(546):161-64, 180-82 (Apr. 1990).

the FIS called for an indefinite and nationwide strike and announced rallies and marches all over the country. The strike was called to protest the government's gerrymandering tactics to give rural districts a greater electoral representation, which would favor the ruling party. They also demanded that presidential elections be held simultaneously with the legislative elections.

After days of disturbances, the Algerian government took new measures to deal with these disturbances: it ordered the reestablishment of all public services and the arrest of those who were obstructing government officials from performing their duties. Clashes between demonstrators and the gendarmerie turned violent, and the security forces used firearms. Finally, on 5 June President Bendjedid ordered a state of siege for four months to restore public order. All gatherings, demonstrations, and marches were banned. A curfew was imposed between 11 p.m. and 3:30 a.m. in the provinces of Algiers, Blida, Tipasa, and Boumerdes, and the military began patrolling the capital in tanks. Legislative elections were postponed, and the government resigned.

After jailing both the leader of the FIS and his deputy and breaking off further negotiations with the Islamicists, the government set the date for legislative elections. On 26 December 1991, elections were held, and the FIS won a landslide victory, capturing 188 seats out of the National Assembly's 430, with 176 seats to be contested in a runoff election three weeks later. The FLN came in third, with only 15 seats. Bendjedid resigned on 11 January, leaving the door open to a confrontation between the army and the FIS. The army created a High Security Council, which canceled the runoff elections and effectively blocked the FIS from coming to power.[12]

Ideologically, the Algerian Muslim fundamentalists are among the most radical in North Africa. They advocate a complete restructuring of society "in an attempt to realize the City of God on Earth."[13] They have pushed for the application of Islamic law, *shari'a*, to replace the code of civil law of Algeria and for reforms based on Islamic principles such as a stricter dress code for women, more religious broadcasts on radio and television, and banning the consumption of alcohol in public places.

RELIGION AND POLITICS IN TUNISIA

The Islamicist movement in Tunisia has its roots in the Quranic Preservation Society, founded in 1970. The Tunisian government permitted its development to counterbalance a growing leftist movement on the campuses of the University of Tunis. Only in the late 1970s did a loose coalition of Islamicists, many of whom had links to the Quranic Preservation Society, emerge as an important element in Tunisian politics, voicing the economic, social, and political grievances of many Tunisians.[14] This coalition, which became known as the Islamic Tendency

Movement (MTI), set up organized committees primarily in urban centers of Tunisia and openly began criticizing the government and calling for economic and political reforms based on a return to the true principles of Islam.

One of the principal ideologues and leaders of the MTI, Rached Ghannouchi, describes the movement in his speeches and writings as one that would save the Islamic nation from domination by the West and by atheist or secular governments allied to the West. Westernization or what he calls "the Western plan" would destroy civilization, religion, morality, the nation, the family, and the tribe. The Islamic movement, on the other hand "would save human civilization from the domination of the Samaritans who worship the golden calf."[15] Ghannouchi, like the leaders of the other militant Islamic movements, believes in the use of force to achieve the ultimate Islamic state. Like others, he calls for *jihad* as a step in liberating the land of Islam, which he believes has been invaded by the West due in part to the weakness of the Islamic *umma* and the collaboration of regional governments with the West.[16] He sees the enormous wealth of the Islamic world as a sacred *waqf* ("Islamic religious endowment") that should be distributed equitably among Muslims and serve to resolve its economic problems.[17]

Realizing that the MTI was developing into a major opposition force,

---

12. *Washington Post*, 15 Jan. 1992.

13. Entelis, *Algeria*, p. 85.

14. On the origins of the movement, see Walz, "Islamist Appeal in Tunisia," pp. 652-54.

15. See Rached Ghannouchi, Speech at the First Islamic Congress on the Palestinian Question, Tehran, 4-6 Dec. 1990, pp. 5-6.

16. Ibid., pp. 15-16, 21.

17. Ibid., pp. 21-22.

the Tunisian government began to crack down on its members as early as 1979. By 1981, MTI members were being arrested in significant numbers and accused of various political crimes. The MTI tried unsuccessfully to gain acceptance as a political party within the constitutional framework of Tunisia throughout the 1980s and resorted to violence to pressure the government to legalize the movement.[18] In August 1987, four tourist hotels were bombed, and MTI members were accused of the crime. When they came to trial a few weeks later, large antigovernment demonstrations took place in protest, and the judge presiding over their trial was sprayed with hydrochloric acid. In September 1987, the State Security Court sentenced 7 of the 90 MTI members to death, Rached Ghannouchi to life imprisonment, and 67 members from two years to life in jail; 14 were acquitted. In October 1987, the first death sentences were carried out, and two MTI members were hanged. Later that month, two MTI leaders, Ali Laaridh and Fadel Beldi, were captured by the security forces, after having been sentenced to death and to hard labor, respectively, in absentia in September.

On the eve of the November 1987 ouster of Bourguiba, it was reported that the Tunisian President was planning on reopening the trials and extending the death penalty to other members of the MTI. Fear that such an action would lead to more violence and bloodshed was apparently behind the timing of the overthrow of

the ailing head of state.[19] In December 1987, the new Tunisian leader, Ben Ali, granted amnesty to 2487 prisoners, including 608 MTI members. He also commuted the death sentence of Ali Laaridh to hard labor and dropped charges against another 60 MTI members. In May 1988, he pardoned Rached Ghannouchi and set him free, and in July a number of MTI members who were imprisoned for crimes "against public rights" were released from jail. In September 1988, Ben Ali allowed the secretary-general of the MTI, Abd al-Fattah Mourou, to return to Tunisia after two years in exile.

In April 1989, the Tunisians went to the polls to elect their president as well as their deputies for parliament. Once again, the Islamicists were not allowed to run as Islamicists and so ran as independents under the banner of the Nahda, or Renaissance Party. They were well organized and able to mobilize significant support. There were reportedly 1200 Islamicist observers in Tunis alone to ensure fair elections. Although the Constitutional Rally, the government party, won all the seats, the Islamicists won 14 percent of the national votes and reportedly almost 30 percent in some urban centers.[20]

In mid-May 1991, the Tunisian government announced that it had

18. Mohammed Elbaki Hermassi, "La société tunisienne au miroir islamiste," *Maghreb-Machrek*, vol. 103 (1984).

19. Marion Boulby, "The Islamic Challenge: Tunisia since Independence," *Third World Quarterly*, 10:613 (1988).

20. For an analysis of the electoral results, see Habib Slim, "Réflections autour des résultats des élections législatives en Tunisie: Implications et perspectives" (Paper delivered at the Twenty-Third Annual Meeting of the Middle East Studies Association of North America, Toronto, Nov. 1989).

uncovered a plot by Islamic fundamentalists to overthrow the government of President Ben Ali. The
Nahda Party was accused of having
masterminded the plot. The alleged
plot consisted of a long-term strategy
to infiltrate the army, the security
forces, and the customs service, and
to destabilize the government by
means of terrorist activities, protests, demonstrations, and the call to
general strikes. The Tunisian government also made public the organizational structure of the Nahda
which was shown to have not only a
political wing but also a paramilitary
wing trained for special operations.[21]
Three hundred people were arrested,
including one hundred military men
and several officers sympathetic to
the Nahda. Its leader, Rached Ghannouchi, denied that such a plot existed and accused the government of
fabricating the story to crack down on
the movement.[22]

MILITANTS AGAINST
REFORMISTS IN LIBYA

Opposition to Qadhdhafi's regime
has come from many sides. Islamic
groups such as the Ikhwan al-
Muslimin (Muslim Brothers) directly
challenged many of Qadhdhafi's
ideas and policies from the start.
Those groups were influenced by
their counterparts in Egypt and ex-

isted in Libya even before Qadhdhafi
came to power.[23]

The Hizb al-Tahrir al-Islami (Islamic Liberation Party) is a major
Islamic organization in Libya rooted
in the Ikhwan movement. It appears
to be linked to similar organizations
in other parts of North Africa, in
Egypt, and in Jordan, where the
movement was originally founded in
the 1950s. It has made deep inroads
into the military and among students
in universities in Tripoli and Benghazi and believes in the restoration
of the original purity and morality of
Islamic society at the time of the first
four Muslim caliphs. It also believes
in the use of violence to achieve its
goals.

The National Front for the Salvation of Libya (NFSL), created in
Khartoum in October 1981, is another movement opposed to the
Qadhdhafi regime that has a strong
Islamic tendency. It is headed by Mohammed Youssef al-Maqaryaf and includes a number of high-level government officials who have defected
from Libya.[24] Some of its members
belonged to the Islamic Association of
Libya, which had ties to the Muslim
Brothers. They publish a magazine
called, appropriately enough, al-
Inqadh (Salvation), which reports
events in Libya and regularly calls
for the overthrow of the government.[25] They also publish a series of

21. Tunisian Republic Radio Network,
Tunis, 22 May 1991, in Foreign Broadcast Information Service, FBIS—NES, 23 May 1991,
pp. 15-16.
22. Interview with Rached Ghannouchi,
Paris Radio France International, 23 May
1991, in Foreign Broadcast Information Service, FBIS—NES, 23 May 1991, p. 16.

23. Mary-Jane Deeb, "Tunisia," in Religion
in Politics, ed. Mews, pp. 268-69.
24. François Burgat, "Libye," Annuaire de
l'Afrique du Nord, 1983 (Paris: Editions du
Centre National de la Recherche Scientifique,
1985), p. 771.
25. This group is discussed in the larger
framework of opposition to the Qadhdhafi re-

pamphlets called Kul al-haqiqat lil-sha'b (The Whole Truth for the People), among which is one on Qadhdhafi's position on Islamic issues. They attack his position as heretical for trying to separate church and state; putting *shari'a*, or Islamic law, on a par with Roman law or the Napoleonic Code; taking the position that the *sunna*, or traditions of the Prophet Muhammad, are not sacred; changing the start of the Islamic calendar, and misunderstanding the concept of *jihad*, or holy war, as being one between believers and unbelievers and adding that Christians and Jews are believers.[26] The pamphlet thus shows how the NFSL views Islam and the relation between state and religion, the role of Islamic law in Libya, and the concept of holy war.

The NFSL, however, is a broad organization with both secular and Islamicist members, as well as a paramilitary wing. Like the other militant organizations discussed earlier in this article, it aims at overthrowing the government in power and has made a number of such attempts. The best known was the May 1984 attack on the Bab al-'Azizya barracks, Qadhdhafi's own headquarters, which was instigated at the behest of the Islamicists in the NFSL.[27]

In September 1986, 26 men were arrested, accused of being members of Jihad al-Islami (Islamic Jihad Organization), which the Libyan government had discovered only a few months earlier. In February 1987, 9 people arrested with them were hanged and their execution televised. They were accused of belonging to the Islamic Jihad Organization, of having carried out two assassinations, and of being involved in acts of sabotage.[28]

Qadhdhafi repressed these groups ruthlessly from the early 1970s through the 1980s, arresting their leaders, hanging their members, and discrediting their views.[29]

In January 1989, unrest spread throughout Tripoli, Benghazi, Ajdabiya, and al-Kufrah with Libyans protesting deteriorating economic conditions, lack of jobs for graduating students, and attacks on religious figures and institutions by government security forces. This unrest followed a raid on the mosque of al-Zurayraq bil-Sabri in Benghazi.[30] The teaching section of the mosque was also closed down because the imam had been publicly critical of Qadhdhafi's views on religion. In Tripoli, a number of mosques were raided in December 1988 and January 1989 during the time of prayer.[31]

Islamic opposition has become more outspoken and more organized. It does not want to compromise or

gime in Lisa Anderson, "Qadhdhafi and His Opposition," *Middle East Journal*, 40:232 (1986).

26. 'Abdallah al-Sadiq, *Tajribat al-Qadhdhafi fi itar al-mawazin al-Islamiyya*, 5th pamphlet in Kul al-haqiqat lil-sha'b (n.p., n.d.).

27. George Joffe, "Islamic Opposition in Libya," *Third World Quarterly*, 10:628 (1988).

28. Tripoli Television Service, 17 Feb. 1987, in Foreign Broadcast Information Service, *FBIS—NES*, 18 Feb. 1987, p. Q1.

29. Amnesty International, "Libya: Summary of Amnesty International's Prisoner Concerns," *Summary* (London), 26 Oct. 1987.

30. *Al-Inqadh*, 7(27):8-9 (Mar. 1989).

31. Mary-Jane Deeb, "New Thinking in Libya," *Current History*, 89(546):151 (Apr. 1990).

cooperate with a regime it perceives as evil.[32] It may become the most important opposition to the Qadhdhafi regime in the near future and prove to be the unifying force that until now has eluded the Libyan opposition domestically and externally.

MILITANCY IN THE
OCCUPIED TERRITORIES

In the 1970s, several Islamic groups emerged in the Occupied Territories, encouraged by the Israeli government's eagerness to undermine the power of the PLO and other nationalists and leftist organizations. Among them were the Islamic Charitable League, led by Shaykh Ahmad Yassin, and the Islamic Society, whose founder was Khalil al-Qoqa. Both movements were part of the Muslim Brothers organization that had been active in the territories since the time of the Egyptian administration. Those organizations centered their efforts around educational institutions and mosques to provide youngsters with an Islamic awareness. They wanted to create an alternative to the PLO, whose leadership they believed was not representative of the Palestinians. Their goal was the establishment of a Muslim state in Palestine.

But it was the Islamic Jihad, which emerged in the mid 1980s in Gaza, that became the most militant Islamic movement in the area. One of the founding members was Imad al-

Saftawi, who rejected both the leadership of the PLO, which he saw as too willing to compromise with Israeli authorities, and the more conservative Islamic Charitable League, which he perceived as ritualistic and inactive on the nationalist front.[33] This movement believed in the use of force to achieve its goals and first became known in 1986 after it attacked Israeli recruits at a ceremony in Jerusalem. Throughout 1987, Islamic Jihad was very active against Israeli forces, which responded by imprisoning several of its members and deporting many of its leaders to Lebanon. In May 1987, al-Saftawi escaped from jail and was next heard of in Baghdad. Damascus also harbors a wing of Islamic Jihad that is often active in Lebanon, where it operates against Israeli forces there.

The Islamic Resistance Movement, Harakat al-Muqawama al-Islamiyya, better known by its Arabic acronym, Hamas, emerged in August 1988, a few months after the start of the *intifada*. It was founded by Shaykh Ahmad Yassin of the Islamic Charitable League and a member of the Ikhwan. Hamas was created in part to steal the thunder of the nationalist movement in the territories and eventually replace its leadership.[34] Like the other Islamic movements, it rejects the leadership of the PLO and believes that it is the duty of every Muslim to struggle for an Islamic state.

For Hamas, the Islamic Jihad, and other Islamic organizations on the West Bank and in Gaza, the political

32. See, for instance, an editorial in *al-Inqadh*, 2(9):7 (June 1984).

33. Ann M. Lesch, "Prelude to Uprising in the Gaza Strip," *Journal of Palestine Studies*, 20:10, 11 (1990).

34. See Lisa Taraki, "The Islamic Resistance Movement in the Palestinian Uprising," *Middle East Report*, p. 30 (1989).

entity they are fighting against and wish to replace is more complex than that of any opponents of the other organizations discussed here. Not only are the Palestinians fighting Israelis, whom they see as foreigners and infidels, but in addition they are up against a nationalist movement that also seeks to liberate the territories. Their weapon against the PLO or the Communist Party in Israel is religion. They see those organizations as secular or even as atheist and attribute their failure to their lack of faith. Hamas is, however, less vocally in opposition to the PLO than are the other organizations; nonetheless, it has asked that the PLO become ideologically more Islamic.[35]

THE PARTY OF GOD IN LEBANON

Hizballah (the Party of God) was founded in the summer of 1982, the brainchild of Muhammad Hussain Fadhlallah, a Shiite clergyman whose family comes from southern Lebanon but who was born and studied in Najaf, Iraq. The leader and ideologue of the party, Fadhlallah was inspired by the Iranian revolution, which has since supported him politically, financially, and militarily, sending both men and arms to strengthen his movement.[36] His closest aides are also Shiite clergymen who studied theology in Najaf.

Like some of the other militant movements in the region, Hizballah has two wings: the political, which

deals with the dissemination of information and the organization's planning and policymaking, and an underground paramilitary wing, which operates under the name "Islamic Jihad." The latter group undertakes all the major terrorist operations associated with the movement.

Ideologically, Hizballah is very close to the Islamic militancy of Khomeini's Iran. In his major political treatise, *al-Islam wa mantiq al-quwwa* (Islam and the logic of force),[37] Fadhlallah put forward the ideas that have become the main tenets of the movement. He believes it is the duty of Muslims to fight *al-dawla al-kafira* ("the heretical state").[38] Like other Islamic militants, he wants to help establish an Islamic republic in Lebanon as well as in other Muslim countries, although, according to him, they are not yet ready for such a state.[39] Like them also, he believes that the Islamic *shari'a* should be the law of the land, but he insists it should also be applicable to Christians living in the Islamic world.

Fadhlallah also believes in organizing Muslims to fight what he calls the unbelievers, whether they be parties or states. According to his writ-

35. Ibid., p. 32.

36. See Marius Deeb, "Shia Movements in Lebanon: Their Formation, Ideology, Social Basis, and Links with Iran and Syria," *Third World Quarterly*, 10:683-98 (1988).

37. Mohammed Hussain Fadhlallah, *al-Islam wa mantiq al-quwwa*, 2d ed. (Beirut: al-Muassasat al-Jami'iyya li-al-Dirasat Wa al-Nashr Wa al-Tawzi', 1981).

38. For an analysis of Hizballah and other Islamic groups in Lebanon, see Marius Deeb, *Militant Islamic Movements in Lebanon: Origins, Social Basis, and Ideology*, Occasional Paper Series (Washington, DC: Georgetown University, Center for Contemporary Arab Studies, Nov. 1986).

39. Malaf al-Shira', *al-Harakat al-Islamiyya fi Lubnan* (Beirut: Dar Sannin, 1984), p. 263.

ings, political forces fall into two categories: *hizballah* (God's party) that unites all believers and *hizb al-Shaytan* (the Devil's party) to which all others belong. This concept, taken from the Iranian revolution, is appealing because of its stark simplicity. There is a commitment that has to be made, as no one can be left on the periphery lest he fall into *hizb al-Shaytan*. Western governments and local governments that cooperate with the West fall within the latter category. Like its Iranian counterparts, Hizballah is profoundly suspicious of the West's intentions and motivations in the region.

Hizballah supports armed struggle to liberate Muslim land and establish an Islamic republic. It has encouraged a number of operations against Israeli forces in southern Lebanon and wants to liberate Jerusalem, arguing that the Palestinian struggle has been a failure until now because of its secular nature.[40]

The social basis of the movement is the poorer areas of Lebanon in the south, the Biqa' region, and the slum areas of Beirut. Hizballah as well as a number of other Islamic organizations have done what their counterparts have done elsewhere in the Middle East: they have provided health care, education, vocational training, and financial support at a time when the state has been incapable of providing that type of assistance.

CONCLUSION

Militant Islamic movements in the Arab world have emerged in the

40. *Al-Nahar* (Beirut), 5 June 1985.

1980s, but all derive from earlier movements that either were suppressed or agreed to play by the rules of the governments in power. Most of the Sunnite militant groups examined here were influenced by, or were offshoots of, organizations having links with the Muslim Brotherhood of Hasan al-Banna in Egypt, which emerged in 1928. The Shiite movements, on the other hand, have their roots in Iran or in the Iraqi holy cities of Shiism like Najaf and Karbala.

Ideologically, they are not very different from their predecessors. What differentiates them is their commitment to achieving their goals not in the distant future but in the present. They are much better organized than earlier movements; they are better financed, as they raise money from their members and from external sources and governments; and they have younger, better-educated, and more active leaders. Most are very secretive about their organizational structures and have separate wings with different names that perform different functions. All have a paramilitary arm for terrorist activities.

Militant Islamic movements are also much more outspoken than their predecessors in their criticisms of governments and leaders in power. They use the difficult economic conditions under which their fellow citizens live to support their allegations of corruption, mismanagement, and kowtowing to the West. They argue that those leaders have failed and that it is time for change, an idea appealing even to those who do not support them.

These movements are militant because they refuse to compromise with the powers that be. They all argue that there can be no compromise with the forces of evil. They are, however, pragmatic and ready, as in Algeria, to maneuver tactically to achieve their goals. The ultimate goal is an Islamic republic that would transcend national borders, but until that time they want to establish Islamic republics within national borders that would assist similar movements elsewhere. Another characteristic of these movements, therefore, is the close links they maintain with each other and the support they give one another.

Because of their unwillingness to compromise, their criticisms of governments in power, their use of force and violence, and their expressed goal of overthrowing ruling elites, they have all been suppressed and their leaders and followers imprisoned. Many have had harsh prison sentences, have suffered torture in captivity, and have been sent or have fled into exile. They have therefore been able to glean a great deal of support as the underdog organization that has stood up to the powerful and corrupt.

ANNALS, *AAPSS*, 524, November 1992

Conservative and Traditional Brotherhoods

By JOHN OBERT VOLL

ABSTRACT: The major Sufi brotherhoods have a significance in the development of political Islam in the modern era that is often under-estimated. The traditional brotherhoods provided the basis for much of the militant opposition to European imperial expansion in the nineteenth century and, through these efforts, created symbols for Islamic authenticity that have remained important throughout the twentieth century. These brotherhoods also were major conservative forces, preserving a sense of an Islamic identity in times of rule by non-Muslims or secularizing and westernizing Muslim elites after independence. The long-term impact of this conservative force is to provide a foundation for popular support for political Islam at the end of the twentieth century. This popular support is a major factor in transforming political Islam from a radical force on the periphery of the political arena into the basic foundation of mainstream politics in many Islamic societies.

John Obert Voll is professor of history at the University of New Hampshire. He is the author of Islam: Continuity and Change in the Modern World *and other publications on Islam in the modern era. He is president-elect of the Middle East Studies Association of North America and serves on the editorial board of the* Encyclopedia of the Modern Islamic World.

POLITICAL Islam in the modern era reflects the influence of the great Sufi brotherhoods, for they play an important role in Islamic society and history. A major force in the life of personal and social Islamic piety, they have also helped shape the definition of Islam in the modern political arena. The position and significance of the brotherhoods have changed in recent years, but the traditional structures have shown a remarkable ability to adapt to the major social and political transformations of the present day.

During the past two centuries, the world historical context within which the Sufi brotherhoods operate has changed dramatically. In each of three phases of historical-political development, the brotherhoods in different areas have been able to respond in significant and usually effective ways. In the first era, that of Western imperialist conquest and establishment of Western dominance, the brotherhoods sometimes performed the active function of providing organization and inspiration for military resistance. Then, when foreign dominance was established, the brotherhoods often provided the means for communication between the rulers and the general Muslim populace, especially the nonliterate, nonelite segments of society.

In the second phase, however, when both foreign rulers and then Western-educated nationalist elites worked to create modern societies utilizing Western secular models, the brotherhoods were a significant conservative force. They provided means whereby traditional identities and modes of operation could be maintained while avoiding open social conflict. Often the brotherhoods became, in this way, the vehicle for expanding the modern awareness of important parts of the general population without creating a total disruption of societal continuity.

Recent years mark the beginning of what many see as a major third phase in this set of experiences and developments. The domination of the West, both in imperial forms and in the form of rule by local, culturally Western elites, has significantly declined. This does not mean that the modernizing transformation has stopped, but that it is assuming often radically new forms. The older liberal Westernist and radical Westernist approaches to modernization no longer represent the only or even the dominant perspective underlying policies and aspirations. In this dramatically changing context, the Sufi brotherhoods face challenges in the redefinition of their role and mission within Muslim societies.

Political establishments themselves, with important lines of continuity in maintaining the more Westernist perspectives, have significantly altered their roles as leaders of Islamic societies. Islamic conceptualizations play an increasingly important role in the politics of established regimes. At the same time, a new style of political Islam, affirmed in a form sometimes called "fundamentalist," reflects the rise of new types of popular and political organizations. As these newer organizations provide the leadership for the affirmation of the new political Islam, the more traditional brotherhoods appear to be more conservative and less openly visible in the political arena. Their impact is, however, still significant in the developing articulation of both the political Islam of political establishments and the new political Islam.

THE CONTINUING IMPACT OF NINETEENTH-CENTURY POLITICAL SUFISM

Political Islam in the nineteenth century was importantly identified with major brotherhoods and brotherhoodlike organizations. Even at the end of the twentieth century, this identification is important in the struggle to define and control the heritage of this activist political Islam. The nineteenth-century brotherhood leaders have been adopted by a variety of twentieth-century groups who claim to be their heirs. Sufi leaders in Algeria, Somalia, Libya, and elsewhere became, in twentieth-century terms, the "first nationalists." In the current Islamic resurgence, the symbolism of these early activists continues to have persuasive power.

In an era when the steady advance of European imperial control in Africa and Asia was a major feature of political history, the resistance movements organized by the Sufi brotherhoods were a significant force. Other major social institutions and structures seemed less well-equipped to provide this organization. The political and military establishments of the existing states were relatively weak and were undertaking major reforms utilizing Western models, thus only strengthening the picture of Western domination.

The 'ulama' were not organized in a way that would encourage military resistance. Their major actions in the political arena tended to be like those of the 'ulama' of Cairo who invited the Ottoman soldier Muhammad Ali to undertake the responsibilities of governing Egypt in order to avoid further invasion or internal disorder. The great schools like al-Azhar in Cairo or Kairouan in Tunisia could provide advice but not political leadership. Major ethnic and tribal groupings of the day could and did provide some resistance, but this was only in particular localities and did not have much of a large-scale impact. It was the major popular organizations of piety, the brotherhoods, that provided models of organization and leadership for the defense of society.

The traditional brotherhood organizational structure was relatively simple and effective. The key is the relationship between the spiritual guide, often called a "shaykh," and his disciples. The disciple is bound to the shaykh by an oath of absolute obedience. There is usually a hierarchy of followers, with designated representatives of the shaykh serving particular groups and in specific areas. After the death of the shaykh who established the group, succession to leadership is sometimes hereditary and sometimes by designation.

The core of the identity is the regulated life of personal and group piety utilizing special collections of prayers and recitations. These devotional materials are "the path," or the *tariqa*, and the brotherhoods are usually identified as being the *tariqa* of the particular individual who initiated the prayers and devotional tradition. The group gathers regularly to recite the prayers and engage in other acts of devotion. The gathering place of the order often becomes a major social center for the members, providing a concrete focus for the lives of the followers of the shaykh. Even at the end of the twentieth century, this type of organization continues to provide an effective foundation for socially and politically influential organizations. It is not as highly visible as the more purely political groups, but this is part of its strength as a continuing force within Muslim societies.

At the beginning of the nineteenth century, there was already an established tradition of Islamic political activism utilizing brotherhood organization in many parts of the Islamic world. In West Africa at the end of the eighteenth century, for example, Uthman dan Fodio began a militant movement of Islamic renewal that resulted in the creation of an important political system, with a sultanate centered in the present northern region of Nigeria. Dan Fodio's initial identification was with a major Sufi brotherhood, and it was as a scholar and a shaykh in this order that he began his movement of renewal. The state that was created by the West African Jihad movement of dan Fodio provided the political organization for northern Nigeria as it came under British control. After independence in 1960, the major Muslim political leaders in Nigeria had ties with the Jihad tradition.

The effort to control the office of sultan in the north, now formally outside of the Nigeria political system, continues to involve major political struggles. The succession of a relatively liberal Islamic modernist, Al-

haj Ibrahim Dasuki, as the sultan of Sokoto in 1988 was the cause for strong protests among the more activist Islamicist groups, who spoke of the "unholy alliance between the Sultanate and secularism."[1] The continuing political importance of the symbols created by the political Islam of the brotherhoods in the nineteenth century is a factor that must be kept in mind when evaluating the contemporary role of the traditional brotherhoods.

During the nineteenth century, many major movements of Islamic renewal and resistance to European expansion arose out of the traditions of the brotherhoods and their organizations. Some of these were tariqas that remained basically traditional orders while performing major functions beyond those of individual and group piety. One important cluster of such brotherhoods was created by the followers of Ahmad ibn Idris (d. 1837). These orders were influential in varying ways from North Africa to the islands of Southeast Asia. The disciples of ibn Idris developed brotherhoods that "were relatively more centralized and less prone to fission than their predecessors; they introduced into the areas where they proselytized new forms of social organization, often based on autonomous agricultural communities, zawiya or jama‘a; recruited en masse, and later were politically active."[2]

1. Ibraheem Sulaiman, "Caesar on a Sacred Throne," *Africa Events*, Dec. 1988, p. 13. See also Kenneth B. Noble, "A Sultan with His Feet Planted in Two Worlds," *New York Times*, 11 Mar. 1989, p. 4.

2. R. S. O'Fahey, *Enigmatic Saint: Ahmad Ibn Idris and the Idrisi Tradition* (London: Hurst, 1990), pp. 4-5.

Among the most important of these brotherhoods was the Sanusiyya, which was established in Libya in the nineteenth century, led the resistance to Italian control in the twentieth century, and provided the basis for the monarchy when Libya became independent in 1951. Another important brotherhood in this tradition was the Khatmiyya in the Sudan. Under the leadership of the Mirghani family, the order became an important political force in the twentieth century, first as a patron for an emerging nationalist movement and then as the basis for one of the major political parties in the postcolonial era. The Khatmiyya-supported political parties were influential forces in the politics of the parliamentary periods in 1956-58, 1964-69, and 1985-89. The traditional brotherhood structure continues to provide an effective basis for mobilization of political support in the context of parliamentary party politics.

There were many other brotherhood-based movements of political Islam in the nineteenth century, and their traditions continue to have an impact on the development of political Islam in the late twentieth century. In the republics of the former Soviet Union in the Caucasus region, for example, there continue to be reflections of the Naqshabandiyya-led resistance to Russian imperial expansion. The Imam Shamil was able to maintain a holy war against the Russians for almost a quarter of a century before his final defeat in 1859. In Somalia, Muhammad Abdallah Hasan (1864-1921) was the leader of the Salihiyya who led a major holy war of resistance to expanding British imperial control. The so-called Mad Mulla became a symbol for later Somali nationalism, and the recent disintegration of independent Somalia shows the importance of having a supratribal principle of political unification in that country.

While the brotherhoods were not the only source of political Islamic activism in the nineteenth century, they did provide important foundations for continuing political Islam in many areas. In concrete terms, the orders were able to provide a structure through which actual military resistance to European imperial expansion organized. Their campaigns helped to define the specific boundaries of the resisting societies. Thus the Qadiriyya resistance to the French led by the Amir Abd al-Qadir helped to provide a historical foundation for the Algerian identity. The Sanusiyya provided a similar basis for Libya, and the Salihiyya for Somalia. The brotherhoods therefore made contributions to the nationalist mode of political Islam as it emerged during the twentieth century.

THE CONSERVATIVE ROLE OF THE BROTHERHOODS

The great brotherhoods also played, and continue to play, an important conservative role in Muslim societies. It is mistaken to identify radical Islamic revolutionism as a "conservative" force in the normal meaning of that term. In broader political discussions, conservatives are people who attempt to preserve the general outlines of the existing social order. They are protectors of the status quo. Modern and premodern fundamentalists, in contrast, are radically dissatisfied with the existing conditions. Some brotherhoods, like the renewalist movement in West Africa led by Uthman dan Fodio, were not conservative. But, within Islamic societies in the modern era, many brotherhoods have served as a profoundly conservative force. Even in their militant opposition to Western imperial expansion, they were primarily working to preserve society as it existed.

Once European imperial control was established in many areas, the brotherhoods were often important vehicles for helping the system operate. Working within the system of imperialist control, the brotherhoods were an important source for maintaining the Muslim identity of the peoples. As the educated elites became increasingly westernized in their thinking and daily lives, the brotherhoods provided an alternative arena within which even the Western educated elite could continue to function as visibly believing Muslims. In some cases, the brotherhoods provided some of the most effective means for preserving an Islamic identity and even spreading Islam beyond previous limits in the context of non-Muslim and sometimes anti-Islamic rulers.

Highly visible examples of this conservative role of the brotherhoods can be found in Africa and in Central Asia. In West Africa, both the militant and the more quietist orders of the nineteenth century were important forces in the territories ruled by the French and the British. As imperial rulers established more stable governing systems, the leaders of the brotherhoods provided "leaders of public opinion" who could be consulted and who could influence the local populations. In the Sudan, the Mirghani family provided an important intermediary between large numbers of people in the northern Sudan and the British rulers. Leaders of these more staid *tariqa*s were thought to be a force that could prevent the resurgence of militant Islamic activism in the country.[3] In Algeria, the French worked with the Sufi organizations; in northern Nigeria, the heirs of Uthman dan Fodio became the Native Administration of British indirect rule.

This role has been criticized by later nationalists and secular radicals because it involved collaboration with the imperial rulers. It provided, however, a vehicle for conservative preservation of the fundamental Islamic identity when militant resistance seemed impossible. Beyond this, in Africa, the "modern state in its colonial form established an institutional framework which allowed the *tariqa* new possibilities of expansion."[4] New means of communication and more open trade patterns were elements in this. In this colonial context, the boundaries of the Islamic world expanded considerably beyond

3. See, for example, the discussions in Gabriel Warburg, "Religious Policy in the Northern Sudan: Ulama and Sufism, 1914-1945," *Asian and African Studies*, 7:163-78 (1971); John O. Voll, "The British, the Ulama, and Popular Islam in the Early Anglo-Egyptian Sudan," *International Journal of Middle East Studies*, 2:212-18 (1971).

4. Donal B. Cruise O'Brien, "Islam and Power in Black Africa," in *Islam and Power*, ed. Alexander S. Cudsi and Ali E. H. Dessouki (Baltimore, MD: Johns Hopkins University Press, 1981), p. 160.

where they had been at the time of the eighteenth-century revivalist holy wars. It was the conservative gradualism of the orders that helped to expand Islam in the twentieth century, making it the most rapidly expanding religion on the African continent.

An even more dramatic case reflecting the power of the conservative brotherhoods can be seen in the Muslim societies of Central Asia. Russian imperial expansion under the czars began a process that continued after the Communist revolution. Both regimes actively sought to discourage adherence to Islam, either through Russification or, under the Communists, through vigorous anti-religion campaigns. Initially, there had been active resistance, much of which was led by Sufi leaders and involved the brotherhoods. There was the Naqshabandiyya resistance in the Caucasus during the nineteenth century, and in the Basmachi revolts following World War I, brotherhood leaders also played an important role. This resistance was crushed, however, and Central Asian Muslims faced the problems of living under non-Muslim and frequently actively anti-Islamic rule.

Soviet leaders engaged in both a frontal assault on the ideas and institutions of religion and a direct attempt to institutionalize and control what Islamic activity could survive the assault. As a result, a government establishment was created that was to regulate Muslim life. There was a structure of councils and directorates with the major regions and republics having muftis and directors appointed. In this way, a Muslim governmental institution came into existence as a structure for bringing the Communist regime and the Muslim peoples more closely together. This religious establishment had some resources available to it but had little control or influence over most of the lives of the majority of Central Asian Muslims.

Under Soviet rule, formal, visible Muslim organizations other than those of the religious establishment were suppressed, and most such groupings disappeared. But the Sufi brotherhoods, based as they are on the private devotional lives of the believers, had the means to maintain an underground religious tradition. Such a phenomenon would reflect great diversity because it would usually be highly localized in structure and following. As these groupings developed, Soviet analysts began to speak of an unofficial, unregulated "parallel Islam," with leaders drawn to a remarkable degree from the Sufi brotherhoods.[5]

The leaders of parallel Islam maintained many of the older social and religious traditions and rituals and, in this way, performed a profoundly conservative function that, in the context of Soviet rule, could have revolutionary implications. After the wars of the 1920s, however, there were few major revolts that had any impact on the direction of Soviet rule. Instead, the Sufi-based parallel Islam simply resisted the ideological expansion of communism in its athe-

5. Alexandre Bennigsen and S. Enders Wimbush, *Mystics and Commissars: Sufism in the Soviet Union* (Berkeley: University of California Press, 1985), p. 86. In many ways, this book is the standard source on Sufism in the former Soviet Union.

istic form and provided a continuing distinctive basis for Central Asian sociocultural identities. Before the collapse of the Soviet Union, Alexandre Bennigsen wrote, "Although Soviet dogma has insisted for nearly seventy years that Islam must be eliminated in the course of producing the 'New Soviet Man,' all evidence points to just the opposite having happened: Islam has strengthened and Marxism-Leninism has failed to inspire and to satisfy."[6]

The continued existence and growing strength of Islam were not the products of fundamentalist activism over the decades. They were primarily the products of the patient and quiet maintenance of Islamic customs and identity, in other words, the products of a strong conservative force, and this force is primarily identified with the traditional Sufi brotherhoods. With the sudden collapse of the Soviet Union at the beginning of the 1990s, the conservative contribution of the brotherhoods has immense significance, regardless of whether or not the brotherhoods will emerge as visible political forces within the Central Asian republics. It may be that the era of necessarily conservative approaches is past, but, if so, the passing is itself the product of the brotherhoods' work.

The general conservative role of the traditional brotherhoods throughout the Muslim world has had significance. It allowed conquered populations to adjust to non-Muslim rulers without losing their own religiocultural identity. Indeed, these brother-

6. Alexandre Bennigsen, "Unrest in the World of Soviet Islam," *Third World Quarterly*, 10:786 (1988).

hoods, at least at times, were the agents for the expansion of Islam and the turning back of the challenges of non-Islamic forces. In contrast to the tradition of the nineteenth-century activist brotherhoods, however, the twentieth-century conservative efforts of the orders were less militant and overcame opposition more by patient and quiet diligence than by violent resistance. The major contribution of these conservative orders is that when non-Muslim rule was withdrawn, there remained a core of Islamic community and identity on which independent Muslim leaders could and can build.

INDEPENDENCE AND THE TRADITIONAL BROTHERHOODS

In most Muslim societies, the era of independence from imperial control was not initially a time of establishment of clearly Islamic regimes. Most of the leaders of the new states were themselves strongly influenced by Western conceptualizations of the nature and needs of political development in the modern world. The great competition was frequently between liberal and radical Western-style approaches to nation building, and more explicitly Islamic approaches to fundamental issues of political order and development were viewed with suspicion.

In the years following World War II, as growing numbers of Muslim societies became independent states, much effort was given to the establishment of liberal parliamentary regimes. When those failed, they were replaced by military governments who often looked more to the example of Mustafa Kemal Ataturk, the secularist reformer of Turkey following World War I, than to more explicitly Islamic models.[7] Later, more explicitly radical programs were developed by leaders in major Muslim countries like Egypt, Syria, and Algeria, and even more traditional monarchs articulated their programs in the terminology of Western concepts of development.

In this context, political Islam was a concept and force that tended to run counter to the political mainstream in most Muslim societies. The more secular leaders made an effort not to appear anti-Islamic and often used Islamic forms and slogans in their programs and pronouncements. The groups that directly advocated programs of Islamization of state and society were, however, actively suppressed or shunted to the periphery of politics by the 1960s. Most leaders of the Muslim Brotherhood in Egypt, for example, were imprisoned by President Nasser, and other branches of this organization or groups inspired by its message had similar experiences in other parts of the Arab world. The activist followers of Mulla Kashani in Iran also had political difficulty, as did groups like the Dar ul-Islam movement in Indonesia.

The traditional brotherhoods were not usually a direct part of this more revolutionary style of political Islam. At least some of the emerging Islamicist movements had had contact with Sufi orders in their early days. The founder of the Muslim

Brotherhood in Egypt, Hasan al-Banna, for example, was strongly influenced by the Hasafiyya *tariqa* and had been involved with this particular order for twenty years and "with Sufism in a special way for most of his life."[8] Groups like the Muslim Brotherhood were not and are not, however, Sufi brotherhoods. They represent a new form of popular Islamic activism, even though they often interact with and resemble the more revivalist brotherhoods of the eighteenth and nineteenth centuries.

The position of the traditional brotherhoods under national rulers with relatively secular perspectives tended to be similar to that adopted under imperial rule. There was a quiet cooperation and an underlying persistent devotion to the older piety. In other words, the response of the traditional orders to both radical and liberal westernizers tended to be conservative rather than militant. Egypt during the 1960s provides an instructive example. While the militant Islamicists of the Muslim Brotherhood were being suppressed, many of the traditional Sufi orders were flourishing. The Rifa'iyya *tariqa*, as just one example, regularly brought significant numbers of people to the Rifa'i mosque for devotional exercises, and a respected philosopher at the University of Cairo, who was a member, was highly regarded by both government officials controlling cultural affairs and teachers at al-Azhar

7. See, for example, the comments in Anwar al-Sadat, *In Search of Identity: An Autobiography* (New York: Harper & Row, 1977), chap. 1.

8. Richard P. Mitchell, *The Society of the Muslim Brothers* (London: Oxford University Press, 1969), p. 2. For Banna's observations on the Hasafiyya and Sufism, see *Memoirs of Hasan Al Banna Shaheed*, trans. M. N. Shaikh (Karachi: International Islamic Publishers, 1981), pp. 67-76.

University.[9] Although people like this scholar were eager to maintain a clearly Islamic tradition in a relatively conservative manner, they were not interested in advocating a program of political activism and were not necessarily concerned with the formal Islamization of the state structures of the day.

The primary role of the traditional *tariqa*s in the context of the liberal and radical modernizers was conservative. This represents a style of political Islam but one that is different from that of the activists like the Muslim Brothers. However, the long-term significance of this conservatism may be great because it helped to maintain the popular sense of the long continuities of the identity of the Islamic community. Just as the early fundamentalist writers and activists, like Hasan al-Banna and Sayyid Qutb in Egypt or Abu al-A'la al-Mawdudi in South Asia, may have laid the conceptual foundations for the Islamic resurgence of the late twentieth century, the conservative persistence of the traditional brotherhoods may have preserved and even created the mass audience for the fundamentalists' message.

9. Based on observations of *dhikr* ceremonies at the Rifa'i mosque during 1960-61 by the author and also on interviews with officials at the Ministry of Awqaf and the Islamic administration of al-Azhar at the time. The professor mentioned was Dr. Muhammad Mustafa Hilmi, who was the author, for example, of a popular booklet published by the Ministry of Culture and National Guidance on Sufism: *al-Hubb al-ilahi fi al-tasawwuf al-Islami*, al-Maktaba al-Thiqafiyya no. 24 (Cairo: Wizara al-Thiqafa wa al-Irshad al-Qawmi, 1970). Comments on Professor Hilmi's views are based on a series of interviews with him during 1960-61.

THE CURRENT RESURGENCE AND TRADITIONAL BROTHERHOODS

In many parts of the Muslim world, there is an increasing sense of affirmation of Islam in an active mode. Political Islam in an activist sense is emerging as a vital part of the politics of Muslim societies. This Islamic resurgence has received much attention, but the role of the traditional brotherhoods has been relatively ignored despite their potential importance. In addition to having preserved a popular audience for emerging Islamicist tendencies, these orders have other roles. They may provide mass support at key moments of crisis and stable continuity in times when the sense of crisis or mission is less acute. The experience of the Sudan in recent years can provide an important example of how these roles can function in the context of the contemporary world.

In the Sudan during the 1980s, the more traditional and conservative brotherhoods played a significant but usually indirect role in the developing Islamization of state and society. A group of younger military officers led by Ja'far Numayri took control of the government in 1969, and the regime of the May Revolution went through many different phases. It began as a relatively radical and secular regime, strongly influenced by the Sudan Communist Party. When the Communists in the military leadership attempted to overthrow Numayri in 1971, he began a shift in his orientation. Eventually, he became fully committed to an activist program of Islamization of state and society in the Sudan, culminating in

1983 in what are now known as the September Laws.[10]

The traditional brotherhoods played some important roles in this process of the transformation of the basic orientation of Numayri and his political system. The most visible of the older orders was the Khatmiyya, which continued to play the political role that had been defined earlier by the Mirghani family. They provided patronage and leadership for one of the major political parties that had been active in the eras of party politics and parliaments. The Khatmiyya-supported party, called the Democratic Unionist Party since the late 1960s, was a major part of the alliance of forces opposed to the Numayri regime during the 1970s. Within the alliance, it was a conservative force countering both the activist Islamicists and the leftist groups.

Traditional brotherhoods also had a more direct impact on the increasingly Islamic orientation of Numayri. Many of the Sudanese brotherhoods had not taken a direct role in the politics of anti-imperialism or the politics of the parliamentary periods. Instead, they had continued to function as local centers of devotional piety and social life. In the times of major social change, they had provided a more conservative focus in the lives of many people, especially in the smaller towns and villages. Often the local leaders of these orders were

seen as obstacles to development, as they might oppose expansion of the modern education system or the extension of certain modern services. By the early 1970s, however, at least some of the local leadership became more active in these types of activities. They also were viewed as a balance to the influence of Islamic leaders like the Mirghani family and so were increasingly consulted by government officials. The evolution of the social and political role of the leader of the local order centered in Um Dubban is a good example of this transition, which involved increasing interaction with government officials. "The close links between state senior policy-makers and religious leaders of *turuq* have provided the latter with immense influence over government officials working in their areas. That has in turn given the religious leaders leverage over local political and social organizations."[11]

In the early 1980s, Numayri began to articulate policies in a more explicitly Islamic mode, and he drew on a number of sources for this. He had initiated a "national reconciliation" in the late 1970s that drew the Sudanese Muslim Brotherhood into the regime. Hasan al-Turabi, the leader of the brotherhood, served in a number of high-level posts and was assigned the task of leading a special committee for the Islamization of Sudanese law. As a result, the emerging Islamization program was strongly

---

10. For Numayri's public account of the early stages of this reorientation, see Ja'far Muhammad Numayri, *al-Nahj al-Islami limadha?* (Cairo: al-Maktab al-Masri al-Hadith, 1980).

11. Idris Salim El Hassan, "On Ideology: The Case of Religion in Northern Sudan" (Ph.D. diss, University of Connecticut, 1980), p. 185. This is a thorough study of the development of a local *tariqa* center, Um Dubban, in the modern era.

influenced by the more activist Islamicist forces in the Sudan.

At the same time, Numayri had developed a strong personal relationship with some leaders of the more traditional and conservative brotherhoods. These people were not organized as a cohesive political faction but were able to encourage the official reaffirmation of Islam by the revolutionary regime. As Numayri moved in the direction of direct and rapid Islamization, he distanced himself somewhat from the leadership of the Muslim Brotherhood and turned to more conservative and directly loyal people from the smaller *tariqas*. By the time of the actual announcement of the implementation of a direct Islamization program, the effort was managed by two younger men, Nayal Abu Groon and Awad el Geed Mohamed Ahmed, who were drawn from smaller orders. The more traditional Sufi tone was emphasized by the initial importance of the oath of allegiance to Numayri that Abu Groon and Awad el Geed defined.[12]

In the Sudan in recent years, the traditional brotherhoods have in these ways provided strong support for the main trends of the Islamic resurgence even though they have not been the most visible forces within those trends. They have had special influence by working in the arena of personal piety to provide personal spiritual comfort as well as political support for a leader like Numayri. This personal dimension of

political Islam is often ignored, but it may be the arena of the most significant contributions of the traditional orders to political Islam in the long run. In the emerging Central Asian republics, for example, leaders long nurtured by the parallel Islam of the orders may be the shapers of political Islam in that region.

The political Islam of the 1990s already may be reflecting the broader influence of the more traditional and conservative Sufi brotherhoods.[13] As the concept and ideal of explicit Islamization of society spreads from the radical fringes of the political system into the mainstream, political Islam becomes a more complex force. This normalization of the original more revolutionary impulse of Islamic resurgence[14] is distinctly influenced by conservatism of the type shown throughout Islamic history by at least some of the traditional Sufi brotherhoods. The contribution of the traditional and conservative brotherhoods to contemporary political Islam is their traditionalism and conservatism, which provide a strong sense of continuity in personal and

13. Relatively little has been published about the continuing and probably growing popular influence of the more traditional brotherhoods. However, works of scholars like Valerie J. Hoffman-Ladd and Albrecht Hofheinz on orders like the Burhaniyya in Egypt and the Majdhubiyya in the Sudan will be making significant contributions as conference papers become published as articles and monographs.

14. For a more complete discussion of this process of normalization in the context of Egypt, see John O. Voll, "Fundamentalism in the Sunni Arab World: Egypt and the Sudan," in *Fundamentalisms Observed*, ed. Martin E. Marty and R. Scott Appleby (Chicago: University of Chicago Press, 1991), pp. 384-90.

12. John Obert Voll, *The Political Impact of Islam in Sudan: Numayri's Islamization Program*, INR/LAR 1722-420140 (Washington, DC: Department of State, 1984), pp. 89-91.

public life. It is not an antimodern force so much as a force that reminds both leaders and the general public that there are devotional and spiritual resources available within the Islamic cumulative tradition for coping with the great problems and issues of the contemporary world.

ANNALS, *AAPSS*, **524**, November 1992

State Islam and Communal Plurality

By NAZIH N. AYUBI

ABSTRACT: The historical Islamic state developed interesting methods of quasi-consociational and semi-corporatist aggregation of communities. From quite early on, Sunnism became the religion of the ruling elite and of the state as well as part of the state's legal and cultural system. Subsequently, the geographical distribution and the political economy of the Islamic sects and of the religious minorities manifested quite distinct features that were mainly a function of their relationship to the state. Whereas the Islamic sects did not come to terms ideologically and organizationally with the state, the religious minorities, on the whole, adjusted themselves mentally and behaviorally to its requirements. By comparison, the contemporary Middle Eastern state, both the secular and the Islamic, is achieving less success in dealing with its communal problem. Certain groups are excluded in the former type in spite of the secularist slogans, and certain groups are excluded in the latter because of the ideological or religious nature of the state. Improvisation is needed, and Muslim statesmen and intellectuals may need to go beyond, and even outside, conventional Islamic jurisprudence in order to deal with this issue.

Nazih N. Ayubi is a reader in politics and director of the Middle East Politics Program at the University of Exeter, United Kingdom. He holds a Jean Monnet Fellowship at the European University Institute in Florence, Italy (1991-92) and will be a Hallsworth Fellow at Manchester University in 1992-93. A graduate of Cairo University, he obtained his doctorate from Oxford University. He is the author of Bureaucracy and Politics in Contemporary Egypt; Political Islam: Religion and Politics in the Arab World; *and* The State and Public Policies in Egypt since Sadat.

M OST contemporary countries with Muslim majorities declare in their constitutions that Islam is the religion of the state, and many of them have increasingly incorporated a further clause to the effect that *shari'a* is a major, or sometimes the major, source of legislation. In so doing, modern politicians are trying to impart to the contemporary state some of the legitimacy that the historical Islamic state used to derive from being perceived as the "guardian of the faith." In that capacity, activist opposition to the historical Islamic state, as for example by the Kharijites ("deviants," "exiters"), or disgruntled withdrawal from public affairs, as for example by the Sufis ("mystics," "gnostics"), were both dealt with severely by the state as being heresies against the religion itself.

Much of Islamic jurisprudence, especially that of the mainstream Sunnite tradition, was consequently related to a doctrine of civil obedience. The *'ulama'* (religious scholars) often taught that the caliph, or in reality anyone in effective possession of political power, had to be obeyed since an unjust ruler was still better for the community than civil strife. Yet the historical Islamic state was not as monolithic a polity as some maintain. Not only did *fiqh* ("jurisprudence") develop into a multiplicity of schools, but the state also developed interesting methods of quasi-consociational and semi-corporatist aggregation of communities that were quite advanced and sophisticated in their time and that should provide the comparativist scholar with very rich material for study and analysis.

The purpose of this article is (1) to illustrate the ways in which Sunnism has developed, historically, as state Islam; (2) to examine the ways in which the Sunnite establishment dealt, historically, with the communal diversity of society, that is, with the existence of Islamic sects and non-Muslim minorities; and (3) to consider the ways in which the modern territorial state in the Middle East has tried to grapple with the contradiction between the principle of state Islam and the reality of communal plurality.

SUNNITE CENTRALIZATION AND SECTARIAN AUTONOMY

From quite early on, Sunnism developed to become the religion of the ruling elite and of the state and to be part and parcel of the state's legal and cultural system. Sunnism developed in close alliance with, and through adjustment to, the requirements of the central state, whereas "sects" (*firaq, nihal, tawa'if*) emerged and developed as ideologies of groups opposed to the central state and concerned with their own cultural and social group autonomy. Sunnism developed historically as *the* religion (*al-din*) and described its doctrine as being that of the entire group or collectivity (*al-jama'a*), whereas sects were variously described as deviationist (*khawarij*), extremist (*ghulat*), or rejectionist (*bughat, rawafid*), and their followers were regarded as discordant "parties" (*ahzab*). It is therefore fairly understandable why Sunnite scholars are to be found, even to this day, classifying Kharijism and its offshoots—for example, Azariqa,

Ibadiyya, and so on—and Shiism and its offshoots—such as Isma'iliyya, Druze, and the like—as "political sects."[1]

Over time, the Sunnites absorbed the accumulated religious heritage and incorporated it more thoroughly with politics, whereas the Shiites— who originally came mostly from the underprivileged groups and tended to extol the virtues of austerity, meekness, and simplicity—had for a long time been excluded from political power. Whereas the Sunnites, usually in government, emphasized agreement and consensus (ijma') and strove to turn religion into "public policy," the Shiites, who were usually subservient, lamented injustice and complained about the arbitrariness of government. Whereas the Sunnites did things publicly and openly, the sects were more inclined to concepts such as al-batin (the inner, hidden truth) and to devices like taqiyya (concealment of real beliefs).[2] Whereas the Sunnites expanded the scope of their authoritative leadership, their religious sources, and their juridical schools, the sects confined these to a few selected leaders, sources, and schools. Whereas the Sunnites have tended, to this day, to admit most people to their mosques, the Shiites confine mosques to their own. Sunnite men often marry Christian or Jewish women; Shiites seldom do. Sunnites eat food slaughtered or prepared by Christians or Jews; Shiites have traditionally regarded this as najas, polluted and impure.[3] In short, the Sunnites have tended to be both expansionist and assimilationist; the sects have tended to be withdrawn and exclusivist.

The Sunnites' dominance over the state has meant their control over the city as well and their preponderance in official and administrative affairs, even in societies where the Sunnites coexist with other important sects, such as in Iraq, Yemen, and Morocco. The sects, which have long maintained their fighting spirit, tend— with the tribes—to be more strongly represented in the military forces: the Zaidis (Zuyud) in Yemen, the Berbers in Morocco, and various minority groups in Syria, Lebanon, and Oman. This is particularly true when the solidarity of sect is reinforced by a solidarity of tribe, as with the Ibadis of Oman, the Zuyud of Yemen, the Druze and Alawites of Syria and Lebanon, and the Yazidis of Iraq.

When the solidarity of sect coincided with the solidarity of tribe, the group was more often capable of achieving an element of political autonomy, especially in times of weakness of the central Islamic state, as happened in the second Abbasid era and in some periods of the Ottoman era and, of course, during the colonial and modern eras. Thus, for example, the settlement of a Kharijite branch, the Ibadis, in Oman toward the end of the second century A.H. (eighth

---

1. See Muhammad Ahmad Abu Zahra, al-Madhahib al-Islamiyya [Islamic sects] (Cairo: Maktabat al-Adab, n.d.), pp. 29-130; Manna' al-Qattan, al-Tashri' wa al-fiqh al-Islami [Islamic legislation and jurisprudence] (Cairo: Wahba, 1979), pp. 280 ff.

2. Fu'ad al-Khuri, Imamat al-shahid wa imamat al-batal [Leadership of the martyr and leadership of the hero] (Beirut: Markaz Dar al-Jami'a, 1988), pp. 29-48, 132.

3. Fouad Ajami, The Vanished Imam: Musa al-Sadr and the Shia of Lebanon (Ithaca, NY: Cornell University Press, 1986), p. 133.

century A.D.) gave the country the distinct political character that it has retained ever since. The settlement of a certain Shiite branch, the Zuyud, in northern and eastern Yemen toward the end of the third century A.H. (ninth century A.D.) has also given that country a certain distinct political personality. In Lebanon, too, the emergence from the beginning of the seventeenth century A.D. of the Ma'ni and Shihabi emirates—the first Druze, the second Maronite, but tribally related—contributed to the development of a certain Lebanese distinctiveness. In modern times, the appearance of new religious sects or movements has also been influential in imparting a certain political character to a particular country, as with the Wahhabis in Arabia during the eighteenth century and the Sanusi in Libya during the nineteenth century.[4]

There has also been a geographical map and a political economy of Muslim sectarianism in the Arab world. The Sunnites, who dominated the state and the city, also dominated the fertile plains and prairies of the whole of the Arab world. Even where they do not form the overwhelming majority of the population, they are to be found in the fertile regions of Lebanon, Oman, Yemen, Iraq, and Bahrain. In most cases, Sunnites have owned the land, whereas Shiites and other sects have tilled it; this applies to Iraq, Syria, Bahrain, Saudi Arabia, and elsewhere. Historically, of course, landownership was an extension of state power, where the urban Sunnites were already dominant.

In Iraq, the Sunnite-Shiite dichotomy has been geographical—the former in the middle and north, the latter in the south—but it also overlapped until the interwar period with class divisions. Thus the most influential landlords of the province of Basrah were Sunnites, while the cultivators of their palm groves were overwhelmingly Shiites. Sunnites were also highly represented among the affluent landowners or merchants of all other southern areas except for the Shiite holy cities of Najaf and Karbala. In Baghdad, too, where the two sects enjoyed almost numerical parity, the socially dominant families were, with some exceptions, Sunnite. In the Iraqi army of the 1930s, the officers were Sunnite but the rank and file was mostly Shiite.[5] The Shiite south had for a long time been more culturally and economically tied to Iran, whereas the Sunnite north had been more culturally and economically tied to Syria and Turkey. From the interwar period, and especially after World War II, the Shiites went through a period of accelerated social mobility, not least in the matter of wealth, which they managed to accumulate through commerce. The Sunnites, however, continued to be more preponderant in holding state offices, both civilian and military.[6]

Smaller sects tend to reside in peripheral and mountainous territo-

    4. Al-Khuri, *Imamat al-shahid*, pp. 53-65; Iliya Harik, "The Origins of the Arab State System," in *The Foundations of the Arab State*, ed. Ghassan Salamé (London: Croom Helm, 1987), pp. 25-30.

    5. Hanna Batatu, *The Old Social Classes and the Revolutionary Movements of Iraq* (Princeton, NJ: Princeton University Press, 1982), pp. 44-45.

    6. Ibid., pp. 47-49.

ries: the Alawites, an offshoot of the Shiites, in the mountainous Latakia region of northwest Syria; the Druze, an offshoot of the Isma'ilis, in Jabal al-Duruz and in Wadi al-Tim in Syria and Lebanon; the Ibadis, a branch of the Kharijites, in the interior of Jabal Oman and in mountainous or oasis areas in Libya, Tunisia, and Algeria; the Zuyud in the mountainous regions of northeast Yemen; and the Yazidis on the Sinjar mountains in northern Iraq. The sects tend to be highly concentrated in their regions; thus 68 percent of the Alawites, 82 percent of the Syrian Druze, and 68 percent of the Ibadis live in their own territory. Similarly, 68 percent of the Lebanese Shiites and 91 percent of the Saudi Arabian Shiites all live within their own region, namely, southern Lebanon and eastern Arabia. Most sects also represent the statistically predominant religious denomination within their own region —for example, over 87 percent of the inhabitants of southern Iraq are Shiites. These sects have not only developed their own religious symbols and constructions in their territories but also tend to possess a fairly comprehensive economy of their own, based on diversified agriculture, local crafts, and small towns. Landownership is often extensively spread among members of the community and so are things such as the ownership of palm trees—the community is obviously striving for economic self-sufficiency in grains and other basic foods, as well as in crafts and small industries. The religious symbols and the self-contained economy reinforce the sense of psychological and cultural distinctiveness from the surrounding society.[7]

SUNNITE-SHIITE DISTINCTIONS

The social and cultural differences between the Sunnites and the other Islamic sects are all reflected in the political realm. The Sunnites tend to look to the state as the organizer of their religious affairs. In their traditional theory, the ruler is the implementer of the Word of God; and in this capacity obedience is due to him from every believer. And that Word of God is specifically translated, by the jurists, into law, the shari'a. Little space is allowed for disagreement: consensus (ijma') is a cardinal principle, based on the decisions of those who "bind and loosen" (ahl al-hal wa al-'aqd), who are mainly the caliph and the 'ulama'. The culture is assimilationist in spite of social diversity, giving an impression of unity and harmony to be derived from the comprehensive translation of religion into public policies. Opposition to the state is therefore almost tantamount to abandoning the faith; it is not only to be condemned by the society but is also to be prevented by the state.[8]

By contrast, the Shiites are not etatists but imamites—their imam or spiritual leader (a term they prefer to the term "caliph," which is more familiar to the Sunnites) is the peak of their religiosity and pious emotions; he is an example to be followed and an inspiration to be striven after. His

7. Al-Khuri, *Imamat al-shahid*, pp. 71-92.
8. See Nazih Ayubi, *Political Islam: Religion and Politics in the Arab World* (London: Routledge, 1991), chap. 1.

is an internal spiritual authority, whereas that of the Sunnite caliph is more of an external political control. Whereas the Sunnites have tended to believe that government is legitimate and just as long as it follows the *shari'a*, the Shiites have on the whole maintained that government can never be legitimate and just as long as the Imam remained absent or "hidden." Their attitude toward government has therefore tended to oscillate between the concealment of their real feelings (*taqiyya*) and the mobilization of forces against the existing illegitimate order. A sense of permanent revolution has thus tended to be part of their ideological and psychological outlook, always kept alive by the memory of their martyrs and by their own readiness to emulate their example. Their rites and rituals are often intense and collective, maintaining group cohesiveness and a certain sense of distinctiveness and moral superiority.[9]

The Sunnite state controls its jurists and clerics tightly. Originally the restricting of juridical schools to four in number—Hanafi, Maliki, Shafi'i, and Hanbali—was a political decision; the Ja'fari school might also have been recognized by al-Mutawakkil (A.H. 232-47) had it not been for the Shiite disturbances during his time. Although the original writings of the jurists of the four Sunnite schools might to some extent have mirrored the environment in which each of them had lived—for example, Abu Hanifa, a liberal, might have reflected the more complex and more advanced Iraqi society in which he functioned, whereas

Malik, a conservative, might have been more representative of the harsher Arabian society—what is more important is the way in which teachings of the various schools were acclimatized in various societies. Thus, with the passing of time, certain countries came to be more favorable to a certain school than others; for example, Malikism was favored in North Africa; Shafi'ism in Egypt, Syria, and Lebanon; Hanafism in Iraq, Turkey, and the Caucasus; and Hanbalism in the Arabian Peninsula.[10]

A rather distinctive feature in Arabia and the Persian Gulf is the greater emphasis attached there to people's *madhhab*, that is, their juridical "sect" or "school"; indeed, in Yemen the Sunnites are commonly known by their juridical sect as *shawafi'*. Apparently, tribal and familial groupings try to distinguish themselves by following a specific *madhhab*. Thus, in Bahrain, for example, tribal lineages would follow the Maliki school; al-Hawla—Sunnite Arabs of Iranian background—the Hanbali; and urban and rural Shiites, the Ja'fari.[11] In other societies, the following of a particular *madhhab* may indicate some professional or social difference. Thus, in Tunisia and other parts of North Africa, most Hanafi families are of Turkish and/or a princely or official background. For that matter, too, Hanafism remains a favorite school among the *'ulama'* in Egypt; sanctioned as the state's official *madhhab*

9. Al-Khuri, *Imamat al-shahid*, pp. 156-63.

10. Hasan Sadiq, *Judhur al-fitna fi al-firaq al-Islamiyya* [Roots of discord in the Islamic sects] (Cairo: Madbuli, 1988), pp. 227-43.
11. Al-Khuri, *Imamat al-shahid*, pp. 222-23.

by the Ottomans, it remains to this day the official juridical school of *ifta'* ("counseling") and *qada'* ("the judiciary"), even though the majority of the population, especially in the rural areas, are non-Hanafis. In northern Lebanon, whereas the distinguished families of merchants and landowners are often Shafi'is, the families of artisans and craftsmen are overwhelmingly Maliki.[12]

The *'ulama'* are an integral part of the state establishment in Sunnite countries, fitting very often within the contours of its administrative organization. They are frequently employed by the government as judges, preachers, and teachers. As state functionaries, they often dissociate themselves from the more ritualistic functions in which less educated and more popular types engage in the countryside, such as circumcision, burial, and chanting. Among the Shiites, on the other hand, the role of the clergy who are directly involved—in a more voluntary way—in the social and cultural affairs of their local communities is much more profound. Religious services and ceremonies are very extensive at the grass-roots levels, with an abundance of festivals to commemorate all kinds of religious occasions, both sad and joyful. The Shiite clergy are also more likely than their Sunnite counterparts to adjudicate in sensitive family conflicts involving adultery, sodomy, violence, or black magic, since on the whole the Shiite clerics are much more socially intimate with their congregations.[13] Among Shiite communities there is a higher percentage of

clergy to attend to all such functions than there is among communities of Sunnites; for instance, there is about one cleric to every 2000 of the population in predominately Sunnite Syria compared to about one to every 300 of the population in predominately Shiite Iran. The intensity of the Shiite rituals is also more remarkable, as for example in the Karbala commemorations, where the public believes that the status of the *mulla* is to be measured by his ability to inspire weeping, agony, and torment in his audience.

This does not mean that the clergy in Shiism do not cooperate with the state, for indeed many of them do. These are the ones whom Ayatollah Khomeini designated as the "jurists of the Sultans" *(fuqaha' al-salatin),* for they interpret religion to suit the requirements of the government even at times when the Imam remains absent and politics therefore continue to be unjust. Their standing, however, is never considered to be as noble as the status of those who work for the autonomy of the religious society, away from government and the central authority, in preparation for and in expectation of the arrival of the just Imam. It should be remembered as well that the political economy of the Shiite establishment is also different. For apart from the religious judges who may work for the state, most Shiite scholars derive their incomes from private popular sources and various tithes and donations or else from religious endowments subject to their direct control. All this gives the Shiite clergy a certain measure of autonomy vis-à-vis the state and enables them in many

12. Sadiq, *Judhur al-fitna*, pp. 229-31.
13. Al-Khuri, *Imamat al-shahid*, pp. 224-52.

instances to voice their protest against government.

To speak about the social, economic, and political distinctiveness of the Muslim sects is not to suggest, however, that such characteristics are permanent or eternal. In the same way in which many of the original aspects of distinction were accentuated by various economic, political, and cultural developments, changes in these latter factors can in turn induce significant changes in the general outlook of the sects. To illustrate this point, two examples concerning the political outlook of the Shiite community in Iraq and in Lebanon can be cited.

The conventional view on the position of the Shiites in Iraq maintains that the traditional supremacy of the Sunnites, inherited from Ottoman and pre-Ottoman times, has been continued in independent Iraq, royal and republican. Because the Shiites were politically disenfranchised, the conventional argument runs, they have come to represent on the whole an oppositional community. While Sunnites have identified with Arab nationalism—the other Arab states are predominantly Sunnite—those Shiites who have adopted modern political ideologies have tended toward leftist orientations, notably the Communist Party. Yet as Sami Zubaida rightly illustrates, the political orientations of the Shiites are diverse, and this diversity is as much the product of political institutions and processes and of class and economic factors as it is of communal solidarity.[14]

Under the monarchy, southern Shiite shaykh-landlords were a predominant part of the political establishment. Different factions of the 'ulama' had different associates: peasants and merchants, conservatives and progressives, domestic patrons and foreign agencies. In due course, Nasserism and Ba'thism did attract many Shiites. Equally, at various points in its history, the Communist Party included many Sunnite Arabs in its leadership. The presence of the Shiites was notable, but their numerical representation was no higher, and perhaps even a little lower, than their representation in the population at large. The remarkable fact about Iraqi Shiites is the extent to which they have been predominant in politics generally: rather than saying that they have a propensity toward communism, it would be more accurate to say that they have a propensity for politics. Moreover, the directions in which this propensity is expressed change often, with yet another shift occurring after the Iranian Revolution, which has politicized the Iraqi Shiites even further.[15]

Another interesting example may be observed with regard to the Lebanese Shiites. For centuries, this community appeared to accept its marginal and downtrodden status. Ritualistic ceremony could provide psychological consolation, but little more. In the collective memory of the Shiites, the seventh-century story of

14. Sami Zubaida, "Class and Community in Urban Politics," in *Urban Crises and Social Movements in the Middle East*, ed. Kenneth

Brown et al. (Paris: Editions l'Harmattan, 1989), pp. 63 ff.

15. Ibid., pp. 63-66; see also Tawfiq al-Shaikh, 'An al-'Iraq wa al-haraka al-Islamiyya [On Iraq and the Islamicist movement] (London: al-Safa, 1988), pp. 60-67.

Husain's martyrdom appeared to have a permanent, sad, and lonely relevance: "Every day is Ashura, and every place is Karbala" was the teaching of Shiite history. This ritualistic reminder of the Shiites' solitude and defeat, however, could also be transformed into a celebration of defiance and moral superiority—both Ayatollah Khomeini in Iran and Musa al-Sadr in Lebanon have managed to turn it in that direction. With the victory of clerics in Iran,

the once embarrassing symbols of [Shiite] Islam were exalted. Men no longer awaited the millennium; they proclaimed that in Iran they had an answer for the ailments of the Muslim world. . . . A political tradition of submission gave way to a messianic movement; [Shiite] clerics who once summoned men to worship, who monitored ritual, were summoning men to arms.[16]

From its inception, Shiite thought did not see the acquisition of power as a prerequisite for a good and pious life. Now, however, in the thinking of the Lebanese Shiite Muhammad Hussain Fadhlallah, as in that of Khomeini himself, there is a new, "curiously [Sunnite] orientation—the sense that taqiyya, dissimulation, should be abandoned, that men should create a Muslim order and defend it."[17]

It is also important to note that the recent politicization of the Shiites has taken different forms, depending on the distinct political conjunctures pertaining in various Arab countries. The contrast between Iraq and Lebanon is again illustrative in this regard, refuting as it does the claim

that communal entities have a permanent, essentialist character. In spite of their exclusion from authority and in spite of the opportunity for rebellion provided for them by the prolonged Iran-Iraq war—the majority of the soldiers being Shiites—the Iraqi Shiites have not opted for a purely Shiite solution, as through secession or segregation, or even for a separate political organization for their community. Exclusively Shiite political parties have always been weak, from the Nahda party in the 1920s to the Da'wa party in the 1980s. The Shiites of Lebanon, on the other hand, have either accepted the confessional framework of Lebanon and tried to enlarge their share within its confines as a community, as Amal has done, or else have rebelled against the entire territorial-state paradigm and declared their identification with the Islamic revolution of Iran, claiming that religion has no geography. The latter is the course chosen by Hizballah.[18]

The idea to be deduced from the previous analysis is that the ideological and political import of religious communal identification does not have an essential, unchanging nature but is contingent upon the sociohistorical environment and on the political conjunctures in which these communities function. It is only with such an idea in mind that one can understand how the Shiite doctrine has been turned, with such people as Khomeini, Sadr, and Fadhlallah, from a doctrine of political quiet-

16. Ajami, Vanished Imam, pp. 141-52, 191.
17. Ibid., pp. 214-15.

18. Ghassan Salama, al-Mujtama' wa al-dawla fi al-Mashriq al-'arabi [Society and state in the Arab Levant] (Beirut: Centre for Arab Unity Studies, 1987), pp. 85-98.

ism and resignation into a doctrine of political action and struggle. This is also how one may understand the way in which the presumably statist Sunnite doctrine, which has been built into the entire tissue of the state in countries such as Saudi Arabia and Morocco, has been able to generate oppositional religiopolitical movements, such as al-Jihad, al-Takfir wa al-Hijra, and Hizb al-Tahrir al-Islami.[19]

THE RELIGIOUS MINORITIES

Following the precepts of the Quran and *hadith*, those *ahl al-kitab* ("People of the Book"—mainly Jews and Christians) who lived within the Islamic dominion (*dar al-Islam*) were normally accorded their freedom of belief and security of life and possessions in return for paying a sort of poll tax (*jizya*). A juridical disagreement eventually emerged as to whether the *jizya* was to be levied as a means of pressure to induce more people to convert to Islam or whether it was enforced in return for the non-Muslims' not being required—owing to their sensitive position—to participate in the activities of war, that is, whether it was a payment in return for their being protected and exempted from the military duties of *jihad*. Christians and Jews, as well as Sabaeans and Magi, were subsequently categorized by the jurists as *ahl al-dhimma* or *dhimmi*s, implying that they were, by accord (*'ahd*), under the protection of the Muslims. Their conditions varied from ruler to ruler, but they were on the whole—given the standards of the day—treated with tolerance, and

many of them did assume fairly influential posts as administrators, accountants, physicians, and the like in the service of the state. Historically, they were also on occasion exempt from paying the *jizya* if the state failed to protect them or if they were recruited for military service.[20]

The Ottomans institutionalized the Islamic tradition with regard to the position of non-Muslims, under the label of the *millet* system, and accorded them a considerable degree of cultural, social, and legal autonomy. Consequently, a Christian or a Jew did not enjoy as an individual whatever rights he had; rather, he enjoyed them as a member of his community. If he deserted his church, for example, he lost his legal status and the rights and duties that went with it. The religious communities represented, therefore, part of the general pattern of unity in diversity, as the historical Islamic state was perhaps almost as much corporatist as it was integrative.[21]

Nonetheless, the religious minorities have developed their lives in close proximity to the Muslim state and have adjusted their perspectives and attitudes to its requirements. Many of the Eastern churches—the Copts as well as the Nestorians,

---

19. For details, see Ayubi, *Political Islam.*

20. See Radwan al-Sayyid, *Mafahim al-jama'at fi al-Islam* [The concept of groups in Islam] (Beirut: Dar al-Tanwir, 1984), pp. 115-30; Victor Sahhab, *Darurat al-turath* [The necessity of the heritage] (Beirut: al-'Ilm li-al-Malayin, 1984), pp. 169-70; Muhammad Hamdi al-Manawi, *al-Wizara wa al-wuzara' fi al-'asr al-Fatimi* [The vizarate and viziers in the Fatimid era] (Cairo: Dar al-Ma'arif, 1970), pp. 38-39, 133 ff.

21. Cf. al-Sayyid, *Mafahim al-jama'at,* pp. 134-40.

Jacobites, and Maronites, which sprang from the Syriac tradition— had originally emerged by way of a kind of national reaction and self-assertion vis-à-vis the Byzantine establishment. Most of them had welcomed the Muslim conquerors as saviors from Byzantine persecution and subsequently learned to adjust themselves to the ideology and institutions of the Islamic state and to play a complementary economic role within it.

As a result, the religious minorities, unlike the Islamic sects, have tended to be geographically dispersed and doctrinally diverse. Thus, among the Christians of the Middle East, there are Orthodox churches known as Coptic, Syriac, Greek, Armenian, Nestorian, Chaldean, and so on as well as the more recent Catholic and Protestant offshoots of the older orthodox churches. The organizational diversity of the religious minorities was partly a function of their residence in the cities and their direct relationship with the central state, which, dominated as it was by the assimilationist Sunnites, was prepared to accept them socially but only as weak, scattered entities deprived of any clear manifestations of cultural distinction.[22] Whereas the Islamic sects opposed the dominant ideology and the central power and existed only by way of resisting or deceiving it, the religious minorities accepted the ideology of the government, however reluctantly, and conformed to its expectations of them; their survival is not as much a func-

tion of their resistance as it is of the tolerance of the Muslims.

The Maronites were almost unique among the religious minorities in their resistance to the *dhimmi* status, an attitude that eventually culminated in their refusal to join the *millet* council organized by the Ottomans in the nineteenth century. Such an attitude, derived as it is from their distinctive history as well as from their collective mythology, makes them different from other religious minorities—to the extent that Fu'ad al-Khuri classifies them, functionally speaking, among the sects (*tawa'if*) and not among the minorities (*aqalliyyat*).[23] Like the sects, the Maronites have historically inhabited the mountains and developed their own semi-autonomous political economy. Their sense of distinctiveness has been reinforced by the fact that they probably originated as a tribe rather than as a church. Indeed, their bishops were, conventionally, representatives of the various sublineages of the tribe and not of various geographic parishes, as is the case with other churches, Eastern and Western.[24]

The specificity of the Maronites becomes all the more obvious when one compares them to the other major Christian communities of the Levant, the Greek Orthodox. From the beginning, the Orthodox adjusted themselves to the requirements of the Byzantine and then the Islamic state. They have always prayed in

---

22. Waddah Sharara, *Isti'naf al-bad'* [Resuming the start] (Beirut: Dar al-Hadatha, 1981), pp. 170-71.

23. Al-Khuri, *Imamat al-shahid*, pp. 13, 109.

24. Salama, *al-Mujtama'wa al-dawla*, p. 109, n. 28 and references; Harik, "Arab State System," pp. 31-33.

their Mass for the ruler of the day and asked God for victory over "the enemy of the land." It is little wonder that the Arabs were to call them the "royalists" (al-Mulukiyyun). Their assimilation into the Arabic culture has been extensive, and their commercial activities have often been complementary to those of the Sunnite Muslim merchants. Many among them have been members of, and even leaders in, the modern and contemporary Arab nationalist movements; examples include Michel 'Aflaq and George Habash.

Within the Islamic state, the religious minorities, while they do not possess their own economy as the Islamic sects do, are often professionally distinct from the majority of Muslims. There has been a certain element of ethnoreligious division of labor in the Muslim state since its early days. The situation continued for many centuries, and some features of it can be detected to this day. Not only do non-Muslims often engage in activities prohibited by Islam, such as the practice of usury and the making of wines, but they have tended historically to be highly represented in professions carrying lower social status, such as tanning, tailoring, smithing, carpentry, jewelry making, and entertainment.

The ethnoreligious division of labor was eventually to be somewhat reversed and to work for the benefit of the religious minorities when, from the eighteenth century but especially from the nineteenth, European colonialism was opening up the Ottoman empire, Egypt, and North Africa to the world capitalist market. Christians and Jews were preferred as commercial agents, possibly because of religious affinity with the Europeans but more importantly because of their commercial and financial expertise as well as their greater proficiency in foreign languages. A new type of ethnoreligious division of labor was to develop, and, indeed, until the interwar period and in some cases until later, an exceptionally high percentage of all people involved in business, commerce, and finance in Turkey and most parts of the Arab world were normally from among the non-Muslim communities. This, in turn, sometimes led to a Muslim backlash against the minorities once national independence had been gained, even though the Christians, in particular, had played a prominent role in the nationalist movements of several countries, including Egypt, Syria, and Palestine.

PROSPECTS FOR THE TERRITORIAL STATE

I have argued here that partly as a result of religious doctrine and partly as a result of the political precedence of the historical Islamic state, Islamic sects and religious minorities have conventionally developed certain distinct characteristics. The geographic distribution as well as the political economy of the sects and of the minorities manifest in reality quite different features, which are in the main a function of their relationship to the state. Whereas the Islamic sects—in varying degrees, of course—have not come to terms ideologically or organizationally with the state, the religious minorities have on the whole—with the possible exception of the Maronites—

adjusted themselves mentally and behaviorally to the requirements of the state.

The modern Middle Eastern state has largely ignored the communal problem, pretending as much as possible that it does not exist. The Islamicists, on the other hand, have remained in this regard the prisoners of early juridical interpretations and political precedents, which are not capable of offering effective solutions to today's problems. If anything, the contemporary Islamicists seem to be less imaginative and innovative than their earlier predecessors. Even the *sahifa* ("constitution") of Medina, prescribed by the Prophet Muhammad himself, was to include the Jews in the definition of the *umma* ("nation"). Yet there is no effective solution to the communal problem in the contemporary state that can be derived literally and ready-made from the conventional jurisprudence of the early Islamic state. The *ahl al-dhimma* formula that was so noble and progressive ten centuries ago is hardly suitable after the centuries of human and constitutional progress that has affected all societies. One can quite understand the alarm with which the Christians of Egypt, for example, receive the incessant calls for a full application of the *shari'a*, which is often taken to mean conventional jurisprudence. Nor is there any provision in the conventional jurisprudence for the position of other Muslim sects within an Islamic state.

Improvisation and innovation are therefore required, and it is thus refreshing to observe a few attempts by contemporary Islamic writers to address such issues in an enlightened way. Islamic sympathizers such as Tariq al-Bishri, Muhammad 'Imara, and 'Adil Husain have produced some interesting improvisations with regard to the position of non-Muslims in a modern Islamic state.[25] Most explicit, however, has been Fahmi Huwaidi, who has put forth a persuasive case for the full citizenship of non-Muslims in a contemporary Islamic state. He derives his argument from Islam's humanitarian inclination, from the shared monotheism of the three major Middle Eastern religions, from the Medina Constitution, and from Muhammad's ruling about *ahl al-kitab*: "To them what is due to us, and from them what is due on us."[26]

25. Tariq al-Bishri, *al-Muslimun wa al-Aqbat* [Muslims and Copts] (Cairo: Hai'at al-Kitab, 1980); Muhammad 'Imara, *al-Islam wa al-sulta al-diniyya* [Islam and religious authority] (Cairo: Dar al-thaqafa al-jadida, 1979); 'Adil Husain, *Nahwa fikr 'arabi jadid* [Toward a new Arab thought] (Cairo: Dar al-Mustaqbal al-'Arabi, 1985).
26. Fahmi Huwaidi, *Muwatinun la dhimiyyun* [Citizens, not protected subjects] (Beirut: Dar al-Shuruq, 1985), pp. 128-45.

ANNALS, *AAPSS*, 524, November 1992

The Clergy's Concepts
of Rule in Egypt and Iran

By SHAHROUGH AKHAVI

ABSTRACT: In the wake of the current cycle of Islamic resurgence, which began at the time of the June 1967 Arab-Israeli war, the question of rule has been at the center of clerical discourse. This article analyzes this question in the debates of the Egyptian and Iranian *'ulama'*. While they agree upon the perception of Islam as both religion and state and upon the need to base public law upon the *shari'a* (the holy law of Islam), they differ on the role of secular rulers, the relevance of *jihad*, identifying apostates, calling for rebellion, authorizing the *'ulama'* to rule society, and endowing Islamic states with extraordinary powers. The debate will continue to focus on these issues in the future, as Islamic groups press the case for full implementation of the *shari'a* in all areas of life, not only in Egypt and Iran but in all Muslim societies.

Shahrough Akhavi is professor of government and international studies, University of South Carolina. He is editor of the Middle East Series of the State University of New York Press and an editor of Oxford University Press's forthcoming Encyclopedia of the Modern Islamic World. *He has published widely on Egyptian and Iranian politics.*

NOTE: Part of the research for this article was undertaken by the author as a Fulbright Research Scholar in Cairo during the autumn of 1991. The author would like to thank the Fulbright Commission of Egypt for its support.

A S in earlier cycles of Islamic resurgence during the modern period, the current one highlights the
question of rule. In Islamic discourse,
the term "rule" is usually rendered
"imamate" or "caliphate," and the
theory pertaining to it was elaborated in the medieval era. Those con-
tributing to the theory had to grapple
with the fact that, although the doctrine held that, after the Prophet's
death, rule should devolve upon the
most learned, just, pious, and capable leader of the community, in fact,
it was increasingly appropriated by
the strongest prince. The Muslim jurists rationalized these arrant sei-
zures of power by tribal chiefs on the
grounds that the continued existence
of the Islamic community depended
upon the acceptance of these actions,
as long as the chiefs upheld the basic
pillars of the faith. However, current
activists—termed here Islamicists—
reject such compromises with power
holders and insist that they are responsible, in great measure, for the
difficulties Muslims face today.

There is consensus that the current Islamic resurgence has its roots
in the disastrous Arab defeat in the
June 1967 Arab-Israeli war.[1] This suggests that it antedates the Iranian
revolution, although it certainly re-

ceived a major impetus from that
shattering event. This article focuses
upon the clergy's discourse on the
question of rule in Egypt and Iran,
where the debates have probably had
the greatest impact in the Islamic
world.

THE EGYPTIAN 'ULAMA'

In Egypt, the 'ulama' ("clergy") of
al-Azhar, the most famous mosque
and Islamic theological college in the
world, have been generally supportive of the state over the generations.
Those clergymen who have opposed
the government's policies have grav-
itated to the Sunnite Islamic world's
most important social movement, the
nonviolent Muslim Brotherhood,
which was established in 1928. It is
predominantly a lay organization of
religiously minded Muslims. The
most radical clergymen, younger in
age and committed to violent opposition, have affiliated with splinter organizations that have split from the
Muslim Brotherhood.

The Shaykh al-Azhar owes his
post to the government and supports
the latter on issues of moment. The
Ministry of Religious Endowments
and al-Azhar Affairs is another government body that exercises authority in the religious field. Within the
ministry is the Supreme Council on
Religious Affairs, on which sit, inter
alia, the Shaykh al-Azhar, the Minister of Religious Endowments and al-
Azhar Affairs, and the Mufti of
Egypt, who is the country's chief Islamic jurist.

Despite the differences between
the state religious institutions, the
Muslim Brotherhood, and the radical

1. Husayn Ahmad Amin, "al-Tayyarat al-
Islamiyya fi Misr khilal al-sab'inat" [Islamic
trends in Egypt during the 1970s], in al-Islam
fi 'alam mutaghayyir wa maqalat Islamiyya
ukhra [Islam in a changing world and other
Islamic essays] (Cairo: Maktaba Madbuli,
1989), p. 169; Hasan Hanafi, "Ahadith fi al-
harakat al-diniyya al-Mu'asira" [Comments
about contemporary religious movements] in
al-Din wa al-dawla fi Misr [Religion and state
in Egypt], vol. 6, al-Usuliyya al-Islamiyya [Is-
lamic fundamentalism] (Cairo: Maktaba
Madbuli, 1989), p. 320.

Islamic groups, all three support the idea of making the holy law—the *shari'a*—the source of law in Egypt. They also agree that Islam is both a religious and a political system: *Islam din wa dawla* ("Islam is religion and state"), according to this view.[2] There may be differences between them as to whether the *shari'a* should be the only source of public law or just the major source, but in any case their position contrasts with that of the regime, which has temporized and failed so far to take a final decision on this crucial matter. However, the regime has accepted the parliament's 1985 amendment to the Personal Status Law, which changed the more liberal version of 1979 on questions of divorce and custody of children by making it more difficult for women to initiate divorce or to have custody over children.

Generally speaking, al-Azhar, the Ministry of Religious Endowments, and the Mufti do not get involved directly in central public policy issues. Occasionally, however, they are implicated in the hurly-burly of what we may term, for lack of a better phrase, religious politics. Between 1979 and 1981, clashes broke out be-

tween Copts (Christians) and Muslims in Egypt over the issue of land and religious activity, and Egyptian President Sadat, the official Islamic bodies, the Muslim Brotherhood, and the militant Islamicists all criticized the Coptic leadership and community.[3]

THE ARGUMENT OF *THE ABSENT PRECEPT*

But perhaps the most interesting intervention by the official Egyptian clergy on a political matter occurred in the aftermath of President Anwar al-Sadat's assassination in October 1981 by radical Islamicists of the Tanzim al-Jihad (Jihad Organization). In this case, the then Mufti (currently Shaykh al-Azhar), Shaykh Jadd al-Haqq 'Ali Jadd al-Haqq, issued a *fatwa* (an authoritative opinion), rejecting arguments made in a pamphlet that apparently was the inspiration of the assassins. This pamphlet, known as *The Absent Precept* (*al-Farida al-gha'iba*), was a 54-page text written by an engineer, Muhammad 'Abd al-Salam Faraj. Because of its importance, it will be discussed in some detail, as will the Mufti's *fatwa* refuting its contents.[4] Although Faraj was not a member of the *'ulama'* stra-

2. This is not a unanimous view, but it certainly is the overwhelmingly majority position of the contemporary clergy. See, for example, Shaykh Muhammad al-Ghazali, *Min huna na'lam* [From here we know], 5th ed. (Cairo: Dar al-Kutub al-Haditha, 1965 [originally published in 1950]); Shaykh 'Umar al-Tilimsani, *Dhikrayat, la mudhakkarat* [Remembrances, not reminders] (Cairo: Dar al-Taba'a wa al-Nashr al Islamiyya, 1985), p. 274; Khalid Muhammad Khalid, *al-Dawla fi al-Islam* [The state in Islam] (Cairo: Dar Thabit, 1981). Interestingly, Khalid had, in 1950, concluded the contrary.

3. Hamied Ansari, "Sectarian Conflict in Egypt and the Political Expediency of Religion," *Middle East Journal*, 38:397-418 (1984); idem, "The Islamic Militants in Egyptian Politics," *International Journal of Middle East Studies*, 16:123-44 (1984); Sa'd Eddine Ibrahim, "The Anatomy of Egypt's Militant Islamic Groups," *International Journal of Middle East Studies*, 12(4):423-53 (Dec. 1980).

4. For an English translation of Faraj's pamphlet and an analysis of al-Haqq's *fatwa*, see J.G.G. Jansen, *The Neglected Duty* (New York: Macmillan, 1986).

tum, some leaders of his organization were clergymen, and, on the whole, this pamphlet represents the thinking of younger-generation militant *'ulama'* who feel betrayed by the formal religious bodies and also by the Muslim Brotherhood.

Faraj's argument was that Muslims had neglected the categorical imperative of *jihad* ("struggle for the faith") at their peril. He noted that the principle of *jihad* was one of the collective obligations of the Muslims, and their abandonment of it had led them to their current difficulties.[5] Faraj insisted that the establishment of an Islamic state was mandated by the Quran and the Prophet.[6] He also held that Muslims must rule according to what Allah has revealed. This is a reference to the so-called *hakimiyya* or sovereignty/rulership verses of the Quran, to which the Pakistani Muslim Abu al-A'la al-Mawdudi (d. 1971) and the Egyptian thinker Sayyid Qutb (d. 1966)—under Mawdudi's influence—had attached such major importance.

Other points made by Faraj included the idea that the current rulers of Islamic countries were like the Mongols at the time of Genghis Khan's invasion of the Middle East in the thirteenth century. Like the Mongols, he argued, the current rulers do not rule according to Islamic laws but according to secular laws into which have been suffused elements of Islamic legislation.[7]

As a consequence, Faraj pointed out, the current rulers of Islamic countries are in a state of apostasy with respect to the faith, even though they preserve some of the outward manifestations of belief, such as upholding prayer and fasting during Ramadan. Apostates are more dangerous than unbelievers who never committed themselves to Islam, and hence it is imperative to pronounce *takfir* (formally stating that they have turned to unbelief) against these rulers. Not only that, but the Islamic law on apostasy sanctions capital punishment.[8]

Faraj argued that the violent overthrow of existing regimes is the only path that could guarantee the establishment of a truly Islamic state. This is more effective than, for example, trying to retake Jerusalem from the Israelis on grounds that, at first, one fights the enemy who is near at hand, for only after defeating him can one move to defeat the opponent who is further afield.[9]

He then cited the sword verse of the Quran (9:5), which proclaims that after the lapse of the months during which no fighting is allowed between the Muslims and their enemies, "slay the idolaters wherever you find them, and take them captive or besiege them, and lie in wait for them at every likely place." In Faraj's opinion, this verse superseded all the 124 verses of the Quran that counsel

5. Muhammad 'Abd al-Salam Faraj, *al-Farida al-gha'iba* [The absent precept], reprinted in Jumhuriyya Misr al-'Arabiyya, Wizara al-Awqaf, al-Majlis al-A'la li al-Shu'un al-Islamiyya, *Al-Fatawa al-Islamiyya min dar al-ifta' al-Islamiyya* [Islamic fatwas from the office of the Mufti] (Cairo: al-Majlis al-A'la li al-Shu'un al-Islamiyya, 1403 H.Q./1984), 10: 3762; 3780 ff.

6. Ibid., pp. 3763-64.

7. Ibid., pp. 3765-66; comparisons with the Mongols continue, pp. 3767-71.

8. Ibid., p. 3766.

9. Ibid., pp. 3775-76.

patience or abjuring armed conflict with the non-Muslims in a spirit of peaceful persuasion.[10]

His last major point is that it would be wrong to suggest that there are stages of *jihad* and to hold that the current stage is simply one of *jihad al-nafs*, or struggling inwardly to purify oneself for the sake of Allah. In fact, such individual cleansing goes hand in hand, in his view, with *al-jihad al-akbar*, or struggling at the community level for the sake of Allah against the enemies of Islam. To say that Muslims are still at the preliminary point of self-*jihad* is to rationalize inaction at a time when the community is in great danger from without. This sort of individualist *jihad* must be simultaneously accompanied by *jihad* at the community level against Islam's enemies, identified as neo-Crusaders, imperialism, and Zionism.[11]

AL-AZHAR'S RESPONSE

In his *fatwa*, the Mufti of Egypt considers first the question of who is a Muslim. He cites the Prophet as having declared that the Muslim is the one who recites the credo "I attest that there is no god but Allah and Muhammad is his prophet" and also commits himself to the remaining four pillars: prayer, alms, fasting, and pilgrimage.[12] When, then, may a

person be said to have abandoned Islam? The Mufti replies by citing the Quran (4:116): "Allah does not forgive one who associates others with Himself; otherwise, He forgives whom He wants." Then, he cites a tradition of the Prophet, who is said to have declared, "The archangel Gabriel came to me and said: 'He of your community who has died but not in any way associated others with Allah will enter paradise.' I said: 'Even if he has committed adultery and theft?' He said: 'Even if he has committed adultery and theft.' "[13] In other words, only arrant polytheists may be apostates, according to the Shaykh.

Consequently, Shaykh al-Haqq concludes that a person who genuinely believes in Islam but can be objectively shown to have violated even a core religious tenet has done no more than commit a sin. While sinning is reprehensible, it does not cause the believer to have renounced his belief in Islam. Thus, although it is true that our actions are the warrants of our beliefs, only Allah, not mere mortals, can punish a sinner.[14]

The Mufti cautions that false accusations of unbelief against Muslims are themselves cause for the most serious breach of Allah's laws. He declares that the Quran commands Muslims to submit disputes among themselves to Allah—that is, to the Quran—and to the Prophet (4:59) and orders the faithful to "ask the keepers of the scripture" when in doubt over a matter of faith (21:7). The Prophet, hearing Muslims dis-

10. Ibid., pp. 3777-78.

11. Ibid., p. 3780.

12. Shaykh Jadd al-Haqq 'Ali Jadd al-Haqq, "al-Mawdu' (1326) Katib al-farida al-gha'iba wa al-radd 'alayhi" [The problem (1326) The absent precept pamphlet and a riposte to it], in Jumhuriyya Misr al-'Arabiyya, Wizara al-Awqaf, al-Majlis al-A'la li al-Shu'un al-Islamiyya, *al-Fatawa al-Islamiyya min dar*

al-ifta' al-Islamiyya [Islamic fatwas from the office of the Mufti], 10:3730.

13. Ibid., pp. 3731-32.

14. Ibid.

puting over verses of the Quran, warned that in the past those who had disputed over Allah's words had perished, and he enjoined them to "say what you know about it [the Quran] and of that about which you are ignorant, assign it to the person who knows."[15]

For the Mufti, not surprisingly, the *'ulama'* are the ones to whom the Quran and the Prophet are referring. Religiosity is the province of all Muslims, he notes, but the clarification of Islam's ordinances and of what is permitted and prohibited is for the specialists—the *'ulama'*—to decide.[16]

As for *jihad*, Shaykh al-Haqq reasons that the law prescribes *jihad* in times of peace and also in times of war. During times of peace, *jihad* is characterized by the individual's struggle to purify his or her soul and distance himself or herself from Satan. In times of war, *jihad* devolves upon the community to fight those who repudiate the oneness of Allah and the prophecy of His messenger.

It is true that *jihad* was the obligation of every individual (*fard 'ayn*) at the time of the Prophet, but after him, it devolved upon the community if necessity called for it. Such necessity existed when the land of the Muslims was occupied by non-Muslims, but even then it would be conducted not only by armed conflict but by means of wealth, words, and heart, in accordance with the saying attributed to the Prophet: "Fight the polytheists by means of your wealth, your hands, and your tongues."[17]

The Mufti acknowledges the sword verse but rejects the view that it supersedes all others counseling patience, dialogue, and persuasion. The latter are more representative, the Mufti opines; examples include the following: "There is no compulsion in matters of religion" (2:256); "call them to the path of your Lord with wisdom and words of good advice, and reason with them in the best way possible" (16:125). As for the *hakimiyya* verses (especially 5:44, 45, and 47: "And those who do not rule[18] according to Allah's revelation are unbelievers/oppressors/dissolutes"), Shaykh al-Haqq counters that, first of all, only he who irrevocably abandons Allah's ordinances is an unbeliever; someone who incidentally and casually happens to have done so is not. Second, given the verses immediately preceding these, it is clear that the antecedent noun of the pronoun "those" are the "people of the book"—in this particular case, the Jews, since it is they who, by worshipping the golden calf, had abandoned the Torah and thus come to be unbelievers. The reference, then, is not to the Muslims.[19]

---

15. Ibid., p. 3735.
16. Ibid.
17. Ibid., pp. 3736-37.

18. "*Wa man lam yahkum.* . . ." Faraj, as with al-Mawdudi and Qutb before him, has rendered the verb *yahkum* as "rule," rather than the traditional "judge." It is interesting that in rebutting Faraj's interpretation of this verse, the Shaykh does not pronounce this newer interpretation to be *bid'a* ("reprehensible innovation") but rather contents himself with reproving him for taking it out of context.
19. Al-Haqq, "al-Mawdu'," pp. 3742-43. The alert reader will have noted a contradiction here. First, the Mufti is saying that only Muslims who totally break with Allah's ordinances may be considered unbelievers, and then he says the verse refers to the Jews who abandoned the Torah.

The Mufti holds that Egypt, more-over, is not the abode of unbelief but rather the abode of Islam, since prayer, alms, pilgrimage to Mecca, and many other aspects of the faith are observed there. The only excep-tions pertain to the Islamic punish-ments, usury, and the like, where positive law has been enacted and implemented. These exceptions do not warrant the conclusion that the rulers and people who accept such a state of affairs are apostates. To the contrary, Shaykh al-Haqq insists, both rulers and ruled believe in the abolition of usury, prostitution, theft, and so on, even though those phe-nomena occur in Egypt. The people of Egypt want Allah's dispensation and His law, and they implement it "within the limits of their capability." As justification for this less than cat-egorical commitment, the Mufti cites the verse, "So fear Allah as much as you can" (64:16).[20]

The Mufti goes as far as to argue that, according to several sayings at-tributed to the Prophet, no insurrec-tion against a Muslim ruler is al-lowed, even if the only religious prescription that such a ruler up-holds is prayer. When the Muslims differ with their ruler, they must counsel him and peacefully try to bring him to their way of thinking, says Shaykh al-Haqq.[21]

The analogy of current Muslim rulers as modern-day versions of Genghis Khan will not wash, argues the Mufti, since such rulers have not made the mosques stables for their animals, nor have they destroyed mosques or shredded the Quran. Ibn

Taymiyya's *fatwa* authorizing *jihad* against the Mongols was due to such behavior and to the fact that, under their aegis, prayer was haphazard, muezzins and imams were missing from the mosques that had not been destroyed, the rulers absconded with the people's wealth, destroyed their villages, and promoted the view that Genghis Khan was the son of Allah.[22]

Shaykh al-Haqq also declares that Faraj's pamphlet is out of touch with the Quran's political tenets. Consul-tation is the basis of rule in Islam, he alleges, citing four different verses (3:159, 42:38, 88:22, and 50:45): "And consult them in affairs"; "their affairs are a matter of counsel"; "you are not a warden over them"; "it is not for you to compel them." These verses, he maintains, make clear that the ruler in Islam is a mere agent of the people, who elect and dismiss him. Accord-ingly, the community is the source of authority in Islam. The implication is that a self-styled group within the community may not, on its own, de-cide the fate of rulership. Further-more, the early Islamic method of appointing leaders is not necessarily the model for today. Since succession is a worldly matter, it is subject to change over time, and it is up to the community to decide the best proce-dure to adopt concerning it.[23]

The important thing is not to have a caliph per se, given the fragmenta-tion of the *umma* into separate states. The important thing, the Mufti holds, is that the ruler in such states be a Muslim and that he tend to the affairs of the Muslims. As for the oath of allegiance to the ruler—

20. Ibid., pp. 3743-44.
21. Ibid., pp. 3744-45.

22. Ibid., pp. 3747-49.
23. Ibid., pp. 3749-51.

the *bay'a*—elections in modern times take its place.[24]

In conclusion, Shaykh al-Haqq contends that if there is a summons to do battle in defense of religion and the country, Muslims will respond, but the army, rather than a self-designated group of private individuals, is their instrument. But there is also *jihad* against oneself and Satan, and this is a continuous type of *jihad* incumbent on every individual Muslim. This allows the Muslim to improve himself or herself to do good works, to be pious, to be true to agreements, and to avoid evil. As one can therefore see, argues the Mufti, *jihad* is hardly an "absent precept." What should be "made absent" is the view that *jihad* entails pronouncing unbelief upon Muslims or violently attacking their community and leaders. Finally, *jihad* is not implemented by interpreting texts in a way that those texts will not bear. For if this were to be allowed, then there would be perversions in the meanings of phrases and concepts—something prohibited by Allah.[25]

SHIISM AND THE
THEORY OF RULE

The theory of *vilayat-i faqih* (the authority of the Imam as exercised by the leading jurist), propounded by Ayatollah Ruhollah Khomeini (d. 1989), is a reconsideration of the classic Shiite theory of rule. Although it would be wrong to intimate that any theory is once and for all set in concrete at its inception, it is nonetheless the case that Khomeini's per-

24. Ibid., pp. 3750-51.
25. Ibid., p. 3761.

spectives on the imamate constitute a radical departure from the views of mainstream Shiism. In looking at the constituent elements of Khomeini's theory of rule, we must stress the following factors: (1) the role of the Imams and the nature of their authority; (2) the significance of the oath of allegiance (*bay'a*); (3) the principle of deputyship; and (4) the role of the clergy. According to Shiism, only the Imam is entitled to rule the Islamic community. The Imams were 'Ali, the cousin of the Prophet, and 'Ali's descendants through his wife, Fatima, the Prophet's daughter. Shiites differ in their interpretation of how many Imams there were, but the dominant view is known as the twelver. According to this view, the twelfth Imam disappeared on Allah's commands, but the faithful believe he will return as the messiah, thereby ushering in the Day of Judgment.

The Imams were all considered "the proofs of Allah" in that the community had always to be led by one of their number as evidence of Allah's existence. The Imams were deemed to be the incarnations of Allah's light and were judged to have special abilities, such as foreknowledge of events to come, immunity from error, and the like. If there were no Imam leading the community, then the religious injunctions would lapse and Muslims would be in a state of ignorance, incapable of carrying out Allah's commands.

It is true that the disappearance of the twelfth Imam left the community without a leader, but the religious injunctions were considered to be still intact because the disappearance was at Allah's command. For him to have remained would have subjected him to murder by his opponents, thereby extinguishing the line of Imams forever. For the Imam was a young lad at the time of his disappearance and had no progeny to succeed him.

During his occultation, the obligation of Shiites to give the Imam their oaths of allegiance was considered to be in abeyance. This crucial fact made it possible for them to tolerate rule by secular leaders—provided that such leaders were just, consulted the people, and heeded the advice of the clergy.

According to the standard view of the doctrine of rule, while the Imam was in occlusion, he was in touch with his community through a series of agents, considered as the Imam's deputies. This period of contact lasted from about A.D. 874 to 940. After the death of the fourth of these agents, the Imam was considered to have entered the period of the greater occultation, which is to last until the end of time. During this period, the clergy are viewed collectively to be the general agents of the Imam.

Neither the four special agents nor the clergy in their capacity as the general agents were ever considered by the doctrine to be entitled to exercise the Imam's full authority on his behalf, however. The authority they wielded was residual in nature and limited them to such things as superintending the care of orphans, widows, the infirm, and the destitute.

What this suggests is that the doctrine did not permit the clergy to exercise substantial authority in the sense of sovereign rule over the community. Khomeini's achievement was

to mount a theoretical argument that empowered precisely the clergy to take over executive power and rule on the Imam's behalf until his return.

In his reasoning, Khomeini tried to adduce evidence from the classic sources of Islamic law. This proved difficult, since the Quran contains no references to the Imams and only vaguely refers to the obligation of Muslims to follow the commands of "those in authority among you" (4:59). Nor could Khomeini find any support for his radical view in the traditions (*sunna*) about the Prophet's behavior and statements.

On the other hand, he claimed to have found a sound tradition relating to the statement of the sixth Imam, Ja'far (d. 765), that allegedly empowered judges to rule the Shiite community should the Imam not be available. On closer inspection, however, it would appear that the tradition in question authorizes the clergy not to exercise sovereign rule but simply to give a ruling in technical disputes over inheritance or debts.[26] Nonetheless, Khomeini invoked reason as a source of law and maintained that, since the sources contained many references to the clergy as the "fortresses of Islam" and the like, they were the logical referents when the sacred texts made mention of leaders of the community after the Prophet's death.

The term *vilayat-i faqih* refers to the leading jurist as the one to carry out the authority of the Imam. At the time of the Iranian revolution and

26. Joseph Eliash, "Misconceptions Regarding the Juridical Status of the Iranian 'Ulama'," *International Journal of Middle East Studies*, 10:9-25 (1979).

during the next decade, this jurist was considered by many to be Khomeini himself, the author of the doctrine. This was so even though, on traditional grounds, other jurists could be said to have been his senior in learning and other qualities normally considered important in designating leaders among the jurists. Some eminent jurists actively disputed Khomeini's concept of *vilayat-i faqih*, but their objections were silenced by the revolutionaries, and the Constitution of 1979 contains several references to Khomeini by name as the *faqih*.

In lionizing Khomeini's role as *faqih* during the years 1979-89, his supporters went to extraordinary lengths. This may be seen, for example, in the following two citations from senior members of the regime, Ayatollah Rabbani 'Amlashi and Ayatollah Mu'min:

"Obedience to *vilayat-i faqih* is an incumbent duty . . . like the daily prayer and fasting, and disobeying it is like disobeying the Islamic sacred law."

"The legitimacy and legality of whatever is done and whatever institutions exist is due to the fact that they are buttressed by *vilayat-i faqih*. As the *vali-yi faqih* is at the head of all affairs and main guarantor of the current laws of the country, it is the *divinely ordained duty of all the people* to follow every law which is passed and given to the Islamic government for execution. Disobeying such a law is as forbidden as drinking wine is forbidden by Islam."[27]

Such sentiments found their practical crystallization in two *fatwas* issued by Khomeini in late 1987 and early 1988 dealing with the hegemonic power of the state. In defending the state's power to impose sanctions on those refusing to obey the laws, Khomeini wrote that the state could even abrogate one of the five pillars of Islam if it saw that this was necessary for the safeguarding of the 1979 revolution. In his reasoning, the Iranian state and the revolution that had spawned it were tantamount to Islam itself.[28]

Upon Khomeini's death, however, a crisis arose, as no individual could be found within the regime who had his stature. Whereas Khomeini both had been a *marja' al-taqlid* (a term referring to the most distinguished jurists of the age) and had been given unprecedented political powers in the 1979 Constitution as the *faqih*, his successor was not even an ayatollah. Therefore, at the time of the constitutional reforms of July 1989— a month after Khomeini's demise— official sources began to use the religiously neutral term *rahbar* ("leader") rather than *faqih* to refer to Khomeini's successor, Sayyid 'Ali Khamanah'i. It is true that this term had also been used to refer to Khomeini, but that did not detract from his towering stature in the eyes of his followers as *vali-yi faqih*.

Moreover, it has been argued that there is no longer a necessity for the leader to be a *marja' al-taqlid* on grounds that learnedness in the religious law does not guarantee "great

27. Cited in Said Arjomand, *The Turban for the Crown* (New York: Oxford University Press, 1988), p. 182. Emphasis added.

28. "The state, which has the full delegated authority of the Prophet . . . takes precedence over other Islamic regulations, even prayer and pilgrimage," asserted Khomeini. *Iran Times* (Washington, DC), 4 Day 1366 H. Sh.; ibid., 25 Day 1366 H. Sh.

capability in management" or "strong political and social perspicacity in regard to the social affairs of the moment." Since the latter qualities are deemed more important, the qualification that the leader be a *marja'* *al-taqlid* lapses "since it is seen as a superfluous requirement."[29]

CONCLUSION

One dimension of the question of rule that unites the Islamic *'ulama'* is the belief that Islam is both religion and politics. Although one may be able to identify religiously minded lay thinkers today who believe the contrary,[30] almost all *'ulama'* insist on the integration of religion and politics. The one reputable contemporary *'alim* ("clergyman") who believed in the necessity of separating religion and state in Islam—Shaykh Khalid Muhammad Khalid—suddenly recanted his views in 1981, after thirty years.[31]

A second dimension of the question of rule upon which the Islamic *'ulama'* have created a consensus is the issue of applying the *shari'a* in public life rather than only in personal matters. The current constitutions of Middle Eastern states are found wanting because they are based on Western models that rule out the possibility for the Quran and the Prophet's traditions to be the source of law.

29. See the comments of Shaykh 'Abdullah Nuri, the Minister of the Interior of the Islamic Republic of Iran, as cited in *Iran Times*, 3 Shahrivar 1368 H. Sh.

30. For example, Muhammad 'Amara, *al-Dawla al-Islamiyya bayn al-'Almaniyya wa al-Sulta al-Diniyya* [The Islamic state between secularism and religious authority] (Cairo: Dar al-Shuruq, 1988), pp. 31-82.

31. It was Shaykh Khalid Muhammad Khalid who argued for their separation in his landmark polemic *Min huna nabda'u* [From here we begin] (Cairo: Dar al-Nil li al-Taba'a, 1950). For two interpretations of why he did so, see Emanual Sivan, *Radical Islam* (New Haven, CT: Yale University Press, 1985), p. 132; Leonard Binder, *Islamic Liberalism: A Critique of Development Ideologies* (Chicago: University of Chicago Press, 1988), pp. 158-61.

ANNALS, *AAPSS*, 524, November 1992

Monarchs, Mullas, and Marshals: Islamic Regimes?

By IBRAHIM A. KARAWAN

ABSTRACT: This article examines three regime types that assert that they represent "Islam in power." They are the conservative dynastic regime of Saudi Arabia, the populist clerical regime of Iran, and the authoritarian military regimes of the Sudan and Pakistan. These regimes articulate different interpretations of Islam that reflect the interests and ideology of those who control the state machinery, the influence of society's historical legacy, and specific characteristics of the immediate situational setting. The Islamic legitimization of all three types has been contested on religiopolitical grounds by domestic rivals for power and external rivals for leadership in the Muslim world. The most effective challenges to regime legitimacy have been manifested in the Islamized military regimes. The predicament of "the Islam of the marshals" is due to several factors: their lack of the political capital available in the Saudi type of "the Islam of wealth," or the legitimacy generated by revolutionary change under charismatic leadership known in the Iranian type of "the Islam of revolution," and their antipolitical character, manifested in their distrust of political movements that supported their Islamization programs and whose leaders aspired to play the roles of its theoreticians and organizers.

Ibrahim A. Karawan teaches Middle Eastern politics at the University of Utah. He has also been a research associate in the Center for Political and Strategic Studies in Cairo. His publications include Beyond Desert Storm: The Middle East after the Gulf War, *coedited with Peter von Sivers (forthcoming) and* Israeli Settlement Policy, *coauthored with Ali Dessouki and K. Qassimiya. He has contributed chapters to a number of volumes including* The Middle East and the Western Alliance *and* Defense Planning in Less-Industrialized States. *His articles have appeared in the* Journal of Arab Affairs; Contention; al-Siyassa al-dawliya; *and* al-Tali'a.

NOTE: I am grateful to Tim Sullivan, F. Gregory Gause, Nikki Keddie, Peter Diamond, and Donald Hanson for offering helpful comments, and to Janessa and Suhayla Karawan for their unlimited support.

IRONICALLY enough, Islamic political movements assessed by modernization theorists as destined to become relics of the past have been presented lately as the most potent sociopolitical force, perhaps even the wave of the future, in many Muslim countries. Instead of the earlier failure to see any sustained political significance for Islamic movements, many commentators now seem to have great difficulty seeing anything else.[1] One possible explanation of such a reversal may be the fact that political action under the banner of Islam has become a widespread phenomenon shared by many actors in Muslim societies. The extensive use of Islamic political discourse by avowed Arab nationalists since the eruption of the gulf conflict in 1990-91 is one clear illustration; for example, many of them described Iraq's battle as a "rage for God" against the "infidel evildoers" and as a "holy war" of "faith" against "atheism." Even the Marxist Left is no exception. In the words of one prominent Arab Marxist addressing fellow leftists, "No political party can ignore the Islamic issue and not use it in the political struggle without suffering a tremendous loss by being isolated from the broad masses . . . as long as religious forces are dominant in the street. . . . Otherwise, you have to import another

nonreligious people to help launch the desired revolution!"[2]

During the 1970s and 1980s, political regimes that were increasingly challenged or threatened by Islamic opposition made frequent attempts to check that threat by finding an Islamic garb or justification for their policies.[3] These attempts included utilizing Islamic symbolism, portraying political leaders as pious adherents of the Islamic faith and regular practitioners of its rituals, interrupting radio and television programs to broadcast the call to prayer, banning alcoholic beverages on national airlines, and forming *lijan muraja'at al-qawanin li-tatamasha ma'a ahkam al-shari'a al-Islamiyya* ("committees to revise the legal system to be in accordance with the rules of Islamic law").

The regime types addressed in this article, however, go beyond the usual resort to religious symbolism. These regimes do not merely suggest that one or another of their policies is congruent with Islamic principles. Their explicit point of departure, as far as legitimacy is concerned, is *la hukma wa la siyada illa li-allah* ("rule and sovereignty belong only to God"). They make an assertion, the essence

---

1. For more on this sharp reversal, see Ali E. Hillal Dessouki, "Islamic Resurgence," in his *Islamic Resurgence in the Arab World* (New York: Praeger, 1982), pp. 2-9; Gilles Kepel, "God Strikes Back: Movements of Re-Islamization in Contemporary History," *Contention*, 2:151-59 (Fall 1992); Ibrahim Karawan, " 'Reislamization Movements' according to Kepel: On Striking Back and Striking Out," ibid., pp. 161-79.

2. The statement was made by Lutfi al-Kholi in *Nadwat al-tataruf al-siyasi al-dini fi Misr* [The workshop on religiopolitical extremism in Egypt], *Fikr li-al-dirasat wa al-abhath* (Cairo), p. 100 (Dec. 1985).

3. See the perceptive analysis by Ali E. Hillal Dessouki, "Official Islam and Political Legitimation in the Arab Countries," in *The Islamic Impulse*, ed. Barbara Stowasser (London: Croom Helm, 1986), pp. 135-41; Sadek Belaid, "Role of Religious Institutions in Support of the State," in *Beyond Coercion*, ed. Adeed Dawisha and I. William Zartman (London: Croom Helm, 1988), pp. 147-63.

of which is that they represent "Islam in power." Such regimes elevate the objective of defending the faith and implementing the totality of the *shari'a* to the level of their very political raison d'être. By striving to approximate a certain image of Islam's founding period or golden age, they claim also to provide other Muslims with an example of how to proceed toward building a genuine Islamic state and society.[4]

My objective in this article is to address the following question: Is there a model of Islamic governance that reveals certain common characteristics among regimes proclaiming themselves to be Islamic? The argument I advance here is that an analytical perspective focusing on diversity of types rather than their unity, historical and societal variety rather than coherent pronouncements on the ideational level, and the multiplicity rather than the oneness of political legitimation patterns may enable us to gain a better understanding of Islamic regimes. Such an understanding should cover the various ways and the broad settings in which they get to power, their formulas for seeking legitimization, and the challenges with which they have to contend.

A consensus already exists among students of Islamic resurgence that what is known as popular Islam has diverse manifestations and components. It includes movements that pursue divergent objectives such as promoting individual religiosity, introducing social reform, and the fundamental restructuring of state-society relations in the image of Islam's founding period. It should come as no surprise that among those self-proclaimed Islamic regimes, diversity is an unmistakable feature of their domestic and foreign policies. After all, each has its historical specificity, varied societal characteristics, and particular attributes of its political leadership. Although all these regimes identify themselves as based on Islam, as Nazih Ayubi has put it, "Islam means different things to different people, and this applies to politics as it applies to other areas of social life. To some, Islam may serve as means for legitimizing . . . the status quo, while for others it may provide . . . a spearhead for revolution."[5]

It may suffice to recall here that both Saudi Arabia's monarchical, conservative, and pro-Western regime and Iran's republican, populist, and anti-Western regime based their political legitimacy on quite different interpretations of Islam. During the 1980s, each of them refused to recognize the Islamic "credentials" of the other and saw in such recognition a challenge to, and perhaps a negation of, its own legitimacy. In fact, each identified the other as posing the greatest danger to "the true Islamic call and movement." Accordingly, Saudi Arabia was both willing and able during most of the decade to ally itself with Iraq's secular pan-Arabist regime, in light of their shared hostil-

---

4. See Mohammed Arkoun, "The Concept of Authority in Islamic Thought," in *Islam: State and Society*, ed. Klaus Ferdinand and Mehdi Mozaffari (London: Curzon Press, 1988), pp. 53-73.

5. Nazih Ayubi, "The Politics of Militant Islamic Movements in the Middle East," *Journal of International Affairs*, 36:271 (Fall-Winter 1982-83).

ity toward the Iranian system after the Islamic revolution.

As William Quandt has accurately pointed out, what worried the Saudi regime most "about the Iranian revolution was not the personal fate of the Shah, but the specter of a mass-based revolution bringing about the downfall of a conservative monarchy." In daily Arabic radio broadcasts directed at Saudi Arabia, Iran's leaders emphasized that "monarchy and Islam are mutually exclusive" and called "for the overthrow of the Saudi dynasty in the name of Islam."[6] The political-ideological confrontation between the two Islamic protagonists continued to escalate. On the one hand, Saudi Arabia denounced the Iranian leadership for launching deliberate campaigns of subversion and political agitation, particularly around the holy places during the pilgrimage (hajj) and within the Shiite minority in the oil-rich Eastern Province of the kingdom. These campaigns, according to Saudi rulers, were not merely misguided acts perpetrated by Iranian militants; rather, they reflected a state ideology that equated the Islamic call with fomenting discord, extremism, terrorism, and bloodshed as a prelude to Iranian regional hegemony.

On the other hand, Khomeini accused the House of Saud of being unfit for the custodianship of Islam's holiest shrines, "which belong to all Muslims," and of attempting to reduce the hajj to a "dry ritual" devoid of any political meaning or responsibility. According to him, the Saudi regime, which he often referred to with disdain as the "government of the Hijaz," was guilty of massacring defenseless Iranian pilgrims, desecrating God's Two Houses, and serving as a surrogate of the "Black House" of the "Great Satan" (read: the White House of the United States). The Islam to which Saudi leaders actually adhered was, in Khomeini's words, "the Islam of money and power . . . deception, compromise, and captivity, the Islam of the sovereignty of capital and capitalists over the oppressed . . . in a word the American Islam."[7]

Islamic regimes not only face external challenges to their legitimacy mounted by other contenders for leadership in the Muslim world; they also have to contend with domestic Islamic opposition groups. Many of these groups call into question the authenticity of the regimes' Islamic claims and denounce the contrast between lofty ideological formulations and concrete realities of social corruption, political repression, and

6. William Quandt, "Saudi Views of the Iranian Revolution," in Iran since the Revolution, ed. Barry Rosen (Boulder, CO: Social Science Monographs, 1985), pp. 53-57; Jacob Goldberg, "Saudi Arabia and the Iranian Revolution: The Religious Dimension," in The Iranian Revolution and the Muslim World, ed. David Menashri (Boulder, CO: Westview Press, 1990), pp. 155-70. See also Hermann F. Eilts, "Saudi Arabia: Traditionalism versus Modernism—A Royal Dilemma," in Ideology and Power in the Middle East, ed. Peter Chelkowski and Robert Pranger (Durham, NC: Duke University Press, 1988), pp. 78-81; David Long, "The Impact of the Iranian Revolution on the Arabian Peninsula and the Gulf States," in The Iranian Revolution, ed. John Esposito (Miami: Florida International University Press, 1990), pp. 100-115.

7. "Imam Khumayni's Message on the First Anniversary of the Makkah Massacre," in al-Tawhid, 6:83-91 (1988).

moral alienation. The historical experience has shown that opposing a certain regime on grounds that it is rigid in its understanding of Islam is not usually very efficacious from the opposition's perspective when compared with alternative strategies, such as criticizing the regime for its *nifaq* ("hypocrisy"), for *tahrif al-shari'a* ("distortion of Islamic law"), or for lacking Islamic resolve and decisiveness.

I shall address the diversity of self-proclaimed Islamic regimes along the aforementioned lines under three subcategories: the conservative dynastic regime of Saudi Arabia; the populist clerical regime of Iran; and Islamized military regimes of the Sudan and Pakistan.

LEGITIMIZING DYNASTIC CONSERVATISM: SAUDI ARABIA

One of the two countries in the Muslim world most identified with Islamic governance is Saudi Arabia. Historically, Saudi Arabia was based on a tribal dynasty, that of the Saudi family, which adopted a religious call, the Wahhabi *Da'wa*. The *Da'wa* was advocated by Muhammad ibn 'Abd al-Wahhab, who was inspired by the strict Hanbali school of Islamic jurisprudence. He called for a return to "true Islam" and condemned any lax or partial implementation of the rules of the *shari'a*. It is in that sense that Wahhabism has been referred to as the first revivalist movement in modern Sunnite Islamic history. Contemporary Saudi rulers emphasize that the country's constitution is the "Book of God and the sayings of His Prophet."[8] Its flag represents more than a national symbol since it has the Islamic *shahada* ("There is no God but Allah and Muhammad is his Prophet") inscribed on it. The state implements the *hudud* ("penalties") on those who violate the rules of Islam. A religious police or a public morality squad of sorts, known as the Organization for the Enforcing of Good and Forbidding of Evil, is assigned the task of ensuring the performance of daily prayers, the observance of fasting during the month of Ramadan, and the ongoing public segregation of the sexes.

Moreover, Saudi Arabia is associated with the holiest birthplaces of Islam, Mecca and Medina, and with one of the pillars of that religion, the *hajj*, which it assumes the responsibility of supervising. Every year Saudi rulers symbolize their commitment to Islam by assisting in the cleaning of its holiest shrine, al-Ka'ba. In October 1986, King Fahd requested that he no longer be addressed as "Majesty" but as *Khadim al-Haramayn al-Sharifayn* (custodian of the two revered sacred places in Mecca and Medina). The kingdom sponsors a host of pan-Islamic organizations such as the Islamic Conference Organization and the Muslim World League. It provides large sums of money to support the activities of Muslim groups, associations, and publications. Since the riyal is Saudi Arabia's currency, some commentators refer to this policy as "riyal-politik"! In short, Islam is proclaimed as the country's sole legitimate ideology; the pivotal foundation of its political system; the exclusive regulator of social, economic, and cultural life;

8. King Fahd's statement in *Middle East Report*, 14 Mar. 1992, p. 2.

the only source of legislation; and the most important factor in shaping Saudi international behavior.

In assessing how Islamic the Saudi regime is, however, three important qualifications must be added to the foregoing characterization. First, the relative influence of Shaykh ibn 'Abd al-Wahhab and his descendants regarding major policymaking issues has tended generally and gradually to decline. This should not be understood as implying that the role of the 'ulama' has become irrelevant. Their role remains important regarding specific issue areas—namely, judicial, educational, and religious matters—and under particular and rather exceptional conditions, such as a serious and open rift in the royal family. On the whole, however, it is not difficult to recognize an "actual imbalance in the joint venture" between the ruling dynasty's political power and the religious establishment's ideological influence.[9] While the Saudi regime, as Lisa Anderson has aptly put it, has been "more solicitous of religious sentiment than most . . . it is the . . . 'ulama' who are closely supervised by the government rather than the reverse."[10]

    9. Ghassan Salamé, "Islam and Politics in Saudi Arabia," *Arab Studies Quarterly*, 9:310 (1987). For other assessments, see Joseph Kechichian, "The Role of the Ulama in the Politics of an Islamic State: The Case of Saudi Arabia," *International Journal of Middle East Studies*, 18:62-66 (1986); William Ochsenwald, "Saudi Arabia," in *The Politics of Islamic Revivalism*, ed. Shireen Hunter (Bloomington: Indiana University Press, 1988), pp. 109-13.
    10. Lisa Anderson, "Absolutism and the Resilience of Monarchy in the Middle East," *Political Science Quarterly*, 106:10 (1991).

Second, the logic and requirements of state-building, consolidation, and development prompted Saudi leaders to form international alliances—such as the alliance of King 'Abd al-'Aziz with Britain—and to pursue domestic policies, such as the education of women, which were not, at least initially, deemed acceptable on purely religious grounds as understood by segments of the 'ulama'. More recently, some of the consequences of the massive inflow of oil wealth, such as greater exposure to Western influences, have periodically strained the relationship between the regime and the men of religion. The latter became critical of the erosion of traditional, austere, and conservative Wahhabi values as a result of that exposure. But such enormous oil-based fortunes also provided the regime with the means of co-opting many of the 'ulama' as salaried employees of the state. For example, the government appointed the members of Dar al-Da'wa wa al-Ifta (the Board of Islamic Research) as well as the Council of the Grand 'Ulama', who issue authoritative religious and legal opinions or judgments.

Third, as an outcome of the 'ulama''s structural dependency, their role in ideological and political legitimation has become conditioned primarily by the interests of what is known as al-dawla ("the state") or al-mulk ("reign" or "rulership"). In fact, this is how that relationship was perceived by Juhayman al-'Utaybi, the leader of the Ikhwan, the group that occupied the Ka'ba at the dawn of the first day of the fifteenth century according to the Islamic calendar (20 November 1979).

The leaders of the Saudi regime, as seen by the group's founder, had been morally corrupt and guilty of consorting and collaborating with the infidels; for example, concerning the Saudi leaders, al-'Utaybi asked, "How can we preach Islam while we take Christians as professors?" The majority of the *'ulama'* tended to be "court clerics," who were subservient to and apologetic for the corrupt rulers. Al-'Utaybi concluded that "if the devil had a state, he would have *'ulama'* . . . working for him as long as he gave them an academic degree, a scholarly title, and a salary" and that the *shari'a* "could not be learned in government controlled institutions."[11]

Al-'Utaybi would have been the last person to be surprised that when the regime needed a religious *fatwa* in support of using force to regain control of the most sacred sanctuary in Islam, where fighting is explicitly prohibited, the *'ulama'* complied with the king's request and authorized the use of force to end the occupation of the Ka'ba. In authorizing the resort to force, they characterized the Ikhwan's action as sedition, insurrection, encroachment on the sacredness of the holy place of God, and utter perversion of Islam committed by *mufsidun fi al-ard* ("those who corrupt on earth") and a clique of religious deviants against rulers who actually apply the *shari'a*.

In August 1990, the Saudi regime needed an Islamic legitimization of the massive deployment of American, European, and other non-Muslim troops to the kingdom in the aftermath of the Iraqi invasion of Kuwait. The stationing of these troops in Saudi Arabia was condemned by a variety of groups in the Muslim world as a violation of the sanctity of the territory where the Ka'ba and the Prophet's mosque are located. Shaykh 'Abd al-'Aziz Bin Baz and other senior religious authorities approved of the king's decision. They concluded that he was authorized, according to the rules of the *shari'a*, to "seek the help of whoever has the power that enables them to perform the task" of defending Muslim land and resisting aggression. Once again, on 18 January 1991, the top Saudi religious authorities issued another *fatwa* in which they described Iraq's President Saddam Hussein as "the enemy of God" and identified the battle that had just been launched against his army in Kuwait and Iraq as a *jihad* ("holy war").[12]

11. Salamé, "Islam and Politics," p. 315; Ayman al-Yassini, *Religion and State in the Kingdom of Saudi Arabia* (Boulder, CO: Westview Press, 1985), pp. 124-29; "Islamic Revival and National Development in the Arab World," *Journal of Asian and African Studies*, 11:105-9 (1986); James Buchan, "Secular and Religious Opposition in Saudi Arabia," in *State, Society and Economy in Saudi Arabia*, ed. Tim Niblock (London: Croom Helm, 1982), pp. 120-23. See also Rif'at Sayyid Ahmad, *Rasa'il Juhayman al-'Utaybi* [The letters of Juhayman al-'Utaybi] (Cairo: Madbuli, 1988), pp. 11-52.

12. Quoted in James Piscatori, "Religion and Realpolitik: Islamic Responses to the Gulf War," in *Islamic Fundamentalisms and the Gulf Crisis*, ed. James Piscatori (Chicago: American Academy of Arts and Sciences, 1991), p. 9. For examples of sharp religious denunciation of the *'ulama'*'s *fatwa* by Safar al-Hawali, dean of Islamic studies at Umm al-Qura University in Mecca, see his "Infidels Without, and Within," *New Perspectives Quarterly*, 8:50-51 (1991); Mamoun Fandy, "The Hawali Tapes," *New York Times*, 24 Nov. 1990; "An Open Letter to al-Shaykh 'Abd al-'Aziz Bin Baz," *al-Gazira al-'arabiyya* [The Arabian pen-

LEGITIMIZING REVOLUTION AND MULLASTROIKA: IRAN

If the Saudi system has been associated with religious and political conservatism, Iran's Islamic Republic has usually been identified as an embodiment of a radical, antimonarchical, antidynastic, and anti-Western type of Islamic activism. In Saudi Arabia, the dynastic "protectors of the holy places" managed to co-opt or subordinate the religious establishment, while in Iran's case the clerical "custodians of the Islamic revolution" led the overthrow of a westernizing dynasty. According to this clerical elite, the only legitimate government is Islamic government, and the sole way to remove the *taghut* ("arrogant, tyrannical earthly power") and establish an Islamic state is through launching an Islamic revolution. Much has been written about the political efficacy with which Khomeini used the "Karbala paradigm," with its evocative symbols and emotive imagery grounded in Shiite traditions, to delegitimize the Shah by describing him as the "Yazid of our time" and to inspire the demonstrators against his regime during a critical stage of the revolution to emulate the courage and martyrdom of Imam Hussein in resisting tyranny.[13]

In addition, the ideology of the movement manifested an Islamic populist emphasis on the theme of social justice. It attacked those living in opulence who lead a life of luxury and moral decadence (*mutrafun*). At the same time, it was presented as backing the dispossessed (*mahrumun*) and the oppressed on earth (*mustaz'afun*), who were politically excluded and socioeconomically marginalized under the Shah; these are the poor urban workers, lower middle classes of the bazaar, and small peasants. Despite repeated denials of being a class-based movement, this populist identification with the disadvantaged or the underprivileged has created a supportive constituency for the Islamic activists during, and in the aftermath of, the Iranian revolution. Leading clerics stressed in their Friday sermons in Tehran that this identification with the downtrodden and disinherited in pursuit of social justice ('*adl*) was a common characteristic of both the Islamic revolution in Iran and the Muhammadan revolution in seventh-century Arabia.[14]

---

insula] (Feb. 1991). For a biting critique of the role of establishmentarian Islam during the crisis, see Magdi Hussein, *Azmat al-khalij bayn ahkam al-Qur'an wa fatawi al-sultan* [The gulf crisis between Quranic rules and sultanic stipulations] (Cairo: Dar al-Sharq al-Awssat, 1990).

13. Said Amir Arjomand, *The Turban for the Crown* (New York: Oxford University Press, 1988), pp. 99-100; Nikki Keddie, "Shi'ism and Revolution," in *Religion, Rebellion, Revolution*,

ed. Bruce Lincoln (New York: St. Martin's Press, 1985), pp. 172-75; Haggy Ram, " 'The Government Myth' of Early Islam: The Legitimation of the Islamic Government in Iran" (Paper delivered at the annual conference of the Middle East Studies Association, Washington, DC, Nov. 1991), pp. 4-6. According to Ram, the sermons delivered at the Friday prayers in Tehran described the victory of Iran's Islamic revolution as "reminiscent of the victory of the Noble Prophet over the infidels." Ibid, pp. 11-13.

14. Ervand Abrahamian, "Structural Causes of the Iranian Revolution," *MERIP Reports*, no. 87, pp. 24-25 (May 1980); Afsaneh Najmabadi, "Iran's Turn to Islam," *Middle East Journal*, 41:213-14 (1987); Ram, " 'Government Myth,' " pp. 13-15. In practice, however, the initial nar-

In less than three years, some fundamental changes have taken place in Iran, particularly regarding the background characteristics of the political elite.[15] The broad coalition that combined its political resources to launch the revolution has disintegrated. The clerical leadership managed to capture the state and control the political society after undermining, even crushing, any effective, organized existence of its national, liberal, leftist, and Islamic rivals. The legitimization of the ideological and political hegemony of the clerical elite, as reflected in the constitution, was based on Khomeini's doctrine of *vilayat-i faqih*, the guardianship of the jurisprudent or the mandate of the Islamic Jurist. In essence, he argued that since any duality of religious and political authority or separation of the spiritual and temporal realms is un-Islamic, and since the main obligation of the Islamic government is the full implementation of the Sacred Law, none other than a fully qualified Islamic jurist, who has the two essential qualities of profound concern with justice and comprehensive knowledge of the *shari'a*, is entitled to be in charge of such government.[16] During the absence of

the "Glorious Lord of the Age," the Islamic jurist, as the representative of the infallible imams, has to be the only authoritative interpreter of God's laws.[17]

Once in power, the Islamic regime presented the revolution itself as model for all Muslims. It called for an immediate overthrow of all the remaining functional equivalents of the Shah and lackeys of "satanical powers" in the Muslim world, particularly in the Persian Gulf area. The triumph of Iran's Islamic revolution seems to have bestowed on its leaders a strong sense of obligation to "make the world safe for Islam," by performing a universal mission that would not be deemed complete until all Muslim communities had undergone revolutionary transformations similar in essence to those witnessed by Iran.[18]

38-40; Marvin Zonis, "The Rule of the Clerics in the Islamic Republic of Iran," *The Annals* of the American Academy of Political and Social Science, 482:85-108 (1985); Mehdi Mozaffari, *Authority in Islam* (London: Sharp, 1987), pp. 49-51.

17. For a discussion of objections as well as amendments to the doctrine expressed by a number of Iranian Shiite religious authorities, see Arjomand, *Turban for the Crown*, pp. 155-60; Ahmad K. Moussavi, "New Interpretation of the Theory of Vilayat-i Faqih," *Middle Eastern Studies*, 28:101-7 (1992).

18. R. K. Ramazani, "Khumayni's Islam in Iran's Foreign Policy," in *Islam in Foreign Policy*, ed. Adeed Dawisha (New York: Cambridge University Press, 1983), pp. 16-23; idem, "Iran's Export of Revolution: Politics, Ends, and Means," in *Iranian Revolution*, ed. Esposito, pp. 40-62. For competing explanations of the resilience of Arab and particularly Persian Gulf regimes characterized by Khomeini as "un-Islamic," see Emmanuel Sivan, "Sunni Radicalism in the Middle East and the Iranian Revolution," *International Journal of Middle East Studies*, 21:1-30 (1989); F. Gregory Gause,

rowing of the income gap between the top and bottom segments in society was ultimately halted in the urban centers and reversed in the countryside. See Sohrab Behdad, "Winners and Losers of the Iranian Revolution," *International Journal of Middle East Studies*, 21:327-58 (1989).

15. Richard Cottam, "Inside Revolutionary Iran," in *Iran's Revolution*, ed. R. K. Ramazani (Bloomington: Indiana University Press, 1990), pp. 3-26; idem, "Charting Iran's New Course," *Current History*, 90:21-24 (1991).

16. Shaul Bakhash, *The Reign of the Ayatollahs* (New York: Basic Books, 1984), pp.

However, the current realities of Iran suggest that although the Islamic regime remains in control and presumably follows the imam's line, the self-righteous revolutionary zeal has been gradually losing ground to a more calculating pragmatic trend. The ascendant pragmatists favor a policy package known as Baz-Sazi (Rebuilding), which includes further liberalization of the economy, enhancing the powers of the presidency, incremental opening to the international economic system by encouraging foreign investment, and normalizing diplomatic relations with the outside world including the Arab regimes that supported Iraq during the first gulf war as well as Western countries.[19] They have been attempting to legitimize this restructuring, or mullastroika, under the banner of what may be described as "Islam in one country." By focusing on the economic development and welfare of Iran, they aspire to consolidate the Islamic Republic and export its revolution by other means, namely, by building a societal model worthy of importation by other Muslims. The outcome of the parliamentary elections of April 1992 indicates that the pragmatists have been gaining

influence at the expense of the ideologues.[20]

The increasing weight of the pragmatic trend cannot be adequately understood by focusing only on the personal characteristics of Khomeini's successors without taking into consideration the impact of the war fatigue stemming from the protracted military confrontation with Iraq and the extremely costly reconstruction of Iran's economy—estimates range from $350 to $600 billion.[21] In other words, the clerical accommodation with reality did not start exactly after June 1989, following Khomeini's death. The antecedents of some of the aforementioned policy reorientation go back to the mid-1980s. Moreover, it was Khomeini who finally decided on 18 July 1988 to accept, without conditions, an end to the war with Iraq as an overriding necessity to safeguard, as he put it, "the interests of the revolution and the system."[22]

"Revolutionary Fevers and Regional Contagion," *Journal of South Asian and Middle Eastern Studies*, 14:1-23 (1991).

19. Hooshang Amirahmadi, *Revolution and Economic Transition: The Iranian Experience* (Albany: State University of New York Press, 1990), pp. 119-24; Judith Miller, "Islamic Radicals Lose Their Tight Grip on Iran," *New York Times*, 8 Apr. 1991. For the radicals' critique of this policy shift as a betrayal of the "line of the imam," see Fahmi Huweidi, "The Mother of All Electoral Battles in Iran," *al-Majalla*, 18-24 Mar. 1992, pp. 22-31.

20. *Al-Majalla* (London), 15-21 Apr. 1992, pp. 24-25. On the significance of the April 1992 elections, see Elaine Sciolino, "For Iran Chief, a Mandate and a Test," *New York Times*, 14 Apr. 1992; Claude van England, "Iran Picks up the Pace of Reform," *Christian Science Monitor*, 17 Apr. 1992.

21. Hooshang Amirahmadi, "War Damage and Reconstruction in the Islamic Republic of Iran," in *Post-Revolutionary Islam*, ed. Hooshang Amirahmadi and Manoucher Parvin (Boulder, CO: Westview Press, 1988), pp. 126-49; G. Hossein Razi, "An Alternative Paradigm to State Rationality in Foreign Policy: The Iran-Iraq War," *Western Political Quarterly*, 41:700-701 (1988).

22. "Imam Khumayni's Message," pp. 99-102. Interestingly enough, two years earlier, Islamic modernists affiliated with the Liberation Movement of Iran led by Mehdi Bazargan argued that the regime's continuation of the war against Iraq and its rejection of peace proposals were "contrary to God's will, the tra-

Even during the early 1980s, Iran's leadership demonstrated that it had enough selective pragmatism to establish a de facto alliance with a secular regime like that of Syria on the basis of common interest and political expediency, regardless of that regime's pan-Arabist ideology or its ruthless suppression of Islamicists.

Needless to say, even more pragmatism was displayed in the early 1990s by the current leadership regarding the second gulf crisis, which exploded after the Iraqi invasion of Kuwait. Calls to join Iraq in a *jihad* against the United States and later to join Iraq's Shiites in another holy war against Saddam's army were made by some in the Iranian leadership.[23] However, Iran did neither. Its

behavior was actually more influenced by the raison d'état than by the ideology of the revolution. The formulation of Iran's policy during the various states of the crisis was, as Arjomand succinctly put it, the outcome of a "sober calculation of its interests as a regional power."[24]

ISLAMIZING MILITARY REGIMES: THE SUDAN AND PAKISTAN

Saudi Arabia and Iran are not the only cases to be studied under the category of Islamic regimes. Claims to have transformed particular regimes along the path of Islamization have been made in the Sudan and Pakistan. Obviously, the Saudi and Iranian regimes exercised and continue to exercise much greater influence within the Islamic world than did Numayri's Sudan or Zia's Pakistan. The latter two lacked the equivalent of the Saudi *tharwa* ("wealth") or the Iranian *thawra* ("revolution"). Moreover, the Sudan's and Pakistan's experiments in Islamization were introduced by military regimes as a means of arresting further erosion of their legitimacy.

Islamization in such cases had a certain instrumental quality best illustrated by the televised scenes of former Sudanese President Numayri pouring bottles of whiskey into the Nile or receiving the *bay'a* ("pledge of allegiance") from army officers as the commander of the faithful.[25] As one

---

ditions of the Prophet, and the record of the Imams." In their open letter to Khomeini, they argued, on the basis of *fiqh* (jurisprudence) sources, that "during the occultation of the Twelfth Imam all offensive wars were unlawful." H. E. Chehabi, *Iranian Politics and Religious Modernism* (Ithaca, NY: Cornell University Press, 1990), pp. 299-300.

23. "Calls for Jihad against U.S.," Radio Tehran, in Persian, Foreign Broadcast Information Service, 13 Sept. 1990, pp. 52-53. Sadeq Khalkhali advocated a military alliance with Iraq in order to "turn the Persian Gulf and Saudi Arabia into graveyards for American soldiers." See ibid., p. 57. Though Shiite holy places in Karbala and Najaf were under fire in March and April 1991 and fellow Shiites were being crushed by Saddam's Republican Guards, Iran's actual support of the Shiite uprising was quite measured. Iran's restraint reflected its leaders' concern that any overt and massive intervention on their part might have increased and prolonged the U.S. presence in the area or led to a large-scale Iranian military confrontation with Iraq, or both. Iran's interests were not going to be served by either outcome. Derek J. Harvey, "Determinants of Iranian Foreign Policy during the Gulf Crisis" (Manuscript, Middle East Center, University of Utah, Aug. 1991), pp. 17-37.

24. Said Amir Arjomand, "A Victory for the Pragmatists: The Islamic Fundamentalist Reaction in Iran," in *Islamic Fundamentalisms and the Gulf Crisis*, ed. Piscatori, pp. 52-69.

25. Gabriel Warburg, "The Shari'a in Sudan: Implementation and Repercussions,

astute Sudanese writer pointed out, the application of the *shari'a* or "the legislative coup d'etat of September 1983" by Numayri was "a natural continuation of [his] politics of sudden new initiatives and shifting alliances with various political factions . . . [and a means of legitimizing] his claim to the absolute powers" of a caliph. Although "Numayri's Islamization program" benefited from a growing Islamic resurgence in the Sudan, it was launched as a palace coup through a set of hastily formulated, poorly drafted, and erratically implemented presidential decrees.

Numayri's declaration, in September 1983, that the Sudan had become an Islamic republic was motivated primarily by considerations of political expediency in a societal setting characterized by a mounting politicization of socioeconomic grievances, frequent outbreaks of food riots in urban centers, resumption of ethnic conflicts in the south, and growing opposition activities in the ranks of army officers. Faced with such challenges and capitalizing on religious sentiments among Sudanese Muslims, the state-controlled media endlessly repeated Numayri's pronouncements about the Sudan's "Islamic revolution," the implementation of the Islamic legal code, replacing the state income tax with the *zakat*, and a plan to turn all banks into interest-free financial institutions.

Despite its initial popularity, Numayri's brand of Islamization was met with growing resistance, mostly by professional associations—such as those of judges, doctors, and aca-

1983-1989," *Middle East Journal*, 44:624-37 (1990).

demics—and a coalition of opposition forces. Prominent political figures, such as Sadiq al-Mahdi, the leader of the Umma Party, saw Numayri's Islamization as opportunistic. They called for reforming an unjust socioeconomic system, fighting endemic and planned corruption in high circles, as well as expanding the narrow scope of political participation prior to, or simultaneously with, the implementation of the Islamic *hudud*. They pointed out that ethnic conflict and economic crisis had escalated further in the Sudan after the implementation of the Islamization program. The religious pretensions of Marshal Numayri, who claimed to have become the imam of the *umma* —after years of identifying himself either as an Arab nationalist or a Sudanese socialist—were also criticized as a mask for dictatorship. This criticism became particularly more credible after Numayri, in response to this opposition, declared a state of emergency in April 1984 and proposed a set of constitutional amendments that would have allowed the president-imam to hold office for life. Even the usually tame parliament managed to resist Numayri's pressures to ratify these amendments immediately.

As the Islamization of the Sudanese regime was introduced from above by presidential decrees, it was suspended mostly through subsequent presidential decrees. Instead of gaining the president more political support, enhancing the regime's viability, and making the Sudan more governable, Numayri's initial introduction and later suspension of his Islamization program ultimately weakened his regime's credibility and undermined its domestic political alliances. They were also among the factors that led to his overthrow in April 1985.[26]

Four years of political confusion and policy immobilism were followed, in June 1989, by a military coup led by General al-Bashir, who allied himself with al-Turabi's National Islamic Front to establish another Islamic government. The new military-Islamic regime imposed a state of emergency, suspended the constitution, dissolved the Constituent Assembly, and banned political parties. In al-Turabi's words, "Muslims themselves sometimes don't even know how to go about their Islam. They have no recent precedent of an Islamic government."[27] After the Sudan's second Islamic revolution in less than six years, however, its eco-

nomic crisis has worsened, and the deeply indebted government's response to it owed much more to International Monetary Fund orthodoxy than to Islamic teachings.[28] The sociopolitical dilemma facing the regime has been compounded further by a prolonged and severe drought, an escalating civil war, a taxing refugee problem, and a sharp decline in Arab and Western aid after the Sudan sided with Iraq during the gulf conflict/crisis in 1990-1991. As of this writing, the protracted and multidimensional crisis of the al-Bashir and al-Turabi regime continues to worsen. To the extent that the regime's performance and political legitimacy are interdependent, the challenges to its very survival are likely to increase.[29]

The case of Islamization in Pakistan is different from the Sudanese case in terms of historical evolution. The very rationale for the emergence of Pakistan as a separate political entity, as stated in its constitution, was to provide an independent homeland for Muslims on the Indian subcontinent. Thus the political identity of the community and the political function of the state were closely tied to Islam. Islamic identity and national self-determination became closely intertwined or, as articulated by the Jama'at-i Islami, "Pakistan came into being in the name of Islam,

26. Abdullahi Ahmad An-Na'im, "Constitutionalism and Islamization in the Sudan," *Africa Today*, 36:11-28 (1989); Nelson Kasfir, "One Full Revolution: The Politics of Sudanese Military Government," in *The Military in African Politics*, ed. John Harbeson (New York: Praeger, 1987), pp. 141-62; John Esposito, "Sudan," in *Politics of Islamic Revivalism*, ed. Hunter, pp. 193-201; Carolyn Fluehr-Lobban, "Islamization in Sudan," *Middle East Journal*, 44: 618-23 (1990); Farag Fouda, *Qabla al-suqut* [Before the fall] (Cairo: n.p., 1985), pp. 121-41; Ann M. Lesch, "The Fall of Numeiri" (Report no. 9, Universities Field Staff International, Indianapolis, 1985). See also Mansour Khalid, *al-Fajr al-kadhib* [The false dawn] (Cairo: Dar al-Hillal, 1986). Khalid is former foreign minister of the Sudan.

27. *Economist*, 18 Apr. 1992, pp. 41-42. For an earlier and more elaborate presentation of his critique of Western notions of popular sovereignty, political pluralism, and competitive politics, see Hassan al-Turabi, "al-Shura wa al-dimuqratiyya" [Shura and democracy], *al-Mustaqbal al-'arabi* [The Arab future], 7:4-22 (1985).

28. See Benaiah Yongo-Bure, "Sudan's Deepening Crisis," *Middle East Report*, pp. 9-13 (Sept.-Oct. 1991); John Voll, "Political Crisis in Sudan," *Current History*, 89:153-56, 178-80 (1990).

29. John Voll has concluded that the "issue may in fact have changed from who will rule Sudan to whether or not Sudan will be able to survive in any meaningful fashion." See Voll, "Political Crisis in Sudan," p. 179.

and it could exist in the name of Islam alone." The Objectives Resolution, approved by the country's first Constituent Assembly, centered around the notion that the very raison d'être of the state in Pakistan was to play an activist, interventionist role in bringing about a social and political order based on Islamic principles.[30] Given this historical legacy of "Pakistan's Islamic mandate," all of that country's successive regimes have sought to legitimize their power and their policies, as well as to contain or weaken their political opponents, on Islamic grounds.

As is to be expected, though, Pakistan's regimes differed in terms of their policy orientation and their interpretation of "Islamic ideology." Zulfikar Ali Bhutto's regime and his Pakistan People's Party (PPP), for example, adopted a populist interpretation of Islam. Under the banner of "Islamic socialism," the PPP pursued policies of socioeconomic redistribution at home and nonalignment abroad. The regime's reformist political discourse emphasized *musawat* ("equality") and social justice as basic Islamic principles and fundamental features of Muslim society and polity under the Prophet Muhammad.[31] Faced with growing urban restlessness in the mid-1970s, the party's platform for the March 1977 elections called for Islamic educational and social reforms and greater recognition of the role of the *'ulama'* and the mosques in society. Bhutto's re-

gime was already in retreat, however, and conservative Islamic organizations, under the umbrella of the Pakistan National Alliance, were increasing their appeal, influence, and protest. The regime was finally overthrown by the military coup of July 1977.

The new regime, under General Zia ul-Haq, was decidedly more conservative socioeconomically, more authoritarian politically, clearly pro-Western, and particularly pro-American in its foreign policy orientation. Divine guidance was invoked by the general regarding the origin of his Islamization program known as *nizam-i mustafa* ("order of the Prophet or the Chosen One"). As he put it, " 'I have a mission, given by God, to bring Islamic order to Pakistan.' "[32] The day selected for introducing the Islamization program was that of the Prophet's birthday. In the economic sphere, the program promised to safeguard private property rights and to abolish bank interest through the establishment of Islamic financial institutions. In the educational sphere, it placed greater emphasis on the Islamic content of textbooks and the expansion of *shari'a* training institutes. Regarding the social sphere, it called for a stricter enforcement of Islamic moral code and the prohibition of gambling and alcohol consumption. As to the legal sphere, Zia's program included the implementation of the *hudud* ordinances, the appointment of *muhtasib-i a'la* (a sort of Islamic ombudsman), and the es-

30. Mumtaz Ahmad, "Pakistan," in *Politics of Islamic Revivalism*, ed. Hunter, pp. 229-32.

31. Gerald Heeger, "Socialism in Pakistan," in *Socialism in the Third World*, ed. Helen Desfosses and Jacques Levesque (New York: Praeger, 1975), pp. 291-309.

32. Interview with the British Broadcasting Corporation, 15 Apr. 1978, as quoted in Omar Noman, *The Political Economy of Pakistan* (London: KPI, 1988), p. 141.

tablishment of a judicial review process by *shari'a* judges to decide whether all laws were in accordance with Islam.[33]

Among the major exceptions regarding the scope of such judicial review were various martial law ordinances. As Mumtaz Ahmad put it, Zia's government insisted on linking "the destiny of both Islam and Pakistan with the continuity of the military regime . . . [consequently] any deviation from the official interpre-

tation . . . becomes both a religious heresy and treason against the state . . . political rebellion and religious dissent become indistinguishable." The regime's main objective in pursuing this linkage was to gain legitimacy particularly among the lower middle classes and in the ranks of the *'ulama'*, as well as among conservative religious political parties. Another major objective of such linkage was to discredit leftist and liberal opposition forces and to portray them to the public as un-Islamic and thus unacceptable alternatives to an Islamic regime. In fact, the interim constitution of March 1981 empowered the President to dissolve any political party "operating in a manner prejudicial to Islamic ideology."[34]

As in the case of the Sudan, the call for Islamization in Pakistan gained what appeared at first to be a significant measure of support. But it also raised popular expectations regarding the prospects of more just and more livable conditions in Pakistan; however, the living conditions of many continued to deteriorate. No *shura* ("consultation") was seriously contemplated by the military-Islamic regime. On the contrary, freedom of expression was subjected to serious restrictions, opposition publications were banned, defiant writers jailed, and uncooperative newsmen flogged.[35]

Once again, as in the Sudanese case, most of the Islamization was concentrated on turning bank inter-

33. See Riaz Hassan, "Islamization: An Analysis of Religious, Political and Social Change in Pakistan," *Middle East Studies*, 21: 263-84 (1985); Charles Kennedy, "Islamization and Legal Reform in Pakistan, 1979-1989," *Pacific Affairs*, 63:62-77 (1990); idem, "Islamization in Pakistan," *Asian Survey*, 28:307-16 (1988). It is interesting to note that while General Zia's Islamization program won the endorsement and support of Saudi Arabia (see Noman, *Political Economy of Pakistan*, p. 150), Iran's media characterized it as " 'the exact antithesis of Islam' " and concluded that Zia " 'could much more readily be likened to the ex-Shah.' " Quoted in Roger Savory, "Ex Oriente Nebula: An Inquiry into the Nature of Khomeini's Ideology," in *Ideology and Power in the Middle East*, ed. Chelkowski and Pranger, p. 352. Iran's leaders, however, opted for a cautious policy toward Pakistan to ensure continued assistance to pro-Iranian groups in the Afghan resistance against the Soviets. See Zalmay Khalilzad, "The Iranian Revolution and the Afghan Resistance," in *Shi'ism, Resistance, and Revolution* (Boulder, CO: Westview Press, 1987), pp. 257-73. However, the Iranian leadership adopted a critical position toward "Numayri's Islamization," which they perceived as lacking credibility in light of his regime's alignment during the 1980s with the United States, Saudi Arabia, and Iraq. The Sudanese President even claimed that the Islamic Republic of Iran attempted to destabilize his regime. See Gehad Auda, "The Foreign Policy of a Fragmented Polity: The Case of Sudan," in *The Foreign Policies of Arab States*, by Bahgat Korany and Ali Dessouki (Boulder, CO: Westview Press, 1991), p. 368.

34. Ahmad, "Pakistan," pp. 231-33; Hassan, "Islamization," p. 269.

35. James Napoli, "Benazir Bhutto and the Issues of Press Freedom in Pakistan," *Journal of South Asian and Middle Eastern Studies*, 14:64 (1991).

est into profits, setting up the *shari'a* courts, and implementing the *hudud*. The initial popular support has gradually given way to disillusionment and cynicism. The political outcome of all this was captured by Hamza Alavi when he concluded that the "regime's strident rhetoric about the Islamic basis of Pakistan's ideology has failed to give it the basis of legitimacy that it has sought . . . its rhetoric has compounded its problems by raising the hopes . . . of Islamic fundamentalists."[36] The regime was in no position to fulfill these hopes, and in February 1984 it had to intervene and curtail a cycle of violence and assassinations that involved the Islamic Society of Students, which was an earlier collaborator with General Zia's regime in suppressing supporters of the PPP, and its leftist opponents on university campuses.[37] The 1988 national elections, which were held after Zia's death in a mysterious airplane crash, brought the PPP back to power in a coalition government led

by Benazir Bhutto. Other changes have occurred since then, but the nature of the regime is no longer what it was under Zia.

CONCLUSION

The core argument of this article can be restated briefly as follows: The diversity characterizing popular and oppositional Islamic movements is also evident in the regimes that base their very identity and legitimacy on Islamic grounds. In pursuing this path, Islamic regimes articulate different interpretations of Islam that reflect the interests and ideology of those who control the state machinery—for example, conservative, reformist, or revolutionary; the influence of society's historical legacy and traditions, such as identity formation, evolution of authority patterns, or crucial formative experiences; and specific characteristics of the immediate situational setting, such as crisis situations. I have examined three types of Islamic regimes, led by monarchs, mullas, and marshals, to illustrate and compare the Islamic legitimation of diverse domestic and foreign policy outcomes. The three are the conservative dynastic regime of Saudi Arabia, the populist clerical regime of Iran, and the military authoritarian regimes of the Sudan and Pakistan.

In all three regime types, the Islamic legitimization of their rule did not proceed uncontested. It has been frequently challenged on religiopolitical grounds by domestic rivals for power and external rivals for leadership in the Muslim world. Among the cases covered in this article, the most effective challenges to regime legiti-

36. Hamza Alavi, "Ethnicity, Muslim Society, and the Pakistan Ideology," in *Islamic Reassertion in Pakistan*, ed. Anita Weiss (Syracuse, NY: Syracuse University Press, 1986), pp. 45-46. For more on the growth of popular dissatisfaction with Zia's program, see Richard Kurin, "Islamization in Pakistan: A View from the Countryside," *Asian Survey*, 25:852-62 (1985); Hassan, "Islamization," pp. 279-80. On the organized opposition by women to particular draft "Islamic ordinances," see Khawar Mumtaz and Farida Shaheed, eds., *Women of Pakistan: Two Steps Forward, One Step Back?* (London: Zed Books, 1987), pp. 123-42.

37. On student political activism during that period, including a reference to the lives of 80 students lost in this wave of violence, see Seyyed Vali Reza Nasr, "Students, Islam, and Politics," *Middle East Journal*, 46:67-68 (1992).

macy have been manifested in the Islamized military regimes of the Sudan and Pakistan. Their predicament can be attributed to the fact that in addition to presiding over societies deeply divided along ethnic and linguistic lines, these regimes lacked the political capital provided by huge oil revenues available in the Saudi case of *al-Islam al-tharawi* ("the Islam of wealth," or, as described by one writer, "petro-Islam").[38] They also lacked the legitimacy generated by revolutionary change under charismatic leadership known in the Iranian case of *al-Islam al-thawri* ("revolutionary Islam").

Whether the Islamization of these military regimes followed a palace coup, as in the Sudan in 1983, or a

---

38. See Fouad Zakariya, *al-Haqiqa wa al-wahm fi al-haraka al-Islamiyya al-mu'asira* [Reality and myth in the contemporary Islamic movement] (Cairo: Dar al-Fikr, 1986), pp. 23-26. On Saudi responses to the challenges posed by socioeconomic change under conditions of the oil boom and oil glut, see Kirin Chaudhry, "The Price of Wealth," *International Organization*, 43:108-19, 123-30, 135-42 (Winter 1989); David Long, "Stability in Saudi Arabia," *Current History*, 90:9-13 (1991).

full-blown army takeover, as in Pakistan in 1977, it did not alter their fundamentally discipline-centered, antipolitical character. This character has been manifested not only in their attempts to silence any opposition to their rule but also in their distrust of the political movements that supported their Islamization programs and whose leaders aspired to play the roles of its theoreticians and organizers; such movements include the Muslim Brotherhood in the Sudan and the Jama'at-i Islami in Pakistan. It is no wonder, then, that these regimes have lost, rather quickly, most of the popular support generated by the promise of Islamization. Whether Saudi Arabia and Iran provide alternative models of Islamic governance worthy of emulation by other Muslim communities is a subject of contention and debate. The Saudi monarchs and Iranian mullas have, however, managed with some degree of success to use available economic, political, and cultural resources in dealing with their diverse challenges. The same cannot be said for the Islam of the marshals.

ANNALS, *AAPSS*, 524, November 1992

Islamicist Utopia and Democracy

By LAHOUARI ADDI

ABSTRACT: This article addresses democratic construction in Islamic societies throughout the Algerian experience. Its main conclusions can be summarized as follows. First, in all Muslim societies, there exists an Islamicist utopia that stands as an obstacle not only to democracy but also to political modernity. Until now, this utopia has been contained only by repression that finally impedes the democratization. Second, Islam presents itself as a public religion that participates in the legitimization of political power. The democratic ideology, however, is compatible with religion to the extent that it is lived as a private concern. Finally, the Islamicist utopia and the public aspect of Islam aim at maintaining society's communal structures. They refuse to make the singularity of the political arena independent and reject differentiation through politics within a society that claims to be fraternal.

Lahouari Addi is professor of political sociology at Oran University, Algeria. He holds a degree from Université des Sciences Sociales de Grenoble and a doctorat d'état from École des Hautes Études en Sciences Sociales de Paris (France). He has written four books: De L'Algerie pre-coloniale à l'Algerie coloniale (1985); Approche methodologique du pouvoir et de l'état dans les sociétés du Tiers-Monde (1990); L'impasse du populisme (1991); and L'Algerie, l'économie et la question du politique, edited by Bouchene Alger (1992). During the year 1991-92, he was a visiting fellow in the Near Eastern Studies Department, Princeton University.

IN the years following the independence of much of the Third
World in the 1950s and 1960s, political sociology examined developing
polities through the concepts of nation building and state building. The
object of this examination focused on
the emergence of a political center or
central power that structured its periphery in order to create a homogeneous nation and a developed economy. The accent was placed on the
autonomy of central power vis-à-vis
the exterior world and on its will and
capacity to create a national society
through the process of modernization
and industrial development.

The record of the decades since
independence, however, has shown
that this approach overestimated the
capacity of the political center to develop a modern economy and to begin
the creation of a society, in the sense
of Ferdinand Tönnies. Scholars realized that the central power, itself belonging to the historical reality it
sought to transform, came to be governed by the dominant political logic.
Setting itself up as a self-contained
end, it created an obstacle to its proclaimed objectives. In the process,
modernization called into question
the dominant ideological interests
and social structures, and the central
power followed its own interests and
entered into the collective image in
order to ensure its own survival.

The concepts of modernization and
of nation building—after Apter and
Abdelmalek—remained incomplete
because they were developed separately from the question of power,
which is the basic question of political science and therefore the essential element in political analysis.

After noting that the political center
is privatized, that is, considered to be
a private patrimony and thus creating the notion of neopatrimonialism,
political sociology leapt over the
problem by focusing on the concept of
democracy building. In order to understand what was going on, all that
the analyst had to do was emerge
from the neopatrimonial logic, face
the question of pluralism, and introduce the laws of free competition and
free enterprise. But the analyst for-
got that neopatrimonialism was the
political effect of a historic situation
where the central power was privatized for ideopolitical reasons, making
the central power the object of public competition. Deprivatizing it will
be possible only if the ideopolitical
factors lose their relevance and
dominance.

POLITICAL CITIZENSHIP
AND PUBLIC RELIGION

The example of Algeria shows that
democratization was conceived as an
operation to justify the disengagement of the state from the economy.
But democratization is above all a
political and ideological struggle; it
implies the emergence of citizenship,
with liberty. Without a central power
to protect public liberty and the exercise of citizenship, there is no democracy. But in Algeria the team in
power, delegitimized by the economic
and social failures for which it was
responsible, could not impose the authority of the state over the dominant
ideological interests and the logic of
the collective image that refused individual autonomy and its juridical
political expression as a subject of

law. The citizen is a legal subject of law who obeys civil laws born out of reasoned public debate. If the individual were to obey only other individuals, depend on the whim of the prince, submit to laws handed down from time immemorial, there would be no citizenship. The citizen is a free person vis-à-vis his or her peers, living and dead. This liberty is no caprice destined to diminish the citizen's human dignity, culture, religion, or history. Indeed, it permits the development, expansion, and liberation of all the potentialities within the human being.

In a society confronted with the process of modernization, the emergence of citizenship arouses suspicion among the religious. However, religious faith is true and sincere only when it is lived in a free social milieu. If the exterior appearances of faith were imposed by social constraint, there would be an unimaginable number of hypocrites among sincere believers. Religious awareness will accept political citizenship only after historical experience shows that citizenship does not diminish religion in the strict sense. Social constraint does not come from religion, however; it is, rather, the effect of the public character of religion, manifested as a social fact of the group and not as a spirituality belonging to the private intimacy of the individual. Religion becomes a political order to which one aspires, a political order whose coming is resisted by immoral beings lacking respect for the word of God.

This political order is not the coming of the kingdom of God on earth or the preparation of believing souls for eternal life. Islam does not permit

this fundamentalism. The Islamicists are not fundamentalists, and, although they proclaim the contrary, they do not confuse the spiritual and the temporal. Their objective is to construct not a divine order but a human order that obeys the prescriptions of the sacred test. This objective, if realized, will not ensure the individual's place in paradise but will permit better life on earth. Access to paradise is an individual and not a collective task.

This spiritual predisposition is shared by all believers in the land of Islam; in other words, Muslim societies are pregnant with a religious utopia from which they would like to draw political order. It is an Islamicist utopia, which stands as an obstacle not only to democracy but also to political modernism in general—at least in the latter's Western formulation. This utopia, latent in all Muslim societies, is politically active in those countries where great expectations have been disappointed, where the conditions of daily life are at the limit of the tolerable, and where repression can go no further. These three conditions applied in Algeria under the rule of Chadli Bendjedid.

But the Islamicist utopia is not an accident of circumstances; on the contrary, it belongs to the long term of history. The Islamic world held itself apart from the social debates that the Renaissance unleashed in Europe. Untouched by the dynamic of social criticism, it remained faithful to apologetic historiography. The Islamic renaissance, or Nahda, which took place in the second half of the nineteenth century beginning with Jamal al-Din al-Afghani, marks the beginning of the intellectual movement's attempt to integrate faith and reason. But, confronted with the expansion of colonialism, the Nahda fell back upon mythification of the past and apologetic discourse. Its last thinker, Rashid Reda, had Hasan al-Banna, founder of the Muslim Brotherhood movement in Egypt, as a disciple. Thus colonization did not help matters, since modernism was delegitimized by the very fact that it had brought with it colonial domination. This explains why, with the exception of a few isolated Arab intellectuals, whose positions were suspect, the paradigms of the Enlightenment had such feeble echoes in Muslim societies. In the rare cultivated milieu of the national liberation movements, the question was put off until after independence, which was supposed to ignite the dynamic of modernism automatically.

Nevertheless, a few decades after independence, national disenchantment appeared. Modernity had not been ignited at the desired speed or in the desired conditions. During the first years of independence—the 1950s and the 1960s—popular Marxism, at least in the universities, opposed the influence of Hobbes, Rousseau, Kant, de Tocqueville, natural law, and political freedom. It delegitimized them, labeling them "ideologies in service to the bourgeoisie, which produce alienation and exploitation." The Islamicist utopia became politically active, therefore, in a social and political context marked by a double disappointment: hopes invested in independence going unfulfilled and dissipation of the illusions of "developmentalism."

In this perspective, the system of education, in its legitimate task of teaching the past, reactivates the epic combat of Islam. In reaction against the West, the past is taught without any critical sense. Its specificity is emphasized to the detriment of universality. Historic events in the origins of modernity are minimized because they do not belong to the history of Islam. The discovery of America—why, in fact, did the Muslims not take part in it?—the Christian Reformation and the wars that followed it; the English, American, Russian, and French revolutions; the recomposition of national borders in Europe in the nineteenth century; the rise of Nazism in Germany—all these major events are considered foreign to the Muslim historical experience and therefore relegated to secondary importance. It is as if the Muslims did not consider themselves as taking part in the universalizing historical process and as if they sought to remake their history without drawing lessons from other people, especially people who set in march the process of modernity and the process of domination of which Muslims—along with other people—have been the victim. From the point of view of Islamic sensitivity, there is no modern reading of the American Revolution, the French Revolution, the Russian Revolution, and Hitlerism. Obviously, this is not a task for high school teachers. It belongs to the university, which should produce historical works from which the public school system can draw its lessons. In the absence of such research, the educational system spreads myths that deform the perception of the contemporary historical process, a deformation that results in a loss of the sense of reality. The system of mass education spreads the myths that feed the utopia, which is itself repressed when it expresses itself politically.

Muslim society is thus enclosed in a logic of ever-deepening repression. In this context, any opening to pluralism and democratization is condemned to failure, because the historical and ideological conditions for the privatization of public power have not been reached. Democratization threatens to change radically the verbal mode of legitimizing the neopatrimonial system. Historical legitimacy risks being replaced by religious legitimacy, but both put central authority above individuals and historical time; both refuse political citizenship and attack the dignity of individuals, making them administrative subjects who bow as the official vehicle passes by. Historical and religious legitimacy are the modality by which the dead exercise their dictatorship on the living. In the twentieth century there is only one legitimacy that conforms to the dignity of the free individual, electoral legitimacy. But electoral legitimacy is an inseparable part of democratic ideology, and the latter requires religion to lose the public character that predisposes it to be a basis of legitimacy and thus a political resource in the competition for power. Without democratic ideology, the political party presenting itself as most Muslim—or perceived as such—would be assured a crushing victory in democratic elections, and this would inaugurate the end of the democratic process.

POLITICAL MODERNITY AND PUBLIC RELIGION

It is necessary to show how political modernity is incompatible with the public character of religion and how modernity is built on the depoliticization of religion. But the notion of depoliticizing religion has a precise content, for the idea that religion must be separated from politics proceeds from a voluntarist, naive, and even religiously hostile vision. Clearly, every social act and collective or public manifestation contains a political dimension. Islam, like any other religion, contains a political dynamic that is impossible to deny. In Christianity, the church does not permit a believer outside the ecclesiastical hierarchy to speak to others in the name of religion. To the contrary, in Islam, the political aspect is limited to no institution, thus permitting any believer to claim religious authority and use it for temporal purposes over other individuals. For reasons deriving from the structure of its dogma, the political character of Islam is obvious. In addition, this character is emphasized by the recent history of Muslim societies struggling against colonial domination, during which Islam was mobilized as a political resource and a factor of identity—so much as to become a constructive element in national ideology and a constituent of nationality. Consequently, it is no longer possible to call for the separation of religion and politics.

But modernity does not require the separation of religion and politics or the marginalization of religion as a precondition. Nobody has the right to prevent the mosque from condemning corruption and arbitrariness or emphasizing the duty to assist widows and orphans. It is even desirable for the mosque to have moral authority in society, in order to appeal to the preservation of human values—fraternity, solidarity, and justice—that accompany the divine message and to denounce flagrant restrictions on human rights and social inequalities. But for the mosque to incarnate this moral authority, it must remain outside of the competition for power. That is, modernity and, more particularly, democratic ideology are incompatible with religion's having a partisan character.

Indeed, under modernity and democratic ideology, public debate about individual autonomy, political citizenship, juridical equality, and political liberty would be considered to be undermined were a party to claim divine authority in making its argument. Democracy means free elections and alternance in power, but it is also the public exercise of reason, as Habermas would say, on all issues concerning the individual and his or her relations with the community. Political parties that compete in elections try to convince their voters on the basis of supposedly rational argumentation. Of course, these parties defend the ideological interests of the group. But these interests, frequently not perceived as such, are theoretically rationalized in order to be presented as in the common interest of all members of society. Political debate, public in its essence, has the purpose of making group interests and political programs attractive

from the point of view of a broad rationality. The voter is supposed to choose, according to reason, the program most satisfactory to his or her own interests and vision of things. Without open public debate, without reference to the rationality of social choice, there can be no democracy.

If religion as such intervenes in the debate, that is to say, if the protagonists claim divine authority, there will no longer be debate or democracy. For citizens, most of whom are believers, cannot opt against the religious prescriptions for society. Once there is a religious party in the electoral competition or a party presenting itself as such, there can be no free national choice on the part of any voter who cannot imagine voting against the divine message. Human nature being what it is, there might even be voters who would vote for religious parties in order to assuage their conscience or to atone for bad behavior in the past (or in the future).

It is not the purpose of the electoral act to be transformed into a religious rite. It is not Islam as a text that transforms the electoral act into a rite; it is the culture of the believer, his or her capacity or incapacity to separate the sacred from the profane. In a society where the level of political culture is low, the theological content of the sacred text is altered. In such a case, the finality of the profane act is transformed: the profane becomes sacralized and the sacred profaned.

There is no contradiction, of course, between textual Islam—the Quran and the *sunna*—and modernism. The contradiction is with the way Islam is lived and practiced today. But a religion's public character is not inevitable or inherent; it is a product of history. Without succumbing to the illusion of hindsight, it can be said that the public character of Islam results from the medieval interpretation of the religion, an interpretation that remains active and formally rejects the notion of political sovereignty—only God is sovereign. It rejects, consequently, the logic of juridical positivism; it rejects political freedom, the abyss of the civil state founded on the Hobbesian-Rousseauistic notion of social contract; in short, as Charles Butterworth notes in his article in this volume, it rejects the modern construction of political life.

The Islamicist utopia is not, however, merely a relic from the past. On the contrary, it expresses, in a contradictory manner, a desire to join with modernism, while at the same time assuring the survival of community values. The Islamicist utopia seeks to construct a City where values of solidarity, equality, and justice will dominate, with respect for the word of God. That is, its goal is a City regulated not by politics—which showcase the ugliness of humankind—but by morality. Political parties are not the expression of preexisting divergences; in its view, they are the cause of these divergences. For the militant of the Islamic Salvation Front (FIS), for example, the so-called Berberist parties create the linguistic issues that serve as their stock in trade. Banning those parties, therefore, would be enough to make the issues go away. The same goes for all other parties

that seek to divide the national community.

Economic battles and the ideological divergences that traverse Muslim societies would not exist except for the fact that humans have turned aside from the work of God. Let us come back to it, and we will once again become brothers, united by the love of God. The interest of the individual as well as the cupidity of the haves would stimulate the productivity of the workers, which would increase the riches to be shared. The Islamicist utopia is rooted in this ethical-religious anthropological optimism and therefore refuses to establish social relations on a juridical-political basis that implies the Kantian categories of civil law, rights and their subject, and individual will. To reorganize society on the basis of the anthropological pessimism of Hobbes, Spinoza, Kant, or Carl Schmitt would, for the Muslim consciousness, be a leap into the great unknown. The Islamicist utopia exists only because the categories of political modernism have not been reworked in the mold of Arab-Islamic culture. But such a creation of modernism by way of Arab-Islamic culture is theoretically possible, for there is no reason—everything else kept the same—why democracy should be inherently Western and absolutism inherently Muslim.

Thus the Muslim world is now in the throes of a debate it missed in the wake of its decadence. But now it is not the venerated thinkers who are forcing the debate. It is being forced by the streets, violently, murderously. As in the past, the thinkers of al-Azhar continue to ponder the immutable rules of grammar and the placement of punctuation marks in the sacred texts, bypassing the fundamental questions. In Algeria, it is the FIS—the street—that poses, unwittingly, the essential questions about the reconstruction of political life in the context of local culture. The Algerian democratic experience would have shown that as long as the Islamicist utopia remained popular, as long as it remained anchored in the collective imagination, it would constitute an obstacle to the influx of modern political categories without which democracy is impossible. This is why the democratic experience in Algeria would have been decisive for the whole Muslim world. Either it would have succeeded, and the Muslim world would have profited; or it would have failed, and the Muslim world would have returned either to the wasting of the oil patrimony in unproductive consumption or to international beggary.

FRATERNAL SOCIETY AS A REFUSAL OF CHANGE

The interruption of the electoral process—and probably of democracy building—in Algeria at best restores the situation before October 1988, when the country went out into the streets to protest government inefficiency. One may ask whether the defense of immediate interests and the fear of eventual sanctions against the ruling elite or the fear of political anarchy by themselves explain this interruption. There may well be deeper reasons related to the very perception of politics revealing fears

of radical breaks with the past and historic changes. This does not mean that the arrival of the FIS to power would provoke a historic change in the FIS's view of itself as the single party of all Algerians; rather, it is itself the refusal to change from the single-party system of the National Liberation Front (FLN). But from the formal point of view, by coming to power neither by riot nor by coup d'état, the FIS would inaugurate a new period of political history for the country, a period that would have its own dynamic in the recomposition of political forces.

But the incumbent leaders did not have the imagination and the courage to enter into the movement of change. In this perspective, the banning of the FIS blocks change; for the FIS, as an organized movement, serves as a magnet for the ideology of the fraternal society. This magnet allows the protagonists to define themselves in relation to each other. Banning the FIS means that the ideology it bears will continue to dominate the entire political space and to be present in all of the political groups. For the FIS, far from being a party, is a sentiment, a prepolitical culture.

From this point of view, all Algerians are members of the FIS to the extent that we all swim in its prepolitical culture. The sense of historical perspective suggests that this prepolitical culture will crystallize itself into a movement expressing a utopian sentiment, even if this movement takes power by democratic rules. Then, upon confronting the contradictions of social life, it will be repulsed to the point of losing any political meaning. It is through political competition, public debate, freedom of expression, and the practice of political citizenship that a large part of the electorate will come to realize that the FIS is only a sentiment and not a management tool of modern political life and social contradictions.

Electoral competition forces the actors to situate themselves politically in the logic of alternance, in a political space defined by ideological rivalries. Political programs are not merely a trick to conquer and occupy central power. Any attempt to recover the adversary becomes futile, because political adversaries clash and publicly declare themselves to be irreconcilable. The bitterness of their struggle does not affect civil peace, however, because the struggle is regulated by democratic institutions and sanctioned by universal suffrage within the framework of an alternance accepted by all. This political game supposes above all that the society is permeated by irreducible political cleavages and that these cleavages are interiorized by the actors. Such a political game also presupposes that the historical subjects of political modernity are in place and that they have a more or less clear awareness of theoretical categories through which they perceive and practice politics. That leading figures of the FLN easily join the FIS or that leaders of the FIS easily participate in power only shows that the actors do not obey a rationality of political modernity that presupposes the insurmountable ideological and political contradictions compatible only in democratic institutions and in alternance in state power.

The refusal of political differentiation is founded on political fraternalism that the interruption of the electoral process destroys. Because it does not conceive of a national collectivity that is irreconcilably divided, fraternalism raises the possibility of recovering the adversary of the moment, allying with him if he is intransigent or sharing power if he is sufficiently strong. One must not believe that political fraternalism is justified by a fear of recourse to physical coercion. To the contrary, to the extent that fraternalism denies the political character of social contradictions, it offers no institutional means of resolution and therefore opens the possibility of bloody riots. In a fraternal society, central power is not the subject of political competition; it is the expression of a momentary relation of force. Maintaining oneself in power or conquering it supposes the use of physical force and violence. Violence is a banal means of political regulation in a fraternal society, as differentiated from a democratic society where parties declare themselves irreconcilable political adversaries without destroying civil peace and citizens' lives, whatever their political opinions.

On the day after the elections of 26 December 1991, Algeria was confronted with the choice of opting either for the fraternal society that had prevailed to this point, with its ideological handicaps and its political lethargy, or for a democratic society, with its competition and implacable logic. It chose fraternal society twice. The first time, it gave the majority to the FIS, which is an expression par excellence of fraternal society; the second time, it stopped the electoral process. Henceforth the great party of fraternal society will have to be reconstructed on the remains of the FLN and the debris of the FIS. The result, necessarily a single party, will have to reproduce the past and put central authority above political competition. Obviously, this does not prevent absolutism, corruption, or—even less—bloody repression of the riots that will arise within the logic of fraternal society.

What to do? There are two possible choices. The first one is to modernize the economy so that the Islamicist utopia cannot be joined to the social discontent that gives it its imprint. For Algeria, this choice will require a radical shuffling of the team in power and financial resources to the tune of $50 billion, earmarked for restructuring the economy. A different team in power—vested with a vision of the future, developing the economy, and releasing a dynamic of accumulation—would have enough authority to effect the necessary ruptures and to transform the education system. The social base of the Islamicist utopia would leave it a minority opinion expressed by a few firebrands whose startling actions would be human-interest stories without any impact on the democratic functioning of political society.

The second choice would be to permit the democratic process to bring about its own termination, by carrying the Islamicists to power. For a utopia, there is no antidote like reality. Utopia is an attempt to replace the real with the imaginary. As long as it is expressed by an opposition party, it can be pertinent and effica-

cious. But once the party comes to power, it becomes reduced to reflecting reality—the harsh reality of concrete causality and human vice. History is the unhappy experiment. It has never followed the wise counsels of the Platonic sage. Westerners did not construct modernism and democracy with an ear to Hobbes, Rousseau, or Kant. Only after having suffered the tragic excesses of absolute power and tyranny, only after being instructed by Robespierre and Napoleon, did the consciousness of common interest prevail. The thinkers were not convoked until afterward, to provide the ideological justification for the new political order. That justification was traced back to Greek antiquity and primitive Christianity. Why could it not be found in the Islamic heritage as well?

It is clear that preference for the first or the second of these choices depends on the position of the chooser. If I, for example, were a Western politician, I would do anything to prevent the Islamicists from acceding to power, because that would provoke regional instability and threaten Western interests. For, after all, in the Islamicist discourse, the Evil Empire is the now-Christian, now-atheist materialist West. If I were an army officer or a high bureaucrat, implicated in the past mismanagement of the state, I would mount a coup d'état to prevent the Islamicists' accession. For, drunk with hatred for those whom they consider to be the enemies of God, would they not wish to throw some heads to the mob?

But I am neither a Western politician nor an officer of the Algerian army. I am an academic-Platonist, and the object of my reflection is the Islamicist utopia and its rootedness in society. As long as this utopia remains active, Algeria will twiddle its thumbs at the doorway of modernism. The Muslim consciousness will not awaken to modernism until after the clash between the Islamicist utopia and the political realities of human anthropology occurs. At what price? one might ask. To this I would be inclined to answer, "I am neither an officer of the Algerian army nor a Western politician."

ANNALS, *AAPSS*, **524**, November 1992

Islam in the States of the Former USSR

By VITALY NAUMKIN

ABSTRACT: Under the Soviet system, the rich intellectual life of Islam was eliminated, but a vigorous if unsophisticated popular tradition remained. After *perestroika*, an Islamic movement emerged as a form of political protest. But secular nationalism and ethnic conflict within and between the new republics also provided political dynamics. Throughout the time of change, Islam has served as a symbol of identity, a force for mobilization, and a pressure for democracy. But if successful politically, it faces economic challenges beyond its grasp.

Professor Vitaly Naumkin received his doctorate from Moscow University and has conducted research and taught in Russia and the Middle East. He is deputy director of the Institute of Oriental Studies of the Russian (formerly Soviet) Academy of Sciences, president of the Russian Center for Strategic Research and International Studies, and author of works in Russian, English, and Arabic on Soviet Central Asia and the Middle East.

THE former USSR held the fifth-largest population of Muslims in the world; according to various estimates, the population was 60-70 million. Since its formation, that state pursued a rigid policy of forcing out religion not only from public and political life but also from the life of the individual. The ideology of the ruling Communist Party was atheistic. Officially, religion was separated from the state, but even outside the framework of the state, the transmission of religious knowledge was extremely inhibited, primarily due to the strict limitation of the printing and distribution of religious literature and the absence of religious schools. The disintegration of the traditional way of life, industrialization, and urbanization also helped to lessen the weight of religion in the life of all peoples of the USSR, including the Muslims.

Muslims are found in Central Asia, Kazakhstan, Azerbaijan, North Caucasus, and the Volga region of Russia itself. The processes taking place before and under way after the disintegration of the USSR differed in each of these areas, though they have many traits in common. With that condition in mind, it is possible to focus on Central Asia and Kazakhstan.

During the years of Soviet power, Islam, though greatly restricted, did not completely lose its place in the life of Central Asian society. It was driven deep down and forced to hide under the surface of social structures. The greatest harm was done to intellectual Islam, represented, in the main, by the highly educated intelligentsia, many of whom in the

early twentieth century were advocating reform and renovation of the religion. This intelligentsia was annihilated, and the intellectual Islamic tradition was fully suppressed.

A different fate fell to the so-called everyday or popular Islam based on the synthesis of classical Islamic values and notions with the elements of pre-Islamic beliefs. This Islam included a tremendous number of rites that were particularly vivid in the activities of the Sufi orders, with the Nakshbandiyya order having the greatest currency in Central Asia and the Volga area. For a number of reasons, this kind of Islam was able to survive within the borders of a very vast region comprising, inter alia, Central Asia. In other areas, this kind of Islam came to naught.

The place of the former stratum of theologians and shaykhs was occupied by official clergy institutionalized and integrated into the system of power and controlled with the help of Councils for Religious Affairs, which, in turn, were controlled by the Party bodies and the KGB. This new official clergy did not present a threat to the Communist regime, but to no small extent it facilitated the stabilization of the political situation in Muslim areas. Some researchers are also of the opinion that popular Islam, too, was organically interwoven into socialist life, also helping to consolidate the power of the party-state elite who did not violate the traditional norms of life and thus helping to strengthen the prestige of the authorities.

According to A. Malashenko, "after the completion of the struggle against the Basmach, the authorities practically stopped interfering with the internal affairs of Muslim communities, leaving them to the keepers of the old patriarchal traditions, i.e., the lowest stratum of the clergy who were ignorant of the canons of classical Islam but well versed in the aspirations and needs of the simple folk."[1] The imams of the underground mosques, unofficial village mullas, readers of the Quran, teachers of the secret *maktabs* ("schools"), and *mazar* shaykhs ("shrine officials") made up the stratum with the help of which religious tradition and knowledge were handed down. It was they who prepared the ground for the religious revival of today in that region.

The village community was one of the principal instruments for the preservation of popular Islam. Both prior to the Revolution and after it, irrigation facilities were in the hands of the state, but land was in the possession of peasants. Despite the large-scale establishment of state and cooperative farms, the state did not control the peasants' individual farms. The domination of that kind of economic life and the spread of private trade, which existed secretly despite formal bans, were instrumental in the preservation of traditional ways of life in the countryside. In the cities the role of the conserving element was played by the *mahalla*, the block community whose chairman acted in the same way as the *rais* ("leader") prior to the Revolution. He controlled the observance of Islamic norms and rites in everyday life.

There were very few mosques in Central Asia, and in most small towns and villages there was none at all. The local population used private or public facilities for prayers. Now village clubs, rest houses, and the like are used for this purpose. The setting up of so-called *hujras*, or agricultural settlements, on individual plots of local dwellers has become a common practice for the same purpose.

The cult of saints, always popular in the region, began developing on a large scale in the 1970s. In practically all Central Asian *kishlaks* there is a *mazar*—the tomb of the local saint—which is considered a holy place. Also considered sacred are almost all the graves of clergy, former members of the Emir and Khan administration, and leaders of the Basmach, the armed movement against Soviet power that was finally suppressed only in early 1941. According to S. Polyakov, there was no case in which a grave of a Soviet regime leader became a *mazar*. The *mazars* were addressed with various requests, mainly about the curing of diseases, barrenness, the evil eye, and the like.[2] In Uzbekistan, Tadzhikistan, and Kazakhstan, especially revered were the graves of Khojas and Sayyids whose families descended from the Prophet Muhammad; in Turkmenia, the graves of the representatives of the "six sacred tribes" and the graves of the Turas, descendants of the Genghisides and also of the heads of the Dervish orders,

1. A. V. Malashenko, "Novy politichesky start Islama" [The 1980s: The new political beginning of Islam] *Oriens* (Moscow) no. 5, p. 54:80-e (1991).

2. S. P. Polyakov, "Tradicionaliam v sovremenom sredneaziatskom obscestve" [Traditionalism, the contemporary Central Asian society] (Moscow, 1989), p.75.

which are especially numerous in Samarkand, are held in special esteem. According to expedition data, the *mazar* shaykhs are usually children of mullas in North Tadzhikistan and members of the "sacred tribes" in Turkmenia; in Uzbekistan, Kazakhstan, and some areas of Tadzhikistan, they are representatives of the Khoja and Sayyid families.[3]

The 1970s and 1980s saw the rapid enhancement of the role of religion in the Islamic republics of the USSR as a result of greater access to information, the deepening of crisis in the society, and the influence of the Islamic revolution in Iran. The Islamic *jihad* of the Afghan opposition served as a strong impetus to that process in the southern part of the USSR, along with the increasing resistance to the Soviet presence in Afghanistan. As was stated at a symposium on Islam in Moscow, by the mid-1980s there were about 11,000 members of Sufi orders in the southern areas of the USSR.

PERESTROIKA AS CATALYST

With the beginning of *perestroika*, an Islamic movement emerged in the Soviet Muslim areas that started under the slogans of religious enlightenment, spreading religious culture among the Muslim peoples of the USSR, building and establishing Islamic traditions, and so forth. The ideas of Islamic enlightenment were quite rapidly adopted by various political forces, well aware that they were a reliable means of political mobilization. Believers expressed dissatisfaction with Party and state control of religious communities and demanded the abolition of the system of councils and the renovation of the official clergy. The supreme Mufti of Central Asia and Kazakhstan, Shamsuddin Babakhan, was accused of godlessness and violation of Islamic laws and removed from his post. The process of splitting communities into smaller units began when they refused to be controlled by large regional religious boards. The democratic processes that started in the country as a whole opened the way to rapidly growing religious activity, which, under the conditions of greater openness and expansion of the Soviet Union's international links, won the support of the leading centers of the Muslim world, which began to help Soviet Muslims.

Alongside the trend of purely cultural enlightenment, the tendency of the politicization of Islam emerged in the USSR's Muslim areas in the mid-1980s. For instance, Tadzhikistan witnessed the call to set up an Islamic state. Some participants in the protest demonstrations in various republics voiced Islamic slogans.

Three main blocs of political forces gradually formed in the Muslim republics: former leaders of the Communist parties and the state apparatus, who changed their political face; new democratic parties and movements; and Islamic fundamentalists. Such movements as the Uzbek Birlik or Tadzhik Rastodhez were secular, but the advocates of the Islamic identity of the republics participated in them.

It is thought that the Islamicist movement emerged in Uzbekistan and Tadzhikistan as far back as the

3. Ibid., p. 76.

1970s among the unofficial clergy. Its followers become known as Wahhabites; although they are not true followers of Muhammad ibn 'Abd al-Wahhab, they are akin to the Arabian Wahhabites because of their religious rigorism and ascetic attitude to life. In Tadzhikistan, the Islamicists found their main support in the less developed areas of the South; prominent positions in the Party and state apparatus were, as a rule, held by persons hailing from the North. In Uzbekistan, the main support was in the Ferghana Valley, known as the main agricultural area of the republic. The comparison of the data on the composition of the Islamic groups in the Ferghana Valley and a number of the Middle East countries yields a substantial difference. In Egypt, where we have concrete data on the composition of such groups, the urban youths—mainly children of migrants from rural areas—form their main social base. In the Ferghana Valley, where Islamic customs and values were preserved over the entire Soviet period, Islamicist groups consist mainly of rural people.

By the late 1980s, young leaders of the Islamicist movement became noticeably active. They accused the official clergy of conformism, collaboration, self-interest, violation of Islamic principles, and so on. In Tadzhikistan, several hundred inhabitants of Kulab, Kurgan-Tube, and Dushanbe attempted to enter the congress of Muslims of Central Asia and Kazakhstan, convened in March 1989.[4] At the same time, they tried repeatedly to depose the imams in the Dushanbe Karamirshiko mosque and the Kulab mosque.

Official Muslim clergy were against the politicization of Islam, rejecting the idea of establishing political parties on an Islamic basis. Evidently, this stand was prompted by the traditional loyalty of that clergy to the authorities and the apprehension that such a step might put unofficial mullas at the head of the Islamic movement. Naturally, the authorities, both in the republics and at the center, did not approve of this idea. Nevertheless, on 9 June 1990, a congress of the representatives of the Muslim communities of the country was convened in Astrakhan, Russia. It declared the establishment of the Islamic Revival Party (IRP) and adopted its platform and constitution. These documents of the party, as well as the speeches of its leaders, were of a moderate tenor, supporting the idea of equality of all religions and the readiness to collaborate with the state structures and other parties.

Among other things, the platform of the party stated that it

defends Islam from the attacks of its adversaries . . . advocates equality between believers and nonbelievers . . . demands an end to the propaganda of atheism . . . favors the enhancement of the role of women in families, believing that a woman is in the first place the mother of her children, and only afterward an industrial worker, public figure, etc. The society must provide them with the opportunity for education and all-round development, but the main thing is to give them real opportunity to be the keepers of the family hearth.[5]

4. *Grajdanskie politicheskie dvijeniya v Tadjikistane* [Civil political movements in Tadzhikistan, 1989-March 1990] (Dushanbe, 1990), p. 5.

5. *Komsomolec tadjikistana* (Dushanbe), 24 Nov. 1990.

The official clergy disapproved of the establishment of an Islamic party. The head of the Central Asia Muslims, Mufti Mohammed Sadik Mohammed Yusuf, declared: "We believe that Islam is a party in itself, having already existed for over 1400 years. We have a Constitution in the Quran and a platform in the Sunna of our Prophet. Moreover, Islam is above all parties."[6]

The authorities in Tadzhikistan, referring to the February 1990 riots in Dushanbe, prohibited the activity of the new party; the Tadzhik Kaziyat prohibited the leaders of the mosque from taking part in the activities of any political parties. But in the autumn of 1991, the IRP nevertheless held its constituent regional conference in the village of Chortut, near the capital of the republic. It formed the Tadzhik branch of the party, apparently with the aim of avoiding accusations of violating the ban. Only after the failure of the August 1991 putsch in Moscow did the republican parliament cancel the ban, and at the congress of the branch in the autumn of 1991 the decision for full independence of the Tadzhikistan party from the all-Union party was adopted.

The members of the branch party discussed the problem of the extent to which the Islamic movement should take into account the national interests of the Muslim peoples of the Soviet Union. The members of Turkic origin advocated the unity of interests of all Muslims. Thus one of the leaders of the party in Moscow, Gheidar Jamal, in his interview on Radio Liberty on 18 January 1991, stated, "Uzbekistan and Tadzhiki-

stan are the result of national partition and the undermining of integration principles in Central Asia. . . . Belonging to the Muslim world without boundaries is more essential than the national identity." Among Tadzhiks, a little apprehensive of the predominance of Turkic leaders, the tendency of the synthesis with national ideas prevails along with some pan-Iranian feelings. In that sense, the establishment of the Tadzhik IRP was in line with the aspirations of Tadzhik Islamicists.

In a short time, the IRP proved able to win some influence in a number of areas of Tadzhikistan, Uzbekistan, and other republics of the USSR. Its total membership was estimated to be 60,000 in early 1991, and after the disintegration of the USSR in December 1991, its membership increased. According to expert opinion, it enjoys the strongest positions in the south of Tadzhikistan. The election campaign showed that in Tadzhikistan, the IRP may be ahead of the democratic movement due to the weakness of the national intelligentsia, low political culture, and contradictions between different areas of the republic. In Uzbekistan, where democratic traditions are much stronger, Islamicists have as yet been unable to win such positions.

The Islamic Party of Turkestan, established in the Turkic republics, combines pan-Turkic nationalist and Islamicist ideas. As yet, that party has not won strong support in these republics, which have a mainly Turkish orientation, while Turkey is not interested in the encouragement of the Islamicist forces. At the same time, neither the Saudi Arabian nor

6. *Izvestiya* (Moscow), 14 Dec. 1990.

the Iranian Islamicists would like to encourage pan-Turkic aspirations. The former prefers mainly the support of purely Islamic forces. The latter, comprising Azerbaijani Shiites, resists the development of nationalist sentiments in Turkestan, for they may affect the population of Iranian Azerbaijan as well as the ethnically close Tadzhiks. The leaders of the Tadzhik IRP regard the activities of the Islamic Party of Turkestan with animosity.

The failure of the August 1991 putsch in the USSR opened up new opportunities for the democratic movement. In 1991, the democratic and Islamicist forces of the Islamic areas tried to make their election platforms more alike: the Islamicists strove to win over the democratically minded electorate and the democrats tried to make use of the religious sentiments of the population. Thus the Democratic Erk Party, of Uzbekistan, made an appeal to the ideas of Islamic revival. In Tadzhikistan, democrats and Islamicists acted jointly against the government and in August 1991 forced the Chairman of the Supreme Soviet, K. Mahkamov, to retire.

EXPLOSION IN TASHKENT

In January 1992, the establishment of the Islamic Democratic Party of Russia was announced in Moscow, but the number of its adherents is very small. In September 1991, before the presidential election in Tadzhikistan, the IRP of that republic decided to support the candidate of the democratic forces, D. Khudonazarov. Not only did their support not

help the candidate, but, in the experts' view, it deprived him of the votes of those apprehensive of the prospect of an Islamic state of the Iranian kind. Assessing the situation, P. Mullojanov writes,

Democrats hoped that with the help of the IRP and the Kaziyat of the republic it would be possible to organize truly mass manifestations and meetings which would create a critical situation for the ruling structures. The Islamicists realized that if democrats were not with them in the square, the authorities would not hesitate to employ force. Using the democrats as their shield, they ensured the neutrality of the Center, the army, and the Ministry of the Interior. Thus, the alliance of democratic organizations and the IRP is rather a forced step prompted by special circumstances.[7]

In some places there was a tendency toward cooperation between the Islamicist leaders and the official clergy. But on the whole, the movement to discredit the official mullas continued. Thus, after returning from their pilgrimage to Mecca in 1991, some imams of Tashkent and the Tashkent region, in Uzbekistan, came out against Mufti Mohammed Yusuf, accusing him of violating Islamic norms and, among other things, of selling Qurans received as a gift of Saudi Arabia to the community. Soon afterward, the imams announced that they did not recognize the Mufti's power as the head of the Religious Board and declared their independence. The Mufti could no longer preach in mosques where the imams served, though his *fatwas* were recognized. By the end of the

7. P. Mullojanov, "Islam i politika v Tadjikistane: Rukopis" [Islam and politics in Tadzhikistan: A manuscript], n.d., p. 29.

year, the relations between a part of the Muslim clergy of Uzbekistan and the Mufti and his adherents had become worse. In January 1992, the information agencies in Moscow announced the "removal of the Mufti by the Islamic leaders of the republic," but the Mufti himself denied the news.

The creation of independent states in the place of former republics, following the disintegration of the Soviet Union, and the beginning of radical economic reforms aggravated the internal situation in Muslim regions, as everywhere else. On 16 January 1992, the day of the announced liberalization of prices in Uzbekistan, there was a clash on the campus of the University of Tashkent between students who rebelled against the government and the internal forces. Finding themselves among the least provided-for of the population strata with the liberalization of prices, the Tashkent student community exploded. The students destroyed and put fire to several objects. As a result, one student died and dozens of people were wounded, including students and members of the internal forces. The youths' newspaper, *Turkestan*, produced two versions of the event. According to one, reported also by the official sources of information, "because of the price rise, students went out into the streets to take part in a meeting." The other version initially stated, "It can be the continuation of the previous, specially organized, bloody events."[8] After a few days, the President of Uzbekistan, I. Kerimov, actually repeated the second version, pointing out that students were

drawn into the political struggle. Both the democratic forces of Uzbekistan and Islamic forces were accused of participating in the riots. The students attending meetings handed their demands to the governmental commission headed by the Prime Minister, A. Mutalov, and vacations were announced early in many higher schools, but the students would not calm down.

The Presidium of the Uzbekistan Supreme Soviet mentioned in their statement that those who were behind the disturbances "are not content with our policy of national harmony. They would like very much to sow discord among people, to spread dissension, to occupy places in the power structures for the performance of their dirty deeds on an even greater scale."[9]

SECULAR NATIONALISM

Alongside the growth of an Islamic movement in the Muslim areas there is a developing secular nationalist movement. On the very eve of the Alma-Ata meeting of the leaders of 11 states of the former USSR, at which the declaration on the creation of the Commonwealth of Independent States was adopted, a special Turkic Assembly was brought to a close. It had been held on 18-20 December 1991, and delegations from the Turkic areas of the Russian Federation and a number of republics took part in it. The main issue discussed at the Assembly was the possibility of the establishment of Turkestan, a state uniting republics with Turkic populations.

8. *Turkestan* (Tashkent), 17 Jan. 1992.

9. *Komsomolskaya pravda*, 21 Jan. 1992.

The necessity of setting up a united Turkic state was the subject of speeches by the representatives of Kazakhstan, Azerbaijan, and Tatarstan. No delegation represented the will of its entire people, nor had any a mandate for adopting decisions on the main issue. Delegates were also unable to decide on the question of the borders of the Turkic state, but they formed branches of the Assembly in the Turkic regions of the former USSR—the Black Sea; Transcaucasus-Caucasus, with Baku as its center; Kazakh; and Central Asia. In addition, the formation of Turkic regions in the territory of the Russian Federation—the Urals, Yakut, and South Siberia—was announced.

It is significant that it was planned to unite regions based exclusively on ethnicity, irrespective of religion, in the proposed Turkic Commonwealth. The Yakuts and Turks of South Siberia, for example, do not practice Islam and are either Buddhist or Christian. In addition, rather than being drawn to their Turkic brothers in Central Asia and Transcaucasia, some gravitate toward Russia, others toward Mongolia. Despite those circumstances and the fact that there are many grave differences between the Turkic peoples, delegates were able to set up a Coordination Council of the Turkic Assembly. It was composed of representatives from all the regions and was to be in charge of relations between them so as to perform some of the functions of a common Turkic body.

The delegates agreed that all Turkic peoples should have one and the same alphabet. Since by then the Turkic peoples of the former Union had already used the same alphabet system for a long time, one based on the Cyrillic alphabet, it was clear that they were not content with it. The secular pan-Turkic orientation of the Assembly was particularly forceful in the decision adopted on that issue and proposed a transfer to the Latin alphabet, but one with 34 letters, following the model of Turkey. This means that political forces participating in the Assembly see Turkic unity not only as a union of all Turks of the former USSR but as a union with Turks living abroad. Moreover, it is evident that this union would be oriented toward Turkey as its leader. But there are no grounds to say that pan-Turkic organizations of Turkey itself took any part in these efforts. These organizations have not up to now enjoyed any support from Turkey's population. Delegates also agreed to set up a united Institute of Common Turkic Problems.

Secular or pro-Turkist concepts of the reform of the alphabet differ from the idea of going back to the Arabic written language. In the case of Muslim peoples, a return to written Arabic would mean a return to their former culture, but using written Arabic would be completely unacceptable to non-Muslim peoples. Though pan-Turkic aspirations do not reflect the views of the majority, they arouse the apprehensions of the non-Turkic peoples of Transcaucasia and also of Tadzhikistan.

Though official authorities in Kazakhstan and the Central Asian and Transcaucasian republics had no direct connection with the Assembly, some observers nevertheless noted their possible interest in the Assembly, held so soon after Russia, Ukraine, and Byelorussia announced in Minsk the creation of the Commonwealth of Independent States. In a way, it reflected the anxiety felt then by the leaders of the states of the southern belt of the former USSR. It was at that time that they decided to join the Commonwealth but expressed apprehensions about not being full-fledged founders of the Commonwealth but simply joining the states of Central Asia and Kazakhstan. The Alma-Ata meeting dispelled their doubts and reassured the political circles of these states, which were especially satisfied with the choice of Alma-Ata as the place to hold such an important meeting.

But other apprehensions were nevertheless expressed at the Turkic Assembly. A number of delegates said that the proposed alliance should defend the Turkic and Muslim world against possible expansion on the part of Russia. As the chairman of the Kazakh National Democratic Party, Hasan Hajiahmetov, stated, "The situation in Russia is very tense and unstable. It is not yet known what turn events in Moscow may take. At any moment the chauvinist Zhirinovsky or others like him may come to power. So here we must be prepared to resist possible intervention."

Shortly before the Assembly, another happening took place in Alma-Ata, affecting the tempestuous political history of the country in late 1991. On 13 December, the day of the Friday prayer, the opposition convened the Majlis of the Islamic community of the city in Alma-Ata. Leaders of the Alash Party of National Independence of Kazakhstan acted

as the conveners. Declaring freedom of enterprise, individual rights, freedom of religious belief, and equality of nations since 1990, the party had been publishing its own newspaper under the slogan of "Turkism is our body, Islam is our spirit." The Majlis adopted the decision to depose the Mufti or head of the Muslim Religious Board of Kazakhstan, Ratbek Nysanbai-uly, for numerous violations of the shari'a. Members of the opposition called the Mufti a KGB agent, and the Majlis formed a working presidium to hold new democratic elections for the position of Mufti.

After that, seven men burst into the office of Nysanbai-uly and demanded that he resign because the people no longer trusted him. The Mufti, who was also a deputy in the Kazakh Parliament, refused to obey and was tied and severely beaten. Later it was discovered that his right arm and collarbone had been broken. While beating the Mufti, his assailants kept saying, "We have here in Kazakhstan two traitors: the President and Nysanbai-uly, a KGB agent." They also beat the bookkeeper of the mosque and took away his keys. The workrooms were searched.

Militia soon set the Mufti free, but the assailants captured the mosque and refused to leave it. The blockade of the mosque lasted from 13 to 15 December. Only on 15 December did a militia detachment for special purposes clear the mosque, detaining 41 persons, including several activists of the Alash Party. The chairman of the Alash Party, Aren Atabek, denied beating the Mufti, saying that the intervention by the militia detachment was similar to the suppression by the authorities of the Alma-Ata youth disturbances in 1986, which later was called unlawful by the new authorities of Kazakhstan. For his part, Mufti Nyusanbai-uly condemned the hooligans, saying that in his opinion they were incited by the mullas "who had been ousted from mosques for violations of the shari'a canons and embezzlement of money." Thus the Mufti clearly wanted to make the conflict look like a clash between the legitimate leadership of the community and the transgressors of law.

But representatives of the authorities gave the conflict a political interpretation. Kazakhstan's Attorney General Tukakbayev was confident that the reason for the attack against the Mufti was "the influence of Islamic fundamentalists." In his opinion, "many do not like the Mufti's attitude of being against the establishment of Islamic parties." Though there were no grounds for Tuyakbayev to speak about the ban of the Alash Party, he hinted about such a possibility: it would be possible to speak about the ban, if actions of that kind were its programmatic tasks, said the Attorney General.[10]

Islamic factors also played a prominent part during the crisis in the Chechen republic, a part of the Russian Federation, which occurred in the autumn of 1991. President Dudayev made active use of Islamic slogans. Pathological anatomical postmortems were prohibited in the republic, and men were forbidden to work as gynecologists.

10. Commersant (Moscow), 16-23 Dec. 1991, no. 49, p. 18.

CONCLUSION

Assessing the situation as a whole, one should point out the following. First, Islam as the symbol of national identity, of the return to the original culture, became extremely popular among the peoples of the former USSR. Second, Islam is used as a means of political mobilization by various political forces, democratic, conservative, and nationalist. Third, the Islamicist movement as such still prefers to appeal to democratic or nationalist ideas. This last factor is due to an awareness of the sentiments of the masses of the population, who, in most Muslim areas today, are not ready to support the idea of an Islamic state in its direct form. But the Islamicist movement gains in impetus. Should present economic difficulties become more aggravated or the economic program of the authorities in the Muslim republics fail, the movement may have a good chance of success, particularly where the democratic alternative is weak.

It is not clear to what extent Islamic and nationalist trends will be combined in political life. In some situations they may unite, and this will make it possible for movements acting in concert with existing moods to become powerful; in other circumstances, they will be prone to act against each other. Nor is it clear what the result of the struggle within the Muslim clergy will be. If the struggle leads to a drastic renewal of the body of mullas and to the unification of the official and nonofficial leaders of the community, that also will enhance the political chances of the Islamicists. But it is hardly prob-

able that, in the extremely complicated economic conditions existing in
all the republics of the former USSR,
Islamicist forces would be able to suggest an alternative capable of solving
the crisis. Nevertheless, in the near
future Islam and political groups
guided by Islamic principles are, in
all events, sure to remain one of the
most influential forces in the region.

ANNALS, *AAPSS*, **524**, November 1992

An African Case Study of Political Islam: Nigeria

By JOHN HUNWICK

ABSTRACT: Since the early nineteenth century, when Uthman b. Fudi established an Islamic state in northern Nigeria, there has been a close symbiosis between religion and political power. Since independence in 1960, the issue of regional or ethnic power sharing in Nigeria has shifted to a contest between Muslims and Christians, with the part-Muslim, part-Christian Yoruba of the southwest helping to hold the balance. Since the 1960s, Saudi Arabia has promoted its own austere interpretation of Islam, to the discomfort of the Sufi groups. More recently, Iran has been a model for younger militant Muslims. Calls by Nigerian Muslims for an Islamic state, and wider application of *shari'a* law, as well as the question of Nigeria's membership in the Organization of Islamic Conference have aroused the antagonism of Christians. Religious issues were behind several outbreaks of violence in the 1980s, some of which threatened the integrity of the Nigerian state.

John Hunwick has his B.A. and Ph.D. from the School of Oriental and African Studies, London. In 1981, after twenty years of teaching in Africa—in the Sudan, Nigeria, Ghana, and Egypt—he was appointed professor of African history and professor of religion (Islam) at Northwestern University. He is author of Shari'a in Songhay *(1985) and editor of* Religion and National Integration in Africa: Islam, Christianity and Politics in the Sudan and Nigeria *(1992).*

I N late 1991, a senior analyst of the
   Bush administration reviewing
the current political situation in Africa was reported as saying that the
most worrisome trend for policymak-
ers was what he called " 'the march
of Islamic fundamentalism.' "[1] This
was shortly before elections in Algeria in which the Islamic Salvation
Front, campaigning under the slogan
"No laws. No constitution. Only the
laws of God and the Quran" gained
victory in the first round of national
legislative elections. The analyst's remarks also came at the end of a decade in which various external forces
have attempted to use sub-Saharan
Africa as a theater for the implementation of political agendas inspired by
or exploiting the emotive appeal of
Islam. Using an eccentric blend of
socialism, Islam, and Arabism, Libya's Muammar Qadhdhafi has wooed
several African governments—notably Gabon, whose president, Omar
Bongo, converted to Islam; the Central African Republic, whose former
president Bokassa briefly adopted
Islam; and Ghana—while at the
same time supporting forces working
for the overthrow of others, such as
Senegal, Niger, and Chad. Saudi Arabia has poured untold sums of money
into sub-Saharan Africa for the prop-
agation of its own austere brand of
Islam. Iraq before the gulf war used
the appeal of both Islamic ideals and
Arab nationalism in Mauritania and
the Sudan to further its political am-
bitions. More recently, Iran, while rebuilding its bridges to the West, has

begun to seek friends and influence
in Africa and perhaps to use the
Sudan for the training of Islamic
militants.

The Sudan in the 1980s under
various governments, but frequently
ideologically guided by Dr. Hasan al-
Turabi, leader of the National Islamic
Front, has flirted with each of these
external forces in turn. Despite an
intractable civil war and virtual economic collapse, it presents itself as a
role model for the establishment of
Islamic states in Africa and is not
without its admirers. Nigeria, launching its third attempt at democratic
politics in 1992, is emerging from a
decade of verbal and physical confrontation between Muslims and Christians, shrill debates over the place of
shari'a (Islamic law) within the national legal framework, and several
outbreaks of murderous violence
sparked off by members of a Muslim
underclass for whom the state had no
meaning. As the most populous state
in Africa and the one with the largest
Muslim population, Nigeria has
great diplomatic and cultural influence in Africa and is potentially the
continent's economic giant. Both for
these reasons and because of the way
in which Nigeria illustrates so many
of the problems associated with
Muslim reassertion within a religiously diverse society, this article
will focus on the relationship of Islam
to politics, in the broad sense, within
Nigeria since independence.

HISTORICAL BACKGROUND

Islam is no stranger to the political
process in West Africa. Nearly a thou-

1. See Barbara Crossette, "U.S. Aide Calls
Muslim Militants' Concern to World," *New York
Times*, 1 Jan. 1992.

sand years ago, Islam was a factor in political change in the kingdom of Takrur on the banks of the river Senegal and a little later in Ancient Ghana and in the kingdom of Kanem near Lake Chad. Under the influence of North African Muslim merchants and itinerant teachers and preachers, many rulers and their courts adopted Islam between the eleventh and the sixteenth centuries, though they generally preserved much of their more ancient non-Islamic social and political praxis. However, rulers such as Mansa Musa of Mali (1312-37), Askiya al-Hajj Muhammad of Songhay (1493-1528), and Mai Idris Aloma of Borno (1564-96) made ceremonial pilgrimages to Mecca and engaged in diplomatic exchanges with various rulers of Morocco and, in the last case, also with the Ottoman sultan.

Trans-Saharan trade and the pilgrimage to Mecca provided continuing avenues of contact between the more or less Islamized kingdoms of West Africa and the heartlands of Islam in North Africa and the Middle East. Political as well as theological and mystical ideas passed along these conduits, and the eighteenth and nineteenth centuries saw a number of attempts—some more successful than others—to establish Islamic states in the area. One of the most successful of these was in the area of what is now northern Nigeria in the early nineteenth century. In 1804, a Fulani scholar and mystic, Shaykh Uthman b. Fudi, led a "withdrawal" (*hijra*) of his followers from the Hausa state of Gobir in northwestern Nigeria, established his own commu-

nity as the touchstone of true Islam, and declared a *jihad* first against Gobir and later against all the other Hausa states whose rulers he proclaimed "unbelievers" (*kuffar*). His efforts led to the unification of the Hausa states of northern Nigeria and the incorporation, more or less loosely, within the new Islamic state of other, non-Hausa lands and various polities to the north and west of Hausaland in what is now the republic of Niger.

Some areas of northern Nigeria, however, remained beyond the pale of this new Islamic state. Principal among these was the ancient Muslim kingdom of Borno in the northeast, which successfully defeated attempts by local Fulani to take control in the name of Shaykh Uthman. Other areas such as the uplands of the central plateau and much of what is loosely called the "Middle Belt," the bulk of whose inhabitants were not Muslims, also remained outside the grasp of the new Islamic state, whose capital was established at Sokoto. Little attempt was made to incorporate them during the nineteenth century; instead, they were exploited as reservoirs for slaves for internal use within the Sokoto state and for export to North Africa.

This new state, however, was not a unitary state. The former polities that were incorporated within it, such as Kano, Katsina, Zaria, Nupe, and Ilorin, retained their individual identities, though now they were governed by mainly Fulani dynasties descended from local warriors or scholars who were given flags and authority to rule by Shaykh Uthman.

These emirs, as they were now called, governed their territories with a large measure of autonomy, despite occasional Sokoto interference in succession, and demonstrated their loyalty to the caliphs of Sokoto by sending twice-yearly tribute.

This federal structure proved to be an ideal vehicle for the colonial policy of indirect rule introduced by Lord Lugard after the British conquest of northern Nigeria in 1902-3. Though controlled by British residents and though their power to enforce law was severely curtailed, the emirs still retained the respect, even the devotion, of their subjects down to Nigerian independence in 1960. Since then, their power and prestige have suffered considerable attrition at the hands of various federal governments, civil and military—a process aided by the creation and multiplication of states within the federation since 1967.

POSTINDEPENDENCE NIGERIA

When Nigeria became independent on 1 October 1960, it had an estimated population of some 50 million, of whom close to half were Muslims. It was a federal state with three regions—North, West, and East—and a political system at both the regional and federal levels modeled on the British parliamentary system. Of the three regions, the North was by far the largest in area, occupying some two-thirds of the land mass. Although its total population was only slightly greater than the combined total of the other two regions, it contained about two-thirds of the total Muslim population. Its Muslim population was distributed unevenly, however, seven provinces having Muslim majorities and five having a minority of Muslims.[2]

It would, of course, be convenient if one could give comparative figures for the present time. Unfortunately, none is available. Although a national census was taken in late 1991, it was decided that no data should be gathered on religious affiliation. The last figures we have that give such a breakdown are those of 1963, which show a total population of 55 million, of whom 49 percent were said to be Muslims, 34 percent Christians, and 17 percent animists.[3] While the percentage of animists has almost certainly decreased dramatically in the intervening period, due to conversion campaigns by both Muslims and Christians, it is not possible to say which faith has gained more converts, nor are figures available that might correlate birthrate with religion.[4]

This review of population statistics is a necessary prelude to what follows inasmuch as the fundamental political problem that has plagued Nigeria since independence has been how to share national wealth and

2. See John N. Paden, *Religion and Political Culture in Kano* (Berkeley: University of California Press, 1973), tab. 3, p. 44. Apart from a small number of converts to the Ahmadiyya sect, all Nigerian Muslims are Sunnites of the Maliki school.

3. Paden, *Religion and Political Culture.* The figures announced for the 1991 census show a total population of 88.5 million.

4. See further Jibrin Ibrahim, "The Politics of Religion in Nigeria: The Parameters of the 1987 Crisis in Kaduna State," *Review of African Political Economy*, 45-46:78 (1989), where attention is also drawn to the dramatic gains of Christianity vis-à-vis animism in the period 1931-63.

access to education, employment opportunities, and political office in a country of multiple ethnic identities and many and diverse regional and local loyalties overlaid by religious loyalties to Islam or Christianity. This has led to what have been termed "prebendal politics" in which individual and group access to education, employment opportunities, and the national wealth was closely linked to the political ascendancy of the political party or ethnic group of those who so benefited.[5] During periods of civilian rule—October 1960 to January 1966, and October 1979 to December 1983—dominance at the federal level, which was in the hands of essentially northern-based Muslim-led parties, was considered to be the key to economic development, jobs, and educational opportunity among the constituencies that voted the politicians into power. For example, at independence the Northern Region, by comparison with the Eastern and Western regions, was economically underdeveloped, virtually devoid of university-trained personnel, and grossly underrepresented in federal ministries and institutions. The regional prime minister, Alhaji Sir Ahmadu Bello, Sardauna of Sokoto, had already begun to take steps within his own region to "northernize" the regional civil service; in the early 1960s the federal government, dominated by the Northern People's Congress (NPC) and led by Sir Abubakar Tafawa Balewa, began to correct the regional imbalance in the federal civil service, often filling po-

sitions with northerners who were less qualified than their southern counterparts.[6] In the nature of things, a high proportion of these new appointees were Muslims.

During the First Republic (1960-66), the struggle for power at the center was essentially between the three regions (a fourth, the Midwest, was created out of the former Western Region in 1963), the politics of each of which was dominated by a single large ethnic group and a regional-based party: in the North by the Hausa and the NPC, in the East by the Igbo and the National Council of Nigerian Citizens and in the West by the Yoruba and the Action Group, though the National Council of Nigerian Citizens initially also had some strength there, too. Although the Eastern and Western—and Midwestern—regions in some sense viewed themselves as constituting the south as opposed to the north—the uproar over the 1963 census was about population balance between north and south—the controversy over power was never pitched in explicitly religious terms. On the one hand, the West was religiously divided with almost as many Muslims as Christians; on the other, the dominant party in the North, the NPC, had as its slogan "One North, One People," despite a 30 percent non-Muslim minority. There is little doubt, however, that the premier, Sir

5. See Richard Joseph, *Democracy and Prebendal Politics in Nigeria* (New York: Cambridge University Press, 1987).

6. Taylor Cole, "Bureaucracy in Transition," in *The Nigerian Political Scene*, ed. Robert O. Tilman and Taylor Cole (Durham, NC: Duke University Press, 1962), p. 109. A regional quota system for recruitment of army officers was also established in which 50 percent of the places were reserved for candidates of northern origin.

Ahmadu Bello, at least latterly, looked forward to an eventual coincidence of northernness with Islam. Hence in 1963-64 he undertook conversion campaigns among the animists of the Middle Belt area and among the Maguzawa, who are non-Muslim Hausa, and hoped to extend these campaigns to other areas of Nigeria.[7]

The power struggle in the civilian realm was superseded in 1966 by a similar one in the military realm. First, a coup brought an Igbo-led military regime to power, and seven months later a second coup thrust a northern—but Christian—officer, Lieutenant Colonel (later General) Yakubu Gowon, into the headship of the Nigerian state. In May 1967, in an attempt to forestall the secession of the Eastern Region, Gowon replaced the four regions composing the federation with 12 states, thus defusing power and allowing ethnic groups other than the "big three" a greater share in their own governance. Since then subsequent decrees by military governments have increased the number of states to a current total of 30 plus a federal territory around the new capital, Abuja. The old North thus disappeared, though its shadow lingered for a decade longer, and with it disappeared what many southerners had perceived as a threat of northern—Muslim—domination.

Civil war, however, was not averted, and between July 1967 and January 1970 a federal army of very mixed ethnic and religious complex-

7. See John N. Paden, *Ahmadu Bello, Sardauna of Sokoto* (London: Hodder & Stoughton, 1986), pp. 566-78; Ibrahim, "Politics of Religion."

ion fought its way into the secessionist Republic of Biafra; this republic was originally the entire old Eastern Region, but finally only the Igbo heartlands. Biafran war propaganda liked to paint the federal attack on it as an Islamic *jihad* against embattled Christians, but the absurdity of this claim was patent. In fact, the war was about retaining a Nigerian federation—very much in the interest of the landlocked Muslim majority states and ethnic minorities in all areas—and federal control over the prime economic asset, oil, of which the former Eastern Region had an abundance.

These events—military rule, civil war, and the abolition of hugely powerful regions in favor of more and weaker states—had a number of consequences. The crushing of secession made it clear that hiving off was not an option no matter how great the grievance. The creation of states, while it diffused some political energies, in the end only underlined the importance of the federal center. The armed forces—and we should remember that the much smaller navy and air force have also shared in government along with the army—who phased themselves out of power in 1979 demonstrated that they were no worse at governing than civilians and were ready to step in again, as they did in 1984. The diffusion of political energy and the absence of normal political life under military rule, however, were contributory factors in the politicization of religion, or, rather, the use of religion as a tool for creating a political constituency. The emergence of a small very wealthy class and the general impoverishment of the urban masses, resultant upon the oil boom of the mid-1970s followed by a sudden slump in the 1980s, created discontent and frustration, and Nigerians—both Muslims and Christians—turned to religion both as a refuge and as a political weapon.

THE *SHARI'A* LAW ISSUE

The first indications that religion might begin to play a major role in national political life came during the 1977 debates in the newly created Constituent Assembly on the draft constitution for the Second Republic. The issue was the creation of a Federal Shari'a Court of Appeal which could hear appeals from state Shari'a Courts of Appeal rather than sending them directly to the Supreme Court of Nigeria. Before the creation of states in 1967, *shari'a* cases, which were confined essentially to matters of personal status, could be sent on appeal to a Northern Region Shari'a Court of Appeal. In other areas of the country, there were neither *shari'a* courts nor Shari'a Courts of Appeal.

The proposal to create a Federal Shari'a Court of Appeal unleashed a storm of protest from Christian members of the assembly who claimed that this privileged Islamic law, created a dual system of law in the country, and opened the door for the creeping Islamization of the Nigerian state. Muslim members countered that the application of *shari'a* lay at the core of their lives as Muslims and to deny them the exercise of the *shari'a* rights to the highest level was discrimination against them and an attack on Islam. In the end, a compro-

mise was fashioned with the support of Yoruba Muslim members—reflecting traditional Yoruba tolerance in religious matters—under which there would be within the Federal Court of Appeal a panel of three judges "versed in Islamic law" who would decide cases sent up by a state Shari'a Court of Appeal.[8]

Despite the dissatisfaction at such a compromise expressed by many Muslim members from northern states, the then head of state, General Olusegun Obasanjo, accepted the amendment and had it written into the constitution. The issue did not, however, die there. It surfaced again with equal or greater passion in similar debates over a constitution for the Third Republic in 1989. This time the then—and current—head of state, General Ibrahim Babangida, simply foreclosed debate on the issue, and the constitution for the Third Republic, published on 3 May 1989, shows no change on this matter from its predecessor. There is little doubt that this issue will continue to surface. Indeed, it would be no surprise if some states with Muslim majorities eventually seek to arrogate to themselves the right to impose *shari'a* as the only form of law within their territories. The imposition of *shari'a* has been at the cutting edge of all recent debates about the Islamic state, whether in Pakistan, Iran, the Sudan, or, now, in Algeria, where the Islamic Salvation Front has made implementation of *shari'a* the cornerstone of its program.

8. On this issue, see David D. Laitin, "The Sharia Debate and the Origins of Nigeria's Second Republic," *Journal of Modern African Studies*, 20(3):411-30 (1982).

While the *shari'a* debate of 1977 first brought Muslim-Christian antagonism into sharp focus, it was the issue of Nigeria's membership in the Organization of Islamic Conference (OIC) in 1986 that caused Nigerian Christians to suggest there was a conspiracy to turn Nigeria into an Islamic state—an issue on which many have since become virtually paranoid. Nigeria had long been an observer at OIC meetings, but suddenly it was rumored that Nigeria had become a full member. Christians argued that the OIC was more than a club of friendly states that mutually aided one another in the economic sphere; rather, it was an organization for the promotion of Islam that required member countries to be headed by Muslims and encouraged movement toward the implementation of Islamic legal and social norms. The brouhaha created was very considerable. The government set up a committee to inquire into the matter, but the affair only quieted down when the government announced that the question of Nigeria's membership in the OIC had been shelved. Christians remained suspicious that the full truth had not been disclosed, and they continue nervously to monitor the actions of Muslim organizations for any hint, real or imagined, that Nigeria may be moving toward an Islamic state.

REGISTERS OF ISLAMIC DISCOURSE

The 1980s witnessed an increasing polarization between Muslims and Christians as symbolic power blocks within Nigeria. In both Muslim and Christian milieus, there were attempts to galvanize and radicalize the faithful and persuade them to give primacy to an identification based on religion. At the same time, there has been considerable infighting among various Muslim groups and an extraordinary multiplication of sects, churches, and charismatic movements among Nigerian Christians.[9] There has also been a sustained attack in some Muslim quarters on the idea of the secular state, which one writer described as " 'a child, albeit a bastard, of Christianity . . . [which] has become a sinister but convenient mechanism to blackmail Muslims and impede the progress of Islam.' "[10]

The principal cleavage between the Muslims of the northern states has been between the proponents of an Islamic discourse dominated by strict adherence to the Quran and the *sunna* largely reflecting the reformist teachings of Uthman b. Fudi and the political legacy of the Sokoto Caliphate, on the one hand, and, on the other, those who belong to Sufi *tariqas*—often, misleadingly, called brotherhoods—in particular the Tijaniyya, which has had its strongholds in Kano and Zaria, with important links to the West African Tijani

---

9. See Rosalind Hackett, ed., *New Religious Movements in Nigeria* (Lewiston, NY: Edwin Mellen Press, 1987). See also Don Ohadike, "Muslim-Christian Conflict and Political Instability in Nigeria," in *Religion and National Integration in Africa: Islam, Christianity and Politics in the Sudan and Nigeria*, ed. John O. Hunwick (Evanston, IL: Northwestern University Press, 1992), pp. 101-24.

10. Ibrahim, "Politics of Religion in Nigeria," p. 77, quoting remarks of Ibrahim Suleiman published in the Nigerian *Sunday Triumph*, 24 Apr. 1986.

headquarters in Kaolack, Senegal.[11] The leader of the first tendency is Alhaji Abubakar Gummi, a close associate of the late Sardauna Sir Ahmadu Bello and for many years Grand Kadi of Northern Nigeria. He accompanied the Sardauna on his twice-annual pilgrimages to Saudi Arabia between 1955 and 1965, formed close relations with members of the Saudi ruling family, and imbibed the austere and anti-Sufi interpretation of Islam preached there. These links have ensured him financial support for his cause and in 1988 earned him the King Faisal Prize—a fitting Islamic riposte, so it was seen, to the award of the Nobel Prize for Literature to the non-Muslim Wole Soyinka.

It was Abubakar Gummi who advised the Sardauna in 1962 to establish the Jama'atu Nasril Islam (Group for the Victory of Islam), conceived of as an umbrella organization to promote Muslim interests. After the Sardauna's assassination in 1966, Gummi, though still a functionary of the Jama'atu Nasril Islam, began to attack the *tariqas* more vociferously. His attacks in fact helped to bring together the Qadiriyya and the Tijaniyya, which had hitherto often been hostile to one another. In 1977, for example, the Kungiyar Jama'ati Ahlis-Sunna was formed as a sort of union of Sufi *tariqas*.[12] Gummi soon began to feel the need for an independent

platform of his own and in particular one upon which he could promote more effectively his Wahhabi views. The result was the emergence of a group that finally became formalized in 1978 as the Jama'at Izalat al-Bid'a wa-Iqamat al-Sunna (Group for the Eradication of Innovation and the Upholding of the Sunna), commonly known as the Izala. In the 1980s, it recruited a large membership, opened branches in many Nigerian towns, and established its own separatist mosques. Using both traditional methods such as open-air preaching, when such was not banned by government, and modern methods of communication such as radio, television—including Quranic exegesis during Ramadan—and recorded audiocassettes, it harangued the Sufis—often in immoderate language—and called on Muslims to follow only the Quran and *sunna*. Gummi himself became notorious for provocative statements including an assertion that no Muslim would join a political party led by a non-Muslim and hence the two-party system announced as the model for democratic politics by General Babangida would become a contest between Islam and Christianity.[13]

Another important Muslim group in Nigeria—more influential than its name would suggest—is the Muslim Students Society. Founded as far back as 1954 in Lagos, its originally Yoruba leadership passed into the hands of northern Nigerian students

11. See Ousmane Kane,"La confrérie 'Tijâniyya Ibrahîmiyya' de Kano et ses liens avec la zâwiya mère de Kaolack," *Islam et sociétés au sud du Sahara*, 3:27-40 (1989).

12. See Muhammad Sani Umar, "Changing Islamic Identity in Nigeria, 1960s-1980s: From Sufism to Anti-Sufism," in *Muslim Identities in Sub-Saharan Africa: Contemporary Transformations in Muslim Societies*, ed.

L. Brenner (London: Christopher Hurst, forthcoming).

13. See Peter Clarke, "Islamic Reform in Contemporary Nigeria: Methods and Aims," *Third World Quarterly*, 10(2):530 (Apr. 1988).

in the 1970s as it entrenched itself and expanded its membership at universities such as Ahmadu Bello University, in Zaria, and Bayero University, in Kano. Its now radical leadership began to call for "total application of the Sharia and its full entrenchment in the constitution."[14]

The overthrow of the Shah and the installation of an Islamic republic in Iran in 1979 had repercussions in Nigeria and in particular among the members of the Muslim Students Society, now led by Aminudeen Abubakar, a student of Gummi. A split occurred, with one wing, the Da'wa, under Abubakar, supported by Saudi and Kuwaiti funds and stressing the fight against "innovations" (bid'a) and with the other, the Umma, taking a stronger line on the implementation of shari'a and the establishment of an Islamic state. The Umma wing itself split again into two groups: one, called Hodaybiya, recalling the Prophet Muhammad's truce with the Meccans, favored an accommodation, at least temporarily, with the secular state, and the other, often referred to as the Yan Shi'a, taking its inspiration directly from events in Iran and from the mujahidin struggle in Afghanistan and preaching a more radical message that brooked no compromise with the ungodly state.[15] Iran has, indeed, been active

in seeking sympathizers to its cause in Nigeria, largely, it would appear, to attempt to neutralize the well-entrenched influence of its archrival Saudi Arabia. Much Iranian Shiite literature in English and Arabic has been distributed, and an Iranian magazine in Hausa, Sakon Islam [The message of Islam] is being published. Given the anti-Sufi stance of the Saudis, it was natural for the Iranians to woo the tariqa leaders as well, and in 1987 a prominent Tijani leader, Dahiru Bauchi, was invited to Iran for the eighth anniversary of the revolution.[16]

RELIGION AND VIOLENCE

None of the foregoing movements is, in and of itself, a real threat to political stability in Nigeria, though each is a breeding ground for the ideologization of various forms of political and social discontent and each represents an attempt to dominate the discourse about what is normative Islam and hence what kind of society Muslims should create for themselves—and perhaps others—in Nigeria. The greatest threat to the state lies in the growing general antagonism between Muslims and Christians, most vividly seen in the frontier areas of northern Nigeria—Kaduna, Plateau, and Bauchi states—where militant Christians—many, especially among university students, "born again"—conduct their own crusades. A Christian preacher,

14. See the press release of the Muslim Students Society of Nigeria, Ahmadu Bello University, Zaria, n.d., in Peter Clarke and Ian Linden, Islam in Modern Nigeria (Mainz-Munchen: Kaiser-Grunewald, 1984), pp. 167-68.
15. On these developments, see the excellent summary in Ousmane Kane, "Mouvements religieux et champ politique au Nigeria septentrional: Le cas de réformisme musulman au Kano," Islam et sociétés au sud du

Sahara, 4:7-24 (1990). The term "Shia" seems to be used loosely in Nigeria, without doctrinal connotations, to stigmatize radical, militant Muslim groups.
16. See Umar, "Changing Islamic Identity."

a convert from Islam,[17] was the focus of rioting in Kaduna State in March 1987 that claimed many lives and caused destruction of millions of dollars' worth of property—in particular, churches and hotels—over a three-day period.[18] While a religious issue was the ostensible cause of this outbreak, the head of state, General Babangida, characterized the riots as "carefully planned and masterminded by evil men who saw the incident in Kafanchan as an opportunity to subvert the Federal Military Government and the Nigerian nation." It was, he said, "the civilian equivalent of an attempted coup d'état organized against the Military Government and the Nigerian nation."[19] He did not elaborate on these sibylline utterances and no "masterminds" were ever indicted.

In 1991, there were other riots that pitted Muslims against Christians with ensuing loss of life. One began near Bauchi over the use of a slaughtering place by adherents of the two religions and spread quickly to Bauchi Town. The other erupted in Kano when foreign evangelists arrived to lead a revival campaign among Christians in the Sabon Gari ("New Town," that is, the strangers' quarter outside the old city), leading to a number of deaths and the burning and looting of property—mainly

that of Igbos—bringing back memories of the 1966 pogroms.[20]

Undoubtedly, the most serious manifestation of Christian resentment of perceived domination by Muslims in Nigeria came with the attempted intra-army coup in April 1990. Fighting, including the use of tanks, raged for some 12 hours in the capital, Lagos, after an army major from the Middle Belt, supported by others from what is now Edo State, set in motion a move to topple the Babangida government and kill its leader—his aide-de-camp was in fact killed in the fighting. In his single broadcast, Major Gideon Orka attacked "those who think it is their birthright to dominate till eternity the political and economic privileges of this great country to the exclusion of the Middle Belt and the South" and threatened to excise the five majority Muslim states of the north from the federation until, as he put it, a delegation would come "to vouch that the feudalistic and aristocratic quest for domination and oppression will never again be practiced in any part of the Nigerian state."[21] General Babangida's loyal troops won the day; had they lost, the country would inevitably have been plunged into a second civil war. It was a close call.

Space precludes full discussion of the most violent religious episodes of the 1980s—the so-called Maitatsine disturbances—which, though they were intra-Islamic rather than interfaith, nevertheless had the potential

17. It may be noted that, had *shari'a* been applicable, the man would have suffered the death penalty for his apostasy from Islam.
18. According to an official inquiry, 19 people and eight animals were killed, and 169 hotels or beer parlors, 152 churches, five mosques, and 95 vehicles were destroyed or damaged. See Ibrahim, "Politics of Religion," p. 67.
19. Ibid., p. 68.

20. A Muslim preacher from South Africa had earlier been denied a permit to hold meetings in Kano.
21. As reported in *Punch* (Lagos), 24 Apr. 1990, p. 8.

for creating considerable political destabilization. The original disturbances took place in Kano in 1980, and subsequent outbreaks occurred over the next five years in Maiduguri, Kaduna, Yola, and Gombe. In these upheavals, groups of poor and mainly illiterate men who had set up a type of commune existence got into—possibly provoked—clashes with the police, effectively using bows and arrows and knives and in return were slaughtered in large numbers by the police. In two instances, the police were backed by army units.

The original leader, Muhammad Marwa, whose nickname Mai Tatsine ("the one who says, 'cursed be!' ") gave the name to these disturbances (although it is unclear to what extent they were all organically linked), was a preacher from Marwa, in Cameroon, but long a resident in Kano. He preached deviant interpretations of Muslim belief and ritual; according to some, they included human sacrifice and magical use of body organs. He was fiercely antagonistic to all Muslims outside his community, extremely anti-elitist, and probably a chiliast. He was killed in the first disturbances in Kano, and his followers refused to talk about him or about his message.

Many varying interpretations of his movement and the copycat disturbances that followed the 1980 Kano riot have been given. What is clear is that those involved were economically and socially marginal men with a strong sense of grievance against the state and its agents and those who had grown rich from association with it or through entrepreneurial activity. In and of themselves, Mai

Tatsine and his followers and emulators were irrelevant to the greater politicoreligious discourse. The question has remained, however, as to whether they were, or could potentially be, manipulated by larger political forces, whether external, as some alleged at the time, or internal, as some have since suggested.[22] The existence of any such thing as a Maitatsine sect or movement seems very doubtful, but it is clear that rapid urbanization in northern Nigeria, the oil boom, and subsequent economic decline have created extraordinary social and economic problems and an atmosphere of uncertainty and anger in which violent movements of protest can flourish. In the Hausa political idiom, it is not surprising that such movements should express themselves within the framework of religious discourse.[23]

PROSPECTS FOR THE 1990s

The prospects for an end to violence between Muslims of different persuasions or between Muslims and Christians do not seem very encouraging. The overall economic situation of Nigeria in a world currently plagued by severe economic troubles is unlikely to improve dramatically in the near future. The planned return to civilian rule in January 1993, provided nothing happens to defer it,

22. Kane, "Mouvements religieux," p. 21.
23. The Maitatsine phenomenon has provoked a literature of explanations. A convenient bibliography of this literature is to be found in Niels Kastfelt, "Rumours of Maitatsine: A Note on Political Culture in Northern Nigeria," *African Affairs*, 88:83-90 (1989), an article that analyzes the power of rumor in political myth-making in the Nigerian context.

ought to provide more multifaceted outlets for political energies, but in fact the religion question in one form or another has been an integral part of Nigerian political discourse since the beginning of party politics. Most constitutional and political thinking has refused to face this stark fact, mainly for fear of the animosity that might be stirred up. Much will depend on how the elections for federal and state assemblies go, since the ban on the participation of former political personalities has been lifted; the crucial test will be the election for an executive president who, in the nature of things, will belong, or be perceived to belong, to either the Muslim or the Christian constituency.

In any future moves to gain greater recognition for *shari'a* at the federal level or to dilute in any way the secular nature of the Nigerian state, the role of the Yoruba will be critical. Historically, there has been a lack of consonance between Yoruba Muslims and northern Muslims, not least because Yoruba religious thinking tends to favor a plurality of views,

even allowing different members of the same family to belong to different religions without divisiveness. It should not be assumed that this situation is incapable of change. Indeed, there are signs that change is occurring. Shifting political alliances, too, might bring Yorubas closer to Hausas, as they did during the latter days of the First Republic.

External influences will also play a role in determining the fortunes of differing political and social interpretations of Islam in Nigeria. There are many and diverse historical links between Nigeria and the Sudan, and one may expect that the experiences of the Sudan in Islamization will be closely studied by activist Muslim groups in Nigeria. Iran and Saudi Arabia will continue, covertly or overtly, to attempt to influence the course of Muslim debates in Nigeria, and, if the Islamic Salvation Front dominates Algerian politics, Algeria, too, can be expected to play a more active role in promoting its own interpretations of Islam in sub-Saharan Africa and not least in Nigeria.

ANNALS, *AAPSS*, 524, November 1992

Political Islam in Asia:
A Case Study

By ALAIN-GÉRARD MARSOT

ABSTRACT: The phenomenon of Islamic resurgence, the so-called fundamentalism, has had important political effects, but it is often viewed as a Middle Eastern issue, just as Islam is essentially perceived as a Middle Eastern religion. In point of fact, the major Muslim nations are found in Asia, where most of the world's Muslims live. Islamic resurgence is also found, in various degrees, in all the countries of Asia where there are Muslims. The intensity and character of this phenomenon, however, depends on several factors, such as geography, historical background, and the relative size of the Muslim communities. While it is both a religious and a political phenomenon, as Islam itself, this Islamic resurgence should also be considered a response to the global issue of modernization and development, in all its complex and unsettling dimensions.

Born in Vietnam of French origin, Alain-G. Marsot received a law degree, took the bar exam, and received a Ph.D. in political science from the University of Paris. He also received an advanced degree from the University of Oxford. Dr. Marsot has taught at different universities in England, France, Egypt, Thailand, and the United States and has lived and traveled in many countries of the Middle East and South and Southeast Asia, which have also been the subject of his publications.

WESTERN stereotypes associate Islam with the Middle East and North Africa, as geographic areas, and with the Arabs as people. Most of the Muslims, however, are found in Asia, where the largest Muslim nations are located: Indonesia, Pakistan, and Bangladesh. Furthermore, there are other nations in Asia where either Islam is the religion of the majority—or of the largest group, as in Malaysia—or there are sizable Muslim minorities, as in India, the Philippines, and Thailand. In point of fact, there are more Muslims in the Indian subcontinent than in all of the Middle East and North Africa. Were it not for Eurocentric notions, the Middle East, more appropriately, would be referred to as West Asia and North Africa. But this article is concerned with regions traditionally considered Asian, such as South and Southeast Asia, keeping in mind that there are also sizable Muslim communities in Central Asia and China.[1]

Just as in the Middle East and North Africa, most Asian countries with Muslim communities were colonized and then again became independent in the aftermath of World War II. Therefore, those communities have been faced with the issue of nationalism and the struggle for independence leading ultimately to decolonization. Following the end of colonization, new problems appeared in the shape of attempts at moderniza-

tion and development. More recently, a major phenomenon has spread through the Muslim world, giving religion—Islam—a major role in political, economic, and social matters. This phenomenon has been characterized, by outsiders, as a resurgence of Islam or, more commonly, as "fundamentalism." This so-called fundamentalism, or, more accurately, Islamic activism, has affected Asian Muslim countries as well as the countries of the Middle East and North Africa. It has become a major political issue, especially in the wake of the establishment of an Islamic regime in Iran, which has had an impact far beyond the borders of that country.

PRELIMINARY OBSERVATIONS

Before discussing the role of Islam in the politics of Asia, a preliminary observation has to be made, as well as some considerations regarding the character of Islam in that part of the world.

First of all, in Islam there is no separation between the realm of the religious and that of the political, or, as commonly stated in the West, between church and state. While all religions affect and are affected by the political, to a greater or lesser degree, Christianity early on claimed such a separation, expressed in the New Testament as "Render unto Caesar the things that are Caesar's, and unto God the things that are God's." The whole history of Christianity contradicts this statement, from the quarrel of the Two Swords in medieval times to the war of religions in the age of the Renaissance and Reformation, to the temporal powers of

---

1. Some of the information and observations in this article are the result of research and interviews conducted between 1988 and 1991 in Southeast Asia—Malaysia, Thailand, Indonesia—and India on the subject of Muslim attitudes toward modernization.

the Papacy and many other instances down to the present time. But in Islam, there has never been such a disclaimer. Islam was political from the very first day, concerned with the governing of the religious community and with any and all political questions, as well as with dogma and religious problems. Over time, and in different historical and geographic contexts, the connection may have loosened, but it is always in the background and ready to reassert itself.

The second question that arises, keeping in mind that Islam originated in the Middle East, is whether the form of Islam practiced in Asia is any different from that practiced in the Middlè East and North Africa. While one can expect that distance from the beginning and source of Islam as well as different geographic and cultural contexts in the areas affected by the spread of Islam might somewhat modify the character of the religion, the essential factors of differentiation between Middle Eastern/ North African Islam and Asian Islam are related to the historical circumstances in which Islam reached various Asian countries.

FACTORS AFFECTING
THE IMPACT OF ISLAM
ON ASIA: CONVERSION

Before discussing the role of Islam in the contemporary politics of Asia, one has to recognize that it is determined, or at least affected, by three sets of factors, which are sometimes intertwined.

The first factor is the way Islam came to Asia. From its birth in the Arabian peninsula in the seventh century, Islam spread its political control through military conquest over the Middle East, Persia, North Africa, and Spain with extreme rapidity. The Islamization of the conquered territories, however, took place progressively, given the tolerance displayed by the Arab conquerors toward the religious beliefs of the conquered peoples, essentially various brands of Christianity, considered worthy of protection (*dhimma*). This first phase in the spread of Islam is marked by a close relationship between the religion, the Arabic language of the conquerors and of the Quran, the fusion of the spiritual and temporal powers of the caliph, and consequently the intertwining of political and religious questions.

South Asia

In the second phase of the spread of Islam, the leadership of the Muslim community had passed from the hands of the Arabs into those of Turks from Central Asia, the Ottomans, following the destruction of the Abbassi Caliphate in Baghdad. It is during this phase that Islam really reached the South Asian subcontinent. The impact of Islam on South Asia was marked by somewhat contradictory factors. The first wave of Arab conquests in the Middle East and North Africa, along with subsequent Islamization, was accompanied, overall, by a fair amount of toleration due to the fundamental closeness of Islam to Christianity. Moreover, the conquered Christians in the Middle East found their Muslim masters more lenient in terms of both taxation and religious dogma than their previous Byzantine overlords, who practiced a different form of Christianity and persecuted them for that reason.

In South Asia, on the other hand, apart from a brief Arab incursion in the Sind province (now Pakistan), conquest was carried out by Turkic bands from Central Asia, who were recent converts to Islam and overzealous, as new converts usually are. Those Turkic elements justified their looting and massacring of the local populations by the fact that Hindus and Buddhists were idolaters, not entitled to the protection afforded the People of the Book—Christians, Jews, and Zoroastrians—and therefore were to be offered only the choice between death and conversion to Islam. Successive Central Asian and Mongol leaders conquered and lost various parts of the northern Indian subcontinent between A.D. 1000 and 1500, but with the passage of time the Muslim conquerors came to some sort of accommodation with the peoples of the Indian peninsula who had remained Hindus.

This modus vivendi was the result of several factors. While quite a few Indians converted to Islam, especially people from the lower castes escaping the oppressive Hindu socioreligious structure, the Muslim ruling class was still very small in number compared to the Hindu masses. Therefore, it had to call upon upper-caste Hindus to serve as officials at its court and in the administration of the country.[2] Because the Muslim

rulers were no longer Arabs and Arabic speaking, they were less knowledgeable of the sacred law and texts and consequently less intransigent regarding Islamic norms. This increasing tolerance reached a high point under the early Mogul emperors, marked by intermarriage with high-caste Hindu princesses, notably Rajput, and most of all by the Mogul Emperor Akbar's attempt to create a syncretic religion combining Islam with local contributions. This attempt, by the greatest of the Moguls, ultimately failed and there were resurgences of intransigence and persecution of non-Muslims, notably by Emperor Aurangzeb.

From the thirteenth century onward, armies of Muslims no longer expanded south and east; instead, the Muslim religion was peacefully introduced by traders and preachers who carried it all the way to the limits of Southeast Asia and to China. In this process, Islamization was helped in no small measure by the appearance of mystics, or Sufis. Sufis attempted to reach the transcendent through inner or intuitive knowledge, rather than book learning, presenting a popular understanding rather than an intellectual one. That approach found a fertile terrain among many mystically inclined people in India and in the Malay world.[3]

Southeast Asia

The progressive Islamization of most of the Malay world thus took place in a peaceful fashion. In many ways, this process was similar to the Indianization of the area in either its

2. Marshall G. S. Hodgson, *The Venture of Islam* (Chicago: University of Chicago Press, 1974), 2:557.

3. Ibid., p. 542.

Hindu or its Buddhist form several centuries earlier. Many of the local potentates were merchant-rulers. Muslim traders would marry into those princely families and spread Islam to the ruling elite, to those who soon found it expedient to adopt the new creed for trading purposes, as well as to others who believed its tenets. The Arab traders, present in the area and in south China since pre-Islamic times, had refrained from proselytizing after the birth of the new religion. Islamization was therefore carried out by Indian Muslim traders from Gujarat and, to a lesser extent, by Tamils from the Coromandel coast in southeast India. Those Gujaratis benefited from the prestige attached to India, in terms of advanced culture and technology, and, like their Hinduizing predecessors, superimposed their creed and culture over the existing beliefs and traditions they found, be they Hindu, Buddhist, or animist, without erasing them.[4]

Thus traditional laws and customs (*adat*) survived in the Indonesian archipelago. One finds there the attitude, so prevalent in most of Asia, of blending new beliefs and cultures with preexisting ones without exercising exclusion, intolerance, or fanaticism (there were always a few exceptions). The result has been a widespread propensity toward syncretism, either formally or simply in practice. It should be added that when Islam arrived in the Malay world, the local Hinduized empires and kingdoms had become exhausted, thereby weakening the Hindu-Bud-

dhist traditions.[5] In other Southeast Asian regions, Islam did not make any inroads, save in Champa (southern Vietnam). Finally, in the Malay world, Islam essentially reached the elites, the coasts, and the port cities. Inland populations were little touched by the new faith, or only progressively so at later periods.[6] Small Islamized communities also appeared in China as a consequence of trade, either on the southern coast or in the far west on the Silk Road.

EUROPEAN COLONIZATION

The arrival of European traders in the sixteenth century and later European colonization constitute the second factor that has had direct and profound effects on the place and role of Islam in Asia. It is ironic that initially the first Europeans, the Portuguese, unwittingly helped the spread of Islam in the Indonesian archipelago.[7] Their missionary zeal was so brutal and heavy-handed, marked by a mix of crusading, Iberian peninsula *reconquista* spirit, visceral anti-Muslim feelings, not to mention the spirit of lucre and plunder, that they often succeeded in unifying the local populations under the banner of Islam, perceived as a barrier against such abuses.

The Western presence, through traders and missionaries, even when it used military means, did not at first lead to outright colonization except in the Philippines. There, the

4. Ibid., p. 548.

5. D.G.E. Hall, *A History of Southeast Asia*, 4th ed. (New York: St. Martin's Press, 1981), p. 221.
6. Ibid., p. 231.
7. Ibid.

Spanish emphasis on proselytizing and the absence of strong religious traditions on the islands led to successful Christianization and to arresting the progress of Islam. Only the large island of Mindanao became Muslim. The Spanish government's commitment and use of violence accounts for this lone victory of the cross over the crescent in Asia. Elsewhere, European interest in the Malay world was of a commercial nature, even if it did occasionally use the argument of Christianization as a pretext for their endeavors; the Portuguese were a case in point. When European governments became involved in South and Southeast Asian affairs in the eighteenth and, most of all, the nineteenth centuries, progressively supplanting private commercial companies instead of simply giving them assistance, the stage was set for outright colonization. This was to have a much greater impact upon the local peoples and their traditional cultures.

South Asia

On the Indian subcontinent, the eighteenth century saw a struggle for power and influence between British and French companies, each supported by its respective government, especially the British, which resulted in the victory of British concerns. In the first part of the nineteenth century, there was a steady increase of British governmental control and interference in Indian affairs, accompanied by high-handed and superior attitudes that increasingly antagonized the locals and were partly responsible for the Sepoy mutiny of 1857. Following the mutiny, which the British tended to blame on the Muslims, the Muslims were ostracized by the colonizers; but the birth of a Hindu nationalist movement led the British to practice a divide-and-rule policy on the subcontinent. Threatened by this Hindu resurgence, the Indian Muslim minority looked to the British for protection against the Hindu majority.

When the British had to grant some measure of self-government to the Indians, they instituted separate electorates for the Muslims and the Hindus. Some of the Indian nationalist leaders, Hindus and Muslims alike, were westernized and secular in attitude, but the utterly fragmented nature of the socioethnic scene in India made it imperative to emphasize religion as a factor of unity. This was true most of all for the Hindus, and, in consequence, the Muslims were forced to adopt the same approach, making impossible a durable alliance between the communities in the struggle for independence.

The outcome, in 1947, was the partition of British India into two states—India and Pakistan—based on communal lines. Partition was accompanied by massive transfers of population and much bloodshed between the communities. Thereafter, while India has attempted with some success to follow a secular and democratic policy, the genesis of the birth of Pakistan, the nature of its political elite, and irredentist claims based on religion, as in Kashmir, have placed Islam squarely at the center of politics in Pakistan. In any case, from the beginning of British rule in India, the Hindus had been more willing to adopt Western ways, while the Muslims, displaced as the ruling elite, had remained somewhat on the sidelines, sulking, so to say. In the first years of independence, Islam had been the common bond between the two wings of Pakistan, until insurmountable differences brought about the breakup of the country and the birth of Bangladesh in the east wing, following the Indo-Pakistani war of 1971.

Southeast Asia

In the Malay world, on the other hand, where the large majority of the population was Muslim and where the colonizers were more interested in profits than conversion to Christianity, the British and the Dutch essentially practiced indirect rule. They maintained at least the facade of the preeminence of the local aristocracies and traditional rulers, taking care not to upset the peoples' beliefs and customs. An Islamic-based political movement, however, appeared in Java in 1825-30 with the Dipo Negoro war, which was based as much on Dutch meddling in dynastic affairs as on the increasing role of the Chinese in the economy. Throughout the nineteenth century, there were numerous instances of 'ulama'-led peasant resistance against Dutch rule, including the long Acheh wars between 1871 and 1908.[8] The founding in 1912 of the Sarekat Islam (Islam Association) in Java was motivated by identical economic rea-

8. Ira M. Lapidus, *A History of Islamic Societies* (New York: Cambridge University Press, 1988), p. 758.

sons. Sarekat Islam had a socialist orientation, but it soon split into several tendencies, and the leadership of the budding nationalist, anticolonial movement in the Dutch East Indies came to be in the hands of more secular leaders, either nationalists or Communists. The Japanese occupation during World War II accelerated the drive toward decolonization and independence throughout Southeast Asia, but Islam per se did not play a major role in this process either in Indonesia or in Malaya. Once independence had been achieved, however, Islam reemerged as a political force, increasingly so in the wake of the so-called Islamic resurgence.

THE MUSLIM POPULATION

The third factor that has affected the place and role of Islam in Asia is the size of the Muslim population in various Asian countries at the present time. With respect to population, there are three categories of countries. Some countries have an overwhelmingly Muslim majority. These include, first, Indonesia, the largest Muslim country in the world and the fifth most populous country, with a total population of 186.9 million people, of which 168.2 million, or 90 percent, are Muslims; second, Pakistan, with a total population of 120.8 million, of which 117.2 million, or 97 percent, are Muslims; and third, Bangladesh, with a total population of 117.8 million, of which 97.8 million, or 83 percent, are Muslims.

The second category comprises one country, Malaysia, which has a bare majority of Muslims: 9.3 million out of 18.6 million.

The third category comprises several countries with a Muslim minority. In India, the minority is nevertheless large in numbers, with 96.3 million geographically dispersed Muslims composing a mere 11 percent of the population. In the Philippines, the Muslims number 3.16 million, constituting 5 percent of the total population of 63.3 million; in Thailand, they are 2.3 million, 4 percent of the total population of 57.6 million; in China, they are 11.4 million, or about 1 percent of the total population of 1,147.6 million.[9] In the case of both the Philippines and Thailand, however, the Muslims are concentrated in specific geographic areas and, in the case of the Thai, Muslims belong to a different ethnic group from that of the Buddhist majority of the population.

All three factors discussed earlier—the spread of Islam, European colonization, and population patterns—have had a direct correlation with the behavior of Muslims and the role of Islam in the various countries of Asia. Looking at the record since independence, one can determine two periods regarding the role of Islam in the politics of Asia. Following independence, with the exception of Pakistan, the leadership in most countries was essentially secular, concerned with problems of foreign policy, nation building, modernization, and development. Then, from the late 1960s, and in some places even earlier, one witnesses the alleged resurgence of Islam, the rise of

9. *World Development Report 1991* (New York: Oxford University Press, 1991). Figures are population projections for 1992, based on statistics in ibid., p. 254.

Islamic fundamentalism. In point of fact, this was not the resurgence of a religion, which had always been there, but an attempt to interpret Islam holistically by using principles derived from Islamic teachings to guide politics and economics, as well as society in general. What attracted the attention of the West was the political dimension, which used Muslim idiom instead of Western terminology and which distanced itself from westernization while preaching reform.

Revivalism or fundamentalism—whatever term one uses—is not a new phenomenon in Islam. It has occurred many times in the past centuries. The present conditions in the world, in terms of rapid change and modern means of communication and transportation, have given this resurgence a global character that it could not have had in the past.

ISLAM IN ASIA: CASE STUDIES

The reappearance of Islamic idiom as a political factor in Asia has taken different forms in different countries, both before and after the watershed constituted by the Iranian revolution.

Pakistan

Religion played an essential role in the birth of Pakistan. After independence, it continued to play a major role in the politics of the country and not just because the official name of the country is "The Islamic Republic of Pakistan." Less westernized than India, or at least less receptive to Western ideas of political and economic organization, Pakistan did not succeed in establishing a durable semidemocratic system within the framework of a secular ideology. The first years of the new state were marked by political instability, aggravated by the successive deaths of its most able leaders, Mohammed Ali Jinnah and Liaqat Ali Khan. The only anchor that could be used to keep the country together was religion, and it was not sufficient to prevent the breakup that produced the new nation of Bangladesh in 1971. Since 1958, Pakistan has been under military rule, except for brief civilian interludes with Zulfikar Ali Bhutto and, more recently, his daughter, Benazir. But whatever type of regime operated, Islam has been used as a guideline in both domestic and international affairs. From the very beginning of the new state, there has been a struggle for influence between the modernists, often coming from the Muslim League and trained at Aligahr Muslim University, a modern institution, and the traditionalists led by the 'ulama'.[10] At least in theory, the traditionalists have been successful in imposing their agenda on the political system, both under civilian and military regimes.

Both types of leaders were under pressure to establish or maintain their Muslim credentials. Military rulers, such as Zia ul-Haq, were eager to preempt the most extreme demands of Muslim traditionalists in

order to justify and maintain their hold on power. While Pakistan's three constitutions (1956, 1962, and 1973) contained Islamic provisions governing, for instance, individual moral or social behavior, General Zia after 1977 attempted to enforce the more extremist interpretations of *shari'a* law in judicial and criminal matters, such as in punishments for theft or adultery, to enforce a strict observance of the Five Pillars of Islam, even forcing a dress code on government employees and women in general.[11] There was also to be the establishment of "Islamic economics and banking," which would prohibit interest and usury. The attempt was to bring about a society fairly similar to that of Khomeini's Iran.

An additional factor on the path of Islamization had been the breakup of Pakistan in 1971 and its reorientation in international affairs toward the traditional Muslim heartland, the Middle East, which was initiated by the secular and socialist Bhutto.[12] This was further reinforced by the 1973 Arab-Israeli war and the subsequent rise in oil prices, which have exacerbated anti-Western feelings and given added leverage and influence to traditional and conservative regimes such as Saudi Arabia. The anti-Soviet, anti-Communist struggle in Afghanistan waged in the name of Islam, the influx of Afghans into Pakistan, and Saudi financial support of the resistance have played in

10. Kemal A. Faruki, "Pakistan: Islamic Government and Society," in *Islam in Asia: Religion, Politics and Society*, ed. John L. Esposito (New York: Oxford University Press, 1987), p. 54. See also Barbara D. Metcalf, "Islamic Arguments in Contemporary Pakistan," in *Islam and the Political Economy of Meaning*, ed. William R. Roff (Berkeley: University of California Press, 1987).

11. Metcalf, "Islamic Arguments in Contemporary Pakistan," p. 74.

12. John L. Esposito, "Pakistan: Quest for Islamic Identity," in *Islam and Development*, ed. John L. Esposito (Syracuse, NY: Syracuse University Press, 1980), pp. 150-51.

the same direction. It remains that ethnic, linguistic, economic, and social differences, and dissensions within Pakistan remain profound and are unlikely to diminish.

Bangladesh

The new state of Bangladesh, born in 1971 as a result of the breakup of Pakistan, initially emphasized national, secular goals.[13] This was understandable, since the secession had broken the bond between the two wings of a union that was based only on the common religion, Islam. Later, especially in the wake of military coups and takeovers, an Islamic fundamentalist orientation somewhat similar to that of Pakistan, but so far not carried to the same length, has appeared. In spite of the phenomenon of Islamic resurgence, which has also reached Bangladesh, the Islamic idiom in the politics of that country has remained moderate because of the circumstances of the country's birth, its connections with India, present rule by a democratic regime, and the existence of a substantial non-Muslim minority.[14] What might give the Islamic political idiom a renewed influence would be a demand for greater social justice, given the extreme poverty of the country, one of the world's poorest, and its vulnerability to recurrent natural disasters such as floods.

13. Lapidus, *History of Islamic Societies*, p. 747.
14. Peter J. Bertocci, "Bangladesh: Composite Cultural Identity and Modernization in a Muslim-Majority State," in *Change and the Muslim World*, ed. Philip H. Stoddard et al. (Syracuse, NY: Syracuse University Press, 1981), pp. 77, 78.

India

Of the three countries of the subcontinent, India is the only one where Muslims constitute a minority. But it is a very large minority in absolute numbers, nearly as large as the Muslim majority in neighboring Bangladesh and twice as large as the Muslim majority in any Middle Eastern country. Nonetheless, the situation of the Muslims in India is a difficult one. First, they suffer from the circumstances of the partition, which has left durable rancors and antagonisms, especially in northern India, where most Muslims are to be found. On the other hand, over most of the postindependence years, the official government ideology has been secular, committed to nondiscrimination on the basis of race, caste, or religion.[15] Some Muslims have reached very high positions in the government structure, up to and including head of state. But the Muslims are also subject to special provisions governing their personal status, such as family matters.

The attempt to combine nondiscriminatory provisions at the public level and a special status at the private level has generated tensions between the communities. In practice, discrimination against the Muslims is widespread, both at the public level—with respect to government jobs, for instance—and at the private, such as with jobs in the private sector, bank loans, and so on.[16] Some, but by no means all, such practices may be justified by the overall lower

15. Syed Shahabuddin and Theodore P. Wright, Jr., "India: Muslim Minority Politics and Society," in *Islam in Asia*, ed. Esposito, p. 155.
16. Ibid., p. 164.

educational achievements of the Indian Muslims. Intercommunal riots and violence have been widespread, exacerbated by a renewed Islamic consciousness on the part of some elements of the Muslim community and accompanied by a renewed Hindu consciousness, communal disputes over the location of a mosque or Hindu temple on the same site, and, lastly, the situation of quasi civil war in the Muslim majority province of Kashmir.

In the recent past, for the Indian Muslims, Islam played a major role at the devotional level, not perforce at the public one, and in fact the more affluent Muslims have reached a fair level of accommodation with the Hindu majority.[17] But the conjunction of the continuing religio-ethnic strife in India—affecting communities other than the Muslim one—and the Islamic resurgence can only increase, albeit in a limited way, the political role of Islam within the Indian Muslim community.

Indonesia

In Southeast Asia, one finds a wide array of situations with respect to the political role of Islam. In Indonesia, governments since independence have managed to maintain a secular approach within the state ideology of Pancasila, whose principles include a belief in God and are acceptable to other communities as well as the Muslims. This secular approach was followed both under Sukarno, in the first years of the Republic, and the military under Suharto and the New

Order, since 1965.[18] It seems paradoxical that the largest Muslim country in the world appears to be one of the least influenced by Islamic political activities. But several reasons account for this situation.

While Muslim parties or movements were active under Dutch colonization, during the Japanese occupation, and in the struggle for independence, the leadership of the independence movement and then of the independent Republic remained in the hands of committed secularists. Under Sukarno, some Muslim parties led secessionist movements;[19] others spent their energy fighting Communist influence. Under the New Order of General Suharto, some fringe Muslim groups have been involved in terrorist acts, giving the military government a pretext for keeping a tight control over all Muslim movements and activities.

The historical and geographic contexts have made the emergence of a strong, unified Islamic political movement difficult. There is the geographic, ethnic, and linguistic diversity of the Indonesian islands and their inhabitants. There is the survival of pre-Islamic, animist, Hindo-Buddhist traditions in a tolerant and syncretic environment. Religious and cultural pluralism is a fact of public life and a matter of pride for many Indonesians.[20] An added factor of fragmentation is resentment in the outer

17. Lapidus, *History of Islamic Societies*, p. 748.

18. Nasir Tamara, "Islam under the New Order," *Prisma* (Jakarta), June 1990, no. 49. pp. 6-31.

19. Anthony H. Johns, "Indonesia: Islam and Cultural Pluralism," in *Islam in Asia*, ed. Esposito, pp. 211-12.

20. Ibid., p. 204.

islands caused by the domination of heavily populated Java. It remains that reformist Muslim movements continue to exist and to advocate a polity more in tune with the precepts of Islam but equally in tune with the demands of a technological world. Devotional Islam is on the increase, as is Islamic education, encouraged but controlled by the authorities. As in many other places in the Muslim world, the tensions created by modernization contribute to a reinforced sense of Islamic identity at the national and global level.

Malaysia

The picture is very different in Malaysia, providing an interesting contrast with Indonesia in terms of the Islamic dimension of politics. In Malaysia, the Muslims constitute a bare majority but control the political system, while the Chinese and Indian communities have long controlled the economic life of the country. As opposed to the autocratic civilian or military regimes that have governed Indonesia since independence, Malaysia has, so far, enjoyed a fairly democratic form of government. That government, based on an alliance of representatives of the various communities, but under the leadership of Malays—which in Malaysia means Muslims—attempted at first to follow a secular policy balancing the interests of the different communities. In more recent years, however, the phenomenon of Islamic resurgence, more obvious in Malaysia than anywhere else in Southeast Asia, has pressured the political system into moving in the direction of a greater

Islamic presence in public life, accompanied by a policy of affirmative action for the Malays.[21] Such a trend might ultimately upset the precarious balance that has kept the communities together.

But the Islamic resurgence, apart from some regional influence, including financial support from the oil-rich countries of the Middle East, is essentially for domestic and global reasons. Under colonization, the Malays were content to remain peasants, and the British had to bring Chinese and Indians to work in the tin mines and on the rubber plantations. In time, those overseas immigrants drifted into cities, which they pretty much populated and whose economy they dominated. When the Malays started to move to the cities, they became exposed to modernization and urbanization in an environment dominated by those communities of foreign origin with different cultures and religions, which generated confrontations. This has led to a reassertion of the Malays' self-identity, naturally centered on Islam.[22]

Increased possibilities for education in this dynamic, partly alien economic environment have exposed young educated Malays to the materialistic, westernized cultural aspects of modernization, which, more often than not, they find offensive to their deep-rooted ethical values. While they realize that modernization is probably a one-way street, they want it to take place within an

21. Margaret Scott, "Where the Quota is King," *New York Times*, 17 Nov. 1991.
22. Fred von der Mehden, "Malaysia: Islam and Multiethnic Politics," in *Islam in Asia*, ed. Esposito, p. 192.

Islamic framework respectful of their values.[23] More in evidence in Malaysia than possibly anywhere else in the Asian Muslim world is the difference between modernization, which is desired, and westernization in its conspicuous-consumption aspects, which is rejected, together with its capitalist, neo-imperialist dimension. Some signs of the Islamic resurgence have been the growth of *dakwah* ("missionary") movements, the increasing place given by the politicians and the media to Islamic issues, and the popularity of the Islamic type of dress.[24] The government's answer has been to co-opt some of the movement's leaders and to try and raise the economic level of the Malays through policies aimed at increasing their share in the economy.

In two other Southeast Asian countries, the Philippines and Thailand, Muslims constitute small minorities, concentrated in specific areas. Policies of either benign neglect or semi-forced cultural assimilation have radicalized the Muslims' resistance, leading to insurgency, often supported from outside. Examples of this resistance are that of the Moros of Mindanao in the Philippines and the Muslims of southern Thailand, who feel greater affinities with their Malay cousins of Malaysia and have been further politicized by the phenomenon of Islamic resurgence.

23. Fred von der Mehden, *Religion and Modernization in Southeast Asia* (Syracuse, NY: Syracuse University Press, 1986), p. 108.

24. Ibid., p. 107. See also Muhammad Kamal Hassan, "The Response of Muslim Youth Organizations to Political Change: HMI in Indonesia and ABIM in Malaysia," in *Islam and the Political Economy of Meaning*, ed. Roff.

CONCLUSION

After this all too brief overview of the most significant countries of Asia with a Muslim population, one can attempt to draw some tentative conclusions as to the role played by Islamic activism in the politics of these countries. First, the phenomenon of Islamic "resurgence," with its holistic approach to politics as inseparable from religion, is not a new one. It has occurred many times before, in different places, at different moments. What is new is its global character, how it is widespread throughout the Muslim world from North Africa to Southeast Asia, from Central Asia to sub-Saharan Africa, and in fact everywhere where there are Muslims. Part of the reason for its ubiquity is the modern means of transportation and communication, which have facilitated contacts and transfers of ideas.

A more profound reason is also rooted in the advent of modernization, due first to the advent of a global society, then to the change from an agricultural society to an industrial one and subsequently to an information society, progressive in the Western world, often partial or telescoped in the developing world, to which most of the Muslim countries belong. This rapid change is profoundly disruptive and even traumatic. While old securities inherent in the stability of traditional societies are vanishing or under considerable challenge, the modern world offers alternatives, which both in their Western and Communist versions—before the latter's collapse—appear exploitative, mindless, and dehumanizing.

On the one hand, modernization seems inevitable to most Muslims.

The only way to "tame the beast" is to have an anchor, a sense of purpose, an ethical foundation, which Islam seems to offer because it is a Weltanschauung with a promise of a just and integrated society. This is why the phenomenon of Islamic resurgence has had, and continues to have, such an impact. In Asia, the extent of that impact has varied depending, as we have seen, on such factors as historical and cultural backgrounds, geography, size of the Muslim community, and government policy. But whatever its degree of intensity, it has affected, affects, or will affect the politics of those countries. In many ways, the rapid political decolonization following World War II did not fulfill widespread expectations for a better life in the former Western colonies. What we may well witness in the making is a political phenomenon of the first magnitude, a second decolonization, a cultural dewesternization spearheaded by resurgent Islam.

ANNALS, *AAPSS*, 524, November 1992

Maghrebi Immigration to Europe: Double Insertion or Double Exclusion?

By RÉMY LEVEAU

ABSTRACT: In Europe, Islam became a significant form of collective behavior among migrants from the Maghreb, Turkey, Western Africa, and India during the 1970s, when that group of people decided to settle abroad and raise their children in what they considered, at the beginning, to be a lasting exile. In that way, Islam appeared as an instrument for building new identities and transnational solidarities for the purpose of negotiating with the states and societies of settlement. But that peaceful approach has been taken as an unacceptable challenge by secular societies, which are no longer used to dealing with religious values as a way of collective self-assertion. In a future open Europe that will include 5 to 6 million Muslims, it will be necessary to establish a new doctrinal framework of cultural pluralism that includes Islam.

Rémy Leveau is professor at the Institut d'Études Politiques de Paris. He has taught at the Universities of Rabat, Michigan, and Beirut (St. Joseph) and New York University. He has spent many years as a civil servant with the Ministry of Foreign Affairs (cultural affairs). He has published Le fellah marocain: défenseur du Trône *(1985);* Les musulmans dans la société française *(with Gilles Kepel) (1987); and many articles on subjects related to the Middle East, the Maghreb, Islam in France, and migration.*

IN today's Europe, everyone's attention is focused on political changes in the East and the potentially important modifications of migratory flows that may go along with these changes. Interest in the Maghreb awakens only when events like the Persian Gulf crisis, martial law in Algeria, or the Islamic Salvation Front's success in legislative elections provoke passionate reactions. But a new social and human alignment has been building up between the Maghreb and Europe as a result of an immigration that was unplanned and largely unrecognized in either place. Since 1970, a slow, sometimes painful awareness of the scale and implications of this migration have developed, along with reactions of rejection in European, particularly French, society.[1]

At the same time, a sense of identity among Maghrebi immigrants

1. Particularly useful works on the topic of the present article are *Être français aujourd'hui et demain* (Paris: La Documentation française, 1988); Gilles Kepel, *Les banlieues de l'islam* (Paris: Le Seuil, 1987); Rémy Leveau and Gilles Kepel, *Les musulmans dans la société française* (Paris: Presses de la Fondation nationale des sciences politiques, 1987); Dominique Schnapper, *La France de l'intégration* (Paris: Gallimard, 1991); Patrick Weil, *La France et ses étrangers: L'aventure d'une politique de l'immigration 1938-1991* (Paris: Calmann-Lévy, 1991); Michel Wieviorka, *La France raciste* (Paris: Le Seuil, 1992); Catherine Wihtol de Wenden, *Les immigrés et la politique* (Paris: Presses de la Fondation nationale des sciences politiques, 1988); Rémy Leveau, "Les partis et l'intégration des 'beurs'" in *Idéologies, partis politiques et groupes sociaux*, ed. Y. Mény (Paris: Presses de la Fondation nationale des sciences politiques, 1989), pp. 247-62; Fathia Dazi and Rémy Leveau, "L'intégration par le politique: Le vote des 'beurs,'" *Études* pp. 179-88 (Sept. 1988).

and their descendants has been developing that focuses on Islam. By choosing Islam, this sense of identity, which has allowed these insecure new immigrants to legitimize their presence within European society, blurs the traditional European boundaries between public and private affairs. On the other hand, the language of the French extreme right, the National Front, represents a typical example of the reaction of a majority group that adopts minority group behavior and redefines its own identity on the basis of cultural and religious values.

The process of collective negotiation that uses Islam as the focal point, however, is in turn affected by the changes that occurred in Europe, particularly the opening to the East and the unification planned for 1993. Competitive, conflictual, and interactive situations are taking shape, presaging a new type of North-South relationship, which could be compared with some of the factors at work in the plans for a common market between the United States, Canada, and Mexico. It may also create conflicts of a new type and magnitude.

To start with, the ambiguity of the situation is amplified by the world's perception of a coincidence between Maghrebi immigration, its assertion of an Islamic cultural identity, and the Iranian revolution of 1979. It is true that the French political system has long been familiar with Islam because of the French colonial history and since the 1930s has known a significant Maghrebi influx. That immigration has continued long after decolonization, although since then talk about going back to the countries of origin has accompanied the move away from them.

Change has been taking place since the 1970s, when, officially, immigration to all the European countries was stopped and Islam became a tool for collective negotiation. First of all, Islam has occupied that private space to which religious behaviors have been confined since the separation between church and state that occurred in France in 1905. However, it has voiced a demand for recognition in the public space, constituting a community capable of becoming a legitimate collective actor to face the various French authorities. The religious factor has become a substitute for political participation, which is lacking, and for economic and cultural integration that is insufficient. Religion is a provocative way to ask for integration, and the French system cannot answer the questions it raises without having to modify itself. On the part of the migrants, the religious demands have been peaceful ones, most often made on the basis of human rights revendications.

Since the 1970s, the phenomenon has taken a pan-European dimension. First of all, the Maghrebi diaspora has not limited itself to France. It has existed in Belgium, in Germany, and in Holland since the 1970s, going through the same changes, especially in becoming a family immigration. A more recent immigration, but nevertheless similar to the previous ones as far as behavior is concerned, is nowadays occurring in Spain and Italy.

The problems linked with the nationality of either the countries of origin or the host countries are creating what will probably become a new type of citizenship in the community. The Maghrebi case is similar to that of the Turks, settled essentially in Germany, and the Indo-Pakistanis in Great Britain.

As a consequence of the groups' immigration, the old nation-states can no longer define the rules of citizenship as they once did.

Communities of a new type are coming into being in the transnational space. Their presence modifies the rules of the game and tends, in the long run, to add to the pressures for a European federal system on the verge of being elaborated, evoking some aspects of the American system and more clearly giving the preference to the *jus solis* (place of birth) over the *jus sanguini* (descendance) as the determinant of citizenship. In the meantime, the developing system is unable to adopt immediately a precise attitude without conflicting with various national heritages.

Moreover, the groups that assert their collective identity by valorizing their cultural and religious heritage nevertheless adopt a cautious behavior in their relationships and display an adhesion to collective rules, especially in French society. Two recent events, the crisis over wearing the so-called Islamic scarf at school in October 1989 and the Persian Gulf crisis, may have, paradoxically, helped to demonstrate that there exists a largely predominant allegiance attitude among Muslims. On the one hand, Muslims are looking for a collective visibility by respecting food taboos, by having identifiable places of worship available, and by searching for a group representation capable of negotiating on their behalf. On the other hand, they see to it that they do not become too provocative in the eyes of the majority of the population. Polls show that more than half of them are against the wearing of the scarf and nearly as many do not want a call for prayer from the mosque. Nearly all favor private practice of Islam, accept intermarriage with a non-Muslim person, and support ongoing relations with a relative who has abandoned Islam. But collective reactions that some perceive as related to the management of a private space appear to the outside world as being characteristic behaviors of a community group and as a kind of intrusion into the public space.

In the same way, during the Persian Gulf crisis, at a time when French society feared particularly the impact of solidarity conflicts, Muslims in France recognized the legitimacy of the right of the President of the Republic to involve France in a war against an Arab and Muslim country, although they preferred negotiations as an alternative. In February 1991, François Mitterrand received favorable opinions from 67 percent of Muslims, while Saddam Hussein found favor with only 26 percent. The discourse of Muslims in France was above all anti-American and anti-Israeli, and Muslims tried, on the contrary, to find excuses for the behavior of French leaders.

Confronting the new situation of a minority trying to negotiate its space without disappearing, in the 1980s the French political system created interlocutors from among the migrants, by converting Maghrebi intellectuals into social workers. Of-

ficially committed to the earlier policy of individual integration, the French political system gradually came to accept dealing with intermediaries acting on behalf of the community. But, in the process, the state got the impression that it no longer had complete control over the norms of society. Other actors, especially local powers, have, since 1982, had greater autonomy and, since 1985-86, with the construction of the new European political space, have been competing with the central state for the definition of values and collective practices.

THE PRESSURES ON EUROPEAN STATES

At a time when the state is doubting its capability and is losing part of its efficacy because of the economic crisis that affects particularly the youth, are there any signs of a policy for the integration of Maghrebi immigrants within the European Community? Officially, there is no policy or institutional answer to this question. For the time being, immigration does not belong to the areas of supranational authority. The only collective actions on the subject concern groups of experts from the Interior Ministries of the 12 countries, who, at first, had been directed to study terrorism and drug problems and then the circulation of nationals from outside the European Community.

More than the others, the northern European states, where outmoded industries—steel, mining, public works, automobile—were in crisis at the end of the 1970s, are directly concerned with the immigration problem. Thus they are the ones that have gone the furthest in coordinating the control of population moves. As with the Turks in Germany, and the Indo-Pakistanis in Great Britain, an economic and social phenomenon—the integration of a population of Mediterranean and Asian origin—is linked with a cultural and political phenomenon comprising the assertion of an Islamic identity. This raises a collective anxiety over an imported and extremist Islamism, and these fears lead to the rise of an extreme-right electorate.

Nevertheless, the simple assertion of an Islam, most of the time peaceful, challenges the principles that are at the basis of centralized states. The Rushdie affair has been an illustration of those tensions at the European level. The opening up of Eastern Europe has led to the confused notion that migratory movements from the East would compete with those of nearby Third World countries. They would discourage questioning the principles defining the relationships between centralized states and the non-European culture's migrant groups. It is very tempting to create a community barrier at the southern and eastern Mediterranean shores, while applying flexible controls on the eastern border. This comes into conflict with the policy of the free movement of capital and goods that accompanies the triumph of the free-market economy and presides over the evolution of today's Europe.

The main obstacle to the free movement of people across borders stems from the fact that immigration has become a major political issue within the northern European countries of France, Germany, and Great

Britain. The coincidence between the North African and West Asian settlement of Europe at the end of the 1970s and the assertion of an Islamic identity has meant, above all, for the migrants, a desire not to be diluted in the mass of the populations of the host countries and, at the same time, a desire to pass on to their children some of their own values and memories. But, because of the 1979 Iranian revolution, that strategy has been perceived as an external threat linked with Middle East terrorism and the taking of European hostages.

For that reason, starting with the communal elections in France in 1983, the immigration problem has become a major political issue, causing the rise of a populist movement under the leadership of Jean-Marie Le Pen. The National Front does not limit itself to the recruiting of a classical, marginal, extreme-right electorate, which may represent about 5 percent of the votes. In 1986, and again in 1988-89, it more than doubled that figure, indicating, according to 25 percent of opinions expressed in opinion polls taken in a time of crisis, that even Socialist and Communist voters were inclined to adopt positions close to the National Front program when it came to immigration problems.

The settlement of Turks in Germany and the de facto disappearance of the myths about the guest workers have given rise, under similar conditions, to the success of the Republican Party in that country. For a long time, Great Britain has been able to manage the tensions created by the integration of an Indo-Pakistani minority, thanks to Britain's acceptance of multiculturalism and to the minority's participation in political life, facilitated by Commonwealth citizenship. For the whole of the European Community, the immigrants of Islamic culture certainly do not represent more than about 6 million people: 2.5 to 3 million in France, 2 million in Great Britain, 1 million in Germany, and a few hundred thousand in Belgium and Holland. In France as well as in Great Britain, the majority of these migrants, or at least their children, are on their way to becoming citizens of the host country. In Germany, that practice is more difficult, but their right to stay is nevertheless recognized.

Taken as a whole, the immigrant group, if one imagines it as a coherent unit, represents only a small segment—2 percent—of the European population. But, in some countries, that share may rise to 5 percent locally, and in other places to 20 percent, due to high concentrations in housing. These concentrations favor the identity reactions translated into communitywide strategies, but also the rejection reactions or a low threshold of tolerance. In France, in the 1970s, these reactions led Communist city councils to enact quotas for dwellings, for entering nurseries, or for access to social services. In this way, the councils dealt with very high concentrations of immigrant populations that often adopt a type of blockbusting strategy and compete with the oldest strata of the working class, which, due to the economic crisis of the late 1970s, can no longer improve their living conditions and find their social mobility blocked. That confrontation has engendered, since the be-

ginning of the 1980s, a slide toward the extreme right, particularly among the middle class.

Thus local tensions coupled with the general decline in the influence of the Communist Party might, during the next municipal elections—in 1994—lead to the crumbling of those traditional Communist Party strongholds that the city councils in the suburbs of big cities—Paris, Lyons, Marseilles, Lille—have represented and where the major part of the immigrant populations undergoing integration are living. If, at that time, the Communists' decline among the working-class electorate has not been compensated for by the involvement in political life of the new generations of Maghrebi immigrants through the Socialist Party, then these city councils risk coming under the control of the National Front. That development will make even more difficult the realization of integration policies on which a reasoned management of local affairs greatly depends.

Decentralization measures taken since 1982 make it extremely difficult for the state to interfere directly in these policies especially when mayors who exclude the immigrants either from entering schools or from getting a home are supported by their electorate. Today, these mayors are able to control either directly or indirectly the housing market, including private housing, through the use of their right to preempt sales. A great number of (illegal) actions to prevent immigrant children from entering nurseries or primary schools lead the immigrants into conflict with state authorities. In the end, their decisions are abrogated by the administrative jurisdiction after the education authorities have initiated a request. But by then, local elected representatives have gained a real popularity and probably discourage immigrants from settling down in their area. In the same way, by broadly interpreting their rights, they now use their control over housing certificates to hinder access to three-month visas.

Their statements about illicit immigration use examples of tourists who settle down, saturate the labor market, and add to the demands for social assistance. They justify in the eyes of their electorate the excessive practices of most of the town councils, whether dominated by the right or the left. Interventions of the same sort tend to develop, aiming at limitations on possible family regrouping.

The state gradually finds itself confronted with a tricky situation in the sense that, if the immigrants continue to be excluded at the local level of government, any rational policy of integration will become impossible. The state might even have to face, here and there, violence engendered by these exclusions. Today, it cannot consider recovering direct control of the areas that, since the 1982 decentralization law, have been delegated to local authorities without provoking a major political crisis. But the evolution toward local management of the problems linked with immigration has given birth, within some decentralized political systems such as Great Britain and Germany, to high concentrations of population that claim, even more than in the French system, a strong and separate iden-

tity, leading in the end to a ghetto phenomenon.

One can witness blockage at the local level in France, but the state is still responsible for integration policies. Integration is advanced when leaders belonging to the immigration association movement become involved in social and political life. In the classical ways of the French political system, that involvement runs through the parties and, primarily, the Socialist Party. It is incarnated essentially in the personality of the President of the Republic, who is viewed positively by migrants as a supreme recourse in the face of misunderstanding and hostility on the part of the local and administrative services. But this integration by political channels, which might be characteristic of the French system and is derived from its history, comes today to a dead end, as much as a consequence of local authorities' reactions as of some of the claims presented by the immigrant populations. The immigrants' felt need to mobilize the community and to accentuate their pressure on the central government increases their tendency to resort to the expression of cultural and religious identities. That strategy comes in conflict with the traditions of hostility toward intermediate groups and of confining religious matters to the private sphere, which are part of the basic principles of the modern French state. Therefore, it becomes difficult to find a satisfactory solution to the crisis on a purely national level. To abandon the principles of state secularism and to recognize that legitimate community actors exist would mean giving birth to a major internal crisis. To assume control of the managing power now exercised by local authorities would equally engender opposition beyond the single issue of immigration.

THE NEED FOR A
COMMUNITY RESPONSE

A broad compromise is needed, establishing a level of decision making that combines local management, state policies, and some forms of pan-European coordination. As for the management of immigration, the absence of a European policy will be an embarrassment, both for the member states and for the Community, on the eve of 1993. The states wish very strongly to keep their authority over any question related to population movements that, in the long run, could affect their own society. They might, though, find it practical for a community authority to be established to present externally a restrictive immigration policy, in order to minimize contradictions between state policies, local authorities, and community groups, the inner logics of which lead to conflict.

There is a real need to define a common policy toward an Islamicist movement based in the Maghreb. Too strong a solitary reaction on the part of the French authorities would provoke opposition on the part of the Islamicist movement's new leaders along the theme of colonialist interference. The expression of a policy on the Community level would be more difficult to condemn. A European policy on immigration could help as much to establish common rules for the management of visas and residence conditions as to define arbitra-

tion terms concerning the methods used by local authorities. A common policy could prevent them from engaging in an opposition game with national authorities. In addition, if the European power gives itself the judiciary and political means necessary to enforce its general lines, then the local authorities would be led more easily to abandon their discriminatory practices. The collective structure may not immediately be as efficient as one wishes, but the blockages of state mechanisms, the fear of external pressures, and the rise of community dangers may force the establishment of new procedures.

The previous analysis of tensions refers essentially to the French case, in which visibility strategies chosen by the immigrants have thrust religion into the public space, thus spurring conflict with the secular tradition at the heart of the political system. While Islam is part of the immigrants' assertions of identity in Germany, its religious presence in the German public space does not appear to conflict with common rules. Rather, the conflict relates to the principle of dual citizenship as requested by Turkish associations, which is as much in opposition to the constitutional rules of the German nation as the contesting of secularism is in France.

Is the implication in both cases that conflict is, in essence, linked to an integration process and aims above all at redefining the terms of a new social contract? If so, it would be even more urgent to contemplate redefining the contract at a global and European level rather than through a series of national adjustment processes that might be contradictory.

A study of group perceptions, collective memory, and values, and not only of security, is the only way to establish a new contract. It can constitute a guideline for the judges who will have to regulate immigration in a legal common space, before the state-level powers take charge of it. Such a study will also give material to political leaders for defining their strategy and will help the negotiation with minority elites who tend increasingly to locate their identity in the European space. Reflection on collective memory and on the way groups are perceived ought to avoid the sort of incoherences and hasty opinions that accompanied both official and popular reactions at the time of the Rushdie affair or the Islamic scarf crisis. Great Britain as well as France appears as a precursor when it comes to those identity crises, inasmuch as they symbolize opposite ways of managing the minority phenomenon.

Germany is probably in a more favorable position because of the federal and decentralized character of its political system and the solidity of its economic system, making it possible to grant economic compensation to those who have no hope of entering the political field. Given a tradition of religious pluralism that is evidently more integrated into Germany than into France, the fact that Islam constitutes the third religion in Germany seems to engender less rejection of immigration than either in France or in Great Britain. The challenge that the Muslims present is related more to the idea of a homogeneous nation seeking incarnation in a state. Turkish and Maghrebi immigrants have settled in industrial cities where their percentages have risen to levels similar to those in France. The fact that the term "foreigner" has been substituted for "guest worker" clearly indicates the idea of a lengthy residence, but it also indicates that the application of *jus solis*, which, in the long run, would grant citizenship to immigrants' children born in Germany, is not even contemplated. That country remains unwilling to accept dual citizenship, a measure capable of facilitating integration.

Meanwhile, one ought to note that, in spite of legal uncertainty, Germany does not expel more foreigners than does France. But German reunification and East German hostility toward Turkish immigration will probably accentuate pressure for them to leave the country; the result will be a move westward rather than a return to Anatolia. Because French citizenship is easier to obtain, it may be used to allow Turks from Germany to move freely in the European space.

The signing, on 19 June 1990, of the Schengen agreement by the five countries of northern Europe—Belgium, France, Germany, Luxembourg, and the Netherlands—might create difficulties. That agreement, which Italy joined in November 1990 and Spain in May 1991, provides for the generalization of visa procedures that are applied by each country. A computer network established for control at the external borders will ensure that the traveler is in possession of all the necessary papers. Such strict measures will permit foreigners to move freely within the whole of the Community space from the Polish border to Algeciras or Bari. The establishment of that Schengen space will create a new type of relationship with the non-Community foreigners.

The consular procedures of the signing countries will be harmonized and made quite dissuasive for those who may be suspected of intending permanent settlement. Administrative controls will be reinforced through the airlines and maritime companies in charge of repatriation, which will have to pay heavy fines in cases where travelers are turned back. Interconnected computerized management ought also to permit identification of those who have extended their legal stay. It is highly probable that overextending one's legal length of time will be punished not only by expulsion but by inclusion on the list of undesirable foreigners who will thereafter not be granted another visa. Indeed, these procedures will affect the relationship between the immigrants settled in Europe and their external bases.

To avoid abuses by overexuberant leaders and their police services, a centralized service in charge of controlling the various national authorities should be established. That would mean moving toward a European authority similar to the American federal Immigration and Naturalization Service, which calls for a strong executive and appropriate legal control. Beyond those technical procedures, the major political issue at stake in the relationships between the European ensemble and its southern

Mediterranean environment is taking shape. It would be illusory to think that the tight barrier that is the aim of the Schengen agreement's procedures may be kept very long, especially because the minorities settled in those countries will wish to keep contact, through family networks, with their countries of origin. Their insertion in Europe would be made easier through a flexible management of interests rather than breaking off with those countries.

On the other hand, it would be contradictory, at a time when Europe is developing a philosophy of the free movement of capital, goods, and persons, to establish a lasting barrier vis-à-vis the South. But, since the free circulation would engender tensions that the European society would not be capable of managing, it appears more appropriate to filter and regulate flows. In the meantime, this could be compensated for through economic assistance so as not to accentuate tensions within southern Mediterranean societies.

The welfare state, along with European television images, which today can be received directly by millions of people in the Maghreb or in Turkey, provokes both a fascination and a frustration inherent in the desire to go elsewhere. But those images reflect, at the same time, an inaccessible society that rejects them and therefore justifies a withdrawal into their own identity—a self-ghettoization—favorable to Islamicist movements. In the short run, that evolution is also translated into a new exodus of middle-class people who, having been educated in a modern system, no longer find a place in Maghrebi societies. It would be futile to believe that one is going to put an end to these cultural, economic, and social flows by using visas, computerized controls, and other repressive measures. Such a policy may, indeed, slow down and delay pressure from southern Mediterranean countries, which tends to become an exodus of middle-class persons. But the gains will be meaningful only if a true policy of economic transfers to those countries is coupled with a policy aimed at the integration of minorities with respect for their double culture and interests. If the only objective is to gain time in order to quiet European fears, then it is very risky, for that might engender situations of tension and violence both in Europe and in those countries.

ANNALS, *AAPSS*, 524, November 1992

Democracy and Islam:
The Cultural Dialectic

By I. WILLIAM ZARTMAN

ABSTRACT: Current history is marked by the meeting of two powerful currents, democracy and political Islam. Islam itself is the subject of a cultural dialectic between a modern and an authentistic form, out of which a synthesis tends to arise, only to be attacked again by a new authentistic antithesis. Political Islam is the current antithesis, attacking the unpopular states for impiety and materialism. Democracy is also rising in popularity as a criterion of good government, with special meaning as the consummation of nationalism for new states recently free from colonial rule. The two currents are not necessarily incompatible, but they have different sources and will have a profound effect on each other whenever they meet.

I. William Zartman is Jacob Blaustein Professor of International Organization and Conflict Resolution and director of African studies at the Nitze School of Advanced International Studies of the Johns Hopkins University in Washington, D.C. His doctorate in international relations is from Yale. He is past president of the Middle East Studies Association and founding president of the American Institute for Maghrib Studies. He is coeditor and coauthor of Beyond Coercion: The Durability of the Arab State *(1988) and* Polity and Society in the Contemporary North Africa *(1992).*

MUCH of the world finds itself today at the crossroads of two historical political currents. They deal with the highest question of political life: How will individuals and societies decide their own future? Will it be by repeated and updated acts of choice in a rapidly evolving world or by a single referendum on faith in millennial verities? One of these currents is democracy; the other, political Islam. It is unlikely that either current will win totally; more probably, the result will be a turbulent mixture of the two in varying proportions. The outcome, however, will have momentous consequences for the people involved and also for the rest of the world.

The confrontation concerns two rising tides of attention, surging from their own sources, spreading through their own dynamics, and flowing together in many places throughout the world. They meet wherever governance is debated in the land of Islam (*dar al-Islam*), but they also meet in the streets of Paris, in the hidden house of Salman Rushdie, author of *The Satanic Verses*,[1] and in the District Building in Washington, D.C., when it was taken over by the Hanafi sect in 1977. From one side, democracy, flowing from the West since classical Athens, has suddenly resurged as a popular demand and a political criterion in response to the failures of authoritarian rule in both the Second and Third worlds. On the other side, Islamic revival and its extension as a political formula have also arisen, in reaction to the failures of modernization and secular socialism in developing countries.

This is not to say that Islam is the successor to communism as a threat to the West, as some U.S. government spokespersons have suggested.[2] Islam as a personal religious belief has no necessary consequences for either domestic governance or foreign relations, despite the inherent unity of social and religious life in Islamic teaching; it is only when the religious beliefs about piety and correct behavior are promoted as the basis of the political system that they shape the practices of domestic governance and international relations.[3] Even then, as previous articles in this volume have shown, regimes that call themselves Islamic may pursue their interests in cooperation with Western states, as governments in Saudi Arabia, Pakistan, and Mauritania have done, whereas others also calling themselves Islamic may see themselves necessarily and primarily in conflict with the West, as governments in Iran and the Sudan have done. Moreover, in all of these states, opposition parties calling themselves Islamic have contested their own governments.

Nonetheless, as currents of political philosophy, and so of practice, both Western democracy and politi-

---

1. Salman Rushdie, *The Satanic Verses* (New York: Viking, 1988).

2. Barbara Crossette, "US Aide Calls Muslim Militants Big Concern in World," *New York Times*, 1 Jan. 1992; David Ignatius, "Islam in the West's Sights: The Wrong Crusade?" *Washington Post*, 9 Mar. 1992.

3. See James Piscatori, ed., *Islam in the Political Process* (New York: Cambridge University Press, 1983); Adeed Dawisha, ed., *Islam in Foreign Policy* (New York: Cambridge University Press, 1983).

cal Islam are systems of thought and action with their own integrity, neither containing the precepts of the other. In reality, in the earthbound workings of politics and governance, the two sets of ideas and practices challenge and contaminate each other wherever they meet. How to be a democrat in an Islamic state? How to be an Islamicist in a democratic state? How democratic can an Islamic state be? How Islamicist can a democratic state be? All are real and important questions for sincere citizens not only in Saudi Arabia, Pakistan, Iran, the Sudan, and Mauritania but also in France, Nigeria, England, India, the Russian Confederation, and the United States.

ISLAM: THE CULTURAL DIALECTIC

Arab writers and Western analysts have long debated two poles of attraction for Muslim society in its search for a model for the kingdom of believers on earth. One is an Arabo-Islamic model of revealed values, calling for a return to religious inspiration to bring the kingdom of God to his followers. The other is a worldly model of materialist values, designed to bring modern success to the community of believers. To some, the first is seen as authentistic but traditional, and hence outmoded; to others, the second is considered as modern but secularist and often foreign, and thus alien. This dichotomy represents not merely a clash of conceptions and of criteria for desirable conduct but the basis of a dynamic process of conflict and creation that acts as a dialectic.

Out of this clash between thesis and antithesis came not simply a clear-cut victory but rather, in time, a synthesis of the two cultures into a political system that combined the material values of the state with religious values for the individual, as Lapidus records in his article in this volume. In time, however, the synthesis itself has come under attack, usually from a new antithesis in the form of a religious revival that castigates the incumbent political culture for its materialism and worldliness. The confrontation reopens, and is resolved in turn not by a clear defeat of one side but by a new synthesis combining elements of both models. The dynamic goes on.

This dialectic was the basis of the famous analysis of the fourteenth-century Arab philosopher Abdurrahman ibn Khaldun,[4] who saw the dynamic of history as a conflict between desert zealots and urban materialists. The rulers of Arab society became caught up in the corrupting material culture of their capitals, arousing the corrective zealotry of the hardy communities living on the desert fringes of the countries. They emerged from the wilds to conquer the cities and install austere government based on religious principles. But in time the urban life got to them and their rule became a synthesis of the two cultures. In a cyclical fashion, new zealot groups, bound together in their coarse life by a strong spirit of

4. Abdurrahman ibn Khaldun, *An Arab Philosophy of History*, ed. Charles Issawi (New York: Grove Press, 1950); idem, *The Muqaddimah: An Introduction to History*, ed. Franz Rosenthal and N. J. Dawood (Princeton, NJ: Princeton University Press, 1967).

solidarity, again came over the mountains to clean out the urban fleshpots and, in turn, fall into them.

In the coming of Western colonialism, the dialectic took on a new meaning. The materialistic thesis became the colonial society, which drew in imitators fascinated by Western material success but which offended the colonized society because of its foreign and secular worldliness. This time the antithesis came from abroad, through contact with Europe, producing reform governments in the Ottoman core—Tanzimat—and in Tunisia at the end of the nineteenth century. In the Arab world, the clash of values produced a notable synthesis of faith and reason in the works of Jamal al-Din al-Afghani at the same time. However, the corruption of this synthesis through association with reinforced colonial rule in World War I produced a new antithesis in the ideas of Hasan al-Banna and the organization he founded in 1928, the Muslim Brotherhood.

Throughout the depression and World War II, Arab nationalism and Islam combined to form a powerful message to be used against colonial rule. The most successful nationalist leaders, however, were those who could wield that message but could also speak the language of the colonizer and negotiate an agreement for independence to create a modern society based on both national and modern values. North African nationalist leaders such as Allal al-Fassi, the 'alim ("doctor of theology") from Qarawiyin University in Fez who led the Moroccan Independence Party, or Habib Bourguiba, the French-trained lawyer from Monastir who founded the New Constitution Party and for thirty years was Tunisia's first president, embodied the new synthesis of modern Western and Arabo-Muslim national values.

In time, however, this synthesis, too, has come under attack from a new wave of corrective zealotry from the margins of modern society. Bourguiba, President Anwar al-Sadat of Egypt, King Hassan II of Morocco, and, outside the Arab world, Shah Reza Pahlevi of Iran have drawn heavy attack for being too modern, materialistic, secular, tied to the West.[5] Their governments have been charged with corruption, impiety, and neglect of the national culture and heritage but also with disrupting traditional national society in the name of modernization without providing the promised benefits in compensation. Basic values have been destroyed, the city has corrupted the soul, but poverty is more pervasive than it ever was in traditional times, the wealth of the few is more ostentatiously flaunted, and yet the developed world surges ahead, mocking the house of Islam. This is the language of the new antithesis, turned against the former national synthesis of modernity and authenticity and carrying the banner of resurgent political Islam.

These moments of confrontation and challenge to a former synthesis

5. Mohammed Tozy, "Islam and the State in North Africa," in *Polity and Society in Contemporary North Africa*, ed. I. William Zartman and W. Mark Habeeb (Boulder, CO: Westview Press, 1992); Douglas Magnuson, "Islamic Reform in Contemporary Tunisia," in *Tunisia: The Political Economy of Reform*, ed. I. William Zartman (Boulder, CO: Lynn Rienner, 1991).

do not arrive by chance, and it is no accident that Islamicism is on the rise at the end of the twentieth century. Such times occur when the current order is in difficulty and no longer a source of stability and satisfaction. When order, identity, and resources collapse, believers flock back to their religion and seek in it not just a means of salvation in the afterlife, in its normal personal role, but also an answer to unsatisfactory conditions in the earthly life. Previous instances in the collapse of regional orders were associated with the coming of colonialism at the turn of the century and then with its destruction in the aftermath of the world wars, both of them strong markers in the disruption of the twentieth-century world order. Steps in the colonization and decolonization of the Muslim world were disruptions in the sense of identity in the region; people literally no longer knew who they were in the clash between authentism and modernity.[6]

But these moments of confrontation are not merely philosophical matters; they concern material conditions as well, and perhaps above all. When the economy is no longer able to fill the needs of its inhabitants, when the disruptions of modernization dismantle the peasant and traditional urban commercial economies, and when the state falls short in assuming the colonial promise of social services as well as general responsibility for welfare, believ-

ers tend to see the cause in divine retribution for the adoption of alien models and for the corrupt deviance of the rulers, and the corrective in a return to the straight path revealed in God's word.

The antithesis, in the words of Addi's article, comes in the form of a religious utopia, which promises jobs and good government here and now, because its economic program "is in the Quran," in the words of Islamicist campaigners from Algeria and Tunisia to the Sudan and Iran. Because the response bears the stamp of religious legitimacy, it must succeed, again not in terms of bringing salvation in the hereafter—where it cannot be verified—but in terms of bringing successful governance in the temporal immediacy. If it does not succeed immediately, it is not because it is wrong but because it is thwarted by the incompletely eradicated forces of impiety. In the best dialectical terms, the antithesis does not seek a compromising synthesis; it seeks to win.

What is required for a new synthesis, therefore, is a vigorous confrontation between the two forces, modernist and Islamicist, and, eventually, a new figure with a following who can combine the best of the two into a nationalist-modernist program for society. That synthesis cannot come too early, or it weakens the force of the debate that is needed to reveal and purge the depths of corruption and irresponsibility in the modernist thesis and the shallowness of utopia and atavism that is in the religious antithesis. Only then can the scientific understanding of modernism and the mobilizing inspiration of nation-

6. See Albert Memmi, *The Colonizer and the Colonized* (Boston: Beacon Press, 1967); Frantz Fanon, *Black Skin, White Masks* (New York: Grove Press, 1967).

alism be combined to produce a program of commitment and productivity that will meet the need for order, identity, and resources in society.

DEMOCRACY: THE CONSUMMATION OF NATIONALISM

There have been many stirring and insightful treatises on democracy, from which it is necessary to draw two apparently contradictory but defining elements into this discussion. On the one hand, democracy is a procedure. It is the provision of a choice of rulers, at regular intervals, from among contending candidates. It does not guarantee results at any particular time; it is not synonymous with good government in the short run. It is the way in which both good results and mistakes are produced, and the procedure cannot be annulled merely because of a momentary mistake. In the longer run, however, it is the only guarantee of accountability and responsibility by the governors, the only way of correcting mistakes, the only way both of getting the rascals out and reducing rascality while they are in. Democracy is the ability to choose *and* the ability to repent.

On the other hand, democracy is not just procedure. It is government conducted by democrats, by people who live within the rules that provide for repeated choice and who believe that losing does not threaten their security, nor winning guarantee their privilege. While it does not guarantee good results at any one election, it is based on the deeper belief that only by open debate will the best alterna-

tive be brought to light and that open debate will—perhaps with a little lag time—produce the best alternatives. Perhaps the most difficult part of democracy lies in the surrounding attributes that allow for its success, attributes that comprise social preconditions such as literacy and urbanization[7] but also include an adherence to such democratic ideals and values as those indicated previously. Literacy and urbanization have independent sources of development, but adherence to democratic values is hard to come by without experience in democracy, posing a chicken-and-egg dilemma.

Colonialism tried to resolve this dilemma by giving a threefold training in democracy to its subjects. It taught colonial peoples about its own ideals of governance, in terms of parliamentary democracy, for example, or liberty, equality, and fraternity. It gave them something to emulate by showing how colonial governments were responsible to settler populations, a process from which the colonized peoples were excluded. Finally, it forced them to create democratic nationalist movements as the means to achieve national self-determination, since masses and then legitimacy were the only instruments of power that the colonial ruler did not monopolize, unlike arms, money, organization, and international support, for example.

As a result, democracy, too, has come in waves across the world. Early waves came with the great rev-

7. Seymour Martin Lipset, *Political Man* (New York: Doubleday, 1960).

olutions—American and French—of the later eighteenth century, and again with the lesser revolutions—Paris Commune, Hungarian rebellion, Italian revolt, Frankfort assembly—of the mid-nineteenth century. More recent waves were brought by Woodrow Wilson's Fourteen Points and the emphasis on national self-determination as the outcome of World War I and then, as the result of colonial training, through the Atlantic Charter and the collapse of the colonial order after World War II. But colonial training in democratization was necessarily skewed and truncated.

Nationalist movements were the embodiment of the mass democracy of Rousseau's General Will, targeted against the colonial order. They were an exercise in national self-determination, taking government into their own hands and restoring it to the people, often using institutions that the colonizer had brought and left them. But the nationalist governments were so heavy with legitimacy and unity that they were unable to carry the democratic argument to the conclusion it required. They were unable to condone division, debate, parties, and repeated elections between competing candidates, and they were therefore unable to provide for successors to the father of the new emancipated countries. The democracy of the colonial succession remained a dead letter, a truncated exercise.

Thus, at the end of the millennium, half a century or so after independence, there is a new wave of democracy sweeping the world, a renewed pressure for popular sovereignty that has a special meaning for developing polities and for the Muslim countries among them. It is the fulfillment of the logic and promise of the nationalist movement and the culmination of self-determination, in which government itself is determined on regular intervals by the people, and not merely the independence of the state determined in a one-time vote. The current wave of democracy, which began in the late 1980s, draws its major impetus from the collapse of the Communist system of social or totalitarian democracy[8] in the Soviet Union and Eastern Europe and from the culmination of the colonial liberation movement in the exhaustion of the apartheid system of hijacked democracy in South Africa. But it is in the Muslim world where it has a special impact, since it meets the historical current of Islamicism, which is rising at the same time.

In addition to its importance as the culmination of the nationalist movement, the current wave of democracy gains significance from two other aspects in the operation of the postcolonial state. One is the enormous expansion of the functions of the state, into areas of socioeconomic services and regulations that far exceed the scope of state activities in the precolonial or even colonial times. Typically, in the Third and especially the Muslim worlds, the state is the largest employer and the largest investor; nearly all university faculties are civil servants and all students live on state subsidies, expecting—

8. J. L. Talmon, *The Origins of Totalitarian Democracy* (Boulder, CO: Westview Press, 1985).

and sometimes guaranteed—state jobs upon graduation. Basic food staples are subsidized to a low consumer price, and medical treatment, like education, is free or low-cost. But it is also a source of intrusive regulations, as a legislator of labor laws, currency controls, exit visas, curriculum reforms, and social norms. As a result, the state is an important prize for democratic—or any other—control and not just a source of privilege for a ruling few.

Yet the other element in the struggle for the state is that in fact it has been viewed in the Arab world—and elsewhere in the Third World—as the hunting preserve of the few, alienated from the people, ruling not so much by coercion as by manipulation, and without the charismatic leaders who dominated Arab politics in the 1950s and 1960s. The decade of the 1980s saw significant outbursts of popular disapproval in most Arab countries, protesting not only shortfalls in goods and services provided by the government but a lack of trust and faith in the leaders themselves. Riots in 1981 and 1984 in Casablanca and 1990-91 in northern Morocco, in 1986 in Constantine and then 1988 throughout Algeria, in 1984 in Tunis, in 1986 in Cairo and other cities of Egypt, in 1989 in Amman, and in 1986 in the Great Mosque in Mecca and, of course, the revolution of 1979 in Iran are all strident and bloody instances of popular protest against the governors of the Muslim Middle East.

Alienated rulers controlling a powerful state and confronting a sudden rise in the pressures for democracy as the consummation of nationalist self-determination have made for a most explosive combination. Unfortunately for a lasting commitment to democratic values, the situation has meant that democracy is not viewed merely as a healthy procedure but as a guarantee of the results that the previous system failed to produce. That is a tough challenge to throw in the face of a new system of government in which its practitioners have had little experience, at a time of falling foreign aid, unfavorable terms of trade, and shrinking and redirected investment. Democracy in the Middle East, and elsewhere in the Third World, is threatened with becoming yet another system of government that did not produce the expected results, because so much is expected of it. If the democratic resurgence threatens incumbent authoritarians in the Muslim world, the charismatic demagogue in turn threatens to deform democracy into xenophobic populism. But the most powerful form of this challenge is political Islam, which promises the restoration of morality, authenticity, and earthly success and the exclusion of corruption and error, backed by God's word as a guide and as a guarantee.

DEMOCRACY AND ISLAM

There is no inherent incompatibility between democracy and Islam. Like all scripture, the Quran can be interpreted to support many different types of political behavior and systems of government. It contains no direct support for democracy, the closest statement being an indication that "what is with God is better and more lasting for those . . . who [conduct] their affairs by mutual consultation [*shura*]."[9] As would be expected, its emphasis lies much more on the pious qualities expected of a ruler than on the way in which rulers should be chosen. As indicated at the outset, each of the two currents comes from different sources and addresses different issues.

The conflict arises when the particular form of political Islam precludes the procedural essence of democracy, the repeated provision of debate and choice between a free range of options. When political Islam, in the name of cleaning out the stables of corruption and alienation, promises to install a system where only those who subscribe to the true path are allowed into the contest for power, then the incompatibility arises. When parties led by devoted leaders inspired by religious beliefs vie among others for a role in government, there is no incompatibility. But when the party arrogates for itself the mantle of the national religion, monopolizing its symbols and delegitimizing its opponents, open democratic debate and the guarantee of future free elections are hard to insure.

Islamic parties and regimes are usually rather straightforward about their intentions, although not always to the Western press. Although the leaders of the Algerian Islamic Salvation Front (FIS) profess their devotion to democracy before Western journalists, they also tell local audi-

9. Quran 42:36, 38; this *sura* ("chapter") is named "*al-shura*" because of the reference to discussion that it contains.

ences that "democracy is heresy" and "all parties who subscribe to the Way can compete freely," clear statements of incompatibility with democracy. It should be remembered that the position of democracy and that of political Islam on the matter of open debate are similar but different in an important way. Both maintain that truth will prevail in open debate, but democrats are proponents of the debate whereas Islamicists are proponents of the Truth.

More complex is the usual division of Islamic parties into a moderate, usually visible leadership and a radical militant wing, often underground, creating a situation where, as in any revolutionary movement, the moderate leadership is controlled and can eventually be replaced by the militants once its usefulness in achieving power is spent. Thus the compatibility of political Islam and democracy must be judged not only by public statements but also by an analysis of probable political dynamics.

While the confrontation is going on, what can be done to create conditions for a functioning synthesis, so that democracy can be preserved in the presence of political Islam rather than being destroyed by it? One way, adopted by most Muslim countries, is through constitutional provisions declaring Islam to be the national religion but prohibiting Islamic parties, often along with ethnic and other religious parties. Many Muslim states' constitutions have both provisions—including Algeria, where the FIS was authorized in 1989 despite its unconstitutionality! A similar method involves the use of a national charter of agreed principles to register a national consensus of values on which participation and competition can be based. This device has been used both in Egypt and in Tunisia, and in the latter case included an Islamicist representative as a signatory but did not permit the legalization of the Islamicist party.

A second measure is the development of a credible opposition. The crisis in the current confrontations between a decrepit authoritarian regime and a new Islamicist opposition arises from the absence of alternatives. In Algeria, in the elections of 1990 and 1991—and the canceled elections of 1992—it was not that the FIS won but that the discredit of the old single party, the National Liberation Front, left no party known and attractive enough to draw the votes. As a result, the FIS, mobilizing all the voters it could, won 47 percent of the votes cast but only 25 percent of the eligible voters. The crisis came from the fact that there was no party that could win majority support from the nation and, more specifically, that could even draw out the majority of the population to vote. In Tunisia and Egypt, strong government parties, even if tied to the old regime, handily overcame Islamicist opposition, running as independents in Tunisia in 1989 and among several parties in Egypt in 1990 and 1991. But in both countries, third parties, try as they did, were too new, inexperienced, and unknown to present a serious challenge to the incumbents, and the old parties were hampered by ties to previous regimes. Yet, as the experience of Iran under the Shah

shows, incumbents are in a poor position to help develop credible oppositions to their own regimes.

A third measure is to use the technicalities of elections to encourage pluralism and limit the hold that an Islamicist party could gain on the government apparatus. An electoral system of proportional representation gives seats to smaller parties and prevents an overemphasis of the majority. It often leads to coalition governments and less coherent policies, however. Majoritarian systems, either for single-member districts or for large-constituency lists, tend to focus on prominent alternatives, to the underrepresentation of small and regional parties. Establishment of a minimum percentage for inclusion, usually set between 5 and 8 percent, keeps tiny parties from producing many splinters and overvalued coalition partners. Parties may be required to show clientele or candidates in all regions or all voting districts, in order to establish their national character. These and other aspects of election laws can be used to limit extremist parties, encourage coalitions, eliminate splinters, and strengthen credible options.

A fourth measure would be to delay political democracy until its preconditions are established or at least begun. Literacy levels and urban concentrations have been mentioned as social requisites, but other political correlates of democracy include a free and pluralistic press, an independent judiciary, autonomous associations including labor unions and public affairs discussion groups, and respect for civil liberties and human rights. The problem is that these conditions are as difficult to establish as free elections themselves and more difficult to maintain. Their existence does not guarantee their continuity, and their imperfection can be too easily used as a pretext to postpone the exercise of democracy that would help perpetuate them. Yet without these conditions, it is hard to maintain the democratic values that undergird free elections. The bundle of measures should go together, and it is important to begin wherever one can.

A fifth measure would be to practice the forms of democracy whenever scheduled, let the most popular—including the Islamicists—win, and let them learn democracy on the job. The lesson of many experiments with radical groups is that responsibility moderates, but that lesson is not absolute. Another lesson is that experiments in moderating revolutionary groups tend to take up to a generation, as the Iranian experience shows. Such experiments make for exciting stuff for social science analysts, but they are hard on the subject populations and disruptive for the world around them. The dialectical conflict within Islam and the confrontation of the two waves of political Islam and democracy also have their costs. Ultimately, it is the populations themselves, acting as masses or as political leaders, who will have to make the choice of which costs to bear.

Book Department

INTERNATIONAL RELATIONS AND POLITICS

OBERDORFER, DON. *The Turn: From the Cold War to a New Era: The United States and the Soviet Union, 1983-1990.* Pp. 514. New York: Poseidon Press, 1991. $25.00.

FEINBERG, RICHARD F. et al. *From Confrontation to Cooperation: U.S. and Soviet Aid to Developing Countries.* Pp. 229. New Brunswick, NJ: Transaction Books, 1991. $24.95. Paperbound, $15.95.

These two very different books share the commonality of looking at the end of the Cold War and its consequences for the operation of the international system. In terms of style, audience, scope, and intent, however, they are quite different.

Don Oberdorfer's *Turn* is the larger of the two, in just about every sense. Oberdorfer is a *Washington Post* correspondent by trade, and in his professional endeavors, he attended and covered many of the events that cumulated to produce the dramatic change—the "turn" —in Soviet-American relations. His methodology, in addition to direct observation, was to read extensively in the secondary literature but, primarily, to interview an astounding array of current and former governmental officials—both American and Soviet—to whom his position gave him access.

The result is a panoramic chronology of the period beginning basically with the rise of Gorbachev and carrying through 1990. Oberdorfer's purpose is "instant," if provisional, history of the kind found in Robert Woodward's *Commanders*, and the book is very similar in style and impact to Woodward's. Undoubtedly, it will receive the same mixture of reaction.

As a first attempt at the history of this epoch—and given that there is more to be added in the future—it is an insightful chronology that adds some richness and detail to what we knew or suspected. His depiction of the Reagan-Gorbachev summit at Reykjavik and how close the two men actually came to agreeing to essential nuclear disarmament reveals how two people at the top can nearly change the world essentially without consulting anyone else. The evolution of the personal relationships between Gorbachev and both Presidents Reagan and Bush adds texture to our understanding of how the world has changed.

This is a very rich, even heavy book, but it is a fascinating read. Small insights abound; I was particularly fascinated to learn that one of the people most responsible for convincing Gorbachev of the need to invest in high technology was no less than Secretary of State George Shultz.

This book will be widely read both for its content and for its highly readable style. Oberdorfer has gone out of his way to avoid interpreting and editorializing on events. Although he recognizes this to be an interim history of the era, it is still a highly valuable source.

The Feinberg et al. volume is a good bit narrower and more specialized. As its subtitle suggests, it is an investigation of how the Americans and Soviets can cooperate in providing developmental assistance to the Third World in the future. Its unique perspective is that it is the product of a conference under the joint auspices of the Overseas Development Council and the Institute of World Economy and International Relations of the USSR Academy of Sciences.

The book is both an analysis and an advocacy of future joint ventures. In the early chapters, Soviet and American scholars look at how they operated competitively in the past and move on to how they may be able to cooperate in the post-Cold War world. When the analysis moves to advocacy, it loses some of its rigor; for instance, the participants argue that funds spent on military competition during the Cold War might now be used for funding developmental assistance.

This book clearly has a much more limited audience. Moreover, the timing of its appearance could hardly have been worse, since its suggestions for collaboration are almost certainly going to evaporate as rapidly as has the former Soviet Union itself. Still, it is an interesting example of just how far the Cold War relationship has moved away from confrontation toward cooperation.

DONALD M. SNOW

University of Alabama
Birmingham

TRACHTENBERG, MARC. *History and Strategy*. Pp. xii, 292. Princeton, NJ: Princeton University Press, 1991. $44.50. Paperbound, $14.92.

In recent years it has been frequently argued that the most interesting scholarship is appearing along the interstices between traditionally defined disciplines. Marc Trachtenberg's brilliant and richly detailed book provides a superb example of this phenomenon. Trachtenberg was trained as a historian, and his first, highly regarded, book dealt with a classic topic in diplomatic history, the issue of reparations after the First World War.

History and Strategy, a series of discrete essays, is in large measure a sophisticated dialogue between diplomatic history and political science, focusing on American nuclear policy and strategy between 1945 and the late 1960s. Included are three important studies of how that strategy was implemented in moments of crisis. Trachtenberg pays close attention to the tremendously important literature on strategic theory, produced by a hybrid breed of intellectuals associated with governmental and private think tanks and various university institutes of advanced study, who are closest to political scientists in method and approach.

The first essay deals with strategic thought in America between 1952 and 1966. It is a powerful and original analysis of the influential writings of such theorists as Bernard Brodie, Thomas Schelling, and Albert Wohlstetter, mostly affiliated with the RAND Corporation. All the other essays, except the second, build upon the premises developed in this more theoretical chapter. The studies of the Berlin Crisis and the Cuban Missile Crisis offer convincing reconstructions of terrifying moments in our recent history. Trachtenberg uses recently declassified material most effectively, and he ingeniously works around key documents that are still classified, making plausible hypotheses about what actually transpired. His inferences—based, of course, upon very different and much less reliable evidence—about Soviet attitudes and responses during various crises are remarkably persuasive.

My one regret is that Trachtenberg— or his editors—felt obliged to include his 52-page essay on the coming of World War I, which in itself is an excellent overview of one of what remains probably the greatest historical controversy of this century, if not of all time. But it does not fit with the rest of the book and should have been published separately. A slimmer but more satisfyingly structured volume would have resulted.

Trachtenberg's book was completed before the dramatic reductions in nuclear weapons put into effect by Presidents Bush and Gorbachev in the fall of 1991. As of this writing, in late November 1991, the Doomsday Clock has just been reset at 17 minutes before midnight, the best setting since this unnerving, if effective, graphic image began to appear in the *Bulletin of the Atomic Scientists* more than forty years ago. Trachtenberg warns us that in the more relaxed climate of the late 1980s Americans were suffering from "what can only be called an extraordinary case of collective nuclear amnesia." This careful, judicious reconstruction of a time when the hands on that clock were much closer to midnight and global catastrophe goes a long way toward helping us recover

from that amnesia. Trachtenberg's book should be widely read and debated by academics and political and military leaders alike.

DAVID L. SCHALK

Vassar College
Poughkeepsie
New York

AFRICA, ASIA, AND LATIN AMERICA

FORESTA, RONALD A. *Amazon Conservation in the Age of Development: The Limits of Providence.* Pp. x, 366. Gainesville: University of Florida Press, 1991. $49.95.

Here is a specialized study that richly deserves a readership far wider than those persons customarily interested in a book by a geographer about conservation in one foreign river valley, albeit the world's largest one. On a topic where advocacy writings often bordering on the polemical have enjoyed much greater attention than those founded on serious and objective scholarship, Ronald Foresta has combined rigorous research with eminently sensible analysis in a readable work that goes far to frame the increasingly salient issue of tropical rain forest preservation in truly meaningful terms. With the 1992 world ecology conference having taken place in June in Rio de Janeiro, this well-grounded study could hardly be more timely. Although it carries the detailed story of Brazilian Amazon programs only through the mid-1980s, Foresta's impressively documented book provides all the elements necessary to place the present policy debate in proper focus and set the broader philosophical issues in perspective.

Foresta is highly concerned with putting biological conservation into a broader sociopolitical context. To this end, he closely examines the programs and activities of Brazil's Forest Development Institute and environment secretary within the immense area of the Amazon basin, always with an eye for lessons from this experience that can be applied to successful strategies for conservation in the future. Following an overview through the 1970s in his first three chapters, Foresta focuses upon the difficult and only partially successful task of developing a continuing political constituency for conservation and consolidating the gains made to 1980. He perceptively portrays the heavy impact of economic and political interests whenever conservation and development clashed frontally. In large part owing to the economic recession of the late part of the 1980s, the long-awaited return to civilian democratic politics after 1985 resulted in loss of headway by the Brazilian conservation movement rather than the gains that environmentalists had expected. Although Foresta does not foresee a major upsurge in domestic political support for conservation in the years immediately ahead, he does believe that external pressures will have a significant positive impact.

Important as this book is to the comparative study of conservation, it is equally valuable as a case study of public policymaking in Brazil over a time span of two decades, for Dr. Foresta has developed a competence with respect to Brazilian government and politics extremely rare among scholars outside the closely related disciplines of political science, sociology, and economics. Indeed, his grasp of political factors involved in policy toward the Amazon—closer to masterful than merely competent—surpasses that of all but the best of the latter and the cream of historians working on Brazil.

RONALD M. SCHNEIDER

Queens College
Flushing
New York

HAERI, SHAHLA. *Law of Desire: Temporary Marriage in Shi'a Islam.* Pp. xiii, 256. Syracuse, NY: Syracuse University Press, 1989. No price.

Shahla Haeri's study of the unique Shi'a Muslim practice of temporary marriage has, in the short time since its publication, already become a classic work. This should ideally be the fate of every well-researched, well-written book. But Haeri's study has the added attraction of being virtually the only study of this social institution—exotic even within the world of Islam, since it is prohibited by Sunni Muslim law.

Haeri's study is masterful because she is able to use the investigation of temporary marriage to explore so many aspects of Iranian society: male-female relationships, Shi'a-Sunni religious divisions, and the nature of contract in Islamic legal codes. She is also able to shed light on processes of social adaptation and modernization through exploration of the ways in which Iranians have adapted this institution to contemporary use.

In Shi'a Islam, men and women may enter into temporary contract marriages (*mut'a*, or, more popularly, *sigheh* marriage) at any time. These marriages differ from "permanent" marriages (*nikah*, or, more popularly, *'aqd*). Here English fails in simple translation, since both *sigheh* and *'aqd* literally mean "contract." It is the nature of the contract that differentiates temporary from permanent marriages.

Sigheh marriages differ from *'aqd* marriages first in that they are contracted for a predetermined length ranging from a few minutes to a hundred years or more. Second, a man may have an unlimited number of these marriages simultaneously, whereas he may contract only four permanent marriages at one time. Third, since the temporary marriages are contracted, the Quranic restrictions and limitations on permanent marriage regarding paternal and spousal permission, inheritance, divorce, and equal treatment of multiple wives are effectively not operative or are constructed differently. The most intriguing aspect of the two forms of contracts, as Haeri demonstrates, is that permanent marriage is constructed as a contract of sale whereas temporary marriage is constructed as a contract of lease. In both cases, specific payment must be made as part of the contract. *Mut'a* marriage, if sexual in nature, carries the additional restriction that the woman must wait nine months before contracting a new relationship, presumably to determine paternity. In terms of control of personal choice, perhaps the crucial difference is that permanent marriage is a contract between the father of the bride and the groom (and his family), publicly written and recorded, whereas temporary marriage is a direct contract between a man and a woman that may be written but that can be only a private verbal agreement.

Sigheh marriage is most often sexual in nature, and it has been institutionalized in a number of ways. Often the marriages are contracted in shrines, one location where the sexes can mix freely. Here men and women approach each other and agree to a relationship. This kind of liaison is often associated with prostitution and is the source of much public ambiguity about *mut'a* marriage.

Not all temporary marriage is suspect, though. One of the most frequent uses of the institution is for the family to hire a maid and make her a *sigheh* wife to the husband of the house or, occasionally, to a teenage son. Haeri reports that for the maid, being a *sigheh* wife confers additional status and solves a social problem concerning the presence of an unrelated female in the house. A *sigheh* marriage can also become a kind of surrogate motherhood in the case where a permanent wife is barren.

The temporary marriage can also be nonsexual in nature. This is a fascinating twist both in human relations and in legal scholarship, for, as Haeri states: "nonsexual *sigheh* is truly a product of popular 'imagination.' It is continually improvised by people who come face to face with moral barriers imposed by the paradigm of sex segregation." In one case cited by Haeri, a family traveling with the wife's widowed aunt contracted a *sigheh* marriage between the elderly woman and the couple's two-year-old son so that they could travel together in a train compartment without the need for the aunt to veil herself before the husband, since the marriage made her his daughter-in-law. In revolutionary Iran, women and men working in rural areas on development projects contracted nonsexual *sigheh* marriages for the duration of their projects so that they could work together with no threat of impropriety. Clearly, the use of this institution is limited only by the imagination. Indeed, in post-Khomeini Iran, *sigheh* marriage is seen by religious officials as a direct benefit of the Iranian revolution. It is also used as a defense against overzealous officials anxious to arrest people for moral impropriety. Haeri reports one Islamic notary who issues *sigheh* documents to his friends to present to the police whenever questioned about their association with a female.

Haeri's book would be excellent if it dealt only with these institutional and legal matters, but she also appends a set of wonderful biographical sketches of women and men who have entered into *sigheh* relationships. This gives the entire institution a human face. The women in Haeri's sketches universally show vulnerability and a need for protection both as a way of attracting men and as a justification for *sigheh* relationships when permanent marriage has not been possible. For both men and women, however, eroticism is an explicit component in the decision to contract these kinds of marriages. Both men and women seem to initiate the suggestion to enter into the relationship.

This book raises some penetrating questions about women in Iran. *Sigheh* marriage uncovers a range of contradiction about women and their status. They are revealed as both active and passive socially and sexually, both helpless and cunning, independent and dependent, controlled and free. There is no easy resolution to the contradictions inherent in these gender issues, but Haeri has used this investigation to provide a unique and provocative view of their complexity.

WILLIAM O. BEEMAN

Brown University
Providence
Rhode Island

HOURANI, ALBERT. *A History of the Arab Peoples*. Pp. xx, 551. Cambridge, MA: Harvard University Press, Belknap Press, 1991. $24.95.

Albert Hourani, a doyen of Middle East scholarship whose previous works have become required for students of the region, has contributed still another volume that should be required reading for those with more than a passing interest in the subject. Unlike his previous studies, this is not a piece of original research but a summary of his own broad perspectives covering not only conventional history but the economic, cultural, and intellectual history of the Arab peoples from the seventh to the late twentieth centuries.

The book distills from the rich history of the Arab world the essence of most major trends and developments since the rise of Islam to the upheavals throughout the region during the 1980s. What emerges is a luxuriant tapestry blending with unique coherence a variety of historical trends. These include descriptions of changes in regimes, governments, leaders, and intellectual currents; scientific progress, literature, and the arts; and the progress of economic development or the lack of it. Few other single-volume surveys of the region have so skillfully integrated these diverse aspects of Arab and Middle Eastern history.

The 26 chapters are divided into five parts covering Islam from the seventh to tenth centuries, medieval Islam from the eleventh to the fifteenth, the Ottoman era from the sixteenth to the eighteenth, European empire building in the region from 1800 to the eve of World War II, and the emergence of independent Arab states since 1939. Within each of these five principal divisions, chapters are devoted to the evolution of Islam, everyday life as lived by the common person, Middle Eastern perspectives of the outer world, and Western perspectives of the Middle East. The role of non-Arabs and non-Muslims is described as is the status of women, themes not generally treated in survey histories of the Middle East.

Subjects such as the Arab-Israeli conflict are covered objectively but not without critical insight. The recent popularization of emphasis on Islamic revival/fundamentalism is avoided. Indeed, a unifying thread in the total history of Arab peoples since the seventh century has been Islam in one form or another, as Hourani and most other scholars make plain.

The book includes over thirty pages of photo illustrations, twenty pages of maps, genealogies of principal dynasties, a general index and index of terms, and a thirty-page, chapter-by-chapter bibliography. Since the book is not intended as a work of original scholarship, notes are sparse, some chapters having none at all.

DON PERETZ

State University of New York
Binghamton

HUNTER, F. ROBERT. *The Palestinian Uprising: A War by Other Means.* Pp. xx, 312. Berkeley: University of California Press, 1991. $24.95.

F. Robert Hunter's analysis of the Palestinian *intifada* from December 1987 through August 1989 focuses on five related topics: the events of the *intifada* itself; the mobilization of the Palestinian community in the occupied territories; the response of the Palestine Liberation Organization and its constituent organizations; Israeli government attempts to combat the *intifada*; and the diplomatic activity aimed at starting negotiations between Israel, Palestinians, and other Arab countries. The work is based primarily on newspaper accounts and on interviews with Palestinian and Israeli informants that Hunter conducted during 1988 and 1989. The broad scope of Hunter's concerns, the limited duration of his investigation, his reliance on available published sources, and questions about his use of informants combine to make his book valuable more for the many questions it raises than for the answers it provides.

Hunter's most interesting discussion focuses on the mobilization of Palestinian society to develop a national and local *intifada* leadership. Hunter argues that one important result of the *intifada* was some restructuring of Palestinian society due to the weakening of many economic links between Israel and the territories, primarily those based on the employment of Palestinians in Israel. But he never presents systematic data that would indicate the extent of this disengagement or the degree to which local initiatives actually compensated Palestinians for losses resulting from the breakdown of cross-Green Line employment and commercial ties.

Hunter recognizes the difficulties of studying history in the making, and his use of Palestinian informants reflects them. It is hard to evaluate the words of anonymous sources, though Hunter makes some attempt to do so. His subtitle, "A War by Other Means," can also apply to what outsiders are told.

Hunter's analysis of Israel often lacks the sensitivity he displays to the intricacies of Palestinian society. His view of "oriental" Jews in Israeli politics, for example, is simplistic. He treats Israel and Palestinians almost exclusively as opposing communities, emphasizing how their long joint history has kept them apart but not appreciating sufficiently how it has also joined them.

A book such as this cannot help being overtaken by events. In an epilogue, Hunter speculates that the *intifada* "has already delivered what it can. Political change can now come only from the brokers outside, the United States, the Soviet Union, and other powers." But the Soviet Union is no more, and its collapse sent more than 350,000 Jews to Israel in the past two years. It remains to be seen whether the peace talks that began in Madrid will reflect these changes.

CHARLES S. KAMEN

University of Connecticut
Storrs

KOHLI, ATUL. *Democracy and Discontent: India's Growing Crisis of Governability.* Pp. xi, 420. New York: Cambridge University Press, 1990. $59.50. Paperbound, $17.95.

Democracy and Discontent is an important book, not only for the study of India but also for comparison with other Third World countries and the operation of democratic systems in the developing world. Atul Kohli states that his study is analytical, but "two policy prescriptions emerge from the discussion: the need to strengthen the organizations of the major parties, and the need to narrow the gap between the state's commitments and capabilities."

In reaching these policy recommendations, Kohli follows a path begun by Myron Weiner in his *Party Building in a New Nation: The Indian National Congress* (Chicago: University of Chicago Press, 1967). Weiner chose five districts for study: Kheda, Gujarat; Belgaun, Karnataka; Guntur, Andhra Pradesh; Madurai, Tamil Nadu; and Calcutta, West Bengal. There was an obvious flaw in this selection in that none of the districts were from the "Hindi heartland." Kohli, deliberately following Weiner, re-studied the same districts. He mentions in a footnote (p. 184) that he also investigated Deoria in Uttar Pradesh but little of the results of the investigation are contained in the note. He does, however, add state-level studies on Bihar, which is often selected as a disaster area for governance; Gujarat; and West Bengal, concluding, as have others, that Communist-led West Bengal now may well be the best-governed state in India. He also looks at two national issues: economic liberalization and the Punjab crisis. His analyses are excellent, as were Weiner's almost 25 years earlier.

Kohli's fieldwork was done in the mid and late 1980s. His conclusions might be even more dismal had he seen the two consecutive failures of the Congress Party to gain parliamentary majorities. Indira Gandhi's populism—displaying the gap between commitments and capabilities—and her failure to maintain the party organization, Sanjay Gandhi's "goons," and Rajiv Gandhi's "incompetence" figure prominently in the analysis, although he adds in reference to Indira: "Would a different leader have done things very differently?"

Kohli cites—correctly in my view—four factors that have been key to the "crisis of governability": poorly organized

and deteriorating political parties, undisciplined mobilization of various groups, conflict between classes, and the weakness of leaders.

Kohli's work should lead the way to further country-specific studies on the ability of state systems to govern and to do so in a democratic framework. South Asia might be a good place to begin, with the laboratories of Bangladesh, Pakistan, and Sri Lanka close at hand and each with some type of democratic system; however, these may be perverted by their leaders.

CRAIG BAXTER

Juniata College
Huntingdon
Pennsylvania

NESTER, WILLIAM R. *The Foundation of Japanese Power: Continuities, Changes, Challenges.* Pp. 418. Armonk, NY: M. E. Sharpe, 1991. $49.95.

William Nester provides an in-depth description and analysis of the Japanese political economy since World War II. He describes in detail the neomercantilist policies designed and implemented by the conservative political, bureaucratic, and corporate elites since 1945. These policies, many of them initiated or made possible by the U.S. occupation, focus almost single-mindedly on spurring Japanese economic growth with little regard to their consequences for other nations, the global environment, or even for the Japanese people.

Nester rejects the currently popular "Japan is unique," "Japan, Inc.," and "Japan as number one" theories as well as neoclassical theories of the Japanese political and economic development "miracles." The neomercantilist policies forged by Japan's elites have drawn upon existing institutions, culture, and values, but they are not in any sense a natural or inevitable outgrowth or carryover of a "samurai ethic," Japanese Confucianism, or the "Japanese spirit." Japanese workers, for example, work the longest hours in the industrialized world not because the workers, imbued with a Japanese spirit, are exceptionally loyal and committed but because the system of labor discipline leaves them little opportunity to resist employers' demands that they work these hours. Similarly, the impressive household savings rate is shown to be the product of government and industrial policies, not culture.

Charges of Japan bashing leveled against any critics of Japanese policies and practices are revealed as a carefully orchestrated lobbying effort that has served well to minimize American and other foreign retaliation against Japan's protectionist trade practices. Myriad complex nontariff barriers, erected expressly to protect the Japanese domestic market from foreign penetration, keep profits high for Japanese businesses, keep foreign countries from obtaining more than a minuscule market share in Japan, and encourage foreign countries to sell their technology to Japanese companies as a substitute for direct access to the Japanese market.

Japanese consumers pay much higher prices than do residents of other industrialized countries. The per capita income of Japanese people is the second highest in the world at $19,500, but the price parity purchasing value of that income reduces them to a more moderate $13,000. Japanese people are convinced to accept these high prices through government- and business-sponsored campaigns portraying foreign goods as inferior, tainted, and dangerous.

The analysis in this book is thorough, accurate, and detailed. Nester draws upon the best of current scholarship in his area and synthesizes and organizes it into a valuable introduction of the Japa-

nese political economy. There is little in the book that would be new to another specialist in the area, but it is an excellent choice for the nonspecialist who really wants to understand how Japan got to where it is today, what lies behind its seeming miracles, and what implications this has for the future for all of us.

CHARLOTTE G. O'KELLY

Providence College
Rhode Island

TAPPER, NANCY. *Bartered Brides: Politics, Gender and Marriage in an Afghan Tribal Society*. Pp. xx, 309. New York: Cambridge University Press, 1991. $54.50.

Nancy Tapper's book describes marriage in detail among the Maduzai, a subtribe of the Durrani Pashtuns of northwestern Afghanistan. The book's aim is to show marriage as a means of managing political conflict. The economic and political ideal of a household, argues Tapper, is independence, self-sufficiency, and noninterference from outsiders. Households compete vehemently for the control of resources and prestige, which are obtained by maintaining male unity and cooperation in a household. Hence marriages, inextricable from politics, are an attempt to maintain this unity, particularly among closest agnates, who constitute the greatest potential threat to each other. Strict endogamy is thus the rule.

Tapper divides the book into four parts. The first is introductory, providing background information on her own fieldwork, on marriage in the Middle East, and on the Durrani of the Saripul region. Part 2 describes the indigenous classification of social groups and how it is reinforced by marriage practices.

Part 3 includes the most detailed description of marriage. First, marriage types are discussed in terms of bride-price and exchange. The direct exchange of women for women, claims Tapper, is done to regulate the increasing competition between households, particularly close agnatic households. Ceremonies, gift exchange, and marriage choice are all discussed as political moves between households.

The last part of the book concerns a household's ability to control its resources, especially in terms of marriage and the behavior of women. The lack of political and economic control in weak household heads is reflected in their corresponding lack of control over their wives and daughters. Powerful men, on the contrary, exercise tight control over their women, who have the fewest means of alternative personal expression or of improving their situation.

Tapper provides a fifty-year marital history between several leading Maduzai families, including bride-prices, feuds, deaths, and consequent marriages. This narrative clearly shows the variety of marriages and how most marriages are contingent on those that have preceded them.

Several issues remain ill defined throughout this work. First, the precise total length of fieldwork, conducted between 1970 and 1977, is not stated. The book reads like a grammar of rules, a myriad of general cultural facts charted onto tables and figures, which are at times difficult and time-consuming to follow. More disturbing is the lack of mention as to informants. It seems that a work dealing with gender would at least specify whether the voice behind quoted statements and opinions is male or female.

This last criticism leads to what is perhaps the book's greatest shortcoming: the lack of any feminine voice. Tapper claims that she worked among women, gained their trust, and even taped much material. Yet, the cases, the marital history, the general voice of the book are all given from male leaders' accounts, with

the assumption that women have no real say. This is surprising and disappointing from a woman researcher who could have had access to, and might have at least mentioned, women's perceptions of marriage. Despite her in-depth discussion of exchange, Tapper speaks of women as objects of exchange, with no mention of exchanges between women. This solely male perspective raises doubts as to how much fieldwork was actually done with women.

Nonetheless, this long-awaited and long-needed book is a great contribution to the literature on marriage practices in the Middle East and certainly increases our awareness of the major differences between Arab and Mediterranean Islamic models, on the one hand, and Eastern Muslim models, on the other.

BENEDICTE GRIMA

University of Pennsylvania
Philadelphia

VAILLANT, JANET G. *Black, French, and African: A Life of Leopold Sedar Senghor.* Pp. 388. Cambridge, MA: Harvard University Press, 1990. $29.95.

Janet G. Vaillant, associate director of the Soviet and East European Language and Area Center at Harvard University, seems well qualified to give the reader a fascinating account of one of Africa's foremost leaders, Léopold Sédar Senghor. Although Africa is not an area of her expertise, Vaillant presents a vivid composite portrait of Senghor, not only as an individual African but also as a national and continental leader in search of solutions to the problems of a continent desperately in need of new directions. The environment that exists at Harvard University to promote international studies has combined with her experiences at Queens College, Barbados, Radcliffe, and

Boston University to give Vaillant an unquestionably high level of knowledge about world leaders, which she has adequately utilized to give the reader a credible narrative of Léopold Senghor.

To understand and appreciate Vaillant's credibility as Senghor's biographer, one needs to follow closely the sequence of events in his life that she discusses so well. His birth in October 1906, his early education in Senegal, the recognition by his teachers of his ability and their assisting him in his endeavors to secure more education in France beginning in 1925, his determination to acquire basic elements of French culture in order to function in the colonial setting, his serving as president of Senegal from 1960 to 1980, and his election to the prestigious Académie française for his literary contribution to the advancement of the French culture are among the major events that Vaillant captures to portray Senghor as a national leader who has demonstrated commitment to the emergence of a democratic society.

In Vaillant's depiction of this aspect of Senghor as his major contribution to the development of postcolonial Africa lies the sad contradiction so characteristic of "successful" Africans who were products of both colonial conditions and their own cultural background. Although Vaillant discusses the relationships that existed between Senghor's personality, his family background, his literary efforts, and his political philosophy and behavior to suggest the organized mind of an individual who sees his place in society as being determined by a combination of what he is and what he does, one is still struck by the extent of the contradiction that is tragically part of the character of most African leaders. This contradiction has taken a heavy toll on Senghor.

On the one hand, Senghor systematically sought to accommodate himself to the French culture in order not only to survive and function under oppressive colonial conditions but also to assert himself in a fashion that compelled him to question the values of his own African cultural identity. From his arrival in France in 1920, Senghor decided that his future was inseparably intertwined with anything French. Any relationships that he might have with his native Senegal were intended to reinforce his perception of himself as a French national whose origins were African. Slowly Senghor began to drift into the dark shadows of the colonial corridors, where his acceptance by the French was by no means certain and his relationships with his own people were strained beyond repair. This is the dilemma that many educated Africans face.

On the other hand, realizing that he had lost contact with himself and his own people, Senghor groped for rescue where there was none. Claiming in 1948 that "Western technology and culture might set in motion change that would shake African society to its foundations," Senghor used his French cultural discomfort to launch a movement he called Negritude to redirect the thought process to stress what he called positive attributes of African culture, including socialist ideological precepts and claims of rejection of the capitalist and material greed of the West. But when he was seeking his own place within the French cultural setting and the African sense of collective destiny, Senghor "castigated as deserters of Negritude those Africans who espoused Marxism." This contradiction alienated Senghor and badly tarnished his image as a continental leader seeking to assert his leadership role in a tragic vacuum created by Nkrumah's demise.

That Senghor would never fully recover from this crushing dilemma suggests the confused mind of an individual whose perception of self had been lost in the inevitable cultural conflict cast in a limiting environment. Senghor was losing both himself and the course he had charted for his nation. Was he French, black, or African? Senghor did not seem to know. This is the reason why Vaillant entitles the book the way she does. In 1984, four years after Senghor had retired as president of Senegal and sensing the predicament in which he found himself, the French did what they thought they had to do to restore the tarnished image of their favorite African cultural agent and give him back some of his lost sense of self: they voted him into the prestigious Académie française, the only African to have this honor. That this further alienated Senghor from the mainstream of African thought process simply compounded the identity crisis he was facing. When Abdou Diouf succeeded Senghor in 1980, he was highly sensitive to the need to bring Senegal back into the circle of the continental family that Africans have been yearning for since the founding of the Organization of African Unity in May 1963.

The power and relevance of this book lie not so much in its biographical insights into one of Africa's foremost leaders but in its perception of what Africa has been in relationship to what it could be in the context of the life of an individual. The limitation of the book is its limited effort to see issues beyond a biographical portrait; however, this is overshadowed by its candid discussion of the controversial African leader. Everyone who has the interest of Africa at heart will read this book with great interest.

DICKSON A. MUNGAZI

Northern Arizona University
Flagstaff

EUROPE

CHRISTIAN, DAVID. *Living Water: Vodka and Russian Society on the Eve of Emancipation*. Pp. x, 447. New York: Oxford University Press, Clarendon Press, 1990. $74.00.

Throughout the nineteenth century, Russia raised about a third of its public revenue from the sale of vodka. With a largely subsistence agriculture and less dependence on foreign trade than most other countries in Europe, Russia had to depend quite heavily on the taxation of commodities traded in the domestic market. Vodka was the obvious choice.

Public revenue from the sale of vodka was acquired by tax farming until 1864, by excise taxation from 1864 to 1894, and by public monopoly of production and sale from 1894 to the present day. *Living Water* is about the organization of the tax farm and the reasons for its eventual replacement by excise taxation.

The choice between these methods of taxation depended for the most part on the impediments to tax collection in nineteenth-century Russia. Excise taxation, such as imposed in most countries on cigarettes today, would presumably have been feasible in Russia during the early years of the nineteenth century, but it was generally considered to be a poor source of revenue in a society where accounting was rudimentary, officials corrupt, and black markets difficult to detect.

The problem with the pure excise system was to find some guarantee that the money would actually reach the government . . . "where the very life of the inspector may be endangered by smugglers determined to make their way with arms if necessary . . . [and where] . . . honest officials will refuse to serve, and those that do agree to serve will aim merely at enriching themselves at the expense of the treasury" (p. 356).

The tax farm was an exclusive right to sell vodka within a certain territory, for a fixed period of time, and subject to restrictions on price and quality. Public revenue was raised from tax farming by putting the farm to auction. Every four years the exclusive right to sell vodka in each district of Russia was granted to the merchant who offered the largest annual revenue to the government. Clearly, public revenue would have been maximized and there would have been a considerable discouragement of drunkenness—one of the professed objects of public policy—if tax farms had been awarded to the highest bidder, with no restrictions on the price or quality of the vodka sold to the public. Restrictions were nonetheless imposed, in part because the czarist government refused to allow the price of vodka to rise as high as it would go in an unconstrained monopoly and perhaps because it was in the nature of that government to regulate wherever possible.

Regulation of the price and quality of vodka gave rise to cheating by tax farmers and to an almost inevitable complicity on the part of public officials. Tax farmers and their agents, the tavern keepers, had every incentive to charge customers more than the maximum allowable price for any grade of vodka, to adulterate vodka, or to sell low-grade vodka as high-grade vodka. Customers surely understood what was going on but were powerless to stop it as long as actual prices were less than the market would bear and officials were unwilling or unable to enforce the regulations. But the profit from cheating, from not adhering to the regulations on price and quality, would be automatically passed back to the government as merchants capitalized these profits in their bids for the right to become the tax farmer. It was inherent in the institution of tax farming that the government became the beneficiary at the expense of the peasants of the violation of its own regulations.

The most effective evader of the rules could afford to offer the highest bid for the tax farm, and the government became increasingly unwilling to prosecute the malfeasant tax farmer once it had accepted from him a sum that he could afford to pay only by breaking the rules. Contemporary observers were under no illusions about how the system worked.

In the words of one commentator, "'under the existing system the government is obliged to accept revenues from tax farmers which it knows are higher than can be recouped by honest means. . . . Such a demand is bound, in reality, to appear as farming out the right to commit abuses.'"

The choice between tax farming and excise taxation was a balancing of considerations. Though the case for tax farming seemed the stronger in the earlier part of the nineteenth century, it appeared less persuasive later on when "the government itself had finally acquired the bureaucratic reach necessary to undertake on its own account the functions it had previously entrusted to tax farmers." A special corps of young, well-trained, well-paid, and well-disciplined officials was established to administer the excise tax.

Christian tells the story of the rise and fall of the tax farm, including accounts of the culture of drinking in czarist Russia, the organization of the taverns, the "sobriety movement" to stop drunkenness, and the "tipling theory," put forward as justification for public sponsorship of drinking. According to this theory, steady drinking, day by day, is salutary as long as one does not allow oneself to go on a binge. The tipling theory can be recognized from its modern counterpart in which, for instance, the government of Ontario, with the same deep respect for its people that the czarist government showed for the peasantry, advertises on billboards and television to encourage people to gamble in the state lottery every single week.

The story is well told. The book is a pleasure to read. The research is, insofar as an amateur like me can tell, thorough and sound. Christian is judicious and fair in his presentation of contemporary opinion. Sometimes, however, material that might usefully have been collected in one place is scattered throughout the book. In particular, I would have liked to have seen an early chapter on the regulation of tax farming and the detail of the auctioning procedure so that when corruption was discussed, the reader would know precisely what rules were being violated. It would have been helpful to include a summary of the Russian public accounts and to express time-series of monetary values in real terms so that the reader could tell when an increase in a monetary value was something more than the normal consequence of inflation.

The book is not improved, in my opinion, by Christian's analysis of Russian society and of the institution of tax farming from a Marxist perspective. The damage is less than it might be because, to a large extent, Christian's Marxism is restricted to pronouncements ex cathedra at the beginnings of chapters, pronouncements that the judicious reader can ignore without losing the thread of the story. We are told, for example, that "the consumers' taste for vodka encountered the retailers' thirst for cash. Before arriving at these institutions, vodka was merely a source of wealth; once it left them, it was merely a source of gratification" and that "taxes, like commercial profits, are a form of revenue—a way in which wealth is transferred to social and political elites."

The real cost of this gratuitous Marxism is that an important question is overlooked. The czarist regime was undoubtedly autocratic and brutal in many respects, but not all of its actions in the fiscal realm were a direct manifestation of its brutality. Some aspects of its tax and expenditure policy might have been appropriate to a government that was not at all brutal or autocratic. The question that Christian might have asked and did not is, Which aspects of the story of the rise and fall of the tax farm are a reflection of policies that any government—good or bad—might have adopted in the economic and technical circumstances of

nineteenth-century Russia, and which are specifically characteristic of the czarist regime?

DAN USHER

Queen's University
Kingston
Ontario
Canada

EDWARDS, JOHN CARVER. *Berlin Calling: American Broadcasters in Service to the Third Reich.* Pp. xi, 288. New York: Praeger, 1991. $21.95.

This is an unusual book. It deals very unevenly and somewhat confusedly with a fascinating subject: American men and women who served Germany during World War II by broadcasting Nazi propaganda to the United States. John Carver Edwards, a university archivist at the University of Georgia, has researched this subject intensely and well. He has made use of a wide variety of sources including trial records and Federal Bureau of Investigation files of his subjects, various manuscript collections, and numerous secondary works in German and English.

Unfortunately, his massive labors have not resulted in a well-rounded, integrated, finished work. He asks all the right questions, but the answers are confusing. We learn that some individuals fared better after the war than others, but we never learn why. We are told a great deal about the different broadcasters, but the context is so loose that it is difficult to understand just where they fit in. "Axis Sally"—one of the best-known of the broadcasters—is dealt with only in passing. The "ballyhoo artist" Edward Delaney is not given a chapter of his own but gets more space than Jane Anderson, who is the subject of a separate case study.

Edwards attempts to make clear why these men and women worked for the Nazis. He raises a series of interesting questions about their disaffection from an increasingly complex American society and about the dissolution of their ties to it after extended stays in Europe. But in the final analysis, it seems that what really moved them was an almost irrational fear of the Soviets and communism, anti-Semitism—although its intensity varied from individual to individual—an increasing hostility to the America being shaped by Franklin Roosevelt, and various individual quirks.

Edwards early on makes the important point that "among the great world powers Germany was the first to employ foreign nationals as propagandists to their respective countries" but does not follow up on it. He does present some very useful examples of the kinds of broadcasts that were made, and he does go into the bureaucratic infighting that hampered the broadcasters. Overall, there is much of interest in the book.

But the material does not hang together as it is presented. There is a lack of consistency. Two of the chapters appeared earlier as articles and are not fully integrated. The subject is an important one, and Edwards is to be commended for his energy, his diligence, and his research. But the finished product is one that probably will be mined by others who will use the material to much better ends.

DANIEL J. LEAB

Seton Hall University
South Orange
New Jersey

GILLINGHAM, JOHN. *Coal, Steel and the Rebirth of Europe, 1945-1955: The Germans and French from Ruhr Conflict to Economic Community.* Pp. xv, 397. New York: Cambridge University Press, 1991. $44.50.

John Gillingham has made an important addition to the recent literature on the reorganization of Europe after World War II. As he himself notes, the European Coal and Steel Community (ECSC), after some initial studies a generation ago, has received little critical analysis; no systematic study of the diplomatic origins of the ECSC, the aims of its founders, or the actual results of the negotiations has appeared. Gillingham has now filled this gap, his analysis extending to the Messina resolution of June 1955. Throughout, he has skillfully interwoven relevant published materials—including his own —with extensive use of public and private archival sources.

According to Gillingham, given the ECSC's historical antecedents during the interwar period, the important story of the ECSC in the post-World War II period is to be found not so much in new policy initiatives as in the constellation of factors and events that made the Paris agreement possible. Unquestionably, the role of the United States was indispensable. Apart from its general support of integration since the inception of the Marshall Plan, its tactical alliance with Monnet influenced the course of the Paris negotiations and helped bring them to a successful conclusion.

Monnet's initial plans were very much traditional French *Ruhrpolitik*, implying control and reform of the Ruhr in order to serve French interests and then gradually ever closer cooperation with Germany. Yet the final product of the Paris negotiations was quite different from this scenario; developments after the ECSC came into operation continued the trend away from the plans of European integrationists.

How can Gillingham claim therefore that the ECSC became all important in the subsequent construction of an integrated Europe? His answer dwells on the paradox that, despite the failure of Monnet's plans, the cause of European integration was nevertheless strengthened by such factors as the growing desire of Europeans for unity, German willingness to make concessions, and the learning process connected with participation in the functioning of ECSC institutions. Still, Gillingham is somewhat diffident about his answer, noting at one point that "the puzzle" calls for "intelligent speculation rather than rigorous structural analysis." His "speculation" should have been given more extended treatment, since it cannot be easily deduced from his detailed treatment of the ECSC's origins. But this observation should not detract from the book's solid merits. This is a superb study and deserves to join the classics by Alan Milward and Michael Hogan.

KARL H. CERNY

Georgetown University
Washington, D.C.

KENNETT, LEE. *The First Air War: 1914-1918.* Pp. xii, 275. New York: Free Press, 1991. $24.95.

This is a most valuable and interesting book. The author is clearly fascinated by his subject, but at the same time very much on his guard against a tendency to make too much of it. If we often nostalgically exaggerate how important the airplane was in World War I, Lee Kennett attempts to set the record straight.

The book is certainly well researched and includes a valuable survey of the literature as an appendix. One finds numerous citations of actual combat records, but also some of the very intriguing speculations at the time on what air power might be able to do, and even such speculations from before World War I (but fewer from after—more on this). The narrative is well written throughout and offers a series of macroscopic overviews and summaries, interspersed with just

enough anecdotal material and detail to make the story quite interesting, but avoiding letting the "flying stories" produce any distortion of the overall picture.

The overarching structure is very logical. Basically, it is organized by the kinds of uses to which airplanes were put, stressing first the supreme importance of the intelligence information-gathering function, and then somewhat debunking the impacts achieved otherwise from 1914 to 1918.

The one criticism that might be made of the book is that, by rejecting a romanticization of this first air war, it may also be understating the impression that bombing raids left on the governments and publics in the major powers between 1919 and 1939. Kennett somewhat quickly concludes, at the end of chapter 3, that the inhabitants of London, matching the pluck they were to display in the World War II blitz, did not show a great fear of the bombing they were suffering from 1914 to 1918. But there are other accounts that come to very different conclusions, and one can find many discussions after 1918 of how unbearable aerial bombardment was to be in the future.

Kennett may be right that World War I was nothing like what we have projected for World War III. But he may be dismissing too much the post-1918 analysts, of whom Douhet is only one example, who were making just such a projection.

GEORGE H. QUESTER

University of Maryland
College Park

MERRIMAN, JOHN M. *The Margins of City Life: Explorations on the French Urban Frontier, 1815-1851.* Pp. x, 318. New York: Oxford University Press, 1991. $45.00.

The city, as many have observed, is a stage, and the play that runs ordinarily is, appropriately enough, called civilization. The metaphor applies also if one enlarges the view to include the surroundings. The backstage or periphery, is often larger, busier, and more populous than the visible stage or city, but it lacks the latter's veneer of glamour, and a rougher drama plays out there than in the limelight.

France as a whole urbanized slowly in the first half of the nineteenth century, although large cities and places touched by emerging industrialization expanded faster. Paris more than doubled in population, Le Havre and Saint-Étienne grew lustily, and such industrial towns as Roubaix emerged from insignificance. While rapid urban growth led to infilling, crowding, and land-use transformation in city centers, it chiefly affected the periphery. Settlement pressed against any remaining barriers before leaping over them or hastening their destruction. Walls or no, the urban fringes accumulated the human and physical by-products of urbanization: vagrants, paupers, outcasts, new arrivals; dumps, noxious processes, shantytowns.

It is this margin of cities, fast-growing or not, that draws John Merriman's attention. Using mainly archival materials —police documents and military surveys that document the seedy side of life much as the press does today—he focuses on marginality as a social, spatial, and political process. His organizing idea is that the urban establishment's concern shifted over the period: feared as a source of disorder, the urban margin—faubourg or suburb—came to be seen as a hatchery for insurrection, the nesting place for a social alternative subversive of the property-respecting bourgeois order.

Given the inescapable parallels with urban issues today—the very adjective has become a code word for social pathology—certain aspects of the story in Restoration and July Monarchy France strike the reader. One is the gap between the aspirations to social control, as defined by what was thought proper and by the minimal legal-political restraints on the use of state power, and the means in fact available to enforce control. Spies and a compliant judiciary did not compensate for tight budgets and the lack of a professional police force. Merriman nonetheless has to draw heavily on establishment fears to flesh out the story, since the actual record of crime and conflict is remarkably spotty. Finally, while the urban margins appeared to threaten society, they, like the sprawl of Los Angeles, also prefigured the urban future. Not only would the agglomeration swallow its one-time outskirts, but, already on the fringe, precapitalistic restrictions on commerce in goods and labor were absent or ineffective, while proto-industry flourished.

Merriman devotes chapters also to well-established peripheral communities and to their conflicts, notably around religion: Red and White Catalans in Perpignan, Protestants and Catholics in Nîmes. Yet even here, his underlying concern is with politics, with the local fact of the contention among regimes and with the struggle of working-class radicalism to recapture the glory of 1792 in a crasser time. While the White Terror and July 1830 occasioned unrest here and there, 1848 and its harsh aftermath come in for the most emphasis. What we can call the Second Thoughts Republic, from June 1848 to the coup of 2 December 1851, saw urban property gradually suppress largely suburban labor, which had mistakenly taken the joint February uprising for the dawn of an age of social justice. Yet even this painful disillusion, Merriman argues, served to integrate new proletarians into the agglomerated world of industrial society.

PAUL M. HOHENBERG

Rensselaer Polytechnic Institute
Troy
New York

UNITED STATES

BELLAH, ROBERT N., RICHARD MADSEN, WILLIAM M. SULLIVAN, ANN SWIDLER, and STEVEN TIPTON. *The Good Society.* Pp. 347. New York: Knopf, 1991. $25.00.

A variety of recent studies have indicated that Americans seem to feel less allegiance to the society at large than in the past. We have in some respects become a nation of individualists with little concern for the common good. A continuation or intensification of this trend can have a devastating effect for the body politic and can lead to a brokered society with races and social and economic classes allied against each other. Results of statewide elections in New Jersey, Louisiana, and Mississippi in 1991 offer evidence that a form of balkanization can indeed be a possibility in our nation.

What is the role of institutions in American society, and how can they be utilized to halt the trend toward an America lacking a central core? This is the key question posed by the five writers of *The Good Society*, who are also the authors of the 1985 volume *Habits of the Heart*, which dealt with the theme of individualism and social commitment in modern society.

It is through institutions, the authors write, that we maintain the delicate balance between individual liberty and social order. Sadly, however, the major American institutions are failing in their task. They have often adopted narrow and parochial viewpoints and advocated single-issue politics at the expense of compromise and common themes. The institutions that matter most are those that deal with religion, international relations, government, education, and political economy.

The authors provide excellent analyses of the decision-making processes of these institutions, and they blast the view that individual autonomy must be the only social goal, arguing that social responsibility should also be a major factor in public life.

They advocate many specific reforms aimed at bringing about greater social responsibility in our national institutions. For instance, they recommend that we examine the European approaches to the issue of abortion; they suggest a greater sharing of authority and responsibility by workers and managers in the workplace; they promote the idea that political parties should be strengthened at the expense of individual candidates in order to promote more responsive candidates and elected officials; and they urge the development of a democratic administrative state able to support and extend a vital public sphere rather than supplant it.

The foregoing are a few of the many suggested reforms that could help make institutions more responsive to the promotion of a greater social harmony. The suggestions are in the most part practical and utilitarian. The question now, however, is to find the mechanisms—whether they be public or private—that could take these suggestions and those from other public policy analysts and begin to implement them with the goal of achieving some very necessary reform in American communal life.

FRED ROTONDARO

Congressional Affairs Press
Alexandria
Virginia

CARSON, MINA. *Settlement Folk: Social Thought and the American Settlement Movement, 1885-1930.* Pp. xiii, 280. Chicago: University of Chicago Press, 1990. No price.

Mina Carson's *Settlement Folk* is a comparative welfare history dealing with the confluence of Victorian English social radicalism and the U.S. urban progressive movement. In this elegantly written and researched academic book, Carson communicates her scholarly passion for the social welfare movement while effectively integrating newer bottom-up social history and gender issues with elite American social thought.

The reaction to crude mid-nineteenth-century English capitalism produced both Karl Marx and the Christian socialism of Thomas Carlyle and John Ruskin, who pioneered "practicable socialism," a mixture of paternalism, idealism, and aesthetic and educational inspiration—an attempt to soften class conflict and the utilitarian Darwinian ethos of Victorian Britain through voluntarism.

When social welfare and social science joined the growing professionalism of the new American university in the mid-1880s, cultural literacy and an obligation to build "character" became the foundation of the new liberal education. Social investigation offered a professional livelihood for the university-educated woman. New religion and new science merged in 1890s Britain when Charles Booth and Mrs. Humphry Ward published popular books that influenced Fabians like Beatrice Potter Webb. Christian socialism's "religion of humanity" was nurtured in American colleges by middle-class women, convinced that social science could solve the problems of an urban industrial ethos. American vernacular "plasticity" helped balance the inherent paternalism of educated outsiders helping the poor.

Lillian Wald's Henry Street settlement, in New York, established a visiting nursing service so that immigrants could avoid unnecessary hospitalization for routine illness; Jane Addams's Hull House, in Chicago, insisted that making the place pretty was more important than establishing "a sociological laboratory." One is more impressed by the courage of the settlement workers than appalled by their naïveté and by the magnitude of the problems they faced, especially with sensitive new immigrants. Addams and President Theodore Roosevelt made a political alliance based on their mutual conviction in "possibilism" as the best way to deal with the threat of social unrest.

With World War I, the generous settlement-folk impulse fragmented. One extreme was the militaristic paternalism of Robert Woods, who saw society's ills through the eyes of the social worker as epidemiologist. For Woods, prohibition was a necessary medicine.

Settlement Folk is an extremely useful study of how well-educated American idealists grappled with the modernism that challenged all of the pre-World War I world. The footnotes—regrettably, located at the back of the book—are as engaging as the well-written text.

RICHARD H. COLLIN

University of New Orleans
Louisiana

CORNELIUS, JANET DUITSMAN. *When I Can Read My Title Clear: Literacy, Slavery, and Religion in the Antebellum South.* Pp. xiii, 215. Columbia: University of South Carolina Press, 1991. $29.95.

Janet Cornelius's important contribution to the literature on African American slavery in the antebellum South explains why literacy was so important to the slave: it was not just for "practical uses—learning to read and write to help facilitate escape—but because literacy, especially the ability to write, signified an establishment of the African's human identity to the European world." After having been defined as inferior and subhuman, the slaves' demonstration of the intellectual capacity to be literate, like the Europeans, was a powerful boost to their self-esteem and pride.

Beyond this, slaves wished to learn to read and write so that they might read the Bible. While the important role played by religion within the African American slave community has already been established, Cornelius takes this discussion one step further by showing the connection of the quest for religious solace with literacy and the connection of both religion and literacy to leadership, secular and spiritual, in the African American community.

Cornelius establishes that a much larger number of slaves than previously estimated could read and write, although problems in determining an accurate rate of literacy remains. Slaves learned to read through their own efforts, picking up words here and there, and sometimes through the efforts of sympathetic whites. The ability to read clearly represented a perceived threat to the autonomy of the white slaveholding establishment, who enforced clear and rigid sanctions against slaves' acquiring such skills. Using Charleston as an example, Cornelius points out how working-class whites as well feared slave literacy, because of the ensuing competition for jobs.

Cornelius has written a well-researched, well-documented, and insightful work that will be must reading for all those interested in African American history, slavery, education, and political leadership. Alongside such works as Loren Schweninger's *Black Property Owners in the South, 1790-1915*, Cornelius's book should cause us to begin rethinking our assumptions about African American slaves and their accomplishments. As both authors reinforce for us, slaves were not merely workers but complex people who, like us, wanted to and did live their lives with dignity and self-respect.

KENNETH W. GOINGS

Florida Atlantic University
Boca Raton

HAYWOOD, C. ROBERT. *Victorian West: Class and Culture in Kansas Cattle Towns*. Pp. ix, 325. Lawrence: University of Kansas Press, 1991. $29.95.

WILLIAMS, MARILYN THORNTON. *Washing "The Great Unwashed": Public Baths in Urban America, 1840-1920*. Pp. xiv, 190. Columbus: Ohio State University Press, 1991. $40.00.

"Cleanliness is next to godliness" and, as John Wesley might have added, "dirt is next to disease and death." It was originally a fear of fever that encouraged philanthropic and then municipal enterprise to provide baths and washhouses in urban centers throughout the Western world in the nineteenth century. In developing the theme of respectability, C. Robert Haywood, in his book on "class and culture in Kansas cattle towns," has something in common with Marilyn Williams's book on public baths. Both are describing aspects of middle-class lives as Victorians strove to better themselves. Both books are also about women's efforts to keep the clothes and the bodies of their families clean.

Victorian West is a labor of love as the author examines the culture of three Kansas cattle towns, Caldwell, Dodge City, and Wichita. Of these, Wichita is the only one to have become a sizable town at the present time, with a population of nearly 300,000 persons. Caldwell is nowadays a village, while Dodge City is a small regional center with 20,000 inhabitants. The book will be warmly welcomed as it examines the social mores of these towns in the wild years after the 1880s.

However, Haywood's espousal of Bernard Bailyn's suggestion, to explain the "presence of great violence coupled with an equally persistent drive for gentility" in American society, such that it might relate to the "high proportion of colonists brought as transported criminals" seems wide of the mark. Surely these "criminals" were in reality the poor, ordinary men and women struggling to survive in the Old World, where draconian laws banished them to the New World for petty offenses. Would it be any more plausible to suggest that the two poles represented male and female elements in society?

Robert Haywood makes much of the divide in cattle-town society between respectable and fallen women. But it was women's low wages that determined their fate; prostitution was for many a necessary—but last—resort. Haywood argues that such women lived wild and hectic lives and died young. But Dr. William Acton, the least sensational and most sensible Victorian English commentator, wrote, "Prostitution is a transitory state through which an untold number of British women are forever on their passage." Were American women very different?

Marilyn Williams develops with skill and understanding the role of the philanthropist in putting pressure on municipal authorities to take on themselves the responsibility for public cleanliness. Her work is illuminating as she demonstrates that the provision of public bathing and washing facilities proved not to be an end but only a beginning as respectable families aimed for private bathrooms within their own homes rather than use public facilities, even good public facilities.

Although Williams examines with care the greater success of the Boston public baths, because they provided for leisure activities, she does not explore the bath, or washing house, as a social center. But in Glasgow, Scotland, the public washing and bathing facilities—never known as anything but "the steamie"— were the center of a strong and sustaining female fellowship that has been wonderfully portrayed in Tony Roper's play The Steamie (circa 1985). A lament for the closing of the last of the public baths and washhouses, this play, written for an all-female cast, reveals the strength of the female community in supporting each

other. As the women scrub and pound on the washing board, soap, and plunge the dolly up and down, wrapped in swirling steam from the glorious hot water, they talk. They help and encourage the elderly widow, they chide the young girls for their silliness, and they consider, endlessly, the behavior of their menfolk. It is a telling image as they mourn the passing of the steamie, a symbol of warmth and indeed comfort in the harsh world they inhabit.

OLIVE CHECKLAND

University of Glasgow
Scotland

SCHUMAKER, PAUL. Critical Pluralism, Democratic Performance, and Community Power. Pp. xvii, 258. Lawrence: University Press of Kansas, 1991. $29.95.

A study of democratic governance in Lawrence, Kansas, this book is likely to be received by specialists as a major contribution to the theory and analysis of community power, and by others of us, perhaps, as a way of enhancing democracy—of a sort—in American cities. This towering achievement in empirical research offers in "comparative issues" an innovative method; and in "responsible representation," "complex equality," and "principle-policy congruence" it suggests analytical tests for evaluating the democratic performance of urban governments.

Critical Pluralism takes us beyond the elitist-pluralist debate and beyond the economistic and regime paradigms—all of which Schumaker examines closely— promising to specify democratic ideals, measure the extent to which they have been achieved, and suggest how they might be more faithfully realized. It is the last part of this promise that is likely to be most controversial. Modestly stated but clear enough, it is Schumaker's claim that his study is a significant step toward making good on the much-heralded but largely neglected postbehavioral project of fusing the empirical and the normative in the study of politics.

I agree that his book is just such a step, and an empirical study of such obvious depth and rigor that is also expressly normative is indeed a welcome achievement. Unreconstructed behavioralists will fulminate, and devout positivists cry heresy. The rest of us, however, while admiring the elegance of his science, may wish to quarrel with his philosophy, to ask, specifically, whether "critical pluralism" is right about democratic ideals.

Complex equality, for example, a concept borrowed from Michael Walzer, seems to me partly misapplied in Schumaker's analysis. Rather than part of a theory of justice that might challenge the reigning conceptions of justice in Lawrence—utilitarian and Rawlsian—both of which are tolerant of a great deal of political passivity and also of just the sort of dominance—money and commodities, here "economic growth"—that Walzer says we need to reduce, complex equality is used mostly to explain (away) the political inequality that Schumaker documents.

Again, principle-policy congruence threatens to mask if not legitimate a kind of majority tyranny, where the majority, formed by the alliance between middle and upper classes, are relatively well off and powerful and the minority are relatively poor and powerless. (The weak and poor win just often enough to make it possible to speak of complex equality.) Representatives, who tend to come from the well-to-do classes, of course "respond" to the "principles" of the majority more often than not. The resulting policies may not always be "progressive," as Schumaker concedes at one point; they may also represent a distorted or corrupted form of democracy when the principles from which they proceed are hardly debated and seem, moreover, tacitly to spurn democratic politics.

Lawrence appears to embody many of Progressivism's characteristic prejudices: economic growth—"progress"—over communal integrity, rule by experts rather than politicians, and a moralistic but unorganized citizenry. We also know that Progressivism rather quickly muted its clamorings for equality as it embraced economic efficiency. Welcome as Schumaker's taking a normative stand is, his political science as a whole seems itself to be rooted in that same Progressivism, certainly in its laudable—in my view—and avowed commitment to democracy but also in its limited and "realistic" view of democracy's possibilities. Schumaker cites as "promising" Stephen Elkin's insistence that a democratic urban regime must, most importantly, cultivate the citizen embedded in every private individual, but this evidently is not one of Schumaker's ideals of democracy. Throughout the study, two kinds of persons are mentioned over and over: those who act, are informed, and make things happen, called notables, representatives, or participants; and those who mostly behave and are passive, uninformed, and the objects, not makers, of policy, called—citizens! In short, critical pluralism is scarcely critical at all of prevailing American political culture, whose celebration of privatism and individualism counsels withdrawal from public life and renders "citizens" a synonym for "masses."

Finally, there is the disquieting suggestion that while a given community may pass the test set for it by critical pluralism, it will be political scientists and not citizens themselves who will have devised the questions and graded the examination. Hence the criticism of Elkin's acceptance of a "subjective" public interest in need of debate and democratic determination and the call instead for one "objectively" ascertained, presumably by the appropriate experts.

Whatever the merit of these observations, they should not obscure the overall point that this is an important book, political science that really matters. It seems certain to set a new agenda for research and thinking about democracy writ small in America.

ROBERT E. CALVERT

DePauw University
Greencastle
Indiana

WHITE, SHANE. *Somewhat More Independent: The End of Slavery in New York City, 1770-1810.* Pp. xxix, 278. Athens: University of Georgia Press, 1991. $35.00.

Shane White, lecturer of history at the University of Sydney, Australia, has written an extraordinary view of the United States' "peculiar institution." He analyzes the public documents and private data on the slaveholders and slaves in New York City during the last decades of slavery's legal existence there. His study also questions traditional assumptions about the benevolence of non-Southern American whites who granted emancipation to blacks.

While data on New York slavery in this period are far from copious, Professor White's use of extant sources reveals that, among Dutch and English New Yorkers, slavery was strongly embraced. Gradual emancipation followed a 1799 state law that stipulated that those already enslaved were to remain so and that the slave children born after 4 July 1799 were bound to the owner of their mother until their middle twenties. After enactment of the law, some New York slaves negotiated with their masters for freedom while others challenged the proprietary rights of slave owners.

Subsequently, slave ownership in New York City became a more complex, ambiguous socioeconomic institution. One example of this was John Jay, who served as president of the New York Manumission Society yet kept his slaves after the passage of the 1799 law. Upper- and middle-class New Yorkers such as Jay were not concerned about the incongruity of ending slavery and owning slaves; to them, slave owning was a symbol of economic achievement.

Professor White also argues that black culture—whether slave or free—significantly influenced the New York colonial society in adjusting to a nonslaveholding status. In this period, white New Yorkers became accustomed to the gradual rearrangement of master-slave relationships. Some New York slaves influenced their owners in the selection of new owners while others found their own buyers. Thus white and black New Yorkers made accommodation with the process of gradual emancipation.

Yet, black New Yorkers had no illusions about the alleged mildness of their slavery before and after the 1799 law. Violence toward slaves and violent resistance—such as the 1712 slave rebellion—were not uncommon. Slaves and free blacks were victimized by working-class white New Yorkers who resented the African presence.

Although this well-crafted book focuses on New York, it suggests that scholars still do not understand the complex social, economic, and political manifestations of chattel slavery in American cities in general. The book is troubling at some points; for example, it provides too little discussion of the black church and the role that Peter Williams of New York played in the establishment of African Methodist Episcopal Zion Church. Despite this, the volume is a useful analysis of New York City in the late eighteenth and early nineteenth century and of how that city maintained institutionalized slavery and, paradoxically, also sought to disestablish it.

JOHN A. HARDIN

Western Kentucky University
Bowling Green

SOCIOLOGY

ANDERSON, ELIJAH. *Streetwise: Race, Class, and Change in an Urban Community.* Pp. xii, 276. Chicago: University of Chicago Press, 1990. $19.95.

In this readable and interesting book, Elijah Anderson offers his insights into the continuing poverty and crime that afflict urban neighborhoods, especially those with a concentration of blacks. His focus is entirely upon the areas adjoining the University of Pennsylvania and Drexel University in Philadelphia, and his approach is exclusively ethnographic.

The book has two unusual assets. During the 1980s, when Anderson carried out his fieldwork, this heterogeneous locale included students from the universities; survivors of the antiwar and counterculture movements of the 1960s; middle-class whites and blacks involved in gentrification; a few newly arrived Asians; the remnants of a previous middle-class black group; and another few blocks with an impoverished black population, a group many would identify as the urban underclass. A unique contribution is Anderson's detailed description of how these groups shared their space, that is, how they behaved toward each other on the streets and in the meetings they held that sought to deal with pressing community issues. Quite clearly, there was a class dimension, but it was complicated by race, by the commitment some residents had to liberal ideologies more popular a generation ago, and by the hope of others for profits as land values went up.

For readers who are interested in public behavior in an intriguing neighborhood, such as how individuals determine whether it is safe to go for a walk or how the police perceive the area or whether a black skin protects a person from street crime, this is the book. It is the work of a perceptive and thorough ethnographer. The portrayal of the values of the struggling black working class is exceptionally good.

Anderson also makes a contribution by carefully examining the idea that structural changes in the economy and in the welfare system produced substantial changes in the values and behavior of those blacks who lacked the training and skills to secure good jobs. As blue-collar employment declined in Philadelphia, a drug culture emerged and some young black men regarded the opportunity to become rich selling drugs much more highly than taking the low-level jobs for which they were qualified. In Anderson's view, this reshaped their views of work and led them to disparage the older black men in the community who held solid blue-collar jobs. Young black women hoped they could marry a man who would work diligently, become a model father, and buy a home in the suburbs. They realized this was improbable, and welfare gave them an opportunity for independence. Thus the availability of payments from Aid to Families with Dependent Children, Anderson suggests, created a new set of values among poor women and helped to further isolate men and women by making them economically more independent.

I stress that Anderson does not prove that the values of lower-class blacks have been fundamentally reshaped by the absence of good blue-collar jobs, by the possibility for wealth by merchandising drugs, or by governmental welfare payments. Rather, he presents a plausible and thoughtful discussion of these issues.

Few social scientists are willing to take on the task of describing how social values change, especially when the new ones are seemingly much more deleterious to everyone than were the previous ones.

Three issues might have been treated differently. First, much of the book focuses upon the lower-class black residents and their interactions with the police or with the gentrifiers, both black and white. Anderson is careful not to generalize, but a reader might infer that he describes a pattern of change common in many black urban neighborhoods. He suggests that the area formerly housed a stable middle- or working-class black population, and readers will infer that what happened in this Philadelphia neighborhood probably occurred elsewhere. In particular, Anderson implies that there was a social cohesion in the black community that disappeared because of job loss, drugs, and welfare. Supposedly, older black men and women once socialized their children, monitored their neighbors' children, and taught young blacks how to be upstanding citizens who would take working-class jobs and raise stable families. Was this ever the case? Perhaps, but there is nothing in this volume to document it. Certainly, the descriptions of Washington's black ghettos a generation ago provided in Elliot Liebow's *Tally's Corner* (Boston: Little, Brown, 1967) and in Ulf Hannerz's *Soulside* (New York: Columbia University Press, 1969) do not match the image Anderson provides. Nor did W.E.B. DuBois, in *The Philadelphia Negro* (Philadelphia: University of Pennsylvania Press, 1899), describe much social cohesion when he lived and wrote about an adjoining Philadelphia area nine decades ago. Philadelphia's black community has been studied extensively, and Anderson might have drawn upon previous investigations and census data to provide several pages or a chapter about the actual status in 1950 or 1960 of the area he studied.

Second, I would appreciate more specification about what distinguishes the values and behaviors of the lower-class blacks in this book. For example, an interesting chapter describes sex codes and family life, reporting that young black men use many verbal games and strategies in their efforts to seduce young women, who have their own wily ways to obtain what they want from a relationship. Perhaps the same game is also played across the street by the middle-class and upper-class college students. Similarly, is there anything unique about the conflict over the functioning of the local public school?

Finally, there are problems in the last chapter, which discusses possible public policies. There is something for everybody in this discussion. Running throughout the book is the powerful idea that young black men with limited skills can no longer locate high-paying jobs, jobs that were readily available to their fathers. This agrees with the idea of William Julius Wilson and John Kasarda that male joblessness is the key cause of current black poverty. But Anderson also states that the work ethic has been lost and that young black men are often reluctant to accept the physically demanding, dirty jobs that may be available. In this regard, he endorses the views of Lawrence Mead. Interestingly, there is little in this book about the apparently improving job prospects for black women. Anderson's interpretation of the consequences of governmental transfer payments—especially benefits for unmarried women with children—seems consistent with those of Charles Murray and George Gilder.

This lucid book is stimulating and will be widely cited in the continuing thriving discussion of black poverty and urban decline. It clearly reports that the process of gentrification will hardly uplift neighboring poor areas. Similar to Alan Kotlowitz's *There Are No Children Here* (New York: Doubleday, 1991), the book is basically very pessimistic. After reading *Streetwise*, one appreciates that there are no easily implemented policies that will facilitate upward mobility by impoverished blacks, that might make urban areas safe, or that might encourage the residential integration of blacks and whites or the rich and the poor.

REYNOLDS FARLEY

University of Michigan
Ann Arbor

GOODWIN, MARJORIE HARNESS. *He —Said—She—Said: Talk as Social Organization among Black Children.* Pp. x, 371. Bloomington: Indiana University Press, 1990. $49.95. Paperbound, $19.95.

For eighteen months, anthropologist Marjorie Goodwin, armed with a tape recorder, followed a group of 49 black youngsters who lived on a street she calls Maple Street in Southwest Philadelphia. Early on, she became an invisible member of the group and diligently recorded their activities and conversations. The 26 boys ranged in age from 5 to 14; the 23 girls, from 4 to 13. The original focus of her investigation, part of a Ph.D. dissertation at the University of Pennsylvania, centered on how children from working-class families interacted and socialized, but, a decade later, after immersing herself in the literature on children by sociologists, anthropologists, psychologists, linguists, folklorists, ethnologists, and others—the appendices, notes, and bibliography of the book under review comprise nearly 20 percent of the volume—Goodwin turned her attention increasingly to how everyday talk could be analyzed to understand the social interaction —and by extension, the social organization—of the Maple Street youngsters.

By examining the conversations of youngsters in their social environment—rather than their speech patterns when they are with adults or in a caretaker setting—the study concentrates on, as Goodwin writes, "children as *actors actively engaged* in the construction of their social worlds rather than as *passive objects* who are recipients of culture." The social world the children created, as revealed in their talk, is discussed under such rubrics as "directives" (how one child attempted to get another to do something); "pretend play" (how boys used a hierarchical social organization to coordinate their activities and girls had minimal concern about status); "disputes and gossip" (how the children dealt with their differences of opinion); "he—said—she—said" gossip disputes, a form used almost exclusively by the girls and including accusations or a particular breach, such as one girl's talking behind another's back; and, perhaps most important, "stories," or how speakers created what was in essence "a vernacular theatrical performance" with the storyteller mimicking the exploits of participants, gesturing to set the scene, and providing necessary background information.

Although at times didactic, and occasionally pedantic, what emerges from the pages of this volume is an analysis of the remarkable diversity and complexity of activities and talk among a group of inner-city youngsters, who, despite age and gender differences, created a social environment that was at once exciting, complicated, engaging, and meaningful. Cooperation and competition existed across age and gender groupings. In the process of socialization, age, sex, and, by inference, race were not as important as what the children had in common—their shared humanity. By focusing on the social world of the children themselves, Goodwin breaks new ground.

LOREN SCHWENINGER

University of North Carolina
Greensboro

JENCKS, CHRISTOPHER and PAUL PETERSON, eds. *The Urban Underclass.* Pp. xiv, 490. Washington, DC: Brookings Institution, 1991. $34.95. Paperbound, $14.95.

This book is a collection of papers presented at a conference on the urban underclass at Northwestern University in 1989. The papers discuss the theories and hypotheses set forth by the sociologist William Julius Wilson. Although other research is also mentioned in the book, most of the papers revolve around Wilson's book *The Truly Disadvantaged.*

The book is divided into five sections. In part 1, Paul Peterson defines the concept of the urban underclass and discusses the paradox of poverty amid plenty. Christopher Jencks reports that, in the 1980s, dropout rates and reading and mathematical skills improved for the urban poor, teenage parenthood and poverty stopped improving, welfare dependency and violence stopped getting worse, and male joblessness and unwed parenthood became more severe. The paper is an excellent survey of the data and literature on the issues discussed throughout the book.

Part 2 deals with the economic conditions of the urban underclass. The titles of the articles are indicative of the issues discussed, for example, Richard Freeman's "Employment and Earnings of Disadvantaged Young Men in a Labor Shortage Economy" and Greg Duncan and Saul Hoffman's "Teenage Underclass Behavior and Subsequent Poverty."

Parts 3 and 4 cover the rationale of inner-city life and the causes and consequences of concentrated poverty. In this section, Elijah Anderson's and James Rosenbaum and Susan Popkins's papers are recommended for their originality.

Part 5 is concerned with the policy responses to poverty and whether the programs to combat it should be targeted exclusively on the poor or should be more universal in their application. Wilson discusses the latter issue in this part, and he restates his views in the last chapter.

Although the book contains valuable research, it lacks coherence. According to Jencks, what is considered underclass can be disaggregated into what he labels the impoverished underclass or undeserving poor, the jobless underclass, the educational underclass, the violent underclass, and the reproductive underclass or unwed mothers. He then finds that some problems are getting better and some are getting worse depending on whether the numbers in each category are increasing or decreasing. Wilson's approach to the phenomenon is holistic. According to him, what differentiates the urban underclass from what is traditionally called the lower class is their neighborhood or social milieu, specifically, living in urban census tracts with poverty rates exceeding 40 percent. He then rightly dismisses Jencks's paper as being irrelevant to the issue. For Wilson, individuals in their spatial context, their neighborhood, are the units that can be referred to as underclass. But as pointed out by Peterson, only 1 percent of the total U.S. population and 9 percent of the poor live in census tracts with poverty rates over 40 percent. Wilson's insistence on restricting the definition of the urban underclass has the effect of doing what he is afraid would happen to the concept, namely, making it a pejorative term for a small part of the poor.

A. REZA VAHABZADEH

University of Pennsylvania
Philadelphia

KADISH, MORTIMER R. *Toward an Ethic of Higher Education.* Pp. viii, 205. Stanford, CA: Stanford University Press, 1991. $29.50.

Mortimer Kadish's thesis posits that "there are choices of higher education that might produce a virtue that puts it to people to choose for themselves the better from the worse." He calls this "education for virtue." In 13 chapters, he tries to lay out his image of the possible shape of an ethic of higher education. Although he succeeds in this venture, many questions arise that need to be addressed.

To begin, questions regarding who has the power to define what is ethical, what is virtuous, what is better or worse are not adequately resolved. For example, in developing his framework, Kadish states that higher education's problem is to determine the objects most deserving appreciation. What he does not discuss is how we go about determining those objects. What power relations are involved in the process of making those decisions? He argues that through rational resolution, differences of opinion will be settled on their merits. But again, where do power, hegemony, and control fit into this equation?

The student's positional self-interest is also a central concept in his framework, but Kadish has not considered the collective interest of students or subgroups of students as alternative ways of defining positional interest. For instance, he states that nationalisms—ethnic or gender—break fraternities apart; however, he never discusses the history of exclusion related to these fraternities. Might these nationalisms be a rational response to historical exclusion?

Although Kadish argues against education for either the cultural connoisseurs or the technological marketplace, he does not adequately describe his education for virtue. What would these institutions look like—their faculties, students, and curricula? Kadish uses the ballet of higher education as a metaphor for describing his education for virtue, but his dance is very individualistic, a dance of positional self-interest. One could argue for a communal dance as an alternate description. For instance, in a polka one might be individually creative, but the real beauty is in its collective creativity: individuals working together for the collective good. Moreover, can one imagine an ethic of higher education without examining the populations served and those not served?

Kadish calls for an opening of the campus in advance of necessity, and the need for and importance of raising divisive issues, instead of waiting for them to strike. Despite this opening, he does not discuss how the critical issues of diversity, ethnic studies, affirmative action, gender, and sexuality on college campuses fit into his ethic of higher education.

Last, if we are working toward an ethic in higher education, then should we be producing students who have a sense of community interest or responsibility? Or should we be developing, as Kadish posits, students who are individualistic and self-interested albeit virtuous, democratic, nonauthoritarian, and nonspecialized—liberal? Kadish asks us what type of human beings we wish to work for. I would hope that we would work for students who have a sense of agency—those who can act on their own behalf—but who do so with a self- and community interest.

DANIEL G. SOLORZANO

University of California
Los Angeles

PESHKIN, ALAN. *The Color of Strangers, the Color of Friends: The Play of Ethnicity in School and Community.* Pp. xiii, 304. Chicago: University of Chicago Press, 1991. Paperbound, $15.95.

Alan Peshkin's study is a readable narrative. In eight chapters, it is "the story of a school and community that transcended a decade and more of ethnic strife to become a place of abiding mingling," with "ethnic conflict" lessened.

Peshkin combines techniques of anthropological ethnography, while using the tools of sociology, namely, theory, survey methods, questionnaires, participant observation, and interviews. He focuses on community residents and their school, with special emphasis on ethnic groups like blacks, Asians, and Hispanics. Peshkin gleans insightful glimpses into the intimacy of this community and school.

Chapter 2 shows the Riverview community to be a pluralistic mixture of ethnic groups. It is not a melting pot of harmony but one of conflict, woven into the belief in Americanization and assimilation. Chapter 3 demonstrates that what happened in Riverview was "what happened in the United States as a whole. Riverview is a microcosm." The rise and fall of ethnic conflict in Riverview from 1968 to 1980 paralleled that in the United States during the civil rights movement and the aftermath of ethnic strife. For Riverview, the change resulting from that period brought about a transformation and a new outlook—that ethnic differences could be tolerated and strife resolved.

The transformation of Riverview and its high school to consistently maintain this acceptance of ethnic differences can be summed up as follows:

1. Academic rather than ethnic considerations emerged, cutting across all ethnic barriers; the standard yardstick of grades, test results, overruled in most cases the intervention of ethnic identity.

2. At Riverview High School, assimilation into the mainstream is neither demanded nor supported by groups seeking to maintain ethnic identity by means of enforcement, but it still exists as a principle to follow.

3. The success of ethnic mingling, with minimal conflict, is due to the circumstances of the school setting. Individuals accept the legitimate authority of the school system to make decisions.

Overall, Alan Peshkin's study has one weakness. The sociological concepts of ethnicity introduced to examine this particular setting are inconsistently applied to the data, presenting a vacillation in the style of presentation. Also, the results of his analysis seem to be dictated by his subjective interpretation of the setting and data. As a participant observer, Peshkin allowed his bias to select informants amenable to his perception. He did, however, admit to his subjective analysis of data, writing, "I run the risk of presenting a study that has become blatantly autobiographical."

Alan Peshkin's book is designed to interest the general public and those concerned about the ongoing problems and turmoil in American communities and high schools. It is well researched and highly readable.

DANIEL MITCHELL

Silver City
New Mexico

SNOW, CATHERINE E., WENDY S. BARNES, JEAN CHANDLER, IRENE F. GOODMAN, and LOWRY HEMPHILL. *Unfulfilled Expectations: Home and School Influences on Literacy.* Pp. 251. Cambridge, MA: Harvard University Press, 1991. $29.95.

While it is obvious that children's skills in reading are developed both at home and in school, the process by which this happens is not at all obvious. How these two sources of reading development complement or compete with one another for children from low-income families— the topic of this excellent book—has been especially poorly understood. The authors, all faculty or students at the Harvard Graduate School of Education, studied intensively a relatively small number of low-income children and families— 32—residing in a small Northeastern city. The children, in second, fourth, and sixth grades at the outset of the study, were followed longitudinally at three time points over two school years; an epilogue describes their academic and family conditions five years after the onset of the study.

This book, the second of two describing the results of this ambitious study, uses both quantitative and qualitative—or ethnographic—methods to relate gains in children's literacy status to factors in their homes and classrooms. (The complementary volume is J. W. Chall, V. A. Jacobs, and L. E. Baldwin, *The Reading Crisis: Why Poor Children Fall Behind* [Cambridge, MA: Harvard University Press, 1990].) The data base is very rich in terms of describing two models of home influence: "the family as educator" and "the resistant family," with case-study portraits of particular families and children provided for each model. Parent-school relationships are given full treatment, again enriched by case-by-case information. While less detailed, the descriptions of the children's classrooms help complete the picture of the two sources of literacy development for this sample of low-income children.

The most interesting findings involve comparisons of gains in reading comprehension for children whose homes were more or less supportive of literacy and whose classroom experiences in literacy development were rated as high, mixed, or low. Home and classroom experiences interacted strongly. All children in classrooms with strong ratings made expected or higher gains in reading comprehension, regardless of their home environment, as did most of those in low or mixed classrooms from highly supportive homes. However, none of the children in low-rated classrooms whose homes were also rated low on support for literacy made expected gains. Only 25 percent of children from low-literacy homes and a mixed classroom environment made expected gains. Two findings are noteworthy. The more important is that, for poor children, strong school experiences may compensate for literacy-poor homes, or vice versa. Second, not all low-income households are impoverished in terms of their support for their children's literacy development.

The very ambitiousness of this study, unfortunately, contributes to its major weakness. The authors were intent on presenting both quantitative and qualitative analyses of the data they had collected. Thirty-two children and families at three grade levels and three time points is a very large sample on which to collect such a wide array of observations, interviews, and elaborate literacy evaluations. On the other hand, 32 is a very small sample for conducting quantitative analysis, particularly considering variation in age, classrooms, schools, or family economic and social conditions. The major method, therefore, is necessarily bivariate—correlation—which provides no opportunity for statistically controlling for the multiple factors that might provide alternative explanations to those findings that the authors report.

Despite the weakness of the quantitative analyses presented in this book, the compelling nature of the findings about the ability of schools to compensate for literacy-poor homes in developing children's reading skills is heartening. The descriptions of the actual classroom experiences of many of these poor children, on the other hand, provides little hope that schools are actually providing the compensatory educational boost that this study shows is especially beneficial for children from low-income families. The long-term educational development of these children, demonstrated by their experiences in high school, is even more disheartening. This study demonstrates clearly that schools can make a difference in the literacy development of poor children, but the schools these children typically attend seldom fulfill this challenging task.

VALERIE E. LEE

University of Michigan
Ann Arbor

TYACK, DAVID and ELISABETH HANSOT. *Learning Together: A History of Coeducation in American Public Schools*. Pp. xii, 369. New Haven, CT: Yale University Press, 1990. No price.

Learning Together analyzes the history of American education from the viewpoint of women or gender policy and practice. Since it wrestles with an issue—coeducation—that most Americans take for granted, the authors imagine that it might have been otherwise. They show that coeducation sometimes became the target of vigorous debates, particularly when "women and men and cultural beliefs about gender were in transition." More specifically, this book explores the emergence of coeducation from the colonial period through recent years, emphasizing the complex relationships between what Tyack and Hansot call "silence, policy talk, and educational practice."

Learning Together shows that the system of coeducation took a variety of paths. Although most communities eventually pursued the pattern of mixing boys and girls in the same classroom, teaching them the same subjects, and subjecting them to the same rules and rewards, mixed schools followed different patterns at the local level. Some districts mixed sexes in the primary grades but separated them in secondary grades; others initiated coeducation in the high schools and only gradually extended it downward to the grammar schools.

This study demonstrates that the education of girls was not only a variegated but also a slow process. During the colonial period, prohibitions against the education of females led to the smuggling in of girls after the boys had completed their lessons in New England towns. Under the impact of the American Revolution and the advent of evangelical Protestantism, however, women gained increasing access to education as consistent with the requirements of life in a republic, piety, and, above all, the fulfillment of conventional female roles as mother and wife. By the eve of the Civil War, the coeducation of boys and girls in rural America had become an established fact, largely devoid of acrimonious debate. While coeducation was much more contentious in the cities, it had nonetheless won out there, too, by 1890.

Although educating boys and girls together had become the norm in American society by the 1890s, Tyack and Hansot show how the Progressive Era posed the greatest challenge to the idea of coeducation. As growing numbers of women entered the teaching profession and as high schools expanded during the period, key educational leaders—particularly Dr. Edward H. Clarke of Harvard Medical School and G. Stanley Hall, president of Clark University—attacked coeducation as too masculine for girls and too feminine for boys and advocated schooling that separated the sexes. Yet, this resistance to coeducation and women teachers failed to halt the rising numbers of women in the profession or to turn the tide against coeducation. Although schools introduced a variety of new programs—especially vocational courses and athletic activities for boys and domestic science classes for girls—designed to segregate children by sex within the structure of coeducational environments, Tyack and Hansot convincingly argue that such efforts had little impact on the prevailing relatively undifferentiated learning experiences of male and female students.

Learning Together also documents the impact of the women's movement of the 1960s and 1970s on American coeducation. It shows how the feminist movement discovered "hidden injury" to women in the coeducational system. Building upon the lessons of the civil rights movement, women activists emphasized the impact of institutional sexism: gender-biased textbooks, classroom interactions that favored males over females, unequal access to athletic programs, and the dearth of women in positions of real power. Still, Tyack and Hansot conclude, because public schools historically provided greater equity for males and females than other institutions did in American society, they "proved to be a more responsive target for feminist reformers than many other institutions." In a brief but telling concluding chapter, Tyack and Hansot analyze the unraveling of this liberal agenda, as traditionalists mobilized against treating boys and girls alike and some feminists lost faith in the efficacy of coeducation itself.

This study provides a valuable synthesis of coeducation in America, but significant aspects of the story are inadequately developed. African American, Southern, and immigrant experiences receive uneven treatment. While the study gives some attention to the South and black education before the 1930s, there is little discussion of this from the 1930s onward. Indeed, the civil rights movement is treated mainly as a model for explaining the feminist attack on gender inequality in the schools. The complicated intersection of race and gender in the development of coeducation during the period is not explored. Much the same is true of immigrants and the question of ethnicity. Asian and Hispanic Americans barely receive a footnote, indicating insufficient attention to the West and Southwest.

Until a variety of neglected groups and regions are brought more fully into the story, our understanding of the history of coeducation is only partial. Thanks to Tyack and Hansot, however, *Learning Together* provides an indispensable scaffolding for building a broader synthesis.

JOE W. TROTTER

Carnegie Mellon University
Pittsburgh
Pennsylvania

ECONOMICS

BURTON, LLOYD. *American Indian Water Rights and the Limits of Law*. Pp. xiii, 174. Lawrence: University Press of Kansas, 1991. $22.50.

Lloyd Burton's sympathetic, carefully researched case law study of the erosion of Indian water rights reminds us that because one purpose of law is sanctifying the rights of particular groups, that which entitles some disenfranchises others. Courts cannot defend without destroying. Three issues are at the center of water conflicts between Native Americans and white settlers: (1) diametrically opposed values—limited-use rights to a resource on behalf of a collective good versus doctrines of perpetual private ownership; (2) states' rights—the federal government has acquiesced in the allocation of surface water rights to non-Indian interests, knowing that states compete with tribes over economic benefits of resources; and (3) a "morally indefensible conflict of interest" within the Department of the Interior between the Bureau of Reclamation, responsible for western water resource development, and the Bureau of Indian Affairs, charged with stewardship over Indian interests. Theories of constituency-based decision making in water policy—sometimes called "subsystem" policymaking—

perhaps explain this third issue better than ethical inconsistency does.

Examining a litany of cases, Burton contends that federal court rulings have in most cases defended the superiority of Indian rights, a position first affirmed in *Winters* v. *United States* (1908). Congress and the executive branch have subverted these rights by being more sympathetic to, and more subject to the influence of, states-rights advocates. Negotiation has not functioned equitably because, in the past, it was used to get tribes to relinquish water; this dilemma is compounded by the fact that unlike whites, indigenous Americans have never been concerned with how much money they could receive for their water but with how much water they could receive through negotiation.

Historically, erosion of Indian rights parallels growth in the white settler population. After the Civil War, westerners won the outright sale of federal lands to private parties for nominal fees, a pattern accelerated after World War II when explosive growth resulted in further disenfranchisement of Indians. With the end of the reclamation era, and decisions over allocation revolving around existing resources such as the Central Arizona Project, the water-rights game cannot be played the same way. While few can disagree with Burton's conclusion that prospects for improving the climate of equitable negotiations toward nonlitigated dispute settlements are better when both sides to a conflict share "similar economic perspectives" over efficiency, it will remain for future studies to determine if regional basin management systems or true water markets based on the environmental costs of misuse could produce fairer outcomes.

DAVID LEWIS FELDMAN

Oak Ridge National Laboratory
Tennessee

University of Tennessee
Knoxville

SLOANE, ARTHUR A. *Hoffa*. Pp. xi, 430. Cambridge: MIT Press, 1991. $24.95.

At a time when American labor finds itself on the fringes of American society, Arthur Sloane's absorbing chronicle of the life and times of James Riddle Hoffa reminds us of the central role labor leaders once played in the equation of American power. Chronologically last on a list that includes Samuel Gompers, John L. Lewis, Phillip Murray, Walter Reuther, and George Meany, Hoffa remains perhaps the best known of all. Unfortunately, this notoriety stems not from his considerable accomplishments in collective bargaining but from his completely amoral exercise of power in the corrupt, Byzantine precincts of the International Brotherhood of Teamsters.

Unlike former books on corruption in the Teamsters, Sloane's is a full-blown biography of an American original—a man who combined a single-minded, often violent pursuit of power with a private life of rectitude and familial devotion. One of the strengths of this biography is Sloane's picture of the private Hoffa, who lived simply, was generous to his friends, cared little for what money could buy, eschewed alcohol and tobacco, and was devoted to his wife and family.

Students of labor relations will appreciate the book because of the attention it pays to Hoffa as a labor leader. Hoffa, with all of his troubles with the law, was probably as popular with his rank and file as any union chief in American history. The reasons for this are not complex. Hoffa delivered for the members. Yet Sloane adeptly shows us that Hoffa's greatest collective bargaining triumph, the nationwide master freight agreement, was fashioned in a decentralized, low-profit, and regulated industry—the perfect setting for a system of union-dominated industrywide bargaining. Nevertheless, it was Hoffa who accomplished it, to the undying gratitude of the truck drivers and the almost universal admiration of the employers.

What Sloane does not solve is the riddle of Jimmy Hoffa. We are taken through Hoffa's rise to power, his feud with Robert Kennedy, his endless legal problems, imprisonment, and, finally, his mysterious disappearance. But the biographer draws few conclusions about the motivations of this complex man. Although Hoffa took advantage of his position in the union to enrich himself to some degree, he had no real interest in money. He used the mob when he needed them, and he accepted their penetration of the union at all levels as normal, but he does not seem to have been their creature. Although he learned organizing tactics and strategy at the feet of the Trotskyists Farrel Dobbs and the Dunne brothers in Minneapolis, he rejected all variants of socialism. When the time came, he ruthlessly destroyed his Minnesota mentors without a second thought.

Nor, in fact, does Hoffa appear to have had any political convictions. He was, in the final analysis, an extreme but logical product of the American system of bread-and-butter unionism. Hoffa relished power. Because of the circumstances of his life, the arena in which he came to exercise it was organized labor. He loved being president of the union, and he knew that as long as he kept the members happy, they would keep him in power. He saw no social reform role for trade unionism and did not want to change society. To Hoffa, a union was a business whose job was to sell the members' labor at the top dollar. In this regard, he resembled John L. Lewis, and it is not surprising that the great leader of the coal miners was one of his role models.

That Hoffa succeeded in his narrow vision of the role of a labor leader is unquestionable. This success allowed him to run the union as he saw fit. Although Sloane shows that there was already plenty of corruption in the union when Hoffa became president, under his leadership the word "Teamster" came to be synonymous with organized crime for most Americans. Whatever Hoffa's considerable success in collective bargaining, it hardly compensated for the damage his tenure at the head of the Teamsters did to the reputation of organized labor in this country.

RONALD L. FILIPPELLI

Pennsylvania State University
University Park

OTHER BOOKS

ABBOTT, DAVID W. and JAMES P. LE-VINE. *Wrong Winner: The Coming Debacle in the Electoral College.* Pp. xiii, 168. New York: Praeger, 1991. Paperbound, $13.95.

ALLARD, C. KENNETH. *Command, Control, and the Common Defense.* Pp. xiii, 317. New Haven, CT: Yale University Press, 1990. $25.00.

AVERCH, HARVEY. *Private Markets and Public Intervention.* Pp. xiii, 221. Pittsburgh, PA: University of Pittsburgh Press, 1990. $29.95. Paperbound, $14.95.

BANERJEE, NIRMALA, ed. *Indian Women in a Changing Industrial Scenario.* Pp. 319. Newbury Park, CA: Sage, 1991. $35.00.

BARKAI, AVRAHAM. *Nazi Economics: Ideology, Theory, and Policy.* Pp. xii, 291. New Haven, CT: Yale University Press, 1990. $27.50.

BAUMAN, ZYGMUNT. *Modernity and Ambivalence.* Pp. vii, 285. Ithaca, NY: Cornell University Press, 1991. $43.50.

BAXTER, CRAIG et al. *Government and Politics in South Asia.* Pp. xv, 416. Boulder, CO: Westview Press, 1990. $55.00. Paperbound, $24.95.

BECKER, THEODORE L. *Quantum Politics: Applying Quantum Theory to Political Phenomena.* Pp. xvi, 232. New York: Praeger, 1991. $45.00.

BIRNBAUM, PIERRE and JEAN LECA, eds. *Individualism: Theories and Methods.* Pp. vi, 340. New York: Oxford University Press, 1990. $79.00.

BOGGS, DAVID L. *Adult Civic Education.* Pp. xii, 140. Springfield, IL: Charles C Thomas, 1991. $29.75.

BOTT, ALEXANDER J. *Handbook of United States Election Laws and Practices: Political Rights.* Pp. xxi, 535. Westport, CT: Greenwood Press, 1990. $75.00.

BOULDING, ELISE et al., eds. *Peace Culture and Society: Transnational Research and Dialogue.* Pp. xii, 308. Boulder, CO: Westview Press, 1991. Paperbound, $29.95.

BRAMS, STEVEN J. *Negotiation Games: Applying Game Theory to Bargaining and Arbitration.* Pp. xviii, 297. New York: Routledge, 1991. $49.50. Paperbound, $15.95.

BROWN, LESTER R. et al., eds. *State of the World.* Pp. xvii, 254. New York: Norton, 1991. Paperbound, $10.95.

BROWN, NEVILLE. *New Strategy through Space.* Pp. xi, 295. London: Pinter, 1989. Distributed by Columbia University Press, New York City. $35.00.

BRYNEN, REX. *Sanctuary and Survival: The PLO in Lebanon.* Pp. xiv, 255. Boulder, CO: Westview Press, 1990. $28.50.

BUELL, EMMETT H., Jr. and LEE SIGELMAN, eds. *Nominating the President.* Pp. xix, 300. Knoxville: University of Tennessee Press, 1991. Paperbound, no price.

CALDWELL, LYNTON KEITH. *International Environmental Policy: Emergence and Dimensions.* 2d ed. Pp. xvii, 460. Durham, NC: Duke University Press, 1991. $35.00. Paperbound, $18.95.

CAPUTO, RICHARD K. *Welfare and Freedom American Style: The Role of the Federal Government, 1900-1940.* Pp. xvi, 174. Lanham, MD: University Press of America, 1991. $41.25.

CASTRO, GINETTE. *American Feminism: A Contemporary History.* Pp. xii, 302. New York: Columbia University Press, 1990. $55.00. Paperbound, $12.50.

CHENG HSIAO-SHIH. *Party-Military Relations in the PRC and Taiwan: Paradoxes of Control.* Pp. xiv, 178. Boulder, CO: Westview Press, 1990. Paperbound, $28.50.

CHRISTEN, YVES. *Sex Differences: Modern Biology and the Unisex Fal-*

lacy. Pp. 141. New Brunswick, NJ: Transaction, 1991. $29.95. Paperbound, $21.95.

CLARK, BARRY. *Political Economy: A Comparative Approach*. Pp. xii, 313. New York: Praeger, 1991. $24.95.

COHEN, BENJAMIN J. *Crossing Frontiers: Explorations in International Political Economy*. Pp. x, 336. Boulder, CO: Westview Press, 1991. $49.95.

DENNIS, EVERETTE E. et al., eds. *Beyond the Cold War: Soviet and American Media Images*. Pp. 180. Newbury Park, CA: Sage, 1991. $36.00. Paperbound, $17.95.

DEVLIN, ROBERT. *Debt and Crisis in Latin America: The Supply Side of the Story*. Pp. xvi, 320. Princeton, NJ: Princeton University Press, 1990. $35.00.

DINNERSTEIN, LEONARD and KENNETH T. JACKSON. *American Vistas*. 6th ed. Pp. x, 371. New York: Oxford University Press, 1991. Paperbound, $14.95.

DONALDSON, THOMAS. *The Ethics of International Business*. Pp. xvi, 196. New York: Oxford University Press, 1989. $24.95.

DREZE, JEAN and AMARTYA SEN. *Hunger and Public Action*. Pp. xviii, 373. New York: Oxford University Press, 1989. No price.

DUNCAN, DAYTON. *Grass Roots: One Year in the Life of the New Hampshire Presidential Primary*. Pp. 436. New York: Viking, 1991. $22.95.

EDWARDS, RICHARD and PAOLO GARONNA. *The Forgotten Link: Labor's Stake in International Economic Cooperation*. Pp. x, 132. Savage, MD: Rowman & Littlefield, 1991. $42.50. Paperbound, $17.95.

ERIKSEN, VIKING OLVER. *Sunken Nuclear Submarines*. Pp. 176. New York: Oxford University Press, 1991. $35.00.

EYERMAN, RON and ANDREW JAMISON. *Social Movements: A Cognitive Approach*. Pp. 184. University Park:

Pennsylvania State University Press, 1991. $35.00. Paperbound, $14.95.

FONES-WOLF, KEN. *Trade Union Gospel: Christianity and Labor in Industrial Philadelphia 1865-1915*. Pp. xx, 266. Philadelphia: Temple University Press, 1989. No price.

GABEL, JOSEPH. *Manheim and Hungarian Marxism*. Pp. xii, 122. New Brunswick, NJ: Transaction, 1991. $34.95. Paperbound, $25.95.

GIAVAZZI, FRANCESCO and ALBERTO GIOVANNINI. *Limiting Exchange Rate Flexibility: The European Monetary System*. Pp. xi, 230. Cambridge: MIT Press, 1989. $27.50.

GIBNEY, MARK, ed. *World Justice? U.S. Courts and International Human Rights*. Pp. xiv, 178. Boulder, CO: Westview Press, 1991. $39.95.

GILL, STEPHEN. *American Hegemony and the Trilateral Commission*. Pp. xiii, 304. New York: Cambridge University Press, 1990. No price.

GOTTFRIED, KURT and PAUL BRACKEN, eds. *Reforging European Security: From Confrontation to Cooperation*. Pp. xiii, 226. Boulder, CO: Westview Press, 1990. Paperbound, $26.95.

GRAZIANI, GIOVANNI. *Gorbachev's Economic Strategy in the Third World*. Pp. xx, 116. New York: Praeger, 1990. $34.95.

HAAS, PETER M. *Saving the Mediterranean: The Politics of International Environmental Cooperation*. Pp. xxiv, 303. New York: Columbia University Press, 1990. $42.00.

HALE, CHARLES A. *The Transformation of Liberalism in Late Nineteenth-Century Mexico*. Pp. xi, 291. Princeton, NJ: Princeton University Press, 1990. $37.50.

HANRIEDER, WOLFRAM F. *Germany, America, Europe: Forty Years of German Foreign Policy*. Pp. xviii, 509. New Haven, CT: Yale University Press, 1991. $35.00. Paperbound, $18.00.

HEADY, FERREL. *Public Administration: A Comparative Perspective*. 4th ed. Pp. x, 472. New York: Marcel Dekker, 1991. $49.75.

HESS, GARY R. *Vietnam and the United States: Origins and Legacy of War.* Pp. xvi, 205. Boston, MA: G. K. Hall, 1990. $26.95.

HIERONYMI, OTTO. *Economic Policies for the New Hungary: Proposals for a Coherent Approach.* Pp. xiii, 121. Boulder, CO: Westview Press, 1990. Paperbound, $18.85.

HIXSON, WALTER L. *George F. Kennan: Cold War Iconoclast.* Pp. xiii, 381. New York: Columbia University Press, 1991. Paperbound, $14.50.

HOLLIS, MARTIN and STEVE SMITH. *Explaining and Understanding International Relations.* Pp. vi, 226. New York: Oxford University Press, 1990. $55.00.

HULME, DERICK L., Jr. *The Political Olympics: Moscow, Afghanistan, and the 1980 U.S. Boycott.* Pp. xi, 179. New York: Praeger, 1990. $39.95.

HUNT, WILLIAM R. *Front-Page Detective: William J. Burns and the Detective Profession 1880-1930.* Pp. 222. Bowling Green, OH: Bowling Green University Popular Press, 1990. $39.95. Paperbound, $19.95.

HUTTMAN, ELIZABETH et al., eds. *Urban Housing Segregation of Minorities in Western Europe and the United States.* Pp. xiii, 431. Durham, NC: Duke University Press, 1991. $59.95.

JACOBS, FRANCIS and RICHARD CORBETT. *The European Parliament.* Pp. xxi, 298. Boulder, CO: Westview Press, 1991. $58.00.

JANOWITZ, MORRIS. *On Social Organization and Social Control.* Pp. vii, 324. Chicago: University of Chicago Press, 1991. $34.95. Paperbound, $17.50.

KEGLEY, CHARLES W., Jr. and KENNETH L. SCHWAB, eds. *After the Cold War: Questioning the Morality of Nuclear Deterrence.* Pp. xi, 276. Boulder, CO: Westview Press, 1991. $55.00. Paperbound, $16.95.

KELLER, WILLIAM W. *The Liberals and J. Edgar Hoover.* Pp. xiii, 215. Princeton, NJ: Princeton University Press, 1989. $25.00.

KELSO, LOUIS O. and PATRICIA HETTER KELSO. *Democracy and Economic Power: Extending the ESOP Revolution through Binary Economics.* Pp. 202. Lanham, MD: University Press of America, Kelso Institute for the Study of Economic Systems, 1991. $45.25. Paperbound, $27.25.

KITSCHELT, HERBERT and STAF HELLEMANS. *Beyond the European Left: Ideology and Political Action in the Belgian Ecology Parties.* Pp. viii, 262. Durham, NC: Duke University Press, 1990. $39.50.

KOBURGER, CHARLES W., Jr. *Narrow Seas, Small Navies, and Fat Merchantmen.* Pp. xxi, 157. New York: Praeger, 1990. $39.95.

KRUGMAN, PAUL R. *Rethinking International Trade.* Pp. viii, 282. Cambridge: MIT Press, 1990. $25.00.

LAIDI, ZAKI. *The Superpowers and Africa: The Constraints of a Rivalry, 1960-1990.* Pp. xxv, 232. Chicago: University of Chicago Press, 1990. $45.00. Paperbound, $14.95.

LASATER, MARTIN L. *A Step toward Democracy: The December 1989 Elections in Taiwan, Republic of China.* Pp. vii, 100. Lanham, MD: AEI Press, 1991. Paperbound, $7.95.

LAVIE, SMADAR. *The Poetics of Military Occupation.* Pp. ix, 397. Berkeley: University of California Press, 1991. No price.

LESSNOFF, MICHAEL, ed. *Social Contract Theory.* Pp. 233. New York: New York University Press, 1990. Paperbound, $19.00.

LIEVEN, DOMINIC. *Russia's Rulers under the Old Regime.* Pp. xxii, 407. New Haven, CT: Yale University Press, 1991. $40.00. Paperbound, $18.95.

LIPARTITO, KENNETH J. and JOSEPH A. PRATT. *Baker and Botts in*

the Development of Modern Houston.
Pp. xi, 253. Austin: University of Texas
Press, 1991. $24.95.
LIPSHITZ, LESLIE and DONOGH Mc-
DONALD, eds. German Unification:
Economic Issues. Pp. xv, 171. Washing-
ton, DC: International Monetary Fund,
1990. Paperbound, $10.00.
MacDONALD, STUART. Technology and
the Tyranny of Export Controls: Whis-
per Who Dares. Pp. xi, 206. New York:
St. Martin's Press, 1990. $55.00.
MARDER, ARTHUR J. et al. Old
Friends, New Enemies. Pp. xxx, 621.
New York: Oxford University Press,
1990. $69.00.
MASTERS, ROGER D. The Nature of
Politics. Pp. xvii, 298. New Haven, CT:
Yale University Press, 1991. $30.00.
Paperbound, $12.95.
MESA-LAGO, CARMELO, ed. Cuban
Studies. Vol. 20. Pp. xi, 245. Pitts-
burgh, PA: University of Pittsburgh
Press, 1990. $32.95.
MINARIK, JOSEPH J. Making Amer-
ica's Budget Policy: From the 1980s to
the 1990s. Pp. xv, 229. Armonk, NY:
M. E. Sharpe, 1990. $39.95. Paper-
bound, $15.95.
MISHEL, LAWRENCE and DAVID M.
FRANKEL. The State of Working
America 1990-91. Pp. xiv, 315.
Armonk, NY: M. E. Sharpe, 1991.
$29.95.
MOLLENKOPF, JOHN H. and MAN-
UEL CASTELLS, eds. Dual City: Re-
structuring New York. Pp. xiv, 477.
New York: Russell Sage, 1991. $39.95.
MORALES-GOMEZ, DANIEL A. and
CARLOS ALBERTO TORRES. The
State, Corporatist Politics, and Educa-
tional Policy Making in Mexico. Pp. xxiv,
197. New York: Praeger, 1990. $39.95.
MULGAN, G. J. Communication and
Control. Pp. 302. New York: Guilford
Press, 1991. $35.00.
NASSAR, JAMAL R. The Palestine Lib-
eration Organization: From Armed
Struggle to the Declaration of Indepen-

dence. Pp. xii, 242. New York: Praeger,
1991. $42.95.
NEEDLER, MARTIN C. The Concepts of
Comparative Politics. Pp. xiii, 156.
New York: Praeger, 1991. $39.95. Pa-
perbound, $14.95.
NIELSEN, KAI. After the Demise of the
Tradition: Rorty, Critical Theory, and
the Fate of Philosophy. Pp. x, 278. Boul-
der, CO: Westview Press, 1991. $38.50.
PATTERSON, GRAEME. History and
Communications. Pp. 251. Buffalo,
NY: University of Toronto Press, 1990.
$40.00. Paperbound, $16.95.
POHLMAN, H. L. Justice Oliver Wendell
Holmes: Free Speech and the Living
Constitution. Pp. ix, 265. New York:
New York University Press, 1991. $45.00.
PROVENZO, EUGENE F., Jr. Religious
Fundamentalism and American Edu-
cation. Pp. xix, 134. Albany: State Uni-
versity of New York Press, 1990.
Paperbound, $10.95.
RABKIN, RHODA P. Cuban Politics: The
Revolutionary Experiment. Pp. xvi,
233. New York: Praeger, 1990. $39.95.
RASKIN, MARCUS G. Essays of a Citi-
zen: From National Security State to
Democracy. Pp. xiii, 321. Armonk, NY:
M. E. Sharpe, 1991. $27.50.
ROGERS, PAUL P. The Bitter Years: Mac-
Arthur and Sutherland. Pp. xvi, 348.
New York: Praeger, 1990. $49.95.
ROGERS, PAUL P. The Good Years: Mac-
Arthur and Sutherland. Pp. xix, 380.
New York: Praeger, 1990. $49.95.
SANDOZ, ELLIS, ed. Eric Voegelin's Sig-
nificance for the Modern Mind. Pp. xi,
218. Baton Rouge: Louisiana State
University Press, 1991. $25.00.
SANDOZ, ELLIS, ed. Political Sermons
of the American Founding Era, 1730-
1805. Pp. xxxvii, 1598. Indianapolis,
IN: Liberty Press, 1991. $38.00. Pa-
perbound, $12.00.
SCHRECKER, JOHN E. The Chinese
Revolution in Historical Perspective.
Pp. xx, 240. New York: Praeger, 1991.
$45.00. Paperbound, $17.95.

SHAH, GHANSHYAM. *Social Movements in India*. Pp. 222. Newbury Park, CA: Sage, 1991. $27.50.

SPRAGENS, THOMAS A., Jr. *Reason and Democracy*. Pp. xi, 281. Durham, NC: Duke University Press, 1990. $39.50. Paperbound, $17.95.

STEPHENSON, D. GRIER, Jr., ed. *An Essential Safeguard: Essays on the United States Supreme Court and Its Justices*. Pp. xii, 178. Westport, CT: Greenwood Press, 1991. $42.95.

STERLING, CLAIRE. *Octopus*. Pp. 384. New York: Simon & Schuster, 1991. Paperbound, $10.95.

STOKES, GALE, ed. *From Stalinism to Pluralism*. Pp. xi, 267. New York: Oxford University Press, 1991. $35.00. Paperbound, $12.95.

STROTHER, RAYMOND. *Cottonwood*. Pp. 285. New York: E. P. Dutton, 1991. $18.95.

VILLE, SIMON P. *Transport and the Development of the European Economy, 1750-1918*. Pp. xiii, 252. New York: St. Martin's Press, 1990. $59.95.

WATANABE, MASAO. *The Japanese and Western Science*. Pp. xiv, 141. Philadelphia: University of Pennsylvania Press, 1991. $28.95.

WATTS, MEREDITH W. et al. *Contemporary German Youth and Their Elders: A Generational Comparison*. Pp. xv, 193. Westport, CT: Greenwood Press, 1989. $39.95.

WENNER, LETTIE McSPADDEN. *U.S. Energy and Environmental Interest Groups: Institutional Profiles*. Pp. xxvii, 358. Westport, CT: Greenwood Press, 1990. $55.00.

WESTON, BURNS H., ed. *Alternative Security: Living without Nuclear Deterrence*. Pp. xv, 283. Boulder, CO: Westview Press, 1990. $45.00. Paperbound, $14.95.

YOON, DAE-KYU. *Law and Political Authority in South Korea*. Pp. xiii, 247. Boulder, CO: Westview Press, 1991. $40.00.

INDEX

ANGUS E. TAYLOR

Professor of Mathematics
University of California
Los Angeles

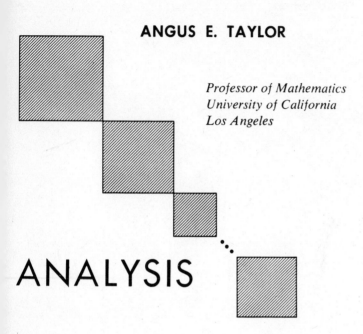

ANALYSIS

New York · John Wiley & Sons, Inc.

London · Chapman & Hall, Ltd.

To GORDON,

KENNETH, and KITTY

PREFACE

This book has been written as a part of my program of teaching at the graduate level. The primary aim of the book is to assist graduate students in learning fundamental ideas and theorems about linear spaces and linear operators and to lead them to an appreciation of the unifying power of the abstract-linear-space point of view in surveying the problems of algebra, classical analysis, the theory of integration, and differential and integral equations. While the book is principally addressed to graduate students, it is also intended to be useful to mathematicians, both pure and applied, who have need of a simple and direct presentation of the fundamentals of the theory of linear spaces and linear operators.

The central theme of the book is the theory of normed linear spaces and of linear operators which map one such space into another. A normed linear space which is complete is called a Banach space; a number of the most important results in linear-space theory depend on completeness, and so we have a Banach space context for these results. However, the hypothesis of completeness is not invoked except as it is needed for effective results. The more specialized theory of inner-product spaces (which, when complete and infinite dimensional are called Hilbert spaces) is carried along within the normed-linear-space context, leaning upon the general theory of normed linear spaces, but with its own characteristic special development where such development can achieve results of a distinctive character.

Although the emphasis is mainly on normed linear spaces, the more general ideas of topological linear spaces are developed to some extent, since an understanding of these is relevant at many places in the theory of normed linear spaces, notably in connection with the weak topologies of such spaces and their conjugate spaces. Part of Chapter 3 provides a brief introduction to the study of general topological linear spaces, both without and with the assumption of local convexity. The geometry of convex sets and linear varieties (especially hyperplanes) is all presented in the context of topological linear spaces.

There are many illustrations and applications of the abstract concepts and methods. The numerous problems serve both to illustrate and to extend the theory, as well as to train the student by having him fill in details omitted in the text. For many of the illustrations and problems the sequence spaces l^p have been chosen, in order to minimize the technical analytical difficulties. There are applications to differential equations, to integral equations, and to the classical theory of analytic functions.

Chapter 5 stresses the importance of complex contour integration and the calculus of residues in the spectral theory of linear operators. The methods apply to all closed linear operators, bounded or not. This chapter also contains the famous Riesz theory of compact (completely continuous) operators, as extended and perfected by later research workers, and its application to obtain the classical "determinant-free" theorems for Fredholm integral equations of the second kind.

Chapter 6 presents the standard elementary theory of self-adjoint, normal, and unitary operators in Hilbert space. There is also the discussion, very important for applications to integral and differential equations, of the theory of compact symmetric operators and symmetric operators with compact resolvent. This discussion does not require the completeness of the inner-product space under consideration. The spectral analysis of self-adjoint operators is performed with the aid of the Riesz representation theorem for linear functionals on a space of continuous functions. The treatment is deliberately kept as close to classical analysis as possible within this framework. After the student is acquainted with the situation from this point of view, he may with great profit go on to a study of B*-algebras, and learn to view the spectral theorem for a normal or self-adjoint operator as a consequence of the Gelfand-Neumark theorem for commutative B*-algebras. For an understanding of these developments Chapter 7 is an essential prepara-

tion.   But there is no room in this book for a treatment of Banach algebras.

   The book is an introduction, not a treatise.   It is meant to open doors
for the student and to give him understanding and preparation which will
help him to push on, if he wishes, to the new frontiers of modern mathematics, carrying with him a clearer realization of the structure of classical mathematics.

ANGUS E. TAYLOR

Los Angeles
August 1957

ACKNOWLEDGMENTS

The first draft of this book was written while I was on sabbatical leave from the University of California, Los Angeles. During part of that time I worked in Geneva, where I was accorded the courtesy of the libraries of the University and of the Mathematical Institute. Then for six months in 1955 I was privileged to be a Fulbright Research Scholar visiting at the Johannes Gutenberg University in Mainz, Germany. I am deeply grateful to Professor Gottfried Köthe, who was at that time Rektor of the University and who graciously furnished me his own office in the Mathematical Institute.

I wish to thank the University of California for a small grant of funds for assistance in the preparation of the manuscript. I also thank Ruthanne Clark for very expert typing and handwork on the formulas.

The book has taken shape in my mind gradually since 1946. I owe a great deal to successive groups of graduate students to whom I have lectured and who have participated in seminars. For various improvements in style and presentation and for the detection of errors of omission and commission, I am especially indebted to my 1956–1957 class, which read the manuscript in its nearly final form.

For helpful conversations and comments I am especially indebted to Professors Richard Arens and Magnus Hestenes. Lastly, I take pleasure in thanking Professor Nelson Dunford for providing me with a manuscript copy of the book by himself and J. T. Schwartz. This voluminoùs and encyclopedic manuscript, available to me after my own first draft was written, made it easier for me to resign myself to the omission of topics which I had originally hoped to be able to include in my own book.

A. E. T.

CONTENTS

INTRODUCTION

It is the purpose of this introduction to explain certain notations and terminologies used throughout the book.

Sets

Let X be a given set. If x is an element of X this fact is expressed in symbols by writing

$$x \in X.$$

The negation of $x \in X$ is written in the form

$$x \notin X.$$

A subset of X is a set E such that if $x \in E$, then also $x \in X$. In particular, X is a subset of itself. A subset of X which is not all of X is called a *proper* subset of X. The statement "E is a subset of X" is expressed in symbols by writing

$$E \subset X, \quad \text{or} \quad X \supset E.$$

Two sets E, F are the same if and only if $E \subset F$ and $F \subset E$.

Among the subsets of a given set is the *empty set*, the set having no elements. We denote the empty set by $\emptyset$.

Let X be a set and let x be a variable element of X. For each x let $P(x)$ denote a proposition concerning x. Then we use the symbol

$$\{x : P(x)\}$$

to denote the set of all $x \in X$ for which $P(x)$ is true. This notation is extended in an obvious manner for more than one proposition. Thus, if $P_1(x)$, $P_2(x)$, $\cdots$ are propositions, $\{x : P_n(x), n = 1, 2, \cdots\}$ denotes the set of all $x \in X$ such that $P_n(x)$ is true for each of the values $n = 1, 2, \cdots$.

Example I. Let X be the set of all continuous real-valued functions of s on the interval $0 \leqslant s \leqslant 1$. Let E be the subset of X consisting of those functions x for which $x(0) = x(1)$. Then

$$E = \{x : x(0) = x(1)\}.$$

Example 2. Let X be the set of all real-valued functions x which are defined and have derivatives of all orders for all real values of s. Let E be the set of those x such that x and all its derivatives have the value 0 at $s = 0$. Then

$$E = \{x : x^{(n)}(0) = 0, \qquad n = 0, 1, 2, \cdots\}.$$

Subsets of a given set can be combined in two ways: by the formation of *unions* and *intersections*. If $E_1, \cdots, E_n$ are subsets of X, the union of $E_1, \cdots, E_n$ is defined as the set of all elements of X which belong to *at least* one of the sets $E_1, \cdots, E_n$. This union is denoted by

$$E_1 \cup E_2 \cup \cdots \cup E_n, \qquad \text{or} \qquad \bigcup_{i=1}^{n} E_i.$$

This definition and notation are extended to arbitrary collections of subsets of X as follows: Suppose $\mathscr{E}$ is a collection (family) of subsets of X. The set of all $x \in X$ such that $x \in E$ for at least one $E \in \mathscr{E}$ is denoted by

$$\bigcup_{E \in \mathscr{E}} E$$

and is called the union of the sets of $\mathscr{E}$. In case $\mathscr{E}$ is a countable set, with members $E_1, E_2, \cdots$, we write the union as

$$\bigcup_{n=1}^{\infty} E_n.$$

If the members of $\mathscr{E}$ are indexed in some manner, say E_α, where α ranges over a set A, we may denote the union by

$$\bigcup_{\alpha \in A} E_\alpha.$$

The *intersection* of a collection $\mathscr{E}$ of subsets E of X is defined as the set of all $x \in X$ such that $x \in E$ for *every* $E \in \mathscr{E}$. It is denoted by

$$\bigcap_{E \in \mathscr{E}} E$$

If the members of $\mathscr{E}$ are indexed, the intersection is represented symbolically in the appropriate manner corresponding to the usage for unions, but with

$$\bigcap \text{ in place of } \bigcup.$$

The intersection of the finite collection $E_1, \cdots, E_n$ is also written in the form

$$E_1 \cap E_2 \cap \cdots \cap E_n.$$

If $E \subset X$, the *complement* of E (relative to X) is defined as the set of all $x \in X$ such that $x \notin E$. We denote the complement of E by E', or, in some cases where the prime notation is inconvenient, by $C(E)$. Observe the following:

$$(E')' = E,$$

and if $E \subset F$, then $F' \subset E'$.

There is an important relation between complements, unions, and intersections; namely: If $\mathscr{E}$ is a collection of subsets of X, the complement of the union of all the members of $\mathscr{E}$ is the intersection of their complements. That is,

$$\left(\bigcup_{E \in \mathscr{E}} E \right)' = \bigcap_{E \in \mathscr{E}} E'.$$

For a finite collection this can be written

$$(E_1 \cup E_2 \cup \cdots \cup E_n)' = E_1' \cap E_2' \cap \cdots \cap E_n'.$$

If we replace E_i by E_i' throughout and then take the complement of both sides, we obtain the equivalent relation

$$(E_1 \cap E_2 \cap \cdots \cap E_n)' = E_1' \cup E_2' \cup \cdots \cup E_n'.$$

The general form of this is

$$\left(\bigcap_{E \in \mathscr{E}} E \right)' = \bigcup_{E \in \mathscr{E}} E'.$$

If E and F are subsets of X, the *difference* $E - F$ is defined as the set of all $x \in X$ which are in E but not in F. In other words,

$$E - F = E \cap F'.$$

Functions

In this book, unless we make special mention to the contrary, we always use the word "function" to mean a single-valued function. Since we shall have a great deal to do with functions whose arguments and values need not be real or complex numbers but may be elements of quite arbitrary sets, we put down here explicitly our general definition of a function.

Let X and Y be arbitrary nonempty sets. Suppose there is some rule whereby to each element $x \in X$ corresponds a uniquely determined element $y \in Y$. Consider the set consisting of all ordered pairs (x, y), where $x \in X$ and y is the corresponding element of Y. This set of pairs is called a *function*. The set X is called the *domain* of the function. The set of y's which occur as correspondents of the x's may or may not comprise all of Y. In any event, this set of y's is called the *range* of the function.

We see by this definition that a function with domain X and range contained in the set Y is a subset of the set of *all* ordered pairs (x, y) with $x \in X$ and $y \in Y$. This latter set of *all* such pairs is denoted by $X \times Y$ and called the *Cartesian product* (or often, just the *product*) of X and Y. Thus, a function with domain X and range in Y is a particular kind of subset of $X \times Y$. The distinguishing property of a function, as contrasted with other subsets of $X \times Y$, is that among the pairs (x, y) which form the distinct elements of the function, *each x in X occurs once and only once*. Any subset of $X \times Y$ with this property is a function with domain X and range in Y. Thus, let F be a subset of $X \times Y$. Then F is a function with domain X and range in Y if and only if the two following conditions are satisfied:

1. To each $x \in X$ corresponds some $y \in Y$ such that $(x, y) \in F$,
2. If (x_1, y_1) and (x_2, y_2) are in F and $y_1 \neq y_2$, then $x_1 \neq x_2$.

Sometimes we have occasion to consider nonempty sets X, Y and a function whose domain is a proper subset of X and whose range is contained in Y. In this case the function is a subset of $X \times Y$ which satisfies the second but not the first of the two foregoing conditions.

If F is a function and $(x, y) \in F$, we write $y = F(x)$; this is the usual functional notation. In general, we find it best to refer to the function by the single letter F, reserving the notation $F(x)$ for the element of the range of F which corresponds to the element x of the domain. Sometimes, however, it is convenient to do otherwise. Thus, in speaking of the exponential function, we may refer to the function e^x, or the function $y = e^x$, instead of using the lengthy phraseology "the function consisting of all pairs (x, y), where $y = e^x$ and x varies over all real numbers."

Inverse Functions

Suppose F is a function with domain D and range R, where $D \subset X$ and $R \subset Y$. Consider the Cartesian product $Y \times X$; note the reversal of order. Consider the subset of $Y \times X$ consisting of those elements (y, x) such that $(x, y) \in F$. It *may* be that this subset of $Y \times X$ is a function (with domain in Y and range in X). If so, we call it the function *inverse* to F, and we often denote it by F^{-1}. The domain of F^{-1} is then R, and its range is D.

Observe that the inverse of F is defined if and only if the correspondence between x and $F(x)$, as x varies over D, is a one-to-one correspondence between the elements of D and the elements of R. Another way of putting it is that F has an inverse if and only if $F(x_1) = F(x_2)$ implies that $x_1 = x_2$.

Also observe that, when F has an inverse, $y = F(x)$ is equivalent to $x = F^{-1}(y)$. Finally, if F has the inverse F^{-1}, then F^{-1} also has an inverse, namely F.

Usage Relating to Real Numbers

The least upper bound (if it exists) of a set S of real numbers is denoted by sup S. The greatest lower bound of S is denoted by inf S. The sup and inf notation is also used in other appropriate situations. For instance, if f is a real-valued function whose domain includes the set E, the least upper bound of the set of all $f(x)$ corresponding to x in E is denoted by

$$\sup_{x \in E} f(x).$$

We follow standard usage with respect to the symbols $+\infty$, $-\infty$ in relation to the real number system.

Inequalities

At a number of places in this book we use some of the standard inequalities concerning sums and integrals. We list the most commonly used ones here. The standard reference work on this subject is the book, *Inequalities*, by Hardy, Littlewood, and Pólya. In what follows we refer to this book as H, L, and P, and cite by number the section in which the stated inequality is discussed. In all inequalities the quantities involved may be either real or complex. Sums are either all from 1 to n or from 1 to ∞, and in the latter case certain evident assumptions and implications of convergence are involved. For simplicity the inequalities for integrals are written for the case in which the functions are defined on a finite or infinite interval of the real axis. The inequalities are valid with more general interpretations of the set over which integration is extended.

Hölder's inequality for sums (H, L, and P, § 2.8): If $1 < p < \infty$ and $p' = \dfrac{p}{p-1}$, then

$$\sum|a_i b_i| \leqslant (\sum|a_i|^p)^{1/p}(\sum|b_i|^{p'})^{1/p'}.$$

The special case when $p = p' = 2$ is called Cauchy's inequality (H, L, and P, § 2.4).

Minkowski's inequality for sums (H, L, and P, § 2.11): If $1 \leqslant p < \infty$, then

$$(\sum|a_i + b_i|^p)^{1/p} \leqslant (\sum|a_i|^p)^{1/p} + (\sum|b_i|^p)^{1/p}.$$

Jensen's inequality (H, L, and P, § 2.10): If $0 < p < q$, then

$$(\sum|a_i|^q)^{1/q} \leqslant (\sum|a_i|^p)^{1/p}.$$

Hölder's inequality for integrals (H, L, and P, § 6.9): If $1 < p < \infty$ and $p' = \dfrac{p}{p-1}$, then

$$\int|f(x)\,g(x)|\,dx \leqslant \left(\int|f(x)|^p\,dx\right)^{1/p}\left(\int|g(x)|^{p'}\,dx\right)^{1/p'}.$$

The special case when $p = p' = 2$ is called the Schwarz inequality (H, L, and P, § 6.5).

Minkowski's inequality for integrals (H, L, and P, § 6.13): If $1 \leqslant p < \infty$, then

$$\left(\int|f(x) + g(x)|^p\,dx\right)^{1/p} \leqslant \left(\int|f(x)|^p\,dx\right)^{1/p} + \left(\int|g(x)|^p\,dx\right)^{1/p}.$$

The Kronecker Delta

The symbol δ_{ij} denotes the number 1 if $i = j$ and the number 0 if $i \neq j$. Here i and j are positive integers.

I

THE ABSTRACT APPROACH TO LINEAR PROBLEMS

I.0 Introductory Statement

The modern treatment of many topics in pure and applied mathematics is characterized by the effort which is made to strip away nonessential details and to show clearly the fundamental assumptions and the structure of the reasoning. This effort often leads to a certain degree of abstraction, the concrete nature of the originally contemplated problem being temporarily put aside, and the aspects of the problem which are of greatest significance being cast into axiomatic form. It is found that in this way there is a considerable gain in transparency and that diverse problems exhibit common characteristics which enable them all to be at least partially solved by the methods of a single general theory.

In this chapter we consider the algebraic aspects of such an abstract approach to linear problems. In essence, all linear problems are viewed in some measure as analogous to the linear problems exhibited in elementary algebra by the theory of systems of linear equations. The linear problems of analysis usually require topological as well as algebraic considerations. However, in this chapter, we exclude all concern with topology; the topological aspects of the abstract approach to linear problems will be taken up in later chapters.

The profoundest results of the chapter are the extension theorems in § 1.71 (Theorems 1.71–A and 1.71–D). They depend on Zorn's lemma. Theorem 1.71–A is needed to demonstrate the existence of certain projections (see Theorem 4.8–A). Theorem 1.71–D is the fundamental tool in proofs concerning the extension of continuous linear functionals and, in particular, in the proof of the Hahn-Banach theorem (see Theorems 3.7–B, 3.8–D, and 4.3–A).

Chapter 1 culminates in § 1.91 with two groups of theorems: one group (the first three theorems) concerning the range of a linear operator and the null manifold of the transpose of the operator and the other group (the last four theorems) concerning the null manifold of the operator and the range of its transpose. These theorems furnish information on existence and uniqueness theorems in the case of certain kinds of linear problems. For the finite-dimensional case these theorems include the standard results concerning algebraic systems of linear systems. In the infinite-dimensional case the results are not as useful as results which can be obtained with the aid of metric or topological tools. Nevertheless, the material of § 1.91 points the way to more incisive results, some of which are given in § 4.6.

1.1 Abstract Linear Spaces

We have as yet made no formal definition of what is meant by the adjective *linear* in the phrase "linear problems." We can cite various particular kinds of linear problems: the problems of homogeneous and inhomogeneous systems of linear equations in *n* "unknowns" in elementary algebra; the problems of the theory of linear ordinary differential equations (existence theorems, particular and general solutions, problems of finding solutions satisfying given conditions at one or two end points); boundary or initial-value problems in the theory of linear partial differential equations; problems in the theory of linear integral equations; linear "transform" problems, e.g., problems related to Fourier and Laplace transforms. This is by no means an exhaustive list of the types of mathematical situation in which linear problems arise.

At the bottom of every linear problem is a mathematical structure called a *linear space*. We shall therefore begin with an axiomatic treatment of abstract linear spaces.

A collection of elements, together with a certain structure of relations between elements or of rules of manipulation and combination, the whole supporting a mathematical development, is often called a *space*. This terminology derives from the model of geometry, in which the elements are points.   We are now going to define what is meant, abstractly, by a *linear space.*

Definition.   Let X be a set of elements, hereafter sometimes called *points,* and denoted by small italic letters: x, y, $\cdots$.   We assume that each pair of elements x, y can be combined by a process called addition to yield another element z denoted by $z = x + y$.   We also assume that each real number α and each element x can be combined by a process called multiplication to yield another element y denoted by $y = \alpha x$.   The set X with these two processes is called a *linear space* if the following axioms are satisfied:

1. $x + y = y + x$.
2. $x + (y + z) = (x + y) + z$.
3. There is in X a unique element, denoted by 0 and called the zero element, such that $x + 0 = x$ for each x.
4. To each x in X corresponds a unique element, denoted by $- x$, such that $x + (- x) = 0$.
5. $\alpha(x + y) = \alpha x + \alpha y$.
6. $(\alpha + \beta)x = \alpha x + \beta x$.
7. $\alpha(\beta x) = (\alpha\beta)x$.
8. $1 \cdot x = x$.
9. $0 \cdot x = 0$.

Anyone who is familiar with the algebra of vectors in ordinary three-dimensional Euclidean space will see at once that the set of all such vectors forms a linear space.   An abstract linear space embodies so many of the features of ordinary vector algebra that the word *vector* has been taken over into a more general context.   A linear space is often called a *vector space,* and the elements of the space are called *vectors.*

In the foregoing list of axioms it was assumed that the multiplication operation was performed with *real* numbers α, β.   To emphasize this, if necessary, we call the space a *real* linear space, or a *real* vector space. An alternative notion of a linear space is obtained if it is assumed that any *complex* number α and any element x can be multiplied, yielding another element αx.   The axioms are the same as before.   The space is then called a *complex* linear space.

The notion of a vector space is defined even more generally in abstract algebra, by allowing the multipliers α, β, $\cdots$ to be elements of an arbitrary commutative field.   In this book, however, we confine ourselves to the two fields of real and complex numbers, respectively.   The elements of the field are called *scalars,* to contrast with the *vector* elements of the linear space.

It is easy to see that $-1 \cdot x = -x$ and that $\alpha \cdot 0 = 0$. We write $x - y$ for convenience in place of $x + (-y)$. The following "cancellation" rules are also easily deduced from the axioms:

(1.1–1) $x + y = x + z$ implies $y = z$;

(1.1–2) $\alpha x = \alpha y$ and $\alpha \neq 0$ imply $x = y$;

(1.1–3) $\alpha x = \beta x$ and $x \neq 0$ imply $\alpha = \beta$.

With respect to addition, a linear space X is an Abelian (commutative) *group*, in the technical algebraic sense.

Definition. A nonempty subset M of a linear space X is called a *linear manifold* in X if $x + y$ is in M whenever x and y are both in M and if also αx is in M whenever x is in M and α is any scalar.

In this definition and generally throughout the book, statements made about linear spaces, without qualification as to whether the space is real or complex, will be intended to apply equally to real spaces and complex spaces.

It will be seen at once that, if M is a linear manifold in X, it may be regarded as a linear space by itself. For, if x is in M, then $-1 \cdot x = -x$ is also in M, and $x - x = 0$ is also in M. The nine axioms for a linear space are now found to be satisfied in M. Another term for a linear manifold in X is *subspace* of X. A subspace of X is called *proper* if it is not all of X.

The set consisting of 0 alone is a subspace. We denote it by (0).

Suppose S is any nonempty subset of X. Consider the set M of all finite linear combinations of elements of S, i.e., elements of the form $\alpha_1 x_1 + \cdots + \alpha_n x_n$, where n is any positive integer (not fixed), $x_1, \cdots, x_n$ are any elements of S, and $\alpha_1, \cdots, \alpha_n$ are any scalars. This set M is a linear manifold. It is called the linear manifold generated, or determined, by S. Sometimes we speak of M as the linear manifold *spanned* by S. It is easy to verify the truth of the following statements: (1) M consists of those vectors which belong to every linear manifold which contains S; i.e., M is the intersection of all such manifolds. (2) M is the smallest linear manifold which contains S; i.e., if N is a linear manifold which contains S, then M is contained in N.

One of the most important concepts in a vector space is that of linear dependence.

Definition. A finite set of vectors $x_1, \cdots, x_n$ in the space X is *linearly dependent* if there exist scalars $\alpha_1, \cdots, \alpha_n$, not all zero, such that $\alpha_1 x_1 + \cdots + \alpha_n x_n = 0$. If the finite set $x_1, \cdots, x_n$ is not linearly dependent, it is called *linearly independent*. In that case, a relation $\alpha_1 x_1 + \cdots + \alpha_n x_n = 0$ implies that $\alpha_1 = \cdots = \alpha_n = 0$. An infinite set S of vectors is called linearly independent if every finite subset of S is linearly independent; otherwise S is called linearly dependent.

Observe that, if a set of vectors contains a linearly dependent subset, the whole set is linearly dependent. Also note that a linearly independent set cannot contain the vector 0.

We note the following simple but important theorem, of which use will be made in later arguments:

Theorem I.1–A. *Suppose $x_1, \cdots, x_n$ is a set of vectors with $x_1 \neq 0$. The set is linearly dependent if and only if some one of the vectors $x_2, \cdots, x_n$, say x_k, is in the linear manifold generated by $x_1, \cdots, x_{k-1}$.*

PROOF. Suppose the set is linearly dependent. There is a smallest integer k, with $2 \leqslant k \leqslant n$, such that the set $x_1, \cdots, x_k$ is linearly dependent. This dependence is expressed by an equation $\alpha_1 x_1 + \cdots + \alpha_k x_k = 0$, with not all the α's equal to zero. Necessarily, then, $\alpha_k \neq 0$, for otherwise $x_1, \cdots, x_{k-1}$ would form a linearly dependent set. Consequently $x_k = \beta_1 x_1 + \cdots + \beta_{k-1} x_{k-1}$, where $\beta_i = -\alpha_i/\alpha_k$. This shows that x_k is in the manifold spanned by $x_1, \cdots, x_{k-1}$. On the other hand, if we assume that some x_k is in the linear manifold spanned by $x_1, \cdots, x_{k-1}$, then an equation of the form $x_k = \beta_1 x_1 + \cdots + \beta_{k-1} x_{k-1}$ shows that the set $x_1, \cdots, x_k$ is linearly dependent, whence the same is true of the set $x_1, \cdots, x_n$.

It is convenient to say that x is a *linear combination* of $x_1, \cdots, x_n$ if it is in the linear manifold spanned by these vectors.

Using the notion of linear dependence, we can define the concept of a finite-dimensional vector space.

Definition. Let X be a vector space. Suppose there is some positive integer n such that X contains a set of n vectors which are linearly independent, while every set of $n + 1$ vectors in X is linearly dependent. Then X is called *finite dimensional*, and n is called the dimension of X. A vector space with just one element (which must then be the zero element) is also called finite dimensional, of dimension zero. If X is not finite dimensional, it is called infinite dimensional.

As we shall see later, the spaces of greatest interest in analysis are infinite dimensional. Nevertheless, it will often be of use to consider finite-dimensional spaces. Such spaces are, moreover, the source of much of our intuitive perception about what to expect in dealing with linear spaces generally.

Definition.   A finite set S in a space X is called a *basis* of X if S is linearly independent and if the linear manifold generated by S is all of X.

If $x_1, \cdots, x_n$ is a basis of X, the definition means that every x in X can be expressed in the form $x = \xi_1 x_1 + \cdots + \xi_n x_n$. Since the basis is a linearly independent set, the coefficients $\xi_1, \cdots, \xi_n$ are uniquely determined by x; that is, x cannot be expressed as a *different* linear combination of the basis elements.

It is readily seen that, if X is n-dimensional, where $n \geqslant 1$, then X has a basis consisting of n elements. For, X certainly contains vectors x_1, $\cdots, x_n$ which form a linearly independent set. Now, for any x, the set of $n + 1$ vectors $x_1, x_2, \cdots, x_n, x$ must be linearly dependent, by the definition of the dimensionality of X. Hence it is clear, by Theorem 1.1–A, that x is in the linear manifold spanned by $x_1, \cdots, x_n$. This shows that $x_1, \cdots, x_n$ form a basis of X.

Next we wish to show that if X has a basis of n elements, then X is n-dimensional. First we prove a lemma.

Lemma 1.1–B.   *If the finite set $x_1, \cdots, x_n$ generates X, and if $y_1, \cdots, y_m$ are elements of X forming a linearly independent set, then $m \leqslant n$.*

PROOF.   If S is any linearly dependent finite ordered set of vectors u_1, $\cdots, u_p$ with $u_1 \neq 0$, let S' denote the ordered set which remains after the deletion of the first u_i which is a linear combination of its predecessors. Also, for any y, let yS denote the ordered set $(y, u_1, \cdots, u_p)$. Now define S_1 to be the set $(y_m, x_1, \cdots, x_n)$, $S_2 = y_{m-1} S_1'$, $S_3 = y_{m-2} S_2'$, and so on. We make several observations: (1) S_1 spans X, is a linearly dependent set, and $y_m \neq 0$. Hence we can form S_1' (see Theorem 1.1–A). (2) S_1' and hence also S_2, spans X. We can continue in this way, constructing new sets S and S' as long as the y's last. Since the set of y's is linearly independent, the discarded element at each step must be an x. Since we can form $S_1', \cdots, S_m'$, it follows that we discard m x's, and hence $n \geqslant m$, as asserted in the lemma.

Theorem 1.1–C.   *If the linear space X has a basis of n elements, X is n-dimensional, and conversely.*

PROOF.   The proof of the converse has already been given (just before Lemma 1.1–B). If X has a basis of n elements, any linearly independent set in X has at most n elements, by Lemma 1.1–B. On the other hand, the basis is a set of n linearly independent elements. Hence X is n-dimensional, by definition.

The following theorem will be useful later on:

Theorem 1.1–D.   *Let X be an n-dimensional vector space, and let the* *set* $y_1, \cdots, y_m$ *be linearly independent, with* $m < n$. *Then there exists a basis of* X *composed of* $y_1, \cdots, y_m$ *and* $n - m$ *other vectors.*

PROOF. Let $x_1, \cdots, x_n$ be a basis of X. Let S_1 be the ordered set $(y_1, \cdots, y_m, x_1, \cdots, x_n)$, and let $S_2 = S_1'$, $S_3 = S_2'$, and so on, where S' is related to S in the manner explained in the proof of Lemma 1.1–B. Observe that S_1 is certainly linearly dependent and that the deleted vector at each step is one of the x's (by Theorem 1.1–A), so that each S_k includes $y_1, \cdots, y_m$. Since S_1 spans X, so does S_1', and so on. We can form S_k' if and only if S_k is linearly dependent. Ultimately we reach a stage where S_k is linearly independent and spans X. It is then a basis of X and includes $y_1, \cdots, y_m$. Since the basis must have n elements, there are $n - m$ vectors in addition to $y_1, \cdots, y_m$.

It is natural to expect that, if X is a linear space of dimension n, every subspace of X has dimension not exceeding n. This is indeed the case.

Theorem 1.1–E. *Suppose the vector space* X *is of dimension* n, *and let* M *be a proper subspace of* X. *Then* M *is of some finite dimension* m, *where* $m < n$.

PROOF. If $M = (0)$, it is of dimension 0, by definition. Since X must contain nonzero elements, $n > 0$, so the assertion of the theorem is true in this case. We now assume that M contains nonzero elements. If x_0 is a nonzero element of M, it forms a linearly independent set in M. On the other hand, a linearly independent set in M cannot contain as many as n elements. For, a linearly independent set of n elements is a basis of X (as we saw following the definition of a basis), so that, in such a case X would be generated by M; this is impossible, since $M \neq X$, and the linear manifold generated by the manifold M is M itself. We now consider the nonempty class of all linearly independent sets in M. Each such set has a finite number of elements p, where $1 \leqslant p < n$. There is therefore a set for which p is largest, say $p = m$. It is immediate that $m < n$ and that M is of dimension m.

Before going on to consider the general form of linear problems in linear spaces, we illustrate to some extent the great variety of possible examples of linear spaces.

1.2 Examples of Linear Spaces

Example 1. The simplest important example of a real linear space is the set of all n-tuples of real numbers, $x = (\dot{\xi}_1, \cdots, \dot{\xi}_n)$. The definitions of addition and multiplication by scalars in this space are as follows:

If $x = (\dot{\xi}_1, \cdots, \dot{\xi}_n)$ and $y = (\eta_1, \cdots, \eta_n)$, then $z = x + y$, where

$z = (\zeta_1, \cdots, \zeta_n)$, $\zeta_k = \xi_k + \eta_k$, $k = 1, \cdots, n$. The vector αx is $(\alpha\xi_1,$ $\cdots, \alpha\xi_n)$. Here the ξ's, η's, and α are arbitrary real numbers, and n is an arbitrary, fixed positive integer. We define $0 = (0, \cdots, 0)$ and $-x = (-\xi_1, \cdots, -\xi_n)$. It is an easy matter to verify that the nine axioms for a linear space are satisfied.

The dimension of this space is n; we prove this by exhibiting a basis consisting of n elements. Let $e_1 = (1, 0, \cdots, 0)$, $e_2 = (0, 1, 0, \cdots, 0)$, $\cdots, e_n = (0, 0, \cdots, 0, 1)$. If $x = (\xi_1, \cdots, \xi_n)$, observe that $x = \xi_1 e_1 + \cdots + \xi_n e_n$. Thus, the set $e_1, \cdots, e_n$ generates the whole space. Moreover, the set is linearly independent, for $\alpha_1 e_1 + \cdots + \alpha_n e_n = (\alpha_1, \cdots, \alpha_n) = 0$ if and only if all the α's are zero. Thus $e_1, \cdots, e_n$ constitute a basis.

We call this space *n-dimensional real arithmetic space*, and denote it by R_n.

The space R_n has a familiar geometrical interpretation, $\xi_1, \cdots, \xi_n$ being the coordinates of the point x in a system of Cartesian coordinates. Thus, R_1 is interpreted as a line, R_2 as a plane, and so on. In the geometrical interpretation of R_n we may regard the element x either as a point or as the vector from 0 (the origin in R_n) to that point. For geometrical interpretations this latter point of view is in many ways the most fruitful.

Example 2. The set of all n-tuples $x = (\xi_1, \cdots, \xi_n)$ of *complex* numbers forms a complex linear space, which we call *n-dimensional complex arithmetic space*, and denote by C_n.

The n vectors $e_1 = (1, 0, \cdots, 0)$, $\cdots, e_n = (0, \cdots, 0, 1)$ form a basis of C_n. It will be observed that the elements of R_n belong to C_n; however, R_n is not a subspace of C_n, for, if α is complex and x is in R_n, then αx is in C_n but not always in R_n (e.g., $i \cdot e_1 = (i, 0, \cdots, 0)$ is not in R_n).

The set C_n can also be regarded as a *real* linear space, by using the real field for scalar multipliers. But then the space is not of dimension n, but of dimension $2n$, one possible basis consisting of the vectors $e_1, \cdots, e_n$ and $ie_1, \cdots, ie_n$. We shall hereafter always regard C_n as a *complex* space.

Example 3. Let $[a, b]$ (with $a < b$) be a finite closed interval of the real axis, and let x denote a continuous real-valued function whose value at the point s of $[a, b]$ is $x(s)$. Let $C[a, b]$ denote the set of all such functions, and define $x_1 + x_2$, αx in the natural manner, i.e., $z = x_1 + x_2$, where the value of z at s is $z(s) = x_1(s) + x_2(s)$; $y = \alpha x$, where the value of y at s is $y(s) = \alpha x(s)$. It is clear that $C[a, b]$ is a real vector space.

We might equally well have considered complex-valued continuous functions of s; in that case we would have obtained a complex vector space. We shall denote this space by $C[a, b]$ also; thus, in speaking of the space $C[a, b]$, we shall have to make clear by an explicit statement whether we are talking about real-valued or complex-valued functions. In either case, $C[a, b]$ is infinite dimensional. For, let $x_0(s) = 1$, $x_n(s) = s^n$, $n = 1, 2, \cdots$. Evidently, $x_0, x_1, \cdots, x_n$ all belong to $C[a, b]$. This set of elements is linearly independent, no matter how large n is; for, by well known properties of polynomials, if $\alpha_0 + \alpha_1 s + \cdots + \alpha_n s^n = 0$ for every s such that $a \leqslant s \leqslant b$, then $\alpha_0 = \alpha_1 = \cdots = \alpha_n = 0$. Therefore $C[a, b]$ cannot be finite dimensional.

The interval $[a, b]$ does not play a very important role in the demonstration that $C[a, b]$ is a vector space and of infinite dimension. For example, we could equally well have considered continuous functions of a complex variable which ranges over some fixed infinite point set in the complex plane. An infinite set is essential to make the space infinite dimensional.

A great many of the linear spaces which are of interest in analysis are spaces whose elements are functions. We shall mention a few further examples.

Example 4. Let f be a function of the complex variable z which is defined (single valued), analytic, and bounded in the open unit circle $|z| < 1$. The class of all such functions becomes a complex vector space when $f + g$ and αf are defined in the natural way. This space is infinite dimensional. As a subspace we mention the class of all those functions f in the space for which $f(0) = 0$. Another subspace is the class of those f's whose definitions can be extended to the boundary $|z| = 1$ in such a way that each f is continuous in the closed circle $|z| \leqslant 1$. Both of these subspaces are infinite dimensional.

Example 5. Consider the complex-valued functions x of the real variable s which are such that $x(s)$, $x'(s)$ and $x''(s)$ are defined and continuous on the closed interval $[0, \pi]$. The set of all such functions is a linear space. It is of interest in considering ordinary second-order linear differential equations with coefficients continuous on $[0, \pi]$. The set of all elements of the space which satisfy the equation $x''(s) + x(s) = 0$ is a subspace of dimension 2. A basis of the subspace is furnished by the functions e^{is}, e^{-is}. Another basis is furnished by $\sin s$ and $\cos s$. Another subspace of interest is that consisting of all elements of the space such that $x(0) = x(\pi) = 0$. This subspace is infinite dimensional, for it contains the infinite linearly independent set consisting of $\sin ns$, $n = 1$, $2, \cdots$.

Example 6. As elements of a space consider infinite sequences $x = \{\xi_n\}$ $(n = 1, 2, \cdots)$ such that $\sum\limits_{n=1}^{\infty} |\xi_n|^2 < \infty$, the ξ's being complex numbers. Define $\alpha x = \{\alpha \xi_n\}$ and $\{\xi_n\} + \{\eta_n\} = \{\xi_n + \eta_n\}$. It is readily seen (by Minkowski's inequality with $p = 2$) that this is an infinite-dimensional complex linear space. We denote it by l^2. It is the space which was first extensively studied by D. Hilbert in his work on quadratic forms in infinitely many variables, with applications to the theory of integral equations. On this account l^2 is the classical prototype of the variety of linear space known today under the name *Hilbert* space. Hilbert spaces are linear spaces with a certain special kind of metrical structure. We discuss them extensively elsewhere in this book.

Example 7. Suppose $p \geqslant 1$ (p not necessarily an integer). Let $\mathscr{L}^p$ denote the class of all functions x of the real variable s such that $x(s)$ is defined for all s, with the possible exception of a set of measure zero, and is measurable and $|x(s)|^p$ is integrable (in the Lebesgue sense) over the range $(-\infty, \infty)$. Instead of $(-\infty, \infty)$ we could equally well consider $(0, \infty)$ or any finite interval (a, b). We write $\mathscr{L}^p(-\infty, \infty)$, $\mathscr{L}^p(0, \infty)$, $\mathscr{L}^p(a, b)$ to distinguish these various situations. Also, we usually omit the index p when $p = 1$, writing $\mathscr{L}$ for $\mathscr{L}^1$.

Let $\mathscr{D}_x$ denote the set on which x is defined. We define αx as the function $(\alpha x)(s) = \alpha x(s)$, with $\mathscr{D}_{\alpha x} = \mathscr{D}_x$, and $x + y$ as the function $(x + y)(s) = x(s) + y(s)$, with $\mathscr{D}_{x+y} = \mathscr{D}_x \cap \mathscr{D}_y$. Clearly $\alpha x \in \mathscr{L}^p$ if $x \in \mathscr{L}^p$; it is also true that $x + y \in \mathscr{L}^p$ if $x, y \in \mathscr{L}^p$. This latter fact follows from the inequality

$$(1.2\text{--}1) \qquad\qquad |A + B|^p \leqslant 2^p[|A|^p + |B|^p],$$

where A and B are any real or complex numbers. For, if w is measurable, if z is integrable, and if $|w(s)| \leqslant |z(x)|$, then w is integrable. To see the truth of (1.2–1), observe that

$$\max\{|A|, |B|\} \leqslant |A| + |B| \leqslant 2 \max\{|A|, |B|\},$$

$$|A + B|^p \leqslant (|A| + |B|)^p \leqslant (2 \max\{|A|, |B|\})^p$$
$$= \max\{2^p|A|^p, 2^p|B|^p\} \leqslant 2^p|A|^p + 2^p|B|^p.$$

If we define $x = y$ to mean that $\mathscr{D}_x = \mathscr{D}_y$ and $x(s) = y(s)$ for every $s \in \mathscr{D}_x$, we may at first think that $\mathscr{L}^p$ is a linear space. It is not, however. For, if $\mathscr{L}^p$ were a linear space, the zero element z would necessarily be the function defined for *all* s, with $z(s) = 0$ for every s. But then $x + (-x) = z$ would not be true for all x, as we see by choosing an x for which $\mathscr{D}_x$ does not include every s. To get around this difficulty we proceed as follows: Define an equivalence relation $=^0$ in $\mathscr{L}^p$ by saying that $x =^0 y$ if $x(s) = y(s)$ a.e. (i.e., almost everywhere, which means except on a set of measure zero). The set of equivalence classes into which $\mathscr{L}^p$ is thus divided is denoted by L^p; here also, we write L for L^1. For the time being we shall denote an element of L^p which contains x by $[x]$. We define $[x] + [y] = [x + y]$. This definition of $[x] + [y]$ is unambiguous, for, if $x =^0 x_1$ and $y =^0 y_1$, it follows that $x_1 + y_1 =^0 x + y$. Likewise, we define $\alpha[x] = [\alpha x]$, noting that $\alpha x =^0 \alpha x_1$ if $x =^0 x_1$. With these definitions the class L^p becomes a linear space; the zero element of L^p is the equivalence class consisting of all $x \in \mathscr{L}^p$ such that $x(s) = 0$ a.e.

In practice we usually ignore the notational distinction between $\mathscr{L}^p$ and L^p and write x instead of $[x]$. When we do this it must be remembered that x really denotes, not a single function, but a class of equivalent functions.

The space L^p is of interest in connection with Fourier transforms and various kinds of integral equation problems. The case $p = 2$ is especially important.

As an example of a subclass of $\mathscr{L}^p$ that is useful in certain applications to first-order ordinary differential equation problems, we mention the following: the class of all x for which $x(s)$ is defined everywhere and is absolutely continuous on every finite interval and both $x(s)$ and $x'(s)$ define elements of $\mathscr{L}^p$.

Example 8. Let $[a, b]$ be a finite closed interval of the real axis. Let $BV[a, b]$ denote the class of real-valued functions of s which are defined and of bounded variation on $[a, b]$. This class is a linear space.

Example 9. Let x be a complex-valued function of the real variable s which is defined and has derivatives of all orders for every value of s. The class of all such functions x is evidently a linear space.

It would be easy to give many more examples of linear spaces whose elements are certain kinds of functions. We shall see later on in this book that the study of linear spaces leads us to introduce still other linear spaces composed of functions defined on the original linear spaces.

1.3 Linear Operators

A linear operator is a certain kind of function whose domain is a linear space and whose range is contained in another linear space (possibly the same as the first one). For the terminology concerning functions we refer the reader to the Introduction. If A is a linear operator, it is customary to omit parentheses and write Ax instead of $A(x)$ whenever it seems convenient.

Definition.   Let X and Y be linear spaces (both real or both complex). Let A be a function with domain X and range contained in Y. Then A is called a linear operator, or more explicitly a linear operator on X into Y, if the following two conditions are satisfied:

(1.3–1) $$A(x_1 + x_2) = Ax_1 + Ax_2,$$

(1.3–2) $$A(\alpha x) = \alpha Ax.$$

Here α is an arbitrary scalar, and x_1, x_2, x are arbitrary vectors from X.

It follows immediately by induction from (1.3–1) and (1.3–2) that

(1.3–3) $$A(\alpha_1 x_1 + \cdots + \alpha_n x_n) = \alpha_1 Ax_1 + \cdots + \alpha_n Ax_n,$$

for arbitrary n.   Also, by taking $\alpha = 0$ in (1.3–2), we see that

(1.3–4) $$A(0) = 0.$$

Sometimes we consider a linear operator A whose domain is a proper subset of a given linear space X. The domain is itself a linear space (by definition), and so it is a subspace of X. Our standard notation for the domain of A is $\mathscr{D}(A)$. We denote the range of A by $\mathscr{R}(A)$.

Theorem 1.3–A.   *Let A be a linear operator with domain $\mathscr{D}(A) \subset X$ and range $\mathscr{R}(A) \subset Y$, where X and Y are linear spaces. Then $\mathscr{R}(A)$ is a linear manifold in Y.*

PROOF.   Suppose $y_1, y_2 \in \mathscr{R}(A)$, and let α be a scalar. We have to prove that $y_1 + y_2$ and αy_1 are in $\mathscr{R}(A)$. Now $y_1 \in \mathscr{R}(A)$ means that there is an $x_1 \in \mathscr{D}(A)$ such that $Ax_1 = y_1$. Likewise $Ax_2 = y_2$ for some $x_2 \in \mathscr{D}(A)$. Then, since A is linear, $A(x_1 + x_2) = Ax_1 + Ax_2 = y_1 + y_2$, and $A(\alpha x_1) = \alpha Ax_1 = \alpha y_1$. The desired conclusions are now evident.

If a linear operator A has an inverse, we denote it by A^{-1}. (The reader should consult the Introduction for the definition of the inverse of a function.) The statement "A^{-1} exists" means the same as "A has an inverse."

Theorem 1.3–B.   *The inverse of a linear operator A exists if and only if $Ax = 0$ implies $x = 0$. When A^{-1} exists it is a linear operator.*

PROOF.   We know by the definition of an inverse function that A^{-1} exists if and only if $Ax_1 = Ax_2$ implies $x_1 = x_2$. Suppose $Ax = 0$ implies $x = 0$, and let $Ax_1 = Ax_2$. Then, by the linearity of A, $A(x_1 - x_2) = 0$, whence $x_1 - x_2 = 0$, or $x_1 = x_2$. Thus A^{-1} exists. Now suppose, vice versa, that A^{-1} exists, and let x be a vector for which $Ax = 0$. Then $A(x) = A(0)$ [see (1.3–4)], and so, by the condition for the existence of A^{-1}, $x = 0$. This finishes the proof of the first statement in the theorem. The proof that A^{-1} is linear, when it exists, is left to the reader.

The linear problems of algebra and analysis are concerned with linear operators on various linear spaces. We mention two kinds of problems in very general terms: *existence* problems and *uniqueness* problems. Suppose A is a given linear operator, with domain a given space X and range in a given space Y. Then we can ask: "For which elements $y \in Y$ does there exist in X an element x such that $Ax = y$?" This is the same as asking: "Which elements of Y belong to $\mathscr{R}(A)$?" Existence problems are of this kind.

Example 1. Let $Y = C[0, 1]$ (real-valued functions). Let X be the subclass of Y consisting of those elements x which have first and second derivatives continuous on $[0, 1]$ and which are, moreover, such that $x(0) = x'(0) = 0$. Let p and q be members of Y, and define A on X by $Ax = y$ where

$$y(s) = x''(s) + p(s)x'(s) + q(s)x(s).$$

Then A is linear on X into Y. Is $\mathscr{R}(A)$ all of Y? This is the question as to whether the differential equation

$$x'' + px' + qx = y$$

has a solution such that $x \in X$, for each choice of $y \in Y$. Note that $x \in X$ implies that $x(0) = x'(0) = 0$. The "initial conditions" have been incorporated into the definition of the domain of A. There is a standard existence theorem in the theory of differential equations which does in fact assure us that $\mathscr{R}(A) = Y$. It also assures us that for a given y there is *only* one x in X such that $Ax = y$. Therefore A^{-1} exists.

Example 2. Let X be the space $BV[0, 1]$ defined in Example 8, § 1.2. Let Y be the space of all bounded sequences $y = \{\eta_i\}$ $(i = 1, 2, \cdots)$ where the definitions of the algebraic processes in Y are made as for the space l^2 of Example 6, § 1.2. Define a linear operator A on X into Y by $Ax = y$, where

$$\eta_k = \int_0^1 s^k \, dx(s).$$

The integral here is a Stieltjes integral. The η_k's are called *moments*. A sequence $\{\eta_k\}$ which arises in this way is called a *moment sequence* arising from x. A moment sequence is certainly bounded, for $|\eta_k|$ cannot exceed the total variation of x. But which bounded sequences are moment sequences? That is, how can we recognize those bounded sequences which are in the range of A? This is a classical problem known as the *moment problem of Hausdorff*. In this case $\mathscr{R}(A)$ is not all of Y. For a description of $\mathscr{R}(A)$ (i.e., of all moment sequences) we refer the reader to Chapter 3 of D. V. Widder, **1**; consult the bibliography.*

In addition to existence problems there are *uniqueness* problems. In the case of any linear operator A we can ask: is the x such that $Ax = y$ unique in all cases in which a solution for x exists? This is the same as the question: does A^{-1} exist? By Theorem 1.3–B this is equivalent to the question: does the equation $Ax = 0$ have a unique solution (namely $x = 0$)? To answer this question for a particular operator we must have a good deal of detailed knowledge about the operator.

Example 3. Let $Y = C[a, b]$ and let X be the subspace of $C[a, b]$ consisting of those functions x which have continuous first and second derivatives on $[a, b]$ and are such that $x(a) = x(b) = 0$. Define A on X into Y by $Ax = x''$, where x'' is the second derivative of x. It is easy to show that A^{-1} exists. For, $Ax = 0$ implies that $x(s) = c_1 s + c_2$, where c_1 and c_2 are constants, and the requirements $x(a) = x(b) = 0$, then lead to the conclusions $c_1 = c_2 = 0$. It is also easy to show that $\mathscr{R}(A) = Y$. For a given $y \in C[a, b]$ the unique x in X such that $Ax = y$ is given by

$$x(s) = \int_a^s du \int_a^u y(t)\, dt - \frac{s - a}{b - a} \int_a^b du \int_a^u y(t)\, dt.$$

With a little manipulation this formula may be put in the form

$$x(s) = \int_a^b K(s, t) y(t)\, dt,$$

where

$$K(s, t) = \begin{cases} \dfrac{(s - b)(t - a)}{b - a} & \text{if } a \leqslant t \leqslant s, \\[2ex] \dfrac{(s - a)(t - b)}{b - a} & \text{if } s \leqslant t \leqslant b. \end{cases}$$

Note that $K(s, t) = K(t, s)$ and that K is continuous on the square where it is defined.

Sometimes there is an important connection between existence problems and uniqueness problems. This connection is simplest in the case of finite-dimensional spaces, as we shall see in Theorem 1.3–E.

* References to the bibliography are made by listing the author's name and a number in boldface type, identifying a book or article by that author.

Lemma 1.3–C. *Let A be a linear operator on X into Y, and let X be of finite dimension n. Then $\mathscr{R}(A)$ is of some finite dimension m, with m ⩽ n.*

PROOF. If $\mathscr{R}(A) = (0)$, then $m = 0$, and there is nothing more to prove. Since $X = (0)$ implies $\mathscr{R}(A) = (0)$, we assume that $n > 0$ and that $\mathscr{R}(A) \neq (0)$. Suppose $y_1, \cdots, y_{n+1}$ are in $\mathscr{R}(A)$. Then, there exist vectors $x_1, \cdots, x_{n+1}$ in X with $Ax_k = y_k$, $k = 1, \cdots, n + 1$. Since X is of dimension n, there exists scalars $\alpha_1, \cdots, \alpha_{n+1}$, not all zero, such that $\alpha_1 x_1 + \cdots + \alpha_{n+1} x_{n+1} = 0$. Then $0 = A(\alpha_1 x_1 + \cdots + \alpha_{n+1} x_{n+1}) = \alpha_1 y_1 + \cdots + \alpha_{n+1} y_{n+1}$, so that the set $y_1, \cdots, y_{n+1}$ is linearly dependent. Now $\mathscr{R}(A)$ certainly contains some finite linearly independent sets, for a single nonzero vector is such a set. Hence, $\mathscr{R}(A)$ contains a finite linearly independent set with the largest possible number of elements, and this number m cannot exceed n, as has been shown. This completes the proof.

Theorem 1.3–D. *In addition to the hypothesis of Lemma 1.3–C, assume that A^{-1} exists. Then $\mathscr{R}(A)$ is of the same dimension as X (the domain of A).*

PROOF. We know $m ⩽ n$, by the lemma. Now $\mathscr{R}(A) = \mathscr{D}(A^{-1})$ and $X = \mathscr{R}(A^{-1})$. Hence, applying the lemma to A^{-1}, $n ⩽ m$. Thus $m = n$.

Theorem 1.3–E. *Let A be a linear operator on X into Y, where X and Y are both of the same finite dimension n. Then $\mathscr{R}(A) = Y$ if and only if A^{-1} exists.*

PROOF. If A^{-1} exists, we know that $\mathscr{R}(A)$ is of the same dimension as X. It follows by Theorem 1.1–E that $\mathscr{R}(A)$ cannot be a proper subset of Y and must, therefore, coincide with Y. On the other hand, suppose that $\mathscr{R}(A) = Y$. Let $y_1, \cdots, y_n$ be a basis of Y. There exist vectors $x_1, \cdots, x_n$ in X such that $Ax_k = y_k$, $k = 1, 2, \cdots, n$, since $\mathscr{R}(A) = Y$. The set of x's is linearly independent. For, if $\alpha_1 x_1 + \cdots + \alpha_n x_n = 0$, it follows that $0 = A(\alpha_1 x_1 + \cdots + \alpha_n x_n) = \alpha_1 y_1 + \cdots + \alpha_n y_n$, whence $\alpha_1 = \cdots = \alpha_n = 0$, since the set of y's is linearly independent. Consequently, the set $x_1, \cdots, x_n$ is a basis of X. Now suppose $Ax = 0$ for some x. We can express x in the form $x = \alpha_1 x_1 + \cdots + \alpha_n x_n$, and so $0 = Ax = \alpha_1 y_1 + \cdots + \alpha_n y_n$. This implies $\alpha_1 = \cdots = \alpha_n = 0$, and so $x = 0$. Therefore A^{-1} exists. The proof is now complete.

Finite dimensionality is essential in Theorem 1.3–E. We can see that this is so by the following example. Let X be the linear space of Example 9, § 1.2, and let $Y = X$. Define A by setting $Ax = y$, where $y(s) = x'(s)$. In this case $\mathscr{R}(A) = X$, for a solution of $Ax = y$ is given by $x(s) = \int_0^s y(t) \, dt$. The inverse A^{-1} does not exist, however, for $Ax = 0$ in the case of every constant function.

PROBLEM

Alternative argument for second part of proof of Theorem 1.3–E: Assume that $\mathscr{R}(A) = Y$ but that A^{-1} does not exist, so that there is an $x_1 \neq 0$ with $Ax_1 = 0$. Choose $x_2, \cdots, x_n$ so that $x_1, \cdots, x_n$ is a basis of X. Let $y_k = Ax_k$, $k = 2, \cdots, n$, and show that the whole of Y is generated by $y_2, \cdots, y_n$.

I.4 Linear Operators in Finite Dimensional Spaces

Let X denote either the real space R_n or the complex space C_n (Examples 1 and 2, § 1.2). Let $Y = R_m$ if $X = R_n$, and $Y = C_m$ if $X = C_n$. Here m and n may be any positive integers. Let

$$(1.4\text{–}1) \qquad (\alpha_{ij}) \equiv \begin{Vmatrix} \alpha_{11} & \alpha_{12} & \cdots & \alpha_{1n} \\ \alpha_{21} & \alpha_{22} & \cdots & \alpha_{2n} \\ \cdots\cdots\cdots\cdots\cdots\cdots \\ \alpha_{m1} & \alpha_{m2} & \cdots & \alpha_{mn} \end{Vmatrix}$$

be any $m \times n$ matrix of scalars (real or complex according as X and Y are real or complex). Such a matrix defines a linear operator A on X into Y as follows: $Ax = y$, where $x = (\xi_1, \cdots, \xi_n)$, $y = (\eta_1, \cdots, \eta_m)$, and

$$(1.4\text{–}2) \qquad \sum_{j=1}^{n} \alpha_{ij}\xi_j = \eta_i \qquad i = 1, \cdots, m.$$

The linear problems connected with the operator A are, in this case, problems connected with the system of m linear equations (1.4–2). The special properties of the operator A must be found by an examination of the particular matrix (1.4–1).

We recall the notation

$$e_1 = (1, 0, \cdots, 0), \cdots, e_n = (0, \cdots, 0, 1)$$

introduced in Example 1, § 1.2. The vectors $e_1, \cdots, e_n$ form a basis of X. Let us write

$$f_1 = (1, 0, \cdots, 0), \cdots, f_m = (0, \cdots, 0, 1)$$

for the analogous basis in Y. Observe that $x = \xi_1 e_1 + \cdots + \xi_n e_n$ and $y = \eta_1 f_1 + \cdots + \eta_m f_m$. Now let us define vectors $u_1, \cdots, u_n$ in Y by $a_k = Ae_k$. Since $\xi_j = \delta_{kj}$ (the Kronecker delta) if $x = e_k$, we see by (1.4–2) that

$$a_k = \sum_{i=1}^{m} \left(\sum_{j=1}^{n} \alpha_{ij}\delta_{kj} \right) f_i = \sum_{i=1}^{m} \alpha_{ik} f_i = (\alpha_{1k}, \alpha_{2k}, \cdots, \alpha_{mk}).$$

In other words, the vector a_k appears as the kth column in the matrix (1.4–1).

In the foregoing situation we started with an arbitrary $m \times n$ matrix and used it to define a linear operator on X into Y. Let us now proceed the other way around. We shall start with an arbitrary linear operator A on X into Y and show that there is an $m \times n$ matrix of the form (1.4–1) such that it defines the operator A, in the sense that $Ax = y$ means precisely that the η's are defined in terms of the ξ's by equations (1.4–2).

If A is the given operator, we define $a_j = Ae_j, j = 1, \cdots, n$. The a's are vectors in Y and can, therefore, be expressed in terms of the basis $f_1, \cdots, f_m$. Let the expression of a_j be $a_j = \alpha_{1j}f_1 + \cdots + \alpha_{mj}f_m$. In this way we arrive at the set of scalars α_{ij}, with which we form the matrix (1.4–1). Now, if $x = (\xi_1, \cdots, \xi_n)$ and $y = Ax = (\eta_1, \cdots, \eta_m)$, we have to show that the equations (1.4–2) are valid. We have $x = \xi_1 e_1 + \cdots + \xi_n e_n$, $Ax = \xi_1 a_1 + \cdots + \xi_n a_n$, or

$$y = \sum_{j=1}^{n} \xi_j \left(\sum_{i=1}^{m} \alpha_{ij} f_i \right) = \sum_{i=1}^{m} \left(\sum_{j=1}^{n} \alpha_{ij} \xi_j \right) f_i.$$

Since the expression of a vector in terms of the basis is unique, this last equation is equivalent to the equations (1.4–2).

The foregoing considerations show that the study of linear operators on R_n into R_m is closely related to the study of matrices of the form (1.4–1) with real elements α_{ij}. If we deal with C_n and C_m the only difference is that the matrix elements are from the complex number field.

If we now turn to a study of linear operators on X into Y, where X and Y are *arbitrary* finite-dimensional spaces, we shall find the same close connection between linear operators and matrices. The reason for this is that every n-dimensional real linear space X is in a certain sense the same as R_n (or the same as C_n if X is complex instead of real). This sense in which two spaces are said to be the same will now be explained.

Definition. Two linear spaces X, Y (with the same scalar field) are said to be *isomorphic* if there exists a linear operator T whose domain is X, whose range is all of Y, and whose inverse T^{-1} exists.

In less technical language, X and Y are isomorphic if there is a one-to-one correspondence between the elements of X and the elements of Y, such that the operations of vector addition and scalar multiplication are preserved under the correspondence. That is, if x_1 and x_2 have correspondents y_1 and y_2, respectively, then $y_1 + y_2$ corresponds to $x_1 + x_2$ and αy_1 corresponds to αx_1.

If X is isomorphic to Y and Y is isomorphic to Z, it is easy to see that X is isomorphic to Z.

Theorem 1.4–A.   *If X and Y are both n-dimensional linear spaces with the same scalar field, they are isomorphic.*

PROOF.   Assume the scalar field is that of the real numbers, for definiteness.   We shall show that X (and hence also Y) is isomorphic to R_n, from which it will follow that X and Y are isomorphic.   Let $x_1, \cdots, x_n$ be a basis of X.   Every x in X has a unique representation $x = \xi_1 x_1 + \cdots + \xi_n x_n$, where $\xi_1, \cdots, \xi_n$ are real numbers.   We define a linear operator T on X into R_n by writing $Tx = (\xi_1, \cdots, \xi_n)$.   The facts that this is a linear operator, that it has all of R_n as its range, and that T^{-1} exists are all easily verified, and we omit the details.   This completes the proof.

If X is n-dimensional, with a basis $x_1, \cdots, x_n$, the coefficients $\xi_1, \cdots, \xi_n$ in the representation $x = \xi_1 x_1 + \cdots + \xi_n x_n$ may be called the *coordinates* (or, also, the *components*) of x with respect to the basis $x_1, \cdots, x_n$.   Thus, the isomorphism of X and R_n is established by correlating x with the point in R_n whose coordinates with respect to the basis $e_1, \cdots, e_n$ of R_n are the same as the coordinates of x with respect to $x_1, \cdots, x_n$.

Suppose now that X and Y are any linear spaces of dimensions n and m, respectively, with the same scalar field.   Let $x_1, \cdots, x_n$ be a basis in X, and $y_1, \cdots, y_m$ a basis in Y.   Let A be a linear operator on X into Y. Since $Ax_j \in Y$, we can write

$$(1.4\text{–}3) \qquad Ax_j = \sum_{i=1}^{m} \alpha_{ij} y_i, \qquad j = 1, \cdots, n.$$

The operator A, in conjunction with the two bases $(x_1, \cdots, x_n)$, $(y_1, \cdots, y_m)$, determines an $m \times n$ matrix (α_{ij}).   With this matrix we can calculate the vector Ax for every $x \in X$.   The calculations are essentially the same as those given earlier in the special case $X = R_n$, $Y = R_m$; the coordinates η_i of Ax are given in terms of the coordinates ξ_j of x by equations (1.4–2).

It must be kept in mind that, although the operator A is represented by the matrix (α_{ij}), *it is not the same thing as the matrix*.   For, the operator A is not dependent on the particular bases which are chosen for X and Y, whereas the matrix *does* depend on these bases, and the same operator is represented by different matrices when different bases are chosen.

To conclude this section we give an example.

Example.   Let X be the complex linear space consisting of all polynomials in the real variable s of degree not exceeding $n - 1$, with complex coefficients.   Let Y be the corresponding space of polynomials with degree not exceeding n. It is readily evident that Z is of dimension n, one possible basis $x_1, \cdots, x_n$ being that defined by

$$x_1(s) = 1, \ x_2(s) = s, \cdots, \ x_n(s) = s^{n-1}.$$

Likewise, Y is of dimension $n + 1$. X is a subspace of Y. For a basis in Y we take $y_1 = x_1, \cdots, y_n = x_n,\ y_{n+1}(s) = s^n$.

Now, consider the operator A on X into Y defined by $Ax = y$, where

$$y(s) = \int_0^s x(t)\, dt.$$

We see that

$$Ax_j = \frac{1}{j} y_{j+1}, \qquad j = 1, \cdots, n.$$

The matrix (α_{ij}) in this case is therefore

$$
\left\|
\begin{array}{ccccccccc}
0 & 0 & \cdot & \cdot & \cdot & \cdot & \cdot & \cdot & \cdot\,0 \\
1 & 0 & \cdot & \cdot & \cdot & \cdot & \cdot & \cdot & \cdot\,0 \\
0 & \tfrac{1}{2} & 0 & \cdot & \cdot & \cdot & \cdot & \cdot & \cdot\,0 \\
0 & 0 & \tfrac{1}{3} & 0 & \cdot & \cdot & \cdot & \cdot & \cdot\,0 \\
\cdot & & & & & & & & \cdot \\
\cdot & & & & & & & & \cdot \\
\cdot & & & & & & & & \cdot \\
\cdot & & & & & & & \cdot & \cdot\,0 \\
\cdot & & & & & & \cdot & \cdot & \cdot \\
0 & 0 & \cdot & \cdot & \cdot & \cdot & \cdot\,0 & \cdot & \tfrac{1}{n}
\end{array}
\right\|
$$

with $n + 1$ rows and n columns.

We observe, incidentally, that the inverse A^{-1} exists. The range $\mathscr{R}(A)$ consists of all polynomials of degree $\leqslant n$ whose constant term is zero. That is, $\mathscr{R}(A)$ is the linear manifold spanned by $y_2, \cdots, y_{n+1}$. With $\mathscr{R}(A)$ as its domain, A^{-1} is defined by $A^{-1}y = x$, where $x(s) = y'(s)$.

PROBLEM

Let X and Y be as in the example, but take $x_k = y_k = P_{k-1}$, $k = 1, \cdots,$ n, $y_{n+1} = P_n$, where P_n is the Legendre polynomial of degree n. Here we have bases for X and Y different from the ones previously mentioned. The recursion formula

$$(2k + 1)P_k(s) = P'_{k+1}(s) - P'_{k-1}(s)$$

and the known values of $P_k(0)$

$$P_k(0) = 0 \text{ if } k \text{ is odd}$$

$$= (-1)^{k/2} \frac{1 \cdot 3 \cdot 5 \cdots (k-1)}{2 \cdot 4 \cdots k} \text{ if } k \text{ is even}$$

make it possible to compute the matrix of the operator A relative to these bases. For $n = 6$ the matrix is

$$\begin{Vmatrix} 0 & \frac{1}{6} & 0 & -\dfrac{1}{2\cdot4} & 0 & \dfrac{1\cdot3}{2\cdot4\cdot6} \\ 1 & 0 & -\frac{1}{5} & 0 & 0 & 0 \\ 0 & \frac{1}{3} & 0 & -\frac{1}{7} & 0 & 0 \\ 0 & 0 & \frac{1}{5} & 0 & -\frac{1}{9} & 0 \\ 0 & 0 & 0 & \frac{1}{7} & 0 & -\frac{1}{11} \\ 0 & 0 & 0 & 0 & \frac{1}{9} & 0 \\ 0 & 0 & 0 & 0 & 0 & \frac{1}{11} \end{Vmatrix}.$$

1.5 Other Examples of Linear Operators

In this section we give a number of illustrations of problems in analysis, as formulated in terms of linear operators.

Example I. Let G be a nonempty, bounded, connected, open set in the Euclidean xy-plane. Let $\bar{G}$ be the closure of G; then the boundary $\bar{G}$–G is nonempty. Let H be the class of all real-valued functions f of x, y which are defined and continuous on $\bar{G}$ and harmonic in G (i.e., each f must satisfy Laplace's equation in G). Let C denote the class of real-valued functions defined and continuous on $\bar{G}$–G. Clearly H and C are both linear spaces.

Now, if $u \in H$, $u(x, y)$ is defined at every point $(x, y) \in \bar{G}$. If we think only of the values of u at the points of $\bar{G}$–G, we arrive at an element f of C defined by $f(x, y) = u(x, y)$ when $(x, y) \in \bar{G}$–G. We call f the restriction of u to the boundary of G. We define a linear operator A on H into C by writing $Au = f$; the fact that A is linear is evident.

Let us consider existence and uniqueness problems for A (see § 1.3 for a general discussion of these problems). In the present example these are problems of potential theory. The uniqueness problem is completely disposed of by the well-known fact that, if $u \in H$ and $u(x, y) = 0$ on $\bar{G}$–G, then $u(x, y) = 0$ at all points of G (since u must attain both its maximum and minimum values on the boundary of G). In our present notation this means that $u = 0$ if $Au = 0$; consequently A^{-1} exists. For the existence problem we want to know if $\mathscr{R}(A)$ is all of C. This is the famous Dirichlet problem: Is there for each $f \in C$ an element $u \in H$ such that f is the restriction of u to the boundary of G? The answer to this question is not always affirmative; $\mathscr{R}(A)$ may be a proper subspace of C. However, under certain conditions involving the nature of the set G and its boundary, it is known that $\mathscr{R}(A) = C$. In particular, under suitable conditions, $\mathscr{R}(A) = C$ and A^{-1} is defined by an integral, involving the Green's function of G, extended over the boundary of G.

Many boundary-value problems of both ordinary and partial differential equations are susceptible of formulation in terms of linear operators, by procedures analogous to those of Example 1.   It is essential that the differential equations be linear and that either the differential equations or the boundary conditions be homogeneous.

Example 2.   Let $X = Y = C[a, b]$ (see Example 3, § 1.2).   Let $k(s, t)$ be defined for $a \leqslant s \leqslant b$, $a \leqslant t \leqslant b$ and such that for each $x \in X$ the Riemann integral

$$(1.5\text{--}1) \qquad\qquad \int_a^b k(s, t)x(t)\, dt$$

exists and defines a continuous function of s on $[a, b]$.   The values of k are to be either real or complex, depending on whether the values of the elements of $C[a, b]$ are taken as real or complex.

The integral (1.5–1) defines a linear operator K on X into X, if we take $Kx = y$ to mean

$$(1.5\text{--}2) \qquad\qquad y(s) = \int_a^b k(s, t)x(t)\, dt.$$

The equation (1.5–2) is called an *integral equation*.   It is of the particular sort known as an equation *of Fredholm type, of the first kind*.

Another operator T is obtained by defining $Tx = y$ to mean

$$(1.5\text{--}3) \qquad\qquad y(s) = x(s) - \int_a^b k(s, t)x(t)\, dt.$$

In this case the integral equation is said to be *of Fredholm type, of the second kind*.   Equations of this sort are of great importance.   There is a well worked-out theory of the existence and uniqueness problems associated with such equations.   The applications of this theory play a vital role in the theory of boundary-value problems in differential equations.

A special situation results if we assume that $k(s, t) = 0$ when $t > s$. The integral (1.5–1) then becomes

$$\int_a^s k(s, t)x(t)\, dt.$$

The equations (1.5–2) and (1.5–3), in this modified form, are said to be *of Volterra type*.   The theory of Volterra equations of the second kind is particularly simple, much more so than the corresponding theory for equations of the Fredholm type.   Later on in this book we shall treat the theory of integral equations of the second kind, using abstract-linear-space methods. For this treatment it is necessary to introduce topological as well as algebraic considerations about linear spaces.

Example 3. Let $X = Y = C[0, \pi]$. In this case we assume specifically that we are dealing with complex-valued continuous functions. If $x \in X$ and if $x'(s)$ exists on $[0, \pi]$, we denote the derived function by x'. Likewise x'' denotes the second derivative if $x''(s)$ exists on $[0, \pi]$. We now define a linear operator A as follows: Let $\mathscr{D}(A) = \{x : x', x'' \in C[0, \pi]$ and $x(0) = x(\pi) = 0\}$. (See the statement in the Introduction about defining subsets of X by the brace notation.) For $x \in \mathscr{D}(A)$ define $Ax = y$ to mean

$$(1.5\text{--}4) \qquad -x''(s) + \lambda x(s) = y(s),$$

where λ is a complex parameter. The operator A thus depends on λ. Clearly $\mathscr{R}(A) \subset X$.

We shall discuss the existence and uniqueness problem for A in some detail. This amounts to a discussion of finding solutions of the differential equation (1.5–4) which satisfy the end conditions $x(0) = x(\pi) = 0$.

Let one of the square roots of λ be denoted by μ. By the method of variation of parameters the general solution of (1.5–4) (disregarding the end conditions) is found to be

$$(1.5\text{--}5) \qquad x(s) = \frac{1}{\mu} \int_0^s y(t) \sinh \mu(t - s)\, dt + C_1 e^{\mu s} + C_2 e^{-\mu s},$$

where C_1 and C_2 are arbitrary constants. This is in case $\lambda \neq 0$. If $\lambda = 0$ the solution may be found by direct integration. If we impose the end conditions $x(0) = x(\pi) = 0$, we find, first, that $C_1 + C_2 = 0$ and then that

$$0 = \frac{1}{\mu} \int_0^\pi y(t) \sinh \mu(t - \pi)\, dt + 2C_1 \sinh \pi\mu.$$

To solve this equation for C_1 we must assume that $\sinh \pi\mu \neq 0$. On substituting into (1.5–5) the values found for C_1, C_2, we have

$$(1.5\text{--}6) \qquad x(s) = \frac{1}{\mu} \int_0^s y(t) \sinh \mu(t - s)\, dt$$
$$- \frac{\sinh \mu s}{\mu \sinh \mu\pi} \int_0^\pi y(t) \sinh \mu(t - \pi)\, dt.$$

The corresponding formula when $\lambda = 0$ is

$$(1.5\text{--}7) \qquad x(s) = \int_0^s y(t)(t - s)\, dt - \frac{s}{\pi} \int_0^\pi y(t)(t - \pi)\, dt.$$

It may now be seen that the equation $Ax = y$ admits a solution $x \in \mathscr{D}(A)$ for every $y \in X$, provided either that $\lambda = 0$ or that $\sinh \pi\mu \neq 0$

if $\lambda \neq 0$. Moreover, the solution is unique, for it may be argued from the standard theory of linear differential equations that (1.5–6) and (1.5–7) give, in their respective cases, the *only* solutions of (1.5–4) satisfying the given end conditions.

There remain to be considered the cases when $\lambda \neq 0$ but $\sinh \pi\mu = 0$. Now, since $\mu^2 = \lambda$ and since $\sinh \pi\mu = 0$ if and only if $\pi\mu = in\pi$, where n is an integer, we see that the exceptional cases are given by $\lambda = -n^2$, $n = 1, 2, 3, \cdots$. In these cases (1.5–4) cannot have a unique solution in $\mathscr{D}(A)$ (i.e., A^{-1} does not exist), for $Ax = 0$ in case $\lambda = -n^2$ and $x(s) = \sin ns$. If we re-examine our earlier work, assuming that $\lambda = -n^2 \neq 0$, we see that the equation $Ax = y$ has all its solutions $x \in \mathscr{D}(A)$ given by

$$(1.5\text{–}8) \qquad x(s) = \frac{1}{n} \int_0^s y(t) \sin n(t - s)\, dt + C \sin ns,$$

where C is an arbitrary constant, if and only if the function y satisfies the condition

$$(1.5\text{–}9) \qquad \int_0^\pi y(t) \sin nt\, dt = 0.$$

This condition serves as a description of $\mathscr{R}(A)$ in this case.

By writing $\int_0^\pi = \int_0^s + \int_s^\pi$ in (1.5–6), and rearranging somewhat, the formula can be written

$$x(s) = \int_0^s y(t) \frac{\sinh \mu t \sinh \mu(\pi - s)}{\mu \sinh \mu\pi}\, dt + \int_s^\pi y(t) \frac{\sinh \mu s \sinh \mu(\pi - t)}{\mu \sinh \mu\pi}\, dt.$$

If we define

$$k(s, t) = \frac{\sinh \mu t \sinh \mu(\pi - s)}{\mu \sinh \mu\pi} \qquad \text{when } 0 \leqslant t \leqslant s$$

and $k(s, t) = k(t, s)$ when $s \leqslant t \leqslant \pi$, (1.5–6) becomes

$$x(s) = \int_s^\pi k(s, t)y(t)\, dt.$$

We note that this formula is of the same type as (1.5–2). In our operator notation this formula is $x = A^{-1}y$. If we regard $x = A^{-1}y$ as an equation to be solved for y, we see that it is an integral equation of Fredholm type, of the first kind. It has a unique solution, for each $x \in \mathscr{D}(A)$, given by (1.5–4).

Example 4. Let $X = Y = L(0, \infty)$ (see Example 7, § 1.2). Let us define an operator A as follows: Consider those functions in $\mathscr{L}(0, \infty)$ which are absolutely continuous on $[0, a]$ for every finite a, with derivatives also belonging to $\mathscr{L}(0, \infty)$. Each such function determines an equivalence class in $\mathscr{L}(0, \infty)$, i.e., an element of $L(0, \infty)$. The set of such elements of $L(0, \infty)$ is going to be $\mathscr{D}(A)$. For convenience we shall drop the notational distinction between an element of $L(0, \infty)$ and one of its representatives in $\mathscr{L}(0, \infty)$. Thus if $x \in L(0, \infty)$, we shall write $x(s)$ to indicate a functional value at s of a representative of x. We then define $Ax = y$ to mean that

$$(1.5\text{--}10) \qquad\qquad -x'(s) + \lambda x(s) = y(s)$$

almost everywhere on $(0, \infty)$. This defines $y \in L(0, \infty)$ uniquely if $x \in \mathscr{D}(A)$. As in Example 3, λ denotes a complex parameter.

To solve the equation $Ax = y$, we proceed formally to solve (1.5–10) by use of the integrating factor $e^{-\lambda s}$. If $x(s)$ is absolutely continuous and satisfies (1.5–10), it is necessarily of the form

$$(1.5\text{--}11) \qquad\qquad x(s) = e^{\lambda s}\left\{ C - \int_0^s y(t)e^{-\lambda t}\, dt \right\},$$

where C is some constant, and, vice versa, the function $x(s)$ so defined, for any C, is absolutely continuous and does satisfy (1.5–10). If $x(s)$ turns out to belong to $\mathscr{L}(0, \infty)$, it is clear from (1.5–10) that $x'(s)$ will also belong, because we assume that $y(s)$ belongs to $\mathscr{L}(0, \infty)$. The problem is then that of seeing whether the constant C can be chosen so that the integral $\int_0^\infty |x(s)|\, ds$ will be convergent. In considering this problem it is convenient to consider three cases, depending upon whether the real part of λ is positive, negative, or zero. We write $\lambda = \alpha + i\beta$, α and β real. Note that

$$|x(s)| = e^{\alpha s}\left| C - \int_0^s y(t)e^{-\lambda t}\, dt \right|.$$

Case I. $\alpha > 0$. Since

$$\int_0^s y(t)e^{-\lambda t}\, dt \to \int_0^\infty y(t)e^{-\lambda t}\, dt \qquad \text{as } s \to \infty,$$

we see that $|x(s)|$ will be of the order of magnitude of $e^{\alpha s}$ when s is large unless

$$(1.5\text{--}12) \qquad\qquad C = \int_0^\infty y(t)e^{-\lambda t}\, dt.$$

This is therefore a necessary condition for $x(s)$ to belong to $\mathscr{L}(0, \infty)$, when $\alpha > 0$. It is also sufficient; for, if it is satisfied, we have

$$(1.5\text{--}13) \qquad x(s) = e^{\lambda s} \int_s^\infty y(t)e^{-\lambda t}\, dt = \int_0^\infty y(s + u)e^{-\lambda u}\, du,$$

from which it is easy to see that $x(s) \in \mathscr{L}(0, \infty)$ if $\alpha > 0$.

Case 2. $\alpha = 0$. The condition (1.5–12) is likewise necessary in this case. It is not sufficient, however, and whether or not $x(s) \in \mathcal{L}(0, \infty)$ will depend on the choice of y. For instance, if

$$y(t) = e^{i\beta t} t^{-2}$$

when t is large, then for large s

$$x(s) = e^{\lambda s} \int_s^\infty y(t) e^{-\lambda t}\, dt = e^{i\beta s} \int_s^\infty t^{-2}\, dt = \frac{e^{i\beta s}}{s},$$

and $x(s)$ is not in $\mathcal{L}(0, \infty)$.

Case 3. $\alpha < 0$. In this case the function $x(s)$ defined by (1.5–11) is in $\mathcal{L}(0, \infty)$, no matter how C and y are chosen. This is easily seen, for $e^{\lambda s}$ is in $\mathcal{L}(0, \infty)$, and

$$\int_0^s y(t) e^{\lambda(s-t)}\, dt$$

is also in $\mathcal{L}(0, \infty)$. In fact,

$$\int_0^\infty \left| \int_0^s y(t) e^{\lambda(s-t)}\, dt \right| ds \leqslant \int_0^\infty ds \int_0^s |y(t)| e^{\alpha(s-t)}\, dt$$

$$= \int_0^\infty e^{-\alpha t} |y(t)|\, dt \int_t^\infty e^{\alpha s}\, ds = -\frac{1}{\alpha} \int_0^\infty |y(t)|\, dt.$$

We can sum up the discussion as follows. The inverse A^{-1} exists if $\alpha \geqslant 0$, and the solution $x = A^{-1}y$ is expressed by (1.5–13). If $\alpha > 0$, $\mathcal{R}(A)$ is all of X, but not so if $\alpha = 0$. When $\alpha < 0$, A^{-1} does not exist, but $\mathcal{R}(A)$ is all of X.

Example 5. Let $X = L(0, 2\pi)$. Let F be the class of functions f analytic in the unit circle $|z| < 1$. For $x \in X$, with representative $x(s) \in \mathcal{L}(0, 2\pi)$, define $Ax = f$ to mean

(1.5–14) $$f(z) = \frac{1}{2\pi} \int_0^{2\pi} \frac{x(s)}{1 - ze^{-is}}\, ds.$$

Then A is a linear operator on X into F. The inverse A^{-1} does not exist, for it is a simple matter to calculate that $Ax = 0$ if $x(s) = e^{-ims}$, $m = 1$, $2, \cdots$ (use the geometric series for $(1 - ze^{-is})^{-1}$, and integrate term by term). The problem of characterizing the range $\mathcal{R}(A)$ has not yet been solved satisfactorily. One would like to know conditions on the analytic function f, necessary and sufficient in order that f can be represented by formula (1.5–14), with some $x \in L(0, \pi)$. A simple *sufficient*, but not necessary, condition is that f be continuous when $|z| \leqslant 1$ as well as analytic when $|z| < 1$. For then, by Cauchy's formula,

$$f(z) = \frac{1}{2\pi i} \int \frac{f(w)}{w - z}\, dw,$$

the complex line integral being extended counterclockwise around the unit circle $|w| = 1$. If we write $w = e^{is}$, $0 \leqslant s \leqslant 2\pi$, this becomes

$$f(z) = \frac{1}{2\pi} \int_0^{2\pi} \frac{f(e^{is})}{1 - ze^{-is}}\, ds.$$

Thus in this case $f = Ax$, where $x(s) = f(e^{is})$.

A less restrictive sufficient condition is known. Suppose $f \in F$, and suppose that there is a constant M such that

(1.5–15)
$$\int_0^{2\pi} |f(re^{i\theta})|\, d\theta \leqslant M$$

when $0 \leqslant r < 1$. Then it may be shown that $\lim_{r \to 1} f(re^{is}) = x(s)$ exists almost everywhere on $0 \leqslant s \leqslant 2\pi$ and that $x(s) \in \mathscr{L}(0, 2\pi)$. It may also be shown that

(1.5–16)
$$\lim_{r \to 1} \int_0^{2\pi} |f(re^{i\theta}) - x(\theta)|\, d\theta = 0.$$

See § 7.56 of Zygmund, **1**; these results are due to F. Riesz, **2**. From these facts it is easy to prove that $Ax = f$. Thus, a sufficient condition that $f \in \mathscr{R}(A)$ is that f be an element of F satisfying (1.5–15) for some constant M and all r such that $0 \leqslant r < 1$.

Example 6. Let X be the class of all infinite arrays of the form $x = (\cdots, \xi_{-2}, \xi_{-1}, \xi_0, \xi_1, \xi_2, \cdots)$, where the ξ_n's are arbitrary complex numbers. We denote these more briefly as $x = \{\xi_n\}$, $n = 0, \pm 1, \pm 2, \cdots$. Define addition and scalar multiplication in the obvious way, i.e.,

$$\{\xi_n\} + \{\eta_n\} = \{\xi_n + \eta_n\}, \quad \alpha\{\xi_n\} = \{\alpha\xi_n\}.$$

Then X is a complex linear space. Now consider the linear operator A on $L(0, \pi)$ into X defined as follows: If $f \in L(0, 2\pi)$ with representative $f(t) \in \mathscr{L}(0, 2\pi)$, let $Af = x$, where $x = \{\xi_n\}$ is defined by

$$\xi_n = \frac{1}{2\pi} \int_0^{2\pi} f(t)e^{-int}\, dt, \qquad n = 0, \pm 1, \pm 2, \cdots.$$

The numbers ξ_n are the complex Fourier coefficients of f.

The inverse A^{-1} exists. This is simply the classical theorem that if $f(t) \in \mathscr{L}(0, 2\pi)$ and if all of its Fourier coefficients vanish, then $f(s) = 0$

almost everywhere [so that $f = 0$ as an element of $L(0, 2\pi)$]. The problem of characterizing $\mathscr{R}(A)$ has never been fully solved, though many things are known about $\mathscr{R}(A)$ from the theory of Fourier series. Many interesting and important results have been found by confining attention to subspaces of $L(0, 2\pi)$ and X. For instance, it is known that if we consider the domain of A to be $L^2(0, 2\pi)$ instead of $L(0, 2\pi)$, the range of A is the subspace of X consisting of all $\{\xi_n\}$ for which the series

$$\sum_{n=-\infty}^{\infty} |\xi_n|^2$$

is convergent.

PROBLEM

Suggestion for showing that $Ax = f$ in the context of the paragraph where (1.5–15) occurs: Let $C(z, \theta) = (1 - ze^{-i\theta})^{-1}$. If $|z| < r < 1$, it may be seen from Cauchy's integral formula that

$$\left| f(z) - \frac{1}{2\pi} \int_0^{2\pi} C(z, \theta)x(\theta) \, d\theta \right|$$

$$\leqslant \frac{1}{2\pi} \int_0^{2\pi} |f(re^{i\theta})| \left| C\left(\frac{z}{r}, \theta\right) - C(z, \theta) \right| d\theta + \frac{1}{2\pi} \int_0^{2\pi} |f(re^{i\theta}) - x(\theta)| \, |C(z, \theta)| \, d\theta.$$

One may then use (1.5–15) and (1.5–16) to obtain $Ax = f$.

1.6 Linear Functionals

The field of real numbers is a real linear space; it is 1-dimensional. Likewise, the field of complex numbers is a 1-dimensional complex linear space.

Let X be a real or complex linear space, and let Y be the linear space composed by the scalar field associated with X. A linear operator on X into Y is then called a *linear functional* on X.

Since we shall have many occasions to deal with linear functionals, we shall make certain conventions of notation concerning them. If X is a linear space and x is a generic symbol for elements of X, we shall often use x' as a generic symbol for linear functionals on X. If $x_1 \in X$ and if x_1' is a linear functional on X, there is no implication of a special relationship between x_1 and x_1'. Since x' is a function, we can speak of its value at the point x; by our previous usage this value would be denoted by

$x'(x)$, or simply $x'x$. It will sometimes be convenient to have another notation. We shall write

$$\langle x, x'\rangle$$

for the value of x' at x. This notation has several advantages, as we shall see, especially when we replace x' by a more complicated symbol representing a linear functional on X.

If x_1' and x_2' are linear functionals on X and α in a scalar, we define $x_1' + x_2'$ and $\alpha x_1'$ by the formulas

(1.6–1) $\langle x, x_1' + x_2'\rangle = \langle x, x_1'\rangle + \langle x, x_2'\rangle$,

(1.6–2) $\langle x, \alpha x_1'\rangle = \alpha \langle x, x_1'\rangle$.

These are the usual definitions for adding functions and multiplying them by scalars. The functional x' such that $x'(x) = 0$ for every x is denoted by 0. Thus, we use 0 to denote the zero scalar, the zero vector in X, and the zero functional; the meaning of 0 in a particular occurrence will be clear from the context.

In addition to the formulas (1.6–1) and (1.6–2), we note the formulas

(1.6–3) $\langle x_1 + x_2, x'\rangle = \langle x_1, x'\rangle + \langle x_2, x'\rangle$,

(1.6–4) $\langle \alpha x, x'\rangle = \alpha\langle x, x'\rangle$.

These are merely the properties (1.3–1), (1.3–2) of linear operators, expressed in the new notation for linear functionals.

Definition. Let X be a linear space. Let X^f be the class of all linear functionals on X. By the foregoing definitions X^f becomes a linear space. We call it the *algebraic conjugate* of X.

We shall see later that the space X^f plays an important role in the study of linear operators with domain X.

Before going further we pause to give some illustrative examples of linear functionals. We refer to the examples of linear spaces in § 1.2.

Example 1. Let X be either R_n or C_n, where $n \geq 1$ (see Examples 1, 2, of § 1.2). Since a linear functional on X is a linear operator with its range in the 1-dimensional space R_1 or C_1 (depending upon whether X is R_n or C_n), we can see from § 1.4 that every linear functional $x' \in X^f$ has a representation

(1.6–5) $\langle x, x'\rangle = \alpha_1\xi_1 + \cdots + \alpha_n\xi_n, \quad x = (\xi_1, \cdots, \xi_n)$,

where $\alpha_1, \cdots, \alpha_n$ are scalars, and conversely, that every n-tuple of scalars

$(\alpha_1, \cdots, \alpha_n)$ can be used to define a functional x' by formula (1.6–5). From this we see that, if we define

$$Ax' = (\alpha_1, \cdots, \alpha_n),$$

then A is a linear operator on X^f into X. We also see that A^{-1} exists and that $\mathcal{R}(A) = X$. Hence, by the definition in § 1.4, X^f and X are isomorphic in case $X = R_n$ or $X = C_n$.

Example 2. Let $X = C[a, b]$ (see Example 3, § 1.2). Let s_0 be a fixed point in the interval $[a, b]$. The formula

(1.6–6) $$\langle x, x' \rangle = x(s_0)$$

defines an element of X^f. Another example of a linear functional is furnished by

(1.6–7) $$\langle x, x' \rangle = \int_a^b x(s)\, df(s),$$

where f is an arbitrary function of bounded variation defined on $[a, b]$ and the integral is a Stieltjes integral. In case f has a continuous derivative, (1.6–7) can be written

$$\langle x, x' \rangle = \int_a^b x(s) f'(s)\, ds,$$

the integral being a Riemann integral.

It may be observed that (1.6–6) is a special case of (1.6–7). If $s_0 = a$, (1.6–7) reduces to (1.6–6) when we define $f(a) = 0$ and $f(s) = 1$ if $a < s \leqslant b$. If $a < s_0 \leqslant b$, (1.6–7) reduces to (1.6–6) by choosing $f(s) = 0$ when $a \leqslant s < s_0$ and $f(s) = 1$ when $s_0 \leqslant s \leqslant b$.

Example 3. Let $X = l^2$ (see Example 6, § 1.2). Suppose that $a = \{\alpha_n\}$ is an element of l^2, and define $x' \in X^f$ by

(1.6–8) $$\langle x, x' \rangle = \sum_{i=1}^{\infty} \alpha_i \xi_i, \qquad \text{where } x = \{\xi_n\}.$$

The series does converge, for, by Cauchy's inequality,

$$\sum_{i=1}^{n} |\alpha_i \xi_i| \leqslant \left(\sum_{i=1}^{n} |\alpha_i|^2 \right)^{\frac{1}{2}} \left(\sum_{i=1}^{n} |\xi_i|^2 \right)^{\frac{1}{2}}$$

for every value of n. Therefore, since $a \in l^2$ and $x \in l^2$, the partial sums of the series $\sum |\alpha_i \xi_i|$ are bounded, and the series in (1.6–8) is absolutely convergent. It is evident that x', so defined, is a member of X^f.

Example 4. Let $X = L(-\infty, \infty)$ (see Example 7, § 1.2). If f is a bounded measurable function defined almost everywhere on $(-\infty, \infty)$, we can use it to define a linear functional on X as follows:

$$(1.6\text{-}9) \qquad \langle x, x' \rangle = \int_{-\infty}^{\infty} x(s)f(s)\, ds,$$

where $x(s)$ is a function in $\mathscr{L}(-\infty, \infty)$ representing the element $x \in L(-\infty, \infty)$, and the integral is a Lebesgue integral.

The reader will note that it was only in the case of Example 1 that we asserted anything about giving a general representation of *all* elements of X^f. Ordinarily, in dealing with the infinite-dimensional spaces arising in analysis, we find it most useful to limit attention to certain subspaces of X^f. These subspaces are arrived at by imposing a topological structure on the space X and then considering only those linear functionals on X which are continuous with respect to the topology in question. We shall see later that the functionals exhibited in Examples 2, 3, and 4 are typical for the respective spaces when suitable topologies are introduced.

Since X^f is a linear space, we may also consider its algebraic conjugate, which we denote by

$$(X^f)^f, \qquad \text{or simply } X^{ff}.$$

We shall denote elements of X^{ff} generically by x'', and we shall use the notations

$$x''(x') = \langle x', x'' \rangle$$

for the value of x'' at x'.

Corresponding to each x in X there is a unique x'' in X^{ff} defined by

$$(1.6\text{-}10) \qquad \langle x', x'' \rangle = \langle x, x' \rangle$$

or equivalently, $x''(x') = x'(x)$. That this formula does in fact define a linear functional on X^f is apparent from (1.6–1) and (1.6–2). The correspondence between x and x'' in (1.6–10) defines a linear operator J on X into X^{ff}: $Jx = x''$. The fact that J is linear is apparent from (1.6–3) and (1.6–4).

Definition. The mapping of X in X^{ff} by the operator J is called the *canonical mapping* of X into X^{ff}.

It will be shown in Theorem 1.71–C that J has an inverse, that is, that $Jx = 0$ implies $x = 0$. If X is finite dimensional, this is shown in Theorem 1.61–B. It follows from this fact that the range of J is isomorphic to X. Hence we may identify X and the range of J, thus permitting ourselves to look upon X as a subspace of X^{ff}. When we adopt this point of view, we speak of the canonical imbedding of X in X^{ff}.

Definition. If $\mathscr{R}(J) = X^{ff}$, we say that X is *algebraically reflexive.*

It turns out, as we shall see later, that X is algebraically reflexive if and only if it is finite dimensional (Theorem 1.72–A).

PROBLEM

Show that, if X is algebraically reflexive, so is X^f. Suggestion: Let J_0 and J_1 be the canonical mappings of X and X^f into X^{ff} and X^{fff} respectively. The problem is to show that $\mathscr{R}(J_1) = X^{fff}$. If $x''' \in X^{fff}$ is given, define $x' \in X^f$ by the formula $\langle x, x' \rangle = \langle J_0 x, x''' \rangle$. Show that $J_1 x' = x'''$.

1.61. Linear Functionals in Finite-Dimensional Spaces

Let X be an n-dimensional linear space, and let $x_1, \cdots, x_n$ be a basis of X. Let $x = \xi_1 x_1 + \cdots + \xi_n x_n$ be the representation of an element $x \in X$. For any $x' \in X^f$ we have

(1.61–1) $$x'(x) = \xi_1 x'(x_1) + \cdots + \xi_n x'(x_n).$$

The coefficients $x'(x_1), \cdots, x'(x_n)$ are independent of x. This set of coefficients may be prescribed arbitrarily; that is, given any n scalars $\alpha_1, \cdots, \alpha_n$, there exists a unique $x' \in X^f$ such that $x'(x_i) = \alpha_i$, $i = 1, \cdots, n$. This x' is given by

(1.61–2) $$x'(x) = \sum_{i=1}^n \alpha_i \xi_i, \qquad \text{where } x = \sum_{i=1}^n \xi_i x_i.$$

The case in which one α_i is 1 and the others are 0 is of especial interest. If $\alpha_1 = 1$, $\alpha_2 = \cdots = \alpha_n = 0$, denote the corresponding x' by x_1'. Then $x_1'(x_1) = 1$, $x_1'(x_2) = \cdots = x_1'(x_n) = 0$. We define $x_2', \cdots, x_n'$ in similar fashion. Specifically, for each $k(k = 1, \cdots, n)$ let $\alpha_i = \delta_{ik}$, and denote the corresponding x' in (1.6–2) by x_k'. The essential character of the functionals $x_1', \cdots, x_n'$ is then exhibited in the equations

(1.61–3) $$\langle x_j, x_k' \rangle = \delta_{jk} \qquad j, k = 1, \cdots, n.$$

To demonstrate this we observe that

$$x_j = \sum_{i=1}^n \delta_{ij} x_i, \quad x_k'(x_j) = \sum_{i=1}^n \delta_{ik} \delta_{ij} = \delta_{jk}.$$

Theorem 1.61–A. *The set $x_1', \cdots, x_n'$ defined in the foregoing discussion is a basis of X^f. Hence the algebraic conjugate of an n-dimensional linear space is n-dimensional.*

PROOF. The set $x_1', \cdots, x_n'$ is linearly independent. For, from $\beta_1 x_1' + \cdots + \beta_n x_n' = 0$ it follows with the aid of (1.61–3) that

$$0 = \left\langle x_j, \sum_{i=1}^{n} \beta_i x_i' \right\rangle = \sum_{i=1}^{n} \beta_i \langle x_j, x_i' \rangle = \sum_{i=1}^{n} \beta_i \, \delta_{ji} = \beta_j,$$

or $\beta_1 = \cdots = \beta_n = 0$. Next, for a given $x' \in X^f$ we define $\alpha_i = x'(x_i)$ and prove that

$$(1.61–4) \qquad\qquad x' = \alpha_1 x_1' + \cdots + \alpha_n x_n',$$

thereby completing the proof of the theorem. The meaning of (1.61–4) is that, for every $x \in X$,

$$(1.61–5) \qquad\qquad x'(x) = \alpha_1 x_1'(x) + \cdots + \alpha_n x_n'(x).$$

The validity of this formula is readily verified with the aid of (1.61–2) and (1.61–3).

Definition. The basis $x_1', \cdots, x_n'$ of X^f, as defined in the foregoing work, is said to be *dual* to the basis $x_1, \cdots, x_n$ of X.

Corresponding to each basis of X there is a uniquely defined dual basis of X^f.

Theorem 1.61–B. *If X is n-dimensional and if $x \in X$ is such that $x'(x) = 0$ for every $x' \in X^f$, it follows that $x = 0$. In other words, $Jx = 0$ implies $x = 0$, so that J^{-1} exists.*

PROOF. We use the basis $x_1, \cdots, x_n$ and its dual $x_1', \cdots, x_n'$. In the notation of (1.61–4) and (1.61–2) we have $\alpha_1 \xi_1 + \cdots + \alpha_n \xi_n = 0$ for all choices of $\alpha_1, \cdots, \alpha_n$. This implies $\xi_1 = \cdots = \xi_n = 0$, and so $x = 0$.

Theorem 1.61–C. *If X is an n-dimensional linear space, it is algebraically reflexive.*

PROOF. We assume $n > 0$, since the case $n = 0$ is trivial. By Theorem 1.61–A both X^f and X^{ff} are n-dimensional. Consider the canonical mapping J of X into X^{ff} (see § 1.6). Since J^{-1} exists, $\mathscr{R}(J)$ is n-dimensional by Theorem 1.3–D. Hence $\mathscr{R}(J) = X^{ff}$, by Theorem 1.1–E. This completes the proof.

Theorem 1.61–D. *Let M be a proper subspace of the n-dimensional linear space X, and suppose $x_0 \in X - M$. Then there exists an element $x_0' \in X^f$ such that $x_0'(x) = 0$ if $x \in M$ and $x_0'(x_0) = 1$.*

PROOF. Suppose M is m-dimensional. The trivial case $m = 0$ is left to the reader, and we consider the case $0 < m < n$. Let $x_1, \cdots, x_m$ be a basis of M, and write $x_{m+1} = x_0$.   The set $x_1, \cdots, x_{m+1}$ is linearly independent.   By Theorem 1.1–D we can find a basis of X whose first $m + 1$ vectors are $x_1, \cdots, x_{m+1}$.   Let $x_1', \cdots, x_n'$ be the dual basis of X^f, and define $x_0' = x'_{m+1}$.   Then the conditions required in the theorem are satisfied.

The proofs of Theorems 1.61–B and 1.61–D have been given by methods depending on finite dimensionality.   But the theorems are true if the assumption of finite dimensionality of X is dropped.   The proofs in this general case require more profound methods, however; see § 1.71.

PROBLEM

If X^f is n-dimensional, so is X.

1.7 Zorn's Lemma

What is commonly known as Zorn's lemma was originally formulated by Zorn as a proposition in the theory of sets, which he showed to be equivalent to the axiom of choice.   Subsequently, this proposition has been given a formulation in terms of partially ordered sets which is extremely convenient for many applications.   In this book we state Zorn's lemma and use it as the need arises.   It is immaterial whether the reader chooses to regard the lemma as an axiom of set theory or as a theorem derived from the axiom of choice.

Our statement of Zorn's lemma depends upon the notion of a partially ordered set.

Definition.   Let P be a set of elements.   Suppose there is a binary relation defined between certain pairs of elements a, b of P, expressed symbolically by $a \prec b$, with the properties:

1. If $a \prec b$ and $b \prec c$, then $a \prec c$.
2. If $a \in P$ then $a \prec a$.
3. If $a \prec b$ and $b \prec a$, then $a = b$.

Then P is said to be *partially ordered* by the relation.

For example, if P is the set of all subsets of a given set X, the set inclusion relation ($A \subseteq B$) gives a partial ordering of P.   The set of all complex numbers $z = x + iy$, $w = u + iv$, $\cdots$ is partially ordered by defining $z \prec w$ to mean that $x \leqslant u$ and $y \leqslant v$, where $\leqslant$ has its usual meaning for real numbers.

If P is partially ordered and if, moreover, for every pair a, b in P either $a \prec b$ or $b \prec a$, then P is said to be *completely* ordered. (The adjectives *linearly*, *totally*, and *simply* are also used in place of *completely*.)

For example, the real numbers are completely ordered by the relation "a is less than or equal to b."

A subset of a partially ordered set P is itself partially ordered by the relation which partially orders P. Also, a subset of P may turn out to be completely ordered by this relation.

If P is a partially ordered set and S is a subset of P, an element $m \in P$ is called an *upper bound* of S if $a \prec m$ for every $a \in S$. An element $m \in P$ is said to be *maximal* if $a \in P$ and $m \prec a$ together imply $m = a$.

Zorn's Lemma. *Let P be a nonempty partially ordered set with the property that every completely ordered subset of P has an upper bound in P. Then P contains at least one maximal element.*

Some applications of this proposition will be found in §§ 1.71, 1.72.

1.71 Extension Theorems for Linear Operators

If X is a set, M a proper subset of X, and f a function defined on M, a function F defined on X is called an *extension* of f if $F(x) = f(x)$ when $x \in M$. In practice, we are usually concerned with extensions which conform to certain additional requirements. Often these requirements are of the sort which state that the extension F is to have certain of the properties possessed by f (e.g., be bounded, or continuous, or differentiable, or analytic, etc.). The question as to whether an extension of the required sort exists may be easy or difficult to answer, depending on the particular nature of the problem. In this section we are concerned with the existence of an extension when X is a linear space, M is a proper subspace, and f is a linear operator on M into a second linear space Y. We require the extension F to be linear on X into Y. There may also be further conditions on f and F.

Theorem 1.71–A. *Let X and Y be linear spaces and M a proper subspace of X. Let f be a linear operator, defined on M into Y. Then, there exists a linear operator F defined on X into Y such that F is an extension of f.*

PROOF. Choose any element $x_0 \in X - M$, and let M_0 be the subspace of X spanned by the set consisting of M and x_0. Any element of M_0 can be written in one and only one way in the form $x + \alpha x_0$, where $x \in M$

and α is some scalar.   The uniqueness of the representation follows from
the fact that, if $x_1 + \alpha_1 x_0 = x_2 + \alpha_2 x_0$, where x_1, $x_2 \in M$, then
$x_1 - x_2 = (\alpha_2 - \alpha_1)x_0$, whence $(\alpha_2 - \alpha_1)x_0 \in M$, since M is a linear
manifold.   But, since $x_0 \notin M$, we are forced to conclude that $\alpha_1 - \alpha_2 = 0$,
since otherwise $x_0 = (\alpha_2 - \alpha_1)^{-1}(\alpha_2 - \alpha_1)x_0$ would also be in M.   Hence
also $x_1 - x_2 = 0$, and the representation is unique.

We now define a linear operator F_0 on M_0 into Y as follows:

$$F_0(x + \alpha x_0) = f(x) + \alpha y_0,$$

where y_0 is some fixed vector in Y.   For our present purpose it does not
matter how y_0 is chosen.   It is readily seen that F_0 is an extension of f
and that it is a linear operator on M_0 into Y.

It now seems plausible to suppose that by a continuation of the
procedure we can arrive at the required extension F defined on all of X.
Indeed, if X is finite dimensional, we shall arrive at the desired goal in a
finite number of steps.   For the general case the argument is made
precise by use of Zorn's lemma.

Let g be a linear operator with domain $\mathscr{D}(g) \subset X$ and range $\mathscr{R}(g) \subset Y$;
suppose M is a proper subspace of $\mathscr{D}(g)$ and that g is an extension of f.
Let P be the class of all such operators g.   If $g, h \in P$, let us define the
relation $g \prec h$ to mean that $\mathscr{D}(g) \subset \mathscr{D}(h)$ and that h is an extension of g.
This relation defines a partial ordering of P.   Moreover, P is nonempty,
for certainly $F_0 \in P$.

Now suppose that Q is a completely ordered subset of P.   We shall
define an element $G \in P$ which is an upper bound of Q.   Let $\mathscr{D}(G)$ be the
union of all the sets $\mathscr{D}(g)$ corresponding to elements $g \in Q$.   This set
$\mathscr{D}(G)$ is a subspace of X.   For, suppose $x_1, x_2 \in \mathscr{D}(G)$.   Then, there exist
elements $g_1, g_2 \in Q$ such that $x_k \in \mathscr{D}(g_k)$ $(k = 1, 2)$.   We may suppose
$g_1 \prec g_2$, since Q is completely ordered.   Then $\mathscr{D}(g_1) \subset \mathscr{D}(g_2)$, and so
$x_1 + x_2 \in \mathscr{D}(g_2) \subset \mathscr{D}(G)$.   Closure of $\mathscr{D}(G)$ under multiplication by
scalars is proved even more simply.   Now, suppose $x \in \mathscr{D}(G)$.   Then
$x \in \mathscr{D}(g)$ for some $g \in Q$.   We shall define $G(x) = g(x)$.   This definition
is unambiguous, for, if $x \in \mathscr{D}(g_1)$ and $x \in \mathscr{D}(g_2)$, where $g_1, g_2 \in Q$, we
have $g_1(x) = g_2(x)$ by the fact that Q is completely ordered.   The proof
that G is linear is like the proof that $\mathscr{D}(G)$ is a linear manifold.   It is
clear that $G \in P$ and that $g \prec G$ for every $g \in Q$.

We now know that P satisfies the conditions of Zorn's lemma and
must, therefore, contain a maximal element, say F.   The domain of F
must be all of X, for otherwise we could regard $\mathscr{D}(F)$ as the M in the first
part of the proof and thus obtain an element $g \in P$ with $g \neq F$, $F \prec g$,
contrary to the maximality of F.   The proof of the theorem is now
complete, for F has the properties required in the theorem.

Theorem 1.71–B.   *Let X_0 be a proper subspace of the linear space X, and suppose $x_1 \in X - X_0$. Then, there exists an element $x_1' \in X^f$ such that $\langle x, x_1' \rangle = 0$ if $x \in X_0$ and that $\langle x_1, x_1' \rangle = 1$.*

PROOF.   We observe that this is the same as Theorem 1.61–D with the hypothesis of finite dimensionality omitted.   To prove the theorem, let M be the subspace of X spanned by the set consisting of X_0 and x_1. Elements of M are uniquely representable in the form $x + \alpha x_1$, where $x \in X_0$ and α is a scalar.   (See the argument at the beginning of the proof of Theorem 1.71–A.)   Let us define $f(x + \alpha x_1) = \alpha$.   Then f is a linear functional on M, and $f(x) = 0$ if $x \in X_0$, whereas $f(x_1) = 1$.   By Theorem 1.71–A (with Y the linear space of scalars) there exists an element of X^f which is an extension of f.   If we denote this element by x_1', we see that it has the required properties.

Theorem 1.71–C.   *Let X be a linear space.   If $x \in X$ and if $\langle x, x' \rangle = 0$ for every $x' \in X^f$, then $x = 0$.   In other words, J^{-1} exists, where J is defined as in § 1.6 [see (1.6–10)].*

PROOF.   Applying Theorem 1.71–B with $X_0 = (0)$ we see that if $x_1 \neq 0$, there exists $x_1' \in X^f$ such that $\langle x_1, x_1' \rangle \neq 0$.   This statement is merely the contrapositive form of Theorem 1.71–C, so the proof is complete. Note that this proposition is the same as Theorem 1.61–B with the hypothesis of finite dimensionality omitted.

Next we consider an extension theorem for linear functionals which are subjected to a special kind of condition.

Definition.   Let X be a real linear space, and let p be a real-valued function defined on X, with the properties

$$u. \quad p(x + y) \leqslant p(x) + p(y),$$
$$b. \quad p(\alpha x) = \alpha p(x) \quad \text{if } \alpha \geqslant 0.$$

We call p a *sublinear* functional on X.

As an example of a sublinear functional we cite the example of the space $X = R_n$ with p defined by $p(x) = |\xi_1| + \cdots + |\xi_n|$, where $x = (\xi_1, \cdots, \xi_n)$.   Another example is that of $X = C[a, b]$, with $p(x) = |x(a)|$ or $p(x) = \max |x(t)|$ for $a \leqslant t \leqslant b$.

Theorem 1.71–D.   *Let X be a real linear space, and let M be a proper subspace of X.   Let p be a sublinear functional defined on X and let f be a linear functional defined on M such that $f(x) \leqslant p(x)$ for each $x \in M$. Then, there exists a linear functional F defined on X such that F is an extension of f and $F(x) \leqslant p(x)$ for each $x \in X$.*

PROOF.   We have arranged the notation so that the proof can be given in a somewhat abbreviated form by referring to the proof of Theorem

1.71-A.   We start with x_0 and M_0 as in that proof.   The first problem is to show that there exists a real number ξ_0 such that the linear functional F_0 defined on M_0 by

(1.71–1) $$F_0(x + \alpha x_0) = f(x) + \alpha \xi_0$$

satisfies the inequality

(1.71–2) $$F_0(x + \alpha x_0) \leqslant p(x + \alpha x_0)$$

for every real α and every $x \in M$.

By taking $\alpha = 1$ in (1.71–1) and (1.71–2) we see that one necessary condition which must be satisfied by ξ_0 is the inequality

(1.71–3) $$\xi_0 \leqslant p(x + x_0) - f(x),$$

which must hold for every $x \in M$.   Another similar necessary condition is obtained by taking $\alpha = -1$ and replacing x by $-x$ in (1.71–1) and (1.71–2).   In this way we see that the inequality

(1.71–4) $$- p(- x - x_0) - f(x) \leqslant \xi_0$$

must hold for every $x \in M$.

Now, conversely, if (1.71–3) and (1.71–4) are valid inequalities for every $x \in M$, it follows that (1.71–2) is always satisfied.   To see this, suppose $\alpha > 0$, and replace x by $\alpha^{-1}x$ in (1.71–3).   Then

$$\xi_0 \leqslant p\left(\frac{x}{\alpha} + x_0\right) - f\left(\frac{x}{\alpha}\right) = \frac{1}{\alpha}p(x + \alpha x_0) - \frac{1}{\alpha}f(x),$$

and so, rearranging,

$$f(x) + \alpha\xi_0 \leqslant p(x + \alpha x_0)$$

for $x \in M$ and $\alpha > 0$.   If $\alpha < 0$, replace x by $\alpha^{-1}x$ in (1.71–4).   Then

$$\xi_0 \geqslant - p\left(-\frac{x}{\alpha} - x_0\right) - f\left(\frac{x}{\alpha}\right) = \frac{1}{\alpha}p(x + \alpha x_0) - \frac{1}{\alpha}f(x),$$

$$- p(x + \alpha x_0) + f(x) \leqslant - \alpha\xi_0,$$

and so

$$f(x) + \alpha\xi_0 \leqslant p(x + \alpha x_0)$$

if $x \in M$ and $\alpha < 0$.   These two results together show that (1.71–2) is always true (the case $\alpha = 0$ is obvious).

Now, suppose x_1 and x_2 are any elements of M.   Then

$$f(x_2) - f(x_1) = f(x_2 - x_1) \leqslant p(x_2 - x_1)$$
$$= p[(x_2 + x_0) + (-x_1 - x_0)] \leqslant p(x_2 + x_0) + p(- x_1 - x_0),$$

whence

(1.71–5) $$- p(- x_1 - x_0) - f(x_1) \leqslant p(x_2 + x_0) - f(x_2).$$

Let

$$c = \sup_{x \in M} \{- p(- x - x_0) - f(x)\},$$

$$C = \inf_{x \in M} \{p(x + x_0) - f(x)\}.$$

We see by (1.71–5) that $c \leqslant C$, both c and C necessarily being finite. There certainly exists a real number ξ_0 such that $c \leqslant \xi_0 \leqslant C$, and it will satisfy (1.71–3) and (1.71–4) by the way in which c and C are defined. We then define F_0 by (1.71–1), and (1.71–2) is satisfied. This completes the first phase in the proof of Theorem 1.71–D.

The proof is completed by use of Zorn's lemma in essentially the same way as in the proof of Theorem 1.71–A. We consider the class P of all linear functionals g with $\mathscr{D}(g) \subset X$ such that M is a proper subspace of $\mathscr{D}(g)$, g is an extension of f, and $g(x) \leqslant p(x)$ when $x \in \mathscr{D}(g)$. The partial ordering of P is defined as before, and the rest of the proof is essentially as before.

1.72 Hamel Bases

The German mathematician Hamel conceived the notion of a "basis" for all real numbers as follows: Let H be a set of real numbers with the properties:

1. If $x_1, \cdots, x_n$ is any finite subset of H and if $r_1, \cdots, r_n$ are rational numbers for which $r_1 x_1 + \cdots + r_n x_n = 0$, then $r_1 = \cdots = r_n = 0$.

2. Every real number x can be expressed as a finite linear combination of elements of H, with rational coefficients.

In terms of such a basis, Hamel (**1**) then discussed real functions f satisfying the equation $f(x + y) = f(x) + f(y)$ for all real x, y. If H is a basis in the foregoing sense, let a real function f be defined as follows: If $x \in H$, assign the values of $f(x)$ arbitrarily. Any real x has a unique representation $x = r_1 x_1 + \cdots + r_n x_n$, where $x_1, \cdots, x_n$ are in H and $r_1, \cdots, r_n$ are rational (n may vary with x, of course). We then define $f(x) = r_1 f(x_1) + \cdots + r_n f(x_n)$, the values $f(x_1), \cdots, f(x_n)$ having already been assigned. With this definition f turns out to satisfy the condition $f(x + y) = f(x) + f(y)$ for every x and y. This procedure gives all possible functions f satisfying this condition.

To show the existence of a basis for all real numbers, Hamel used an argument based on the proposition that every set can be well ordered. This proposition is equivalent to the axiom of choice, or to Zorn's lemma.

Hamel's whole procedure can be adapted to the purpose of showing the nature of all possible linear functionals on a linear space X.

Definition. Let X be a linear space with some nonzero elements. A set $H \subset X$ is called a *Hamel basis* of X if:

1. H is a linearly independent subset of X.
2. The linear manifold spanned by H is all of X.

To show the existence of a Hamel basis, let P be the class whose members are the linearly independent subsets of X. Let P be partially ordered by the relation of set inclusion (i.e., $M \prec N$ if M, $N \in P$ and $M \subset N$). It is easy to see that P satisfies the conditions of Zorn's lemma. For, if $x_1 \neq 0$, the set consisting of x_1 alone is in P, and, if Q is a completely ordered subset of P, the subset of X obtained by taking the union of all the subsets of X comprised in Q is in P and is an upper bound for Q. Hence P must contain a maximal element, say H. Then the linear manifold spanned by H must be X. For, otherwise, some element x of X is not in the linear manifold spanned by H, and the set consisting of x and the elements of H is linearly independent and contains H as a proper subset, contrary to the maximal character of H. Thus H is a Hamel basis of X.

If $x' \in X^f$, we have $x'(x) = \alpha_1 x'(x_1) + \cdots + \alpha_n x'(x_n)$ whenever $x = \alpha_1 x_1 + \cdots + \alpha_n x_n$, the α's being any scalars. Conversely, suppose H is a Hamel basis of X. Define x' by assigning the value of $x'(x)$ arbitrarily when $x \in H$, and define $x'(x) = \alpha_1 x'(x_1) + \cdots + \alpha_n x'(x_n)$ if x is any element of X, uniquely represented in the form $x = \alpha_1 x_1 + \cdots + \alpha_n x_n$ where $x_1, \cdots, x_n$ are in H and $\alpha_1, \cdots, \alpha_n$ are scalars. Then $x' \in X^f$, as is easily seen.

By using the concept of a Hamel basis, we can show that no infinite-dimensional space is algebraically reflexive. First we observe that, if S is a linearly independent subset of X, there is a Hamel basis H of X such that S is a subset of H. This is shown by use of Zorn's lemma, taking P to be the class of all linearly independent subsets of X which contain S.

Theorem 1.72–A. *If X is infinite dimensional, it is not algebraically reflexive. Consequently (see Theorem 1.61–B), a linear space is algebraically reflexive if and only if it is finite dimensional.*

PROOF. Let $H = \{x_i : i \in I\}$ be a Hamel basis of X. Then I is an infinite index set, and $x_i \neq x_j$ if $i \neq j$. Define $x_i' \in X^f$ by $x_i'(x_i) = 1$, $x_i'(x_j) = 0$ if $i \neq j$. Then the set $\{x_i' : i \in I\}$ is a linearly independent set in X^f. For, if we suppose that $\sum_{\nu=1}^{n} \alpha_\nu x_{i(\nu)}' = 0$, we have $0 = \sum_{\nu=1}^{n} \alpha_\nu x_{i(\nu)}'(x_{i(\mu)})$ $= \alpha_\mu$ when $\mu = 1, \cdots, n$. Now let H' be a Hamel basis of X^f which contains the set $\{x_i' : i \in I\}$.

Let $\{\beta_i : i \in I\}$ be a set of numbers such that $\beta_i \neq 0$ for infinitely many indices i. Define $x'' \in X^{ff}$ by setting $x''(x_i') = \beta_i$ and $x''(x') = 0$ if $x' \in H'$ but x' is not one of the elements x_i'. Consider an element $x_0'' \in X^{ff}$ of the form $x_0'' = Jx$, $x \in X$. We have $x_0''(x_i') = x_i'(x) = \alpha_i$, where α_i is the coefficient of x_i in the representation of x in terms of the Hamel base H. Since $\alpha_i = 0$ for all but a finite number of indices i, it follows that the set of α_i's cannot be the same as the set of β_i's, and therefore $x'' \neq x_0''$. This shows that X^{ff} contains elements not in the range of J, so that X is not algebraically reflexive.

PROBLEMS

1. If H_1 and H_2 are any two Hamel bases for X, they have the same cardinal number. For each $x \in H_1$ let $H_2(x)$ be the finite set of those elements of H_2 which are needed to represent x by using the basis H_2. Show that, if $y \in H_2$, then $y \in H_2(x)$ for some $x \in H_1$, and hence that

$$H_2 = \bigcup_{x \in H_1} H_2(x).$$

The cardinality argument from here on is like that used in another context later in this book; see the last part of the proof of Theorems 3.2–0, following (3.2–11).

2. The cardinal number of a Hamel basis of X is called the dimension of X. In the case of a space X of infinite dimension, the cardinal of X itself can be shown to be the product $C \cdot \dim X$, where C is the cardinal of the set of all real numbers and $\dim X$ is the dimension of X. Since this product is just the larger of the two factors, the cardinal of X is C if $\dim X < C$ and $\dim X$ if $C \leqslant \dim X$. See Jacobson, **1**, Chapter 9, and Löwig, **1**, p. 20.

3. The dimensions of X and X^f are related as follows, provided that $\dim X$ is infinite:

$$\dim X^f = C^{\dim X}.$$

See the reference to Jacobson in the foregoing problem. It follows that X cannot be algebraically reflexive if $\dim X$ is infinite, for in that case $\dim X < \dim X^f$. We can also write $\dim X^f = 2^{\dim X}$ in this case. For, we have $C = 2^{\aleph_0}$, and $\aleph_0 \aleph = \aleph$ for any infinite cardinal $\aleph$, whence $C^{\aleph} = 2^{\aleph}$.

1.8 The Transpose of a Linear Operator

Suppose X and Y are linear spaces, and let A be a linear operator on X into Y. Let X^f and Y^f be the algebraic conjugates of X and Y respectively. We use the notations introduced in § 1.6. To each $y' \in Y^f$ let us make correspond the element $x' \in X^f$ defined by

$$(1.8\text{--}1) \qquad\qquad \langle x, x' \rangle = \langle Ax, y' \rangle,$$

where x varies over all of X, and let us denote the function so defined by $A^T : A^T y' = x'$. It is easy to check that A^T is a linear operator on Y^f into X^f. We leave the verifications to the reader. Equation (1.8–1) may now be written in the form

$$(1.8-2) \qquad \langle x, A^T y' \rangle = \langle Ax, y' \rangle, \qquad x \in X, \; y' \in Y^f.$$

This formula defines A^T.

Definition. The operator A^T defined by (1.8–2) is called the *transpose* of A.

To see the motivation for this terminology, let us consider the case in which X and Y are finite dimensional. Let X be n-dimensional, with basis $x_1, \cdots, x_n$, and let Y be m-dimensional, with basis $y_1, \cdots, y_m$. Let the corresponding dual bases in X^f and Y^f be $x_1', \cdots, x_n'$ and $y_1', \cdots, y_m'$ respectively (see § 1.61). We know from § 1.4 that the operator A determines, and is determined by, a matrix

$$(1.8-1) \qquad \begin{Vmatrix} \alpha_{11} & \alpha_{12} & \cdots & \alpha_{1n} \\ \alpha_{21} & \alpha_{22} & \cdots & \alpha_{2n} \\ \multicolumn{4}{c}{\dotfill} \\ \multicolumn{4}{c}{\dotfill} \\ \alpha_{m1} & \alpha_{m2} & \cdots & \alpha_{mn} \end{Vmatrix}$$

The basic formulas are [see (1.4–3)]

$$(1.8-2) \qquad Ax_j = \sum_{i=1}^{m} \alpha_{ij} y_i \qquad j = 1, \cdots, n.$$

Since A^T is a linear operator on Y^f into X^f, it follows that A^T is determined by a certain matrix

$$(1.8-3) \qquad \begin{Vmatrix} \beta_{11} & \beta_{12} & \cdots & \beta_{1m} \\ \beta_{21} & \beta_{22} & & \beta_{2m} \\ \cdots & \cdots & \cdots & \cdots \\ \cdots & \cdots & \cdots & \cdots \\ \beta_{n1} & \beta_{n2} & \cdots & \beta_{nm} \end{Vmatrix}$$

and the set of equations

$$(1.8-4) \qquad A^T y_i' = \sum_{k=1}^{n} \beta_{ki} x_k', \qquad i = 1, \cdots, m.$$

If we use the relations between a basis and the dual basis, we shall be able to find the relation which the matrix (1.8–3) bears to the matrix

(1.8–1). We know that $\langle x_j, x_k' \rangle = \delta_{jk}$ [see (1.61–3)] and likewise that $\langle y_k, y_i' \rangle = \delta_{ki}$. Consequently by (1.8–2),

$$\langle Ax_j, y_i' \rangle = \left\langle \sum_{k=1}^{m} \alpha_{kj} y_k, y_i' \right\rangle = \sum_{k=1}^{m} \alpha_{kj}\, \delta_{ki} = \alpha_{ij}.$$

But also, by (1.8–4),

$$\langle Ax_j, y_i' \rangle = \langle x_j, A^T y_i' \rangle = \left\langle x_j, \sum_{k=1}^{n} \beta_{ki} x_k' \right\rangle = \sum_{k=1}^{n} \beta_{ki}\, \delta_{jk} = \beta_{ji}.$$

Therefore

(1.8–5) $\alpha_{ij} = \beta_{ji}.$

In other words, the matrix (1.8–3) has for its kth row the kth column of the matrix (1.8–1). In the customary terminology of matrix algebra, the matrix (1.8–3) is the *transpose* of the matrix (1.8–1). It is on this account that the operator A^T is called the transpose of A.

The main reason for introducing the notion of the transpose of a linear operator is that the discussion of the existence of A^{-1} and the description of the range $\mathscr{R}(A)$ are facilitated by considering the transpose operator A^T. We shall see this in § 1.91.

1.9 Annihilators

The material of this section will be used in the following section, § 1.91, where we discuss certain relations between a linear operator A and its transpose A^T. In the present section we do not consider linear operators. Instead, we are concerned with certain linear manifolds in X and X^f, where X is a linear space and X^f is its algebraic conjugate.

Definition. Suppose S is a nonempty subset of X. Then S^0 denotes the set of all $x' \in X^f$ such that $\langle x, x' \rangle = 0$ if $x \in S$. This set S^0 is called the *annihilator* of S in X^f.

Several obvious facts may be noted:

S^0 *is a linear manifold, whether S is or not.*

(1.9–1) $(0)^0 = X^f, \qquad X^0 = (0);$

(1.9–2) $S_1 \subset S_2$ implies $S_2^0 \subset S_1^0.$

It will be of particular interest to us to consider the annihilator of the range of a linear operator.

If we consider a nonempty subset S of X^f, it will have an annihilator in X^{ff}, namely, the set of all $x'' \in X^{ff}$ such that $\langle x', x'' \rangle = 0$ if $x' \in S$. However, it is also useful to consider another notion, as follows:

Definition. If S is any nonempty subset of X^f, we use the symbol ^0S to denote the set of all $x \in X$ such that $\langle x, x' \rangle = 0$ if $x' = S$. This set ^0S is called the annihilator of S in X.

We observe the facts:

^0S *is a linear manifold, whether S is or not.*

(1.9–3) $\qquad\qquad ^0(0) = X, \qquad ^0(X^f) = (0).$

(1.9–4) $\qquad\qquad S_1 \subset S_2$ implies $^0S_2 \subset {}^0S_1$.

The relation $^0(X^f) = (0)$ in (1.9–3) follows from Theorem 1.71–C.

If $S \subset X^f$, there is a very simple relation between the annihilator of S in X and the annihilator of S in X^{ff}. If we think of X as a subspace of X^{ff}, via the canonical imbedding (see § 1.6), then ^0S is just that part of S^0 which lies in X. If we use the canonical imbedding operator J, the exact relationship between S^0 and ^0S is expressed in the formula

(1.9–5) $\qquad\qquad J(^0S) = J(X) \cap S^0.$

The verification of this formula is left to the reader. It is an immediate consequence of the definitions.

The first important theorem about annihilators is as follows; it concerns the annihilator of an annihilator:

Theorem 1.9–A. *If S is a nonempty subset of X, then $^0(S^0)$ is the linear manifold spanned by S. In particular, if M is a subspace in X, we have*

(1.9–6) $\qquad\qquad ^0(M^0) = M.$

PROOF. Let M be the linear manifold spanned by S. If $x = \alpha_1 x_1 + \cdots + \alpha_n x_n$, where $x_1, \cdots, x_n \in S$, and if $x' \in S^0$, we have

$$\langle x, x' \rangle = \alpha_1 \langle x_1, x' \rangle + \cdots + \alpha_n \langle x_n, x' \rangle = 0,$$

so that $x \in {}^0(S^0)$. Thus $M \subset {}^0(S^0)$. If we suppose $x_0 \in {}^0(S^0) - M$, we know by Theorem 1.71–B that there exists an element $x_0' \in X^f$ such that $\langle x, x_0' \rangle = 0$ if $x \in M$, but $\langle x_0, x_0' \rangle \neq 0$. The first of these two conditions on x_0' implies that $x_0' \in S^0$, because $S \subset M$. But then $\langle x_0, x_0' \rangle = 0$, because $x_0 \in {}^0(S^0)$. We have now reached a contradiction. Therefore $^0(S^0) \subset M$, and the proof is complete.

Corollary 1.9–B. *If M_1 and M_2 are subspaces of X such that $M_1{}^0 = M_2{}^0$, it follows that $M_1 = M_2$.*

PROOF.   By (1.9–6) we have $M_1 = {}^0(M_1{}^0) = {}^0(M_2{}^0) = M_2$.
In case of finite-dimensional spaces we have:

Theorem 1.9–C. *Let X be a linear space of dimension n, and let M be a subspace of X, of dimension m.   Then the annihilator M^0 has dimension $n - m$.*

PROOF.   We assume that $n > 1$ and that M is different from (0) and from X, so that $0 < m < n$.   The proof is very simple otherwise, and we leave the verification to the reader in these other cases.   Let $x_1, \cdots, x_n$ be a basis for X such that $x_1, \cdots, x_m$ is a basis for M.   Let $x_1', \cdots, x_n'$ be the dual basis of X^f.   Suppose $x \in M$.   Then $x = \xi_1 x_1 + \cdots + \xi_n x_n$, where $\xi_i = 0$ if $m < i \leqslant n$.   Hence, if $m < j \leqslant n$, $\langle x, x_j' \rangle = \xi_1 \langle x_1, x_j' \rangle + \cdots + \xi_m \langle x_m, x_j' \rangle = 0$, because of the relations (1.61–3).   This shows that $x_j' \in M^0$.   On the other hand, if $x' \in M^0$, we have $\dot{x}' = \xi_1' x_1' + \cdots + \xi_n' x_n'$ and, if $1 \leqslant i \leqslant m$, $0 = \langle x_i, x' \rangle = \xi_1' \langle x_i, x_1' \rangle + \cdots + \xi_n' \langle x_i, x_n' \rangle = \xi_i'$, again by (1.61–3).   Thus x' is in the linear manifold spanned by $x_{m+1}', \cdots, x_n'$.   These two results together show that $x_{m+1}', \cdots, x_n'$ constitute a basis for M^0, which therefore has dimension $n - m$.

Next we consider the situation analogous to that of Theorem 1.9–A when we start with a subset of X^f.

Theorem 1.9–D. *Suppose S is a nonempty subset of X^f, and let M be the linear manifold spanned by S.   Then*

$$(1.9–7) \qquad\qquad M \subset ({}^0S)^0.$$

The proof is simple; we leave it to the reader.
Unlike the situation in Theorem 1.9–A, it can happen that $M \neq ({}^0M)^0$ when M is a subspace of X^f.   An example will be given presently.

Theorem 1.9–E. *Let M be a proper subspace of X^f.   Then $M = ({}^0M)^0$ if and only if to each $x' \in X^f - M$ corresponds some $x \in {}^0M$ such that $\langle x, x' \rangle \neq 0$.*

PROOF.   By (1.9–7) we know that $M \subset ({}^0M)^0$.   Hence $({}^0M)^0 = M$ if and only if $({}^0M)^0 \subset M$.   For a given $x' \in X^f$ the statement "to x' corresponds some $x \in {}^0M$ such that $\langle x, x' \rangle \neq 0$" is equivalent to the statement "x' is not in $({}^0M)^0$."   Thus the theorem can be rephrased as follows: $({}^0M)^0 \subset M$ if and only if $x' \in X^f - M$ implies $x' \in X^f - ({}^0M)^0$.   In this form the assertion is obviously true, since a set-theoretic inclusion relation is reversed when we pass from the sets to their complements.

Definition. A subspace M of X^f is called *algebraically saturated* if $M = (^0M)^0$.

We see by (1.9–3) and (1.9–1) that (0) and X^f are both algebraically saturated subspaces of X^f. Also, it follows from (1.9–6) that, if M is any subspace of X, its annihilator M^0 is an algebraically saturated subspace of X^f.

Theorem 1.9–F. *If M_1 and M_2 are algebraically saturated subspaces of X^f and $^0M_1 = {}^0M_2$, it follows that $M_1 = M_2$.*

PROOF. $M_1 = (^0M_1)^0 = (^0M_2)^0 = M_2$.

Theorem 1.9–G. *If X is finite dimensional, every subspace of X^f is algebraically saturated.*

PROOF. Let M be a subspace of X^f, we can assume $M \neq X^f$, since we already know that X^f is saturated. Suppose $x_0' \in X^f - M$. By Theorem 1.61–D there exists an element $x_0'' \in M^0$ such that $x_0''(x_0') = 1$. But X is algebraically reflexive, and so there is an element $x_0 \in X$ such that $Jx_0 = x_0''$. Then $\langle x_0, x_0' \rangle = \langle x_0', x_0'' \rangle = 1$. The fact that $x_0'' \in M^0$ implies that $\langle x_0, x' \rangle = \langle x', x_0'' \rangle = 0$ if $x' \in M$; therefore $x_0 \in {}^0M$. Consequently M is algebraically saturated, by Theorem 1.9–E. We now give an example in which $M \neq (^0M)^0$.

Example 1. Let X be the space consisting of all convergent sequences $x = \{\xi_n\}$, with addition and scalar multiplication defined in the natural way. Let M be the subspace of X^f consisting of all linear functionals x' expressible in the form

$$(1.9\text{–}8) \qquad \langle x, x' \rangle = \sum_{i=1}^{\infty} \xi_i \xi_i' \qquad \text{where} \quad \sum_{i=1}^{\infty} |\xi_i'| < \infty.$$

Let x_0' be the particular element of X^f defined by

$$(1.9\text{–}9) \qquad \langle x, x_0' \rangle = \lim_{n \to \infty} \xi_n.$$

We shall show that $x_0' \in (^0M)^0 - M$. First we show that $(^0M)^0 = X^f$, so that certainly $x_0' \in (^0M)^0$. Suppose that $x \in {}^0M$, i.e., that $\langle x, x' \rangle = 0$ for each $x' \in M$. For any given positive integer n let $\xi_i' = 0$ if $i \neq n$, $\xi_n' = 1$, and let x' be the corresponding element of M, as in (1.9–8). Then $0 = \langle x, x' \rangle = \xi_n$; this is true for $n = 1, 2, \cdots$, and so $x = 0$. This shows that $^0M = (0)$; it follows that $(^0M)^0 = X^f$. Next we show that x_0' is not in M. For, if we suppose $x_0' \in M$, we have a representation

$$(1.9\text{–}10) \qquad \langle x, x_0' \rangle = \sum_{i=1}^{\infty} \xi_i \alpha_i, \qquad \sum_{i=1}^{\infty} |\alpha_i| < \infty.$$

For a given k let x be chosen with $\xi_n = 0$ if $n \neq k$, $\xi_k = 1$. Then, comparing (1.9–9) and (1.9–10), we see that $\alpha_k = 0$. This holds for each k, so (1.9–10) tells us that $\langle x, x_0' \rangle = 0$ for every x. This is false, for (1.9–9) shows that $\langle x, x_0' \rangle = 1$ when x is defined by $\xi_1 = \xi_2 = \cdots = 1$. We have thus shown that $x_0' \in ({}^0M)^0 - M$. Therefore M is not algebraically saturated.

1.91 Ranges and Null Manifolds

In this section we consider an arbitrary linear operator A on X into Y, where X and Y are linear spaces with the same field of scalars. In § 1.3 we discussed in general terms two important questions which arise in connection with a linear operator: (1) For which elements $y \in Y$ does the equation $Ax = y$ have a solution x? (2) Is the solution unique in all cases in which a solution exists? The first question leads us to seek various ways of characterizing the range $\mathscr{R}(A)$. The second question is the same as the question: "Does the inverse A^{-1} exist?" In the present section we investigate these questions with the aid of the transpose operator A^T (see § 1.8) and the annihilator concepts developed in § 1.9.

Definition. By the *null manifold* of A is meant the set of all $x \in X$ such that $Ax = 0$. We denote this set by $\mathscr{N}(A)$.

It is evident that $\mathscr{N}(A)$ is a linear manifold in X.

The definition of null manifold can be applied to the transpose A^T, so that $\mathscr{N}(A^T)$ is the set of all $y' \in Y^f$ such that $A^T y' = 0$.

We recall that the inverse A^{-1} exists if and only if $Ax = 0$ implies $x = 0$, that is, if and only if $\mathscr{N}(A) = (0)$.

Our first results deal with the relations between $\mathscr{R}(A)$ and $\mathscr{N}(A^T)$.

Theorem 1.91–A. $\{\mathscr{R}(A)\}^0 = \mathscr{N}(A^T)$.

PROOF. By definition of A^T we have $\langle Ax, y' \rangle = \langle x, A^T y' \rangle$ for $x \in X$, $y' \in Y^f$. If $y' \in \{\mathscr{R}(A)\}^0$ we see that $\langle Ax, y' \rangle = 0$ for each $x \in X$, and so $A^T y' = 0$, or $y' \in \mathscr{N}(A^T)$. The reasoning is reversible, and so the theorem is proved.

Theorem 1.91–B. $\mathscr{R}(A) = {}^0\{\mathscr{N}(A^T)\}$.

PROOF. $\mathscr{R}(A) = {}^0\{\mathscr{R}(A)^0\} = {}^0\{\mathscr{N}(A^T)\}$, by Theorems 1.9–A and 19.1–A.

Theorem 1.91–C. $\mathscr{R}(A) = Y$ *if and only if* $(A^T)^{-1}$ *exists.*

PROOF. $\mathscr{R}(A) = Y$ implies $\mathscr{N}(A^T) = Y^0 = (0)$, by Theorem 1.91–A and (1.9–1). But $\mathscr{N}(A^T) = (0)$ is equivalent to the existence of $(A^T)^{-1}$. Thus, $\mathscr{R}(A) = Y$ implies the existence of $(A^T)^{-1}$. Conversely, $\mathscr{N}(A^T) = (0)$ implies $\mathscr{R}(A) = {}^0(0) = Y$, by Theorem 1.91–B and (1.9–3).

The foregoing theorems give us what we want with respect to $\mathscr{R}(A)$. Next we seek to obtain information about $\mathscr{N}(A)$ by considering $\mathscr{R}(A^T)$.

Theorem 1.91–D. $\mathscr{N}(A) = {}^0\{\mathscr{R}(A^T)\}$.

PROOF. The formula $\langle x, A^T y' \rangle = \langle Ax, y' \rangle$, valid for $x \in X$ and $y' \in Y^f$, shows at once that $\mathscr{N}(A) \subset {}^0\{\mathscr{R}(A^T)\}$. The same formula shows that $x \in {}^0\{\mathscr{R}(A^T)\}$ implies $\langle Ax, y' \rangle = 0$ for every $y' \in Y^f$. But then $x \in \mathscr{N}(A)$ by Theorem 1.71–C. This completes the proof.

Theorem 1.91–E. *We always have* $\mathscr{R}(A^T) \subset \{\mathscr{N}(A)\}^0$. *We have* $\mathscr{R}(A^T) = \{\mathscr{N}(A)\}^0$ *if* $\mathscr{R}(A^T)$ *is algebraically saturated. This is certainly the case if* X *is finite dimensional.*

PROOF. By Theorem 1.91–D we have $\{{}^0\{\mathscr{R}(A^T)\}\}^0 = \{\mathscr{N}(A)\}^0$. Then $\mathscr{R}(A^T) \subset \{\mathscr{N}(A)\}^0$, by Theorem 1.9–D. For the rest of the theorem we use the definition of "algebraically saturated" and Theorem 1.9–G.

Theorem 1.91–F. *If* $\mathscr{R}(A^T) = X^f$, *then* A^{-1} *exists.*

PROOF. This follows by Theorem 1.91–D and (1.9–3).

Theorem 1.91–G. *If* A^{-1} *exists, it follows that* $\{{}^0\mathscr{R}(A^T)\}^0 = X^f$. *If* $\mathscr{R}(A^T)$ *is algebraically saturated (hence certainly if* X *is finite dimensional), we can conclude further that* $\mathscr{R}(A^T) = X^f$.

PROOF. If A^{-1} exists, $\mathscr{N}(A) = (0)$. Then $\{{}^0\{\mathscr{R}(A^T)\}\}^0 = (0)^0 = X^f$ by Theorem 1.91–D and (1.9–1). The rest of the theorem follows at once (see Theorem 1.91–E).

We emphasize that, if X is finite dimensional, A^{-1} exists if and only if $\mathscr{R}(A^T) = X^f$.

PROBLEM

If X^f is algebraically reflexive, so is X. Prove this without resort to questions of finite dimensionality, using the following suggestions: Let J_0 be the canonical mapping of X into X^{ff}, J_1 the canonical mapping of X^f into X^{fff}. By Theorem 1.91–C, X is algebraically reflexive if and only if $(J_0^T)^{-1}$ exists. By hypothesis $\mathscr{R}(J_1) = X^{fff}$. Show that $J_1^{-1} = J_0^T$, whence $(J_0^T)^{-1}$ exists $(= J_1)$.

1.92 Conclusions

The theorems of § 1.91 involve the ranges and null manifolds of the operator A and its transpose A^T. If we suppose that the spaces X, Y and the operator A come to us as known things, the theorems will be effectively useful to us in furnishing information about $\mathscr{R}(A)$ and $\mathscr{N}(A)$ only to the extent that we know or can find out the relevant information about $\mathscr{R}(A^T)$ and $\mathscr{N}(A^T)$. For this, we must, at the very least, know some things about the spaces X^f, Y^f and the operator A^T.

In the case in which X and Y are finite dimensional, the spaces X^f and Y^f are also finite dimensional. In this case the operator A is fully represented by a matrix, and the transpose A^T is represented by the transposed matrix. For the finite-dimensional case all the results of § 1.91 are well known in algebra (though perhaps in a different terminology) as part of the theory of systems of linear equations or of the theory of matrices.

For infinite-dimensional spaces the results of § 1.91 are not as useful as could be wished, because the algebraic conjugate of an infinite-dimensional space is not as amenable to study as the algebraic conjugate of a finite-dimensional space. The theory for finite-dimensional spaces is much simplified by the fact that we have simple "concrete representations" of such spaces. If X is an n-dimensional linear space with real scalars, it is isomorphic to the arithmetic space R_n (see the proof of Theorem 1.4–A), and we can regard R_n as a concrete representation of X. Likewise, if A is a linear operator on X into Y (spaces of dimensions n and m respectively), we have a concrete representation of A by a certain $m \times n$ matrix. The purpose of such a representation is to replace one object of study by another object whose properties are more readily apparent because the structure of the object is more familiar or more susceptible to intuitive perception.

In order to obtain results of the type presented in § 1.91, but more useful, it seems essential to abandon the purely algebraic approach to linear problems for infinite-dimensional spaces and to bring in topological considerations. If we impose a specified topological structure on a linear space X, it is natural to consider those linear functionals on X which are continuous with respect to the topology. These form a subspace of the algebraic conjugate space X^f; this subspace may be called the *topological conjugate* of X. In a good many interesting special cases the topological conjugate of a given topological linear space X can be studied more effectively than the algebraic conjugate of X. This may be the case, for one thing, because the topological conjugate is significantly smaller than the algebraic conjugate (i.e., has fewer elements). It may also turn out that there is a useful concrete representation of the topological conjugate space. Thus, for example, if X is the space of real-valued continuous functions defined on $0 \leqslant t \leqslant 1$, with a certain natural topology for X, the topological conjugate of X is isomorphic to a certain space whose elements form a subclass of the class of all real-valued functions of bounded variation defined on $0 \leqslant t \leqslant 1$; see Theorem 4.32–C.

This necessarily somewhat vague and general discussion is intended to suggest in part why the abstract approach to linear problems, as far as infinite-dimensional spaces are concerned, is more fruitful if suitable topological as well as algebraic methods are employed. There are still other reasons why it is useful to take account of a topology for a given linear space. A given linear operator may have important properties which find their appropriate expression in terms of the topological or metric notions of "nearness," "small variations," and other related ideas.

The greatest successes of the abstract approach to linear problems have been achieved in the study of Hilbert space. A Hilbert space is a very special type of linear space with a topology. It has many of the properties of Euclidean space and is, therefore, amenable to the use of geometric reasoning guided by intuition. But perhaps the decisive reason for the importance of Hilbert space, and for the greater success which has been achieved with Hilbert space than with other spaces, is the fact that the topological conjugate of a Hilbert space is isomorphic with the given Hilbert space.

SUGGESTED READING

Banach, **1**, especially Chapter 2.
Bourbaki, **1**, especially p. 37 in connection with Zorn's lemma.
Bourbaki, **3**.
Halmos, **1**.
Hamburger and Grimshaw, **1**.
Jacobson, **1**, especially Chapters 1, 2, 9.
Kelley, **1**, especially pp. 31–36 in connection with Zorn's lemma.
Zaanen, **1**, especially Chapter 8.

2

TOPOLOGIES

2.0 Scope of the Chapter

This chapter is intended primarily for reference purposes. It contains the definitions and theorems relating to general topological matters which are needed at various places throughout the book. Since this is not a book on general topology, the selection of topics and the treatment of them conform to our primary interest in linear spaces.

Although the reader is not presumed to have made an extensive study of abstract topology as a prerequisite for studying this book, some acquaintance with the ideas of abstract topology is needed. The student with some experience in topology should proceed directly to Chapter 3 after a preliminary scanning of Chapter 2. Thereafter he can refer back to Chapter 2 as needed. The student who has never studied abstract general topology will probably find it best to read parts of Chapters 2 and 3 in close conjunction, paying especial attention to the examples in Chapter 3. It is not necessary to master all of these chapters before going on to later chapters.

2.1 Topological Spaces

The very general concept of a topological space has evolved by abstraction from various special situations; the original model for a topological space is the real axis, i.e., Euclidean 1-dimensional space. The basic notion in the general definition of a topological space is that of axiomatizing the properties of open sets. A topological space is a set of elements in which certain subsets are designated as "open sets." The class of these open sets must satisfy certain axioms.

Definition. A set X with a family $\mathscr{T}$ of subsets is called a *topological space* if $\mathscr{T}$ satisfies the following conditions:

(a) The empty set $\emptyset$ and the whole space X belong to $\mathscr{T}$.
(b) The union of any number of members of $\mathscr{T}$ (even uncountably many) is again a member of $\mathscr{T}$.
(c) The intersection of any finite number of members of $\mathscr{T}$ is again a member of $\mathscr{T}$.

The family $\mathscr{T}$ is called a *topology* for X, and the members of $\mathscr{T}$ are called the *open sets* of X in this topology.

Example 1. If X is any nonempty set and $\mathscr{T}$ consists of $\emptyset$ and X, $\mathscr{T}$ is evidently a topology for X.

Example 2. If X is any nonempty set and $\mathscr{T}$ consists of *all* subsets of X ($\emptyset$ and X are of course included), $\mathscr{T}$ is evidently a topology for X. It is called the *discrete* topology for X.

Example 3. Let X be the set of all real numbers x. A subset T of X will be called open if to each x_0 in T corresponds some $h > 0$ such that $x \in T$ if $|x - x_0| < h$. Evidently X is open, and $\emptyset$ satisfies vacuously the condition of being open. The axioms (a), (b), (c) for open sets are satisfied. The topology thus defined for X is the one regularly used in analysis.

It is clear from Examples 1 and 2 that the general definition of a topology for a set X leaves the way open for situations quite different from those encountered in the customary topology of the real axis or of the Euclidean plane.

A set S in the topological space X is called *closed* if its complement S' is open. It will be seen that the empty set $\emptyset$ and the whole space X are both open and closed. Because of the complementation rules, it follows that any intersection of closed sets is closed and that any finite union of closed sets is closed. Also, since $(S')' = S$, a set is open if and only if its complement is closed.

If $S \subset X$, the intersection of all closed subsets of X which contain S is called the *closure* of S and denoted by $\bar{S}$. Clearly $\bar{S}$ is closed and $S \subset \bar{S}$. Moreover, it is easy to see that $S = \bar{S}$ if and only if S is closed.

If $S \subset X$, the union of all the open subsets of S is called the *interior* of S and denoted by int (S). Evidently int (S) is open and int $(S) \subset S$. Moreover, S is open if and only if $S = $ int (S).

The *boundary* of a set S is defined as the intersection of the closures of S and its complement S'.

Any open set which contains a point x is called a *neighborhood* of x. Likewise, if $S \subset X$, an open set U such that $S \subset U$ is called a neighborhood of S.

A point x is called an *accumulation point* of a set S if every neighborhood of x contains a point of S distinct from x. It is not hard to see that a set S is closed if and only if it contains all its accumulation points.

When we set out to construct a topology for a given set we often achieve this end by selecting certain sets which turn out to be open and which are used in determining all the other open sets. For example, in our definition of the topology of the real axis, in Example 3, we made use of the *open intervals* with a given point x_0 as center. This idea finds its general expression in the concept of a *base*.

A family $\mathscr{B}$ of open sets is called a *base at the point* x if $x \in B$ whenever $B \in \mathscr{B}$ and if to each neighborhood U of x corresponds some $B \in \mathscr{B}$ such that $B \subset U$. A family of open sets is called a *base for the space* X (or simply a base) if for each $x \in X$ there is a subfamily which is a base at x. A family $\mathscr{B}$ is thus a base for X if and only if to each $x \in X$ and each neighborhood U of x there is a set $B \in \mathscr{B}$ such that $x \in B$ and $B \subset U$. The subfamily of all elements of $\mathscr{B}$ which are neighborhoods of x is then a base at x. Clearly the same family $\mathscr{B}$ cannot be a base for two different topologies on X.

Example 4. Consider the topology for the axis of real numbers defined in Example 3. The set of all open intervals of lengths $2/n$ ($n = 1$, 2, $\cdots$) is a base for this topological space, and the open intervals $\{x : |x - x_0| < 1/n\}$ ($n = 1, 2, \cdots$) form a base at x_0.

If $\mathscr{B}$ is a base for a topological space X, the following assertions are evidently true:

(a) To each $x \in X$ corresponds some $B \in \mathscr{B}$ such that $x \in B$.
(b) If $B_1, B_2 \in \mathscr{B}$ and $x \in B_1 \cap B_2$, there exists some $B_3 \in \mathscr{B}$ such that $x \in B_3 \subset (B_1 \cap B_2)$.

Now let us suppose that X is a set, initially without any specified topology, and suppose that there is a family $\mathscr{B}$ of subsets of X satisfying the two conditions a, b just given. Let us then *define* a set $S \subset X$ to be open if for each $x \in S$ there is some $B \in \mathscr{B}$ with $x \in B \subset S$. The class

$\mathcal{T}$ of open sets is a topology for X.   The verification is easy.   The empty set $\emptyset$ is open, since it satisfies the condition vacuously.   The set X is open, by (a).   Condition (b) assures that finite intersections of open sets are open, and unions of open sets are seen to be open by the definition. The members of $\mathcal{B}$ are themselves open, according to the definition, and $\mathcal{B}$ is a base for the topological space X whose topology $\mathcal{T}$ was defined by means of $\mathcal{B}$.   This illustrates an important method of introducing a topology on a set.

Example 5.   In R_n (Example 1, § 1.2) let $\mathcal{B}$ be the family of sets B of the following sort: Choose an arbitrary point $x_0 = (\xi_1{}^0, \cdots, \xi_n{}^0)$ and an arbitrary positive number r; let B be the set of points $x = (\xi_1, \cdots, \xi_n)$ such that $(\xi_1 - \xi_1{}^0)^2 + \cdots + (\xi_n - \xi_n{}^0)^2 < r^2$.   This family $\mathcal{B}$ has the properties (a) and (b) mentioned in the preceding discussion; the topology for R_n determined by $\mathcal{B}$ as a base in the standard topology for R_n.

Sometimes we consider several topologies for the same set X.   If two topologies $\mathcal{T}_1$ and $\mathcal{T}_2$ for X are such that every member of $\mathcal{T}_1$ is also a member of $\mathcal{T}_2$ (i.e., $\mathcal{T}_1 \subset \mathcal{T}_2$), we say that $\mathcal{T}_1$ is *weaker* than $\mathcal{T}_2$ and that $\mathcal{T}_2$ is *stronger* than $\mathcal{T}_1$.   The stronger topology has more open sets. Other terminologies in this situation are: $\mathcal{T}_1$ is *coarser* than $\mathcal{T}_2$ and $\mathcal{T}_2$ is *finer* than $\mathcal{T}_1$; also, $\mathcal{T}_2$ is *larger* than $\mathcal{T}_1$.

If $\mathcal{F}$ is any nonempty family of topologies for X, the intersection of all these topologies is a topology for X, and it is weaker than all the topologies in $\mathcal{F}$.   Suppose that $\mathcal{A}$ is any nonempty class of subsets of X.   There certainly is a topology for X which includes the members of $\mathcal{A}$, namely the discrete topology for X.   Hence there is a well-defined topology for X which is the intersection of all those topologies for X which include the members of $\mathcal{A}$.   We call it *the topology generated by $\mathcal{A}$*.   The open sets in this topology are: $\emptyset$, X, and all unions of finite intersections of members of $\mathcal{A}$.   The family $\mathcal{A}$ is called a *subbase* for the topology which it generates.

In our definition of a topological space there are no *separation* axioms. It can happen that, given two distinct points x_1, x_2, every neighborhood of x_1 contains x_2.   This implies that x_1 is an accumulation point of the set consisting of x_2 alone and, thus, that the latter set is not closed.   There are various separation axioms that may be imposed on a topological space.   One such axiom provides that, if x_1 and x_2 are distinct points, there exists an open set S_1 such that S_1 contains x_1 but not x_2.   This is equivalent to the requirement that every set consisting of a single point be closed.

Definition.   A topological space is called a T_1-space if each set consisting of a single point is closed.

A more stringent separation axiom requires that, if $x_1 \neq x_2$, there shall exist open sets S_1, S_2 such that $x_1 \in S_1$, $x_2 \in S_2$, and $S_1 \cap S_2 = \emptyset$. Spaces with this property are called T_2-spaces, or Hausdorff spaces. They are discussed in § 2.3.

PROBLEMS

1. If $S \subset X$ and $x \in X$, $x \in \bar{S}$ if and only if every neighborhood of x intersects S.

2. A point x is in the boundary of a set S if and only if every neighborhood of x intersects both S and S'.

3. A set S is open if and only if to each point x in S corresponds some neighborhood U of x such that $U \subset S$.

4. The closure of a set consists of the set together with all its accumulation points.

5. If $\mathscr{B}$ is a base for X, every open set in X is the union of certain (perhaps uncountably many) members of the base.

6. If $\mathscr{T}$ is the discrete topology for X (see Example 2), every subset of X is both open and closed. The discrete topology is stronger than every other topology.

7. The weakest possible topology for X is that one in which consists solely of $\emptyset$ and X.

8. In the xy-plane let $\mathscr{A}$ be the family of sets A of the following sort: Each A is determined by two distinct parallel lines and consists of all points of the xy-plane lying strictly between these two lines. What is the nature of the topology generated by $\mathscr{A}$? In particular, how is this topology related to the topology defined in Example 5 if we regard the xy-plane as the space R_2?

2.11 Relative Topologies

Suppose X is a topological space with topology $\mathscr{T}$, and let X_0 be a subset of X. Then we can define a topology $\mathscr{T}_0$ for X_0 by taking for $\mathscr{T}_0$ the family of sets of the form $T \cap X_0$, where $T \subset \mathscr{T}$. The topology $\mathscr{T}_0$ is called the *relative topology for X_0 induced by* (or *inherited from*) *the topology $\mathscr{T}$*.

When it is clear from the context in a certain situation that we are talking about the topology of X and the relative topology $\mathscr{T}_0$ for X_0, a subset of X_0 which is open (or closed) in the topology $\mathscr{T}_0$ is called *relatively open* (or *relatively closed*). A set $S \subset X_0$ is relatively closed if and only if it is of the form $A \cap X_0$, where A is closed. For, S is relatively closed if and only if its complement relative to X_0 is relatively open, so that S itself must be of the form $X_0 - (T \cap X_0)$, where T is open. But

$$X_0 - (T \cap X_0) = X_0 \cap (T \cap X_0)' = X_0 \cap (T' \cup X_0')$$
$$= (X_0 \cap T') \cup (X_0 \cap X_0') = X_0 \cap T'.$$

Since T' is closed, this shows that S has the form asserted.

It is useful to observe that, if X_0 is a closed subset of X and if $S \subset X_0$ is relatively closed, then S is closed in the topology of X. We can see the truth of this as follows: If $S \subset X_0$, we have $X_0' \subset S'$, and hence $X_0' \cap S' = X_0'$ so that

$$S' = (S' \cap X_0') \cup (S' \cap X_0) = X_0' \cup (S' \cap X_0).$$

But, if S is relatively closed, we have $X_0 - S = X_0 \cap S' = T \cap X_0$, where T is open.   Thus

$$S' = X_0' \cup (T \cap X_0) = X_0' \cup T,$$

whence S' is open (for X_0' is open) and S is closed.

2.12 Continuous Functions

Let X and Y be topological spaces, and let f be a function with domain X and range Y. If $S \subset X$, we denote by $f(S)$ the set of all $f(x) \in Y$ corresponding to $x \in S$. If $T \subset Y$, we denote by $f^{-1}(T)$ the set of all $x \in X$ such that $f(x) \in T$. There is no implication in this notation that an inverse function exists.

Definition.   The function f is said to be continuous at the point $x_0 \in X$ if to each neighborhood V of $f(x_0)$ in Y there corresponds a neighborhood U of x_0 in X such that $f(U) \subset V$. An equivalent rewording of this definition is convenient for some purposes: f is continuous at x_0 if, for each neighborhood V of $f(x_0)$, the set $f^{-1}(V)$ contains a neighborhood of x_0. We further say that f is continuous on X if it is continuous at each point of X.

Theorem 2.12–A.   *Suppose f is a function with domain X and range Y, where X and Y are topological spaces. Then f is continuous on X if and only if $f^{-1}(V)$ is an open set in X whenever V is an open set in Y.*

PROOF.   Suppose $f^{-1}(V)$ is open whenever V is open.   Let x_0 be any point in X and V any neighborhood of $f(x_0)$. Then $f^{-1}(V)$ is open and contains x_0, so that $f^{-1}(V)$ is a neighborhood of x_0. Thus f is continuous at x_0, by the second form of the definition.   For the argument in the other direction, suppose f is continuous on X, and let V be an open set in Y. Then, if $x \in f^{-1}(V)$, V is a neighborhood of $f(x)$, and hence $f^{-1}(V)$ must include a neighborhood of x.   This implies that $f^{-1}(V)$ is open.

If f has domain X and range Y and $T \subset Y$, it is easy to see that

(2.12–1) $f^{-1}(T') = [f^{-1}(T)]'$.

From this formula and Theorem 2.12–A we see that f is continuous on X if and only if $f^{-1}(S)$ is a closed set in X whenever S is a closed set in Y.

Sometimes we have the situation that X and Y are topological spaces and f is a function with domain $\mathscr{D}(f) \subset X$ and range $\mathscr{R}(f) \subset Y$.   In this case continuity of f at a point of $\mathscr{D}(f)$ is defined by considering $\mathscr{D}(f)$ and $\mathscr{R}(f)$ as spaces with the relative topologies inherited from X and Y respectively.

Suppose that X and Y are topological spaces and that f is a function with domain X and range Y such that the inverse function f^{-1} exists.   If both f and f^{-1} are continuous on their domains, f is called a *homeomorphism* of X onto Y, and X and Y are said to be *homeomorphic*.

2.2 Compact Sets

Let X be a set, S a subset of X, and $\mathscr{F}$ a family of subsets of X such that each point of S belongs to at least one member of $\mathscr{F}$.   Then the family $\mathscr{F}$ is said to *cover* S, or to be a *covering* of S.   If X is a topological space and if all the sets in $\mathscr{F}$ are open, $\mathscr{F}$ is called an *open covering* of S.

Definition.   A subset S of a topological space X is called *compact* if every open covering of S includes a finite subfamily which covers S.

It is readily seen that S is compact as a subset of X if and only if S is compact when we consider S itself to be the whole space and use the relative topology.

The empty set is compact.   So is any finite set.

Theorem 2.2–A.   *A set $S \subset X$ is compact if and only if in every family of relatively closed subsets of S, the intersection of all of which is $\emptyset$, there is a finite subfamily with this same property.*

PROOF.   A family of relatively open sets covers S if and only if their complements (relative to S) form a family of relatively closed sets with intersection $\emptyset$.   The theorem follows from this remark.

Theorem 2.2–B.   *A closed subset of a compact space is compact.*

PROOF.   Let X be a compact space and S a closed subset of X.   Let $\mathscr{F}$ be a family of relatively closed subsets of S whose intersection is $\emptyset$.   If $F \in \mathscr{F}$, F is closed as a subset of X (this follows by an observation made in § 2.11).   Hence, by Theorem 2.2–A (applied to the compact set X), $\mathscr{F}$ includes a finite subfamily whose intersection is $\emptyset$.   Hence, again by Theorem 2.2–A, S is compact.

Theorem 2.2–C.   *Let f be a continuous function whose domain is compact.   Then its range is also compact.*

PROOF.   We can assume that the domain of f is all of X and the range is all of Y.   If $\mathscr{V}$ is a family of open sets V and if $\mathscr{V}$ covers Y, the family $\mathscr{U}$ of sets $U = f^{-1}(V)$ certainly covers X.   Moreover, each U is open, by Theorem 2.12–A.   Since X is compact, $\mathscr{U}$ includes a finite subfamily $U_1, \cdots, U_n$ which covers X.   The corresponding finite subfamily $V_1, \cdots, V_n$ clearly covers Y, and so Y is compact.

We remind the reader that a point set on the real axis (or in n-dimensional Euclidean space) is compact if and only if it is closed and bounded.   It follows from Theorem 2.2–C that, if f is real valued and continuous on a compact topological space, the values of f are bounded.   Moreover, the set of values is closed, so that the function actually attains its least upper bound and its greatest lower bound.   In other words, the function has a maximum value at some point of the space, and likewise a minimum value.

Sometimes we consider sets S with the property that the closure $\bar{S}$ is compact.   A set of this kind is called *conditionally* compact (or, also, *relatively* compact).

2.21 Category. Separability

Suppose X is a topological space.   If $S \subset X$ and $\bar{S} = X$, we say that S is *dense* in X.   If the interior of $\bar{S}$ is empty, we say that S is *nowhere dense*.

Definition.   A set $S \subset X$ is said to be of the *first category* if S is the union of a countable family of nowhere dense sets.   If S is not of the first category, it is said to be of the *second category*.   If $S \subset X$ and $x \in X$, we say that S is of the first category at x if there is a neighborhood U of x such that $U \cap S$ is of the first category; otherwise $U \cap S$ is of the second category for every neighborhood U of x, and S is said to be of the second category at x.

It can be verified that if S is of the first category it is of the first category at every point of X, and conversely.

Definition. A topological space X is called *perfectly separable* if there exists a countable family of sets forming a base for X (or, briefly, if X has a countable base). A space with a finite base will also be called perfectly separable.

The Euclidean plane, for example, is perfectly separable. As a countable base we may take the family of all interiors of circles with rational radii and rational coordinates for the centers.

If the space X is perfectly separable, it contains an at most countable set S which is dense in X. In fact, if $\mathscr{B}$ is a finite or countable base for X and if S is a set formed by selecting one element from each of the sets in $\mathscr{B}$, then S is at most countable and $\bar{S} = X$. For, if we assume $X - \bar{S}$ to be nonempty, it is an open set containing some point x, and hence (since $\mathscr{B}$ is a base) there exists some $B \in \mathscr{B}$ with $x \in B \subset X - \bar{S}$. Some point of B must belong to S, however, and this is a contradiction, since $B \cap \bar{S} = \emptyset$.

Definition. A topological space X is called *separable* if there exists a finite or countable set S which is dense in X.

The foregoing argument shows that a perfectly separable space is separable. The converse is not true in general, though it is true for certain types of spaces (e.g., metric spaces; see § 2.4).

Some spaces, though not perfectly separable, have the property that *at each point* there is a countable base. The requirement that this be so is called the *first axiom of countability*. The requirement of perfect separability is called the *second axiom of countability*.

2.3 Separation Axioms. Hausdorff Spaces

In § 2.1 we gave the definition of a T_1-space: a topological space in which sets consisting of a single point are closed. We now define several other types of spaces, each of which is characterized by the addition of one or more separation axioms to the axioms for a topological space.

Before stating these definitions we remark that two sets A, B are called *disjoint* if $A \cap B = \emptyset$.

Hausdorff Spaces. A topological space is called a *Hausdorff space* if for each pair of distinct points x_1, x_2 in the space there exists disjoint neighborhoods U_1, U_2 of x_1 and x_2 respectively.

Regular Spaces. A topological space is called *regular* if for each point x and each closed set A not containing x there exists disjoint neighborhoods of x and A respectively. An equivalent formulation: For each point x

and each neighborhood U of x there exists a neighborhood V of x such that $\bar{V} \subset U$.

Normal Spaces. A topological space is called *normal* if for each pair of disjoint closed sets A, B there exist disjoint neighborhoods U, V of A and B respectively.

Every Hausdorff space is a T_1-space, but some T_1-spaces are not Hausdorff spaces. A space can be regular or normal without being a T_1-space. However, as applied to T_1-spaces, the types Hausdorff, regular, normal, form a hierarchy: Every normal space is regular and every regular space is a Hausdorff space. There is a nomenclature according to which spaces are classified as T_1, T_2, T_3, T_4. The definitions for T_2, T_3, T_4 are as follows:

T_2-space: a Hausdorff space.
T_3-space: a regular T_1-space.
T_4-space: a normal T_1-space.

The class of T_3-spaces is a proper subclass of the class of T_2-spaces. Likewise for T_4 and T_3.

Compact Hausdorff spaces of a rather general sort play an important role in certain parts of functional analysis. Nearly all of the topologies which are used in connection with linear spaces are such as to make the spaces regular; they are usually assumed to be T_1-spaces also, so that they are T_3-spaces.

Later on we shall need certain facts about Hausdorff spaces and normal spaces. We present these facts here as theorems.

Theorem 2.3–A. *If C_0 and C_1 are disjoint compact sets in a Hausdorff space X, there exist disjoint neighborhoods W_0 and W_1 of C_0 and C_1 respectively.*

PROOF. We suppose at first that C_0 consists of a single point x_0 (such a set, in fact any finite set, is compact). Then for every point x in C_1 there exist disjoint neighborhoods U and V of x_0 and x respectively. The family of all the V's covers C_1, and hence some finite subfamily $V_1, \cdots,$ V_n covers C_1. Let $U_1, \cdots, U_n$ be the corresponding U's and let $W_0 = U_1 \cap \cdots \cap U_n$, $W_1 = V_1 \cup \cdots \cup V_n$. This gives what is wanted for this special case. In the general case suppose x is any point of C_0. By what has just been proved there exist disjoint neighborhoods U, V of x and C_1 respectively. The family of all the U's covers C_0, and hence some finite subfamily $U_1, \cdots, U_m$ also covers C_0. If $V_1, \cdots, V_m$ are the corresponding V's, we let $W_0 = U_1 \cup \cdots \cup U_m$, $W_1 = V_1 \cap \cdots \cap V_m$ and attain the desired result.

Theorem 2.3–B.   *A compact subset of a Hausdorff space is closed.*

PROOF.   Suppose C is compact and $x \in \bar{C}$.   Then $x \in C$.   For, if not, Theorem 2.3–A implies the existence of a neighborhood of x which doesn't intersect C.   This in turn implies that $x \notin \bar{C}$ (see § 2.1).   From this contradiction we conclude that $\bar{C} \subset C$; hence $\bar{C} = C$, and C is closed.

A Hausdorff space is sometimes defined (as was originally done by Hausdorff) by a separate set of axioms.   Let X be a set of elements, and suppose there is given a family $\mathscr{N}$ of ordered pairs (N, x), where N is a subset of X and $x \in N$, satisfying the following axioms:

1. For each $x \in X$ there is at least one $N \subset X$ such that $(N, x) \in \mathscr{N}$.
2. If (N_1, x) and (N_2, x) are in $\mathscr{N}$, there exists an $(N_3, x) \in \mathscr{N}$ with $N_3 \subset N_1 \cap N_2$.
3. If $(N_1, x_1) \in \mathscr{N}$ and $x_2 \in N_1$, there exists an $N_2 \subset X$ such that $(N_2, x_2) \in \mathscr{N}$ and $N_2 \subset N_1$.
4. If $x_1 \neq x_2$, there exist sets N_1, N_2 in X with (N_1, x_1) and (N_2, x_2) belonging to $\mathscr{N}$, and $N_1 \cap N_2 = \emptyset$.

We now define a set S to be open if to each $x \in S$ there corresponds an element $(N, x) \in \mathscr{N}$ with $N \subset S$.   Axioms 1 and 2 guarantee that the open sets thus defined actually yield a topology for X.   Axiom 3 assures us that all the sets N occurring in the elements of $\mathscr{N}$ are open.   They evidently form a base for X.   Finally, axiom 4 guarantees us that the space is a Hausdorff space.   Conversely, a Hausdorff space satisfies axioms 1–4 if we take for the elements of $\mathscr{N}$ all the pairs (U, x), where U is an open set containing x.

There is a property called *complete regularity* which a topological space may possess and which is useful in the expression of certain ideas.

Definition.   A space X is called *completely regular* if for each $x_0 \in X$ and each neighborhood U of x_0 there can be defined on X a real-valued continuous function f, all of whose values lie on the closed interval $[0, 1]$, such that $f(x_0) = 0$ and $f(x) = 1$ if $x \in X - U$.

A completely regular space is certainly regular.   For, if x_0, U, and f are as in the definition of complete regularity, the set $\{x : f(x) < \frac{1}{2}\}$ is a neighborhood of x_0 whose closure lies in U.

Every T_4-space is completely regular.   This fact is implied by the following more general result:

Theorem 2.3–C.   *Let E and F be disjoint closed sets in a T_4-space X. Then, there can be defined on X a real-valued continuous function f, all of whose values lie on the closed interval $[0, 1]$, such that $f(x) = 0$ if $x \in E$ and $f(x) = 1$ if $x \in F$.*

This theorem is commonly known as Urysohn's lemma. We omit the proof in order to save space for other things. For proofs see Loomis, **1**, page 6, or Kelley, **1**, page 115.

We also observe the following:

Theorem 2.3–D. *A compact Hausdorff space is normal.*

PROOF. An immediate consequence of Theorems 2.3–A and 2.2–B.

2.31 Locally Compact Spaces

Definition. A topological space is called *locally compact* if every point has a neighborhood whose closure is compact.

Any topological space X can be imbedded in another topological space Y, having just one more point than X, in such a way that Y is compact and the relative topology of X as a subset of Y is just the original topology of X. It is done in this way: Let y_0 be any element distinct from the points of X. Let $\mathscr{W}$ be the class of open sets W in X such that W' is compact. Observe that $X \in \mathscr{W}$. Let Y be the set consisting of the points of X and the point y_0. A set in Y will be called open if either (*a*) it does not contain y_0 and is open as a subset of X, or (*b*) it does contain y_0 and its intersection with X is a member of $\mathscr{W}$. These sets in Y meet the requirements for defining a topology; we leave verification to the reader. It is evident that the relative topology of X coincides with its original topology.

Now Y is compact. For, supposing $\mathscr{V}$ to be a family of open sets which covers Y, there must be some member of $\mathscr{V}$ of the form $W_0 \cup (y_0)$, where $W_0 \in \mathscr{W}$. Then W_0' is compact as a subset of X. It is covered by the sets $V \cap X$, V varying over $\mathscr{V}$. Hence some finite set $V_1 \cap X, \cdots,$ $V_n \cap X$ covers W_0'. Then $V_1, \cdots, V_n$ and $W_0 \cup (y_0)$ cover Y, so that Y is compact.

The space Y constructed in this way is called the *one-point compactification* of X.

If X is a T_1-space, so is Y. It can happen that Y is not a Hausdorff space, even though X is. However, if X is a locally compact Hausdorff space, Y will be a Hausdorff space. To verify that Y fulfills the Hausdorff separation condition in this case, it is enough to consider pairs of points of which one is y_0, for, if both points are in X, the separation is accomplished by using the same sets as if we were dealing entirely with the space X. If $x \in X$, there exists a neighborhood U of x such that $\bar{U}$ is compact. Then $\bar{U}' \cup (y_0)$ is a neighborhood of y_0 which is disjoint from U, and the separation requirement is satisfied.

It is easy to see, conversely, that, if X and Y are both Hausdorff spaces, then X is locally compact.

Theorem 2.31–A. *Let X be a locally compact Hausdorff space, and let C_0, C_1 be disjoint compact sets in X. Then, there exist disjoint neighborhoods W_0 and W_1 of C_0 and C_1 respectively such that the closures of W_0 and W_1 are compact.*

We state this theorem formally for later reference. Its proof differs but slightly from that of Theorem 2.3–A. One need only observe that, if U and V are neighborhoods of a point and V has compact closure, $U \cap V$ is a neighborhood of the point having the same property. One can then make sure that all the neighborhoods obtained in the earlier proof have compact closures.

Theorem 2.31–B. *Let X be a locally compact Hausdorff space. Let C be a compact set in X, and U a neighborhood of C. Then, there can be defined on X a real-valued continuous function f such that $0 \leqslant f(x) \leqslant 1$ for every x, $f(x) = 1$ if $x \in C$, and $f(x) = 0$ if $x \in U'$.*

PROOF. Let Y be the one-point compactification of X, and in Y let $E = U' \cup (y_0)$, $F = C$. Then E and F are disjoint closed sets in Y, and we can apply Theorem 2.3–C, since Y is normal.

2.4 Metric Spaces

If X is any set, we denote by $X \times X$ the set of all ordered pairs (x_1, x_2), where x_1 and x_2 are in X. A function d with domain $X \times X$ and range in the real number field is called a *distance function* on X if it satisfies the conditions:

(a) $d(x_1, x_2) = d(x_2, x_1)$.
(b) $d(x_1, x_3) \leqslant d(x_1, x_2) + d(x_2, x_3)$.
(c) $d(x_1, x_2) = 0$ if and only if $x_1 = x_2$.
(d) $d(x_1, x_2) \geqslant 0$.

A set X with a distance function is called a *metric space*. We note, incidentally, that (d) is a consequence of (a), (b), and (c) [put $x_1 = x_3$ in (b)]. The number $d(x_1, x_2)$ is called the distance between x_1 and x_2. Property (c) is called the triangular law of distances.

With each point x_0 in a metric space X and with each positive number r we associate the set of all $x \in X$ such that $d(x, x_0) < r$. We call this set the *sphere* with center x_0 and radius r. In some spaces a sphere may contain no points other than the center. The set $\mathscr{N}$ of all pairs (N, x), where N is any sphere with center at x and x is any point of X, satisfies the four Hausdorff axioms (see § 2.3) and thus defines a topology for the metric space, the set of all spheres being a base.   The space is, moreover, a Hausdorff space.   Whenever we speak of a metric space, it is understood that its topology is defined in this way.   Verification that the four Hausdorff axioms are satisfied is left to the reader.

A metric space has a countable base at each point (the set of spheres with positive rational radii and centers at the point).   The space is perfectly separable if and only if there exists a finite or countable set which is dense in the space.   We already know that such a set exists if the space is perfectly separable (see § 2.21).   On the other hand, if we suppose that an at most countable set exists which is dense in the space, the set of all spheres with positive rational radii and centers at the points of this dense set provides a countable base for the space, as is readily verified. Thus, for a metric space, the notions of perfect separability and separability are equivalent.

A sequence $\{x_n\}$ of points in a metric space X is called *convergent* if there is a point $x \in X$ such that $d(x_n, x) \to 0$ as $n \to \infty$; this x is unique if it exists.   We then write $x_n \to x$ and call x the *limit* of the sequence.

Theorem 2.4–A.   *In a metric space a set S is closed if and only if the situation: $x_n \in S$, $x_n \to x$ implies that $x \in S$.*

PROOF.   If $x_n \to x$, where $\{x_n\}$ is a sequence in S, every neighborhood of x intersects S, and so $x \in \bar{S}$.   If S is closed, $\bar{S} = S$, and so $x \in S$.   On the other hand, suppose S has the property that $x \in S$ whenever $x_n \to x$ and all the x_n are in S.   Choose any $x \in \bar{S}$.   Then, for each n the sphere of center x and radius $1/n$ intersects S at least in one point, say x_n.   Then $d(x_n, x) < 1/n$, and so $x_n \to x$, whence $x \in S$.   Thus $\bar{S} \subset S$, and S is closed.

Theorem 2.4–B.   *In a metric space a point x is an accumulation point of a set S if and only if there exists a convergent sequence $\{x_n\}$ of distinct points of S with x as limit.*

The proof of this theorem is left to the reader.

Sometimes a set X can be made into a metric space in different ways by different definitions of a distance function.   For example, if X is the xy-plane, any one of the expressions

$$[(x - a)^2 + (y - b)^2]^{\frac{1}{2}},$$

$$|x - a| + |y - b|,$$

$$\max \{|x - a|, |y - b|\},$$

can be taken as the definition of the distance between (x, y) and (a, b). It turns out that the topology for X determined by any one of these distance functions is the same as that determined by either of the others.

If d_1 and d_2 are two distance functions on a set X and if $\mathcal{T}_1$ and $\mathcal{T}_2$ are the resulting topologies for X, it is easily proved that $\mathcal{T}_1 = \mathcal{T}_2$ if and only if, for all $\{x_n\}$, $d_1(x_n, x) \to 0$ is equivalent to $d_2(x_n, x) \to 0$.

If X and Y are metric spaces and f is a function with domain $\mathscr{D}(f)$ in X and range $\mathscr{R}(f)$ in Y, the topological definition of continuity (in § 2.12) is equivalent to the familiar $\epsilon\delta$-formulation of continuity: f is continuous at $x_0 \in \mathscr{D}(f)$ if to each $\epsilon > 0$ corresponds a $\delta > 0$ such that $d(f(x), f(x_0)) < \epsilon$ whenever $x \in \mathscr{D}(f)$ and $d(x, x_0) < \delta$. Here we have used the same symbol d for the distance functions in X and Y. Just as in classical analysis, we have the proposition: *f is continuous at x_0 if and only if $f(x_n) \to f(x_0)$ whenever $x_n \to x_0$, $\{x_n\}$ being a sequence of points in $\mathscr{D}(f)$.*

The concept of uniform continuity can be defined for a function with domain and range in metric spaces: f is uniformly continuous on its domain if to each $\epsilon > 0$ there corresponds a $\delta > 0$ such that $d(f(x_1), f(x_2)) < \epsilon$ whenever $x_1, x_2 \in \mathscr{D}(f)$ and $d(x_1, x_2) < \delta$.

A subset S in a metric space X can be considered as a metric space by itself, using the same distance function as that defined on X, but confining attention to distances between pairs of points in S. The resulting topology of the metric space S is the same as the relative topology of S induced by the topology of X.

A set in a metric space is called *bounded* if it is contained in some sphere.

Theorem 2.4–C. *In a metric space a compact set is closed and bounded.*

PROOF. We already know that a compact set is closed, since a metric space is a Hausdorff space (see Theorem 2.3–B). Hence we have only to prove that a compact set is bounded. We may assume the set is nonempty. If the compact set is S and if $x \in S$, let V_n be the (open) sphere of center x and radius n. The family of all the V_n's covers S (in fact, covers the space). Since S is compact, a finite number of the V_n's suffice to cover S, and hence $S \subset V_N$ for some index N. Thus S is bounded.

Theorem 2.4–D. *If S is a compact set in a topological space, every infinite subset of S has an accumulation point in S.*

PROOF. In this theorem the space need not be metric, nor even a Hausdorff space. Suppose T is an infinite subset of S but that T has no accumulation point in S. Then to each $x \in S$ there corresponds some neighborhood U of x which intersects T at most in the one point x (if x happens to be in T). The set of all these neighborhoods covers S, and so a finite number of them, $U_1, \cdots, U_n$, suffice to cover S. Since

$T \subset U_1 \cup \cdots \cup U_n$ and at most one point of T is in each U_k, it follows that T is finite.   This contradiction completes the proof.

Theorem 2.4–E.   *If S is a subset of a metric space X with the property that every infinite subset of S has an accumulation point in X, there exists a countable family $\mathcal{N}$ of open sets in X such that, if U is any open set in X and $x \in S \cap U$, there is some set $N \in \mathcal{N}$ for which $x \in N \subset U$.*

PROOF.   We assert that for each positive integer n there is some finite set of points $x_1, \cdots, x_{N(n)}$ in S such that the set of spheres of radii $1/n$ with centers at $x_1, \cdots, x_{N(n)}$ covers S.   For, if this were not so, there would be some n and a sequence of points $x_1, x_2, \cdots$ in S such that $d(x_i, x_j) \geqslant 1/n$ if $i \neq j$.   The infinite set of all these x's could not have any accumulation point, contrary to the hypothesis on S.   Now let $\mathcal{N}$ be the countable family of all these finite sets of spheres.   It is easy to see that this family $\mathcal{N}$ has the property asserted for it.

Theorem 2.4–F.   *A compact metric space is separable.*

PROOF.   We see by Theorems 2.4–D and 2.4–E that, if the metric space X is compact, it has a countable base.

Theorem 2.4–G.   *If S is a set in a metric space with the property that every infinite subset of S has an accumulation point in S, then S is compact.*

PROOF.   Suppose $\mathcal{U}$ is an open covering of S.   Now, Theorem 2.4–E applies to S; hence let $\mathcal{N}$ be a countable family of open sets with the property specified in Theorem 2.4–E.   Let $\mathcal{N}^*$ be the subfamily of $\mathcal{N}$ defined as follows: $N \in \mathcal{N}^*$ if and only if $N \in \mathcal{N}$ and there is some $U \in \mathcal{U}$ with $N \subset U$.   By the property of $\mathcal{N}$ and the fact that $\mathcal{U}$ covers S, we see that $\mathcal{N}^*$ covers S.   Now let $\mathcal{U}^*$ be a subfamily of $\mathcal{U}$ obtained by taking from $\mathcal{U}$ just one U such that $N \subset U$, for each $N \in \mathcal{N}^*$.   Then $\mathcal{U}^*$ is at most countable, and it covers S.   It remains to prove that some finite subfamily of $\mathcal{U}^*$ covers S.   Let the sets in $\mathcal{U}^*$ be indexed: $U_1, U_2, \cdots$.   Suppose, contrary to what we wish to prove, that for each n the finite union $U_1 \cup \cdots \cup U_n$ fails to cover S, so that there is some point $x_n \in S - (U_1 \cup \cdots \cup U_n)$.   The set of x_n's must be infinite, and hence must have an accumulation point, say x_0, in S.   Then $x_0 \in U_N$ for some index N, and by Theorem 2.4–B $x_n \in U_N$ for infinitely many values of n, in particular for some $n > N$.   This contradicts the fact that $x_n \in S - (U_1 \cup \cdots \cup U_n)$, and so the proof is complete.

Theorems 2.4–D and 2.4–G together show us that, *in a metric space, a set S is compact if and only if every infinite subset of S has an accumulation point in S.*   For many purposes the following criterion for compactness is convenient:

Theorem 2.4–H. *In a metric space, a set S is compact if and only if every sequence in S contains a convergent subsequence with limit in S.*

The proof of this theorem is left to the reader.

Let S be a nonempty set in the metric space X, and let x_0 be any point in X. The distance between S and x_0 is denoted by $d(S, x_0)$ and defined as

$$d(S, x_0) = \operatorname*{glb}_{x \in S} d(x, x_0).$$

If S_1 and S_2 are two nonempty sets in X, the distance between them is denoted by $d(S_1, S_2)$ and defined as

$$d(S_1, S_2) = \operatorname{glb} d(x_1, x_2) \qquad (x_1 \in S_1, x_2 \in S_2).$$

Evidently $d(S_1, S_2) = d(S_2, S_1)$. It is not difficult to see that

$$(2.4\text{--}1) \qquad d(S_1, S_2) = \operatorname*{glb}_{x \in S_2} d(S_1, x) = \operatorname*{glb}_{x \in S_1} d(S_2, x).$$

For any x_0, $d(x, x_0)$ is a continuous function of x. For, it is readily seen by the properties of the distance function that

$$|d(x, x_0) - d(x', x_0)| \leqslant d(x, x'),$$

whence the asserted continuity follows. It is also true that $d(x_1, x_2)$ is a continuous function of both x_1 and x_2. For, it may be seen that

$$(2.4\text{--}2) \qquad |d(x, x') - d(x_0, x_0')| \leqslant d(x, x_0) + d(x', x_0').$$

It follows from the continuity of $d(x, x_0)$ as a function of x that, if S is a nonempty compact set, there is a point $x \in S$ such that $d(S, x_0) = d(x, x_0)$ (see Theorem 2.2–C and the remarks following it). If S is a fixed nonempty set, then $d(S, x)$ is a continuous function of x; we leave the proof of this to the reader. It follows that, if S_1 is any nonempty set and S_2 is a nonempty compact set, there is a point $x_2 \in S_2$ such that $d(S_1, S_2) = d(S_1, x_2)$. Hence, if S_1 and S_2 are both compact, there exist points $x_1 \in S_1$, $x_2 \in S_2$ such that $d(S_1, S_2) = d(x_1, x_2)$. A different proof of this last assertion can be made using Theorem 2.4–H, and we give this proof in the next paragraph to illustrate the convenience of the characterization of compact sets in the last mentioned theorem.

If S_1 and S_2 are any nonempty sets, there exist sequences $\{x_n'\}$, $\{x_n''\}$ in S_1 and S_2 respectively such that

$$d(S_1, S_2) = \lim_{n \to \infty} d(x_n', x_n'').$$

If S_1 is compact, $\{x_n'\}$ contains a convergent subsequence with limit

$x_1 \in S_1$. Let this subsequence be denoted by $\{y_n'\}$, and let the corresponding subsequence of $\{x_n''\}$ be denoted by $\{y_n''\}$. Thẹn

$$d(S_1, S_2) = \lim_{n\to\infty} d(y_n', y_n'').$$

If S_2 is also compact, $\{y_n''\}$ contains a convergent subsequence with limit $x_2 \in S_2$. Let this subsequence be denoted by $\{z_n''\}$, and let the corresponding subsequence of $\{y_n'\}$ be denoted by $\{z_n'\}$. Then $z_n' \to x_1$, $z_n'' \to x_2$, and

$$d(S_1, S_2) = \lim_{n\to\infty} d(z_n', z_n''),$$

whence $d(S_1, S_2) = d(x_1, x_2)$.

If $d(S_1, S_2) > 0$, it follows that $S_1 \cap S_2 = \emptyset$. The converse is not true, however, even if S_1 and S_2 are closed. For example, in the xy-plane, the sets $S_1 = \{(x, y) : y \geqslant e^x\}$ and $S_2 = \{(x, y) : y \leqslant 0\}$ are closed and disjoint, and yet $d(S_1, S_2) = 0$.

Suppose S is any nonempty set in a metric space. Then $d(S, x) = 0$ if and only if $x \in \bar{S}$, as is easily seen. This result can be generalized as follows:

Theorem 2.4–I. *Suppose that S_1, S_2 are nonempty sets and that S_2 is compact. Then $d(S_1, S_2) = 0$ if and only if $\bar{S}_1 \cap S_2 \neq \emptyset$.*

PROOF. As we saw previously, $d(S_1, S_2) = d(S_1, x_2)$, where x_2 is some point in S_2. Thus $d(S_1, S_2) = 0$ implies $d(S_1, x_2) = 0$, which in turn implies $x_2 \in \bar{S}_1$, so that $\bar{S}_1 \cap S_2 \neq \emptyset$. Conversely, if $x_2 \in \bar{S}_1 \cap S_2$, it follows that $d(S_1, x_2) = 0$, and this implies $d(S_1, S_2) = 0$, by (2.4–1).

Theorem 2.4–J. *A metric space is normal.*

PROOF. Suppose S_1 and S_2 are nonempty closed sets in a metric space. For each point $x \in S_1$ construct the sphere with center x and radius $^1/_2 d(S_2, x)$. Let U_1 be the union of all such spheres as x varies over S_1. Likewise construct a set U_2, related to S_2 as U_1 is related to S_1. Then U_1 and U_2 are open, and clearly $S_k \subset U_k$ $(k = 1, 2)$. It remains only to prove that $U_1 \cap U_2 = \emptyset$. Suppose that $x \in U_1 \cap U_2$. Then, there exist points x_1 and x_2 in S_1 and S_2 respectively such that $d(x, x_1) < {}^1/_2(S_2, x_1)$, $d(x, x_2) < {}^1/_2 d(S_1, x_2)$. Consequently, by the triangular law,

(2.4–3) $\qquad d(x_1, x_2) < \tfrac{1}{2} d(S_2, x_1) + \tfrac{1}{2} d(S_1, x_2).$

Now

(2.4–4) $\qquad d(S_2, x_1) \leqslant d(x_2, x_1)$ and $d(S_1, x_2) \leqslant d(x_1, x_2).$

Consequently, we see from (2.4–3) that $d(S_2, x_1) \leqslant d(S_1, x_2)$ and $d(S_1, x_2) \leqslant d(S_2, x_1)$, whence $d(S_2, x_1) = d(S_1, x_2)$. But then (2.4–3) becomes $d(x_1, x_2) < d(S_2, x_1)$, which contradicts (2.4–4). We conclude that $U_1 \cap U_2 = \emptyset$. Therefore the space is normal.

2.41 Completeness

If X is a metric space and $\{x_n\}$ is a convergent sequence in X, with limit x, then $d(x_n, x_m) \leqslant d(x_n, x) + d(x, x_m)$, whence it follows that $d(x_n, x_m) \to 0$ as $m \to \infty$ and $n \to \infty$. It can happen, however, that a sequence $\{x_n\}$ is such that $d(x_n, x_m) \to 0$ as $m \to \infty$ and $n \to \infty$, and yet the sequence has no limit. A sequence $\{x_n\}$ is called a *Cauchy sequence* if $d(x_n, x_m) \to 0$ as m and $n \to \infty$ (i.e., if to each $\epsilon > 0$ corresponds an N such that $d(x_n, x_m) < \epsilon$ when $N \leqslant m$ and $N \leqslant n$).

Definition. If a metric space X has the property that every Cauchy sequence in X has a limit in X, then X is said to be *complete*.

The property of completeness is very important in the construction of existence proofs. The fundamental difference between the fields of real and rational numbers, respectively, is that the real field is complete and the rational field is not when these fields are considered as metric spaces with $d(x_1, x_2) = |x_1 - x_2|$ as the distance function.

Definition. Two metric spaces X and Y are said to be *isometric* if there is a function f with domain X and range Y such that the inverse function f^{-1} exists and furthermore such that $d(x_1, x_2) = d(f(x_1), f(x_2))$ for every pair of points $x_1, x_2 \in X$.

It is a fact of fundamental importance that an incomplete metric space can always be regarded as a dense subset in a complete metric space. The precise statement is as follows:

Theorem 2.41–A. *Let X be an incomplete metric space. There exists a complete metric space Y and a subset Y_0 dense in Y such that Y_0 and X are isometric.*

PROOF. Let $\{x_n\}$ and $\{x_n'\}$ be two Cauchy sequences in X. We write $\{x_n\} \sim \{x_n'\}$ and say that the two sequences are *equivalent* if $d(x_n, x_n') \to 0$ as $n \to \infty$. Equivalence, thus defined, is reflexive, symmetric, and transitive, so that the set of all Cauchy sequences in X is divided into equivalence classes. We denote by Y the set of all these equivalence classes. We shall define a distance function on Y.

First we observe that if $\{x_n\}$ and $\{x_n'\}$ are Cauchy sequences in X, $d(x_n, x_n')$ is a Cauchy sequence of real numbers. For, by (2.4–2)

$$|d(x_n, x_n') - d(x_m, x_m')| \leqslant d(x_n, x_m) + d(x_n', x_m'),$$

whence we see the truth of the assertion just made. Next we assert that $\lim_{n \to \infty} d(x_n, x_n')$ (which exists, since the real numbers form a complete space) is unchanged if we replace $\{x_n\}$ by any equivalent Cauchy sequence, and likewise with $\{x_n'\}$. This is because, if $\{x_n\} \sim \{a_n\}$ and $\{x_n'\} \sim \{a_n'\}$,

$$|d(x_n, x_n') - d(a_n, a_n')| \leqslant d(x_n, a_n) + d(x_n', a_n').$$

We leave the rest of this argument to the reader. Now, if $y, y' \in Y$, let $\{x_n\}$ and $\{x_n'\}$ be Cauchy sequences from the equivalence classes y, y' respectively. We define $d(y, y') = \lim_{n \to \infty} d(x_n, x_n')$. By what has been said, this limit exists and is uniquely determined by y, y'. It is not hard to show that the function d thus defined on $Y \times Y$ is a distance function, so that Y is a metric space. We leave these details to the reader.

Let Y_0 be the subset of Y consisting of those equivalence classes which contain a Cauchy sequence $\{x_n\}$ for which $x_1 = x_2 = x_3 = \cdots$. There cannot be two different Cauchy sequences of this kind in the same equivalence class. If $y, y' \in Y_0$ and if corresponding Cauchy sequences are $\{x_n\}$ and $\{x_n'\}$, with $x_n = x$, $x_n' = x'$ for every n, we see that $d(y, y') = d(x, x')$. It is then clear that Y_0 and X are isometric. Next we show that $\bar{Y}_0 = Y$. If $y \in Y$, let $\{x_n\}$ be a Cauchy sequence from the class y, and suppose $\epsilon > 0$. There exists an integer N such that $d(x_n, x_N) < \epsilon/2$ if $N \leqslant n$. Let $y_0 \in Y_0$ be the class containing the repetitive sequence $x_N, x_N, \cdots$. Then $d(y, y_0) = \lim_{n \to \infty} d(x_n, x_N) \leqslant \epsilon/2 < \epsilon$. This shows that $y \in \bar{Y}_0$, and hence that $Y = \bar{Y}_0$.

Finally, we show that Y is complete. Suppose $\{y_n\}$ is a Cauchy sequence in Y. For each n choose $z_n \in Y_0$ so that $d(y_n, z_n) < 1/n$; we can do this since Y_0 is dense in Y. Now

$$d(z_n, z_m) \leqslant d(z_n, y_n) + d(y_n, y_m) + d(y_m, z_m)$$

$$< \frac{1}{n} + \frac{1}{m} + d(y_n, y_m),$$

and so $\{z_n\}$ is a Cauchy sequence. Let x_n be the element in X which is matched with z_n in the isometric correspondence between X and Y_0. Then $\{x_n\}$ is a Cauchy sequence in X. Accordingly, there is a unique equivalence class $y \in Y$ which contains $\{x_n\}$. Now

$$d(y_n, y) \leqslant d(y_n, z_n) + d(z_n, y) < \frac{1}{n} + d(z_n, y),$$

and since $d(z_n, y) = \lim_{m \to \infty} d(x_n, x_m)$, it is clear that $y_n \to y$. This proves that Y is complete and finishes the proof of the theorem.

In practice we identify X with Y_0 and regard X as a dense set in Y. The space Y is called the *completion* of X. We can, if we choose, adjoin the elements of $Y - Y_0$ to X and form a space isometric to Y in which X is genuinely a dense set.   When this is done we shall denote the completion of X by $\hat{X}$.

A nonempty set S in a metric space is said to have finite diameter if $d(x, x')$ is bounded as x and x' vary over S.   The diameter of S is then defined as the least upper bound of the distances $d(x, x')$.   We denote the diameter of S by diam (S).   A nonempty set has finite diameter if and only if it is bounded.

Theorem 2.41–B.   *Let X be a complete metric space.   Suppose $\{S_n\}$ is a sequence of nonempty closed sets in X such that $S_1 \supset S_2 \supset S_3 \supset \cdots$ and such that* diam$(S_n) \to 0$ *as $n \to \infty$.   Then the intersection of all the sets S_n is nonempty.*

PROOF.   This theorem is commonly known as Cantor's intersection theorem.   To prove the theorem, choose a point $x_n \in S_n$ for each n.   If $m < n$, x_m and x_n are both in S_m and so $d(x_n, x_m) \leqslant$ diam(S_m).   Thus $\{x_n\}$ is a Cauchy sequence, and, since X is complete, the sequence has a limit x in X.   It is a simple matter to prove that $x \in S_m$ for every m.   We leave the completion of the proof to the reader.

Theorem 2.41–C.   *Let X be a nonempty complete metric space.   Then X is of the second category as a subset of itself.   Moreover, X is of the second category at every one of its points.*

PROOF.   We shall refer to this theorem, and especially to the first assertion in the theorem, as Baire's category theorem.   If $x_0 \in X$ and $r > 0$, let us write $K(x_0, r) = \{x : d(x, x_0) \leqslant r\}$.   This set is closed; we call it the closed sphere with center x_0 and radius r.   The set $\{x : d(x, x_0) < r\}$, which we have previously called the sphere of center x_0 and radius r, may for emphasis be referred to as an *open* sphere.   It is clear that any open sphere with center x_0 contains a closed sphere with the same center, and vice versa.

Now suppose that X is of the first category, so that X is the union of nowhere dense sets $S_1, S_2, S_3, \cdots$.   The fact that S_k is nowhere dense can be expressed by the statement that any closed sphere contains another closed sphere which does not intersect S_k.   Hence we see by induction that there exists a sequence of closed spheres $K_n = K(x_n, r_n)$ such that $K_n \cap S_n = \emptyset$, $0 < r_n < 1/n$, and $K_{n+1} \subset K_n$.   Now diam$(K_n) \leqslant 2/n$; hence we can apply Cantor's intersection theorem to assert that there exists a point x in the intersection of all the closed spheres K_n.   But then x is not in any S_n and hence not in X, which is a contradiction.   Therefore X is of the second category.

To prove the second assertion in the theorem, suppose some point $x \in X$ has a neighborhood V which is of the first category, so that $V = \bigcup_{n=1}^{\infty} S_n$, where S_n is nowhere dense. Let K be a nonempty closed sphere contained in V. Then (see Theorem 2.41–E) K in itself is a complete metric space. Now $K = \bigcup_{n=1}^{\infty} (S_n \cap K)$. It is easily verified that $S_n \cap K$ is nowhere dense in K, and hence K is of the first category in itself, contrary to the fact that it is a complete space. This contradiction completes the proof.

The next theorem has applications in the study of linear operators, as well as elsewhere in analysis.

Theorem 2.41–D. , *Let X be a metric space and S a set of the second category in X. Let $\mathscr{F}$ be a family $\{f\}$ of real-valued, continuous functions defined on X such that for each $x \in S$ there exists a real number $m(x)$ with the property that $f(x) \leqslant m(x)$ for every $f \in \mathscr{F}$. Then, there exists a real constant N and an open sphere K in X such that $f(x) \leqslant N$ if $x \in K$ and $f \in \mathscr{F}$.*

PROOF.   For each positive integer n let $S_n = \{x : f(x) \leqslant n \text{ when } f \in \mathscr{F}\}$. The continuity of f insures that S_n is closed. The condition on S and $\mathscr{F}$ insures that $S \subset \bigcup_{n=1}^{\infty} S_n$. Let $T_n = S \cap S_n$. Then $\bar{T}_n \subset \bar{S}_n = S_n$, and $S = \bigcup_{n=1}^{\infty} T_n$. Since S is of the second category, at least one of the sets T_n, say T_N, is such that $\bar{T}_N$ contains a nonempty open set and hence contains an open sphere, say K. Then $K \subset S_N$. This means that $f(x) \leqslant N$ if $x \in K$ and $f \in \mathscr{F}$. The proof is now complete.

Theorem 2.41–E. *Let X be a complete metric space, and X_0 a closed set in X. Then X_0, considered as a metric space by itself, is complete.*

The proof is left to the reader.

Theorem 2.41–F. *Let S be a compact set in a metric space. Then S, considered as a metric space by itself, is complete.*

The proof is left to the reader.   Use Theorem 2.4–H.

Suppose that S is a set in the metric space X, and let $\hat{X}$ be the completion of X. If we regard S by itself as a metric space, the completion of S, denoted by $\hat{S}$, can be identified with a subset of $\hat{X}$, and we shall suppose this to be done. If $\bar{S}$ is the closure of S in X, it is easily seen that $\bar{S} = \hat{S} \cap X$. The closure of S in $\hat{X}$ is $\hat{S}$.

Definition.   A set S is called *precompact* if $\hat{S}$ is compact.

It is readily seen that S and $\bar{S}$ have the same closure in $\hat{X}$, and therefore the same completion. If S is conditionally compact (see § 2.2), i.e., if $\bar{S}$ is compact, then $\bar{S}$ is complete, and so coincides with its completion $\hat{S}$. Hence a conditionally compact set is precompact. If the space X is complete, $\bar{S}$ coincides with $\hat{S}$. Hence in this case (but not in general) a precompact set is conditionally compact.

Theorem 2.41–G.   *A nonempty set S in a metric space X is precompact if and only if to each $\epsilon > 0$ corresponds some finite set $x_1, \cdots, x_n$ of points of X such that S is contained in the union of the spheres of radius ϵ with centers at $x_1, \cdots, x_n$.*

PROOF.   If $x_0 \in X$, the sphere in $\hat{X}$ with center x_0 and radius ϵ intersects X in the sphere in X with center x_0 and radius ϵ. Consider the set $\mathscr{F}$ of all spheres in $\hat{X}$ with centers in S, each sphere of radius $\epsilon > 0$. If $x \in \hat{S}$, the sphere in $\hat{X}$ of radius ϵ and center x will contain some point $y \in S$, and hence the sphere in $\hat{X}$ of center y and radius ϵ will contain x. Thus $\mathscr{F}$ covers $\hat{S}$. Assuming now that $\hat{S}$ is compact, we conclude that a finite number of the members of $\mathscr{F}$ suffice to cover $\hat{S}$. Hence the intersections of these spheres with X cover S. Thus one half of the theorem is proved. Note that the centers of the spheres can be taken in S.

Now let us assume that S has the property stated in the theorem, and let us prove that $\hat{S}$ is compact. First we shall show that every sequence of elements from S contains a Cauchy subsequence. Starting with a given sequence $\{x_n\}$, we know that there exists a finite number of spheres in X of radius 1, with centers in X, whose union contains S; therefore, some one of these spheres must contain a subsequence from $\{x_n\}$. Denote this subsequence by $x_{11}, x_{12}, x_{13}, \cdots$. Next we consider spheres of radius $\frac{1}{2}$, and conclude that some sphere of radius $\frac{1}{2}$ must contain a subsequence of the foregoing subsequence. We proceed by induction, obtaining sequences $x_{k1}, x_{k2}, x_{k3}, \cdots, (k = 1, 2, \cdots,)$ each a subsequence of its predecessor, and the kth sequence contained in a sphere of radius $1/k$. The diagonal sequence $x_{11}, x_{22}, x_{33}, \cdots$ is then a Cauchy sequence and a subsequence of the original sequence $\{x_n\}$. Now consider a sequence $\{y_n\}$ from $\hat{S}$. Since $\hat{S}$ is closed in $\hat{X}$ and $\hat{X}$ is complete, $\hat{S}$ will be proved compact if we show that $\{y_n\}$ contains a Cauchy sequence. Now, there exists a point $x_n \in S$ such that $d(x_n, y_n) < 1/n$. The sequence $\{x_n\}$ contains a Cauchy subsequence $\{x_{n(k)}\}$, and the corresponding subsequence $\{y_{n(k)}\}$ will also have the Cauchy property, as is readily seen by the triangular inequality. Thus the proof is complete.

2.5 Product Spaces

If X and Y are nonempty sets, the Cartesian *product* set $X \times Y$ is by definition the set of all ordered pairs (x, y), where $x \in X$ and $y \in Y$. If X and Y are topological spaces, there is a standard method of assigning a topology to $X \times Y$. Let $\mathscr{A}$ be the family of subsets of $X \times Y$ of the form $U \times V$, where U and V are any nonempty open sets in X and Y respectively. Then, we take as the standard topology of $X \times Y$ the topology generated by $\mathscr{A}$ (see § 2.1). The open sets in $X \times Y$ are thus $\emptyset$ and unions of members of $\mathscr{A}$. This definition extends in an obvious manner to products $X_1 \times \cdots \times X_n$ of a finite number of topological spaces.

It is sometimes necessary to define the Cartesian product of an infinite number of topological spaces. This is done as follows. Let I be an index set and $\{X_i\}$ $(i \in I)$ a family of sets. The product set $X = \prod_{i \in I} X_i$ is by definition the set of all functions x with domain I and range $\bigcup_{i \in I} X_i$ such that the value of x at i [denoted by $x(i)$] is in X_i. This definition is consistent with the one already given if I is a finite set. If each X_i is a topological space, let $\mathscr{A}$ be the family of product sets of the form $\prod_{i \in I} S_i$, where for some *finite* subset of the indices i, S_i is an arbitrary nonempty open set in X_i, and $S_i = X_i$ for the rest of the indices. The topology of X is then taken to be that generated by $\mathscr{A}$, and with this topology X is called the Cartesian product of the X_i.

If $x \in X$, the value $x(i)$ is called the *coordinate* of x in X_i. Let f_i be the function with domain X and range X_i defined by $f_i(x) = x(i)$. If (for a fixed i) T_i is an open set in X_i, $f_i^{-1}(T_i)$ is the product set $\prod_{j \in I} S_j$ in which $S_i = T_i$ and $S_j = X_j$ if $j \neq i$. This set is open in X, and so f_i is continuous. Actually, it can be shown that the topology we have assigned to X is the weakest topology such that all the functions f_i are continuous. If S is a set in X, the set $f_i(S)$ is called the *projection* of S onto X_i.

It is easily seen that if all the spaces X_i are Hausdorff spaces, their Cartesian product is also a Hausdorff space.

Suppose for a moment that I is the finite set of integers $1, \cdots, n$. Let us write $x(i) = x_i$. The value $f(x)$ of a function defined on X is often written $f(x_1, \cdots, x_n)$. If the values of f are in a topological space Y, f is continuous at $a = (a_1, \cdots, a_n)$ if and only if to each neighborhood V

of $f(a_1, \cdots, a_n)$ there correspond neighborhoods $U_1, \cdots, U_n$ of $a_1, \cdots,$ a_n in $X_1, \cdots, X_n$, respectively, such that $f(x_1, \cdots, x_n) \in V$ if $x_1 \in U_1, \cdots,$ $x_n \in U_n$.

If $X_1, \cdots, X_n$ is a finite set of metric spaces, the product set $X = X_1 \times \cdots \times X_n$ can be made into a metric space in a number of ways. For example, if $x = (x_1, \cdots, x_n)$ and $a = (a_1, \cdots, a_n)$ are points of X, we can define

$$d(x, a) = d_1(x_1, a_1) + \cdots + d_n(x_n, a_n),$$

where d_i is the distance function in X_i. Other workable definitions of distance in X are

$$d(x, a) = \max_{1 \leqslant i \leqslant n} d_i(x_i, a_i)$$

and

$$d(x, a) = [\{d_1(x_1, a_1)\}^2 + \cdots + \{d_n(x_n, a_n)\}^2]^{\frac{1}{2}}.$$

All three of these definitions of distance yield the same topology for X, and it is the same as the topology of the Cartesian product.

Later on in the book we shall need the following theorem, due to Tychonoff:

Theorem 2.5–A. *The Cartesian product of compact spaces is compact.*

For reasons of space we omit the proof of Theorem 2.5–A. For proofs we refer to Loomis, **1**, page 11, and Kelley, **1**, page 143.

SUGGESTED READING

Banach, **1**, especially the Introduction.
Bourbaki, **2**.
Fréchet, **1**.
Hall and Spencer, **1**, especially Chapters 1–4.
Kelley, **1**.
Loomis, **1**, especially Chapter 1.
Ljusternik and Sobolew, **1**, especially Chapter 1.

3

TOPOLOGICAL LINEAR SPACES

3.0 Introduction

The concept of a topological linear space is the result of combining in a suitable way the concept of a linear space and the concept of a topological space. The phrase "in a suitable way" means that we set up a certain relation between two concepts. The essence of this relation is that we require the topology of the space to be such that the algebraic operations native to the linear space are continuous as functions of the elements which enter into these operations. We state this requirement more precisely as follows:

Definition. Let X be a linear space which is also a topological space in the sense of §2.1. Let A be the space of scalars associated with X, with its usual topology (that of the real or complex number system). Then $x_1 + x_2$ is a function defined on the product space $X \times X$ and αx is a function defined on $A \times X$. We say that X is a *topological linear space* if $x_1 + x_2$ is a continuous function on $X \times X$ and αx is a continuous function on $A \times X$. The product spaces are given the usual topologies for Cartesian products (see §2.5).

Purely from a logical point of view it might be appropriate to begin our consideration of topological linear spaces with a study of general

features common to all such spaces.   We might then proceed to classify
topological linear spaces in some way and to study the various classifications in some order determined by a scheme of progressive specialization.
Our procedure will be quite different from this.   We shall begin with
consideration of *normed linear spaces*.   These are spaces in which the
topology is introduced, by means of a metric, in a simple and natural way
by assuming that each vector in the linear space has a *length* and that the
rules governing the lengths of vectors conform to a few simple and natural
geometrical principles.   Most of the later part of this book is concerned
with the use of normed linear spaces in functional analysis.   Some
knowledge of topological linear spaces of more general type is advanta-
geous, even if one restricts his attention mainly to normed linear spaces.
On this account we have given some attention to the general fundamental
notions about topological linear spaces in the latter half of this chapter.
In particular, the study of convex sets is made in the context of general
topological linear spaces.   A good deal of this material is of importance
for applications in connection with normed linear spaces, but for various
reasons it seems better to present it in the general form as part of the
theory of topological linear spaces.   The reader who is interested mainly
in normed linear spaces need not have an extensive knowledge of the more
general theory in order to get what he needs out of §§ 3.4–3.7.   The
general form of the Hahn-Banach theorem is given as Theorem 3.7–B.
The special form of it needed in normed linear spaces occurs in Chapter 4
as Theorem 4.3–A.   For locally convex topological linear spaces the
appropriate form is that of Theorem 3.8–D.

Kolmogoroff's criterion for normability of a topological linear space
is given in Theorem 3.41–D.   In § 3.81 are given some of the fundamental
notions about weak topologies for linear spaces.   The main use of these
ideas in the book is in connection with normed linear spaces (see
especially, §§ 4.41, 4.61, 4.62).

Of especial interest among normed linear spaces are the inner-product
spaces, in which the length, or *norm*, of a vector is defined in terms of
a certain function of two vectors, called the *inner product*.   If the vectors
are x, y, the inner product is denoted by (x, y).   It is formally analogous
to the dot product of ordinary vector analysis; in fact, an n-dimensional real
inner-product space is congruent to the Euclidean space R_n, in which the
inner product ($=$ dot product) of $x = (\xi_1, \cdots, \xi_n)$ and $y = (\eta_1, \cdots, \eta_n)$ is

$$(x, y) = \xi_1\eta_1 + \cdots + \xi_n\eta_n.$$

The relation of the norm to the inner product is that expressed in the
formula

$$\|x\| = (x, x)^{\frac{1}{2}}.$$

For R_n this gives

$$\|x\| = (\xi_1{}^2 + \cdots + \xi_n{}^2)^{\frac{1}{2}};$$

this is the usual expression for the length of x in Euclidean geometry.

A complete, infinite-dimensional inner-product space is called a Hilbert space. The name is in honor of David Hilbert, who studied a particular space of this sort in connection with his investigations of the theory of integral equations.

In some of those sections in this chapter where there are a great many theorems, a statement will be found early in the section calling attention to the principal theorems.

3.1 Normed Linear Spaces

A *norm* on a linear space X is a real-valued function, whose value at x we denote by $\|x\|$, with the properties:

(a) $\|x_1 + x_2\| \leqslant \|x_1\| + \|x_2\|$.
(b) $\|\alpha x\| = |\alpha| \, \|x\|$.
(c) $\|x\| \geqslant 0$.
(d) $\|x\| \neq 0$ if $x \neq 0$.

Actually, property (c) is a consequence of properties (a) and (b). For $\|0\| = 0$ by (b) (put $\alpha = 0$), and from (a) and (b) $0 = \|x - x\| \leqslant \|x\| + \|-x\| = 2\|x\|$, whence $0 \leqslant \|x\|$.

A linear space on which a norm is defined becomes a metric space if we define $d(x_1, x_2) = \|x_1 - x_2\|$, as is easily verified. A linear space which is a metric space in this way is called a *normed linear space*, or a *normed vector space*. If we regard x as a vector, its length is $\|x\|$; the length $\|x_1 - x_2\|$ of the vector difference $x_1 - x_2$ is the distance between the end points of the vectors x_1, x_2.

If f is a function with domain $\mathscr{D}(f) \subset X$ and range $\mathscr{R}(f) \subset Y$, where X and Y are normed linear spaces, continuity of f at $x_0 \in \mathscr{D}(f)$ is expressed by the condition: to each $\epsilon > 0$ corresponds some $\delta > 0$ such that $\|f(x) - f(x_0)\| < \epsilon$ if $x \in \mathscr{D}(f)$ and $\|x - x_0\| < \delta$.

The set $\{x : \|x - x_0\| < r\}$, where $r > 0$, is the (open) sphere of radius r with center x_0; the closure of this set is $\{x : \|x - x_0\| \leqslant r\}$, which we call the closed sphere of radius r with center x_0. By the *surface* of this sphere we mean the set $\{x : \|x - x_0\| = r\}$.

A set S in a normed linear space is bounded if and only if it is contained in some sphere; an equivalent condition is that S be contained in some sphere with center at 0, which means that $\|x\|$ is bounded for $x \in S$.

The field of scalars associated with a normed linear space may be either the real field or the complex field, and the space itself is called real or complex according to which of these scalar fields is used. Definitions and theorems in which no particular specification is made concerning the scalar field are applicable to both real and complex spaces.

We make free use of the definitions and terminology concerning linear spaces as given in Chapter 1. A subspace of a normed linear space is itself a normed linear space. However, a subspace of a normed linear space may or may not be closed, and the distinction between closed and nonclosed subspaces is often important. The terms *subspace* and *linear manifold* are used interchangeably.

A linear space can be a metric space without being a normed linear space. Also, a linear space can have a topology and yet not be a metric space.

Let X be a normed linear space and let A denote the scalar field associated with X (either the real or the complex field). We observe that A itself is a normed linear space, with the absolute value as norm. Vector addition in X is a function on the Cartesian product $X \times X$. This function is continuous, as we see from the inequality

$$\|(x_1 + x_2) - (y_1 + y_2)\| \leqslant \|x_1 - y_1\| + \|x_2 - y_2\|.$$

Multiplication of vectors by scalars is a function on $A \times X$. This function is continuous, as we see from the relations

$$\|\alpha x - \alpha_0 x_0\| = \|\alpha(x - x_0) + (\alpha - \alpha_0)x_0\|$$
$$\leqslant |\alpha| \, \|x - x_0\| + |\alpha - \alpha_0| \, \|x_0\|.$$

As a result of the continuity of $x_1 + x_2$ and αx, it is easy to see that, if M is a linear manifold in X, the closure $\bar{M}$ is also a linear manifold. If S is any set in X, the closure in X of the linear manifold generated by S (as defined in § 1.1) is called the closed linear manifold generated by S. The word "generated" in this definition is sometimes replaced by "determined" or "spanned."

It is also to be observed that $\|x\|$ is a continuous function of x. This follows from the inequality

$$\big| \, \|x_1\| - \|x_2\| \, \big| \leqslant \|x_1 - x_2\|,$$

which follows easily from property (a) of the norm.

Definition. Two normed linear spaces X and Y are said to be *isometrically isomorphic* or, more briefly, congruent, if there is a one-to-one correspondence between the elements of X and Y which makes the two spaces isomorphic in the sense defined in § 1.4 and isometric in the sense defined in § 2.41.

In order that X and Y be congruent it is necessary and sufficient that there exist a linear operator T with domain X and range Y, such that T^{-1} exists and $\|Tx\| = \|x\|$ for every $x \in X$. Here we use the same symbol for the norm in X as for the norm in Y. We shall meet examples of congruent spaces when we deal with concrete representations of various linear spaces whose elements are linear operators.

Definition. Two normed linear spaces X and Y are said to be *topologically isomorphic* if there is a linear operator T (with inverse T^{-1}) which establishes the isomorphism of X and Y and which furthermore has the property that T and T^{-1} are continuous on their respective domains. In other words, X and Y are topologically isomorphic provided there is a homeomorphism T of X onto Y which is also a linear operator. For this reason X and Y may be called *linearly homeomorphic*.

As we see later, there exist examples of pairs of spaces which are topologically isomorphic but not congruent.

It is convenient at this point to consider a few facts about continuous linear operators in normed linear spaces. Linear operators, without regard to continuity, were defined in § 1.3.

Theorem 3.1–A. *Let X and Y be normed linear spaces and T a linear operator on X into Y. Then T is continuous either at every point of X or at no point of X. It is continuous on X if and only if there is a constant M such that $\|Tx\| \leqslant M\|x\|$ for every x in X.*

PROOF. Let x_0 and x_1 be any points of X, and suppose T is continuous at x_0. Then to each $\epsilon > 0$ corresponds $\delta > 0$ such that $\|Tx - Tx_0\| < \epsilon$ if $\|x - x_0\| < \delta$. Now suppose $\|x - x_1\| < \delta$. Then $\|(x + x_0 - x_1) - x_0\| < \delta$, and so $\|T(x + x_0 - x_1) - Tx_0\| < \epsilon$. But $T(x + x_0 - x_1) - Tx_0 = Tx - Tx_1$, and so $\|Tx - Tx_1\| < \epsilon$. This shows that, if T is continuous at x_0, it is also continuous at x_1; thus, the first assertion of the theorem is proved.

If $\|Tx\| \leqslant M\|x\|$ for all x, it is clear that T is continuous at 0 [recall that $T(0) = 0$]. Conversely, if T is continuous at 0, $\|Tx\|$ can be kept as small as we please by keeping x sufficiently small. Thus, in particular, there is some $\delta > 0$ such that $\|Tx\| < 1$ if $\|x\| < \delta$. Now, if $x \neq 0$, let $x_0 = (\delta x)/(2\|x\|)$, so that $\|x_0\| = \delta/2 < \delta$. Then $\|Tx_0\| < 1$. But $Tx_0 = [\delta/(2\|x\|)]Tx$, and so

$$\|Tx\| = \frac{2\|x\|}{\delta} \|Tx_0\| < \frac{2}{\delta}\|x\|.$$

Thus, if we take $M = 2/\delta$, we have $\|Tx\| \leqslant M\|x\|$ if $x \neq 0$, and this inequality evidently is true as well when $x = 0$. The proof is thus complete.

If $\|Tx\| \leqslant M\|x\|$ for every x, it is plain that $\|Tx\| \leqslant M$ when $\|x\| \leqslant 1$. Vice versa, if $\|Tx\| \leqslant M$ for every x such that $\|x\| \leqslant 1$ (or even for every x such that $\|x\| = 1$), then $\|Tx\| \leqslant M\|x\|$ for every x. This is proved by an argument like that used in the last part of the foregoing proof. The smallest admissible value of M in the inequality $\|Tx\| \leqslant M\|x\|$ is called the *bound* of T. It is also called the *norm* of T and denoted by $\|T\|$. The reason for this terminology and notation will appear later. The following formulas for the norm of T are useful:

$$(3.1\text{--}1) \qquad\qquad \|T\| = \sup_{\|x\| \leqslant 1} \|Tx\|,$$

$$(3.1\text{--}2) \qquad\qquad \|T\| = \sup_{\|x\| = 1} \|Tx\|,$$

$$(3.1\text{--}3) \qquad\qquad \|T\| = \sup_{x \neq 0} \frac{\|Tx\|}{\|x\|}.$$

For (3.1–2) and (3.1–3) we assume, of course, that X contains some x such that $x \neq 0$.

When T is a continuous linear operator on X into Y, it is clear from Theorem 3.1–A that a set S lying in the sphere $\|x\| \leqslant r$ in X is carried into the set $T(S)$ lying in the sphere $\|y\| \leqslant \|T\|r$ in Y. Hence $T(S)$ is bounded if S is bounded. Conversely, if T is linear and has the property that $T(S)$ is a bounded set whenever S is a bounded set, it follows that T is continuous. We leave verification of this assertion to the reader.

Theorem 3.1–B. *Suppose T is a linear operator on X to Y, where X and Y are normed linear spaces. Then, the inverse T^{-1} exists and is continuous on its domain of definition if and only if there exists a constant $m > 0$ such that*

$$(3.1\text{--}4) \qquad\qquad m\|x\| \leqslant \|Tx\|$$

for every $x \in X$.

PROOF. If (3.1–4) holds and $Tx = 0$, it follows that $x = 0$. Then T^{-1} exists, by Theorem 1.3–B. Now $y = Tx$ is equivalent to $x = T^{-1}y$. Hence (3.1–4) is equivalent to $m\|T^{-1}y\| \leqslant \|y\|$, or $\|T^{-1}y\| \leqslant \dfrac{1}{m}\|y\|$, for all y in the range of T, which is the domain of T^{-1}. This implies that T^{-1} is continuous, by Theorem 3.1–A. We leave the converse proof to the reader.

Theorem 3.1–C. *If X and Y are normed linear spaces, they are topologically isomorphic if and only if there exists a linear operator T with domain X and range Y, and positive constants m, M such that*

$$(3.1\text{--}5) \qquad\qquad m\|x\| \leqslant \|Tx\| \leqslant M\|x\|$$

for every x in X.

PROOF. This theorem is a direct corollary of Theorems 3.1–A and 3.1–B.

Theorem 3.1–D. *Let X be a linear space, and suppose two norms $\|x\|_1$ and $\|x\|_2$ are defined on X. These norms define the same topology on X if and only if there exist positive constants m, M such that*

$$(3.1\text{–}6) \qquad m\|x_1\| \leqslant \|x\|_2 \leqslant M\|x\|_1$$

for every x in X.

PROOF. Let X_i be the normed linear space which X becomes with the norm $\|x\|_i$ $(i = 1, 2)$. Let $Tx = x$, and consider T as an operator with domain X_1 and range X_2. Condition (3.1–6) is precisely the condition that T and T^{-1} both be continuous. They are both continuous if and only if the open sets in X_1 are the same as the open sets in X_2 (Theorem 2.12–A). The conclusion now follows.

3.11 Examples of Normed Linear Spaces

In this section we define and establish standard notations for a number of spaces which will be referred to at various places throughout the book. In defining the norms in these various spaces we frequently leave it for the reader to verify that the norm, as defined, actually has the properties required of a norm.

In many of our examples, the elements of the spaces are functions defined on some set T. The values of the functions may be either real or complex; we get a real or complex space according to whether the values of the functions are real or complex. It is always to be understood that, if x_1, x_2 and x are functions defined on T, the functions $x_1 + x_2$ and αx are defined by

$$(x_1 + x_2)(t) = x_1(t) + x_2(t), \qquad (\alpha x)(t) = \alpha x(t), \qquad t \in T.$$

Example I. The spaces R_n and C_n (defined in Examples 1 and 2, § 1.2) can be made into normed linear spaces in a variety of ways. Let us consider C_n. If $x = (\xi_1, \cdots, \xi_n) \in C_n$ and $p \geqslant 1$, let us define

$$(3.11\text{–}1) \qquad \|x\| = (|\xi_1|^p + \cdots + |\xi_n|^p)^{1/p}.$$

The triangularity property $\|x_1 + x_2\| \leqslant \|x_1\| + \|x_2\|$ is the same as Minkowski's inequality for finite sums, namely

$$\left(\sum_{i=1}^{n} |\xi_i + \eta_i|^p \right)^{1/p} \leqslant \left(\sum_{i=1}^{n} |\xi_i|^p \right)^{1/p} + \left(\sum_{i=1}^{n} |\eta_i|^p \right)^{1/p}$$

For reference to Minkowski's inequality see the Introduction. When C_n is considered as a normed linear space with the norm (3.11–1), we denote the space by $l^p(n)$. We can make the real space R_n into a normed space in the same way. We shall use $l^p(n)$ for both the real and the complex space with norm (3.11–1); whether the real or complex space is under discussion at a given time will either be clear from the context, or we shall make a specific statement if necessary.

We can also define a norm in R_n and C_n by the formula

$$\|x\| = \max\,[|\xi_1|, \cdots, |\xi_n|].$$

The notation for the space with this norm is $l^\infty(n)$. This notation is natural, since

$$(3.11\text{–}2) \qquad \max_{1 \leqslant k \leqslant n} |\xi_k| = \lim_{p \to \infty} (|\xi_1|^p + \cdots + |\xi_n|^p)^{1/p}.$$

Example 2. We also have spaces analogous to $l^p(n)$ and $l^\infty(n)$ for *infinite* sequences. The space l^p, where $p \geqslant 1$, is defined to consist of all sequences $x = \{\xi_n\}$ such that $\sum_{n=1}^{\infty} |\xi_n|^p < \infty$. The norm in l^p is defined by

$$(3.11\text{–}3) \qquad \|x\| = \left(\sum_{n=1}^{\infty} |\xi_n|^p \right)^{1/p}.$$

Minkowski's inequality for infinite sums is used in showing that the requisite properties of a norm are fulfilled.

The space l^∞ is defined to consist of the *bounded* sequences $x = \{\xi_n\}$, with the norm

$$\|x\| = \sup_{n} |\xi_n|.$$

For any $x \in l^\infty$ we have

$$(3.11\text{–}4) \qquad \sup_{n} |\xi_n| = \lim_{n \to \infty} \left[\lim_{p \to \infty} (|\xi_1|^p + \cdots + |\xi_n|^p)^{1/p} \right].$$

Some interest attaches to various subspaces of l^∞. We mention in particular the space of all *convergent* sequences $x = \{\xi_n\}$. We denote this space by (c).

Sometimes it is convenient to denote the norm in l^p by $\|x\|_p$, and that in l^∞ by $\|x\|_\infty$. It is worth noticing that the elements of l^p form a subclass of the elements of l^q if $1 \leqslant p < q \leqslant \infty$, and that then $\|x\|_q \leqslant \|x\|_p$ if $x \in l^p$ (see Jensen's inequality in the Introduction).

The space l^p is separable if $1 \leqslant p < \infty$. To see that this is so let us first introduce some terminology. A point $x \in l^p$ will be called rational if $x = \{\xi_n\}$ and each ξ_n is rational. In the case of the complex field a number ξ_n is called rational if its real and imaginary parts are rational. A point $x = \{\xi_n\}$ will be called of *finite type* if the set of n for which $\xi_n \neq 0$ is finite. The set of all rational points of finite type is readily seen to be countable. It is also everywhere dense in l^p. For, suppose $\epsilon > 0$ and $x \in l^p$. We choose N so that $\sum\limits_{n=N+1}^{\infty} |\xi_n|^p < \epsilon^p/2$, and then we choose a rational point of finite type, say $y = \{\eta_n\}$, such that $\eta_n = 0$ if $n > N$, and $|\xi_k - \eta_k| < (2N)^{-1/p}\epsilon$ if $k = 1, \cdots, N$. Then

$$\|x - y\|^p = \sum_{n=1}^{N} |\xi_n - \eta_n|^p + \sum_{n=N+1}^{\infty} |\xi_n|^p < N \frac{\epsilon^p}{2N} + \frac{\epsilon^p}{2} = \epsilon^p,$$

so that $\|x - y\| < \epsilon$. Thus l^p is separable.

The space l^∞ is not separable, however. For, if $\{x_n\}$ is any countable set in l^∞, with $x_n = (\xi_1^{(n)}, \xi_2^{(n)}, \cdots)$, let $x = \{\xi_n\}$ be the element of l^∞ defined by $\xi_k = \xi_k^{(k)} + 1$ if $|\xi_k^{(k)}| \leqslant 1$ and $\xi_k = 0$ if $|\xi_k^{(k)}| > 1$. Then the kth component of $x - x_k$ is $\xi_k - \xi_k^{(k)}$, and $|\xi_k - \xi_k^{(k)}| \geqslant 1$, so that $\|x - x_k\| \geqslant 1$. Thus the set $\{x_k\}$ cannot be dense in l^∞, and l^∞ is not separable.

Example 3.   Let T be any nonempty set, and let $B(T)$ be the class of all bounded functions x defined on T, with either real or complex values. Then $B(T)$ becomes a normed linear space if we define

$$\|x\| = \sup_{t \in T} |x(t)|.$$

The scalar field for $B(T)$ will be the same as the field in which the function values are required to lie.

Observe that l^∞ is the special case of $B(T)$ in which T is the set of positive integers. In the special case where T is an interval $[a, b]$ of the real axis, we shall denote $B(T)$ by $B[a, b]$.

If T is an infinite set, $B(T)$ is not separable. This is shown by the same kind of argument that was used in showing the nonseparability of l^∞.

Example 4.   Suppose T is a topological space. Let $C(T)$ denote the class of bounded and continuous functions x defined on T. Then $C(T)$ is a linear manifold in $B(T)$, and we consider $C(T)$ as a normed linear space on its own account, with the norm as defined in $B(T)$. If T is compact, the requirement that the values $x(t)$ be bounded is fulfilled automatically as a consequence of the assumption that x is continuous on T. This is because of Theorem 2.2–C and the fact that a compact set of real or complex numbers is bounded. It is moreover true that, if $x \in C(T)$, there is some point $t_m \in T$ such that

$$|x(t_m)| = \max_{t \in T} |x(t)| = \|x\|.$$

This is because $|x(t)|$ is continuous on T and a compact set of real numbers is closed as well as bounded.

If T is a finite closed interval on the real axis, we shall usually denote $C(T)$ by $C[a, b]$ (see Example 3, § 1.2).

Example 5. The class $\mathscr{L}^p = \mathscr{L}^p(-\infty, \infty)$ and the corresponding linear space L^p were defined in Example 7, § 1.2. Here we assume $1 \leqq p < \infty$. If $x \in \mathscr{L}^p$ we write

$$(3.11\text{--}5) \qquad \|x\|_p = \left(\int_{-\infty}^{\infty} |x(t)|^p \, dt \right)^{1/p}.$$

Evidently $\|x\|_p = 0$ is equivalent to $x(t) = 0$ a.e. and $\|x\|_p = \|y\|_p$ if $x =^0 y$. Minkowski's inequality for integrals (see the Introduction) states that

$$\|x + y\|_p \leqslant \|x\|_p + \|y\|_p$$

if $x, y \in \mathscr{L}^p$. Hence, if $[x] \in L^p$ and we define $\|[x]\| = \|x\|_p$, L^p becomes a normed linear space. As stated in § 1.2, we shall usually write x in place of $[x]$. Also, we shall write $\|x\|$ instead of $\|x\|_p$ if the situation is such that the use of the index is not essential.

Instead of functions defined on $(-\infty, \infty)$, we can consider any measurable set E in n-dimensional Euclidean space. The classes $\mathscr{L}^p$ and L^p are then defined with reference to Lebesgue integrals over E, and we indicate the dependence on E, if necessary, by writing $\mathscr{L}^p(E)$ and $L^p(E)$. Still more generally, as we shall see later, it is possible and desirable to consider the case in which E is replaced by a more general measure space and the integrals are defined in terms of a more general measure.

The space $L^p(E)$ is separable. See problem 5, § 7.3.

Example 6. Let (a, b) be an interval, finite or infinite of the real axis. A measurable function x defined on (a, b), with real or complex values, is called *essentially* bounded if there is some $A \geqslant 0$ such that the set $\{t : |x(t)| > A\}$ has measure 0 [i.e., such that $|x(t)| \leqslant A$ almost everywhere on (a, b)]. If such a constant exists, there is a least one; we call this smallest possible A the *essential least upper bound* of x, and denote it by $\sup^0 |x(t)|$. The notation $\sup^0$ distinguishes $\sup^0 |x(t)|$ from the ordinary least upper bound $\sup |x(t)|$. It can of course happen that $\sup^0 |x(t)| < \sup |x(t)|$, and it can even happen that $\sup^0 |x(t)| < \infty$ but $\sup |x(t)| = \infty$. Another characterization of $\sup^0 |x(t)|$ is the following: It is the largest number B such that if $\epsilon > 0$ the set $\{t : |x(t)| > B - \epsilon\}$ has positive measure.

Let $\mathscr{L}^\infty$ denote the class of all measurable and essentially bounded functions x defined on (a, b). If $x, y \, \mathscr{L}^\infty$, we write $x =^0 y$ if $x(t) = y(t)$

a.e. We then define the linear space L^∞ in relation to $\mathscr{L}^\infty$ just as we
defined L^p in relation to $\mathscr{L}^p$ (see Example 7, § 1.2). If $x =^0 y$, it is clear
that $\sup^0 |x(t)| = \sup^0 |y(t)|$. Hence, if we define

$$\|[x]\| = \sup^0 |x(t)|,$$

L^∞ becomes a normed linear space.

The space L^∞ is not separable. For, if $a < s < b$, let x_s be the characteristic function of the interval (a, s) as a subset of (a, b). Then it is clear
that $\|[x_s] - [x_t]\| = 1$ if $a < s < t < b$. Now consider the family of
spheres $\|[x] - [x_s]\| < \frac{1}{2}$ with centers at $[x_s]$ in L^∞, for various values of
s. No two of these spheres have points in common, and there are
uncountably many of them. It is therefore clear that any set which is
everywhere dense in L^∞ cannot be countable, so that L^∞ cannot be
separable.

If (a, b) is a finite interval and $x \in \mathscr{L}^\infty$, then $x \in \mathscr{L}^p$ for every $p > 0$,
and it can be proved that

$$(3.11\text{–}6) \qquad \lim_{p \to \infty} \left(\int_a^b |x(t)|^p \, dt \right)^{1/p} = \sup^0 |x(t)|.$$

In fact, if $A < \sup^0 |x(t)|$ and E is the set where $|x(t)| > A$, we have
$m(E) > 0$ and

$$A[m(E)]^{1/p} \leqslant \left(\int_a^b |x(t)|^p \, dt \right)^{1/p} \leqslant (b - a)^{1/p} \sup^0 |x(t)|.$$

Letting $p \to \infty$, we see that

$$A \leqslant \underline{\lim} \left(\int_a^b |x(t)|^p \, dt \right)^{1/p} \leqslant \overline{\lim} \left(\int_a^b |x(t)|^p \, dt \right)^{1/p} \leqslant \sup^0 |x(t)|.$$

Since A can be as near $\sup^0 |x(t)|$ as we please, this justifies (3.11–6). If
the interval (a, b) is infinite, (3.11–6) is replaced by

$$(3.11\text{–}7) \qquad \lim_{n \to \infty} \lim_{p \to \infty} \left(\int_{E_n} |x(t)|^p \, dt \right)^{1/p} = \sup^0 |x(t)|,$$

where E_n is a sequence of finite intervals such that $E_1 \subset E_2 \subset \cdots$, each
E_n lies in (a, b), and $\bigcup_n E_n = (a, b)$.

Example 7. The linear space $BV[a, b]$ of functions of bounded
variation on $[a, b]$ was defined in Example 8, § 1.2. If $x \in BV[a, b]$ and
$V(x)$ denotes the total variation of $x(t)$ for $a \leqslant t \leqslant b$, we can define a
norm by

$$(3.11\text{–}8) \qquad \|x\| = |x(a)| + V(x).$$

The space BV[a, b] is not separable. This may be shown by the same kind of argument that was used in showing the nonseparability of L^∞.

Many interesting spaces can be formed from classes of analytic functions of a complex variable. Let $\mathfrak{A}$ denote the class of all functions $f(z)$ which are defined, single valued, and analytic in the unit circle $|z| < 1$ of the complex plane. This class is a complex linear space. We shall in the next two examples describe some subspaces of $\mathfrak{A}$ which become normed linear spaces with appropriately defined norms.

Example 8. Suppose $0 < p < \infty$. For any $f \in \mathfrak{A}$ and $0 \leqslant r < 1$ let

$$(3.11\text{--}9) \qquad \mathfrak{M}_p[f; r] = \left(\frac{1}{2\pi} \int_0^{2\pi} |f(re^{i\theta})|^p \, d\theta \right)^{1/p}.$$

The class H^p is by definition composed of those $f \in \mathfrak{A}$ such that $\sup_{0 \leqslant r < 1} \mathfrak{M}_p[f; r] < \infty$. If $1 \leqslant p$ it is clear by Minkowski's inequality that $f + g$ is in H^p if f and g are in H^p. If $0 < p < 1$, this same conclusion follows from the following inequality [Hardy, Littlewood, and Pólya, **1**, formula (6.13–6)]:

$$(3.11\text{--}10) \quad \int_0^{2\pi} |f(re^{i\theta}) + g(re^{i\theta})|^p \, d\theta \leqslant \int_0^{2\pi} |f(re^{i\theta})|^p \, d\theta + \int_0^{2\pi} |g(re^{i\theta})|^p \, d\theta.$$

It is thus seen that H^p is a linear space. If $1 \leqslant p$ we define

$$(3.11\text{--}11) \qquad \|f\| = \sup_{0 \leqslant r < 1} \mathfrak{M}_p[f; r].$$

This has the properties of a norm; thus H^p is a normed linear space if $1 \leqslant p$. If $0 < p < 1$, (3.11–11) does not define a norm, for the triangularity condition $\|f + g\| \leqslant \|f\| + \|g\|$ is not always satisfied.

It is natural to define H^∞ as the class of those $f \in \mathfrak{A}$ such that the values $f(z)$ are bounded. We define a norm on H^∞ by

$$\|f\| = \sup_{|z| < 1} |f(z)|.$$

That H^∞ is a natural notation for this space is seen from the fact that, if $f \in \mathfrak{A}$ and $0 \leqslant r < 1$, then

$$\max_{|z|=r} |f(z)| = \lim_{p \to \infty} \mathfrak{M}_p[f; r],$$

while, if $f \in H^\infty$, then

$$\|f\| = \sup_{0 \leqslant r < 1} \left\{ \max_{|z|=r} |f(z)| \right\}.$$

For complete uniformity of notation we define

$$\mathfrak{M}_\infty[f; r] = \max_{|z|=r} |f(z)|.$$

Then (3.11–11) is the definition of the norm in H^p for $1 \leqslant p \leqslant \infty$, and H^p consists of those $f \in \mathfrak{A}$ such that $\|f\| < \infty$.

The space H^p is separable if $1 \leqslant p < \infty$. This may be shown in various ways. If one makes use of the fact that L^p is separable, the separability of H^p follows at once from the following facts: If $f \in H^p$, then $\lim\limits_{r \to 1} f(re^{i\theta})$ exists for almost all values of θ, thus defining a function which we denote by $f(e^{i\theta})$. Moreover, the latter function belongs to $L^p(0, 2\pi)$, and

$$\|f\| = \left(\frac{1}{2\pi} \int_0^{2\pi} |f(e^{i\theta})|^p \, d\theta \right)^{1/p}$$

For these facts about H^p, we refer the reader to F. Riesz, **2**, and A. Zygmund, **1**, pages 158–162. Thus H^p is in isometric correspondence with a subset of L^p. Since any subset of a separable metric space is itself separable, we see that H^p is separable.

The space H^∞ is not separable, however. To show this, it suffices to show that the set of all $f \in H^\infty$ such that $\|f\| = 1$ is not separable. Let $\{f_n\}$ be any sequence from this set. Then $\mathfrak{M}_\infty[f_n; r] \to 1$ as $r \to 1$, for each n. Choose $r_n > 0$ so that $r_n \leqslant r < 1$ implies $\mathfrak{M}_\infty[f_n; r] \geqslant \frac{1}{2}$. Let $\rho_n = \max\{r_n, 1 - 1/n^2\}$, and choose points α_n so that $|\alpha_n| = \rho_n$ and $|f_n(\alpha_n)| = \mathfrak{M}_\infty[f_n; \rho_n]$. Thus $1 - 1/n^2 \leqslant |\alpha_n| < 1$ and $|f_n(\alpha_n)| \geqslant \frac{1}{2}$. Now define $f(z)$ by the Blaschke product

$$f(z) = \prod_{k=1}^{\infty} |\alpha_k| \frac{1 - (z/\alpha_k)}{1 - \bar{\alpha}_k z}.$$

Then $f \in H^\infty$, $f(\alpha_k) = 0$, and $\|f\| = 1$, for it is known that $|f(e^{i\theta})| = 1$ for almost all values of θ. (See pages 160–161 and pages 163–164 of Zygmund, **1**, or F. Riesz, **2**.) Finally, $\|f_n - f\| \geqslant |f_n(\alpha_n) - f(\alpha_n)| \geqslant \frac{1}{2}$. Thus H^∞ cannot be separable.

Example 9. Let CA denote the class of functions f which are defined (single valued) and continuous when $|z| \leqslant 1$ and analytic when $|z| < 1$. Evidently CA is a linear subclass of H^∞ and is a normed linear space with the norm defined as in H^∞. Because of the maximum modulus theorem and the fact that f is continuous, it is clear that for $f \in CA$

(3.11–12) $$\|f\| = \max_{|z|=1} |f(z)|.$$

The space CA is separable. In fact, the linear combinations of the functions $1, z, z^2, \cdots, z^n, \cdots$, with complex rational coefficients, form a set everywhere dense in CA.   This can be seen, for instance, from Fejér's theorem on the $(C, 1)$ summability of Fourier series.   If

$$f(z) = \sum_0^\infty a_n z^n$$

is in CA, the Fourier series of $f(e^{i\theta})$ is

$$\sum_0^\infty a_n e^{in\theta},$$

and this series is uniformly $(C, 1)$ summable to $f(e^{i\theta})$ (Zygmund, **1**, page 45).   This implies that

$$\sum_{k=0}^{n-1} (1 - k/n) a_k z^k$$

converges to $f(z)$ uniformly in $|z| \leqslant 1$ as $n \to \infty$.

The spaces H^p with $1 \leqslant p \leqslant \infty$ and the space CA have been investigated in connection with more general studies of Banach spaces composed of functions which are analytic in the unit circle.   See Taylor, **4**.

PROBLEMS

1. The complex space $C(T)$ is separable if and only if the corresponding *real* space is separable.

2. The real space $C[a, b]$ is separable if $[a, b]$ is a finite closed interval of the real axis.   One way of seeing this may be outlined as follows: For each positive integer n and each set of $n + 1$ rational numbers $r_0, r_1, \cdots, r_n$, divide $[a, b]$ into $2n$ equal parts by points $t_0, t_1, \cdots, t_{2n}$ (in order from a to b); then define a function x by setting $x(t) = r_k$ if $t_{2k} \leqslant t \leqslant t_{2k+1}$, $k = 0, 1, \cdots, n - 1$, $x(t_{2n}) = r_n$, making $x(t)$ linear in each of the remaining subintervals in such a way that it is continuous at all points.   The set of such functions is everywhere dense in $C[a, b]$.

3. The separability of $C[a, b]$ may also be established by relying on the known theorem of Weierstrass which states (in effect) that those elements of $C[a, b]$ which are polynomials in t are dense in $C[a, b]$.   One then shows that the polynomials with rational coefficients are also dense in $C[a, b]$.

3.12 Finite-Dimensional Normed Linear Spaces

We saw in Theorem 1.4–A that two linear spaces of the same finite dimension n over the same scalar field are isomorphic.   Now we shall see that, if each of the two spaces has a norm, the spaces are topologically isomorphic according to the definition of § 3.1.

Theorem 3.12–A.   *Let X_1 and X_2 be two normed linear spaces of the same finite dimension n, with the same scalar field.   Then X_1 and X_2 are topologically isomorphic.*

PROOF.   The case $n = 0$ is trivial, and we assume $n \geqslant 1$.   It will suffice to prove that, if X is an n-dimensional normed linear space, it is topologically isomorphic to $l^1(n)$, for the relation of topological isomorphism is transitive (as well as being reflexive and symmetric).   Suppose that $x_1, \cdots, x_n$ is a basis for X.   If $x = \xi_1 x_1 + \cdots + \xi_n x_n$ is the representation of an arbitrary $x \in X$, we know from § 1.4 that the correspondence $x \leftrightarrow (\xi_1, \cdots, \xi_n)$ defines an isomorphism of X and $l^1(n)$.   By Theorem 3.1–C, all we have to prove is that there exists positive constants m and M such that

$$(3.12–1) \qquad \|\xi_1 x_1 + \cdots + \xi_n x_n\| \leqslant M(|\xi_1| + \cdots + |\xi_n|)$$

and

$$(3.12–2) \qquad m(|\xi_1| + \cdots + |\xi_n|) \leqslant \|\xi_1 x_1 + \cdots + \xi_n x_n\|$$

for all possible sets of values $(\xi_1, \cdots, \xi_n)$.   Now (3.12–1) is evidently true if we choose for M the maximum of $\|x_1\|, \cdots, \|x_n\|$.   To prove (3.12–2) it suffices to show that $m \leqslant \|\xi_1 x_1 + \cdots + \xi_n x_n\|$ if $|\xi_1| + \cdots + |\xi_n| = 1$, for (3.12–2) certainly holds if $\xi_1 = \cdots = \xi_n = 0$, and, if $c = |\xi_1| + \cdots + |\xi_n| > 0$, we can define $\eta_i = c^{-1}\xi_i$, whence $|\eta_1| + \cdots + |\eta_n| = 1$, and $\|\eta_1 x_1 + \cdots + \eta_n x_n\| = c^{-1}\|\xi_1 x_1 + \cdots + \xi_n x_n\|$, so that (3.12–2) holds if $m \leqslant \|\eta_1 x_1 + \cdots + \eta_n x_n\|$.

Now let $f(\xi_1, \cdots, \xi_n) = \|\xi_1 x_1 + \cdots + \xi_n x_n\|$.   The function f is continuous on $l^1(n)$, as a consequence of (3.12–1).   In fact, since $|\|x\| - \|y\|| \leqslant \|x - y\|$, we see that

$$|f(\xi_1, \cdots, \xi_n) - f(\eta_1, \cdots, \eta_n)| \leqslant \|(\xi_1 - \eta_1)x_1 + \cdots + (\xi_n - \eta_n)x_n\|$$
$$\leqslant M(|\xi_1 - \eta_1| + \cdots + |\xi_n - \eta_n|),$$

whence the continuity of f is clear.   Now the surface of the unit sphere in $l^1(n)$ (the set S for which $|\xi_1| + \cdots + |\xi_n| = 1$) is compact, as we see, for example, by the use of Theorem 2.4–H and the Bolzano-Weierstrass theorem for scalars.   Hence f, being continuous on S, attains a minimum value $m \geqslant 0$ on S.   But $m > 0$, for $m = 0$ would imply that $x_1, \cdots, x_n$ are linearly dependent, contrary to the fact that they form a basis for X.   The proof of (3.12–2) and of Theorem 3.12–A is now complete.

It is clear from Theorem 3.1–C that, if X and Y are topologically isomorphic normed linear spaces and if one of them is complete (as a metric space), the other is also complete.   Now $l^1(n)$ is evidently complete (as a consequence of the completeness of $l^1(1)$, the real number field).   Thus we have:

Theorem 3.12–B. *A finite-dimensional normed linear space is complete.*

As a corollary of this we have:

Theorem 3.12–C. *If X is a normed linear space, any finite-dimensional subspace of X is necessarily closed.*

Another important result is the following:

Theorem 3.12–D. *If X is a finite-dimensional normed linear space, each closed and bounded set in X is compact.*

PROOF. This proposition is true (by classical analysis) for the particular finite-dimensional space $l^1(n)$. It then follows, by virtue of Theorem 3.12–A, that the theorem is true for any finite-dimensional space X, for the properties of being bounded and closed are transferred from a set S to its image S_1 in $l^1(n)$ by the topological isomorphism, and the compactness is then carried back from S_1 to S.

The converse of Theorem 3.12–D is also true. Before proving the converse, we consider a general theorem due to F. Riesz which is useful in many arguments.

Theorem 3.12–E (Riesz's Lemma). *Suppose X is a normed linear space. Let X_0 be a subspace of X such that X_0 is closed and a proper subset of X. Then for each θ such that $0 < \theta < 1$ there exists a vector $x_\theta \in X$ such that $\|x_\theta\| = 1$ and $\|x - x_\theta\| \geqslant \theta$ if $x \in X_0$.*

PROOF. Select any $x_1 \in X - X_0$ and let

$$d = \inf_{x \in X_0} \|x - x_1\|.$$

Since X_0 is closed, it follows that $d > 0$. There exists $x_0 \subset X_0$ such that $\|x_0 - x_1\| \leqslant \theta^{-1}d$ (because $\theta^{-1}d > d$). Let $x_\theta = h(x_1 - x_0)$, where $h = \|x_1 - x_0\|^{-1}$. Then $\|x_\theta\| = 1$. If $x \in X_0$, then $h^{-1}x + x_0 \in X_0$ also, and so

$$\|x - x_\theta\| = \|x - hx_1 + hx_0\| = h\|(h^{-1}x + x_0) - x_1\| \geqslant hd.$$

But $hd = \|x_1 - x_0\|^{-1}d \geqslant \theta$, by the way in which x_0 was chosen. Thus $\|x - x_\theta\| \geqslant \theta$ if $x \in X_0$, and the proof is complete.

We can restate Riesz's lemma as follows: *If X_0 is a closed and proper subspace of X, there exist on the surface of the unit sphere in X points whose distance from X_0 is as near 1 as we please.* This is the most that can be said in general however. It need not be true that there are points on the unit sphere whose distance from X_0 is *equal* to 1.

Example. Let X be that subspace of the real space $C[0, 1]$ (see § 3.11, Example 4) consisting of all continuous functions x on $[0, 1]$ such that $x(0) = 0$. For X_0 we take the subspace of all $x \in X$ such that $\int_0^1 x(t)\, dt = 0$. Now suppose that $x_1 \in X$, $\|x_1\| = 1$, and $\|x_1 - x\| \geqslant 1$ if $x \in X_0$. Corresponding to each $y \in X - X_0$ let

$$c = \frac{\int_0^1 x_1(t)\, dt}{\int_0^1 y(t)\, dt}.$$

Then $x_1 - cy \in X_0$, and so $1 \leqslant \|x_1 - (x_1 - cy)\| = |c|\,\|y\|$, or

$$\left| \int_0^1 y(t)\, dt \right| \leqslant \left| \int_0^1 x_1(t)\, dt \right| \|y\|$$

for each $y \in X$. Now, we can make $\left| \int_0^1 y(t)\, dt \right|$ as close to 1 as we please while maintaining $\|y\| = 1$ (e.g., let $y_n(t) = t^{1/n}$ and let $n \to \infty$). Thus we see that

$$1 \leqslant \left| \int_0^1 x_1(t)\, dt \right|.$$

But, since $\|x_1\| = \max_{0 \leqslant t \leqslant 1} |x_1(t)| = 1$ and $x_1(0) = 0$, the continuity of x_1 shows that we must have

$$\left| \int_0^1 x_1(t)\, dt \right| < 1,$$

and thus we have a contradiction.   Therefore, with X_0 and X as here given, there is no point on the surface of the unit sphere in X at unit distance from X_0.

We come now to the converse of Theorem 3.12–D.

Theorem 3.12–F. *Let X be a normed linear space, and suppose the surface S of the unit sphere in X is compact. Then X is finite dimensional.*

Suppose that X is not finite dimensional.   Choose $x_1 \in S$, and let X_1 be the subspace generated by x_1.   Then X_1 is a proper subspace of X, and it is closed (by Theorem 3.12–C).   Hence, by Riesz's lemma, there exists $x_2 \in S$ such that $\|x_2 - x_1\| \geqslant 1/2$.   Let X_2 be the (closed and proper) subspace of X generated by x_1, x_2; then, there must exist $x_3 \in S$ such that $\|x_3 - x\| \geqslant 1/2$ if $x \in X_2$.   Proceeding by induction, we obtain an infinite sequence $\{x_n\}$ of elements of S such that $\|x_n - x_m\| \geqslant 1/2$ if $m \neq n$.   This sequence can have no convergent subsequence.   This contradicts Theorem 2.4–H, since S is compact.   Thus X must be finite dimensional.

Another proof, using the definition of compactness directly, may be given as follows: The family of all open spheres of radius $^1/_2$ with centers on S is an open covering of S. Since S is compact, there must exist a finite number of points $x_1, \cdots, x_n$ on S such that S is covered by the set of open spheres of radius $^1/_2$ with centers at $x_1, \cdots, x_n$. Let M be the finite dimensional, and therefore closed, subspace of X generated by $x_1, \cdots, x_n$. Then M must be all of X. For, if not, by Riesz's lemma there exists a point $x_0 \in S$ whose distance from M is greater than $^1/_2$, and this point x_0 cannot be in any of the spheres which cover S. Since $M = X$, X is finite dimensional.

PROBLEM

If X and Y are normed linear spaces, if X is finite dimensional, and if T is a linear operator on X into Y, T is necessarily continuous.

3.13 Banach Spaces

If a normed linear space is complete, it is called a *Banach space*. While many propositions about normed linear spaces do not require the hypothesis of completeness, a number of theorems of critical importance do depend upon completeness. In particular, there are some important theorems in the theory of linear operators which make use of the theorem of Baire (Theorem 2.41–C), and this is made possible by the assumption of completeness for the normed linear spaces under consideration. In some work it is necessary to construct elements of a normed linear space by means of infinite series or integrals, and completeness is then needed to insure the existence of limits.

If a normed linear space is not complete, we may complete it as a metric space by the process described in the proof of Theorem 2.41–A. It is important to know that we can complete X, not merely as a metric space, but also as a normed linear space. That is, using the notation of Theorem 2.41–A, where X is the normed linear space and Y is its completion as a metric space, the space Y can be made into a linear space in such a way that the subset Y_0 (which is isometric with X and dense in Y) is congruent to X as a normed linear space.

Suppose y, $v \in Y$, and let $\{x_n\}$, $\{u_n\}$ be Cauchy sequences from X which are in the equivalence classes y, v respectively. Then $\{x_n + u_n\}$ is a Cauchy sequence, since

$$\|(x_n + u_n) - (x_m + u_m)\| \leqslant \|x_n - x_m\| + \|u_n - u_m\|.$$

Moreover, if $\{a_n\}$ and $\{b_n\}$ are Cauchy sequences equivalent to $\{x_n\}$ and $\{u_n\}$ respectively, then $\{a_n + b_n\}$ is equivalent to $\{x_n + u_n\}$, because

$$\|(x_n + u_n) - (a_n + b_n)\| \leqslant \|x_n - a_n\| + \|u_n - b_n\|.$$

Thus we can define $y + v$ as that equivalence class which contains $\{x_n + u_n\}$, and the definition depends only on y, v, not on the particular choice of $\{x_n\}$, $\{u_n\}$. Likewise we define αy as the equivalence class which contains $\{\alpha x_n\}$, and we define $\|y\| = \lim_{n \to \infty} \|x_n\|$. The zero element of Y is the unique equivalence class all of whose members $\{x_n\}$ are such that $x_n \to 0$. It is a routine matter to verify that Y is a normed linear space and that Y_0 (defined in the proof of Theorem 2.41–A) is a linear manifold in Y congruent to X. Finally, the metric defined in Y by the norm is the same as the metric defined in Y by the completion process of Theorem 2.41–A when the metric of X is defined by the norm in X.

It is convenient to adopt a standard notation and terminology regarding the completion of a space X. It is evident that we can adjoin certain "ideal" elements to X so as to obtain a complete space in which X is everywhere dense. This complete space will be called the completion of X, and denoted by $\hat{X}$. The important feature of this arrangement is that X is actually a subspace of $\hat{X}$, whereas in the original process of completing a metric space, we obtain a complete space Y whose elements are equivalence classes of Cauchy sequences from X, so that X is not actually a subset of Y. A space X is complete if and only if $X = \hat{X}$.

There is a particular kind of extension theorem for linear operators which we shall need later and which is convenient to discuss here.

Theorem 3.13–A. *Let X and Y be normed linear spaces, and let T be a continuous linear operator on X into Y. Then there is a uniquely determined continuous linear operator $\hat{T}$ on $\hat{X}$ into $\hat{Y}$ such that $\hat{T}x = Tx$ if $x \in X$. The relation $\|\hat{T}\| = \|T\|$ is valid.*

PROOF. To define $\hat{T}$ we suppose $\hat{x} \in \hat{X}$, and select a sequence $\{x_n\}$ from X such that $x_n \to \hat{x}$. Then $\{x_n\}$ is a Cauchy sequence, and

$$\|Tx_n - Tx_m\| = \|T(x_n - x_m)\| \leqslant \|T\| \, \|x_n - x_m\|,$$

so that $\{Tx_n\}$ is a Cauchy sequence in Y. Consequently $Tx_n \to \hat{y}$, where $\hat{y}$ is some element of $\hat{Y}$. It is readily proved that $\hat{y}$ depends only on $\hat{x}$ and T, not on the particular sequence $\{x_n\}$. We define $\hat{T}\hat{x} = \hat{y}$. It is a simple matter to verify that $\hat{T}x = Tx$ if $x \in X$ and that $\hat{T}$ is linear. We see that $\|x_n\| \to \|\hat{x}\|$, $\|Tx_n\| \leqslant \|T\| \, \|x_n\|$, and hence $\|\hat{T}\hat{x}\| \leqslant \|T\| \, \|\hat{x}\|$. Thus $\hat{T}$ is continuous and $\|\hat{T}\| \leqslant \|T\|$ (see § 3.1). On the other hand, if $x \in X$, we have $\|Tx\| = \|\hat{T}x\| \leqslant \|\hat{T}\| \, \|x\|$, so that $\|T\| \leqslant \|\hat{T}\|$. Hence $\|\hat{T}\| = \|T\|$. The uniqueness assertion about $\hat{T}$ is easily justified by using the fact that X is dense in $\hat{X}$.

Theorem 3.13–B. *If X is a Banach space and X_0 is a closed linear manifold in X, then X_0, considered as a normed linear space by itself, is a Banach space.*

PROOF.   This is a special case of Theorem 2.41–E.

It is useful to note that a Cauchy sequence $\{x_n\}$ in a metric space is bounded, irrespective of whether or not the space is complete.   Hence, if $\{x_n\}$ is a Cauchy sequence in a normed linear space, the sequence of norms $\|x_n\|$ is bounded.

One simple but important property of Banach spaces is shown in the following theorem:

Theorem 3.13–C.   *Let X be a Banach space, and let $\{x_n\}$ be a sequence of elements of X such that $\sum\limits_{1}^{\infty} \|x_n\| < \infty$.   Then, the infinite series $\sum\limits_{1}^{\infty} x_n$ is convergent and defines an element of X.*

PROOF.   Let $y_n = x_1 + \cdots + x_n$.   Then $\{y_n\}$ is a Cauchy sequence, for, if $m < n$, $\|y_n - y_m\| \leqslant \|x_{m+1}\| + \cdots + \|x_n\|$, and we can employ the Cauchy criterion on the series $\sum\|x_n\|$.   Since X is complete, it follows that $\lim\limits_{n \to \infty} y_n$ exists.

We turn to a discussion of completeness for the examples of normed linear spaces given in § 3.11.   We already know (Theorem 3.12–B) that every finite-dimensional normed linear space is complete.

The space l^p, where $p \geqslant 1$, is complete.   Let $\{x_n\}$ be a Cauchy sequence in l^p, with $x_n = (\xi_1^{(n)}, \xi_2^{(n)}, \cdots)$.   For each fixed k, $\{\xi_k^{(n)}\}$ is a Cauchy sequence, because

$$|\xi_k^{(n)} - \xi_k^{(m)}| \leqslant \left(\sum_{i=1}^{\infty} |\xi_i^{(n)} - \xi_i^{(m)}|^p \right)^{1/p} = \|x_n - x_m\|.$$

Let $\xi_k = \lim\limits_{n \to \infty} \xi_k^{(n)}$.   We shall first prove that the sequence $\{\xi_k\}$ is an element of l^p.   We know that $\|x_n\|$ is bounded, say $\|x_n\| \leqslant M$.   Now, for any k,

$$\left(\sum_{i=1}^{k} |\xi_i^{(n)}|^p \right)^{1/p} \leqslant \|x_n\| \leqslant M.$$

Letting $n \to \infty$, we obtain

$$\left(\sum_{i=1}^{k} |\xi_i|^p \right)^{1/p} \leqslant M.$$

Since k is arbitrary, this shows that $\{\xi_k\} \in l^p$ and that its norm does not exceed M. Let $x = \{\xi_k\}$. It remains to prove that $\|x_n - x\| \to 0$. Suppose $\epsilon > 0$. Then there exists an integer N such that $\|x_n - x_m\| < \epsilon$ if $N \leqslant m$ and $N \leqslant n$. Therefore, for any k,

$$\left(\sum_{i=1}^{k} |\xi_i^{(n)} - \xi_i^{(m)}|^p \right)^{1/p} \leqslant \|x_n - x_m\| < \epsilon$$

if $N \leqslant m$ and $N \leqslant n$. Keeping k and n fixed, let $m \to \infty$. This gives

$$\left(\sum_{i=1}^{k} |\xi_i^{(n)} - \xi_i|^p \right)^{1/p} \leqslant \epsilon$$

if $N \leqslant n$. Since this is true for all k, we can let $k \to \infty$, and we obtain the result that $\|x_n - x\| \leqslant \epsilon$ if $N \leqslant n$. This finishes the proof that l^p is complete.

The form of the foregoing argument is such that it can be adapted to proving the completeness of a number of spaces. To avoid much repetition of essentially the same argument we shall formulate a general theorem which embodies the principle of the argument.

Theorem 3.13–D. *Let Y be a linear space. Let S be a certain class of sequences $\{y_n\}$ of elements of Y, and let $\mathscr{F}$ be a certain family of real-valued functions defined on Y. We assume that S and $\mathscr{F}$ satisfy the following conditions:*

1. With each $\{y_n\} \in S$ is associated a certain element $y \in Y$. This association is indicated by writing $y_n \to y$.

2. If $\{y_n\} \in S$, with $y_n \to y$, then for each fixed k the sequence $\{z_n\}$ with $z_n = y_k - y_n$ is in S, and $z_n \to y_k - y$.

3. If $\{y_n\} \in S$, with $y_n \to y$, then $f(y_n) \to f(y)$ for each $f \in \mathscr{F}$.

4. The class X of $x \in Y$ such that $\sup\limits_{f \in \mathscr{F}} f(x) < +\infty$ is a linear manifold in Y and the function $\|x\|$ on X defined by

$$\|x\| = \sup_{f \in \mathscr{F}} f(x)$$

is a norm on X.

5. If $\{x_n\}$ is a Cauchy sequence in X [relative to the metric topology defined by the norm of (4)], then $\{x_n\} \in S$.
With these assumptions, X is a Banach space (i.e., it is complete).

PROOF. Suppose that $\{x_n\}$ is a Cauchy sequence in X. Then there is some M such that $\|x_n\| \leqslant M$ for all values of n. By (1) and (5) there is some $x \in Y$ such that $x_n \to x$, and by (3) it follows that $f(x_n) \to f(x)$ for each $f \in \mathscr{F}$. Now $f(x_n) \leqslant \|x_n\| \leqslant M$ for each $f \in \mathscr{F}$, by the definition of the norm. Letting $n \to \infty$, we see that $f(x) \leqslant M$. Since this is true for every $f \in \mathscr{F}$, we see by (4) that $x \in X$ and $\|x\| \leqslant M$. Now, if $\epsilon > 0$, there exists an integer N such that $\|x_n - x_m\| < \epsilon$ if $N \leqslant n$ and $N \leqslant m$. Therefore, for each $f \in \mathscr{F}$, $f(x_n - x_m) < \epsilon$ under the same conditions on m and n. Letting $m \to \infty$, we see by (2) and (3) that $f(x_n - x_m) \to f(x_n - x)$, and so $f(x_n - x) \leqslant \epsilon$. This is true for each $f \in \mathscr{F}$ and each $n \geqslant N$. Therefore $\|x_n - x\| \leqslant \epsilon$ if $N \leqslant n$. This finishes the proof that X is complete.

To see the application of this theorem to l^p let Y be the linear space of *all* sequences $y = \{\eta_i\}$, where $\eta_1, \eta_2, \cdots$ are scalars. Let S be the class of all sequences $\{y_n\}$ in Y (where $y_n = \{\eta_i^{(n)}\}$) such that $\lim_{n \to \infty} \eta_i^{(n)} = \eta_i$ exists for $i = 1, 2, \cdots$, and let the associated $y \in Y$ be $\{\eta_i\}$. Let $\mathscr{F}$ be the countable family of functions $f_1, f_2, \cdots$, with f_k defined by

$$f_k(y) = \left(\sum_{i=1}^{k} |\eta_i|^p \right)^{1/p}, \qquad y \in Y.$$

Then Theorem 3.13–D can be applied with $X = l^p$. Our proof that l^p is complete follows exactly the same lines as the proof of Theorem 3.13–D.

It is easy to give examples of incomplete normed linear spaces. Consider, for example, the subset X of l^p $(1 \leqslant p < \infty)$ consisting of sequences $x = \{\xi_n\}$ such that the set of n for which $\xi_n \neq 0$ is finite. This subset of l^p is a linear manifold and can be regarded as a space by itself. It is not complete. For, let x be an element of l^p that is not in X. If $x = \{\xi_n\}$, let $x_n = (\xi_1, \xi_2, \cdots, \xi_n, 0, 0, \cdots)$. Then $x_n \in X$, and $\{x_n\}$ is a Cauchy sequence in X. But the sequence has no limit in X, for, if it did, say $x_n \to y$, we should have $y = x$, since it is readily seen that $x_n \to x$, and the limit of a convergent sequence is unique. But $y \in X$ and $x \notin X$. Thus we have a contradiction, and we have proved that X is not complete.

The essential principle in the foregoing argument shows us the truth of the following statement: If X is a linear manifold in a normed linear space Y such that X is dense in Y but a proper subset of Y, then X, considered as a normed linear space by itself, is not complete.

PROBLEMS

1. Theorem 3.13–D may be used to prove that a number of spaces are complete. Indications of procedure are given below. Details are left to the reader.

a. B(T) is complete (see Example 3, § 3.11). Let Y be the linear space of *all* scalar-valued functions y defined on T. Let S be the class of sequences $\{y_n\}$

from Y such that $\lim_{n\to\infty} y_n(t) = y(t)$ exists for each $t \in T$; then write $y_n \to y$. Let $\mathscr{F}$ be the family of functions f_t, $t \in T$, defined by $f_t(y) = y(t)$.

b. *$BV[a, b]$ is complete* (see Example 7, § 3.11). Choose Y and S as in (a), with $T = [a, b]$. For $\mathscr{F}$ take the class of all function f_Δ, defined by

$$f_\Delta(y) = |y(a)| + \sum_{i=1}^{n} |y(t_i) - y(t_{i-1})|,$$

where Δ is the partition of $[a, b]$ by the points $t_0, t_1, \cdots, t_n$ ($a = t_0 < t_1 < \cdots < t_n = b$); $\mathscr{F}$ is generated by taking all possible Δ's.

c. *H^p is complete*, $1 \leq p \leq \infty$ (see Example 8, § 3.11). Let Y be the class $\mathfrak{A}$ (defined previously) of all functions y of the complex variable t, defined and analytic when $|t| < 1$. Let S be the class of sequences $\{y_n\}$ from Y such that $y_n(t)$ is convergent to a limit $y(t)$ as $n \to \infty$, uniformly with respect to t in every compact set lying in the open unit circle $|t| < 1$. For $\mathscr{F}$ we take the family of functions f_r, defined by

$$f_r(y) = \mathfrak{M}_p[y; r], \qquad 0 \leq r < 1.$$

The meaning of $\mathfrak{M}_p$ is explained in § 3.11; we are now using y where f was used in § 3.11. The X of Theorem 3.13–D is H^p in this case. For $x \in X$ it may be proved that

$$|x(t)| \leq \frac{\|x\|}{1 - |t|}$$

if $|t| < 1$, and from this it follows that condition 5 in Theorem 3.13–D is satisfied. The proof of the inequality runs as follows: Let

$$x(t) = \sum_{n=0}^{\infty} \xi_n t^n$$

$$\xi_n = \frac{1}{2\pi r^n} \int_0^{2\pi} x(re^{i\theta})e^{-in\theta}\, d\theta, \qquad 0 < r < 1.$$

Then

$$r^n|\xi_n| \leq \mathfrak{M}_p[x; r] \leq \|x\|,$$

whence $|\xi_n| \leq \|x\|$ and

$$|x(t)| \leq \sum_{n=0}^{\infty} \|x\|\, |t|^n = \frac{\|x\|}{1 - |t|}.$$

If $p = \infty$ we have the stronger inequality

$$|x(t)| \leq \|x\|.$$

d. *The space $C(T)$ is complete* (Example 4, § 3.11). It suffices to show that $C(T)$ is closed in $B(T)$. This follows from the fact that in $B(T)$ $\|x_n - x\| \to 0$ signifies uniform convergence of $x_n(t)$ to $x(t)$.

e. *The space CA is complete* (Example 9, § 3.11). Argument as in (d), with H^∞ in place of $B(T)$.

2. *The space $L^p(E)$ is complete* (Example 5, § 3.11). Here $1 \leq p < \infty$ and E is a measurable set in Euclidean space of n-dimensions. This fundamental theorem in the theory of Lebesgue integration goes back to work of Fischer and F. Riesz; see, e.g., Titchmarsh, **1**, § 12.5. For the result in a more abstract setting see § 7.1.

3. *The space L^∞ is complete* (Example 6, § 3.11). The argument is left to the reader.

3.14 Quotient Spaces

Let X be a linear space, and M a linear manifold in X. Two elements x_1, $x_2 \in X$ are said to be *equivalent modulo M* if $x_1 - x_2 \in M$. We write $x_1 \equiv x_2 \pmod{M}$. It is clear that this kind of equivalence has the usual properties of an equivalence relation, namely reflexivity, symmetry, and transitivity. Hence X is divided into mutually disjoint equivalence classes, two elements being in the same equivalence class if and only if they are equivalent modulo M. The set of all these equivalence classes is denoted by X/M. We shall explain how to define addition and multiplication by scalars in X/M so that it becomes a linear space. Let $[x]$ denote the equivalence class which contains the element x; thus $[x_1] = [x_2]$ if and only if $x_1 \equiv x_2 \pmod{M}$. We make the definition $[x] + [y] = [x + y]$. To show that $[x] + [y]$ is unambiguously defined we have to show that $[u + v] = [x + y]$ if $[u] = [x]$ and $[v] = [y]$. This is at once evident, however, because $(x + y) - (u + v) = (x - u) + (y - v)$ and M is a linear manifold. We also define $\alpha[x] = [\alpha x]$, observing that $[\alpha x] = [\alpha y]$ if $[x] = [y]$. It is a routine matter to verify that X/M becomes a linear space as a result of these definitions. The zero element of X/M is $[0]$, which is the same as M.

Definition. The linear space X/M, as described in the foregoing paragraph, is called the *quotient space* of X modulo M. The mapping ϕ of X onto X/M defined by $\phi(x) = [x]$ is called the *canonical mapping* of X onto X/M.

To get an intuitive geometric appreciation of the definition of X/M, consider the case in which X is three dimensional and the points of X are represented in a three-dimensional rectangular-coordinate system, the point $x = (\xi_1, \xi_2, \xi_3)$ having ξ_1, ξ_2, ξ_3 as its coordinates. If M is the linear manifold of points $(\xi_1, 0, 0)$ (i.e., the ξ_1-axis), the elements of X/M are the straight lines parallel to the ξ_1-axis. Each such line is uniquely determined by the point $(0, \xi_2, \xi_3)$ in which it intersects the plane $\xi_1 = 0$, and it is readily seen that X/M is isomorphic to the linear manifold of points $(0, \xi_2, \xi_3)$. Again, if M is the linear manifold of points $(\xi_1, \xi_2, 0)$, the elements of X/M are the planes parallel to the plane $\xi_3 = 0$. Each such plane is uniquely determined by the point $(0, 0, \xi_3)$ in which it is pierced by the ξ_3-axis, and X/M is isomorphic to the one-dimensional linear manifold of points $(0, 0, \xi_3)$. The isomorphism between X/M and a certain subspace of X, which is apparent in these particular cases, persists in general, but we shall not pursue this aspect of the situation further.

If X is a normed linear space and the linear manifold M is closed, it is possible to define a norm on X/M.

Theorem 3.14–A. *Let M be a closed linear manifold in the normed linear space X.   For each element $[x] \in X/M$ we define*

$$(3.14–1) \qquad\qquad \|[x]\| = \inf_{y \in [x]} \|y\|.$$

Then $\|[x]\|$ is a norm on X/M.   If X is a Banach space, so is X/M.

PROOF.   We have

$$\|[x_1] + [x_2]\| = \|[x_1 + x_2]\| = \inf_{y \in [x_1 + x_2]} \|y\| = \inf_{u \in [x_1], \, v \in [x_2]} \|u + v\|$$

$$\leqslant \inf_{u \in [x_1]} \|u\| + \inf_{v \in [x_2]} \|v\| = \|[x_1]\| + \|[x_2]\|.$$

Also

$$\|\alpha[x]\| = \|[\alpha x]\| = \inf_{y \in [\alpha x]} \|y\| = \inf_{u \in [x]} \|\alpha u\| = |\alpha| \inf_{u \in [x]} \|u\| = |\alpha| \, \|[x]\|.$$

To show that $\|[x]\|$ is a norm it remains only to show that $[x]$ is the zero element of X/M (i.e., that $x \in M$) if $\|[x]\| = 0$.   Now M is a closed set, and from this it follows that each of the equivalence classes $[x]$ is closed. In fact, $[x]$ is homeomorphic to M by the mapping $y = x + m$ (x fixed, $m \in M$, $y \in [x]$).   If $\|[x]\| = 0$ there is a sequence $\{y_n\}$ such that $y_n \in [x]$ and $\|y_n\| \to 0$.   But then $y_n \to 0$, and so $0 \in [x]$, which means that $x \in M$.   Thus $\|[x]\|$ is a norm on X/M.

Now suppose that X is a Banach space, that is, that X is complete as a metric space.   To show that X/M is complete it suffices to show that every Cauchy sequence in X/M contains a convergent subsequence.   For, if a subsequence of a Cauchy sequence has a limit, it is an easy matter to verify that the sequence itself has this limit.   Let $\{U_n\}$ denote a Cauchy sequence in X/M.   By induction it is possible to select a subsequence $\{U_{n(i)}\}$ such that $\|U_{n(i+1)} - U_{n(i)}\| < 1/2^i$, $i = 1, 2, \cdots$.   For convenience we write $V_i = U_{n(i)}$.   Now select $w_i \in V_{i+1} - V_i$ (this is a vector difference, not a set-theoretic difference) so that $\|w_i\| < 1/2^{i-1}$, $i = 1, 2, \cdots$. This is possible by the way in which the norm is defined in X/M.   Select $v_1 \in V_1$, and, if $v_1, \cdots, v_i$, have been chosen, choose $v_{i+1} \in V_{i+1}$ so that

$w_i = v_{i+1} - v_i$. Then, if $m < n$, $v_n - v_m = (v_n - v_{n-1}) + (v_{n-1} - v_{n-2})$

$+ \cdots + (v_{m+1} - v_m)$, $\|v_n - v_m\| \leqslant \|w_{n-1}\| + \|w_{n-2}\| + \cdots + \|w_m\| < \dfrac{1}{2^{m-1}}$

$+ \cdots + \dfrac{1}{2^{n-2}} < \dfrac{1}{2^{m-2}}$. Therefore $\{v_n\}$ is a Cauchy sequence in X,

and $v = \lim\limits_{n \to \infty} v_n$ exists. Let $V = [v]$. Then

$$\|V_n - V\| = \|[v_n - v]\| \leqslant \|v_n - v\|,$$

so that $V_n \to V$. This finishes the proof that X/M is complete.

For instances of the use of the quotient-space concept, see Theorem 4.3–F and problems 5, 6 in § 4.6.

3.2 Inner-Product Spaces

Definition. A complex linear space X is called an inner-product space if there is defined on $X \times X$ a complex-valued function (x_1, x_2) (called the *inner product* of x_1 and x_2) with the following properties:

1. $(x_1 + x_2, x_3) = (x_1, x_3) + (x_2, x_3)$.
2. $(x_1, x_2) = (\overline{x_2, x_1})$ (the bar denoting complex conjugate).
3. $(\alpha x_1, x_2) = \alpha(x_1, x_2)$.
4. (x, x) is $\geqslant 0$ [it must be real by (2)], and $(x, x) \neq 0$ if $x \neq 0$.

A *real* linear space X is called an inner-product space if there is defined on $X \times X$ a real-valued function (x_1, x_2) with the properties 1–4, except that (2) is to be written without the bar over (x_2, x_1).

Observe that, as a consequence of the properties listed, (x_1, x_2) has the further properties:

$$(x_1, x_2 + x_3) = (x_1, x_2) + (x_1, x_3),$$

$$(x_1, \alpha x_2) = \bar{\alpha}(x_1, x_2),$$

where the bar over α is to be omitted in the case of a real space.

There are fifteen theorems in this section; the last twelve of them refer to orthonormal systems. Of these latter theorems, the principal ones are 3.2–D (the generalized Bessel inequality), 3.2–G (the abstract counterpart of the classical Riesz-Fischer theorem), 3.2–H [one form of the projection theorem; see also problem 4, § 4.81, and § 4.82], 3.2–K (the Parseval identity), and 3.2–L (the Gram-Schmidt orthogonalization process).

The first important fact to be noted about inner-product spaces is that we can use the inner product to define a norm. We must first prove the following theorem.

Theorem 3.2–A. *If X is an inner-product space, then*

$$(3.2–1) \qquad |(x_1, x_2)| \leqslant \sqrt{(x_1, x_1)} \sqrt{(x_2, x_2)}.$$

The equality holds in (3.2–1) *if and only if* x_1 *and* x_2 *are linearly dependent.*

PROOF. For any α and β we have $(\alpha x + \beta y, \alpha x + \beta y) = \alpha \bar{\alpha}(x, x) + \alpha \bar{\beta}(x, y) + \bar{\alpha}\beta(y, x) + \beta \bar{\beta}(y, y) \geqslant 0$. The idea of the proof is to reduce this to an inequality of the form $At^2 + 2Bt + C \geqslant 0$, with A, B, C real constants and t a real variable. We choose $\alpha = t$ (real) and define

$$\beta = \frac{(x, y)}{|(x, y)|} \qquad \text{if } (x, y) \neq 0,$$

$$\beta = 1, \text{ otherwise.}$$

Thus $\bar{\beta}(x, y) = |(x, y)|$ and $\beta \bar{\beta} = 1$. Therefore

$$(3.2–2) \qquad t^2(x, x) + 2t|(x, y)| + (y, y) \geqslant 0$$

for all real t. We conclude that

$$|(x, y)|^2 - (x, x)(y, y) \leqslant 0,$$

which is equivalent to (3.2–1). The equality $|(x, y)|^2 = (x, x)(y, y)$ can hold when $x \neq 0$ if and only if there is a real value of t for which the quadratic form in (3.2–2) takes on the value 0. But, because of the origin of the quadratic form, we see that this occurs if and only if $tx + \beta y = 0$ for some real t and some β such that $|\beta| = 1$. This relation implies and is implied by the statement that x and y are linearly dependent, provided that $x \neq 0$. When $x = 0$ the equality holds in (3.2–1), of course, and also x and y are linearly dependent. Thus the proof is complete.

The inequality (3.2–1) is known as *Schwarz's inequality*.

Theorem 3.2–B. *If X is an inner-product space,* $\sqrt{(x, x)}$ *has the properties of a norm.*

PROOF. We write $\|x\| = \sqrt{(x, x)}$. The only requisite property of $\|x\|$ that is not immediately apparent is the triangular inequality property. Now

$$\|x + y\|^2 = (x, x) + (x, y) + (y, x) + (y, y).$$

For complex A we write $\operatorname{Re} A = \frac{1}{2}(A + \bar{A}) = $ real part of A. Since $|\operatorname{Re} A| \leqslant |A|$, we see that

$$\|x + y\|^2 \leqslant \|x\|^2 + 2|(x, y)| + \|y\|^2.$$

With (3.2–1) this gives

$$\|x + y\|^2 \leqslant \|x\|^2 + 2\|x\| \, \|y\| + \|y\|^2 = (\|x\| + \|y\|)^2.$$

Consequently $\|x + y\| \leqslant \|x\| + \|y\|$, and the proof is complete.

While the norm is expressible in terms of the inner product, it is also true that the inner product is expressible in terms of the norm.   If X is a *real* inner-product space, we have

(3.2–3) $(x, y) = \frac{1}{4}[\|x + y\|^2 - \|x - y\|^2]$.

If X is a *complex* inner-product space, the real and imaginary parts of (x, y) are expressible in the forms

(3.2–4) $\text{Re}\,(x, y) = \frac{1}{4}[\|x + y\|^2 - \|x - y\|^2]$,

(3.2–5) $\text{Im}\,(x, y) = -\,\frac{1}{4}[\|ix + y\|^2 - \|ix - y\|^2]$.

The validity of these formulas is readily verified by direct simplification of the expressions on the right, using the properties of the inner product.

Throughout the rest of this section the discussion and theorems are concerned with inner-product spaces, and we shall not repeat this fact every time in stating theorems.   It is furthermore assumed that an inner-product space is given the topology of a normed linear space, using the norm $\|x\| = \sqrt{(x, x)}$.

Theorem 3.2–C.   *The inner product (x_1, x_2) is a continuous function on $X \times X$.*

PROOF.   Let $x_1 - u_1 = v_1$, $x_2 - u_2 = v_2$, where x_1, x_2, u_1, u_2 are arbitrary.   Then

$$(x_1, x_2) - (u_1, u_2) = (u_1 + v_1, u_2 + v_2) - (u_1, u_2)$$
$$= (u_1, v_2) + (v_1, u_2) + (v_1, v_2).$$

Therefore, using (3.2–1) and the definitions of v_1, v_2, we have

$$|(x_1, x_2) - (u_1, u_2)| \leqslant \|u_1\|\,\|x_2 - u_2\|$$
$$+ \|x_1 - u_1\|\,\|u_2\| + \|x_1 - u_1\|\,\|x_2 - u_2\|.$$

The asserted continuity is now evident.

Examples of inner-product spaces.   The space l^2 is an inner-product space, with inner product

$$(x, y) = \sum_{n=1}^{\infty} \xi_n \bar{\eta}_n,$$

where $x = \{\xi_n\}$, $y = \{\eta_n\}$.

The space $L^2(a, b)$ is an inner-product space, with inner product

$$(x, y) = \int_a^b x(t)\,\overline{y(t)}\, dt.$$

The two spaces just mentioned are complete.   We can get many examples of *incomplete* inner-product spaces by selecting nonclosed linear manifolds in the aforementioned spaces.   For instance, the subspace of $L^2(a, b)$ which is composed of elements corresponding to functions continuous on $[a, b]$ is an incomplete inner-product space.

The n-dimensional space $l^2(n)$ is an inner-product space, with

$$(x, y) = \sum_{k=1}^{n} \xi_k \bar{\eta}_k.$$

One of the most important notions in an inner-product space is that of orthogonality.

Definition.   We say that x and y are *orthogonal* if $(x, y) = 0$.   The statement "x and y are orthogonal" is often expressed symbolically in the form $x \perp y$.

Observe that $x \perp y$ is equivalent to $y \perp x$; also, $x \perp 0$ for every x.

Definition.   A set S of vectors is called an *orthogonal set* if $x \perp y$ for every pair x, y for which $x \in S$, $y \in S$, and $x \neq y$.   If in addition $\|x\| = 1$ for every $x \in S$, the set is called an *orthonormal set*.

The remainder of this section is devoted to a discussion of orthonormal sets.   One of the main goals of the discussion is the determination of the nature of the closed linear manifold generated by a given orthonormal set: How is it related to the whole space?   How may an element of the manifold be expressed in terms of the elements of the orthonormal set? We find here the inequality of Bessel and the Parseval identity.   These are the general forms of the relations bearing these names which occur in the theory of Fourier series.

Theorem 3.2–D.   *Let S be an orthonormal set.   If $u_1, \cdots, u_n$ is any finite collection of distinct elements of S, and $x \in X$, then*

(3.2–6)
$$\sum_{i=1}^{n} |(x, u_i)|^2 \leqslant \|x\|^2.$$

The set of those $u \in S$ such that $(x, u) \neq 0$ (x any fixed element of X) is either finite or countably infinite.   If $x, y \in X$,

(3.2–7)
$$\sum_{u \in S} |(x, u)\,(\overline{y, u})| \leqslant \|x\|\,\|y\|,$$

it being understood that the sum on the left includes all $u \in S$ for which $(x, u)(\overline{y, u}) \neq 0$, and is, therefore, either a finite series or an absolutely convergent series with a countable infinity of terms.

PROOF. To prove (3.2–6) we write $\xi_i = (x, u_i)$. Then

$$0 \leqslant \left(x - \sum_1^n \xi_i u_i, \ x - \sum_1^n \xi_j u_j \right)$$

$$= (x, x) - \sum_1^n \bar{\xi}_j(x, u_j) - \sum_1^n \xi_i(u_i, x) + \sum_i \sum_j \xi_i \bar{\xi}_j(u_i, u_j).$$

But $(u_i, u_j) = \delta_{ij}$, since S is orthonormal. If we take into account the definition of ξ_i, we see that

$$0 \leqslant \|x\|^2 - \sum_j |\xi_j|^2 - \sum_i |\xi_i|^2 + \sum_i |\xi_i|^2 = \|x\|^2 - \sum_j |\xi_j|^2,$$

and this is equivalent to (3.2–6).

It follows from (3.2–6) that, if $x \in X$ and n is a positive integer, the number of elements u of S such that $|(x, u)| \geqslant 1/n$ cannot exceed $n^2\|x\|^2$. Since $|(x, u)| \geqslant 1/n$ for some n if $(x, u) \neq 0$, the set of those $u \in S$ such that $(x, u) \neq 0$ is a countable union of finite sets and is, therefore, either finite or countably infinite. The inequality (3.2–7) now follows from (3.2–6), for, if $u_1, \cdots, u_n$ is a finite collection of distinct elements of S, we have

$$\sum_{i=1}^n |(x, u_i)\overline{(y, u_i)}| \leqslant \left(\sum_{i=1}^n |(x, u_i)|^2 \right)^{\frac{1}{2}} \left(\sum_{i=1}^n |(y, u_i)|^2 \right)^{\frac{1}{2}} \leqslant \|x\| \, \|y\|,$$

by (3.2–6) and Cauchy's inequality.

Examples of orthonormal sets. In the space l^2 let $e_k(k = 1, 2, \cdots)$ be that element $x = \{\xi_n\}$ for which $\xi_n = 0$ if $n \neq k$, and $\xi_k = 1$. The set of all the e_k's, or any nonempty subset of this set, is an orthonormal set.

In the complex space $L^2(0, 2\pi)$ let u_n be the element corresponding to the function $(1/\sqrt{2\pi})e^{int}(n = 0, \pm 1, \pm 2, \cdots)$. Since

$$\frac{1}{2\pi} \int_0^{2\pi} e^{imt} \, e^{-int} \, dt = \begin{cases} 1 & \text{if } m = n \\ 0 & \text{if } m \neq n \end{cases}$$

we see that the various elements u_n form an orthonormal set.

If we deal with the *real* space $L^2(0, 2\pi)$, the elements determined by the functions

$$\frac{1}{\sqrt{2\pi}}, \qquad \frac{1}{\sqrt{\pi}} \cos t, \qquad \frac{1}{\sqrt{\pi}} \cos 2t, \qquad \cdots$$

$$\frac{1}{\sqrt{\pi}} \sin t, \qquad \frac{1}{\sqrt{\pi}} \sin 2t, \qquad \cdots$$

form an orthonormal set.

Other examples of orthonormal sets are mentioned in § 3.22.

Theorem 3.2–E.   *Suppose X is separable and that S is an orthonormal set in X.   Then S is either a finite or a countably infinite set.*

PROOF.   If $x \perp y$ and $\|x\| = \|y\| = 1$, we have

$$(x - y, x - y) = (x, x) - (x, y) - (y, x) + (y, y) = 2,$$

or $\|x - y\| = \sqrt{2}$.   Thus, in an orthonormal set, each pair of distinct elements are a distance $\sqrt{2}$ apart.   Now let $\{y_n\}$ be a denumerable set everywhere dense in X.   Then to each $x \in S$ corresponds some n, depending on x, such that $\|x - y_n\| < \sqrt{2}/3$.   If x and u are distinct members of S and if $\|u - y_m\| < \sqrt{2}/3$, then

$$\sqrt{2} = \|x - u\| \leqslant \|x - y_n\| + \|y_n - y_m\| + \|y_m - u\|$$

$$< \frac{2\sqrt{2}}{3} + \|y_n - y_m\|,$$

or

$$\frac{\sqrt{2}}{3} < \|y_n - y_m\|,$$

so that $n \neq m$.   There is thus a one-to-one correspondence between the elements of the orthonormal set S and the elements of a subset of the countable set $\{y_n\}$.   This proves the theorem.

Theorem 3.2–F.   *Let $u_1, \cdots, u_n$ be a finite orthonormal set in the space X, and let M be the subspace of X generated by $u_1, \cdots, u_n$.   Then $u_1, \cdots, u_n$ is a basis for M, and the coefficients in a representation $x = \xi_1 u_1 + \cdots + \xi_n u_n$ of an element of M are related to x by the formulas $\xi_i = (x, u_i)$.*

PROOF.   If $x = \xi_1 u_1 + \cdots + \xi_n u_n$, then

$$(x, u_i) = \xi_1(u_1, u_i) + \cdots + \xi_n(u_n, u_i) = \xi_i,$$

by the orthonormality relations.   If $x = 0$ it follows that $\xi_1 = \cdots = \xi_n = 0$.   Hence we see that the u_i's form a linearly independent set and, hence, form a basis for the subspace which they generate.

Theorem 3.2–G.   *Suppose X is complete, and let $\{u_n\}$ be a countably infinite orthonormal set in X.   Then a series of the form $\sum_{1}^{\infty} \xi_n u_n$ is convergent if and only if $\sum_{1}^{\infty} |\xi_n|^2 < \infty$, and in that case we have the relations*

$$\xi_n = (x, u_n), \qquad x = \sum_{1}^{\infty} \xi_n u_n,$$

between the coefficients ξ_n and the element x defined by the series.

PROOF.   Let $s_n = \xi_1 u_1 + \cdots + \xi_n u_n$. Then, if $m < n$, the orthonormality relations and the relation between the norm and inner product lead to the formula

$$\|s_n - s_m\|^2 = \left\| \sum_{i=m+1}^{n} \xi_i u_i \right\|^2 = \sum_{i=m+1}^{n} |\xi_i|^2.$$

Since X is complete, it is now clear that the sequence $\{s_n\}$ is convergent in X if and only if $\sum_1^{\infty} |\xi_i|^2 < \infty$.   If this latter condition is satisfied, and if $x = \lim\limits_{n \to \infty} s_n$, we prove that $\xi_i = (x, u_i)$ as follows: By Theorem 3.2–F we know that $\xi_i = (s_n, u_i)$ if $1 \leqslant i \leqslant n$.   But $s_n \to x$ and hence $(s_n, u_i) \to (x, u_i)$ when $n \to \infty$, by the continuity of the inner product.   Therefore $\xi_i = (x, u_i)$.   This completes the proof.

The Riesz-Fischer theorem in the theory of Fourier series is a concrete instance of Theorem 3.2–G.   This theorem asserts that, if $a_0, a_1, a_2, \cdots$ and $b_1, b_2, \cdots$ are sequences of real constants such that

$$\frac{a_0^2}{2} + \sum_1^{\infty} (a_n^2 + b_n^2) < \infty,$$

there exists a function x of class $\mathscr{L}^2(0, 2\pi)$ having a_n and b_n as its Fourier coefficients, i.e.,

$$a_n = \frac{1}{\pi} \int_0^{2\pi} x(t) \cos nt \, dt, \qquad b_n = \frac{1}{\pi} \int_0^{2\pi} x(t) \sin nt \, dt.$$

We take X to be $L^2(0, 2\pi)$ and for $u_1, u_2, u_3, u_4, u_5, \cdots$ the elements of X corresponding to

$$\frac{1}{\sqrt{2\pi}}, \qquad \frac{\cos t}{\sqrt{\pi}}, \qquad \frac{\sin t}{\sqrt{\pi}}, \qquad \frac{\cos 2t}{\sqrt{\pi}}, \qquad \frac{\sin 2t}{\sqrt{\pi}}, \cdots.$$

The coefficients $\xi_1, \xi_2, \cdots$ in Theorem 3.2–G are related to the standard Fourier coefficients by the formulas

$$\xi_1 = a_0 \sqrt{\pi/2}, \qquad \xi_2 = a_1 \sqrt{\pi}, \qquad \xi_3 = b_1 \sqrt{\pi}, \cdots.$$

If x is orthogonal to each element of a set S, we say that x is orthogonal to S, and write $x \perp S$.   Since the inner product is continuous, it follows that if $x \perp y_n$ and $y_n \to y$, then also $x \perp y$.   Also, if $x \perp y$ and $x \perp z$, then $x \perp (y + z)$ and $x \perp (\alpha y)$ for every scalar α.   Hence, if $x \perp S$, then x is also orthogonal to the linear manifold generated by S, and to the closure of this linear manifold.

Theorem 3.2–H.   *Let S be an orthonormal set in the space X. If S is* *infinite, assume further that X is complete. For each $x \in X$ there is an element of X unambiguously defined by*

$$x_S = \sum_{u \in S} (x, u)u.$$

Let M be the closed manifold generated by S. Then $x \in M$ if and only if $x = x_S$. In any case, $x_S \in M$ and $(x - x_S) \perp M$.

PROOF. If $x \in X$, we know by Theorem 3.2–D that $(x, u) \neq 0$ for at most a countably infinite number of elements $u \in S$. If we index the u's for which $(x, u) \neq 0$, in some arbitrary order, say $u_1, u_2, \cdots$, the series $\sum_n (x, u_n)u_n$, if infinite, is convergent (by Theorems 3.2–D and 3.2–G). Moreover, the series remains convergent, no matter how its terms are rearranged, as may be seen by the first part of the proof of Theorem 3.2–G, using the fact that the series $\sum_n |(x, u_n)|^2$ is absolutely convergent. We may then show that the series $\sum_n (x, u_n)u_n$ converges to the same element, no matter how the terms are rearranged. For, if $\{v_n\}$ is a rearrangement of $\{u_n\}$, and

$$x_1 = \sum_n (x, u_n)u_n, \qquad x_2 = \sum_n (x, v_n)v_n,$$

we have $(x_1, u_n) = (x, u_n)$ and $(x_2, v_n) = (x, v_n)$, by Theorem 3.2–G. Thus, if $u_n = v_{m(n)}$, we have $(x_1 - x_2, u_n) = (x_1, u_n) - (x_2, u_n) = (x, u_n) - (x_2, v_{m(n)}) = (x, u_n) - (x, u_n) = 0$, and from this it follows, on setting $\alpha_n = (x, u_n)$, $\beta_n = (x, v_n)$, that

$$\|x_1 - x_2\|^2 = \left(x_1 - x_2, \sum_n \alpha_n u_n - \sum_n \beta_n v_n\right)$$

$$= \sum_n \bar{\alpha}_n(x_1 - x_2, u_n) - \sum_n \bar{\beta}_n(x_1 - x_2, v_n) = 0,$$

whence $x_1 = x_2$. These considerations show us that the notation $\sum_{u \in S} (x, u)u$ has an unambiguous meaning and defines an element which we denote by x_S. Evidently $x_S \in M$. To prove $(x - x_S) \perp M$ it suffices to prove $(x - x_S) \perp S$. Let v be an arbitrary element of S. Then

$$(x - x_S, v) = (x, v) - \sum_{u \in S} (x, u)(u, v)$$

$$= (x, v) - (x, v) = 0,$$

and hence $(x - x_S) \perp S$.

Since $x_S \in M$, it remains only to prove that $x_S = x$ if $x \in M$. Now, if $x \in M$, then $x - x_S \in M$, and since $(x - x_S) \perp M$, we have

$$\|x - x_S\|^2 = (x - x_S, x - x_S) = 0,$$

whence $x = x_S$. It is clear from a scrutiny of the proof that we need not assume the completeness of X if S is a finite set, for in that case no convergence questions arise, and the linear manifold generated by S, being finite dimensional, is closed.

Definition. An orthonormal set S in the space X is called *complete* if there exists no orthonormal set of which S is a proper subset. In other words, S is called complete if it is maximal with respect to the property of being orthonormal.

Theorem 3.2–I. *Every inner-product space X having a nonzero element contains a complete orthonormal set. Moreover, if S is any orthonormal set in X, there is a complete orthonormal set containing S as a subset.*

PROOF. Let S be an orthonormal set in X. Such sets certainly exist; for instance, if $x \neq 0$, the set consisting merely of $x/\|x\|$ is orthonormal. Let P be the class of all orthonormal sets having S as a subset. It is easily verified that P satisfies the conditions of Zorn's lemma (§ 1.7). Thus P contains a maximal member.

Theorem 3.2–J. *Let S be an orthonormal set in X, and let M be the closed linear manifold generated by S. If $M = X$, it follows that S is complete. If the space X is complete and the orthonormal set S is complete (i.e., maximal), then $M = X$.*

PROOF. If S is not complete, there exists some $x \neq 0$ such that $x \perp S$, and hence also $x \perp M$. Now, if $M = X$, we have $x \perp x$, which implies $x = 0$. Thus, if S is not complete, we must conclude that $M \neq X$. This proves the first part of the theorem. Let us now assume that X is complete. Then, if $M \neq X$, suppose $x \in X - M$ and construct x_S as in Theorem 3.2–H. Then let

$$y = \frac{x - x_S}{\|x - x_S\|}.$$

Then the set consisting of S and y is orthonormal, and $y \notin S$, so that S cannot be complete. This completes the proof.

The assumption that X is complete in the second part of the theorem is essential, for it has been shown by an example that, if X is incomplete, it can happen that there is no orthonormal set in X such that the closed linear manifold generated by the set is all of X (see Dixmier, **2**).

Example of a complete orthonormal set. We have already mentioned the orthonormal set composed of $e_1, e_2, e_3, \cdots$ in the space l^2. This is a complete orthonormal set, as we now prove. If $x = \{\xi_n\}$ let $x_n = \xi_1 e_1 + \cdots + \xi_n e_n$. Then

$$\|x - x_n\|^2 = \sum_{k=n+1}^{\infty} |\xi_k|^2,$$

and so $\|x - x_n\| \to 0$. It follows that the closed linear manifold generated by the elements $e_1, e_2, \cdots$ is all of l^2. Hence, by Theorem 3.2–J the orthonormal set is complete. In this example we observe that $\xi_n = (x, e_n)$ and hence that

$$\|x\|^2 = \sum_{n=1}^{\infty} |(x, e_n)|^2.$$

In the next theorem we see that this formula is a special case of a relation which is characteristic of complete orthonormal sets, provided we deal with complete spaces.

Theorem 3.2–K. *Let S be an orthonormal set in X. Suppose that*

$$(3.2\text{–}8) \qquad \|x\|^2 = \sum_{u \in S} |(x, u)|^2$$

for every $x \in X$. Then S is complete. On the other hand, if we assume that X is a complete space and that S is a complete orthonormal set, it follows that (3.2–8) holds true for every $x \in X$.

PROOF. If S is not complete, there exists some $x \neq 0$ such that $x \perp S$. But (3.2–8) then gives $\|x\|^2 = 0$. This proves the first assertion. Now suppose that X is complete (as a metric space) and that S is complete (as an orthonormal set). For each $x \in X$ there is some finite or countable set $\{u_n\}$ in S such that

$$x = \sum_{u \in S} (x, u)u = \sum_{n} \xi_n u_n, \qquad \xi_n = (x, u_n).$$

Here we use Theorems 3.2–H and 3.2–J. Now

$$\|x\|^2 = \left(\sum_{n} \xi_n u_n, \sum_{m} \xi_m u_m \right) = \sum_{n} \sum_{m} \xi_n \bar{\xi}_m (u_n, u_m) = \sum_{n} |\xi_n|^2,$$

by the orthonormality relations. The equality just obtained is equivalent to (3.2–8).

The equality (3.2–8) is called *Parseval's formula.*   The inequality

$$(3.2\text{–}9) \qquad \sum_{u \in S} |(x, u)|^2 \leqslant \|x\|^2,$$

which holds for *all* orthonormal systems, complete or not (see Theorem 3.2–D), is called *Bessel's inequality.*

The same method which was used to derive (3.2–8) may be used to prove Parseval's formula in the more general form

$$(3.2\text{–}10) \qquad (x, y) = \sum_{u \in S} (x, u)(\overline{y, u}),$$

where S is a complete orthonormal set, and x, y are arbitrary elements of X.   It is assumed that X is a complete space.

There is an important constructive process for obtaining an orthonormal set from a finite or countable linearly independent set.

Theorem 3.2–L.   *Suppose $\{x_n\}$ is a finite or countable linearly independent set.   Then, there exists an orthonormal set having the same cardinal number and generating the same linear manifold as the given set.*

PROOF.   Certainly $x_1 \neq 0$.   We define y_1, y_2, $\cdots$ and u_1, u_2, $\cdots$ recursively, as follows:

$$y_1 = x_1 \qquad\qquad u_1 = \frac{y_1}{\|y_1\|},$$

$$y_2 = x_2 - (x_2, u_1)u_1 \qquad\qquad u_2 = \frac{y_2}{\|y_2\|},$$

$$\cdots \qquad\qquad\qquad \cdots$$

$$y_{n+1} = x_{n+1} - \sum_{k=1}^{n} (x_{n+1}, u_k)u_k, \qquad u_{n+1} = \frac{y_{n+1}}{\|y_{n+1}\|},$$

$$\cdots \qquad\qquad\qquad \cdots$$

The process terminates if the set of x's is finite.   Otherwise it continues indefinitely.   It is clear by induction that u_n is a linear combination of $x_1, \cdots, x_n$, and vice versa.   Thus, the linear manifold generated by the u's is the same as that generated by the x's.   Observe that $y_n \neq 0$, because the set $x_1, \cdots, x_n$ is linearly independent.   By direct calculation we see that $(y_{n+1}, u_i) = 0$ if $i = 1, \cdots, n$.   From this it follows that the u's form an orthonormal set.

This process of constructing the u's from the x's is called the Gram-Schmidt orthogonalization process.

For a finite-dimensional space we obtain the following result:

Theorem 3.2–M. *If X is a space of finite dimension $n \geqslant 1$, it has a basis which is an orthonormal set.   Moreover, every complete orthonormal set in X is a basis.*

PROOF.   If $x_1, \cdots, x_n$ is any basis of X, the Gram-Schmidt process gives us an orthonormal basis $u_1, \cdots, u_n$.   An orthonormal set is linearly independent, as we saw in the proof of Theorem 3.2–F.   It follows from Theorem 3.2–J that a complete orthonormal set in X is necessarily a basis.

Theorem 3.2–N. *Suppose X is infinite dimensional and separable (though not necessarily complete).   Then, there exists in X a countable complete orthonormal set S such that the closed linear manifold generated by S is X.*

PROOF.   Since X is separable, there exists a countable set $\{x_n\}$ which is everywhere dense in X.   Let y_1 be the first nonzero element in the sequence $\{x_n\}$, y_2 the first x_n which is not in the linear manifold generated by y_1, and y_{k+1} the first x_n which is not in the linear manifold generated by $y_1, \cdots, y_k$.   It is clear that the x's and the y's generate the same linear manifold and hence the same closed linear manifold.   This manifold is the whole space X, because the set of x's is dense in X.   Applying the Gram-Schmidt process to the y's, we obtain an orthonormal set which generates the closed linear manifold X and which must therefore be complete, by the first part of Theorem 3.2–J.   The orthonormal set cannot be finite, since X is not finite dimensional.

The assumption in Theorem 3.2–N that X is separable is essential, even if we omit the word "countable" in the conclusion.   This can be shown by an example; see the remarks following the proof of Theorem 3.2–J.

Theorem 3.2–O. *Let X be an inner-product space, and let S_1 and S_2 be two complete orthonormal sets in X.   Then S_1 and S_2 have the same cardinal number (i.e., there is a one-to-one correspondence between the elements of S_1 and S_2).*

PROOF.   Suppose that one of the sets S_1, S_2, say S_1, is finite, and let M be the closed linear manifold determined by S_1.   Then $M = X$, for otherwise the set S_1 would not be complete, as we can see readily with the aid of Theorem 3.2–H.   Hence X is finite dimensional.   But then S_1 and S_2 are both bases for X, by Theorem 3.2–M, and the sets S_1, S_2 must both have the same finite number of elements.   For the remainder of the proof we therefore assume that S_1 and S_2 are both infinite sets.   For each $x \in S_1$ let $S_2(x)$ be the set of those elements $y \in S_2$ such that $(x, y) \neq 0$.   We know by Theorem 3.2–D that $S_2(x)$ is an at most countably infinite set. If $y \in S_2$, then $\|y\| = 1$, and it follows from the completeness of S_1 that there is some $x \in S_1$ such that $y \in S_2(x)$ (since otherwise S_1 together with y would be an orthonormal set). Hence we see that

$$(3.2\text{–}11) \qquad\qquad S_2 = \bigcup_{x \in S_1} S_2(x).$$

Now let A_1, A_2 be the cardinal numbers of the sets S_1, S_2 respectively, and let A_0 be the cardinal number of the set of positive integers. The relation (3.2–11) shows that $A_2 \leqslant A_0 A_1$. But it is known that, if A is any infinite cardinal number, then $A_0 A = A$ (see, for example, Sierpinski, 1, § 103). Thus, we see that $A_2 \leqslant A_1$. So far we have used only the completeness of S_1. If S_2 is also complete, we can exchange the roles of S_1 and S_2 and so conclude $A_1 \leqslant A_2$. But then $A_1 = A_2$, and the proof is finished.

PROBLEM

If X is a complex complete inner-product space, there exists an operator C of the following sort: The domain of C is X, the range of C is in X, and C has the properties

$$C(x + y) = Cx + Cy, \qquad C(\alpha x) = \bar{\alpha} Cx,$$
$$C^2 x = x, \qquad\qquad \|Cx\| = \|x\|.$$

Such an operator may be called a *conjugation* of X, and the notation $\bar{x} = Cx$ is appropriate. The further property $(Cx, Cy) = \overline{(x, y)}$ may be deduced, using (3.2–4) and (3.2–5). Furthermore, the range of C is *all* of X, and C has the inverse $C^{-1} = C$. To obtain such an operator, let S be a complete orthonormal set in X, and if $x = \sum_{u \in S} (x, u)u$ is the representation of x, let

$$Cx = \sum_{u \in S} (\overline{x, u})u.$$

3.21 Hilbert Spaces

Definition. An inner-product space which is infinite dimensional and complete is called a *Hilbert space* (real or complex, according to whether the scalar field is real or complex). If X is a finite-dimensional inner-product space, we shall call it a *Euclidean space*.

In the early literature on Hilbert spaces, it was usual to assume separability as part of the definition of a Hilbert space, and separability was used in proving some of the most important theorems. But it was subsequently discovered that these theorems could be proved without the hypothesis of separability, and the current practice is to invoke this hypothesis when it is needed, but not otherwise.

Some writers have used the adjective *Euclidean* for any complete inner-product space, or even for incomplete inner-product space. Also, *complex* inner-product spaces of finite dimension are frequently called *unitary* spaces.

An incomplete inner-product space X, being a normed linear space, can be completed in the manner described in § 3.13. Moreover, if Y is the completion of X, we can define an inner product on $Y \times Y$ by

$$(y, z) = \lim_{n \to \infty} (x_n, u_n),$$

where y, z are equivalence classes of Cauchy sequences from X containing $\{x_n\}$ and $\{u_n\}$, respectively. The existence of the limit defining (y, z) may be seen with the aid of the formulas (3.2–3)–(3.2–5). We leave it for the reader to take care of the details of showing that (y, z) has all the requisite properties of an inner product. We see then that any incomplete inner-product space X can be extended to form a Hilbert space in which X is everywhere dense. Because of this fact, an incomplete inner-product space may be descriptively called a *pre-Hilbert space*. This terminology has been used by a number of writers.

We now give some theorems about concrete representations of Euclidean and Hilbert spaces.

Theorem 3.21–A. *Every Euclidean space X of finite dimension $n(n \geqslant 1)$ is congruent to $l^2(n)$.*

PROOF. For the definition of congruence see § 3.1. We can choose for X an orthonormal basis $u_1, \cdots, u_n$. Then, if $x = \xi_1 u_1 + \cdots + \xi_n u_n$, the correspondence $x \leftrightarrow (\xi_1, \cdots, \xi_n)$ establishes the congruence of X and $l^2(n)$. The isometric character of the correspondence follows by direct calculation, for, if $y = \eta_1 u_1 + \cdots + \eta_n u_n$, we have

$$(x, y) = \xi_1 \bar{\eta}_1 + \cdots + \xi_n \bar{\eta}_n.$$

Hence

$$\|x\| = (|\xi_1|^2 + \cdots + |\xi_n|^2)^{\frac{1}{2}},$$

and the right member of this equation is the norm of $(\xi_1, \cdots, \xi_n)$ in $l^2(n)$.

It is interesting to observe that, if two inner-product spaces X and Y are congruent and if T is the operator which maps X isomorphically and isometrically onto Y, we not only have $\|Tx\| = \|x\|$, but also $(Tx_1, Tx_2) = (x_1, x_2)$, for every pair x_1, x_2 in X. That this is so follows directly from formulas (3.2–3)–(3.2–5).

Theorem 3.21–B. *Let X be a separable Hilbert space. Then X is congruent to l^2.*

PROOF. We know (Theorem 3.2–N) that X contains a countable complete orthonormal set $\{u_n\}$. If $x \in X$, let $\xi_n = (x, u_n)$. Then the sequence $\{\xi_n\}$ belongs to l^2 and

$$\|x\|^2 = \sum_{n=1}^{\infty} |\xi_n|^2,$$

by Parseval's formula (3.2–8). Moreover, every $\{\xi_n\} \in l^2$ arises from some $x \in X$ in this way, by Theorem 3.2–G. The correspondence $x \leftrightarrow \{\xi_n\}$ clearly establishes an isometric and isomorphic correspondence between the elements of X and l^2, so that these spaces are congruent.

In order to get a result like that of Theorem 3.21–B for nonseparable Hilbert spaces we must first construct a space somewhat like l^2, but of such a character that it need not be separable.

Definition of the Space $l^2[Q]$. Let Q be any nonempty set of elements. Let $l^2[Q]$ be the class of all complex-valued functions x defined on Q such that the set of $q \in Q$ for which $x(q) \neq 0$ is either finite or countable and, moreover,

$$\sum_{q \in Q} |x(q)|^2 < \infty.$$

This class becomes a complex inner-product space if we define $x + y$ and αx as usual with functions and define the inner product by

$$(x, y) = \sum_{q \in Q} x(q)\overline{y(q)}.$$

Moreover, the space is complete. This is clear if Q is a finite set with n elements or if Q is countable, for in these cases $l^2[Q]$ is congruent to $l^2(n)$ and to l^2 respectively (in fact $l^2[Q]$ is $l^2(n)$ if Q is the set of integers $1, \cdots, n$ and $l^2[Q]$ is l^2 if Q is the set of *all* positive integers). If Q is uncountable, the fact that $l^2[Q]$ is complete follows readily from the fact that l^2 is complete (see § 3.13).

We have defined the *complex* space $l^2[Q]$; it is clear that, if we require all the functions x to be real-valued, we get a real inner-product space.

Now, for each $p \in Q$ let x_p be the function defined by $x_p(q) = 0$ if $p \neq q$, $x_p(p) = 1$. The set of all the x_p's is an orthonormal set; clearly its cardinal number is the same as that of the set Q. Hence, by Theorem 3.2–E, $l^2[Q]$ is not separable if Q is uncountable. The orthonormal set formed by the x_p's is complete. For, if $x \in l^2[Q]$, the definition of the inner product shows that $(x, x_p) = x(p)$, and thus, by the definition of the norm,

$$\|x\|^2 = \sum_{p \in Q} |(x, x_p)|^2.$$

Therefore the orthonormal set is complete, by Theorem 3.2–K.

This example shows that there exist Hilbert spaces having complete orthonormal sets whose cardinal number is any specified infinite cardinal.

Theorem 3.21–C. *Let X be a Hilbert space for which the cardinal number of any one (and hence of every) complete orthonormal set is A. Let Q be any set the cardinal number of whose elements is A. Then X is congruent to $l^2[Q]$.*

The proof is just like that of Theorem 3.21–B.

3.22 The Completeness of Certain Orthonormal Sets

Example I. It was mentioned in § 3.2 that the functions $(1/\sqrt{2\pi})e^{int}$ $n = 0, \pm 1, \pm 2, \cdots$ determine an orthonormal set in the complex space $L^2(0, 2\pi)$. It is a fact of paramount importance in the theory of Fourier series that this orthonormal set is complete, i.e., that, if

$$\int_0^{2\pi} x(t)e^{int}\, dt = 0$$

for all integers n, then $x(t) =^0 0$. For a proof see Zygmund, **1**, § 1.5. By Theorem 3.2–K the completeness also finds its expression in the Parseval relation

(3.22–1) $$\frac{1}{2\pi} \int_0^{2\pi} |x(t)|^2\, dt = \sum_{n=-\infty}^{\infty} |c_n|^2$$

where

$$c_n = \frac{1}{2\pi} \int_0^{2\pi} x(t)e^{-int}\, dt.$$

The real functions

$$(1/\sqrt{2\pi}), \qquad (1/\sqrt{\pi}) \cos t, \qquad (1/\sqrt{\pi}) \cos 2t,$$
$$(1/\sqrt{\pi}) \sin t, \qquad (1/\sqrt{\pi}) \sin 2t, \qquad \cdots$$

also form a complete orthonormal system. The Parseval relation here (for real functions), in terms of the usual Fourier coefficients, is

(3.22–2) $$\frac{1}{\pi} \int_0^{2\pi} \{x(t)\}^2\, dt = \frac{a_0^2}{2} + \sum_1^{\infty} (a_n^2 + b_n^2).$$

Example 2.   In the space $L^2(-\infty, \infty)$ one example of a complete ortho-normal system is furnished by the elements corresponding to the Hermite functions, which are defined in terms of the Hermite polynomials.   These polynomials are

$$H_n(t) = (-1)^n e^{t^2} \frac{d^n}{dt^n} e^{-t^2}, \qquad n = 0, 1, 2, \cdots,$$

and the Hermite function ψ_n is defined as

$$\psi_n(t) = (2^n n! \sqrt{\pi})^{-\frac{1}{2}} H_n(t) e^{-t^2/2}.$$

The fact that the ψ_n's are pairwise orthogonal is a consequence of the fact that

$$\psi_n''(t) - t^2 \psi_n(t) = -(2n + 1)\psi_n(t).$$

For proofs that the ψ_n's form a complete orthonormal set see Wiener, **1**, page 64, and Achieser and Glasmann, **1**, pages 27–28.

Example 3.   Another interesting example is that of the Laguerre functions

$$\phi_n(t) = \frac{1}{n!} e^{-t/2} L_n(t), \qquad n = 0, 1, 2, \cdots$$

where

$$L_n(t) = e^t \frac{d^n}{dt^n} (t^n e^{-t})$$

is the Laguerre polynomial of degree n.   The functions $\{\phi_n\}$ determine a complete orthonormal system in the space $L^2(0, \infty)$.   See Courant and Hilbert, **1**, volume I, page 81; this proof shows that the closed linear manifold determined by the functions $\{\phi_n\}$ contains all the elements of $L^2(0, \infty)$ corresponding to piecewise continuous functions in $\mathscr{L}^2(0, \infty)$. Since elements of $L^2(0, \infty)$ corresponding to functions of this latter type are dense in $L^2(0, \infty)$ it follows by Theorem 3.2–J that the Laguerre functions determine a complete orthonormal system.

Example 4.   The Legendre polynomial of degree n may be defined as

$$P_n(t) = \frac{1}{2^n n!} \frac{d^n}{dt^n} (t^2 - 1)^n.$$

The functions

$$\{\sqrt{n + \tfrac{1}{2}}\, P_n(t)\} \qquad n = 0, 1, 2, \cdots$$

determine a complete orthonormal set in the space $L^2(-1, 1)$.   The argument in Churchill, **1**, pages 185–186, can be modified so as to prove this assertion.

We shall see later on (see Theorem 6.4–D and the latter part of § 5.5) that certain types of integral equations lead to the determination of complete orthonormal sets.   This situation occurs, in particular, when certain types of boundary value problems for differential equations are recast as problems of integral equations (see § 6.41).

3.3 Topological Linear Spaces

The general definition of a topological linear space was given in § 3.0. In this section we give a rather brief discussion of such spaces, with emphasis upon the way in which the topology is determined by systems of neighborhoods of 0.   Throughout the section X denotes a topological linear space.

The principal theorems are 3.3–E, 3.3–F, and 3.3–G.   The first two of these theorems are concerned with fundamental aspects of systems of neighborhoods of 0 in a topological linear space; the third theorem brings out the important fact that in a topological linear space the weak T_1-separation axiom implies that the space is a Hausdorff space (and even somewhat more than this).

One important preliminary comment is this: The function f defined by $f(x) = \alpha x + x_0$, where α and x_0 are fixed, is continuous.   Moreover, if $\alpha \neq 0$, then f is a homeomorphism of X onto all of X.   It therefore maps open sets onto open sets.   In particular, if S is a neighborhood of 0, $f(S)$ is a neighborhood of x_0.

If S, S_1, S_2 are sets in X, B is a set of scalars, x_0 is a fixed vector and α is a fixed scalar, we write

$$S_1 + S_2 = \{x_1 + x_2 : x_1 \in S_1, x_2 \in S_2\},$$
$$x_0 + S = \{x_0 + x : x \in S\},$$
$$BS = \{\beta x : \beta \in B, x \in S\},$$
$$\alpha S = \{\alpha x : x \in S\}.$$

Since $S_1 - S_2$ is regularly used for set-theoretic difference, it is necessary to distinguish carefully between $S_1 - S_2$ and $S_1 + (-1) \cdot S_2$.   We *do* denote $(-1) \cdot S$ by $-S$, however, when this symbol stands alone.

Definition.   A set S in X is called *symmetric* if $x \in S$ implies $-x \in S$, i.e., if $-S \subset S$.   This is equivalent to $-S = S$.

Every neighborhood U of 0 contains a symmetric neighborhood of 0, e.g., $U \cap (-U)$.

Definition.   A set S in X is called *balanced* (in the Bourbaki books the term is *équilibré*) if $ES \subset S$, where E is the set of all scalars α such that

$|\alpha| \leqslant 1$. If T is any nonempty set in X, the set ET is balanced. It is called the *balanced hull* of T. A balanced set coincides with its balanced hull.

The intersection of balanced sets is balanced. The balanced hull of S is the intersection of all balanced sets which contain S.

Observe that a balanced set is symmetric and contains 0.

The three following theorems are stated formally for purposes of later reference.

Theorem 3.3–A. *Let $\mathscr{U}$ be a base at 0 in X. Then, the family of sets $x_0 + U$, U varying over $\mathscr{U}$, is a base at x_0.*

The simple proof is left to the reader.

Theorem 3.3–B. *If $\mathscr{U}$ is a base at 0 and $U \in \mathscr{U}$, there exists $V \in \mathscr{U}$ such that $V + V \subset U$.*

PROOF. Use the facts that $0 + 0 = 0$ and that addition is continuous. We omit the details.

Theorem 3.3–C. *If S is a neighborhood of 0, the balanced hull of S is open.*

The simple proof is left to the reader. It may be observed that, if S is open but does not contain 0, the balanced hull of S may not be open. However, if the point 0 is deleted from the balanced hull, the set which remains is open.

The following theorem shows that there exists a family of balanced neighborhoods of 0 constituting a base at 0.

Theorem 3.3–D. *If $\mathscr{U}$ is a base at 0 and $\mathscr{V}$ is the family of balanced hulls of the members of $\mathscr{U}$, then $\mathscr{V}$ is a base at 0.*

PROOF. Suppose $U \in \mathscr{U}$. From $0 \cdot 0 = 0$ and the continuity of products it is possible to obtain a neighborhood of 0, say W_1, whose balanced hull W_2 is contained in U. Since W_2 is a neighborhood of 0 (by Theorem 3.3–C), there exists $U_1 \in \mathscr{U}$ such that $U_1 \subset W_2$. If V is the balanced hull of U_1, we have $V \subset W_2$, and hence $V \subset U$. This completes the proof.

Definition. A set S in X is called *absorbing* if to each $x \in X$ corresponds some $\epsilon > 0$ such that $\alpha x \in S$ if $0 < |\alpha| \leqslant \epsilon$. An equivalent formulation is: S is absorbing if to each $x \in X$ there corresponds some $r > 0$ such that $x \in \alpha S$ if $|\alpha| \geqslant r$.

It is clear at once from the continuity of products and the fact that $0 \cdot x = 0$ for every x that each neighborhood of 0 is absorbing.

The concepts of balanced sets and absorbing sets do not require a topology for their definition; they make sense in any linear space. As we shall presently see, a suitable family of balanced and absorbing sets in a linear space can be used to define a topology for the space.

A balanced set S is absorbing if and only if to each $x \in X$ there corresponds some $\alpha \neq 0$ such that $\alpha x \in S$.

Theorem 3.3–E. *If X is a topological linear space, there exists a family $\mathcal{U}$ of open sets forming a base at 0 and having the properties:*

1. *Each member of the family is balanced and absorbing.*
2. *If $U \in \mathcal{U}$ and $\alpha \neq 0$, then $\alpha U \in \mathcal{U}$.*
3. *If $U \in \mathcal{U}$, there exists $V \in \mathcal{U}$ such that $V + V \subset U$.*

PROOF.   Let $\mathcal{U}$ be the family of all balanced neighborhoods of 0, which is the same as the family of balanced hulls of *all* neighborhoods of 0. We leave the verification of properties 1–3 to the reader.

In a normed linear space X the sets $\{x : \|x\| < r\}$, r varying over all positive numbers, form a family with the properties specified for $\mathcal{U}$ in Theorem 3.3–E.   In proving theorems about topological linear spaces, a base with these properties is frequently used to pattern arguments after proofs using norms.

The next theorem shows how a topology may be constructed for a linear space.

Theorem 3.3–F. *Let X be a linear space.   Let $\mathcal{U}$ be a nonempty family of nonempty subsets of X with the following properties:*

1. *Each member of $\mathcal{U}$ is balanced and absorbing.*
2. *If $U \in \mathcal{U}$, there exists $V \in \mathcal{U}$ such that $V + V \subset U$.*
3. *If U_1 and U_2 are in $\mathcal{U}$, there exists $U_3 \in \mathcal{U}$ such that $U_3 \subset U_1 \cap U_2$.*
4. *If $U \in \mathcal{U}$ and $x \in U$, there exists $V \in \mathcal{U}$ such that $x + V \subset U$.*

Then there is a unique topology for X such that X is a topological linear space with $\mathcal{U}$ as a base at 0.

PROOF.   A nonempty balanced set contains 0.   Hence $x \in x + U$ for each $U \in \mathcal{U}$.   We shall define a set S to be open if to each $x \in S$ there corresponds some $U \in \mathcal{U}$ such that $x + U \subset S$.   The elements of $\mathcal{U}$ are open, by (4), and (3) shows that the intersection of two open sets is open. The class of open sets, as defined, obviously has the remaining properties required in order for it to be a topology for X.   The set $\mathcal{U}$ is evidently a base at 0.

The fact that addition is continuous follows at once from (2).   Before proving continuity of multiplication we observe the following:

5. *If $U \in \mathcal{U}$ and $\alpha \neq 0$, there exists $V \in \mathcal{U}$ such that $\alpha V \subset U$.*

To prove this we observe by (2) and induction that, if $U \in \mathscr{U}$ and n is any positive integer, there exists $V \in \mathscr{U}$ such that $2^n V \subset U$. Now consider U and α in (5). Choose n so that $|\alpha| < 2^n$, and $V \in \mathscr{U}$ so that $2^n V \subset U$. Since U is balanced it is readily seen that $\alpha V \subset U$. Thus (5) is proved.

Now suppose that α_0 and x_0 are fixed. We shall show that, if $U \in \mathscr{U}$ there is a $V \in \mathscr{U}$ and an $\epsilon \mathbin{\char`\~} 0$ such that $\alpha x \in \alpha_0 x_0 + U$ if $|\alpha - \alpha_0| < \epsilon$ and $x \in x_0 + V$. Choose W in $\mathscr{U}$ so that $W + W + W \subset U$ [by double use of (2) and observing that $0 \in W$]. If $\alpha_0 = 0$, let $V = W$; if $\alpha_0 \neq 0$, choose $W_1 \in \mathscr{U}$ so that $\alpha_0 W_1 \subset W$ [by (5)], and then choose $V \in \mathscr{U}$ so that $V \subset W \cap W_1$. By (1) there is some $\epsilon > 0$ such that $\beta x_0 \in V$ if $|\beta| < \epsilon$. We can assume that $\epsilon \leqslant 1$. Now suppose that $|\alpha - \alpha_0| < \epsilon$ and $x \in x_0 + V$, or $x - x_0 \in V$. We know that $(\alpha - \alpha_0)x_0 \in V$, and $(\alpha - \alpha_0)(x - x_0) \in V$ as a result of the fact that V is balanced. Finally, $\alpha_0(x - x_0) \in \alpha_0 V \subset W$. Consequently, from

$$\alpha x - \alpha_0 x_0 = (\alpha - \alpha_0)x_0 + \alpha_0(x - x_0) + (\alpha - \alpha_0)(x - x_0)$$

we see that $\alpha x - \alpha_0 x_0 \in W + W + W \subset U$. This completes the proof that multiplication is continuous.

The uniqueness assertion in Theorem 3.3–F follows from Theorem 3.3–A and the fact that a base determines its topology uniquely.

The definition of a topological linear space makes no provision for separation axioms. Thus, the space need not be a T_1-space. Consider, for instance, a linear space X having more than one point, with $\emptyset$ and X as the only open sets. The next theorem shows, however, that a T_1-topological linear space must necessarily be a T_3-space, and so, in particular, a Hausdorff space.

Theorem 3.3–G. *A topological linear space is regular. Hence, if it is a T_1-space, it is also a Hausdorff space.*

PROOF. Regularity is defined in § 2.3. We choose a base $\mathscr{U}$ at 0 having the property 3 in Theorem 3.3–E. Suppose $U, V \in \mathscr{U}$ and $V + V \subset U$, and suppose $x \in \bar{V}$. Now $x + (-1) \cdot V$ is a neighborhood of x, and therefore $\{x + (-1) \cdot V\} \cap V \neq \emptyset$. Suppose $y \in \{x + (-1) \cdot V\} \cap V$, and write $y = x - z$, $z \in V$. Then $x = y + z \in V + V \subset U$. This proves $\bar{V} \subset U$. The complete proof of the theorem now follows from Theorem 3.3–A and the fact that the closure of a set $x + V$ is $x + \bar{V}$.

It is also true that a topological linear T_1-space is completely regular (definition in § 2.3). For a proof of a somewhat more general result which is easily rephrased for the present situation, see Weil, **1**, page 13.

Definition. Two topological linear spaces X and Y are called *topologically isomorphic*, or *linearly homeomorphic*, if there exists a linear operator T which establishes a homeomorphic mapping of X onto all of Y.

Are all n-dimensional topological linear spaces with the same scalar field linearly homeomorphic to one another (and so in particular to $l^2(n)$)? Not necessarily so, for, if X is n-dimensional, we may give it the topology in which the only open sets are $\emptyset$ and X, and then it is certainly not homeomorphic to $l^2(n)$. However, this anomalous situation is avoided if we deal with T_1-spaces.

Theorem 3.3–H. *All n-dimensional topological linear T_1-spaces with the same scalar field are linearly homeomorphic.*

This is a generalization of Theorem 3.12–A. The proof is left for the problems at the end of the section.

Since the concept of distance is not available to us in discussing the general theory of topological linear spaces, the concept of a bounded set must be defined in a manner different from that for metric spaces.

Definition. In a topological linear space a set S is said to be *bounded* if for each neighborhood U of 0 there is some scalar α such that $S \subset \alpha U$.

In view of the fact that there exists a base at 0 composed of balanced neighborhoods, we may say "some positive scalar α" instead of "some scalar α," and the modified definition is equivalent to the original.

It is clear that a subset of a bounded set is bounded.

In the particular case in which the space is a normed linear space, the foregoing definition is easily seen to be equivalent to the definition of boundedness in terms of the norm; that is, S is bounded if and only if there is some positive β such that $\|x\| < \beta$ for each x in S.

The concept of boundedness is important in connection with the question of whether a topological linear space is normable (see Theorem 3.41–D).

In this book no extensive use is made of the general theory of topological linear spaces. Apart from normed linear spaces, the topological linear spaces studied in this book are mainly those which arise from the introduction of "weak topologies" into normed linear spaces. However, the general theory is a subject of growing interest, and much research is being done on it.

PROBLEMS

1. To prove Theorem 3.3–H it suffices to show that an n-dimensional topological linear T_1-space X is linearly homeomorphic to $l^2(n)$. If we write $x = \xi_1 x_1 + \cdots + \xi_n x_n$, where $x_1, \cdots, x_n$ is a basis for X, the main difficulty lies in proving that the point $(\xi_1, \cdots, \xi_n)$ of $l^2(n)$ depends continuously on x. The following suggestions should enable the reader to make the proof. If

$\epsilon > 0$ is given, let K be the set of points in $l^2(n)$ for which $|\xi_1|^2 + \cdots + |\xi_n|^2 = \epsilon^2$, and let S be the corresponding set in X. The fact that X is a T_1-space is used in proving that S is closed. It is possible to choose a balanced neighborhood of 0 in X, say U, such that $U \cap S = \emptyset$. One can then show that $x \in U$ implies $|\xi_1|^2 + \cdots + |\xi_n|^2 < \epsilon^2$.

2. If X and Y are topological linear spaces and X is a finite-dimensional T_1-space, every linear operator on X into Y is continuous.

3. A set T is said to absorb a set S if there is some $r > 0$ such that $S \subset \alpha T$ when $|\alpha| \geqslant r$. Show that a set S is bounded if and only if each balanced neighborhood of 0 absorbs S.

4. A set S is bounded if and only if it has the following property: If $\{\alpha_n\}$ is a sequence of scalars such that $\alpha_n \to 0$ and if $\{x_n\}$ is a sequence of elements of S, the sequence $\{\alpha_n x_n\}$ is convergent to 0.

5. Let X be the linear space of real-valued functions x which are defined and continuous on the real axis. Corresponding to each $\epsilon > 0$ and each compact set S of real numbers, let

$$U_{\epsilon, S} = \{x : |x(s)| < \epsilon \text{ if } s \in S\}.$$

As ϵ and S vary, the family $\mathscr{U}$ of the sets $U_{\epsilon, S}$ satisfies the conditions 1–4 of Theorem 3.3–F, and hence $\mathscr{U}$ is a base at 0 for a topology on X, making X into a topological linear space. Is it a T_1-topology?

6. On occasion it is useful to have an alternative to Theorem 3.3–F for the construction of a topological linear space. Here is such an alternative. Let X be a linear space, and let $\mathscr{W}$ be a nonempty family of nonempty sets with the following properties:

a. Each W in $\mathscr{W}$ is balanced and absorbing.
b. If W_1 and W_2 are in $\mathscr{W}$, there exists $W_3 \in \mathscr{W}$ such that $W_3 \subset W_1 \cap W_2$.
c. If $W_1 \in \mathscr{W}$, there exists $W_2 \in \mathscr{W}$ such that $W_2 + W_2 \subset W_1$.

Let a set S in X be defined as an open set if to each $x \in S$ there corresponds some $W \in \mathscr{W}$ such that $x + W \subset S$. With this family of open sets, X is a topological linear space. Verification of this assertion is left to the reader.

If we compare this situation with that in Theorem 3.3–F, we observe that property 4 of Theorem 3.3–F is not assumed as a property of the family $\mathscr{W}$. Otherwise the situations are the same. As a consequence, we are not able to assert that the members of $\mathscr{W}$ are open sets. Suppose, for instance, that X is the Euclidean plane and that $\mathscr{W}$ is the family of sets W_ϵ of the form

$$W_\epsilon = \{(\xi_1, \xi_2) : \xi_1^2 + \xi_2^2 \leqslant \epsilon^2\},$$

where ϵ can vary over all positive numbers. The resulting topology for X is the usual topology of the plane.

7. Consider $L^p(a, b)$, where $0 < p < 1$. We write

$$\|x\| = \left(\int_a^b |x(s)|^p \, ds \right)^{1/p},$$

just as when $p \geqslant 1$. With $0 < p < 1$ $\|x\|$ is not a norm, for the triangular inequality fails to hold. Instead, we have the inequality

$$\|x + y\| \leqslant \max \{2\|x\|, 2\|y\|\}.$$

However, let $W_\epsilon = \{x : \|x\| \leq \epsilon\}$. The family $\mathscr{W}$ of all such sets W_ϵ, for all $\epsilon > 0$, satisfies conditions a–c of 6. Hence L^p becomes a topological linear space if open sets are defined as follows: S is open if to each $x \in S$ there corresponds some $\epsilon > 0$ such that $y \in S$ whenever $\|y - x\| \leq \epsilon$.

8. If X and Y are topological linear spaces, a linear operator T on X into Y is continuous at all points of X if it is continuous at some point of X.

9. There is a generalization of the concept of completeness for a topological linear space. Since the topology may not be that of a metric space, it turns out to be desirable to use Moore-Smith convergence instead of sequential convergence in defining completeness. We rely on the terminology concerning *directed sets* and *nets* used by Kelley, **1**, Chapter 2, in connection with Moore-Smith convergence. Suppose X is a topological linear space. A net f in X (i.e., a function with range in X and domain some directed set D) is called a *Cauchy net* if for each neighborhood U of 0 in X there is some $d_0 \in D$ such that $f(d_1) - f(d_2) \in U$ if $d_0 < d_1$ and $d_0 < d_2$. The net is said to converge to x if for each neighborhood U of 0 there is some $d_0 \in D$ such that $f(d) - x \in U$ when $d_0 < d$. If a net converges to a point, it is a Cauchy net. If every Cauchy net in X converges to a point in X, we say that X is complete. An alternative approach to completeness is through the concept of *Cauchy filters* (see Bourbaki, **2**, Chapter II).

a. If X and Y are topological linear spaces which are topologically isomorphic, they are both complete if one is.

b. For a normed linear space the present definition of completeness is equivalent to the notion of completeness for metric spaces, as defined in § 2.41.

c. Let M be a closed subspace of the topological linear space X. If X is complete, so is M. If X is a T_1-space and if M is complete, it is closed in X, regardless of whether X is complete. For the proof it is necessary to know that, if $S \subset X$, a point x is in $\bar{S}$ if and only if there is a net in S converging to x. Also, when X is T_1, it is also T_2, and then a net in X cannot converge to two different points.

d. If X is a topological linear space which is locally compact and T_1, it is finite dimensional. We sketch the argument. Using the local compactness, we obtain a balanced neighborhood of 0, say V, such that $\bar{V}$ is balanced and compact. Then, for each neighborhood W of 0 we obtain as follows an $\alpha \neq 0$ such that $\alpha \bar{V} \subset W$. Choose a balanced neighborhood W_1 of 0 such that $W_1 + W_1 \subset W$. Choose points $x_1, \cdots, x_k \in \bar{V}$ so that $x_1 + W_1, \cdots, x_k + W_1$ cover $\bar{V}$. Choose $\alpha_i \neq 0$ so that $\alpha_i x_i \in W_1$. Then take α so that $|\alpha| \leq 1$ and $0 < |\alpha| \leq \min|\alpha_i|$. One can show $\alpha \bar{V} \subset W$. Since $\bar{V}$ is compact we can choose $y_1, \cdots, y_n \in \bar{V}$ so that $y_1 + {}^1/_2 \bar{V}, \cdots, y_n + {}^1/_2 \bar{V}$ cover $\bar{V}$. Let M be the linear manifold generated by $y_1, \cdots, y_n$. Evidently $\bar{V} \subset M + {}^1/_2 \bar{V}$. Since X is T_1, M is topologically isomorphic to $l^2(m)$ for some $m \leq n$. Hence M is complete and therefore closed in X. Finally, $M = X$. For, assume $x_0 \in X - M$. Let A be the set of all nonzero scalars α such that $(x_0 + \alpha \bar{V}) \cap M \neq \emptyset$. Then A is not empty, as a result of the fact that $\bar{V}$ is absorbing. Let $\delta = \inf |\alpha|$ for $\alpha \in A$. The following argument shows that $\delta > 0$. Since $X - M$ is open there exists a neighborhood W of 0 such that $x_0 + W \subset X - M$. There exists a nonzero scalar α_1 such that $\alpha_1 \bar{V} \subset W$. Then, using the fact that $\bar{V}$ is balanced, we show that α is not in A if $0 < |\alpha| \leq |\alpha_1|$, and so $\delta \geq |\alpha_1|$. Now choose $\alpha \in A$ so that $|\alpha| < 2\delta$ and choose $x \in (x_0 + \alpha \bar{V}) \cap M$. Then $(x - x_0)/\alpha \in \bar{V} \subset M + {}^1/_2 \bar{V}$, and so we can write $x - \alpha y_0 = x_0 + (\alpha/_2)v$ with $y_0 \in M$ and $v \in \bar{V}$. We conclude that $(\alpha/2) \in A$, which is a contradiction. Hence $M = X$ and X is finite dimensional.

e. Every finite-dimensional subspace of X is closed if X is a T_1-space.

10. Let M be a closed subspace of the topological linear space X. With the quotient space X/M and the canonical mapping ϕ of X onto X/M as defined in § 3.14, define a set S in X/M to be open if $\phi^{-1}(S)$ is open in X. This makes X/M a topological linear T_1-space. If the topology of X arises from a norm, this topology for X/M is the same as that generated by the norm defined in Theorem 3.14–A.

▲

3.4 Convex Sets

Let X be a real linear space. If x_1 and x_2 are distinct points of X, the set of all points $(1 - \alpha)x_1 + \alpha x_2$ for which $0 \leqslant \alpha \leqslant 1$ is called the *line segment* joining x_1 and x_2, or simply the line segment x_1x_2.

Definition. A set S in X is called *convex* if S contains the line segment x_1x_2 whenever x_1 and x_2 are distinct points of S. This is equivalent to the requirement that, if x_1, $x_2 \in S$, then also $\alpha_1 x_1 + \alpha_2 x_2 \in S$ whenever α_1 and α_2 are positive numbers such that $\alpha_1 + \alpha_2 = 1$.

The empty set and a set consisting of one point are convex, since the conditions of the definition are vacuously satisfied by such sets. Notice that a linear manifold is convex and that the intersection of a family of convex sets is a convex set.

In a normed linear space an open sphere is a convex set. Likewise the closed sphere $\{x : \|x - x_0\| \leqslant r\}$ is convex.

The notion of a convex set is independent of topology, but convex sets play an important part in the theory of topological linear spaces. The first five theorems of this section make no use of topology. The remaining theorems involve topological ideas. The student who is interested in normed linear spaces, to the exclusion of more general types of topological linear spaces, may ignore Theorem 3.4–H.

If X is a complex linear space, it can also be regarded as a real linear space, and it is this point of view which is taken when we define the concept of a convex set in a complex linear space.

Theorem 3.4–A. *Let X be a linear space (real or complex). Let S and T be convex sets in X, and let α and β be any scalars. Then the set $\alpha S + \beta T$ is convex.*

We omit the proof, which is immediate.

Theorem 3.4–B. *Let S be a convex set in X, and let α, β be positive. Then $\alpha S + \beta S = (\alpha + \beta)S$.*

PROOF.   It is evident that $(\alpha + \beta)S \subset \alpha S + \beta S$, regardless of convexity. If S is convex, and $y = \alpha x_1 + \beta x_2$, where $x_1, x_2 \in S$, then

$$\frac{1}{\alpha + \beta} y = \frac{\alpha}{\alpha + \beta} x_1 + \frac{\beta}{\alpha + \beta} x_2 \in S,$$

since

$$\frac{\alpha}{\alpha + \beta} + \frac{\beta}{\alpha + \beta} = 1.$$

Thus $y \in (\alpha + \beta)S$, and $\alpha S + \beta S \subset (\alpha + \beta)S$.   This completes the proof.

Definition.   If S is any set in X, the *convex hull* of S is defined to be the intersection of all convex sets which contain S.   We sometimes denote it by S_c.

Theorem 3.4–C.   *The convex hull of S consists of all points which are expressible in the form $\alpha_1 x_1 + \cdots + \alpha_n x_n$, where $x_1, \cdots, x_n$ are any points of S, $\alpha_k > 0$ for each k and $\sum_k \alpha_k = 1$.   The index n is not fixed.*

PROOF.   Let T be the set of points expressible in the manner described in the theorem.   It is readily seen by the definition of convexity that T is convex.   Since T clearly contains S, it follows that $S_c \subset T$.   We shall show that T is contained in every convex set which contains S.   We do this by induction on the number of points of S occurring in the representation of a point of T.   Let W be a convex set containing S.   If $x = \alpha_1 x_1$ is a point of T for which $n = 1$, it is clear that $\alpha_1 = 1$ and $x \in S$.   Let us assume that a point of T is in W if it is represented in terms of $n - 1$ points of S.   Then, let $x = \alpha_1 x_1 + \cdots + \alpha_n x_n$ be in T. Let $\beta = \alpha_1 + \cdots + \alpha_{n-1}$, $\beta_k = \alpha_k/\beta$ $(k = 1, \cdots, n - 1)$, $y = \beta_1 x_1 + \cdots + \beta_{n-1} x_{n-1}$.   Then $y \in W$, by the induction hypothesis.   But $x_n \in W$, $\alpha_n = 1 - \beta$, and $x = \beta y + (1 - \beta)x_n \in W$, since W is convex.   This completes the induction.   Thus $T \subset W$, and it follows that $T \subset S_c$. The proof is now complete.

We shall later on have occasion to deal with sets which are both balanced and convex.   The concept of a balanced set involves considering all scalars α such that $|\alpha| \leqslant 1$.   Accordingly, if X is a complex linear space, a set in X which is balanced when complex scalars are considered is also balanced when only real scalars are considered and X is viewed as a real linear space.   But a set may be balanced from this latter point of view and *not* balanced when complex scalars are considered.   To avoid confusion, we shall always understand that, when balanced sets are

mentioned without explicit mention of the field of scalars under consideration, the sets are balanced relative to the field of scalars associated with
the space.

Theorem 3.4–D. *A convex set in a real linear space is balanced if
and only if it is symmetric.*

PROOF.   Since every balanced set is symmetric, it suffices to show that
a convex and symmetric set S is balanced. Suppose $x \in S$. Then
$- x \in S$. Hence, since S is convex, $(1 - \alpha)(- x) + \alpha x = (2\alpha - 1)x$ is
in S if $0 \leqslant \alpha \leqslant 1$. Thus $\beta x \in S$ if $- 1 \leqslant \beta \leqslant 1$, and S is balanced, by
definition.

Let X be a linear space, either real or complex. If $S \subset X$, let S_b denote
the balanced hull of S, and let S_c denote the convex hull of S.

Definition.   The set $(S_b)_c$ is called the *balanced and convex hull* of S.
We denote it simply by S_{bc}.

Theorem 3.4–E.   *If X is a real or complex linear space, the set S_{bc}
consists of all finite sums $\sum \alpha_k x_k$, where the x_k's are elements of S and
$\sum |\alpha_k| \leqslant 1$. S_{bc} is the intersection of all sets which are both balanced and
convex and contain S.*

PROOF.   Let T be the set described in the theorem.   We recall that S_b
is the set of all elements αx, where $|\alpha| \leqslant 1$ and $x \in S$. If $x \in S_{bc}$, we
know by Theorem 3.4–C that x is a finite sum $\sum \beta_k \alpha_k x_k$, where $x_k \in S$,
$|\alpha_k| \leqslant 1$, $\beta_k > 0$, and $\sum \beta_k = 1$. It is thus clear that $S_{bc} \subset T$.   On the
other hand, suppose $x \in T$. Then $x = \sum \alpha_k x_k$, where $x_k \in S$, and
$\sum |\alpha_k| \leqslant 1$. If $\sum |\alpha_k| = 0$ it is clear that $x = 0 \in S_b$ and so $x \in S_{bc}$. If
$\sum |\alpha_k| = \alpha \neq 0$, let $\beta_k = |\alpha_k|/\alpha$. Then $\beta_k \geqslant 0$, $\sum \beta_k = 1$. We can write
$\alpha_k = |\alpha_k|\gamma_k$, where γ_k is a scalar (real or complex) such that $|\gamma_k| = 1$.
Let $y_k = \alpha \gamma_k x_k$. Then $\beta_k y_k = \alpha_k x_k$, and $x = \sum \beta_k y_k$. But $|\alpha \gamma_k| = \alpha \leqslant 1$,
so $y_k \in S_b$. Thus $x \in S_{bc}$, by Theorem 3.4–C. We now know that
$T \subset S_{bc}$ and therefore that $T = S_{bc}$. It is clear from the form of the
elements of T that S_{bc} is balanced. It is of course convex. Verification
of the last assertion in the theorem is left to the reader.

It may be remarked that $(S_c)_b$ is not always the same as $(S_b)_c$.   Indeed,
$(S_c)_b$ can fail to be convex.

Next we consider convex sets in a topological linear space.

Theorem 3.4–F.   *Let S be a convex set in a topological linear space.
Then the closure $\bar{S}$ is also convex.*

PROOF.   Suppose x_0, $y_0 \in \bar{S}$ and $0 < \alpha < 1$. Consider the function
$f(x, y) = (1 - \alpha)x + \alpha y$. It is continuous. Let U be any neighborhood

of $(1 - \alpha)x_0 + \alpha y_0$. If we show that U contains points of S, it will follow that $(1 - \alpha)x_0 + \alpha y_0 \in \bar{S}$ and hence that $\bar{S}$ is convex. Now, since f is continuous, there exist neighborhoods V and W of x_0 and y_0 respectively such that $f(x, y) \in U$ if $x \in V$ and $y \in W$. Since $x_0 \in \bar{S}$, V contains some point $x_1 \in S$; likewise W contains some point $y_1 \in S$. Thus, since S is convex, $f(x_1, y_1) \in S$. But $f(x_1, y_1) \in U$ also. Thus the proof is complete.

If S is any set, the closure of the convex hull of S is called the *closed convex hull* of S. It is the intersection of all closed and convex sets which contain S. The sets S and $\bar{S}$ have the same closed convex hull.

Theorem 3.4–G. *If S is an open set, its convex hull S_c is also open.*

PROOF. Suppose $x \in S_c$, then x is a finite sum $\sum \alpha_k x_k$, where $x_k \in S$, $\alpha_k > 0$, and $\sum \alpha_k = 1$. Since S is open, there exist neighborhoods V_k of x_k such that $V_k \subset S$. Let T be the set $\sum \alpha_k V_k$, i.e., the set of all elements $\sum \alpha_k v_k$, where $v_k \in V_k$. Clearly $x \in T \subset S_c$, so all that is needed is to show that T is open. Now each $\alpha_k V_k$ is open, since $\alpha_k \neq 0$. Hence T will be open, by induction, once we know that $U + V$ is open if U and V are open. Now $x + V$ is open for each fixed x, and $U + V$ is the union of all $x + V$ as x varies over U. Thus $U + V$ is open.

The next theorem is used in the proof of Theorem 3.41–D. The result would be obvious and a formal statement unnecessary if we confined ourselves to normed linear spaces.

Theorem 3.4–H. *If X is a topological linear space and U is a convex neighborhood of 0, then U contains a balanced and convex neighborhood of 0.*

PROOF. We know from the proof of Theorem 3.3–D that U contains a balanced neighborhood V of 0. Let W be the convex hull of V. Then W is a neighborhood of 0, by Theorem 3.4–G. Since V is its own balanced hull, W is the balanced and convex hull of V and is therefore balanced (Theorem 3.4–E). Since U is convex, it follows that $W \subset U$. Thus W meets the requirements of the theorem. This argument works for both real and complex spaces. For real spaces we could obtain a satisfactory W by taking $W = U \cap (- U)$ (see Theorem 3.4–D).

PROBLEMS

1. Let S be a convex set in the topological linear space X. Suppose $x_0 \in \text{int } (S)$ and $y_0 \in \bar{S}$. Then, every point y expressible in the form $y = \alpha x_0 + (1 - \alpha)y_0$, $0 < \alpha < 1$, is an interior point of S.

2. Under the conditions on S and X in problem 1, the set int (S) is convex. If int $(S) \neq \emptyset$, we have $\overline{\text{int } (S)} = \bar{S}$ and int $(S) = \text{int } (\bar{S})$.

3. Let $A_1, \cdots, A_n$ be compact convex sets in the topological linear space X. Let $A = A_1 \cup \cdots \cup A_n$. Then A_c is compact. Begin by showing that A_c is composed of all the points x which are expressible in the form $x = \alpha_1 x_1 + \cdots + \alpha_n x_n$, with $x_k \in A_k$, $0 \leqslant \alpha_k$, and $\alpha_1 + \cdots + \alpha_n = 1$. Then, let P be the compact set in $l^2(n)$ composed of all points $(\alpha_1, \cdots, \alpha_n)$ with $\alpha_k \geqslant 0$ and $\alpha_1 + \cdots + \alpha_n = 1$. Observe that A_c is the image in X of the product set $P \times A_1 \times \cdots \times A_n$ by the mapping $(\alpha_1, \cdots, \alpha_n, x_1, \cdots, x_n) \rightarrow \alpha_1 x_1 + \cdots + \alpha_n x_n$.

4. In a normed linear space X the convex hull of a precompact set S is precompact. The argument depends on Theorem 2.41–G and problem 3. If $\epsilon > 0$, choose $x_1, \cdots, x_n$ in X so that S is contained in the union B of the open spheres of radii $\epsilon/2$ with centers $x_1, \cdots, x_n$. Let A be the finite set $x_1, \cdots, x_n$. Show that B_c is contained in the union of the open spheres of radii $\epsilon/2$ with centers in A_c. Then observe that A_c is compact and so deduce that S_c is precompact.

5. In a Banach space X the closed convex hull of a compact set is compact. Use problem 4.

3.4I Minkowski Functionals

In this section we assume that X is a real linear space and that K is a convex set in X. We assume further that K is an absorbing set and that $0 \in K$.

Definition. For each $x \in X$ let A_x be the set of those real α such that $\alpha > 0$ and $x \in \alpha K$. Since K is absorbing, A_x is not empty. We then define

$$(3.41–1) \qquad p(x) = \inf A_x.$$

The functional p is called the Minkowski functional of the set K. Evidently $0 \leqslant p(x) < \infty$. This functional is useful in dealing analytically with K. We shall see in § 3.7 that there is a close relation between Minkowski functionals and seminorms, which are used in connection with the topology of certain topological linear spaces.

If X is a normed linear space and $K = \{x : \|x\| < r\}$, where r is fixed and positive, it is easy to see that $p(x) = \|x\|/r$. If K is a closed and bounded convex set in Euclidean space of n dimensions, if 0 is an interior point of K and $x \neq 0$, we can think of $p(x)$ as follows: Let y be that unique positive multiple of x in which the ray from 0 through x intersects the boundary of K. Then $x = p(x)y$, and $p(x)$ is the ratio of the distance $0x$ to the distance $0y$.

Theorem 3.4I–A. *Let K be a convex, absorbing set which contains 0. The Minkowski functional of K has the properties*

$$(3.41–2) \qquad p(0) = 0, \qquad p(\lambda x) = \lambda p(x) \qquad if \ \lambda > 0$$

(3.41–3) $p(x + y) \leqslant p(x) + p(y)$.

If K is balanced, then, for any scalar λ,

(3.41–4) $p(\lambda x) = |\lambda| p(x)$.

This last relation holds even for complex λ if X happens to be a complex space and K is balanced in the complex sense.

PROOF.   If x and y are given and α, β are arbitrary elements of A_x, A_y respectively, we have $x + y \in \alpha K + \beta K$. This last set is $(\alpha + \beta)K$, by Theorem 3.4–B, and so $\alpha + \beta \in A_{x+y}$. It follows that $p(x + y) \leqslant \alpha + \beta$. Owing to the arbitrariness of α and β, (3.41–3) now follows.   The relation $p(0) = 0$ is evident, since $0 \in K$. To prove the other relation in (3.41–2) suppose $\lambda > 0$ and $x \in X$. Take any $\alpha \in A_x$. Then $x \in \alpha K$, $\lambda x \in \lambda \alpha K$, and so $\lambda \alpha \in A_{\lambda x}$, whence $p(\lambda x) \leqslant \lambda \alpha$. By the arbitrariness of α we conclude that $p(\lambda x) \leqslant \lambda p(x)$. Now replace x by λx and λ by λ^{-1}, thus obtaining $p(x) \leqslant \lambda^{-1} p(\lambda x)$, or $\lambda p(x) \leqslant p(\lambda x)$. Consequently $p(\lambda x) = \lambda p(x)$. If K is balanced, if $\lambda \neq 0$ and $x \in X$, suppose $\alpha \in A_x$. Then $x \in \alpha K$, $(\lambda/|\lambda|\alpha)x \in K$, $\lambda x \in |\lambda|\alpha K$, $p(\lambda x) \leqslant |\lambda|\alpha$, and so $p(\lambda x) \leqslant |\lambda| p(x)$. The reverse inequality is obtained by the same device as before, and so (3.41–4) is proved.

As a result of (3.41–3) we note the following inequalities, which will be used later:

(3.41–5) $- p(y - x) \leqslant p(x) - p(y) \leqslant p(x - y)$.

Theorem 3.41–B.   *Let K be a convex, absorbing set which contains 0. If p is the Minkowski functional of K, then $p(x) \leqslant 1$ whenever $x \in K$, and $p(x) < 1$ implies that $x \in K$.*

PROOF.   If $x \in K$, then $1 \in A_x$ and so $p(x) \leqslant 1$. If $p(x) < 1$, there exists $\alpha \in A_x$ such that $0 < \alpha < 1$. Now, since 0 and $\alpha^{-1}x$ are in K and K is convex, it follows that $\alpha \cdot \alpha^{-1}x + (1 - \alpha)\cdot 0 = x \in K$.

Next we add the assumption that X is a topological linear space.

Theorem 3.41–C.   *Let X be a topological linear space, and let p be the Minkowski functional of a set K in X, where K is convex, absorbing, and contains 0. Let $K_1 = \{x : p(x) < 1\}$, $K_2 = \{x : p(x) \leqslant 1\}$.   Then*

a. int $(K) \subset K_1 \subset K \subset K_2 \subset \bar{K}$.
b. $K = K_1$ *if K is open.*
c. $K = K_2$ *if K is closed.*
d. *If p is continuous,* $K_1 = \text{int } (K)$ *and* $K_2 = \bar{K}$.
e. *p is continuous if and only if* $0 \in \text{int } (K)$.
f. *If K is bounded and X is a T_1-space, $p(x) = 0$ implies $x = 0$.*

PROOF. Suppose $x \in \text{int}\,(K)$. Then $\alpha x \in K$ when α is sufficiently near 1, and hence we can find some $\alpha > 1$ such that $\alpha x \in K$. Then $\alpha^{-1} \in A_x$ and $p(x) \leqslant \alpha^{-1} < 1$, so $x \in K_1$. We know $K_1 \subset K \subset K_2$ from Theorem 3.41–B. To prove $K_2 \subset \bar{K}$ it suffices to consider an x for which $p(x) = 1$. Then $\alpha x \in K_1 \subset K$ if $0 < \alpha < 1$. Letting $\alpha \to 1$ we see that $\alpha x \to x$, whence $x \in \bar{K}$. We have now finished with (a); (b) and (c) are immediate consequences. If p is continuous, K_1 is open by Theorem 2.12–A; hence, in view of (a), $K_1 = \text{int}\,(K)$; it also follows that K_2 is closed and so $K_2 = \bar{K}$. We observe that $0 \in K_1$. Then $0 \in \text{int}\,(K)$ if p is continuous, by (d). On the other hand, if $0 \in \text{int}\,(K)$, let U be a neighborhood of 0 such that $U \subset \text{int}\,(K)$. Then $p(x) < 1$ if $x \in U$. Now, if $\epsilon > 0$, then ϵU is a neighborhood of 0, and we have $p(x) < \epsilon$ if $x \in \epsilon U$, because $\epsilon^{-1} x \in U$ and $p(\epsilon^{-1} x) = \epsilon^{-1} p(x) < 1$. This shows that p is continuous at 0. The inequalities (3.41–5) then show that p is continuous at all other points (recall that every neighborhood of 0 contains a symmetric neighborhood of 0). Finally, suppose that X is a T_1-space and that K is bounded. If $x \neq 0$, there exists a balanced neighborhood of 0 which does not contain x. Let U be this neighborhood. Since K is bounded, $K \subset \beta U$ for some $\beta > 0$. Now suppose $\alpha \in A_x$. Then $x \in \alpha K$ and so $x/\alpha \in \beta U$, or $(1/\alpha\beta)x \in U$. Since U is balanced and x is not in U, it follows that $\alpha\beta > 1$, for $\alpha\beta \leqslant 1$ would imply $x = \alpha\beta(1/\alpha\beta)x \in U$. But $\alpha > 1/\beta$ implies $p(x) \geqslant 1/\beta$, and so $p(x) > 0$. This finishes the proof of the theorem.

Definition. A topological linear space X is said to be *normable* if there exists (i.e., if it is possible to define) a norm on X such that the resulting topology for X as a normed linear space is the same as the given topology for X.

Theorem 3.41–D. *A topological linear space X is normable if and only if* (1) *X is a T_1-space and* (2) *there exists in X a convex and bounded neighborhood of* 0.

PROOF. The conditions are evidently necessary, for a metric space is a T_1-space, and the set $\{x : \|x\| < 1\}$ in a normed linear space is both convex and bounded. Suppose, on the other hand, that X satisfies conditions 1 and 2 of the theorem. Let U be a bounded and convex neighborhood of 0. There exists a neighborhood V of 0 such that $V \subset U$ and V is balanced as well as convex and bounded (Theorem 3.4–H). Let p be the Minkowski functional of V. By Theorem 3.41–A we see that p has all the properties of a norm except possibly for the property that $p(x) \neq 0$ if $x \neq 0$, and this property follows by Theorem 3.41–C, part f. Thus p is a norm on S.

We now complete the proof by showing that the topology of X is the same as the topology defined on X by the norm p. We know by Theorem 3.41–C, part b, that $V = \{x : p(x) < 1\}$. If $\alpha > 0$, $\alpha V = \{x : p(x) < \alpha\}$. It suffices to prove that the family of sets $\{\alpha V\}$ (α the parameter) is a base at 0 in the given topology of X. Suppose U is any neighborhood of 0. There exists a balanced neighborhood of 0, say W, such that $W \subset U$. Since V is bounded, there exists some $\epsilon > 0$ such that $V \subset \epsilon W$. Thus $\epsilon^{-1} V \subset U$. This shows that $\{\alpha V\}$ is a base at 0, and the proof is complete.

3.5 Linear Varieties

Throughout this section X denotes a linear space; except where specific mention is made of the nature of the scalar field, it may be either the real or the complex field.

The considerations of this section are geometric in character. If we suppose that X is Euclidean space of three dimensions, a linear variety is either a point, a line, a plane, or the whole space. The general notion of linear variety requires merely a linear space for its setting, with no need of considerations of topology or finite dimensionality. The most interesting linear varieties are those known as *hyperplanes*. A hyperplane M through 0 in X can be characterized in two ways: (1) It is the set of elements x such that $x'(x) = 0$, where x' is some nonzero linear functional on X; (2) it has the property that X can be expressed as the direct sum of M and a one-dimensional subspace.

Definition. A set $M \subset X$ is called a *linear variety* if $M = x_0 + M_0$, where x_0 is a fixed vector and M_0 is a subspace of X.

We call M a translation of M_0. Note that $x_0 \in M$, because $0 \in M_0$. It is easy to see that, if $M = x_0 + M_0$ and $x_1 \in M$, then also $M = x_1 + M_0$. This follows at once from the fact that, if x_1 and x_2 are in M, then $x_1 - x_2 \in M_0$.

A linear variety is a convex set. A set consisting of a single point is a linear variety, for (0) is a subspace.

A subspace X_0 of X will be called *maximal* if it is not all of X and if there exists no subspace X_1 of X such that $X_0 \neq X_1$, $X_1 \neq X$ and $X_0 \subset X_1$. A linear variety which results from the translation of a maximal subspace is called a *hyperplane*. In particular, a hyperplane containing 0 is the same thing as a maximal subspace. All of the hyperplanes obtained by translating a particular one are said to be parallel to this one.

At this point we recall the notation X^f for the linear space of all linear functionals on X (see § 1.6).

Theorem 3.5–A. *If* $x' \in X^f$, $x' \neq 0$, *and* α *is any fixed scalar, the set* $M = \{x : x'(x) = \alpha\}$ *is a hyperplane. It contains the origin* 0 *if and only if* $\alpha = 0$. *To each hyperplane* M *containing* 0 *corresponds an* $x' \in X^f$ *such that* $x' \neq 0$ *and* $M = \{x : x'(x) = 0\}$.

PROOF. Consider the first assertion. Since $x' \neq 0$, there exists x_1 such that $x'(x_1) = \beta \neq 0$. Let $x_0 = (\alpha/\beta)x_1$. Then $x'(x_0) = \alpha$, so $x_0 \in M$. Let $M_0 = -x_0 + M$. It is quickly verifiable that $M_0 = \{x : x'(x) = 0\}$. Clearly M_0 is a subspace, and so M is a linear variety. Now $M_0 \neq X$. If $y \in X - M_0$, every element of X can be written as the sum of an element of M_0 and a multiple of y. In fact, if $x \in X$ and

$$z = x - \frac{x'(x)}{x'(y)}\, y,$$

we see that $x'(z) = 0$, so that x has the required form. If we now suppose that M_1 is a subspace of X for which $M_0 \subset M_1$ and $M_1 \neq M_0$, we can choose $y \in M_1 - M_0$. The foregoing argument then shows that $X \subset M_1$, so that $M_1 = X$. This shows that M_0 is maximal and that M is a hyperplane. Evidently M contains 0 if and only if $\alpha = 0$.

Now suppose that M is any hyperplane containing 0. Theorem 1.71–B shows that there exists an $x' \neq 0$ such that $M \subset \{x : x'(x) = 0\}$. But then we must have $M = \{x : x'(x) = 0\}$; otherwise M would not be maximal. This completes the proof.

In the course of the proof of Theorem 3.5–A we obtained the following result:

Theorem 3.5–B. *Suppose* $x' \in X^f$, $x' \neq 0$, *and* $M = \{x : x'(x) = 0\}$. *Then, if* $x_0 \in X - M$, *every* $x \in X$ *can be expressed in the form*

(3.5–1) $$x = \frac{x'(x)}{x'(x_0)}\, x_0 + m, \qquad m \in M.$$

This is a convenient place at which to insert the following useful theorem:

Theorem 3.5–C. *Suppose that* $x_1', \cdots, x_n'$ *are linearly independent elements of* X^f, *and let* $y' \in X^f$ *be such that* $y'(x) = 0$ *whenever* $x_1'(x) = \cdots = x_n'(x) = 0$. *Then* y' *is a linear combination of* $x_1', \cdots, x_n'$.

PROOF. For the case $n = 1$ we get the proof directly from (3.5–1). If $x_1' \neq 0$, and if $y'(x) = 0$ whenever $x_1'(x) = 0$, we have

$$y' = \frac{y'(x_0)}{x_1'(x_0)}\, x_1',$$

where x_0 is any element for which $x_1'(x_0) \neq 0$. We now proceed inductively, assuming the theorem true for a set of $n - 1$ linearly independent elements of X^f. It then follows, since $x_1', \cdots, x_n'$ are linearly independent, that for each $k (k = 1, \cdots, n)$ there exists an x_k such that $x_k'(x_k) \neq 0$ and $x_j'(x_k) = 0$ if $j \neq k$. Because of homogeneity we may arrange to have $x_k'(x_k) = 1$. Now let

$$y = x - \sum_{k=1}^{n} x_k'(x)x_k.$$

We then see that $x_j'(y) = 0$ for each j; hence also $y'(y) = 0$, by our assumption. But then

$$y'(x) = \sum_{k=1}^{n} x_k'(x)y'(x_k);$$

this is equivalent to

$$y' = \sum_{k=1}^{n} y'(x_k)x_k',$$

and the theorem is proved.

Theorem 3.5–D. *Let X be a topological linear space. The closure of a linear variety in X is a linear variety.*

PROOF. Suppose first that M is a linear subspace. Now, the following general proposition is true: If f is a continuous function which maps one topological space into another and S is any set in the first space, $f(\bar{S}) \subset \overline{f(S)}$. This is easily proved, directly from the definition of continuity. Now consider f to be the function which maps $X \times X$ into X, the value of f at (x, y) being $x + y$. We know that f is continuous. Hence $f(\bar{M} \times \bar{M}) \subset \overline{f(M \times M)}$. But, since M is a subspace, $f(M \times M) \subset M$. Thus $f(\bar{M} \times \bar{M}) \subset \bar{M}$. This shows that $x + y \in \bar{M}$ if $x \in \bar{M}$ and $y \in \bar{M}$. A similar argument, using the continuity of αx, shows that $\alpha x \in \bar{M}$ if $x \in \bar{M}$. Thus $\bar{M}$ is a subspace. A translation is a homeomorphism; therefore the closure of any linear variety is a linear variety.

Theorem 3.5–E. *Let X be a topological linear space and M a hyperplane containing 0. Then, either M is a closed set, or it is everywhere dense in X. Suppose $M = \{x : x'(x) = 0\}$, where x' is a fixed element of X^f. Then M is closed if and only if x' is continuous.*

PROOF. We have $M \subset \bar{M} \subset X$, and $\bar{M}$ is a subspace. Since M is maximal, we have either $M = \bar{M}$ or $\bar{M} = X$. This proves the first assertion. If x' is continuous, M is closed, for it is the inverse image (by x') of a single point in the scalar field. Suppose, on the other hand, that M is closed but that x' is not continuous. Then it is not continuous at 0, and there is some $\epsilon > 0$ such that every neighborhood U of 0 contains some point for which $|x'(x)| \geq \epsilon$. Now let $L = \{x:x'(x) = \epsilon/2\}$. The set L is obtained from M by translation. In fact, if $x_0 \in X - M$, L is the set of all elements of the form $[\epsilon/2x'(x_0)]x_0 + m$, $m \in M$, as we see by (3.5–1). Therefore L is closed. Hence there exists a neighborhood of 0 which does not meet L. We can choose a balanced neighborhood U of this kind, by Theorem 3.3–E. Now U must contain a point x_1 such that $|x'(x_1)| \geq \epsilon$. Let $\alpha = [\epsilon/2x'(x_1)]$. Then $\alpha x_1 \in U$, for U is balanced. But $x'(\alpha x_1) = \epsilon/2$, so that $\alpha x_1 \in L$, and we have a contradiction. Therefore x' is continuous.

We remark, for later use, that, if a hyperplane is closed, all the translations of it are likewise closed and that, if it is not closed, each of these translations is everywhere dense in X.

3.6 Convex Sets and Hyperplanes

In this section we assume throughout that X is a real linear space; all scalars which occur are real.

Our object in this section is to discuss certain geometrical relationships between convex sets and hyperplanes. Some of the theorems have important uses in connection with applications.

If $M = \{x:x'(x) = \alpha\}$ is a hyperplane ($x' \neq 0$, α fixed), each of the sets

$$\{x:x'(x) < \alpha\}, \quad \{x:x'(x) > \alpha\}, \quad \{x:x'(x) \leq \alpha\}, \quad \{x:x'(x) \geq \alpha\}$$

is convex. Each of these sets is called a *half space* determined by M. If X is a topological linear space and x' is continuous, the first two of these half spaces are open and the last two are closed.

We say that a set S *lies on one side* of M if S lies entirely in one of the four half spaces determined by M. If S lies on one side of M and does not intersect M, we say that S is *strictly* on one side of M.

Theorem 3.6–A. *In order that a convex set S lie strictly on one side of a hyperplane M, it is necessary and sufficient that the intersection $S \cap M$ be empty.*

PROOF. The condition is necessary, by definition. Let $M = \{x:x'(x) = \alpha\}$, suppose that x_1 and x_2 are in S and that $x'(x_1) < \alpha < x'(x_2)$. Now $\lambda x_1 + (1 - \lambda)x_2$ lies in S if $0 \leq \lambda \leq 1$, and $x'(\lambda x_1 + (1 - \lambda)x_2) = \lambda x'(x_1) + (1 - \lambda)x'(x_2)$ is a continuous function of λ which has the value $x'(x_2)$ at $\lambda = 0$ and the value $x'(x_1)$ at $\lambda = 1$. It must then have the value α at some λ for which $0 < \lambda < 1$. But then $\lambda x_1 + (1 - \lambda)x_2 \in S \cap M$. Hence $S \cap M = \emptyset$ implies that S lies strictly on one side of M.

Theorem 3.6–B.   *Let K be a convex, absorbing set which contains 0, and let p be its Minkowski functional* (see § 3.41).   *Let M be a hyperplane which does not intersect K.   There exists $x' \in X^f$ such that $M = \{x : x'(x) = 1\}$, and for this x' we have*

$$(3.6\text{–}1) \qquad\qquad -p(-x) \leqslant x'(x) \leqslant p(x)$$

if $x \in X$.

PROOF.   Any M which does not contain 0 can be represented in the form $M = \{x : x'(x) = \alpha\}$ where $\alpha \neq 0$.   This follows readily from Theorem 3.5–A.   We can then, on multiplying x' by a suitable constant if necessary, assume that $\alpha = 1$.   Since $0 \in K$ and $x'(0) = 0$, we see (Theorem 3.6–A) that K lies strictly on one side of M and in the half space $\{x : x'(x) < 1\}$.   Thus $x'(x) < 1$ if $x \in K$.   Now consider any $x \in X$, and suppose $\alpha \in A_x$ (notation as in § 3.41).   Then $0 < \alpha$, $\alpha^{-1}x \in K$, $x'(\alpha^{-1}x) < 1$, and $x'(x) < \alpha$.   But then $x'(x) \leqslant p(x)$, by the definition of $p(x)$.   We also have $x'(-x) \leqslant p(-x)$, whence $-p(-x) \leqslant -x'(-x) = x'(x)$.   This completes the proof.

Theorem 3.6–C.   *Let X be a topological linear space and M a hyperplane.   Suppose that S is a set having at least one interior point and lying on one side of M.   Then M is closed; the interior of S lies strictly on one side of M, and the closure $\bar{S}$ also lies on one side of M.*

PROOF.   Let $M = \{x : x'(x) = \alpha\}$.   We can suppose that S lies in the half space $\{x : x'(x) \leqslant \alpha\}$ (otherwise replace x' by $-x'$ and α by $-\alpha$).   Now M must be closed, for otherwise the hyperplane $\{x : x'(x) = \alpha + 1\}$ would be everywhere dense and would, therefore, intersect S (since S has an interior point).   Consequently x' is continuous (Theorem 3.5–E).   But then the set $\{x : x'(x) < \alpha\}$ is open, and it is the interior of the closed set $\{x : x'(x) \leqslant \alpha\}$, for it is easy to see that x is *not* an interior point of the latter set if $x'(x) = \alpha$ (if $\alpha \neq 0$ merely consider λx for λ sufficiently near 1; otherwise use a preliminary translation).   The assertions about the interior and closure of S now follow at once.

Theorem 3.6–D.   *Let K be a convex absorbing set which contains 0, and let p be its Minkowski functional.   Let L be a linear variety which does not intersect K.   Then there exists a hyperplane M with equation $x'(x) = 1$ such that M contains L and $x'(x) \leqslant p(x)$ for every x.   The set K lies in the half space $\{x : x'(x) \leqslant 1\}$.   If X is a topological linear space and K has interior points, x' is continuous and M is closed.   In this case the closure of K lies in the half space $\{x : x'(x) \leqslant 1\}$, and the interior of K lies in the open half space $\{x : x'(x) < 1\}$.   In particular, if K is open, K does not intersect the closed hyperplane M.*

PROOF.   Choose $x_0 \in L$ and let $L_0 = -x_0 + L$.   Observe that x_0 is not in L_0, for, if it were, we should have $L = L_0$; then $0 \in L \cap K$, whereas $L \cap K$ is empty.   Let X_0 be the set of all elements of the form $x = \alpha x_0 + y$, $y \in L_0$. X_0 is a subspace, and L_0 is a maximal subspace of X_0.   For, suppose L_1 is a subspace such that $L_0 \subset L_1 \subset X_0$ and $L_0 \neq L_1$. Choose $x_1 \in L_1 - L_0$.   Then $x_1 = \alpha_1 x_0 + y_1$, where $y_1 \in L_0$ and $\alpha_1 \neq 0$. Now, if $x = \alpha x_0 + y \in X_0$, we can write $x = (\alpha/\alpha_1)x_1 + z$, where $z = -(\alpha/\alpha_1)y_1 + y$.   Since $z \in L_0$, we see that $x \in L_1$.   Thus $L_1 = X_0$. This shows the maximality of L_0 in X_0.   Now consider $K \cap X_0$.   It is a convex and absorbing set in X_0; it contains 0, and its Minkowski functional is the restriction of p to X_0.   Since $K \cap X_0$ does not intersect L, we know by Theorem 3.6–B that there exists $g \in (X_0)^f$ such that $L = \{x : x \in X_0, \ g(x) = 1\}$ and $g(x) \leqslant p(x)$ if $x \in X_0$.   By Theorem 1.71–D there exists $x' \in X^f$ such that $x'(x) = g(x)$ if $x \in X_0$ and $x'(x) \leqslant p(x)$ if $x \in X$.   The hyperplane $M = \{x : x'(x) = 1\}$ evidently contains L.   Theorem 3.41–B shows that $x'(x) \leqslant 1$ if $x \in K$.   If we assume that X is a topological linear space, the last assertions of the theorem follow from Theorem 3.6–C.

Theorem 3.6–E.   *Let K be a nonempty open convex set in a topological linear space X, and let L be a linear variety which does not intersect K. Then, there exists a closed hyperplane M which contains L and is such that K lies strictly on one side of M.*

PROOF.   The theorem is true if it is true for the case in which $0 \in K$, as we see by making suitable translations.   But, if $0 \in K$, K is absorbing, and the theorem results at once from Theorem 3.6–D.

PROBLEMS

A general X referred to in these problems is a real topological linear space.

1. If K_1 and K_2 are nonempty, nonintersecting convex sets and if K_1 is open, there exists a closed hyperplane M such that K_1 is in one of the two closed half spaces determined by M and K_2 is in the other.   If K_2 is also open, M can be chosen so that K_1 and K_2 are strictly on opposite sides of M.   Argument: $K = K_1 + (-1)K_2$ is convex, nonempty, open, and does not contain 0.   Hence there exists a closed hyperplane through 0 and not intersecting K_2.   A suitable parallel hyperplane can be chosen for M.

2. If $S \subset X$, a *support* of S is a hyperplane M such that S lies on one side of M and $S \cap M \neq \emptyset$.   If $x_0 \in S \cap M$, we say that S is supported by M at x_0. A closed convex set with a nonvacuous interior is called a *convex body*.   Show that a support of a convex body is closed and that the body is supported at every boundary point.   (See problem 2, § 3.4.)

3. Let K be a convex body in X and not all of X. Consider the closed half spaces containing K, and determined by the supports of K (see problem 2). The intersection of all these half spaces is K.

4. There exists a nonzero continuous linear functional x' defined on X if and only if in X there is at least one convex set which is open and contains 0 but is not all of X. For the "if" part, use Theorem 3.6–E, taking L to be a point not in the convex set. M. M. Day (see Day, **1**) has shown that there exists no nonzero continuous linear functional on $L^p(a, b)$ if $0 < p < 1$. For the topology of $L^p(a, b)$ see § 3.3, problem 7.

3.7 Seminorms

The concept of a seminorm plays an important role in the study of topological linear spaces. Seminorms are analytical devices for dealing with convex sets of a special sort. Seminorms are useful in describing the topology of a linear space if it is of the special type known as a locally convex topological linear space (see § 3.8).

Definition. Let X be a linear space (real or complex), and let p be a function with real values defined on X such that

(a) $\qquad\qquad p(x_1 + x_2) \leqslant p(x_1) + p(x_2)$ $\qquad$ if $x_1, x_2 \in X$,

(b) $\qquad\qquad p(\alpha x) = |\alpha| p(x)$ $\qquad$ if $x \in X$ and α is any scalar.

Then p is called a *seminorm* on X.

If p has the further property that $p(x) \neq 0$ if $x \neq 0$, p is a *norm* (see § 3.1). As with a norm, the properties of p imply the further properties

$(3.7–1)$ $\qquad\qquad\qquad p(0) = 0,$

$(3.7–2)$ $\qquad\qquad\qquad p(x) \geqslant 0,$

and

$(3.7–3)$ $\qquad\qquad |p(x_1) - p(x_2)| \leqslant p(x_1 - x_2).$

As we see by Theorem 3.41–A, if p is the Minkowski functional of a convex, balanced, and absorbing set K, then p is a seminorm. The following theorem shows that the converse is also true.

Theorem 3.7–A. *Let X be a linear space and p a seminorm on X. Let V be the set $\{x : p(x) < 1\}$. Then V is convex, balanced, and absorbing, and p is the Minkowski functional of V. If we suppose in addition that X is a topological linear space and that p is continuous, the set V is open.*

PROOF. Suppose $x_1, \ x_2 \in V$ and $0 \leqslant \alpha \leqslant 1$. Then $p(x_1) < 1$, $p(x_2) < 1$, and

$$p[(1 - \alpha)x_1 + \alpha x_2] \leqslant (1 - \alpha)p(x_1) + \alpha p(x_2) < 1,$$

by the properties a and b of p. Thus V is convex. The fact that V is balanced and absorbing follows from the homogeneity property b of p. Let q be the Minkowski functional of V. By definition, this means that $q(x)$ is the infimum of positive numbers α such that $x \in \alpha V$. But $\alpha > 0$ and $x \in \alpha V$ are together equivalent to $\alpha > 0$ and $p(x) < \alpha$. It is therefore clear that $p(x) = q(x)$. The final assertion of the theorem, about V being open, is true as a consequence of Theorem 2.12–A.

Before considering the next theorem we shall make some general observations about linear functionals on complex linear spaces. Suppose that X is a complex linear space. Then, we can also regard X as a real linear space simply by restricting our attention to real scalars. Let us denote by X_r the real linear space obtained from X by adopting this point of view. Now consider a linear functional $x' \in X^f$. If $x \in X$ let us denote the real and imaginary parts of $x'(x)$ by $x_1'(x)$ and $x_2'(x)$, respectively, so that $x'(x) = x_1'(x) + ix_2'(x)$. Since $x'(ix) = ix'(x)$, we have

$$x_1'(ix) + ix_2'(ix) = ix_1'(x) - x_2'(x),$$

whence $x_2'(x) = - x_1'(ix)$, and so

(3.7–4) $$x'(x) = x_1'(x) - ix_1'(ix).$$

It is readily verified that $x_1' \in (X_r)^f$, i.e., that x_1' is a *real*-valued linear functional on the *real* linear space X_r. Conversely, if we start with *any* element $x_1' \in (X_r)^f$ and define x' by (3.7–4), it is easy to verify that $x'(\alpha x) = \alpha x'(x)$ for all *complex* scalars and that $x' \in X^f$.

Theorem 3.7–B. *Let X be a linear space, and let p be a seminorm defined on X. Let M be a linear manifold in X and f a linear functional defined on M such that $|f(x)| \leqslant p(x)$ if $x \in M$. Then, there exists a linear functional F defined on X such that $|F(x)| \leqslant p(x)$, if $x \in X$, and $F(x) = f(x)$ if $x \in M$.*

PROOF. Observe that the seminorm p is a sublinear functional (defined just preceding Theorem 1.71–D). Since $p(- x) = p(x)$, it may be noted that, for a linear F, $F(x) \leqslant p(x)$ for all x implies $|F(x)| \leqslant p(x)$. For $- F(x) = F(- x) \leqslant p(- x) = p(x)$, or $- p(x) \leqslant F(x)$. The two inequalities yield $|F(x)| \leqslant p(x)$.

For the case in which X is a real space, the present theorem is a direct application of Theorem 1.71–D. If X is a complex space, we proceed as follows: Denote X by X_r when we consider it as a linear space with real scalars; likewise with M and M_r. We write $f(x) = f_1(x) - if_1(ix)$, with $f_1(x)$ the real part of $f(x)$. Then f_1 is a real linear functional on M_r [by the discussion accompanying (3.7–4)]. Now, $|f_1(x)| \leqslant |f(x)| \leqslant p(x)$ if $x \in M$. Hence, by what we already know for the real case, there exists a real linear functional F_1 on X_r such that $F_1(x) = f_1(x)$ if $x \in M_r$ and $|F_1(x)| \leqslant p(x)$ if $x \in X$. We define $F(x) = F_1(x) - iF_1(ix)$. Then F is a linear functional on the complex space X, and $F(x) = f(x)$ if $x \in M$. For any given x let $F(x) = re^{i\theta}$ $(r \geqslant 0)$. Then $F(e^{-i\theta}x) = e^{-i\theta}F(x) = r$. Since this is a real value, $F(e^{-i\theta}x) = F_1(e^{-i\theta}x)$. Then $|F(x)| = F_1(e^{-i\theta}x) \leqslant p(e^{-i\theta}x) = p(x)$. This completes the proof.

Theorem 3.7–C. *Let X be a topological linear space, x_0 a point of X, and p a seminorm on X which is continuous. Then, there exists a continuous linear functional F defined on X, such that $F(x_0) = p(x_0)$ and $|F(x)| \leqslant p(x)$ if $x \in X$.*

PROOF. Let M be the set of all elements αx_0, and define f on M by $f(\alpha x_0) = \alpha p(x_0)$. Then f is linear on M and $|f(\alpha x_0)| = p(\alpha x_0)$. Hence, by Theorem 3.7–B, there exists a linear functional F defined on X such that F is an extension of f and $|F(x)| \leqslant p(x)$. This inequality shows that F is continuous at 0 (and hence continuous at all points) because p is continuous. Clearly $F(x_0) = f(x_0) = p(x_0)$.

Theorem 3.7–D. *Let X be a topological linear space, and let V be a subset of X which is closed, balanced, convex, and of which 0 is an interior point. Let x_0 be a point on the boundary of V. Then, there exists a continuous linear functional F defined on X such that $F(x_0) = 1$ and $|F(x)| \leqslant 1$ if $x \in V$.*

PROOF. Let p be the Minkowski functional of V (see § 3.41). The properties of V assure us that p is a seminorm (by Theorem 3.41–A), and by Theorem 3.41–C we see that $V = \{x:p(x) \leqslant 1\}$, that p is continuous, and that the interior of V is the set $\{x:p(x) < 1\}$. Consequently $p(x_0) = 1$, since x_0 is on the boundary of V. The conclusions now follow from Theorem 3.7–C.

One of the important uses of this theorem is in the proof of Theorem 4.7–C.

3.8 Locally Convex Spaces

Among topological linear spaces which are not normed linear spaces, there is a class of spaces for which theoretical developments along the lines drawn for normed linear spaces seem to be more satisfactory than is possible without restriction of attention to this class. This class of spaces is characterized by the existence of a base at 0 composed of convex sets. The spaces are said to be locally convex. The main reason for singling out locally convex spaces for special attention lies in the fact that for such spaces we can prove certain important theorems about the existence of continuous linear functionals. In this section we discuss briefly a few of the main features of locally convex spaces.

Definition. A topological linear space X is called *locally convex* if every neighborhood of 0 contains a convex neighborhood of 0.

If X is locally convex and $\mathscr{U}$ is the family of all balanced and convex neighborhoods of 0, this family is a base at 0 (see Theorem 3.4–H). It is easily verified that, if $U \in \mathscr{U}$, then $\alpha U \in \mathscr{U}$ when $\alpha \neq 0$; also, there exists $V \in \mathscr{U}$ such that $V + V \subset U$ (use Theorem 3.4–B).

One way of constructing a locally convex topology is described in the following theorem.

Theorem 3.8–A. *Suppose that X is a linear space and that $\mathscr{U}$ is a nonempty family of nonempty subsets of X with the properties:*

1. *Each member of $\mathscr{U}$ is balanced, convex, and absorbing.*
2. *If $U \in \mathscr{U}$, there exists some α such that $0 < \alpha \leqslant {}^1\!/_2$ and $\alpha U \in \mathscr{U}$.*
3. *If U_1 and U_2 are in $\mathscr{U}$, there exists $U_3 \in \mathscr{U}$ such that $U_3 \subset U_1 \cap U_2$.*
4. *If $U \in \mathscr{U}$ and $x \in U$, there exists $V \in \mathscr{U}$ such that $x + V \subset U$.*

Then there is a unique topology for X such that X is a locally convex topological linear space with $\mathscr{U}$ as a base at 0.

PROOF. If we compare this theorem with Theorem 3.3–F, we see that it suffices to prove that, if $U \in \mathscr{U}$, there exists $V \in \mathscr{U}$ such that $V + V \subset U$. With U given we select α as in (2), and let $V = \alpha U$. Then $V + V = \alpha U + \alpha U = 2\alpha U \subset U$ as a result of the fact that $2\alpha \leqslant 1$ and that U is convex and balanced.

Next we show how seminorms may be used to define a locally convex topology.

Theorem 3.8–B. *Let P be a nonempty family of seminorms defined on the linear space X. For each $p \in P$ let $V(p)$ be the set $\{x : p(x) < 1\}$. Let $\mathscr{U}$ be the family of all finite intersections*

$$r_1 V(p_1) \cap r_2 V(p_2) \cap \cdots \cap r_n V(p_n), \qquad r_k > 0, \qquad p_k \in P.$$

Then $\mathscr{U}$ satisfies the conditions of Theorem 3.8–A.

PROOF. The sets $V(p)$ are balanced, convex, and absorbing (Theorem 3.7–A). The members of $\mathscr{U}$ also have these properties. Verification of conditions 2 and 3 in Theorem 3.8–A is left to the reader. As for (4), if $U = r_1 V(p_1) \cap \cdots \cap r_n V(p_n)$ and $x \in U$, it suffices to take $V = \alpha_1 V(p_1) \cap \cdots \cap \alpha_n V(p_n)$, where $\alpha_k = r_k - p_k(x)$.

Observe that $rV(p) = \{x : p(x) < r\}$.

Definition.   The topology for X determined by taking the family $\mathscr{U}$ of Theorem 3.8–B as a base at 0 is called the topology generated by the family P of seminorms.

Observe that, if P contains just one element p and if p is a norm, $\mathscr{U}$ is the family of all spheres $\{x:p(x) < r\}$, and the topology for X generated by P is the topology of X as a normed linear space with norm p.

If X is a locally convex space and P is the family of all continuous seminorms on X, the topology of X is exactly the topology generated by P.   The fact that P is not empty follows from the results of § 3.41 (see especially Theorem 3.41–C, part e).

If $p_1, \cdots, p_n$ are seminorms on X and if $\alpha_1, \cdots, \alpha_n$ are positive, let us define

$$p(x) = \max \{\alpha_1 p_1(x), \cdots, \alpha_n p_n(x)\}.$$

Then p also is a seminorm.   If $p_1, \cdots, p_n$ are continuous, so is p.   These observations are useful in connection with the formulation of the continuity of a linear operator by means of conditions involving seminorms.

Theorem 3.8–C.   *Let X and Y be locally convex topological linear spaces, and let Q be a family of seminorms which generates the topology of Y.   Let T be a linear operator on X into Y.   Then T is continuous on X if and only if to each $q \in Q$ there corresponds some continuous seminorm p on X such that $q(Tx) \leqslant p(x)$ for each $x \in X$.*

PROOF.   We prove the "only if" assertion and leave the rest of the proof to the reader.   Let T be continuous, and suppose $q \in Q$.   Then $\{y:q(y) < 1\}$ is a neighborhood of 0 in Y.   Hence there exists a set $V = r_1 V(p_1) \cap \cdots \cap r_n V(p_n)$ (in the notation of Theorem 3.8–B), determined by continuous seminorms $p_1, \cdots, p_n$ on X and positive numbers $r_1, \cdots, r_n$, such that $q(Tx) < 1$ if $x \in V$.   Then

$$p(x) = \max_k \frac{1}{r_k} p_k(x)$$

defines a continuous seminorm p.   If x is arbitrary in X and α is chosen so that $p(x) < \alpha$, it follows that $x/\alpha \in V$ and hence $q(Tx) < \alpha$.   Since α can be as close to $p(x)$ as we please, we infer that $q(Tx) \leqslant p(x)$.

The reader will note that the condition for continuity in the foregoing theorem specializes to the condition $\|Tx\| \leqslant M\|x\|$ of Theorem 3.1–A in case the space is a normed linear space.

We come now to the theorems about the existence of continuous linear functionals in certain situations.

Theorem 3.8–D. *Let X be a locally convex topological linear space. Let M be a linear manifold in X, and let f be a continuous linear functional on M. Then, there exists a continuous linear functional F on X which is an extension of f.*

PROOF. Since f is continuous and X is locally convex, there exists a balanced and convex neighborhood of 0, say V, such that $|f(x)| < 1$ if $x \in M \cap V$. Let p be the Minkowski functional of V. Then p is a seminorm, it is continuous, and $V = \{x : p(x) < 1\}$ (Theorems 3.41–A and 3.41–C). For any $x \in M$ choose α so that $\alpha > p(x)$. Then $p(x/\alpha) < 1$ and so $|f(x/\alpha)| < 1$, or $|f(x)| < \alpha$. By letting $\alpha \to p(x)$ we see that $|f(x)| \leqslant p(x)$. Applying Theorem 3.7–B, we obtain a linear functional F on X which is an extension of f and such that $|F(x)| \leqslant p(x)$ for every x. This inequality and Theorem 3.8–C show that F is continuous, so the proof is complete.

Theorem 3.8–E. *Let X be a locally convex topological linear space. Let X_0 be a closed subspace of X, and suppose $x_1 \in X - X_0$. Then, there exists a continuous linear functional x' on X such that $x'(x_1) = 1$ and $x'(x) = 0$ if $x \in X_0$.*

PROOF. Consider the subspace M generated by x_1 and X_0, and represent elements of M uniquely in the form $m = \alpha x_1 + x$, $x \in X_0$. The set $x_1 + X_0$ (i.e., the set of elements of M for which $\alpha = 1$) is closed and does not contain 0. Hence there exists a balanced convex neighborhood of 0, which we denote by V, such that V does not intersect $x_1 + X_0$. Let p be the Minkowski functional of V; p is a continuous seminorm and $V = \{x : p(x) < 1\}$. We then have $p(x_1 + x) \geqslant 1$ if $x \in X_0$. Let us define a functional m' on M by setting $m'(m) = \alpha$. We assert that $|m'(m)| \leqslant p(m)$. If $\alpha = 0$, this is clear, and if $\alpha \neq 0$, we have $p(m) = p(\alpha x_1 + x) = |\alpha| p(x_1 + \alpha^{-1}x) \geqslant |\alpha| = |m'(m)|$, because $\alpha^{-1}x \in X_0$. Since p is continuous it now follows that m' is continuous. Observe that $m'(m) = 0$ if $m \in X_0$ and that $m'(x_1) = 1$. Applying Theorem 3.8–D we finish the proof.

Theorem 3.8–F. *Let X be a locally convex topological linear space which is a T_1-space. Then, if $x_0 \neq 0$, there exists a continuous linear functional x' on X such that $x'(x_0) = 1$.*

PROOF. We can take $X_0 = (0)$ and apply Theorem 3.8–E; X_0 will be closed, since X is a T_1-space.

The next theorem gives a simple criterion for a space to be a T_1-space.

Theorem 3.8–G. *If X is a locally convex topological linear space with* *topology generated by a family P of seminorms, then X is a T_1-space if and only if to each $x \neq 0$ corresponds $p \in P$ such that $p(x) \neq 0$.*

The proof is left to the reader.

The main reference to locally convex spaces in this book comes in connection with the study of "weak" topologies; one aspect of this subject is introduced in the following example, and other aspects are considered in § 3.81.

Example I. Let T be any nonempty set. Let X be a linear space composed of elements which are real-valued (or complex-valued) functions x defined on T. X need not comprise *all* functions defined on T. For example, X might consist of all bounded functions or of all functions meeting some prescribed condition, provided that $x + y$ and αx meet the condition whenever x and y do. As a family of seminorms take

$$p_t(x) = |x(t)|$$

for each $t \in T$. This family of seminorms generates a locally convex topology for X. With this topology X is a T_1-space, by Theorem 3.8–G. We note that $x_n \to x$ (convergence in the sense of this topology) means that $x_n(t) \to x(t)$ (convergence in the usual sense for scalars) for each $t \in T$.

There is an aspect of this topology for X which is interesting and significant, namely, the following: For a given $t \in T$ consider $x(t)$ as a function of x, with x varying over X. This function is continuous on X in the topology just defined. For, if $x_0 \in X$ and $\epsilon > 0$ and U is the neighborhood of 0 defined by $U = \{x : p_t(x) < \epsilon\}$, we see that $|x(t) - x_0(t)| < \epsilon$ means the same thing as $x \in x_0 + U$. Suppose for a moment that we consider any topology for X which is such that $x(t)$ is continuous as a function of x, no matter how t is chosen in T. Then, if $\epsilon > 0$, the set $\{x : |x(t)| < \epsilon\}$ is open, for it is the inverse image of an open set of scalars. But

$$\{x : |x(t)| < \epsilon\} = \{x : p_t(x) < \epsilon\}.$$

Hence the given topology for X contains among its open sets the base at 0 in the topology for X generated by the family of seminorms. This shows that the latter topology is the weakest topology for X with respect to which $x(t)$ is continuous as a function of x for each t. It is called the *weak topology of X as a space of functions*. One specific example of T and X is that in which T is the set of positive integers and X is the space of *all* sequences $x = \{\xi_1, \xi_2, \cdots\}$. The weak topology of X arises from the demand that each ξ_n be a continuous function of x.

We conclude this section with an example of a different sort.

Example 2. Suppose c is either a positive real number or $+\infty$. Let X be the linear space of all functions x of the complex variable t representable as a power series

$$x(t) = \sum_{0}^{\infty} \dot{\xi}_n t^n$$

which is convergent if $|t| < c$. The coefficients $\dot{\xi}_n$ are to be complex. For each R such that $0 < R < c$ let

$$p_R(x) = \sum_{0}^{\infty} |\dot{\xi}_n| R^n.$$

It is readily evident that p_R is a norm on X. The family of these norms, obtained by varying R, generates a locally convex topology for X and makes X a T_1-space. Convergence in this topology is equivalent to uniform convergence on each compact subset of the set $\{t : |t| < c\}$. This is easily verified if we recall that when $0 < b < c$ and $M_b = \max |x(t)|$ for $|t| = b$, then

$$|\dot{\xi}_n| \leqslant \frac{M_b}{b^n}.$$

It may also be verified that a set S in this space X is bounded, in the sense defined in § 3.3, if and only if the family of functions forming the set S is uniformly bounded on each compact subset of the set $\{t : |t| < c\}$. It is a well-known theorem (due to Montel) of classical function theory that from every infinite sequence in such a family of functions there can be selected a subsequence which converges uniformly on each compact subset of the domain on which the family is defined. This leads (by means of the fact that X is metrizable and that when metrized it is complete) to the conclusion that the space under consideration has the property that all of its closed and bounded subsets are compact. Since the space is not finite dimensional, the situation is in strong contrast with the situation for normed linear spaces (see Theorem 3.12–F). For information about metrizability, see § 3.9, especially Theorem 3.9–B.

PROBLEMS

1. Let P be the family of all seminorms on the linear space X, where $X \neq (0)$. This family is nonempty, and the topology it generates is the strongest locally convex topology on X. Moreover, it is a T_1-topology. Suggestion: Given $x_0 \neq 0$, choose a Hamel basis for X of which x_0 is a member. For any $x \in X$ let $p(x)$ be the absolute value of the coefficient of x_0 in the representation of x in terms of the Hamel basis.

2. If S is a set in the locally convex topological linear space X, S is bounded if and only if each continuous seminorm is bounded on S. Instead of *all* continuous seminorms it is sufficient to consider those in a family which generates the topology.

3. For the next problem we require the following result: Let A and B be disjoint sets in the topological linear space X (not necessarily locally convex). Assume A compact and B closed. Then, there exists a neighborhood of 0, say V, such that $A + V$ and $B + V$ are disjoint. Outline of argument: Assume $(A + V) \cap (B + V) \neq \emptyset$, no matter how V is chosen (as a neighborhood of 0). If V is symmetric, this implies that $A \cap (B + V + V) \neq \emptyset$, for we can choose $a \in A, b \in B, v_1 \in V, v_2 \in V$ so that $a + v_1 = b + v_2$, whence $a \in A \cap (B + V + V)$.

Show that, if $V_1, \cdots, V_n$ are symmetric neighborhoods of 0, $\bigcap_{i=1}^{n} [A \cap (B + V_i + V_i)] \neq \emptyset$, and deduce the existence of $x_0 \in A \cap \bigcap_V [\overline{A \cap (B + V + V)}]$.

Hence, for any symmetric V, $x_0 + V$ must intersect $A \cap (B + V + V)$. From this deduce that $x_0 \in B$, a contradiction.

4. Let X be a real locally convex topological linear space. Let K_1, K_2 be nonempty, nonintersecting convex sets in X, with K_1 closed and K_2 compact. Then, there exists a closed hyperplane M such that K_1 and K_2 lie strictly on opposite sides of M. Argument: Let V be a convex neighborhood of 0. Then $K_1 + V$ and $K_2 + V$ are open and convex. By problem 3 we may choose V so that $(K_1 + V) \cap (K_2 + V) = \emptyset$. Now apply the result of problem 1, § 3.6.

5. If K is a closed convex set in the real locally convex topological linear space X, then K is the intersection of all the closed half spaces which contain it. Can we also assert this for open half spaces?

6. Let K be a nonempty compact convex set in the real locally convex topological linear T_1-space. Consider the closed half spaces which contain K and which are determined by the supports of K (see problem 2, § 3.6). *The intersection of these half spaces is K.* It suffices to show that, if x_0 is a point not in K, there exists a support M of K such that x_0 and K are not in the same one of the two closed half spaces determined by M. Choose (x_0) and K as the K_1 and K_2 of problem 4, and obtain a separating closed hyperplane, say with equation $x'(x) = \alpha$. By considering the values of x' on K, a suitable support of K may be found as a hyperplane $x'(x) = \beta$.

3.81 Weak Topologies for Linear Spaces. Duality

In this section we consider briefly the basic notions about a class of topologies, called *weak topologies*, for a linear space. These notions are developed further in connection with normed linear spaces, in Chapter 4.

Suppose that X is any linear space (real or complex), and let F be a nonempty set in X^f. In what follows immediately hereafter we use A, A_1, A_2, etc. to denote nonempty finite subsets of F. For any such A and any $\epsilon > 0$ let

$$U(A; \epsilon) = \{x : |x'(x)| < \epsilon \qquad \text{if } x' \in A\}.$$

It is no trouble to verify that $0 \in U(A; \epsilon)$, that $U(A; \epsilon)$ is balanced, convex, and absorbing, that $U(A_1 \cup A_2; \min [\epsilon_1, \epsilon_2]) \subset U(A_1; \epsilon_1) \cap U(A_2; \epsilon_2)$, and that $\alpha U(A; \epsilon) = U(A; |\alpha| \epsilon)$ if $\alpha \neq 0$. If $x \in U(A; \epsilon)$, let $\delta = \sup_{x' \in A} |x'(x)|$, so that $0 \leqslant \delta < \epsilon$. Then $x + U(A; \epsilon - \delta) \subset U(A; \epsilon)$. It follows by Theorem 3.8–A that the family of all sets $U(A; \epsilon)$ is a base at 0 for a uniquely defined locally convex topology on X. We denote this topology by $\mathscr{T}(X, F)$. If p is the Minkowski functional of $U(A; \epsilon)$, it is a seminorm which is continuous on X in the topology just defined. It is easy to demonstrate that

$$p(x) = \frac{1}{\epsilon} \sup_{x' \in A} |x'(x)|.$$

The following theorem is of basic importance to an understanding of the nature of the topology $\mathscr{T}(X, F)$.

Theorem 3.81–A. *An element x' of X^f is continuous on X with the topology $\mathscr{T}(X, F)$ if and only if x' is in the linear manifold generated by F.*

PROOF. The proof that x' is continuous if $x' \in F$ is easy, and we leave it to the reader. The "if" assertion follows at once. Now assume that $y' \in X^f$ and that y' is continuous in the $\mathscr{T}(X, F)$ topology. By Theorem 3.8–C, with Y the space of scalars, we see that there exists some finite subset A of F and some $\epsilon > 0$ such that

$$|y'(x)| \leqslant \frac{1}{\epsilon} \sup_{x' \in A} |x'(x)|$$

for every x in X. It follows that $y'(x) = 0$ whenever $x'(x) = 0$ for every x' in A. If $x_1', \cdots, x_n'$ is a maximal linearly independent subset of A, it follows by Theorem 3.5–C that y' is a linear combination of $x_1', \cdots, x_n'$. This completes the proof.

If A is a set consisting of a single element x', then $U(A; \epsilon)$ is the inverse image, under x', of the set of scalars α for which $|\alpha| < \epsilon$. It follows easily from this remark and Theorem 3.81–A that $\mathscr{T}(X, F)$ is the weakest topology for X which makes it a topological linear space and which makes all the elements of F continuous on X. This is the reason why $\mathscr{T}(X, F)$ is called a weak topology for X.

It follows from the foregoing remarks that, if M is the linear manifold generated by F, the topologies $\mathscr{T}(X, F)$ and $\mathscr{T}(X, M)$ are the same. Also, if M_1 and M_2 are linear manifolds in X^f, with M_1 a proper subset of M_2, the topology $\mathscr{T}(X, M_2)$ is strictly stronger than $\mathscr{T}(X, M_1)$.

An explanation of the conditions under which $\mathscr{T}(X, F)$ makes X a T_1-space depends upon the concept of a *total* set of linear functionals.

Definition.   A set $F \subset X^f$ is called total if to each $x \neq 0$ in X there corresponds some x' in F such that $x'(x) \neq 0$.   Or, equivalently, F is total if $x'(x) = 0$ for each $x' \in F$ implies $x = 0$.

For example, if $X = C[a, b]$ and F is the set of functionals of the form $x'(x) = x(r)$, where $a \leqslant r \leqslant b$ and r is rational, then F is total.

Theorem 3.81–B.   *The topology $\mathscr{T}(X, F)$ makes X a T_1-space if and only if F is total.*

This follows directly from Theorem 3.8–G.

When F is total, we may identify X with a certain space of functions defined on F.   We identify x with the function whose value at x' in F is $x'(x)$.   The topology $\mathscr{T}(X, F)$ is then the same as the weak topology described in Example 1, § 3.8, where T is taken to be F.

Suppose now that M is a subspace of X^f.   If x is a fixed element of X and x' is a variable element of M, the expression $x'(x)$ defines an element of M^f, and the set G of such elements is a linear manifold and a total set in M^f.   Hence the weak topology $\mathscr{T}(M, G)$ for M makes M a locally convex topological linear space and a T_1-space.   If M itself is total as a subset of X^f, we can identify X and G (i.e., the correspondence between x and the element of G which it defines establishes an isomorphism of X and G as linear spaces).   In this case we shall write $\mathscr{T}(M, X)$ in place of $\mathscr{T}(M, G)$.   There is a kind of *duality* here: M is the class of all linear functionals on X which are continuous in the topology $\mathscr{T}(X, M)$, and X is identified with the class G of all the linear functionals on M which are continuous in the topology $\mathscr{T}(M, X)$.

It sometimes happens that we consider weak topologies for a linear space X which is already a locally convex topological linear space, say with a topology $\mathscr{T}_0$.   Let M be the class of all those elements of X^f which are continuous on X with respect to the topology $\mathscr{T}_0$.   As we have already noted, the topology $\mathscr{T}(X, M)$ is weaker than $\mathscr{T}_0$ (though not necessarily strictly weaker).   We observe, as a consequence of Theorem 3.8–F, that, if X is a T_1-space, then M will be total.

Theorem 3.81–C.   *Let X, $\mathscr{T}_0$, and M be as described in the foregoing paragraph (X need not be a T_1-space).   Then, a linear manifold in X is closed relative to the topology $\mathscr{T}_0$ if and only if it is closed relative to the topology $\mathscr{T}(X, M)$.*

PROOF.   Let L be the linear manifold in question.   We prove that L is closed relative to $\mathscr{T}(X, M)$ if it is closed relative to $\mathscr{T}_0$.   The other half of the proof is evident by taking the complement of L and using the fact that $\mathscr{T}(X, M)$ is weaker than $\mathscr{T}_0$.   Suppose $x_0 \in X - L$.   By

Theorem 3.8–E there exists $x' \in M$ such that $x'(x_0) = 1$ and $x'(x) = 0$ if $x \in L$. Suppose $0 < \epsilon < 1$. The set $\{x : |x'(x - x_0)| < \epsilon\}$ is a neighborhood of x_0 in the topology $\mathscr{T}(X, M)$. This neighborhood lies in $X - L$, and therefore $X - L$ is open relative to $\mathscr{T}(X, M)$. Then L is closed relative to $\mathscr{T}(X, M)$.

PROBLEMS

1. Let X be any linear space and M any subspace of X^f. A nonempty subset $S \subset X$ is bounded relative to the topology $\mathscr{T}(X, M)$ if and only if $\sup_{x \in S} |x'(x)| < \infty$ for each $x' \in M$.

2. Let X be a locally convex topological linear T_1-space. Let M be the set of those $x' \in X^f$ which are continuous on X. Let V_0 be a balanced and convex neighborhood of 0 which is bounded relative to the topology $\mathscr{T}(X, M)$, and let p_0 be the Minkowski functional of V_0. Then p_0 is a norm. It can be shown that the topology generated by p_0 is the same as the given topology of X. See problem 8, § 4.4.

3. Let X be a complex linear space, and let X_r be the associated real linear space (as in § 3.7). If $x' \in X^f$ and $x'(x) = x_1'(x) - ix_1'(ix)$, where $x_1' \in (X_r)^f$ [see (3.7–4)], we may look upon x' as an element of $(X^f)_r$, and the correspondence $x' \leftrightarrow x_1'$ establishes an isomorphism of $(X^f)_r$ and $(X_r)^f$. Let M be a complex linear manifold in X^f, and let M_1 be the corresponding real linear manifold in $(X_r)^f$. Show that the topology $\mathscr{T}(X, M)$, as applied to X_r, coincides with $\mathscr{T}(X_r, M_1)$.

4. Let X be a locally convex topological T_1-space, and let S be a convex set in X. Let X' be the set of all the continuous linear functionals on X. Then, the closure of S with respect to the given topology of X is the same as the closure of S with respect to the weak topology $\mathscr{T}(X, X')$. Use Theorem 3.81–C and problem 5 in § 3.8.

3.9 Metric Linear Spaces

Suppose that X is a linear space and that there is a metric $d(x_1, x_2)$ defined on X. If the metric has the property

$$(3.9\text{–}1) \qquad\qquad d(x_1 + y, x_2 + y) = d(x_1, x_2)$$

for every choice of x_1, x_2 and y, we call it an *invariant metric*. If the metric is invariant, the choice $y = -x_2$ shows that

$$(3.9\text{–}2) \qquad\qquad d(x_1 - x_2, 0) = d(x_1, x_2).$$

Conversely, if (3.9–2) holds for all choices of x_1, x_2, the metric is invariant, as we see at once.

Definition. We shall say that X is a *metric linear space* if it is a topological linear space with topology derived from an invariant metric $d(x_1, x_2)$.

A normed linear space is a metric linear space, for the metric $d(x_1, x_2) = \|x_1 - x_2\|$ derived from a norm is certainly invariant. However, there are metric linear spaces in which the metric is not derived from a norm. In order to see the similarities and differences when comparing metric linear spaces with normed linear spaces, it is convenient to abbreviate $d(x, 0)$ by the notation $|x|$. We see from the properties of the invariant metric that

$$(3.9\text{–}3) \qquad\qquad |x + y| \leqslant |x| + |y|,$$

$$(3.9\text{–}4) \qquad\qquad |-x| = |x|,$$

$$(3.9\text{–}5) \qquad\qquad |x| = 0 \qquad \text{if and only if } x = 0.$$

There is nothing to guarantee that $|\alpha x| = |\alpha|\,|x|$, however, and so $|x|$ may not be a norm. An example will be given presently. Of course, $d(x, 0)$ is a continuous function of x and αx is a continuous function of α and x; therefore $|\alpha x|$ is a continuous function of α and x. It follows that

$$(3.9\text{–}6) \qquad |\alpha_n x| \to 0 \qquad \text{if } |\alpha_n| \to 0,$$

$$(3.9\text{–}7) \qquad |\alpha x_n| \to 0 \qquad \text{if } |x_n| \to 0,$$

$$(3.9\text{–}8) \qquad |\alpha_n x_n| \to 0 \qquad \text{if } |\alpha_n| \to 0 \text{ and } |x_n| \to 0.$$

The following theorem shows how a metric linear space may be characterized by specifying properties of $|x|$ rather than properties of a metric.

Theorem 3.9–A. *Let X be a linear space, and suppose $|x|$ is a real-valued function on X with the six properties* (3.9–3)–(3.9–8). *Make the definition $d(x_1, x_2) = |x_1 - x_2|$. Then d is an invariant metric on X, and, with this metric, X is a metric linear space.*

The proof is left to the reader. For continuity of scalar multiplication we observe that

$$|\alpha_n x_n - \alpha x| \leqslant |(\alpha_n - \alpha)x| + |\alpha(x_n - x)| + |(\alpha_n - \alpha)(x_n - x)|.$$

Some simple examples of nonnormed, but metric, linear spaces are based on the inequality

$$(3.9\text{–}9) \qquad\qquad \frac{|A + B|}{1 + |A + B|} \leqslant \frac{|A|}{1 + |A|} + \frac{|B|}{1 + |B|},$$

which is valid if A and B are arbitrary real or complex numbers. A proof of (3.9–9) follows readily from the observation that $x(1 + x)^{-1}$ increases as the real variable x increases, if $x > -1$ (check by computing the derivative).

Example 1. The space (s). The class of all sequences $x = \{\xi_n\}$ becomes a metric linear space if we define

$$(3.9–10) \qquad |x| = \sum_{n=1}^{\infty} \mu_n \frac{|\xi_n|}{1 + |\xi_n|},$$

where $\{u_n\}$ is any fixed sequence of positive numbers such that $\sum_{1}^{\infty} \mu_n$ is convergent. We denote this space by (s).

Convergence in (s) is merely componentwise convergence. That is, if $x^{(i)} = \{\xi_n^{(i)}\}$, then $\|x^{(i)} - x\| \to 0$ as $i \to \infty$ if and only if $\lim_{i \to \infty} \xi_n^{(i)} = \xi_n$ for each n. Proof is left to the reader. It follows that (s) is a complete metric space.

Example 2. *The space S.* Let $[a, b]$ be a finite closed interval of the real axis. Consider the family of all real-valued functions defined on $[a, b]$ which are measurable in the Lebesgue sense, but not necessarily bounded. By using almost-everywhere equality as an equivalence relation this family gives rise to a family of equivalence classes which we make into a linear space (see, e.g., the discussion of $\mathscr{L}^p$ and L^p in Example 7, § 1.2). If x is one of the equivalence classes, we define

$$(3.9–11) \qquad |x| = \int_a^b \frac{|x(t)|}{1 + |x(t)|} \, dt,$$

where $x(t)$ denotes a representative function for x. We then obtain a metric linear space, which we denote by S. We can also consider the case in which the functions are complex-valued.

Convergence in S is interpretable in terms of convergence *in measure*. We recall the definition: $x_n(t)$ converges in measure to $x(t)$ if for each $\epsilon > 0$ the measure of the set $\{t : |x_n(t) - x(t)| \geq \epsilon\}$ converges to zero as $n \to \infty$. Let $E_n(\epsilon)$ be the set in question. By decomposing $[a, b]$ into the union of $E_n(\epsilon)$ and its complement we see from (3.9–11) that

$$|x_n - x| \leq m(E_n(\epsilon)) + \epsilon(b - a),$$

where m refers to Lebesgue measure. Also, since $\alpha(1 + \alpha)^{-1}$ is an increasing function of α when $\alpha > -1$, we see that

$$|x_n - x| \geq \int_{E_n(\epsilon)} \frac{|x_n(t) - x(t)|}{1 + |x_n(t) - x(t)|} \, dt \geq \frac{\epsilon}{1 + \epsilon} m(E_n(\epsilon)).$$

From the foregoing considerations it is clear that $|x_n - x| \to 0$ as $n \to \infty$ is equivalent to convergence in measure of $x_n(t)$ to $x(t)$. From a well-known fact about convergence in measure it then follows that S is a complete metric space (see, e.g., Halmos, **2**, Theorem E, page 93).

A complete metric linear space has been called a space of type (F) by Banach (Banach, **1**, Chapter III). The F is for Fréchet, who made important contributions in the early studies of linear spaces with a metric. Currently, however, the designation "a space of type (F)" is sometimes used with the additional assumption that the space is locally convex (see, e.g., Dieudonné, **2**, page 499).

We say that a topological linear space X is *metrizable* if its topology is metrizable, i.e., if there is a metric in X such that the metric topology is the same as the given topology of X. Now, in a metric space there is a countable base of neighborhoods at each point (e.g., the interiors of spheres of radii $1/n$ with centers at the point, $n = 1, 2, \cdots$). Moreover, a metric space is of course a T_1-space. Hence, in order that a topological linear space be metrizable, it is *necessary* that it be a T_1-space and that there exist a countable base at 0. These necessary conditions are also *sufficient*, not merely to guarantee that the space is metrizable, but that it be metrizable with an invariant metric. We state this formally:

Theorem 3.9–B. *Let X be a T_1-topological linear space in which there exists a countable base at 0. Then X is metrizable with an invariant metric.*

We omit the rather lengthy proof of this theorem. See Kelley, **1**, pages 185–186 and p. 210.

In a metric linear space the concept of boundedness, as defined in § 3.3 for a topological linear space, does not need to coincide with the concept of boundedness for a metric space, as defined in § 2.4. A set may be metrically bounded but not bounded in the sense of § 3.3. This is easily shown to be possible in the space (s) of Example 1. In fact, the space as a whole is metrically bounded, but not bounded as a topological linear space.

PROBLEMS

1. A topological linear T_1-space is metrizable if there exists a bounded neighborhood of 0. The converse is not true. A space is called *locally bounded* if there exists in it a bounded neighborhood of 0.

2. Let X be a linear space, and suppose M is a subspace of X^f. Then the topology $\mathcal{T}(X, M)$ defined in § 3.81 is metrizable if and only if M is total and possesses an at most countable Hamel basis. The topology is normable if and only if M is total and finite dimensional.

3. Consider $L^p = L(a, b)$, where (a, b) is any interval of the real axis and $0 < p < 1$. For $x \in L^p$ let

$$|x| = \int_a^b |x(s)|^p \, ds.$$

Then L^p becomes a complete locally bounded metric linear space according to the prescription of Theorem 3.9-A. For the inequality $|x + y| \leqslant |x| + |y|$ see Hardy, Littlewood and Pólya **1**, Theorem 199, page 147. The space is not locally convex; in fact, the only nonempty open convex set in L^p is the whole space (see problem 4, § 3.6).

4. Consider H^p, where $0 < p < 1$ (see Example 8, § 3.11). For $f \in H^p$ define

$$|f| = \sup_{0 \leqslant r < 1} \int_0^{2\pi} |f(re^{i\theta})|^p \, d\theta = \int_0^{2\pi} |f(e^{i\theta})|^p \, d\theta.$$

Then H^p may be regarded as a closed subspace of $L^p(0, 2\pi)$. In contrast to the situation for L^p, H^p possesses many continuous nonzero linear functionals. In fact, for a fixed z with $|z| < 1$, $f(z)$ is a continuous linear functional of f. Also, the Taylor coefficients in the power series expansion of f are such functionals. For discussion of H^p when $0 < p < 1$, see Walters, **1, 2**. A. E. Livingston, **1**, has shown that the space is not locally convex and hence certainly not normable.

5. If x' is a continuous linear functional defined on the space (s), there exists a finite set $\alpha_1, \cdots, \alpha_N$ such that $x'(x) = \sum_{n=1}^{N} \alpha_n \xi_n$ for each $x \in (s)$.

SUGGESTED READING

For normed linear spaces

Banach, **1**, especially Chapter 4.
Dunford and Schwartz, **1**, Chapters 1, 4, 5.
Fréchet, **1**.
Ljusternik and Sobolew, **1**, Chapter 2.
Zaanen, **1**, Chapter 6.

For Inner-product spaces

Achieser and Glasmann, **1**, Chapter 1.
Bourbaki, **4**, especially Chapter 5 of No. 1229.
Cooke, **1**, Chapter 1.
Halmos, **3**, Chapter 1.
Jacobson, **1**, Chapter 6.
Julia, **1**, Chapters 1–3.
Nagy, **1**, Chapter 1.
Schmeidler, **1**, Chapter 1.
Stone, **1**, Chapters 1–3.
von Neumann, **1**, Chapters 1–2.
Zaanen, **1**, Chapter 6.

For topological linear spaces

Bourbaki, 4.
Dieudonné, 1, 2.
Hyers, 1.
Mackey, 1, 2.
von Neumann, 2.
Wehausen, 1.

GENERAL THEOREMS
ON
LINEAR OPERATORS

4.0 Introduction

In this chapter the emphasis is principally on the study of continuous linear operators in normed linear spaces. Completeness of the spaces is assumed only where it seems to be essential for decisive results. Some important results, especially those concerning closed operators in § 4.2, are valid in complete metric linear spaces, where the metric need not be that defined by a norm. The middle portion of the chapter (§§ 4.5–4.71) is concerned with conjugate spaces and conjugate operators and presents the more intricate counterpart, for Banach spaces, of the purely algebraic study made in §§ 1.8–1.91 of the relations between an operator and its transpose. The later part of the chapter, beginning with § 4.8, is devoted to inner-product spaces, the special aim being to present some of the fundamental facts about continuous linear functionals and the adjoint of a bounded linear operator in Hilbert space. The theory of adjoint operators closely resembles the theory of conjugate operators but has certain special features because of the fact that the normed conjugate space of a complete inner-product space is congruent in a special way to the space itself.

There are many far-reaching results in this chapter. The massive

Theorem 4.2–G is the fount from which spring many of the most important results in the theory of linear spaces.   Theorems 4.2–H and 4.2–I, both very important, follow directly from 4.2–G.   Theorem 4.2–I is the often used "closed-graph theorem."   From it we deduce the highly important and useful theorems which express, in one form or another, the principle of uniform boundedness.   Our most general formulations of this principle are given in Theorems 4.4–B and 4.4–E.

The normed-linear-space form of the Hahn-Banach theorem is given in 4.3–A.   This theorem is an indispensable tool in the proofs of many subsequent theorems.   As an illustration of its more direct use in analysis we show, at the end of § 4.3, how the Hahn-Banach theorem can be used to give an existence proof in connection with the Dirichlet problem.

Weak topologies are of significant importance in the theory of normed linear spaces.   We mention here especially Theorems 4.61–A, 4.61–C, and 4.62–A.

A large block of material in this chapter deals with a bounded linear operator and its conjugate.   There are many theorems, and it is hard to single out any selected few of them as being the most important.   Those in § 4.7 are more profound than those in § 4.6.   The pooling of all the results about an operator and its conjugate, using theorems from §§ 4.2, 4.6, and 4.7, leads to the "state diagram" in § 4.71, which is a complete tabulation of all the relations of a certain kind which can exist between an operator and its conjugate.

In the last part of the chapter the central theorems are the representation theorem for continuous linear functionals on a Hilbert space (4.81–C), and the closely associated Theorem 4.82–A, on orthogonal complements (often called "the projection theorem").

4.1 Spaces of Linear Operators

Linear operators were defined in § 1.3.   If X and Y are linear spaces (with the same scalar field), the set of all linear operators on X into Y is a linear space if we define addition of operators and multiplication of operators by scalars in the natural way, namely

$$(A + B)x = Ax + Bx, \qquad (\alpha A)x = \alpha(Ax).$$

The operator which maps every $x \in X$ into the zero element of Y is the zero of the linear space of operators; without serious danger of confusion with other zeros we denote this zero operator by 0.

If X and Y are topological linear spaces, those linear operators on X into Y which are continuous on X form a subspace of the space of *all* linear operators on X into Y. We shall denote the linear space of all *continuous* linear operators on X into Y by $[X, Y]$.

If $Y = X$, the space of all linear operators on X into Y is not merely a linear space; it is an *algebra*, according to the following definition of that term.

Definition. A set X is called an algebra if it is a linear space in which to each ordered pair x, y corresponds an element of X denoted by xy and called the product "x times y," subject to the following axioms:

   1. $(xy)z = x(yz)$.
   2. $x(y + z) = xy + xz$.
   3. $(x + y)z = xz + yz$.
   4. $(\alpha x)(\beta y) = (\alpha\beta)(xy)$.

Here it is understood that x, y, z are arbitrary elements of X and α, β are arbitrary scalars. The algebra is called real or complex according as the scalar field is real or complex.

If the algebra X contains an element e such that $ex = xe = x$ for every x, e is called the *unit* of the algebra; it is necessarily unique if it exists.

An algebra is called commutative if $xy = yx$ for every pair x, y. An algebra need not be commutative.

If X_0 is a subset of an algebra X and if $x + y$, αx and xy are in X_0 whenever x, y are any elements of X_0 and α is any scalar, then X_0 is called a *subalgebra* of X. Observe that X_0 is also a linear manifold, or subspace, in X.

If A and B are linear operators on X into X, where X is any linear space, we define AB as the linear operator such that $(AB)x = A(Bx)$ for each $x \in X$. With this definition it is clear that the set of *all* linear operators on X into X is an algebra. Moreover, this algebra has a unit, namely, the operator I defined by $Ix = x$ for every x. The *continuous* linear operators on X into X also form an algebra with this same unit I. Instead of the notation $[X, X]$ we shall use the simpler notation $[X]$ for this algebra of all continuous linear operators on X into X.

If X and Y are normed linear spaces, a linear operator A on X into Y is continuous on X (i.e., $A \in [X, Y]$) if $\sup_{\|x\| \leqslant 1} \|Ax\| < \infty$. For such an A we define

(4.1–1) $$\|A\| = \sup_{\|x\| \leqslant 1} \|Ax\|.$$

These matters were discussed in § 3.1; see especially Theorem 3.1–A and formulas (3.1–1)–(3.1–3); the latter formulas give useful alternative formulas for $\|A\|$.

Theorem 4.1–A.   *If X and Y are normed linear spaces, $[X, Y]$ is a normed linear space with the norm defined by* (4.1–1).   *If Y is complete so is $[X, Y]$.*

PROOF.   We leave to the reader the simple verification that $\|A\|$ is a norm on $[X, Y]$.   We shall prove the assertion about completeness.   Let $\{A_n\}$ be a Cauchy sequence in $[X, Y]$.   For given $\epsilon > 0$ let N be such that $\|A_m - A_n\| < \epsilon$ if $N \leqslant m$ and $N \leqslant n$.   Then also, for each x, $\|A_m x - A_n x\| \leqslant \|A_m - A_n\| \|x\| < \epsilon\|x\|$.   It is thus clear that $\{A_n x\}$ is a Cauchy sequence in Y.   Since Y is complete, $A_n x$ has a limit which depends on x; we define $Ax = \lim_{n \to \infty} A_n x$.   It is readily seen that A is a linear operator on X into Y.   Now $\{\|A_n\|\}$ is a bounded sequence (since every Cauchy sequence in a normed linear space is bounded), and we have $\|A_n\| \leqslant M$ for all n, where M is some constant.   Then $\|A_n x\| \leqslant M\|x\|$ for every x; it follows that $\|Ax\| \leqslant M\|x\|$.   Therefore A is a member of $[X, Y]$, by Theorem 3.1–A.   If we now return to the inequality $\|A_m x - A_n x\| < \epsilon\|x\|$ and let $n \to \infty$, we see that $\|A_m x - Ax\| \leqslant \epsilon\|x\|$ for every x if $N \leqslant m$.   This means that $\|A_m - A\| \leqslant \epsilon$ if $N \leqslant m$.   But then $A_m \to A$ in the topology defined on $[X, Y]$ by the norm.   Consequently $[X, Y]$ is complete.

Suppose that A_n and A are in $[X, Y]$ and that $\|A_n - A\| \to 0$.   This is equivalent to the statement that $\|A_n x - Ax\| \to 0$ uniformly for all $x \in X$ such that $\|x\| \leqslant 1$.   For this reason the topology for $[X, Y]$ defined by the norm (4.1–1) is sometimes called the *uniform topology* for $[X, Y]$.

For the case $Y = X$, $[X, Y] = [X]$, we have the following theorem:

Theorem 4.1–B.   *Suppose X is a normed linear space.   Then*

$$(4.1\text{–}2) \qquad\qquad \|AB\| \leqslant \|A\| \|B\|$$

for each pair A, B in $[X]$.   Also

$$(4.1\text{–}3) \qquad\qquad \|I\| = 1.$$

PROOF.   For each x, $\|(AB)x\| = \|A(Bx)\| \leqslant \|A\| \|Bx\| \leqslant \|A\| \|B\| \|x\|$, and (4.1–2) is a consequence.   The truth of (4.1–3) is immediate from the definition of the norm.

From (4.1–2) it follows that AB is a continuous function of the pair A, B.

When X and Y are normed linear spaces, it is a common practice to call the elements of $[X, Y]$ *bounded linear operators*.   The use of the adjective "bounded" as an equivalent for "continuous" is explained by the remarks following formula (3.1–3).

The next two theorems furnish very important information about the existence and nature of inverse operators under certain conditions. Formula (4.1–4) is closely related to an old result in the theory of integral equations, generally known as the Neumann expansion (named after C. Neumann, cf. Hellinger and Toeplitz, **1**, page 1347), though the method goes back as far as Liouville.

Theorem 4.1–C. *Let X be a Banach space, and suppose $A \in [X]$ and $\|A\| < 1$. Then the range of $I - A$ is X, $(I - A)^{-1}$ exists and belongs to $[X]$, and*

$$(4.1\text{–}4) \qquad (I - A)^{-1} = I + A + A^2 + \cdots + A^n + \cdots,$$

the series converging in the uniform topology of the space $[X]$. Furthermore,

$$(4.1\text{–}5) \qquad \|(I - A)^{-1}\| \leqslant \frac{1}{1 - \|A\|}.$$

PROOF. Since $\|A\| < 1$, the series $\sum_0^\infty \|A\|^n$ converges. But $\|A^n\| \leqslant \|A\|^n$, by (4.1–2), and hence the series $\sum_0^\infty A^n$ converges in $[X]$, owing to the completeness of the latter space (see Theorem 4.1–A). If we let $B = \sum_0^\infty A^n$, we see that

$$AB = BA = \sum_0^\infty A^{n+1},$$

and hence

$$(I - A)B = B(I - A) = I.$$

This implies that $(I - A)^{-1}$ exists and is equal to B. The inequality (4.1–5) is now evident, and so the proof is complete.

Theorem 4.1–D. *Let X be a Banach space. Let R be the set of elements $A \in [X]$ such that $\mathscr{R}(A) = X$ and A^{-1} exists and is continuous. If $A \in R$, $B \in [X]$, and $\|A - B\| < 1/\|A^{-1}\|$, then $B \in R$, and*

$$(4.1\text{–}6) \qquad \|B^{-1}\| \leqslant \frac{\|A^{-1}\|}{1 - \|A^{-1}\| \|A - B\|},$$

$$(4.1\text{–}7) \qquad \|B^{-1} - A^{-1}\| \leqslant \frac{\|A^{-1}\|^2 \|A - B\|}{1 - \|A^{-1}\| \|A - B\|}.$$

Thus, in particular, R is an open set in $[X]$ and A^{-1} is a continuous function of A.

PROOF.   We can write

$$B = A - (A - B) = A[I - A^{-1}(A - B)].$$

Since $\|A^{-1}(A - B)\| \leqslant \|A^{-1}\|\,\|A - B\| < 1$, it follows by Theorem 4.1–C that $[I - A^{-1}(A - B)]^{-1}$ exists, is in $[X]$, and is given by

$$(4.1\text{–}8) \qquad [I - A^{-1}(A - B)]^{-1} = \sum_{n=0}^{\infty} \{A^{-1}(A - B)\}^n.$$

It follows readily that B^{-1} exists, belongs to $[X]$, and is given by

$$B^{-1} = [I - A^{-1}(A - B)]^{-1}A^{-1}.$$

The inequalities (4.1–6) and (4.1–7) follow readily from the series (4.1–8), and we omit the details.   It may be remarked that

$$\|B^{-1} - A^{-1}\| \leqslant \frac{\|A^{-1}\|\,\|I - A^{-1}B\|}{1 - \|I - A^{-1}B\|}.$$

This will in general be a sharper inequality than (4.1–7), since $\|I - A^{-1}B\| = \|A^{-1}(A - B)\| \leqslant \|A^{-1}\|\,\|A - B\|$.   Likewise (4.1–6) can be sharpened.

PROBLEM

Suppose that X, Y, and Z are normed linear spaces, that X is a subspace of Z dense in Z, and that Y is complete.   Show that $[X, Y]$ is congruent to $[Z, Y]$ by mapping $T \in [Z, Y]$ into $A \in [X, Y]$, where A is the restriction of T to X.

4.11 Integral Equations of the Second Kind.   The Neumann Expansion

We start out by referring back to Example 2 in § 1.5, where integral equations of Fredholm and Volterra type were defined.   Such equations can be considered in various function spaces; at first we shall deal with the space of continuous functions.   Let X be the Banach space $C[a, b]$, and let K be the element of $[X]$ defined by $Kx = y$, where

$$(4.11\text{–}1) \qquad y(s) = \int_a^b k(s, t)x(t)\, dt,$$

and the function $k(s, t)$ (called the kernel) is subjected to certain restrictions. There are various sets of restrictions which are adequate for the purposes of the developments which are to follow.   The simplest restrictions are as follows:

a. $k(s, t)$ is continuous in both variables when $a \leqslant s \leqslant b$ and $a \leqslant t \leqslant b$.

b. If M is the maximum of $|k(s, t)|$ on the square $[a, b] \times [a, b]$, then $M(b - a) < 1$.

These restrictions may be made less severe, but at the cost of some complication in statements and proofs.   Our main purpose is to give an exposition of the formal aspects of part of the theory of integral equations of the second kind, and the conditions *a, b* will serve conveniently for the rigorous justification of the formal procedures.

We are concerned with the equation

$$y(s) = x(s) - \int_a^b k(s, t)x(t)\, dt;$$

as an equation in the space X it can be written

(4.11–2) $y = x - Kx.$

According to Theorem 4.1–C, this equation has a unique solution x for each given y if $\|K\| < 1$.   (We do not assert that $\|K\| < 1$ is a *necessary* condition; only that it is sufficient.)   The solution is

(4.11–3) $x = y + Ky + K^2y + \cdots + K^ny + \cdots.$

Now, from (4.11–1) and the definition of M in condition *b*, we see that

(4.11–4) $\|K\| \leqslant M(b - a).$

Condition *b* then assures us that $\|K\| < 1$.

We are going to show that each of the operators $K^2, K^3, \cdots$ is of the same sort as K, with a suitable kernel.   We shall define

(4.11–5) $\begin{cases} k_1(s, t) = k(s, t) \\ k_n(s, t) = \displaystyle\int_a^b k_1(s, u)k_{n-1}(u, t)\, du, \quad n > 1. \end{cases}$

By definition, $z = K^2y$ means $z = K(Ky)$, or

$$z(s) = \int_a^b k(s, t)\, dt \int_a^b k(t, u)y(u)\, du.$$

We invert the order of integration, obtaining

$$z(s) = \int_a^b y(u)\, du \int_a^b k(s, t)k(t, u)\, dt,$$

$$z(s) = \int_a^b k_2(s, u)y(u)\, du.$$

Thus K^2 is defined in terms of the kernel k_2 just as K is defined in terms of k_1.   It is easily proved by induction that $z = K^n y$ is expressed by

$$(4.11\text{–}6) \qquad z(s) = \int_a^b k_n(s, t)y(t)\, dt,$$

so that k_n is the kernel used to determine K^n.   For $n > 1$, k_n is called the nth iterated kernel.

The series (4.11–3) now takes the form

$$(4.11\text{–}7) \qquad x(s) = y(s) + \sum_{n=1}^{\infty} \int_a^b k_n(s, t)y(t)\, dt.$$

The convergence of (4.11–3) as a series of elements in the Banach space $C[a, b]$ means that (4.11–7) is uniformly convergent on $[a, b]$.   Now consider the function h defined by

$$(4.11\text{–}8) \qquad h(s, t) = \sum_{n=1}^{\infty} k_n(s, t).$$

It is easily proved by induction from (4.11–5) that

$$|k_n(s, t)| \leqslant M^n(b - a)^{n-1}, \qquad n > 1.$$

Since we have assumed $M(b - a) < 1$, it follows that the series (4.11–8) converges uniformly; thus h is a continuous function of s and t.   Moreover, we can exchange the order of summation and integration in (4.11–7) and obtain

$$(4.11\text{–}9) \qquad x(s) = y(s) + \int_a^b h(s, t)y(t)\, dt.$$

We shall define an operator H with h as kernel, so that $z = Hy$ means

$$z(s) = \int_a^b h(s, t)y(t)\, dt.$$

Then (4.11–9) becomes

$$x = y + Hy.$$

We thus arrive at the conclusion that, when conditions a and b are satisfied, there is an operator H determined by a kernel h in such a way that

$$(4.11\text{–}10) \qquad (I - K)^{-1} = I + H.$$

The kernel h is sometimes called the *reciprocal* kernel corresponding to k.   It has also been called the *resolvent* kernel, but in modern operator theory the word resolvent is used in a slightly different way.

An operator K defined by a kernel k as in (4.11–1) is called a Fredholm-type operator. The name goes back to the Swede, Fredholm, who developed a comprehensive theory for integral equations of the second kind at the beginning of the twentieth century.

The theory of Volterra integral equations may be developed independently, or it may be regarded as a special case, with important special features, of the theory of Fredholm integral equations. A Volterra-type operator K is defined by $y = Kx$, where

$$y(s) = \int_a^s k(s, t)x(t)\, dt.$$

We shall assume that the kernel $k(s, t)$ is continuous in both variables in the triangular region defined by the inequalities $a \leqslant t \leqslant s \leqslant b$. If we define k to have the value 0 in the part of the square $[a, b] \times [a, b]$ where $t > s$, we can regard K as a Fredholm-type operator with this special feature of the kernel k. Since $k(s, s)$ need not be 0, there may be discontinuities of the kernel at points along the diagonal $t = s$ of the square. These discontinuities have no adverse effects on the earlier developments in this section, however.

It may be verified by induction from (4.11–5) that, when k is a Volterra kernel, the iterated kernels k_n are also Volterra kernels; that is, $k_n(s, t) = 0$ if $t > s$. The iterative formula for k_n becomes

(4.11–11) $k_n(s, t) = \int_t^s k_1(s, u)k_{n-1}(u, t)\, du,$ $n > 1,$ $t \leqslant s.$

From this it can readily be proved by induction that

(4.11–12) $|k_n(s, t)| \leqslant M^n \dfrac{(s - t)^{n-1}}{(n - 1)!}$

where M is the maximum of $|k(s, t)|$. Hence certainly

$$|k_n(s, t)| \leqslant M^n \frac{(b - a)^{n-1}}{(n - 1)!}.$$

This inequality shows that the series (4.11–8) converges uniformly. The function $h(s, t)$ is also a Volterra kernel; it is continuous in the triangle $a \leqslant t \leqslant s \leqslant b$, and $h(s, t) = 0$ if $t > s$.

From (4.11–12) and the formula for K^n in terms of k_n it follows that

(4.11–13) $\|K^n\| \leqslant M^n \dfrac{(b - a)^n}{n!}.$

Consequently the series $\displaystyle\sum_{n=0}^{\infty} K^n$ converges in the uniform topology of the space $[X]$. A perusal of the proof of Theorem 4.1–C shows that the assertion made in connection with (4.1–4) remains valid under any conditions which insure the convergence of the series in (4.1–4). As a consequence, it follows that the equation $y = x - Kx$ has a unique solution for each y, the solution being

$$x = \sum_{n=0}^{\infty} K^n y.$$

Furthermore, this solution may be expressed in the form

$$x(s) = y(s) + \int_a^s h(s, t)y(t)\, dt.$$

The very important fact about Volterra integral equations of the second kind is, then, that such an equation is always uniquely solvable. The special nature of the Volterra-type operator K insures that the Neumann expansion is always convergent, regardless of the magnitude of the kernel k. This is not true in general in the case of a Fredholm-type operator.

4.12 $\mathscr{L}^2$ Kernels

In this section we consider the space $L^2(a, b)$ (hereafter in this section written simply as L^2). Suppose $k(s, t)$ belongs to the class $\mathscr{L}^2(E)$, where E is the square $[a, b] \times [a, b]$. Then we call k an $\mathscr{L}^2$ kernel. Such a kernel defines a bounded operator K on L^2 in the following way: If $x \in L^2$ let $y = Kx$, where this means

$$y(s) = {}^0\!\!\int_a^b k(s, t)x(t)\, dt.$$

Since

$$|y(s)|^2 \leqslant {}^0\!\!\int_a^b |k(s, t)|^2\, dt \int_a^b |x(t)|^2\, dt,$$

we see that

$$\int_a^b |y(s)|^2\, ds \leqslant \int_a^b \int_a^b |k(s, t)|^2\, ds\, dt \int_a^b |x(t)|^2\, dt.$$

This shows that

$$\|y\| = \|Kx\| \leqslant \left(\int_a^b \int_a^b |k(s, t)|^2\, ds\, dt \right)^{\frac{1}{2}} \|x\|,$$

and hence that

(4.12–1) $$\|K\| \leqslant \left(\int_a^b \int_a^b |k(s, t)|^2\, ds\, dt \right)^{\frac{1}{2}}.$$

As a member of $\mathscr{L}^2(E)$, $k(s, t)$ determines an element of the Hilbert space $L^2(E)$. We denote this element by k and its norm in $L^2(E)$ by $\|k\|$:

(4.12–2) $$\|k\| = \left(\int_a^b \int_a^b |k(s, t)|^2 \, ds \, dt \right)^{\frac{1}{2}}.$$

From (4.12–1) we see that $\|K\| \leqslant \|k\|$.

The equation $y = x - Kx$ in L^2 corresponds to a Fredholm integral equation

$$y(s) =^0 x(s) - \int_a^b k(s, t)x(t) \, dt$$

in $\mathscr{L}^2$. By Theorem 4.1–C we know that $y = x - Kx$ has a unique solution x in L^2 for each choice of y in L^2, provided that $\|K\| < 1$. This will certainly be the case if $\|k\| < 1$.

In the case of $\mathscr{L}^2$ kernels we can define the iterated kernels k_n and the reciprocal kernel h in a manner formally the same as we did in § 4.11 with continuous kernels. The details are somewhat different, however. The iterated kernels are defined essentially as before: $k_1(s, t) = k(s, t)$ and

$$k_n(s, t) =^0 \int_a^b k_1(s, u)k_{n-1}(u, t) \, du,$$

where $=^0$ refers to the exception of a set of two-dimensional measure zero. It is not difficult to show by induction that we also have

(4.12–3) $$k_n(s, t) =^0 \int_a^b k_{n-1}(s, u)k(u, t) \, du.$$

Also, by induction and the Schwarz inequality we find that k_n is an $\mathscr{L}^2$ kernel, with

$$\int_a^b \int_a^b |k_n(s, t)|^2 \, ds \, dt \leqslant \left(\int_a^b \int_a^b |k(s, t)|^2 \, ds \, dt \right)^n,$$

or

$$\|k_n\| \leqslant \|k\|^n.$$

It is a more delicate matter to estimate the numerical magnitude of $k_n(s, t)$. Let us write

$$u(s) =^0 \left(\int_a^b |k(s, t)|^2 \, dt \right)^{\frac{1}{2}}$$

$$v(t) =^0 \left(\int_a^b |k(s, t)|^2 \, ds \right)^{\frac{1}{2}}.$$

Now, for each t except on a set of measure 0, $k(s, t)$ as a function of s

determines an element k_t of L^2.   Likewise $k_n(s, t)$ determines an element $k_t^{(n)}$.   Formula (4.12–3) shows that

$$k_t^{(n)} = K^{n-1}k_t = Kz,$$

where $z = K^{n-2}k_t$.   Thus

$$k_n(s, t) = {}^0 \int_a^b k(s, u)z(u) \, du,$$

$$|k_n(s, t)| \leqslant {}^0 \left(\int_a^b |k(s, u)|^2 \, du \right)^{\frac{1}{2}} \left(\int_a^b |z(u)|^2 \, du \right)^{\frac{1}{2}},$$

$$|k_n(s, t)| \leqslant {}^0 u(s) \, \|z\|.$$

But

$$\|z\| = \|K^{n-2}k_t\| \leqslant \|K\|^{n-2} \, \|k_t\| = \|K\|^{n-2}v(t),$$

and so

(4.12–4) $$|k_n(s, t)| \leqslant {}^0 \|K\|^{n-2}u(s)v(t), \qquad n \geqslant 2.$$

This inequality shows that the series (4.11–8) converges and defines a function $h(s, t)$ almost everywhere on $E = [a, b] \times [a, b]$, provided that $\|K\| < 1$.   The inequality (4.12–4) also enables us to conclude that h is an $\mathscr{L}^2$ kernel, that the series (4.11–7) converges almost everywhere, and that we can reverse the order of summation and integration to obtain

$$x(s) = {}^0 y(s) + \int_a^b h(s, t)y(t) \, dt$$

as the solution of the integral equation in $\mathscr{L}^2$ (all this when $\|K\| < 1$).

Observe that in this case the Banach space theory tells us merely that

$$x = y + Ky + K^2y + \cdots + K^ny + \cdots,$$

the series being convergent in L^2.   The additional information that

$$x(s) = y(s) + \int_a^b k(s, t)y(t) \, dt + \cdots + \int_a^b k_n(s, t)y(t) \, dt + \cdots$$

is convergent almost everywhere, with its terms dominated as in (4.12–4), is more than was obtained directly from Theorem 4.1–C.

4.13 Differential Equations and Integral Equations

In order to indicate some of the reasons why integral equations are of significant interest, we shall show how certain types of questions concerning differential equations can be recast as questions about integral equations.   For simplicity we confine attention to second-order linear ordinary differential equations. The discussion could be extended to cover ordinary equations of higher order.

Consider the equation

$$(4.13\text{–}1) \qquad y''(s) + a_1(s)y'(s) + a_2(s)y(s) = x(s),$$

where a_1 and a_2 are fixed continuous functions of s, defined when $a \leqslant s \leqslant b$. Let $X = C[a, b]$. The *initial-value problem* for (4.13–1) is the problem of finding $y \in X$, with y' and y'' also in X, so that (4.13–1) is satisfied and so that $y(a)$ and $y'(a)$ have preassigned values, say $y(a) = \alpha_0$, $y'(a) = \alpha_1$. The function x is to be an arbitrarily assigned member of X. The fact that this initial-value problem always has a solution (and a unique one), no matter how α_0, α_1, and x are chosen, is a consequence of standard existence theorems in the theory of differential equations. But we can also demonstrate the fact by using what we have learned in § 4.11 about Volterra integral equations.

We write $y''(s) = z(s)$, assuming for the moment that y is a solution of the initial value problem. Then

$$\int_a^u z(t)\, dt = y'(u) - \alpha_1,$$

$$(4.13\text{–}2) \qquad \int_a^s du \int_a^u z(t)\, dt = y(s) - \alpha_0 - \alpha_1(s - a).$$

The iterated integral in this last formula can be expressed in the form

$$\int_a^s z(t)\, dt \int_t^s du = \int_a^s (s - t)z(t)\, dt.$$

On replacing y, y', and y'' in (4.13–1) by their expression in terms of z, we obtain

$$(4.13\text{–}3) \qquad z(s) + a_1(s)\left\{\alpha_1 + \int_a^s z(t)\, dt\right\}$$

$$+ a_2(s)\left\{\alpha_0 + \alpha_1(s - a) + \int_a^s (s - t)z(t)\, dt\right\} = x(s).$$

This equation is satisfied by z if y is a solution of the initial-value problem. Conversely, if z satisfies (4.13–3) and y is defined by (4.13–2), y is a solution of the initial-value problem.

If we define

$$k(s, t) = -a_1(s) - a_2(s)(s - t),$$

$$w(s) = x(s) - \alpha_0 a_2(s) - \alpha_1\{a_1(s) + a_2(s)(s - a)\},$$

the equation (4.13–3) can be written in the form

$$z(s) - \int_a^s k(s, t)z(t)\, dt = w(s).$$

This is a Volterra integral equation of the second kind. As we know from § 4.11, it has a unique solution $z \in X$ for each $w \in X$. *Therefore, the initial value problem for* (4.13–1) *always has a unique solution.*

There is another important class of problems related to the differential equation (4.13–1), namely the two-point problems. For a *two-point problem* we ask for a solution of the differential equation which satisfies a certain specified condition at $s = a$ and another condition at $s = b$. A common form of condition is one in which we specify the value at an end point of some predetermined linear combination of y and y'. We shall illustrate by discussing the problem with the conditions $y(a) = \alpha$, $y(b) = \beta$. We refer back to Example 3 of § 1.3 for certain things which we need. There it was shown (we change the notation slightly) that if $x \in C[a, b]$ and if

$$c(s, t) = \begin{cases} \dfrac{(b - s)(t - a)}{b - a} & \text{when } a \leqslant t \leqslant s \\[2ex] \dfrac{(s - a)(b - t)}{b - a} & \text{when } s \leqslant t \leqslant b, \end{cases}$$

then the function

$$z(s) = -\int_a^b c(s, t)x(t)\, dt$$

satisfies the conditions

$$z''(s) = x(s), \qquad z(a) = z(b) = 0.$$

Consequently the function

$$(4.13\text{–}4) \qquad y(s) = \alpha\frac{b - s}{b - a} + \beta\frac{s - a}{b - a} - \int_a^b c(s, t)x(t)\, dt$$

satisfies the conditions

$$y''(s) = x(s), \qquad y(a) = \alpha, \qquad y(b) = \beta.$$

In (4.13–4) let us replace $x(t)$ by

$$x(t) - a_1(t)y'(t) - a_2(t)y(t).$$

In this way we see that y will be a solution of our two-point problem if and only if it has a continuous derivative and satisfies the equation

$$(4.13\text{–}5) \qquad y(s) = \alpha\frac{b - s}{b - a} + \beta\frac{s - a}{b - a}$$

$$- \int_a^b c(s, t)\{x(t) - a_1(t)y'(t) - a_2(t)y(t)\}\, dt.$$

The discussion of this equation is much simplified if we assume that $a_1(t) \equiv 0$.   For this special case let us write

$$k(s, t) = c(s, t)a_2(t),$$

$$w(s) = \alpha \frac{b - s}{b - a} + \beta \frac{s - a}{b - a} - \int_a^b c(s, t)x(t)\, dt.$$

Then (4.13–5) becomes

$$y(s) - \int_a^b k(s, t)y(t)\, dt = w(s).$$

This is a Fredholm integral equation of the second kind.   It will certainly have a unique solution $y \in C[a, b]$ if $\|K\| < 1$, where K is the Fredholm-type operator with kernel k.   (The condition $\|K\| < 1$ is sufficient; it may not be necessary.)   We know from § 4.11 that $\|K\| \leqslant M(b - a)$, where M is the maximum value of $|k(s, t)|$.   Now, the maximum value of $(b-a)\,|c(s, t)|$ is readily found to be $(b-a)^2/4$.   Let A be the maximum value of $|a_2(t)|$.   Then certainly $\|K\| < 1$ if $(b - a)^2 A < 4$.   We summarize the conclusions:

The two-point problem for the equation

$$y''(s) + a_2(s)y(s) = x(s)$$

with the end conditions $y(a) = \alpha$, $y(b) = \beta$, is always uniquely solvable, with arbitrarily assigned α, β, x, provided that

$$(b - a)^2 \max |a_2(s)| < 4.$$

(For what may happen if this inequality is not satisfied, see problem 14 in § 5.5.)
We return to the case when $a_1(t) \neq 0$.   One way to handle this is to make a change of variable.   If $a_1'(s)$ is continuous, we can define

$$q(s) = e^{-\frac{1}{2}\int_a^s a_1(t)\, dt}$$

and set $y = uq$.   Then, with u as the new unknown, we have the equation

$$u''(s) + \{a_2(s) - \tfrac{1}{2}a_1'(s) - \tfrac{1}{4}[a_2(s)]^2\}u(s) = \frac{x(s)}{q(s)}.$$

The new end conditions are

$$u(a) = \frac{\alpha}{q(a)} = \alpha, \qquad u(b) = \frac{\beta}{q(b)}.$$

Since the $u'(s)$ term does not appear in the differential equation, the previous method may be used to recast the problem as an integral equation problem.

If a_1 cannot be eliminated, so that the y' term is actually present in (4.13–5), we have what is called an *integro-differential* equation. It is a more complicated matter to discuss the possibility of solution of such an equation, and we shall leave the matter at this point.

In some later sections (§ 6.11 and § 6.41) we shall discuss another phase of the relation between differential and integral equations, with applications to eigenvalue problems of differential equations of Sturm-Liouville type.

4.2 Closed Linear Operators

For the purposes of applications to analysis it is essential to consider some linear operators which are not continuous. However, many of the most important discontinuous linear operators have a property which in some respects compensates for the absence of the property of continuity. This property is most naturally described in terms of the concept of the graph of a function.

Definition. Let X and Y be topological spaces. Let f be a function with domain $\mathscr{D}$ and range $\mathscr{R}$ such that $\mathscr{D} \subset X$ and $\mathscr{R} \subset Y$. The set $\{(x, f(x)) : x \in \mathscr{D}\}$ in the product space $X \times Y$ is called the *graph* of f. The function is called *closed* in case the graph is a closed set in $X \times Y$ (with the topology of the product space as defined in § 2.5).

Observe that the graph of f is the set of all ordered pairs $(x, f(x))$, where $x \in \mathscr{D}$.

In case X and Y are metric spaces, the topology of $X \times Y$ can also be defined by a metric. From Theorem 2.4–A we obtain the following theorem:

Theorem 4.2–A. *If X and Y are metric spaces a function f with domain $\mathscr{D} \subset X$ and range $\mathscr{R} \subset Y$ is closed if and only if the situation $x_n \in \mathscr{D}$, $x_n \to x$, $f(x_n) \to y$ implies that $x \in \mathscr{D}$ and $f(x) = y$.*

For many purposes the criterion for a closed function which we find it convenient to use is that given in Theorem 4.2–A.

Example 1. *A discontinuous but closed operator*: Let $X = C[0, 1]$ and let $X = Y$. Let $\mathscr{D}$ be the set of $x \in X$ such that the derivative $x'(t)$ is defined and continuous on $[0, 1]$; let T be the operator with domain $\mathscr{D}$ defined by $Tx = x'$. It is evident that T is linear. If $x_n(t) = t^n$, then $\|x_n\| = 1$, $x_n'(t) = nt^{n-1}$, and so $\|Tx_n\| = \|x_n'\| = n$ ($n = 1, 2, \cdots$). Thus T is not continuous, because $\sup_{\|x\|=1} \|Tx\| = \infty$. But T is closed. In fact, suppose $x_n \in \mathscr{D}$, $x_n \to x$, $Tx_n \to y$. Then $x_n'(t)$ converges uniformly to

$y(t)$, and y is continuous.   It follows by a standard convergence theorem that $x(t)$ is differentiable, with derivative equal to $y(t)$.   Therefore $x \in \mathscr{D}$, $Tx = y$, and T is closed.

One of the important fields of application of functional analysis is in the theory of differential equations.   Operators defined by means of ordinary or partial differentiation are frequently discontinuous, but in the applications it is often possible to arrange matters so that the differential operators to be dealt with are closed.

Example 2.   Let $X = L^2(0, 1)$.   Let T be an operator with domain and range in X, defined as follows: $\mathscr{D}(T)$ is the class of those $x \in X$ for which a representative function in $\mathscr{L}^2(0, 1)$ can be found such that $x(s)$ is absolutely continuous on $[0, 1]$, $x(0) = x(1)$, and $x'(s)$ is in $\mathscr{L}^2(0, 1)$. This means that $x(s)$ is of the form

$$x(s) = \alpha + \int_0^s u(t) \, dt,$$

where $u(t) \in \mathscr{L}^2(0, 1)$, α is a scalar, and

$$\int_0^1 u(t) \, dt = 0.$$

We then define $Tx = x'$.

We shall demonstrate that T is closed.   Assume that $x_n \in \mathscr{D}$, x, $y \in X$, $x_n \to x$, $Tx_n \to y$.   We can write

(4.2–1) $$x_n(s) = x_n(0) + \int_0^s x_n'(t) \, dt.$$

Now

$$\left| \int_0^s x_n'(t) \, dt - \int_0^s y(t) \, dt \right| \leqslant \int_0^s |x_n'(t) - y(t)| \, dt$$

$$\leqslant \int_0^1 |x_n'(t) - y(t)| \, dt \leqslant \left(\int_0^1 |x_n'(t) - y(t)|^2 \, dt \right)^{\frac{1}{2}} \left(\int_0^1 1^2 \, dt \right)^{\frac{1}{2}}.$$

Therefore $\int_0^s x_n'(t) \, dt$ converges to $\int_0^s y(t) \, dt$; the convergence on $[0, 1]$ is uniform with respect to s.   In particular, $\int_0^1 y(t) \, dt = 0$, since $\int_0^1 x_n'(t) \, dt = 0$.   Next,

$$x_n(0) - x_m(0) = x_n(s) - x_m(s) - \int_0^s [x_n'(t) - x_m'(t)] \, dt$$

$$|x_n(0) - x_m(0)| = \left(\int_0^1 |x_n(0) - x_m(0)|^2 \, dt \right)^{\frac{1}{2}}$$

$$\leqslant \left(\int_0^1 |x_n(s) - x_m(s)|^2 \, ds \right)^{\frac{1}{2}} + \left\{ \int_0^1 \left| \int_0^s [x_n'(t) - x_m'(t)] \, dt \right|^2 ds \right\}^{\frac{1}{2}}.$$

It then follows that $\{x_n(0)\}$ is a Cauchy sequence, with some limit α. Returning to (4.2–1), we see that $x_n(s)$ converges uniformly to the limit $z(s)$, where

$$z(s) = \alpha + \int_0^s y(t) \, dt.$$

Hence $z \in \mathscr{D}(T)$. Also, $z'(s) = {}^0 y(s)$. The uniform convergence of $x_n(s)$ to $z(s)$ implies that

$$\int_0^1 |x_n(s) - z(s)|^2 \, ds \to 0.$$

That is, $x_n \to z$. Since $x_n \to x$, we must have $x = z$. But then $z'(s) = {}^0 y(s)$ means that $Tx = y$. Hence T is closed.

We now present a group of four very elementary theorems which it is useful to have on record for later use.

Theorem 4.2–B.   *Let X be a topological space, and let Y be a Hausdorff space. Suppose f is a continuous function, with range in Y, whose domain is a closed set in X. Then f is closed.*

PROOF.   Let $\mathscr{R}$ be the range of f. If we suppose that f is not closed, the complement in $X \times Y$ of the graph is not open, so there must be a point (x_0, y_0) in this complement such that every neighborhood of (x_0, y_0) contains a point of the graph. This implies that every neighborhood of x_0 (in X) contains a point of $\mathscr{D}$ and thus that $x_0 \in \overline{\mathscr{D}}$. But then $x_0 \in \mathscr{D}$, since $\mathscr{D}$ is closed. Then $y_0 \neq f(x_0)$, since otherwise (x_0, y_0) would be in the graph. Since Y is a Hausdorff space, we can find disjoint neighborhoods V_1 and V_2 of $f(x_0)$ and y_0 respectively. From the continuity of f it follows that there is some neighborhood U of x_0 such that $f(x) \in V_1$ if $x \in \mathscr{D} \cap U$. Now $U \times V_2$ is a neighborhood of (x_0, y_0) and must contain a point $(x_1, f(x_1))$ of the graph. Then $x_1 \in \mathscr{D} \cap U$, and so $f(x_1) \in V_1$. But $f(x_1) \in V_2$, and so we reach a contradiction.

Theorem 4.2–C.   *If f is closed and f^{-1} exists, f^{-1} is also closed.*

PROOF.   The graph of f^{-1} is the set $\{(f(x), x) : x \in \mathscr{D}\}$ in $Y \times X$. The result follows readily from this.

Theorem 4.2–D.   *Let X and Y be normed linear spaces, with Y complete. Let A be a linear operator with domain $\mathscr{D} \subset X$ and range $\mathscr{R} \subset Y$. Suppose that A is both closed and continuous. Then $\mathscr{D}$ is closed.*

PROOF.   Suppose $x \in \overline{\mathscr{D}}$. Then there exists a sequence $\{x_n\}$ from $\mathscr{D}$ with $x_n \to x$. The sequence $\{Ax_n\}$ is a Cauchy sequence, for $\|Ax_n - Ax_m\| \leqslant C\|x_n - x_m\|$, where C is the norm of A as an operator on the space $\mathscr{D}$.

Hence $\{Ax_n\}$ has some limit $y \in Y$. But then $x \in \mathscr{D}$ and $Ax = y$, since A is closed.

Theorem 4.2–E. *Let X and Y be normed linear spaces, with X complete. Let A be a closed linear operator with domain $\mathscr{D} \subset X$ and range $\mathscr{R} \subset Y$. Suppose that A^{-1} exists and is continuous. Then $\mathscr{R}$ is closed.*

PROOF. A^{-1} is closed (Theorem 4.2–C), and $\mathscr{R}$ is its domain. Hence $\mathscr{R}$ is closed, by Theorem 4.2–D.

There are certain conditions under which it may be concluded that a closed linear operator is continuous.   One of the most important theorems of this type is that, if X and Y are complete metric linear spaces (and hence in particular if X and Y are Banach spaces), a linear operator whose domain is all of X and whose range is in Y is continuous if it is closed. This theorem is a consequence of the series of theorems which we shall now consider.

Theorem 4.2–F. *Let X and Y be topological linear spaces. Let T be a linear operator on X into Y, and suppose that the range of T is a set of the second category in Y. Then, to each neighborhood U of 0 in X there corresponds some neighborhood V of 0 in Y such that $V \subset \overline{T(U)}$.*

PROOF.   For the convenience of readers who are primarily interested in normed linear spaces, we first give the proof for the case in which X is a normed linear space.   Afterwards we shall indicate how to adapt the method of proof for the general case.

If U is a neighborhood of 0 in the normed linear space X, there is an $\epsilon > 0$ such that the open sphere $\|x\| < 2\epsilon$ lies in U.   Let W be the open sphere $\|x\| < \epsilon$.   Then nW is the open sphere $\|x\| < n\epsilon$, and the union of the sets $T(nW)$ for $n = 1, 2, \cdots$ is the range of T.   Consequently, since this range is of the second category in Y, there is some positive integer n such that the interior of $\overline{T(nW)}$ is not empty.   But $\overline{T(nW)} = \overline{nT(W)} = n\overline{T(W)}$, and, since $n\overline{T(W)}$ and $\overline{T(W)}$ are homeomorphic sets, the latter also has a nonempty interior.   Therefore there exists some point $y_0 \in T(W)$ which is an interior point of $\overline{T(W)}$.   It follows that 0 is an interior point of $- y_0 + \overline{T(W)}$.   Now let V be a neighborhood of 0 in Y such that $V \subset - y_0 + \overline{T(W)}$.   Since $y_0 \in T(W)$, we can write $y_0 = Tx_0$, where $x_0 \in W$.   Elements of $- y_0 + T(W)$ have the form $- y_0 + T(w) = T(w - x_0)$, $w \in W$.   But $w - x_0 \in U$, because of the way in which W and U are related.   Thus $- y_0 + T(W) \subset T(U)$.   The closure of $- y_0 + T(W)$ is $- y_0 + \overline{T(W)}$.   Therefore $- y_0 + \overline{T(W)} \subset \overline{T(U)}$, and so also $V \subset \overline{T(U)}$.   This finishes the proof in this case.

For the case in which X is an arbitrary topological linear space the only difference in the proof concerns the way in which W is chosen. We choose for W a balanced neighborhood of 0 such that $W + W \subset U$ (see Theorem 3.3–E). The fact that W is balanced and absorbing assures that X is the union of the sets nW, $n = 1, 2, \cdots$. Since $-x_0 \in W$ if $x_0 \in W$, it follows in the proof that $w - x_0 \in W + W \subset U$. All the rest of the argument is unchanged.

In the next several theorems we deal with metric linear spaces, as defined in § 3.9. We shall denote the distance from 0 to x by $\|x\|$, rather than by $|x|$, as was done in § 3.9. But the reader must remember that we do not have the property $\|\alpha x\| = |\alpha| \|x\|$ at our disposal, since $\|x\|$ need not be a norm. We *do* have $\|-x\| = \|x\|$ and the continuity properties (3.9–6)–(3.9–8). Because we are dealing with metric linear spaces it is necessary, in a few places, to proceed in a manner more roundabout and cumbersome than if we were dealing with normed linear spaces.

Theorem 4.2–G. *Let X and Y be metric linear spaces, and let X be complete. Let T be a closed linear operator with domain $\mathscr{D}$ in X and range $\mathscr{R}$ a set of the second category in Y. For each $\alpha > 0$ let B_α be the closed sphere $\|x\| \leqslant \alpha$ in X and let C_α be the closed sphere $\|y\| \leqslant \alpha$ in Y. We draw the following conclusions:*

1. *To each $\alpha > 0$ corresponds some $\beta > 0$ such that $C_\beta \subset T(\mathscr{D} \cap B_\alpha)$.*
2. *The range $\mathscr{R}$ is all of Y.*
3. *If S is a relatively open subset of $\mathscr{D}$, then $T(S)$ is an open set in Y.*
4. *If T^{-1} exists, it is continuous.*
5. *In particular, if X and Y are normed linear spaces, we can conclude from conclusion 1 that there exists some $m > 0$ such that each $y \in Y$ is of the form $y = Tx$, where $x \in \mathscr{D}$ and $\|x\| \leqslant m\|y\|$.*

PROOF. If $\alpha > 0$ is given, let U be the open sphere $\|x\| < \alpha/2$ in X. Then $U \subset B_{\alpha/2}$. By Theorem 4.2–F there exists an open sphere V in Y, defined by $\|y\| < 2\beta$ for some $\beta > 0$, such that $V \subset \overline{T(\mathscr{D} \cap U)}$ (we take $\mathscr{D}$ for the X in Theorem 4.2–F). Thus certainly $V \subset \overline{T(\mathscr{D} \cap B_{\alpha/2})}$. We shall show that $V \subset T(\mathscr{D} \cap B_\gamma)$ if $\alpha/2 < \gamma$. Choose a sequence $\{\epsilon_n\}$ with

$$\epsilon_n > 0 \text{ and } \sum_1^\infty \epsilon_n < \gamma - \alpha/2.$$ Let U_n be the open sphere $\|x\| < \epsilon_n$ in X.

We know by Theorem 4.2–F that there exists a positive number δ_n such that $V_n \subset \overline{T(\mathscr{D} \cap U_n)}$ if V_n is the open sphere $\|y\| < \delta_n$ in Y. We can evidently impose on the sequence $\{\delta_n\}$ the further requirement that $\delta_n \to 0$. Now suppose $y \in V$. There exists a point of $T(\mathscr{D} \cap B_{\alpha/2})$, which we can write as $y_0 = Tx_0$, with $x_0 \in \mathscr{D} \cap B_{\alpha/2}$, such that $\|y - y_0\|$

$< \delta_1$. Then $y - y_0 \in V_1$ and hence there exists a point $y_1 = Tx_1$ with $x_1 \in \mathscr{D} \cap U_1$ such that $\|y - y_0 - y_1\| < \delta_2$. Proceeding in this way, by induction we define sequences $\{x_n\}$ and $\{y_n\}$ such that $y_n = Tx_n$, $x_n \in \mathscr{D} \cap U_n$, and $\|y - y_0 - y_1 - \cdots - y_n\| < \delta_{n+1}$, $n = 1, 2, \cdots$. Since $\delta_n \to 0$ we see that $y = \sum_0^\infty y_n$. Now $\|x_n\| < \epsilon_n$ if $n \geq 1$, and

$$\sum_0^\infty \|x_n\| < \sum_1^\infty \epsilon_n < \gamma - \alpha/2.$$ Since X is complete, the series $\sum_1^\infty x_n$ is convergent, and there is a point x of X defined by $x = \sum_0^\infty x_n$. Moreover,

$$\|x\| < \|x_0\| + \sum_1^\infty \epsilon_n < \gamma,$$ since $x_0 \in B_{\alpha/2}$. Thus $x \in B_y$. The fact that T is closed enables us to infer that $x \in \mathscr{D}$ and $Tx = y$ (see Theorem 4.2–A). We have now shown that $V \subset T(\mathscr{D} \cap B_y)$. If we take $\gamma = \alpha$, the fact that $C_\beta \subset V$ now shows that $C_\beta \subset T(\mathscr{D} \cap B_\alpha)$. This proves (1).

To prove (2) observe that, for any $y \in Y$, $(1/n)y \to 0$ as $n \to \infty$, and hence $\|(1/n)y\| < \beta$ if n is large enough. Then $(1/n)y \in C_\beta$, $(1/n)y = Tx$, where $x \in \mathscr{D} \cap B_\alpha$, and $y = T(nx)$, whence $y \in \mathscr{R}$. Thus (2) is proved.

To prove (3) we write $S = \mathscr{D} \cap W$, where W is an open set in X. Suppose $y_0 \in T(S)$, so that $y_0 = Tx_0$, $x_0 \in S$. The set $-x_0 + W$ is a neighborhood of 0, and so contains B_α for some $\alpha > 0$. Then $\mathscr{D} \cap B_\alpha \subset \mathscr{D} \cap (-x_0 + W) = -x_0 + \mathscr{D} \cap W$, and, by (1), $C_\beta \subset T(\mathscr{D} \cap B_\alpha) \subset T(-x_0 + \mathscr{D} \cap W) = -y_0 + T(S)$. It follows that $y_0 + C_\beta \subset T(S)$. Since $y_0 + C_\beta$ contains a neighborhood of y_0, $T(S)$ is open. Thus (3) is proved.

The proof of (4) follows at once from (3) by Theorem 2.12–A, because $(T^{-1})^{-1} = T$. For proof of (5), which is concerned with the particular case in which X and Y are normed linear spaces, observe that, if $y \in Y$ and $y \neq 0$, then $\|\beta y/\|y\| \| = \beta$. Hence, by (1), there exists $u \in \mathscr{D}$ with $\|u\| \leq \alpha$ and $Tu = \beta y/\|y\|$. Let $x = (\|y\|/\beta)u$. Then $Tx = y$ and $\|x\| \leq \alpha\|y\|/\beta$. Thus we can take $m = \alpha/\beta$.

Part 3 of the conclusion of Theorem 4.2–G is sometimes referred to as "*the interior-mapping principle.*"

Several important theorems follow readily from Theorem 4.2–G. We cite two such theorems, which will be used repeatedly in later parts of this book.

Theorem 4.2–H. *Let X and Y be complete metric linear spaces. Let T be a linear operator whose domain is X and whose range is all of Y. Suppose that T is continuous and that T^{-1} exists. Then T^{-1} is continuous.*

PROOF. T is closed, by Theorem 4.2–B.   The range of T is of the second category in Y, since Y is complete.   The conclusion now follows from Theorem 4.2–G.

Theorem 4.2–I.   *Let X and Y be complete metric linear spaces.   Let T be a closed linear operator whose domain is all of X and whose range is in Y.   Then T is continuous.*

PROOF.   Form the product space $X \times Y$.   It becomes a complete metric linear space if we define

$$\|(x, y)\| = \|x\| + \|y\|, \qquad (x, y) \in X \times Y.$$

Since T is closed, its graph is a closed linear manifold in $X \times Y$ and can therefore be regarded as a complete metric linear space by itself.   We define a linear operator A, with the graph of T as its domain and with X as its range, as follows:

$$A(x, Tx) = x.$$

Since $\|x\| \leqslant \|(x, Tx)\|$, A is continuous at $(0, 0)$ and hence at every point of its domain.   Evidently A^{-1} exists and is defined by $A^{-1}x = (x, Tx)$.   Then A^{-1} is continuous, by Theorem 4.2–H.   It follows that T is continuous.

Theorem 4.2–I has many applications and is used in many arguments.   It is commonly referred to as the "*closed-graph theorem.*"

We now consider some concrete applications of the last two theorems.

Example 3.   Let Y be the Banach space $C[a, b]$, and let X be a linear space consisting of those functions in $C[a, b]$ which have continuous first and second derivatives on $[a, b]$ and satisfy some definitely specified linear end conditions (e.g., $x(a) = 0$ and $x'(a) = 0$, or $x(a) = x(b) = 0$).   Let T be the linear differential operator with domain X and range in Y defined by $Tx = y$, where

(4.2–2) $a_0(s)x''(s) + a_1(s)x'(s) + a_2(s)x(s) = y(s).$

The fixed coefficients a_0, a_1, a_2 are assumed to be in Y.   We can make X into a Banach space by defining $\|x\|$ to be the greatest of the maximum values on $[a, b]$ of $|x(s)|$, $|x'(s)|$, $|x''(s)|$, respectively.   The operator T is continuous, for if

$$M = \|a_0\| + \|a_1\| + \|a_2\|,$$

where $\|a_k\|$ is the norm of a_k as an element of Y, we see that $\|y\| = \|Tx\| \leqslant M\|x\|$.

Now let us suppose that the differential equation (4.2–2) has a unique solution $x \in X$ (i.e., satisfying the specified end conditions) for each choice of $y \in Y$. That is, we assume $\mathscr{R}(T) = Y$ and that T^{-1} exists. It then follows by Theorem 4.2–H that T^{-1} is continuous. The continuous dependence of x on y offers a certain assurance that "perturbation-theory" methods for approximating the solution of the differential equation are satisfactory. That is, a small perturbation of the function y will result in a small perturbation of the solution x and of its first and second derivatives. The striking thing about this result is that it is obtained without any detailed knowledge of the behavior of the co-efficients a_0, a_1, a_2 or of the nature of the end conditions. There is, of course, the strong assumption that the problem always has a unique solution.

The principle involved in the foregoing example can be applied to partial differential equations also.

Example 4. Suppose $1 < p < \infty$, and suppose a sequence of scalars α_1, α_2, α_3, $\cdots$ is given, with the assumption that the series

$$\sum_{1}^{\infty} \alpha_k \xi_k$$

is convergent whenever $x = \{\xi_k\}$ is an element of the space l^p. We shall prove that the sequence $\{\alpha_k\}$ belongs to $l^{p'}$, where $p' = p/(p-1)$.
For each x and i let

(4.2–3) $$\eta_i = \sum_{k=1}^{i} \alpha_k \xi_k \qquad i = 1, 2, \cdots.$$

The sequence $\{\eta_i\}$ is bounded, since it is convergent. Hence equations (4.2–3) can be regarded as defining a linear mapping T of l^p into l^∞, where $y = \{\eta_i\}$ and $y = Tx$. This operator T is closed, as we shall see. For, suppose $x_n \to x$ and $Tx_n \to z$, where x_n and x are in l^p and $z \in l^\infty$. Let $z = \{\zeta_i\}$ and $x_n = \{\xi_k^{(n)}\}$. Then $Tx_n \to z$ means that $\sum_{k=1}^{i} \alpha_k \xi_k^{(n)}$ converges uniformly to ζ_i as $n \to \infty$. Now, by Hölder's inequality,

$$\left| \sum_{k=1}^{i} \alpha_k \xi_k^{(n)} - \sum_{k=1}^{i} \alpha_k \xi_k \right| \leqslant \left(\sum_{k=1}^{i} |\xi_k^{(n)} - \xi_k|^p \right)^{1/p} \left(\sum_{k=1}^{i} |\alpha_k|^{p'} \right)^{1/p'}$$

$$\leqslant \|x_n - x\| \left(\sum_{k=1}^{i} |\alpha_k|^{p'} \right)^{1/p'}.$$

Hence, since $x_n \to x$, the uniqueness of limits shows that

$$\zeta_i = \sum_{k=1}^{i} \alpha_k \xi_k.$$

In other words, $Tx = z$. Thus T is closed. But then it is continuous, by the closed-graph theorem. It then follows that for any x and all i we have

(4.2–4)
$$\left| \sum_{k=1}^{i} \alpha_k \xi_k \right| \leqslant \|T\| \left(\sum_{k=1}^{\infty} |\xi_k|^p \right)^{1/p}.$$

Now let us make a special choice of x as follows:

$$\xi_k = \bar{\alpha}_k |\alpha_k|^{p'-2} \qquad \text{if } 1 \leqslant k \leqslant i \text{ and } \alpha_k \neq 0,$$
$$\xi_k = 0 \qquad \text{otherwise.}$$

Then

$$\alpha_k \xi_k = |\xi_k|^p = |\alpha_k|^{p'} \qquad \text{if } 1 \leqslant k \leqslant i.$$

[Observe that $(p' - 1)p = p'$]. When these results are placed in (4.2–4), we have

$$\sum_{k=1}^{i} |\alpha_k|^{p'} \leqslant \|T\| \left(\sum_{k=1}^{i} |\alpha_k|^{p'} \right)^{1/p},$$

whence

$$\left(\sum_{k=1}^{i} |\alpha_k|^{p'} \right)^{1/p'} \leqslant \|T\|.$$

This holds for all i, so it follows that $\{\alpha_k\}$ belongs to $l^{p'}$.

Example 5. Suppose $1 \leqslant p \leqslant \infty$ and $1 \leqslant q \leqslant \infty$. Let $\{\alpha_{ij}\}$ be an infinite matrix ($i, j = 1, 2, \cdots$) of scalars with the following property: For each $x = \{\xi_j\}$ in l^p the series

$$\eta_i = \sum_{j=1}^{\infty} \alpha_{ij} \xi_j,$$

is convergent for each i, and the sequence $y = \{\eta_i\}$ belongs to l^q. Then the operator A defined by $y = Ax$ is a continuous linear mapping of l^p into l^q.

To prove this we observe first of all that

$$x_i'(x) - \sum_{j=1}^{\infty} \alpha_{ij} \xi_j$$

defines a continuous linear functional x_i' on l^p. If $1 < p < \infty$, this follows from the result established in Example 4, for

$$|x_i'(x)| \leqslant \left(\sum_{j=1}^{\infty} |\alpha_{ij}|^{p'}\right)^{1/p'} \left(\sum_{j=1}^{\infty} |\dot{\xi}_j|^p\right)^{1/p},$$

so that x_i' is continuous, with

$$\|x_i'\| \leqslant \left(\sum_{j=1}^{\infty} |\alpha_{ij}|^{p'}\right)^{1/p'} < \infty.$$

(Actually, the last $\leqslant$ can be replaced by $=$, but we do not need this fact here.) If $p = 1$ we have

$$\|x_i'\| \leqslant \sup_j |\alpha_{ij}| < \infty;$$

if $p = \infty$ we have

$$\|x_i'\| \leqslant \sum_{j=1}^{\infty} |\alpha_{ij}| < \infty.$$

These latter facts result from problems 4 and 5 at the end of this section. Now, to prove that A is continuous, it suffices to prove that it is closed, by Theorem 4.2–I. Suppose that $x_n \to x$ and $Ax_n \to y$, where x_n, $x \in l^p$ and $y \in l^q$. From $x_n \to x$ we conclude $x_i'(x_n) \to x_i'(x)$ as $n \to \infty$, since x_i' is continuous. Now, if $z = \{\zeta_i\}$ is any member of l^q, ζ_i is a continuous function of z, as we see from the fact that $|\zeta_i| \leqslant \|z\|$. Since $Ax_n = \{x_i'(x_n)\}$ and $y = \{\eta_i\}$, we conclude from $Ax_n \to y$ that $x_i'(x_n) \to \eta_i$. But then $\eta_i = x_i'(x)$. This means that $y = Ax$. Thus A is closed, and the argument is complete.

PROBLEMS

1. Suppose that X is a linear space in which two invariant metrics are defined, in such a way that X is a complete metric linear space with respect to each metric. Suppose that the two topologies are $\mathscr{T}_1$, $\mathscr{T}_2$, and that $\mathscr{T}_1$ is stronger than $\mathscr{T}_2$ (or, equivalently, that if $x_n \to x$ in the sense of $\mathscr{T}_1$, then $x_n \to x$ in the sense of $\mathscr{T}_2$). Then, the two topologies are actually the same. Use Theorem 4.2–H and the identity mapping of X on itself, with the topology $\mathscr{T}_1$ for the domain and $\mathscr{T}_2$ for the range.

2. Let X be a linear space with two norms $\|x\|_1$, $\|x\|_2$, and let X be complete with respect to each norm. Suppose there exists M such that $\|x\|_2 \leqslant M\|x\|_1$ for every x. Then, there is also an m such that $\|x\|_1 \leqslant m\|x\|_2$.

3. Prove Theorem 4.2–I by defining another invariant metric on X, with $\|x\|_1 = \|x\| + \|Tx\|$. Then use problem 1.

4. If $\sum_1^\infty \alpha_k \xi_k$ is convergent whenever $\sum_1^\infty |\xi_k| < \infty$, then $\sup_k |\alpha_k| < \infty$.

5. If $\sum_1^\infty \alpha_k \xi_k$ is convergent whenever $\lim_{k \to \infty} \xi_k = 0$, then $\sum_1^\infty |\alpha_k| < \infty$.

6. For each $x \in L(0, 2\pi)$ let

$$\xi_n = \frac{1}{2\pi} \int_0^{2\pi} x(t) e^{-int} \, dt, \qquad n = 0, \pm 1, \pm 2, \cdots.$$

Suppose X is some closed subspace of $L(0, 2\pi)$ such that $\sum_{-\infty}^\infty |\xi_n| < \infty$ for each $x \in X$.   Show that there is some constant M such that

$$\sum_{-\infty}^\infty |\xi_n| \leq M \int_0^{2\pi} |x(t)| \, dt$$

for each $x \in X$.

7. Suppose $x \in L(0, 2\pi)$ and

$$y(t) = \frac{1}{2\pi} \int_0^{2\pi} \frac{x(\theta)}{1 - te^{-i\theta}} \, d\theta,$$

where t is complex and $|t| < 1$.   The two following propositions are true (A. E. Taylor, **4**, p. 41 and p. 45):

a. If $1 < p < \infty$ and $x \in L^p(0, 2\pi)$, then $y \in H^p$ (see Example 8, § 3.11 for the definition of H^p).

b. There exists a constant M_p, depending only on p, such that

$$\left(\frac{1}{2\pi} \int_0^{2\pi} |y(re^{i\theta})|^p \, d\theta \right)^{1/p} \leq M_p \left(\int_0^{2\pi} |x(\theta)|^p \, d\theta \right)^{1/p}$$

for all $x \in L^p(0, 2\pi)$ and all r, $0 \leq r < 1$.

Show that *b* is a consequence of *a*, by means of the closed-graph theorem.

8. Prove that the operator A of Example 4, § 1.5, is closed, with domain and range in $L(0, \infty)$.   It suffices to deal with the case when $\lambda = 0$, since the addition of a scalar multiple of I to a closed operator leaves a closed operator.

4.3 The Normed Conjugate of a Normed Linear Space

Let X be a normed linear space, and let A be the associated scalar field. This field is itself a Banach space, with the absolute value $|\alpha|$ as the norm of α.   A continuous linear operator on X into A, that is, a continuous linear functional on X, is an element of the space $[X, A]$, as defined in § 4.1.   We shall denote this space by X'.   It is a subspace of X^f.   The space X' becomes a Banach space if

(4.3–1) $$\|x'\| = \sup_{\|x\| \leq 1} |x'(x)|.$$

When X is normed in this way, we call it the *normed conjugate* of X.

Some authors call X' the *dual* of X; others call it the *adjoint* of X. Sometimes it is denoted by X^* or by $\bar{X}$.

Our first concern is to establish the fact that X' has sufficiently many elements to meet our needs in some situations which will soon arise. For what follows the reader will need to refer back to § 3.7.

Theorem 4.3–A. *Suppose M is a proper subspace of the normed linear space X. If $m' \in M'$, X' contains an element x' such that $\|x'\| = \|m'\|$ and $x'(x) = m'(x)$ if $x \in M$.*

PROOF. We define $p(x) = \|m'\|\,\|x\|$, $x \in X$. Then p is a norm on X. We observe that $|m'(x)| \leqslant p(x)$ if $x \in M$. We apply Theorem 3.7–B, taking m' and x' in place of the f and F of the theorem referred to. Then $|x'(x)| \leqslant \|m'\|\,\|x\|$ for each x in X. This implies that $x' \in X'$ and $\|x'\| \leqslant \|m'\|$. But $\|m'\| \leqslant \|x'\|$, as a result of the fact that x' is an extension of m'. Thus all is proved.

Theorem 4.3–A is commonly called the Hahn-Banach theorem.

A number of simple but important consequences follow rapidly from Theorem 4.3–A.

Theorem 4.3–B. *If X is a normed linear space, and $x_0 \in X$ with $x_0 \neq 0$, then there exists $x' \in X'$ such that $\|x'\| = 1$ and $x'(x_0) = \|x_0\|$. As a consequence we have*

$$(4.3\text{–}2) \qquad\qquad \sup_{\|x'\|=1} |x'(x)| = \|x\|$$

for each $x \in X$.

PROOF. Let M be the subspace of X generated by x_0. If $x = \alpha x_0$, define $m'(x) - \alpha\|x_0\|$. It is clear that $m' \in M'$ and $\|m'\| = 1$. The existence of the required x' now follows from Theorem 4.3–A. Verification of (4.3–2) is left to the reader.

Theorem 4.3–C. *Suppose x is an element of the normed linear space X such that $x'(x) = 0$ for every $x' \in X'$. Then $x = 0$.*

PROOF. Apply (4.3–2).

Theorem 4.3–D. *Let X be a normed linear space, and let X_0 be a subspace of X. Suppose there exists an x_1 in X at a positive distance h from X_0. (This will be the case if X_0 is closed and a proper subset of X, in which case x_1 may be any element of $X - X_0$.) Then, there exists $x' \in X'$ such that $x'(x_1) = h$, $\|x'\| = 1$, and $x'(x) = 0$ if $x \in X_0$.*

PROOF. First we give a demonstration, based on Theorem 4.3–A. This argument is most convenient for readers interested primarily in normed linear spaces, if they have not studied §§ 3.5, 3.6 in detail.   After that we show the relation of Theorem 4.3–D to Theorem 3.6–E and in so doing indicate an alternative proof.

Let M be the subspace generated by X_0 and x_1.   Elements of M are representable in the form $m = \alpha x_1 + x$, $x \in X_0$; α and x are uniquely determined by m, because x_1 is not in X_0.   Let us define m' by $m'(m) = \alpha h$.   We shall show that $m' \in M'$ and $\|m'\| = 1$.   If $\alpha \neq 0$ we have $\|m\| = \|\alpha x_1 + x\| = \| -\alpha(- \alpha^{-1}x - x_1)\| \geqslant |\alpha|h$, because $- \alpha^{-1}x \in X_0$ and the distance from x_1 to X_0 is h.   Thus $|m'(m)| = |\alpha|h \leqslant \|m\|$ if $\alpha \neq 0$.   This inequality is obviously true if $\alpha = 0$.   Consequently $m' \in M'$ and $\|m'\| \leqslant 1$.   Now, if $\epsilon > 0$ there exists $x \in X_0$ such that $\|x - x_1\| < h + \epsilon$.   Let

$$y = \frac{x - x_1}{\|x - x_1\|}.$$

Then $y \in M$, $\|y\| = 1$, and

$$|m'(y)| = \frac{h}{\|x - x_1\|} > \frac{h}{h + \epsilon}.$$

Consequently $\|m'\| > \dfrac{h}{h + \epsilon}$.   Since $h \neq 0$ and this is true for every $\epsilon > 0$, we conclude that $\|m'\| \geqslant 1$.   Observe that $m'(x_1) = h$ and that $m'(x) = 0$ if $x \in X_0$.   The existence of the required $x' \in X'$ now follows from Theorem 4.3–A.

To show the relation of Theorem 4.3–D to Theorem 3.6–E, let $K = \{x : \|x - x_1\| < h\}$.   Then K and X_0 do not intersect.   Theorem 3.6–E shows that there exists a closed hyperplane which contains X_0 and is such that K lies strictly on one side of it.   Since $0 \in X_0$, by Theorem 3.5–E the hyperplane is the set $\{x : x'(x) = 0\}$, where x' is some element of X'.   By replacing x' with some constant multiple of itself, we can arrange matters so that $x'(x_1)$ has any specified nonzero value.   We choose to make $x'(x_1) = h$.   Then $x'(x) > 0$ if $x \in K$.   The remainder of the proof consists in showing that $\|x'\| = 1$.   Suppose that y is any vector for which $\|y\| < 1$.   Then $x_1 \pm hy \in K$, and so $0 < x'(x_1 \pm hy) = h \pm hx'(y)$.   From this we obtain $-1 < x'(y) < 1$.   It follows that $|x'(x)| \leqslant 1$ if $\|x\| \leqslant 1$.   Hence $\|x'\| \leqslant 1$.   On the other hand, we can choose a sequence $\{y_n\}$ from X_0 so that $\|y_n - x_1\| \to h$.   Let $z_n = \|y_n - x_1\|^{-1}(y_n - x_1)$.   Then $\|z_n\| = 1$ and $x'(z_n) = - h\|y_n - x_1\|^{-1}$, so that $|x'(z_n)| \to 1$.   Hence $\|x'\| \geqslant 1$, and the proof is complete.

The next two theorems show some uses of the Hahn-Banach theorem and its immediate consequences.

Theorem 4.3–E.   *If X' is separable, so is X.*

PROOF.   Let $\{x_n'\}$ be a countable set which is everywhere dense on the set $\{x':\|x'\| = 1\}$ in X'.   Choose $x_n \in X$ so that $\|x_n\| = 1$ and $|x_n'(x_n)| \geqslant {}^3/_4$.   Let M be the closed linear manifold in X generated by the sequence $\{x_n\}$.   Suppose $M \neq X$ and $x_0 \in X - M$.   Then Theorem 4.3–D tells us that there exists $x' \in X'$ such that $\|x'\| = 1$, $x'(x_0) \neq 0$, and $x'(x) = 0$ if $x \in M$.   Then $x'(x_n) = 0$ if $n = 1, 2, \cdots$, and

$$\tfrac{3}{4} \leqslant |x_n'(x_n)| \leqslant |x_n'(x_n) - x'(x_n)| + |x'(x_n)|,$$

whence

$$\tfrac{3}{4} \leqslant \|x_n' - x'\| \, \|x_n\| = \|x_n' - x'\|.$$

This contradicts the fact that $\|x_n' - x'\|$ can be made as small as we please by suitable choice of n.   Hence $M = X$.   It then follows that linear combinations formed from $\{x_n\}$ with rational scalar coefficients constitute a countable set everywhere dense in X, so that X is separable.

We shall see that X can be separable and X' not, so that the converse of Theorem 4.3–E is false.   For example, l^1 is separable, but it turns out (see Theorem 4.32–A) that $(l^1)'$ is congruent to l^∞, which is not separable.

The next theorem involves the concept of a quotient space as a normed linear space (see § 3.14).

Theorem 4.3–F.   *Let X be a normed linear space and M a subspace of it.   Let $M^0 = \{x' \in X' : x'(x) = 0$ if $x \in M\}$.   Then M^0 is a closed subspace of X', and the conjugate space M' is congruent to X'/M^0.*

PROOF.   It is evident that M^0 is a closed subspace.   In what follows we use m and m' for typical elements of M and M', respectively.   A typical element of X'/M^0 is $[x']$, where $x' \in X'$.   We have $y' \in [x']$ if and only if $y' - x' \in M^0$, i.e., $y'(m) = x'(m)$ for every m.   With $[x']$ given we define m' by $m'(m) = y'(m)$, where $y' \in [x']$.   Clearly m' depends only on $[x']$ and not on the particular y' chosen.   Also, $m' \in M'$.   Now $|m'(m)| \leqslant \|y'\| \, \|m\|$, and so, by the way in which $\|[x']\|$ is defined, we conclude that $\|m'\| \leqslant \|[x']\|$.   On the other hand, Theorem 4.3–A shows that there exists some $y' \in [x']$ with $\|y'\| = \|m'\|$.   Therefore

$$\|[x']\| = \inf_{y' \in [x']} \|y'\| \leqslant \|m'\|.$$

Thus $\|m'\| = \|[x']\|$.   If we write $m' = T([x'])$, we see that T defines a linear and isometric mapping of X'/M^0 into M'.   The range of T is in fact all of M', for if $m' \in M'$, and $x' \in X'$ is such that $x'(m) = m'(m)$ when $m \in M$, we have $m' = T([x'])$.   Such an x' exists, by Theorem 4.3–A. This completes the proof.

The Hahn-Banach theorem can be used to prove an existence theorem for Green's function for the Dirichlet problem, under certain conditions.

We present a brief sketch of the line of argument of this proof.   For simplicity we consider the two-dimensional case.

Let D be a bounded, connected open set in the plane, with boundary C consisting of a finite number of smooth curves.   Let B be the real Banach space of continuous functions f defined on C, with $\|f\| =$ the maximum value of $|f|$ on C.   Let B_0 be the linear manifold in B consisting of those f for which the Dirichlet problem for the region D is solvable (see the discussion of Example 1, § 1.5).   With each point $Q \in D$ we associate a continuous linear functional l defined on B_0, the value of l at $f \in B_0$ being $u(Q)$, where u is the solution of the Dirichlet problem for the boundary-value function f.   That is, u is harmonic in D, continuous in $\bar{D}$, and $u = f$ on C.   This functional l is linear.   Since $u \equiv 1$ if $f \equiv 1$, and since $|u(Q)| \leqslant$ maximum of $|f|$ on C (by the maximum-value theorem for harmonic functions), it is evident that $l \in B_0'$ and $\|l\| = 1$.   By Theorem 4.3–A there exists an element L of B' which is an extension of l and for which $\|L\| = 1$.   We shall denote L by L_Q to exhibit its dependence on Q.

Now let P be any point not on C in the plane.   If t represents a point on C, let $g_P(t) = \log \overline{tP}$.   Note that $g_P \in B_0$ if P is in the complement of $\bar{D}$.   The value at Q of the corresponding solution of the Dirichlet problem is $u(Q) = l(g_P) = \log \overline{QP}$.   Now, for any fixed P not on C, g_P is an element of B, and so we can apply L_Q to g_P; we define

$$k(P, Q) = L_Q(g_P).$$

If P is on C (and Q is in D), we define

$$k(P, Q) = \log \overline{QP}.$$

We then define

$$G(P, Q) = - \log \overline{QP} + k(P, Q)$$

for $Q \in D$ and any P.   We assert that G is Green's function (to be considered as a function of P with singularity, or "pole," at Q).   To show this it is merely necessary to prove that, as a function of P, $k(P, Q)$ is continuous on the set $\bar{D}$ and harmonic in D.   Let Δ_P denote the Laplacian operator.   Then, for P in D,

$$\Delta_P k(P, Q) = L_Q(\Delta_P g_P) = L_Q(0) = 0.$$

The commuting of Δ_P and L_Q is justified by the fact that L_Q is a bounded operator, just as in differentiating under an integral sign.   Hence $k(P, Q)$ is harmonic in D.   All that remains is to prove continuity of $k(P, Q)$ at points P on C.

We know that $L_Q(g_P) = \log \overline{QP}$ if $Q \in D$ and P is *not* in $\bar{D}$. Hence, if $P_0 \in C$ and $R \to P_0$ from outside of $\bar{D}$, it follows that $k(R, Q) \to \log \overline{QP_0} = k(P_0, Q)$. We want to prove that $k(P, Q) \to k(P_0, Q)$ as $P \to P_0$ from inside C. It will suffice to show that, with each point P sufficiently near P_0 and in D, we can associate a point R not in $\bar{D}$ such that $R \to P_0$ and $k(P, Q) - k(R, Q) \to 0$ as $P \to P_0$. We demonstrate this as follows. With P given, draw a straight line from P to a nearest point N of C; this line is normal to C at N. Continue the line beyond N to a point R such that $\overline{PN} = \overline{NR}$. If P is sufficiently near P_0, R will not be in $\bar{D}$. We have

$$k(P, Q) - k(R, Q) = L_Q(g_P - g_R),$$

$$g_P(t) - g_R(t) = \log \frac{\overline{tP}}{\overline{tR}}.$$

It can be proved that, as $P \to P_0$, $R \to P_0$ and

$$\frac{\overline{tP}}{\overline{tR}} \to 1$$

uniformly with respect to t on C. Thus $\|g_P - g_R\| \to 0$. The desired result now follows, owing to the continuity of the linear functional L_Q.

For more details on this subject, see the papers by P. D. Lax and C. Miranda listed in the bibliography.

If X is an incomplete normed linear space, and $\hat{X}$ is the completion of X (see § 3.13), it turns out that X' and $\hat{X}'$ are congruent, and it is convenient to regard X' and $\hat{X}'$ as being the same space. The fact that they are congruent follows from Theorem 3.13–A, with Y the space of scalars.

PROBLEMS

1. If X is a normed linear space of finite dimension n, the dimension of X' is also n. Prove this by showing that $X' = X^f$. See Theorem 1.61–A and the proof of Theorem 3.12–A.

2. The proposition in (1) can be generalized. If X is an n-dimensional topological linear T_1-space, all the elements of X^f are continuous, and X^f is n-dimensional. See problems 1 and 2 of § 3.3.

3. If X is a complex normed linear space and X_r is the associated real linear space, we write $x'(x) = x_1'(x) - ix_1'(ix)$, where $x_1' \in (X_r)'$ and $x' \in X'$ (see § 3.7). Show that $\|x_1'\| = \|x'\|$.

4. Suppose M is a subspace of the normed linear space X. Let $G = M \cap \{x : \|x\| \leqslant 1\}$. Suppose $x_0' \notin M^0$. Show that the distance from x_0' to M^0 is $\sup_{x \in G} |x_0'(x)|$ and that there is in M^0 an element x' such that $\|x' - x_0'\| = d(x_0', M^0)$.

5. If X is a Banach space of infinite dimension, its dimension (see problem 2, § 1.72) is at least as great as the cardinality C of the set of all real numbers. The proof is made (a) by observing that the dimension of l^∞ is at least as great as C, and (b) by constructing a one-to-one linear mapping of l^∞ into X. For (a) consider the elements $(t, t^2, t^3, \cdots)$ of l^∞, where $0 < t < 1$. For (b) construct a sequence $\{x_n\}$ of elements of X and a sequence $\{M_n\}$ of closed subspaces of X such that $\sum_n \|x_n\| < \infty$, $x_n \notin M_n$, $x_k \in M_n$ if $k > n$. Then, if $y = \{\xi_k\} \in l^\infty$, define $Ty = x = \sum_1^\infty \xi_k x_k$; T is the desired mapping of l^∞ into X. To obtain $\{M_n\}$ and $\{x_n\}$ let $M_0 = X$ and for $n \geqslant 1$ choose $m_n' \in M_{n-1}$ with $m_n' \neq 0$; then define $M_n = \{x \in M_{n-1} : m_n'(x) = 0\}$ and choose $x_n \in M_{n-1} - M_n$ in a suitable way.

6. If X is an infinite-dimensional separable Banach space, its dimension is C. This can be shown by using the results of the foregoing problem and of problem 2, § 1.72, for the cardinality of X cannot exceed C.

7. If X is a Banach space of infinite dimension, the weak topology $\mathcal{T}(X, X')$ for X is not metrizable. Use problem 5 and § 3.9, problem 2.

8. Let X be a normed linear space and M a subspace of X'. If M is not closed, then $\mathcal{T}(X, \bar{M})$ is strictly stronger than $\mathcal{T}(X, M)$ (see § 3.81). However, if S is a bounded subset of X, the relative topologies induced on S by $\mathcal{T}(X, M)$ and $\mathcal{T}(X, \bar{M})$ are the same. To prove this it suffices to show that, if $\epsilon > 0$ and $x_1', \cdots, x_n'$ are in $\bar{M}$, the set $V \cap S$, where $V = \{x : |x_i'(x)| < \epsilon, i = 1, \cdots, n\}$, is open in the topology induced on S by $\mathcal{T}(X, M)$.

4.31 The Second Normed Conjugate Space

If X is a normed linear space, we denote the normed conjugate of X' by X''. We shall use x'' as a typical notation for elements of X'', and we shall often write $\langle x', x'' \rangle$ in place of $x''(x')$.

Note that, although X' is a subspace of X^f, X'' is not in general a subspace of X^{ff} (though it is a subspace of $(X')^f$). There is, however, a canonical mapping of X into X'' which is similar to the canonical mapping of X into X^{ff}, as defined in § 1.6. We shall use the symbol J for this canonical mapping of X into X'', in spite of the fact that it is not the same as the J of § 1.6. Since we do not consider both mappings at the same time, no confusion need arise.

The definition of the canonical mapping of X into X'' is expressed by the formula

$$(4.31\text{--}1) \qquad \langle x', Jx \rangle = \langle x, x' \rangle, \qquad x \in X, \qquad x' \in X'.$$

That is, $Jx = x''$, where $x''(x') = x'(x)$. It is evident that $x'' \in (X')^f$, and since $|x''(x')| \leqslant \|x'\| \|x\|$, it is clear that $x'' \in X''$ and $\|x''\| \leqslant \|x\|$. Actually, we can prove that $\|x''\| = \|x\|$. This is obviously so if $x = 0$, and so we assume $x \neq 0$. Then, there exists $x' \in X'$ such that $\|x'\| = 1$ and $x'(x) = \|x\|$ (Theorem 4.3–B). By the formula for $\|x''\|$ corresponding to (4.3–1) we see then that $\|x''\| \geqslant \|x\|$. Hence $\|x''\| = \|x\|$. We state this result for reference in the form

$$(4.31–2) \qquad \|Jx\| = \|x\|.$$

Evidently J sets up a congruence between X and a subspace of X''.

Definition. If the range of J is all of X'', we say that X is *norm reflexive*. If the exact context is clear, we may use the simpler term *reflexive* instead of *norm reflexive*. But it should be recalled that we have already (in § 1.6) defined a concept of *algebraic reflexivity* for a linear space. In contrast to the situation with algebraic reflexivity, we shall see that there exist infinite-dimensional spaces which are norm reflexive.

Since X'' is complete, whether X is or not, it is clear from (4.31–2) that, if X is incomplete, it cannot be reflexive.

Theorem 4.31–A. *If X is norm reflexive, so is X'.*

PROOF. The argument is very straightforward. Denote by J_0 the canonical mapping of X into X'', and by J_1 that of X' into X'''. We assume $\mathcal{R}(J_0) = X''$, and we wish to prove $\mathcal{R}(J_1) = X'''$. Suppose $x''' \in X'''$, and define x' by $\langle x, x' \rangle = \langle J_0 x, x''' \rangle$, x varying over X. The proof is then completed by proving that $x' \in X'$ and $J_1 x' = x'''$. We leave the last details to the reader.

It will be shown in § 4.6 (problem 4) that, if X is complete and X' is norm reflexive, so is X.

Theorem 4.31–B. *If X is norm reflexive, the same is true of each closed subspace of X.*

PROOF. Let M be a closed subspace of X. We use Theorem 4.3–F and the notation employed in its proof. In particular, we use the operator T which maps X'/M^0 isometrically and linearly onto M'. Suppose $m'' \in M''$. Define $x'' \in X''$ by setting $x''(x') = m''\{T([x'])\}$ for each x' in X'. Since X is reflexive, there exists $x \in X$ such that $x''(x') = x'(x)$ for each x'. We assert that $x \in M$. For, if not, the fact that M is closed enables us to infer that there exists $x' \in X'$ such that $x' \in M^0$ and $x'(x) \neq 0$ (by Theorem 4.3–D). Then $[x']$ is the zero element of X'/M^0, and so $T([x']) = 0$, whence $x'(x) = x''(x') = m''\{T([x'])\} = 0$, contrary to fact. Let us now denote x by m, since $x \in M$. If $m' = T[x']$ is any element of M', we have $m'(m) = x'(m)$, by the way in which T is defined. Thus $m''(m') = x''(x') = x'(m) = m'(m)$. This proves that M is reflexive.

PROBLEMS

1. A finite-dimensional normed linear space is norm reflexive.

2. The range of J is closed in X'' if and only if X is complete.

3. If X is complete but not norm reflexive, $J(X)$ is of the first category in X.

4.32 Some Representations of Linear Functionals

In this section we shall obtain representation theorems for linear functionals on certain particular normed linear spaces.   These represent-ation theorems are of the following sort: If X is a certain given space, we find another normed linear space Y which is congruent to X' in such a way that, if $x' \in X'$ and if the corresponding element of Y is y, for each $x \in X$ the value of $x'(x)$ is expressed in a well-determined way by an analytical process involving x and y.   This process usually involves an infinite series or some kind of an integral.

Several important results are given as problems.

THE NORMED CONJUGATE OF l^p, $1 \leqslant p < \infty$

The spaces l^p were discussed in § 3.11.   With each p we associate p', defined as follows:

$$p' = \frac{p}{p-1} \qquad \text{if } 1 < p < \infty,$$

$$p' = \infty \qquad \text{if } p = 1,$$

$$p' = 1 \qquad \text{if } p = \infty.$$

Note that $(p')' = p$ and that

(4.32–1) $$\frac{1}{p} + \frac{1}{p'} = 1 \quad \text{if } 1 < p < \infty.$$

Note also that $p' = 2$ if and only if $p = 2$, and that $1 < p < 2$ implies $2 < p' < \infty$.

For general use, here and elsewhere, we define

$$\operatorname{sgn} c = \begin{cases} 0 & \text{if } c = 0 \\ \dfrac{c}{|c|} & \text{if } c \neq 0. \end{cases}$$

Here c may be any real or complex number.   Sometimes it is convenient in printing to denote sgn $\bar{c}$ by $\overline{\operatorname{sgn}} \, c$, especially if c is replaced by a lengthy or bulky expression.   Observe that $c \operatorname{sgn} \bar{c} = |c|$, and that $|\operatorname{sgn} c| = 0$ or 1 according to whether c is 0 or $\neq 0$.

If $x = \{\xi_n\} \in l^p$, we denote by u_k that x for which $\xi_k = 1$ and $\xi_n = 0$ if $n \neq k$. If $1 \leqslant p < \infty$, we see that for any $x \in l^p$

$$\left\| x - \sum_1^n \xi_k u_k \right\| = \left(\sum_{n+1}^\infty |\xi_k|^p \right)^{1/p} \to 0$$

as $n \to \infty$, so that

(4.32–2)
$$x = \sum_1^\infty \xi_k u_k.$$

It follows that

(4.32–3)
$$x'(x) = \sum_1^\infty \xi_k x'(u_k)$$

if $x' \in X'$.   The condition $p < \infty$ is essential for (4.32–2).

The problem of representing x' is now seen to be the problem of describing what sets of values are admissible for $x'(u_k)$, $k = 1, 2, \cdots$, and of giving a formula for $\|x'\|$ in terms of these values.   The solution of the problem is given in the following theorem.

Theorem 4.32–A.   *Suppose $1 \leqslant p < \infty$.   Every continuous linear functional on l^p is representable in one and only one way in the form*

(4.32–4)
$$x'(x) = \sum_1^\infty \alpha_k \xi_k,$$

where the sequence $a = \{\alpha_n\}$ is an element of $l^{p'}$.   Every element a of $l^{p'}$ can be used in this way to define an element of $(l^p)'$, and the correspondence between x' and a is a congruence of $(l^p)'$ and $l^{p'}$.   In particular,

(4.32–5)
$$\|x'\| = \begin{cases} \left(\sum_1^\infty |\alpha_k|^{p'} \right)^{1/p'} & \text{if } 1 < p < \infty \\[2mm] \sup_k |\alpha_k| & \text{if } p = 1. \end{cases}$$

PROOF.   Suppose $x' \in (l^p)'$ given.   Define $\alpha_k = x'(u_k)$.   Then $x'(x)$ is given by (4.32–3), or (4.32–4).   Suppose first that $1 < p < \infty$.   The case $p = 1$ is considered later.   For a given positive integer n, choose x as follows:

(4.32–6)
$$\xi_k = \begin{cases} |\alpha_k|^{p'-1} \operatorname{sgn} \bar\alpha_k & \text{if } 1 \leqslant k \leqslant n \\ 0 & \text{if } n < k. \end{cases}$$

Then, if $1 \leqslant k \leqslant n$,

$$\alpha_k \xi_k = |\alpha_k|^{p'} = |\xi_k|^p,$$

and so

$$\|x\| = \left(\sum_1^n |\alpha_k|^{p'} \right)^{1/p}, \qquad x'(x) = \sum_1^n |\alpha_k|^{p'}.$$

But $|x'(x)| \leqslant \|x'\| \|x\|$, and so

$$\sum_1^n |\alpha_k|^{p'} \leqslant \|x'\| \left(\sum_1^n |\alpha_k|^{p'} \right)^{1/p}.$$

It follows that

$$\left(\sum_1^n |\alpha_k|^{p'} \right)^{1/p'} \leqslant \|x'\|.$$

Hence $a = \{\alpha_n\}$ is in $l^{p'}$, and $\|a\| \leqslant \|x'\|$.

Suppose, on the other hand, that $a = \{\alpha_n\}$ is a given element of $l^{p'}$. We can define $x' \in (l^p)'$ by (4.32–4). By Hölder's inequality we have

$$|x'(x)| \leqslant \left(\sum_1^\infty |\alpha_k|^{p'} \right)^{1/p'} \left(\sum_1^\infty |\xi_k|^p \right)^{1/p} = \|a\| \|x\|,$$

so that $\|x'\| \leqslant \|a\|$. Since $x'(u_k) = \alpha_k$ in this case it follows from the preceding work that $\|a\| \leqslant \|x'\|$. Hence $\|a\| = \|x'\|$, and all is clear when $1 < p < \infty$.

If $p = 1$ we replace (4.32–6) by

$$\xi_k = \begin{cases} \operatorname{sgn} \bar{\alpha}_n & \text{if } k = n \\ 0 & \text{if } k \neq n. \end{cases}$$

Then $\|x\| \leqslant 1$, and (4.32–4) becomes $x'(x) = |\alpha_n|$, so that $|\alpha_n| \leqslant \|x'\| \|x\| \leqslant \|x'\|$, whence $a = \{\alpha_n\} \in l^\infty$, with $\|a\| \leqslant \|x'\|$. The rest of the argument for $p = 1$ is left to the reader.

Theorem 4.32–A is not true for the case $p = \infty$. If it were, $(l^\infty)'$ would be congruent to the separable space l^1. Since l^∞ is not separable, this would contradict Theorem 4.3–E.

THE NORMED CONJUGATE OF $C[a, b]$

For the definition of $C[a, b]$ see Example 3, § 1.3 and Example 4, § 3.11. We shall also have to consider $B[a, b]$ (Example 3, § 3.11), of which $C[a, b]$ is a subspace.

Our problem is to discover an analytic representation for all continuous linear functionals on $C[a, b]$. We shall see that to each such functional x' corresponds a function of bounded variation v such that the values of the functional are given by the Riemann-Stieltjes integral

(4.32–7) $$x'(x) = \int_a^b x(t)\, dv(t).$$

Theorem 4.32–B. *Suppose $x' \in X'$, where $X = C[a, b]$. Then, there exists a function of bounded variation v, defined on $[a, b]$ and with values in the scalar field associated with X, such that (4.32–7) is valid for each x and also such that the total variation of v on $[a, b]$ is $\|x'\|$.*

PROOF.   Let f be a continuous linear functional on $B[a, b]$ which is an extension of x' and such that $\|f\| = \|x'\|$.   Such an f exists, by Theorem 4.3–A.   If s is any point of $[a, b]$, let x_s be defined by $x_a(t) \equiv 0$ (for $s = a$) and by

$$x_s(t) = \begin{cases} 1 & \text{if } a \leqslant t \leqslant s \\ 0 & \text{if } s < t \leqslant b \end{cases}$$

in case $a < s \leqslant b$.   Then $x_s \in B[a, b]$.   We define v by

$$(4.32\text{–}8) \qquad\qquad v(s) = f(x_s).$$

We now proceed to show that v is of bounded variation and that $V(v) \leqslant \|x'\|$, where $V(v)$ is the total variation of v.   Consider any partition of $[a, b]$:

$$a = t_0 < t_1 < \cdots < t_n = b.$$

Using the $\overline{\text{sgn}}$ notation explained earlier, we let

$$\epsilon_i = \overline{\text{sgn}} \, [v(t_i) - v(t_{i-1})], \qquad i = 1, \cdots, n,$$

and we construct the function

$$y(t) = \begin{cases} \epsilon_1 & \text{if } t_0 \leqslant t \leqslant t_1 \\ \epsilon_i & \text{if } t_{i-1} < t \leqslant t_i, \end{cases} \qquad i = 2, \cdots, n.$$

Then $y \in B[a, b]$ and $\|y\| \leqslant 1$.   We can write

$$y(t) = \sum_{i=1}^{n} \epsilon_i [y_i(t) - y_{i-1}(t)],$$

where $y_k = x_{t_k}$.   Thus

$$f(y) = \sum_{i=1}^{n} \epsilon_i [f(y_i) - f(y_{i-1})] = \sum_{i=1}^{n} \epsilon_i [v(t_i) - v(t_{i-1})]$$

$$= \sum_{i=1}^{n} |v(t_i) - v(t_{i-1})|.$$

But $|f(y)| \leqslant \|f\| \, \|y\| \leqslant \|f\| = \|x'\|$.   Therefore

$$\sum_{i=1}^{n} |v(t_i) - v(t_{i-1})| \leqslant \|x'\|.$$

This shows that v is of bounded variation, with $V(v) \leqslant \|x'\|$.

Now we proceed to prove the validity of (4.32–7). With the same notation as before for an arbitrary partition, and with any given x in $C[a, b]$, we define $z \in B[a, b]$ as follows:

$$z(t) = \sum_{i=1}^{n} x(t_{i-1})[y_i(t) - y_{i-1}(t)].$$

Then

$$(4.32–9) \quad f(z) = \sum_{i=1}^{n} x(t_{i-1})[v(t_i) - v(t_{i-1})].$$

Also,

$$|z(t) - x(t)| = \begin{cases} |x(t_0) - x(t)| & \text{if } a \leqslant t \leqslant t_1 \\ |x(t_{i-1}) - x(t)| & \text{if } t_{i-1} < t \leqslant t_i, i = 2, \cdots, n. \end{cases}$$

Let $\varDelta$ denote the partition, and let

$$|\varDelta| = \max \{|t_1 - t_0|, \cdots, |t_n - t_{n-1}|\}.$$

Then we see (by the uniform continuity of x) that $\|z - x\| \to 0$ when $|\varDelta| \to 0$. Since f is continuous, $f(z) \to f(x)$. But also, it is clear from (4.32–9) and the definition of a Stieltjes integral that

$$f(z) \to \int_a^b x(t)\, dv(t).$$

We therefore conclude that

$$f(x) = \int_a^b x(t)\, dv(t).$$

This is the same as (4.32–7), since f is an extension of x'. It is a standard property of Stieltjes integrals that

$$(4.32–10) \quad \left| \int_a^b x(t)\, dv(t) \right| \leqslant \|x\| V(v).$$

Consequently $\|x'\| \leqslant V(v)$. We already know that $V(v) \leqslant \|x'\|$, and so $V(v) = \|x'\|$.

Theorem 4.32–B makes no assertion about the uniqueness of v, nor does it assert that X' is congruent to some space of which v is a member. We observe in the first place that there is no unique function of bounded variation which makes (4.32–7) true for all $x \in C[a, b]$. For, we can add an arbitrary constant to v without affecting (4.32–7). It is also easy to see that the values of v at its points of discontinuity in the interior of the interval $[a, b]$ can be altered without affecting the value of the integral in (4.32–7).   For, if w is a function of bounded variation which is equal to v at a, b and at all points t in the interior of $[a, b]$ at which v is continuous, the approximating sums which define

$$\int_a^b x(t)\, dv(t) \qquad \text{and} \qquad \int_a^b x(t)\, dw(t)$$

can be formed exclusively by use of values of v and w at points of the aforementioned kind, so that the integrals must be equal in value.

In order to obtain a congruence between the space X' and a suitable space of functions of bounded variation, we proceed in the following manner.   As in Example 7, § 3.11, we denote by $BV[a, b]$ the Banach space of functions of bounded variation defined on $[a, b]$, with

$$\|v\| = |v(a)| + V(v).$$

We can define an equivalence relation in $BV[a, b]$ by writing $v_1 \sim v_2$ if

$$\int_a^b x(t)\, dv_1(t) = \int_a^b x(t)\, dv_2(t)$$

for each $x \in C[a, b]$.   We assert that $v \sim 0$ if and only if $v(a) = v(b)$ and $v(c - 0) = v(c + 0) = v(a)$ if $a < c < b$.   To see this we observe first of all that $v \sim 0$ implies

$$0 = \int_a^b dv(t) = v(b) - v(a).$$

Next we observe the following: If $v \in BV[a, b]$ and $a \leqslant c < b$, then

$$(4.32\text{–}11) \qquad \frac{1}{h} \int_c^{c+h} v(t)\, dt \to v(c + 0)$$

as $h \to 0$.   Likewise, if $a < c \leqslant b$,

$$(4.32\text{–}12) \qquad \frac{1}{h} \int_{c-h}^c v(t)\, dt \to v(c - 0)$$

as $h \to 0$.   We leave the simple proofs of these facts to the reader.   Now suppose that $a \leqslant c < b$, $0 < h < b - c$, and define

$$x(t) = \begin{cases} 1, & a \leqslant t \leqslant c \\ 1 - \dfrac{t - c}{h}, & c \leqslant t \leqslant c + h \\ 0, & c + h \leqslant t \leqslant b. \end{cases}$$

Then $v \sim 0$ implies

$$0 = \int_a^b x(t)\, dv(t) = v(c) - v(a) + \int_c^{c+h} x(t)\, dv(t).$$

On integration by parts we obtain

$$\int_c^{c+h} x(t) \, dv(t) = -v(a) + \frac{1}{h} \int_c^{c+h} v(t) \, dt.$$

Using (4.32–11), we obtain the result $v(c + 0) = v(a)$. A similar argument shows that $v(c - 0) = v(b)$ if $a < c \leqslant b$. [We remark that $v(a + 0) = v(a)$ is a consequence of $v(c + 0) = v(a)$ for $a < c < b$, because there exists a sequence c_n such that $a < c_n < b$, $c_n \to a$, and $v(c_n + 0) = v(c_n)$; likewise for $v(b - 0) = v(b)$.]

Conversely, it is evident that, if $v \in BV[a, b]$ and $v(a) = v(b) = v(c + 0) = v(c - 0)$ when $a < c < b$, then $v \sim 0$. For then $v(t) = v(a)$ at $t = a$, $t = b$, and all interior points of $[a, b]$ at which v is continuous, so that, if $x \in C[a, b]$,

$$\int_a^b x(t) \, dv(t) = \int_a^b x(t) \, dw(t) = 0,$$

where $w(t) \equiv v(a)$.

Now let $X = C[a, b]$. We wish to associate with each $x' \in X'$ a unique $v \in BV[a, b]$ in such a way that the association makes X' congruent to a subspace of $BV[a, b]$, and such that x' and v are related by the formula (4.32–7). We do this by introducing the concept of a normalized function of bounded variation. We shall say that v is *normalized* if $v(a) = 0$ and if $v(t + 0) = v(t)$ when $a < t < b$. Other definitions of normalization can be used; we might alternatively require $v(t - 0) = v(t)$, or

$$v(t) = \tfrac{1}{2}[v(t + 0) + v(t - 0)].$$

Our choice is governed by consideration of some future applications.

The normalized functions form a linear manifold in $BV[a, b]$. Each equivalence class contains at most one normalized function. These facts are readily evident. From any $v \in BV[a, b]$ we can define another member v^* of $BV[a, b]$ as follows:

$$v^*(a) = 0, \qquad\qquad v^*(b) = v(b) - v(a)$$
$$v^*(t) = v(t + 0) - v(a), \qquad a < t < b.$$

Then one can easily verify that v^* is normalized and that $v^* \sim v$. Thus each equivalence class contains *exactly* one normalized function. Finally, one may show that $V(v^*) \leqslant V(v)$. For, suppose $a = t_0 < t_1 < \cdots < t_n = b$. If $\epsilon > 0$ we can choose points $s_1, \cdots, s_{n-1}$ at which v is continuous, with s_k so close to t_k (on the right) that

$$|v(t_k + 0) - v(s_k)| < \epsilon/2n.$$

It is then readily seen that, if $s_0 = a$ and $s_n = b$, we have

$$\sum_{k=1}^{n} |v^*(t_k) - v^*(t_{k-1})| \leqslant \sum_{k=1}^{n} |v(s_k) - v(s_{k-1})| + \epsilon \leqslant V(v) + \epsilon,$$

and so $V(v^*) \leqslant V(v) + \epsilon$.   But then $V(v^*) \leqslant V(v)$.

We can now state:

Theorem 4.32–C.   *Let $X = C[a, b]$.   Then X' is congruent to the subspace of $BV[a, b]$ consisting of all normalized functions of bounded variation.   If v is such a normalized function, the corresponding x' is given by*

$$(4.32\text{--}13) \qquad x'(x) = \int_a^b x(t)\, dv(t).$$

PROOF.   Formula (4.32–13) defines a linear mapping $x' = Tv$, where v is normalized and $x' \in X'$.   We evidently have $\|x'\| \leqslant V(v)$ [see (4.32–10)]. For a normalized v, $V(v)$ is the norm of v, because $v(a) = 0$.   Now consider any $x' \in X'$.   Theorem 4.32–B tells us that there is some $u \in BV[a, b]$ such that

$$x'(x) = \int_a^b x(t)\, du(t)$$

and $V(u) = \|x'\|$.   The integral is not changed if we replace u by u^*. Then $x' = Tu^*$ and $\|x'\| \leqslant V(u^*)$.   Also, $V(u^*) \leqslant V(u) = \|x'\|$.   Therefore $\|x'\| = V(u^*)$.   Since there is just one normalized function in each equivalance class, we see that the theorem is proved.

The following theorem is of interest, especially in relation to § 7.5.

Theorem 4.32–D.   *Suppose the functional x' is defined by formula (4.32–7), where v is of bounded variation.   Suppose also that $x'(x) \geqslant 0$ if $x \in C[a, b]$ and $x(t) \geqslant 0$ for all values of t on $[a, b]$.   Then $v(a) \leqslant v(s + 0) \leqslant v(b)$ if $a \leqslant s < b$ and $v(s_1 + 0) \leqslant v(s_2 + 0)$ if $a \leqslant s_1 < s_2 < b$.   In particular, v is nondecreasing if it is normalized.*

PROOF.   We shall not go into full detail with the argument.   The fundamental idea of the proof rests on the following consideration: If $a \leqslant s < b$ and $0 < h < b - s$, let x be the function defined by $x(t) = 1$ if $a \leqslant t \leqslant s$, $x(t) = (s + h - t)/h$ if $s \leqslant t \leqslant s + h$,   and $x(t) = 0$ if $s + h \leqslant t \leqslant b$.   Then $x'(x) \geqslant 0$.   A rather easy calculation shows that, as $h \to 0$,

$$\int_a^b x(t)\, dv(t) \to v(s + 0) - v(a).$$

Thus $v(a) \leqslant v(s + 0)$.   The rest of the proof is left to the reader.

PROBLEMS

1. Let (c) denote the space of sequences $x = \{\xi_n\}$ such that $\lim\limits_{n\to\infty} \xi_n = \xi_0$ exists. Let $\|x\| = \sup\limits_{n} |\xi_n|$. Then (c) is a subspace of l^∞. Show that it is complete. Let u_0 be the x for which $\xi_n = 1$ for every n, and let $u_1, u_2, \cdots$ be as in the discussion of l^p. Show that

$$x = \xi_0 u_0 + \sum_1^\infty (\xi_k - \xi_0) u_k.$$

If $x' \in (c)'$ and $x'(u_k) = \alpha_k$, show by special choice of x that $\sum\limits_1^\infty |\alpha_k| < \infty$. Then in general we can write

$$x'(x) = \left(\alpha_0 - \sum_1^\infty \alpha_k \right) \xi_0 + \sum_1^\infty \alpha_k \xi_k.$$

Show that $(c)'$ is congruent to l^1 under the correspondence $x' \leftrightarrow b = \{\beta_n\}$, where

$$x'(x) = \sum_1^\infty \beta_n \xi_{n-1}.$$

2. Let (c_0) be the closed subspace of (c) consisting of those $x \in (c)$ for which $\xi_n \to 0$. Show that $(c_0)'$ is congruent to l^1 under the correspondence $x' \leftrightarrow a = \{\alpha_n\}$, where $x'(x) = \sum\limits_1^\infty \alpha_k \xi_k$.

3. If $1 < p < \infty$, then l^p is norm reflexive.

4. l^1 is not norm reflexive.

5. (c) and (c_0) are not norm reflexive.

6. State and prove a representation theorem for $l^p(n)$, $1 \leqslant p \leqslant \infty$.

7. Let (a, b) be a finite or infinite interval of the real axis. The general representation of a continuous linear functional on $L^p(a, b)$, if $1 \leqslant p < \infty$, is

$$x'(x) = \int_a^b v(t) x(t) \, dt,$$

where $v \in L^{p'}(a, b)$. The correspondence $x' \leftrightarrow v$ is a congruence of $(L^p)'$ and $L^{p'}$. See Banach, **1**, pages 61–65 and Riesz and Nagy, **1**, page 78. A more general form of this representation theorem is given in § 7.4.

4.4 The Principle of Uniform Boundedness

In this section we have several theorems, in each of which the conclusion is that a certain set in a certain normed linear space is bounded. In some cases the space is a space of continuous linear operators. It is convenient to state several theorems, even though, in a certain sense, they are all derivable from one general theorem. For the purpose of applications it is better to state the results in various forms adapted to easy recognition in the various situations where they are needed. But there is a single fundamental principle underlying all the theorems. This principle goes back to the fact that a complete metric space is of the second category in itself. Our proofs use this fact through the medium of the closed-graph theorem (Theorem 4.2–I).

To avoid trivial situations we assume throughout that we deal with linear spaces which contain some nonzero elements.

Theorem 4.4–A. *Let X be a normed linear space, and let F be a nonempty subset of X. Suppose that $\sup_{x\in F} |x'(x)| < \infty$ for each $x' \in X'$. Then $\sup_{x\in F} \|x\| < \infty$ (i.e., F is a bounded set).*

This theorem is merely a special case of the next theorem, but we state Theorem 4.4–A separately to make the nature of the principle of uniform boundedness stand out clearly before we embark upon more general theorems.

Theorem 4.4–A can be given a geometric interpretation by using the notion of a hyperplane. A closed hyperplane through 0 is a set of the form $\{x:x'(x) = 0\}$, where x' is some element of X'. The set $\{x:|x'(x)| < \alpha\}$ (where $\alpha > 0$) is then the set of all points between the two closed hyperplanes $\{x:x'(x) = \alpha\}$, $\{x:x'(x) = -\alpha\}$, which are parallel to one through the origin, and at equal distances from it on opposite sides of 0. Theorem 4.4–A states that, if for every closed hyperplane L through 0 the set F lies in some open "slab" between two closed hyperplanes parallel to L, then F is bounded.

To generalize Theorem 4.4–A we propose to draw the same conclusion as before but with the weaker assumption that $\sup_{x\in F} |x'(x)| < \infty$ for each $x' \in M$, where M is merely a subset of X' but of a suitably special nature.

Definition. If M is a linear manifold in X' and $x \in X$, let

(4.4–1) $p_M(x) = \sup |x'(x)|$ for $x' \in M$ and $\|x'\| = 1$.

Let

(4.4–2) $\nu(M) = \inf p_M(x)$ for $x \in X$ and $\|x\| = 1$.

We call $\nu(M)$ the *characteristic* of M. If $\nu(M) > 0$, M is said to be *norm-determining* for X.

It is evident that

(4.4–3) $$\nu(M)\|x\| \leqslant p_M(x) \leqslant \|x\|$$

and that $0 \leqslant \nu(M) \leqslant 1$. If $\nu(M) > 0$, then p_M is evidently a norm on X, and the topology for X defined by using this norm is the same as the topology for X defined by using $\|x\|$ as norm.

Theorem 4.4–B. *Let F be a nonempty subset of the normed linear space X, and let M be a closed linear manifold in X' which is norm-determining for X. Suppose that $\sup_{x \in F} |x'(x)| < \infty$ for each $x' \in M$. Then F is a bounded set.*

PROOF. Consider $B(F)$, the Banach space of all bounded scalar-valued functions f defined on F, with $\|f\| = \sup_{x \in F} |f(x)|$. Define a linear operator T with domain M and range in $B(F)$ by defining Tx' to be the element of $B(F)$ whose value at x is $x'(x)$. The hypothesis assures that $Tx' \in B(F)$, and T is obviously linear. Since $\|x_n' - x'\| \to 0$ implies $x_n'(x) \to x'(x)$ for each $x \in X$, it is a simple matter (using Theorem 4.2–A) to verify that T is a closed operator. But, since M and $B(F)$ are both complete, it follows by the closed-graph theorem that T is continuous. Hence $|x'(x)| \leqslant \|T\| \|x'\|$ if $x \in F$ and $x' \in M$. It follows that $\nu(M)\|x\| \leqslant p_M(x) \leqslant \|T\|$ if $x \in F$. Since $\nu(M) > 0$, the fact that F is bounded now follows at once.

If $M = X'$, then $p_M(x) = \|x\|$, by (4.3–2). Hence $\nu(M) = 1$ in this case. It is then clear that Theorem 4.4–A is just a special case of Theorem 4.4–B.

Next we consider X' and X''. If J is the operator which maps X canonically into X'', the range of J is a subspace of X'' which is norm-determining for X'. In fact, the characteristic of $\mathcal{R}(J)$ is 1, as we see by examining the definition of $\nu\{\mathcal{R}(J)\}$ and recalling the definition of $\|x'\|$. It is furthermore true that, if X is complete, $\mathcal{R}(J)$ is closed in X''. We can therefore apply Theorem 4.4–B to subsets of X', using $\mathcal{R}(J)$ for the role of M. This gives us the result:

Theorem 4.4–C. *Let X be a Banach space, and let F be a subset of X'. Suppose that $\sup_{x' \in F} |x'(x)| < \infty$ for each $x \in X$. Then $\sup_{x' \in F} \|x'\| < \infty$.*

As immediate application of Theorems 4.4–A and 4.4–C we have:

Theorem 4.4–D. *(a) Let $\{x_n\}$ be a sequence in the normed linear space X such that $\lim_{n \to \infty} x'(x_n)$ exists for each $x' \in X$. Then the sequence of norms $\|x_n\|$ is bounded.*

(b) *Let* X *be a Banach space, and let* $\{x_n'\}$ *be a sequence in* X' *such that* $\lim\limits_{n\to\infty} x_n'(x)$ *exists for each* $x \in X$. *Then, the sequence of norms* $\|x_n'\|$ *is bounded.*

We can formulate a theorem similar to Theorem 4.4–B, dealing with uniform boundedness of a set of bounded linear operators. Let X and Y be normed linear spaces, and let Z be a subspace of X. If $T \in [X, Y]$, define

$$q_Z(T) = \sup \|Tx\| \qquad \text{for } x \in Z \text{ and } \|x\| = 1.$$

Then define

$$\mu(Z) = \inf q_Z(T) \qquad \text{for } T \in [X, Y] \text{ and } \|T\| = 1.$$

If $\mu(Z) > 0$, we shall say that Z is norm-determining for $[X, Y]$. [Note that $\mu(X) = 1$.]   Evidently $0 \leqslant \mu(Z) \leqslant 1$ and

$$\mu(Z)\| T\| \leqslant q_Z(T) \leqslant \|T\|.$$

We have the following result:

Theorem 4.4–E.   *Suppose* X *is a Banach space, and let* Y *be a normed linear space.   Let* Z *be a closed subspace of* X *which is norm-determining for* $[X, Y]$. *Let* G *be a nonempty subset of* $[X, Y]$ *such that* $\sup\limits_{T\in G} \|Tx\| < \infty$ *for each* $x \in Z$. *Then* $\sup\limits_{T\in G} \|T\| < \infty$.

PROOF.   The argument is essentially similar to that in the proof of Theorem 4.4–B.   First of all, we observe that it suffices to prove the theorem with the added assumption that Y is complete.   For, if Y is not complete and $\hat{Y}$ is its completion, we can just as well look upon G as a subset of $[X, \hat{Y}]$.   This does not affect $\|Tx\|$ or $\|T\|$.   Now, assuming that Y is complete, we consider the class of all bounded functions g with domain G and range in Y, with $\|g\| = \sup\limits_{T\in G} \|g(T)\|$.   This space is complete.   For each $x \in Z$ let Ax be the function on G with value Tx at T.   Then A is a linear operator with domain Z.   It is easily proved that A is closed and hence continuous.   The proof that G is a bounded set in $[X, Y]$ is then just like the last part of the proof of Theorem 4.4–B.

It is possible to regard Theorem 4.4–B as a special case of Theorem 4.4–E.   The parts of X, Y, $[X, Y]$, Z, and G in Theorem 4.4–E are played by X', A (the space of scalars), X'', M and $J(F)$ in Theorem 4.4–B.   Saying that $J(F)$ is bounded in X'' is equivalent to saying that F is bounded in X (J the canonical mapping).

As a particular case of Theorem 4.4–E we note the following (with assumptions on X and Y as in the theorem): *If $T_n \in [X, Y]$ and if $Tx = \lim\limits_{n\to\infty} T_n x$ exists for each $x \in X$, then $T \in [X, Y]$; that is, T is not only linear, but also continuous.*

One of the striking applications of the principle of uniform boundedness is concerned with the notion of analyticity for vector-valued functions of a complex variable. If X is a complex Banach space and Δ is an open set in the complex plane, we shall say that a function f defined on Δ, with values in X, is *locally analytic* on Δ if $f(\lambda)$ is differentiable with respect to the complex variable λ at each point of Δ. If $f'(\lambda_0)$ is the derivative of $f(\lambda)$ at λ_0, this means that

$$\left\| \frac{f(\lambda) - f(\lambda_0)}{\lambda - \lambda_0} - f'(\lambda_0) \right\| \to 0 \qquad \text{as } \lambda \to \lambda_0.$$

A necessary condition for this to be true is that

$$\lim_{\lambda\to\lambda_0} x' \left\{ \frac{f(\lambda) - f(\lambda_0)}{\lambda - \lambda_0} \right\}$$

exist for each $x' \in X'$ (the limit, of course, will be $x'\{f'(\lambda_0)\}$). The remarkable fact is that this, apparently weak, necessary condition is in fact also a sufficient condition for the local analyticity of f.

Theorem 4.4–F. *Let X be a complex Banach space, and let f be a function with values in X, defined on an open set Δ in the complex λ-plane. Let M be a closed linear manifold in X' which is norm-determining for X. Suppose that, for each $x' \in M$, $x'[f(\lambda)]$ is differentiable at each point of Δ. Then f is locally analytic on Δ.*

PROOF. Since X is complete, it will suffice to prove that for each point λ_0 in Δ the expression

$$\frac{f(\lambda) - f(\lambda_0)}{\lambda - \lambda_0} - \frac{f(\mu) - f(\lambda_0)}{\mu - \lambda_0}$$

approaches 0 as λ and μ independently approach λ_0. Let $r > 0$ be such that $\lambda \in \Delta$ if $|\lambda - \lambda_0| \leqslant r$. Suppose $0 < |\lambda - \lambda_0| < r$ and $0 < |\mu - \lambda_0| < r$. By Cauchy's formula we have, for each $x' \in M$,

$$x'(f(\lambda)) = \frac{1}{2\pi i} \int_C \frac{x'(f(\xi))}{\xi - \lambda} \, d\xi,$$

where C is the circle $|\xi - \lambda_0| = r$, positively oriented. Corresponding formulas hold with λ_0 and μ in place of λ.   A straightforward calculation leads to the formula

$$(4.4\text{-}4) \quad x'\left\{\frac{f(\lambda) - f(\lambda_0)}{\lambda - \lambda_0} - \frac{f(\mu) - f(\lambda_0)}{\mu - \lambda_0}\right\} =$$

$$\frac{1}{2\pi i}\int_C x'[f(\xi)]\,\frac{\lambda - \mu}{(\xi - \lambda)(\xi - \mu)(\xi - \lambda_0)}\,d\xi.$$

Now $x'[f(\xi)]$ is continuous, and hence bounded, on C.   Therefore, by Theorem 4.4–B, there is some constant A such that $\|f(\xi)\| \leqslant A$ when ξ is on C.   If we now require that $|\lambda - \lambda_0| \leqslant \tfrac{1}{2}r$, $|\mu - \lambda_0| \leqslant \tfrac{1}{2}r$, so that $|\xi - \lambda| \geqslant \tfrac{1}{2}r$ when ξ is on C (and likewise for μ in place of λ), we readily see that the absolute value of the left member of (4.4–4) does not exceed $4r^{-2}A\|x'\|\,|\lambda - \mu|$.   It follows from (4.4–1) and (4.4–3) that

$$\left\|\frac{f(\lambda) - f(\lambda_0)}{\lambda - \lambda_0} - \frac{f(\mu) - f(\lambda_0)}{\mu - \lambda_0}\right\| \leqslant \frac{4A|\lambda - \mu|}{r^2 v(M)}$$

if $0 < |\lambda - \lambda_0| \leqslant \tfrac{1}{2}r$ and $0 < |\mu - \lambda_0| \leqslant \tfrac{1}{2}r$.   The   desired   conclusion now follows.

In order to emphasize the remarkable quality of Theorem 4.4–F, we point out explicitly that, if $\{x_n\}$ is a sequence in X such that $x'(x_n) \to x'(x)$ for each $x' \in X'$, it *does not necessarily follow* that $\|x_n - x\| \to 0$.   For example, take $X = l^2$ and $x_1 = (1, 0, 0, \cdots)$, $x_2 = (0, 1, 0, \cdots)$, $x_3 = (0, 0, 1, 0, \cdots)$, etc.   Then $x'(x_n) \to 0$ for each $x' \in X'$.   For, we know by Theorem 4.32–A that x' is representable in the form $x'(x) = \sum_1^\infty \alpha_k \xi_k$, with $\sum_1^\infty |\alpha_k|^2 < \infty$.   Hence $x'(x_n) = \alpha_n \to 0 = x'(0)$ for each x'.   But it is not true that $\|x_n\| \to 0$.

There is a theorem which is related to Theorem 4.4–F in much the same way that Theorem 4.4–E is related to Theorem 4.4–B.

Theorem 4.4–G.   *Let X and Y be complex Banach spaces, and let Δ be an open set in the complex plane.   For each λ in Δ let A_λ be an element of $[X, Y]$.   Suppose that $A_\lambda x$ is a locally analytic function on Δ, with values in Y, for each x in X.   Then A_λ is a locally analytic function on Δ, with values in $[X, Y]$.*

We have here an inference from differentiability in the metric of Y to differentiability in the metric of $[X, Y]$.   Or, to put it another way, if $A_\lambda x$ is differentiable for each x, it is differentiable uniformly for all x such that $\|x\| \leqslant 1$.   As in Theorem 4.4–E, it is sufficient to make the assumption for all x in a closed subspace of X which is norm-determining for $[X, Y]$.   The proof is left to the reader.

PROBLEMS

1. It is essential that X be complete in Theorem 4.4–C.   To show this let X be the subset of those $x \in l^2$ for which $x = \{\xi_k\}$ and $\xi_k = 0$ if k exceeds some integer depending on x.   Let $x_n'(x) = n\xi_n$, and let F be the countable set of the elements $x_1', x_2', \cdots$.

2. *a.* A Banach space X is said to have a *countable basis* $\{u_n\}(n = 1, 2, \cdots)$ if each $x \in X$ can be represented in one and only one way as a series $x = \sum_1^\infty \omega_k u_k$. Show that no u_n is 0 and that $\{u_n/\|u_n\|\}$ is also a countable basis.

b. Let W be the class of all sequences $w = \{\omega_n\}$ such that $\sum_1^\infty \omega_k u_k$ is con-vergent.   Define

$$\|w\| = \sup_n \left\| \sum_1^n \omega_k u_k \right\|.$$

Show that with this norm W is a Banach space.   [First show that $|\omega_n| \leqslant 2(\|w\|/\|u_n\|)$.   Now define $Tw = \sum_1^\infty \omega_k u_k$.   Show that T is a linear homeo-morphism of W onto all of X.

c. Define $u_k' \in X'$ by $u_k'(x) = \omega_k$.   Show that $\|u_k'\| \leqslant 2\|T^{-1}\|/\|u_k\|$.

d. Let Y be the space of all scalar sequences $y = \{\eta_k\}$ such that $\sum_1^\infty \omega_k \eta_k$ is convergent whenever $w = \{\omega_k\} \in W$.   Define

$$\|y\| = \sup_{\|x\| \leqslant 1} \left| \sum_1^\infty \omega_k \eta_k \right|, \text{ where } x = Tw.$$

Show that Y is congruent to X', with $y \leftrightarrow x'$, where $x'(x) = \sum_1^\infty \omega_k \eta_k$.

3. Show that a Banach space with a countable basis is separable.

4. There is an alternative way of proving Theorem 4.4–B without using the closed-graph theorem.   For each $x \in F$ consider $|x'(x)|$ as a continuous, real-valued function of x', defined on M.   Since M is complete we can apply Theorem 2.41–D to conclude that $|x'(x)|$ is uniformly bounded as x varies over F and x' varies over some closed sphere in M.   Suppose $K > 0$, $\delta > 0$, and that $|x'(x)| \leqslant K$ if $x \in F$ and $\|x' - x_0'\| \leqslant \delta$ (x' and $x_0' \in M$).   Show that $p_M(x) \leqslant 2K/\delta$ if $x \in F$ and hence that $\|x\| \leqslant 2K/\delta\nu(M)$ if $x \in F$.

5. Let $X = l^p$, $1 \leqslant p < \infty$.   Let $\{\phi_n\}$ be a sequence of complex-valued functions defined on the open set $\varDelta$ in the complex plane.   Then $f(\lambda) = \{\phi_n(\lambda)\}$ defines a function on $\varDelta$ into X which is locally analytic on $\varDelta$ if and only if each ϕ_n is locally analytic and the series $\sum_1^\infty |\phi_n(\lambda)|^p$ is convergent and bounded on each compact subset of $\varDelta$.   Use Theorem 4.32–A.

6. Let S be a nonempty subset of the normed linear space X, and let M be a subspace of X'. Consider the topology $\mathcal{T}_0$ for X defined by the norm and the topology $\mathcal{T}(X, M)$ as defined in § 3.81. If S is bounded relative to $\mathcal{T}_0$, it is bounded relative to $\mathcal{T}(X, M)$. Show that the converse statement is true if M is norm-determining for X.

7. Let p_1 and p_2 be two norms on the linear space X, generating topologies $\mathcal{T}_1$ and $\mathcal{T}_2$ respectively. Let M_i be the subspace of all $x' \in X^f$ such that x' is continuous relative to $\mathcal{T}_i (i = 1, 2)$. Now $\mathcal{T}_2$ is stronger than $\mathcal{T}_1$ if and only if there is some $C > 0$ such that $p_1(x) \leqslant Cp_2(x)$ for all x. Show that this is equivalent to having $M_1 \subset M_2$. As a result, $\mathcal{T}_1 = \mathcal{T}_2$ if and only if $M_1 = M_2$.

8. Let X be a locally convex topological linear T_1-space, with topology $\mathcal{T}$. Let M be the class of all $x' \in X^f$ which are continuous relative to $\mathcal{T}$. Suppose there is in $\mathcal{T}$ a neighborhood of 0, say V_0, which we may as well assume is balanced and convex, which is bounded relative to $\mathcal{T}(X, M)$. Then $\mathcal{T}$ is the topology generated by the Minkowski functional of V_0 (call it p_0), this functional being in fact a norm (see problem 2, § 3.81). First observe the following: if p is any continuous seminorm on X, let $q(x) = \max\{p(x), p_0(x)\}$, and let Q be the family of seminorms q obtained in this way. Then Q generates $\mathcal{T}$, and each q is a norm. Let $\mathcal{T}_q$ be the topology generated by the norm q, and let M_q be the set of those $x' \in X^f$ which are continuous relative to $\mathcal{T}_q$. Then $M_q \subset M$. As a result, V_0 is bounded relative to $\mathcal{T}_q$ (see problem 6). It can then be shown that p_0 and q generate the same topology, which must be $\mathcal{T}$.

9. Let M be a norm-determining linear manifold in X', with characteristic $v = v(M)$. Let $S_\alpha = \{x: \|x\| \leqslant \alpha\}$. Show that, relative to the topology $\mathcal{T}(X, M)$, the closure of S_1 lies in $S_{1/v}$. Hence, if $v = 1$, S_1 is closed in this topology. For further study of $v(M)$ and $\mathcal{T}(X, M)$ see Dixmier, **1**.

10. If J is the canonical mapping of X into X'', $J(X)$ is norm-determining for X' and of characteristic 1. Hence $\{x': \|x'\| \leqslant 1\}$ is closed in X' with respect to $\mathcal{T}(X', J(X))$.

11. The space X is norm reflexive if and only if the topologies $\mathcal{T}(X', X'')$ and $\mathcal{T}(X', J(X))$ for X' are the same. (A clue will be found in § 3.81.)

4.41 Weak Convergence

Suppose X is a normed linear space, and consider the weak topology $\mathcal{T}(X, M)$ for X, as defined in § 3.81, on the supposition that M is a total subspace of X'. If $\{x_n\}$ is a sequence in X, we shall say that $\{x_n\}$ is M-weakly convergent to x (where $x \in X$) if $\{x_n\}$ converges to x in the sense of the topology $\mathcal{T}(X, M)$. In view of the definition of $\mathcal{T}(X, M)$, this means the same as saying that $x'(x_n) \to x'(x)$ for each $x' \in M$. The requirement that M be total makes the limit x unique, for then $\mathcal{T}(X, M)$ is a Hausdorff topology (Theorems 3.81–B and 3.3–G). Theorem 4.4–B shows that an M-weakly convergent sequence is bounded in norm if M is a closed subspace of X' which is norm-determining for X.

In the case of X'-weak convergence (i.e., when $M = X'$) it is the common practice to drop the reference to X' and speak merely of weak convergence.

If J is the canonical mapping of X into X'', then $J(X)$ is a total subset of X''. We shall habitually write $\mathscr{T}(X', X)$ in place of $\mathscr{T}(X', J(X))$. See the remarks about duality in § 3.81; we have here an instance of this kind of duality when we consider the topology $\mathscr{T}(X, X')$ for X and the topology $\mathscr{T}(X', X)$ for X'. The topology $\mathscr{T}(X', X)$ is what is often called the w^* (or weak-*) topology for X' in current literature.

If $\{x_n'\}$ is a sequence in X' which is convergent to x' (where $x' \in X'$) in the sense of the topology $\mathscr{T}(X', X)$, we say that $\{x_n'\}$ is X-weakly convergent to x'. This happens if and only if $x_n'(x) \to x'(x)$ for each $x \in X$. When X is complete this implies that $\{\|x_n'\|\}$ is bounded [Theorem 4.4–D(b)].

Theorem 4.41–A. *If X is separable, every bounded sequence in X' contains an X-weakly convergent subsequence.*

PROOF.   Let $\{x_n'\}$ be a bounded sequence in X', and let $\{x_k\}$ be a sequence which is dense in X. Since $\{x_n'(x_1)\}$ is a bounded sequence of scalars, it contains a bounded subsequence, which we denote by $\{x_{n1}'(x_1)\}$. Likewise $\{x_{n1}'(x_2)\}$ contains a convergent subsequence, which we denote by $\{x_{n2}'(x_2)\}$. Continuing by induction, we obtain a "diagonal sequence" $\{x_{nn}'\}$ such that $\lim_{n\to\infty} x_{nn}'(x_k)$ exists for each k. It is then easy to see that $\{x_{nn}'(x)\}$ is a Cauchy sequence for each x, thus defining $x' \in X'$ such that $\{x_{nn}'\}$ is X-weakly convergent to x'.

If we suppose that $\{x_n\}$ is X'-weakly convergent to x, it follows that $\|x\| \leqslant \lim \inf_{n\to\infty} \|x_n\|$. For, $|x'(x_n)| \leqslant \|x'\| \|x_n\|$, whence $|x'(x)| \leqslant \|x'\| \lim \inf_{n\to\infty} \|x_n\|$. The desired result now follows from (4.3–2). In particular, if $\|x_n\| \leqslant C$, it follows that $\|x\| \leqslant C$ also.

Theorem 4.41–B. *If X is norm reflexive, each bounded sequence from X contains an X'-weakly convergent subsequence. In particular, if $\{x_n\}$ is a sequence for which $\|x_n\| \leqslant 1$, it contains a subsequence converging X'-weakly to a limit x for which $\|x\| \leqslant 1$.*

PROOF.   In view of the remarks preceding the theorem, it suffices to prove the first assertion. Suppose $x_n \in X$ and $\sup_n \|x_n\| = C < \infty$. Let X_0 be the closed linear manifold generated by $x_1, x_2, \cdots$. It is easy to see that X_0 is separable. It is reflexive, also (Theorem 4.31–B). Hence X_0'' is separable, and therefore X_0' is separable (Theorem 4.3–E). The canonical mapping of X_0 onto X_0'' carries $\{x_n\}$ into a bounded sequence in X_0''. By Theorem 4.41–A this latter sequence contains an X_0'-weakly convergent subsequence. This subsequence corresponds to a subsequence of $\{x_n\}$ which is X_0'-weakly convergent to a limit in X_0. Since every element of X', when restricted to X_0, determines an element of X_0', it is clear that the subsequence in question is X'-weakly convergent. This completes the proof.

Weak convergence is used in various contexts in the calculus of variations and in the general theory of differential equations.

PROBLEMS

1. If M is a total subspace of X', $\{x_n\}$ is M-weakly convergent to x provided that $\sup_n \|x_n\| < \infty$ and that $x'(x_n) \to x'(x)$ for each $x' \in G$, where G is some dense subset of M.

2. If $\{x_n'\}$ is X-weakly convergent to x', then $\|x'\| \leqslant \lim_{n \to \infty} \inf \|x_n'\|$.

3. If $x_n = \{\xi_k^{(n)}\} \in l^p$, where $1 < p < \infty$, $\{x_n\}$ is X'-weakly convergent to $x = \{\xi_k\}$ (where $X = l^p$) if and only if $\sup_n \|x_n\| < \infty$ and $\lim_{n \to \infty} \xi_k^{(n)} = \xi_k$ for each k.

4. In $X = l^1$, $\{x_n\}$ converges X'-weakly to x if and only if $\|x_n - x\| \to 0$ (see Banach **1**, page 137). In spite of this, the topology $\mathscr{T}(X, X')$ is not the same as the topology generated by the norm.

5. If $X = C[a, b]$, a sequence $\{x_n\}$ is X'-weakly convergent to x if and only if $\sup_n \|x_n\| < \infty$ and $x_n(t) \to x(t)$ for each t. The necessity of these conditions is evident. The sufficiency is clear from standard convergence theorems as soon as one knows how to represent elements of X' with the aid of a suitable signed measure. See § 7.7; also see Banach, **1**, page 134.

6. For $X = L^p(a, b)$, where $1 < p < \infty$, $\{x_n\}$ converges X'-weakly to x if and only if $\sup_n \|x_n\| < \infty$ and $\int_E x_n(t)\, dt \to \int_E x(t)\, dt$ for each measurable set E of finite measure on (a, b). (Use problem 1 and the known representation of elements of X' in this case.) For $p = 1$ the result breaks down, the conditions being necessary but not sufficient for weak convergence. This is because the finite linear combinations of characteristic functions of sets of finite measure are not dense in $L^\infty(a, b)$. For a further discussion see Banach **1**, page 136.

7. A space X is called X'-weakly sequentially complete if the existence of $\lim_{n \to \infty} x'(x_n)$ for each $x' \in X'$ implies the existence of $x \in X$ such that $\{x_n\}$ converges X'-weakly to x. The space $C[a, b]$ is not X'-weakly sequentially complete. However, any norm-reflexive space is X'-weakly sequentially complete. The nonreflexive spaces $L^1(a, b)$ and l^1 are X'-weakly sequentially complete. See Banach **1**, page 141.

4.42 An Application of Vector-Valued Analytic Functions

Many features of the classical theory of analytic functions are retained in the theory of analytic functions whose values lie in a complex Banach space. In Chapter 5 we use the theorems of Cauchy, Liouville, and Laurent in this more general setting. In this section we present an interesting application of the theory of Banach-space-valued analytic functions to prove some classical theorems about mean values of complex-valued analytic functions.

Analyticity of a vector-valued function may be defined in terms of differentiability, as in the latter part of § 4.4. We may also use the theory of power series in a complex variable, with Banach space elements as coefficients.

We begin by observing the generalization of certain standard theorems. Here X denotes a complex Banach space.

Theorem 4.42–A. *Suppose Δ is a connected open set in the complex λ-plane. Let F be holomorphic (single valued and analytic) on Δ, with values in X, and suppose that $\|F(\lambda)\|$ is not constant on Δ. Then $\|F(\lambda)\|$ cannot attain an absolute maximum at any point of Δ.*

PROOF. We could imitate one of the classical proofs which uses Cauchy's integral formula. Instead, we shall give a proof using linear functionals. Suppose the theorem false, so that for some $\lambda_0 \in \Delta$ we have $\|F(\lambda)\| \leqslant \|F(\lambda_0)\|$ for each λ. Using Theorem 4.3–B, we choose $x' \in X'$ so that $\|x'\| = 1$ and $x'[F(\lambda_0)] = \|F(\lambda_0)\|$. Then $x'[F(\lambda)]$ is a complex-valued holomorphic function such that $|x'[F(\lambda)]| \leqslant |x'[F(\lambda_0)]|$ at all points $\lambda \in \Delta$. The classical counterpart of Theorem 4.42–A then implies that $x'[F(\lambda)]$ is constant in Δ, its value being $\|F(\lambda_0)\|$. But $|x'[F(\lambda)]| \leqslant \|F(\lambda)\|$, and, since $\|F(\lambda)\| < \|F(\lambda_0)\|$ at some points of Δ, we have a contradiction.

Now consider the special case in which Δ is the circular region $\{\lambda : |\lambda| < R\}$, where $R > 0$. Let $M(r) = \max_{|\lambda|=r} \|F(\lambda)\|$, $0 \leqslant r < R$. Theorem 4.42–A implies the following theorem.

Theorem 4.42–B. *If F is holomorphic when $|\lambda| < R$, then $M(r)$ is a nondecreasing function of r. Furthermore, $0 < r_1 < r_2$ and $M(r_1) = M(r_2)$ imply that $M(r)$ is constant when $0 \leqslant r \leqslant r_2$.*

We also have the generalization of Hadamard's three-circles theorem:

Theorem 4.42–C. *If F is holomorphic and not identically 0 when $|\lambda| < R$, then $\log M(r)$ is a convex function of $\log r$ when $0 < r < R$.*

This theorem may be proved exactly as in one of the standard proofs for the complex-valued case (e.g., Titchmarsh 1, § 5.3 and § 5.32), except that norms are written instead of absolute values.

Let us now turn to the definition of the means $\mathfrak{M}_p[f; r]$ in (3.11–9), where f is a complex-valued function which is holomorphic in the unit circle of the complex plane. We are going to assume that $1 \leqslant p < \infty$ and prove:

1. $\mathfrak{M}_p[f; r]$ is, for $0 \leqslant r < 1$, a strictly increasing function of r, unless f is a constant.

2. If f is not identically 0, $\log \mathfrak{M}_p[f; r]$ is a convex function of $\log r$ when $0 < r < 1$.

These propositions go back to G. H. Hardy, **1**. Very beautiful proofs of the propositions were given by F. Riesz, **3**, using the principle of subharmonic functions. The propositions are true for all $p > 0$, but our proofs require $p \geqslant 1$, because we depend on the fact that H^p is a Banach space if $p \geqslant 1$. See § 3.11 and problem 1c in § 3.13.

If f is holomorphic when $|z| < 1$ and if $|\lambda| < 1$, let f_λ be the function defined by $f_\lambda(z) = f(\lambda z)$. Then f_λ is holomorphic in a domain which includes the closed disk $|z| \leqslant 1$, so that $f_\lambda \in H^p$. Hence the function F defined by $F(\lambda) = f_\lambda$ is a function of λ with values in H^p. It is a fact of crucial importance for us that F is holomorphic when $|\lambda| < 1$. See problems 1–3 for a discussion of this matter. If we compute $\|F(\lambda)\| = \|f_\lambda\|$, using (3.11–11), we find that $\|F(\lambda)\| = \|F(|\lambda|)\|$. Thus $\|F(\lambda)\|$ is constant on the circle $|\lambda| = r$; we denote it by $M(r)$. Theorems 4.42–B and 4.42–C apply to $M(r)$ for $r < 1$. The computation of $\|F(\lambda)\|$ also shows that

(4.42–1) $$M(r) = \sup_{0 \leqslant x < 1} \mathfrak{M}_p[f; rx].$$

From this we shall be able to show that

(4.42–2) $$M(r) = \mathfrak{M}_p[f; r].$$

First we take note of the fact that

(4.42–3) $$\mathfrak{M}_p[f; 0] = |f(0)| \leqslant \mathfrak{M}_p[f; r]$$

if $0 < r < 1$ and that the inequality here is strict unless f is a constant function. For, by Cauchy's formula,

$$f(0) = \frac{1}{2\pi} \int_0^{2\pi} f(re^{i\theta})\, d\theta,$$

whence $|f(0)| \leqslant \mathfrak{M}_1[f; \theta]$. The inequality here is easily seen to be strict unless f is constant. But then $\mathfrak{M}_1[f; r] \leqslant \mathfrak{M}_p[f; r]$ if $1 < p$ (see Hardy, Littlewood and Polya, **1**, page 143), whence (4.42–3) follows.

Now let $\phi(r) = \mathfrak{M}_p[f; r]$; we know that ϕ is continuous. Evidently $M(0) = \phi(0)$ and $\phi(r) \leqslant M(r)$, because of (4.42–1). Suppose that for some r_0 we have $0 < r_0 < 1$ and $\phi(r_0) < M(r_0)$. Consider the maximum

of $\phi(r)$ for $0 \leqslant r \leqslant r_0$. It occurs for some r_1 on the interval and is equal
to $M(r_0)$, by (4.42–1). That is, $\phi(r_1) = M(r_0)$. Hence $r_1 < r_0$, because
$\phi(r_1) \neq \phi(r_0)$. We see that $M(r_0) \leqslant M(r_1)$. But $M(r_1) \leqslant M(r_0)$, by the
first conclusion in Theorem 4.42–B. Hence $M(r_1) = M(r_0)$, and it follows
from the second conclusion in Theorem 4.42–B that $M(r)$ is constant on
$[0, r_0]$. Then $\phi(r_0) < M(r_0) = M(0) = \phi(0)$. This contradicts (4.42–3).
Hence (4.42–2) is established.

Proposition 2 now follows at once from (4.42–2) and Theorem 4.42–C.
From Theorem 4.42–B we infer that $\mathfrak{M}_p[f; r]$ is a nondecreasing function
of r. Actually, $\mathfrak{M}_p[f; r]$ must be strictly increasing, unless f is constant,
for otherwise, by Theorem 4.42–B we would have $M(r)$ constant on some
interval $[0, r_1]$, whence $\mathfrak{M}_p[f; 0] = \mathfrak{M}_p[f; r_1]$, in contradiction to the
statement made in connection with (4.42–3).

PROBLEMS

1. Let $u_n(z) = z^n$, $n = 0, 1, \cdots$. Show that u_n, as an element of H^p, has
$\|u_n\| = 1$.

2. If $h \in H^p$ and $h(z) = \sum_0^\infty c_n z^n$, use Cauchy's formulas for c_n to show that
$r^n|c_n| \leqslant \mathfrak{M}_p[h; r]$ if $0 < r < 1$, and hence $|c_n| \leqslant \|h\|$. Deduce that $|h(z)| \leqslant
\|h\|\,(1 - |z|)^{-1}$ if $|z| < 1$.

3. If $f(z) = \sum_0^\infty a_n z^n$ converges when $|z| < 1$, show that $\sum_0^\infty a_n \lambda^n u_n$ is convergent
to f_λ in the metric of H^p (with u_n as in problem 1). First show that the series
converges to some element $g \in H^p$. Then use problem 2 to show that
$\sum_0^\infty a_n \lambda^n z^n = g(z)$, whence $g = f_\lambda$. The conclusion is that $F(\lambda)$ is given by a
power series in λ with coefficients from H^p. Hence F is holomorphic. For
this and more general results of the same type see Taylor **3, 4**.

4.5 The Conjugate of a Bounded Linear Operator

The notion of the conjugate of a bounded linear operator is closely
related to the notion of the transpose of a linear operator, as defined
in § 1.8.

Let X and Y be normed linear spaces, and suppose $A \in [X, Y]$. If
$y' \in Y'$, the linear functional x' defined on X by $x'(x) = y'(Ax)$ is clearly
continuous. We write $x' = A'y'$. The operator A', which is linear and

maps Y' into X', is called the *conjugate* of A.   The definition of A' is expressed by the formula

$$(4.5\text{–}1) \qquad \langle x, A'y' \rangle = \langle Ax, y' \rangle, \qquad x \in X, y \in Y'.$$

If $Y' = Y^f$ (which is the case if Y is finite dimensional), A' is the same thing as the transpose A^T.   However, Y' is a proper subspace of Y^f in general, so A^T is an extension of A', or A' is the restriction of A^T to the space Y'.

If $A'y' = x'$, we have $|x'(x)| = |y'(Ax)| \leqslant \|y'\| \|Ax\| \leqslant \|y'\| \|A\| \|x\|$, and so $\|x'\| \leqslant \|A\| \|y'\|$.   This shows that A' is continuous on Y' and that $\|A'\| \leqslant \|A\|$.   On the other hand,

$$|y'(Ax)| = |x'(x)| \leqslant \|x'\| \|x\| = \|A'y'\| \|x\|.$$

Hence, by (4.3–2) and the definition of $\|A'\|$,

$$\|Ax\| = \sup_{\|y'\| \leqslant 1} |y'(Ax)| \leqslant \sup_{\|y'\| \leqslant 1} \|A'y'\| \|x\| = \|A'\| \|x\|.$$

Therefore $\|A\| \leqslant \|A'\|$.   We have thus proved the formula

$$(4.5\text{–}2) \qquad\qquad\qquad \|A\| = \|A'\|.$$

Other notations and terminologies have been used for A'.   It has been denoted by $\bar{A}$ or A^*; it has been called the *adjoint* of A and also the *dual* of A.   In this book the notation A^* and the name "adjoint" are reserved for use in connection with linear operators in Hilbert space.   In that situation A^* is closely related to A', but is not the same as A'.   It is troublesome to have A^* mean one thing when we deal with Hilbert space and another thing in the general theory of normed linear spaces.   Hence our distinction between A^* and A'.

We sometimes need some formal algebraic rules for handling conjugate operators.   If A and B are in $[X, Y]$, then

$$(4.5\text{–}3) \qquad (A + B)' = A' + B' \qquad \text{and} \qquad (\alpha A)' = \alpha A'.$$

If $B \in [X, Y]$ and $A \in [Y, Z]$, then

$$(4.5\text{–}4) \qquad\qquad\qquad (AB)' = B'A'.$$

If $A \in [X, Y]$ and if A^{-1} exists and belongs to $[Y, X]$, then $(A')^{-1}$ exists, belongs to $[X', Y']$, and is the same as $(A^{-1})'$.   We leave it for the reader to verify these assertions.

If we are studying the operator A, a knowledge of certain facts about A' can be helpful to us.   In general A' is more amenable to investigation than A^T.   In studying A' we usually need representation theorems for elements of Y' and X' (as in § 4.32, for example).   We also need representation theorems for bounded linear operators. For instance, suppose $X = Y = l^p$, where $1 \leqslant p < \infty$. We know from Theorem 4.32–A that X' is congruent in a natural way to $l^{p'}$. In the problems at the end of § 4.51 we shall see that, if $A \in [l^p]$, A can be represented by an infinite matrix and that A', which we identify with an element of $[l^{p'}]$, is representable by the transposed matrix. Likewise, if $X = Y = L^2(a, b)$ and if K is the Fredholm-type operator defined as $y = Kx$ by

$$y(s) = {}^0\!\int_a^b k(s, t)x(t)\, dt,$$

where k is an $\mathscr{L}^2$ kernel (see § 4.12), we can identify X' with $L^2(a, b)$ and K' with the Fredholm-type operator determined by the transpose kernel $k'(s, t) = k(t, s)$. This identification is a consequence of the general representation theorem for linear functionals on a Hilbert space (see § 4.81).

PROBLEMS

1. Suppose X and Y are normed linear spaces, and let A be a linear operator with domain X and range in Y. Suppose that Y' contains a closed linear manifold M which is norm-determining for Y and such that $A^T(M) \subset X'$. Then A is continuous. Apply Theorem 4.4–B to the set $\{Ax : \|x\| \leqslant 1\}$ in Y.

2. If A maps X congruently onto all of Y, then A' maps Y' congruently onto all of X'.

3. Suppose $A \in [X_1, X_2]$. Then $(A')' \equiv A'' \in [X_1'', X_2'']$. Let J_1 and J_2 be the operators defining the canonical mappings of X_1 and X_2 into X_1'' and X_2'' respectively. Then $A''J_1 = J_2A$. If we identify X_1 with $J_1(X_1)$ and X_2 with $J_2(X_2)$, this means that A'' is an extension of A. In particular, A'' coincides with A if X_1 is norm reflexive.

4. If X_1 is norm reflexive and X_1 is congruent to X_2, then X_2 also is norm reflexive.

4.51 Some Representations of Bounded Linear Operators

In this section we discuss the representation of bounded linear operators on X into Y, especially for the case in which X and Y are chosen in various ways from the spaces l^p, (c) and (c_0). The discussion is based on a theorem of very general scope about the representation of linear operators.

For the purpose of our first general theorem we make the following assumptions: X is an arbitrary Banach space; Z is an arbitrary normed linear space; S is an arbitrary nonempty set of elements of unspecified nature; Y is a Banach space which is a subspace of the linear space of all functions defined on S, with values in Z. If $s \in S$ and $y \in Y$, we call $y(s)$ the component of y at s, and we assume that $y(s)$ is a continuous function of y. A possible choice for Y is l^p ($1 \leqslant p \leqslant \infty$), with S the set of positive integers and Z the space of scalars. Again, the space $B(S)$ of bounded scalar-valued functions on S, for an arbitrary S, is a possible choice for Y.

In what follows we refer to the space $[X, Z]$. This is X' if Z happens to be the space of scalars; it is this choice of Z that we shall use mainly in the applications of these general considerations.

Theorem 4.51–A. *Assume X, Y, Z, S as in the foregoing remarks. Then, to each $A \in [X, Y]$ there corresponds a function on S to $[X, Z]$, whose value at s we denote by $a(s)$, such that, if $y = Ax$ then $y(s) = a(s)x$ for each s. Conversely, if $a(\cdot)$ is any function with domain S and range in $[X, Z]$ such that for each $x \in X$ the formula $y(s) = a(s)x$ defines an element of Y, this dependence of y on x defines an element A of $[X, Y]$.*

PROOF. If $A \in [X, Y]$ is given and $y = Ax$, we define $a(s)$ by $a(s)x = y(s)$. Then $a(s) \in [X, Z]$ for each s. The linearity of $a(s)$ is evident, and the continuity of $a(s)x$ with respect to x follows from the fact that $y(s)$ is a continuous function of y. For the converse part of the proof, the linearity of A is evident, and its continuity will follow from Theorem 4.2–I if we prove that A is closed. Suppose that $x_n \to x$. Then $a(s)x_n \to a(s)x$, because $a(s) \in [X, Z]$. Suppose also that $Ax_n \to y$. Then $(Ax_n)(s) \to y(s)$ for each s, by the continuous dependence of components on vectors. But $(Ax_n)(s) = a(s)x_n$. Hence $a(s)x = y(s)$, so that $y = Ax$; that is, A is closed.

A situation of some especial interest is that in which the space Y is of such a nature that the norm of an element in Y is given by

$$(4.51–1) \qquad \qquad \|y\| = \sup_{s \in S} \|y(s)\|_Z.$$

Here $\|y(s)\|_Z$ denotes the norm of $y(s)$ as an element of Z, s being fixed. Among the examples of spaces Y of this type, all with Z the space of scalars, we cite l^∞, (c), (c_0), $B(S)$, and, if S is a topological space, the subspace $C(S)$ of $B(S)$.

Theorem 4.51–B. *With the hypotheses as in Theorem 4.51–A, suppose the norm in Y is given by (4.51–1). Then $a(\cdot)$ is a bounded function on S to $[X, Z]$, and*

$$(4.51–2) \qquad \qquad \|A\| = \sup_{s \in S} \|a(s)\|.$$

*If Z is complete and if Y consists of all bounded functions on S to Z, any
bounded function a($\cdot$) on S to $[X, Z]$ determines an operator belonging to
$[X, Y]$.*

The proof is left to the reader.   The assumption in the last part, that
Z is complete, is made to insure that Y is complete, this being needed in
Theorem 4.51–A.

Let us denote by $B_Z(S)$ the Banach space of all bounded functions on
S to the Banach space Z, with norm as in (4.51–1).   Using this notation
for arbitrary Z, we see that Theorem 5.51–B implies that $[X, B_Z(S)]$ is
congruent to $B_{[X, Z]}(S)$ in a natural way.   If Y is a closed subspace of
$B_Z(S)$, the theorem states that $[X, Y]$ is congruent to a subspace of
$B_{[X, Z]}(S)$, but the theorem does not describe this subspace.   A certain
description of the subspace may be inferred from Theorem 4.51–A.

We can now give representation theorems for elements of $[X, Y]$,
where X is one of the spaces (c_0), (c), or $l^p(1 \leqslant p < \infty)$ and Y is one of the
spaces l^∞, (c), or (c_0).   For this purpose we need Theorem 4.32–A and
the results stated in problems 1 and 2 at the end of § 4.32.   We take Z
as the space of scalars and S as the set of positive integers.

Theorem 4.51–C.   *Each bounded linear operator A on (c_0) into l^∞,
(c), or (c_0) determines and is determined by an infinite matrix of scalars
$\alpha_{ij}(i, j = 1, 2, \cdots)$, $y = Ax$ being expressed by the equations*

$$(4.51\text{–}3) \qquad\qquad \eta_i = \sum_{j=1}^{\infty} \alpha_{ij}\xi_j \qquad i = 1, 2, \cdots.$$

The norm of A is given by

$$(4.51\text{–}4) \qquad\qquad \|A\| = \sup_i \sum_{j=1}^{\infty} |\alpha_{ij}|.$$

*For the case of mapping into l^∞ the only restriction on the matrix (α_{ij}) is
that the expression defining $\|A\|$ be finite.   For the case of mapping into (c)
the only additional requirement is that the limits*

$$(4.51\text{–}5) \qquad\qquad \alpha_j = \lim_{i \to \infty} \alpha_{ij} \qquad j = 1, 2, \cdots$$

*must exist.   Finally, the mapping is into (c_0) if and only if, in addition,
$\alpha_1 = \alpha_2 = \cdots = 0$.*

PROOF.   For the case of mapping into l^∞, the theorem results immediately
from problem 2, § 4.32, and Theorems 4.51–A, 4.51–B.   For the case of
mapping into (c) the further requirement is that $\lim_{i \to \infty} \eta_i$ exist for each
choice of x in (4.51–3).   An obvious special choice of x shows the

necessity for the existence of the limits in (4.51–5).   On the other hand, if
these limits exist, it is easy to prove that

$$(4.51\text{–}6) \qquad\qquad \lim_{i \to \infty} \eta_i = \sum_{j=1}^{\infty} \alpha_j \xi_j.$$

For, we know that $\sum_{j=1}^{n} |\alpha_{ij}| \leqslant \|A\|$ for all i and n.   Letting first i and then
n become infinite we see that $\sum_{j=1}^{\infty} |\alpha_j| \leqslant \|A\|$.   Then, for each n,

$$\left| \eta_i - \sum_{1}^{\infty} \alpha_j \xi_j \right| = \left| \sum_{j=1}^{\infty} (\alpha_{ij} - \alpha_j)\xi_j \right| \leqslant$$

$$\sum_{=1}^{n} |\alpha_{ij} - \alpha_j| \, |\xi_j| + 2\|A\| \sup_{j > n} |\xi_j|.$$

From this it follows that (4.51–6) is true, so that $y \in (c)$ if $x \in (c_0)$.   We
leave to the reader the proof of the last assertion in the theorem.

The next theorem concerns operators $A \in [(c), Y]$, where Y is either l^{∞},
(c), or (c_0).   It is slightly different from the foregoing theorem, because
of the intervention of the limit $\xi_0 = \lim_{j \to \infty} \xi_j$ when $x = \{\xi_j\} \in (c)$.

Theorem 4.51–D.   *Each bounded linear operator A on (c) into l^{∞}, (c),
or (c_0) determines and is determined by a matrix of scalars α_{ij} ($i = 1, 2, \cdots$,
$j = 0, 1, 2, \cdots$), $y = Ax$ being expressed by the equations*

$$(4.51\text{–}7) \qquad\qquad \eta_i = \sum_{j=0}^{\infty} \alpha_{ij} \xi_j \qquad i = 1, 2, \cdots.$$

The norm of A is given by

$$(4.51\text{–}8) \qquad\qquad \|A\| = \sup_{i} \sum_{=0}^{\infty} |\alpha_{ij}|.$$

*For $A \in [(c), l^{\infty}]$ the sole condition on the matrix (α_{ij}) is that the expression
defining $\|A\|$ be finite.   For $A \in [(c), (c)]$ there is the additional requirement
that the limit*

$$(4.51\text{–}9) \qquad\qquad \alpha = \lim_{i \to \infty} \sum_{j=0}^{\infty} \alpha_{ij}$$

exist and that the limits

$$(4.51\text{–}10) \qquad\qquad \alpha_j = \lim_{i \to \infty} \alpha_{ij}$$

exist if $j = 1, 2, \cdots$ (no requirement when $j = 0$).   Finally, the range of A is in (c_0) if and only if, in addition, $\alpha = 0$ and $\alpha_1 = \alpha_2 = \cdots = 0$.

Proof is left to the reader, who should refer to problem 1, § 4.32. We note, incidentally, that, if $A \in [(c), (c)]$ and $\lim_{i \to \infty} \eta_i = \eta_0$, then

$$(4.51\text{--}11) \qquad \eta_0 = \overset{\text{\tiny o}}{\xi}_0 \alpha + \sum_{j=1}^{\infty} (\overset{\text{\tiny o}}{\xi}_j - \overset{\text{\tiny o}}{\xi}_0)\alpha_j.$$

For, from problem 1, § 4.32 we have

$$Ax = \overset{\text{\tiny o}}{\xi}_0 Au_0 + \sum_{j=1}^{\infty} (\overset{\text{\tiny o}}{\xi}_j - \overset{\text{\tiny o}}{\xi}_0)Au_j.$$

If u_0' is the continuous linear functional defined by $u_0'(x) = \overset{\text{\tiny o}}{\xi}_0$, we have

$$u_0'(Ax) = \overset{\text{\tiny o}}{\xi}_0 u_0'(Au_0) + \sum_{j=1}^{\infty} (\overset{\text{\tiny o}}{\xi}_j - \overset{\text{\tiny o}}{\xi}_0)u_0'(Au_j),$$

and a little checking shows that this result is equivalent to (4.51–11). We see from (4.51–11) that $\eta_0 = \overset{\text{\tiny o}}{\xi}_0$ for every choice of x if and only if $\alpha = 1$ and $\alpha_1 = \alpha_2 = \cdots = 0$.

When X and Y both are spaces with a countable basis, they may be regarded as spaces whose elements are sequences.   This latter is then true of the conjugate spaces X', Y'.   (For basic facts about X and X' when X has a countable basis see problem 2, § 4.4.)   In such cases an element $A \in [X, Y]$ is representable by an infinite matrix, and the conjugate operator A' is then representable by the transpose of this matrix.   For more precise details see problem 6.

PROBLEMS

1. Each bounded linear operator A on l^p $(1 \leqslant p < \infty)$ into l^∞, (c), or (c_0) is representable by an infinite matrix (α_{ij}) of scalars, where $y = Ax$ is expressed by equations (4.51–3).   The norm of A is

$$\|A\| = \begin{cases} \sup_i \left(\sum_{j=1}^{\infty} |\alpha_{ij}|^{p'} \right)^{1/p'} & \text{if } 1 < p < \infty \\[2mm] \sup_i \sup_j |\alpha_{ij}| & \text{if } p = 1. \end{cases}$$

Except for the difference in the expression for $\|A\|$, the rest of the assertion here is just like that in Theorem 4.51–C.

2. A matrix (α_{ij}) $(i, j = 1, 2, \cdots)$ defines a bounded linear operator A on l^∞ into l^∞, by means of equations (4.51–3) if the following expression, which then defines the norm of A, is finite:

$$\|A\| = \sup_i \sum_{j=1}^{\infty} |\alpha_{ij}|.$$

This is not, however, the most general form for an element of $[l^\infty, l^\infty]$, for elements of $(l^\infty)'$ are not all expressible by an infinite series. The operator has its range in (c) or c_0) (subspaces of l^∞) under the same conditions for these things as are stated in Theorem 4.51–C.

3. If X is any Banach space, the general form of $A \in [X, l^q]$, where $1 \leqslant q < \infty$, is $y = Ax$, where $y = \{\eta_i\}$ and $\eta_i = x_1'(x)$, $\{x_i'\}$ being a sequence of elements of X' such that $\{x_i'(x)\} \in l^q$ for each x.

4. Suppose $X = l^p$ $(1 < p < \infty)$ in problem 3. The form of x_i' is

$$x_i'(x) = \sum_{j=1}^{\infty} \alpha_{ij}\xi_j, \text{ where}$$

$$\|x_i'\| = \left(\sum_{j=1}^{\infty} |\alpha_{ij}|^{p'}\right)^{1/p'}, \qquad p' = \frac{p}{p-1}.$$

No direct condition on the matrix elements α_{ij} have been discovered which are necessary and sufficient for the matrix to yield an operator A in $[l^p, l^q]$. Nor is there any known explicit representation of $\|A\|$ as a function of the matrix elements. For $p = 1$ see problem 5.

5. Each bounded linear operator A on l^1 into l^q $(1 \leqslant q < \infty)$ is representable as in (4.51–3) by a matrix (α_{ij}). The only condition on the matrix is that the following expression, defining $\|A\|$, be finite.

$$\|A\| = \sup_j \left(\sum_{i=1}^{\infty} |\alpha_{ij}|^q\right)^{1/q}.$$

Conversely, any matrix satisfying this condition determines an A in $[l^1, l^q]$.

6. Let X and Y be Banach spaces with countable bases $\{u_n\}$ and $\{v_n\}$ respectively $(n = 1, 2, \cdots)$. See problem 2, § 4.4. Let $\{u_n'\}$ and $\{v_n'\}$ be the corresponding sequences of coefficient functionals, so that

$$x = \sum_1^{\infty} \xi_j u_j \qquad u_j'(x) = \xi_j, \qquad x \in X$$

$$y = \sum_1^{\infty} \eta_i v_i \qquad v_i'(y) = \eta_i, \qquad y \in Y.$$

By the problem referred to, elements of X' and Y' are representable in the respective forms

$$x'(x) = \sum_1^{\infty} \lambda_j \xi_j, \qquad y'(y) = \sum_1^{\infty} \mu_i \eta_i.$$

Suppose $A \in [X, Y]$, $\alpha_{ij} = v_i'(Au_j)$, so that $y = Ax$ is expressed by

$$\eta_i = \sum_{j=1}^{\infty} \alpha_{ij}\xi_j, \qquad i = 1, 2, \cdots.$$

Show that $x' = A'y'$ is expressed by

$$\lambda_j = \sum_{i=1}^{\infty} \alpha_{ij}\mu_i \qquad j = 1, 2, \cdots.$$

Note that this result means that, if A is represented by a certain infinite matrix, A' is represented by the transposed matrix.

7. Suppose $A \in [(c), (c)]$ is defined by (4.51–7).   Let

$$\alpha_{00} = \alpha - \sum_{j=1}^{\infty} \alpha_j$$

$$\alpha_{0j} = \alpha_j, \qquad j = 1, 2, \cdots,$$

where α and α_j are defined by (4.51–9) and (4.51–10).   If x' and y' are elements of $(c)'$ defined by

$$x'(x) = \sum_{j=0}^{\infty} \lambda_j\xi_j, \qquad y'(y) = \sum_{i=0}^{\infty} \mu_i\eta_i,$$

show that $Ay' = x'$ means

$$\lambda_j = \sum_{i=0}^{\infty} \alpha_{ij}\mu_i \qquad j = 0, 1, 2, \cdots.$$

4.52 The M. Riesz Convexity Theorem

Consider a matrix (α_{ij}) of complex numbers, not all 0, with m rows and n columns.   Let $\xi_1, \cdots, \xi_n$ and $\zeta_1, \cdots, \zeta_m$ be complex numbers, and let $x = (\xi_1, \cdots, \xi_n)$, $z = (\zeta_1, \cdots, \zeta_m)$.   If $\mu \geqslant 0$, define

$$M_\mu(x) = \begin{cases} \left(\sum_{j=1}^{n} |\xi_j|^{1/\mu}\right)^\mu & \text{if } \mu > 0 \\[2mm] \sup_j |\xi_j| & \text{if } \mu = 0. \end{cases}$$

If $v \geqslant 0$, define $N_v(z)$ in a similar manner.   Let

(4.52–1) $$M(\mu, v) = \sup \left| \sum_{i=1}^{m} \sum_{j=1}^{n} \alpha_{ij}\zeta_i\xi_j \right|,$$

the supremum being taken for all x and z such that $M_\mu(x) \leqslant 1$ and $N_v(z) \leqslant 1$.   Then $\log M(\mu, v)$ is *a convex function of the point* (μ, v) *in the* *part of the (μ, ν)-plane defined by the inequalities $\mu \geqslant 0$, $\nu \geqslant 0$.* This means that if (μ_1, ν_1) and (μ_2, ν_2) are admissible points,

$$\log M[(1 - t)\mu_1 + t\mu_2, (1 - t)\nu_1 + t\nu_2]$$

is a convex function of t when $0 \leqslant t \leqslant 1$.

We shall refer to this result as the M. Riesz convexity theorem. M. Riesz's proof of this theorem was given in his paper **1**, subject to the more restrictive conditions $0 \leqslant \mu \leqslant 1$, $0 \leqslant \nu \leqslant 1$, $\mu + \nu \geqslant 1$. See also Hardy, Littlewood and Polya, **1**, pages 214–219. In the more general form the result is due to Thorin, **1**. If the matrix elements α_{ij} are real and if the vectors x, z are assumed to have real components, the convexity property of $\log M(\mu, \nu)$ obtains when $0 \leqslant \mu$, $0 \leqslant \nu$, and $\mu + \nu \geqslant 1$. This was shown partly by Riesz and partly by Thorin.

We shall not prove the Riesz convexity theorem. Our concern is to discuss the application of it to continuous linear mappings of l^p into l^q. For a more far-reaching discussion of the development of such ideas, with various important applications to integrals, Fourier coefficients, and other topics, see Dunford and Schwartz, **1**, §§ 10, 11 in Chapter VI, and Zygmund, **1**, Chapter XI, especially pages 189–202.

Suppose $1 \leqslant p \leqslant \infty$, $1 \leqslant q \leqslant \infty$, and consider the m by n matrix (α_{ij}) as representing a linear operator A mapping $l^q(n)$ into $l^q(m)$, with $y = Ax$ meaning $x = (\xi_1, \cdots, \xi_n)$, $y = (\eta_1, \cdots, \eta_m)$, and

$$\eta_i = \sum_{j=1}^{n} \alpha_{ij}\xi_j.$$

With the aid of Theorem 4.3–B we see that $\|A\| = \sup |y'(Ax)|$, the supremum being taken for all $x \in l^p(n)$ with $\|x\| \leqslant 1$ and all linear functionals y' on $l^q(m)$ with $\|y'\| \leqslant 1$. Since $y'(y)$ has a representation

$$y'(y) = \sum_{i=1}^{m} \zeta_i\eta_i,$$

we see that

$$(4.52\text{–}2) \qquad \|A\| = \sup \left| \sum_{i=1}^{m} \sum_{j=1}^{n} \alpha_{ij}\zeta_i\xi_j \right|,$$

the supremum being taken for all x such that $\|x\| \leqslant 1$ and all $(\zeta_1, \cdots, \zeta_m)$ determining a functional y' with $\|y'\| \leqslant 1$. Now, the normed conjugate of $l^q(m)$ is congruent to $l^{q'}(m)$. Hence, comparing (4.52–1) and (4.52–2), we see that

$$\|A\| = M(1/p, 1/q'),$$

where $1/p$ is understood to be 0 if $p = \infty$, and likewise for $1/q'$. To emphasize the dependence of $\|A\|$ on p and q we shall write it as $\|A\|_{p,\,q}$.

It is clear that, when $\nu \leqslant 1$, convexity as a function of (μ, ν) is the same as convexity as a function of $(\mu, 1 - \nu)$. Hence, by Riesz's theorem, $\log \|A\|_{p,\,q}$ is convex as a function of $(1/p, 1/q)$. In the complex case this is true for $p \geqslant 1, q \geqslant 1$. In the real case there is the additional restriction $(1/p) + (1/q') \geqslant 1$, which is the same as $q \geqslant p$. We summarize:

Theorem 4.52–A. *If $A \in [l^p(n),\ l^q(m)]$, then $\log \|A\|_{p,\,q}$ is a convex function of $(1/p, 1/q)$ for all $p \geqslant 1, q \geqslant 1$ in the complex case and for $q \geqslant p \geqslant 1$ in the real case.*

In order to display more directly the implication of this theorem, suppose $\psi(t)$ is a positive function such that $\log \psi(t)$ is convex when $0 \leqslant t \leqslant 1$. In particular, when $0 < t < 1$, the point $(t, \log \psi(t))$ on the graph of $\log \psi(t)$ is on or below the straight line joining the points $(0, \log \psi(0))$ and $(1, \log \psi(1))$. When the condition for this is worked out, it is found to be

$$(4.52\text{–}3) \qquad \psi(t) \leqslant [\psi(0)]^{1-t}[\psi(1)]^t.$$

Suppose now that we are given pairs (p_1, q_1), (p_2, q_2) which are admissible under the conditions stated in Theorem 4.52–A. Let p and q be defined in terms of t by

$$(4.52\text{–}4) \qquad \frac{1}{p} = \frac{1-t}{p_1} + \frac{t}{p_2}, \quad \frac{1}{q} = \frac{1-t}{q_1} + \frac{t}{q_2}, \qquad 0 < t < 1.$$

Let $\psi(t) = \|A\|_{p,\,q}$. Then (4.52–3) becomes

$$(4.52\text{–}5) \qquad \|A\|_{p,\,q} \leqslant (\|A\|_{p_1,\,q_1})^{1-t}(\|A\|_{p_2,\,q_2})^t.$$

As t varies from 0 to 1, p varies from p_1 to p_2; likewise for q. Formula (4.52–5) expresses the content of Theorem 4.52–A. For example, if $p_1 = 1, q_1 = 2, p_2 = 2, q_2 = \infty$, we find that

$$p = \frac{2}{2-t}, \qquad q = \frac{2}{1-t} = \frac{2p}{2-p}.$$

In this case (4.52–5) becomes

$$\|A\|_{p,\,2p/(2-p)} \leqslant (\|A\|_{1,\,2})^{(2-p)/p}(\|A\|_{2,\,\infty})^{2(p-1)/p}.$$

Here p may vary from 1 to 2.

Now let us consider an infinite matrix (α_{ij}), $i, j = 1, 2, \cdots$. Let $A_{n,\,m}$ be the mapping of $l^p(n)$ into $l^q(m)$ defined by considering α_{ij} for $1 \leqslant i \leqslant n$, $1 \leqslant j \leqslant m$. It is easily proved that the infinite matrix defines a continuous linear mapping A of l^p into l^q if and only if $\|A_{n,\,m}\|_{p,\,q}$ is bounded as m and n vary and that, when such is the case,

$$(4.52\text{--}6) \qquad\qquad \|A\|_{p,\,q} = \sup_{m,\,n} \|A_{n,\,m}\|_{p,\,q}.$$

We write $\|A\|_{p,\,q}$ rather than $\|A\|$, because we now wish to consider the possibility that A may be regarded as belonging to $[l^p,\,l^q]$ for various values of p and q.

Theorem 4.52–B. *Suppose that (α_{ij}) is an infinite matrix of scalars. Let (p_1, q_1) and (p_2, q_2) be admissible pairs according to the conditions of Theorem 4.52–A. Suppose the matrix defines an A belonging both to $[l^{p_1}, l^{q_1}]$ and to $[l^{p_2}, l^{q_2}]$. Then A belongs to $[l^p, l^q]$ for each (p, q) given by (4.52–4), and the norms in these various cases satisfy the inequality (4.52–5).*

The proof is immediate, by applying (4.52–5) to $A_{n,\,m}$ and taking note of the assertion made in connection with (4.52–6).

PROBLEMS

1. If the infinite matrix (α_{ij}) defines an operator $A \in [l^p]$, denote its norm by $\|A\|_p$. Show that, if the operator defined by the matrix belongs to $[l^1]$ and $[l^\infty]$, it belongs to l^p for $1 < p < \infty$, and $\|A\|_p \leqslant (\|A\|_1)^{1/p}(\|A\|_\infty)^{1-(1/p)}$. For a different approach to the case $p = 2$, see § 6.12.

2. Carry out the proof of (4.52–6).

4.6 Annihilators, Ranges, and Null Manifolds

We are now ready to take up the study of matters corresponding to the subject matter of §§ 1.9, 1.91, but with X', Y' replacing X^f, Y^f and A' replacing A^T. The differences are due mainly to the intervention of topological matters: the continuity of functionals and operators, and the distinction between closed and arbitrary linear manifolds.

The spaces X and Y referred to in this section are understood, without further mention, to be normed linear spaces. Completeness is not needed except in some of the problems. Many of the ideas and results apply to general topological linear spaces and especially to locally convex ones, but we shall not concern ourselves with the greater generality of such spaces.

In this section, and in applications based on it, the definitions of annihilators are as follows: If $G \subset X$, the annihilator of G in X' is the set

$$G^0 = \{x' \in X' : x'(x) = 0 \qquad \text{if } x \in G\}.$$

If $H \subset X'$, the annihilator of H in X is the set

$$^0H = \{x \in X : x'(x) = 0 \quad \text{if } x' \in H\}.$$

It is assumed that G and H are nonempty.

The annihilator G^0 is a closed linear manifold in X'; it coincides with M^0, where M is the closed linear manifold generated by G. Similar remarks apply to ^0H.

In certain proofs in §§ 1.9, 1.91 we used Theorems 1.71–B and 1.71–C. For present purposes, in the corresponding circumstances, we can appeal to Theorems 4.3–D and 4.3–C. For later use we state the following theorems, leaving the proofs to the reader.

Theorem 4.6–A. *If $G \subset X$ and M is the closed linear manifold in X generated by G, then $^0(G^0) = M$. In particular, $^0(M^0) = M$ if M is any closed linear manifold in X.*

Theorem 4.6–B. *If $H \subset X'$ and N is the closed linear manifold in X' generated by H, then $N \subset (^0H)^0$. In particular, $N \subset (^0N)^0$ if N is any closed linear manifold in X'.*

A linear manifold N in X' will be called *saturated* if $N = (^0N)^0$. Such an N is necessarily closed. But a closed linear manifold is not necessarily saturated. To see this we refer to problem 1, § 4.32 and to the example at the end of § 1.9. If $X = (c)$, every $x' \in X'$ is representable in the form

$$x'(x) = \sum_0^\infty \alpha_{k+1}\xi_k, \qquad \text{with} \qquad \sum_1^\infty |\alpha_k| < \infty.$$

The space $(c)'$ is congruent in a natural way to l^1. Now let N be the set of those x' for which $\alpha_1 = 0$. This is a proper closed subspace of X'. But $^0N = (0)$ (argument given in § 1.9) and hence $(^0N)^0 = X'$. Thus N is not saturated.

In the case of any X there do exist saturated subspaces of X'; (0) and X' are examples. So is H^0, where H is any nonempty set in X.

In view of Theorem 4.6–B we note that, if N is any linear manifold in X', it is saturated if and only if $(^0N)^0 \subset N$. This is equivalent to

$$\text{complement of } N \subset \text{complement of } (^0N)^0.$$

Hence, a proper subspace N of X' is saturated if and only if to each $x' \in X' - N$ corresponds an $x \in {}^0N$ for which $x'(x) \neq 0$. Thus, a saturated subspace of X' is what has been called a *regularly closed* subspace (see Banach, **1**, pages 115–117). The notion of a saturated subspace is closely related to the weak topology $\mathscr{T}(X', X)$ for X' [$\mathscr{T}(X', X)$ is defined in the second paragraph after Theorem 3.81–B]. In fact, as we show later, in § 4.62, a subspace N of X' is saturated if and only if it is closed in the weak topology $\mathscr{T}(X', X)$.

We now turn to an examination of theorems analogous to those of § 1.91. When A is a continuous linear operator, the null manifold $\mathscr{N}(A)$ is a closed subspace; it is closed because it is the inverse image, by A, of a closed set. However, the range of A need not be closed.

Example. Let $X = Y = l^1$, and define $A \in [X]$ by $Ax = y$, where $y = \{\eta_k\}$, $x = \{\xi_k\}$, and $\eta_k = k^{-1}\xi_k$. Clearly $\mathscr{R}(A)$ contains all y's for which $\eta_k = 0$ except for a finite number of indices k, and so $\overline{\mathscr{R}(A)} = X$. But $\mathscr{R}(A) \neq X$; for instance, the vector y with $\eta_k = k^{-2}$ is in $X - \mathscr{R}(A)$, because $\xi_k = k^{-1}$ does not define an element of X. It follows that $\mathscr{R}(A)$ is not closed.

In the theorems which correspond to those of §1.91, it is the closure of the range of an operator which takes the place of the range itself. This is because of two things: (1) an annihilator is always closed, and (2) a linear manifold and its closure possess the same annihilator.

For later reference we state the following three theorems, leaving the proofs to the reader. It is assumed that $A \in [X, Y]$; X and Y need not be complete.

Theorem 4.6–C. $\{\overline{\mathscr{R}(A)}\}^0 = \mathscr{N}(A')$.

Theorem 4.6–D. $\overline{\mathscr{R}(A)} = {}^0\{\mathscr{N}(A')\}$.

Theorem 4.6–E. $\overline{\mathscr{R}(A)} = Y$ *if and only if* $(A')^{-1}$ *exists.*

At this point we are saying nothing about the continuity of $(A')^{-1}$. In § 4.7 we have some deeper theorems which relate the situation $\mathscr{R}(A) = Y$ to the existence and continuity of $(A')^{-1}$. These deeper theorems involve the issue of completeness.

When we exchange the roles of A and A' we do not get quite as much information as in the foregoing set of theorems. The following results are easily proved, and we leave proofs to the reader.

Theorem 4.6–F. ${}^0\{\overline{\mathscr{R}(A')}\} = \mathscr{N}(A)$.

Theorem 4.6–G. $\overline{\mathscr{R}(A')} \subset \{\mathscr{N}(A)\}^0$.

Theorem 4.6–H. *If* $\overline{\mathscr{R}(A')} = X'$, *then* A^{-1} *exists.*

Theorem 4.6–I. *If* A^{-1} *exists, then* $({}^0\{\overline{\mathscr{R}(A')}\})^0 = X'$.

In connection with Theorem 4.6–G we observe that, if $\overline{\mathscr{R}(A')}$ is saturated in X', we have the equality $\overline{\mathscr{R}(A')} = \{\mathscr{N}(A)\}^0$. This happens, for instance, if X is norm reflexive or if $\overline{\mathscr{R}(A')}$ is finite dimensional (see problems 1, 2 at the end of this section).   Likewise, when A^{-1} exists and we have reason to know that $\overline{\mathscr{R}(A')}$ is saturated, we can conclude from Theorem 4.6–I that $\overline{\mathscr{R}(A')} = X'$.

PROBLEMS

1. If X is norm reflexive, every closed subspace of X' is saturated.

2. A finite-dimensional subspace of X' is saturated (see Theorem 3.5–C).

3. If $\{\alpha_n\}$ is a sequence of scalars with $\sup\limits_n |\alpha_n| < \infty$, let $X = l^1$, and let A be the operator $A \in [l^1]$ defined by $Ax = y$, where $\eta_k = \alpha_k \xi_k$. Then $\|A\| = \sup\limits_n |\alpha_n|$.   The inverse A^{-1} exists if and only if $\alpha_n \neq 0$ for every n, and then $\overline{\mathscr{R}(A)} = X$.   Show that $\mathscr{R}(A) = X$ and A^{-1} is continuous if and only if $\inf\limits_n |\alpha_n| > 0$.

4. If X is complete and X' is norm reflexive, so is X.   Let J_0 and J_1 be the canonical mappings of X and X' into X'' and X''', respectively.   Show that $(J_1)^{-1} = J_0'$, as a result of the reflexivity of X'.   Then use Theorem 4.6–E.

5. Let M be a closed subspace of the normed linear space X.   Let $F = X/M$ (normed as in § 3.14).   Then F' is congruent to M^0.   The congruence is established by the mapping $Tf = x'$, where $f \in F'$ and $x'(x) = f([x])$, $x \in X$, $x' \in X'$, $[x] \in X/M$.   It is to be shown that T is linear and isometric, with range M^0.

6. Suppose M is a closed subspace of the norm-reflexive space X.   Then the quotient space X/M is norm reflexive.   The argument is that X' is norm reflexive and hence also, in turn, M^0, $(X/M)'$, and X/M.   See the two preceding problems and problem 4, § 4.5.

7. Suppose that X is complete and that $\mathscr{R}(A)$, as a normed linear space on its own account, is complete [as it is, for example, if Y is complete and $\mathscr{R}(A)$ is closed].   Then $\mathscr{R}(A') = \{\mathscr{N}(A)\}^0$.   In view of Theorem 4.6–G it suffices to show that $\{\mathscr{N}(A)\}^0 \subset \mathscr{R}(A')$.   If $x' \in \{\mathscr{N}(A)\}^0$ and $y \in \mathscr{R}(A)$, then $x'(x)$ has the same value for each x such that $y = Ax$.   Hence define $f(y) = x'(x)$, using such an x.   Use Theorem 4.2–G(5) to show that $f \in \{\mathscr{R}(A)\}'$.   Then extend f to obtain $y' \in Y'$ and show that $A'y' = x'$.

4.61 Weak Compactness in Normed Linear Spaces

The use of weak topologies sheds light on various questions which arise in relation to normed linear spaces.   In this section we consider compactness, using weak topologies.

Throughout the section X denotes a normed linear space, X' its normed conjugate, and J the canonical mapping of X into X''.   We shall be concerned with the topology $\mathcal{T}(X, X')$ for X and the topology $\mathcal{T}(X', X)$ for X' (see the third paragraph of § 4.41). We also consider the topology $\mathcal{T}(X'', X')$ for X''.

The first main result is the following:

Theorem 4.61–A. *Suppose $S \subset X'$. Let S be bounded with respect to the norm in X' and closed with respect to $\mathcal{T}(X', X)$. Then S is compact with respect to $\mathcal{T}(X', X)$. In particular, $\{x': \|x'\| \leqslant 1\}$ is compact in this sense.*

PROOF. Suppose $C = \sup\limits_{x \in S} \|x'\|$. For each $x \in X$ let $A_x = \{\alpha : |\alpha| \leqslant C\|x\|\}$. Let $A = \prod\limits_{x \in X} A_x$ (the Cartesian product as in § 2.5). Then A is compact, by Theorem 2.5–A. Now, any element $x' \in S$ is determined by the set of values $x'(x)$, $x \in X$; since $|x'(x)| \leqslant \|x'\| \|x\| \leqslant C\|x\|$, we see that $x' \in A$ or $S \subset A$. Moreover, it is easily verified that the topology induced on S by $\mathcal{T}(X', X)$ is the same as the topology induced on S by the Cartesian product topology for A. Hence, for the first assertion in the theorem, it suffices to prove that S is closed as a subset of A (see Theorem 2.2–B). Suppose f is an element of the closure of S in A. Consider any $\epsilon > 0$ and any $x, y \in X$. The set of all $g \in A$ such that

$$|g(x) - f(x)| < \epsilon, \qquad |g(y) - f(y)| < \epsilon,$$

and
$$|g(x + y) - f(x + y)| < \epsilon,$$

is a neighborhood of f in A. This neighborhood contains some point $x' \in S$, and, since x' is linear, we have

$$|f(x + y) - f(x) - f(y)| \leqslant |f(x + y) - x'(x + y)| \\ + |x'(x) - f(x)| + |x'(y) - f(y)| < 3\epsilon,$$

whence it follows that $f(x + y) = f(x) + f(y)$. In a similar way we prove that $f(\beta x) = \beta f(x)$. Now, by the fact that $f \in A$, we know that $f(x) \in A_x$ or $|f(x)| \leqslant C\|x\|$. Hence $f \in X'$. Then $f \in S$, for S is closed in X' relative to $\mathcal{T}(X', X)$. This proves that S is closed in A and hence that S is compact relative to $\mathcal{T}(X', X)$. The last assertion of the theorem follows from the fact that $\{x': \|x'\| \leqslant 1\}$ is closed in X' relative to $\mathcal{T}(X', X)$ (see problems 9 and 10 in § 4.4).

The next main result is Theorem 4.61–C, for the proof of which we need the following lemma:

Lemma 4.61–B. *Consider $S \subset X$ and $S'' \subset X''$ defined as follows:*

$$S = \{x : \|x\| \leqslant 1\}, \quad S'' = \{x'' : \|x''\| \leqslant 1\}.$$

Also consider the canonical image $J(S)$ of S in X''.   This set $J(S)$ is dense in S'' with respect to the topology $\mathcal{T}(X'', X')$.

PROOF.   Suppose $x_0'' \in S''$, and suppose $\epsilon > 0$, $x_1', \cdots, x_n' \in X'$.   We shall produce an $x_0 \in S$ such that Jx_0 is in the neighborhood of x_0'' defined by $\epsilon, x_1', \cdots, x_n'$.   That is, x_0 will be such that

$$(4.61\text{-}1)\qquad |x_i'(x_0) - x_0''(x_i')| < \epsilon, \qquad i = 1, \cdots, n.$$

Let M be the set of all $x \in X$ such that $x_i'(x) = 0$ if $i = 1, \cdots, n$.   Then M is a subspace of X, closed in the norm topology.   By Theorem 3.5–C, M^0 is the subspace of X' generated by $x_1', \cdots, x_n'$ (it suffices to work with a maximal linearly independent subset of $x_1', \cdots, x_n'$).   Consider the quotient space X/M.   The fact that the dimension of M^0 does not exceed n implies the same property for X/M.   In fact, $(X/M)'$ is congruent to M^0 (problem 5, § 4.6), so that $(X/M)'$, and so also X/M, have the same finite dimension as M^0.   Now, the space X/M, being finite dimensional, is reflexive.   We utilize the congruence of $(X/M)'$ and M^0 under the mapping $x' = T(V')$, where $V' \in (X/M)'$, $x' \in M^0$, and $x'(x) = V'([x])$.   Using the given $x_0'' \in S''$, we define $V'' \in (X/M)''$ by $V''(V') = x_0''(TV')$.   Evidently $\|V''\| \leqslant 1$, because T is norm-preserving.   Because of the reflexivity of X/M there exists $V \in X/M$ such that $V''(V') = V'(V)$ for every V', and $\|V\| = \|V''\| \leqslant 1$.   Now choose $C > \sup_i \|x_i'\|$.   By the definition of norms in X/M, there exists $x \in V$ such that $\|x\| < \|V\| + \epsilon/C \leqslant 1 + (\epsilon/C)$.   By the definition of T, $x'(x) = V'(V)$, where $x' = TV'$.   Therefore $x'(x) = x_0''(x')$ for every $x' \in M^0$.   Now let $x_0 = Cx/(C + \epsilon)$.   We see that $\|x_0\| < 1$ and $\|x - x_0\| = \epsilon\|x\|/(C + \epsilon) < \epsilon/C$.   Also, if $x' \in M$,

$$|x_0''(x') - x'(x_0)| = |x'(x) - x'(x_0)| \leqslant \|x'\|\,\|x - x_0\| < \epsilon\|x'\|/C;$$

therefore, by the definition of C, it follows that (4.61–1) holds.   This proves the theorem.

We observe that, if X is given the topology $\mathcal{T}(X, X')$ and the canonical image $J(X)$ of X in X'' is given the topology induced on it by $\mathcal{T}(X'', X')$, then J is a linear homeomorphism of X onto $J(X)$.   This is clear directly from the way in which the bases at 0 are defined for the topologies in question.

Theorem 4.61–C.   *The normed linear space X is norm reflexive if and only if the set $S = \{x : \|x\| \leqslant 1\}$ is compact with respect to the weak topology $\mathcal{T}(X, X')$.*

PROOF.   If S is compact, $J(S)$ is compact relative to the topology $\mathcal{T}(X'', X')$, since J is continuous, as noted above.   Hence, by Theorem

2.3–B, $J(S)$ is closed in X''. It then follows from Lemma 4.61–B that $J(S) = S''$, for S'' is closed with respect to $\mathcal{T}(X'', X')$ (see problem 10, § 4.4). It now follows easily that $J(X) = X''$, so that X is norm reflexive.

On the other hand, if X is norm reflexive, $J^{-1}(S'') = S$. Now S'' is compact relative to $\mathcal{T}(X'', X')$ (Theorem 4.61–A), and hence S is compact relative to $\mathcal{T}(X, X')$, since J^{-1} is continuous.

In the older literature dealing with Banach spaces, before the systematic development of the weak topologies, a good deal of attention was paid to the concept of weak convergence of sequences, even though the weak topologies themselves were not investigated. In particular, the following concept was used (though with different terminology):

Definition. In the normed linear space X, a set S is called conditionally sequentially X'-weakly compact if every sequence from S contains a subsequence which is X'-weakly convergent to some limit in X.

We see from Theorem 4.41–B that if X is norm reflexive, every bounded set in X is conditionally sequentially X'-weakly compact. This proposition has a valid converse, as follows:

Theorem 4.61–D. *If X is a Banach space such that every bounded sequence contains an X'-weakly convergent subsequence, then X is norm reflexive.*

We shall not give a complete proof of this theorem. It was first proved under the additional assumption that X is separable (Banach **1**, pages 189–191). After a great deal of development of the subject of weak topologies it was proved that, *if X is a Banach space and S is a set in X which is closed relative to the topology $\mathcal{T}(X, X')$ and conditionally sequentially X'-weakly compact, then S is compact relative to $\mathcal{T}(X, X')$* (Eberlein, **1**). Theorem 4.61–D is a consequence of this result, in view of Theorem 4.61–C and the fact that $\{x : \|x\| \leqslant 1\}$ is closed relative to $\mathcal{T}(X, X')$ (see problem 9, § 4.4).

A partial outline of the proof of Eberlein's result runs as follows: consider the canonical image $J(S)$ of S in X''. Since S is bounded (in the norm sense), so is $J(S)$. The difficult thing to prove is that $J(S)$ is closed relative to the topology $\mathcal{T}(X'', X')$. Once this is done, Theorem 4.61–A shows that $J(S)$ is compact relative to $\mathcal{T}(X'', X')$. Finally, S itself is compact relative to $\mathcal{T}(X, X')$, because J^{-1} is continuous in the relevant topologies. The proof that $J(S)$ is closed relative to $\mathcal{T}(X'', X')$ makes use of the important theorem 4.62–B, which we state, but do not prove, in the next section. Use is also made of the interesting fact (see problem 4, § 3.81) that, if K is a convex set in X, its closure in the norm topology coincides with its closure in the topology $\mathcal{T}(X, X')$.

For further information about compactness relative to the topology $\mathcal{T}(X, X')$, see Dunford and Schwartz, **1**, Chapter V, § 6.

PROBLEMS

1. Let X be a normed linear space, and suppose $x_1', \cdots, x_n' \in X'$. Suppose $\alpha_1, \cdots, \alpha_n$ are scalars, that $B > 0$, and that $|\lambda_1\alpha_1 + \cdots + \lambda_n\alpha_n| \leqslant B\|\lambda_1 x_1' + \cdots + \lambda_n x_n'\|$ for every set of scalars $\lambda_1, \cdots, \lambda_n$. Then, to each $\delta > 0$ corresponds some x with $\|x\| \leqslant B + \delta$ and $x_i'(x) = \alpha_i$, $i = 1, \cdots, n$. Outline of proof: Let T be the mapping of X into $l^2(n)$ defined by $Tx = [x_1'(x), \cdots, x_n'(x)]$. Let $K = \{x : \|x\| \leqslant B + \delta\}$. Show that there exists a linear functional on $l^2(n)$ with value 1 at $(\alpha_1, \cdots, \alpha_n)$ and of absolute value not exceeding 1 on $T(K)$. If the value of this functional at $(\xi_1, \cdots \xi_n)$ is $\lambda_1\xi_1 + \cdots + \lambda_n\xi_n$, deduce the contradiction $\lambda_1\alpha_1 + \cdots + \lambda_n\alpha_n = 0$. This is Y. Mimura's proof of a result due originally to E. Helly. See Kakutani, **1**, page 171.

2. Use the result in problem 1 to arrive at (4.61–1) in a different way, thus giving an alternative proof of Lemma 4.61–B. Take $B = \|x_0''\|$, $\alpha_i = x_0''(x_i')$. Then x_0 can be chosen as a suitable multiple of the x obtained by using problem 1.

3. A normed linear space X is called *uniformly* convex if to each $\epsilon > 0$ corresponds $\delta(\epsilon) > 0$ such that $\|x + y\| \leqslant 2(1 - \delta(\epsilon))$ when $\|x\| \leqslant 1$, $\|y\| \leqslant 1$ and $\|x - y\| \geqslant \epsilon$. This concept is due to Clarkson, **1**. Every uniformly convex Banach space is norm reflexive. This has been proved in different ways by Milman, **1**, Pettis, **1**, and Kakutani, **1**. Kakutani's argument depends on problem 1. It will suffice to show that, if $x_0'' \in X''$ and $\|x_0''\| = 1$, then $x_0'' \in \mathcal{R}(J)$, J being the canonical mapping of X into X''. Choose $x_k' \in X'$ so that $\|x_k'\| = 1$ and $x_0''(x_k') > 1 - (1/k)$. Applying problem 1 with $B = 1$ and $\alpha_i = x_0''(x_i')$, $i = 1, \cdots, n$, we obtain $x_n \in X$ so that $\|x_n\| < 1 + (1/n)$ and $x_i'(x_n) = x_0''(x_i')$, $i = 1, \cdots, n$. Use uniform convexity to deduce a contradiction if one assumes that $\{x_n\}$ is not a Cauchy sequence. Then $x_n \to x_0$, and it follows easily that $\|x_0\| = 1$, $x_n'(x_0) = x_0''(x_n)$ for $n = 1, 2, \cdots$. Using uniform convexity again, it can be seen that these last mentioned conditions determine x_0 uniquely. Now suppose $x_0' \in X'$. Proceeding from problem 1 again, we obtain $y_n \in X$ so that $\|y_n\| < 1 + (1/n)$ and $x_i'(y_n) = x_0''(x_i')$ if $i = 0, 1, \cdots, n$. Then $\{y_n\}$ is a Cauchy sequence with limit y_0 such that $\|y_0\| = 1$, $x_n'(y_0) = x_0''(x_n')$ if $n = 0, 1, \cdots$. By the uniqueness, $y_0 = x_0$ and hence $Jx_0 = x_0''$.

4.62 Saturated Subspaces of a Conjugate Space

If X is a normed linear space, the topology $\mathcal{T}(X', X)$ is weaker than $\mathcal{T}(X', X'')$, which in turn is weaker than the topology generated by the norm in X'. A subspace of X' is closed relative to $\mathcal{T}(X', X'')$ if and only if it is closed in the norm topology (by Theorem 3.81–C). Because $\mathcal{T}(X', X)$ is weaker than $\mathcal{T}(X', X'')$, it follows that a subspace of X' which is closed relative to $\mathcal{T}(X', X)$ is also closed relative to $\mathcal{T}(X', X'')$.

The converse is not true in general; in fact, as we shall see, if X has the property, that every subspace of X' which is closed relative $\mathcal{T}(X', X'')$ is also closed relative to $\mathcal{T}(X', X)$, then X must be norm reflexive.

Theorem 4.62–A. *A subspace M of X' is closed relative to $\mathcal{T}(X', X)$ if and only if it is saturated.*

PROOF.   Suppose M is saturated and that $x_0' \in X' - M$. Then there exists some $x_1 \in {}^0M$ such that $x_0'(x_1) \neq 0$. Choose ϵ so that $0 < \epsilon < |x_0'(x_1)|$. Then $\{x' : |x'(x_1) - x_0'(x_1)| < \epsilon\}$ is a neighborhood of x_0' in the topology $\mathcal{T}(X', X)$. This neighborhood does not intersect M, and so M is closed.

Now suppose that M is closed relative to $\mathcal{T}(X', X)$. We can assume $M \neq X'$, for X' is saturated. Suppose $x_0' \in X' - M$. The fact that M is closed means that there exists $\epsilon > 0$ and $x_1, \cdots, x_n \in X$ such that, if $x' \in M$, then

$$(4.62\text{–}1) \qquad |x'(x_i) - x_0'(x_i)| \geqslant \epsilon, \qquad i = 1, 2, \cdots, n.$$

Let T be the linear mapping of X' into $l^2(n)$ defined by $Tx' = \{x'(x_1), \cdots, x'(x_n)\}$. Then $T(M)$ is a closed subspace of $l^2(n)$, and it does not contain Tx_0'. Hence there exists a linear functional on $l^2(n)$ which has the value 0 on $T(M)$ and a nonzero value at Tx_0'. Let $\sum_{i=1}^{n} \alpha_i \xi_i$ be the value of this functional at the point $(\xi_1, \cdots, \xi_n)$. Define $x_0 = \sum_{i=1}^{n} \alpha_i x_i$. Then $x'(x_0) = 0$ if $x' \in M$, and $x_0'(x_0) \neq 0$. This proves that M is saturated.   The proof is now complete.

We have not the space or the need in this book to push very far with a study of saturated subspaces. However, we mention without proof the following very important theorem.

Theorem 4.62–B. *Let X be a Banach space. Let M be a subspace of X' such that $M \cap \{x' : \|x'\| \leqslant 1\}$ is compact relative to $\mathcal{T}(X', X)$. Then M is saturated.*

In view of Theorem 4.61–A, the word "compact" may be replaced by "closed" in the statement of Theorem 4.62–B. This theorem, due to Dieudonné (**1**, Théorème 23), is closely related to Lemma 2, page 119 in the book **1** of Banach.

PROBLEMS

1. Suppose $x'' \in X''$, and let $M = \{x' : x''(x') = 0\}$. Then $x'' \in J(X)$ if and only if M is saturated. In proving the "if" part use Theorem 3.5–C.

2. The space X is norm reflexive if every subspace of X' which is closed in the norm topology is saturated.   See problem 1 of § 4.6 for the converse.

3. Use Theorem 4.62–B to prove the "if" part of Theorem 4.61–C without using Lemma 4.61–B.   Using the notation of these propositions, observe that $J(S) = J(X) \cap S''$, and deduce that $J(X)$ is saturated, whence $J(X) = X''$.

4. Let M be a subspace of X', and let $\bar{M}$ be its closure in the topology $\mathscr{T}(X', X)$.   Then $\bar{M} = X'$ if and only if M is total.   Note that "M is total" can be expressed in the form $^0M = (0)$.

4.7 Theorems about Continuous Inverses

Throughout this section we assume that X and Y are normed linear spaces and that $A \in [X, Y]$, whence $A' \in [Y', X']$.   In some cases we assume completeness for X or Y; these assumptions are made explicit in each case.   The conjugate spaces X', Y' are complete, in any event.

Theorem 4.7–A. $\mathscr{R}(A') = X'$ if and only of A^{-1} exists and is continuous.

PROOF.   Suppose that $\mathscr{R}(A') = X'$ but that A does not have a continuous inverse.   Then, by Theorem 3.1–B, there is a sequence $\{x_n\}$ such that $x_n \neq 0$ and $\|Ax_n\|/\|x_n\| \to 0$.   Let

$$\alpha_n = \max\left\{\left(\frac{\|Ax_n\|}{\|x_n\|}\right)^{\frac{1}{2}},\ n^{-\frac{1}{2}}\right\}, \qquad u_n = \frac{x_n}{\alpha_n\|x_n\|}.$$

Then $\|u_n\| = \dfrac{1}{\alpha_n} \to \infty$, and

$$\|Au_n\| = \frac{\|Ax_n\|}{\alpha_n\|x_n\|} \leqslant \left(\frac{\|Ax_n\|}{\|x_n\|}\right)^{\frac{1}{2}} \to 0.$$

But then $y'(Au_n) \to 0$ for each $y' \in Y'$.   Since $\mathscr{R}(A') = X'$ and $y'(Au_n) = \langle Au_n, y'\rangle = \langle u_n, A'y'\rangle$, this implies that $x'(u_n) \to 0$ for each $x' \in X'$.   But then, Theorem 4.4–Da implies that $\{\|u_n\|\}$ is bounded, which is a contradiction.

Now suppose, conversely, that A has a continuous inverse.   If x' is fixed in X' and y is variable in $\mathscr{R}(A)$, $x'(A^{-1}y)$ defines a continuous linear functional on $\mathscr{R}(A)$.   This functional can be extended to all of Y, the extension being a member of Y' (Theorem 4.3–A).   That is, there exists $y' \in Y'$ such that $y'(y) = x'(A^{-1}y)$ when $y \in \mathscr{R}(A)$.   Thus $y'(Ax) = x'(x)$ for each $x \in X$.   This means that $x' = A'y'$.   Therefore $\mathscr{R}(A')$ is all of X'.   The proof is now complete.

Theorem 4.7–B. *Suppose that Y is complete and that $\mathcal{R}(A) = Y$. Then A' has a continuous inverse.*

PROOF. The argument is very much like that in the first part of the proof of Theorem 4.7–A. If A' did not have a continuous inverse, we should be able to assert the existence of a sequence $\{y_n'\}$ such that $\|y_n'\| \to \infty$ and $\|A'y_n'\| \to 0$. Then $\langle x, A'y_n' \rangle \to 0$ for each $x \in X$. Since $\langle x, A'y_n' \rangle = \langle Ax, y_n' \rangle$ and $\mathcal{R}(A) = Y$, this means that $y_n'(y) \to 0$ for each $y \in Y$. Since Y is complete, we see by Theorem 4.4–Db that $\{\|y_n'\|\}$ is bounded. This is a contradiction, so the theorem is proved.

The next theorem is in the nature of a converse of Theorem 4.7–B. But the proof is more complicated, and we need to assume that X is complete.

Theorem 4.7–C. *Suppose that X is complete and that A' has a continuous inverse. Then $\mathcal{R}(A) = Y$. Moreover, it follows that Y is complete. Finally, A^{-1} is continuous, if it exists.*

PROOF. For each $\alpha > 0$ let $B_\alpha = \{x : \|x\| \leqslant \alpha\}$. We first prove that the set $\overline{A(B_\alpha)}$ contains a neighborhood of 0 in Y. This part of the proof does not require X to be complete. The set B_α is convex and balanced, so the same is true of $A(B_\alpha)$ and $\overline{A(B_\alpha)}$. Suppose that, for some α, $\overline{A(B_\alpha)}$ does not contain a neighborhood of 0. Then there exists a sequence $\{y_n\}$ in Y such that $y_n \to 0$ and $y_n \notin \overline{A(B_\alpha)}$. Let d_n be the distance between y_n and $\overline{A(B_\alpha)}$. If $y_0 \in \overline{A(B_\alpha)}$, consider the closed sphere $\{y : \|y - y_0\| \leqslant d_n/2\}$, and (for a fixed n) the union S_n of all such spheres corresponding to all choices of y_0. Let $V_n = \bar{S}_n$. By a very simple argument the convexity of $\overline{A(B_\alpha)}$ implies that of S_n, and hence V_n is convex. Likewise, V_n is balanced. Since $0 \in A(B_\alpha)$, V_n contains 0 as an interior point. Hence $\epsilon y_n \in V_n$ if ϵ is sufficiently small. However, $y_n \notin V_n$; therefore, if ϵ_n is the largest positive value of ϵ such that $\epsilon y_n \in V_n$, we know that $\epsilon_n < 1$ and that $\epsilon_n y_n$ is on the boundary of V_n. By Theorem 3.7–D there exists an element $y' \in Y'$ such that $y'(\epsilon_n y_n) = 1$ and $|y'(y)| \leqslant 1$ if $y \in V_n$. In particular, $|y'(Ax)| \leqslant 1$ if $\|x\| \leqslant \alpha$, and $|y'(Ax)| \leqslant \alpha^{-1}$ if $\|x\| \leqslant 1$. This means that $\|A'y'\| \leqslant \alpha^{-1}$. Now, the fact that A' has a continuous inverse means that $\|(A')^{-1}x'\| \leqslant m\|x'\|$ for each $x' \in \mathcal{R}(A')$, where m is some positive constant. If $x' = A'y'$ we then have $\|y'\| \leqslant m\alpha^{-1}$. Then $1 = y'(\epsilon_n y_n) \leqslant \|y'\| \|\epsilon_n y_n\| < m\alpha^{-1}\|y_n\|$, because $0 < \epsilon_n < 1$. But $\|y_n\| \geqslant \alpha/m$ contradicts the fact that $y_n \to 0$. This shows that $\overline{A(B_\alpha)}$ contains a neighborhood of 0.

The rest of the proof is much like the last part of the argument used in proving assertion 1 of Theorem 4.2–G. There is some $\beta > 0$ such that $\{y : \|y\| \leqslant \beta\} \subset \overline{A(B_\alpha)}$. Choose the values $1, 2^{-1}, 2^{-2}, \cdots, 2^{-n}, \cdots$ for

α, and denote corresponding values of β by $\beta_0, \beta_1, \cdots, \beta_n, \cdots$. Choose any y_0 for which $\|y_0\| \leqslant \beta_0$. Then $y_0 \in \overline{A(B_\alpha)}$ for $\alpha = 1$, and hence there exists an element $y_1 = Ax_1$, with $\|x_1\| \leqslant 1$, such that $\|y_0 - y_1\| \leqslant \beta_1$. This implies $y_0 - y_1 \in \overline{A(B_\alpha)}$ with $\alpha = 2^{-1}$. By induction we obtain elements $y_n = Ax_n$, with $\|x_n\| \leqslant 1/2^{n-1}$, such that $\|y_0 - y_1 - \cdots - y_n\| \leqslant \beta_n$, and hence $y_0 - y_1 - \cdots - y_n \in \overline{A(B_\alpha)}$ with $\alpha = 2^{-n}$. Now $\|Ax\| \leqslant \|A\|\alpha$ if $\|x\| \leqslant \alpha$. Therefore $\|y\| \leqslant \|A\|\alpha$ if $y \in \overline{A(B_\alpha)}$. This shows that $\beta_n \to 0$, and hence that

$$ y_0 = \sum_1^\infty y_n. $$

Since X is complete and $\sum_1^\infty \|x_n\|$ is convergent, the series $\sum_1^\infty x_n$ converges

and defines an element $x_0 \in X$. Moreover, $Ax_0 = \sum_1^\infty Ax_n = y_0$. This

shows that $\{y : \|y\| \leqslant \beta_0\} \subset \mathscr{R}(A)$; it follows by homogeneity that $\mathscr{R}(A) = Y$.

It remains to prove that Y is complete. Let $\hat{Y}$ be the completion of Y, and define $\hat{A} \in [X, \hat{Y}]$ by writing $\hat{A}x = Ax$ if $x \in X$. As we remarked in § 4.3, we can identify $\hat{Y}'$ with Y'; hence we can identify $(\hat{A})'$ with A'. It follows that $(\hat{A})'$ has a continuous inverse, and so, by what has already been proved, we know that $\mathscr{R}(\hat{A}) = \hat{Y}$. But $\mathscr{R}(\hat{A}) = \mathscr{R}(A)$, and so $\hat{Y} = Y$; it follows that Y is complete. The fact that A^{-1} is continuous, if it exists, now follows from Theorem 4.2–H.

4.71 The States of an Operator and its Conjugate

The theorems in § 4.7, together with some of those in §§ 4.2, 4.6, make it possible for us to tabulate in diagrammatic form a large number of interesting and useful implications involving a bounded linear operator and its conjugate. In order to tabulate information concisely, we make a ninefold classification of what we shall call the *state* of an operator. If $A \in [X, Y]$, we list three possibilities for $\mathscr{R}(A)$, labelling them I, II, III, as follows:

    I. $\mathscr{R}(A) = Y$.

    II. $\overline{\mathscr{R}(A)} = Y$, but $\mathscr{R}(A) \neq Y$.

    III. $\overline{\mathscr{R}(A)} \neq Y$.

As regards A^{-1} we also list three possibilities, labelling them 1, 2, 3:

1. A^{-1} exists and is continuous.
2. A^{-1} exists but is not continuous.
3. A^{-1} does not exist.

By combining these possibilities in all possible ways we obtain nine different situations. For instance, it may be that $\overline{\mathscr{R}(A)} = Y$, $\mathscr{R}(A) \neq Y$, and that A^{-1} exists but is discontinuous. We shall describe this as state II_2 for A; alternatively, we shall say that A is in state II_2. There are nine states in all: I_1, I_2, I_3, II_1, $\cdots$, III_2, III_3.

The notion of the state of an operator can be applied, in particular, to A'. Here A' replaces A and X' replaces Y in the description of the states; to say that A' is in state I_3 means that $\mathscr{R}(A') = X'$ and A' does not have an inverse.

It is possible for A to be in any one of the nine states if no restrictions are placed on X and Y. But, if we assume that X and Y are both complete, it is impossible for A to be in state I_2; this is a consequence of Theorem 4.2–H. Since X' and Y' are always complete, this shows that A' can never be in state I_2. Likewise, if X is complete, A can never be in state II_1. For, it follows by Theorem 4.2–B that A is closed; hence, if X is complete and A has a continuous inverse, Theorem 4.2–E shows that $\mathscr{R}(A)$ is closed, so that $\overline{\mathscr{R}(A)} = Y \neq \mathscr{R}(A)$ is impossible. Applying this result to A' (noting that Y' is complete), we see that A' can never be in state II_1.

Next we define the *state of the pair* (A, A'); this is the ordered pair of the states of A and A', respectively, with the state of A listed first. We shall now proceed to construct a diagram which shows the states of the pair (A, A') which are demonstrated to be impossible because of various theorems in §§ 4.2, 4.6, and 4.7. This diagram is a large square, divided into eighty-one smaller squares arranged in rows and columns. We label each column by a state symbol placed at the bottom; this denotes a certain state for A. We label each row by a state symbol placed at the left; this denotes a certain state for A'. The square which is the intersection of a certain column and row denotes a state of the pair (A, A') [the intersection of the I_2 column and III_1 row denoting the state $(\text{I}_2, \text{III}_1)$, and so on].

We cross out a small square by its diagonals if the corresponding state is impossible by virtue of our theorems, *without requiring X or Y to be complete*. The reader should now examine the state diagram, as it appears on page 237. We shall explain briefly the reasons for the crossing out of those squares which are crossed out. All squares in the I_2 and II_1 rows are crossed out, since A' can never be in these states; this was

THE STATE DIAGRAM

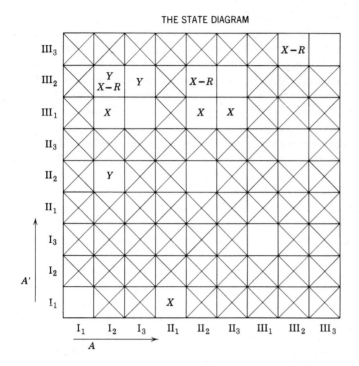

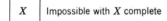

	X	Impossible with X complete
	Y	Impossible with Y complete
	$X-R$	Impossible with X norm reflexive

explained earlier.   Theorem 4.6–E says that, if A is in a I or II state, A' must be in a 1 or 2 state, and vice versa.   Thus any state of the pair with I or II for A and 3 for A' is impossible; also, III for A and 1 or 2 for A' is impossible.   Theorem 4.6–H says that a state of the pair with 3 for A and I or II for A' is impossible.   Theorem 4.7–A says that we have 1 for A if and only if we have I for A'.   This eliminates states with 1 for A and II or III for A' and also those with 2 or 3 for A and I for A'.   All but sixteen of the eighty-one squares are crossed out as a result of the foregoing considerations.   These sixteen remaining states for the pair (A, A') are all possible, if no restrictions are placed on X or Y; this has been shown by the construction of examples (see Taylor and Halberg, **1**). Some of these examples are considered in the problems.   Many implications can now be read from the state diagram.   Samples: The state of A is III_1 if and only if the state of A' is I_3; if the state of A is III_2, the state of A' is either II_3 or III_3.

Next we consider the effect of assuming that X is complete.   Theorem 4.7–C tells us, in this case, that any state except I_1 and I_3 for A is impossible if we have 1 for A'.   Of the sixteen states previously not crossed out, this rules out (I_2, III_1), (II_1, I_1), (II_2, III_1), and (II_3, III_1).   These exclusions are indicated on the state diagram by putting the letter X in the corresponding square.

Now consider the effect of assuming that Y is complete.   Theorem 4.7–B says, in this case, that I for A makes 2 and 3 impossible for A'. This rules out (I_2, II_2), (I_2, III_2), and (I_3, III_2), in addition to some states already crossed out.   These exclusions are indicated by putting a Y in the appropriate square on the state diagram.

With X and Y both assumed to be complete, there are nine states still left as apparently possible for the pair (A, A').   Examples exist which show that these states are actually possible.

If we assume that X is norm reflexive, but make no restrictions on Y, Theorem 4.6–I and problem 1 of § 4.6 tell us that we must have I or II for A' if we have 1 or 2 for A.   Hence, if X is norm reflexive, in addition to the states ruled out because X is complete, this rules out (I_2, III_2), (II_2, III_2) and (III_2, III_3) from the sixteen states which are not crossed out by their diagonals.   These three exclusions are indicated by $X - R$ in the corresponding square on the state diagram.

It is now interesting to observe, on the state diagram, that when X is norm reflexive and Y is complete, there are seven state squares left blank. Also, there is at most one blank square in any one row or column.   Hence, with these conditions on X and Y, the state of either A or A' determines uniquely the state of the other.   These seven states for the pair (A, A') do actually occur; examples can be constructed with $X = Y = l^2$.

PROBLEMS

In the first nine problems are given examples of operators A which provide illustrations of various states for the pair (A, A'). In these examples X and Y are chosen from the spaces $l^p (1 \leqslant p < \infty)$ and (c_0). In each of these spaces we denote the vector $(0, \cdots 0, 1, 0, \cdots)$ (with 1 in the kth place) by u_k. In l^p, with $1 \leqslant p < \infty$, and (c_0) the set $\{u_k\}$ is a countable basis, and in defining A on these spaces it suffices to define Au_k for each k. If X and Y are both spaces in which $\{u_k\}$ is a countable basis, A' is determined by the transpose of the infinite matrix which represents A. In each problem it is left for the reader to show that the state of the pair (A, A') is as indicated.

1. $X = Y = l^2$. $Au_k = 2^{1-k} u_k$. The state is $(\text{II}_2, \text{II}_2)$.

2. $X = l^1$, $Y = l^2$, A as in problem 1. The state is $(\text{II}_2, \text{III}_2)$.

3. $X = Y = l^2$. $Au_1 = 0$, $Au_k = u_k$ if $k \geqslant 2$. The state is $(\text{III}_3, \text{III}_3)$.

4. $X = Y = l^2$. $Au_1 = 0$, $Au_k = u_{k-1}$, $k \geqslant 2$. The state is $(\text{I}_3, \text{III}_1)$.

5. $X = Y = l^2$. $Au_k = u_{k+1}$. The state is $(\text{III}_1, \text{I}_3)$.

6. $X = Y = l^2$. $Au_1 = 0$, $Au_k = \displaystyle\sum_{i=k-1}^{\infty} 2^{1-i} u_i$. The state is $(\text{II}_3, \text{III}_2)$. Note

that $A(u_k - u_{k+1}) = 2^{2-k} u_{k-1}$ if $k \geqslant 2$. Also that $\displaystyle\sum_1^{\infty} 2^{1-k} u_{2k}$ is not in $\mathscr{R}(A)$.

7. $X = Y = l^2$. $Au_k = 2^{1-k} (u_2 + \cdots + u_{k+1})$. The state is $(\text{III}_2, \text{II}_3)$. We can also take $X = Y = (c_0)$ in this case.

8. $X = Y = l^2$. $Au_1 = u_2$, $Au_k = u_{k-1} + u_{k+1}$ if $k \geqslant 2$. The state is $(\text{II}_2, \text{II}_2)$. Note that u_{2k} is in $\mathscr{R}(A)$, but u_{2k-1} is not. But it can be shown that $u_{2k-1} \in \overline{\mathscr{R}(A)}$.

9. $X = Y = (c_0)$. $Au_1 = 2u_1 - u_2$, $Au_k = -u_{k-1} + 2u_k - u_{k+1}$ if $k \geqslant 2$. The state is $(\text{II}_2, \text{II}_2)$.

10. Suppose $A \in [X, Y]$ and $\mathscr{R}(A) = Z \neq Y$. Define $B \in [X, Z]$ by setting $Bx = Ax$ when $x \in X$. Suppose also that Y is complete and $\overline{\mathscr{R}(A)} = Y$. Then we can identify Z' with Y' and B' with A'. The states of A' and B' are the same, but, if the state of A is II_i ($i = 1, 2, 3$), that of B is I_i. In this way we can produce examples of states $(\text{I}_2, \text{II}_2)$, $(\text{I}_2, \text{III}_2)$, and $(\text{I}_3, \text{III}_2)$ from some of the earlier examples.

11. X the subspace of l^2 generated by $\{u_k\}$, $Y = l^2$. A as in problem 4, but with this change in X. The state is $(\text{II}_3, \text{III}_1)$.

12. X the subspace of (c_0) generated by $\{u_k\}$, Y either X or (c_0) itself. $Au_1 = u_1$, $Au_k = -2u_{k-1} + u_k$ if $k \geqslant 2$. The state is $(\text{II}_2, \text{III}_1)$ if $Y = (c_0)$ and $(\text{I}_2, \text{III}_1)$ if $Y = X$.

13. If Y is a complete space and X is a proper but dense subspace of Y, let $Ax = x$ for $x \in X$. Then $A \in [X, Y]$ and the state of the pair is $(\text{II}_1, \text{I}_1)$.

14. X the subspace of l^1 generated by $\{u_k\}$, Y either X or l^1 itself. $Au_1 = \displaystyle\sum_1^{\infty} 2^{-k} u_k$, $Au_k = u_{k-1}$ if $k \geqslant 2$. The state is $(\text{II}_2, \text{III}_1)$ or $(\text{I}_2, \text{III}_1)$ according to whether Y is l^1 or X.

15. Let Y be any Banach space of infinite dimension, and let H be a Hamel basis for Y with all elements h of H such that $\|h\| \leqslant 1$.   If $y \in Y$ and $y = \alpha_1 h_1 + \cdots + \alpha_n h_n$, let $N(y) = \sum_{i=1}^{n} |\alpha_i|$.   Let X be the space with the same elements as Y, but with N as a norm.   Let $Ay = y$, and consider A as an element of $[X, Y]$. The state is (I_2, III_1).

16. If X and Y are linearly homeomorphic and X is norm reflexive, so is Y. Suggestion: Let A be the linear homeomorphism of X onto Y.   Determine the state of A'' by using the state diagram.   Consider the canonical mappings: J_1 of X onto X'' and J_2 of Y into Y''.   Express J_2 in terms of J_1, A'' and A^{-1}.

17. Suppose $A \in [X, X']$.   Assume that $\overline{\mathscr{R}(A)} = \mathscr{R}(A')$. If X is norm reflexive, show that the only possible states are (I_1, I_1), (II_2, II_2), (III_3, III_3).

18. Suppose $A \in [X, X']$, that $A = A'J$, and that X is norm reflexive.   Then, the states of A and A' are the same, and the only possible states of A are I_1, II_2, III_3.

19. Suppose $A \in [X]$.   Let B be a linear homeomorphism of X onto X', and suppose $A = B^{-1}A'B$.   Then, the only possible states for A are I_1, II_2, III_3.

4.8 Projections

Operations of a special type, called *projections*, play an important role in the systematic study of linear operators.   The notion of a projection is closely related to the concept of a *direct sum of linear manifolds*, and it is with this concept that we begin this section.

Let $M_1, \cdots, M_n (n \geqslant 2)$ be linear manifolds in a linear space X.   We say that this set of linear manifolds is linearly independent if no M_i contains a nonzero vector which is in the linear manifold determined by the remaining $n - 1$ linear manifolds.   An equivalent condition is that if $x_i \in M_i$ and $\alpha_1 x_1 + \cdots + \alpha_n x_n = 0$, then $x_k = 0$ if $\alpha_k \neq 0$.   The linear manifold generated by the elements of $M_1 \cup \cdots \cup M_n$ is denoted by $M_1 \oplus \cdots \oplus M_n$ and called the *direct sum* of $M_1, \cdots, M_n$.   Elements x of the direct sum are representable uniquely in the form $x = x_1 + \cdots + x_n$, with $x_i \in M_i$.

Whenever we use the $\oplus$ notation, it is to be understood implicitly that the manifolds in question are linearly independent.

If $X = M_1 \oplus \cdots \oplus M_n$, the representation $x = x_1 + \cdots + x_n$, with $x_i \in M_i$, determines operators $P_1, \cdots, P_n$, defined by $P_i x = x_i$.   These operators are linear, and they satisfy the relations

$$(4.8\text{–}1) \qquad \begin{cases} P_i P_j = 0 \quad \text{if } i \neq j, \quad P_i{}^2 = P_i, \\ \quad I = P_1 + \cdots + P_n. \end{cases}$$

Conversely, if the linear operators $P_1, \cdots, P_n$ are given, with domains X

and ranges $M_1, \cdots, M_n$ in X, and if they satisfy the conditions (4.8–1), it follows that $X = M_1 \oplus \cdots \oplus M_n$.

Definition.   A linear operator P with domain X and range in X is called a *projection* (of X) if $P^2 = P$.   If M is the range of P, then P is called a projection of X onto M.

It is easily seen that, if P is a projection of X, then

$$(4.8–2) \qquad\qquad X = \mathscr{R}(P) \oplus \mathscr{N}(P).$$

The direct sum representation of an element is

$$x = Px + (x - Px).$$

The operator $Q = I - P$ is also a projection; its range is $\mathscr{N}(P)$. Elements x of $\mathscr{R}(P)$ are characterized by the fact that $Px = x$.

When $X = M_1 \oplus M_2$, we say that M_2 is a complement of (or is complementary to) M_1.   Thus, (4.8–2) says that, if P is a projection, $\mathscr{N}(P)$ is complementary to $\mathscr{R}(P)$.   There can be more than one complement of a given linear manifold.

As for the existence of complements of a given linear manifold, we have the following result:

Theorem 4.8–A.   *If M is a linear manifold in the linear space X, there exists a projection P of X whose range is M.*

PROOF.   The cases $M = (0)$ or X are obvious, so we set them aside. Let f be the linear operator with domain and range M, defined by $f(x) = x$. Take $Y = M$ in Theorem 1.71–A.   Then the F of Theorem 1.71–A will serve as P for our present purpose.

Thus far nothing has been said about topology in connection with projections.

Theorem 4.8–B.   *If X is a topological linear space and if P is a projection of X which is closed, the range of P is closed.*

PROOF.   Suppose $y \in \overline{\mathscr{R}(P)}$.   If V is any neighborhood of y, it contains a point of $\mathscr{R}(P)$, say $z = Px$.   Then $Pz = z$, and (z, z) is a point of the graph of P.   But also, $(z, z) \in V \times V$, which is a neighborhood of (y, y) in the product space $X \times X$.   Hence, since V is arbitrary and the graph of P is closed, (y, y) is in the graph.   That is, $Py = y$, and so $y \in \mathscr{R}(P)$. Hence $\mathscr{R}(P)$ is closed.

Theorem 4.8–C.   *Suppose X is a topological linear T_1-space.   Suppose P is a continuous projection of X.   Then $\mathscr{R}(P)$ is closed.*

PROOF. $\mathscr{R}(P)$ is the null space of the continuous operator $I - P$. Since (0) is closed, so is the inverse image $\{x : x - Px = 0\}$.

Theorem 4.8–D.   *Let X be a complete metric linear space.   Let P be a projection of X such that both $\mathscr{R}(P)$ and $\mathscr{N}(P)$ are closed.   Then P is continuous.*

PROOF.   Because of Theorem 4.2–I it suffices to prove that P is closed. Suppose $x_n \to x$ and $Px_n \to y$.   Then $x_n - Px_n \to x - y$.   Since $Px_n \in \mathscr{R}(P)$ and $x_n - Px_n \in \mathscr{N}(P)$, it follows that $y \in \mathscr{R}(P)$ and $x - y \in \mathscr{N}(P)$. Then $Px - Py = 0$, or $Px = Py = y$.   Thus P is closed.

If X is a Banach space and M is a closed subspace of X, there may be no continuous projection of X whose range is M.   In view of (4.8–2) and Theorem 4.8–D, this is the same as saying that there may be no *closed* linear manifold which is complementary to M.   Examples have been given, even in reflexive spaces, by F. J. Murray, **1** and by A. Sobczyk, **1**. It can also occur, even in Hilbert space, that $M_1 \oplus M_2$ is not closed, even though M_1 and M_2 are closed and linearly independent subspaces.   In this case the associated projections of $M_1 \oplus M_2$ onto M_1 and M_2 are not continuous.   For an example, see Stone, **1**, pages 21–22.

For inner-product spaces the notion of direct sum of linear manifolds is of particular importance in connection with the concept of mutually orthogonal linear manifolds.

Definition.   Two linear manifolds M, N in the inner-product space X are said to be orthogonal if $(x, y) = 0$ whenever $x \in M$ and $y \in N$.   A family of linear manifolds is called an orthogonal family if each pair of distinct manifolds from the family are orthogonal.

If $M_1, \cdots, M_n$ is an orthogonal family of linear manifolds, the manifolds are linearly independent.   For, if $\alpha_1 x_1 + \cdots + \alpha_n x_n = 0$, with $x_k \in M_k$, the orthogonality shows that $0 = (\alpha_1 x_1 + \cdots + \alpha_n x_n, x_k) = \alpha_k \|x_k\|^2$, and hence $x_k = 0$ if $\alpha_k \neq 0$.

A direct sum of orthogonal closed linear manifolds in a complete space is closed.   We state this formally.

Theorem 4.8–E.   *If X is a complete inner-product space and if M, N are orthogonal closed linear manifolds, $M \oplus N$ is closed.*

PROOF.   If $x \in M$ and $y \in N$, an easy calculation shows that $\|x + y\|^2 = \|x\|^2 + \|y\|^2$.   Now suppose that $z_n \in M \oplus N$ and that $z_n \to z$.   We can write $z_n = x_n + y_n$, $x_n \in M$, $y_n \in N$.   Then

$$\|z_n - z_m\|^2 = \|x_n - x_m\|^2 + \|y_n - y_m\|^2.$$

Since $\{z_n\}$ is a Cauchy sequence, so are $\{x_n\}$ and $\{y_n\}$.   If $x_n \to x$ and $y_n \to y$, we have $z = x + y$.   But $x \in M$, $y \in N$, since M and N are closed.   Hence $z \in M \oplus N$, and the proof is complete.

PROBLEMS

1. Suppose X is a Banach space, $M_1, \cdots, M_n$ are closed and linearly independent subspaces of X, and $M = M_1 \oplus \cdots \oplus M_n$. Suppose that the projections $P_1, \cdots, P_n$ of M onto $M_1, \cdots, M_n$ respectively, associated with the direct sum, are continuous. Then M is closed.

2. If X is a complete metric linear space, if $M = M_1 \oplus M_2$, where M_1 and M_2 are closed and linearly independent subspaces, and if M is closed, the associated projections of M onto M_1 and M_2 are continuous. This does not generalize for more than two M_i's.

3. If X is a Banach space and M_1, M_2 are closed and linearly independent subspaces of X, then $M_1 \oplus M_2$ is closed if and only if there exists a $d > 0$ such that $\|x_1 - x_2\| \geqslant d$ whenever $x_1 \in M_1$, $x_2 \in M_2$, and $\|x_1\| = \|x_2\| = 1$.

4. Let X be a normed linear space. Let P_1 and P_2 be continuous projections of X such that $I = P_1 + P_2$. Let M_k be the range of P_k, so that $X = M_1 \oplus M_2$. Then P_k' is a continuous projection of X'. The range of P_1' is M_2^0, and the range of P_2' is M_1^0. Finally, $X' = M_1^0 \oplus M_2^0$.

5. If P is a projection on any linear space, show that $(\lambda - P)^{-1} = \lambda^{-1}I + \lambda^{-1}(\lambda - 1)^{-1}P$ if $\lambda(\lambda - 1) \neq 0$.

4.81 Continuous Linear Functionals on a Hilbert Space

We have seen, in Theorem 4.32–A, that every continuous linear functional on l^2 is representable in the form

$$x'(x) = \sum_1^\infty \alpha_n \xi_n, \qquad x = \{\xi_n\} \in l^2,$$

where

$$\|x'\| = \left(\sum_1^\infty |\alpha_n|^2 \right)^{\frac{1}{2}} < \infty.$$

This result can be restated as follows, by defining $y = \{\bar{\alpha}_n\}$ as an element of l^2: to each $x' \in (l^2)'$ corresponds a unique $y \in l^2$ such that $x'(x) = (x, y)$ for each $x \in l^2$. In this form the result is valid for an arbitrary Hilbert space, or, since it is true for finite-dimensional as well as for infinite-dimensional spaces, it is valid for all complete inner-product spaces. To prove this we need two preliminary theorems. In each of the three following theorems it is assumed that X is a complete inner-product space.

Theorem 4.81–A. *Let S be a nonempty closed convex set in X, and suppose $d = \inf_{x \in S} \|x\|$. Then, there exists a unique $x \in S$ such that $\|x\| = d$.*

PROOF. From the way in which the norm is defined in terms of the inner product, it follows that

(4.81–1) $$\|x + y\|^2 + \|x - y\|^2 = 2(\|x\|^2 + \|y\|^2)$$

for all pairs x, y in X. Now suppose that $x_n \in S$ and $\|x_n\| \to d$. Since S is convex, $1/2(x_n + x_m) \in S$, and so

$$\left\| \frac{x_n + x_m}{2} \right\| \geqslant d.$$

From this inequality and (4.81–1) we have

$$\|x_n - x_m\|^2 = 2(\|x_n\|^2 + \|x_m\|^2) - \|x_n + x_m\|^2$$
$$\leqslant 2(\|x_n\|^2 + \|x_m\|^2) - 4d^2,$$

whence, since $\|x_n\|^2 \to d^2$, it appears that $\{x_n\}$ is a Cauchy sequence. If $x_n \to x$, it follows that $x \in S$ and $\|x\| = d$. To see that x is unique, suppose x and y are in S and that $\|x\| = \|y\| = d$. Then, since S is convex,

$$d \leqslant \left\| \frac{x + y}{2} \right\| \leqslant \tfrac{1}{2}\|x\| + \tfrac{1}{2}\|y\| = d.$$

It then follows by (4.81–1) that

$$4d^2 + \|x - y\|^2 = 4d^2.$$

whence $x = y$.

Theorem 4.81–B. *Let H be the closed hyperplane $\{x : y'(x) = 1\}$ where y' is a fixed nonzero element of X'. Then, there is a unique $z \in H$ such that $(x, z) = 0$ whenever $y'(x) = 0$.*

PROOF. H is nonempty, closed, and convex. Hence, by Theorem 4.81–A, there exists $z \in H$ such that $\|z\| = \inf_{x \in H} \|x\|$. Now choose any x such that $x \neq 0$ and $y'(x) = 0$. We wish to prove that $(x, z) = 0$. Define

(4.81–2) $$z_1 = \frac{(z, x)}{\|x\|^2} x, \qquad z_2 = z - z_1.$$

Then $y'(z_1) = 0$, and so $y'(z_2) = y'(z) = 1$ (since $z \in H$). Hence $z_2 \in H$. It follows that $\|z_2\| \geqslant \|z\|$. But, from (4.81–2) it follows that $(z_1, z_2) = 0$ and hence that

(4.81–3) $$\|z\|^2 = (z_1 + z_2, z_1 + z_2) = \|z_1\|^2 + \|z_2\|^2,$$

whence $\|z_2\| \leqslant \|z\|$. Therefore $\|z_2\| = \|z\|$, and consequently, by (4.81–3), $z_1 = 0$. Since $x \neq 0$, this implies $(x, z) = 0$. To see that z is unique, suppose that w also has the properties asserted for z. Then $y'(w - z) = y'(w) - y'(z) = 1 - 1 = 0$, and hence $(w - z, z) = (w - z, w) = 0$. But then $\|w - z\|^2 = 0$, or $w = z$.

We now come to the main representation theorem.

Theorem 4.81–C.   *To each $y' \in X'$ corresponds a unique $y \in X$ such that $y'(x) = (x, y)$ for every x.*

PROOF.   It is clear that there cannot be more than one such y, for if y_1 and y_2 meet the requirement, it follows that $(x, y_1 - y_2) = 0$ for every x, so that, in particular, $\|y_1 - y_2\|^2 = 0$ and $y_1 = y_2$. If $y' = 0$ we can take $y = 0$, so we assume $y' \neq 0$. Choose z as in Theorem 4.81–B. Now, (x, z) is a linear functional of x; hence, by Theorem 3.5–C, there is some scalar α such that $(x, z) = \alpha y'(x)$ for every x. Putting $x = z$, we obtain $\|z\|^2 = \alpha y'(z) = \alpha$. Hence $y'(x) = (x, z)/\|z\|^2$ for every x. We now let $y = z /\|z\|^2$, and the proof is complete.

PROBLEMS

1. If y', y, and z are related as in the proof of Theorem 4.81–C, show that $\|y'\| = \|y\| = 1/\|z\|$. Thus the distance from 0 to the set $\{x : y'(x) = 1\}$ is $1/\|y'\|$.

2. If X is a complete inner-product space, X and X' are congruent. For the complex case use the result at the end of § 3.2.

3. A Hilbert space is norm reflexive.

4. Let M be a closed linear manifold in the complete inner-product space X. If $x \in X$, define Qx as the unique element of $N = x + M$ such that $\|Qx\| = \inf_{y \in N} \|y\|$ (use Theorem 4.81–A). From $\|Qx\|^2 \leqslant \|Qx + \alpha m\|^2$ if $m \in M$, show that Qx is orthogonal to M [choose $\alpha = - (Qx, m)/\|m\|^2$]. Note that $x = (x - Qx) + Qx$ and that $x - Qx \in M$. The element $x - Qx$ is called the *orthogonal projection of x onto M*. Observe that $Qx = 0$ if $x \in M$.

5. Use the result of problem 4 to give an alternative proof of Theorem 4.81–B. Take $M = \{x : y'(x) = 0\}$.

4.82 Orthogonal Complements

In this section X denotes an inner-product space. Completeness is not assumed except as stated explicitly.

Definition.   If S is a nonempty subset of X, the set of all x such that $(x, y) = 0$ if $y \in S$ is called the *orthogonal complement* of S, and is denoted by $S^{\perp}$.

A number of simple facts are at once evident:

$$(0)^{\perp} = X, \quad X^{\perp} = (0),$$
$$S_1 \subset S_2 \text{ implies } S_2^{\perp} \subset S_1^{\perp},$$
$$x \in S \cap S^{\perp} \text{ implies } x = 0.$$

The set $S^\perp$ is a closed linear manifold.   If M is the closed linear manifold generated by S, then $M^\perp = S^\perp$.

We denote $(S^\perp)^\perp$ by $S^{\perp\perp}$.   It is obvious that $S \subset S^{\perp\perp}$.

The main theorem about orthogonal complements is the following:

Theorem 4.82–A. *If X is complete and if M is a closed subspace of X, then $X = M \oplus M^\perp$.*

PROOF.   Choose any $y \in X$.   The inner product (x, y), as x varies over M, defines an element of M'.   Since M can be regarded as a complete inner-product space, Theorem 4.81–C asserts the existence of an element $y_1 \in M$ such that $(x, y) = (x, y_1)$ if $x \in M$.   Let $y_2 = y - y_1$.   Then $y_2 \in M^\perp$, for $(x, y_2) = (x, y) - (x, y_1) = 0$ if $x \in M$.   Writing $y = y_1 + y_2$, we have the proof of the theorem.

If we write $Py = y_1$ in the foregoing notation, P is a projection with range M.   It is called *the orthogonal projection of X onto M*, because of the fact that $x - Px \in M^\perp$.   We note that a different proof of Theorem 4.82–A is indicated in problem 4 of § 4.81.

PROBLEM

Suppose X is a complete inner-product space.   If $y' \in X'$ is represented by $y'(x) = (x, y)$, let $Ey = y'$, so that E is an operator which maps X onto X'. Show that annihilators (as in § 4.6) and orthogonal complements are related as follows: If $S \subset X$, then

$$S^0 = E(S^\perp), \qquad S^\perp = E^{-1}(S^0),$$

and $^0(S^0) = S^{\perp\perp}$.

4.83 Dirichlet's Principle

The subject matter of this section illustrates the usefulness, in potential theory, of the notion of the direct sum of two orthogonal subspaces of an inner-product space.

Let R be a bounded open set with boundary $B(R)$, in Euclidean space of three dimensions.   We suppose, furthermore, that $B(R)$ is smooth enough to enable us to apply the divergence theorem to vector fields which are continuously differentiable in $\bar{R}$.   In particular, then, with adequate continuity and differentiability we have the identity of Green

$$(4.83\text{--}1) \qquad \int_R g\nabla^2 h \, dV + \int_R \nabla g \cdot \nabla h \, dV = \int_{B(R)} g \frac{\partial h}{\partial n} \, dS,$$

where g and h are real-valued functions defined in R, ∇^2 denotes the Laplacian, ∇ the gradient, and n the outward normal to $B(R)$.

We define a real inner-product space $\mathscr{F}$ as follows: The elements f of $\mathscr{F}$ are the real-valued functions which are twice continuously differentiable in $\bar{R}$. The inner product is

$$(4.83\text{--}2) \qquad (f_1, f_2) = \int_{B(R)} f_1 f_2 \, dS + \int_R \nabla f_1 \cdot \nabla f_2 \, dV.$$

The space $\mathscr{F}$ is not complete. Let $\mathscr{G}$ be the subspace of those elements $g \in \mathscr{F}$ which vanish on $B(R)$, and let $\mathscr{H}$ be the subspace of those elements $h \in \mathscr{F}$ which are harmonic (i.e., $\nabla^2 h = 0$) in R. From (4.83–1) and (4.83–2) we see that $(g, h) = 0$ if $g \in \mathscr{G}$ and $h \in \mathscr{H}$; that is, $\mathscr{G}$ and $\mathscr{H}$ are orthogonal.

Now consider any $h \in \mathscr{H}$ and any $f \in \mathscr{F}$ such that $f = h$ on $B(R)$. Let $g = f - h$. Then $g \in \mathscr{G}$. Since $f = g + h$, the orthogonality shows that

$$\|f\|^2 = \|g\|^2 + \|h\|^2,$$

and hence $\|h\| \leqslant \|f\|$. Thus, among all elements of $\mathscr{F}$ which are equal to the given h on $B(R)$, h has the smallest norm. This characterization of h by a minimal property is what is known as *Dirichlet's principle* (though originally the principle was not stated in the language of norms).

In the early work in the calculus of variations, attempts were made to use Dirichlet's principle to prove the existence of a solution of the Dirichlet problem. Let us see how we might attempt to give an existence proof by linear-space methods. Suppose f_0 is a given element of $\mathscr{F}$. Denote by K the set of elements of $\mathscr{F}$ which coincide with f_0 on $B(R)$. This set is precisely the set $f_0 + \mathscr{G}$. Since $\mathscr{G}$ is a closed linear manifold in $\mathscr{F}$, K is a closed-linear variety in $\mathscr{F}$; in particular, K is convex. If f_0 does not vanish identically on $B(R)$, the distance d from 0 to K is positive, and there exists a sequence $\{f_n\}$ in K such that $\|f_n\| \to d$. Just as in the proof of Theorem 4.81–A we see that $\{f_n\}$ is a Cauchy sequence. But, since $\mathscr{F}$ is not complete, we cannot be certain that the sequence has a limit in $\mathscr{F}$. (It is precisely here that this method fails in its attempt to provide an existence proof for the Dirichlet problem.) If a limit h *does* exist in $\mathscr{F}$, then $h \in K$. In this case, the fact that h is the element of K with minimal norm allows us to conclude, by the standard reasoning of the calculus of variations, that h satisfies Laplace's equation, which is the Euler equation for this situation. Thus we can say: If $f_0 \in \mathscr{F}$, the Dirichlet problem for the region R, with the values of f_0 on $B(R)$ as assigned boundary values, is solvable if and only if there is a point of $f_0 + \mathscr{G}$ at minimal distance from 0. This "point" is then the solution of the Dirichlet problem.

It is interesting to observe that, if the Dirichlet problem is solvable, in the sense just described, for each $f \in \mathscr{F}$, we can write

$$\mathscr{F} = \mathscr{G} \oplus \mathscr{H}.$$

Hence, if $f = g + h$, where $g \in \mathscr{G}$ and $h \in \mathscr{H}$, then h is the solution of the Dirichlet problem with boundary values of f. We can describe h as the orthogonal projection of $\mathscr{F}$ on $\mathscr{H}$.

This concept of orthogonal projections in connection with the Dirichlet problem became very well known in the 1930's and was utilized in various ways by research workers in the calculus of variations. It led naturally to various schemes for overcoming the difficulties arising from an incomplete space. One line of development was that in which the space was taken to be complete and the basic Dirichlet problem was modified by generalizing the sense in which a function takes on prescribed values at the boundary of a region. We present a brief exposition of a paper by Weyl (**1**, especially pages 411–414). We now let R be any open set in Euclidean 3-space. We consider vector fields F of class $\mathscr{L}^2$ in R and form a Hilbert space $\mathscr{F}$ with the inner product

$$(F_1, F_2) = \int_R F_1 \cdot F_2 \, dV,$$

by the usual formation of equivalence classes. We shall be interested in several subspaces of $\mathscr{F}$. First we consider the vector-valued functions defined in R, each of which has the value zero outside of some compact subset of R and has continuous first derivatives in R. If G is such a function, its curl $\nabla \times G$ determines an element of $\mathscr{F}$; we denote by $\mathscr{C}$ the closed linear manifold in $\mathscr{F}$ generated by all such $\nabla \times G$. Next we consider real-valued functions defined and continuously differentiable in R, each of which vanishes outside of some compact subset of R. The gradients ∇v of functions v of this kind generate a certain closed linear manifold in $\mathscr{F}$, which we denote by $\mathscr{G}$. The elements of $\mathscr{F}$ which are orthogonal to $\mathscr{C}$ are called *irrotational*; those which are orthogonal to $\mathscr{G}$ are called *solenoidal*. These are extensions of the ordinary meanings of these terms. We write $\mathscr{F}_i$ for the class of irrotational elements and $\mathscr{F}_s$ for the class of solenoidal elements. Note, in particular, that $\mathscr{G} \subset \mathscr{F}_i$ and $\mathscr{C} \subset \mathscr{F}_s$. That is, $(\nabla v, \nabla \times G) = 0$ for any v and G of the sort mentioned above. This would be obvious from the relation

$$\nabla \cdot (G \times \nabla v) = \nabla v \cdot (\nabla \times G) - G \cdot (\nabla \times \nabla v)$$

if v were twice continuously differentiable. With the weaker conditions here placed on v a deeper examination of the situation is required. The discussion given by Weyl attends to this matter.

By Theorem 4.82–A we have $\mathscr{F} = \mathscr{G} \oplus \mathscr{F}_s$, since $\mathscr{F}_s = \mathscr{G}^\perp$. Now consider the elements of $\mathscr{F}_i$ which are orthogonal to $\mathscr{G}$. These are precisely the elements of $\mathscr{F}_i \cap \mathscr{F}_s$. Hence

$$\mathscr{F}_i = \mathscr{G} \oplus (\mathscr{F}_i \cap \mathscr{F}_s).$$

The relation of all this to the Dirichlet problem (as well as to other problems of potential theory) depends on the following fundamental fact, which is proved in the reference already cited: If $F \in \mathscr{F}_i \cap \mathscr{F}_s$, then F has derivatives of all orders in R, and the divergence and curl of F are both identically zero in R. It follows that the components of F are harmonic functions. Also, F is the gradient of a harmonic function; however, the latter function may be multiple valued, owing to the fact that R need not be simply connected. Suppose now that we start with a given scalar function f such that $F = \nabla f$ is in $\mathscr{F}$. Then $F \in \mathscr{F}_i$, and we can write $F = G + H$, where $H = \nabla h$, h being harmonic, $G = \lim_{n\to\infty} \nabla g_n$, and g_n vanishes outside of some compact subset of R. It can be shown that this behavior of g_n implies that, in a generalized sense, $f - h$ is zero at the boundary of R. Thus h is the solution of a generalized Dirichlet problem.

4.9 Adjoint Operators

Throughout this section X and Y will denote arbitrary complete inner-product spaces. We use the same symbol (parentheses) for the inner product in both spaces. If $A \in [X, Y]$, we have defined A' so that $A' \in [Y', X']$. However, because of Theorem 4.81–C, it is possible for us to identify X' with X and Y' with Y. In so doing, we are led to an operator belonging to $[Y, X]$ which it is natural to consider in place of A'. Suppose y_0 is fixed in Y. Let $x'(x) = (Ax, y_0)$. Then $x' \in X'$, and hence (by Theorem 4.81–C) there is a unique $x_0 \in X$ such that $x'(x) = (x, x_0)$. We write $x_0 = A^*y_0$, thus defining an operator A^* on Y into X. The definition of A^* is fully expressed by the equation

(4.9–1) $(Ax, y) = (x, A^*y), \quad x \in X, y \in Y.$

The operator A^* is called the *adjoint* of A.

It is easy to see that A^* is linear. It is also continuous, and

(4.9–2) $\|A^*\| = \|A\|.$

For hints as to the proof of this, see problem 1.

The following formal properties of adjoints are easily verified:

$$(A + B)^* = A^* + B^*, \qquad (\alpha A)^* = \bar{\alpha} A^*, \qquad 0^* = 0.$$

If I is the identity operator on X to itself, $I^* = I$. If A^{-1} exists and belongs to $[Y, X]$, then $(A^*)^{-1}$ exists, belongs to $[X, Y]$, and

(4.9–3) $$(A^*)^{-1} = (A^{-1})^*.$$

If X, Y, Z are all complete inner-product spaces and if $A \in [Y, Z]$ and $B \in [X, Y]$, then $AB \in [X, Z]$ and

(4.9–4) $$(AB)^* = B^* A^*.$$

We write $(A^*)^* = A^{**}$. We often use the relation

(4.9–5) $$A^{**} = A,$$

which follows easily from (4.9–1).

The relations between annihilators, ranges, and null manifolds, as set forth in § 4.6, have counterparts in relations between orthogonal complements, ranges, and null manifolds. The situation is simpler than that of § 4.6, owing to the identification of X' with X. A complete inner-product space is reflexive, and there are no nonsaturated subspaces of X'. We list the following results, leaving verification to the reader.

(4.9–6) $\{\overline{\mathscr{R}(A)}\}^{\perp} = \mathscr{N}(A^*); \qquad \overline{\mathscr{R}(A)} = \mathscr{N}(A^*)^{\perp}.$

(4.9–7) $\{\overline{\mathscr{R}(A^*)}\}^{\perp} = \mathscr{N}(A); \qquad \overline{\mathscr{R}(A^*)} = \mathscr{N}(A)^{\perp}.$

Next we state two simple but useful theorems.

Theorem 4.9–A. $\mathscr{N}(A^*) = \mathscr{N}(AA^*)$, and $\overline{\mathscr{R}(A)} = \overline{\mathscr{R}(AA^*)}$.

PROOF.   Obviously $\mathscr{N}(A^*) \subset \mathscr{N}(AA^*)$. If $AA^*y = 0$, we have $(A^*y, A^*y) = (AA^*y, y) = 0$, and so $A^*y = 0$. Hence $\mathscr{N}(AA^*) \subset \mathscr{N}(A^*)$. The first part of the theorem is now proved. Next, we observe that $(AA^*)^* = A^{**}A^* = AA^*$. Hence, by (4.9–6) and the first part of our theorem, $\overline{\mathscr{R}(AA^*)} = \mathscr{N}(AA^*)^{\perp} = \mathscr{N}(A^*)^{\perp} = \overline{\mathscr{R}(A)}$. This finishes the proof.

Theorem 4.9–B. $\|A^*A\| = \|A\|^2 = \|AA^*\|$.

PROOF. $\|A^*Ax\| \leqslant \|A^*\|\,\|Ax\| \leqslant \|A^*\|\,\|A\|\,\|x\| = \|A\|^2\|x\|$, by (4.9–2). Therefore $\|A^*A\| \leqslant \|A\|^2$. But also, $\|Ax\|^2 = (Ax, Ax) = (x, A^*Ax) \leqslant \|x\|\,\|A^*Ax\| \leqslant \|A^*A\|\,\|x\|^2$, whence $\|A\|^2 \leqslant \|A^*A\|$. Thus $\|A^*A\| = \|A\|^2$.

We apply this result with A^* in place of A, obtaining $\|A^{**}A^*\| = \|AA^*\| = \|A^*\|^2 = \|A\|^2$.   Thus all is proved.

Let us now recall from § 4.71 the terminology about the nine possible *states* of a bounded linear operator.   Since we are now considering A^* instead of A', it is important to know that the state of A^* is always the same as the state of A'.   That this is so follows from the very close relationship between A^* and A'; we leave verification to the reader.   As a consequence, A^* may replace A' in the state diagram in § 4.71.   Since X and Y are reflexive, there are just seven possible states for the pair (A, A^*).

We say that A is *normal* if $AA^* = A^*A$ and *self-adjoint* if $A^* = A$. Clearly a self-adjoint operator is normal, but the converse does not always hold.   For a normal operator the number of possible states is severely limited.

Theorem 4.9–C.   *For a normal operator A the only possible states are* I_1, II_2, *and* III_3.   *The state of A^* is the same as that of A.*

PROOF.   By Theorem 4.9–A, applied to A^*, we have $\overline{\mathscr{R}(A^*)} = \overline{\mathscr{R}(A^*A)}$. Since A is normal, we then have $\overline{\mathscr{R}(A)} = \overline{\mathscr{R}(A^*)}$.   It follows from this that neither of the operators A, A^* can be in a III state unless the other is also.   If we now examine the state diagram (with A^* in place of A'), we see that four of the seven possible states for the pair (A, A^*) are ruled out, leaving only three states for the pair as indicated in the theorem.

The results of this section are used in Chapter 6.

PROBLEMS

1. Put $x = A^*y$ in (4.9–1) to prove $\|A^*\| \leqslant \|A\|$.   Put $y = Ax$ to prove the reverse inequality.

2. Verify (4.9–3), (4.9–4), and (4.9–5).

3. Prove (4.9–6).   Then use (4.9–5) to get (4.9–7).

4. Let E be the operator defined in the problem at the end of § 4.82, and let F be the corresponding operator for Y.   Show that $A^* = E^{-1}A'F$.   Use this to prove that the states of A^* and A' are the same.   Notice that E and F are norm-preserving operators.

5. $\mathscr{R}(A) = Y$ if and only if A^* has a continuous inverse. $\mathscr{R}(A^*) = X$ if and only if A has a continuous inverse.

6. Let X be a Banach space, and suppose $A \in [X]$.   Then, there exists $B \in [X]$ such that $BA = I$ if and only if (a) A has a continuous inverse, and (b) there exists a continuous projection P of X onto $\mathscr{R}(A)$.   If X is a complete inner-product space, (b) is satisfied whenever (a) is.   Give details of the argument, noting that, if P is known, we can take $B = A^{-1}P$ and that, if B is known, we can take $P = AB$.

SUGGESTED READING

Achieser and Glasmann, **1**, Chapters 2, 3, 4.
Banach, **1**, Chapters 3–11.
Cooke, **1**, Chapters 2, 3.
Dunford and Schwartz, **1**, Chapters 2, 4, 5, 6.
Friedman, **1**, Chapter 1.
Halmos, **3**, parts of Chapters 1, 2.
Hellinger and Toeplitz, **1**, Parts I, II.
Hille, **1**, Chapters 2, 3.
Julia, **1**, Chapters 4, 5.
Ljusternik and Sobolew, **1**, Chapters 2, 3.
Loomis, **1**, Chapter 2.
Riesz and Nagy, **1**, parts of Chapters 4, 5.
Stone, **1**, Chapters 2, 3.
Wintner, **1**, Chapter 3.
Zaanen, **1**, Chapters 6, 7, 9, 10.

SPECTRAL ANALYSIS OF LINEAR OPERATORS

5.0 Introduction

In this preliminary section we shall indicate the main trend of the ideas to be developed in this chapter. We consider a normed linear space X and a linear operator T whose domain $\mathscr{D}(T)$ and range $\mathscr{R}(T)$ lie in X. Then we consider the operator $\lambda I - T$, where λ is a scalar parameter and I is the identity operator. For convenience we usually suppress the I and write $\lambda - T$ in place of $\lambda I - T$.

Definition. If λ is such that the range of $\lambda - T$ is dense in X and if $\lambda - T$ has a continuous inverse, we say that λ is in the *resolvent set* of T; this set of values of λ is denoted by $\rho(T)$. All scalar values of λ not in $\rho(T)$ comprise the set called the *spectrum* of T; it is denoted by $\sigma(T)$.

In a broad sense, spectral theory, or spectral analysis, of linear operators is the systematic study of the relations between the operators T, $(\lambda - T)^{-1}$, the sets $\rho(T)$, $\sigma(T)$, and various other operators and linear manifolds which enter the picture naturally.

If X is of finite dimension n and if $\mathscr{D}(T) = X$, we can represent T by an $n \times n$ matrix, say (t_{ij}); then $\lambda - T$ is also represented by a matrix, and $\sigma(T)$ is composed of those scalars λ which are the roots of the equation

253

$$\begin{vmatrix} \lambda - t_{11} & -t_{12} & \cdots & -t_{1n} \\ -t_{21} & \lambda - t_{22} & \cdots & -t_{2n} \\ \cdot & \cdot & & \cdot \\ \cdot & \cdot & & \cdot \\ \cdot & \cdot & & \cdot \\ -t_{n1} & \lambda - t_{n2} & \cdots & \lambda - t_{nn} \end{vmatrix} = 0.$$

The determinant here is a polynomial of degree n in λ. Hence, if the scalars associated with X are complex, then $\sigma(T)$ contains at least one point, and it may contain as many as, but not more than, n distinct points. If the scalar field is the real field, however, it may be that $\sigma(T)$ is empty. In spectral theory we usually deal with complex scalars, for by so doing we get a richer theory in which we can utilize much of the machinery of the classical theory of functions of a complex variable.

For nearly all of the extensive developments of spectral theory we assume that X is complete and that T is closed. In this case, if $\lambda \in \rho(T)$, the fact that $\lambda - T$ has a continuous inverse implies (see Theorem 4.2–E) that $\mathscr{R}(\lambda - T)$ is closed; since it is dense in X, it is all of X. Hence in this case, when $\lambda \in \rho(T)$ the operator $(\lambda - T)^{-1}$ belongs to $[X]$. It turns out that $\rho(T)$ is an open set in the space of scalars and that $(\lambda - T)^{-1}$ is developable as a power series in $\lambda - \lambda_0$ about each point $\lambda_0 \in \rho(T)$. This power series has coefficients in $[X]$, and it converges in the norm topology of the space of operators. Thus we can regard $(\lambda - T)^{-1}$ as an analytic function defined on $\rho(T)$, with values in $[X]$. This function is called the *resolvent* of T. Any point of $\sigma(T)$ which is a point of accumulation of $\rho(T)$ may be regarded as a "singularity" of the resolvent. If the scalar field is complex, the relation between $(\lambda - T)^{-1}$ and the spectrum can be investigated with the aid of contour integrals in the complex plane.

In the finite-dimensional case, for instance, the spectrum consists of one or more isolated points each of which is, in a certain definite sense, a *pole* of $(\lambda - T)^{-1}$. By using the Laurent expansion of $(\lambda - T)^{-1}$ about each pole, we find certain projections, with the aid of which we express X as a direct sum of linearly independent subspaces, say $X = M_1 \oplus \cdots \oplus M_k$. These subspaces are invariant under T; that is, $T(M_i) \subseteq M_i$. Part of the interest of this decomposition of X as a direct sum lies in the fact that, when we restrict attention to T as it operates merely on the subspace M_i, we find that its spectrum consists of a single point. If we choose a suitable basis for M_i, the matrix representation of T takes on an especially simple form. In the general case (X not finite dimensional) matters are usually much more complicated, but the pattern of developments in the finite-dimensional case still indicates a certain direction for investigations.

Spectral theory includes the study of eigenvalue problems.   If λ is a scalar such that $\lambda - T$ has no inverse, this means that there is at least one nonzero vector x such that $Tx = \lambda x$.   In this case λ is called an *eigenvalue* of T, and x is a corresponding *eigenvector*.   The null manifold of $\lambda - T$ is called the *eigenmanifold* corresponding to λ.   An eigenvalue of T is a point in the spectrum of T.   In general, however, $\sigma(T)$ will contain points which are not eigenvalues.

Certain parts of the classical theory of integral equations can be developed within the framework of abstract spectral theory.   A Fredholm-type integral operator, acting in the space $C[a, b]$, has certain special properties which can be described in terms which are meaningful in any Banach space, and it turns out that these properties furnish a basis for a general theory (the theory of compact operators) which includes important parts of the theory of Fredholm integral equations of the second kind.

There are certain special features of great interest in the spectral analysis of linear operators in inner-product spaces; this is especially so for Hilbert spaces.   The most highly developed spectral theory is that for self-adjoint operators, which are in a certain sense like operators T in $l^2(n)$ which are represented by matrices (t_{ij}) with Hermitian symmetry: $t_{ji} = \bar{t}_{ij}$.   For the finite-dimensional case of the space $l^2(n)$ the dominant fact about such operators is that there is a certain orthonormal basis for the space such that the matrix representation of the operator takes the form

$$\left\|\begin{array}{ccccc} \lambda_1 & 0 & \cdots & & 0 \\ & & & & \cdot \\ 0 & \lambda_2 & & & \cdot \\ \cdot & & \cdot & & \cdot \\ \cdot & & & \cdot & 0 \\ \cdot & & & & \cdot \\ 0 & \cdot & \cdot & 0 & \lambda_n \end{array}\right\|,$$

where $\lambda_1, \cdots, \lambda_n$ are the points (not necessarily all distinct) forming the spectrum of the operator.   The basis vectors in this case are eigenvectors, and $l^2(n)$ is the direct sum of eigenmanifolds corresponding to distinct eigenvalues.   The appropriate generalization of these things for operators in Hilbert space is taken up in Chapter 6.

The main theorems on the spectrum and the resolvent of a linear operator are 5.1–B, 5.1–C, 5.2–A, 5.2–B and 5.2–E.   The principal theorems in the spectral theory of compact operators are 5.5–F, 5.5–G, 5.5–H, and 5.5–I.   Section 5.5 concludes with a summary of applications of the theory of compact operators to the study of integral equations of the second kind.   In the latter part of the chapter, where the spectral analysis is carried on by means of the operational calculus founded on contour integrals, the principal theorems are 5.6–A, 5.7–A, 5.71–A, 5.8–A, and 5.8–B.

5.1 The Resolvent Operator

Once and for all we assume, in this chapter, that X is a normed linear space which contains some nonzero elements. The scalar field may be either real or complex, except as explicitly stated otherwise.

If T is a linear operator with domain and range in X, we adopt the following notations as a convenience in stating some of the next few theorems:

$$T_\lambda = \lambda - T, \qquad \mathscr{R}_\lambda = \text{range of } T_\lambda,$$

$M(\lambda) = $ norm of T_λ^{-1} as an operator on $\mathscr{R}_\lambda$ if T_λ^{-1} exists and is continuous. Our first fundamental results are as follows:

Theorem 5.1–A. *Suppose μ is such that $\mu - T$ has a continuous inverse. Then $\lambda - T$ has a continuous inverse if $|\lambda - \mu|M(\mu) < 1$. Moreover, $\overline{\mathscr{R}_\lambda}$ is not a proper subset of $\overline{\mathscr{R}_\mu}$.*

PROOF. Suppose $x \in \mathscr{D}(T)$. Then $T_\lambda x = \lambda x - Tx = (\lambda - \mu)x + T_\mu x$, and so

$$\|T_\lambda x\| \geqslant \|T_\mu x\| - |\lambda - \mu| \|x\|.$$

Now $\|x\| = \|T_\mu^{-1} T_\mu x\| \leqslant M(\mu)\|T_\mu x\|$. Therefore

$$M(\mu)\|T_\lambda x\| \geqslant M(\mu)\|T_\mu x\| - |\lambda - \mu|M(\mu)\|x\|$$
$$\geqslant \{1 - |\lambda - \mu|M(\mu)\}\|x\|.$$

Because of the inequality assumed in the theorem, this last inequality shows that $x = 0$ if $T_\lambda x = 0$; hence T_λ^{-1} exists. If we write $y = T_\lambda x$, or $x = T_\lambda^{-1}y$, we see that

$$(5.1–1) \qquad \|T_\lambda^{-1}y\| \leqslant \frac{M(\mu)\|y\|}{1 - |\lambda - \mu|M(\mu)}.$$

This shows that T_λ^{-1} is continuous. To prove that $\overline{\mathscr{R}_\lambda}$ is not a proper subset of $\overline{\mathscr{R}_\mu}$, assume the contrary. If θ is chosen so that $|\lambda - \mu|M(\mu) < \theta < 1$, there must exist an element $y_0 \in \overline{\mathscr{R}_\mu}$ such that $\|y_0\| = 1$ and $\|y - y_0\| \geqslant \theta$ if $y \in \overline{\mathscr{R}_\lambda}$ (by Theorem 3.12–E). Now choose $y_n \in \mathscr{R}_\mu$ so that $y_n \to y_0$. Let $x_n = T_\mu^{-1}y_n$, $y_n = T_\mu x_n$. Then $T_\lambda x_n = (\lambda - \mu)x_n + T_\mu x_n$, whence

$$\|T_\lambda x_n - T_\mu x_n\| = |\lambda - \mu| \|x_n\| \leqslant |\lambda - \mu|M(\mu)\|y_n\|.$$

But $T_\lambda x_n \in \mathcal{R}_\lambda$, and so

$$\theta \leqslant \|y_0 - T_\lambda x_n\| \leqslant \|y_0 - T_\mu x_n\| + \|T_\mu x_n - T_\lambda x_n\|,$$

or

$$\theta \leqslant \|y_0 - y_n\| + |\lambda - \mu| M(\mu) \|y_n\|.$$

If we now let $n \to \infty$ we obtain the contradiction $\theta \leqslant |\lambda - \mu| M(\mu)$. This finishes the proof.

Theorem 5.1–B.   *The resolvent set $\rho(T)$ is open, and hence the spectrum $\sigma(T)$ is closed.*

PROOF.   If $\mu \in \rho(T)$, T_μ^{-1} exists and is continuous, and $\overline{\mathcal{R}_\mu} = X$. Theorem 5.1–A shows that, if λ is sufficiently near μ, then T_λ^{-1} also exists and is continuous, and $\overline{\mathcal{R}_\lambda}$ is not a proper subset of X.   Hence $\overline{\mathcal{R}_\lambda} = X$. Then $\lambda \in \rho(T)$.

It was noted in § 5.0 that, if X is complete and T is closed, the range of $\lambda - T$ is all of X when $\lambda \in \rho(T)$.   For certain results about the inverse operator T_λ^{-1} we shall assume directly that $\mathcal{R}_\lambda = X$ when $\lambda \in \rho(T)$, since this is the essential condition for obtaining these results.   When $\lambda \in \rho(T)$, we shall regularly denote T_λ^{-1} by R_λ; as stated in § 5.0, R_λ is called the *resolvent operator* (of T).   The following theorem is of fundamental importance.

Theorem 5.1–C.   *Suppose T is such that $\mathcal{R}_\lambda = X$ if $\lambda \in \rho(T)$.   Then, if λ and μ are any two points in $\rho(T)$, R_λ and R_μ satisfy the relations*

$$(5.1-2) \qquad\qquad R_\lambda - R_\mu = (\mu - \lambda) R_\lambda R_\mu,$$

$$(5.1-3) \qquad\qquad R_\lambda R_\mu = R_\mu R_\lambda.$$

If $\mu \in \rho(T)$ and $|\mu - \lambda| \, \|R_\mu\| < 1$, then $\lambda \in \rho(T)$ and

$$(5.1-4) \qquad\qquad R_\lambda = \sum_0^\infty (\mu - \lambda)^n R_\mu^{n+1},$$

the series converging according to the metric in $[X]$.   As a function on $\rho(T)$ to $[X]$, R_λ has derivatives of all orders, with

$$(5.1-5) \qquad\qquad \frac{d^n}{d\lambda^n} R_\lambda = (-1)^n n! R_\lambda^{n+1}.$$

PROOF.   To prove (5.1–2), suppose $y \in X$ and $x = R_\mu y$, so that $y = T_\mu x$. Then, since

$$T_\mu x - T_\lambda x = \mu x - Tx - (\lambda x - Tx) = (\mu - \lambda) x,$$

we have

$$y - T_\lambda R_\mu y = (\mu - \lambda) R_\mu y.$$

Hence, applying R_λ to both sides, we obtain

$$R_\lambda y - R_\mu y = (\mu - \lambda)R_\lambda R_\mu y.$$

This proves (5.1–2). By symmetry the result holds with λ and μ exchanged; from this we conclude that (5.1–3) holds.

We know from Theorem 5.1–A that $\mu \in \rho(T)$ and $|\lambda - \mu|\,\|R_\mu\| < 1$ imply $\lambda \in \rho(T)$. To prove (5.1–4) with this condition on λ and μ we use (5.1–2), (5.1–3), and induction to prove that

$$R_\lambda = \sum_{k=0}^{n} (\mu - \lambda)^k R_\mu^{k+1} + (\mu - \lambda)^{n+1} R_\mu^{n+1} R_\lambda$$

if $n \geqslant 0$. Thus (5.1–4) is equivalent to

(5.1–6) $$\lim_{n \to \infty} |\mu - \lambda|^{n+1} \|R_\mu^{n+1} R_\lambda\| = 0.$$

Since $\|R_\mu^{n+1} R_\lambda\| \leqslant \|R_\mu\|^{n+1} \|R_\lambda\|$, and $|\mu - \lambda|\,\|R_\mu\| < 1$, we see that (5.1–6) is true.

To prove (5.1–5) when $n = 1$, perhaps the easiest method is to start with (5.1–2) and show that

$$\|(R_\lambda - R_\mu)/(\lambda - \mu) + R_\mu^2\| = \|(\lambda - \mu)R_\lambda R_\mu^2\| \leqslant |\lambda - \mu|\,\|R_\lambda\|\,\|R_\mu^2\|.$$

Then, from (5.1–1) we see that when $|\lambda - \mu|$ is sufficiently small

$$\|R_\lambda\| \leqslant \|R_\mu\|(1 - |\lambda - \mu|\,\|R_\mu\|)^{-1}.$$

Hence $(R_\lambda - R_\mu)/(\lambda - \mu) \to -R_\mu^2$ as $\lambda \to \mu$. For higher values of n, (5.1–5) may be proved by induction. See problem 2.

If $\lambda - T$ has a continuous inverse, λ need not be in $\rho(T)$, for the range of $\lambda - T$ may not be dense in X (for an example see problem 4). The following theorem tells us that, if T is closed and X is complete, such a value of λ must be at a positive distance from $\rho(T)$.

Theorem 5.1–D. *Suppose that X is complete and that T is closed. Suppose $\mu - T$ has a continuous inverse and that $\mu \in \overline{\rho(T)}$. Then $\mu \in \rho(T)$.*

PROOF. Choose $\lambda_n \in \rho(T)$ so that $\lambda_n \to \mu$. For convenience let A_n denote R_λ when $\lambda = \lambda_n$. We know that $\mathscr{R}_\lambda = X$ when $\lambda \in \rho(T)$. Hence, by (5.1–2),

$$\|A_n - A_m\| \leqslant |\lambda_n - \lambda_m|\,\|A_n\|\,\|A_m\|.$$

It follows from (5.1–1) that $\|A_n\|$ is bounded as $n \to \infty$. Hence, since

$[X]$ is complete, we see that there exists some $A \in [X]$ such that $\|A_n - A\| \to 0$.   If $\lambda \in \rho(T)$ we have

$$A_n - R_\lambda = (\lambda - \lambda_n)R_\lambda A_n,$$

and so

(5.1–7) $$A = R_\lambda + (\lambda - \mu)R_\lambda A.$$

This shows that the range of A lies in the range of R_λ, which is $\mathcal{D}(T)$. We shall show that $T_\mu Ay = y$ if $y \in X$, thus proving that the range of T_μ is all of X, whence $\mu \in \rho(T)$.   Now, if $\lambda \in \rho(T)$,

(5.1–8) $$T_\mu Ay = (\mu - \lambda)Ay + T_\lambda Ay.$$

By (5.1–7) we have $T_\lambda Ay = y + (\lambda - \mu)Ay$.   When this is substituted in (5.1–8) we obtain $T_\mu Ay = y$, and the proof is finished.

PROBLEMS

1. Prove that $M(\lambda)$ is continuous on the open set of values of λ for which $\lambda - T$ has a continuous inverse.   Hint: use (5.1–1) and show that, if λ and μ are in the open set referred to and $|\lambda - \mu|$ is sufficiently small, then

$$\frac{M(\mu)}{1 + |\lambda - \mu|M(\mu)} \leqslant M(\lambda) \leqslant \frac{M(\mu)}{1 - |\lambda - \mu|M(\mu)}.$$

2. To complete the proof of (5.1–5) by induction it suffices to prove that $(d/d\lambda)R_\lambda{}^n = -nR_\lambda^{n+1}$.   Do this (at $\lambda = \mu$) by factoring $R_\lambda{}^n - R_\mu{}^n$.

3. Suppose that, for each λ in a nonempty set S of scalars, A_λ is a linear operator on X into X such that $A_\lambda - A_\mu = (\mu - \lambda)A_\lambda A_\mu$ if $\lambda, \mu \in S$.   Suppose also that $A_\lambda{}^{-1}$ exists for at least one $\lambda \in S$.   Show that $A_\lambda{}^{-1}$ exists for every $\lambda \in S$, that all the operators A_λ have the same range $\mathcal{D}$, and that there exists a linear operator T on $\mathcal{D}$ into X such that $\lambda - T = A_\lambda{}^{-1}$ for each $\lambda \in S$.   Show further that, if A_λ is closed for at least one λ, then T is closed and A_λ is closed for every $\lambda \in S$.

4. Consider the operator $T \in [l^1]$ defined by $y = Tx$, where $y = \{\eta_k\}$, $x = \{\xi_k\}$, $\eta_1 = 0$, and $\eta_k = -\xi_{k-1}$ if $k \geqslant 2$.   Show that $(\lambda - T)^{-1}$ exists for all λ, that $\rho(T)$ consists of all λ for which $|\lambda| > 1$, and that $\|R_\lambda\| = (|\lambda| - 1)^{-1}$. Use problem 5, § 4.51.   If $|\lambda| \leqslant 1$ the range of $\lambda - T$ is not dense in l^1.   The inverse is continuous if $|\lambda| < 1$, but not if $|\lambda| = 1$.

5. Let $\hat{X}$ be the completion of X (X itself if X is complete).   Assume $\rho(T)$ not empty, and for each $\lambda \in \rho(T)$ let A_λ be the unique extension of $T_\lambda{}^{-1}$ to all of $\hat{X}$.   Show that $A_\lambda - A_\mu = (\mu - \lambda)A_\lambda A_\mu$ if λ and μ are in $\rho(T)$.   We shall say here that T has a closed linear extension if there exists a closed linear operator T_1, with domain and range in $\hat{X}$, which is an extension of T.   Show that such a closed linear extension exists if and only if A_λ has an inverse for some $\lambda \in \rho(T)$ (and hence for *all* such λ, by problem 3).   The next problem shows that T can fail to have a closed linear extension.

6. Take $X = l^1$. Let $\mathscr{D}(T)$ be the set of $x = \{\xi_n\}$ such that $\xi_n = 0$ except for a finite number of indices. Define $Tx = y$ by $\eta_k = k^{-2} \sum_{i=k}^{\infty} i^2 \xi_i$. Then T defines a one-to-one mapping of $\mathscr{D}(T)$ onto itself; T^{-1} is continuous and T is discontinuous. The extension A of T^{-1} to all of X is defined by $Ay = x$, where $k^2\xi_k = k^2\eta_k - (k + 1)^2\eta_{k+1}$. But A has no inverse. Hence T has no closed linear extension (see problem 5).

7. Let T be a linear operator with domain and range in X (not necessarily complete). Let G be the graph of T and $\bar{G}$ the closure of G (in the product space $X \times X$). If there is some closed linear operator T_0 with domain and range in X, such that T_0 is an extension of T, then $\bar{G}$ is the graph of a uniquely defined "minimal" closed extension of T, which we denote by $\bar{T}$; $\mathscr{D}(T)$ and $\mathscr{R}(T)$ are dense in $\mathscr{D}(\bar{T})$ and $\mathscr{R}(\bar{T})$, respectively. If X is complete and T is continuous on $\mathscr{D}(T)$, $\bar{G}$ is the graph of an operator $\bar{T}$ which is continuous, with $\mathscr{D}(\bar{T}) = \overline{\mathscr{D}(T)}$.

8. If X is complete and if T has a closed linear extension, the operator $\bar{T}$ (see problem 7) has the same resolvent set and spectrum as T.

5.2 The Spectrum of a Bounded Linear Operator

In all of the theorems of this section we assume that $T \in [X]$. The main results are concerned with the finding of the smallest constant r such that $|\lambda| \leqslant r$ if $\lambda \in \sigma(T)$, and with the expression of $(\lambda - T)^{-1}$ in terms of λ and T when $|\lambda| > r$.

Theorem 5.2–A. *If $T \in [X]$ and $|\lambda| > \|T\|$, $(\lambda - T)^{-1}$ exists and is continuous, and*

$$5.2–1) \qquad (\lambda - T)^{-1}y = \sum_{1}^{\infty} \lambda^{-n}T^{n-1}y$$

for each y in the range of $\lambda - T$. If X is complete, $|\lambda| > \|T\|$ implies $\lambda \in \rho(T)$, and then

$$(5.2–2) \qquad (\lambda - T)^{-1} = R_\lambda = \sum_{1}^{\infty} \lambda^{-n}T^{n-1},$$

the series converging in the space $[X]$.

PROOF. If $|\lambda| > \|T\|$, we have

$$\|\lambda x - Tx\| \geqslant |\lambda| \|x\| - \|Tx\| \geqslant (|\lambda| - \|T\|) \|x\|.$$

The existence and continuity of $(\lambda - T)^{-1}$ now follows by Theorem 3.1–B. If $y = (\lambda - T)x$, we find by induction that

$$x = \lambda^{-1}y + \cdots + \lambda^{-n}T^{n-1}y + \lambda^{-n}T^n x.$$

Formula (5.2–1) follows from this, because $\lambda^{-n}T^n x \to 0$ when $|\lambda| > \|T\|$. The assertion about (5.2–2), when X is complete, follows by taking $A = \lambda^{-1}T$ in Theorem 4.1–C.

We see from Theorem 5.2–A that, when X is complete, $\lambda \in \sigma(T)$ implies $|\lambda| \leqslant \|T\|$. Since $\sigma(T)$ is closed, this shows that $\sigma(T)$ is compact when $T \in [X]$ and X is complete. If we are given some compact set, there is some bounded linear operator having this compact set as its spectrum. See problem 1.

Before going further we note this useful fact: *If $T \in [X]$ and if the series $\displaystyle\sum_1^\infty \lambda^{-n}T^{n-1}$ converges in $[X]$ for some value of λ, then $\lambda \in \rho(T)$ and the operator defined by the series is R_λ.* For, denoting the series by A, it is easily seen that $(\lambda - T)A = A(\lambda - T) = I$.

For the remainder of this section we need to assume that X is a complex Banach space. The reasons for this are not superficial. We need the theory of analytic functions of a complex variable, with values in $[X]$. We cannot relate the convergence of the series (5.2–2) to the extent of the set $\rho(T)$ unless we think of λ as a complex variable, for somewhat the same reason that the radius of convergence of the power series expansion of a real analytic function cannot be discovered merely by looking for singularities of the function on the real axis.

In §§ 4.4 and 4.42 we commented on the concept of an analytic function of a complex variable with values in a complex Banach space. We must now make some use of the theory of such functions. A great deal of the standard classical theory can be taken over intact, proofs and all. Cauchy's integral theorem, the integral formulas for a function and its derivatives, Taylor's theorem, Laurent's theorem, Liouville's theorem, and many other theorems retain their validity. The proofs are just as in classical theory, except that norms replace absolute values. Some further discussion of these matters is indicated in the problems. For our immediate purposes we need the theorems of Liouville and Laurent.

The key fact is that, when T is closed and X is a complex Banach space, R_λ depends analytically on λ as λ varies in $\rho(T)$. This is true by Theorem 5.1–C.

Theorem 5.2–B. *If $T \in [X]$ and X is a complex Banach space, $\sigma(T)$ is not empty.*

PROOF. It appears from the proof of Theorem 5.2–A that $\|R_\lambda\| \leqslant (|\lambda| - \|T\|)^{-1}$ if $|\lambda| > \|T\|$. Hence $\|R_\lambda\| \to 0$ as $|\lambda| \to \infty$. If $\sigma(T)$ were empty, it would follow that R_λ is analytic and bounded on the whole plane. But then it would be constant, by Liouville's theorem, and the constant would be the zero operator. This is impossible, by the fact that R_λ sets up a one-to-one mapping of X onto itself, for X is assumed to have some nonzero elements (see the beginning of § 5.1).

Theorem 5.2–B remains valid even if X is not complete, as may be shown by an argument involving the completion $\hat{X}$ and an extension of the operator. See problem 2.

Definition.   Supposing $\sigma(T)$ nonempty and bounded, we define

$$(5.2–3) \qquad\qquad r_\sigma(T) = \sup_{\lambda \in \sigma(T)} |\lambda|,$$

and call $r_\sigma(T)$ the *spectral radius* of T.

Theorem 5.2–C.   *If $T \in [X]$ and X is a complex Banach space, the resolvent is given by*

$$(5.2–4) \qquad\qquad R_\lambda = \sum_{1}^{\infty} \lambda^{-n} T^{n-1}$$

if $|\lambda| > r_\sigma(T)$.   This series also represents R_λ if the series converges and $|\lambda| = r_\sigma(T)$.   The series diverges if $|\lambda| < r_\sigma(T)$.

PROOF.   We know that R_λ is analytic when $|\lambda| > r_\sigma(T)$. Hence it has a unique Laurent expansion in positive and negative powers of λ, convergent when $|\lambda| > r_\sigma(T)$. Now, we already know that (5.2–4) is valid when $|\lambda| > \|T\|$. By the uniqueness, then, this must be the Laurent expansion (it may also be called the Taylor expansion about the point $\lambda = \infty$). The second assertion in the theorem follows from the italicized statement in the second paragraph after the proof of Theorem 5.2–A. For the same reason, the series (5.2–4) cannot converge if $\lambda \in \sigma(T)$. Hence it cannot converge at λ_0 if $|\lambda_0| < r_\sigma(T)$, because, if it did, it would follow, as in the general theory of power series, that the series converges when $|\lambda| > |\lambda_0|$, and so, in particular, for some $\lambda \in \sigma(T)$.

Theorem 5.2–C enables us to write a formula for the spectral radius of T. If we consider the series (5.2–4) as a power series in λ^{-1}, the standard formula for the radius of convergence of a power series tells us that

$$(5.2–5) \qquad\qquad r_\sigma(T) = \limsup_{n \to \infty} \|T^n\|^{1/n}.$$

Actually, as we shall presently prove, $\{\|T^n\|^{1/n}\}$ is a convergent sequence, so that the limit superior in (5.2–5) is a limit. To prove this, we first prove what is called the *spectral-mapping theorem* for polynomials. Suppose

$$F(\lambda) = \alpha_n \lambda^n + \alpha_{n-1} \lambda^{n-1} + \cdots + \alpha_n$$

is a polynomial with complex coefficients. If $T \in [X]$, positive integral powers of T have a clear meaning, and we define

$$F(T) = \alpha_n T^n + \alpha_{n-1} T^{n-1} + \cdots + \alpha_n I.$$

By the rules of algebra for operators it is clear that, if the polynomial $F(\lambda)$ is factored, there is a corresponding factored form of $F(T)$.

Now $F(T) \in [X]$, and we can consider its spectrum.

Theorem 5.2–D. *Suppose $T \in [X]$, where X is a complex Banach space. If F is a polynomial, the spectrum of $F(T)$ consists precisely of those points μ such that $F(\lambda) = \mu$ for some $\lambda \in \sigma(T)$. In symbolic form, $\sigma\{F(T)\} = F\{\sigma(T)\}$.*

PROOF. We can assume that $n \geqslant 1$ and $\alpha_n = 1$, leaving the case $n = 0$ to the reader. For a fixed μ let the zeros of $F(\lambda) - \mu$ be $\beta_1, \cdots, \beta_n$, so that

$$(5.2\text{–}6) \qquad F(T) - \mu I = (T - \beta_1) \cdots (T - \beta_n).$$

If $T - \beta_1, \cdots, T - \beta_n$ each have continuous inverses defined on all of X, so does $F(T) - \mu I$, the inverse of the latter being the product of the inverses of the former in the reverse order. Hence, if $\mu \in \sigma\{F(T)\}$, there must be some β_k such that $\beta_k \in \sigma(T)$. Since $F(\beta_k) = \mu$, this shows that $\sigma\{F(T)\} \subset F\{\sigma(T)\}$. Suppose, on the other hand, that some β_k, say β_1, is in $\sigma(T)$. If $T - \beta_1$ has an inverse, the range of $T - \beta_1$ is not all of X, and (5.2–6) shows that the range of $F(T) - \mu I$ is likewise not all of X; hence $\mu \in \sigma\{F(T)\}$. If $T - \beta_1$ has no inverse, we see by exchanging the positions of the factors $T - \beta_1$ and $T - \beta_n$ in (5.2–6) that $F(T) - \mu I$ also has no inverse, and again $\mu \in \sigma\{F(T)\}$. This argument works just as well for any β_k as for β_1, and so the proof is complete.

Theorem 5.2–E. *Suppose $T \in [X]$, where X is a complex Banach space. Then $r_\sigma(T) \leqslant \|T^n\|^{1/n}$ for every positive integer n. Also, $\|T^n\|^{1/n}$ converges to $r_\sigma(T)$ as $n \to \infty$.*

PROOF. Theorem 5.2–D shows that $\sigma(T^n)$ consists of the nth powers of points of $\sigma(T)$. Hence $r_\sigma(T^n) = [r_\sigma(T)]^n$. We know (Theorem 5.2–A) that $r_\sigma(T^n) \leqslant \|T^n\|$. Hence $r_\sigma(T) \leqslant \|T^n\|^{1/n}$. It follows that

$$r_\sigma(T) \leqslant \liminf_{n \to \infty} \|T^n\|^{1/n}.$$

This, together with (5.2–5), leads to the final conclusion of the theorem.

PROBLEMS

1. Let S be a compact set in the plane. Let $\{\alpha_n\}$ be a sequence of points of S everywhere dense in S. Define $T \in [l^2]$ by $Tx = y$, where $x = \{\xi_n\}$,

$y = \{\alpha_n \xi_n\}$. Then $S = \sigma(T)$. Each α_n is an eigenvalue; for the other points $\lambda \in S$, the range of $\lambda - T$ is dense in l^2 and the inverse is discontinuous.

2. To prove Theorem 5.2-B when X is incomplete, let $\hat{T}$ be the unique linear extension of T to all of the completion $\hat{X}$. Prove that $\rho(T) \subset \rho(\hat{T})$, and hence $\sigma(\hat{T}) \subset \sigma(T)$, in two steps: (a) if $\lambda \in \rho(T)$, $\lambda - \hat{T}$ has an inverse; (b) the range of $\lambda - \hat{T}$ is all of $\hat{X}$, and hence the inverse is continuous.

3. Instead of proving theorems about Banach-space-valued analytic functions by repeating the classical proofs, it is sometimes possible to make use of linear functionals. For instance, to prove Liouville's theorem, assume that f, with values in X, is differentiable at all points of the complex plane and bounded. Then $x'[f(\lambda)]$ is a scalar-valued function with the same properties, for each $x' \in X'$ and is therefore constant. Thus $x'[f(\lambda) - f(0)] = 0$ for each x' and each λ. But then $f(\lambda) \equiv f(0)$. Cauchy's theorem may be proved in a similar way, by noting that $x'\left\{\int_C f(\lambda)\, d\lambda\right\} = \int_C x'[f(\lambda)]\, d\lambda$.

4. If $X = C[a, b]$ and T is a Volterra-type integral operator (see § 4.11), $\sigma(T)$ is the single point $\lambda = 0$.

5. If T does not belong to $[X]$, $\sigma(T)$ may not be compact. Example 3, § 1.5 illustrates a situation in which the spectrum of a certain differential operator consists of the points $-n^2$, $n = 0, 1, 2, \cdots$. Example 4, § 1.5 shows a differential operator whose spectrum is composed of all λ whose real part is $\leqslant 0$.

6. Suppose A, B, $C \in [X]$, $\lambda \neq 0$, and $C(\lambda - BA) = (\lambda - BA)C = I$. Let $D = \lambda^{-1} + \lambda^{-1}ACB$. Then $D(\lambda - AB) = (\lambda - AB)D = I$. Thus, when X is complete, the nonzero points of $\rho(AB)$ and $\rho(BA)$ are the same. Hence AB and BA have the same spectral radius.

7. If X is a complex Banach space and $AB = BA$, where A and B are in $[X]$, then $r_\sigma(AB) \leqslant r_\sigma(A)r_\sigma(B)$.

8. Suppose $A \in [X]$, $A^n \neq 0$ for all n, and let $\|A^n\|^{1/n}$ be monotonic in n. Show that $\|A^{n+1}\|/\|A^n\| \leqslant \|A^n\|^{1/n}$, whence it can be inferred that $\overline{\lim} (\|A^{n+1}\|/\|A^n\|) = \lim \|A^n\|^{1/n}$. For a case in which $\|A^n\|^{1/n}$ is not monotone, let $A \in [l^1]$ be defined by $Ax = y$, where $\eta_1 = 0$, $\eta_{2k} = \xi_{2k-1}$, $\eta_{2k+1} = 2\xi_{2k}$, $k = 1, 2, \cdots$.

5.3 Subdivisions of the Spectrum

We can classify the various values of the parameter λ according to the state of the operator $\lambda - T$, using the definitions of "states" as made in § 4.71. We say that λ is in one of the classes I_1, I_2, $\cdots$, III_2, III_3 if $\lambda - T$ is in the corresponding state, as an operator on $\mathscr{D}(T)$ into X. For this classification we do not insist that T be continuous or even closed. According to the definitions, $\lambda \in \rho(T)$ if and only if λ is in class I_1 or II_1. It has been customary to group the remaining classes as follows, thus dividing the spectrum into three mutually exclusive parts:

Classes I_2 and II_2 = the continuous spectrum, denoted by $C\sigma(T)$;
Classes III_1 and III_2 = the residual spectrum, denoted by $R\sigma(T)$;

Classes I_3, II_3, and III_3 = the point spectrum (eigenvalues), denoted by $P\sigma(T)$.

When $T \in [X]$, the operator T' is defined, and $(\lambda - T)' = \lambda - T'$. The results of § 4.71, and the state diagram in particular, can be applied to show exactly how the classification of λ in relation to T affects its classification in relation to T', and vice versa. We note the following result:

Theorem 5.3–A.   *If $T \in [X]$, then T and T' have the same resolvent set and the same spectrum.*

For illustrative purposes we shall discuss two operators, each of which may be considered as a bounded operator on l^p into l^p for any selected value of p, $1 \leqslant p \leqslant \infty$. We shall analyze the spectrum of each operator and see how the resulting classification of each spectral value λ depends on the value of p. Some of the details are left for the problems. We always write $x = \{\xi_n\}$, $y = \{\eta_n\}$, $n = 1, 2, \cdots$.

Example 1.   Let T on l^p into l^p be defined by the infinite matrix

$$\begin{Vmatrix} 0 & 1 & 0 & 0 & 0 & \cdots \\ 0 & 0 & 1 & 0 & 0 \\ 0 & 0 & 0 & 1 & 0 \\ & & & & \cdot \\ & \cdots & & & & \cdot \end{Vmatrix}$$

so that $(\lambda - T)x = y$ means $\eta_k = \lambda\xi_k - \xi_{k+1}$, $k = 1, 2, \cdots$. It is easy to see that $\|T\| = 1$ for each value of p. Hence $|\lambda| > 1$ implies $\lambda \in \rho(T)$. It is readily seen that when $p = \infty$ and $|\lambda| \leqslant 1$, λ is an eigenvalue; the corresponding eigenmanifold is generated by the vector $(1, \lambda, \lambda^2, \cdots)$. When $1 \leqslant p < \infty$ we have this same eigenvalue and eigenmanifold if $|\lambda| < 1$. But $(\lambda - T)^{-1}$ exists if $|\lambda| = 1$ and $1 \leqslant p < \infty$, for $(1, \lambda, \lambda^2, \cdots)$ is not an element of l^p in this case. Since $\sigma(T)$ is closed, we see that, for each value of p, $\sigma(T)$ is the set $\{\lambda : |\lambda| \leqslant 1\}$. When $|\lambda| = 1$ and $1 \leqslant p < \infty$, the inverse cannot be continuous, by Theorem 5.1–D.

To investigate the range of $\lambda - T$ we find by induction from $\eta_k = \lambda\xi_k - \xi_{k+1}$ that

$$\xi_{k+1} = \lambda^k\xi_1 - \lambda^{k-1}\eta_1 - \lambda^{k-2}\eta_2 - \cdots - \eta_k$$

and that

$$\xi_1 = \lambda^{-1}\eta_1 + \cdots + \lambda^{-k}\eta_k + \lambda^{-k}\xi_{k+1} \text{ if } \lambda \neq 0.$$

Note that $\lambda^{-k}\xi_{k+1} \to 0$ as $k \to \infty$ if $|\lambda| \geqslant 1$ and $1 \leqslant p < \infty$ or if $|\lambda| > 1$ and $p = \infty$. This enables us to find x in terms of y when $y = (\lambda - T)x$.

In particular, we get the formulas for the resolvent operator when $|\lambda| > 1$. When $|\lambda| = 1$ and $1 \leqslant p < \infty$, the range of $\lambda - T$ is dense in l^p, for it is easily seen to contain y if the number of nonzero components of y is finite. The range cannot be all of l^p in this case, however. Why not? We leave it until later to show that the range is *not* dense in l^p for the case $|\lambda| = 1$ and $p = \infty$. When $\lambda = 0$, the range of $\lambda - T$ is obviously all of l^p, for each p. When $0 < |\lambda| < 1$ and y is in the range of $\lambda - T$, any x such that $(\lambda - T)x = y$ is given by $x = \dot{\xi}_1(1, \lambda, \lambda^2, \cdots) - \lambda^{-1}z$, where $z = \{\zeta_k\}$, $\zeta_1 = 0$, and

$$(5.3\text{--}1) \qquad \zeta_{k+1} = \lambda^k \eta_1 + \lambda^{k-1}\eta_2 + \cdots + \lambda\eta_k \qquad \text{if } k \geqslant 1.$$

After discussing Example 2 we shall see that the range of $\lambda - T$ is all of l^p in this case, for each p.

Example 2. Let A on l^p into l^p be defined by the infinite matrix

$$\begin{Vmatrix} 0 & 0 & 0 & 0 & \cdots \\ 1 & 0 & 0 & 0 & \cdots \\ 0 & 1 & 0 & 0 & \\ 0 & 0 & 1 & 0 & \\ & & & \cdot & \\ & & & & \cdot \\ \cdots & & & \cdot & \end{Vmatrix}$$

This is the transpose of the matrix of Example 1. When $p = \infty$, A can be identified with the conjugate operator T', T being the operator of Example 1, with $p = 1$. If $1 < p < \infty$ and $p' = p/(p - 1)$, A for p' can be identified with the conjugate T' of T for p. Finally, T for $p - \infty$ can be identified with the conjugate A' of A for $p = 1$. These remarks, and the state diagram of § 4.71, will help us in analyzing the spectrum of A. In particular, the relations between an operator and its conjugate assure us that $\|A\| = 1$ (which we can of course see directly) and that $\sigma(A) = \sigma(T) = \{\lambda : |\lambda| \leqslant 1\}$.

The equation $(\lambda - A)x = y$ is expressed by the equations $\eta_1 = \lambda\xi_1$, $\eta_{k+1} = -\xi_k + \lambda\xi_{k+1}$, $k \geqslant 1$. When $\lambda = 0$ we see that the inverse of $\lambda - A$ exists and is continuous, for $\|Ax\| = \|x\|$. The range is not dense in l^p, however, for $y = -Ax$ implies $\eta_1 = 0$; the range is a proper closed subspace of l^p. When $\lambda \neq 0$ the inverse of $\lambda - A$ exists; $x = (\lambda - A)^{-1}y$, for y in the range of $\lambda - A$, is expressed by

$$(5.3\text{--}2) \qquad \xi_k = \lambda^{-k}\eta_1 + \lambda^{1-k}\eta_2 + \cdots + \lambda^{-1}\eta_k.$$

In particular, these equations define the resolvent of A when $|\lambda| > 1$.

We can use equations (5.3–2) in discussing the range of $\lambda - T$. A scrutiny of (5.3–1) and (5.3–2) shows that the z of (5.3–1) can be written in the form $z = A(\lambda^{-1} - A)^{-1}y$. The solutions of $(\lambda - T)x = y$ are then $x = \xi_1(1, \lambda, \lambda^2, \cdots) - \lambda^{-1}A(\lambda^{-1} - A)^{-1}y$, where ξ_1 is arbitrary. If $0 < |\lambda| < 1$, this formula is applicable for every y in l^p, for all p, and so we see that the range of $\lambda - T$ is all of l^p in this case. The result is valid for $0 \leqslant |\lambda| < 1$ if we write it in the form $x = \xi_1(1, \lambda, \lambda^2, \cdots) + A(\lambda A - I)^{-1}y$.

Next we show that, for $p = \infty$, the range of $\lambda - A$ is not dense in l^∞ if $|\lambda| = 1$. In fact, we show that y is not in the range if $\|y - w\| = \epsilon < 1$, where $w = (\lambda^{-1}, \lambda^{-2}, \lambda^{-3}, \cdots)$. If we assume that $x \in l^\infty$ and $(\lambda - A)x = y$, we can write $y = w + (\theta_1, \theta_2, \cdots)$, where $|\theta_n| \leqslant \epsilon$, and we have, from (5.3–2),

$$\xi_n = n\lambda^{-n-1} + \lambda^{-n-1}(\lambda\theta_1 + \lambda^2\theta_2 + \cdots + \lambda^n\theta_n),$$

so that

$$|n^{-1}\xi_n - \lambda^{-n-1}| = n^{-1}|\lambda\theta_1 + \cdots + \lambda^n\theta_n| \leqslant \epsilon.$$

Letting $n \to \infty$, we obtain the contradiction $1 \leqslant \epsilon$.

An argument of a similar kind will show for the case $p = \infty$, $|\lambda| = 1$, that the range of $\lambda - T$ is not dense in l^∞. If $y = (\lambda - T)x$, it may be verified that $y = (\lambda\xi_1, 0, 0, \cdots) - (\lambda^{-1} - A)T(\lambda x)$, and from this it may be shown that y is not in the range of $\lambda - T$ if $\|y - w\| = \epsilon < 1$, where $w = (\lambda, \lambda^2, \lambda^3, \cdots)$.

It is now possible to make a complete classification of the points of the spectra of T and A for all values of p. See the problems.

PROBLEMS

1. For the T of Example 1 there is the following classification of points of $\sigma(T)$. (a) $\lambda = 0:I_3$; (b) $0 < |\lambda| < 1:I_3$; (c) $|\lambda| = 1:II_2$ if $1 \leqslant p < \infty$, and III_3 if $p = \infty$.

2. For the A of Example 2 there is the following classification of points of $\sigma(A)$. (a) $|\lambda| < 1:III_1$; (b) $|\lambda| = 1:II_2$ if $1 < p < \infty$, and III_2 if $p = 1$ or ∞. Some of these results are obtained by using problem 1 and the state diagram.

3. When $p = 1$ and $0 \leqslant |\lambda| < 1$ in Example 2, show that $\|(\lambda - A)x\| \geqslant (1 - |\lambda|)\|x\|$, so that $(\lambda - A)^{-1}$ is continuous.

4. If $(\lambda - A)x = y$ in Example 2, show that $\eta_1 + \lambda\eta_2 + \cdots + \lambda^k\eta_{k+1} = \lambda^{k+1}\xi_{k+1}$. This may be used to show that the range of $\lambda - A$ is not dense in l^p if $|\lambda| < 1$ and $p = \infty$, or if $|\lambda| \leqslant 1$ and $p = 1$.

5. If $|\lambda| = 1$ and $1 \leqslant p < \infty$ in Example 2, take $x_n = (1, \lambda^{-1}, \cdots, \lambda^{1-n}, 0, 0, \cdots)$, and show that $(\lambda - A)^{-1}$ is not continuous.

6. Let α_1, α_2, $\cdots$ be scalars such that $\sup_k |\alpha_k| < \infty$. Let β_2, β_3 $\cdots$ be scalars such that $\sum_2^\infty |\beta_k| < \infty$. Define $T \in [l^1]$ by $\eta_1 = \sum_1^\infty \alpha_i \xi_i$, $\eta_k = \beta_k \xi_1$ if $k \geqslant 2$. Discuss $\sigma(T)$ and find the resolvent operator.

7. Let $T \in [l^1]$ be defined by the infinite matrix

$$\begin{Vmatrix} 0 & 1 & 1 & 1 & \cdots \\ 1 & 0 & 0 & 0 & \cdots \\ 0 & 1 & 0 & 0 & \cdots \\ 0 & 0 & 1 & 0 & \cdots \\ & & & & \\ \cdots & & & \end{Vmatrix}.$$

Show that $\sigma(T)$ consists of $\lambda = (1 + \sqrt{5})/2$ and all λ such that $|\lambda| \leqslant 1$. Classify the points of $\sigma(T)$. This operator has an interesting connection with the Fibonacci numbers, as may be seen by computing the matrix representation of T^n. The operator has been studied by Halberg, **1**, pages 21–29.

8. The operator $A \in [l^1]$ defined by the matrix (α_{ij}) with $\alpha_{ij} = 1$ if $|i - j| = 1$, $\alpha_{ij} = 0$ otherwise, is interesting. Its spectrum consists of the interval $-2 \leqslant \lambda \leqslant 2$ of the real axis. The points $\lambda = \pm 2$ are classified II$_2$; the rest of $\sigma(A)$ is classified III$_2$ (see Halberg, **1**, pages 29–36). We may also consider A as an element of $[l^2]$. The spectrum is the same as before, but now all points are classified II$_2$ (Hellinger, **1**, pages 231–232).

5.4 Reducibility

Let T be a linear operator with domain and range in the linear space X. For convenience we shall sometimes write $\mathcal{D}$ instead of $\mathcal{D}(T)$ for the domain of T. A subspace M of X is said to be *invariant* under T if $T(\mathcal{D} \cap M) \subset M$. We can then talk about the *restriction* of T to M, with M in place of X and $\mathcal{D} \cap M$ in place of $\mathcal{D}$.

Definition. The operator T is said to be *completely reduced* by the pair of subspaces (M_1, M_2) if these subspaces are linearly independent (see § 4.8) and invariant under T, such that $X = M_1 \oplus M_2$ and such that $P_i \mathcal{D} \subset \mathcal{D}$ $(i = 1, 2)$, where P_1 and P_2 are the projections defined by $P_i x = x_i$, where $x = x_1 + x_2$ $(x_i \in M_i)$ is the direct sum representation of an arbitrary x.

This definition can be extended in an obvious manner to give meaning to the statement "T is completely reduced by the set of subspaces M_1, $\cdots$, M_n."

Let us see the meaning of the foregoing concepts in terms of the matrix representation of T when X is n-dimensional and $\mathcal{D} = X$. Suppose that

M_1 is r-dimensional ($1 \leqslant r < n$), and let us choose a basis for X such that the first r elements of the basis form a basis for M_1. Then, if M_1 is invariant under T, the matrix which represents T will have all zero elements in the intersection of the first r columns and the last $n - r$ rows. If M_2 is the subspace generated by the last $n - r$ basis elements and if T is completely reduced by (M_1, M_2), all of the elements in the intersection of the first r rows and the last $n - r$ columns will also be zeros.

If an operator is completely reduced by a pair of subspaces, the operator may be studied by studying the restrictions of it to these subspaces. If these restrictions can also be completely reduced, the study of the operator may be simplified further.   Evidently, if X is n-dimensional and $\mathscr{D} = X$, the greatest simplification will occur if we can find a set of n subspaces $M_1, \cdots, M_n$, each of them one dimensional, which completely reduce the operator. This is the same as asking that X have a basis $u_1, \cdots, u_n$, each element of which is an eigenvector. The matrix representing the operator will then have eigenvalues down its main diagonal, and all other elements will be zero.   This situation can occur only for operators of a very special sort.

We are speaking here of finite sets of subspaces which completely reduce an operator.   There are important generalizations of this concept for infinite sets of subspaces.   For the present we do not try to develop such generalizations, but we mention the following concrete example.

Let $X = L^2(0, 2\pi)$.   Let $\mathscr{D}$ be the subspace of X determined by those functions $x(t)$ in $\mathscr{L}^2(0, 2\pi)$ which are absolutely continuous on $[0, 2\pi]$ and are such that $x(0) = x(2\pi)$ and such that the derivative $x'(t)$ is also in $\mathscr{L}^2(0, 2\pi)$.   We then define $Tx = y$, where $y(t) = x'(t)$.   Let $u_n(t) = (1/\sqrt{2\pi})e^{int}$, $n = 0, \pm 1, \pm 2, \cdots$.   The u_n's form a complete orthonormal set in X.   Observe that $u_n \in \mathscr{D}$ and that the closed linear manifold generated by each u_n is invariant under T; the same is true of the closed linear manifold generated by any finite or infinite subset of the u_n's. Hence T is completely reduced by $(M, M^\perp)$, where M is the closed linear manifold generated by any set of the u_n's   In a certain sense T is completely reduced by the infinite set of subspaces $\{M_n\}$, where M_n is generated by u_n.

If $X = M_1 \oplus M_2$ and if P_1, P_2 are the projections determined by this direct sum representation of X, an operator T with domain $\mathscr{D}$ is completely reduced by (M_1, M_2) if and only if $P_1\mathscr{D} \subset \mathscr{D}$ and $P_1Tx = TP_1x$ when $x \in \mathscr{D}$.   The corresponding conditions will then be satisfied by P_2.   The simple verification of these assertions is left to the reader.   It is then easily proved that, if T is completely reduced by (M_1, M_2) and if T^{-1} exists, then T^{-1} also is completely reduced by (M_1, M_2).

For formal reference we now state several theorems.

Theorem 5.4–A. *Let T be completely reduced by (M_1, M_2). Let T_k be the restriction of T to M_k. Then (a) $\mathscr{D}(T) = \mathscr{D}(T_1) \oplus \mathscr{D}(T_2)$; (b) $\mathscr{R}(T) = \mathscr{R}(T_1) \oplus \mathscr{R}(T_2)$; (c) T^{-1} exists if and only if T_1^{-1} and T_2^{-1} exist; (d) $\mathscr{R}(T) = X$ if and only if $\mathscr{R}(T_k) = M_k$ for $k = 1$ and 2.*

The proof is left to the reader.

Theorem 5.4–B. *Consider the situation of Theorem 5.4–A, supposing now that X is a normed linear space and that the projections P_1, P_2 determined by the direct sum $X = M_1 \oplus M_2$ are continuous. Then $\mathscr{R}(T)$ is dense in X if and only if $\mathscr{R}(T_1)$ and $\mathscr{R}(T_2)$ are dense in M_1 and M_2 respectively. If T^{-1} exists, it is continuous if and only if T_1^{-1} and T_2^{-1} are continuous.*

The proof is left to the reader. We remark that P_1 and P_2 will certainly be continuous if X is complete and M_1 and M_2 are closed; see problem 2, § 4.8.

When the conditions of Theorems 5.4–A and 5.4–B are satisfied, we can rephrase most of the results of these theorems as follows, using the terminology of § 4.71 regarding the classifications I, II, III and 1, 2, 3:

T is classified as 1 if and only if T_1 and T_2 are both classified as 1.
T is classified as I if and only if T_1 and T_2 are both classified as I.
T is classified as 3 if and only if at least one of T_1, T_2 is classified as 3.
T is classified as III if and only if at least one of T_1, T_2 is classified as III.

From these statements, as applied to $\lambda - T$, which is completely reduced by (M_1, M_2) if T is, we have the following theorem, verification of which is left to the reader.

Theorem 5.4–C. *Under the conditions of Theorem 5.4–B we have*

  a. $\sigma(T) = \sigma(T_1) \cup \sigma(T_2)$.
  b. $P\sigma(T) = P\sigma(T_1) \cup P\sigma(T_2)$.

If it is furthermore assumed that $\sigma(T_1)$ and $\sigma(T_2)$ have no points in common, it follows that

  c. $C\sigma(T) = C\sigma(T_1) \cup C\sigma(T_2)$
and
  d. $R\sigma(T) = R\sigma(T_1) \cup R\sigma(T_2)$.

PROBLEMS

1. Verify the assertions made in the paragraph immediately before Theorem 5.4–A.

2. Write out the proofs of Theorems 5.4–A and 5.4–B.

3. Write out the proof of Theorem 5.4–C.

4. If $T \in [X]$, where X is a normed linear space, if T is completely reduced by (M_1, M_2), and if the corresponding projections P_1, P_2 are continuous, then T' is completely reduced by (M_1^0, M_2^0).   See problem 4, § 4.8.

5.41 The Ascent and Descent of an Operator

In this section X denotes a linear space, and T is a linear operator with $\mathscr{D}(T)$ and $\mathscr{R}(T)$ in X.   The considerations are all algebraic.   We define T^n by induction, with $T^0 = I$, $T^1 = T$.   If $n \geqslant 1$, $\mathscr{D}(T^n)$ is the set of x such that $x, Tx, \cdots, T^{n-1}x$ are all in $\mathscr{D}(T)$.   If $n \geqslant 2$, $\mathscr{D}(T^n) = \{x : x$ and Tx are in $\mathscr{D}(T^{n-1})\}$.   For convenience we write $\mathscr{D}(T^n) = \mathscr{D}_n(T)$; observe that $\mathscr{D}_0(T) = X$.   In general we have $\mathscr{D}_n(T) \subset \mathscr{D}_{n-1}(T)$; the inclusion may be proper.

We generalize a previous notation and terminology by defining the *null manifold* of T^n as the set of $x \in \mathscr{D}_n(T)$ such that $T^n x = 0$.   We denote this subspace of X by $\mathscr{N}(T^n)$.   Evidently $\mathscr{N}(T^0) = (0)$.

Theorem 5.41–A. $\mathscr{N}(T^n) \subset \mathscr{N}(T^{n+1})$, $n = 0, 1, \cdots$.   *If* $\mathscr{N}(T^k) = \mathscr{N}(T^{k+1})$ *for some* k, *then* $\mathscr{N}(T^k) = \mathscr{N}(T^n)$ *when* $n \geqslant k$.

PROOF.   The first statement is evident.   Suppose that $\mathscr{N}(T^n) = \mathscr{N}(T^{n+1})$ for some n and that $x \in \mathscr{N}(T^{n+2})$.   Then $x \in \mathscr{D}_{n+2}(T)$ and $T^{n+2}x = 0$.   Hence $Tx \in \mathscr{D}_{n+1}(T)$ and $T^{n+1}(Tx) = 0$, so that $Tx \in \mathscr{N}(T^{n+1}) = \mathscr{N}(T^n)$.   Then $T^n(Tx) = T^{n+1}x = 0$.   This shows that $\mathscr{N}(T^{n+2}) \subset \mathscr{N}(T^{n+1})$.   The reverse inclusion also holds, and so $\mathscr{N}(T^{n+1}) = \mathscr{N}(T^{n+2})$.   The second assertion of the theorem now follows by induction.

Definition.   If there is some integer $n \geqslant 0$ such that $\mathscr{N}(T^n) = \mathscr{N}(T^{n+1})$, the smallest such integer is called the *ascent* of T and denoted by $\alpha(T)$.   If no such integer exists we say that $\alpha(T) = \infty$.

Next we consider the ranges $\mathscr{R}(T^n)$.   Note that $\mathscr{R}(T^0) = X$.

Theorem 5.41–B. $\mathscr{R}(T^{n+1}) \subset \mathscr{R}(T^n)$, $n = 0, 1, \cdots$.   *If* $\mathscr{R}(T^{k+1}) = \mathscr{R}(T^k)$ *for some* k, *then* $\mathscr{R}(T^n) = \mathscr{R}(T^k)$ *when* $n \geqslant k$.

PROOF.   If $y \in \mathscr{R}(T^{n+1})$, $y = T^{n+1}x$, where $x \in \mathscr{D}_{n+1}(T)$.   Then $Tx \in \mathscr{D}_n(T)$ and $y = T^n(Tx)$, so that $y \in \mathscr{R}(T^n)$.   This proves the first statement.   Before proving the next assertion we observe that

$$(5.41–1) \qquad \mathscr{R}(T^{n+1}) = T\{\mathscr{R}(T^n) \cap \mathscr{D}(T)\}, \qquad n = 0, 1, 2, \cdots.$$

Now suppose that $\mathscr{R}(T^{n+1}) = \mathscr{R}(T^n)$ for some n, and suppose $y \in \mathscr{R}(T^{n+1})$. By (5.41–1) we can write $y = Tx$, where $x \in \mathscr{R}(T^n) \cap \mathscr{D}(T) = \mathscr{R}(T^{n+1}) \cap \mathscr{D}(T)$. Thus, again by (5.41–1), $y \in \mathscr{R}(T^{n+2})$. This shows that $\mathscr{R}(T^{n+1}) \subset \mathscr{R}(T^{n+2})$, and the proof is finished just as in the case of the previous theorem.

Definition. If there is some integer $n \geqslant 0$ such that $\mathscr{R}(T^{n+1}) = \mathscr{R}(T^n)$, the smallest such integer is called the *descent* of T and denoted by $\delta(T)$. If there is no such integer, we say that $\delta(T) = \infty$.

Observe that $\alpha(T) = 0$ if and only if T^{-1} exists and that $\delta(T) = 0$ if and only if $\mathscr{R}(T) = X$.

There are certain relations between the ascent and descent of an operator, provided that certain auxiliary conditions are satisfied.

Theorem 5.41–C. *If $\alpha(T)$ is finite and $\delta(T) = 0$, then $\alpha(T) = 0$ also.*

PROOF. Suppose that $0 < \alpha(T)$ and $\delta(T) = 0$. Then $\mathscr{R}(T) = X$ and T^{-1} does not exist. Choose $x_1 \neq 0$ so that $Tx_1 = 0$. By induction we define $x_2, x_3, \cdots$ so that $x_{n+1} \in \mathscr{D}(T)$ and $Tx_{n+1} = x_n$. Then we see that $x_{n+1} \in \mathscr{D}_{n+1}(T)$, $T^n x_{n+1} = x_1$, $T^{n+1} x_{n+1} = 0$. Thus $x_{n+1} \in \mathscr{N}(T^{n+1}) - \mathscr{N}(T^n)$. Hence $\alpha(T) = \infty$. This proves the theorem.

Theorem 5.41–D. *If $\alpha(T)$ and $\delta(T)$ are both finite, then necessarily $\alpha(T) \leqslant \delta(T)$.*

PROOF. Let $p = \delta(T)$. Then (5.41–1) shows that

(5.41–2) $$\mathscr{R}(T^p) = T\{\mathscr{R}(T^p) \cap \mathscr{D}(T)\}.$$

Now define a space X_1 and an operator T_1 as follows: $X_1 = \mathscr{R}(T^p)$, $\mathscr{D}(T_1) = \mathscr{R}(T^p) \cap \mathscr{D}(T)$, $T_1 x = Tx$ if $x \in \mathscr{D}(T_1)$. Equation (5.41–2) shows that $\mathscr{R}(T_1) = X_1$, so that $\delta(T_1) = 0$. It is easy to see that $\mathscr{D}(T_1{}^n) = \mathscr{R}(T^p) \cap \mathscr{D}_n(T)$ and $T_1{}^n x = T^n x$ if $x \in \mathscr{D}(T_1{}^n)$. This may be done by induction, using the fact that $\mathscr{R}(T^p) = \mathscr{R}(T^{p+1})$. Now clearly $\mathscr{N}(T_1{}^{n+1}) \subset \mathscr{N}(T^{n+1})$, and $\mathscr{N}(T^n) \cap \mathscr{D}(T_1{}^{n+1}) \subset \mathscr{N}(T^n) \cap \mathscr{D}(T_1{}^n) \subset \mathscr{N}(T_1{}^n)$. It therefore follows that

$$\mathscr{N}(T_1{}^{n+1}) - \mathscr{N}(T_1{}^n) \subset \mathscr{N}(T^{n+1}) - \mathscr{N}(T^n).$$

Consequently $\alpha(T_1) \leqslant \alpha(T)$. Since $\alpha(T)$ is finite, so is $\alpha(T_1)$. But then $\alpha(T_1) = 0$, by Theorem 5.41–C, and so $T_1{}^{-1}$ exists. Now suppose that $x \in \mathscr{N}(T^{p+1})$, and let $y = T^p x$. Then $y \in \mathscr{R}(T^p) \cap \mathscr{D}(T) = \mathscr{D}(T_1)$. But $T_1 y = Ty = T^{p+1} x = 0$. Since $T_1{}^{-1}$ exists we conclude that $y = 0$, or $x \in \mathscr{N}(T^p)$. We thus have $\mathscr{N}(T^{p+1}) \subset \mathscr{N}(T^p)$, whence $\mathscr{N}(T^{p+1}) = \mathscr{N}(T^p)$. This means that $\alpha(T) \leqslant p = \delta(T)$, so the proof is complete.

Theorem 5.41–E.   *If $\mathcal{D}(T) = X$ and the ascent and descent of T are both finite, they are equal.*

PROOF.   We have only to prove $\alpha(T) \geqslant \delta(T)$, because of Theorem 5.41–D.   The case $\delta(T) = 0$ is covered by Theorem 5.41–C; therefore we assume $p = \delta(T) \geqslant 1$.   Then there exists an element $y \in \mathcal{R}(T^{p-1}) - \mathcal{R}(T^p)$.   We can write $y = T^{p-1}x$ for some x.   Let $z = Ty = T^p x$, so that $z \in \mathcal{R}(T^p)$.   Now $T^p\{\mathcal{R}(T^p)\} = \mathcal{R}(T^{2p}) = \mathcal{R}(T^p)$.   Therefore, there exists some $u \in \mathcal{R}(T^p)$ such that $T^p u = z$.   Let $v = x - u$.   Then

$$T^p v = T^p x - T^p u = z - z = 0,$$

and

$$T^{p-1}v = T^{p-1}x - T^{p-1}u = y - T^{p-1}u.$$

Now $T^{p-1}u \in \mathcal{R}(T^{2p-1}) = \mathcal{R}(T^p)$, because $u \in \mathcal{R}(T^p)$.   Therefore $y - T^{p-1}u \neq 0$, because y is not in $\mathcal{R}(T^p)$.   We see then that $v \in \mathcal{N}(T^p) - \mathcal{N}(T^{p-1})$, and this implies $\alpha(T) \geqslant p = \delta(T)$.

Our main interest in the ascent and descent of an operator arises from the facts set forth in the next two theorems.

Theorem 5.41–F.   *Suppose that $\alpha(T)$ and $\delta(T)$ are both finite, and let $p = \delta(T)$.   Then $\mathcal{R}(T^p)$ and $\mathcal{N}(T^p)$ are linearly independent linear manifolds, and*

$$(5.41\text{–}3) \qquad \mathcal{D}_p(T) = \{\mathcal{R}(T^p) \cap \mathcal{D}_p(T)\} \oplus \mathcal{N}(T^p).$$

PROOF.   Suppose $y \in \mathcal{R}(T^p) \cap \mathcal{N}(T^p)$.   We can write $y = T^p x$, $T^p y = 0$, so that $T^{2p}x = 0$.   Then $x \in \mathcal{N}(T^{2p})$.   But $\alpha(T) \leqslant p$, and so $\mathcal{N}(T^{2p}) = \mathcal{N}(T^p)$.   Hence $x \in \mathcal{N}(T^p)$, and $y = 0$.   This proves that $\mathcal{R}(T^p) \cap \mathcal{N}(T^p) = (0)$, as required.   For the proof of (5.41–3) we define X_1 and T_1 as in the proof of Theorem 5.41–D.   Since $\mathcal{R}(T_1) = X_1$, it follows by Theorem 5.41–B that $\mathcal{R}(T_1{}^p) = X_1$.   Hence, if $x \in \mathcal{D}_p(T)$, there is some $x_1 \in \mathcal{D}(T_1{}^p) = \mathcal{R}(T^p) \cap \mathcal{D}_p(T)$ such that $T_1{}^p x_1 = T^p x_1 = T^p x$.   Then $x - x_1 \in \mathcal{N}(T^p)$.   Let $x_2 = x - x_1$.   Then $x = x_1 + x_2$ shows that

$$\mathcal{D}_p(T) \subset \{\mathcal{R}(T^p) \cap \mathcal{D}_p(T)\} \oplus \mathcal{N}(T^p).$$

The reverse inclusion is evident, and so (5.41–3) is proved.

Theorem 5.41–G.   *Suppose that $\mathcal{D}(T) = X$ and that $\alpha(T)$ and $\delta(T)$ are both finite (and hence equal).   Let $p = \delta(T)$.   Then T is completely reduced by the pair of manifolds $\mathcal{R}(T^p)$, $\mathcal{N}(T^p)$, and T maps $\mathcal{R}(T^p)$ in a one-to-one manner onto all of itself.*

PROOF.   The fact that $\mathcal{R}(T^p) \cap \mathcal{N}(T^p) = (0)$ and

$$(5.41\text{–}4) \qquad\qquad X = \mathcal{R}(T^p) \oplus \mathcal{N}(T^p)$$

is known from Theorem 5.41–F, since $\mathcal{D}_p(T) = X$ in this case. The invariance of $\mathcal{N}(T^p)$ under T is obvious; that of $\mathcal{R}(T^p)$ follows from (5.41–2). The restriction of T to $\mathcal{R}(T^p)$ is T_1, as defined in the proof of Theorem 5.41–D. The asserted property of T_1 was established in this previous argument.

We use the results of this section in the study of compact operators, in § 5.5.

PROBLEMS

1. It can happen that $\delta(T) = 0$ and $\alpha(T) = \infty$. Consider $X = l^2$, $\mathcal{D}(T) = X$, and $x = (\xi_1, \xi_2, \cdots)$, $Tx = (\xi_2, \xi_3, \cdots)$.

2. If $\mathcal{D}(T) \neq X$ it can happen that $\alpha(T) < \delta(T)$ when both are finite. Take $\mathcal{D}(T) \neq X$, $Tx = x$ if $x \in \mathcal{D}(T)$. Then $\alpha(T) = 0$, $\delta(T) = 1$.

3. Suppose that X is a Banach space and T is a closed linear operator with domain and range in X. Then points λ of $\rho(T)$ are characterized by $\alpha(\lambda - T) = \delta(\lambda - T) = 0$; points of $P\sigma(T)$ by $\alpha(\lambda - T) \neq 0$; and points of $C\sigma(T) \cup R\sigma(T)$ by $\alpha(\lambda - T) = 0$ and $\delta(\lambda - T) > 0$.

5.5 Compact Operators

In our study of compact operators we shall prove theorems which, when applied to Fredholm integral equations of the second kind, yield a great part of the most fundamental information about such equations.

Definition. Let X and Y be normed linear spaces. Suppose T is a linear operator with domain X and range in Y. We say that T is *compact* if, for each bounded sequence $\{x_n\}$ in X, the sequence $\{Tx_n\}$ contains a subsequence converging to some limit in Y.

A compact operator is also called *completely continuous* (in French, *complètement* or *totalement continue*; in German, *vollstetig*). We note at once that a compact linear operator is continuous. For, discontinuity of T would imply the existence of a sequence $\{x_n\}$ such that $\|x_n\| \leqslant 1$ and $\|Tx_n\| \to \infty$, and this cannot occur if T is compact.

We call explicit attention to the important general facts about compact operators which are stated in problems 1–5 at the end of this section. Some other important facts are stated in the next two theorems.

Theorem 5.5–A.   *If $T \in [X, Y]$ and T is compact, $\mathcal{R}(T)$ is separable.*

PROOF.   Observe that $\mathcal{R}(T) = \bigcup_{n=1}^{\infty} T(S_n)$, where $S_n = \{x : \|x\| \leqslant n\}$. It will suffice to prove that $T(S_n)$ is separable. Now, since T is compact, it is easy to see that every infinite subset of $T(S_n)$ has an accumulation point in Y. Consequently (see the proof of Theorem 2.4–E) for each postive integer $\dot{k}$ there exists a finite set of points in $T(S_n)$ such that the spheres of radius $1/k$ with centers at these points cover $T(S_n)$. The aggregate of such finite sets, one set for each k, is evidently everywhere dense in $T(S_n)$.

Theorem 5.5–B. *If* $T \in [X, Y]$ *and* T *is compact, the conjugate operator* T' *is compact also.*

PROOF. Let $\{y_n\}$ be a sequence everywhere dense in $\mathscr{R}(T)$, and let $\{y_k'\}$ be a bounded sequence in Y', say with $\|y_k'\| \leqslant M$. Since the numerical sequence $y_1'(y_n), y_2'(y_n), \cdots$ is bounded for each n, we can use the diagonal procedure to obtain a subsequence of $\{y_k'\}$, which we shall denote by $\{z_k'\}$, such that $\lim_{k \to \infty} z_k'(y_n)$ exists for each n. It is then true that $\lim_{k \to \infty} z_k'(y)$ exists for each y in $\overline{\mathscr{R}(T)}$; this is easily seen from the inequalities

$$|z_k'(y) - z_j'(y)| \leqslant |z_k'(y) - z_k'(y_n)|$$

$$+ |z_k'(y_n) - z_j'(y_n)| + |z_j'(y_n) - z_j'(y)|$$

$$\leqslant (\|z_k'\| + \|z_j'\|)\, \|y - y_n\| + |z_k'(y_n) - z_j'(y_n)|,$$

since $\{y_n\}$ is everywhere dense in $\overline{\mathscr{R}(T)}$ as well as in $\mathscr{R}(T)$. Now let $x_k' = T'z_k'$. If $x \in X$, we have $x_k'(x) = z_k'(Tx)$. Therefore $\lim_{k \to \infty} x_k'(x)$ exists for each $x \in X$, and the limit defines an element $x' \in X'$. Our proof will be complete if we show that $T'z_k' \to x'$. We assume this is not the case. Then for some $\epsilon > 0$ there will exist a subsequence of $\{z_k'\}$, which we shall denote by $\{w_k'\}$, such that $\|T'w_k' - x'\| \geqslant \epsilon$ for every k. Now $w_k'(Tx) - x'(x)$ is the value at x of the functional $T'w_k' - x'$. Hence there exists $x_k \in X$, with $\|x_k\| = 1$, such that

$$(5.5-1) \qquad |w_k'(Tx_k) - x'(x_k)| \geqslant \tfrac{1}{2}\|T'w_k' - x'\| \geqslant \epsilon/2.$$

By the compactness of T, some subsequence of $\{Tx_k\}$ is convergent. Denote this subsequence by $\{Tu_i\}$, and let $\{v_i'\}$ be the corresponding subsequence of $\{w_k'\}$. Let $Tu_i \to v$. Then $v \in \overline{\mathscr{R}(T)}$. Consequently $\lim_{k \to \infty} v_k'(v) = \alpha$ exists. Now $x'(u_i) = \lim_{k \to \infty} z_k'(Tu_i)$, by definition. Hence also $x'(u_i) = \lim_{k \to \infty} v_k'(Tu_i)$, for $\{v_k'\}$ is a subsequence of $\{z_k'\}$. Next,

$$|v_k'(v) - v_k'(Tu_i)| \leqslant \|v_k'\|\, \|v - Tu_i\| \leqslant M\|v - Tu_i\|,$$

and so

$$(5.5-2) \qquad |\alpha - x'(u_i)| \leqslant M\|v - Tu_i\|.$$

Now $|v_i'(Tu_i) - x'(u_i)| \geqslant \epsilon/2$, in view of (5.5–1). But

$$|v_i'(Tu_i) - x'(u_i)| \leqslant |v_i'(Tu_i) - v_i'(v)| + |v_i'(v) - \alpha| + |\alpha - x'(u_i)|$$
$$\leqslant 2M\|Tu_i - v\| + |v_i'(v) - \alpha|,$$

in view of (5.5–2). The right-hand member of this last inequality tends to 0 as $i \to \infty$, and so we reach a contradiction. The proof is then complete.

The converse of Theorem 5.5–B is valid if Y is complete. See problem 5.

Before going further with our general study of compact operators, let us consider some examples.

Example 1. Let $X = C[a, b]$, where $[a, b]$ is a finite closed interval. The scalars may be either real or complex. Let $k(s, t)$ be a continuous function of s and t on $[a, b] \times [a, b]$, and let $K \in [X]$ be defined as the Fredholm-type integral operator with kernel k [see (4.11–1)]. Then K is compact. The proof of this fact depends on a theorem known as Ascoli's theorem, which involves the notion of an *equicontinuous family*. A family F of elements of $C[a, b]$ is called equicontinuous if to each $\epsilon > 0$ corresponds a $\delta > 0$ such that $|x(t_1) - x(t_2)| < \epsilon$ whenever $x \in F$ and t_1, t_2 are points of $[a, b]$ such that $|t_1 - t_2| < \delta$.

Ascoli's Theorem. *If $\{x_n\}$ is a bounded sequence from $C[a, b]$ such that the x_n's form an equicontinuous family, then $\{x_n\}$ contains a convergent subsequence (convergent in the topology of $C[a, b]$).*

This is a standard theorem. For reference see Graves, **1**, page 122, or McShane, **1**, page 336.

Now consider any bounded sequence $\{x_n\}$ in $C[a, b]$, and let $y_n = Kx_n$. Clearly $\{y_n\}$ is bounded, for $\|y_n\| \leqslant \|K\| \|x_n\|$. Hence K will be proved compact if we can show that the y_n's form an equicontinuous family. Now $k(s, t)$ is uniformly continuous, and hence to each $\epsilon > 0$ there corresponds some $\delta > 0$ such that $|k(s_1, t) - k(s_2, t)| < \epsilon/(b - a)M$ for all t if $|s_1 - s_2| < \delta$; here M denotes $\sup_n \|x_n\|$. Then for each n we have

$$|y_n(s_1) - y_n(s_2)| = \left| \int_a^b [k(s_1, t) - k(s_2, t)]x_n(t)\, dt \right| \leqslant \epsilon$$

if $|s_1 - s_2| < \delta$; thus the proof is completed.

The operator K will still be compact with certain less severe restrictions on the kernel k. If $k(s, t)$ is of class $\mathscr{L}^2(a, b)$ as a function of t for each s, if

$$\int_a^b |k(s, t)|^2\, dt$$

is a bounded function of s, and, if

$$\int_a^b |k(s_1, t) - k(s_2, t)|^2 \, dt \to 0 \qquad \text{as} \qquad |s_1 - s_2| \to 0,$$

the operator K will be compact as an operator acting in $C[a, b]$. It is also compact as an operator acting in $L^2(a, b)$. The proof that K maps a bounded sequence into an equicontinuous sequence is made by using the Schwarz inequality.

Example 2. If $k(s, t)$ is an $\mathscr{L}^2$ kernel (see § 4.12), the corresponding integral operator K, acting in the space $L^2(a, b)$, is compact. We prove this as follows. Choose a complete orthonormal set $u_1, u_2, \cdots$ for $L^2(a, b)$. With the usual notation for inner products, let $\alpha_{ij} = (Ku_j, u_i)$, and let $v_j = Ku_j$. Since $\overline{k(s, t)}$ is of class $\mathscr{L}^2$ as a function of t for almost all s, we have

$$\int_a^b |k(s, t)|^2 \, dt = {}^0\sum_{j=1}^{\infty} \left| \int_a^b \overline{k(s, t)} \, \overline{u_j(t)} \, dt \right|^2 = \sum_{j=1}^{\infty} |v_j(s)|^2.$$

Integrating with respect to s, we get

$$\int_a^b \int_a^b |k(s, t)|^2 \, dt \, ds = \sum_{j=1}^{\infty} \|Ku_j\|^2.$$

But

$$\|Ku_j\|^2 = \sum_{i=1}^{\infty} |(Ku_j, u_i)|^2 = \sum_{i=1}^{\infty} |\alpha_{ij}|^2.$$

Therefore

(5.5–3)
$$\int_a^b \int_a^b |k(s, t)|^2 \, ds \, dt = \sum_{i,j=1}^{\infty} |\alpha_{ij}|^2.$$

Now define an operator K_n by the formula

$$K_n x = \sum_{i,j=1}^{n} \alpha_{ij}(x, u_j)u_i, \qquad x \in L^2(a, b).$$

This operator has the $\mathscr{L}^2$ kernel

$$k_n(s, t) = \sum_{i,j=1}^{n} \alpha_{ij} u_i(s)\overline{u_j(t)}.$$

It is easily verified that

$$(K_n u_j, u_i) = \begin{cases} \alpha_{ij} & \text{if } i \leqslant n \text{ and } j \leqslant n \\ 0 & \text{if } i \text{ or } j > n. \end{cases}$$

Hence, by (5.5–3) applied to $K - K_n$ instead of K, we have

$$\int_a^b \int_a^b |k(s, t) - k_n(s, t)|^2 \, ds \, dt = \sum_{i,j=1}^{\infty} |\alpha_{ij}|^2 - \sum_{i,j=1}^{n} |\alpha_{ij}|^2 \to 0$$

as $n \to \infty$. But, as we know from § 4.12,

$$\|K - K_n\|^2 \leqslant \int_a^b \int_a^b |k(s, t) - k_n(s, t)|^2 \, ds \, dt.$$

Hence $\|K - K_n\| \to 0$. Now, K_n is compact, for its range is finite dimensional (see problem 2). The fact that $K_n \to K$ then assures us that K is compact (see problem 3).

Example 3. If $1 \leqslant q < \infty$, a continuous linear operator A on l^1 into l^q is represented by an infinite matrix (α_{ij}), where the condition on the matrix is that

$$\|A\| = \sup_j \left(\sum_{i=1}^{\infty} |\alpha_{ij}|^q \right)^{1/q}.$$

be finite (see problem 5, § 4.51). The operator will be compact if and only if, in addition,

$$(5.5–4) \qquad \sum_{i=n}^{\infty} |\alpha_{ij}|^q \to 0 \qquad \text{as } n \to \infty, \text{ uniformly in } j.$$

That this is a sufficient condition for compactness of A may be seen by using the result of problem 7, for, if $y = Ax$ it follows from Minkowski's inequality that

$$\left(\sum_{i=n}^{\infty} |\eta_i|^q \right)^{1/q} \leqslant \|x\| \left(\sum_{i=n}^{\infty} |\alpha_{ij}|^q \right)^{1/q}.$$

The condition (5.5–4) is also necessary, again by problem 7, for the vectors $v_j = (\alpha_{1j}, \alpha_{2j}, \cdots)$ must form a conditionally sequentially compact set, owing to the compactness of A (note that $v_j = Au_j$, where u_j is the vector whose ith component is δ_{ij}).

We now turn to the study of a compact linear operator T which belongs to $[X]$. We start by investigating the null manifold and range of $(\lambda - T)^n$ when $\lambda \neq 0$. We do not require that X be complete. For convenience we write $T_\lambda = \lambda - T$.

Theorem 5.5–C. *Suppose $T \in [X]$, T compact, and $\lambda \neq 0$. Then the null manifolds $\mathcal{N}(T_\lambda^n)(n = 1, 2, \cdots)$ are finite dimensional.*

PROOF. We begin with $n = 1$. By Theorem 3.12–F it suffices to show that the set $\{x : \|x\| = 1\} \cap \mathcal{N}(T_\lambda)$ is compact or that every sequence from it contains a convergent subsequence. Suppose $\|x_n\| = 1$ and $x_n \in \mathcal{N}(T_\lambda)$, so that $x_n = \lambda^{-1}Tx_n$. Since T is compact it is now evident that $\{x_n\}$ contains a convergent subsequence. For $n > 1$ we write

$$T_\lambda{}^n = (\lambda - T)^n = \lambda^n - n\lambda^{n-1}T + \cdots + (-1)^n T^n = \lambda^n - TA,$$

where A is a certain member of $[X]$. Now TA is compact, since T is (see problem 4). The foregoing reasoning, applied to $\lambda^n - TA$, shows that $\mathcal{N}(T_\lambda{}^n)$ is finite dimensional.

Theorem 5.5–D.   *Suppose $T \in [X]$, T compact, and $\lambda \neq 0$. Then the ranges $\mathcal{R}(T_\lambda{}^n)$ are all closed.*

PROOF.   Just as in the foregoing proof it suffices to treat the case $n = 1$. We suppose that $\mathcal{R}(T_\lambda)$ is not closed; hence there is a sequence $\{T_\lambda x_n\}$ converging to a limit y, with y not in $\mathcal{R}(T_\lambda)$. Then $y \neq 0$, and hence x_n is not in $\mathcal{N}(T_\lambda)$ if n is sufficiently large. We may therefore suppose that no x_n is in $\mathcal{N}(T_\lambda)$. Since $\mathcal{N}(T_\lambda)$ is closed, the distance d_n from x_n to $\mathcal{N}(T_\lambda)$ is positive. Choose $u_n \in \mathcal{N}(T_\lambda)$ so that $\|x_n - u_n\| < 2d_n$. Let $\theta_n = \|x_n - u_n\|$. We shall prove that $\theta_n \to \infty$. If this were not so, $\{x_n - u_n\}$ would contain a bounded subsequence, and hence $T(x_n - u_n)$ would contain a convergent subsequence. But

$$x_n - u_n = (\lambda^{-1})\,[T_\lambda(x_n - u_n) + T(x_n - u_n)],$$

and $T_\lambda(x_n - u_n) = T_\lambda x_n \to y$, so that $\{x_n - u_n\}$ would also contain a convergent subsequence with some limit x. The corresponding subsequence of $\{T_\lambda(x_n - u_n)\}$ would then converge both to $T_\lambda x$ and to y, whence $y = T_\lambda x \in \mathcal{R}(T)$, contrary to assumption. Thus $\theta_n \to \infty$. Now let $v_n = (x_n - u_n)/\theta_n$. Observe that

(5.5–5) $T_\lambda v_n = (1/\theta_n)T_\lambda x_n \to 0.$

Now

$$v_n = (\lambda^{-1})[T_\lambda v_n + T v_n]$$

and $\|v_n\| = 1$. From (5.5–5) and the compactness of T it follows that $\{v_n\}$ contains a convergent subsequence with some limit v. From (5.5–5) it follows that $T_\lambda v = 0$, i.e., $v \in \mathcal{N}(T_\lambda)$. Now let $w_n = u_n + \theta_n v$. Observe that $w_n \in \mathcal{N}(T_\lambda)$, so that $d_n \leqslant \|x_n - w_n\|$. On the other hand, $x_n - w_n = \theta_n(v_n - v)$, so that $\|x_n - w_n\| < 2d_n\|v_n - v\|$, since $\theta_n < 2d_n$. We see in this way that $1 < 2\|v_n - v\|$, which contradicts the fact that $\{v_n\}$ contains a subsequence converging to v. We must therefore conclude that $\mathcal{R}(T_\lambda)$ is closed.

Theorem 5.5–E.   *Suppose $T \in [X]$, T compact, and $\lambda \neq 0$. Then the ascent and descent of $\lambda - T$ are both finite (and hence equal).*

PROOF. Suppose $\alpha(\lambda - T) = \infty$. Then $\mathcal{N}(T^{n-1})$ is a proper closed subset of $\mathcal{N}(T_\lambda^n)$ for $n = 1, 2, \cdots$. By Theorem 3.12–E there exists $x_n \in \mathcal{N}(T_\lambda^n)$ such that $\|x_n\| = 1$ and $\|x_n - x\| \geqslant {}^1/_2$ if $x \in \mathcal{N}(T^{n-1})$. Assume $1 \leqslant m < n$ and let

$$z = x_m + \lambda^{-1}T_\lambda x_n - \lambda^{-1}T_\lambda x_m.$$

Then

$$T_\lambda^{n-1}z = T_\lambda^{n-1}x_m + \lambda^{-1}T_\lambda^n x_n - \lambda^{-1}T_\lambda^n x_m = 0,$$

and so $z \in \mathcal{N}(T_\lambda^{n-1})$. Consequently $\|x_n - z\| \geqslant {}^1/_2$. But we easily calculate that $Tx_n - Tx_m = \lambda(x_n - z)$, and so $\|Tx_n - Tx_m\| \geqslant |\lambda|/2 > 0$. This shows that $\{Tx_n\}$ can have no convergent subsequence, in contradiction to the fact that T is compact. Thus $\alpha(\lambda - T)$ must be finite.

The proof that $\delta(\lambda - T)$ is finite is similar. If it were not, $\mathcal{R}(T_\lambda^n)$ would be a proper closed subset of $\mathcal{R}(T_\lambda^{n-1})$ for $n = 1, 2, \cdots$. We choose $y_n \in \mathcal{R}(T_\lambda^n)$ so that $\|y_n\| = 1$ and $\|y_n - y\| \geqslant {}^1/_2$ if $y \in \mathcal{R}(T_\lambda^{n+1})$. If $1 \leqslant m < n$ let

$$w = y_n - \lambda^{-1}T_\lambda y_n + \lambda^{-1}T_\lambda y_m.$$

We can write $y_k = T^k x_k$ for some x_k. Thus

$$w = T_\lambda^n x_n - \lambda^{-1}T_\lambda^{n+1}x_n + \lambda^{-1}T_\lambda^{m+1}x_m,$$

from which we see that $w \in \mathcal{R}(T_\lambda^{m+1})$. Therefore $\|y_m - w\| \geqslant {}^1/_2$. But $Ty_m - Ty_n = \lambda(y_m - w)$ and so $\|Ty_m - Ty_n\| \geqslant |\lambda|/2$, and we obtain a contradiction, just as in the earlier argument. This completes the proof.

Our next main objective is to show that when $\lambda \neq 0$ and T is compact, λ is either an eigenvalue of T or in the resolvent set of T. For this purpose we prove that there exists a constant M such that if $d(x)$ is the distance from x to $\mathcal{N}(T_\lambda)$ (x arbitrary), then

(5.5–6) $$d(x) \leqslant M\|T_\lambda x\|.$$

If we suppose this not true, there exists a sequence $\{x_n\}$ of points not in $\mathcal{N}(T_\lambda)$ such that $d(x_n)/\|T_\lambda x_n\| \to \infty$. Since $\mathcal{N}(T_\lambda)$ is finite dimensional, there exists $u_n \in \mathcal{N}(T_\lambda)$ such that $\|x_n - u_n\| = d(x_n)$. Let $y_n = (x_n - u_n)/d(x_n)$. Then $\|y_n\| = 1$ and $T_\lambda y_n \to 0$. From the equation

$$y_n = \lambda^{-1}(T_\lambda y_n + Ty_n)$$

and the compactness of T we infer that $\{y_n\}$ contains a subsequence converging to a limit y. Then the fact that $T_\lambda y_n \to 0$ implies $T_\lambda y = 0$. Then $u_n + d(x_n)y \in \mathcal{N}(T_\lambda)$, and so

$$\|y_n - y\| = \frac{\|x_n - [u_n + d(x_n)y]\|}{d(x_n)} \geqslant 1.$$

This contradicts the fact that $\{y_n\}$ contains a subsequence converging to y. Thus (5.5–6) is proved.

Theorem 5.5–F. *Suppose $T \in [X]$, T compact, and $\lambda \neq 0$. If M is the constant in (5.5–6), then, to each $y \in \mathscr{R}(T_\lambda)$ there corresponds an x such that $T_\lambda x = y$ and $\|x\| \leqslant M\|y\|$. Hence $(\lambda - T)^{-1}$ is continuous if it exists. The point λ is either in $\rho(T)$, in which case $\mathscr{R}(T_\lambda) = X$, or it is in $P\sigma(T)$, in which case $\mathscr{R}(T_\lambda)$ is a proper closed subspace of X.*

PROOF. To prove the first assertion, suppose $y = T_\lambda x_1$. Choose $u \in \mathscr{N}(T_\lambda)$ so that $\|x_1 - u\| = d(x_1)$, and let $x = x_1 - u$. Then $T_\lambda x = y$ and $\|x\| = d(x_1) \leqslant M\|T_\lambda x_1\| = M\|y\|$. We know that either $\alpha(\lambda - T) = \delta(\lambda - T) = 0$ or $0 < \alpha(\lambda - T) = \delta(\lambda - T) < \infty$. In the first case $(\lambda - T)^{-1}$ exists and $\mathscr{R}(T_\lambda) = X$, as we know from the definitions of ascent and descent. In the second case $(\lambda - T)^{-1}$ does not exist and $\mathscr{R}(T_\lambda) \neq X$. The rest of the assertions are evident from what has been shown.

The next question which arises naturally is this: How many points can there be in $P\sigma(T)$? This question is answered in the next theorem.

Theorem 5.5–G. *Suppose $T \in [X]$ and T compact. Then $P\sigma(T)$ contains at most a countable set of points, and these have no accumulation point except possibly the point $\lambda = 0$.*

PROOF. We first observe the following: If $Tx_k = \lambda_k x_k (k = 1, \cdots, n)$, where $x_k \neq 0$ and the λ_k's are all distinct, then $x_1, \cdots, x_n$ are linearly independent. For, if not, let x_m be the first x_k which is a linear combination of its predecessors, say $x_m = \alpha_1 x_1 + \cdots + \alpha_{m-1} x_{m-1}$. From $Tx_m - \lambda_m x_m = 0$ we obtain

$$0 = \alpha_1(\lambda_1 - \lambda_m)x_1 + \cdots + \alpha_{m-1}(\lambda_{m-1} - \lambda_m)x_{m-1}.$$

Hence $\alpha_1 = \cdots = \alpha_{m-1} = 0$, whence $x_m = 0$, which is a contradiction.

Now, to prove the theorem it suffices to show that, if $\epsilon > 0$, the points λ of $P\sigma(T)$ for which $|\lambda| \geqslant \epsilon$ form a finite set. Suppose the contrary for some ϵ, and let $\{\lambda_n\}$ be an infinite sequence of distinct points in $P\sigma(T)$ with $|\lambda_n| \geqslant \epsilon$. Then $Tx_n = \lambda_n x_n$, where $x_n \neq 0$. The set of all the x_n's is linearly independent. Let M_n be the linear manifold generated by $x_1, \cdots, x_n$. Then M_{n-1} is a proper closed subset of M_n. By Theorem 3.12–E there exists $u_n \in M_n$ such that $\|u_n\| = 1$ and $\|u_n - x\| \geqslant \frac{1}{2}$ if $x \in M_{n-1}$. Now $Tu_n \in M_n$, since $Tx_k = \lambda_k x_k$ and u_n is a linear combination of $x_1, \cdots, x_n$. But if $x = \alpha_1 x_1 + \cdots + \alpha_n x_n$ we see that

$$(\lambda_n - T)x = \alpha_1(\lambda_n - \lambda_1)x_1 + \cdots + \alpha_{n-1}(\lambda_n - \lambda_{n-1})x_{n-1},$$

so that $(\lambda_n - T)(M_n) \subset M_{n-1}$. In particular, $(\lambda_n - T)u_n \in M_{n-1}$. Therefore $z = (\lambda_n - T)u_n + Tu_m \in M_{n-1}$ if $1 \leqslant m < n$, and so also $\lambda_n^{-1}z \in M_{n-1}$.   Now

$$Tu_n - Tu_m = \lambda_n u_n - (\lambda_n u_n - Tu_n + Tu_m) = \lambda_n(u_n - \lambda_n^{-1}z),$$

and so $\|Tu_n - Tu_m\| \geqslant |\lambda_n|/2 \geqslant \epsilon/2$. This contradicts the fact that $\{Tu_n\}$ must contain a convergent subsequence and completes the proof of the theorem.

By various examples it may be shown that when T is compact the point $\lambda = 0$ can belong to $P\sigma(T)$, $C\sigma(T)$, or $R\sigma(T)$; it cannot belong to $\rho(T)$ if X is infinite dimensional.   See problems 9–12.

The next phase of our study concerns the conjugate operator T'.   We know that it is compact (Theorem 5.5–B).   From Theorem 5.3–A we know that T and T' have the same spectrum.   Hence, if $\lambda \neq 0$, then λ is an eigenvalue of T if and only if it is an eigenvalue of T'.   But more than this is true.

Theorem 5.5–H.   *Suppose $T \in [X]$, T compact, and $\lambda \neq 0$. Then for each n the null spaces of T_λ^n and $(T_\lambda')^n$ have the same dimension, and hence $\lambda - T$ and $\lambda - T'$ have the same ascent.*

PROOF.   It suffices to give the proof for $n = 1$, because $(T_\lambda^n)' = (T_\lambda')^n$ and $T_\lambda^n = \lambda^n - B$, where B is compact (see the proof of Theorem 5.5–C). Suppose $\mathcal{N}(T_\lambda)$ and $\mathcal{N}(T_\lambda')$ are of dimensions m and n, respectively. We can assume $m \geqslant 1$, $n \geqslant 1$, because $m = 0$ implies $n = 0$ and conversely.   Let $x_1, \cdots, x_m$ and $u_1', \cdots, u_n'$ be bases for $\mathcal{N}(T_\lambda)$ and $\mathcal{N}(T_\lambda')$, respectively.   It follows easily from Theorem 3.5–C that there exists a set of elements $u_1, \cdots, u_n$ in X such that

(5.5–7) $$u_i'(u_j) = \delta_{ij}.$$

Also, there is a set of elements $x_1', \cdots, x_m'$ in X' such that

(5.5–8) $$x_i'(x_j) = \delta_{ij}.$$

This follows from Theorem 3.8–E (or from Theorem 4.3–D).

We assume $m < n$ and deduce a contradiction.   We define an operator A by the equation

$$Ax = Tx + \sum_{i=1}^{m} x_i'(x)u_i;$$

A is compact, by problems 2 and 3.   Applying Theorem 4.6–C to T_λ, we see that

(5.5–9) $$u_j'(T_\lambda x) = 0, \qquad x \in X, \qquad j = 1, \cdots, n.$$

We now prove that $(\lambda - A)^{-1}$ exists.   For,

$$(5.5\text{-}10) \qquad (\lambda - A)x = T_\lambda x - \sum_{i=1}^{m} x_i'(x)u_i.$$

If $(\lambda - A)x = 0$, we conclude from (5.5-10), (5.5-9) and (5.5-8) that $x_1'(x) = \cdots x_m'(x) = 0$, whence $T_\lambda x = 0$.   But then x is a linear combination of $x_1, \cdots, x_m$, say $x = \alpha_1 x_1 + \cdots + \alpha_m x_m$.   Applying x_i' to x, we find that $\alpha_i = 0$, whence $x = 0$.   Thus $(\lambda - A)^{-1}$ exists.   By Theorem 5.5–F, applied to A, we conclude that $\mathcal{R}(\lambda - A) = X$.   We then choose x so that $(\lambda - A)x = u_{m+1}$.   Now $u'_{m+1}(u_{m+1}) = 1$.   But by (5.5-10), (5.5-9) and (5.5-7) we have

$$u'_{m+1}(u_{m+1}) = u'_{m+1}(T_\lambda x) - \sum_{i=1}^{m} x_i'(x)u'_{m+1}(u_i) = 0.$$

From this contradiction we must conclude that $m \geqslant n$.

Next we assume that $m > n$ and deduce a contradiction.   We define an operator B on X' by

$$Bx' = T'x' + \sum_{i=1}^{n} x'(u_i)x_i',$$

and observe that it is compact.   This time we use Theorem 4.6–F to observe that $x_i \in {}^0\{\mathcal{R}(T_\lambda')\}$, and from this we prove that $(\lambda - B)^{-1}$ exists. We then choose x' so that $(\lambda - B)x' = x'_{n+1}$ and obtain a contradiction of the fact that $x'_{n+1}(x_{n+1}) = 1$.   The reader can easily supply the details. Thus, finally, we conclude that $m = n$.

The last of the theorems of this section tells us the exact relation between $\mathcal{R}(T_\lambda)$ and $\mathcal{N}(T_\lambda')$, with a dual result when T_λ and T_λ' are exchanged.

Theorem 5.5–I.   *Suppose $T \in [X]$, T compact, and $\lambda \neq 0$.   Then $\mathcal{R}(T_\lambda) = {}^0\{\mathcal{N}(T_\lambda')\}$, and $\mathcal{R}(T_\lambda') = \{\mathcal{N}(T_\lambda)\}^0$.*

PROOF.   The first relation follows from Theorem 4.6–D, because we know that $\mathcal{R}(T_\lambda)$ is closed.   For the second relation we have only to prove that $\{\mathcal{N}(T_\lambda)\}^0 \subset \mathcal{R}(T_\lambda')$, because of Theorem 4.6–G.   Hence we start by assuming $y' \in \{\mathcal{N}(T_\lambda)\}^0$.   If $y \in \mathcal{R}(T_\lambda)$, define $f(y) = y'(x)$, where x is any element such that $T_\lambda x = y$.   The value of $y'(x)$ is the same, no matter which x is chosen, because $y' \in \{\mathcal{N}(T_\lambda)\}^0$.   Clearly f is a linear functional on $\mathcal{R}(T_\lambda)$.   Now, with y given, we can choose x so that $T_\lambda x = y$ and $\|x\| \leqslant M \|y\|$ (Theorem 5.5–F).   From this it follows easily that f is continuous.   If we now choose $x' \in X'$ so that x' is an extension of f

(and we can do this), we have $x'(T_\lambda x) = y'(x)$ for every $x \in X$, and so $y' = T_\lambda' x'$. Thus $y' \in \mathscr{R}(T_\lambda')$, and the proof is complete.

We conclude this section with a brief summary of the application of the theory of compact operators to the study of integral equations. We consider Fredholm equations of the second kind, in the form

$$(5.5\text{--}11) \qquad y(s) = x(s) - \lambda \int_a^b k(s, t)x(t)\, dt,$$

where the kernel k is of such a sort that the integral operator K defined by it is compact when acting in a certain specified normed linear function space X. We think primarily of $X = C[a, b]$ or $X = L^2(a, b)$. We can write (5.5–11) in the form $y = x - \lambda Kx$. Note that the parameter λ here occupies a different position than it does in our previous work, where we have been studying the equation $y = \lambda x - Tx$. There is no interest in the equation (5.5–11) when $\lambda = 0$, so we can assume $\lambda \neq 0$ and rewrite the equation as

$$\lambda^{-1}y = \lambda^{-1}x - Kx.$$

Since $\lambda^{-1} \neq 0$, our theory of compact operators now tells us the following:

For a given $\lambda \neq 0$, either (5.5–11) has a unique solution x corresponding to each choice of $y \in X$, or else the homogeneous equation

$$(5.5\text{--}12) \qquad 0 = x(s) - \lambda \int_a^b k(s, t)x(t)\, dt$$

has a solution $x \neq 0$. In this latter case the number of linearly independent solutions of (5.5–12) is finite. The number λ^{-1} is then an eigenvalue of the integral operator K. It is customary to call λ itself a *characteristic value* of K. *The set of characteristic values is at most countable. If there is an infinite sequence $\{\lambda_n\}$ of such values, $|\lambda_n| \to \infty$.*

If the function space in question is $C[a, b]$, the conjugate operator K' acts in a different space. But, if we are dealing with $L^2(a, b)$ and if k is an $\mathscr{L}^2$ kernel, we can identify K' with the integral operator in $L^2(a, b)$ such that $K'x$ is represented by

$$\int_a^b k(t, s)x(t)\, dt.$$

In this case the theory goes on to tell us that (5.5–12) and the equation

$$(5.5\text{--}13) \qquad 0 = x(s) - \lambda \int_a^b k(t, s)x(t)\, dt$$

have the same number of linearly independent solutions. Furthermore, if

λ *is a characteristic value,* (5.5–11) *has a solution in L^2 corresponding to a given $y \in L^2$ if and only if*

$$\int_a^b y(t)\overline{x(t)} \, dt = 0$$

whenever x is a solution of (5.5–13).

Even when we are interested in the space $C[a, b]$ the L^2 theory may be useful to us.   Suppose that k is an $\mathscr{L}^2$ kernel such that Kx and $K'x$ are in $C[a, b]$ whenever $x \in L^2(a, b)$.   This is the case, for instance, if $k(s, t)$ is continuous in both variables (we assume that $[a, b]$ is a finite interval). Then, if $y \in C[a, b]$ and $x \in L^2(a, b)$ is a solution of (5.5–11), it follows that $x \in C[a, b]$.   Hence, in particular, the solutions of (5.5–12) are continuous, and the same is true of (5.5–13).   Therefore it follows that all of the foregoing italicized assertions remain valid if we regard the $\mathscr{L}^2$ kernel as defining an operator in $C[a, b]$ rather than in $L^2(a, b)$ and restrict x and y accordingly.

The theory of Fredholm integral equations of the second kind, in the form here presented, can be applied to obtain a solution of the Dirichlet problem in two dimensions, provided the region in question is of a sufficiently simple character (the essential restrictions are on the smoothness of the boundary).   The same method can be applied to other boundary-value problems associated with the Laplace operator, e.g., the Neumann problem.   For the Dirichlet problem in spaces of higher dimension, the procedure is slightly more complicated, because one has to deal with an integral operator which may not be compact.   However, a certain power of the operator turns out to be compact, and this is sufficient to obtain the results stated in the first two sentences in connection with (5.5–12) (see the remarks following the proof of Theorem 5.8–F). These are the decisive results for the application to the Dirichlet problem. For more details see Riesz and Nagy, **1**, pages 189–192 and Kellogg, **1**, pages 311–315.

PROBLEMS

1. If X is finite dimensional and T is linear on X into Y, then T is compact.

2. If $T \in [X, Y]$ and Y is finite dimensional, then T is compact.

3. The set of compact linear operators on X into Y is a linear manifold in $[X, Y]$.   If Y is complete, this manifold is closed.   For proof of the last assertion assume A_k compact and in $[X, Y]$, $B \in [X, Y]$, and $\|A_k - B\| \to 0$. If $\{x_n\}$ is a bounded sequence in X, use the diagonal procedure to obtain a subsequence of $\{x_n\}$, denoted by $\{u_n\}$, such that $\lim_{n \to \infty} A_k(u_n)$ exists for each k. Then show that $\{Bu_n\}$ is a Cauchy sequence in Y.

4. If $A, B \in [X]$ and A is compact, so are AB and BA.

5. If $T \in [X, Y]$, Y is complete, and T' is compact, then T is compact. For the proof use the relation $T''J_1 = J_2T$ (using notation as in problem 3, § 4.5) and the fact that T'' is compact.

6. If $X = l^2$ and (α_{ij}) is an infinite matrix such that $\sum\limits_{i,j=1}^{\infty} |\alpha_{ij}|^2 < \infty$, the equations $\eta_i = \sum\limits_{j=1}^{\infty} \alpha_{ij}\xi_j$ define a compact linear mapping $y = Ax$ of X into itself, with $\|A\| \leqslant \left(\sum\limits_{i,j=1}^{\infty} |\alpha_{ij}|^2 \right)^{\frac{1}{2}}$.

7. A set S in a normed linear space X is called conditionally sequentially compact if every sequence from S contains a convergent subsequence. If $X = l^p$, where $1 \leqslant p < \infty$, a set S in X has this property if and only if (a) S is bounded, and (b) $\sum\limits_{i=n}^{\infty} |\xi_i|^p \to 0$ as $n \to \infty$, uniformly for all $x = \{\xi_i\}$ in S. To prove the sufficiency of these conditions use a diagonal procedure on the components of the given sequence $\{x_n\}$. Boundedness of S is clearly necessary; the necessity of (b) may be proved by the method of contradiction.

8. Show from Theorem 5.5-F that $\lambda - T$ takes open sets in X into sets which are open in the induced topology of $\mathscr{R}(T_\lambda)$.

9. The point $\lambda = 0$ has a status different from other points in relation to T if $T \in [X]$, T is compact, and X is infinite dimensional. In this case 0 can never be in $\rho(T)$. To show this, assume the contrary, so that $\overline{\mathscr{R}(T)} = X$ and T has a continuous inverse. Suppose $\|y_n\| = 1$. Choose $z_n = Tx_n$ so that $\|z_n - y_n\| < 1/n$. Use the compactness of T to deduce that $\{y_n\}$ contains a convergent subsequence and hence that X is finite dimensional.

10. Define $T \in [l^1]$ by $y = \{k^{-1}\xi_k\}$, where $x = \{\xi_k\}$. Then T is compact, and $0 \in C\sigma(T)$. What are the eigenvalues?

11. Define $T \in [l^1]$ by the matrix (t_{ij}) with $t_{i1} = 2^{1-i}$, $i \geqslant 2$, $t_{ii} = 2^{1-i}$, $i \geqslant 2$, and all other $t_{ij} = 0$. Then T is compact, and $0 \in R\sigma(T)$. What are the eigenvalues?

12. Suppose $x_0 \in X$, $x_0' \in X'$, $x_0'(x_0) \neq 0$. Define $Tx = x_0'(x)x_0$. Show that $\sigma(T)$ consists of the eigenvalues $\lambda = 0$, $\lambda = x_0'(x_0)$ and that $R_\lambda y = \lambda^{-1}y + \lambda^{-1}[\lambda - x_0'(x_0)]^{-1}Ty$.

13. Suppose X is not complete, and let $T \in [X]$ be compact. Let $\hat{T}$ be the unique continuous extension of T to all of the completion $\hat{X}$. Then $\hat{T}$ is compact and $\mathscr{R}(\hat{T}) \subset X$. If $\lambda \neq 0$, T_λ^n and $\hat{T}_\lambda^n$ have the same null manifold, and so T_λ and $\hat{T}_\lambda$ have the same ascent; also, $\mathscr{R}(T_\lambda^n) = \mathscr{R}(\hat{T}_\lambda^n) \cap X$ and $\hat{T}_\lambda^n(\hat{X} - X) \subset \hat{X} - X$. Finally, $\sigma(T) = \sigma(\hat{T})$.

14. Suppose $f \in C[a, b]$. Consider the inhomogeneous two-point problem
$$y''(s) + \lambda f(s)y(s) = x(s), \qquad y(a) = \alpha, \qquad y(b) = \beta,$$
and the corresponding homogeneous problem in which the function x is identically zero. Show that, for a given λ, either the inhomogeneous problem has a unique twice continuously differentiable solution corresponding to each $x \in C[a, b]$, or else the homogeneous problem has a nonzero twice continuously differentiable solution. Also, the λ's for which the latter situation occurs form

an at most countable set with no finite point of accumulation in the extended complex plane. Use the discussion in § 4.13, with $\lambda f(s)$ replacing $a_2(s)$.

15. Given $T \in [X, Y]$ (X and Y normed linear spaces) and T compact, then $Tx_n \to Tx$ whenever $\{x_n\}$ is X'-weakly convergent to x. The essential thing to show is that, if $\{x_n\}$ is X'-weakly convergent to x, a subsequence of $\{Tx_n\}$ converges to Tx. This can be done with the aid of the conjugate operator T'. One can then conclude that $Tx_n \to Tx$, by assuming this false and deducing a contradiction.

16. Suppose $T \in [X, Y]$, where X is norm reflexive and T has the property that $Tx_n \to Tx$ whenever $\{x_n\}$ is X'-weakly convergent to x. Then T is compact. For operators in Hilbert space, this is the form in which the concept of a *vollstetig* operator was originally introduced. The proposition does not remain true if the hypothesis that X is norm reflexive is dropped. Example: take $X = Y = l^1$. Then the identity mapping is not compact, whereas X'-weak convergence is identical with convergence according to the norm (Banach, **1**, page 137).

5.6 An Operational Calculus

If X is a complex Banach space and T is a closed operator with domain and range in X, the fact that the resolvent operator $R_\lambda \equiv (\lambda - T)^{-1}$ is analytic as a function of λ enables us to obtain some important results by the use of contour integrals in the complex λ-plane. Since X is complete, so is $[X]$; the completeness of these spaces assures us of the existence of the contour integrals with which we deal. These integrals, of functions with values in X or $[X]$, may be defined just as in classical analysis.

First let us consider some aspects of the situation when $T \in [X]$. In this case $\sigma(T)$ is bounded, and we have a power series formula for R_λ when $|\lambda| > r_\sigma(T)$; see (5.2–4). If C denotes a simple closed contour, oriented counterclockwise, enclosing the circle $|\lambda| = r_\sigma(T)$, we can integrate (5.2–4) term by term around the contour, and we obtain

$$(5.6\text{–}1) \qquad\qquad I = \frac{1}{2\pi i} \int_C R_\lambda \, d\lambda,$$

because of the fact that the integral of each term of the series is 0, except for the first one. In a similar way,

$$(5.6\text{–}2) \qquad T^p = \frac{1}{2\pi i} \int_C \lambda^p R_\lambda \, d\lambda \qquad p = 0, 1, 2, \cdots.$$

Since R_λ is analytic except at the points of $\sigma(T)$, it is clear that the integral in (5.6–2) is unchanged in value if we deform the contour C in any manner, so long as it continues to enclose $\sigma(T)$. We may even replace the single contour C by several nonintersecting closed contours, provided that no one of them is inside any other and $\sigma(T)$ lies in the union of their interiors.

We now propose to define a certain class of complex-valued analytic functions and to associate with each such function f an element of the operator space $[X]$. The operator associated with f will be denoted by $f(T)$. The feature of greatest importance in this association is that the correspondence between f and $f(T)$ preserves the basic algebraic operations. That is, the operators corresponding to $f + g$, αf, and fg, respectively, are $f(T) + g(T)$, $\alpha f(T)$, and $f(T)g(T)$. In particular, then, since $fg = gf$, the operators $f(T)$ and $g(T)$ commute.

In what follows we use $\Delta(f)$ to denote the domain of definition of f.

Definition.   Suppose $T \in [X]$. Let $\mathfrak{A}(T)$ be the class of complex-valued functions f such that: (1) $\Delta(f)$ is an open set in the complex plane, and it contains $\sigma(T)$; (2) f is differentiable at each point of $\Delta(f)$.

We do not insist that $\Delta(f)$ be connected. If $\Delta(f)$ has two components, for example, it is legitimate to have $f(\lambda) = \lambda^2$ on one component and $f(\lambda) = 0$ on the other. The definition means that f is analytic, in the sense of classical function theory, on each component of $\Delta(f)$, but there is no necessary connection, by analytic continuation or otherwise, between the values of f in different components. We say that f is *locally analytic* on $\sigma(T)$.

Next we introduce some terminology and notation in connection with contour integrals.

Definition.   A set D in the complex plane is called a *Cauchy domain* if: (1) it is open; (2) it has a finite number of components, the closures of any two of which are disjoint; (3) the boundary of D is composed of a finite positive number of closed rectifiable Jordan curves, no two of which intersect.

If C is one of the curves forming part of the boundary of D, the positive orientation of C is clockwise or counterclockwise according to whether the points of D near a point of C are outside or inside of C. The positively oriented boundary of D is denoted by $+ B(D)$; with the reverse orientation it is denoted by $- B(D)$.

For our purposes the following are typical examples of bounded Cauchy domains. Unbounded Cauchy domains will be used later.

Example I.   The set $\{\lambda : |\lambda| < 1\} \cup \{\lambda : 2 < |\lambda| < 3\}$.

Example 2.   The set $\{\lambda : |\lambda| < 1\} \cup \{\lambda : |\lambda - 3| < 1\} \cup \{\lambda : |\lambda - 6| < 1\}$.

We are now ready to define an operator $f(T)$ corresponding to $f \in \mathfrak{A}(T)$. The definition is

$$(5.6\text{-}3) \qquad f(T) = \frac{1}{2\pi i} \int_{+B(D)} f(\lambda) R_\lambda \, d\lambda,$$

where D is any bounded Cauchy domain such that $\sigma(T) \subset D$ and $\bar{D} \subset \Delta(f)$. Concerning this definition several comments are needed. (1) When f is given, there exists a Cauchy domain of the required sort. This is intuitively plausible; a detailed proof may be based on the construction given in Taylor, **2** (Theorem 3.3 and proof, page 65).   (2) The integral in (5.6–3) has a value independent of the particular choice of D. This is so by an application of Cauchy's theorem.   For, if D_1 and D_2 are two Cauchy domains of the sort considered, we have $\sigma(T) \subset D_1 \cap D_2$, and there exists a bounded Cauchy domain D such that $\sigma(T) \subset D$ and $\bar{D} \subset D_1 \cap D_2$. Now $D_1 - \bar{D}$ is a bounded Cauchy domain, and its oriented boundary consists of $+ B(D_1)$ and $- B(D)$. Moreover, $f(\lambda) R_\lambda$ has no singularities in $D_1 - \bar{D}$ or on its boundary, and hence, by Cauchy's theorem, the integral of $f(\lambda) R_\lambda$ over $+ B(D_1)$ is equal to the integral over $+ B(D)$. The same result holds with D_2 in place of D_1, and so our assertion is justified.   (3) The integral in (5.6–3) is unchanged in value if we replace f by any other member of $\mathfrak{A}(T)$, say g, such that $f(\lambda) = g(\lambda)$ at each point λ of an open set containing $\sigma(T)$.   This follows from the foregoing remarks.

We now show that the operator corresponding to $f_1 f_2$ is $f_1(T) f_2(T)$. The proof depends heavily on the equation $R_\lambda - R_\mu = (\mu - \lambda) R_\lambda R_\mu$ (see Theorem 5.1–C).   Choose bounded Cauchy domains D_1, D_2 such that $\sigma(T) \subset D_1$, $\bar{D}_1 \subset D_2$, $\bar{D}_2 \subset \Delta(f_1) \cap \Delta(f_2)$.   Then we express $f_1(T)$ as an integral with respect to λ over $+ B(D_1)$ and $f_2(T)$ as an integral with respect to μ over $+ B(D_2)$.   Then we can write

$$(5.6\text{-}4) \qquad f_1(T) f_2(T) = \frac{1}{2\pi i} \int_{+B(D_1)} f_1(\lambda) \left\{ \frac{1}{2\pi i} \int_{+B(D_2)} f_2(\mu) R_\lambda R_\mu \, d\mu \right\} d\lambda.$$

In this expression we replace $R_\lambda R_\mu$ by

$$\frac{R_\lambda - R_\mu}{\mu - \lambda} = \frac{R_\lambda}{\mu - \lambda} + \frac{R_\mu}{\lambda - \mu},$$

and invert the order of the iterated integration where the second fraction is concerned.   Since $\lambda \in D_2$ and μ is not in $\bar{D}_1$, we have

$$\frac{1}{2\pi i} \int_{+B(D_2)} \frac{f_2(\mu)}{\mu - \lambda} \, d\lambda = f_2(\lambda), \qquad \frac{1}{2\pi i} \int_{+B(D_1)} \frac{f_1(\lambda)}{\lambda - \mu} \, d\lambda = 0.$$

Hence we obtain from (5.6–4) the desired result

$$f_1(T)f_2(T) = \frac{1}{2\pi i}\int_{+B(D_1)} f_1(\lambda)f_2(\lambda)R_\lambda \, d\lambda = (f_1 f_2)(T).$$

It is obvious from (5.6–3) that $(f + g)(T) = f(T) + g(T)$ and $(\alpha f)(T) = \alpha f(T)$.

It is instructive to regard the association of $f(T)$ with f as an algebraic homomorphism. But in order to be precise about this it is first of all necessary to convert $\mathfrak{A}(T)$ into an algebra by an appropriate equivalence relation. We define two functions f, g as being equivalent (relative to T) if $f(\lambda) = g(\lambda)$ on some open set containing $\sigma(T)$. Then $\mathfrak{A}(T)$ is divided into equivalence classes, and these classes form a commutative algebra with a unit element if we define the algebraic operations in an obvious way, using representative functions. We have already noted that $f(T)$ is unchanged if f is replaced by an equivalent function.

Theorem 5.6–A. *The mapping $f \to f(T)$ by the formula (5.6–3) is an algebraic homomorphism of the algebra of the equivalence classes of $\mathfrak{A}(T)$ into the algebra $[X]$. This mapping carries the function $f(\lambda) \equiv 1$ into I and the function $f(\lambda) \equiv \lambda$ into T.*

The proof is covered by the preceding discussion. The last two assertions are justified by (5.6–1) and 5.6–2).

The reader may have noticed that the formula defining $f(T)$ has a striking appearance when for heuristic effect we write R_λ in the form $\frac{1}{\lambda - T}$:

$$f(T) = \frac{1}{2\pi i}\int_{+B(D)} \frac{f(\lambda)}{\lambda - T} d\lambda.$$

In formal structure this is just Cauchy's formula, with T in place of a complex number. We refer to the use of the homomorphism $f \to f(T)$ and the consequences flowing out of it as an operational calculus for T.

One use of the operational calculus is that it enables us to compute inverse operators in certain situations.

Theorem 5.6–B. *Suppose $T \in [X]$ and $f \in \mathfrak{A}(T)$. Suppose $f(\lambda) \neq 0$ when $\lambda \in \sigma(T)$. Then $f(T)$ sets up a one-to-one mapping of X onto all of X, with inverse $g(T)$, where g is any member of $\mathfrak{A}(T)$ equivalent to the reciprocal of $f(\lambda)$.*

PROOF. From $f(\lambda)g(\lambda) \equiv 1$ on a neighborhood of $\sigma(T)$ we infer $f(T)g(T) = g(T)f(T) = I$, and the conclusion follows.

We now give an example which illustrates the operational calculus for a particular operator.

Example 3. Let $X = C[0, 1]$, and consider the very special Volterra-type operator T, where $Tx = y$ means

$$y(s) = \int_0^s x(t)\, dt.$$

It is easily verified by induction that $T^{n+1}x = y$ means

$$y(s) = \frac{1}{n!} \int_0^s (s - t)^n x(t)\, dt.$$

In this case the series (5.2–4) for R_λ converges whenever $\lambda \neq 0$ (i.e., $\sigma(T)$ is the single point $\lambda = 0$). By using this series we find that $x = R_\lambda y$ means

$$(5.6\text{–}5) \qquad x(s) = \frac{1}{\lambda} y(s) + \frac{1}{\lambda^2} \int_0^s e^{(s-t)/\lambda} y(t)\, dt.$$

In this case $\mathfrak{A}(T)$ consists of functions analytic in a neighborhood of $\lambda = 0$. If f is such a function, we can deduce the meaning of $f(T)$ from (5.6–3) and (5.6–5). The relation $y = f(T)x$ can be written

$$y(s) = \frac{1}{2\pi i} \oint f(\lambda) \left\{ \frac{1}{\lambda} x(s) + \frac{1}{\lambda^2} \int_0^s e^{(s-t)/\lambda} x(t)\, dt \right\} d\lambda,$$

or

$$(5.6\text{–}6) \qquad y(s) = f(0)x(s) + \int_0^s x(t) \left\{ \frac{1}{2\pi i} \oint \frac{f(\lambda)}{\lambda^2} e^{(s-t)/\lambda}\, d\lambda \right\} dt,$$

where $\oint$ denotes integration counterclockwise around some sufficiently small circle $|\lambda| = r$. We also write this in the form

$$(5.6\text{–}7) \qquad y(s) = f(0)x(s) + \int_0^s F(s - t)x(t)\, dt,$$

where

$$(5.6\text{–}8) \qquad F(u) = \frac{1}{2\pi i} \oint \frac{f(\lambda)}{\lambda^2} e^{u/\lambda}\, d\lambda.$$

The function F turns out to be an entire function of exponential type. If $f(\lambda)$ is expressed as a power series in λ, with radius of convergence α, the type of F is exactly $1/\alpha$. See problem 1 for more on this subject.

We can use the operational calculus for this particular operator to solve the differential equation

$$y^{(n)}(s) + a_1 y^{(n-1)}(s) + \cdots + a_n y(s) = x(s)$$

with the initial conditions

$$y(0) = y'(0) = \cdots = y^{(n-1)}(0) = 0,$$

where $x \in C[0, 1]$ and the coefficients $a_1, \cdots, a_n$ are constants. It is easy to see that y is a solution of this differential equation and satisfies the initial condition if and only if

$$(I + a_1 T + \cdots + a_n T^n)y = T^n x.$$

Now let $g(\lambda) = 1 + a_1 \lambda + \cdots + a_n \lambda^n$. The problem is to solve $g(T)y = T^n x$ for y. Since $g(0) \neq 0$, we know by Theorem 5.6–B that $g(T)$ has an inverse. The operational calculus shows that $y = f(T)x$, where $f(\lambda) = \lambda^n / g(\lambda)$. Hence, by (5.6–6), the solution of the problem is

$$y(s) = \int_0^s x(t) \left\{ \frac{1}{2\pi i} \oint \frac{\lambda^{n-2}}{g(\lambda)} e^{(s-t)/\lambda} \, d\lambda \right\} dt,$$

where the contour encloses $\lambda = 0$, and all the zeros of $g(\lambda)$ are outside of the contour. By the change of variable $z = \lambda^{-1}$ this solution can be put in the form

$$y(s) = \int_0^s x(t) \left\{ \frac{1}{2\pi i} \oint \frac{e^{(s-t)z}}{z^n + a_1 z^{n-1} + \cdots + a_n} \, dz \right\} dt,$$

where the contour is counterclockwise and encloses all the zeros of the polynomial in the denominator. The integral may be evaluated by computing residues.

It is desirable to develop a generalization of the formula (5.6–3) so as to yield an operational calculus for T when T is any closed linear operator with domain and range in X. It turns out that such a development is possible provided that the resolvent set $\rho(T)$ is not empty. When we give up the condition that $T \in [X]$, the spectrum of T need no longer be compact; it might be empty or it might be the whole plane. However, we assume explicitly that $\sigma(T)$ is *not* the whole plane; we also assume that T is closed. This permits us to utilize Theorem 5.1–C.

Definition. By $\mathfrak{A}_\infty(T)$ we mean the class of complex-valued functions f such that: (1) $\Delta(f)$ is an open set in the complex plane which contains $\sigma(T)$ and is such that the complement of $\Delta(f)$ is compact; (2) f is differentiable in $\Delta(f)$ and $f(\lambda)$ is bounded as $|\lambda| \to \infty$.

We know from function theory that $f(\lambda)$ approaches a finite limit as $|\lambda| \to \infty$, and we denote this limit by $f(\infty)$. We may then say that f is locally analytic on $\sigma(T)$ and at ∞.

We may define an equivalence relation in $\mathfrak{A}_\infty(T)$: two functions are equivalent if they agree on a neighborhood of $\sigma(T)$ and also on a neighborhood of ∞. As before, the equivalence classes form a commutative algebra in an obvious way. The function $f(\lambda) \equiv 1$ determines a unit for the algebra.

In seeking the proper replacement for (5.6–3) we observe that Cauchy's formula for an element of $\mathfrak{A}_\infty(T)$ holds in the form

$$(5.6\text{–}9) \qquad f(\xi) = f(\infty) + \frac{1}{2\pi i} \int_{+B(D)} \frac{f(\lambda)}{\lambda - \xi} \, d\lambda,$$

where D is an *unbounded* Cauchy domain such that $\bar{D} \subset \Delta(f)$ and $\xi \in D$. Note that the complement of an unbounded Cauchy domain is compact; in fact, there is just one unbounded component of such a domain, and its complement is compact.

The appropriate definition of $f(T)$ when $f \in \mathfrak{A}_\infty(T)$ is

$$(5.6\text{–}10) \qquad f(T) = f(\infty)I + \frac{1}{2\pi i} \int_{+B(D)} f(\lambda) R_\lambda \, d\lambda,$$

where D is an unbounded Cauchy domain such that $\sigma(T) \subset D$ and $\bar{D} \subset \Delta(f)$. The three comments made after (5.6–3) have counterparts in the present situation. Observe that $f(T) \in [X]$ even though T need not be in $[X]$.

As an illustration of $\Delta(f)$ and D, suppose $\sigma(T)$ is the entire real axis. Then, for some positive r and ϵ, $\Delta(f)$ must include all points for which $|\lambda| > r$ and all points for which the imaginary part of λ is in absolute value less than ϵ. We could then take D to be the union of the sets $\{\lambda : |\lambda| > 2r\}$, $\{\lambda : |\lambda| \leqslant 2r \text{ and } Im \, |\lambda| < \epsilon/2\}$.

As in the case of Theorem 5.6–A, the mapping $f \rightarrow f(T)$ defined by (5.6–10) is an algebraic homomorphism of the algebra of equivalence classes of $\mathfrak{A}_\infty(T)$ into the algebra $[X]$, and the algebra preserves the unit element, i.e., $f(\lambda) \equiv 1$ maps into $f(T) = I$. To see the truth of this last assertion let D_1 be the complement of the D in (5.6–10). Then D_1 is a bounded Cauchy domain, $\bar{D}_1 \subset \rho(T)$, and $+ B(D) = - B(D_1)$. Since R_λ is analytic on $\rho(T)$, the integral in (5.6–10) vanishes if $f(\lambda) \equiv 1$. In this case $f(\infty) = 1$, and we get $f(T) = I$. The proof that $(f_1 f_2)(T) = {}_1(T)f_2(T)$ is similar to the corresponding proof based on (5.6–3), and we leave the argument to the reader. One must use (5.6–9).

If T is not in $[X]$, we must use (5.6–10) instead of (5.6–3). But, if $T \in [X]$ and $f \in \mathfrak{A}_\infty(T)$, the operator $f(T)$ given by (5.6–10) is the same as that given by (5.6–3). To prove this, choose for the D in (5.6–10) the union of a bounded Cauchy domain D_1 and the exterior of a very large circle C which encloses D_1, where $\sigma(T) \subset D_1$ and $\bar{D}_1 \subset \Delta(f)$. Then the integral over $+ B(D)$ in (5.6–10) becomes the integral over $+ B(D_1)$ plus an integral around C. Since $\|R_\lambda\| \rightarrow 0$ as $|\lambda| \rightarrow \infty$ (when $T \in [X]$), it is easy to prove by standard methods that the integral around C cancels the term $f(\infty)I$.

Corresponding to Theorem 5.6–B we have:

Theorem 5.6–C. *If* T *is closed,* $f \in \mathfrak{A}_\infty(T)$ *and* f *has no zeros on* $\sigma(T)$ *or at* ∞, *the operator* $f(T)$ *has an inverse which belongs to* $[X]$. *This inverse is* $g(T)$, *where* g *is any member of* $\mathfrak{A}_\infty(T)$ *equivalent to the reciprocal of* $f(\lambda)$.

The proof is the same as for Theorem 5.6–B.

A polynomial of degree $n \geqslant 1$ does not belong to $\mathfrak{A}_\infty(T)$.   Nevertheless, it is convenient to be able to deal with polynomials in connection with the operational calculus.   We consider now how this is to be done.

If $P(\lambda)$ is a polynomial of degree n, we define $P(T)$ in the obvious way, by putting T^k in place of λ^k in the expression for $P(\lambda)$; the domain of $P(T)$ is $\mathscr{D}_n(T)$, as defined at the beginning of § 5.41.   We have several lemmas which are useful in dealing with polynomials.

Lemma 5.6–D. *Suppose* $f \in \mathfrak{A}_\infty(T)$, *and suppose either* (a) *that* f *has a zero of order* m *at* ∞, *or* (b) *that* f *vanishes identically in a neighborhood of* ∞. *Let* P *be a polynomial of degree* n, *where* $0 < n \leqslant m$ *in case a and* $0 < n$ *in case b. Let* $F(\lambda) = P(\lambda)f(\lambda)$. *Then* $F \in \mathfrak{A}_\infty(T)$, *the range of* $f(T)$ *lies in* $\mathscr{D}_n(T)$, *and* $F(T) = P(T)f(T)$.

For an indication of the proof see problem 6.

Lemma 5.6–E. *Suppose* $f \in \mathfrak{A}_\infty(T)$, $\alpha \in \rho(T)$, *and an integer* $n \geqslant 0$ *are given, and suppose that* $g \in \mathfrak{A}_\infty(T)$, *where* $g(\lambda) = (\alpha - \lambda)^n f(\lambda)$. (*Note that this hypothesis is essentially a condition on the behavior of* f *near* $\lambda = \infty$.) *Then* $f(T)\mathscr{D}_k(T) \subset \mathscr{D}_{k+n}(T)$ *when* $k \geqslant 0$.

PROOF.   If $x \in \mathscr{D}_k(T)$ we can write $x = (R_\alpha)^k y$ for some y.   Then $f(T)x = (R_\alpha)^n g(T)(R_\alpha)^k y = (R_\alpha)^{n+k} g(T) y \in \mathscr{D}_{n+k}(T)$.

Lemma 5.6–F. *If* $f \in \mathfrak{A}_\infty(T)$ *and* $P(\lambda)$ *is a polynomial of degree* $n \geqslant 1$, *then* $f(T)P(T)x = P(T)f(T)x$ *if* $x \in \mathscr{D}_n(T)$.

PROOF.   Let $G(\lambda) = (\alpha - \lambda)^{-n}P(\lambda)$.   Then $G(T) = P(T)(R_\alpha)^n$ (see problem 6).   If $x \in \mathscr{D}_n(T)$, we can write $x = (R_\alpha)^n y$.   We know $f(T)x \in \mathscr{D}_n(T)$ (Lemma 5.6–E).   Then $P(T)f(T)x = P(T)f(T)(R_\alpha)^n y = G(T)f(T)y = f(T)P(T)(R_\alpha)^n y$, and the proof is complete.

We see next how to express $P(T)x$ as an integral.

Theorem 5.6–G. *Suppose* $\alpha \in \rho(T)$. *Let* D *be any unbounded Cauchy domain such that* $\sigma(T) \subset D$ *and* α *is not in* $\bar{D}$. *Then, if* $P(\lambda)$ *is a polynomial of degree* n *and* $x \in \mathscr{D}_n(T)$,

$$(5.6\text{--}11) \qquad P(T)x = \frac{1}{2\pi i} \int_{+B(D)} \frac{P(\lambda)}{(\lambda - \alpha)^{n+1}} (T - \alpha)^{n+1} R_\lambda x \, d\lambda.$$

If $f \in \mathfrak{A}_\infty(T)$ we can also compute $f(T)$ by this formula for any $n \geqslant 0$, by putting $f(\lambda)$ in place of $P(\lambda)$ and $f(T)$ in place of $P(T)$, provided we choose D so that $\sigma(T) \subset D$ and $\bar{D} \subset \Delta(f)$.

PROOF.   We start from the formula

$$(T - \alpha)^{n+1}R_\lambda x = (\lambda - \alpha)^{n+1}R_\lambda x - \sum_{k=0}^{n} (\lambda - \alpha)^{n-k}(T - \alpha)^k x,$$

which is easily established by induction.   The evaluation of the integral in (5.6–11) then becomes a matter of evaluation of familiar integrals, from which the final results are easily obtained.   We leave details to the reader.

The next theorem is a generalization of Theorem 5.6–C.

Theorem 5.6–H.   *Suppose $f \in \mathfrak{A}_\infty(T)$ and $f(\lambda) \neq 0$ if $\lambda \in \sigma(T)$, but that $f(\infty) = 0$, the zero at ∞ being of finite order m.   Then $f(T)$ has an inverse, the range of $f(T)$ is $\mathscr{D}_m(T)$, and for $x \in \mathscr{D}_m(T)$ we have*

$$(5.6\text{--}12) \quad [f(T)]^{-1}x = \frac{1}{2\pi i} \int_{+B(D)} \{f(\lambda)(\lambda - \alpha)^{m+1}\}^{-1}(T - \alpha)^{m+1}R_\lambda x \, d\lambda.$$

Here $\alpha \in \rho(T)$; α and the unbounded Cauchy domain D are to be chosen so that $\sigma(T) \subset D$, $\bar{D} \subset \Delta(f)$, α is not in $\bar{D}$, and $f(\lambda) \neq 0$ if $\lambda \in \bar{D}$.

PROOF.   Let $g(\lambda) = (\alpha - \lambda)^m f(\lambda)$.   Then g has no zeros on $\sigma(T)$ or at ∞, so that $g(T)$ has an inverse belonging to $[X]$.   Now $f(T) = (R_\alpha)^m g(T)$. Hence $f(T)$ has the inverse $[g(T)]^{-1}(\alpha - T)^m$ with domain $\mathscr{D}_m(T)$.   We calculate $[f(T)]^{-1}x = [g(T)]^{-1}(\alpha - T)^m x$ by using (5.6–11), putting $n = 0$, $1/g(\lambda)$ in place of $P(\lambda)$, and $(\alpha - T)^m x$ in place of x.   The result is (5.6–12).

We now consider an example of a closed operator with unbounded spectrum.

Example 4.   Let $X = C[0, 2\pi]$.   Let $\mathscr{D}(T)$ be the set of continuously differentiable functions $x \in X$ such that $x(0) = x(2\pi)$, and let $Tx = y$ mean $y(s) = -ix'(s)$.   To compute R_λ we solve the differential equation

$$x'(s) - i\lambda x(s) = -iy(s)$$

with the condition $x(0) = x(2\pi)$ on the solution.   We find that the values $\lambda = 0, \pm 1, \pm 2, \cdots$ are in the point spectrum, the eigenfunctions corresponding to $\lambda = n$ being multiples of e^{ins}.   All other values of s are in $\rho(T)$, with $x = R_\lambda y$ expressed by

$$(5.6\text{--}13) \quad x(s) = \frac{e^{i\pi\lambda}}{2 \sin \pi\lambda} \int_0^{2\pi} e^{i\lambda(s-t)} y(t) \, dt - i \int_0^s e^{i\lambda(s-t)} y(t) \, dt.$$

Now suppose $f \in \mathfrak{A}_\infty(T)$. This means that f is analytic at ∞ and also in some neighborhood of each of the points of $\sigma(T)$. For the purpose of computing $f(T)$ we may assume that $f(\lambda) = \sum_0^\infty a_n \lambda^{-n}$ when $|\lambda| > N + 1/3$, where N is some positive integer, and that near $\lambda = k$ $(k = 0, \pm 1, \cdots, \pm N)$ f is given by $f(\lambda) = g_k(\lambda)$, where g_k is analytic at $\lambda = k$. In computing $f(T)$ by formula (5.6–10) we can take D to consist of the exterior of the circle $C: |\lambda| = N + 1/2$ and the union of the interiors of circles $C_k: |\lambda - k| < 1/4$, $k = 0, \pm 1, \cdots, \pm N$. The contribution to $f(T)x$ from integration around C_k turns out to be

$$\frac{g_k(k)}{2\pi} \int_0^{2\pi} x(t)e^{ik(s-t)} \, dt = g_k(k)\xi_k e^{iks},$$

where ξ_k is the Fourier coefficient of $x(t)$ with respect to e^{ikt}. The general formula for $y = f(T)x$ is a bit lengthy, and we forego writing it out here. However, in the special case where $f(\lambda) \equiv a_0$ when $|\lambda| > N + 1/3$, things are much simpler, and $y = f(T)x$ is expressed by

$$(5.6–14) \qquad y(s) = a_0 x(s) + \sum_{k=-N}^N (b_k - a_0)\xi_k e^{iks},$$

where $b_k = g_k(k)$. The coefficients a_0 and b_k can be assigned arbitrarily. From Theorem 5.6–C we get the interesting result that, if a_0 and the b_k's are all different from zero, the solution of (5.6–14) for x is

$$x(s) = \frac{1}{a_0} y(s) + \sum_{k=-N}^N \left(\frac{1}{b_k} - \frac{1}{a_0}\right)\eta_k e^{iks},$$

where the η_k's are the Fourier coefficients of y.

If we impose special conditions on T, there may be various other ways besides that indicated by (5.6–10) for developing an operational calculus. The cases in which T is such that $\sigma(T)$ lies in a half plane (Hille, **1**, Chapter 15) or in a strip (Bade, **1**) are of great interest, and in these cases very interesting and useful operational calculi have been developed.

PROBLEMS

1. If $f(\lambda) = \sum_0^\infty a_n \lambda^n$ in (5.6–6), show that $F(u) = \sum_0^\infty a_{n+1}(u^n/n!)$ in (5.6–8). If the radius of convergence of the f series is α, F is of exponential type $1/\alpha$. See R. P. Boas, **1**, page 839. We see that f determines F; conversely, F

determines f, except that a_0 is left arbitrary.   Any Volterra-type integral operator with kernel $F(s - t)$, where F is an entire function of exponential type, is an operator $f(T)$, where f is analytic at $\lambda = 0$ and $f'(0) = 0$.

2. If $f(\lambda) = \sum_0^\infty a_n \lambda^n$ in (5.6–6), show that $f(T) = \sum_0^\infty a_n T^n$, the series converging in $[X]$.

3. Let $X = C[a, b]$ (a finite interval).   Let T be the differentiation operator, $Tx = x'$, where $\mathscr{D}(T)$ is the set of those $x \in X$ such that $x(a) = 0$ and the derivative x' also belongs to X.   This operator is closed, and $\sigma(T)$ is empty. Show that $x = R_\lambda y$ means

$$x(s) = - \int_a^s e^{\lambda(s-t)} y(t)\, dt.$$

If $f \in \mathfrak{A}_\infty(T)$ is defined by $f(\lambda) = \sum_0^\infty a_n \lambda^{-n}$, show that $f(T)x = y$ means

$$y(s) = a_0 x(s) + \int_a^s F(s - t)x(t)\, dt,$$

where $F(u) = \sum_0^\infty a_{n+1}(u^n/n!)$.   The situation here is closely related to that in Example 3, because $y = T^{-1}x$ means $y(s) = \int_a^s x(t)\, dt$.

4. When T is closed and $\rho(T)$ is not empty, $P(T)$ is closed.   Outline of proof: If $\alpha \in \rho(T)$, let $A = (T - \alpha)^{-1}$.   Write $P(\lambda) = \sum_0^n b_k(\lambda - \alpha)^{n-k}$, $p(\mu) = \sum_0^n b_k \mu^k$, $b_0 \neq 0$.   Then $P(T)x = p(A)(T - \alpha)^n x$ if $x \in \mathscr{D}_n(T)$.   Now $(T - \alpha)^n$ is closed, for it is the inverse of A^n.   It can then be proved that $P(T)$ is closed.   See Taylor, 2, Theorem 6.1.   If $\rho(T)$ is void, it can occur that T is closed but T^2 is not.   Here is an example: Let $X = l^2 \times l^2$.   If $(x, y) \in X$ let $\|(x, y)\|^2 = \|x\|^2 + \|y\|^2$.   If $x = \{\xi_k\}$ and $y = \{\eta_k\}$, define $T(x, y) = (\{k^{-2}\eta_k\}, \{k\xi_k\})$, with $\mathscr{D}(T)$ consisting of all (x, y) with $y \in l^2$ and $\{k\xi_k\} \in l^2$.

5. Suppose $\alpha \in \rho(T)$.   Then the function $f(\lambda) = (\alpha - \lambda)^{-n}(n \geqslant 1)$ belongs to $\mathfrak{A}_\infty(T)$, and $f(T) = (R_\alpha)^n$.   Prove this for $n = 1$ directly from (5.6–10), using the fact that $R_\lambda = R_\alpha + (\alpha - \lambda)R_\lambda R_\alpha$.   For general n the result can be proved by induction.

6. To prove Lemma 5.6–D let $g(\lambda) = (\alpha - \lambda)^n f(\lambda)$, where $\alpha \in \rho(T)$.   Then $f(T) = (R_\alpha)^n g(T)$ (use problem 5).   Let $G(\lambda) = (\alpha - \lambda)^{-n}P(\lambda)$ and show that $G(T) = P(T)(R_\alpha)^n$ by expressing $P(\lambda)$ as a sum of powers of $\alpha - \lambda$.   The relation $F(T) = P(T)f(T)$ now follows at once.

7. Let $P(\lambda)$ by a polynomial of degree $n \geqslant 1$ all of whose zeros lie in $\rho(T)$. Then $P(T)$ has X for its range, and it has an inverse belonging to $[X]$ and given by

$$[P(T)]^{-1} = \frac{1}{2\pi i} \int \frac{1}{P(\lambda)} R_\lambda\, d\lambda,$$

the integration being extended clockwise around a set of nonoverlapping circles, one centered at each zero of $P(\lambda)$, each circle and its interior lying in $\rho(T)$. Method of proof: Let $f(\lambda) = 1/P(\lambda)$ and apply Theorem 5.6–H.   A comparison of (5.6–12) for this case with (5.6–11) shows that $[f(T)]^{-1}x = P(T)x$, whence $[P(T)]^{-1} = f(T)$. Then apply (5.6–10).

8. Let T be the operator of problem 3.   Use the formula in problem 7 to solve $P(T)y = x$ for y, where $P(\lambda)$ is a polynomial of degree n.   Compare with the last part of Example 3.

9. Let $X = H^2$ (see Example 8, § 3.11).   Define $Tx(t) = tx(t)$ ($x \in X$, t the complex variable).   Then $T \in [X]$, $\sigma(T) = \{\lambda : |\lambda| \leqslant 1\}$.   If $f \in \mathfrak{A}(T)$, $f(T)x(t) = f(t)x(t)$.

10. Let $X = L(0, \infty)$, and let T be the differentiation operator $Tx = x'$, with $\mathscr{D}(T)$ determined by those functions in $\mathscr{L}(0, \infty)$ which are absolutely continuous on $[0, a]$ for every finite $a > 0$ and whose derivative is again in $\mathscr{L}(0, \infty)$.   It can be seen from Example 4 in § 1.5 that $\sigma(T)$ consists of all λ for which the real part of λ is $\leqslant 0$.   Also, $x = R_\lambda y$ is expressed by

$$x(s) = \int_0^\infty y(t)e^{\lambda(s-t)}\, dt.$$

Discuss the nature of $\mathfrak{A}_\infty(T)$ and the form of $f(T)$ in this case.

5.7 Spectral Sets and Projections

The results of this section are related to the concept of reducibility (see § 5.4).   As we shall see, we can obtain a pair of subspaces which reduce T completely if we can split the spectrum of T into two parts of a suitable nature.   We assume throughout the section that X is a complex Banach space and that T is a closed linear operator with domain and range in X.   We also assume as always that $\rho(T)$ is not empty.

In addition to the concept of the spectrum of T, we need the concept of the *extended spectrum* of T.   This is a point set in the *extended* complex plane (i.e., the one-point compactification of the ordinary plane, by adjunction of the point ∞).   We denote the extended spectrum of T by $\sigma_e(T)$.   It is defined to be the same as $\sigma(T)$ if $T \in [X]$ and to consist of $\sigma(T)$ and the point ∞ if T is not in $[X]$.   Observe that $\sigma_e(T)$ is always closed and nonempty.

Definition.   A subset σ of $\sigma_e(T)$ is called a *spectral set* of T if it is both open and closed in the relative topology of $\sigma_e(T)$ as a subset of the extended plane.   This is the same as requiring that both σ and $\sigma_e(T) - \sigma$ be closed in the extended plane.

An isolated point of $\sigma_e(T)$ is of course a spectral set.   If σ is a spectral set and if one of the sets σ, $\sigma_e(T) - \sigma$ contains ∞, then the other one is bounded as a subset of the ordinary plane.

If σ is a spectral set of T, we can define an $f \in \mathfrak{A}_\infty(T)$ such that $f(\lambda) = 1$ on a neighborhood of σ while $f(\lambda) = 0$ on a neighborhood of $\sigma_e(T) - \sigma$. We then denote the operator $f(T)$ by E_σ. When σ_1 occurs as a subscript on E or X in what follows, we write $\sigma(1)$ instead of σ_1, for convenience in printing. Likewise with σ_2. Since $f(\lambda)f(\lambda) = f(\lambda)$, the homomorphism shows that $E_\sigma E_\sigma = E_\sigma$, so that E_σ is a projection. We call it *the projection associated with* σ. Evidently the function $1 - f(\lambda)$ is related to $\sigma_e(T) - \sigma$ in the way that f is related to σ; consequently $I - E_\sigma$ is the projection associated with the spectral set $\sigma_e(T) - \sigma$. If we denote σ and $\sigma_e(T) - \sigma$ by σ_1 and σ_2 respectively, we see that $E_{\sigma(1)} + E_{\sigma(2)} = I$, and $E_{\sigma(1)}E_{\sigma(2)} = E_{\sigma(2)}E_{\sigma(1)} = 0$. Let $X_{\sigma(i)}$ be the range of $E_{\sigma(i)}$; it is a closed subspace. We see that $X_{\sigma(1)} \cap X_{\sigma(2)} = (0)$ and $X_{\sigma(1)} \oplus X_{\sigma(2)} = X$.

To show that T is completely reduced by $(X_{\sigma(1)}, X_{\sigma(2)})$ it suffices to show that $E_{\sigma(1)}\mathscr{D}(T) \subset \mathscr{D}(T)$ and $E_{\sigma(1)}Tx = TE_{\sigma(1)}x$ if $x \in \mathscr{D}(T)$ (see § 5.4). These things follow from Lemmas 5.6–E (with $n = 0$, $k = 1$) and 5.6–F.

The foregoing considerations can easily be generalized to the extent stated in the following theorem, proof of which is left to the reader.

Theorem 5.7–A. *Suppose* $\sigma_e(T) = \sigma_1 \cup \cdots \cup \sigma_n$, *where* $\sigma_1, \cdots, \sigma_n$ *are pairwise disjoint spectral sets of* T. *Let* $E_{\sigma(i)}$ *be the projection associated with* σ_i *and let* $X_{\sigma(i)}$ *be the range of* $E_{\sigma(i)}$. *Then* T *is completely reduced by* $(X_{\sigma(1)}, \cdots, X_{\sigma(n)})$, *i.e.,* $I = E_{\sigma(1)} + \cdots + E_{\sigma(n)}$, $E_{\sigma(i)}E_{\sigma(j)} = 0$ *if* $i \neq j$, $\mathscr{D}(T)$ *is invariant under* $E_{\sigma(i)}$, *and* $X_{\sigma(i)}$ *is invariant under* T.

In the next theorem we examine the restriction of T to the range of E_σ.

Theorem 5.7–B. *Let* σ *be a spectral set of* T, *and let* T_1 *be the restriction of* T *to the range* X_σ *of* E_σ *(with* $\mathscr{D}(T_1) = \mathscr{D}(T) \cap X_\sigma$*). Then*

a. $\sigma = \sigma_e(T_1)$.
b. $\sigma \cap P\sigma(T) = P\sigma(T_1)$.
c. $\sigma \cap C\sigma(T) = C\sigma(T_1)$.
d. $\sigma \cap R\sigma(T) = R\sigma(T_1)$.
e. If σ *does not contain* ∞, *then* $X_\sigma \subset \mathscr{D}_n(T)$ *for each* $n \geqslant 1$, *and* T_1 *is continuous on* X_σ.

PROOF. It is convenient to prove (*e*) first. When σ does not contain ∞, we have $E_\sigma = f(T)$, where one property of f is that $f(\lambda) = 0$ on a neighborhood of ∞. We can then apply Lemma 5.6–E, with $k = 0$ and n arbitrary, to conclude that $X_\sigma \subset \mathscr{D}_n(T)$. But now T_1 is defined on all of X_σ, and hence it is continuous, for T_1 is closed (since T is) and X_σ is complete. Here we use Theorem 4.2–I.

Next we prove (*a*). Here it is convenient to write $\sigma_1 = \sigma$, $\sigma_2 = \sigma_e(T) - \sigma_1$ and to denote by T_2 the restriction of T to $X_{\sigma(2)}$. Select any finite point μ not in σ_1. If f is the function used in obtaining $f(T) = E_{\sigma(1)}$, let $g(\lambda) = (\mu - \lambda)^{-1}f(\lambda)$. Then $g \in \mathfrak{A}\infty(T)$, $fg = g$, and so $(\mu - T)g(T) = E_{\sigma(1)}$ and $E_{\sigma(1)}g(T) = g(T)$, from which it appears that $\mu - T$ and $g(T)$ are inverse to each other when restricted to $X_{\sigma(1)}$. Consequently $\mu \in \rho(T_1)$. This shows that every point of $\sigma(T_1)$ is a finite point of σ_1; likewise for $\sigma(T_2)$ and σ_2. Hence $\sigma(T_1) \cap \sigma(T_2)$ is empty. Now $\sigma(T) = \sigma(T_1) \cup \sigma(T_2)$ (by Theorem 5.4–Ca). It therefore follows that $\sigma(T_1)$ is identical with the set of finite points of σ_1; likewise for $\sigma(T_2)$ and σ_2. In view of (e) this proves (a) for the case in which ∞ is not in σ_1. If ∞ is in σ_1, then T is not in $[X]$. Also, ∞ is not in σ_2, so T_2 is continuous on $X_{\sigma(2)}$, by e. It follows that T_1 cannot belong to $[X_{\sigma(1)}]$, for otherwise T would be in $[X]$. Therefore $\infty \in \sigma_e(T_1)$, and (a) is completely proved. Assertions b, c and d now follow from Theorem 5.4–C.

The following simple example is instructive.

Example I. Let $X = l^1$ (l^2 would do just as well). Let $\{\lambda_n\}$ be a sequence of distinct nonzero numbers such that $\lambda_n \to 0$, and define Tx by $T\{\xi_k\} = \{\lambda_k\xi_k\}$. Then $\sigma(T)$ consists of the points $\lambda_1, \lambda_2, \cdots$ and 0. The resolvent is defined by $R_\lambda\{\xi_k\} = \{(\lambda - \lambda_k)^{-1}\xi_k\}$. Let E_k be the projection associated with the spectral set formed by the single point λ_k, and let Q_N be the projection associated with the spectral set consisting of λ_{N+1}, $\lambda_{N+2}, \cdots$ and 0. Let $\{u_n\}$ be the standard countable basis for l^1, i.e., $u_1 = (1, 0, 0, \cdots)$, $u_2 = (0, 1, 0, \cdots)$ etc. Then we have

$$x = \sum_1^\infty \xi_k u_k, \qquad E_k x = \xi_k u_k, \qquad Q_N x = \sum_{N+1}^\infty \xi_k u_k.$$

Note that $I = E_1 + \cdots + E_N + Q_N$. Also, $TE_k = \lambda_k E_k$, and so $T = \lambda_1 E_1 + \cdots + \lambda_N E_N + TQ_N$. It is interesting to see what happens as $N \to \infty$. We have $\|Q_N x\| \to 0$ for each x, and so, for each x,

$$x = \sum_1^\infty E_k x \qquad \text{(convergence in } X\text{)}.$$

But $\|Q_N\| = 1$, and so we *cannot* write $I = \sum_1^\infty E_k$ (with convergence in $[X]$). However, $\|TQ_N\| \to 0$, and so we *do* have

$$T = \sum_1^\infty \lambda_k E_k \qquad \text{(convergence in } [X]\text{)}.$$

We also have

$$R_\lambda x = \sum_1^\infty \frac{E_k x}{\lambda - \lambda_k}, \qquad \text{but not } R_\lambda = \sum_1^\infty \frac{E_k}{\lambda - \lambda_k}.$$

For another instructive example we revert to § 5.6.

Example 2. Consider the operator T of Example 4, § 5.6, where the space X is $C[0, 2\pi]$. For this operator $\sigma_e(T)$ consists of the points $0, \pm 1, \pm 2, \cdots$ and ∞. If E_n is the projection associated with the spectral set consisting of the single point $\lambda = n$, we easily find from (5.6–13) that $E_n x(s) = \xi_n e^{ins}$, where ξ_n is the Fourier coefficient of $x(t)$ with respect to e^{int}. If Q_N is the projection associated with the spectral set consisting of $\pm (N + 1), \pm (N + 2), \cdots$ and ∞, we find that

$$Q_N x(s) = x(s) - \sum_{k=-N}^{N} \xi_k e^{iks}.$$

In this case it is not *always* true that $Q_N x \to 0$ as $N \to \infty$. It *is* true, however, if $x \in \mathscr{D}(T)$, by a standard theorem on Fourier series. Thus we can write

$$(5.7\text{–}1) \qquad\qquad x = \sum_{-\infty}^{\infty} E_n x$$

when $x \in \mathscr{D}(T)$. We have $TE_n = nE_n$. In general it is not true that

$$(5.7\text{–}2) \qquad\qquad Tx = \sum_{-\infty}^{\infty} nE_n x$$

when $x \in \mathscr{D}(T)$. But this is true if $x \in \mathscr{D}_2(T)$, since $E_n Tx = TE_n x = nE_n x$, and in this case we can use (5.7–1) with Tx in place of x.

It is interesting to see what happens in the foregoing example if we change the basic space X in which the operator T works. Suppose we take $X = L^2(0, 2\pi)$ and define $Tx = -ix'$, with $\mathscr{D}(T)$ the subspace of X determined by those x such that $x(s)$ is absolutely continuous on $[0, 2\pi]$, with $x(0) = x(2\pi)$ and such that $x'(s)$ belongs to $\mathscr{L}^2(0, 2\pi)$. The spectrum and the formula for the resolvent are just as before, and the formulas for E_n and Q_N are unchanged. But now (5.7–1) holds for all $x \in L^2(0, 2\pi)$. For, if we let $u_n(s) = e^{ins}/\sqrt{2\pi}$, the set $\{u_n\}(n = 0, \pm 1, \pm 2, \cdots)$ is a complete orthonormal set (see § 3.22), and (5.7–1) is just the standard expansion of x with respect to this orthonormal set. That is, $E_n x = (x, u_n)u_n$. Formula (5.7–2) is now true for every x in $\mathscr{D}(T)$, for $(Tx, u_n)u_n = (x, Tu_n)u_n = (x, nu_n)u_n = nE_n x$.

We return again to the general theory. It is easily seen that, if σ is a spectral set of T, then $E_\sigma = 0$ if and only if σ is empty, and $E_\sigma = I$ if and only if $\sigma = \sigma_e(T)$. Now, if $\mathscr{D}(T) \neq X$ and if $\sigma(T)$ is nonempty and bounded, then $\sigma(T)$ and (∞) are complementary nonempty spectral sets.

In this case, therefore, the projection associated with $\sigma(T)$ is neither 0 nor I.

We conclude this section with a theorem which is in a way a companion to Theorem 5.6–H.

Theorem 5.7–C. *Suppose that $\sigma(T)$ is bounded and that f is an element of $\mathfrak{A}_\infty(T)$ which vanishes on a neighborhood of ∞ but has no zeros on $\sigma(T)$. Then $f(T)$ has the same range and null manifold as the projection associated with $\sigma(T)$. In particular, $f(T)$ has no inverse if $\mathscr{D}(T) \neq X$.*

PROOF. We consider two disjoint parts of $\Delta(f)$: the component containing ∞, in which $f(\lambda) \equiv 0$, and the rest of $\Delta(f)$, which is a neighborhood of $\sigma(T)$. We define two functions g and h: $g(\lambda) = 0$ and $h(\lambda) = 1$ on the first part of $\Delta(f)$, $g(\lambda) = 1$ and $h(\lambda) = f(\lambda)$ on the other part. Note that h has no zeros on $\sigma(T)$ or at ∞, so that $h(T)$ has an inverse belonging to $[X]$. Note also that $g(T) = E_\sigma$, where $\sigma = \sigma(T)$. Now $fg = f$ and $gh = f$. Hence $f(T)E_\sigma = E_\sigma f(T) = f(T)$ and $E_\sigma h(T) = h(T)E_\sigma = f(T)$. The truth of the theorem follows from these relations, in view of the fact about the inverse of $h(T)$.

5.71 The Spectral Mapping Theorem

The following generalization of Theorem 5.2–D will be needed in § 5.8. We assume T closed.

Theorem 5.71–A. *If $f \in \mathfrak{A}_\infty(T)$, the spectrum of $f(T)$ is exactly the set of values assumed by $f(\lambda)$ as λ varies over the set $\sigma_e(T)$. In symbols, $\sigma[f(T)] = f[\sigma_e(T)]$.*

PROOF. To show that $f[\sigma_e(T)] \subseteq \sigma[f(T)]$, suppose $\mu \in \sigma(T)$ and define $g(\lambda) = (\lambda - \mu)^{-1}(f(\lambda) - f(\mu))$ if $\lambda \neq \mu$, while $g(\mu) = f'(\mu)$. Then $(\mu - \lambda)g(\lambda) = f(\mu) - f(\lambda)$, and so $(\mu - T)g(T) = f(\mu) - f(T)$, by Lemma 5.6–D. We can permute $\mu - T$ and $g(T)$ on $\mathscr{D}(T)$. It now follows either that the range of $f(\mu) - f(T)$ is not all of X, or that this operator has no inverse; hence $f(\mu) \in \sigma[f(T)]$. It remains to prove that $f(\infty) \in \sigma[f(T)]$ if T is not in $[X]$, or, what is the same thing, if $\mathscr{D}(T) \neq X$. We can assume $f(\infty) - f(\lambda) \neq 0$ if $\lambda \in \sigma(T)$, for otherwise the situation is covered by what has been proved. We can now apply either Theorem 5.6–H or Theorem 5.7–C to the function $f(\infty) - f(\lambda)$ and conclude either that the range of $f(\infty) - f(T)$ is not all of X or that this operator has no inverse. In either event $f(\infty) \in \sigma[f(T)]$.

We now have to prove that $\sigma[f(T)] \subseteq f[\sigma_e(T)]$. Consider first a point $\beta \in \sigma[f(T)]$ such that $\beta \neq f(\infty)$ and suppose, contrary to what is to be proved, that $f(\lambda) - \beta$ has no zeros on $\sigma(T)$. Define $h(\lambda) = [\beta - f(\lambda)]^{-1}$ on a suitable neighborhood of $\sigma(T)$. Then $h \in \mathfrak{A}_\infty(T)$, and $h(T)$ and $\beta - f(T)$ are inverse to each other, so that $\beta \in \rho[f(T)]$, which is a contradiction. If $\beta = f(\infty)$ and T is not in $[X]$, we know that $\infty \in \sigma_e(T)$, and hence $\beta \in f[\sigma_e(T)]$. It remains only to consider the case $\beta = f(\infty) \in \sigma[f(T)]$, $T \in [X]$. In this case we can replace f by another function g, agreeing with f on a neighborhood of $\sigma(T)$, but such that $g(\infty) \neq \beta$. Then $g(T) = f(T)$ and $g[\sigma_e(T)] = f[\sigma_e(T)]$, and the earlier argument shows that $\beta \in g[\sigma_e(T)]$. This completes the proof.

We also need the following theorem, for the general case of a closed T with nonempty resolvent set. For $T \in [X]$ this is the same as Theorem 5.2–D.

Theorem 5.71–B. *If $P(\lambda)$ is a polynomial, $P[\sigma(T)] = \sigma[P(T)]$.*

The proof can be patterned after that of Theorem 5.71–A. At one stage in the argument the result of § 5.6, problem 7, is needed.

The next theorem increases the scope of the operational calculus by enabling us to deal with composition of functions.

Theorem 5.71–C. *Suppose $f \in \mathfrak{A}_\infty(T)$, $S = f(T)$, and $g \in \mathfrak{A}_\infty(S)$. Suppose also that $f(\infty) \in \Delta(g)$ (if $T \in [X]$ we may always suppose f modified near $\lambda = \infty$, if necessary, to make $f(\infty) \in \Delta(g)$). Define F by $F(\lambda) = g[f(\lambda)]$ if $f(\lambda) \in \Delta(g)$. Then $F \in \mathfrak{A}_\infty(T)$ and $F(T) = g(S)$.*

PROOF. Using Theorem 5.71–A, we see that $\sigma(T) \subset \Delta(F)$. Choose a bounded Cauchy domain D such that $\sigma(S) \subset D$, $\bar{D} \subset \Delta(g)$, and $f(\infty) \in D$. Choose an unbounded Cauchy domain D_1 such that $\sigma(T) \subset D_1$, $\bar{D}_1 \subset \Delta(f)$, and $f(\bar{D}_1) \subset D$. Then

$$F(T) = F(\infty)I + \frac{1}{2\pi i} \int_{+B(D_1)} g[f(\xi)]R_\xi \, d\xi$$

and, if $\xi \in B(D_1)$,

$$g[f(\xi)] = \frac{1}{2\pi i} \int_{+B(D)} \frac{g(\lambda)}{\lambda - f(\xi)} \, d\lambda.$$

If $h(\xi) = [\lambda - f(\xi)]^{-1}$ [λ fixed on $B(D)$], we see that $h(T) = (\lambda - S)^{-1}$. Since

$$F(\infty) = \frac{1}{2\pi i} \int_{+B(D)} \frac{g(\lambda)}{\lambda - f(\infty)} \, d\lambda$$

and

$$g(S) = \frac{1}{2\pi i} \int_{+B(D)} g(\lambda)(\lambda - S)^{-1} \, d\lambda,$$

the conclusion of the theorem follows by easy calculations, which we leave to the reader.

One important application of the preceding theorem is to prove the next theorem, which is used in proving Theorem 5.8–F.

Theorem 5.71–D. *Suppose $f \in \mathfrak{A}_\infty(T)$, $S = f(T)$, and let τ be a spectral set of S. Let $\sigma = \sigma_e(T) \cap f^{-1}(\tau)$. Then σ is a spectral set of T, and the projection E_σ associated with σ and T is the same as the projection F_τ associated with τ and S.*

PROOF. Let us write $\sigma' = \sigma_e(T) - \sigma$, $\tau' = \sigma(S) - \tau$. From Theorem 5.71–A we see that $f(\sigma \cup \sigma') = \tau \cup \tau'$. Hence $\sigma' = \sigma_e(T) \cap f^{-1}(\tau')$, and it follows that σ and σ' are complementary spectral sets of T. Since $E_\sigma + E_{\sigma'} = I$ and $F_\tau + F_{\tau'} = I$, the relation $E_\sigma = F_\tau$ is implied by $E_{\sigma'} = F_{\tau'}$. Hence, in proving the theorem, it is allowable to assume that σ is a bounded set in the ordinary plane and that $f(\infty)$ is not in τ, for, if this is not true, we can deal instead with σ' and τ'. Now let U_1, U_2, U_3, U_4 be open sets with the following properties: $\bar{U}_1$ and $\bar{U}_2$ are disjoint, and so are $\bar{U}_3$, $\bar{U}_4$; U_1 and U_3 are bounded neighborhoods of τ and σ respectively; U_2 contains $\tau', f(\infty)$, and a neighborhood of ∞; U_4 contains σ' and a neighborhood of ∞; $\bar{U}_3$ and $\bar{U}_4$ are in $\Delta(f)$ and $f(\bar{U}_3) \subset U_1$, $f(\bar{U}_4) \subset U_2$. Such sets do exist. Define $f_\tau = 1$ on U_1, $f_\tau = 0$ on U_2, $f_\sigma = 1$ on U_3, $f_\sigma = 0$ on U_4. Then $f_\tau[f(\lambda)] = f_\sigma(\lambda)$ on $U_3 \cup U_4$. But $f_\tau(S) = F_\tau, f_\sigma(T) = E_\sigma$, and so $F_\tau = E_\sigma$, by Theorem 5.71–C.

PROBLEMS

1. Suppose $\alpha \in \rho(T)$ and let $A = R_\alpha$. Use Theorem 5.71–A to show that if $\mu(\alpha - \lambda) = 1$, $\mu \in \sigma(A)$ if and only if $\lambda \in \sigma(T)$. If $\mu \in \rho(A)$ and $\mu(\alpha - \beta) = 1$, use Theorem 5.71–C to show that $(\mu - A)^{-1} = \mu^{-1} + \mu^{-2}R_\beta$. Take $f(\lambda) = (\alpha - \lambda)^{-1}$, $g(\lambda) = (\mu - \lambda)^{-1}$. Show also that $R_\beta = \mu A(\mu - A)^{-1}$.

2. Suppose $\alpha \in \rho(T)$ and $A = R_\alpha$. Make the transformation $\mu = (\alpha - \lambda)^{-1}$ from the λ-plane to the μ-plane. If $f \in \mathfrak{A}_\infty(T)$ and g is defined by $g(\mu) = f(\lambda)$, $g(0) = f(\infty)$, show that $g(A) = f(T)$.

3. Suppose X a complex Banach space, A and B in $[X]$, $A \neq B$ and $AB = BA$. Then, if $\lambda_0 \in \sigma(A)$, there exists $\lambda_1 \in \sigma(B)$ with $|\lambda_1 - \lambda_0| \leqslant \|A - B\|$. Suggestion: Suppose the proposition false, and let $C = I - (\lambda_0 - A)(\lambda_0 - B)^{-1} = (A - B)(\lambda_0 - B)^{-1}$. Let $r = \|A - B\|$. Show that $r_\sigma[(\lambda_0 - B)^{-1}] < 1/r$ and hence (see problem 7, § 5.2) that $r_\sigma(C) < 1$, whence $1 \in \rho(C)$. From this follows readily that $\lambda_0 \in \rho(A)$, a contradiction.

4. Consider the operator A of Example 2, § 5.3, with X taken as any fixed l^p. Suppose $\sum_0^\infty |\alpha_n| < \infty$, and let $f(\lambda) = \sum_0^\omega \alpha_n \lambda^n$, $|\lambda| \leqslant 1$. Also let $P_n(\lambda) = \sum_0^n \alpha_k \lambda^k$. Define $S = \sum_0^\infty \alpha_n A^n$ (series convergent in $[X]$). Show that $\sigma(S) = f[\sigma(A)]$. This is not a direct application of Theorem 5.71–A, in general. Why not? For $f[\sigma(A)] \subset \sigma(S)$ use Theorem 4.1–D, and for $\sigma(S) \subset f[\sigma(A)]$ use problem 3 (above) on S and $P_n(A)$.

5.8 Isolated Points of the Spectrum

As in several preceding sections, we assume here that X is a complex Banach space and that T is closed. Then R_λ is analytic as a function of λ on $\rho(T)$, and an isolated point λ_0 of $\sigma(T)$ is an isolated singular point of R_λ. Hence there is a Laurent expansion of R_λ in powers of $\lambda - \lambda_0$. We write this in the form

$$(5.8\text{--}1) \qquad R_\lambda = \sum_0^\infty (\lambda - \lambda_0)^n A_n + \sum_1^\infty (\lambda - \lambda_0)^{-n} B_n.$$

The coefficients A_n and B_n are members of $[X]$, and this series representation of R_λ is valid when $0 < |\lambda - \lambda_0| < \delta$ for any δ such that all of $\sigma(T)$ except λ_0 lies on or outside the circle $|\lambda - \lambda_0| = \delta$. These coefficient operators are given by the usual standard formulas:

$$A_n = \frac{1}{2\pi i} \int_C (\lambda - \lambda_0)^{-n-1} R_\lambda \, d\lambda,$$

$$(5.8\text{--}2)$$

$$B_n = \frac{1}{2\pi i} \int_C (\lambda - \lambda_0)^{n-1} R_\lambda \, d\lambda,$$

where C is any counterclockwise circle $|\lambda - \lambda_0| = h$ with $0 < h < \delta$.

It turns out that there are several important relationships among these coefficient operators. The demonstration of these relationships can be made conveniently by using the operational calculus. Choose $r > 0$ so that $2r < \delta$. Define functions f_n as follows:

$$n \geqslant 0 : f_n(\lambda) = \begin{cases} 0 & \text{if } |\lambda - \lambda_0| < r \\ (\lambda - \lambda_0)^{-n-1} & \text{if } |\lambda - \lambda_0| > 2r \end{cases}$$

$$(5.8\text{--}3)$$

$$n < 0 : f_n(\lambda) = \begin{cases} (\lambda - \lambda_0)^{-n-1} & \text{if } |\lambda - \lambda_0| < r \\ 0 & \text{if } |\lambda - \lambda_0| > 2r. \end{cases}$$

These functions all belong to $\mathfrak{A}_\infty(T)$, and $f_n(\infty) = 0$. If we compare the definition of $f_n(T)$ with formulas (5.8–2) we see that

$$(5.8\text{--}4) \qquad \begin{aligned} A_n &= -f_n(T), & n \geqslant 0, \\ B_n &= f_{-n}(T), & n \geqslant 1. \end{aligned}$$

We note in particular that B_1 is the projection E_σ for the case in which σ is the spectral set consisting of the single point λ_0.   Since σ is not empty, we know that $B_1 \neq 0$.   The only case in which $B_1 = I$ is that in which $\mathscr{D}(T) = X$ and $\sigma(T)$ consists of the single point λ_0.   (See the remarks preceding Theorem 5.7–C.)

Now let us observe that

$$(\lambda - \lambda_0)f_{n+1}(\lambda) = f_n(\lambda), \qquad n \geqslant 0,$$
$$(\lambda - \lambda_0)f_{-n}(\lambda) = f_{-(n+1)}(\lambda), \qquad n \geqslant 1,$$
$$(\lambda - \lambda_0)f_0(\lambda) + f_{-1}(\lambda) = 1.$$

From these relations and Lemma 5.6–D we obtain the formulas

(5.8–5) $$(T - \lambda_0)A_{n+1} = A_n,$$

(5.8–6) $$(T - \lambda_0)B_n = B_{n+1} = (T - \lambda_0)^n B_1,$$

(5.8–7) $$(T - \lambda_0)A_0 = B_1 - I.$$

The second part of (5.8–6) is obtained from the first part by induction. Some further facts are indicated in problem 1.

As in the classical theory of functions, we shall say that λ_0 is a pole of R_λ of order m if and only if $B_m \neq 0$ and $B_n = 0$ when $n > m$.   From (5.8–6) we see that $B_{n+1} = 0$ if $B_n = 0$.   Hence λ_0 is a pole of order m if and only if $B_m \neq 0$ and $B_{m+1} = 0$.   In that case $B_1, \cdots, B_m$ are all $\neq 0$.   If λ_0 is an isolated point of $\sigma(T)$ but not a pole of R_λ, we call it an isolated essential singularity of R_λ.

The case of a pole is of particular interest.

Theorem 5.8–A.   *If λ_0 is a pole of R_λ of order m, then λ_0 is an eigenvalue of T.   The ascent and descent of $\lambda_0 - T$ are both equal to m.   The range of the projection B_1 is the null space of $(\lambda_0 - T)^m$, and the range of $I - B_1$ is the range of $(\lambda_0 - T)^m$, so that*

(5.8–8) $$X = \mathscr{R}(T_0^m) \oplus \mathscr{N}(T_0^m) \qquad (T_0 = \lambda_0 - T).$$

The operator T is completely reduced by the two manifolds occurring in this direct sum.

PROOF.   Let $X_1 = \mathscr{N}(B_1) = \mathscr{R}(I - B_1)$, $X_2 = \mathscr{R}(B_1)$.   Then $X = X_1 \oplus X_2$; both subspaces are closed, since B_1 is continuous.   We know from the early part of § 5.7 that T is completely reduced by (X_1, X_2), for $I - B_1$ and B_1 are projections associated with complementary spectral sets of T.   For convenience we denote the null space and range of $(\lambda_0 - T)^k$ by $\mathscr{N}_k$ and $\mathscr{R}_k$ respectively.   If $x \in \mathscr{N}_n$, where $n \geqslant 1$, we see by (5.8–5), induction, and (5.8–7) that $0 = A_{n-1}(T - \lambda_0)^n x =$

$(T - \lambda_0)^n A_{n-1} x = (T - \lambda_0) A_0 x = B_1 x - x$, so that $x = B_1 x \in X_2$. Thus $\mathcal{N}_n \subset X_2$ if $n \geqslant 1$. On the other hand, it follows from (5.8–6) that, if $x \in X_2$, we have $x = B_1 x$ and $(T - \lambda_0)^n x = B_{n+1} x$. Since $B_{n+1} = 0$ if $n \geqslant m$, it follows that $X_2 \subset \mathcal{N}_n$, and hence $\mathcal{N}_n = X_2$, if $n \geqslant m$. But $\mathcal{N}_{m-1}$ is a proper subset of $\mathcal{N}_m$, for $B_m \neq 0$, and $\mathcal{N}_{m-1} = \mathcal{N}_m = X_2$ would imply $B_m = 0$, because of the relation $B_m = (T - \lambda_0)^{m-1} B_1$. We have now proved that the ascent of $\lambda_0 - T$ is m and that $\mathcal{N}_m = X_2$. In particular, since $m > 0$, λ_0 is an eigenvalue of T.

Now let T_1 and T_2 be the restrictions of T to X_1 and X_2 respectively. We know by Theorem 5.7–Ba that λ_0 is not in $\sigma(T_1)$, for it is in $\sigma(T_2)$. Hence the descent of $\lambda_0 - T_1$ is 0, and the range of $(\lambda_0 - T_1)^n$ is X_1 when $n \geqslant 1$. Hence certainly $X_1 \subset \mathcal{R}_n$. Now, if $n \geqslant m$, the only point common to $\mathcal{R}_n$ and $\mathcal{N}_n$ is 0. For, if $x \in \mathcal{R}_n \cap \mathcal{N}_n$, we can write $x = (\lambda_0 - T)^n y$ and $(\lambda_0 - T)^n x = 0$, whence $y \in \mathcal{N}_{2n} = \mathcal{N}_n$, and therefore $x = 0$. Now suppose $n \geqslant m$ and $x \in \mathcal{R}_n$. Write $x = x_1 + x_2$, where $x_i \in X_i$. Then $x_2 = x - x_1 \in \mathcal{R}_n$, because $X_1 \subset \mathcal{R}_n$. But $x_2 \in X_2 = \mathcal{N}_n$, and so $x_2 = 0$, whence $x = x_1 \in X_1$. Thus $\mathcal{R}_n \subset X_1$ if $n \geqslant m$. We now know that $\mathcal{R}_n = X_1$ if $n \geqslant m$ and, therefore, that the descent of $\lambda_0 - T$ is less than or equal to m. Theorem 5.41–D then shows that the descent is exactly m, which we know to be the ascent. This completes the proof of the theorem.

The next theorem is concerned with conditions on f such that $f(T) = 0$, where $f \in \mathfrak{A}_\infty(T)$. When this theorem is applied to the special case in which X is finite dimensional and $T \in [X]$, it yields the conditions which determine the minimal polynomial associated with T, i.e., the polynomial $P(\lambda)$ of lowest degree such that $P(T) = 0$.

Theorem 5.8–B. *Suppose $f \in \mathfrak{A}_\infty(T)$. In order that $f(T) = 0$ it is necessary and sufficient that the following conditions be satisfied:*

a. If λ_0 is a pole of R_λ of order m, either $f(\lambda) \equiv 0$ in some neighborhood of λ_0 or f has a zero of order at least m at λ_0.

b. $f(\lambda) \equiv 0$ in some neighborhood of each isolated essential singularity of R_λ.

c. $f(\lambda) \equiv 0$ in each component of $\Delta(f)$ which contains infinitely many points of $\sigma(T)$.

d. $f(\lambda) \equiv 0$ in some neighborhood of ∞ if $\mathcal{D}(T) \neq X$.

PROOF. As a preliminary to the proof let us suppose that λ_0 is an isolated point of $\sigma(T)$, that $f \in \mathfrak{A}_\infty(T)$, and that there is no neighborhood of λ_0 in which $f(\lambda) \equiv 0$. There will then be some smallest integer $k \geqslant 0$ such that $f^{(k)}(\lambda_0) \neq 0$. Now choose r as in (5.8–3), and define g_k so that it is analytic at λ_0 and $g_k(\lambda) = (\lambda - \lambda_0)^{-k} f(\lambda)$ if $0 < |\lambda - \lambda_0| < r$,

$g_k(\lambda) = (\lambda - \lambda_0)^{-k-1}$ if $|\lambda - \lambda_0| > 2r$. We may also restrict r so that f is analytic and $f(\lambda) \neq 0$ when $0 < |\lambda - \lambda_0| < r$. Then $g_k \in \mathfrak{A}_\infty(T)$ and $[g_k(T)]^{-1}$ exists, by Theorem 5.6-H. Referring to (5.8-3), we see that $(\lambda - \lambda_0)^k g_k(\lambda) f_{-1}(\lambda) = f(\lambda) f_{-1}(\lambda)$. Hence $(T - \lambda_0)^k g_k(T) B_1 = f(T) B_1$. We can write this in the forms

$$(5.8-9) \qquad\qquad g_k(T)(T - \lambda_0)^k B_1 = f(T) B_1,$$

$$(5.8-10) \qquad\qquad B_{k+1} = [g_k(T)]^{-1} f(T) B_1;$$

to get the second form we make use of (5.8-6).

   With these preliminaries established, let us now assume that $f(T) = 0$. If λ_0 is a pole of order m of R_λ and if there is no neighborhood of λ_0 in which $f(\lambda_0) \equiv 0$, we see from (5.8-10) that $B_{k+1} = 0$, where k has the significance explained in the preceding paragraph. Hence, since $B_m \neq 0$, we conclude that $m \leqslant k$. This shows that condition a in the theorem is satisfied. We also see that b is satisfied. For, if λ_0 is an isolated essential singularity of R_λ, then $B_n \neq 0$ for every n, and this is incompatible with (5.8-10) if $f(T) = 0$. Next we observe that $\sigma[f(T)]$ consists of the single point 0 when $f(T) = 0$. Since $\sigma[f(T)] = f[\sigma_e(T)]$, we conclude that $f(\lambda) = 0$ at all points of $\sigma_e(T)$. That condition c must be satisfied now follows from the fact that f is locally analytic on $\Delta(f)$ and at ∞, for $\sigma_e(T)$ is closed and the extended plane is compact. Finally, suppose $\mathscr{D}(T) \neq X$. Then $f(\infty) = 0$, since $\infty \in \sigma_e(T)$. If ∞ is an accumulation point of $\sigma(T)$, it follows that $f(\lambda) \equiv 0$ in the component of $\Delta(f)$ which contains ∞. If ∞ is isolated in $\sigma_e(T)$ and $f(\lambda)$ is not identically zero in any neighborhood of ∞, this means that ∞ is a zero of f of some finite order k. Let $g(\lambda) = \lambda^k f(\lambda)$. Then $g \in \mathfrak{A}_\infty(T)$ and $g(\infty) \neq 0$. But $g(T) = T^k f(T) = 0$, and therefore $g(\infty) = 0$, for $\sigma[g(T)] = (0) = g[\sigma_e(T)]$. Thus (d) must be satisfied if $f(T) = 0$.

   Now, conversely, suppose that f satisfies conditions a–d in the theorem; we shall show that $f(T) = 0$. We may suppose that there is at least one component of $\Delta(f)$ in which $f(\lambda) \not\equiv 0$, since otherwise the conclusion $f(T) = 0$ is a direct consequence of the defining formula (5.6-10). Because of the conditions on f, the fact that $\sigma(T)$ is closed and $\sigma(T) \subset \Delta(f)$, it follows that there are at most a finite number of points of $\sigma(T)$, say $\lambda_1, \cdots, \lambda_p$, all of them poles of R_λ, in the union of those components of $\Delta(f)$ where $f(\lambda) \not\equiv 0$. Now, if $\mathscr{D}(T) \neq X$, condition d shows that the definition of $f(T)$ can be put in the form

$$(5.8-11) \qquad\qquad f(T) = \sum_{j=1}^{p} \frac{1}{2\pi i} \int_{C_j} f(\lambda) R_\lambda \, d\lambda,$$

where $C_1, \cdots, C_p$ are small nonoverlapping counterclockwise circles with centers at $\lambda_1, \cdots, \lambda_p$. If no such points as $\lambda_1, \cdots, \lambda_p$ exist, then $f(T) = 0$ by Cauchy's theorem. If $\mathscr{D}(T) = X$, formula (5.8–11) is still valid, for the behavior of f near ∞ is irrelevant in this case. Let E_j be the projection associated with the spectral set consisting of the single point λ_j. It is then clear by the definition of E_j and the homomorphism rules of the operational calculus that (5.8–11) becomes

$$f(T) = \sum_{j=1}^{p} f(T)E_j.$$

It therefore remains only to prove that $f(T)E_j = 0$ for each j. Let λ_j be a pole of order m_j of R_λ, and let its order as a zero of f be k_j, so that $m_j \leqslant k_j$, by condition a. If we apply (5.8–6) with λ_j in place of λ_0 and E_j in place of B_1, the fact that λ_j is a pole of order m_j implies $(T - \lambda_j)^{k_j}E_j = 0$. Formula (5.8–9), applied with this change in notation, shows that $f(T)E_j = 0$. This finishes the proof.

Our next principal result is Theorem 5.8–D, which is a sort of converse of Theorem 5.8–A. An important tool in the proof of this theorem is furnished by the following lemma.

Lemma 5.8–C. *Let λ_0 be an isolated point of $\sigma(T)$, and let B_1 be the projection associated with λ_0 as a spectral set. Then $x \in \mathscr{R}(B_1)$ if and only if $\lim_{n\to\infty} (T - \lambda_0)^n \epsilon^{-n} x = 0$ for every $\epsilon > 0$ (or, equivalently, if and only if $\|(T - \lambda_0)^n x\|^{1/n} \to 0$). In order that this be so it is sufficient to have it true for a single ϵ such that $\lambda \in \rho(T)$ if $0 < |\lambda - \lambda_0| \leqslant \epsilon$.*

PROOF. If $x \in \mathscr{R}(B_1)$ we have $x = B_1 x$. It follows from (5.8–6) that $B_{n+1}x = (T - \lambda_0)^n x$. Then, by (5.8–2),

$$(T - \lambda_0)^n \epsilon^{-n} x = \frac{1}{2\pi i} \int_C (\lambda - \lambda_0)^n \epsilon^{-n} R_\lambda x \, d\lambda,$$

where the radius of C may be taken less than ϵ. Consequently, $(T - \lambda_0)^n \epsilon^{-n} x \to 0$. For the converse the motivation is that of finding an operator which is nearly the same as B_1 but has an inverse. We define

$$h_n(\lambda) = \{1 - (\lambda - \lambda_0)^n \epsilon^{-n}\}^{-1},$$

where ϵ is prescribed as in the last sentence of the lemma. Then Theorem 5.6–H applies to h_n; $h_n(T)$ has an inverse, which is evidently $I - (T - \lambda_0)^n \epsilon^{-n}$. To calculate $h_n(T)$ as an integral, let C_1 be the circle $|\lambda - \lambda_0| = r_1$, C_2 the circle $|\lambda - \lambda_0| = r_2$, where $0 < r_1 < \epsilon < r_2$ and

$\lambda \in \rho(T)$ if $0 < |\lambda - \lambda_0| \leqslant r_2$. Then, with proper orientation of the circles,

$$h_n(T) = \frac{1}{2\pi i} \int_{C_1} h_n(\lambda) R_\lambda \, d\lambda - \frac{1}{2\pi i} \int_{C_2} h_n(\lambda) R_\lambda \, d\lambda.$$

We can also write

$$B_1 = \frac{1}{2\pi i} \int_{C_1} R_\lambda \, d\lambda.$$

From these formulas it is easy to see that $\|h_n(T) - B_1\| \to 0$. If now $(T - \lambda_0)^n \epsilon^{-n} x \to 0$, we can write $x = h_n(T)[I - (T - \lambda_0)^n \epsilon^{-n}]x$, and so

$$x - B_1 x = [h_n(T) - B_1]x - h_n(T)(T - \lambda_0)^n \epsilon^{-n} x \to 0.$$

Thus $x = B_1 x \in \mathscr{R}(B_1)$, as was to be proved.

In the next theorem we consider a fixed λ_0, and we denote the range and null space of $(\lambda_0 - T)^n$ by $\mathscr{R}_n$ and $\mathscr{N}_n$ respectively.

Theorem 5.8–D.   *Suppose there is an integer n such that $\mathscr{R}_n \cap \mathscr{N}_n = (0)$, that $\mathscr{R}_n$ is closed and $X = \mathscr{R}_n \oplus \mathscr{N}_n$, and that the smallest integer for which all these things are true is m, with $m \geqslant 1$. Then λ_0 is a pole of R_λ of order m.*

PROOF.   We observe at the outset that $\mathscr{N}_m$ contains nonzero elements. For, if $\mathscr{N}_m = (0)$, then $\mathscr{N}_{m-1} = (0)$ also. Then $X = \mathscr{R}_m \oplus \mathscr{N}_m = \mathscr{R}_m \subset \mathscr{R}_{m-1}$, whence $X = \mathscr{R}_{m-1}$. Then $\mathscr{R}_{m-1} \cap \mathscr{N}_{m-1} = (0)$, $\mathscr{R}_{m-1}$ is closed, and $X = \mathscr{R}_{m-1} \oplus \mathscr{N}_{m-1}$, contrary to the definition of m.

First we shall show that T is completely reduced by $(\mathscr{R}_m, \mathscr{N}_m)$. We leave to the reader the easy verification that $T\mathscr{N}_m \subset \mathscr{N}_m$ and $T[\mathscr{R}_m \cap \mathscr{D}(T)] \subset \mathscr{R}_m$. If we write $x = x_1 + x_2$, where $x_1 \in \mathscr{R}_m, x_2 \in \mathscr{N}_m$, let $E_1 x = x_1$, $E_2 x = x_2$. The projections E_1, E_2 are continuous, by Theorem 4.8–D. Clearly $\mathscr{D}(T)$ is invariant under E_2, since $\mathscr{N}_m \subset \mathscr{D}(T)$. Also, $\mathscr{D}(T)$ is invariant under E_1, because $x \in \mathscr{D}(T)$ implies $E_1 x = x - E_2 x \in \mathscr{D}(T)$. This finishes the demonstration that T is completely reduced by $(\mathscr{R}_m, \mathscr{N}_m)$. Let T_1 and T_2 denote the restrictions of T to $\mathscr{R}_m$ and $\mathscr{N}_m$ respectively. Then T_2 is defined on all of $\mathscr{N}_m$ and is therefore continuous, for T_2 is closed. Also, Theorem 5.4–C is applicable here, and in particular, $\sigma(T) = \sigma(T_1) \cup \sigma(T_2)$.

The next step is to show that λ_0 is a pole of the resolvent of T_2. Choose a fixed point $\alpha \in \rho(T)$ [then $\alpha \in \rho(T_2)$ also], and let $f(\lambda) = (\lambda_0 - \lambda)^m (\alpha - \lambda)^{-m-1}$. Then $f(T) = (\lambda_0 - T)^m R_\alpha^{m+1}$. Now f is in $\mathfrak{A}_\infty(T_2)$ as well as in $\mathfrak{A}_\infty(T)$, and it is easily verified that $f(T_2)$ is the restriction of $f(T)$ to $\mathscr{N}_m$. But, if $x \in \mathscr{N}_m, f(T)x = R_\alpha^{m+1}(\lambda_0 - T)^m x = 0$, and so $f(T_2) = 0 \cdot$ We now apply Theorem 5.8–B. The conclusion is that $\sigma(T_2)$ consists of the single point λ_0, which is a pole of some order m_1 of $(\lambda - T_2)^{-1}$, with $1 \leqslant m_1 \leqslant m$.

Next we prove that $\lambda_0 \in \rho(T_1)$. From this it will follow that λ_0 is an isolated point of $\sigma(T)$. Let $P(\lambda) = (\lambda_0 - \lambda)^m$. We shall show that $P(T_1) = (\lambda_0 - T_1)^m$ has an inverse with domain all of $\mathscr{R}_m$. If $x \in \mathscr{R}_m \cap \mathscr{D}_m(T)$ and $P(T_1)x = 0$, this means that $x \in \mathscr{R}_m \cap \mathscr{N}_m$, and hence that $x = 0$. Therefore $P(T_1)$ has an inverse. If $y \in \mathscr{R}_m$, we can write $y = (\lambda_0 - T)^m x$ for some $x \in \mathscr{D}_m(T)$, by definition. If we write $x = E_1 x + E_2 x$, it follows that $y = (\lambda_0 - T)^m E_1 x = P(T_1)E_1 x$. Thus the range of $P(T_1)$ is all of $\mathscr{R}_m$. Now $P(T_1)$ is closed (see problem 4, § 5.6), and so the inverse of $P(T_1)$ is a closed operator defined on all of $\mathscr{R}_m$; it is therefore continuous, by the closed-graph theorem. This means that $0 \in \rho[P(T_1)]$. But $\sigma[P(T_1)] = P[\sigma(T_1)]$ (Theorem 5.71–B). Consequently $P(\lambda)$ has no zeros on $\sigma(T_1)$; i.e., λ_0 is not in $\sigma(T_1)$.

Now we can regard the single point λ_0 as a spectral set of T and obtain the corresponding projection B_1. We shall prove that $\mathscr{R}(B_1) = \mathscr{N}_m$. For this we use Lemma 5.8–C. It is clear that $\mathscr{N}_m \subset \mathscr{R}(B_1)$, for $(\lambda_0 - T)^n \epsilon^{-n} x = 0$ if $\epsilon > 0$, $n \geqslant m$, and $x \in \mathscr{N}_m$. Let $H = (\lambda_0 - T_1)^{-1}$. We have just seen that $\lambda_0 \in \rho(T_1)$. Choose $\epsilon > 0$ so that $\epsilon \|H\| < 1$, and suppose $x \in \mathscr{R}(B_1)$. Then $(\lambda_0 - T)^n \epsilon^{-n} x \to 0$. Now certainly $(\lambda_0 - T)^n E_2 x = 0$ if $n \geqslant m$, and hence $(\lambda_0 - T)^n \epsilon^{-n} E_1 x \to 0$. Let $y_n = (\lambda_0 - T)^n \epsilon^{-n} E_1 x$. Then $y_n \in \mathscr{R}_m$ and $H^n y_n = \epsilon^{-n} E_1 x$. Hence $\|E_1 x\| = \|\epsilon^n H^n y_n\| \leqslant (\epsilon \|H\|)^n \|y_n\|$. We conclude that $E_1 x = 0$, whence $x \in \mathscr{N}_m$. Thus $\mathscr{R}(B_1) = \mathscr{N}_m$.

Now, the fact that λ_0 is a pole of order m_1 of $(\lambda - T_2)^{-1}$, the underlying space being $\mathscr{N}_m$, enables us to conclude that λ_0 is also a pole of order m_1 of R_λ. The details of this inference are indicated in problem 2 at the end of the section. It remains only to show that $m = m_1$. We know that $m_1 \leqslant m$; $m_1 < m$ is impossible, as we see by Theorem 5.8–A and the assumed minimal character of m. Thus, finally, the proof of Theorem 5.8–D is complete.

We now have the following result:

Theorem 5.8–E. *If T belongs to $[X]$ and is compact, each nonzero point of $\sigma(T)$ is a pole of R_λ.*

PROOF. Suppose $\lambda_0 \in \sigma(T)$, $\lambda_0 \neq 0$. Then $\alpha(\lambda_0 - T) = \delta(\lambda_0 - T) = m \geqslant 1$ (Theorem 5.5–E). The fact that λ_0 is a pole of order m of R_λ now follows by Theorems 5.5–D, 5.41–G, 5.8–D, 5.8–A. Detailed verification is left to the reader.

A different proof of this theorem can be had by way of the next theorem.

Since a pole of R_λ is an eigenvalue of T (Theorem 5.8–A), it is useful to have some means of deciding whether a point of $\sigma(T)$ is a pole of R_λ. One important result along such lines is contained in the following theorem, in which T can be any closed operator with nonempty resolvent set.

Theorem 5.8–F.   *Suppose $f \in \mathfrak{A}_\infty(T)$, and let $f(T)$ be compact. Then, if $\lambda_0 \in \sigma(T)$ and $f(\lambda_0) \neq 0$, λ_0 is a pole of R_λ. Moreover, if B_1 is the projection associated with the spectral set (λ_0), the range of B_1 is finite dimensional, and hence the eigenmanifold corresponding to λ_0 is finite dimensional.*

PROOF.   Let $S = f(T)$, $\mu = f(\lambda_0)$.   We know that $\mu \in \sigma(S)$, by Theorem 5.71–A.   Let $\sigma = \sigma_e(T) \cap f^{-1}(\mu)$.   We know from § 5.5 that μ is isolated in $\sigma(S)$, so that (μ) is a spectral set of S.   Then σ is a spectral set of T, and the projection associated with (μ) and S is E_σ (associated with σ and T), by Theorem 5.71–D.   Let $X_\sigma = \mathscr{R}(E_\sigma)$, and let S_0 be the restriction of S to X_σ.   Then $\sigma(S_0) = (\mu)$ (Theorem 5.7–B), and so $0 \in \rho(S_0)$, whence $x = S_0 S_0^{-1} x$ if $x \in X_\sigma$.   Since S_0 is compact, this implies (by means of Theorem 3.12–F) that X_σ is finite dimensional.   Now let T_1 be the restriction of T to X_σ.   We know from Theorem 5.7–B that $\sigma = \sigma_e(T_1)$. We also know that $\sigma_e(T_1)$ cannot be the entire extended plane, for $\sigma_e(T_1) \subseteq \sigma_e(T)$ and $\rho(T)$ is not empty, by assumption.   It then follows that $X_\sigma \subseteq \mathscr{D}(T)$, for otherwise we could conclude from the finite dimensionality of X_σ that for no λ can the range of $\lambda - T_1$ be all of X_σ and hence that $\sigma_e(T_1)$ is the entire extended plane.   Consequently $T_1 \in [X_\sigma]$ and $\sigma = \sigma(T_1)$ is a finite set.   Since $\lambda_0 \in \sigma$, this means that λ_0 is isolated in $\sigma(T)$.   It is easily seen that $E_\sigma = B_1 + P$, $PB_1 = 0$, where P is the projection associated with $\sigma - (\lambda_0)$ and B_1 is defined as in the theorem.   Hence $\mathscr{R}(B_1) \subseteq X_\sigma$, and so $\mathscr{R}(B_1)$ is finite dimensional.   When T is restricted to $\mathscr{R}(B_1)$, its resolvent must have a pole at λ_0, because of the finite dimensionality.   But then λ_0 is a pole of R_λ (see problem 2). Since the eigenmanifold corresponding to λ_0, namely $\mathscr{N}(\lambda_0 - T)$, is contained in $\mathscr{R}(B_1)$, it must be finite dimensional.

The foregoing proof uses certain facts about the spectrum of an operator in a finite-dimensional space.   These facts are evident as soon as we introduce a basis and represent the operator as a matrix, using determinants to find the spectrum and the resolvent.   A discussion which covers these matters without appeal to determinants appears in § 5.9.

One important application of Theorem 5.8–F is to the case in which $T \in [X]$ and T^n is compact for some positive integer n.   Clearly we can choose $f \in \mathfrak{A}_\infty(T)$ so that $f(\lambda) = \lambda^n$ on a neighborhood of $\sigma(T)$, and then $f(T) = T^n$.   Hence, *if T^n is compact for some n, every nonzero point in $\sigma(T)$ is a pole of R_λ, and the corresponding eigenmanifold is finite dimensional.* It can happen, for example, that T^2 is compact though T is not.

Example. Take $X = L(a, b)$, where (a, b) is a finite or infinite interval. Let $k(s, t)$ be a measurable function on $(a, b) \times (a, b)$ such that $|k(s, t)| \leqslant h(s)$ almost everywhere, where $h \in X$. Define $Kx = y$ to mean $y(s) = \int_a^b k(s, t)x(t)\, dt$. Then $K \in [X]$; K need not be compact, but K^2 is compact. See Zaanen, **1**, pages 322–323. Also Dunford and Pettis, **1**, page 370 and Phillips, **1**, page 536.

Another important application is to the case of an operator (not necessarily a member of $[X]$) whose resolvent is compact. We note that as a result of (5.1–2), if R_λ is compact for one λ in $\rho(T)$, it is compact for every such λ (see problems 3 and 4 in § 5.5). Suppose $\alpha \in \rho(T)$ and that R_α is compact. Now $R_\alpha = f(T)$, where $f(\lambda) = (\alpha - \lambda)^{-1}$. *Theorem 5.8–F then shows that in this case every point of $\sigma(T)$ is a pole of R_λ.* This is the situation which prevails in the case of certain differential operators, that of Example 4, § 5.6, for instance.

PROBLEMS

1. Show that the coefficients in (5.8–1) satisfy the relations (a) $A_m A_n = - A_{m+n+1}$, (b) $B_m B_n = B_{m+n-1}$, (c) $A_m B_n = 0$, (d) $A_n = (-1)^n A_0^{n+1}$. Show also that $\mathscr{R}(A_n) \subset \mathscr{D}_{n+1}(T)$ if $n \geqslant 0$ and $\mathscr{R}(B_n) \subset \mathscr{D}_k(T)$ if $n \geqslant 1$ and $k \geqslant 0$.

2. Let λ_0 be an isolated point of $\sigma(T)$, and consider the Laurent expansion (5.8–1). Show that $\sum_1^\infty (\lambda - \lambda_0)^{-n} B_n$ converges if $\lambda \neq \lambda_0$. Let $X_0 = \mathscr{R}(B_1)$, and let T_0 be the restriction of T to X_0. Then $T_0 \in [X_0]$. Let C_n be the restriction of B_n to X_0, and let $S_\lambda = \sum_1^\infty (\lambda - \lambda_0)^{-n} C_n$. Using (5.8–6), show that $S_\lambda = (\lambda - T_0)^{-1}$ if $\lambda \neq \lambda_0$. Note that $B_n B_1 = B_n$ and so conclude that λ_0 is a pole of order m of R_λ if and only if it is a pole of order m of S_λ.

3. Take $X = l^1$ and define $A \in [X]$ by the matrix (α_{ij}), where $\alpha_{ii} = \beta_i$, $\alpha_{12} = \alpha_{34} = \alpha_{56} = \cdots = 1$, and all other entries in the matrix are 0. Suppose $\beta_i \to 0$. Then A is not compact, but A^2 is compact. Discuss $\sigma(A)$ and the resolvent.

4. If $\mathscr{D}(T) \neq X$ there exists no polynomial $P(\lambda) \neq 0$ such that $P(T)x = 0$ for every $x \in \mathscr{D}_n(T)$ (n the degree of P). If such a polynomial P did exist, choose $\alpha \in \rho(T), f(\lambda) = (\alpha - \lambda)^{-n-1} P(\lambda)$, and show that $f(T) = 0$. Then use Theorem 5.8–B.

5. Suppose that $\sigma(T)$ is bounded and that $\mathscr{D}(T) \neq X$. Then R_λ has an expansion in powers of λ valid when $|\lambda| > r_\sigma(T)$, say $R_\lambda = \sum_1^\infty \lambda^{-n} A_n + \sum_0^\infty \lambda^n B_n$. Show that $TB_0 + I = A_1$, $TB_n = B_{n-1}$, $TA_n = A_{n+1}$. Show that $B_n \neq 0$ for each n and that A_1 is the projection associated with the spectral set $\sigma(T)$.

5.9 Operators with Rational Resolvent

Let X be a complex Banach space. A function f of the complex variable λ, with values in X, is called a rational function if it is expressible in the form $f(\lambda) = p(\lambda)/Q(\lambda)$, where $p(\lambda)$ is a polynomial in λ with co-efficients in X and $Q(\lambda)$ is a polynomial with complex coefficients. We assume that $p(\lambda)$ and $Q(\lambda)$ are never zero at the same point. A rational function also has a partial-fractions representation. Just as in classical analysis it may be proved with the aid of Liouville's theorem that, if the function f is holomorphic on the whole plane except for a finite number of poles and if $f(1/\lambda)$ has a pole or a removable singularity at $\lambda = 0$, then f is rational. This is done by expressing $f(\lambda)$ as the sum of a poly-nomial and the singular parts of its Laurent expansions at the various poles.

In this section we consider operators T for which the resolvent R_λ is a rational function with values in $[X]$. If $T \in [X]$ and $\sigma(T)$ consists of a finite number of points, each a pole of R_λ, then R_λ is rational, for $\|R_\lambda\| \to 0$ as $\lambda \to \infty$. It is impossible to have R_λ rational if T is closed but not in $[X]$ (see problem 5, § 5.8, which indicates that R_λ has an essential singularity at ∞ in this case). Our discussion of operators with rational resolvents includes a determinant-free treatment of the situation when X is finite dimensional.

We begin with consideration of the question as to when $P(T) = 0$ if $T \in [X]$ and $P(\lambda)$ is a scalar polynomial. We could appeal to Theorem 5.8–B, but we prefer a more elementary argument.

Theorem 5–9A. *Suppose $T \in [X]$, and let $P(\lambda)$ be a scalar polynomial of degree $\geqslant 1$. Then $P(T) = 0$ if and only if there exists a polynomial $q(\lambda)$ with coefficients in $[X]$ such that*

(5.9–1)
$$P(\lambda)R_\lambda = q(\lambda)$$

when $\lambda \in \rho(T)$.

PROOF. Let $Q(\lambda, \mu)$ be the polynomial in λ and μ such that $P(\lambda) - P(\mu) \equiv (\lambda - \mu)Q(\lambda, \mu)$. With T in place of μ we have $P(\lambda) - P(T) = Q(\lambda, T)(\lambda - T)$. Multiplication by R_λ gives $P(\lambda)R_\lambda - P(T)R_\lambda = Q(\lambda, T)$. Suppose now that $P(T) = 0$. Then we obtain (5.9–1), with $q(\lambda) = Q(\lambda, T)$. On the other hand, if we start from (5.9–1), we see that $P(T)R_\lambda = q(\lambda) - Q(\lambda, T)$, and hence

$$\|q(\lambda) - Q(\lambda, T)\| \leqslant \|P(T)\| \, \|R_\lambda\|.$$

Since $\|R_\lambda\| \to 0$ as $\lambda \to \infty$, we conclude by Liouville's theorem that

$q(\lambda) - Q(\lambda, T)$ is a polynomial in λ which is identically zero.   It follows that $P(T)R_\lambda = 0$, and hence $P(T) = P(T)R_\lambda(\lambda - T) = 0$.

Theorem 5.9–B.   *Suppose $T \in [X]$.   There exists a scalar polynomial $P(\lambda)$ of degree $\geqslant 1$ such that $P(T) = 0$ if and only if R_λ is rational.*

PROOF.   If R_λ is a rational function of λ, it is expressible in the form $R_\lambda = q(\lambda)/P(\lambda)$, where q and P are polynomials with no common zeros. We know that $\sigma(T)$ is not empty (Theorem 5.2–B); hence the degree of $P(\lambda)$ is at least 1, for $\sigma(T)$ is precisely the set of singular points of R_λ, i.e., the set of zeros of $P(\lambda)$.   It now follows from Theorem 5.9–A that $P(T) = 0$.   Suppose, on the other hand, that $P(\lambda)$ is some polynomial of degree $\geqslant 1$ such that $P(T) = 0$.   By Theorem 5.9–A we know there exists a polynomial $q(\lambda)$ (with coefficients in $[X]$) such that (5.9–1) holds when $\lambda \in \rho(T)$.   It remains to show that there exist polynomials P_1 and q_1 such that $\rho(T) = \{\lambda : P_1(\lambda) \neq 0\}$, P_1 and q_1 have no common zeros, and $R_\lambda = q_1(\lambda)/P_1(\lambda)$.   It is not necessarily true that we can take $P_1 = P$ and $q_1 = q$.

If $\lambda_0 \in \rho(T)$ and if λ_0 is a common zero of P and q, its multiplicity m as a zero of P is the same as its multiplicity n as a zero of q.   For, if we let $r = \min(m, n)$, divide both sides of (5.9–1) by $(\lambda - \lambda_0)^r$, and let $\lambda \to \lambda_0$, we get a contradiction unless $m = n$ (observe that $R_\lambda \neq 0$ when $\lambda \in \rho(T)$, as a result of our standing assumption that X has at least two elements).   Now let P_0 and q_0 be the polynomials obtained from P and q respectively, by removal of the factors arising from common zeros in $\rho(T)$.   Then $P_0(\lambda)$ has no zeros in $\rho(T)$ and

$$(5.9-2) \qquad\qquad R_\lambda = \frac{q_0(\lambda)}{P_0(\lambda)}$$

if $\lambda \in \rho(T)$.

Next we show that $\sigma(T)$ is precisely the set of zeros of $P_0(\lambda)$.   If $\pi = \{\lambda : P_0(\lambda) \neq 0\}$, we know that $\rho(T) \subset \pi$.   Now π is connected and $\rho(T)$ is open, so that, if $\pi - \rho(T)$ were nonempty, it would have to contain an accumulation point of $\rho(T)$, say α.   Let $A = q_0(\alpha)/P_0(\alpha)$.   If $\{\lambda(n)\}$ is a sequence in $\rho(T)$ such that $\lambda(n) \to \alpha$, we see from (5.9–2) that $R_{\lambda(n)} \to A$. From this we easily conclude that $A(\alpha - T) = (\alpha - T)A = I$, so that $\alpha \in \rho(T)$ and $A = R_\alpha$.   We must therefore have $\pi = \rho(T)$.

Now, finally, there may be common zeros of P_0 and q_0 *not* in $\rho(T)$. However, the multiplicity of such a zero for P_0 must exceed its multiplicity for q_0, for a contrary assumption would lead us to the conclusion that the zero is in $\rho(T)$, by an argument like the foregoing.   For each such zero β, of multiplicity n as a zero of q_0, let us divide $P_0(\lambda)$ and $q_0(\lambda)$ by $(\lambda - \beta)^n$.   Let $P_1(\lambda)$ and $q_1(\lambda)$ be the polynomials which result from

$P_0(\lambda)$ and $q_0(\lambda)$ after the elimination of all such factors $(\lambda - \beta)^n$. Then P_1 and q_1 have no common zeros, $\sigma(T)$ is precisely the set of zeros of P_1, and $R_\lambda = q_1(\lambda)/P_1(\lambda)$. This shows that R_λ is a rational function, and completes the proof of the theorem.

The foregoing proof shows that, if $P(T) = 0$, then $P(\lambda)$ is divisible by the denominator $P_1(\lambda)$ of the rational function R_λ. Hence, if R_λ is rational, with distinct poles $\lambda_1, \cdots, \lambda_k$ of orders $m_1, \cdots, m_k$, among all polynomials $P(\lambda)$ of degree $\geqslant 1$ such that $P(T) = 0$ there is a unique one of lowest degree with leading coefficient 1, and this unique one is

$$(\lambda - \lambda_1)^{m_1} \cdots (\lambda - \lambda_k)^{m_k}.$$

This polynomial is called the *minimal polynomial* associated with T. We recall from Theorem 5.8–A that m_i is the ascent of $\lambda_i - T$.

For finite-dimensional spaces we have:

Theorem 5.9–C.   *Suppose X is of finite dimension $n(n \geqslant 1)$ and that $T \in [X]$. Then R_λ is rational.*

PROOF.   We deliberately avoid the use of determinants. Let us write $T(\lambda) = \lambda - T$. The ascent and descent of $T(\lambda)$ must be finite, because of the finite dimensionality. They are equal, by Theorem 5.41–E. If the ascent is 0, then $\lambda \in \rho(T)$; otherwise $\lambda \in P\sigma(T)$. Now, eigenvectors corresponding to distinct eigenvalues are linearly independent (see the first part of the proof of Theorem 5.5–G). Hence, since X is n-dimensional, $\sigma(T)$ cannot contain more than n points. We know that $\sigma(T)$ is not empty. Let the distinct points of $\sigma(T)$ be $\lambda_1, \cdots, \lambda_k$, and let the ascent of $T(\lambda_i)$ be m_i. We define $P(\lambda) = (\lambda - \lambda_1)^{m_1} \cdots, (\lambda - \lambda_k)^{m_k}$. Select any $x \neq 0$. Since X is n-dimensional, there exist scalars $\alpha_0, \alpha_1, \cdots, \alpha_n$ (perhaps depending on x) not all 0, such that $\alpha_0 x + \alpha_1 T x + \cdots + \alpha_n T^n x = 0$. Let $Q(\lambda) = \alpha_0 + \alpha_1\lambda + \cdots + \alpha_n\lambda^n$, and let the factored form of Q be $\alpha(\lambda - \beta_1)^{\nu_1} \cdots (\lambda - \beta_r)^{\nu_r}$, where $\beta_1, \cdots, \beta_r$ are the distinct zeros, and $\alpha \neq 0$. Then

$$(5.9\text{-}3) \qquad (T - \beta_1)^{\nu_1} \cdots (T - \beta_r)^{\nu_r} x = 0.$$

From this we propose to conclude that $P(T)x = 0$. For any β_i that is not one of the points $\lambda_1, \cdots, \lambda_k$ we can omit the factor $(T - \beta_i)^{\nu_i}$ from (5.9–3) without impairing the equality, because $(T - \beta_i)^{\nu_i}$ has an inverse in this case. On the other hand, for any λ_j that is not one of the points $\beta_1, \cdots, \beta_r$ we can insert the factor $(T - \lambda_j)^{m_j}$ in (5.9–3) without destroying the equality. It remains to consider the case of a β_i which *is* one of the points $\lambda_1, \cdots, \lambda_k$. For simplicity of notation suppose $\beta_1 = \lambda_1$. If $\nu_1 < m_1$ we can evidently replace ν_1 by m_1 in (5.9–3), and the equation will still hold. The same is true if $m_1 < \nu_1$, the reason being that

$\mathcal{N}[T(\beta_1)^{\nu_1}] = \mathcal{N}[T(\beta_1)^{m_1}]$ in this case, because m_1 is the ascent of $\beta_1 - T$. It is now clear that $P(T)x = 0$.   But then $P(T) = 0$, since $P(T)$ is independent of x and x was arbitrary.   Hence R_λ is rational, by Theorem 5.9–B.

We now turn to some general considerations which will lead us to a result about reducibility in the case of operators for which R_λ is rational. We shall obtain in a more elementary way a result which is obtainable from Theorems 5.7–A and 5.8–A.   In the immediately following theorem no topology is needed.

Theorem 5.9–D.   *Let X be any complex linear space, and suppose T is a linear operator on X into X.   (a) Let $P_1(\lambda)$ and $P_2(\lambda)$ be scalar polynomials without common zeros.   Let $P(\lambda) = P_1(\lambda)P_2(\lambda)$, and let M_1, M_2, M be the null manifolds of $P_1(T)$, $P_2(T)$, $P(T)$ respectively.   Then $M_1 \cap M_2 = (0)$ and $M = M_1 \oplus M_2$.   (b) Let $\lambda_1, \cdots, \lambda_k$ be distinct complex numbers, and let $m_1, \cdots, m_k$ be positive integers.   Let $P(\lambda) = (\lambda - \lambda_1)^{m_1} \cdots (\lambda - \lambda_k)^{m_k}$.   Let M_i be the null manifold of $(T - \lambda_i)^{m_i}$, and let M be the null manifold of $P(T)$.   Then $M_1, \cdots, M_k$ are linearly independent, and $M = M_1 \oplus \cdots \oplus M_k$.*

PROOF. (a) Since P_1 and P_2 are relatively prime, there exist polynomials Q_1 and Q_2 such that

$$Q_1(\lambda)P_1(\lambda) + Q_2(\lambda)P_2(\lambda) \equiv 1$$

and hence

(5.9–4) $$Q_1(T)P_1(T) + Q_2(T)P_2(T) = I.$$

It follows that

(5.9–5) $$Q_1(T)[P_1(T)]^2 + Q_2(T)P(T) = P_1(T).$$

From (5.9–4) we see that $M_1 \cap M_2 = (0)$.   Now suppose $x \in M$, and let $y = Q_1(T)P_1(T)x$.   Then (5.9–5) shows that $P_1(T)y = P_1(T)x$, or $y - x \in M_1$.   Also, $P_2(T)y = Q_1(T)P(T)x = 0$, so that $y \in M_2$.   Then $x = (x - y) + y$ shows that $M \subset M_1 \oplus M_2$.   It is evident that $M_1 \subset M$ and $M_2 \subset M$, and hence $M = M_1 \oplus M_2$.   This finishes (a).   The truth of (b) follows from (a) by induction.

We now revert to the case in which X is a complex Banach space and $T \in [X]$.

Theorem 5.9–E.   *Suppose R_λ is rational, with $P(\lambda) = (\lambda - \lambda_1)^{m_1} \cdots (\lambda - \lambda_k)^{m_k}$ the minimal polynomial for T.   Then, in the notation of Theorem 5.9–Db, $X = M_1 \oplus \cdots \oplus M_k$, and T is completely reduced by $(M_1, \cdots, M_k)$.*

PROOF. The fact that $T(M_i) \subset M_i$ is evident from $(T - \lambda_i)^{m_i}T = T(T - \lambda_i)^{m_i}$, and $M = X$, because $P(T) = 0$.

The direct-sum decomposition of X described in Theorem 5.9–E determines projections E_i defined by $E_i x = x_i$ if $x = x_1 + \cdots + x_k$, $x_i \in M_i$. The projection E_i may be described as the residue of R_λ at the pole λ_i; it is the projection associated with the spectral set (λ_i). Let

$$N = \sum_{i=1}^{k} (T - \lambda_i)E_i,$$

and let $p = \max(m_1, \cdots, m_k)$. It is easily seen that

$$N^p = \sum_{i=1}^{k} (T - \lambda_i)^p E_i = 0,$$

so that N is nilpotent. (Observe that $N = 0$ if $m_1 = \cdots = m_k = 1$.) We can write

(5.9–6) $$T = \sum_{i=1}^{k} \lambda_i E_i + N.$$

This representation of T is a consequence of the fact that R_λ is rational. There is a converse to this, as the following theorem shows.

Theorem 5.9–F. *Suppose X is a complex Banach space. Let $E_1, \cdots,$ E_k be elements of $[X]$ which are projections such that $E_i E_j = 0$ if $i \neq j$, and $I = E_1 + \cdots + E_k$. Let T be defined by (5.9–6), where $\lambda_1, \cdots, \lambda_k$ are complex constants, and N is a nilpotent member of $[X]$ such that $NE_i = E_i N$ for each i. Then R_λ is rational.*

PROOF. Suppose $N^p = 0$. Now, $(T - \lambda_i)E_i = NE_i$, as we see from (5.9–6). Hence $(T - \lambda_i)^p E_i = N^p E_i = 0$. It now follows from $I = E_1 + \cdots + E_k$ that $(T - \lambda_1)^p \cdots (T - \lambda_k)^p = 0$. Therefore, by Theorem 5.9–B, R_λ is rational.

PROBLEMS

I. Let X be n-dimensional and suppose $T \in [X]$. Let $u_1, \cdots, u_n$ be a basis for X, and let $D(\lambda)$ be the determinant of the matrix corresponding to $\lambda - T$ when this basis is used. Then $D(T) = 0$. (This is the Hamilton-Cayley theorem.) Use Theorem 5.9–A and Cramer's rule. See problem 6 also.

2. Suppose that R_λ is rational, and adopt the notation of Theorem 5.9–E and Theorem 5.9–Db. Let N_i be the null manifold of $\lambda_i - T$, and let Y be the subspace generated by $N_1 \cup \cdots \cup N_k$. Then $Y = X$ if and only if $m_1 = \cdots = m_k = 1$.

3. Suppose that R_λ is rational.   Using the notation of Theorem 5.9–E and the paragraph which follows it, show that, if f is locally analytic on $\sigma(T)$,

$$f(T) = \sum_{i=1}^{k} \sum_{j=0}^{m_i-1} \frac{f^{(j)}(\lambda_i)}{j!}(T - \lambda_i)^j E_i.$$

In particular, suppose m is fixed, $1 \leqslant m \leqslant k$, and let $f(\lambda)$ be a polynomial such that $f^{(j)}(\lambda_i) = 1$ if $i = m, j = 0$, while $f^{(j)}(\lambda_i) = 0$ otherwise as it occurs in the formula for $f(T)$.   Then $f(T) = E_m$.   Since a polynomial of this kind exists (of degree at most $m_1 + \cdots + m_k - 1$), each E_m is expressible as a polynomial in T.   See Hamburger and Grimshaw, **1**, page 111.

4. Suppose $T \in [X]$ and that $X_0 = \mathscr{R}(T)$ is finite dimensional, but $X_0 \neq X$. Then $0 \in \sigma(T)$.   Observe that $T(X_0) \subset X_0$.   Let T_0 be the restriction of T to X_0, and let S_λ be the resolvent of T_0.   In order to see how to express R_λ in terms of S_λ, write $y = \lambda x - Tx$, $Ty = \lambda Tx - T_0(Tx)$, whence $Tx = S_\lambda Ty$ if $\lambda \notin \sigma(T_0)$.   Then $y = \lambda x - S_\lambda Ty$, and $x = \lambda^{-1}[I + S_\lambda T]y$.   This suggests that $R_\lambda = \lambda^{-1}[I + S_\lambda T]$ and that $\sigma(T) = (0) \cup \sigma(T_0)$.   Verify that this is correct. Observe that R_λ is rational, since S_λ is.   An important type of operator with a finite-dimensional range is an integral operator with "degenerate" kernel $k(s, t) = \alpha_1(s)\beta_1(t) + \cdots + \alpha_n(s)\beta_n(t)$.

5. If X is finite dimensional, formula (5.9–6) plus certain well-known facts about nilpotent operators provide the basis for obtaining the *Jordan normal form* matrix representation of the operator T.   Choose a basis $u_1, \cdots, u_n$ for X in such a way that successive sets of u's form bases for $M_1, \cdots, M_k$.   Then the matrix representation of T takes the form shown here in the adjacent diagram,

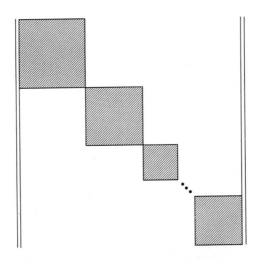

where the only nonzero elements are inside the shaded blocks.   The ith block, counting down the diagonal, is the matrix representation of the restriction of T to M_i.   Owing to the nilpotency of N, whose restriction to M_i is the same as that of $T - \lambda_i$, the basis for M_i may be chosen in such a way that the matrix representation of the restriction of N to M_i has no nonzero elements except for the possibility of 1's in a certain arrangement along the diagonal directly below the main diagonal. There will be some such 1's if $m_i > 1$, but not if $m_i = 1$. Thus the matrix for T has

$$\underbrace{\lambda_1, \cdots, \lambda_1;}_{\nu_1} \quad \underbrace{\lambda_2, \cdots, \lambda_2;}_{\nu_2} \quad \cdots; \quad \underbrace{\lambda_k, \cdots, \lambda_k}_{\nu_k}$$

down the main diagonal, where ν_i is the dimension of M_i. The only other nonzero elements are the 1's already referred to, on the diagonal just below the main diagonal. For more details on the matrix representation of nilpotent operators see Halmos, **1**, pages 164–165.

6. Using the results in problem 5, show that the determinant $D(\lambda)$ in problem 1 is $(\lambda - \lambda_1)^{\nu_1} \cdots (\lambda - \lambda_k)^{\nu_k}$.

SUGGESTED READING

Bade, **1**.
Courant and Hilbert, **1**, parts of Chapter 3.
Dunford, **3**, **4**.
Dunford and Schwartz, **1**, Chapter 7.
Friedman, **1**, Chapter 2.
Halmos, **1**, Chapter 2.
Hamburger and Grimshaw, **1**, Chapter 4.
Hille, **1**, Chapters 5, 11, 15 and many parts of other chapters.
Lorch, **1**.
Ljusternik and Sobolew, **1**, Chapter 4.
Riesz, F., **1**, Chapter 4.
Riesz and Nagy, **1**, Chapters 4, 5, 11.
Stone, **1**, Chapter 4.
Taylor, **1**, **2**.
Titchmarsh, **2**.
Zaanen, **1**, Chapters 11, 13.

SPECTRAL ANALYSIS IN HILBERT SPACE

6.0 Introduction

The principal aim of this chapter is to study the more elementary properties of symmetric linear operators (also called Hermitian operators if the scalar field is complex) and especially the properties of self-adjoint and normal operators in Hilbert space. The theory of compact symmetric operators is developed without requiring the space to be complete. This material has applications to the Hilbert-Schmidt theory of integral equations with symmetric kernel and to symmetric differential operators with compact resolvent; in particular, to the classical Sturm-Liouville differential-equation problems. The spectral theorem is proved for bounded self-adjoint operators and for unitary operators. The state of affairs for unbounded self-adjoint operators is sketched without proofs.

The "big" theorems of the chapter are: 6.4–B, 6.4–C, and 6.4–D for compact symmetric operators; 6.5–A and 6.5–C for the spectral theorem for bounded self-adjoint operators and the operational calculus founded on it; and 6.5–B, the spectral theorem for unitary operators. Theorems 6.5–D and 6.5–E are of fundamental interest, since they relate the spectral classification of a point (in relation to a bounded self-adjoint operator) to the function-theoretic character of the resolution of the identity at that point.

Theorem 6.2–C, comparatively simple in itself, is of crucial importance in the proof of Theorem 6.5–A.

6.1 Bilinear and Quadratic Forms

Throughout this section X denotes a not necessarily complete inner-product space. The scalar field may be either real or complex, except when we specify one or the other explicitly. If no such explicit specification is made, a bar indicating the complex conjugate of a number is to be ignored if the situation under consideration is being regarded from the point of view of real scalars.

Suppose A is a linear operator with domain X and range in X. Then the inner product (Ax, y) is a linear functional of x for each fixed y. As a function of y, (Ax, y) is linear when the scalar field is real; in the complex case, however, we do not quite have linearity with respect to y, for $(Ax, \alpha y) = \bar{\alpha}(Ax, y)$, the scalar factor coming outside as $\bar{\alpha}$ rather than as α. However, for convenience in embracing both the real and complex cases in one terminology, we shall say that (Ax, y) is *bilinear* in x and y.

For some purposes it is desirable to study bilinearity directly, instead of through the medium of a linear operator. Hence we make the following definition: A scalar-valued function ϕ on $X \times X$ is called a *bilinear form* if $\phi(x, y)$ is linear in x for each y, while $\overline{\phi(x, y)}$ is linear in y for each x. With ϕ we associate the functional ψ on X defined by $\psi(x) = \phi(x, x)$. We call ψ the *quadratic form* corresponding to ϕ. Observe that $\psi(\alpha x) = |\alpha|^2\psi(x)$.

One important relation between ϕ and ψ is expressed by the formula

$$(6.1–1) \qquad \tfrac{1}{2}\{\phi(x, y) + \phi(y, x)\} = \psi\left(\frac{x + y}{2}\right) - \psi\left(\frac{x - y}{2}\right).$$

It may be verified by expanding the terms on the right, using the bilinearity. When the scalar field is complex we have

$$(6.1–2) \quad \phi(x, y) = \psi\left(\frac{x + y}{2}\right) - \psi\left(\frac{x - y}{2}\right) + i\psi\left(\frac{x + iy}{2}\right) - i\psi\left(\frac{x - iy}{2}\right).$$

In the complex case, therefore, ϕ can be expressed entirely in terms of ψ. This is not always true in the real case, however, for in this case the left member of (6.1–1) is a bilinear form, in general not the same as ϕ, whose corresponding quadratic form is the same as the one corresponding to ϕ.

A bilinear form ϕ is continuous jointly in its two variables if and only if $|\phi(x, y)|$ is bounded for all x and y such that $\|x\| \leqslant 1$, $\|y\| \leqslant 1$ (proof similar to that of Theorem 3.1–A).   When ϕ is continuous we define

$$\|\phi\| = \sup \frac{|\phi(x, y)|}{\|x\| \, \|y\|} \qquad \text{(for } x \neq 0, \, y \neq 0\text{)},$$

or, equivalently, we may take the supremum merely for all x and y with $\|x\| = \|y\| = 1$.   To avoid trivialities we are assuming that the space X does not reduce to (0).   For the corresponding quadratic form we define

$$\|\psi\| = \sup_{\|x\|=1} |\psi(x)| = \sup_{x \neq 0} \frac{|\psi(x)|}{\|x\|^2}.$$

Obviously $\|\psi\| \leq \|\phi\|$.   When the field of scalars is complex it is easily seen with the aid of (6.1–2) and (4.81–1) that $\|\phi\| \leq 2\|\psi\|$.   Hence

(6.1–3) $$\|\psi\| \leq \|\phi\| \leq 2\|\psi\|$$

in the complex case.

A bilinear form ϕ is called *symmetric* if $\phi(x, y) = \overline{\phi(y, x)}$ (in the complex case such a form is also called *Hermitian*).   If ϕ is symmetric we can prove that

(6.1–4) $$\|\phi\| = \|\psi\|.$$

We have only to prove that $\|\phi\| \leq \|\psi\|$.   Owing to the symmetry we have from (6.1–1) and (4.81–1):

$$|\text{Re } \phi(x, y)| \leq \tfrac{1}{2}\|\psi\| \, (\|x\|^2 + \|y\|^2)$$

(with the Re symbol, for the "real part," superfluous in the real case). For fixed x and y with $\|x\| = \|y\| = 1$ we can choose α so that $|\alpha| = 1$ and $\alpha\phi(x, y) = |\phi(x, y)|$, whence

$$|\phi(x, y)| = \phi(\alpha x, y) = |\text{Re } \phi(\alpha x, y)| \leq \|\psi\|,$$

and so $\|\phi\| \leq \|\psi\|$.

Theorem 6.1–A.   *Suppose $\phi(x, y) = (Ax, y)$, where A is linear on X into X.   Then ϕ is continuous if and only if A is continuous, and then $\|A\| = \|\phi\|$.*

PROOF.   If A is continuous, $|(Ax, y)| \leq \|Ax\| \, \|y\| \leq \|A\| \, \|x\| \, \|y\|$.   If ϕ is continuous, $\|Ax\|^2 = (Ax, Ax) \leq \|\phi\| \, \|x\| \, \|Ax\|$, or $\|Ax\| \leq \|\phi\| \, \|x\|$.   The conclusions now follow.

Theorem 6.1–B.   *Suppose that X is complete and that ϕ is a continuous bilinear form.   Then there exists $A \in [X]$ such that $\phi(x, y) = (Ax, y)$.*

PROOF.   For fixed x, $\overline{\phi(x, y)}$ is a continuous linear functional of y. Hence, by Theorem 4.81–C, we can represent the functional in the form

$\overline{\phi(x, y)} = (y, Ax)$, where Ax is some vector depending on x. This defines an operator A on X; the linearity of A is easily verified, since $(Ax, y) = \phi(x, y)$. That A is continuous follows from Theorem 6.1–A.

PROBLEM

Suppose A is linear on X into X, where X is a complex inner-product space. Then, if $(Ax, x) = 0$ for each $x \in X$, it follows that $A = 0$. Is this true for real inner-product spaces?

6.11 Symmetric Operators

A linear operator A with domain and range in the inner-product space X is called *symmetric* if

$$(6.11-1) \qquad (Ax, y) = (x, Ay)$$

for each x and y in $\mathscr{D}(A)$. In case X is a complex space, a symmetric linear operator is also called a *Hermitian* operator. If we regard $\mathscr{D}(A)$ by itself as an inner-product space, $\phi(x, y) = (Ax, y)$ is a bilinear form on $\mathscr{D}(A) \times \mathscr{D}(A)$, and ϕ is symmetric (as defined in § 6.1) if and only if A is symmetric. The corresponding quadratic form, defined on $\mathscr{D}(A)$, is (Ax, x).

We assume that A is symmetric, with $\mathscr{D}(A) \neq (0)$. Then (Ax, x) is real, even when X is a complex space, and we define

$$(6.11-2) \qquad m(A) = \inf_{\|x\|=1} (Ax, x), \qquad M(A) = \sup_{\|x\|=1} (Ax, x).$$

The possibilities $m(A) = -\infty$, $M(A) = +\infty$ are not excluded.

Theorem 6.11–A. *If A is symmetric and λ is an eigenvalue of A, then λ is real, and $m(A) \leqslant \lambda \leqslant M(A)$. Eigenvectors corresponding to distinct eigenvalues are orthogonal.*

PROOF. Suppose $\|x\| = 1$ and $Ax = \lambda x$. Then $(Ax, x) = (\lambda x, x) = \lambda$, so λ is real and $m(A) \leqslant \lambda \leqslant M(A)$. If $Ax = \lambda x$ and $Ay = \mu y$, where $\lambda \neq \mu$, we have $\lambda(x, y) = (\lambda x, y) = (Ax, y) = (x, Ay) = (x, \mu y) = \mu(x, y)$, or $(\lambda - \mu)(x, y) = 0$, whence $(x, y) = 0$.

Next we consider the question as to whether the bounds $m(A)$ and $M(A)$ can be attained by values of (Ax, x) when $\|x\| = 1$. If $\lambda = m(A)$ happens to be an eigenvalue of A, there is an x with $\|x\| = 1$ and $Ax = \lambda x$. Then $(Ax, x) = (\lambda x, x) = m(A)$. A similar thing is true if $M(A)$ is an eigenvalue. There is a valid converse if $\mathscr{D}(A)$ is dense in X.

Theorem 6.11-B. *Suppose that A is symmetric and that $\mathscr{D}(A)$ is dense in X. Suppose $y \in \mathscr{D}(A)$, $\|y\| = 1$, and $(Ay, y) = \lambda$, where λ is either $m(A)$ or $M(A)$. Then $Ay = \lambda y$, so that λ is an eigenvalue of A.*

PROOF. Suppose for example that $\lambda = m(A)$. Let $B = A - \lambda$. Then B is symmetric, with $(By, y) = 0$ and $m(B) = 0$, so that $(Bx, x) \geqslant 0$ for every x in $\mathscr{D}(A)$. Let $\alpha = \theta(By, x)$, where x is arbitrary in $\mathscr{D}(A)$ and θ is an arbitrary real number. Then

$$0 \leqslant (B[y + \alpha x], y + \alpha x) = (By, y) + \alpha(Bx, y) + \bar{\alpha}(By, x) + |\alpha|^2(Bx, x),$$

or

$$0 \leqslant \theta |(x, By)|^2 \{2 + \theta(Bx, x)\}.$$

Since the right member of the inequality changes sign with θ when θ is small, unless $(x, By) = 0$, we conclude that $(x, By) = 0$. This is true for each $x \in \mathscr{D}(A)$, and, since $\mathscr{D}(A)$ is dense in X, we conclude that $By = 0$ or $Ay = \lambda y$. If $\lambda = M(A)$, we put $B = \lambda - A$, and the same argument applies.

When X is complete and A is symmetric, with $\mathscr{D}(A) = X$, we can prove (see § 6.2) that A is continuous and that $\sigma(A)$ lies on the interval $m(A) \leqslant \lambda \leqslant M(A)$ of the real axis, with $m(A)$ and $M(A)$ actually belonging to $\sigma(A)$.

In the next theorem we consider the situation in which $\mathscr{D}(A) = X$, though X need not be complete.

Theorem 6.11-C. *If A is symmetric, with $\mathscr{D}(A) = X$, then A is continuous if and only if $m(A)$ and $M(A)$ are both finite, and in that case*

(6.11-3) $$\|A\| = \max \{|m(A)|, |M(A)|\}.$$

PROOF. We know from Theorem 6.1-A that A is continuous if and only if $|(Ax, y)|$ is bounded for all x and y for which $\|x\| = \|y\| = 1$; and, as we see in conjunction with (6.1-4), this is the same as demanding that $\sup_{\|x\|=1} |(Ax, x)|$ be finite, this supremum then being equal to $\|A\|$. Formula (6.11-3) now follows from the definitions (6.11-2).

Example I. Let X be the Hilbert space $L^2(0, 2\pi)$. Let $\mathscr{D}(A)$ be the subspace of X determined by those functions $x(t)$ which are absolutely continuous on $[0, 2\pi]$, such that $x(0) = x(2\pi)$ and such that the derivative $x'(t)$ is of class $\mathscr{L}^2(0, 2\pi)$. For $x \in \mathscr{D}(A)$ define $Ax = y$ to mean $y(t) = -ix'(t)$. Then A is symmetric. For, if $x, y \in \mathscr{D}(A)$,

$$i \frac{d}{dt} \{x(t)\overline{y(t)}\} = ix(t)\overline{y'(t)} + ix'(t)\overline{y(t)},$$

and so

$$0 = ix(t)\overline{y(t)} \Big|_0^{2\pi} = (x, Ay) - (Ax, y).$$

Example 2. An important type of symmetric operator arises in connection with certain boundary-value problems for second-order ordinary differential equations. The symmetry of the operator in such problems depends both on the nature of the boundary conditions and on certain formal properties of the differential operator which occurs. The space X is taken to be either $L^2(a, b)$ or some subspace of $L^2(a, b)$, with the usual inner product of $L^2(a, b)$. When the domain $\mathscr{D}(A)$ is suitably defined, $Ax = u$ is expressed by

$$(6.11\text{–}4) \qquad u(t) = -\frac{d}{dt}[p(t)x'(t)] + q(t)x(t)$$

where p and q are certain *real-valued* functions. This formula exhibits the essential formal structure of the differential operator. There must be conditions on p, q and $\mathscr{D}(A)$ which insure that Ax is a well-defined member of X when $x \in \mathscr{D}(A)$. For instance, if (a, b) is a finite interval and if X consists of those elements of $L^2(a, b)$ which correspond to functions continuous on $[a, b]$, we might require q to be continuous and p to be continuously differentiable. We could then take $\mathscr{D}(A)$ to consist of those functions which are twice continuously differentiable and satisfy certain boundary conditions. If X is taken to be all of $L^2(a, b)$, we might require that q be measurable and bounded and that p be absolutely continuous. Then $\mathscr{D}(A)$ could be taken to consist of those elements of $L^2(a, b)$ corresponding to functions $x(t)$ which are such that both $x(t)$ and $p(t)x'(t)$ are absolutely continuous, $p(t)x'(t)$ has a derivative of class $\mathscr{L}^2(a, b)$, and $x(t)$ satisfies certain boundary conditions.

If $Ax = u$ and $Ay = v$, it is easily verified that we have

$$u(t)\overline{y(t)} - x(t)\overline{v(t)} = \frac{d}{dt}\{p(t)[x(t)\overline{y'(t)} - x'(t)\overline{y(t)}]\}.$$

Thus

$$(Ax, y) - (x, Ay) = p(t)[x(t)\overline{y'(t)} - x'(t)\overline{y(t)}]\Big|_a^b.$$

The operator A is then seen to be symmetric, provided that the definition of $\mathscr{D}(A)$ insures that

$$(6.11\text{–}5) \quad p(b)[x(b)\overline{y'(b)} - x'(b)\overline{y(b)}] = p(a)[x(a)\overline{y'(a)} - x'(a)\overline{y(a)}].$$

In case the interval is infinite, this condition must be interpreted appropriately. For a finite interval the boundary conditions are of the form

$$\alpha_{11}x(a) + \alpha_{12}x'(a) + \beta_{11}x(b) + \beta_{12}x'(b) = 0$$
$$\alpha_{21}x(a) + \alpha_{22}x'(a) + \beta_{21}x(b) + \beta_{22}x'(b) = 0$$

where the α's and β's are certain real scalars. For these boundary conditions it can be shown that condition (6.11–5) is equivalent to the condition

$$(6.11\text{–}6) \qquad p(a)\begin{vmatrix} \beta_{11} & \beta_{12} \\ \beta_{21} & \beta_{22} \end{vmatrix} = p(b)\begin{vmatrix} \alpha_{11} & \alpha_{12} \\ \alpha_{21} & \alpha_{22} \end{vmatrix}.$$

It is not our intent in this book to discuss in detail the spectral analysis of a symmetric operator A of the type just described. However, in § 6.4, as an application of the theory of compact symmetric operators, we do discuss the solution of boundary-value problems of this type in the special case in which A^{-1} is a compact operator belonging to $[X]$.

We return now to the general consideration of symmetric operators. Suppose A is symmetric, and that $(Ax, x) \geqslant 0$ for each $x \in \mathscr{D}(A)$. Let us write $\{x, y\} = (Ax, y)$. Then $\{x, y\}$, as a function on $\mathscr{D}(A) \times \mathscr{D}(A)$, has all the properties of an inner product except possibly the property that $\{x, x\} = 0$ implies $x = 0$. This last property is not needed in the derivation of the Schwarz inequality $|\{x, y\}|^2 \leqslant \{x, x\}\{y, y\}$, however (see Theorem 3.2–A), and so we obtain the inequality

$$(6.11\text{–}7) \qquad |(Ax, y)|^2 \leqslant (Ax, x)(Ay, y), \qquad x, y \in \mathscr{D}(A)$$

under the stated conditions on A. This result is used in the proof of Theorem 6.2–B.

PROBLEMS

1. Let A be linear on X into X, where X is a complex inner-product space. Suppose (Ax, x) is real for every x. Then A is symmetric. Use (6.1–2).

2. Suppose A is linear on X into X and symmetric. Then, if $(Ax, x) = 0$ for each x, it follows that $A = 0$. Compare with the problem at the end of § 6.1.

6.12 A Theorem of Schur

A bounded linear operator A with domain l^2 and range in l^2 is representable by an infinite matrix (α_{ij}); see Example 5, § 4.2 and problems 3 and 4, § 4.51. There is a useful theorem, due to I. Schur, **1**, which gives conditions on an infinite matrix sufficient to insure that it defines an element A of $[l^2]$. Schur's theorem also gives an estimate of $\|A\|$. The proof makes use of some facts about symmetric operators in finite-dimensional spaces.

Theorem 6.12–A. *Let (α_{ij}) be an infinite matrix of scalars such that*

$$(6.12\text{–}1) \qquad \sum_{j=1}^{\infty} |\alpha_{ij}| \leqslant M_1, \qquad i = 1, 2, \cdots$$

and

$$(6.12\text{–}2) \qquad \sum_{i=1}^{\infty} |\alpha_{ij}| \leqslant M_2, \qquad j = 1, 2, \cdots.$$

Then the matrix represents an operator A on l^2 to l^2 such that

$$(6.12\text{–}3) \qquad \|A\| \leqslant (M_1 M_2)^{\frac{1}{2}}.$$

PROOF. From (6.12–2) it is clear that $\sum_{k} |\alpha_{kj}|^2 < \infty$ for each j. Hence the series

$$\beta_{ij} = \sum_{k=1}^{\infty} \alpha_{ki} \bar{\alpha}_{kj}$$

is convergent. Now consider the linear operator B_n on $l^2(n)$ defined by

$$\eta_i = \sum_{j=1}^{n} \beta_{ij} \xi_j, \qquad i = 1, \cdots, n.$$

That is, B_n maps $x = (\xi_1, \cdots, \xi_n)$ into $y = (\eta_1, \cdots, \eta_n)$. The inner product of $B_n x$ and x is

$$(B_n x, x) = \sum_{i=1}^{n} \sum_{j=1}^{n} \beta_{ij} \xi_j \bar{\xi}_i = \sum_{i} \sum_{j} \sum_{k=1}^{\infty} \alpha_{ki} \bar{\alpha}_{kj} \xi_j \bar{\xi}_i,$$

or

$$(6.12\text{–}4) \qquad (B_n x, x) = \sum_{k=1}^{\infty} \left| \sum_{i=1}^{n} \alpha_{ki} \xi_i \right|^2.$$

Observe that B_n is symmetric, because $\beta_{ij} = \bar{\beta}_{ji}$. The eigenvalues of B_n are nonnegative, since $(B_n x, x) \geqslant 0$. Suppose λ is an eigenvalue, say $B_n x = \lambda x$, where $x = (\xi_1, \cdots, \xi_n) \neq 0$. Let $|\xi_p|$ be the largest of the values $|\xi_1|, \cdots, |\xi_n|$. Then

$$\lambda \xi_p = \sum_{j=1}^{n} \beta_{pj} \xi_j, \qquad \lambda |\xi_p| \leqslant \sum_{j=1}^{n} |\beta_{pj}| \, |\xi_p|,$$

and so

$$\lambda \leqslant \sum_{j=1}^{n} |\beta_{pj}| = \sum_{j=1}^{n} \left| \sum_{k=1}^{\infty} \alpha_{kp} \bar{\alpha}_{kj} \right|,$$

$$\lambda \leqslant \sum_{k=1}^{\infty} |\alpha_{kp}| \sum_{j=1}^{n} |\alpha_{kj}| \leqslant M_1 M_2.$$

Now, the largest eigenvalue of B_n is given by

$$\lambda = \max_{\|x\|=1} (B_n x, x);$$

we know this from Theorems 6.11–A, 6.11–B.   We have thus proved that $(B_n x, x) \leqslant M_1 M_2$ if $\|x\| = 1$, which implies that

$$(B_n x, x) \leqslant M_1 M_2 \sum_{j=1}^{n} |\dot{\xi}_j|^2$$

for arbitrary $(\dot{\xi}_1, \cdots, \dot{\xi}_n)$.   In view of (6.12–4) we infer that

$$\sum_{k=1}^{\infty} \left| \sum_{i=1}^{\infty} \alpha_{ki} \dot{\xi}_i \right|^2 \leqslant M_1 M_2 \sum_{j=1}^{\infty} |\dot{\xi}_j|^2$$

for each vector $x = \{\dot{\xi}_j\}$ in l^2.   This proves (6.12–3).

The inequality (6.12–3) is a special case of the result of problem 1, § 4.52.

6.2 Normal and Self-adjoint Operators

Throughout this section X denotes a complete inner-product space, and all of the operators which we consider in the theorems belong to $[X]$. We assume $X \neq (0)$.   If $A \in [X]$, then $A^* \in [X]$ also (see § 4.9); the definition of A^* is fully expressed by the relation

(6.2–1) $(Ax, y) = (x, A^*y)$ $x, y \in X.$

We recall from § 4.9 that A is called *normal* if $AA^* = A^*A$, and *self-adjoint* if $A = A^*$.   We see that a self-adjoint operator is symmetric.   Conversely, a symmetric operator whose domain is all of X (with X complete) must be self-adjoint.   The proof of this fact hinges upon the closed-graph theorem, or alternatively, upon the principle of uniform boundedness. See problem 1 at the end of this section.   For a related matter in a more general setting see problem 1, § 4.5.

There is a generalization of the definition of self-adjointness, so that certain unbounded operators with domains dense in X are called self-adjoint.   These operators are symmetric, but not all symmetric operators are self-adjoint in this extended sense.   See § 6.7.

If $X = L^2(a, b)$ and if K is an operator defined by an $\mathscr{L}^2$-kernel $k(s, t)$, the adjoint K^* is defined by the kernel $\overline{k(t, s)}$.   In this case, therefore, K is self-adjoint if and only if $k(s, t) =^0 \overline{k(t, s)}$.

If $X = l^2$ and if $A \in [l^2]$ is represented by the infinite matrix (α_{ij}), the adjoint is represented by $(\bar{\alpha}_{ji})$ (i.e., the conjugate of the transposed matrix). Hence $A = A^*$ means that $\alpha_{ij} = \bar{\alpha}_{ji}$ for each i and j.

Our first theorem concerns the localization of the spectrum of any member of $[X]$.

Definition. If $A \in [X]$, let $V(A)$ be the closure of the set of values of (Ax, x) for all x with $\|x\| = 1$.

Theorem 6.2–A. *If $A \in [X]$, $\sigma(A) \subset V(A)$. If the distance d from λ to $V(A)$ is positive, then*

$$(6.2\text{–}1) \qquad\qquad \|(\lambda - A)^{-1}\| \leqslant d^{-1}.$$

PROOF.   Suppose λ is not in $V(A)$, the distance from λ to $V(A)$ being $d > 0$. Then $|(Ax, x) - \lambda| \geqslant d$ if $\|x\| = 1$. We can write this as $|(Ax, x) - \lambda(x, x)| = |(Ax - \lambda x, x)| \geqslant d$ if $\|x\| = 1$, whence $|(Ax - \lambda x, x)| \geqslant d\|x\|^2$ for every x. But then $d\|x\|^2 \leqslant \|Ax - \lambda x\| \|x\|$, or $d\|x\| \leqslant \|Ax - \lambda x\|$. This shows that $(\lambda - A)^{-1}$ exists and is continuous, with

$$(6.2\text{–}2) \qquad\qquad \|(\lambda - A)^{-1}y\| \leqslant d^{-1}\|y\|$$

for every y in the range of $\lambda - A$. We know, then, that λ is either in $\rho(A)$ or $R\sigma(A)$. It remains only to show that λ cannot be in $R\sigma(A)$. Now, if $\lambda \in R\sigma(A)$, the first of the relations (4.9–6) shows that the null space of $(\lambda - A)^* = \bar{\lambda} - A^*$ contains a nonzero vector, i.e., that $\bar{\lambda}$ is an eigenvalue of A^*. Suppose $\|x\| = 1$ and $A^*x = \bar{\lambda}x$. Then $(Ax, x) = (x, A^*x) = (x, \bar{\lambda}x) = \lambda$, so that $\lambda \in V(A)$. This contradiction finishes the proof.

It can be shown that $V(A)$ is a convex set (see Stone, **1**, pages 130–133). In the case when A is normal, $V(A)$ is the smallest closed convex set containing $\sigma(A)$ (see A. Wintner, **2**, page 248, and Stone, **1**, pages 327–328). For finite-dimensional spaces these results go back to Toeplitz and Hausdorff; see Wintner, **1**, pages 33–38.

Theorem 6.2–B. *Suppose A is a bounded self-adjoint operator. Then $\sigma(A)$ lies on the closed interval $[m(A), M(A)]$ of the real axis. The end points of this interval belong to $\sigma(A)$.*

PROOF.   The first assertion is a consequence of Theorem 6.2–A, for it follows from (6.11–2) that $V(A)$ lies on the closed interval in question. (In fact, $V(A)$ *is* the closed interval $[m(A), M(A)]$, as a result of the fact that $V(A)$ is convex; but we do not need this information.) To see that $m(A)$ is in $\sigma(A)$ let $\lambda = m(A)$ and observe that $([A - \lambda]x, x) \geqslant 0$ for each x. Therefore, by (6.11–7), with $A - \lambda$, x, and $(A - \lambda)x$ in place of A, x, and y respectively, we have

$$\|(A - \lambda)x\|^4 \leqslant ([A - \lambda]x, x)([A - \lambda]^2x, [A - \lambda]x)$$
$$\leqslant ([A - \lambda]x, x) \|A - \lambda\|^3\|x\|^2.$$

If $\|A - \lambda\| = 0$ it is clear that $\lambda \in \sigma(A)$. Otherwise we see from the foregoing that

$$\inf_{\|x\|=1} \|(A - \lambda)x\| = 0,$$

whence $\lambda \in \sigma(A)$. This is because $\inf\limits_{\|x\|=1} ([A - \lambda]x, x) = 0$, by the definition of $m(A)$. The proof that $M(A)$ is in $\sigma(A)$ is similar.

If λ is not on the interval $[m(A), M(A)]$ we can estimate the norm of $(\lambda - A)^{-1}$ in terms of the distance from λ to the interval, using (6.2–1). In particular, if X is a complex space and λ is not real, the distance in question is not less than the absolute value of the imaginary part of λ. Hence

(6.2–3) $$\|(\lambda - A)^{-1}\| \leqslant 2/|\lambda - \bar\lambda|.$$

Theorem 6.2–C. *If $A \in [X]$ and $A = A^*$, the spectral radius of A is* $\|A\|$.

PROOF. This is an immediate consequence of (6.11–3) and Theorem 6.2–B.

This result, which is of crucial importance in our proof of the fundamental spectral theorem for self-adjoint operators (Theorem 6.5–A), can be proved in other ways (see problem 2). The property is true, more generally, of normal operators in complex spaces, as we shall see presently.

Theorem 6.2–D. *If $A \in [X]$, A is normal if and only if $\|Ax\| = \|A^*x\|$ for every x.*

PROOF. We have

$$\|Ax\|^2 = (Ax, Ax) = (x, A^*Ax),$$

and

$$\|A^*x\|^2 = (A^*x, A^*x) = (x, A^{**}A^*x) = (x, AA^*x).$$

Thus $\|Ax\| = \|A^*x\|$ if and only if $(x, A^*Ax) = (x, AA^*x)$. But this is true for every x if and only if $A^*A = AA^*$. For, we can set $B = A^*A - AA^*$, and then $B^* = B$. The desired result now follows by noting that $(Bx, x) = 0$ for all x is equivalent to $B = 0$. See § 6.11, problem 2.

Theorem 6.2–E. *If the space is complex and A is normal, the spectral radius of A is exactly* $\|A\|$.

PROOF. We first prove that $\|A^2\| = \|A\|^2$. We have $\|A^2x\| = \|A^*Ax\|$ for every x, by Theorem 6.2–D. Thus $\|A^2\| = \|A^*A\|$. But we know that $\|A^*A\| = \|A\|^2$ (by Theorem 4.9–B). Since powers of A are normal, it now follows by induction that $\|A^p\| = \|A\|^p$ if p is a positive integer of the form 2^n. The fact that the spectral radius of A is $\|A\|$ now follows from Theorem 5.2–E.

Next we consider the ascent of a normal operator.

Theorem 6.2–F. *If A is normal, its ascent is either 0 or 1.*

PROOF. We give the proof first on the assumption that $A = A^*$. If $x \in \mathcal{N}(A^2)$, we have $0 = (A^2x, x) = (Ax, Ax)$, whence $Ax = 0$. We conclude that $\mathcal{N}(A^2) \subset \mathcal{N}(A)$, whence $\mathcal{N}(A^2) = \mathcal{N}(A)$, and the ascent of A does not exceed 1. For the case of an arbitrary normal A, let $B = AA^* = A^*A$, so that $B^* = B$. If $x \in \mathcal{N}(A^2)$, then $B^2x = (AA^*)^2x \overset{.}{=} (A^*)^2A^2x = 0$. Hence $Bx = 0$, by the first part of the proof. Then $0 = (A^*Ax, x) = (Ax, Ax)$, or $Ax = 0$, and so $\mathcal{N}(A^2) = \mathcal{N}(A)$, as before. This finishes the proof.

We also have:

Theorem 6.2–G. *If A is normal, $\overline{\mathcal{R}(A)}$ and $\mathcal{N}(A)$ are orthogonal complements, so that $X = \overline{\mathcal{R}(A)} \oplus \mathcal{N}(A)$.*

PROOF. We know from Theorem 6.2–D that $\mathcal{N}(A) = \mathcal{N}(A^*)$. We then see from (4.9–6) that $\overline{\mathcal{R}(A)} = \mathcal{N}(A)^\perp$, and the result follows from Theorem 4.82–A.

Now suppose that X is a complex space. If A is normal, so is $\lambda - A$. Let R_λ be the resolvent of A when $\lambda \in \rho(A)$. If λ_0 is a pole of R_λ, it follows by Theorems 5.8–A, 6.2–F, and 6.2–G that the pole is of first order, that $\mathcal{R}(\lambda_0 - A)$ is closed and that $\mathcal{R}(\lambda_0 - A)$ and $\mathcal{N}(\lambda_0 - A)$ are orthogonal complements. In this case, of course, λ_0 is an eigenvalue of A. Conversely, suppose that A is normal and that $\mathcal{R}(\lambda_0 - A)$ is a closed and proper subspace of X. Then, by Theorem 5.8–D, λ_0 is a first order pole of the resolvent of A.

If X is complex and finite dimensional and if A is normal, with the distinct eigenvalues $\lambda_1, \cdots, \lambda_k$, the ascent of $\lambda_i - A$ is 1 for each i (by Theorem 6.2–F). If M_i is the null manifold of $\lambda_i - A$, it follows that $X = M_1 \oplus \cdots \oplus M_k$ and that $A = \lambda_1E_1 + \cdots + \lambda_kE_k$, where E_i is the projection of X onto M_i determined by this particular direct sum decomposition of X. The reader is referred to Theorem 5.9–E and formula (5.9–6); in this case $N = 0$. The null manifolds $M_1, \cdots, M_k$ are mutually orthogonal (see problem 8). We have here a special case of the spectral theorem for normal operators.

PROBLEMS

1. Suppose A and B are linear on X into X and that $(Ax, y) = (x, By)$ for all x and y. Then $A \in [X]$ and $B = A^*$. One method of proof starts by showing that A is closed, whence $A \in [X]$. Another method: $|(Ax, y| = |(x, By)| \leqslant$

$\|x\| \, \|By\| \leqslant \|By\|$ for each y if $\|x\| \leqslant 1$.   Then A is continuous, by the principle of uniform boundedness.

2. If $A \in [X]$ and $A = A^*$, prove that $r_\sigma(A) = \|A\|$, starting as follows: Let $\alpha = \|A\|$.   Show that

$$\|(\alpha^2 - A^2)x\|^2 = \alpha^4\|x\|^2 - 2\alpha^2\|Ax\|^2 + \|A^2x\|^2.$$

Choose x_n so that $\|x_n\| = 1$ and $\|Ax_n\| \to \|A\|$, and deduce that $\alpha^2 \in \sigma(A^2)$. Explain why either $\alpha \in \sigma(A)$ or $-\alpha \in \sigma(A)$, and finish the proof.

3. If A is normal, so is $\lambda - A$.

4. Suppose A and B are normal and that $AB^* = B^*A$.   Then $A^*B = BA^*$, and AB, BA, and $A + B$ are all normal.

5. If $A \in [X]$, we can write A in the form $A = H + iK$, where H and K are self-adjoint, in one and only one way, namely with $H = {}^1/_2(A + A^*)$, $K = (1/2i)(A - A^*)$.   Then A is normal if and only if $HK = KH$.

6. Suppose $A \in [X]$.   Then (a) $\lambda \in \rho(A)$ if and only if $\bar\lambda \in \rho(A^*)$; (b) $\lambda \in C\sigma(A)$ implies $\bar\lambda \in C\sigma(A^*)$; (c) $\lambda \in R\sigma(A)$ implies $\bar\lambda \in P\sigma(A^*)$; (d) $\lambda \in P\sigma(A)$ implies $\bar\lambda \in P\sigma(A^*) \cup R\sigma(A^*)$.

7. Suppose A is normal.   Then λ is in the resolvent set, the continuous spectrum, or the point spectrum of A if and only if $\bar\lambda$ is in the corresponding set associated with A^*.   The residual spectrum of A is empty.   Moreover, λ is an eigenvalue of A if and only if the range of $\lambda - A$ is not dense in X.   This follows from Theorem 4.9–C, applied to $\lambda - A$.   A proof without recourse to the state diagram can be based on the three following facts (for an arbitrary λ): (a) $\mathscr{R}(\lambda - A)$ and $\mathscr{R}(\bar\lambda - A^*)$ have the same closure; (b) $\|(\lambda - A)x\| = \|(\bar\lambda - A^*)x\|$; (c) $\overline{\mathscr{R}(\lambda - A)}^\perp = \mathscr{N}(\bar\lambda - A^*)$.

8. Suppose A is normal.   If λ is an eigenvalue of A and M is the corresponding eigenmanifold, M is also the eigenmanifold corresponding to $\bar\lambda$ as an eigenvalue of A^*.   Eigenvectors corresponding to distinct eigenvalues of A are orthogonal.

9. Suppose A is normal and $A = H + iK$, where H and K are self-adjoint and $HK = KH$ (see problem 5).   Then A^{-1} exists and belongs to $[X]$ if and only if $(H^2 + K^2)^{-1}$ exists and belongs to $[X]$.   In that case $A^{-1} = A^*(H^2 + K^2)^{-1}$.

10. If A is normal, $\overline{\mathscr{R}(A^2)} = \overline{\mathscr{R}(A)}$.

11. If A is normal and its descent is finite, the range of A is closed [use Theorem 5.41–G and (5.41–4)].

6.3 Orthogonal Projections

Suppose that X is an inner-product space and that P is a projection defined on X.   We know that $X = \mathscr{R}(P) \oplus \mathscr{N}(P)$ (see § 4.8).   If $\mathscr{R}(P)$ and $\mathscr{N}(P)$ are orthogonal, we say that P is an *orthogonal projection*.

Theorem 6.3–A.   *A projection is orthogonal if and only if it is symmetric.*

PROOF.   Write $x = Px + u$, $y = Py + v$, with u and v in $\mathscr{N}(P)$.   Then

$$(Px, y) = (Px, Py) + (Px, v),$$
$$(x, Py) = (Px, Py) + (u, Py).$$

If $\mathscr{R}(P)$ and $\mathscr{N}(P)$ are orthogonal, we see that $(Px, y) = (Px, Py) = (x, Py)$, so that P is symmetric.

On the other hand, if P is symmetric and $x \in \mathscr{R}(P)$, $y \in \mathscr{N}(P)$, then $Px = x$, $Py = 0$, so that $(x, y) = (Px, y) = (x, Py) = (x, 0) = 0$, so that P is orthogonal.

Theorem 6.3–B. *An orthogonal projection is continuous, and* $0 \leqslant (Px, x) \leqslant 1$ *if* $\|x\| = 1$. *If* $0 \neq P$, *then* $\|P\| = 1$; *if also* $P \neq I$, *then* $m(P) = 0$ *and* $M(P) = 1$.

PROOF. By the orthogonality of P, $x = Px + u$, with $(u, Px) = 0$. Then $\|x\|^2 = \|Px\|^2 + \|u\|^2$, whence $\|Px\|^2 \leqslant \|x\|^2$ and $\|P\| \leqslant 1$. From $P = P^2$ we see that $\|P\| \leqslant \|P\|^2$, whence $1 \leqslant \|P\|$ and so $\|P\| = 1$ if $P \neq 0$. If $\|x\| = 1$, we have $(Px, x) = (P^2x, x) = (Px, Px) \leqslant \|P\|^2 \leqslant 1$. Hence $0 \leqslant m(P)$ and $M(P) \leqslant 1$ [see (6.11–2)]. If $0 \neq P$, $Px = x$ can occur with $x \neq 0$, so $M(P) = 1$; if $P \neq I$, $Px = 0$ can occur with $x \neq 0$, so $m(P) = 0$.

For symmetric linear operators defined on X it is useful to introduce a partial-order relation. If A and B are symmetric and $(Ax, x) \leqslant (Bx, x)$ for every x, we write $A \leqslant B$. This is equivalent to $m(B - A) \geqslant 0$. If $A \leqslant B$, then $\alpha A \leqslant \alpha B$ when $\alpha > 0$, and $A + C \leqslant B + C$ for every symmetric C. If $A \leqslant B$ and $B \leqslant A$, then $A = B$, by problem 2, § 6.11.

Observe, by Theorem 6.3–B, that $0 \leqslant P \leqslant I$ if P is a symmetric projection.

Theorem 6.3–C. *If* P_1 *and* P_2 *are symmetric projections,* $P_1 \leqslant P_2$ *is equivalent to* $P_2 P_1 = P_1$. *In this case* $P_2 P_1 = P_1 P_2$, *and* $P_2 - P_1$ *is also a symmetric projection.*

PROOF. From $P_2 P_1 = P_1$ we have $(P_1 P_2 x, y) = (P_2 x, P_1 y) = (x, P_2 P_1 y) = (x, P_1 y) = (P_1 x, y)$, whence $P_1 P_2 = P_1$. It is now easy to verify that $P_2 - P_1$ is a symmetric projection, whence $0 \leqslant P_2 - P_1$, or $P_1 \leqslant P_2$. Conversely, suppose $P_1 \leqslant P_2$. Then $I - P_2 \leqslant I - P_1$. Let $Q_k = I - P_k$. Then $Q_2 = Q_2{}^2$, $Q_2 \leqslant Q_1$, $Q_1 P_1 = 0$, and so $(Q_2 P_1 x, Q_2 P_1 x) = (Q_2 P_1 x, P_1 x) \leqslant (Q_1 P_1 x, P_1 x) = 0$, whence $Q_2, P_1 = 0$. This is the same as $P_1 - P_2 P_1 = 0$, or $P_2 P_1 = P_1$.

The foregoing theorem is used in the proof of Theorem 6.5–A.

6.4 Compact Symmetric Operators

For this section we assume that X is a real or complex inner-product space, with $X \neq (0)$. Completeness is assumed only as needed. We consider an operator $A \in [X]$, assuming that it is compact and symmetric.

To avoid trivialities we assume $A \neq 0$.   For the definition of a compact operator see § 5.5.   The present section is largely independent of § 5.5.

The basic fact about the type of operator here considered is that it possesses a finite or countably infinite set of nonzero eigenvalues (and *at least one* such eigenvalue); moreover, the structure of the operator can be completely analyzed in terms of the eigenmanifolds corresponding to these eigenvalues.   The exact story is told by Theorem 6.4–B.   What we have here is a generalization of the fact that, if X is finite dimensional and A is a symmetric member of $[X]$, a basis consisting of eigenvectors can be chosen for X in such a way that the matrix representing A is a diagonal matrix with each diagonal element an eigenvalue.

The initial step is that of proving the existence of at least one nonzero eigenvalue.

Theorem 6.4–A.   *Suppose A compact, symmetric, and $A \neq 0$.   Then either $\|A\|$ or $-\|A\|$ is an eigenvalue of A, and there is a corresponding eigenvector x such that $\|x\| = 1$ and $|(Ax, x)| = \|A\|$.*

PROOF.   In view of (6.11–2) and (6.11–3) there exists a sequence $\{x_n\}$ such that $\|x_n\| = 1$ and $(Ax_n, x_n) \to \lambda$, where λ is real and $|\lambda| = \|A\|$.   Now

$$0 \leqslant \|Ax_n - \lambda x_n\|^2 = \|Ax_n\|^2 - 2\lambda(Ax_n, x_n) + \lambda^2\|x_n\|^2$$
$$\leqslant \|A\|^2 - 2\lambda(Ax_n, x_n) + \lambda^2.$$

But then we see that $Ax_n - \lambda x_n \to 0$.   Since A is compact, $\{Ax_n\}$ contains a convergent subsequence, which we denote by $\{Ay_k\}$, $\{y_k\}$ being a subsequence of $\{x_n\}$.   The sequence $\{y_k\}$ is then convergent also, because $\lambda \neq 0$.   Suppose $y_k \to x$ as $k \to \infty$.   Then $\|x\| = 1$ and $Ay_k \to Ax$, whence $Ax = \lambda x$.   Evidently $|(Ax, x)| = |\lambda| \|x\|^2 = \|A\|$, so the proof is complete.

We now apply Theorem 6.4–A repeatedly.   Denote the eigenvalue and eigenvector of Theorem 6.4–A by λ_1 and x_1 respectively.   Let $X = X_1$, and let $X_2 = \{x : (x, x_1) = 0\}$.   Then X_2 is a subspace invariant under A, for $x \in X_2$ implies $(Ax, x_1) = (x, Ax_1) = (x, \lambda_1 x_1) = \lambda_1(x, x_1) = 0$.   The restriction of A to X_2 is compact and symmetric.   If the restriction is not the zero operator, we can assert the existence of λ_2 and x_2 such that $x_2 \in X_2$, $\|x_2\| = 1$, $Ax_2 = \lambda x_2$, and $|\lambda_2|$ is the norm of the restriction of A to X_2.   Evidently $|\lambda_2| \leqslant |\lambda_1|$.   Continuing in this way we obtain the nonzero eigenvalues $\lambda_1, \cdots, \lambda_n$, with corresponding eigenvectors $x_1, \cdots, x_n$ of unit norm.   We also obtain $X_1, \cdots, X_{n+1}$, with X_{k+1} the set of elements of X_k which are orthogonal to $x_1, \cdots, x_k$.   At each step $x_k \in X_k$ and $|\lambda_k|$ is the norm of the restriction of A to X_k, so $|\lambda_1| \geqslant |\lambda_2| \geqslant \cdots \geqslant |\lambda_n|$.   The process stops with λ_n, x_n and X_{n+1} if and only if the restriction of A to X_{n+1} is 0.   In that case the range of A lies in the linear manifold generated by $x_1, \cdots, x_n$.   For, if $x \in X$, let

$$(6.4\text{--}1) \qquad y_n = x - \sum_{k=1}^{n} (x, x_k)x_k.$$

Then $(y_n, x_i) = 0$ if $i = 1, \cdots, n$, so that $y_n \in X_{n+1}$, and therefore $Ay_n = 0$, or

$$(6.4\text{--}2) \qquad Ax = \sum_{k=1}^{n} (x, x_k)Ax_k = \sum_{k=1}^{n} \lambda_k(x, x_k)x_k.$$

This situation may occur even if X is infinite dimensional.   It will certainly occur eventually if X is finite dimensional, because $x_1, \cdots, x_n$ are linearly independent.

The foregoing considerations lead us to the statement of the fundamental theorem:

Theorem 6.4–B.   *Suppose A compact, symmetric, and $A \neq 0$.   The procedure described in the foregoing discussion yields a possibly terminating sequence of nonzero eigenvalues $\lambda_1, \lambda_2, \cdots$ and a corresponding orthonormal set of eigenvectors $x_1, x_2, \cdots$.   If the sequences do not terminate, then $|\lambda_n| \to 0$.   The expansion*

$$(6.4\text{--}3) \qquad Ax = \Sigma(Ax, x_k)x_k = \Sigma\lambda_k(x, x_k)x_k$$

is valid for each $x \in X$, the summation being extended over the entire sequence, whether finite or infinite.   Each nonzero eigenvalue of A occurs in the sequence $\{\lambda_n\}$.   The eigenmanifold corresponding to a particular λ_i is finite dimensional and its dimension is exactly the number of times this particular eigenvalue is repeated in the sequence $\{\lambda_n\}$.

PROOF.   Since $|\lambda_k| \geqslant |\lambda_{k+1}|$, we either have $\lambda_n \to 0$ or $|\lambda_n| \geqslant \epsilon > 0$ for some ϵ and all n.   Suppose the latter and that the sequence is infinite. Then $\{x_n/\lambda_n\}$ is a bounded sequence, and $A(x_n/\lambda_n) = x_n$, so that $\{x_n\}$ must contain a convergent subsequence.   This is impossible, for the ortho-normality yields $\|x_n - x_m\|^2 = 2$.   Hence $\lambda_n \to 0$ when the sequence is infinite.   If the sequence of λ_k's terminates with λ_n, (6.4–3) is equivalent to (6.4–2).   In the nonterminating case we define y_n by (6.4–1) and obtain

$$\|y_n\|^2 = \|x\|^2 - \sum_{k=1}^{n} |(x, x_k)|^2 \leqslant \|x\|^2.$$

Since $y_n \in X_{n+1}$ and $|\lambda_{n+1}|$ is the norm of the restriction of A to X_{n+1}, we have

$$\|Ay_n\| \leqslant |\lambda_{n+1}| \, \|y_n\| \leqslant |\lambda_{n+1}| \, \|x\|.$$

Hence $Ay_n \to 0$.   But

$$Ay_n = Ax - \sum_{k=1}^{n} (x, x_k)Ax_k,$$

and so we obtain (6.4–3) [note that $Ax_k = \lambda_k x_k$ and $(Ax, x_k) = (x, Ax_k) = \lambda_k(x, x_k)$].

If λ is a nonzero eigenvalue of A which is not in the sequence $\{\lambda_k\}$, there is a corresponding eigenvector x of unit norm, and it must be orthogonal to x_n for every n, by Theorem 6.11–A.   Then $Ax = 0$, by (6.4–3).   This contradicts $Ax = \lambda x \neq 0$.   An eigenvalue cannot be repeated infinitely often in the sequence $\{\lambda_n\}$, because $\lambda_n \to 0$.   Suppose that λ_k occurs p times.   Then the corresponding eigenmanifold contains an orthonormal set of p eigenvectors, and is therefore at least p-dimensional. It cannot be of dimension greater than p, for this would entail the existence of an x such that $Ax = \lambda_k x$, $\|x\| = 1$, and $(x, x_n) = 0$ for every n.   But such a thing is impossible, by an argument given at the beginning of this paragraph.   The proof of Theorem 6.4–B is now complete.

The next theorem describes the inverse of $\lambda - A$.

Theorem 6.4–C.   *Let A, $\{\lambda_n\}$, $\{x_n\}$ be as in Theorem 6.4–B.   Then, if $\lambda \neq 0$ and if $\lambda \neq \lambda_k$ for each k, $\lambda - A$ has a continuous inverse defined on all of X and given by $x = (\lambda - A)^{-1}y$, where*

(6.4–4)
$$x = \frac{1}{\lambda} y + \frac{1}{\lambda} \sum \lambda_k \frac{(y, x_k)}{\lambda - \lambda_k} x_k.$$

PROOF.   We can discover the foregoing formula as follows.   Suppose x and y given, such that $\lambda x - Ax = y$.   Then $Ax = \lambda x - y$, and so from (6.4–3) we have

$$\lambda x - y = \sum \lambda_k(x, x_k)x_k.$$

We form the inner product with x_i and obtain

$$(\lambda x, x_i) - (y, x_i) = \lambda_i(x, x_i).$$

Thus

$$(x, x_i) = \frac{(y, x_i)}{\lambda - \lambda_i},$$

and so

$$\lambda x = y + \sum \lambda_k \frac{(y, x_k)}{\lambda - \lambda_k} x_k,$$

which gives (6.4–4).   This shows that the solution of $(\lambda - A)x = y$ is unique, if it exists.   On the other hand, if the series in (6.4–4) is convergent, the element x defined by (6.4–4) certainly satisfies $(\lambda - A)x = y$, for then

$$\lambda x - Ax = y + \sum_k \lambda_k \frac{(y, x_k)}{\lambda - \lambda_k} x_k - \frac{1}{\lambda} Ay - \frac{1}{\lambda} \sum_k \lambda_k \frac{(y, x_k)}{\lambda - \lambda_k} Ax_k.$$

We put $Ax_k = \lambda_k x_k$ in the last sum and use (6.4–3) with y in place of x; the result is $\lambda x - Ax = y$.

We now show that the series in (6.4–4) *does* converge, no matter how y is chosen. For this purpose let

$$\alpha = \sup_k \left| \frac{\lambda_k}{\lambda - \lambda_k} \right|, \qquad \beta = \sup_k \frac{1}{|\lambda - \lambda_k|}.$$

Also let

$$u_n = \sum_{k=1}^n \lambda_k \frac{(y, x_k)}{\lambda - \lambda_k} x_k, \qquad v_n = \sum_{k=1}^n \frac{(y, x_k)}{\lambda - \lambda_k} x_k.$$

Now, if $m < n$,

$$\|u_n - u_m\|^2 = \sum_{k=m+1}^n \left| \frac{\lambda_k}{\lambda - \lambda_k} \right|^2 |(y, x_k)|^2 \leqslant \alpha^2 \sum_{k=m+1}^n |(y, x_k)|^2.$$

Therefore $\{u_n\}$ is a Cauchy sequence, because $\sum |(y, x_k)|^2$ is convergent (see § 3.2). If X were complete, this would be enough for our purpose. If X is not complete we continue the argument as follows:

$$\|v_n\|^2 = \sum_{k=1}^n \frac{|(y, x_k)|^2}{|\lambda - \lambda_k|^2} \leqslant \beta^2 \sum_{k=1}^n |(y, x_k)|^2 \leqslant \beta^2 \|y\|^2,$$

so that $\{v_n\}$ is bounded. Now $Av_n = u_n$. Hence, the compactness of A shows that $\{u_n\}$ contains a convergent subsequence. Being a Cauchy sequence, $\{u_n\}$ must then be convergent to the same limit as the subsequence. Hence the series in (6.4–4) converges. We see from (6.4–4) that

$$\|x\| \leqslant \frac{1}{|\lambda|} \|y\| + \frac{1}{|\lambda|} \alpha \|y\|.$$

Thus we see that $(\lambda - A)^{-1}$ is continuous and defined on all of X, with

$$(6.4–5) \qquad \|(\lambda - A)^{-1}\| \leqslant \frac{1}{|\lambda|} \left[1 + \sup_k \left| \frac{\lambda_k}{\lambda - \lambda_k} \right| \right].$$

We round out the foregoing discussion by considering the null manifold and range of A. The situation is clearest if X is complete.

Theorem 6.4–D. (a) *Let A, $\{\lambda_n\}$ and $\{x_n\}$ be as in Theorem 6.4–B, and let M be the closed linear manifold generated by the eigenvectors $x_1, x_2, \cdots$.*

Then $M^{\perp} = \mathcal{N}(A)$. Hence the orthonormal set $\{x_n\}$ is complete if and only if 0 is not an eigenvalue of A. When X is complete we have $X = M \oplus \mathcal{N}(A)$.
(b) Suppose X is complete. Then the range of A is composed of those elements y in M which are such that the series

(6.4–6)
$$\sum \frac{(y, x_k)}{\lambda_k} x_k$$

is convergent.

PROOF. (a) It follows from (6.4–3) that $M^{\perp} \subset \mathcal{N}(A)$. On the other hand, $x \in \mathcal{N}(A)$ implies $(x, x_k) = \lambda_k^{-1}(x, Ax_k) = \lambda_k^{-1}(Ax, x_k) = 0$, so that $x \in M^{\perp}$. Hence $M^{\perp} = \mathcal{N}(A)$. The orthonormal set $\{x_n\}$ is complete if and only if $M^{\perp} = (0)$, which then means that 0 is not an eigenvalue of A. If X is complete, we have $X = M \oplus \mathcal{N}(A)$, by Theorem 4.82–A. For the proof of (b) suppose $Ax = y$. Then from (6.4–3) we see that y is in M. From the orthonormality it follows that $(y, x_i) = \lambda_i(x, x_i)$. We can write $x = u + v$, $u \in M$, $v \in \mathcal{N}(A)$. Then $(x, x_k) = (u, x_k)$, since $v \perp M$, and so (see Theorem 3.2–H)

$$u = \sum (u, x_k)x_k = \sum (x, x_k)x_k = \sum \frac{(y, x_k)}{\lambda_k} x_k,$$

the series necessarily being convergent if in fact it is infinite. Conversely, suppose $y \in M$ and that the series (6.4–6) is convergent, with u as its sum. Then

$$Au = \Sigma(y, x_k)x_k = y,$$

so that $y \in \mathcal{R}(A)$. This completes the proof.

We now examine formula (6.4–3) and express it in a somewhat different way, for the purpose of showing the relation between the formula and the general spectral representation theorem (of § 6.5) for self-adjoint operators. For the purpose of the following discussion it is assumed that X is complete.

The series (6.4–3) remains convergent, with the same sum, no matter how the terms are rearranged in order (see the proof of Theorem 3.2–H). It is convenient to rearrange the terms, if necessary, in such a way that all the terms for which λ_k has one particular value are brought so that they occur consecutively in the series. We shall now assume that the notation has been arranged so that this is true. For each λ_k let P_k be the operator defined by

$$P_k x = \sum_{\lambda_i = \lambda_k} (x, x_i)x_i.$$

Then $P_j = P_k$ if $\lambda_j = \lambda_k$. It is easy to verify that $P_j P_k = 0$ if $\lambda_j \neq \lambda_k$, that $P_k{}^2 = P_k$, and that P_k is symmetric. The series (6.4–3) can now be written

(6.4–7) $$Ax = \sum{}' \lambda_k P_k x,$$

where the prime mark on the summation sign indicates that the sum is extended over the distinct values of λ_k. In like manner, (6.4–4) can be put in the form

(6.4–8) $$(\lambda - A)^{-1}y = \frac{1}{\lambda}y + \frac{1}{\lambda}\sum{}' \frac{\lambda_k}{\lambda - \lambda_k} P_k y.$$

This equation shows that λ_k is a first-order pole of $(\lambda - A)^{-1}y$, the residue being $P_k y$. It is easy to verify that P_k is the projection associated with the spectral set (λ_k) (as in § 5.8).

If we use the decomposition $X = M \oplus \mathcal{N}(A)$ (see Theorem 6.4–D), and write $x = u + v$, $u \in M$, $v \in \mathcal{N}(A)$, we have $P_k x = P_k u$ and

$$u = \sum{}' P_k x.$$

If we define P_0 by $P_0 x = v$, we see that

(6.4–9) $$x = \sum{}' P_k x + P_0 x.$$

The operator P_0 is a symmetric projection, and $P_0 P_k = P_k P_0 = 0$ if $k \neq 0$.

Now let us define a one-parameter family of operators E_λ as follows (λ real, x arbitrary):

(6.4–10)
$$\begin{cases} E_\lambda x = \displaystyle\sum_{\lambda_k \leqslant \lambda}{}' P_k x & \text{if } \lambda < 0 \\[2ex] E_\lambda x = x - \displaystyle\sum_{\lambda_k > \lambda}{}' P_k x & \text{if } \lambda \geqslant 0. \end{cases}$$

It is understood that the meaning of a sum is 0 if there exists no points λ_k satisfying the indicated inequality. By separate consideration of the cases $\lambda \leqslant \mu < 0$, $\lambda < 0 \leqslant \mu$, $0 \leqslant \lambda \leqslant \mu$, it is easy to verify that $E_\mu E_\lambda = E_\lambda E_\mu = E_\lambda$ if $\lambda \leqslant \mu$. Hence in particular $E_\lambda{}^2 = E_\lambda$. Moreover, E_λ is symmetric. The operator E_λ is continuous from the right, in the sense that

(6.4–11) $$\lim_{\lambda \to \mu^+} E_\lambda x = E_\mu x,$$

where $\lambda \to \mu^+$ means that we consider values $\lambda > \mu$. This is clear if we examine closely the definition of E_λ. The only possible point of accumulation of the points λ_k is at 0. As we move to the right from a given point μ, E_λ does not change in value except as λ reaches one of the points λ_k or the point 0. Thus (6.4–11) is evident if $\mu \neq 0$, and for $\mu = 0$ it is true as a result of the convergence of the series defining E_0.

Since $\sigma(A)$ lies on $[m(A), M(A)]$, it is easy to see that $E_\lambda = 0$ if $\lambda < m(A)$ and $E_\lambda = I$ if $\lambda \geqslant M(A)$.

We shall denote $\lim_{\lambda \to \mu^-} E_\lambda x$ by $E_{\mu-0}x$. It is easy to see from (6.4–10) that

$$E_\lambda - E_{\lambda-0} = P_k \quad \text{if } \lambda = \lambda_k$$

and that

$$E_0 - E_{0-0} = P_0.$$

Formula (6.4–7) can now be written in the form

(6.4–12) $$Ax = \int_\alpha^\beta \lambda \, dE_\lambda x,$$

where $[\alpha, \beta]$ is any closed interval such that $\alpha < m(A)$ and $M(A) \leqslant \beta$. The integral here is defined by the usual procedure for a Riemann-Stieltjes integral, involving sums of the type

$$\sum \mu_i[E(\mu_i) - E(\mu_{i-1})]x,$$

with $\alpha = \mu_0 < \mu_1 < \cdots < \mu_n = \beta$. (Here we have written $E(\mu_i)$ instead of E with subscript μ_i, to simplify printing.) Formula (6.4–8) can also be expressed in integral form. First we modify (6.4–8) by use of (6.4–9) with y in place of x. In this way we find

$$(\lambda - A)^{-1}y = \sum{}' \frac{1}{\lambda - \lambda_k} P_k y + \frac{1}{\lambda - 0} P_0 y.$$

Then we have

$$(\lambda - A)^{-1}y = \int_\alpha^\beta \frac{1}{\lambda - \mu} \, dE_\mu y.$$

The results of this section have, as their most important application, the theory of integral equations with symmetric (or Hermitian) kernels, where the spaces and the kernels are such that the corresponding integral operators are compact. Compact integral operators were discussed in § 5.5. For symmetry of the operator, the condition on the kernel is $\overline{k(s, t)} = k(t, s)$. For a classical exposition of the theory of symmetric integral equations see Courant and Hilbert, 1, pages 104–118. For an historical account, with many references, see Hellinger and Toeplitz, 1, part III.

PROBLEMS

1. If $\lambda = \lambda_j$ for some j, show that the range of $\lambda - A$ consists of all vectors orthogonal to the eigenmanifold corresponding to λ_j. For such a vector y the general solution of $(\lambda - A)x = y$ is

$$x = \frac{1}{\lambda} y + \frac{1}{\lambda} \sum_{\lambda_k \neq \lambda} \lambda_k \frac{(y, x_k)}{\lambda - \lambda_k} + w,$$

where w is an arbitrary element of the eigenmanifold corresponding to λ_j

2. Suppose X is complete.   Let $\{x_n\}$ be an orthonormal set, and let $\{\lambda_n\}$ be any sequence of real numbers such that $\lambda_n \to 0$.   Let A be defined by $Ax =$ $\sum_{k=1}^{\infty} \lambda_k(x, x_k)x_k$.   Then A is self-adjoint and compact.   For the compactness, start with any bounded infinite sequence of vectors.   Then the sequence contains a weakly convergent subsequence (see Theorem 4.41–B), which we denote by $\{y_n\}$.   Suppose $\|y_n\| \leqslant C$.   Then

$$\|Ay_n - Ay_m\|^2 = \sum_{k=1}^{\infty} |\lambda_k|^2 |(y_n - y_m, x_k)|^2.$$

If $\epsilon > 0$, choose p so that $|\lambda_k| < \epsilon$ if $k > p$.   Then

$$\sum_{k=p+1}^{\infty} |\lambda_k|^2 |(y_n - y_m, x_k)|^2 \leqslant \epsilon^2 \sum_{k=p+1}^{\infty} |(y_n - y_m, x_k)|^2 \leqslant \epsilon^2 \|y_n - y_m\|^2 \leqslant 4C^2\epsilon^2.$$

The weak convergence then enables us to show that $\{Ay_n\}$ is convergent, whence A is compact.

3. Suppose X is a complex inner-product space (not necessarily complete). Suppose S and T are compact members of $[X]$ such that $ST = TS$ and $(Sx, y) = (x, Ty)$ for all x and y.   Then, there exists a finite or infinite orthonormal set $\{u_n\}$ and a corresponding sequence $\{\lambda_n\}$ such that $\lambda_n \neq 0$, $Su_n = \lambda_n u_n$, $Tu_n = \bar{\lambda}_n u_n$, $\|y\|^2 = \Sigma_n |(y, u_n)|^2$ for each $y \in \mathcal{R}(S)$, and $\lambda_n \to 0$ if the sequences are infinite.   Method: Put $S + T = 2A$, $S - T = 2iB$, and consider A, B. They are symmetric and compact, $AB = BA$, and $S = A + iB$.

The foregoing proposition can be used to prove the completeness of the orthonormal set $\{v_\lambda\}$, where $v_\lambda(t) = e^{i\lambda t}$ and λ takes on all real values, in the space of continuous almost-periodic functions, with

$$(x, y) = \lim_{h \to \infty} \frac{1}{h} \int_0^h x(t)\overline{y(t)}\, dt.$$

This is an important example of a non-separable incomplete inner-product space. For this application of the abstract proposition $Sx = y$ is taken to mean

$$y(s) = \lim_{h \to \infty} \frac{1}{h} \int_0^h z(s - t)x(t)\, dt,$$

and $Tx = y$ means

$$y(s) = \lim_{h \to \infty} \frac{1}{h} \int_0^h \overline{z(s - t)}x(t)\, dt,$$

where z is a fixed continuous almost-periodic function.   In this case the ortho- normal set $\{u_n\}$ is a set $\{v_{\nu(n)}\}$, where $\nu(n)$ runs through all the values of λ for which $(z, v_\lambda) \neq 0$.   The λ_n corresponding to u_n is $(z, v_{\nu(n)})$.   For details see Rellich, **1**, pages 351–355.

6.41 Symmetric Operators with Compact Resolvent

As in § 6.4, we assume that X is an inner-product space, not necessarily complete.   We also assume that X is not finite dimensional.

Theorem 6.41–A. *Suppose that T is a symmetric linear operator with domain and range in X, and suppose that T^{-1} exists, belongs to $[X]$, and is compact. Let $\{\lambda_n\}$, $\{x_n\}$ be the sequences of eigenvalues and eigenvectors associated with $A = T^{-1}$, as explained in connection with Theorem* 6.4–B, *and let $\mu_n = 1/\lambda_n$. The sequence $\{\mu_n\}$ is infinite, and $|\mu_n| \to \infty$. The orthonormal set $\{x_n\}$ is complete, and*

$$(6.41\text{–}1) \qquad\qquad x = \sum_{k=1}^{\infty} (x, x_k)x_k$$

for each $x \in \mathscr{D}(T)$. A point μ is in $\sigma(T)$ if and only if it is one of the μ_k's. We have $Tx_n = \mu_n x_n$. If μ is not in $\sigma(T)$,

$$(6.41\text{–}2) \qquad\qquad (\mu - T)^{-1}y = \sum_{k=1}^{\infty} \frac{(y, x_k)}{\mu - \mu_k}\, x_k$$

for each $y \in X$. This inverse operator is compact.

PROOF.   The symmetry of T implies that of A; hence we can apply the results of § 6.4.   We observe that $Ax_n = \lambda_n x_n$ is equivalent to $x_n = \lambda_n Tx_n$, or $Tx_n = \mu_n x_n$.   The orthonormal set $\{x_n\}$ is complete, by Theorem 6.4–D*a*, because 0 is not an eigenvalue of A (since A^{-1} exists).   The orthonormal set must therefore be infinite, since X is infinite dimensional. Hence $|\mu_n| \to \infty$, for we know that $\lambda_n \to 0$.   The range of A is the domain of T; since each $x \in \mathscr{D}(T)$ is of the form $x = Ay$, (6.41–1) is a consequence of (6.4–3).   Next we show that

$$(6.41\text{–}3) \qquad\qquad (\mu - T)^{-1} = \mu^{-1}A\left(A - \frac{1}{\mu}\right)^{-1}$$

if μ is different from 0 and all of the μ_n's.   First suppose that $x \in \mathscr{D}(T)$ and $(\mu - T)x = y$.   Then $\mu Ax - x = Ay$, $(A - \mu^{-1})x = \mu^{-1}Ay$, and $x = \mu^{-1}(A - \mu^{-1})^{-1}Ay$.   On the other hand, if $y \in X$ and $x = \mu^{-1}A(A - \mu^{-1})^{-1}y$, then $x \in \mathscr{D}(T)$ and it is easily verified that $(\mu - T)x = (A - \mu^{-1})(A - \mu^{-1})^{-1}y = y$.   Since A permutes with $(A - \mu^{-1})^{-1}$, this proves (6.41–3).   The compactness of $(\mu - T)^{-1}$ follows from this formula (see problem 4, § 5.5).   To obtain the formula (6.41–2) we use (6.4–4).   First we have

$$\left(\frac{1}{\mu} - A\right)^{-1} y = \mu y + \mu^2 \sum_{k=1}^{\infty} \frac{(y, x_k)}{\mu_k - \mu}\, x_k.$$

Then

$$\frac{1}{\mu}A\left(A - \frac{1}{\mu}\right)^{-1} y = -Ay + \mu \sum_{k=1}^{\infty} \frac{(y, x_k)}{\mu_k(\mu - \mu_k)}\, x_k.$$

If we express Ay by (6.4–3) and simplify, we obtain (6.41–2) from this result and (6.41–3). This finishes the proof.

We observe that the operator T of Theorem 6.41–A is not continuous, because $\|x_n\| = 1$ and $\|Tx_n\| = \|\mu_n x_n\| = |\mu_n| \to \infty$. However, T is closed, because $T = A^{-1}$ and A is closed.

Theorem 6.41–A can be applied to certain kinds of differential equation problems. For instance, consider the type of second-order differential operator discussed in Example 2, § 6.11, with boundary conditions such that the operator is symmetric. We shall now denote the operator by T instead of A. Then $Tx = u$ means that $x \in \mathscr{D}(T)$ (which includes specification of the boundary conditions) and

$$-\frac{d}{dt}[p(t)x'(t)] + q(t)x(t) = u(t).$$

Also, $(\mu - T)x = y$ means $x \in \mathscr{D}(T)$ and

$$(6.41\text{–}3)\qquad \frac{d}{dt}[p(t)x'(t)] + [\mu - q(t)]x(t) = y(t).$$

In order to be able to apply Theorem 6.41–A to this operator T, we have to show that T^{-1} exists and is a compact operator defined on all of X. This can be shown to be true in certain cases by construction of a Green's function $k(s, t)$. The service provided by the Green's function is that of being the kernel for an integral operator which turns out to be T^{-1}. If one can show that the Green's function exists and that the corresponding integral operator is compact, then Theorem 6.41–A is applicable. The Green's function is Hermitian (i.e., $\overline{k(t, s)} = k(s, t)$) as a consequence of the symmetry of the operator T.

There is not space in this book for a detailed treatment of boundary-value problems for second-order ordinary differential equations. For an extensive discussion, using the full power of spectral-theory methods in Hilbert space, see Stone, **1**, pages 448–530. Another useful discussion of differential operators from the Hilbert space viewpoint is to be found in Achieser and Glasmann, **1**, pages 304–356. For an extensive discussion of eigenfunction expansions associated with the equation (6.41–3) [for the special case in which $p(t) = 1$] see Titchmarsh, **2**. Titchmarsh does not employ abstract operator-theory methods; however, his use of contour integrals and the calculus of residues is closely related to the fact that $(\lambda - T)^{-1}$ is an analytic function of λ on the resolvent set of T.

It is not always true that T has a compact resolvent. When it does not, there may be continuous spectrum in addition to or in place of point spectrum, and then the series expansions (6.41–1), (6.41–2) are replaced by integral representations.

PROBLEM

Suppose that H is a continuous symmetric operator such that H^{-1} exists and belongs to $[X]$. Let T and $A = T^{-1}$ be as in Theorem 6.41–A. Let $B = HAH$ (a compact and symmetric operator), and let $\{\lambda_n\}$ be the nonzero eigenvalues and $\{x_n\}$ the corresponding eigenvectors associated with B, just as in § 6.4. Show that $(\mu_n H^2 - T)(H^{-1}x_n) = 0$, where $\mu_n = 1/\lambda_n$. The orthonormal set $\{x_n\}$ is complete, and $x = \sum_1^\infty (x, Hx_n)H^{-1}x_n$ for each $x \in \mathscr{D}(T)$. If μ is different from every μ_n, $\mu H^2 - T$ has a bounded inverse defined on all of X and given by

$$(\mu H^2 - T)^{-1}y = \sum_1^\infty \frac{(y, H^{-1}x_n)}{\mu - \mu_n} H^{-1}x_n.$$

To show this, show first that

$$(\mu H^2 - T)^{-1} = \frac{1}{\mu} H^{-1}\left(B - \frac{1}{\mu}\right)^{-1} HA = \frac{1}{\mu} AH\left(B - \frac{1}{\mu}\right)^{-1} H^{-1}$$

if $\mu \neq 0$.

This problem has an application to the boundary-value problem corresponding to the equation (6.41–3) with $\mu\rho(t)$ in place of μ, where $\rho(t)$ is a positive real function such that, if H maps $x(t)$ into $\sqrt{\rho(t)}x(t)$, then H and H^{-1} are bounded operators on X.

6.5 The Spectral Theorem for Bounded Self-adjoint Operators

In this section we consider an arbitrary bounded self-adjoint operator A on a complex Hilbert space X. These assumptions about A and X apply to all the theorems of this section.   Our aim is to obtain generalizations of the formula (6.4–12) and to use the results to establish a useful operational calculus.   The methods are quite different from those used in § 6.4, for now we do not assume that A is compact, and the spectrum can be much more complicated.

Before stating the first theorem we call the reader's attention to the definitions of $m(A)$ and $M(A)$ in (6.11–2).   Since A is continuous, $m(A)$ and $M(A)$ are finite.

Theorem 6.5–A.   *There exists a family of orthogonal projections E_λ defined for each real λ, with the properties*

a. $E_\lambda E_\mu = E_\mu E_\lambda = E_\lambda$ *if* $\lambda \leqslant \mu$.
b. $\lim\limits_{\mu \to \lambda^+} E_\mu x = E_\lambda x$.
c. $E_\lambda = 0$ *if* $\lambda < m(A)$, $E_\lambda = I$ *if* $M(A) \leqslant \lambda$.
d. $E_\lambda A = AE_\lambda$.

For each x and y in X, $(E_\lambda x, y)$ is of bounded variation as a function of λ, and

(6.5–1) $$(p(A)x, y) = \int_\alpha^\beta p(\lambda)\, d(E_\lambda x, y)$$

for each polynomial $p(\lambda)$ with real coefficients. The integral is an ordinary Stieltjes integral over any interval $[\alpha, \beta]$ such that $\alpha < m(A)$, $M(A) \leqslant \beta$.

PROOF.   Let $p(\lambda)$ be any polynomial with real coefficients.   Then $p(A)$ is self-adjoint, and therefore the spectral radius of $p(A)$ is $\|p(A)\|$ (Theorem 6.2–C).   Now $\sigma[p(A)]$ is the set of values of $p(\lambda)$ for $\lambda \in \sigma(A)$ (Theorem 5.2–D); consequently

(6.5–2) $$\|p(A)\| = \sup_{\lambda \in \sigma(A)} |p(\lambda)|.$$

Now let C be the real Banach space of real-valued continuous functions f defined on the closed interval $m(A) \leqslant \lambda \leqslant M(A)$, with $\|f\|$ defined as the maximum of $|f(\lambda)|$ on the interval.   If we consider the polynomial p as a member of C, we evidently have $\|p(A)\| \leqslant \|p\|$, by (6.5–2) and Theorem 6.2–B.   We can consider the class P of polynomials p with real coefficients as a subspace of C.   Since any member of C can be approximated uniformly as closely as we please by a member of P (the Weierstrass theorem), the subspace P is dense in C.

Now consider any two vectors x, y, and let

$$L(p) = (p(A)x, y).$$

It is readily evident that L is a complex-valued linear functional defined on P and that

(6.5–3) $$|L(p)| \leqslant \|p\|\, \|x\|\, \|y\|.$$

Thus L is continuous on P and may be extended in a unique way by continuity to give a continuous linear functional defined on C.   We denote the extension by L also.   We now refer to § 4.32 for the representation of continuous linear functionals on the space C.   We write $L(f) = L_1(f) + iL_2(f)$, where L_1 and L_2 have real values.   On applying Theorem 4.32–B to L_1 and L_2 and then combining results, we see that there exists a complex-valued function of bounded variation $V(\lambda; x, y)$, depending on x and y as parameters, such that

(6.5–4) $$(p(A)x, y) = \int_{m(A)}^{M(A)} p(\lambda)\, dV(\lambda; x, y)$$

for each p in P.   In order to have $V(\lambda; x, y)$ uniquely determined by the functional L, we agree to have $V(\lambda; x, y)$ normalized in the manner explained in § 4.32, i.e., $V[m(A); x, y] = 0$ and $V(\lambda; x, y) = V(\lambda + 0; x, y)$ if $m(A) < \lambda < M(A)$.

In several parts of subsequent arguments we shall need the following uniqueness principle: If v is a function of bounded variation on $[a, b]$, normalized as in § 4.32, and if $\int_a^b t^n \, dv(t) = 0$ for $n = 0, 1, 2, \cdots$, it follows that $\int_a^b x(t) \, dv(t) = 0$ for every continuous function. This depends on the Weierstrass theorem about approximating continuous functions uniformly by polynomials. Then $v \sim 0$ and hence $v(t) \equiv 0$ (see § 4.32).

The next step is to show that for each λ, $V(\lambda; x, y)$ is a continuous symmetric bilinear form in x and y, in the sense of § 6.1. If α is any scalar and $n = 0, 1, 2, \cdots$, we have

$$\int \lambda^n \, dV(\lambda; \alpha x, y) = (A^n \alpha x, y) = \alpha(A^n x, y) = \alpha \int \lambda^n \, dV(\lambda; x, y)$$

$$= \int \lambda^n \, d[\alpha V(\lambda; x, y)].$$

We omit the limits on the integral signs, for convenience. The uniqueness principle mentioned above now shows that $V(\lambda; \alpha x, y) = \alpha V(\lambda; x, y)$. Similar arguments show that $V(\lambda; x_1 + x_2, y) = V(\lambda; x_1, y) + V(\lambda; x_2, y)$ and $V(\lambda; y, x) = \overline{V(\lambda; x, y)}$. For this last relation we use the fact that A^n is symmetric. The inequality (6.5–3) enables us to assert that the total variation of $V(\lambda; x, y)$ does not exceed $2\|x\| \|y\|$, for the real and imaginary parts of V have variations equal to $\|L_1\|$ and $\|L_2\|$ respectively. Hence $|V(\lambda; x, y)| \leqslant 2\|x\| \|y\|$; this shows that the bilinear form is continuous. By Theorem 6.1–B we now see that for each λ on $[m(A), M(A)]$ there exists a bounded linear operator $F(\lambda)$ such that $V(\lambda; x, y) = (F(\lambda)x, y)$. Since the bilinear form is symmetric, so is $F(\lambda)$. The fact that $V[m(A); x, y] = 0$ implies that $F[m(A)] = 0$. If we put $p(\lambda) \equiv 1$ in (6.5–4), we see that $V[M(A); x, y] = (x, y)$. Hence $F[M(A)] = I$. Next we prove that

(6.5–5) $F(\lambda)F(\mu) = F(\mu)F(\lambda) = F(\lambda)$ if $\lambda \leqslant \mu$.

In particular, $[F(\lambda)]^2 = F(\lambda)$, so that $F(\lambda)$ is a symmetric (and orthogonal) projection. The proof involves use of the following easily proved theorem about Stieltjes integrals: *Suppose f and g are continuous and v is of bounded variation on $[a, b]$. Let*

$$u(t) = \int_a^t g(s) \, dv(s).$$

Then

$$\int_a^b f(t) \, du(t) = \int_a^b f(t) g(t) \, dv(t).$$

We also need to know that, if v is normalized, so is u.   Now let

$$U(\lambda; x, y) = \int_a^\lambda \mu^m \, dV(\mu; x, y),$$

where we have set $a = m(A)$, $b = M(A)$.   Then

$$\int_a^b \lambda^n \, dU(\lambda; x, y) = \int_a^b \lambda^{m+n} \, dV(\lambda; x, y) = (A^{m+n}x, y)$$

$$= (A^n x, A^m y) = \int_b^b \lambda^n \, dV(\lambda; x, A^m y).$$

By the uniqueness principle we have

$$U(\lambda; x, y) = V(\lambda; x, A^m y).$$

Now

$$V(\lambda; x, A^m y) = (F(\lambda)x, A^m y) = (A^m F(\lambda)x, y) = \int_a^b \mu^m \, dV[\mu; F(\lambda)x, y].$$

Consequently

$$\int_a^\lambda \mu^m \, d(F(\mu)x, y) = \int_a^b \mu^m \, d(F(\mu)F(\lambda)x, y).$$

The integral on the left can be written as

$$\int_a^b \mu^m \, dW(\mu; x, y),$$

where

$$W(\mu; x, y) = \begin{cases} (F(\mu)x, y) & \text{if } a \leqslant \mu \leqslant \lambda \\ (F(\lambda)x, y) & \text{if } \lambda \leqslant \mu \leqslant b. \end{cases}$$

Thus, using the uniqueness principle again, we find that $(F(\mu)F(\lambda)x, y) = (F(\nu)x, y)$, where $\nu = \min(\lambda, \mu)$.   This implies the result (6.5–5).

Lastly, as regards $F(\lambda)$, we assert that $F(\mu)x \to F(\lambda)x$ as $\mu \to \lambda^+$ if $a < \lambda < b$.   We write $F(\lambda + 0)x = \lim_{\mu \to \lambda^+} F(\mu)x$, by definition, so that our assertion is

(6.5–6) $F(\lambda + 0)x = F(\lambda)x,$ $a < \lambda < b.$

To prove this we observe by (6.5–5) and Theorem 6.3–C that $F(\mu) - F(\lambda)$ is a symmetric projection if $\lambda < \mu$.   Therefore

$$\|F(\mu)x - F(\lambda)x\|^2 = (F(\mu)x - F(\lambda)x, x) = (F(\mu)x, x) - (F(\lambda)x, x).$$

This expression approaches 0 as $\mu \to \lambda^+$ if $a < \lambda < b$, because $V(\lambda; x, y)$ is normalized.   Thus (6.5–6) is proved.   Likewise, if $a < \lambda_1 < \lambda_2$,

$$\|F(\lambda_2)x - F(\lambda_1)x\|^2 = (F(\lambda_2)x, x) - (F(\lambda_1)x, x) \to 0$$

as λ_1 and $\lambda_2 \to a^+$, because $(F(\lambda)x, x) = V(\lambda; x, x) \to V(a + 0; x, x)$ as $\lambda \to a^+$. Therefore $\lim_{\lambda \to a^+} F(\lambda)x$ exists and defines an operator $F(a + 0)$. We now know that

$$(6.5\text{-}7) \qquad\qquad (p(A)x, y) = \int_a^b p(\lambda)\, d(F(\lambda)x, y).$$

We define $E_\lambda = 0$ if $\lambda < a$, $E_\lambda = I$ if $b \leqslant \lambda$, and $E_\lambda = F(\lambda + 0)$ if $a \leqslant \lambda < b$. This makes $E_\lambda = F(\lambda)$ if $a < \lambda \leqslant b$. It is easy to verify that conditions a, b, and c in Theorem 6.5–A are fulfilled. Since E_λ may differ from $F(\lambda)$ at $\lambda = a$, we cannot replace $F(\lambda)$ by E_λ in (6.5-7). But, if $\alpha < a$ and $b \leqslant \beta$, simple calculations show that

$$\int_b^\beta p(\lambda)\, d(E_\lambda x, y) = 0$$

and that

$$\int_\alpha^a p(\lambda)\, d(E_\lambda x, y) + \int_a^b p(\lambda)\, d\{(E_\lambda x, y) - (F(\lambda)x, y)\} = 0.$$

Thus we obtain (6.5–1).

The fact that $AE_\mu = E_\mu A$ is easily deduced from (6.5–1). We have

$$(E_\mu A x, y) = (Ax, E_\mu y) = \int_\alpha^\beta \lambda d(E_\lambda x, E_\mu y),$$

$$(AE_\mu x, y) = \int_\alpha^\beta \lambda\, d(E_\lambda E_\mu x, y) = (E_\mu A x, y),$$

because $(E_\lambda E_\mu x, y) = (E_\mu E_\lambda x, y) = (E_\lambda x, E_\mu y)$. Thus $E_\mu A = AE_\mu$. Theorem 6.5–A is now proved.

We observe that $(E_\lambda x, x)$ is a nondecreasing function of λ. This is equivalent to $E_\lambda \leqslant E_\mu$ if $\lambda < \mu$, which is equivalent to the known relation $E_\lambda E_\mu = E_\lambda$, by Theorem 6.3–C. Just as in a previous argument about $F(\lambda)$, we can also conclude that $\lim_{\lambda \to \mu^-} E_\lambda x$ exists and defines an operator $E_{\mu-0}$, which is evidently a symmetric projection.

The next theorem shows that (6.5–1) is matched by a direct formula for $p(A)$, without intervention of x and y.

Theorem 6.5–B.   *The formula*

$$(6.5\text{-}8) \qquad\qquad p(A) = \int_\alpha^\beta p(\lambda)\, dE_\lambda$$

holds, the integral on the right being defined in the usual way as a limit of Riemann-Stieltjes sums, with convergence in the norm topology of the operator space $[X]$.

PROOF. We recall that $\alpha < m(A)$, $M(A) \leqslant \beta$. Suppose that $\alpha = \lambda_0 < \lambda_1 < \cdots < \lambda_n = \beta$ and that $\lambda_{k-1} \leqslant \mu_k \leqslant \lambda_k$, $k = 1, 2, \cdots, n$. Let

$$B = \sum_{k=1}^{n} p(\mu_k)[E(\lambda_k) - E(\lambda_{k-1})].$$

Let $\epsilon_k = \max |p(\lambda) - p(\mu)|$ as λ and μ vary over $[\lambda_{k-1}, \lambda_k]$, and let $\epsilon = \max (\epsilon_1, \cdots, \epsilon_n)$. Now

$$(p(A)x, x) = \sum_{k=1}^{n} \int_{\lambda_{k-1}}^{\lambda_k} p(\lambda)\, d(E_\lambda x, x),$$

$$(Bx, x) = \sum_{k=1}^{n} \int_{\lambda_{k-1}}^{\lambda_k} p(\mu_k)\, d(E_\lambda x, x).$$

Since $(E_\lambda x, x)$ is nondecreasing, we see that

$$(p(A)x, x) - (Bx, x) \leqslant \sum_{k=1}^{n} \int_{\lambda_{k-1}}^{\lambda_k} \epsilon\, d(E_\lambda x, x) = \epsilon(x, x),$$

and hence that $M[p(A) - B] \leqslant \epsilon$ [see (6.11–2)]. In a similar way we see that $-\epsilon \leqslant m[p(A) - B]$. But then $\|p(A) - B\| \leqslant \epsilon$, by (6.11–3). Now $\epsilon \to 0$ as we carry out the usual limiting process in connection with a Stieltjes integral, because of the continuity of p. We see in this way that (6.5–8) is true in the sense asserted.

The family of projections E_λ having the properties specified in Theorem 6.5–A is unique. This follows as a result of the uniqueness principle for normalized functions of bounded variation which was mentioned in the course of the proof of Theorem 6.5–A. It can even be shown, though we do not give the details, that, if G_λ is a family of symmetric projections satisfying conditions a, b, and c of Theorem 6.5–A and if the equation

$$(Ax, x) = \int_{\alpha}^{\beta} \lambda\, d(G_\lambda x, x)$$

holds for every x, then $G_\lambda = E_\lambda$ for every λ. Because of this uniqueness, the operator A fully determines the family E_λ (and is, of course, fully determined by the family). This family of projections is called the *resolution of the identity* corresponding to A.

Next we consider the integral

(6.5–9) $$\int_{\alpha}^{\beta} f(\lambda)\, dE_\lambda,$$

where f is an arbitrary complex-valued continuous function defined on the interval $m(A) \leqslant \lambda \leqslant M(A)$. We extend the definition of f by setting

$f(\lambda) = f[m(A)]$ if $\alpha \leqslant \lambda \leqslant m(A)$ and $f(\lambda) = f[M(A)]$ if $M(A) \leqslant \lambda \leqslant \beta$. In order to show that the Stieltjes integral (6.5–9) exists (as a limit of sums in the topology of $[X]$), we can proceed as follows: First suppose that f has real values.   Referring back to the proof of Theorem 6.5–A, we can now see that

$$L(f; x, y) = \int_\alpha^\beta f(\lambda) \, d(E_\lambda x, y),$$

and that this is a continuous symmetric bilinear form in x and y.   Hence there exists a uniquely determined self-adjoint operator, which we denote by $f(A)$, such that

$$(f(A)x, y) = \int_\alpha^\beta f(\lambda) \, d(E_\lambda x, y).$$

It is now easy, just as in the proof of Theorem 6.5–B, to show that

(6.5–10) $$f(A) = \int_\alpha^\beta f(\lambda) \, dE_\lambda.$$

If f is complex valued, the integral in (6.5–10) exists, as we see by separating f into its real and imaginary parts.   In this case also we denote the value of the integral by $f(A)$.

Theorem 6.5–C.   *The correspondence between the continuous function f and the operator $f(A)$ indicated in formula (6.5–10) has the properties:*

  a. $(f + g)(A) = f(A) + g(A)$.
  b. $(\alpha f)(A) = \alpha f(A)$.
  c. $(fg)(A) = f(A)g(A)$.
  d. $f(A)B = Bf(A)$ if $B \in [X]$ and $BE_\lambda = E_\lambda B$ for every λ.
  e. $f(A)$ is normal, with $f(A)^*$ corresponding to the function with values $\overline{f(\lambda)}$.
  f. $f(A)$ is self-adjoint if f is real-valued, and $f(A) \geqslant 0$ if $f(\lambda) \geqslant 0$ for every λ.
  g. $\|f(A)\| \leqslant \max |f(\lambda)|$ $\{\lambda$ varying over $[m(A), M(A)]\}$.
  h. $\|f(A)x\|^2 = \int_\alpha^\beta |f(\lambda)|^2 d\|E_\lambda x\|^2$.

PROOF.   Properties *a* and *b* are obvious.   To prove (*c*) we use an approximating sum for $f(A)$:

$$\sum_{k=1}^n f(\lambda_k) \, [E(\lambda_k) - E(\lambda_{k-1})],$$

and the exactly corresponding sum for $g(A)$. On multiplying the sums, the fact that

$$[E(\lambda_k) - E(\lambda_{k-1})]\,[E(\lambda_j) - E(\lambda_{j-1})] = \begin{cases} E(\lambda_k) - E(\lambda_{k-1}) & \text{if } j = k \\ 0 & \text{if } j \neq k \end{cases}$$

yields us the sums

$$\sum f(\lambda_k)g(\lambda_k)\,[E(\lambda_k) - E(\lambda_{k-1})].$$

The limit of this sum is evidently $(fg)(A)$; but it is also $f(A)g(A)$. Thus (c) is proved. Property d may also be proved by using the approximating sums. We leave (e) and (f) to the reader. For (g) let $\|f\| = \max |f(\lambda)|$, and suppose $\alpha = \lambda_0 < \lambda_1 < \cdots < \lambda_n = \beta$. Then

$$x = [E(\lambda_n) - E(\lambda_0)]x = \sum_{k=1}^{n} [E(\lambda_k) - E(\lambda_{k-1})]x,$$

and by the orthogonality relations among the projections $E(\lambda_k) - E(\lambda_{k-1})$, we find that

$$(6.5\text{-}11) \qquad \|x\|^2 = \sum_{k=1}^{n} \|[E(\lambda_k) - E(\lambda_{k-1})]x\|^2.$$

Also,

$$\|f(A)x\|^2 = \lim \left(\sum_k f(\lambda_k)[E(\lambda_k) - E(\lambda_{k-1})]x, \sum_j f(\lambda_j)[E(\lambda_j) - E(\lambda_{j-1})]x \right)$$

$$= \lim \sum_k |f(\lambda_k)|^2 \,\|[E(\lambda_k) - E(\lambda_{k-1})]x\|^2$$

$$\leqslant \|f\|^2 \,\|x\|^2,$$

by (6.5-11). This proves (g) and at the same time proves (h), for

$$\|[E(\lambda_k) - E(\lambda_{k-1})]x\|^2 = ([E(\lambda_k) - E(\lambda_{k-1})]x, x) = \|E(\lambda_k)x\|^2 - \|E(\lambda_{k-1})x\|^2.$$

We can also obtain h from c and e. This completes the proof.

Theorem 6.5–C exhibits a homomorphism of the algebra of continuous functions on $[m(A), M(A)]$ into the algebra $[X]$. As in the case of the homomorphism referred to in Theorem 5.6–A, the present homomorphism furnishes what may be called an operational calculus.

Next we shall see that the behaviour of E_λ as a function of λ is closely correlated with $\sigma(A)$.

Theorem 6.5–D. *If λ_0 is real, then $\lambda_0 \in \rho(A)$ if and only if there is some $\epsilon > 0$ such that E_λ is constant when $\lambda_0 - \epsilon \leqslant \lambda \leqslant \lambda_0 + \epsilon$.*

PROOF. We prove the "if" part first. Let $f(\lambda) = \lambda_0 - \lambda$, and define $g(\lambda) = (\lambda_0 - \lambda)^{-1}$ except when $\lambda_0 - \epsilon \leqslant \lambda \leqslant \lambda_0 + \epsilon$; the values of g on this latter interval can be assigned arbitrarily, except for the requirement that g be continuous. Then $f(\lambda)g(\lambda) = 1$ except on the interval $[\lambda_0 - \epsilon, \lambda_0 + \epsilon]$. Since E_λ is constant on this interval, it follows that

$$f(A)g(A) = \int_\alpha^\beta f(\lambda)g(\lambda) \, dE_\lambda = \int_\alpha^\beta dE_\lambda = I.$$

Therefore $g(A)$ is the inverse of $\lambda_0 - A = f(A)$. This implies that $\lambda_0 \in \rho(A)$.

For the "only if" part we can assume $m(A) < \lambda_0 < M(A)$, because of Theorem 6.2–B and the known facts about E_λ for $\lambda < m(A)$ and $M(A) < \lambda$. Suppose, no matter how small ϵ is, that there are points λ_1 and λ_2 in the interval $[\lambda_0 - \epsilon, \lambda_0 + \epsilon]$ such that $\lambda_1 < \lambda_2$ and $E(\lambda_1) \neq E(\lambda_2)$. Since $E(\lambda_2)E(\lambda_1) = E(\lambda_1)$, the range M_1 of $E(\lambda_1)$ is properly contained in the range M_2 of $E(\lambda_2)$, and we can choose an element y in $M_2 - M_1$ and orthogonal to M_1. Then $E(\lambda_2)y = y$ and $E(\lambda_1)y = 0$. If $\lambda \leqslant \lambda_1$, then $E_\lambda y = E_\lambda E(\lambda_1)y = 0$; if $\lambda_2 \leqslant \lambda$, then $E_\lambda y = E_\lambda E(\lambda_2)y = E(\lambda_2)y = y$. Thus, since $E_\lambda y$ is constant if $\lambda \leqslant \lambda_1$ and also if $\lambda_2 \leqslant \lambda$, part h of Theorem 6.5–C shows that

$$\|(\lambda_0 - A)y\|^2 = \int_{\lambda_1}^{\lambda_2} (\lambda_0 - \lambda)^2 \, d\|E_\lambda y\|^2 \leqslant \epsilon^2 \|y\|^2.$$

The last inequality follows from the fact that $(E_\lambda y, y) = \|E_\lambda y\|^2$ is nondecreasing and never exceeds $\|y\|^2$. We now see that

$$\inf_{\|x\|=1} \|(\lambda_0 - A)x\| = 0,$$

which implies that $\lambda_0 \in \sigma(A)$. This completes the proof of Theorem 6.5–D.

We see readily, somewhat as in the first part of the proof of Theorem 6.5–D, that the resolvent of A is given by

(6.5–12) $$(\lambda_0 - A)^{-1} = \int_\alpha^\beta \frac{1}{\lambda_0 - \lambda} \, dE_\lambda$$

if λ_0 is not on the interval $[m(A), M(A)]$. If λ_0 is a point of $\rho(A)$ on the aforementioned interval, (6.5–12) is still valid; the singularity of $(\lambda_0 - \lambda)^{-1}$ at λ_0 causes no trouble because of the fact that E_λ is constant on a neighborhood of λ_0.

Theorem 6.5–E.   *The point spectrum $P\sigma(A)$ consists of those points μ for which $E_\mu \neq E_{\mu-0}$. The corresponding eigenmanifold is then the range of the projection $E_\mu - E_{\mu-0}$. The continuous spectrum $C\sigma(A)$ consists of those points μ for which $E_\mu = E_{\mu-0}$ but which are such that E_λ is not constant in any neighborhood of μ.*

PROOF.   (For the definition of $E_{\mu-0}$ see the remarks following the proof of Theorem 6.5–A.)   From the fact that $E_\lambda E_\mu = E_\lambda$ if $\lambda \leqslant \mu$ we easily deduce that $E_\lambda E_{\mu-0} = E_{\mu-0}$ if $\mu \leqslant \lambda$ and $E_\lambda E_{\mu-0} = E_\lambda$ if $\lambda < \mu$.   Hence also $E_{\mu-0}$ and $E_\mu - E_{\mu-0}$ are projections (see Theorem 6.3–C).   Suppose $E_\mu \neq E_{\mu-0}$.   Let $y = (E_\mu - E_{\mu-0})x$, with $y \neq 0$.   The foregoing relations show that $E_\lambda y = 0$ if $\lambda < \mu$ and $E_\lambda y = y$ if $\mu \leqslant \lambda$.   Then, using Theorem 6.5–Ch, we have

$$\|(\mu - A)y\|^2 = \int_\alpha^\beta (\mu - \lambda)^2 \, d\|E_\lambda y\|^2 = \int_\alpha^\mu (\mu - \lambda)^2 \, d\|E_\lambda y\|^2 = 0.$$

The vanishing of the last integral depends on the fact that $(\mu - \lambda)^2 = 0$ at $\lambda = \mu$.   We see that μ is an eigenvalue of A.

Suppose, conversely, that $\mu \in P\sigma(A)$, $y \neq 0$, $Ay = \mu y$.   Then

$$0 = \int_\alpha^\beta (\mu - \lambda)^2 \, d\|E_\lambda y\|^2.$$

We may suppose $M(A) < \beta$, since the integral is independent of β as long as $M(A) \leqslant \beta$.   Now $\alpha < m(A) \leqslant \mu < \beta$, so we may choose $\epsilon > 0$ so that $\alpha < \mu - \epsilon$ and $\mu + \epsilon < \beta$.   We use the facts that $(\mu - \lambda)^2 \geqslant 0$ and $\|E_\lambda y\|^2 = (E_\lambda y, y)$ is nondecreasing to conclude that

$$\int_\alpha^{\mu-\epsilon} (\mu - \lambda)^2 \, d\|E_\lambda y\|^2 = 0.$$

This integral, however, is not smaller than

$$\epsilon^2(\|E_{\mu-\epsilon}y\|^2 - \|E_\alpha y\|^2) = \epsilon^2\|E_{\mu-\epsilon}y\|^2.$$

Therefore $E_{\mu-\epsilon}y = 0$, whence $E_{\mu-0}y = 0$.   We also conclude that

$$\int_{\mu+\epsilon}^\beta (\mu - \lambda)^2 \, d\|E_\lambda y\|^2 = 0,$$

and from this that

$$0 = \epsilon^2(\|E_\beta y\|^2 - \|E_{\mu+\epsilon}y\|^2) = \epsilon^2(\|y\|^2 - \|E_{\mu+\epsilon}y\|^2),$$

whence $E_{\mu+\epsilon}y = y$ and finally that $E_\mu y = y$.   Therefore $E_\mu \neq E_{\mu-0}$. Also, $y = (E_\mu - E_{\mu-0})y$, so that the assertion of the theorem is proved as far as $P\sigma(A)$ is concerned.   The part about $C\sigma(A)$ follows with the aid of Theorem 6.5–D.

The actual determination of the resolution of the identity for a given operator A is not an easy matter, in general.   In some comparatively simple cases it may be inferred or conjectured from (6.5–1) or 6.5–4).   This is so with problems 5 and 6 at the end of this section.   A methodical procedure is furnished by the following formula.   Suppose $\alpha < m(A)$ and $\epsilon > 0$.   Then

$$(6.5\text{–}13) \qquad \tfrac{1}{2}[(E_{\mu-0}x, y) + (E_\mu x, y)] = \lim_{\epsilon \to 0} \frac{1}{2\pi i} \int_\Gamma ((\lambda - A)^{-1}x, y) \, d\lambda,$$

where Γ is the polygonal line joining $\mu + i\epsilon$, $\alpha + i\epsilon$, $\alpha - i\epsilon$, and $\mu - i\epsilon$ in that order.   See Dunford, **3**, page 58.   The proof of (6.5–13) depends on the use of (6.5–12).

PROBLEMS

1. Let X be a complete inner-product space, with either real or complex scalars.   Let $\{A_n\}$ be a sequence of self-adjoint operators such that $A_n \leqslant A_{n+1}$ and $(A_n x, x) \leqslant \alpha\|x\|^2$ for each n, where α is a real constant.   Then there exists a self-adjoint operator A such that $A_n x \to Ax$ for each x.   A similar proposition is valid if all the inequalities are reversed.   For the proof, first show that the sequence $\{\|A_n\|\}$ is bounded.   Then apply (6.11–7) to $H = A_n - A_m$, where $n > m$, treating H like $A - \lambda$ in the proof of Theorem 6.2–B.   The result is

$$\|A_n x - A_m x\|^4 \leqslant [(A_n x, x) - (A_m x, x)]k\|x\|^2,$$

where k is a constant.   The rest of the argument is left to the reader.

2. Let X be as in problem 1.   Let $\{A_n\}$ be a sequence of self-adjoint operators such that $A_n \leqslant A_{n+1}$ for each n, and let A be an operator such that $(A_n x, x) \to (Ax, x)$ for each x.   Then $A_n x \to Ax$.   Instead of $A_n \leqslant A_{n+1}$ we may have $A_{n+1} \leqslant A_n$, and the conclusion is the same.   For the proof the first step is to prove that $\lim_{n \to \infty} (A_n x, y)$ exists for each x and y.   Next, show that $\{\|A_n\|\}$ is bounded.   Then problem 1 is applicable to obtain $A_n x \to Bx$ for some B and each x.   Finally, $A = B$.

3. Let X, A and E_λ be as in Theorem 6.5–A.   Then for each λ there exists a sequence p_n of polynomials such that $p_n(A)x \to E_\lambda x$ for each x.   This is readily evident for $\lambda < m(A)$ or $M(A) \leqslant \lambda$.   Suppose $\alpha < m(A) \leqslant \mu < M(A) \leqslant \beta$, $0 < h < \beta - \mu$, and define $f(\lambda) = 1$, $1 - h^{-1}(\lambda - \mu)$, or 0 according as $\alpha \leqslant \lambda \leqslant \mu$, $\mu \leqslant \lambda \leqslant \mu + h$, or $\mu + h \leqslant \lambda \leqslant \beta$.   Then using (6.5–10) we find

$$(f(A)x, x) = (E_\mu x, x) + \int_\mu^{\mu+h} f(\lambda)\, d(E_\lambda x, x).$$

It follows from this and problem 2 that $f(A)x \to E_\mu x$ as $h \to 0$.   If $h = 1/n$, let the corresponding f be f_n.   Choose a polynomial p_n such that $|p_n(\lambda) - f_n(\lambda)| < 1/n$ if $\alpha \leqslant \lambda \leqslant \beta$.   With the aid of Theorem 6.5–Cg it can then be shown that $p_n(A)x \to E_\mu x$.

4. Show from problem 3 that, if $B \in [X]$ and $AB = BA$, then $BE_\lambda = E_\lambda B$.

5. With $X = l^2$, let $Ax = y$ be defined by $\eta_i = \alpha_i \xi_i$, where α_i is real and $\sup_i |\alpha_i| < \infty$.   Then $\sigma(A)$ is the closure of the set of the α_i's, and the α_i's form $P\sigma(A)$.   The resolution of the identity corresponding to A is defined by $(E_\lambda x, y) = \sum_{\alpha_i \leqslant \lambda} \xi_i \overline{\eta_i}$.   This means that the matrix representing E_λ is a diagonal matrix with 1 in the ith diagonal position if $\alpha_i \leqslant \lambda$, and 0 there otherwise.

6. Consider $X = L^2(a, b)$, where (a, b) is a finite interval.   Let $Ax = y$ be defined by $y(t) = tx(t)$.   Then $\sigma(A)$ is the closed interval $[a, b]$, and $P\sigma(A)$ is empty.   The resolution of the identity corresponding to A is defined by $E_\lambda x = u$, where (for $a \leqslant \lambda \leqslant b$), $u(t) = x(t)$ if $a \leqslant t \leqslant \lambda$, $u(t) = 0$ if $\lambda < t \leqslant b$.

7. Consider $X = L^2(-\infty, \infty)$, and suppose $a(t) \in \mathscr{L}^1(-\infty, \infty)$. Suppose also that $a(t)$ is real and that $a(-t) =^0 a(t)$. Define $Ax = y$ by

$$y(s) = \int_{-\infty}^{\infty} a(s - t)x(t)\, dt.$$

Then A is self-adjoint and $\|A\| \leqslant \int_{-\infty}^{\infty} |a(t)|\, dt$. Let

$$b(s) = \int_{-\infty}^{\infty} e^{-ist} a(t)\, dt.$$

Then $\sigma(A)$ is the closure of the range of b, and $\lambda \in P\sigma(A)$ if and only if $b(s) = \lambda$ on a set of positive measure. The resolvent of A can be expressed in terms of Fourier transforms and then the resolution of the identity can be computed from (6.5–13). See Dunford, **3**, pages 60–64, and Pollard, **1**.

6.6 Unitary Operators

Let X be a complete complex inner-product space.

Definition.   An operator $U \in [X]$ is called *unitary* if $UU^* = U^*U = I$.

Note that a unitary operator is normal and that $U^* = U^{-1}$. We have $(Ux, Uy) = (x, U^*Uy) = (x, y)$ for every x and y. It follows that U maps X isometrically onto all of X.

Theorem 6.6–A.   *If U is unitary, $\sigma(U)$ lies on the circle $|\lambda| = 1$.*

PROOF.   Since U and U^* are isometric, we see that $\|U\| = \|U^*\| = 1$. Hence $\lambda \in \rho(U) \cap \rho(U^*)$ if $|\lambda| > 1$. We know $0 \in \rho(U)$, because $U^{-1} = U^*$. Suppose $0 < |\lambda| < 1$. Then $\lambda^{-1} \in \rho(U^*)$. Now $\lambda - U = \lambda U(U^* - \lambda^{-1})$, and it follows that $(\lambda - U)^{-1} = \lambda^{-1}(U^* - \lambda^{-1})^{-1}U^*$, so that $\lambda \in \rho(U)$. This completes the proof.

Example I.   With $X = L^2(a, b)$ and α real let $Ux = y$ mean $y(t) = e^{i\alpha t}x(t)$. Then U is unitary. The set $\sigma(U)$ consists of the closure of the set of values of $e^{i\alpha t}$, $a < t < b$. The interval may be infinite.

There is a spectral theorem for unitary operators, corresponding closely to Theorem 6.5–A. In order to state the theorem we consider trigonometric polynomials, i.e., functions of the form

(6.6–1) $$p(e^{it}) = \sum_{k=-n}^{n} c_k e^{ikt},$$

with the complex coefficients c_k, and arbitrary $n(n = 0, 1, 2, \cdots)$. We define

(6.6–2) $$p(U) = \sum_{k=-n}^{n} c_k U^k,$$

where $U^k = (U^{-1})^{-k}$ if $k < 0$.   Then

$$p(U)^* = \sum_{k=-n}^{n} \bar{c}_k U^{-k}.$$

It is clear that $p(U)$ is normal.

Theorem 6.6–B.   *Corresponding to the unitary operator U there is a family of symmetric projections E_t such that*

a. $E_s E_t = E_t E_s = E_s$ if $s \leqslant t$.
b. $E_{t+0} = E_t$.
c. $E_t = 0$ if $t \leqslant 0$, $E_t = I$ if $2\pi \leqslant t$.
d. $E_t U = U E_t$.

For each x and y, $(E_t x, y)$ is of bounded variation in t, and $(E_t x, x)$ is a nondecreasing function of t.   For each trigonometric polynomial $p(e^{it})$

(6.6–3) $$(p(U)x, y) = \int_0^{2\pi} p(e^{it}) \, d(E_t x, y).$$

PROOF.   Let $P[0, 2\pi]$ be that subspace of the complex Banach space $C[0, 2\pi]$ which is obtained by selecting out those functions f such that $f(0) = f(2\pi)$.   We need to know how to represent the normed conjugate of $P[0, 2\pi]$ as a subspace of the space $BV[0, 2\pi]$.   By Theorems 4.3–A and 4.32–B, each continuous linear functional on $P[0, 2\pi]$ is representable in the form

(6.6–4) $$L(f) = \int_0^{2\pi} f(t) \, dv(t),$$

where the total variation of v is $\|L\|$.   Let us define an equivalence relation in $BV[0, 2\pi]$, $w_1 \sim w_2$ meaning that

$$\int_0^{2\pi} f(t) \, dw_1(t) = \int_0^{2\pi} f(t) \, dw_2(t)$$

for each $f \in P[0, 2\pi]$.   It turns out that $w \sim 0$ means $w(0) = w(2\pi)$ and $w(t + 0) = w(t - 0) = w(0 + 0) = w(2\pi - 0)$ if $0 < t < 2\pi$.   We shall now say that w is normalized (relative to $P[0, 2\pi]$) if $w(0) = 0$ and $w(t + 0) = w(t)$ when $0 \leqslant t < 2\pi$.   Then, much as in § 4.32, it can be shown that the normed conjugate of $P[0, 2\pi]$ is congruent to the subspace of normalized members of $P[0, 2\pi]$, under the correspondence $L \leftrightarrow v$ exhibited in (6.6–4).

If $p(e^{it})$ is a trigonometric polynomial, it is an element of $P[0, 2\pi]$, and as such has a norm $\|p\| = \max |p(e^{it})|$.   We wish to show that $\|p(U)\| \leqslant \|p\|$.   For this purpose we define a function F by $F(\lambda) = p(\lambda)$

if $0 < |\lambda| < 2$, $F(\lambda) = 0$ if $3 < |\lambda|$.   We can then compute $F(U)$ by the operational calculus based on formula (5.6–10), for $F \in \mathfrak{A}_\infty(U)$, by Theorem 6.6–A.   It is necessary to integrate over two circles, say $|\lambda| = \frac{1}{2}$ and $|\lambda| = \frac{3}{2}$.   For $|\lambda| > 1$ we have

$$(\lambda - U)^{-1} = \sum_0^\infty \frac{U^n}{\lambda^{n+1}};$$

for $|\lambda| < 1$ we use $\lambda - U = (\lambda U^{-1} - 1)U$ and find

$$(\lambda - U)^{-1} = - U^{-1} \sum_0^\infty \lambda^n U^{-n}.$$

It is then easily verified that $F(U)$ coincides with $p(U)$ as defined in (6.6–2).   It then follows from Theorem 5.71–A that $\sigma[p(U)]$ is the set of values assumed by $p(\lambda)$ for $\lambda \in \sigma(U)$.   The spectral radius of $p(U)$ is $\|p(U)\|$, by Theorem 6.2–E.   It then follows that $\|p(U)\| \leqslant \|p\|$.

The proof now proceeds much as in the case of a self-adjoint operator. Since

$$|(p(U)x, y)| \leqslant \|p\|\, \|x\|\, \|y\|,$$

$(p(U)x, y)$ is a continuous linear functional on the trigonometric polynomials, viewed as a subspace of $P[0, 2\pi]$.   Since this subspace is dense in $P[0, 2\pi]$, $(p(U)x, y)$ determines uniquely a continuous linear functional $L(f; x, y)$ on $P[0, 2\pi]$.   Let $V(t; x, y)$ be the normalized function of bounded variation corresponding to this functional.   Then

$$(6.6\text{–}5) \qquad (p(U)x, y) = \int_0^{2\pi} p(e^{it})\, dV(t; x, y).$$

The normalization ensures $V(0; x, y) = 0$, and $V(2\pi; x, y) = (x, y)$ follows by putting $p(\lambda) \equiv 1$.   We leave to the reader the proof that $V(t; x, y)$ is a continuous bilinear form.   Then there exists a family of symmetric operators E_t, defined when $0 \leqslant t \leqslant 2\pi$, such that $V(t; x, y) = (E_t x, y)$.   Evidently $E_0 = 0$ and $E_{2\pi} = I$.   We define $E_t = 0$ if $t < 0$ and $E_t = I$ if $2\pi < t$.   The rest of the proof is similar to the argument in § 6.5, and we leave it to the reader.

Next comes the counterpart of Theorem 6.5–B.

Theorem 6.6–C.   *The formula*

$$(6.6\text{–}6) \qquad p(U) = \int_0^{2\pi} p(e^{it})\, dE_t$$

holds, the integral being defined as a limit in the norm topology of the space $[X]$.

PROOF. It will suffice to prove (6.6–6) for the special case $p(e^{it}) = e^{int}$; the general case will then follow by linearity. Form a subdivision $0 = t_0 < t_1 < \cdots < t_m = 2\pi$ and choose arbitrary points s_k such that $t_{k-1} \leqslant s_k \leqslant t_k$. Let

$$B = \sum_{k=1}^{m} e^{ins_k}[E(t_k) - E(t_{k-1})],$$

and write $A = U^n - B$. Now $(U^n x, U^n x) = (x, x)$. The operator $P_k = E(t_k) - E(t_{k-1})$ is a projection, and $P_j P_k = 0$ if $j \neq k$. From this we see that

$$BB^* = B^*B = \sum_{k=1}^{m} |e^{ins_k}|^2 P_k = I,$$

so that B is unitary. Therefore

(6.6–7) $\qquad \|Ax\|^2 = 2(x, x) - (Bx, U^n x) - (U^n x, Bx).$

Next,

(6.6–8) $\qquad (E_s x, U^n x) = \int_0^s e^{-int} \, d(E_t x, x).$

This is because

$$(E_s x, U^n x) = (U^{-n} E_s x, x) = \int_0^{2\pi} e^{-int} \, d(E_t E_s x, x),$$

and we can use (a) of Theorem 6.6–B. We can now write

$$(Bx, U^n x) = \sum_{k=1}^{m} e^{ins_k}(E(t_k)x - E(t_{k-1})x, U^n x)$$

$$= \sum_{k=1}^{m} e^{ins_k} \int_{t_{k-1}}^{t_k} d(E_s x, U^n x)$$

$$= \sum_{k=1}^{m} \int_{t_{k-1}}^{t_k} e^{in(s_k - t)} \, d(E_t x, x).$$

We used (6.6–8) at the last step. We now have

$$(U^n x, Bx) + (Bx, U^n x) = 2 \sum_{k=1}^{m} \int_{t_{k-1}}^{t_k} \cos n(s_k - t) \, d(E_t x, x).$$

Therefore from (6.6–7) we see that

$$\|Ax\|^2 = 2 \sum_{k=1}^{m} \int_{t_{k-1}}^{t_k} [1 - \cos n(s_k - t)] \, d(E_t x, x).$$

If $\epsilon > 0$, we can make all the intervals (t_{k-1}, t_k) so short that $1 - \cos n(s_k - t) < \epsilon/2$ if $t_{k-1} \leqslant t \leqslant t_k$. Then

$$\|Ax\|^2 < \epsilon \sum_{k=1}^{m} \int_{t_{k-1}}^{t_k} d(E_t x, x) = \epsilon \|x\|^2.$$

This completes the proof.

There are developments parallel to the later part of § 6.5. To each $f \in P[0, 2\pi]$ there corresponds a uniquely determined operator U_f such that

$$(U_f x, y) = \int_0^{2\pi} f(t) \, d(E_t x, y),$$

$$\|U_f x\|^2 = \int_0^{2\pi} |f(t)|^2 \, d(E_t x, x),$$

and

$$U_f = \int_0^{2\pi} f(t) \, dE_t.$$

We write U_f rather than $f(U)$, because in a formal sense U_f results from putting U in place of e^{it}, not in place of t [e.g., $U_f = 1 - U^{-2}$ if $f(t) = 1 - e^{-2it}$]. We have $\|U_f\| \leqslant \|f\|$, and the mapping $f \to U_f$ has the properties corresponding to (a)–(d) of Theorem 6.5–C. In particular, if $|\lambda| \neq 1$,

(6.6–9) $$(\lambda - U)^{-1} = \int_0^{2\pi} \frac{1}{\lambda - e^{it}} \, dE_t.$$

A point e^{is} is in $\sigma(U)$ if and only if s is not interior to an interval of constancy of E_t; if $0 < t \leqslant 2\pi$, $e^{it} \in P\sigma(U)$ if and only if $E_{t-0} \neq E_t$. We omit the details.

The family E_t is called the resolution of the identity for U.

Example 2. The Fourier-Plancherel transform defines a unitary operator F in $L^2(-\infty, \infty)$. The definition of F is $Fx = y$, where

$$y(t) = {}^0 \frac{1}{\sqrt{2\pi}} \frac{d}{dt} \int_{-\infty}^{\infty} \frac{e^{-ist} - 1}{-is} x(s) \, ds.$$

An alternative formula is

$$y(t) = {}^0 \, \text{l.i.m.}_{\alpha \to \infty} \frac{1}{\sqrt{2\pi}} \int_{-\alpha}^{\alpha} e^{-ist} x(s) \, ds,$$

where l.i.m. means "limit in mean," i.e., the limit in the metric of $L^2(-\infty, \infty)$. It turns out that $F^4 = I$, and with the aid of this it is rather easy to show that $\sigma(F)$ consists of the four eigenvalues $\pm 1, \pm i$. The resolution of the identity for F is $E_t = 0$ if $t < \pi/2$, $E_t = P_1$ if

$\pi/2 \leqslant t < \pi$, $E_t = P_1 + P_2$ if $\pi \leqslant t < 3\pi/2$, $E_t = P_1 + P_2 + P_3$ if $3\pi/2 \leqslant t < 2\pi$, and $E_t = I$ if $2\pi \leqslant t$, where

$$P_1 = \tfrac{1}{4}(I - iF - F^2 + iF^3), \qquad P_2 = \tfrac{1}{4}(I - F + F^2 - F^3),$$

$$P_3 = \tfrac{1}{4}(I + iF - F^2 - iF^3).$$

See Riesz and Nagy, **1**, pages 291–292.

PROBLEMS

1. If $A \in [X]$ and $\|Ax\| = \|x\|$ for every x, then A is called isometric. Show that $A^*A = I$ in this case. An isometric operator is not necessarily unitary. Consider $X = l^2$ and $A(\xi_1, \xi_2, \cdots) = (0, \xi_1, \xi_2, \cdots)$.

2. If A is isometric but not unitary, then $\mathscr{R}(A)$ is a proper closed subspace of X. If X is finite dimensional, every isometric operator is unitary.

3. Discuss $\sigma(U)$ and $(\lambda - U)^{-1}$ if $U(\xi_1, \xi_2, \cdots) = (\xi_2, \xi_1, \xi_4, \xi_3, \cdots)$, with $X = l^2$.

6.7 Unbounded Self-adjoint Operators

In this section we shall discuss briefly the adjoints of unbounded operators and certain facts about unbounded symmetric operators, especially unbounded self-adjoint operators. The purpose of the section is to orient the student who desires to study these matters further elsewhere. There is not space in this book for an extensive treatment of these topics. The subject matter leads on naturally into applications to symmetric differential operators, and there are important applications to quantum mechanics.

We assume that X is a complex Hilbert space. Some parts of the considerations can be developed for real spaces and also for incomplete spaces.

Let T be a linear operator with range in X and with domain dense in X; this assumption is retained in all the following discussion. If y, z is a pair such that $(Tx, y) = (x, z)$ when $x \in \mathscr{D}(T)$, we say $y \in \mathscr{D}(T^*)$ and $T^*y = z$. This defines T^*. We now describe things which can be proved, without giving the proofs. The adjoint operator T^* is closed. If $\mathscr{D}(T^*)$ is dense in X, $(T^*)^* \equiv T^{**}$ is defined and is an extension of T. This occurs if and only if T has a closed linear extension, and then T^{**} is the minimal such extension. Hence $T = T^{**}$ if T is closed.

If T is symmetric, T^* is an extension of T, and hence $\mathscr{D}(T^*)$ is dense in X. The operator T^{**} turns out to be symmetric, but T^* is symmetric if and only if $T^* = T^{**}$. In general T^* is a proper extension of T^{**}.

If T is symmetric, $P\sigma(T)$ and $C\sigma(T)$ are confined to the real axis, but there may be nonreal points in $R\sigma(T)$.   However, if λ is nonreal and in $\sigma(T)$, all points on the same side of the real axis as λ are in $R\sigma(T)$.   The relation $T^* = T^{**}$ holds if and only if $\sigma(T)$ is confined to the real axis.

Definition. T is called *self-adjoint* if $T = T^*$.

If T is self-adjoint, it is closed, and $\sigma(T)$ is confined to the real axis. Conversely, if T is closed and symmetric and if $\sigma(T)$ is confined to the real axis, T is self-adjoint.

If T is closed and symmetric, but not self-adjoint, the operators $T \pm i$ have bounded inverses, and hence the ranges of these operators are closed. The dimensions of $\mathscr{R}(T - i)^{\perp}$ and $\mathscr{R}(T + i)^{\perp}$ are called the *deficiency indices* of T.

Various investigations of symmetric operators may be made with the aid of operators called *Cayley transforms*.   If T is symmetric, the Cayley transform of T is the operator

$$V = (T - i)(T + i)^{-1}.$$

The domain of V is $\mathscr{R}(T + i)$, and V maps this domain isometrically onto $\mathscr{R}(T - i)$; V is unitary if and only if T is self-adjoint.

When T is self-adjoint, we can use the spectral representation of its Cayley transform to obtain a spectral representation of T and a generalization of the results of § 6.5.   Applying Theorem 6.6–B to V, let us write

$$(Vx, y) = \int_0^{2\pi} e^{i\theta}\, d(F_\theta x, y),$$

where F_θ is the resolution of the identity for V.   The relation between V and T then permits us to deduce (after some details which we omit) the relation

$$(6.7\text{--}1) \quad (Tx, y) = -\int_0^{2\pi} \operatorname{ctn} \frac{\theta}{2}\, d(F_\theta x, y), \qquad x \in \mathscr{D}(T),\, y \in X.$$

This integral is improper at 0 and 2π.   We then define $E_\lambda = F_\theta$, where $\lambda = -\operatorname{ctn}(\theta/2)$.   Then (6.7–1) becomes

$$(Tx, y) = \int_{-\infty}^{\infty} \lambda\, d(E_\lambda x, y).$$

The family of symmetric projections E_λ has properties much as in Theorem 6.5–A, but we have $E_\lambda x \to 0$ as $\lambda \to -\infty$, $E_\lambda x \to x$ as $\lambda \to +\infty$, in place of property c in this earlier theorem.   The domain of T consists exactly of those x for which

$$\int_{-\infty}^{\infty} \lambda^2\, d(E_\lambda x, x)$$

is convergent; the value of the integral is then $\|Tx\|^2$.   The behavior of E_λ near a particular λ_0 indicates the classification of this point in $\rho(T)$ or $\sigma(T)$ just as in the bounded case.   Finally, an operational calculus can be developed, generalizing Theorem 6.5–C.

Example I.   The operator A of Example 1, § 6.11 is self-adjoint.   Its spectrum is made up of the points $\lambda_n = n$, $n = 0, \pm 1, \pm 2, \cdots$; λ_n is an eigenvalue corresponding to the eigenvector u_n, where $u_n(s) = (2\pi)^{-1/2}e^{ins}$. In this case the resolution of the identity corresponding to A is given by

$$[E(\lambda_n) - E(\lambda_n - 0)]x = (x, u_n)u_n.$$

For $x \in \mathcal{D}(A)$ the formula

$$Ax = \sum_{-\infty}^{\infty} (Ax, u_n)u_n = \sum_{-\infty}^{\infty} n(x, u_n)u_n$$

is just the same as the formula

$$Ax = \int_{-\infty}^{\infty} \lambda \, dE_\lambda x,$$

and $x \in \mathcal{D}(A)$ is equivalent to the convergence of

$$\int_{-\infty}^{\infty} \lambda^2 \, d(E_\lambda x, x) = \sum_{-\infty}^{\infty} n^2|(x, u_n)|^2.$$

The reader should refer to the discussion of Example 2, § 5.7; there, however, E_n is the operator now denoted by $E(\lambda_n) - E(\lambda_n - 0)$.   See also Stone, **1**, pages 428–435.

Example 2.   Let $X = L^2(-\infty, \infty)$.   Let $\mathcal{D}(T)$ be the subspace of X determined by those functions $x(t)$ which are absolutely continuous on every finite interval, with $x(t)$ and $x'(t)$ belonging to $\mathcal{L}^2(-\infty, \infty)$.   Let $Tx = y$ mean $y(t) = ix'(t)$.   The operator T is closely related to the operator S for which $Sx = y$ means $y(t) = tx(t)$, $\mathcal{D}(S)$ being the subset of X for which $x(t)$ and $tx(t)$ are both in $\mathcal{L}^2(-\infty, \infty)$.   The operators S and T are self-adjoint, and $T = FSF^{-1}$, where F is the Fourier-Plancherel operator (see Example 2, § 6.6).   The entire real axis belongs to $\sigma(T)$, and it is all continuous spectrum.   The same is true for S.   The resolution of the identity for S is given by $E_\lambda x = y$, where $y(t) = x(t)$ if $t \leqslant \lambda$, $y(t) = 0$ if $\lambda < t$.   For T the resolution of the identity is given by

$$(E_\lambda - E_\mu)x(t) = \frac{1}{2\pi} \int_{-\infty}^{\infty} \frac{e^{i\lambda(s-t)} - e^{i\mu(s-t)}}{i(s - t)} \, ds.$$

Another item of interest is the following, which relates to the operational calculus as it applies to T: Suppose $f \in \mathscr{L}^2(-\infty, \infty)$, and let g be the Fourier-Plancherel transform of f. Then the operator $f(T)$ corresponding to f is given by $f(T)x = y$, where

$$y(t) \doteq \frac{1}{\sqrt{2\pi}} \int_{-\infty}^{\infty} g(t - s)x(s) \, ds.$$

For details see Achieser and Glasmann, **1**, pages 118–120 and 227–232 and Stone, **1**, pages 441–446.

SUGGESTED READING

Achieser and Glasmann, **1**, Chapters 4, 5, 6, 7.
Cooke, **1**, Chapters 4, 5.
Dunford, **3**, especially pp. 41–64.
Friedman, **1**.
Halmos, **3**, Chapter 2.
Hellinger, **1**.
Hellinger and Toeplitz, **1**.
Ljusternik and Sobolew, **1**, Chapter 5.
Nagy, **1**.
von Neumann, **1**.
Riesz and Nagy, **1**, Chapters 6, 7, 8, 9.
Schmeidler, **1**, Parts II, III.
Stone, **1**, Chapters 5, 6, 8, 9, 10.
Wintner, **1**, Chapters 4, 5, 6.
Zaanen, **1**, Chapter 12.

7

INTEGRATION AND LINEAR FUNCTIONALS

7.0 Explanatory Remarks

In the earlier parts of this book we have from time to time referred to the function classes $\mathscr{L}^p$ and the associated spaces L^p. The functions in question were assumed to be defined and measurable in the Lebesgue sense on some measurable set in Euclidean space of one or more dimensions. The attendant integrals were Lebesgue integrals. A knowledge of classical Lebesgue theory would be sufficient to cope with these previous references to measure and integration.

In modern analysis some form of general theory of measure and integration is essential for proper understanding of numerous developments. Classical theory of functions of a real variable is being swallowed up by topology and abstract functional analysis. It is not one of the objectives of this book to develop the generalization of the Lebesgue theory in detail from its axiomatic foundations. Instead, we assist the reader not already acquainted with such generalizations by outlining one form which the development may take, leaving him to read the details elsewhere. The close relationship between the theory of integration and linear spaces is stressed, and the use of integrals in the representation of certain linear functionals is developed in detail.

Modern forms of the theory of measure and integration play a central role in the theory of topological groups and elsewhere in topological algebra, notably in certain parts of the theory of Banach algebras. Generalizations of the spectral analysis of self-adjoint and normal operators in Hilbert space are prominent in this respect.

The sections prior to § 7.3 are expository, with few proofs given. In § 7.3 the space L^p is defined, and it is proved to be complete (Theorem 7.3–A). Theorem 7.3–D is an important theorem about approximation of elements of L^p by integrable simple functions. Theorem 7.3–E is a sort of converse of Hölder's inequality which is very important in proving the fundamental representation theorem for continuous linear functionals on L^p (Theorems 7.4–A and 7.4–B).

The next portion of the chapter (§§ 7.5–7.7) is devoted to the study of measures in locally compact Hausdorff spaces and the representation of linear functionals on certain spaces of continuous functions. If T is the Hausdorff space and $C_\infty(T)$ is the normed linear space of all real-valued continuous functions on T, with compact support, the relation between regular Borel measures on T and positive linear functionals on $C_\infty(T)$ is sketched, with reference to other sources for proofs. After a discussion of signed Borel measures and vector lattices, we come ultimately to the fundamental theorem (7.7–G) which identifies the normed conjugate of $C_\infty(T)$ with the vector lattice of finite regular signed Borel measures on T (i.e., on the σ-ring of Borel sets in T).

Finally, in § 7.8 and § 7.9 we obtain representation theorems (7.8–A and 7.9–A) for continuous linear functionals on spaces, respectively, of bounded and essentially bounded functions. These representation theorems involve integrals with respect to finitely additive set functions.

7.1 The Space $L(\mu)$

In defining the integral of a real-valued function with respect to a measure μ we follow the exposition of Halmos, **2**, Chapters II, IV, V. The reader will need to have some familiarity with general measure theory and with the general form of the theory of integration with respect to a postulated measure. Our primary aim in this section is to view the definition of the class of integrable functions as a process of completing a normed linear space. In order to assist the reader who is not thoroughly acquainted with the theory of measure and integration from the point of view taken here, we indicate the principal definitions and steps in the development of the theory. For proofs the reader can refer to the book of Halmos or to other standard texts.

Definition. A nonempty class R of sets is called a *ring* if $E \cup F$ and $E - F$ belong to R whenever E and F do. The ring is called a σ-ring if it contains the union of every countable collection of its members.

A ring contains the empty set, and it contains the union and intersection of any finite number of its members.

Definition. A *measure* is a function μ defined on a ring R, the values of μ being either real numbers or $+\infty$, subject to the conditions

a. $\mu(E) \geqslant 0$ if $E \in R$.
b. $\mu(\emptyset) = 0$.
c. If $\{E_n\}$ is a sequence of pairwise disjoint members of R whose union is in R, then $\mu\left(\bigcup_{n=1}^{\infty} E_n\right) = \sum_{n=1}^{\infty} \mu(E_n)$ (with the usual conventions about $+\infty$ in relation to the series).

A measure also has the following properties, as a consequence of the definition:

d. If $E, F \in R$ and $E \subset F$, then $\mu(E) \leqslant \mu(F)$.
e. In the situation of (d), if $\mu(E) < \infty$, then $\mu(F - E) = \mu(F) - \mu(E)$.

Definition. If T is any nonempty set, if S is a σ-ring of subsets of T such that T is the union of all members of S, and if μ is a measure defined on S, we call (T, S, μ) a *measure space*. The members of S are called *measurable sets*.

The set T itself need not belong to S, and the complement of a measurable set need not be measurable.

For the development of the theory of integration based on a measure space it is not necessary to know where the measure came from. In various particular instances of the abstract general theory it is usually the case that a measure is constructed from some set function that has some, but not all, of the properties of a measure.

Example 1. If T is Euclidean space of n-dimensions, S is the class of Lebesgue measurable sets in T, and μ is Lebesgue measure, then (T, S, μ) is a measure space. In this case $T \in S$ and $\mu(T) = +\infty$. The ring S and the measure μ are constructed by starting with the definition and construction of an *outer measure*.

Example 2. Let T be the set of positive integers, S the class of all subsets of T, with $\mu(E)$ equal to the number of elements in E (either an integer or $+\infty$).

A measure space determines a class of functions called *integrable*, and with each such function x there is associated a real number, called its integral, and denoted by

$$\int_T x \, d\mu \quad \text{or} \quad \int x \, d\mu.$$

We frequently omit the symbol T on the integral sign, if the context is such that there is no ambiguity. In order to define the class of integrable functions we begin with the concept of a *measurable function*. This concept involves only T and S, not the measure μ.

First we must define "Borel set of real numbers." We give the definition so that it can be used for any locally compact Hausdorff space.

Definition. If C is the class of all compact subsets of a locally compact Hausdorff space, the elements of the smallest σ-ring containing C are called the *Borel sets* of the space. This smallest σ-ring is the intersection of all σ-rings which contain C.

For Euclidean space an equivalent definition of the Borel sets is obtained if we use the class of all open sets instead of the class of all compact sets.

Now consider functions x defined on T, with values $x(t)$ in the set consisting of the real numbers and the symbols $+\infty$, $-\infty$. We define $N(x)$ as the set of $t \in T$ such that $x(t) \neq 0$.

Definition. The function x is called measurable (with respect to S) if $N(x) \cap x^{-1}(M) \in S$ for each Borel set M of real numbers and if also the sets $\{t : x(t) = +\infty\}$, $\{t : x(t) = -\infty\}$ belong to S.

If T belongs to S and if all values of x are real (*not* $\pm\infty$), it can be shown that x is measurable if and only if $x^{-1}(M) \in S$ for every Borel set M.

This definition of measurability is equivalent to the definition of measurability in the classical Lebesgue theory for the case in which T is Euclidean space and μ is Lebesgue measure.

For the (T, S, μ) of Example 2, all functions are measurable.

If $E \in S$, the characteristic function of E is measurable. We denote it by x_E. For convenience in printing it is best to avoid subscripts on subscripts whenever possible; hence, we shall write $x_{E(n)}$ for the characteristic function of E_n.

Definition. The function x is called *simple* if there exists a finite collection of pairwise disjoint sets $E_1, \cdots, E_n$ in S such that the value of x on E_k is a real constant α_k (not $\pm\infty$) and the value of x is 0 on $T - (E_1 \cup \cdots \cup E_n)$. Then $x = \alpha_1 x_{E(1)} + \cdots + \alpha_n x_{E(n)}$.

The simple functions form a real linear space. The absolute value of a simple function is simple, and the product of two simple functions is simple. It is frequently useful to know that, if x is measurable, there exists a sequence $\{x_n\}$ of simple functions such that $x_n(t) \to x(t)$ for each $t \in T$. If $x(t) \geqslant 0$ for each t, it may be arranged to have $x_n(t) \geqslant 0$ and $x_n(t) \leqslant x_{n+1}(t)$.

Definition. A simple function x is called *integrable* if $\mu[N(x)] < \infty$. If x is an integrable simple function with the distinct nonzero values $\alpha_1, \cdots, \alpha_n$, assumed on sets $E_1, \cdots, E_n$ respectively, the integral of x is defined to be

(7.1–1) $$\int x \, d\mu = \alpha_1 \mu(E_1) + \cdots + \alpha_n \mu(E_n).$$

If $x(t) \equiv 0$, we define the integral of x to be 0.

It is easy to see that the integrable simple functions form a linear space and that the integral is a linear functional on this space. It is also easy to see that

(7.1–2) $$\left| \int x \, d\mu \right| \leqslant \int |x| \, d\mu.$$

If x is an integrable simple function and $E \in S$, the product function xx_E is also simple and integrable; we define the integral of x over the set E as

(7.1–3) $$\int_E x \, d\mu = \int_T xx_E \, d\mu.$$

If x and y are measurable functions, we write $x(t) =^0 y(t)$ and say that $x(t) = y(t)$ almost everywhere (abbreviated as a.e.) provided that the measure of the set $\{t : x(t) \neq y(t)\}$ is 0. It is clear that $=^0$ is an equivalence relation on the class of integrable simple functions and that we can form a linear space whose elements are equivalence classes of integrable simple functions. Equivalent functions have equal integrals. A function x is equivalent to the identically zero function if and only if $\int |x| \, d\mu = 0$. It then follows easily that the space of equivalence classes becomes a normed linear space if we define the norm of an element of the space to be $\int |x| \, d\mu$, where x is any member of the equivalence-class element. All of this depends on just a few of the elementary properties of integrals of integrable simple functions.

Let us denote by W the normed linear space of equivalence classes of integrable simple functions, as described in the foregoing paragraph. For convenience we ignore the notational distinction between an integrable simple function and the equivalence class to which it belongs. It is clear from (7.1–2) that the integral is a continuous linear functional on W. If $\hat{W}$ is the completion of W, the integral, as a continuous linear functional on W, has a uniquely determined extension which is a continuous linear functional on $\hat{W}$. Our aim is to show how $\hat{W}$ can be regarded as a space whose elements are equivalence classes of functions more general than the integrable simple functions. These functions are what we call *integrable* (but not necessarily simple) functions, and the extended linear functional defines the integral for such functions.

The essential concept which is needed at this stage is that of *convergence in measure*.

Definition. A sequence $\{x_n\}$ of measurable functions whose values are a.e. finite (i.e., real, not $\pm\infty$) is called a Cauchy sequence in measure if for each $\epsilon > 0$ the measure of the set $\{t : |x_n(t) - x_m(t)| \geq \epsilon\}$ converges to 0 as m and n become infinite. If x is a function of the same type as the x_n's, the sequence is said to converge to x in measure if for each $\epsilon > 0$ the measure of $\{t : |x_n(t) - x(t)| \geq \epsilon\}$ converges to 0 as $n \to \infty$. For brevity we write

$$x_n - x_m \overset{\mu}{\to} 0 \qquad \text{and} \qquad x_n \overset{\mu}{\to} x$$

respectively in these situations.

It is not a complicated matter to show that, if $x_n \overset{\mu}{\to} x$ and $x_n \overset{\mu}{\to} y$, then $x(t) =^0 y(t)$. A sequence is Cauchy in measure if and only if it has a limit in measure.

Suppose now that $\{x_n\}$ is a sequence of integrable simple functions such that

$$\int |x_n - x_m| \, d\mu \to 0 \qquad \text{as } m \text{ and } n \to \infty.$$

If $E_{mn} = \{t : |x_n(t) - x_m(t)| \geq \epsilon\}$, it follows that

$$\int |x_n - x_m| \, d\mu \geq \int_{E_{mn}} |x_n - x_m| \, d\mu \geq c\mu(E_{mn}),$$

and so $\{x_n\}$ is Cauchy in measure. Hence there exists a measurable and a.e. finite valued x such that $x_n \overset{\mu}{\to} x$. Next, suppose that $\{y_n\}$ is a sequence of integrable simple functions such that

$$\int |y_n - y_m| \, d\mu \to 0 \qquad \text{as } m, n \to \infty,$$

and hence, for a certain y, $y_n \overset{\mu}{\to} y$. Suppose also that $\int |x_n - y_n| \, d\mu \to 0$. Then it is easy to show that $x(t) =^0 y(t)$. Conversely (and this is more difficult to prove), if $\{x_n\}$ and $\{y_n\}$ are sequences of integrable simple functions such that $\int |x_n - x_m| \, d\mu \to 0$, $\int |y_n - y_m| \, d\mu \to 0$, $x_n \overset{\mu}{\to} x$, $y_n \overset{\mu}{\to} y$, and $x(t) =^0 y(t)$, then

(7.1-4) $$\int |x_n - y_n| \, d\mu \to 0.$$

We shall prove this converse assertion.

First we note that to each $\epsilon > 0$ corresponds a $\delta > 0$ such that for all n

$$\int_F |x_n|\, d\mu < \epsilon \qquad \text{if } \mu(F) < \delta.$$

A similar thing holds for $\{y_n\}$. See Halmos, **2**, Theorem C, page 100. Now, for any given $\epsilon > 0$, let

$$E_n = \{t: |x_n(t) - y_n(t)| \geqslant \epsilon\}, \qquad F_n = \{t: |x_n(t) - x(t)| \geqslant \epsilon/3\},$$

$$G_n = \{t: |y_n(t) - y(t)| \geqslant \epsilon/3\}, \qquad H = \{t: |x(t) - y(t)| \geqslant \epsilon/3\}.$$

From the inequality

$$|x_n(t) - y_n(t)| \leqslant |x_n(t) - x(t)| + |x(t) - y(t)| + |y(t) - y_n(t)|$$

it is clear that $E_n \subset F_n \cup G_n \cup H$, and hence that $\mu(E_n) \leqslant \mu(F_n) + \mu(G_n) + \mu(H)$. But $\mu(H) = 0$ and $\mu(F_n) \to 0$, $\mu(G_n) \to 0$, whence $\mu(E_n) \to 0$. If now E is any measurable set of finite measure and $D_n = E \cap E_n$, we have

$$\int_E |x_n - y_n|\, d\mu \leqslant \int_{E-E_n} |x_n - y_n|\, d\mu + \int_{D_n} |x_n|\, d\mu + \int_{D_n} |y_n|\, d\mu.$$

The first term on the right does not exceed $\epsilon\mu(E)$. Then, since $\mu(D_n) \leqslant \mu(E_n) \to 0$, we see that

$$\int_E |x_n - y_n|\, d\mu \to 0$$

for every measurable set E of finite measure.

Next, if E is *any* measurable set, the limit

$$\nu(E) = \lim_{n\to\infty} \int_E |x_n - y_n|\, d\mu$$

exists, as is evident from the inequality

$$\left| \int_E (|x_n - y_n| - |x_m - y_m|)\, d\mu \right| \leqslant \int |x_n - x_m|\, d\mu + \int |y_n - y_m|\, d\mu.$$

It is easily proved that ν is a countably additive set function on S; we omit the details of this part of the argument. Since $\nu(E) = 0$ if $\mu(E)$ is finite, it follows that $\nu(E) = 0$ if E is any countable union of sets of finite measure. In particular, $\nu(E) = 0$ if E is the union of all the sets $N(x_n)$, $N(y_n)$, $n = 1, 2, \cdots$. With this last meaning of E we have

$$\int_T |x_n - y_n|\, d\mu = \int_E |x_n - y_n|\, d\mu \to \nu(E) = 0.$$

Thus (7.1–4) is proved.

A consequence of the conclusion just reached is that, with $\{x_n\}$ and $\{y_n\}$ as given,

$$(7.1\text{–}5) \qquad \lim_{n\to\infty} \int x_n \, d\mu = \lim_{n\to\infty} \int y_n \, d\mu.$$

The limits exist, for

$$\left| \int x_n \, d\mu - \int x_m \, d\mu \right| \leqslant \int |x_n - x_m| \, d\mu \to 0,$$

and likewise for the integrals involving $\{y_n\}$. The truth of (7.1–5) follows from

$$\left| \int x_n \, d\mu - \int y_n \, d\mu \right| \leqslant \int |x_n - y_n| \, d\mu \to 0.$$

This brings us to the general definition of an integral.

Definition. An a.e. finite-valued measurable function x is called integrable if there exists a sequence of integrable simple functions $\{x_n\}$ such that

$$(7.1\text{–}6) \qquad \int |x_n - x_m| \, d\mu \to 0 \qquad \text{and} \qquad x_n \overset{\mu}{\to} x.$$

The integral of x is then defined as

$$(7.1\text{–}7) \qquad \int x \, d\mu = \lim_{n\to\infty} \int x_n \, d\mu.$$

The foregoing considerations justify this definition by showing that the limit in (7.1–7) exists and has the same value for any choice of $\{x_n\}$ satisfying (7.1–6). Moreover, equivalent integrable functions have equal integrals. It is easily verified that the integral in (7.1–7) has the same value as that defined earlier if x happens to be simple and integrable; in that case we can take $x_n = x$ for every n.

Suppose that x is an integrable function which originates from the sequence of integrable simple functions $\{x_n\}$ as in (7.1–6). Then $|x|$ originates in the same manner from $\{|x_n|\}$; therefore $|x|$ is integrable, and

$$(7.1\text{–}8) \qquad \int |x_n| \, d\mu \to \int |x| \, d\mu.$$

We can conclude from this that $\int |x| \, d\mu = 0$ implies $x(t) = {}^0 0$. For, it certainly implies $x_n \overset{\mu}{\to} 0$; since $x_n \overset{\mu}{\to} x$ also, we have $x(t) = {}^0 0$.

We denote the class of integrable functions by $\mathscr{L}(\mu)$. The set of classes of equivalent integrable functions is denoted by $L(\mu)$; $L(\mu)$ is a normed linear space with $\int |x| \, d\mu$ as the norm of the element corresponding to the integrable function x.

We leave it for the reader to verify in detail the correlation between the process of completing the space W and our procedure in defining $\mathscr{L}(\mu)$ and $L(\mu)$. This correlation shows that $L(\mu)$ can be identified with the completion $\hat{W}$. We know that W is dense in $\hat{W}$ and that $\hat{W}$ is complete. In terms of functions, these facts can be stated as follows: *If x is integrable, there exists a sequence $\{x_n\}$ of integrable simple functions such that $\int |x_n - x| \, d\mu \to 0$. If $\{y_n\}$ is a sequence of integrable functions such that $\int |y_n - y_m| \, d\mu \to 0$, there exists an integrable function y such that $\int |y_n - y| \, d\mu \to 0$.*

By using Lebesgue's theorem on dominated convergence (Halmos, **2**, Theorem D, page 110), it is easy to prove the following: *If x is measurable and $|x(t)| \leqslant y(t)$ a.e., where y is integrable, then x is integrable. In particular, if constant functions are integrable, then every bounded measurable function is integrable.* A constant function on T is integrable if and only if T is measurable and $\mu(T)$ is finite.

PROBLEMS

1. With (T, S, μ) as in Example 2, show that convergence in measure is the same as uniform convergence.

2. With (T, S, μ) as in Example 2 and functions x on T expressed as sequences $x = \{\xi_n\}$, discuss the meaning of "simple function," "integrable simple function," and "integrable function." Show that x is integrable if and only if $\sum_1^\infty |\xi_n| < \infty$. What is $\int x \, d\mu$?

3. If (T, S, μ) is a measure space and z is a complex-valued function defined on T, let $z = x + iy$, where x and y are real valued. We say that z is measurable if x and y are both measurable, and likewise for integrability. If z is integrable, we define its integral as

$$\int z \, d\mu = \int x \, d\mu + i \int y \, d\mu.$$

Show that $|z|$ is integrable if z is. Show that, if z is integrable, there exists a sequence $\{z_n\}$ of integrable simple functions such that $\int |z_n - z| \, d\mu \to 0$. Discuss $\mathscr{L}(\mu)$ and $L(\mu)$ for complex functions, and show that $L(\mu)$ is a complex Banach space.

7.2 Signed and Complex Measures

It is useful to generalize the concept of a measure by allowing the function μ to assume values which are negative or complex. However, to avoid the ambiguity of $\infty - \infty$, it is necessary to require that μ can take on at most one of the values $+\infty$, $-\infty$.

Definition. Suppose T is a nonempty set, S is a σ-ring of subsets of T such that T is the union of all the members of S, and μ is a function on S with values in a set consisting of all real numbers and *just one* of the symbols $+\infty$, $-\infty$. Then, if $\mu(\emptyset) = 0$ and if μ is countably additive, μ is called a *signed measure*. Being countably additive means that, for each sequence $\{E_n\}$ of pairwise disjoint members of S such that $\bigcup\limits_{n=1}^{\infty} E_n \in S$, then $\mu\left(\bigcup\limits_{n=1}^{\infty} E_n\right) = \sum\limits_{n=1}^{\infty} \mu(E_n)$.

When we speak of a measure without a qualifying adjective such as "signed" or "complex" we mean a measure in the sense defined at the beginning of § 7.1.

With a signed measure μ we can associate two measures μ^+, μ^- defined as follows:

$$(7.2\text{–}1) \qquad \begin{cases} \mu^+(E) = \sup \mu(F) \\ \mu^-(E) = -\inf \mu(F), \end{cases}$$

where F varies over all members of S such that $F \subset E$. It turns out that

$$(7.2\text{–}2) \qquad \mu(E) = \mu^+(E) - \mu^-(E).$$

This formula expresses what is called the *Jordan decomposition* of μ (see Halmos, **2**, pages 120–123, especially problem 3, page 123; see also Saks, **1**, pages 10–11). If μ happens to be a measure (i.e., if $\mu(E) \geqslant 0$ always), then $\mu = \mu^+$.

We define a function $|\mu|$ by the formula

$$(7.2\text{–}3) \qquad |\mu|(E) = \mu^+(E) + \mu^-(E).$$

This function is a measure on S. It is called the *total variation* measure associated with μ. Observe that $|\mu|(E)$ is in general not the same as $|\mu(E)|$. It can be proved that $|\mu|$ is obtainable from μ in a different way. If $E \in S$, let π_E denote any finite collection of pairwise disjoint sets $E_1, \cdots, E_n$ from S such that $E_k \subset E$. Then it can be shown that

$$(7.2\text{–}4) \qquad |\mu|(E) = \sup_{\pi_E} \sum_{k=1}^{n} |\mu(E_k)|.$$

A signed measure is called *finite* if all the values of μ are real numbers (not $+\infty$ or $-\infty$). When μ is finite, $|\mu|$ is finite also, and the values of $|\mu|$ are bounded, as a result of the fact that S is a σ-ring. The class of finite signed measures becomes a real linear space in an obvious way. The function defined by

$$(7.2\text{–}5) \qquad \|\mu\| = \sup_{E \in S} |\mu|(E)$$

is a norm on this space of measures, and it is easy to prove that the space of measures is complete (see problem 1).

Let μ be a signed measure, and let x be a real-valued function which is defined on T and measurable with respect to the σ-ring S. If x is integrable with respect to $|\mu|$, it is readily seen that x is also integrable with respect to μ^+ and μ^-. We then define the integral of x with respect to μ by the formula

$$(7.2\text{--}6) \qquad \int x\, d\mu = \int x\, d\mu^+ - \int x\, d\mu^-.$$

It is easily shown that

$$(7.2\text{--}7) \qquad \left| \int x\, d\mu \right| \leqslant \int |x|\, d|\mu|.$$

Definition. If T and S are as in the definition of a signed measure, by a *complex measure* we understand a function $\mu = \mu_1 + i\mu_2$, where μ_1 and μ_2 are signed measures on S.

For a complex measure μ we can *define* the associated total variation $|\mu|$ by (7.2–4). It turns out that $|\mu|$ is a measure. If μ_1 and μ_2 are finite we say that μ is finite. Finite complex measures form a complex Banach space with the norm defined by (7.2–5).

We can define integrals with respect to a complex measure μ. Let z be a complex-valued function defined on T, and let $z = x + iy$, x and y having real values. Suppose that x and y are integrable with respect to $|\mu|$. Then they are also integrable with respect to $|\mu_1|$ and $|\mu_2|$, and we define

$$(7.2\text{--}8) \qquad \int z\, d\mu = \int x\, d\mu_1 - \int y\, d\mu_2 + i\int y\, d\mu_1 + i\int x\, d\mu_2.$$

The inequality (7.2–7) is valid with μ a complex measure and x replaced by a complex-valued function z. Likewise, the result of problem 2 extends to the case of complex functions and complex measures.

PROBLEMS

1. Let $\{\mu_n\}$ be a sequence of finite signed measures such that $\|\mu_n - \mu_m\| \to 0$. Show that $\lim_{n\to\infty} \mu_n(E) = \mu(E)$ exists uniformly with respect to E, that μ is a finite signed measure, and that $\|\mu_n - \mu\| \to 0$.

2. If μ is a signed measure and $|\mu|(E) < \infty$, show that

$$|\mu|(E) = \sup_{|x|\leqslant 1} \left| \int_E x\, d\mu \right|$$

(supremum over all real-valued $|\mu|$-integrable functions x for which $|x(t)| \leqslant 1$ on T). Use (7.2–7) and (7.2–4). The integral over E is defined by (7.1–3).

7.21 The Radon-Nikodym Theorem

Suppose that (T, S, μ) is a measure space and that x is an integrable function with values which are either real numbers or $\pm\infty$ (x is necessarily a.e. finite valued). Let

$$(7.21\text{-}1) \qquad\qquad \nu(E) = \int_E x \, d\mu, \qquad E \in S.$$

It is known from the theory of integration that ν is a finite signed measure. It is also known that $\mu(E) = 0$ implies $\nu(E) = 0$.

We now consider a converse situation.

Definition. A signed measure ν on the σ-ring S is said to be *absolutely continuous* with respect to the measure μ on S if $\nu(E) = 0$ whenever $\mu(E) = 0$. If ν is a finite signed measure, it can be shown that this requirement is equivalent to the requirement that to each $\epsilon > 0$ correspond a $\delta > 0$ such that $|\nu(E)| < \epsilon$ if $\mu(E) < \delta$.

In § 7.4 we shall need the following theorem:

Theorem 7.21–A. (Radon-Nikodym). *Suppose that T itself is measurable and that it is the union of a countable family of measurable sets of finite measure. Let ν be a finite signed measure which is absolutely continuous with respect to the measure μ. Then, there exists an integrable function x such that $\nu(E)$ is given by* (7.21–1).

For a proof of this theorem the reader is referred to Halmos, **2**, Theorem B and proof, pages 128–130. We have stated the theorem in the form appropriate for our use, which is not the most general known form of the theorem.

7.3 The Real Space $L^p(\mu)$

Let (T, S, μ) be a measure space as in § 7.1. If $p > 0$, a measurable function x is said to belong to $\mathscr{L}^p(\mu)$ if $|x|^p$ is integrable. We can argue just as in Example 7, § 1.2, to show that $\mathscr{L}^p(\mu)$ contains the sum of any two of its members. We denote by $L^p(\mu)$ the linear space whose elements are the classes of equivalent members of $\mathscr{L}^p(\mu)$. If $p \geqslant 1$, the space $L^p(\mu)$ becomes a normed linear space with

$$(7.3\text{-}1) \qquad\qquad \|x\|_p = \left(\int |x|^p \, d\mu \right)^{1/p}$$

as the norm of the element represented by the function x. The inequalities of Hölder and Minkowski are valid for these general $L^p(\mu)$ spaces (see Halmos, **2**, pages 175–176).   We drop the superscript altogether if $p = 1$.   From now on we confine attention to values of p such that $p \geqslant 1$.   For convenience we write $\mathscr{L}^p$ and L^p instead of $\mathscr{L}^p(\mu)$ and $L^p(\mu)$.

Theorem 7.3–A.   *If $p \geqslant 1$, the space L^p is a Banach space (i.e., it is complete).*

PROOF.   For $p = 1$ the result is known from § 7.1.   For the general case we have to prove the following: Suppose $\{x_n\}$ is a sequence of members of $\mathscr{L}^p$ such that

(7.3–2) $\int |x_n - x_m|^p \, d\mu \to 0$ as m and $n \to \infty$.

Then there exists a function $x \in \mathscr{L}^p$ such that

(7.3–3) $\int |x_n - x|^p \, d\mu \to 0$ as $n \to \infty$.

Now, (7.3–2) implies that $\{x_n\}$ is a Cauchy sequence in measure.   For, if $\epsilon > 0$, let $E_{mn} = \{t : |x_n(t) - x_m(t)| \geqslant \epsilon\}$.   Then

$$\int |x_n - x_m|^p \, d\mu \geqslant \epsilon^p \mu(E_{mn}),$$

and the result follows.   Hence there is a measurable function x such that $\{x_n\}$ converges in measure to x.   Also, a subsequence converges a.e. to $x(t)$.   Denote this subsequence of $\{x_n\}$ by $\{u_n\}$.   If $\epsilon > 0$, choose $K = K(\epsilon)$ so that

$$\int |u_j - u_k|^p \, d\mu < \epsilon \qquad \text{if } j \text{ and } k \geqslant K.$$

For a fixed $j \geqslant K$ let $y_k = |u_j - u_k|^p$, $y = |u_j - x|^p$.   Then $y_k(t) \to y(t)$ a.e., and

$$\int y_k \, d\mu < \epsilon$$

if $k \geqslant K$.   Hence, by Fatou's lemma (Halmos, **2**, Theorem F, page 113), y is integrable and

$$\int y \, d\mu \leqslant \epsilon.$$

This shows that $u_j - x \in \mathscr{L}^p$ if $j \geqslant K$.   Thus $x \in \mathscr{L}^p$ also.   We also conclude that

$$\int |u_j - x|^p \, d\mu \to 0 \qquad \text{as } j \to \infty.$$

From this, using (7.3–2) and Minkowski's inequality, we deduce (7.3–3), by the same argument as in showing that, if a subsequence of a Cauchy sequence has a certain limit, the whole sequence has this limit.

In working with the space L^p it is often convenient to know that the elements of L^p which correspond to integrable simple functions are everywhere dense in the space. We prove this by an argument in several stages. (For $p = 1$, of course, this result is implicit in the very definition of $\mathscr{L}$). Observe that a simple function is in $\mathscr{L}^p$ if and only if it is integrable.

In what follows the reader will need to recall that $N(x) = \{t : x(t) \neq 0\}$.

Lemma 7.3–B.   *If $x \in \mathscr{L}^p$, there exists a sequence $\{x_n\}$ with $x_n \in \mathscr{L}^p$, $\mu[N(x_n)] < \infty$, $|x_n(t)| \leqslant |x(t)|$ for every n and t, and $\|x_n - x\| \to 0$.*

PROOF.   It is known (Halmos, **2**, Theorem F, page 105) that for any integrable x the set $N(x)$ is contained in the union of a countable family of measurable sets of finite measure. Since $N(x)$ is measurable, we can then express $N(x)$ as the union of a countable family of pairwise disjoint sets of finite measure. Now $N(x) = N(|x|^p)$, and so this applies to x if $x \in \mathscr{L}^p$. Hence let $N(x) = \bigcup_{n=1}^{\infty} E_n$ be such a representation of $N(x)$. Now define x_n by

$$x_n(t) = \begin{cases} x(t) & \text{on } E_1 \cup \cdots \cup E_n \\ 0 & \text{elsewhere in } T. \end{cases}$$

Let $N(|x_n - x|) = F_n$; note that $F_n \subset N(x) - (E_1 \cup \cdots \cup E_n)$. Now $x_n \in \mathscr{L}^p$, because $|x_n| \leqslant |x|$. Then

$$\int |x_n - x|^p \, d\mu = \int_{F_n} |x|^p \, d\mu \leqslant \sum_{k=n+1}^{\infty} \int_{E_k} |x|^p \, d\mu.$$

But

$$\int |x|^p \, d\mu = \int_{N(x)} |x|^p \, d\mu = \sum_{k=1}^{\infty} \int_{E_k} |x|^p \, d\mu,$$

the series being convergent, since an integral is a countably additive set function. Therefore it is clear that $\|x_n - x\|_p \to 0$. Also, $N(x_n) \subset E_1 \cup \cdots \cup E_n$, so that $\mu[N(x_n)] < \infty$. This finishes the proof.

Lemma 7.3–C.   *If $x \in \mathscr{L}^p$ and $\epsilon > 0$, there exists $y \in \mathscr{L}^p$ such that $\mu[N(y)] < \infty$, $|y(t)| \leqslant |x(t)|$ for each t, the values $|y(t)|$ are bounded, and $\|y - x\|_p < \epsilon$.*

PROOF.   We first choose $z \in \mathscr{L}^p$ as one of the x_n's in Lemma 7.3–B so that $\|x - z\|_p < \epsilon/2$. We shall now show how to choose $y \in \mathscr{L}^p$ so that $\mu[N(y)] < \infty$, $|y| \leqslant |z|$, the values of $|y|$ are bounded, and $\|z - y\|_p < \epsilon/2$.

The y will then have the properties we seek, by Minkowski's inequality. Let us define z_n by

$$z_n(t) = \begin{cases} z(t) & \text{if } |z(t)| \leqslant n \\ n \operatorname{sgn} z(t) & \text{if } |z(t)| > n. \end{cases}$$

(See § 4.32 for the meaning of sgn.) Then z_n is measurable, $|z_n| \leqslant n$, and $|z_n| \leqslant |z|$. Note that $N(z_n) = N(z)$, whence $\mu[N(z_n)] < \infty$. Let E_n be the set where $|z(t)| > n$. Then

$$\int |z|^p \, d\mu \geqslant \int_{E_n} |z|^p \, d\mu \geqslant n^p \mu(E_n),$$

and so $\mu(E_n) \to 0$. Then

$$\int |z_n - z|^p \, d\mu = \int_{E_n} |z_n - z|^p \, d\mu \leqslant \int_{E_n} (|z_n| + |z|)^p \, d\mu \leqslant 2^p \int_{E_n} |z|^p \, d\mu.$$

From this it follows that $\|z_n - z\|_p \to 0$. We can choose y as z_n for some n large enough to make $\|z_n - z\|_p < \epsilon/2$, and the proof is complete.

Theorem 7.3–D. *If $x \in \mathscr{L}^p$ and $\epsilon > 0$, there exists an integrable simple function y such that $|y(t)| \leqslant |x(t)| + \epsilon$ for all values of t, and $\|x - y\|_p < \epsilon$.*

PROOF. By Lemma 7.3–C we can choose $z \in \mathscr{L}^p$ so that $\mu[N(z)] < \infty$, z is bounded, $|z| \leqslant |x|$, and $\|x - z\|_p < \epsilon/2$. Then we show how to choose an integrable simple function y such that $|y| \leqslant |z| + \epsilon$ and $\|z - y\|_p < \epsilon/2$. This will be enough to prove the theorem.

Let $A = \sup |z(t)|$. Divide the interval $(-A, A)$ of the real axis into n equal parts by points $\alpha_0, \alpha_1, \cdots, \alpha_n$, where $-A = \alpha_0 < \alpha_1 < \cdots < \alpha_n = A$. We define z_n as follows: $z_n(t) = 0$ if $z(t) = 0$, and, if $z(t) \neq 0$, then

$$z_n(t) = \begin{cases} \alpha_0 & \text{if } \alpha_0 \leqslant z(t) \leqslant \alpha_1 \\ \alpha_k & \text{if } \alpha_k < z(t) \leqslant \alpha_{k+1}, \quad k = 1, \cdots, n-1. \end{cases}$$

Then $N(z_n) \subset N(z)$, and z is an integrable simple function. It is evident that $|z_n(t) - z(t)| \leqslant 2A/n$ for every t. Then

$$\int |z_n - z|^p \, d\mu = \int_{N(z)} |z_n - z|^p \, d\mu \leqslant (2A/n)^p \, \mu[N(z)]$$

and $|z_n(t)| \leqslant |z(t)| + (2A/n)$. By taking n large enough the choice $y = z_n$ will be satisfactory.

We shall presently need the following theorem, which is a sort of converse of Hölder's inequality; we adopt the notation of § 4.32 as regards p and p'.

Theorem 7.3–E. *Suppose* $1 < p < \infty$. *Suppose that* T *itself is measurable and that it is expressible as a countable union of measurable sets of finite measure. Let* y *be a real-valued function which is defined a.e. on* T. *Suppose the product function* xy *is integrable whenever* x *is a bounded and measurable function on* T *such that* $\mu[N(x)] < \infty$. *Moreover, suppose that there exists a real constant* M *such that*

$$(7.3\text{--}4) \qquad\qquad \left| \int xy\, d\mu \right| \leqslant M\|x\|_p$$

for every such x. *Then* $y \in \mathscr{L}^{p'}$ *and*

$$(7.3\text{--}5) \qquad\qquad \int |y|^{p'}\, d\mu \leqslant M^{p'}.$$

PROOF. Let E be any measurable set of finite measure, and let x_E be its characteristic function. Then $x_E y$ is integrable, by hypothesis. Let $T = \bigcup\limits_{n=1}^{\infty} E_n$, where the sets E_n are measurable, pairwise disjoint, and of finite measure. Let $F(n) = E_1 \cup \cdots \cup E_n$, and define $y_n(t) = y(t)$ on $F(n)$, $y(t) = 0$ on $T - F(n)$. Then $y_n = y x_{F(n)}$ is measurable, and $y_n(t) \to y(t)$ a.e., so that y is measurable. In what follows we shall prove that $x_E |y|^{p'}$ is integrable for every E of finite measure, and that

$$(7.3\text{--}6) \qquad\qquad \int x_E |y|^{p'}\, d\mu \leqslant M^{p'}.$$

It will then follow by Fatou's lemma that $y \in \mathscr{L}^{p'}$ and that (7.3–5) holds, for, in the notation used above,

$$x_{F(n)}(t) |y(t)|^{p'} \to |y(t)|^{p'} \quad \text{a.e.}$$

If E is any set of finite measure, define $x_n(t) = 0$ if $t \in T - E$, and, if $t \in E$, define

$$x_n(t) = \begin{cases} |y(t)|^{p'-1} \operatorname{sgn} y(t) & \text{if } |y(t)|^{p'-1} \leqslant n^{1/p} \\ n^{1/p} \operatorname{sgn} y(t) & \text{if } |y(t)|^{p'-1} > n^{1/p}. \end{cases}$$

Then x_n is measurable, $|x_n| \leqslant n^{1/p}$, $N(x_n) = N(y) \cap E$, and so $\mu[N(x_n)] < \infty$. Also, if $t \in E$,

$$|x_n(t)|^p = \begin{cases} |y(t)|^{p'} & \text{if } |y(t)|^{p'} \leqslant n \\ n & \text{if } |y(t)|^{p'} > n, \end{cases}$$

and

$$x_n(t)y(t) = \begin{cases} |y(t)|^{p'} & \text{if } |y(t)|^{p'} \leqslant n \\ n^{1/p}|y(t)| & \text{if } |y(t)|^{p'} > n. \end{cases}$$

Note that $x_n(t)y(t) \geqslant |x_n(t)|^p$ for every t.   Therefore, by (7.3–4),

$$\int |x_n|^p \, d\mu \leqslant \int x_n y \, d\mu \leqslant M \Big(\int |x_n|^p \, d\mu \Big)^{1/p},$$

and it follows that

$$\Big(\int |x_n|^p \, d\mu \Big)^{1/p'} \leqslant M.$$

But $|x_n(t)|^p \to x_E(t)| y(t)|^{p'}$ a.e.   Therefore, by Fatou's lemma, $x_E| y|^{p'}$ is integrable and (7.3–6) holds.   In view of remarks made earlier, this completes the proof.

PROBLEMS

1. In Example 6, § 3.11, we defined the function class $\mathscr{L}^\infty$ and the space L^∞ for the case of Lebesgue measure on the real axis.   These definitions can be extended at once, and we obtain $\mathscr{L}^\infty(\mu)$ and $L^\infty(\mu)$ in relation to an arbitrary measure space (T, S, μ).   Show that $L^\infty(\mu)$ is complete.

2. Let the assumptions on y be as in Theorem 7.3–E, except that now we assume $p = 1$.   Then we can conclude that $y \in \mathscr{L}^\infty(\mu)$ and that $\sup^0 |y(t)| \leqslant M$.

3. State and prove a theorem corresponding to Theorem 7.3–E for the case $p = \infty$, $p' = 1$, the conclusion being that y is integrable and $\int |y| \, d\mu \leqslant M$.

4. Let $\mathfrak{M}$ be the class of sets of finite measure in S.   Let $\varDelta$ be a binary operation on sets, defined as follows:

$$E \varDelta F = (E - F) \cup (F - E) = (E \cup F) - (E \cap F).$$

If E and F are in $\mathfrak{M}$, let $d(E, F) = \mu(E \varDelta F)$.   Then, with $d(E, F)$ as distance between E and F, $\mathfrak{M}$ is a complete metric space (see Halmos, **2**, pages 168–169).

5. With $\mathfrak{M}$ the metric space defined as in problem 4, show that $L^p(\mu)$ is separable if $\mathfrak{M}$ is separable and if $1 \leqslant p < \infty$.   Start with a countable dense subset $\mathfrak{M}_0 \subset \mathfrak{M}$.   Then finite linear combinations with rational coefficients, of characteristic functions of members of $\mathfrak{M}_0$, lead to a countable dense subset of $L^p(\mu)$.   Use Theorem 7.3–D.

6. Let (T, S, μ) be a measure space such that $T \in S$ and T is a countable union of measurable sets of finite measure.   Furthermore, assume that there is a countable collection of members of S such that S coincides with the smallest σ-ring containing this collection.   Then the metric space $\mathfrak{M}$ defined in problem 4 is separable.   See Halmos, **2**, Theorem B, page 168.   Show that the conditions here imposed on (T, S, μ) are fulfilled if T is a Lebesgue measurable subset (not necessarily proper) of Euclidean space of n-dimensions and μ is Lebesgue measure on the measurable subsets of T.   Hence $L^p(\mu)$ is separable in this case.

7.4 Continuous Linear Functions on L^p

We work with L^p as defined in § 7.3.   To begin with it is convenient to assume $T \in S$ and $\mu(T) < \infty$.   This restriction is partially relaxed later.

Theorem 7.4–A. *Suppose* $1 \leqslant p < \infty$. *Suppose* $T \in S$ *and* $\mu(T) < \infty$. *Then there is a one-to-one, linear, norm-preserving correspondence between the normed conjugate space of* L^p *and the space* $L^{p'}$, *such that, if* $x' \in (L^p)'$ *and* $y \in \mathscr{L}^{p'}$ *is a function which represents the element of* $L^{p'}$ *corresponding to* x', *we have*

$$(7.4–1) \qquad\qquad x'(x) = \int xy\, d\mu$$

for each $x \in \mathscr{L}^p$. *The norm-preserving feature of the correspondence means that*

$$(7.4–2) \qquad\qquad \|x'\| = \left(\int |y|^{p'}\, d\mu \right)^{1/p'}$$

if $1 < p$, *and*

$$(7.4–3) \qquad\qquad \|x'\| = \sup^0 |y(t)|$$

in case $p = 1$ (*in which case* $p' = \infty$).

PROOF. Let us start with $y \in \mathscr{L}^{p'}$ and define x' by (7.4–1). Then x' is linear and continuous, with $\|x'\| \leqslant \|y\|_{p'}$. This inequality comes from Hölder's inequality if $1 < p < \infty$ and from the fact that $|x(t)y(t)| \leqslant |x(t)| \, \|y\|_\infty$ a.e. in case $\mathrm{p} = 1$, $p' = \infty$. The mapping $y \to x'$ plainly defines a continuous linear mapping of $L^{p'}$ into $(L^p)'$. Also, it is clear by Theorem 7.3–E if $1 < p$, and by problem 2 of § 7.3 if $p = 1$, that if $x'(x) = 0$ for every x, then $\|y\|_{p'} = 0$ and so $y(t) = 0$ a.e. Thus the mapping is one-to-one. It remains to prove that every $x' \in (L^p)'$ is the image of some $y \in L^{p'}$ and that $\|x'\| = \|y\|_{p'}$.

So, suppose $x' \in (L^p)'$. For any $E \in S$ let $\nu(E) = x'(x_E)$, where x_E is the characteristic function of E. Note that $\|x_E\|_p = [\mu(E)]^{1/p}$. Hence

$$(7.4–4) \qquad\qquad |\nu(E)| \leqslant \|x'\|[\mu(E)]^{1/p}.$$

The set function ν is finitely additive; for, if E and F are disjoint measurable sets and $G = E \cup F$, we have $x_G = x_E + x_F$, whence $\nu(E \cup F) = \nu(E) + \nu(F)$. The countable additivity of ν can now be proved with the aid of (7.4–4). Suppose $\{E_n\}$ is a sequence of pairwise disjoint measurable sets. Then, if

$$E = \bigcup_{k=1}^{\infty} E_k \qquad \text{and} \qquad F_n = E - \bigcup_{k=1}^{n} E_k,$$

we have

$$\nu(E) = \sum_{k=1}^{n} \nu(E_k) + \nu(F_n).$$

But $\mu(F_n) \to 0$, since μ is countable additive, and hence $\nu(F_n) \to 0$, by

(7.4–4). Therefore ν is countably additive. It also follows from (7.4–4) that ν is absolutely continuous. We can now use the Radon-Nikodym theorem to assert the existence of an integrable function y such that

$$\nu(E) = \int_E y \, d\mu$$

for every $E \in S$. Since $\nu(E) = x'(x_E)$, it now follows at once that

(7.4–5) $$x'(x) = \int xy \, d\mu$$

for any simple function x. We wish to show next that this same formula holds for any bounded measurable function. If x is bounded and measurable (and hence in $\mathscr{L}^p$), Theorem 7.3–D shows that there exists a uniformly bounded sequence $\{x_n\}$ of simple functions such that $\|x_n - x\|_p \to 0$. The proof of Theorem 7.3–D shows that for the case now before us, in which x is bounded and $\mu(T) < \infty$, we can also require of the sequence $\{x_n\}$ that $x_n(t) \to x(t)$ for each t. It then follows by Lebesgue's theorem of dominated convergence that

$$\int x_n y \, d\mu \to \int xy \, d\mu.$$

Thus, since $x'(x_n) = \int x_n y \, d\mu$, we see that (7.4–5) holds for every bounded measurable x. Since $|x'(x)| \leqslant \|x'\| \, \|x\|_p$, the converse of Hölder's inequality tells us that $y \in \mathscr{L}^{p'}$ and $\|y\|_{p'} \leqslant \|x'\|$ (Theorem 7.3–E if $1 < p$, problem 2, § 7.3 if $p = 1$). Finally, since the elements of L^p corresponding to bounded x are dense in L^p (Lemma 7.3–C), and since $\int xy \, d\mu$ defines a continuous linear functional on *all* of L^p (now that we know $y \in \mathscr{L}^{p'}$), it is clear that (7.3–5) is valid for *all* $x \in \mathscr{L}^p$. We showed that $\|x'\| \leqslant \|y\|_{p'}$ at the outset. Hence $\|x'\| = \|y\|_{p'}$, and the proof is complete.

We now relax the condition $\mu(T) < \infty$.

Theorem 7.4–B.   *Theorem 7.4–A remains true as stated if the hypothesis that $\mu(T) < \infty$ is replaced by the hypothesis that T is the union of a countable family of measurable sets of finite measure.*

PROOF. Let G be any fixed measurable set of finite measure. Those elements $E \in S$ such that $E \subset G$ form a σ-ring containing G, and, if we restrict μ to these sets E, it is a measure on this new σ-ring. Let us write $\mathscr{L}^p(T)$ and $\mathscr{L}^p(G)$ to distinguish the function classes which arise when we talk about functions defined over T and G respectively, using the measure μ and its restriction as just described. If g is a function defined on G, let us denote by g^e the function defined on T by

$$g^e(t) = \begin{cases} g(t) & \text{on } G \\ 0 & \text{on } T - G. \end{cases}$$

Evidently $g \in \mathscr{L}^p(G)$ implies $g^e \in \mathscr{L}^p(T)$ and

$$\int_G |g|^p \, d\mu = \int_T |g^e|^p \, d\mu.$$

Let us now suppose that x' is a continuous linear functional on $L^p(T)$. If $g \in \mathscr{L}^p(G)$, let us define $f(g) = x'(g^e)$. It is easily verified that f is a continuous linear functional on $L^p(G)$ and that, as such, its norm satisfies the inequality $\|f\| \leqslant \|x'\|$. By Theorem 7.4–A there exists a function $y \in \mathscr{L}^{p'}(G)$ such that

$$f(g) = \int_G gy \, d\mu$$

for each $g \in \mathscr{L}^p(G)$. Moreover, $\|y\|_{p'} = \|f\| \leqslant \|x'\|$.

Now let us write $T = \bigcup_{n=1}^{\infty} E_n$, where E_n has finite measure. Let $G_n = E_1 \cup \cdots \cup E_n$. We apply the foregoing reasoning to each G_n and obtain corresponding functionals f_n and functions y_n. For any fixed n suppose $g \in \mathscr{L}^p(G_n)$, and let h be the restriction of g^e to G_{n+1}. Then $g^e = h^e$, and we have

$$\int_{G_n} g y_n \, d\mu = x'(g^e) = x'(h^e) = \int_{G_{n+1}} h y_{n+1} \, d\mu = \int_{G_n} g y_{n+1} \, d\mu.$$

The last equality comes from the fact that $h(t) = 0$ on $G_{n+1} - G_n$. We thus have

$$\int_{G_n} g(y_n - y_{n+1}) \, d\mu = 0$$

for each $g \in \mathscr{L}^p(G_n)$. From this we conclude by Theorem 7.4–A that $y_n(t) - y_{n+1}(t) = 0$ a.e. on G_n. Hence, if for each t we define $y(t) = y_m(t)$, where m is the smallest integer for which $t \in G_m$, we see that $y(t) = y_n(t)$ a.e. on G_n for each n. We can conclude that $y \in \mathscr{L}^{p'}(T)$ and $\|y\|_{p'} \leqslant \|x'\|$. If $p' = \infty \, (p = 1)$, this is immediate, for we know that

$$\sup_{t \in G_n} |y_n(t)| = \|f_n\| \leqslant \|x'\|$$

for each n, whence $\sup_{t \in G}^0 |y(t)| \leqslant \|x'\|$. If $p' < \infty \, (1 < p)$, we have

$$\int_{G_n} |y|^{p'} \, d\mu = \int_{G_n} |y_n|^{p'} \, d\mu = \|f_n\|^{p'} \leqslant \|x'\|^{p'},$$

and the desired result follows by application of Fatou's lemma to the sequence $v_n|y|^{p'}$ (where v_n is the characteristic function of G_n).

Finally, suppose $x \in \mathscr{L}^p(T)$, and let g_n be the restriction of x to G_n. Then $g_n^e = xv_n$, and so

$$x'(xv_n) = f_n(g_n) = \int_{G_n} g_n y_n \, d\mu = \int xv_n y \, d\mu.$$

But

$$\int |xv_n - x|^p \, d\mu = \int_{T-G_n} |x|^p \, d\mu \to 0,$$

as a result of the fact that the set function $\int_E |x|^p \, d\mu$ is countably additive. It then follows that $x'(xv_n) \to x'(x)$, since x' is continuous. It also follows, by Hölder's inequality, that

$$\int xv_n y \, d\mu \to \int xy \, d\mu.$$

Thus we find that $x'(x) = \int xy \, d\mu$ for every $x \in \mathscr{L}^p(T)$.

We have now shown that each x' determines a $y \in \mathscr{L}^{p'}$ with $\|y\|_{p'} \leqslant \|x'\|$. That each such y determines an x' with $\|x'\| \leqslant \|y\|_{p'}$ and that the correspondence between x' and y is one-to-one are shown as in the proof of Theorem 7.4–A. This finishes the argument for Theorem 7.4–B.

For a discussion of the L^p spaces and of the representation of continuous linear functionals on them, using the Daniell approach to the theory of integration, see Loomis, **1**, Chapter III, especially pages 41–43. If $1 < p < \infty$, but not if $p = 1$, Theorem 7.4–A can be extended to the case in which (T, S, μ) is any measure space. The key fact is that for any $x \in L(\mu)$ the set $N(x)$ is contained in a countable union of measurable sets of finite measure (Halmos, **2**, Theorem F, page 105).

PROBLEMS

1. Under the conditions on T stated in Theorem 7.4–B, L^p is norm reflexive if $1 < p < \infty$.

2. Discuss the possibility of $L(\mu)$ being norm reflexive.

7.41 Complex L^p Spaces

If (T, S, μ) is a measure space, we can define complex L^p spaces just as we did in the real case, except that we consider functions with complex values. The results developed in §§ 7.3, 7.4 can all be carried over to the complex case. In some parts of the work the complex case can be treated by separation of the functions into real and imaginary parts; in some instances the best procedure seems to be to imitate the proofs of the real case, making a few necessary modifications here and there (such as writing sgn $\bar{z}$ instead of sgn z in certain places).

7.5 Measures in Locally Compact Hausdorff Spaces

In this section we sketch the subject of measures in locally compact Hausdorff spaces, primarily with a view to indicating the fundamental connection between regular Borel measures and positive linear functionals. Our interest is not to develop the subject systematically, with proofs, but to outline the structure of what we need to know in order to obtain a representation theorem for continuous linear functionals on a certain kind of space of continuous functions.

Throughout this section we let T denote a locally compact Hausdorff space. Let S be the σ-ring of Borel sets in T (defined in § 7.1). A real-valued function x defined on T is called *Borel-measurable* if it is measurable with respect to S in the sense defined in § 7.1. It can be shown, in particular, that x is Borel-measurable if it is continuous and if the set $N(x) = \{t : x(t) \neq 0\}$ is contained in a countable union of compact sets.

Definition. A measure μ on S is called a *Borel measure* if $\mu(C) < \infty$ for each compact set C. The measure is called *regular* if for every Borel set E we have

a. $\mu(E) = \sup_C \mu(C)$ (C compact, $C \subset E$).

b. $\mu(E) = \inf_U \mu(U)$ ($E \subset U$, U an open Borel set).

An open set may fail to be a Borel set; however, an open set *is* a Borel set if it is contained in a countable union of compact sets.

We use the following notations:

C: the family of compact sets in T.

U: the family of open Borel sets in T.

R: the family of sets such that each is contained in a countable union of compact sets.

Note that R is a σ-ring and that every subset of a member of R is itself a member of R.

If T happens to be compact, all open sets are Borel sets, and R is the class of all subsets of T.

If x is a function defined on T, the closure of the set $N(x)$ is called the *support* of x.

Definition.   We denote by $C_\infty(T)$ the class of all real-valued continuous functions x defined on T, such that the support of x is compact. We denote by P the class of those $x \in C_\infty(T)$ such that $x(t) \geqslant 0$ for each $t \in T$.

Evidently $C_\infty(T)$ is a linear space. It is a normed linear space with norm defined by

$$\|x\| = \sup_{t \in T} |x(t)|.$$

The finiteness of $\|x\|$ stems from the fact that x has compact support. If T is compact, then $C_\infty(T)$ is the same as the space $C(T)$ defined in Example 4, § 3.11. The space $C_\infty(T)$ is complete if T is compact.

We write $x \geqslant y$ if $x - y \in P$. Thus $x \geqslant 0$ and $x \in P$ mean the same thing.

Definition.   If x' is a linear functional on $C_\infty(T)$ such that $x'(x) \geqslant 0$ whenever $x \geqslant 0$, we say that x' is *positive*. We denote by P' the class of such x'.

If $x \in C_\infty(T)$ and μ is a Borel measure, then x is integrable with respect to μ. For, if C is the support of x and $M = \sup_{t \in C} |x(t)|$, it is clear that $|x(t)| \leqslant M x_C(t)$. But the characteristic function x_C is an integrable simple function; hence x is integrable (see the end of § 7.1).

If μ is a Borel measure and if we define x' on $C_\infty(T)$ by

$$(7.5\text{–}1) \qquad\qquad x'(x) = \int x \, d\mu,$$

it is evident that $x' \in P'$. The rest of this section is devoted to a discussion of this formula. We indicate how it is established that, if we confine attention to *regular* Borel measures, there is a one-to-one correspondence between P' and the class of regular Borel measures, with corresponding elements x' and μ related by (7.5–1). Our exposition is in outline only, with proofs omitted. For details we refer the reader to Halmos, **2**, Chapter X.

Let us begin with an $x' \in P'$. For each $C \in \boldsymbol{C}$ let

$$(7.5\text{–}2) \qquad\qquad \lambda(C) = \inf x'(x),$$

the infimum being taken over all $x \in P$ such that $x(t) \geqslant 1$ on C. The fact that functions x of this kind do exist is shown by Theorem 2.31–B. It can then be shown that this function λ is what is called a *content*. That is, (a) $0 \leqslant \lambda(C)$; (b) $\lambda(C_1) \leqslant \lambda(C_2)$ if $C_1 \subset C_2$; (c) $\lambda(C_1 \cup C_2) \leqslant \lambda(C_1) + \lambda(C_2)$; (d) $\lambda(C_1 \cup C_2) = \lambda(C_1) + \lambda(C_2)$ if $C_1 \cap C_2 = \emptyset$. Theorem 2.31–A is used in the proof of (d).

Now, there is a procedure by which a content induces a regular Borel measure. The steps in this procedure are as follows: First define $\lambda_*(U)$ for each $U \in U$ by

(7.5-3) $\qquad \lambda_*(U) = \sup_C \lambda(C) \qquad (C \text{ compact}, C \subset U).$

Then define $\mu^*(E)$ for each $E \in R$ by

(7.5-4) $\qquad \mu^*(E) = \inf \lambda_*(U) \qquad (U \in U, E \subset U).$

The function μ^* turns out to be an *outer measure*. That is, (a) $\mu^*(E) \geqslant 0$;

(b) $\mu^*(\emptyset) = 0$; (c) $\mu^*(E) \leqslant \mu^*(F)$ if $E \subset F$; (d) $\mu^* \left(\bigcup_{n=1}^{\infty} E_n \right) \leqslant \sum_{n=1}^{\infty} \mu^*(E_n).$

From the outer measure μ^* a measure is constructed in the standard way. A set $E \in R$ is called μ^*-measurable (hereafter just measurable) if

$$\mu^*(A) = \mu^*(A \cap E) + \mu^*(A \cap E')$$

for each $A \in R$. The measurable sets form a σ-ring, and on this σ-ring μ^* is a measure which we denote by μ. All sets of outer measure 0 are measurable. Every Borel set is measurable, and μ is a regular Borel measure on the σ-ring of Borel sets. This measure μ, obtained by starting from (7.5-2) is called the regular Borel measure induced by x'. One of the important facts is that

(7.5-5) $\qquad\qquad \mu(C) = \lambda(C)$

for every compact C.

The next major step is to show that, if μ is induced by x', the formula (7.5-1) is valid for each $x \in C_\infty(T)$. Finally, it must be shown that, if we *define* x' by (7.5-1), where μ is a given regular Borel measure and if ν is the regular Borel measure induced by x', then $\nu = \mu$. For this uniqueness proof the regularity of both μ and ν is needed.

An important feature of the correspondence between x' and μ is that, if y' and ν also correspond and if $y' - x' \in P'$, then $\mu(E) \leqslant \nu(E)$ for each $E \in S$. This is clear from (7.5-2), (7.5-5), and the regularity of μ and ν.

7.5l Signed and Complex Borel Measures

As in § 7.5 we consider a locally compact Hausdorff space and the σ-ring S of Borel sets in T.

Definition. By a signed Borel measure on S we mean a signed measure μ (defined in § 7.2) such that $|\mu(C)| < \infty$ if C is compact. This is equivalent to requiring that μ^+ and μ^- both be Borel measures. A complex measure such that its real and imaginary parts are signed Borel measures is called a complex Borel measure.

We shall need the concept of regularity for signed and complex Borel measures. One way to extend this concept would be simply to say that a signed Borel measure μ is regular if μ^+ and μ^- are regular and that a complex Borel measure is regular if its real and imaginary parts are regular. However, we prefer to confine our attention to finite measures and to give the definition in a different way.

Definition. Let μ be a finite complex or signed Borel measure. Then μ is said to be regular if, corresponding to each Borel set E and each $\epsilon > 0$, there exists a compact set C and an open Borel set U such that $C \subset E \subset U$ and such that

$$(7.51\text{--}1) \qquad\qquad |\mu(E) - \mu(F)| < \epsilon$$

whenever F is a Borel set such that $C \subset F \subset U$.

If μ is nonnegative, this definition of regularity is equivalent to the definition given in § 7.5; this is readily seen from the fact that μ is monotone, so that $\mu(C) \leqslant \mu(F) \leqslant \mu(U)$.

The sum of finite regular real or complex Borel measures is again such a measure. For, if $\mu = \mu_1 + \mu_2$ and if we choose C_k and U_k so that (7.51–1) is satisfied for μ_k ($k = 1, 2$), we can define $C = C_1 \cup C_2$, $U = U_1 \cap U_2$, and μ will then turn out to satisfy (7.51–1) with 2ϵ in place of ϵ. Likewise, regularity is preserved if we multiply μ by a scalar. Using the norm defined by (7.2–5), we can form a normed linear space of real or complex finite regular Borel measures. This space is complete. The completeness will appear later as a by-product of a representation theorem for linear functionals (see Theorem 7.7–G).

Theorem 7.51–A. *If μ is a finite regular signed Borel measure and $\mu = \mu^+ - \mu^-$ is its Jordan decomposition, then μ^+, u^-, and $|\mu|$ are finite regular Borel measures.*

PROOF. It is enough to show that μ^+ is regular, since $\mu^- = (-\mu)^+$, and $-\mu$ is regular if μ is. The regularity of $|\mu|$ follows, since $|\mu| = \mu^+ + \mu^-$. Now let E be a Borel set, and suppose $\epsilon > 0$. Choose a compact set C and an open Borel set U such that $C \subset E \subset U$ and such that $|\mu(E) - \mu(F)| < \epsilon/2$ if $C \subset F \subset U$. Let G be any Borel set contained in $U - C$. Let $A = E \cup (G - E)$, $B = E - G$. Then $C \subset A \subset U$, $C \subset B \subset U$, and so

$$|\mu(E) - \mu(A)| < \epsilon/2, \qquad |\mu(E) - \mu(B)| < \epsilon/2.$$

But

$$\mu(G) = \mu(G \cap E) + \mu(G - E),$$
$$\mu(E) = \mu(G \cap E) + \mu(B),$$
$$\mu(A) = \mu(E) + \mu(G - E),$$

so

(7.51–2) $|\mu(G)| \leqslant |\mu(E) - \mu(B)| + |\mu(A) - \mu(E)| < \epsilon.$

It now follows from (7.2–1) that

$$\mu^+(U - C) = \sup_{G \subset U-C} \mu(G) \leqslant \epsilon.$$

Now $E = C \cup (E - C)$ and $\mu^+(E - C) \leqslant \mu^+(U - C) \leqslant \epsilon$, so

$$\mu^+(C) = \mu^+(E) - \mu^+(E - C) \geqslant \mu^+(E) - \epsilon.$$

Likewise

$$\mu^+(U) = \mu^+(E) + \mu^+(U - E) \leqslant \mu^+(E) + \mu^+(U - C) < \mu^+(E) + \epsilon.$$

These results show that μ^+ is regular.

Theorem 7.51–B. *If μ is a finite regular complex Borel measure, the total variation $|\mu|$ is a finite regular Borel measure.   The real and imaginary parts of μ are finite regular signed Borel measures.*

PROOF.   First we show that, for any Borel set E,

(7.51–3) $|\mu|(E) \leqslant 4 \sup_{F \subset E} |\mu(F)|.$

Let $\mu = \mu_1 + i\mu_2$, where μ_1 and μ_2 have real values.   Denote the Jordan decompositions of μ_1 and μ_2 in the usual way.   Now, for any Borel set E,

$$\mu_1^+(E) = \sup_{F \subset E} \mu_1(F) \leqslant \sup_{F \subset E} |\mu(F)|,$$

$$\mu_1^-(E) = \sup_{F \subset E} \{- \mu_1(F)\} \leqslant \sup_{F \subset E} |\mu(F)|,$$

with corresponding results for μ_2^+ and μ_2^-.   Thus, if $E_1, \cdots, E_n$ are pairwise disjoint Borel sets contained in E, and $G = E_1 \cup \cdots \cup E_n$,

$$\sum_{k=1}^{n} |\mu(E_k)| \leqslant \sum_{k=1}^{n} \mu_1^+(E_k) + \sum_{k=1}^{n} \mu_1^-(E_k) + \sum_{k=1}^{n} \mu_2^+(E_k) + \sum_{k=1}^{n} \mu_2^-(E_k)$$

$$= \mu_1^+(G) + \mu_1^-(G) + \mu_2^+(G) + \mu_2^-(G)$$

$$\leqslant \mu_1^+(E) + \mu_1^-(E) + \mu_2^+(E) + \mu_2^-(E) \leqq 4 \sup_{F \subset E} |\mu(F)|.$$

In view of the definition of $|\mu|$ [see (7.2–4)], this proves (7.51–3).

Now, to prove that $|\mu|$ is regular, we proceed as in the proof of Theorem 7.51–A as far as (7.51–2), and it then follows from (7.51–3) that $|\mu|(U - C) \leqslant 4\epsilon$.   The rest of the proof is then as before, with $|\mu|$ in place of μ^+.

The fact that the real and imaginary parts of μ are regular is seen at once from the defining condition (7.51–1).

7.6 Vector Lattices

In § 7.7, in the discussion of continuous linear functionals on $C_\infty(T)$, we shall find it convenient to use notions which find their general expression in the context of vector lattices. Hence this section is devoted to a brief discussion of vector lattices.

Let A be a partially ordered set with elements $a, b, \cdots$ (see § 1.7), and let the order relation be denoted by $\leqslant$ instead of $\prec$. If $a \leqslant c$ and $b \leqslant c$, we call c an upper bound for a and b. If furthermore $c \leqslant d$ whenever d is an upper bound for a and b, we call c the *least upper bound* of a and b, and write $c = \sup(a, b)$. This element of A is unique, if it exists. In a similar way we define the greatest lower bound of a and b, and denote it by $\inf(a, b)$. If $\sup(a, b)$ and $\inf(a, b)$ exist for every pair a, b in A, A is called a *lattice*.

Definition. By a partially ordered linear space we mean a linear space A which is partially ordered by a relation $\leqslant$ in such a way that the two following conditions are satisfied:

$a \leqslant b$ implies $a + c \leqslant b + c$ for every c.
$a \leqslant b$ implies $\alpha a \leqslant \alpha b$ for every $\alpha > 0$.

If A is moreover a lattice we call it a *vector lattice*.

For each element in a vector lattice we define

(7.6–1) $$a^+ = \sup(a, 0), \qquad a^- = -\inf(a, 0).$$

Theorem 7.6–A. *In a vector lattice A we always have*

(7.6–2) $$a = a^+ - a^-,$$

(7.6–3) $$\inf(a^+, a^-) = 0.$$

PROOF. To prove (7.6–2) we show that $a - a^+ = \inf(a, 0)$. We know that $0 \leqslant a^+$ and $a \leqslant a^+$, by the definition of a^+. Equivalently, then, $a - a^+ \leqslant a$ and $a - a^+ \leqslant 0$. To complete the proof we suppose that $b \leqslant a$ and $b \leqslant 0$ and show that $b \leqslant a - a^+$; it will then follow that $a - a^+ = \inf(a, 0)$. Now $b \leqslant a$ and $b \leqslant 0$ are equivalent to $0 \leqslant a - b$ and $a \leqslant a - b$. Hence, by the definition of a^+, we have $a^+ \leqslant a - b$, or $b \leqslant a - a^+$. This finishes the proof of (7.6–2). The representation of a by (7.6–2) is called the Jordan decomposition of a.

To prove (7.6–3) we note first that $0 \leqslant a^+$ and $0 \leqslant a^-$. Hence (7.6–3) will be proved if we show that $c \leqslant a^+$ and $c \leqslant a^-$ together imply $c \leqslant 0$. We rewrite $c \leqslant a^+$ and $c \leqslant a^-$ in the forms $0 \leqslant a^+ - c$, $a \leqslant a^+ - c$.

It then follows that $a^+ \leqslant a^+ - c$, or $c \leqslant 0$, by the definition of a^+. This completes the proof of Theorem 7.6–A.

It is useful to know the following formulas, which are valid in any vector lattice:

$$(7.6\text{–}4) \qquad \inf{(a, b)} = - \sup{(- a, - b)},$$

$$(7.6\text{–}5) \qquad \sup{(a, b)} + \inf{(a, b)} = a + b,$$

$$(7.6\text{–}6) \qquad \sup{(a, b)} = a + \sup{(b - a, 0)}.$$

We omit the proofs, which are much like the proofs of (7.6–2) and (7.6–3).

If A is a partially ordered linear space such that $\sup{(a, 0)}$ exists for every $a \in A$, then A is a vector lattice. For, it is then easy to show that $\sup{(a, b)}$ exists for every pair (a, b), being given by (7.6–6); and $\inf{(a, b)}$ exists, being given by (7.6–4). These remarks are useful when it comes to verifying that we have a vector lattice in various concrete situations.

The space $C_\infty(T)$ is a vector lattice, with the partial ordering $x \leqslant y$ defined to mean that $x(t) \leqslant y(t)$ for every $t \in T$. In this case $z = \sup{(x, y)}$ is the function defined by $z(t) = \max{\{x(t), y(t)\}}$. Then $x^+(t) = \max{[x(t), 0]}$ and $x^-(t) = - \min{[x(t), 0]}$.

The finite signed measures on a fixed σ-ring form a vector lattice, the partial ordering $\mu \leqslant \nu$ being understood to mean $\mu(E) \leqslant \nu(E)$ for every E in the ring. The Jordan decomposition $\mu = \mu^+ - \mu^-$ described in § 7.2 is what (7.6–2) becomes for this case. The finite regular signed Borel measures on the Borel sets of a locally compact Hausdorff space also form a vector lattice (see Theorem 7.51–A).

In § 7.7 we shall see that the continuous linear functionals defined on $C_\infty(T)$ also form a vector lattice. Here the partial ordering $x' \leqslant y'$ means that $x'(x) \leqslant y'(x)$ whenever $x \geqslant 0$.

7.7 Linear Functionals on $C_\infty(T)$

In this section we use the notations of § 7.5. Our principal aim is to show that we can identify the normed conjugate of the real space $C_\infty(T)$ with the Banach space of all finite regular signed Borel measures on S. This identification is actually, of course, a congruence of the two Banach spaces in question. The Banach spaces are vector lattices, and the linear correspondence is order preserving.

In the course of our work we go somewhat further than a study of the continuous linear functionals on $C_\infty(T)$; we examine linear functionals which may not be continuous, but which have a property which we call *relative boundedness*. It turns out that these linear functionals are precisely those which can be expressed as the difference of two positive linear functionals (as defined in § 7.5). If T is compact, relative bounded-ness is the same as continuity. A relatively bounded linear functional is called a Radon measure by some authors; see Bourbaki, **5**.

Definition. A linear functional x' defined on $C_\infty(T)$ is said to be relatively bounded if to each compact subset T_0 of T there corresponds a nonnegative number $m(T_0)$ such that

$$(7.7–1) \qquad\qquad |x'(x)| \leqslant m(T_0)\|x\|$$

whenever $x \in C_\infty(T)$ and the support of x is contained in T_0.

It is easily seen that the relatively bounded linear functionals form a linear space.

Theorem 7.7–A. *A positive linear functional on $C_\infty(T)$ is relatively bounded.*

PROOF. Given a positive x' and a compact set T_0, we choose a neighbor-hood U of T_0 having compact closure and a function $y \in C_\infty(T)$ such that $y(t) = 1$ on T_0, $y(t) = 0$ on U', and $0 \leqslant y(t) \leqslant 1$ for all t (Theorem 2.31–B). If the support of x is contained in T_0, it is clear that $-\|x\|y(t) \leqslant x(t) \leqslant \|x\|y(t)$ and, therefore, that $-\|x\|x'(y) \leqslant x'(x) \leqslant \|x\|x'(y)$, since x' is positive. We can then choose $m(T_0) = |x'(y)|$ to show that x' is relatively bounded.

Our next main objective is to show that every relatively bounded linear functional is the difference of two positive linear functionals. For this we need some preliminary results.

Lemma 7.7–B. *If f is a real-valued function on $C_\infty(T)$ such that $f(x + y) = f(x) + f(y)$ for every x and y and if $f(x) \geqslant 0$ whenever $x \geqslant 0$, then $f(\alpha x) = \alpha f(x)$ for each real α.*

PROOF. This theorem is actually valid with any vector lattice in place of $C_\infty(T)$, as the proof will show. From $f(0) + f(0) = f(0)$ follows $f(0) = 0$. Then $f(x) + f(- x) = f(0) = 0$, so $f(- x) = - f(x)$. Hence it suffices to prove $f(\alpha x) = \alpha f(x)$ for $\alpha > 0$. It also suffices to show this for $x \geqslant 0$, since every x can be written as $x = x^+ - x^-$ with $x^+ \geqslant 0$, $x^- \geqslant 0$. Now it is easy to deduce that $f(\alpha x) = \alpha f(x)$ if α is positive and rational; we omit the details. It is for the case of irrational α that we need to know that $f(x) \geqslant 0$ if $x \geqslant 0$. Let $\{\alpha_n\}$ and $\{\beta_n\}$ be sequences of positive rationals converging to α such that $\alpha_n < \alpha < \beta_n$. Then, if $x \geqslant 0$, $\alpha_n x \leqslant \alpha x \leqslant \beta_n x$ and $\alpha_n f(x) = f(\alpha_n x) \leqslant f(\alpha x) \leqslant f(\beta_n x) = \beta_n f(x)$. Letting $n \to \infty$, we obtain $\alpha f(x) \leqslant f(\alpha x) \leqslant \alpha f(x)$. This completes the proof.

Lemma 7.7–C. *If f is a real-valued function which is defined, with nonnegative values, for each $x \in C_\infty(T)$ such that $x \geqslant 0$, and if $f(x + y) = f(x) + f(y)$ for each x and y of this kind, there is a unique linear functional F defined on $C_\infty(T)$ such that $F(x) = f(x)$ if $x \geqslant 0$.*

PROOF.   This result also holds for any vector lattice, not merely on $C_\infty(T)$.   Each x can be written in the form $x = x_1 - x_2$ with $x_1 \geqslant 0$ and $x_2 \geqslant 0$.   If we have another such representation $x = y_1 - y_2$, then $x_1 + y_2 = x_2 + y_1$,   whence   it   easily   follows   that $f(x_1) - f(x_2) = f(y_1) - f(y_2)$.   Consequently, if we define $F(x) = f(x_1) - f(x_2)$, the value of $F(x)$ depends only on x and not on the way in which x is decomposed.   (We note, incidentally, that this is the only value that $F(x)$ could have if it is to be linear and an extension of f.   Hence the uniqueness part of the assertion in the theorem.)   It is easily verified that $F(x + y) = F(x) + F(y)$, and $F(\alpha x) = \alpha F(x)$ follows by Lemma 7.7–B. Thus the proof is finished.

Theorem 7.7–D.   *The relatively bounded linear functionals on $C_\infty(T)$ form a vector lattice.   If x' is such a functional, then the Jordan decomposition of x' is*

(7.7–2) $$x' = (x')^+ - (x')^-,$$

where $(x')^+$ and $(x')^-$ are defined as follows:

(7.7–3) $$(x')^+(y) = \sup_{x \in P_y} x'(x),$$

(7.7–4) $$(x')^-(y) = - \inf_{x \in P_y} x'(x),$$

where $y \geqslant 0$ and P_y is the set of all $x \in C_\infty(T)$ such that $0 \leqslant x \leqslant y$.

PROOF.   Observe that $\|x\| \leqslant \|y\|$ if $x \in P_y$.   Also, if T_0 is the support of y, the support of x is contained in T_0.   Hence, by (7.7–1), we have

(7.7–5) $$|x'(x)| \leqslant m(T_0)\|y\|$$

if $x \in P_y$.   At this stage we define $f(y) = \sup_{x \in P_y} x'(x)$ if $y \geqslant 0$.   Clearly $f(y)$ is finite, by (7.7–5); and $f(y) \geqslant 0$, for $0 \in P_y$.   If $0 \leqslant x_1 \leqslant y_1$ and $0 \leqslant x_2 \leqslant y_2$, we have $0 \leqslant x_1 + x_2 \leqslant y_1 + y_2$ and therefore $x'(x_1) + x'(x_2) - x'(x_1 + x_2) \leqslant f(y_1 + y_2)$.   It   follows   that $f(y_1) + f(y_2) \leqslant f(y_1 + y_2)$.   To prove the reverse of this inequality, suppose that x, y_1, and y_2 are given, with $x \in P_{y_1+y_2}$.   We define

$$x_1(t) = \min \{x(t), y_1(t)\}$$
$$x_2(t) = \max \{0, x(t) - y_1(t)\}.$$

Then x_1 and x_2 are in $C_\infty(T)$ and $x = x_1 + x_2$. It is evident that $0 \leqslant x_1 \leqslant y_1$. It is also true that $0 \leqslant x_2 \leqslant y_2$. For, if $x(t) < y_1(t)$, we have $x_2(t) = 0 \leqslant y_2(t)$, and if $x(t) \geqslant y_1(t)$, we have $x_2(t) = x(t) - y_1(t) \leqslant y_1(t) + y_2(t) - y_1(t) = y_2(t)$. But then $x'(x) = x'(x_1) + x'(x_2) \leqslant f(y_1) + f(y_2)$, and so $f(y_1 + y_2) \leqslant f(y_1) + f(y_2)$. It is now clear that f satisfies the conditions of Lemma 7.7–C and hence that it can be extended in a unique way to give a positive linear functional on $C_\infty(T)$. We denote this extension by $(x')^+$; thus $(x')^+$ is determined by (7.7–3).

It is clear that $C_\infty(T)$ is a partially ordered linear space, and it is seen directly from (7.7–3) that $(x')^+$ is sup $(x', 0)$. As was remarked in § 7.6, the existence of sup $(x', 0)$ for each x' insures that we have a vector lattice. As for $(x')^-$, we can either define $(x')^-$ in terms of x' and $(x')^+$ by (7.7–2) and then prove (7.7–4), or we can define $(x')^-$ by (7.7–4), verify that $(x')^-$ is in fact $-\inf(x', 0)$ in the lattice sense, and then obtain (7.7–2) as a special case of (7.6–2). We leave details to the reader.

We define a positive linear functional $|x'|$ by the formula

$$(7.7\text{–}6) \qquad |x'| = (x')^+ + (x')^-.$$

We must be careful to distinguish $|x'|(x)$ from $|x'(x)|$. Of course we have $(x')^+ = |x'| = x'$ if $x' \geqslant 0$. It may be shown without great difficulty (see problem 2) that

$$(7.7\text{–}7) \qquad |x'|(y) = \sup_{|x| \in P_y} x'(x)$$

if $y \geqslant 0$. Here $|x|$ denotes the function whose values are $|x(t)|$.

As a consequence of (7.7–7) we see that

$$(7.7\text{–}8) \qquad |x'(x)| \leqslant |x'|(|x|).$$

For, $x'(x) \leqslant |x'|(|x|)$; on combining this with what is obtained when x is replaced by $-x$, we obtain (7.7–8).

Definition. If x' is any relatively bounded linear functional on $C_\infty(T)$, we define

$$(7.7\text{–}9) \qquad \|x'\| = \sup_{\|x\| \leqslant 1} |x'(x)|.$$

It may of course happen that $\|x'\| = \infty$ (though not if T is compact). The condition $\|x'\| < \infty$ is satisfied if and only if x' is continuous on $C_\infty(T)$ as a normed linear space. The triangular inequality $\|x' + y'\| \leqslant \|x'\| + \|y'\|$ is valid, with the usual conventions about ∞.

Theorem 7.7–E. *The following relations hold:*

$$(7.7\text{–}10) \qquad \|x'\| = \sup_{0 \leqslant y \leqslant 1} |x'|(y),$$

$$(7.7\text{–}11) \qquad \| \, |x'| \, \| = \|x'\|.$$

If $x' \geqslant 0$ and $y' \geqslant 0$, then

$$(7.7\text{--}12) \qquad \qquad \|x' + y'\| = \|x'\| + \|y'\|.$$

PROOF. We remark that the function with value 1 at all points of T does not belong to $C_\infty(T)$ unless T is compact. Nevertheless, it is convenient to write $y \leqslant 1$ if $y(t) \leqslant 1$ for all t. Suppose that $0 \leqslant y \leqslant 1$ and $|x| \leqslant y$. Then $\|x\| \leqslant 1$. By combining (7.7–7) and (7.7–9) we see that $|x'|(y) \leqslant \|x'\|$. Thus $\sup\limits_{0 \leqslant y \leqslant 1} |x'|(y) \leqslant \|x'\|$. On the other hand, $\|x\| \leqslant 1$ implies $|x| \leqslant 1$; hence (7.7–8) implies

$$|x'(x)| \leqslant \sup_{0 \leqslant y \leqslant 1} |x'|(y)$$

if $\|x\| \leqslant 1$, and from this we infer that

$$\|x'\| \leqslant \sup_{0 \leqslant y \leqslant 1} |x'|(y).$$

This proves (7.7–10). The truth of (7.7–11) follows at once from (7.7–10) and the fact that $|y'| = y'$ if $y' = |x'|$.

To prove (7.7–12) it suffices to prove that $\|x' + y'\| \geqslant \|x'\| + \|y'\|$ under the given conditions, for the reverse inequality is always true. If $0 \leqslant x \leqslant 1$ and $0 \leqslant y \leqslant 1$, let $z(t) = \max\{x(t), y(t)\}$. Then $0 \leqslant z \leqslant 1$, $x \leqslant z$, $y \leqslant z$. Since x' and y' are positive, we have $x'(x) \leqslant x'(z)$, $y'(y) \leqslant y'(z)$, and therefore

$$x'(x) + y'(y) \leqslant (x' + y')(z) \leqslant \|x' + y'\|.$$

Since $x' = |x'|$ and $y' = |y'|$, we now infer from (7.7–10) that $\|x'\| + \|y'\| \leqslant \|x' + y'\|$. Thus (7.7–12) is proved.

Now suppose that x' is a relatively bounded linear functional on $C_\infty(T)$. By the results described in § 7.5 we know that to the positive linear functional $(x')^+$ there corresponds a unique regular Borel measure, which we denote by μ_+, such that

$$(7.7\text{--}13) \qquad \qquad \int x \, d\mu_+ = (x')^+(x)$$

for each $x \in C_\infty(T)$. Likewise, to $(x')^-$ corresponds a unique regular Borel measure μ_- and a formula corresponding to (7.7–13). Hence x' has the representation

$$(7.7\text{--}14) \qquad x'(x) = \int x \, d\mu_+ - \int x \, d\mu_-, \qquad x \in C_\infty(T).$$

The representation of $|x'|$ is

$$(7.7\text{--}15) \qquad \qquad |x'|(x) = \int x \, d\nu,$$

where $\nu = \mu_+ + \mu_-$.

It should be noted that we do not at this juncture define a signed measure $\mu = \mu_+ - \mu_-$, for we have no assurance that the situation $\mu_+(E) = \mu_-(E) = +\infty$ cannot arise, and thus the unambiguous definition of μ may be impossible. Presently we shall see that in the case when x' is continuous, $\mu_+ - \mu_-$ is indeed the Jordan decomposition of a finite signed measure μ.

We have the following theorem.

Theorem 7.7–F. *If x' is any relatively bounded linear functional on $C_\infty(T)$ and if ν is the regular Borel measure corresponding to $|x'|$, then*

$$(7.7\text{–}16) \qquad\qquad \|x'\| = \sup_{E \in S} \nu(E).$$

PROOF. Because of (7.7–11) it suffices to give the proof on the assumption that $x' \geqslant 0$. In this case $\nu = \mu_+$ and $\mu_- = 0$. Consider any $y \in C_\infty(T)$ with $0 \leqslant y \leqslant 1$, and let C be the support of y. There exists a neighborhood U of C with compact closure (so that U is a Borel set) and a function $x \in C_\infty(T)$ such that $0 \leqslant x \leqslant 1$, $x(t) = 1$ on C and $x(t) = 0$ on $T - U$. Then $y \leqslant x$ and $x'(y) \leqslant x'(x)$. Also

$$x'(x) = \int x \, d\nu \leqslant \nu(U).$$

Thus, if M denotes the supremum on the right in (7.7–16), we have $x'(y) \leqslant M$, whence $\|x'\| \leqslant M$, by (7.7–10). On the other hand, if C is *any* compact set, there exists $x \in C_\infty(T)$ such that $x(t) = 1$ on C and $0 \leqslant x \leqslant 1$. Then, by (7.5–2) and (7.5–5) we see that $\nu(C) \leqslant x'(x)$; also, of course, $x'(x) \leqslant \|x'\|$. By the regularity of ν it then follows that $\nu(E) \leqslant \|x'\|$ for every $E \in S$. This completes the proof of (7.7–16).

If x' is not merely relatively bounded, but continuous, $(x')^+$ and $(x')^-$ are continuous also. This is clear from (7.7–12) as applied to (7.7–6), in view of (7.7–11). Hence the continuous linear functionals on $C_\infty(T)$ form a vector lattice.

We come now to the representation of the normed conjugate of $C_\infty(T)$.

Theorem 7.7–G. *The normed conjugate of $C_\infty(T)$ is congruent as a Banach space to the Banach space of all finite regular signed Borel measures on S. The correspondence between a continuous linear functional x' and a finite regular signed Borel measure μ is established by the formula*

$$(7.7\text{–}17) \qquad\qquad x'(x) = \int x \, d\mu \qquad x \in C_\infty(T).$$

These Banach spaces are also vector lattices, and the correspondence set up by (7.7–17) is order-preserving, so that it is a lattice isomorphism.

PROOF. Starting with x', we obtain the representation (7.7–14). The norm of x' is given by (7.7–16), and since $\nu = \mu_+ + \mu_-$, it is clear from this that the values of μ_+ and μ_- are always finite, because $\|x'\| < \infty$. Hence we can define $\mu = \mu_+ - \mu_-$, and μ is a finite regular signed Borel measure. At this stage we do not yet know that $\mu_+ = \mu^+$ and $\mu_- = \mu^-$. It is not at once evident that the mapping $x' \to \mu$ is linear, but we shall show that it is. From (7.7–3) it is readily apparent that $(x' + y')^+ \leqslant (x')^+ + (y')^+$. Let us write

$$z' = (x')^+ + (y')^+ - (x' + y')^+,$$

so that $z' \geqslant 0$. From (7.7–2) we see that

$$z' = (x')^- + (y')^- - (x' + y')^-$$

also. Now let μ_+, ν_+, ω_+ denote the regular Borel measures associated with $(x')^+$, $(y')^+$, $(x' + y')^+$, respectively, and similarly for μ_-, $(x')^-$, and so on. The measure associated with z' can be expressed either as $\mu_+ + \nu_+ - \omega_+$ or as $\mu_- + \nu_- - \omega_-$. (The fact that $\mu_+ + \nu_+ - \omega_+$ has nonnegative values follows from the fact that the correspondence between positive linear functionals and regular measures is order-preserving; see the very end of § 7.5). But then

$$\omega_+ - \omega_- = (\mu_+ - \mu_-) + (\nu_+ - \nu_-),$$

and this shows that the mapping $x' \to \mu$ is additive. Next, it is evident from (7.7–3) and (7.7–4) that $(\alpha x')^+ = \alpha(x')^+$ and $(\alpha x')^- = \alpha(x')^-$ if $\alpha \geqslant 0$, while $(\alpha x')^+ = -\alpha(x')^-$ and $(\alpha x')^- = -\alpha(x')^+$ if $\alpha < 0$. In either case we see that if $x' \to \mu$ then $\alpha x' \to \alpha\mu$. Thus the mapping is linear. It is clear from (7.7–14) that $\mu = 0$ implies $x' = 0$. Consequently, it will be established that we have a one-to-one mapping onto the space of all finite regular signed Borel measures if we show that every μ is the image of some x'.

We therefore let μ be given, and let its Jordan decomposition be $\mu^+ - \mu^-$. We define x' by (7.7–17) [see (7.2–6)]. If C is the support of x,

$$|x'(x)| \leqslant \int |x| \, d|\mu| \leqslant \|x\| \, |\mu|(C) \leqslant \|x\| \, \|\mu\|$$

[where $\|\mu\|$ is defined by (7.2–5)]. This shows that x' is continuous. Applying (7.7–14) to x', we have

$$\int x \, d\mu_+ - \int x \, d\mu_- = \int x \, d\mu^+ - \int x \, d\mu^-,$$

and hence also

$$\int x \, d(\mu_+ + \mu^-) = \int x \, d(\mu^+ + \mu_-)$$

for each $x \in C_\infty(T)$. But then, by the uniqueness feature of the correspondence between positive linear functionals and regular Borel measures (described in § 7.5), we infer that $\mu_+ + \mu^- = \mu^+ + \mu_-$, or $\mu = \mu_+ - \mu_-$. Hence μ is the image of x' under the mapping described at the outset of the proof.

The fact that the mapping is order-preserving follows from the fact that it is one-to-one plus the fact that every positive functional is representable with the aid of a nonnegative measure. The mapping then preserves least upper bounds and greatest lower bounds. From this it follows that $\mu_+ = \mu^+$, for μ_+ is the image of $(x')^+ = \sup (x', 0)$, while $\mu^+ = \sup (\mu, 0)$. Likewise $\mu_- = \mu^-$.

Finally, the mapping is norm-preserving. This follows from (7.7–16) and (7.2–5), for we now know that $\mu_+ + \mu_- = |\mu|$. Since the normed conjugate of $C_\infty(T)$ is complete, it follows that the space of finite regular signed Borel measures is also complete.

PROBLEMS

1. Carry out at least one of the suggestions for dealing with $(x')^-$ as indicated at the end of the proof of Theorem 7.7–D.

2. Prove (7.7–7). Suggestions: If $0 \leqslant |x| \leqslant y$, note that $0 \leqslant x^+ \leqslant y$ and $0 \leqslant x^- \leqslant y$. Then $x'(x) \leqslant |x'|(y)$ follows from (7.7–3) and (7.7–4). On the other hand, if $\epsilon > 0$, choose x_1 and x_2 in P_y so that $x'(x_1) > (x')^+(y) - (\epsilon/2)$ and $x'(x_2) < - (x')^-(y) + (\epsilon/2)$. Then consider $x = x_1 - x_2$.

3. Prove that $\|x'\| = \|(x')^+\| + \|(x')^-\|$.

4. Prove that $\|x'\| \leqslant \|y'\|$ if $0 \leqslant x' \leqslant y'$. Use (7.7–12).

5. If T is compact and x' is a continuous linear functional on $C_\infty(T)$ $[\equiv C(T)]$, show that $\|x'\| = |x'|(1)$, where 1 denotes the function of all whose values are unity.

6. If (μ_1, μ_2) and (ν_1, ν_2) are two pairs of regular Borel measures on S, we define these pairs to be equivalent if $\mu_1(E) + \nu_2(E) = \mu_2(E) + \nu_1(E)$ for every $E \in S$. Show that

$$\int x \, d\mu_1 - \int x \, d\mu_2 \quad \text{and} \quad \int x \, d\nu_1 - \int x \, d\nu_2$$

define the same relatively bounded linear functional on $C_\infty(T)$ if and only if (μ_1, μ_2) and (ν_1, ν_2) are equivalent. Show that there is a one-to-one correspondence between the set of all relatively bounded linear functionals on $C_\infty(T)$ and the set of all equivalence classes of pairs of regular Borel measures.

7. For the purpose of extending some of the results of § 7.7 to the complex case, let $C_\infty(T)$ denote the set of complex-valued continuous functions on T, each with compact support. Denote the corresponding space of real functions by $RC_\infty(T)$. If z' is a relatively bounded complex linear functional on $C_\infty(T)$, if we write $z' = x' + iy'$, where x' and y' have real values, and if we write elements of $C_\infty(T)$ in the form $z = x + iy$ with x and $y \in RC_\infty(T)$, show that

$$z'(z) = x'(x) - y'(y) + iy'(x) + ix'(y).$$

Show that $z'(z)$ is representable in terms of eight real integrals involving four regular Borel measures. Show also that

$$\sup_{\|z\| \le 1} |z'(z)| = \sup_{\|z\| \le 1} |x'(x) - y'(y)|.$$

Then prove that $\|z'\|$, defined by the foregoing supremum, which may be infinite, satisfies the inequalities

$$(\|x'\|^2 + \|y'\|^2)^{\frac{1}{2}} \le \|z'\| \le \|x'\| + \|y'\|.$$

Both extremes are attainable.

8. Continuing along the lines begun in (7), show that the normed conjugate of $C_\infty(T)$, in the complex case, is congruent to the space of finite regular complex Borel measures on S. The principal difficulty is in showing that the one-to-one correspondence is norm preserving. It suffices to show that, if z' and μ correspond by the formula $z'(z) = \int z \, d\mu$, then $\|z'\| \ge \|\mu\|$, for the reverse inequality is evident. We outline the argument. With $\epsilon > 0$ given, choose a Borel set E so that $|\mu|(E) > \|\mu\| - (\epsilon/3)$. Then choose pairwise disjoint Borel sets $E_1, \cdots, E_k$ such that $E_k \subset E$ and

$$\sum_{k=1}^{n} |\mu(E_k)| > |\mu|(E) - (\epsilon/3).$$

Now, if $\|z\| \le 1$,

$$\|z'\| \ge \left| \int z \, d\mu \right| \ge \sum_{k=1}^{n} |\mu(E_k)| - \left| \int z \, d\mu - \sum_{k=1}^{n} |\mu(E_k)| \right|$$

$$\ge \|\mu\| - \tfrac{2}{3}\epsilon - \left| \int z \, d\mu - \sum_{k=1}^{n} |\mu(E_k)| \right|.$$

Hence it suffices to be able to choose z so that $\|z\| \le 1$ and

$$\left| \int z \, d\mu - \sum_{k=1}^{n} |\mu(E_k)| \right| < \epsilon/3.$$

For each k let C_k and U_k be, respectively, compact and open Borel sets such that $C_k \subset E_k \subset U_k$ and such that $|\mu(E_k) - \mu(F_k)| < (\epsilon/27n)$ if F_k is a Borel set for which $C_k \subset F_k \subset U_k$. One can then show, just as in the proof of the regularity of $|\mu|$ in Theorem 7.51–B, that $|\mu|(U_k - C_k) \le (8/27n)$. It also follows that

$$\left| \sum_{k=1}^{n} |\mu(C_k)| - \sum_{k=1}^{n} |\mu(E_k)| \right| \le \sum_{k=1}^{n} |\mu(C_k) - \mu(E_k)| < \epsilon/27.$$

For each i and j with $i \ne j (i, j = 1, \cdots, n)$ there exist disjoint neighborhoods V_{ij} and V_{ji} of C_i and C_j respectively, with compact closures. Let V_k be the intersection of U_k and all the V_{kj} for which $j \neq k$. Then $C_k \subset V_k \subset U_k$, V_k is open with compact closure, and $V_k \cap V_l = \emptyset$ if $k \neq l$. Choose $x_k \in RC_\infty(T)$ so that $0 \leqslant x_k \leqslant 1$, $x_k(t) = 1$ on C_k and $x_k(t) = 0$ on $T - V_k$. Let $\alpha_k = \overline{\operatorname{sgn}} \, \mu(C_k)$ and $z = \sum_{k=1}^{n} \alpha_k x_k$. This element of $C_\infty(T)$ will do what is required for the completion of the proof.

7.8 Finitely Additive Set Functions

In the proof of Theorem 7.4–A we used the fact that $p < \infty$ in proving that the set function ν is countably additive; the fact that ν is finitely additive remains true even in the case $p = \infty$. Finitely additive set functions turn out to be of interest in connection with the study of linear functionals on spaces of bounded or essentially bounded functions.

Definition. Let T be a nonempty set, R a ring of subsets of T, and μ a finitely additive set function on R with real or complex values. If the values of μ on R are bounded, we call μ a *charge* on R. If μ is a charge and $T \in R$, we call (T, R, μ) a *totally charged space.*

This terminology concerning charges is due to Rosenbloom, **1**.

Being finitely additive means that $\mu(E \cup F) = \mu(E) + \mu(F)$ if E and F are disjoint members of R. Of course R contains the empty set $\emptyset$, and hence $\mu(\emptyset) = 0$.

A real-valued charge μ has a Jordan decomposition $\mu = \mu^+ - \mu^-$, just like a signed measure (§ 7.2). With a charge μ we associate the total variation $|\mu|$, given by (7.2–4), just as with a signed or complex measure; $|\mu|$ is a nonnegative charge. We define the norm $\|\mu\|$ of a charge μ just as in (7.2–5). The charges on R form a Banach space. If the space is totally charged, $\|\mu\| = |\mu|(T)$.

Charges can be used to represent the normed conjugate of the space $B(T)$ (defined in Example 3, § 3.11). First we must define a type of integral with respect to a charge. This integral is to some extent analogous to the classical Riemann-Stieltjes integral and is defined with the aid of the notion of Moore-Smith convergence. For terminology about directed sets, nets, and Moore-Smith convergence see Kelley, **1**, Chapter 2.

Suppose that (T, R, μ) is a totally charged space. By a *partition* of T we mean a finite collection $E_1, \cdots, E_n$ of pairwise disjoint nonempty members of R such that $T = E_1 \cup \cdots \cup E_n$. If $\pi_1 = (E_1, \cdots, E_m)$ and $\pi_2 = (F_1, \cdots, F_n)$ are partitions, we define $\pi_1 \leqslant \pi_2$ to mean that each F_j is a subset of some E_k (π_2 is a "refinement" of π_1). This gives a partial ordering of partitions, and every pair of partitions has an upper bound, e.g., the "superposition" of the two partitions. Hence partitions form a

directed set.   Now suppose that x is a scalar-valued function defined on
T.   If $\pi = (E_1, \cdots, E_n)$ is a partition, choose points $t_k \in E_k$ and write

$$(7.8\text{--}1) \qquad f(\pi; t_1, \cdots, t_n) = \sum_{k=1}^{n} x(t_k)\mu(E_k).$$

The (many-valued) function f is a net on the directed set of partitions.   If
the net converges to a limit I, this limit is called the S-integral of x with
respect to μ:

$$I = S \int x \, d\mu.$$

This means, of course, that for every $\epsilon > 0$ there is some partition π_ϵ
such that $f(\pi; t_1, \cdots, t_n)$ differs from I by less than ϵ if $\pi_\epsilon \leqslant \pi$.

The function x is called measurable if $x^{-1}(M) \in R$ for each semi-open
interval $M = \{t : \alpha < t \leqslant \beta\}$.   This is for the real case.   In the complex
case we use semi-open rectangles.   It can then be proved that when
(T, R, μ) is a totally charged space and x is a bounded measurable function
on T, then x is S-integrable.   The argument depends on a Cauchy
condition for the convergence of nets.   We give the argument for the
complex case.

Choose a semi-open rectangle M whose interior contains all the values
of x.   Suppose $\epsilon > 0$, and partition M into disjoint semi-open rectangles
$M_1, \cdots, M_m$, all of diagonal less than ϵ.   Let $F_k = x^{-1}(M_k)$, and let
$E_1, \cdots, E_n$ be the distinct nonempty sets among $F_1, \cdots, F_m$.   Then
$\pi = (E_1, \cdots, E_n)$ is a partition of T.   Suppose now that $\pi_1 = (G_1, \cdots)$
and $\pi_2 = (H_1, \cdots)$ are partitions of T such that $\pi \leqslant \pi_1$ and $\pi \leqslant \pi_2$, and
choose points $s_i \in G_i$, $t_j \in H_j$.   We can write

$$\mu(G_i) = \sum_j \mu(G_i \cap H_j), \quad \sum_i x(s_i)\mu(G_i) = \sum_{i,j} x(s_i)\mu(G_i \cap H_j),$$

and so we see that

$$(7.8\text{--}2) \quad \sum_i x(s_i)\mu(G_i) - \sum_j x(t_j)\mu(H_j) = \sum_{i,j} \{x(s_i) - x(t_j)\}\mu(G_i \cap H_j).$$

We need only consider those terms for which $\mu(G_i \cap H_j) \neq 0$, and for
such terms G_i and H_j are both contained in the same E_k, which means that
$x(s_i)$ and $x(t_j)$ are contained in the same M_l, and hence that $|x(s_i) - x(t_j)|$
$< \epsilon$.   Consequently, the absolute value of the expression in (7.8–2) does
not exceed

$$\epsilon \sum_{i,j} |\mu(G_i \cap H_j)| \leqslant \epsilon |\mu|(T).$$

This shows that the net satisfies a Cauchy condition and is therefore convergent.

The S-integral evidently satisfies the inequality

$$(7.8\text{--}3) \qquad \left| S \int x \, d\mu \right| \leqslant \sup_{t \in T} |x(t)| \, |\mu|(T).$$

Now consider the Banach space $B(T)$, where T is any nonempty set. Let R be the ring of *all* subsets of T. Then any member of $B(T)$ is S-integrable with respect to any charge on R.

Theorem 7.8–A. *With T and R as just described, the normed conjugate of $B(T)$ is congruent to the space of all charges on R, the correspondence between a continuous linear functional x' and its associated charge μ being indicated by the two formulas*

$$(7.8\text{--}4) \qquad x'(x) = S \int x \, d\mu, \qquad x \in B(T),$$

$$(7.8\text{--}5) \qquad \mu(E) = x'(x_E), \qquad E \in R,$$

where x_E is the characteristic function of E.

PROOF. Each charge μ defines an $x' \in \{B(T)\}'$ by formula (7.8–4). From (7.8–3) we see that $\|x'\| \leqslant \|\mu\|$. Formula (7.8–5) clearly holds if E is $\emptyset$ or T. For any other E it suffices to observe that, if π_0 is any partition of T and $\pi = (E_1, \cdots, E_n)$ is the superposition of π_0 and the partition $(E, T - E)$, the expression in (7.8–1) is equal to $\mu(E)$. From (7.8–5) we see that $x' = 0$ implies $\mu = 0$.

On the other hand, if we start with x' and define μ by (7.8–5), it is easy to see that μ is a charge. We wish to show that (7.8–4) holds. If $\epsilon > 0$ and $x \in B(T)$, choose $M, M_1, \cdots, M_m$ and $E_1, \cdots, E_n$ as in the earlier proof of integrability of a bounded measurable function. Choose any $t_k \in E_k$ and form the sum (7.8–1). Since $\mu(E) = x'(x_E)$, we see that

$$\sum_k x(t_k)\mu(E_k) = x' \left(\sum_k x(t_k)y_k \right),$$

where y_k is the characteristic function of E_k. On the other hand, if $t \in E_j$,

$$\left| x(t) - \sum_k x(t_k)y_k(t) \right| = |x(t) - x(t_j)|,$$

so that

$$(7.8\text{--}6) \qquad \left\| x - \sum x(t_k)y_k \right\| \leqslant \epsilon$$

and therefore

$$\left| x'(x) - \sum_k x(t_k)\mu(E_k) \right| \leqslant \epsilon \|x'\|.$$

This inequality evidently remains valid for any sums based on partitions obtained by further subdivision of the E_k's and so (7.8-4) is true.

Finally, to show that $\|\mu\| \leqslant \|x'\|$ in the context of the foregoing paragraph, suppose $\epsilon > 0$ and choose a partition $(E_1, \cdots, E_n)$ of T such that

$$\sum_{k=1}^{n} |\mu(E_k)| > \|\mu\| - \epsilon;$$

this is possible, by the definition of $\|\mu\|$. Then define x by setting $x(t) = \overline{\operatorname{sgn}} \, \mu(E_k)$ on E_k. Then $\|x\| \leqslant 1$ and

$$x'(x) = S\!\int x \, d\mu = \sum_{k} |\mu(E_k)|.$$

Consequently $\|x'\| \geqslant \|\mu\| - \epsilon$. Thus $\|x'\| \geqslant \|\mu\|$. This establishes everything necessary for the proof of Theorem 7.8–A.

7.9 Lebesgue Integrals with Respect to a Charge

Let T be any nonempty set, and let S be a σ-ring of subsets of T such that $T \in S$. Let N be a nonempty proper subclass of S which is closed under the formation of countable unions and which has the property that any subset of a member of N is again a member of N. Evidently N is closed under the formation of differences and intersections and contains the empty set $\emptyset$. One possibility is that N consists solely of the set $\emptyset$. However, the situation we have in mind as a model is that in which S is the class of Lebesgue measurable sets in Euclidean space and N is the class of sets of measure 0.

If x is a real-valued function on T which is measurable with respect to S, we say that x is N-bounded if $\{t : |x(t)| > \alpha\} \in N$ for some $\alpha \geqslant 0$. The smallest α for which this is true is denoted by $\|x\|$ (the existence of this smallest α requires the countable union closure property of N). If x and y are N-bounded, measurable and if $\|x - y\| = 0$, we call them N-equivalent. Just as in the case of L^∞, we construct a Banach space whose elements are equivalence classes of such functions. We permit ourselves the abuse of language whereby we identify x and the equivalence class to which it belongs, and we denote the Banach space here described by $B_N(T)$. If N contains only the set $\emptyset$ and S is the σ-ring of all subsets of T, $B_N(T)$ is just $B(T)$, as previously defined. If μ is a measure on S such that the sets of zero measure form a class N with the required properties, $B_N(T)$ coincides with $L^\infty(\mu)$, as previously defined [problem 1, § 7.3].

Now suppose that μ is a charge on S such that $\mu(E) = 0$ if $E \in N$, and suppose $x \in B_N(T)$. We can define an integral of x with respect to μ by the classical procedure of Lebesgue. Write $\alpha = - \|x\|, \beta = \|x\|$, assuming that $\|x\| > 0$. Suppose $\alpha = \alpha_0 < \alpha_1 < \cdots < \alpha_n = \beta$ and let

$$E_0 = \{t : \alpha_0 = x(t)\}, \qquad E_k = \{t : \alpha_{k-1} < x(t) \leqslant \alpha_k\}, \qquad k = 1, \cdots, n.$$

If $\xi_0 = \alpha_0$ and if $\xi_1, \cdots, \xi_n$ are chosen so that $\alpha_{k-1} \leqslant \xi_k \leqslant \alpha_k$, the sums

$$\sum_{k=0}^{n} \xi_k \mu(E_k)$$

converge to a limit as $\max_k |\alpha_k - \alpha_{k-1}| \to 0$, the limit being independent of how the points $\xi_1, \cdots, \xi_n$ are chosen within the specified subintervals. This limit is by definition the L-integral of x with respect to μ; we denote it by

$$L \int x \, d\mu.$$

The fact that the integral exists can be proved much as in the classical Lebesgue case, and we omit details.

The fact that we assumed $\mu(E) = 0$ if $E \in N$ shows that the value of the integral depends only on the equivalence class represented by the particular N-bounded function, not on the function itself. The definition of the L-integral does not require the introduction of the class N, provided we assume that x is bounded and measurable. Nor is it necessary to have S a σ-ring; merely a ring is enough. However, when we introduce N, we assume that S is a σ-ring.

We can also deal with complex-valued functions, either directly or by separating into real and imaginary parts.

It follows from the form of the sums defining the integral that

$$\left| L \int x \, d\mu \right| \leqslant \|x\| \, \|\mu\|.$$

It may be proved much as in the classical Lebesgue theory that the integral is a linear function of x. Linearity in μ is evident, but linearity in x is not as evident here as with the S-integral. Because of the linearity in μ it is enough, in proving the linearity in x, to treat the case in which μ has nonnegative values, for the general case can be reduced to this by the Jordan decomposition of μ. We omit the details. See, for example, Titchmarsh, **1**, or Rosenbloom, **1**.

If x is measurable and bounded, it is easy to prove that

$$(7.9\text{–}1) \qquad\qquad L \int x \, d\mu = S \int x \, d\mu.$$

For, if we use the simple function

$$y = \sum_k x(t_k) y_k$$

related to x as in the construction leading up to (7.8–6), we see that

$$L\int y \, d\mu = \sum_k x(t_k) \mu(E_k),$$

$$\left| L\int x \, d\mu - L\int y \, d\mu \right| = \left| L\int (x - y) \, d\mu \right| \leqslant \|x - y\| \, \|\mu\| \leqslant \epsilon \|\mu\|,$$

$$\left| S\int x \, d\mu - L\int y \, d\mu \right| \leqslant \epsilon \|\mu\|,$$

and (7.9–1) follows from these results.

Theorem 7.9–A.   *The normed conjugate of* $B_N(T)$ *and the subspace of the space of all charges, consisting of those charges* μ *such that* $\mu(E) = 0$ *if* $E \in N$, *are congruent under the correspondence indicated by the formula*

$$x'(x) = L\int x \, d\mu.$$

The argument is much the same as in the proof of Theorem 7.8–A. Note that, when μ is obtained from x' by the formula $\mu(E) = x'(x_E)$, it follows that $\mu(E) = 0$ if $E \in N$, for $\|x_E\| = 0$ in that case.

SUGGESTED READING

Banach, **1**, pp. 59–65.
Birkhoff, **1**, Chapter 15.
Bourbaki, **5**.
Dunford, **3**, pp. 31–41.
Dunford and Schwartz, **1**, Chapters 3, 4.
Fichtenholz and Kantorovitch, **1**.
Halmos, **2**, Chapters 2, 4, 5, 6, 10.
Hildebrandt, **1**.
Loomis, **1**, Chapter 3.
Riesz and Nagy, **1**, parts of Chapters 2, 3.
Rosenbloom, **1**.
Yosida and Hewitt, **1**.
Zaanen, **1**, Chapter 5 and part of Chapter 7.

BIBLIOGRAPHY

N. I. Achieser and I. M. Glasmann
1. *Theorie der linearen Operatoren im Hilbert-Raum*, Akademie Verlag, Berlin, 1954.

W. G. Bade
1. An operational calculus for operators with spectrum in a strip, *Pacific J. Math.*, 3 (1953), 257–290.

S. Banach
1. *Opérations linéaires*, Monografje Matematyczne, Warsaw, 1932.

G. Birkhoff
1. *Lattice Theory*, revised edition, American Mathematical Society Colloquium Publications, vol. 25, New York, 1948.

R. P. Boas
1. Entire functions of exponential type, *Bull. Amer. Math. Soc.*, 48 (1942), 839–849.

N. Bourbaki
Each of the following is in the series, *Éléments de mathématique, Actualités Sci. Ind.*, Hermann, Paris. Each title is identified by a serial number.
1. *Théorie des ensembles.* No. 846 (1939).
2. *Topologie générale.* No. 858 (1940).
3. *Algèbre linéaire.* No. 1032 (1947).
4. *Espaces vectoriels topologiques.* No. 1189 (1953) and No. 1229 (1955).
5. *Intégration.* No. 1175 (1952).

R. V. Churchill
1. *Fourier Series and Boundary Value Problems*, McGraw-Hill, New York, 1941.

J. A. Clarkson
1. Uniformly convex spaces, *Trans. Amer. Math. Soc.*, 40 (1936), 396–414.

R. G. Cooke
1. *Linear Operators*, Macmillan, London, 1953.

R. Courant and D. Hilbert
1. *Methoden der mathematischen Physik*, vol. I, Springer, Berlin, 1931.

M. M. Day
1. The spaces L^p with $0 < p < 1$, *Bull. Amer. Math. Soc.*, 46 (1940), 816–823.

J. Dieudonné
1. La dualité dans les espaces vectorielles topologiques, *Ann. Sci. Ecole Norm. Sup.* (3), 59 (1942), 107–139.
2. Recent developments in the theory of locally convex vector spaces, *Bull. Amer. Math. Soc.*, 59 (1953), 495–512.

J. Dixmier
1. Sur un théorème de Banach, *Duke Math. J.*, 15 (1948), 1057–1071.
2. Sur les bases orthonormales dans les espaces préhilbertiens, *Acta Sci. Math. Szeged*, 15 (1953), 29–30.

N. Dunford
1. Spectral theory I. Convergence to projections, *Trans. Amer. Math. Soc.*, 54 (1943), 185–217.
2. Spectral theory, *Bull. Amer. Math. Soc.*, 49 (1943), 637–651.
3. Spectral theory in abstract spaces and Banach algebras, *Proceedings of the Symposium on Spectral Theory and Differential Problems*, Oklahoma Agricultural and Mechanical College, 1951.
4. Spectral theory II. Resolutions of the identity, *Pacific J. Math.*, 2 (1952), 559–614.
5. Spectral operators, *Pacific J. Math.*, 4 (1954), 321–354.

N. Dunford and B. J. Pettis
1. Linear operators on summable functions, *Trans. Amer. Math. Soc.*, 47 (1940), 323–392.

N. Dunford and J. T. Schwartz
1. *Linear Operators*, vol. I. *General Theory*, Interscience, New York, 1958.

W. F. Eberlein
1. Weak compactness in Banach spaces I, *Proc. Nat. Acad. Sci.*, *U.S.A.*, 33 (1947), 51–53.

G. Fichtenholz and L. Kantorovitch
1. Sur les opérations dans l'espace des fonctions bornées, *Studia Math.*, 5 (1934), 69–98.

M. Fréchet
1. *Les espaces abstraits*, Gauthier-Villars, Paris, 1928.

B. Friedman
1. *Principles and Techniques of Applied Mathematics*, John Wiley, New York, 1956.

L. M. Graves
1. *The Theory of Functions of Real Variables*, 2nd ed., McGraw-Hill, New York, 1956.

C. J. A. Halberg Jr.
1. Spectral theory of linked operators in the spaces l^p, Doctoral dissertation, University of California, Los Angeles, 1955.

D. W. Hall and G. L. Spencer
1. *Elementary Topology*, John Wiley, New York, 1955.

P. R. Halmos
1. *Finite Dimensional Vector Spaces*, Princeton University Press, 1948.
2. *Measure Theory*, D. Van Nostrand, New York, 1950.
3. *Introduction to Hilbert Space and the Theory of Spectral Multiplicity*, Chelsea, New York, 1951.

H. L. Hamburger and M. E. Grimshaw
1. *Linear Transformations in n-dimensional Vector Space*, Cambridge University Press, 1951.

G. Hamel
1. Eine Basis aller Zahlen und die unstetige Lösungen der Funktionalgleichung $f(x + y) = f(x) + f(y)$, *Math. Ann.*, 60 (1905), 459–462.

G. H. Hardy
1. The mean value of the modulus of an analytic function, *Proc. London Math. Soc.*, 14 (1914), 269–277.

G. H. Hardy, J. E. Littlewood, and G. Pólya
1. *Inequalities*, Cambridge University Press, 1934.

E. D. Hellinger
1. Spectra of quadratic forms in infinitely many variables, *Mathematical Monographs* I (1941), Northwestern University Studies.

E. Hellinger and O. Toeplitz
1. *Integralgleichungen und Gleichungen mit unendlichvielen Unbekannten*, Chelsea, New York, 1953. (A reprint of Part II C13 of the *Encyklopädie der mathematischen Wissenschaften*.)

E. Hille
1. *Functional analysis and semi-groups*, American Mathematical Society Colloquium Publications, vol. 31, New York, 1948.

T. H. Hildebrandt
1. On bounded linear transformations, *Trans. Amer. Math. Soc.*, 36 (1934), 868–875.

D. H. Hyers
1. Linear topological spaces, *Bull. Amer. Math. Soc.*, 51 (1945), 1–24.

N. Jacobson
1. *Lectures in abstract algebra*, vol. II, *Linear Algebra*, D. Van Nostrand, New York, 1953.

G. Julia
1. *Introduction mathématique aux théories quantiques* (second part), Gauthier-Villars, Paris, 1938.

S. Kakutani
1. Weak topology and regularity of Banach spaces, *Proc. Imp. Acad. Tokyo*, 15 (1939), 169–173.

J. L. Kelley
1. *General Topology*, D. Van Nostrand, New York, 1955.

O. D. Kellogg
1. *Foundations of Potential Theory*, Springer, Berlin, 1929.

P. D. Lax
1. On the existence of Green's function, *Proc. Amer. Math. Soc.*, 3 (1952), 526–531.

A. E. Livingston
1. The space H^p, $0 < p < 1$, is not normable, *Pacific J. Math.*, 3 (1953), 613–616.

L. A. Ljusternik and W. I. Sobolew
1. *Elemente der Funktionalanalysis*, Akademie Verlag, Berlin, 1955.

L. H. Loomis
1. *An Introduction to Abstract Harmonic Analysis*, D. Van Nostrand, New York, 1953.

E. R. Lorch
1. The spectrum of linear transformations, *Trans. Amer. Math. Soc.*, 52 (1942), 238–248.

H. Löwig
1. Über die Dimension Linearer Räume, *Studia Math.*, 5 (1934), 18–23.

G. W. Mackey
1. On infinite dimensional linear spaces, *Trans. Amer. Math. Soc.*, 57 (1945), 155–207.
2. On convex topological linear spaces, *Trans. Amer. Math. Soc.*, 60 (1946), 519–537.

E. J. McShane
1. *Integration*, Princeton University Press, 1947.

D. Milman
1. On some criteria for the regularity of spaces of the type (B), *C. R. (Doklady) de l'Acad. Sci. de l'URSS*, 20 (1938), 243–246.

C. Miranda
1. Sul principio di Dirichlet per le funzioni armoniche, *Atti Accad. Naz. Lincei, Rend. Cl. Sci. Fis. Mat. Nat.* (8), 3 (1947), 55–59.

F. J. Murray
1. On complementary manifolds and projections in spaces L_p and l_p, *Trans. Amer. Math. Soc.*, 41 (1937), 138–152.

B. v. Sz. Nagy
1. *Spektraldarstellung linearer Transformationen des Hilbertschen Raumes, Ergebnisse der Mathematik und ihrer Grenzgebiete*, Springer, Berlin, 1942.

J. von Neumann
1. *Mathematische Grundlagen der Quantenmechanik*, Springer, Berlin, 1932.
2. On complete topological spaces, *Trans. Amer. Math. Soc.*, 37 (1935), 1–20.

B. J. Pettis
1. A proof that every uniformly convex space is reflexive, *Duke Math. J.*, 5 (1939), 249–253.

R. S. Phillips
1. On linear transformations, *Trans. Amer. Math. Soc.*, 48 (1940), 516–541.

H. Pollard
1. Integral transforms, *Duke Math. J.*, 13 (1946), 307–330.

F. Rellich
1. Spektraltheorie in nichtseparablen Räumen, *Math. Ann.*, 110 (1934), 342–356.

F. Riesz
1. *Les systèmes d'équations lineairés à une infinité d'inconnues*, Gauthier-Villars, Paris, 1913.
2. Über die Randwerte einer analytischen Funktion, *Math. Zeit.*, 18 (1923), 87–95.
3. Sur les valeurs moyennes du module des fonctions harmoniques et des fonctions analytiques, *Acta Sci. Math. Szeged*, 1 (1922), 27–32.

F. Riesz and B. v. Sz. Nagy
1. *Leçons d'analyse fonctionelle*, 3rd ed. Gauthier-Villars, Paris, 1955.

M. Riesz
1. Sur les maxima des formes bilinéaires et sur les fonctionelles linéaires, *Acta Math.*, 49 (1927), 465–497.

P. C. Rosenbloom
1. Quelques classes de problèmes extrémaux, *Bull. Sci. Math. France*, 79 (1951), 1–58, and 80 (1952), 183–215.

S. Saks
1. *Theory of the Integral*, 2nd ed., Monografje Matematyczne, Warsaw-Lwów, 1937.

W. Schmeidler
1. *Lineare Operatoren in Hilbertschen Raum*, Teubner, Stuttgart, 1954.

I. Schur
1. Bemerkungen zur Theorie der beschränkten Bilinearformen mit unendlichvielen Veränderlichen, *J. Reine Angew. Math.*, 151 (1921), 79–111.

A. Sobczyk
1. Projections in Minkowski and Banach spaces, *Duke Math. J.*, 8 (1941), 78–106.

W. Sierpinski
1. *Leçons sur les nombres transfinis*, Gauthier-Villars, Paris, 1950.

M. H. Stone
1. *Linear transformations in Hilbert space*, American Mathematical Society Colloquium Publications, vol. 15, New York, 1932.

A. E. Taylor
1. Analysis in complex Banach spaces, *Bull. Amer. Math. Soc.*, 49 (1943), 652–669.
2. Spectral theory of closed distributive operators, *Acta Math.*, 84 (1950), 189–224.
3. New proofs of some theorems of Hardy by Banach space methods, *Math. Mag.*, 23 (1950), 115–124.
4. Banach spaces of functions analytic in the unit circle, *Studia Math.*, 11 (1950), 145–170 and 12 (1951), 25–50.

A. E. Taylor and C. J. A. Halberg Jr.
1. General theorems about a bounded linear operator and its conjugate, *J. Reine Angew. Math.*, 198 (1957), 93–111.

G. O. Thorin
1. *Convexity theorems generalizing those of M. Riesz and Hadamard, with some applications*, University of Lund thesis, Uppsala, 1948.

E. C. Titchmarsh
1. *Theory of Functions*, 2nd ed., Oxford University Press, 1939.
2. *Eigenfunction expansions*, Oxford University Press, 1946.

S. S. Walters
1. The space H^p with $0 < p < 1$, *Proc. Amer. Math. Soc.*, 1 (1950), 800–805.
2. Remarks on the space H^p, *Pacific J. Math.*, 1 (1951), 455–471.

J. V. Wehausen
1. Transformations in topological linear spaces, *Duke Math. J.*, 4 (1938), 157–169.

A. Weil
1. *Sur les espaces à structure uniforme*, Actualités Sci. Ind., No. 551, Hermann, Paris, 1937.

H. Weyl
1. The method of orthogonal projection in potential theory, *Duke Math. J.*, 7 (1940), 411–444.

D. V. Widder
1. *The Laplace Transform*, Princeton University Press, 1946.

N. Wiener
1. *The Fourier Integral*, Cambridge University Press, 1933.

A. Wintner
1. *Spektraltheorie der unendlichen Matrizen*, Hirzel Verlag, Leipzig, 1929.
2. Zur Theorie der beschränkten Bilinearformen, *Math. Zeit.*, 30 (1929), 228–282.

K. Yosida and E. Hewitt
1. Finitely additive measures, *Trans. Amer. Math. Soc.*, 72 (1952), 46–66.

A. C. Zaanen
1. *Linear analysis*, North Holland, Amsterdam, 1953.

A. Zygmund
1. *Trigonometrical Series*, Monografje Matematyczne, Warsaw-Lwów, 1935.

LIST OF SPECIAL SYMBOLS

$[x]$	Equivalence class notation, 17, 104
$BV[a, b]$	Space of functions of bounded variation, 17, 91
$\mathscr{D}(A)$	Domain of A, 18
$\mathscr{R}(A)$	Range of A, 18
$\langle x, x' \rangle$	Linear functional notation, 34
X^f	Algebraic conjugate of X, 34
X^{ff}	Algebraic conjugate of X^f, 36
dim X	Dimension of X, 46
A^T	Transpose of A, 47
S^0	Annihilator, 48, 224
^0S	Annihilator, 49, 225
J	Canonical mapping operator, 36, 191
$\mathscr{N}(A)$	Null manifold of A, 52
$\bar{S}$	Closure of S, 57
int (S)	Interior of S, 58
$f^{-1}(T)$	Inverse image of T, 61
T_1- space	A type of topological space, 59
T_1, T_2, T_3 — spaces	Types of topological spaces, 65
$d(x_1, x_2)$	Distance, 68
$\hat{X}$	Completion of X, 76, 99
Π	Cartesian product, 79
$\|T\|$	Norm of T, 86
$l^p(n), l^\infty(n)$	Minkowski spaces, 88
l^p, l^∞	Sequence spaces, 88
(c)	A sequence space, 88, 201
$B(T)$ and $B[a, b]$	Function spaces, 89
$C(T)$	A space of continuous functions, 89
$\sup^0$	Essential supremum, 90
$\mathscr{L}^\infty$	A class of functions, 90
L^∞	A space formed from $\mathscr{L}^\infty$, 91
$V(x)$	Total variation of x, 91
$\mathfrak{M}_p[f; r]$	A mean value, 92
$\mathfrak{M}_\infty[f; r]$	A maximum value, 92
$\mathfrak{A}$	A class of analytic functions, 92
H^p, H^∞	Spaces of analytic functions, 93
CA	A space of analytic functions, 93
(x_1, x_2)	Inner product, 106
$\mathscr{T}(X, M)$	A weak topology, 152
(s)	A sequence space, 156
S	A function space, 156

Discussions Relating to Particular Spaces

INDEX

417